The Salomon Smith Barney Guide to World Equity Markets 1998

The Salomon Smith Barney Guide to World Equity Markets 1998

Research Editors
Robert Irish, Luciano Mondellini

Editors
Jacqueline Grosch Lobo, David Rathborne

Editorial Adviser
Jim Leman (Salomon Smith Barney)

Published by Euromoney Publications PLC
and Salomon Smith Barney

Published by Euromoney Publications PLC.
Nestor House, Playhouse Yard,
London EC4V 5EX
Tel: (44) 171 779 8860
Fax: (44) 171 779 8541
E-mail: embks@dial.pipex.com
Website: www.euromoneyplc.com

ISBN 1 85564 659 5

Typeset by Euromoney Publications
Printed and bound in Great Britain by Biddles Limited

Foreword

Equity markets worldwide continue to develop and expand. As mature markets converge and new markets emerge, the need for a single reference source providing a global overview increases. The Salomon Smith Barney Guide to World Equity Markets, produced annually and now in its twelfth year, builds on previous editions to provide an updated guide to 78 of the world's equity markets.

In order to meet investor demand for increased coverage of Eastern European markets, chapters on Lithuania, Romania and Ukraine have been included for the first time this year. This 1998 edition has also witnessed the expansion and standardisation of the "Summary Information" section, with the addition of data on market capitalisation and inflation rates.

As regards the global ranking of countries by market value (calculated on the market capitalisation, in US dollar terms, of domestic listed companies), the major changes between 1996 and 1997 took place in Asia, with the economic crisis there leading to dramatic plunges throughout the region.

Euromoney Books and Salomon Smith Barney are proud to have worked together on this twelfth edition and are looking forward to starting work on the 1999 edition.

Each chapter follows a uniform structure in its profile of a country's market. The introduction provides a general overview of the character of the market followed by a review of the chief economic and political influences at work. A review of market performance highlights the key factors and the year-end status of key indicators: equity yields, price earnings ratios, share prices and currency movements. A summary table gives vital market statistics such as global ranking, growth in market value over five years, number of companies listed, market value as a percentage of GDP, the market P/E ratio, MSCI total returns and the variation in the MSCI Index. Key economic indicators such as budget deficit as a percentage of GDP, short-term interest rates, long-term bond yields and the dollar exchange rate are also given in this easy-reference table. Subsequent sections detail:

Role of the Central Bank: Relationship with government, reponsibilities with regards to monetary policy, foreign exchange markets, supervision of banking sector and other financial institutions, preparation of monetary, financial and exchange statistical data. Main objectives with regards to stability of currency, economic growth, and inflation.

The Stock Market: background information, structure and organisation of the securities market(s) and a list of the exchanges and their contact details and operating hours.

Market Size: with particular focus on equities, this section outlines the growth of the market in terms of market capitalisation, trading volume, the number of listed securities, details of the largest companies and the most actively traded shares.

Types of share: details of the types of equity (ordinary, preference, preferred ordinary, deferred, convertible etc.) traded and the rights which apply to each share.

Other markets: the operation of additional markets.

Investors: this section indicates (where available) who the key market participants are.

Operations: details of the settlement and transfer structures, brokerage rates and taxation and other costs likely to be incurred. A list of major banks and/or brokers operating in this market.

Taxation and regulation affecting foreign investors: this section explains the principal restricitons which apply on inward equity investment, including any relevant exchange controls and/or rate of withholding taxes.

Reporting, research other information: the final section of each chapter looks at the reporting requirements for listed companies, the level of protection for shareholders and the type and availability of research. As appropriate, prospective changes are also discussed.

The charts of stock market indices featured in the country chapters have been provided by Datastream and are presented in local currency terms for markets in which inflation is relatively stable. For markets where inflation is more volatile the charts are presented in US dollars in order to avoid large fluctuations of the index.

Morgan Stanley Capital International have provided charts of their World Indices in US dollar terms for each of the markets, for regions and for the world. These appear in an appendix at the back of the book.

Also included are Salomon Smith Barney World Equity Index charts for individual markets, regions and the world, showing large capitalisation versus small capitalisation total returns in local currency terms. See introductory chapter: *International Equity Indices.*

Euromoney Books 1998

Acknowledgements

The editors would like to thank the following organisations for their contribution and particularly the invaluable assistance of the people mentioned below, in the compilation of ***The Salomon Smith Barney Guide to World Equity Markets 1998:***

ARGENTINA
ABN AMRO – Walter Kiceleff
Buenos Aires Stock Exchange – Carlos Oscar Terribile
Price Waterhouse & Co. – Hugo Almono

AUSTRALIA
J B Were & Son – Fernando Nivanka
Australian Stock Exchange Ltd – Rory Collins
Minter Ellison Lawyers – Andrew Bullock & Callen O'Brien

AUSTRIA
RZB Austria – Hans Krendel
Wiener Börse – Edith Franc
Law Offices of Dr F Schwank – Friedrich Schwank

BAHRAIN
ABC Investment & Services Co. – Hassan Al Aali
Bahrain Stock Exchange – Ebrahim Jenahi
Norton Rose – David Drake
Clifford Chance – Alexandra McDowall

BANGLADESH
Union Capital Limited – Mahboob Hossain
Dhaka Stock Exchange – Razaur Rehman

BELGIUM
Petercam SA – Benoît t'Kint de Roodenbeke
Brussels Stock Exchange – Daniel Maertens
De Bandt, Van Hecke & Lagae – Inge Basteleurs & Chris Sunt

BERMUDA
Bermuda Monetary Authority – Debra Goins & Antoine Blackburn
Bermuda Stock Exchange – William Woods
Appleby, Spurling & Kempe – Roberta Montefia

BOTSWANA
Stockbrokers Botswana Ltd – Rupert McCammon & Martinus Seboni

BRAZIL
IMF Editoria Ltd – Ronaldo A da Frota Nogueira
Rio de Janeiro Stock Exchange – Ricardo Pinto Nogueira
São Paulo Stock Exchange – Moema Unis
Pinheiro Neto-Advogados – Raphael de Cunto & Kate Sawyer

BULGARIA
ING Sofia – Rumiana Sotirova & Nicolae Stoykov
Bulgarian Stock Exchange-Sofia – Danteleg Karasmaonov
Boteva & Kantutis – Nina Boteva

CANADA
Nesbitt Burns – Ben Joyce & Dwaine Krpan
Montreal Stock Exchange – Concetta Savoia
Toronto Stock Exchange – Catherine McGravey
Vancouver Stock Exchange – Lori Last
Fasken Campbell Godfrey – C L Sugiyama

CHILE
Merrill Lynch – Marco Vargas
Santiago Stock Exchange – Sandra Diaz
Carey y Cia Abogados – Alfonso Silva

CHINA
Daiwa Securities – Alan Caskett
Shanghai Securities Exchange – Gang Zheng
Shenzhen Stock Exchange – Dai Xiaoling
Freshfields China – Matthew Cosans

COLOMBIA
Corredores Asociados – Juan Carlos Gonzales & Leonardo Bravo
Bogota Stock Exchange – Oscar Uruena
Raisbeck, Lara, Rodriquez & Rueda – Jorge Lara-Urbaneja

COSTA RICA
Aldesa Valores SA – Lanzo Luconi
Costa Rica Stock Exchange – Johanna Castro
Pacheco Coto – Umberto Pacheco & Silvia Moreno

CROATIA
Auctor Securities – Michael Glazer
Zagreb Stock Exchange – Zeljko Kardum

CZECH REPUBLIC
Citicorp Securities – Radek Maly & Christina Lenkova
CA IB Securities – Sibilla Wehren
Prague Stock Exchange – Tomas Jursik
Kocián Solc Balastík – Petra Widdess

DENMARK
Alfred Berg – ABN AMRO – Stig Haldan
Copenhagen Stock Exchange – Ellen-Magrethe Solberg
Plesner & Grønborg Advokatfirma – Casper Münter

ECUADOR
Transfiec (Banco Popular) – Enrique Orti & Jeronimo Davalos
Quito Stock Exchange – Patricia Guerrero
Izurieta, Mora, Bowen – Ricardo Izurieta

EGYPT
Hermes Financial – Amr El-Kadi
Capital Market Authority – Ashraf Shams El Din
Baker & McKenzie Law Firm – Samir Hamza

FINLAND
Merita Securities – Tanya Lounevirta
Helsingin Arvopaperiporssi – Sade Juselius
Procopé & Hornborg – Katarina Kujala

FRANCE
Paribas – David Dixon & Howard Jones
Paris Stock Exchange – Marc Outin
Gide Loyrette Nouel – Jean Thibaud

GERMANY
LGT Bank in Liechtenstein (Frankfurt) GmbH – Susanne Reichert
Deutsche Börse AG – Sylvia Kramm & Walter Allwicher
Bruckhaus Westrick Stegemann Rechtsanwälte – Thomas Emde & Gunnar Schuster

GHANA
National Trust Holding Co. – Gladys Odoi
Ghana Stock Exchange – Diana Okine
Bentsi-Enchill, Letsa & Mate – Kojo Bentsi-Enchill

GREECE
Egnatia Securities – George Polites
Athens Stock Exchange – Sofie Athanassopulu
Chrysses Demetriades & Co. – George Economou

HONG KONG
Templeton International – Alister Hill
Hong Kong Stock Exchange – Essie Tsoi
Baker & McKenzie – Anna Chong

HUNGARY
CA IB Securities – Katalin Dani
Raffeisen Securities & Investment Hungary – Zolten Radnoty & Zoltan Torok
Budapest Stock Exchange – Beatrix Jancso
Baker & McKenzie – Cameron Young

INDIA
CIFCO Finance – Mayank Dalal
Bombay Stock Exchange – K G Karekar
Dave & Girish & Co. – G M Dave

INDONESIA
Sigma Batara – Fadjar L Sutandi
Jakarta Stock Exchange – Justarina Naiborhu
Wiriadinata & Widyawan – David Dawborn

IRELAND
Davy Stockbrokers – W Scott Rankin
A & L Goodbody Solicitors – Mark Ward
Irish Stock Exchange – Mark Scully

ISRAEL
Bank Leumi le-Israel – Ruth Heltman
Tel Aviv Stock Exchange – Irit Harel
Herzog, Fox & Neeman Advocates – Danny Chinn

ITALY
Banca Commerciale Italiana – Marco Ratti
Italian Stock Exchange – Luca Filippa & Marco Accorsi
Alegi & Associates – Peter Alegi

JAMAICA
Mayberry Investments Ltd – Christopher Berry
Jamaica Stock Exchange – Ray Johnson
Myers, Fletcher & Gordon – Monica Ladd

JAPAN
Nikko Europe – Roy Young
Tokyo Stock Exchange – Hiroyuki Tokimune
Nakagawa & Takashina Attorneys-at-Law – Noburu Nakagawa

JORDAN
National Securities Company – Amer Mou'asher
Amman Financial Market – Wahid Shair

KENYA
Equity Stockbrokers Ltd – Robert Bunyi
Nairobi Stock Exchange – Francis Wambugu
Daly & Figgis – Hamish Keith

KOREA
Templeton International – Alister Hill
Korea Stock Exchange – Sangho Ha
Kim & Chang – Joon Park

LEBANON
Banque Audi – Marwan Barakat
Lebanon Invest – Najib Maalouf
Beirut Stock Exchange – Eleia Abi Antoun

LITHUANIA
Suprema Securities Brokerage House – Daiva Rakauskaite & Aidas Galubickas
Lithuania Stock Exchange – Arminta Lauzadyte & Lina Levickajta
Lideika, Petrauskas, Valiunas & Partners – Alwida Janulaitiene

LUXEMBOURG
Banque Internationale à Luxembourg – Jean-Charles Schiltz
Luxembourg Stock Exchange – Carlo Mouschang
Arendt & Medernach – François Kremer

MALAYSIA
CLSA Global Emerging Markets – Mark Faulkner
Kuala Lumpur Stock Exchange – Winnie Choong
Rashid & Lee – Christopher Lee

MAURITIUS
General Brokerage – Thierry Hugnin
Mauritius Stock Exchange – Michael Ling
Chambers of Sir Hamid Moolian – Ben L Daby Seesaram

MEXICO
ING Barings México – Felix Boni
Mexico Stock Exchange – Angeles Hewett
Creel, Garcia-Cuellar y Müggenburg – Carlos Creel

MOROCCO
Casablanca Finance Group – Muna Lahlou
Casablanca Stock Excchange – Driss Bencheikh

NETHERLANDS
MeesPierson – Marc Pauwels
Amsterdam Stock Exchange – Suzanne Bierhoff
Loeff Claeys Verbeke – Niels Van de Vijver & Pim Horsten

NEW ZEALAND
Credit Suisse First Boston – Jason Wong
New Zealand Stock Exchange – Kathy Gruschow
Phillips Fox – Tony Agar

NIGERIA
Nigeria Stockbrokers – A S Moore & Jaiye-Oyidotun
Nigerian Stock Exchange – Rasaki Oladejo
Nnenna Ejekam & Associates – Nnenna Ejekam

NORWAY
Alfred Berg – Knut Harald
Oslo Stock Exchange – Bernt Bangstad
Vogt & Co. – Frithjof Herlosfsen & Kristian Ostberg

OMAN
Al Ahlia Portfolio Securities Co – Zohair Abdullah
Muscat Securities Market – Mahmoud Al-Jarwani
Trowers & Hamlins – David Wilson

PAKISTAN
Kausar Abbas Bhayani – Mohammad Zubair Ellahi
Karachi Stock Exchange – Mohammed Farooque
Chambers of Sir Patrick Neill QC and Richard Southwell QC – Khawar Qureshi

PANAMA
Capital Traders of Panama – Dulcidio de la Guardia
Panama Stock Exchange – Ivan Díaz
Ernst & Young – Amanda Barrasa & José Mann

PERU
Peruval – Augusto Larco & Lorenzo Sousa Debarbieri
Lima Stock Exchange – Luccia Reynoso Paz
Rodrigo, Elias & Medrano Abogados – Maria Teresa Quiñones

PHILIPPINES
Central Bank of the Philippines – Diwa C Guinigundo
Manila Stock Exchange – Sergio S Marquez
SyCip Salazar Hernandez & Gatmaitan – Rose Marie King

POLAND
CA IB Securities – Sibilla Wehren
Warsaw Stock Exchange – Leonard Furga
Hogan & Harston – Robert Karwoski & Steven Ballew

PORTUGAL
Banco Cisf – Goncalo Rocha
Lisbon Stock Exchange – Sofia Duarte Silva & Tiago Gomes
Carlos de Sousa e Brito & Associados – Diego Leónidas Rocha

ROMANIA
General Investment Group – Vlad Vasiliu
Bucuresti International Securities – Alexander Menche & Adriano Rus
Bucharest Stock Exchange – Mihai Popescu
Coopers & Lybrand Romania – Emilian Radu

RUSSIA
Russian Brokerage House CA & Co – Valery Mironov & Eugene Schukine
AK & M – Andrey Yakushin
Clifford Chance – Kevin Bell

SINGAPORE
J M Sassoon & Co. – Yin Sze Liew
Singapore Stock Exchange – Patricia Lim
Allen & Gledhill – Gay Tan Tze

SLOVAKIA
CA IB Securities – Sibilla Wehren
Bratislava Stock Exchange – Maria Kunikova
Cernejova & Hrbek – Igor Palka

SLOVENIA
CA IB Securities – Gregor Kastelic, Klemen Hauko & Dana Svetina
Ljubljana Stock Exchange – Lidija Gabrijelcic
Pensa Jadek – Pavle Pensa

SOUTH AFRICA
Société Générale Frankel Pollak – Simon Oliver
Johannesburg Stock Exchange – Leanne Parsons
Edward Nathan & Friedland Inc. – Miranda Feinstein

SPAIN
Santander Investment – Roberto Fernandez
Barcelona Stock Exchange – Antonio Giralt Serra
Madrid Stock Exchange – Domingo Garcia
Prol & Asociados – Francisco Prol

SRI LANKA
CDIC Sassoon Cumberbatch Stockbrokers – Sarath Rajapakse
Colombo Stock Exchange – Rajeeva Bandaranaike
Julius & Creasy – B M Ameresekera & G R M Bandara

SWEDEN
Svenska Handelsbanken – Elizabeth Krämbring
Stockholm Stock Exchange – Leif Vindevåg
Lagerlöf & Leman Advokatbyrå – Peder Hammarskiold & Sophie Degenne

SWITZERLAND
Schweizerische Nationalbank – Gabriel Juri
Swiss Stock Exchange – Marc Berthoud
Baker & McKenzie – Urs Schenker

TAIWAN
Templeton International – Alister Hill
Taiwan Stock Exchange – Paul C Y Huang
Baker & McKenzie – Pauline Jen

THAILAND
Kleinwort Benson – Russell J Kopp
Thailand Securities Depository – Annie D Putthkayon
Ukrit Mongkolnavin Law Office Co. – Suwit Suwan

TRINIDAD AND TOBAGO
Central Bank of Trinidad and Tobago – Dominic Stodard
Trinidad & Tobago Stock Exchange – Sharon Manoo
J D Sellier &Co. – Charmaine Pemberton

TUNISIA
International Mahgreb Merchant Bank – Lillia Abdelwahet
Tunis Stock Exchange – Raouf Budabbous

TURKEY
TEB Ekonomi Arastirmalari AS – Zeynep Turkeri
Istanbul Stock Exchange – Eren Kiliclioglu
White & Case – Emre Derman

UKRAINE
Wood & Company – Ivan Kompan
KPMG/Barents Group LLC – Geoff Elkind
Frischberg & Partners Ltd – Alex Schay

UNITED KINGDOM
London Stock Exchange – Brian Bartholomew
HSBC James Capel – Stewart Breed, Adam Cole & David Bloom
Clifford Chance – Mark Everett

UNITED STATES OF AMERICA
Morgan Stanley – Scott Reed
Nasdaq Stock Market, Inc – Mike Shokouhi
American Stock Exchange – Ryan Ciociola
New York Stock Exchange – Jean Tobin
Weil, Gotshal & Manges – Marvin E Jacob

URUGUAY
Bank of America – Andrew Freris
Montevideo Stock Exchange – Diego Alvares
Hughes & Hughes Abogados – Haroldo Espalter

VENEZUELA
Marino Recio Asociados CA – Eduardo Recio
Caracas Stock Exchange – Miguel Blessing Isava
Rodriguez & Mendoza – Ronaldo Hellmund & Oswaldo Anzola

VIETNAM
Templeton International – Alister Hill

ZAMBIA
ING Barings – James Whittington & Kristina Quatter
Lusaka Stock Exchange – Charles Mate
Christopher Russell Cook & Co – Kanti K Patel

ZIMBABWE
Fleming Martin Edwards Securities – B Msuuaka, Sean Senior & Wellington Chikwata
Zimbabwe Stock Exchange – Tony Barfoot
Midzi, Ziweni and Partners – Oscar Razawe

Euromoney Publications would like to thank the following organisations and people for their assistance in preparing the introductory sections and throughout the book: Datastream International Ltd, London; Dick Frase; Micropal and particularly the assistance of Josh Martin; William P. Miller II; Morgan Stanley Capital International and particularly the assistance of Nick Shellard and Sarah Bullimore; Price Waterhouse; Salomon Smith Barney and particularly the assistance of Jim Leman, Mary Athridge and Marc de Luise.

Euromoney Publications *The Guide to World Equity Markets 1998:* Jacqueline Grosch Lobo and David Rathborne Editors; Robert Irish and Luciano Mondellini Research Editors; Kim Gross Production Editor; Simon Perry and Victoria Barber Editorial.

Contents

INTRODUCTION

MARKETS

APPENDICES

Introduction

December 1997 marked the closing of the merger of Salomon Smith Barney and the birth of a new bulge-bracket firm. In the summer of 1997, top management at Salomon Brothers, Smith Barney, and their parent companies evaluated their strengths and their prospects for becoming a top-tier investment bank. They concluded that the combined firm would be better poised to succeed in the market-place than could each firm on its own. The new Salomon Smith Barney is a prime example of strategic changes that financial services firms have made in order to compete in a new global market-place.

Over the past decade, competitive forces have collapsed boundaries, integrated markets and allowed competitors from around the globe to compete head-to-head in each other's backyards. Deregulation, expanded trade and new technology have linked previously disparate markets, made established markets more efficient and broadened significantly the range of financial products and strategies available to companies worldwide. With new opportunity comes sharply increased competition, which in turn brings the need for new strategic solutions.

Salomon Brothers' global reach, strength in emerging markets and leadership in institutional sales and trading, and Smith Barney's distribution network, Private Client Group, asset management business, and strength in equities and municipal finance were perfect complements to one another. Salomon Smith Barney provides a full range of financial advisory, capital raising, research, and sales and trading services to corporations, governments and individuals. The firm also provides a full range of investment products, including stocks, bonds, CDs, mutual funds, IRAs and annuities.

Salomon Smith Barney boasts an extensive distribution network. The firm has 513 offices in 26 countries around the world. Salomon Smith Barney's 10,300 financial consultants, located in nearly 430 offices across the US, service over five million client accounts representing more than US$590 billion in assets.

INVESTMENT BANKING

Salomon Smith Barney is a global investment banking powerhouse with top-tier strength in numerous industry franchises and in all major product categories: equity, taxable and tax-exempt debt, and mergers and acquisitions. Professionals on five continents provide a full range of investment banking services to supranationals, governments, financial institutions, and large and mid-cap corporate clients.

Many services set Salomon Smith Barney apart from its competitors. Industry franchise bankers provide clients with industry-specific knowledge that is second to none. Salomon Smith Barney maintains a sizeable Financial Strategies Group, the sole purpose of which is to develop innovative financing strategies for the firm. A number of investment bankers are stationed on its trading floors – a structure that adds value to our clients' capital raising decisions.

Equity platform

Smith Barney and Salomon Brothers had two first-class equity platforms with distinctly different and complementary strengths. The combined entity offers equity issuers access to the second-largest retail brokerage in the US and comprehensive penetration of middle-market and large-market institutions worldwide. The firm has one of Wall Street's largest capital bases. It is able to price securities aggressively and to maintain a deep commitment to aftermarket support of clients' shares. Salomon Smith Barney is a market leader in management of equity deals and initial public offerings, the execution of block trades and the creation of innovative convertible securities.

Fixed-income platform

Salomon Smith Barney has a pre-eminent fixed-income platform. The firm's global fixed-income breadth enables it to execute complex financings in multiple currencies and to distribute clients' securities to institutional and retail investors around the world. A dominant position in underwriting, sales and trading, research, foreign exchange operations and risk management gives clients significant flexibility in bringing a debt or bank loan issue to market.

The firm is a long-standing leader in the investment grade, emerging markets Eurobond and Yankee bond sectors. It is a significant player in the high-yield market, especially in telecommunications and gaming. Salomon Brothers invented mortgage-backed securities and alone ranked number one in lead managing mortgage-backed agency securities in 1997. Salomon Smith Barney's Structured Finance Group has won awards for the application of securitisation technology to new asset types. The combined firm also has significant experience in tax-exempt securities; Smith Barney was the number one underwriter in both negotiated and competitive US long-term municipals in 1997.

Advisory services/mergers and acquisitions

Salomon Smith Barney integrates industry, product and regional specialisation to offer clients a comprehensive array of advisory services. This matrix is designed to help address the key strategic issues facing clients and to help them formulate and execute dynamic business planning. Salomon Smith Barney offers clients timely transaction execution, innovative deal and financing structures, and aggressive price negotiation skills. In 1997, Salomon Smith Barney advised on over 270 completed mergers and acquisitions worth over US$200 billion.

RESEARCH CAPABILITIES

Salomon Smith Barney is a front runner in both equity and fixed-income research in the US and around the world. Research analysts cover approximately 2,800 equities, funds and trusts, as well as taxable and tax-exempt fixed-income securities.

Salomon Smith Barney analysts track nearly all of the S&P sectors and more than 90% of the 500 largest US companies, as well as hundreds of middle-market and small-capitalisation stocks. Internationally, Salomon Smith Barney covers approximately 900 companies in Latin America, Europe, Asia-Pacific and Japan.

Equity research

According to an annual survey from Nelson Information Inc, the newly merged Salomon Smith Barney ranks number one among brokerages for the total number of US companies its analysts cover. Over the years, more than half the firm's analysts have been accorded the highest professional recognition, including numerous placements in *Institutional Investor* magazine's All America Research Team, high rankings in peer surveys sponsored by Greenwich Associates, and honours for stock selection and accuracy in earnings estimates in *The Wall Street Journal.*

The Research Department is able to evaluate both industry-based and geographic determinants of profitability and value as companies are impacted by globalisation. Among these factors are capacity, the state of labour markets, competitors' positioning and cost of capital. Equity research is organised into fundamental, technical and investment strategy disciplines. A proprietary equity rating system includes two components – a performance ranking (which includes total return potential) and a risk evaluation.

Fixed-income research

Salomon Brothers created the first Fixed-Income Research Department on Wall Street and the Salomon Smith Barney team intends to continue the tradition of fixed-income product innovation. Unparalleled quantitative skills and commitment to state-of-the-art technology have enabled us to develop a unique approach to fixed-income research.

Leading-edge services are offered to individual investors, institutions and multinational corporations. Salomon Smith Barney's approach involves sophisticated financial modelling; in-depth analysis of corporate and sovereign credit risk; comprehensive portfolio analysis; relative-value judgement strategies for both taxable and non-taxable investments; and an extensive family of global fixed-income indices. One of its best known products is The Yield Book, a proprietary analytical system that is used by 76 of the top 100 US fixed-income investment managers. Others include government bond research, cutting-edge mortgage security and asset-backed security models and detailed corporate/high-yield coverage of 1,200 companies worldwide.

SALES AND TRADING

Backed by one of Wall Street's largest capital bases and securities inventories, Salomon Smith Barney formulates and executes strategies across every major asset category in every major market around the world. The firm provides liquidity 24 hours a day, effectively manages risk and serves clients in a consistently creative fashion.

Equity

Salomon Smith Barney buys and sells equity and equity derivative securities on most of the world's listed exchanges and in the over-the-counter dealer markets. The firm is a dominant trader of NYSE, OTC and listed stocks, handling on a typical day approximately 7–10% of transactions on the NYSE and 10–15% on the Nasdaq.

Our institutional equity sales force maintains a long-standing dialogue with thousands of institutional investors across the globe. Nearly 10,300 financial consultants in more than 430 offices throughout the US provide advice on more than five million customer accounts.

Salomon Smith Barney has used cutting-edge technology to deliver research and global transaction capabilities to our equity trading and brokerage clients. The firm continually works to find new ways to maximise flexibility, convenience and performance for equity trading and brokerage clients, which seamlessly deliver, on a single platform, every key ingredient of successful trading, investment and settlement. Salomon Smith Barney recognises and supports a multi-vendor, multi-broker concept to provide clients with flexibility, and is committed to evolving with our clients' needs.

Taxable fixed-income

Salomon Smith Barney is among the world's premier market-makers in taxable fixed-income securities. Superior securities analytics and a worldwide presence allows the firm to assess relative value across the credit and asset spectrums and to capture value for clients in a 24-hour global market-place. The firm's institutional fixed-income sales-force maintains long-standing relationships with thousands of accounts in the US, Canada, Europe and Asia. In addition, financial consultants serve over 29,000 retail accounts representing nearly US$64 billion in assets through the Fixed-Income High Net Worth Programme.

Salomon Smith Barney is a primary dealer in the US, Canada, the UK, Italy and Japan, and a powerful presence in other government markets such as France and Germany. The firm trades the world's highest volume of mortgage pass-through securities. Salomon Smith Barney is also a leading secondary market-maker in US investment grade and high-yield debt, US agency and non-agency securities, collateralised mortgage obligations and international securities in the Euro and global markets.

Through a unique financial communications tool called Salomon Smith Barney DIRECT, the firm offers customers two-way, real-time access to fixed-income salespeople, traders, researchers and strategists. Easily personalised to provide relevant information on demand, Salomon Smith Barney DIRECT allows customers to view up-to-the-minute information on offerings and trades, market commentary, pricing models, research and news headlines.

Tax-exempt securities

Salomon Smith Barney maintains the industry's largest network of regional sales and trading offices and consistently ranks among the leaders in distribution and trading of tax-exempt fixed-income securities. In 1997, Salomon Smith Barney was ranked number one in lead managed municipal bond offerings.

Derivatives

Salomon Smith Barney is a leader in assisting sovereigns, corporations, financial institutions and investors in using exchange-traded and over-the-counter derivatives to manage interest rate, currency and equity risk. The firm's global derivatives capability is driven by highly sophisticated quantitative portfolio analysis, superior market research, a large capital base and strong credit ratings for Salomon Smith Barney (A/A2) Travelers Group (AA-/Aa3) and the world's largest structured derivatives subsidiary, Salomon Swapco Inc (AAA/Aaa). Customers have a choice of legal entities and guarantees for over-the-counter derivatives.

Foreign exchange

The firm's global team of salespeople, traders, economists, and technology and support staff work together across time zones to provide a full range of products and comprehensive service to clients investing and hedging in the foreign exchange market. The firm offers confidentiality, 24-hour trading and client coverage, in-depth analysis, responsive solutions, competitive pricing and efficient execution in spot, forward and OTC options transactions in all major and emerging market currencies. Additional foreign exchange services include global margin trading and netting capabilities, an option valuation model allowing clients to perform options analytics, and a currency and option market database providing information to assist clients in creating trading strategies.

PRIVATE CLIENT GROUP

With its breadth of knowledge, wide range of products and services, and deep commitment to client satisfaction, the Private Client Group ranks as one of the world's most influential financial advisers. The PCG network services over five million accounts held by high net worth individuals and corporations. In fact, the PCG currently advises one out of every six affluent investors in the US.

The firm's Financial Management Account (FMA) system is the most comprehensive central asset account available today. It offers clients free Internet access, unlimited cheque writing, competitive money market fund rates, dividend reinvestment and automatic daily reinvestment of cash.

The PCG has a full range of retirement planning services including traditional IRAs, Roth IRAs, SIMPLE IRAs and Simplified Employee Pensions (SEPs). Since 1993, we have reigned as the number one distributor of annuities sold through full-service brokerage firms. The TRAK programme, a leader in the mutual fund wrap-fee market, now has assets of over US$10 billion.

The Consulting Group services more than 200,000 accounts for individuals, institutions and retirement plans. The Group offers unambiguous opinions on 700 investment managers and nearly 2,200 investment options daily, providing clients with sophisticated, ongoing monitoring services.

The Estate & Trust Services group helps clients preserve and protect their wealth with an array of planning analyses and insurance, trust and gifting strategies. Using state-of-the-art resources, estate planning teams develop a customised Estate Tax Analysis enabling clients to identify potential estate planning concerns and a wide range of planning strategies.

The Corporate Client Group is a fast-growing group that works with businesses to develop creative benefit services. The Corporate Retirement Group works with businesses to develop innovative defined benefit and defined contribution retirement plan products, custodying more than US$35 billion in qualified plan assets and managing more than 4,000 proprietary 401(k) or other defined contribution plans. The group has emerged as a leader in stock plan services. The Executive Financial Services Group builds relationships with high net worth executives who own large blocks of control and restricted stock.

With over US$7 billion in international client assets, the International Private Client Group provides all of the investment products and services to meet the needs of high net worth clients from around the globe. Products include global equities, fixed-income and structured products, offshore mutual funds, offshore TRAK, offshore unit investment trusts and offshore managed futures.

ASSET MANAGEMENT

Smith Barney Asset Management

As of December 1997, Smith Barney Asset Management Division had assets under fee-based management totalling US$224 billion, of which US$164 billion was managed by Smith Barney. Smith Barney provides clients with a large number of asset management offerings, including mutual funds, private portfolio management to clients who meet certain criteria, and fiduciary services, offered on a wrap-fee basis and covering over 20 investment styles.

In 1997, Smith Barney introduced the Structured Portfolio Group to meet the growing demand for quantitative investment strategies, investment themes and market sector opportunities that emphasise a structured approach to investing. The Strategic Portfolio's Service, for clients with minimum investments of US$50,000 or more, individually manages that client's account. Unit Investment Trusts is a unique capability bolstered by a strong tie with the firm's research division.

Smith Barney manages nearly US$36 billion in assets for US and non-US based institutional clients, offering a variety of styles and capitalisation levels in fixed-income and equity products. Smith Barney also offers a number of non-traditional investment vehicles including hedge funds, private equity funds, exchange funds and real estate funds.

In terms of assets under management, Smith Barney Mutual Funds ranks in the top 10 in the US, with more than US$98 billion under management and more than 3.3 million accounts. Its asset management capabilities range from money market funds to high-yield fixed-income and aggressive growth equities. Among Smith Barney's Mutual Funds portfolio managers is Joseph P. Deane, Morningstar's 1996 Fixed-Income Portfolio Manager of the Year.

Salomon Brothers Asset Management

Salomon Brothers Asset Management is an investment management organisation comprised of several wholly owned subsidiaries in New York, London, Frankfurt and Hong Kong. Salomon manages over US$25 billion for a variety of clients, including pension funds, banks, investment companies, insurance companies, foundations, endowments, governments and individuals. Salomon portfolios cover an array of financial disciplines from US and international equity to fixed-income, convertible securities, municipal bonds, emerging market debt and global advisory.

Salomon's design and implementation of its investment philosophy begins with the Investment Policy Committee, which meets monthly to discuss broad economic and financial trends. Within each asset class or market sector, portfolios are managed according to appropriate investment guidelines. From its inception, Salomon's goal has been superior, risk-adjusted performance over the long term. Salomon delivers such performance through a team approach that brings together experienced portfolio managers and senior analysts with investment perspective, sophisticated risk management practices, a strong commitment to research, a carefully developed investment strategy and a commitment to service that helps build close client relationships.

Though it is a relatively young group, Salomon Brothers Asset Management has been highly ranked. Salomon was ranked as number one in overall marketing and operational support and number two in general opinion ratings in the Dalbar Mutual Funds Broker/Dealers Survey. In 1997, Salomon was named Defined Benefit Manager of the Year by *Plan Sponsor* magazine. Peter Wilby's Emerging Markets Income Fund was named the "best diversified international fund of 1996", and Rick White's Salomon Brothers Investor's Fund has a five-star rating from Morningstar.

The Robinson-Humphrey Company LLC

A wholly owned subsidiary of Smith Barney, 104-year-old Atlanta-based Robinson-Humphrey maintains a distinctive identity as the foremost research, investment banking and brokerage firm in the south-east. The firm is internationally recognised for equity research and market-making, and is a leading presence is middle-market mergers and acquisitions. Robinson-Humphrey is one of the oldest and most respected regionally based brokerage firms in the US, with an exceptionally loyal and satisfied client base.

Overview

The world markets as represented by the Salomon Smith Barney World Equity Index continued to demonstrate healthy total returns in1997, with the Broad Market Index (BMI) World advancing by 17.10% in US dollar terms. The large-cap Primary Market Index (PMI) gained 19.17%, while the small-cap Extended Market Index (EMI), however, gained only 8.40% in the face of Asian economic and financial turmoil. Total world capitalisation, measured in US dollars, rose 14.62%, from US$16,443 billion to US$18,847 billion. The US market, while posting a BMI US total return of 31.12% during 1997, led the field in total market capitalisation growth – from US$7,476 billion at the end of 1996 to US$9,889 billion at the close of 1997 – as small investors defied the predictions of some experts and continued to direct significant investment dollars into the equity markets in the aftermath of the still unresolved Asia crisis.

Conversely, the BMI Japan declined by 28.36% in US dollar terms during 1997, as government plans to instigate economic resurgence continue to languish. Total Japanese market capitalisation, as represented by the BMI Japan, declined by 27.25% – from US$3,068 billion to US$2,232 billion. The BMI Asia Ex Japan registered a total return decline of 28.20% for the year. The BMI Europe advanced by 23.76% in US dollar terms. Meanwhile, the Europe BMI total market capitalisation expanded to US$5,444 billion from US$4,407 billion.

SALOMON SMITH BARNEY WORLD EQUITY INDEX (SSBWEI) TOTAL RETURNS, 1990–97

	No. of	*US$ bn total*	*US$ bn avail.*	*BMI total returns (%) in US$ terms*							
Country	*cos.*	*MCAP 1997*	*MCAP 1997*	*1990*	*1991*	*1992*	*1993*	*1994*	*1995*	*1996*	*1997*
North America	3,459	10,365	8,429	-3.88	33.99	7.90	10.49	0.48	36.03	23.65	30.09
Canada	319	475	339	-14.15	11.16	-10.80	26.51	-5.38	17.89	27.71	9.44
US	3,140	9,890	8,090	-3.29	35.22	8.73	9.89	0.76	36.95	23.46	31.12
Asia-Pacific	2,185	3,038	1,681	-34.31	10.77	-19.98	33.56	14.17	1.55	-8.51	-28.32
Australia	195	275	203	-16.47	34.15	-12.02	39.17	4.48	14.79	23.03	-5.19
Hong Kong	190	333	185	7.67	51.47	32.72	119.06	-30.95	25.47	38.70	-19.51
Japan	1,397	2,232	1,212	-35.80	8.57	-23.13	24.44	21.50	-1.08	-17.01	-19.75
Malaysia	287	82	36	-9.53	5.70	24.51	127.57	-17.39	1.29	24.68	-73.27
New Zealand	25	25	14	-35.20	13.63	-3.11	67.43	8.36	19.44	24.29	-13.84
Singapore	91	92	31	-10.74	40.87	3.23	78.87	2.18	11.80	2.70	-45.99
Europe	1,654	5,444	4,126	-0.84	12.83	-4.01	29.02	2.65	22.53	23.32	23.76
Austria	32	32	15	9.39	-17.93	-18.46	40.83	-3.68	-2.55	4.05	0.35
Belgium	40	121	65	-7.39	13.28	-1.77	26.67	9.73	27.70	16.51	17.67
Denmark	56	80	52	-0.91	13.75	-27.44	35.34	4.63	20.21	24.55	30.81
Finland	42	67	51	-24.21	-20.57	-14.54	80.36	51.24	4.09	39.64	17.60
France	190	634	390	-13.05	15.62	2.17	25.34	-4.74	12.72	21.88	15.34
Germany	163	781	477	-6.70	5.08	-9.05	36.61	4.53	15.03	18.54	21.83
Ireland	33	44	36	-19.12	19.98	-16.29	39.83	9.69	31.52	31.43	32.63
Italy	84	322	192	-14.00	-0.04	-27.43	26.36	12.03	-2.16	11.99	37.73
Netherlands	96	454	364	-2.27	16.92	1.55	35.52	11.39	29.24	29.70	22.98
Norway	59	56	35	-5.79	-9.16	-22.53	31.56	21.87	13.15	32.11	14.69
Spain	65	206	131	-9.78	14.73	-23.56	26.62	-3.17	31.01	38.60	29.99
Sweden	93	244	177	-17.15	14.52	-7.96	32.34	18.77	33.96	39.00	12.29
Switzerland	104	533	467	-4.21	11.27	11.82	43.59	3.83	42.67	3.02	44.02
UK	597	1,870	1,674	9.29	15.94	-2.06	23.81	-0.01	23.13	28.10	21.48
World	7,298	18,847	14,236	-15.07	21.19	-2.98	20.26	4.77	22.42	15.67	17.10

Source: Salomon Smith Barney.

International equity indices

Globally, stock market investors are faced with a plethora of equity market indices. Despite their importance in influencing cross-border investment flows and compensation, their construction methodologies vary. They are price-weighted, cap-weighted, fixed-share weighted, or float-weighted. Some indices include only blue chips, others are cross-sections of the market, while others are comprehensive. Yet, all are used in much the same fashion – for asset allocation, universe definition, risk analysis, performance measurement, indexing, backtesting, derivatives and portfolio trading.

The primary purpose of a financial market index is to measure the return of the market-place as accurately and fairly as possible. Calculation of correlation and other statistical measurements are secondary concerns. Accuracy of return is achieved best by index membership and weighting rules that are simple, clear and concise. These rules should be known in advance and apply equally to all members of the universe. The index should be a meritocracy whereby all companies meeting the index criteria are included, and those that do not are excluded.

The opening of markets to cross-border investors, share class consolidations, and other structural shifts in the market-place should be reflected in the index as they occur. The index should not misrepresent the structure of the market-place. There are numerous examples of major indices weighting stocks and entire countries without regard to their actual investable wealth.

In sum, the index is a "scorekeeper" not a "gatekeeper". While an active selection process may be desirable for the creation of a portfolio, it does not suit the goals and uses of an index.

THE CASE FOR INDEXING

Indexing is based on an elegantly simple argument. If the index fund holds what the aggregate managers hold and in the same proportions, then the index fund's performance will equal that of the average active manager minus costs. Thus, index funds will outperform the average active manager over time. The index fund holds a little bit of every stock, has low management fees, little idle cash and only trades when necessary. Because typical active management fees and trading costs run at about 2–3% annually, over time the odds are against the active manager. Over a 10-year period, the typical active manager has to outperform the index by 20–30% just to cover fees. In addition, most index funds keep cash levels below 1% compared to 5–10% for the typical active manager. High cash levels can mean significant outperformance in bear markets but cause "cash drag" in rising markets. Because markets generally tend to rise over time (why else invest?), on balance "cash drag" tends to hurt active managers.

To work its "magic", the case for indexing requires two conditions. The index underlying the fund must be *comprehensive* and *proportionate*. Indexing only works for certain if the index fund holds a little bit of *every* stock in *proportion* to the amount held by active managers. If one or both of these conditions is missing, then the premise of indexing is undermined and one cannot be sure that the indexing strategy will work. In this case, indexing reduces to a low overhead, low-cost trading strategy that may not outperform the average active manager. The "index fund" becomes an active portfolio with a low-cost structure.

EVALUATING INDICES

Not all indices are created equal. In order to make good decisions regarding their use and application, we provide a framework in which to evaluate the merits of the different types of indices. We delineate desirable attributes of indices and identify those that are flawed.

If the index is to measure the scope and return of the "market", then we must determine what comprises the market and from whose perspective. Does the market include all listed securities in their market capitalisation weightings? For most institutional investors, the market reasonably represents only what a cross-border investor can realistically own. If you can't buy it or own it, you shouldn't be benchmarked to it. With these thoughts in mind, we propose in Exhibit 1 a set of characteristics by which to judge indices.

Exhibit 1:
DESIRABLE AND UNDESIRABLE CHARACTERISTICS OF INDICES

Desirable	*Undesirable*
Objective	Arbitrary
Exact	Estimate
Simple rules	Complex and/or secret rules
Membership earned	Membership given
Complete coverage	Sample
Robust in all dimensions	Robust in some dimensions
Float-weighted	Total-cap weighted
Market determines the index	Committee determines the index

Objective vs arbitrary

The ultimate aim of an index is to measure the return of the market-place. The index should reflect reality – the investable market-place as it truly exists – not one party's unique perspective. If there are 50 highly correlated regional banking stocks in the south-east of the US and one could safely overweight some and exclude others in an index tracking portfolio, then that is fine for constructing a portfolio; however, to accurately measure the return of this part of the universe, all 50 should still be represented in the index, because, invariably, their returns will differ. The index should measure the market and not second-guess and attempt to reshape it.

Exact vs estimate

Once again, the primary purpose of the index is to measure the return of the market-place as accurately as possible. A high level of correlation between the true universe and a sampled index does not ensure that the returns will be similar or even close. When all the dust settles, investors can only spend the return (and principal of course) on their portfolios, they can't spend high correlation. It's no consolation to know that your portfolio's correlation with its benchmark is 0.99 if it underperformed by 500 basis points.

Just as no one would base an incentive fee arrangement on a coin flip, having an index that does not exactly measure the manager's universe introduces an arbitrary element into the performance measurement and manager compensation process.

Ultimately, the primary objective of the index is to measure the return of the target universe and its relevant sub-indices accurately. Merely creating an index with similar summary statistics is not enough. The only way to measure the exact return of the universe is to include all investable companies. This is especially true for sub-categories such as industry indices.

Simple vs complex rules

Index rules for membership and weighting should be simple, clear and concise. The rules should be known in advance to all interested parties and should be applied equally to all members of the universe. There should not be special rules for special groups of shares. Given the rules, it should be possible to accurately predict in advance the stocks going into and out of the index. If the index rules are too secret or complex, then the index is likely to be flawed. The definition of the investable market contains few qualifications and so too should the index.

EXHIBIT 2: SALOMON SMITH BARNEY WORLD EQUITY INDEX VS MSCI WORLD EQUITY INDEX; RATE OF RETURN IN US DOLLARS, 30 JUNE 1989 TO 31 DECEMBER 1997

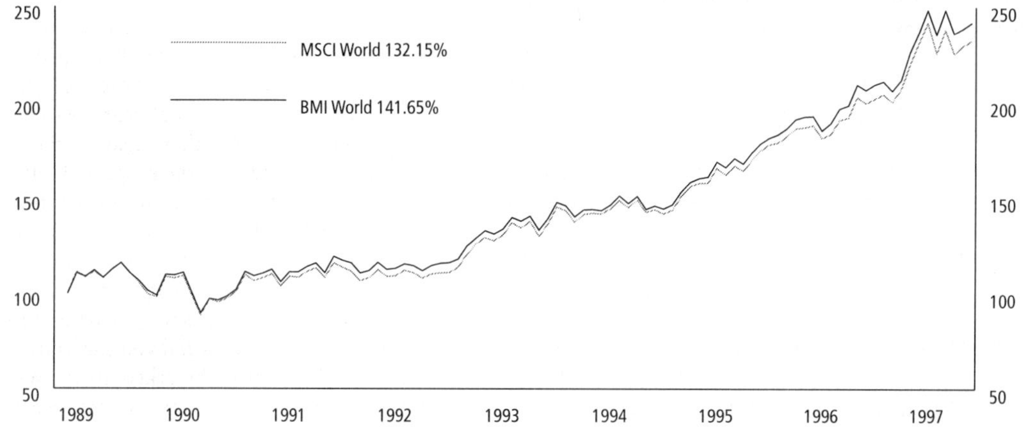

Source: Salomon Smith Barney.

Membership earned vs given

Only the attributes of each company should determine its membership of the index. In essence, the index should be a meritocracy whereby all companies meeting the criteria are included, and those that don't are excluded. Membership of the index should not be handed out based on corporate or personal relationships. The index should follow a *laissez-faire* membership philosophy. Ultimately, the index is a scorekeeper, not a gatekeeper.

Comprehensive vs sampled coverage

To portray a market accurately, a properly constructed index should completely cover its intended universe. The indices should measure the universe as exactly as possible, have complete coverage for the given size companies and allow for robust sub-indices – growth/value, industry, sector, etc.

Sampling techniques are appropriate for constructing indexed portfolios, but not for defining and measuring the scope, size and performance of the universe itself. A by-product of sampling is tracking error – the mismatch between the performance of the target universe and that of the sample. A manager attempting to track a sampled index with a sampled portfolio is often only compounding the portfolio's true tracking error relative to the intended target universe. In effect, that manager is taking a sample of a sample. To ensure correct representation and a valid sample, the sample should be taken from the full universe – a technique that will lead to a better understanding of the sample's inherent biases.

Robust in all vs some dimensions

To meet the needs of an increasingly complex investment management process, the benchmark index must be robust in all dimensions. Among large pension plans, equity management is increasingly handled by specialty managers. Whereas, 15 years ago, a large pension fund may have had 2 categories of equities – domestic and foreign – now there are multiple categories, such as US large-cap, Japanese small-cap, European property, global telecoms, global gold, etc. Ideally, the overall benchmark can be segmented to provide an appropriate benchmark for each market sector. Each sub-sector of the benchmark should possess the same desirable attributes as the overall benchmark.

Float vs total-capitalisation weighted

Float-weighted indices are becoming increasingly important, particularly in manager performance evaluations and asset allocation, due to the drawbacks of total-capitalisation weighted indices (for non-US benchmarks in particular). In theory, float-weighting is superior to a total-capitalisation weighting because it only measures

EXHIBIT 3: SALOMON SMITH BARNEY WORLD BROAD MARKET INDEX (BMI) FLOAT AS A PERCENTAGE OF TOTAL CAPITALISATION, 31 DECEMBER 1997

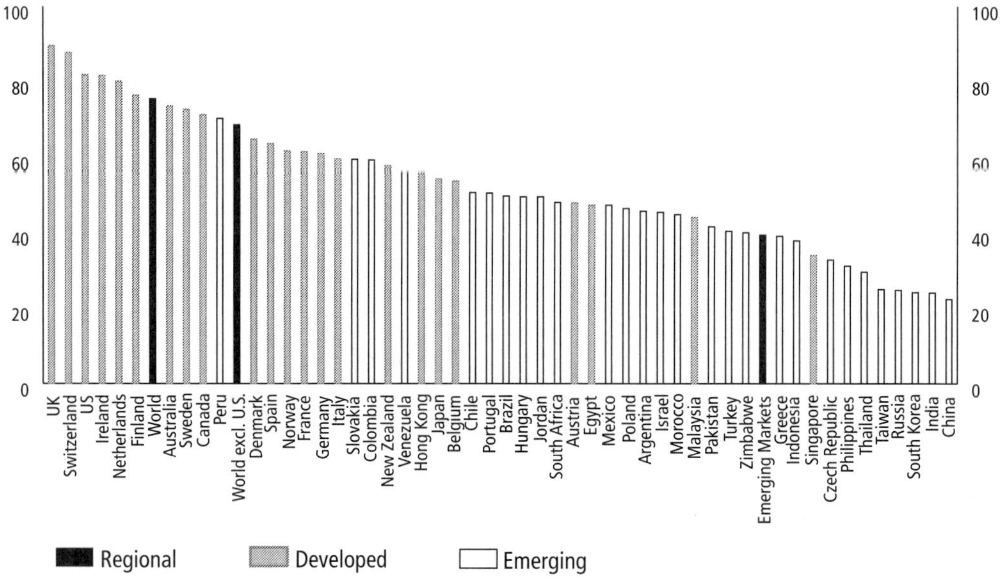

Source: Salomon Smith Barney.

the "investable" portion of each stock. When weighting any company, compilers of total-cap weighted indices have two unappealing alternatives – either a 0% weighting or a 100% total-cap weighting. This is the case whether the true float is 10%, 25%, 50%, 75%, 90% or any number in between. For most companies outside the US and the UK the 0%/100% solution is very likely wrong. Thus, with total-capitalisation weighted indices, companies are either grossly overweighted or terribly underweighted. There is no middle ground.

Compilers of float-weighted indices include companies at their estimated free float weightings. The unpleasant dilemma of what to do about large companies with small float (such as Deutsche Telekom) – they're too big to ignore but including them at their total-cap weighting grossly distorts the index – does not happen with a float-weighted index. These companies are simply included at their relative float-weighting. Even without perfect accuracy, a float-weighted index comes far closer to reality and produces a more accurate benchmark than a total-cap weighted index.

Market determined vs committee determined

To truly serve as a benchmark rather than an indicator, the market must be the final judge determining index membership. An index membership committee that second-guesses the market-place has no role in the construction of financial market benchmarks. Companies gain and lose their value because the market wills it. In an increasingly complex world, winners and losers should not be arbitrarily hand-picked by committee. The market is an evolving phenomenon. Attempts to "stabilise" indices relative to the dynamic nature of the market ultimately prove counter-productive.

THE SALOMON SMITH BARNEY WORLD EQUITY INDICES

With these thoughts in mind, we created the Salomon Smith Barney World Equity Indices (SSBWEI). The SSB-

EXHIBIT 4: SALOMON SMITH BARNEY WORLD EXCLUDING US LARGE-CAP (PMI) VS SMALL-CAP (EMI) INDICES; TOTAL RATE OF RETURN IN US DOLLARS 30 JUNE 1989 TO 31 DECEMBER 1997

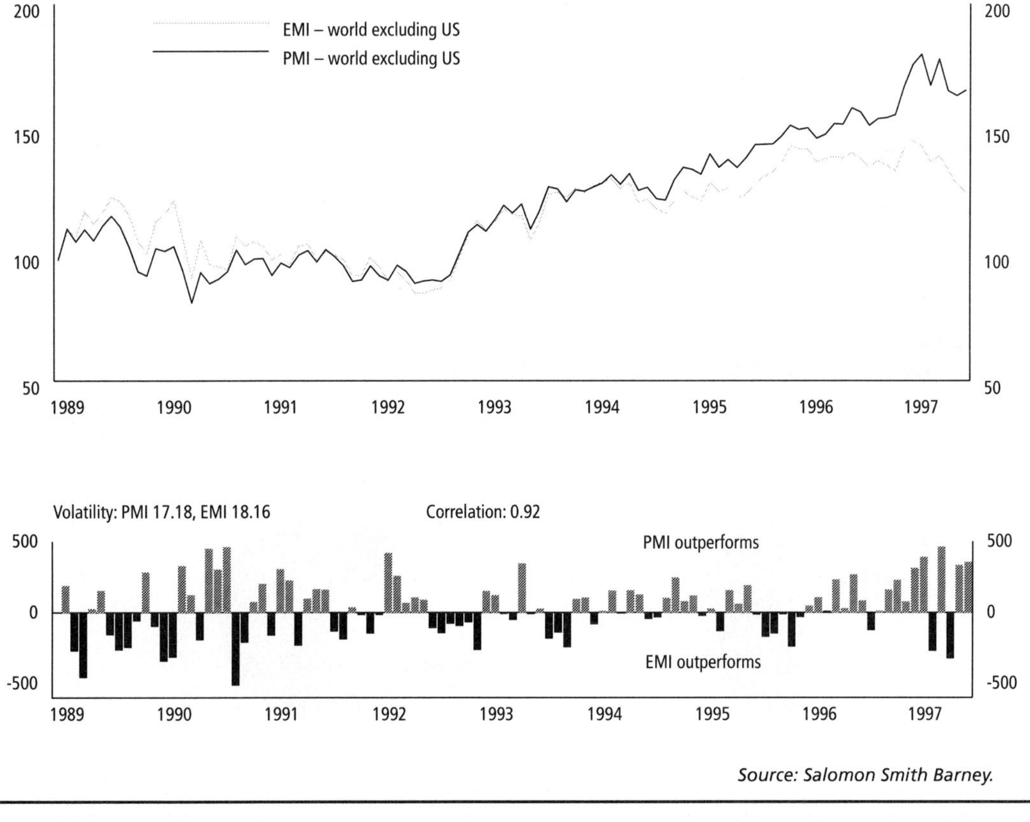

Source: Salomon Smith Barney.

WEI are a series of indices covering all levels of market capitalisation with consistent rules spanning 49 countries across the globe. The SSBWEI are designed to measure the institutional investable equity universe without the biases inherent in stock selection; the indices represent a meritocracy. The final product is the most comprehensive, consistent and accurate global index family for all types of investors. As a result, the SSBWEI are the fastest growing family of global equity indices.

The SSBWEI flagship index is the Broad Market Index (BMI). The BMI includes all companies with an available market capitalisation (float) of at least US$100 million. The index is reconstituted annually, each 30 June, to keep current with the market-place. On 31 December 1997, the SSBWEI included the shares of about 8,300 companies accounting for approximately US$20 trillion in total market capitalisation and US$15 trillion in float.

The SSBWEI is a top-down index that captures the entire global institutional equity universe. As a result, all segments of the world equity market-place, including all industry and economic sectors and capitalisation ranges, are fully represented in their market-place proportions. The SSBWEI approach eliminates unintended biases and distortions caused by stock selection.

We have two sets of size indices – relative size indices as exemplified by the large-cap Primary Market Index (PMI) and the small-cap Extended Market Index (EMI), and absolute size indices known as the "Cap-Range" Indices (all of which are described below).

Relative size indices: PMI/EMI

To create our relative size indices, the BMI is segmented into two mutually exclusive components by country – the Primary Market Index (PMI) and the Extended Market Index (EMI). The PMI contains roughly 1,900 companies, approximately 20% of the total number of issues, and defines the large-capitalisation stock universe. The PMI represents the top 80% of float of the BMI in each country. The EMI defines the small-capitalisation stock universe, the bottom 20% of the float of each country, and includes the remaining 80% of BMI issues (almost 6,400 companies). The split is based on float capital.

Companies are ranked by total capital rather than available capital, because absolute size, not float, is the characteristic we wish to identify. This process ensures that only large-capitalisation companies are included in the PMI and small-capitalisation companies are included in the EMI, regardless of float.

As Exhibit 4 illustrates, over time, despite relatively high statistical correlation, the returns of large and small-cap companies can differ dramatically.

Absolute size indices: Cap-Range Indices

Where the PMI/EMI divides the BMI into large and small-cap indices by country, our "Cap-Range Indices" divide the BMI universe by absolute company size. Because the BMI includes all companies with a float of at least US$100 million, we can create an index family for virtually any capitalisation size range, complete with its own country and industry weightings and returns. For example, our Under US$1 Billion North American Index will include all US and Canadian companies with a total capitalisation of US$1 billion or less. Determination of membership for each index is made annually at reconstitution based on each company's US dollar total market capitalisation.

Within these "Cap-Range Indices', the country weightings of the different capitalisation slices can vary

EXHIBIT 5: TOTAL VS FLOAT WEIGHTINGS: BROAD MARKET INDEX (BMI) GLOBAL REGION ALLOCATIONS 31 DECEMBER 1997

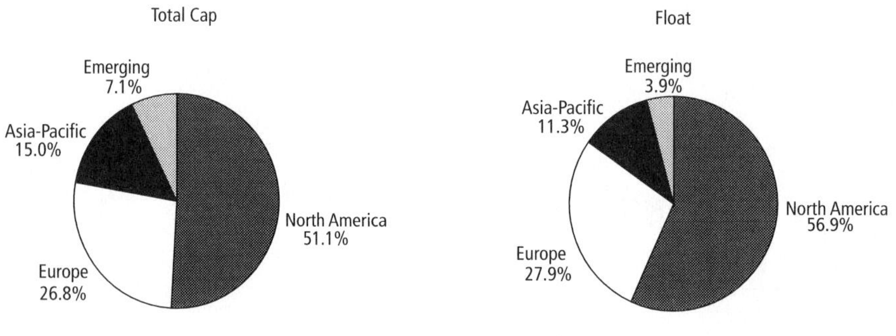

Source: Salomon Smith Barney.

dramatically. For example, in the BMI Under US$1 Billion World Ex US Index, the weighting of the Asia-Pacific region is 31% while it is only 25% of the EMI World Ex US Index. These indices generally appeal to small-cap money managers with specific company size mandates.

Salomon Smith Barney float measurement methodology

Outlined below is a brief description of the Salomon Smith Barney float-weighting methodology and several questions and answers concerning float weighting.

All issues in the SSBWEI are assigned an availability factor. This factor is a measurement of its float (available capital) as a percentage of total capitalisation. When applied to the total capitalisation of an issue, the availability factor is the determinant of each issue's weighting in the Broad Market Index (BMI). The availability factor is 100% minus the net sum of the following four factors: corporate cross-holdings; 10% or greater controlling blocks; government holdings; and legally restricted shares.

Some factors may override others. For example, an overriding foreign ownership percentage limitation may pre-empt an adjustment for a large private holder. What follows are specific examples of how, in practice, each of the four factors are implemented. Adjusting for float has a significant impact on relative country and region weightings as shown in Exhibit 5.

Corporate cross-holdings

The exclusion of corporate cross-holdings eliminates double counting of capitalisation. Corporate cross-holdings are all identifiable stakes of any size (in practice only holdings greater than 0.5% of shares outstanding are generally identified) held in an index company by any other company in the index.

Private control blocks

All verifiable private control block capital that equals or exceeds 10% of an issue's total shares outstanding is removed from the capital of the index. Private control blocks are entities (individual, corporate, family or trust) acting alone or in concert to form a block of holdings.

Government holdings

All identifiable domestic government (or government institution) held shares of each company are deducted. Generally, an official act of government is required to float government held shares.

Legally restricted shares

Companies may be limited by charter or government decree as to the aggregate amount of total shares outstanding that foreign investors can own. These companies generally are involved in industries of strategic national interest such as defence and communications. In some countries, such as Singapore and Malaysia, companies have designated dual classes of shares – free vs restricted or alien versus local – explicitly to segregate free from restricted capital. The "local" designation of shares prohibits non-domiciled ownership. Because these shares are unavailable to foreign investors, they are assigned a 0% availability factor and have no weight in the index but are included to "size" each company correctly. Often, a company may not segregate legally restricted capital into separate classes. In such cases, the restricted percentage is simply deducted from the total capitalisation as represented in the single share class.

Thomas Nadbielny, CFA
Salomon Smith Barney
World Equity Index

The impact of monetary policies on world markets

A key theme for 1998 is the potential impact of slowing emerging economies on the industrial world. The series of market shocks that originated in the summer of 1997 in Asia have reverberated around the globe, triggering declines in equity prices and benchmark bond yields. The developments in emerging economies transmit a disinflationary impulse to the industrial world through global trade and financial links: they dampen net demand and impose downward pressure on dollar prices of traded goods, while muting the profit outlook for industrial country banks and non-financial corporations with direct local exposure.

In addition, heightened risk aversion probably is driving the global financial market link, against a background of high equity valuations in the US and Europe. This second mechanism also can have real effects: the further equity prices plunge, the greater the risk of private sector retrenchment, both because of tighter financing conditions and reduced household wealth.

Against this background, investors face a series of critical questions about industrial country economies and policies in 1998. Will the shocks in emerging economies affect the industrial economies differently? In particular, is the US Goldilocks expansion seriously threatened, or will the "new age" persist? How large is the risk of deflation in Japan and how would policymakers respond? And in Europe, is the ongoing cyclical improvement at risk – as it proved to be in the 1994 mini-boom – or is there hope for a spread of the "new age" phenomenon?

OUTLOOK SUMMARY

The impact of 1997's shocks in emerging economies will be disproportionately large on Japan, where recession and deflation remain a risk. Thus, despite record low yen government bond yields, a substantial market setback appears doubtful in 1998, while a further sharp rally is possible.

At the same time, fears that the emerging market shocks and subsequent equity market declines will seriously blunt the US or European expansions are exaggerated (see Exhibit 1). In the United States, barring a new equity plunge, the external headwinds will mute and delay price pressures, thus extending the life of the "new age" expansion. In effect, 1998 will represent another "soft landing", in which economic growth will average close to trend – slower in the first half and a gradual pick-up in the second – with inflation held to cyclical lows.

As a result, US long-term inflation expectations, which currently exceed actual inflation, will continue their secular decline (see Exhibit 2). The trading range for the long-term Treasury yield in 1998 will fall to about 5.5–6.5%, down from the 6–7% range that has prevailed for the past two years. Moreover, within a few years, a

Exhibit 1:
EMU-11, JAPAN AND THE UNITED STATES – KEY MACROECONOMIC PROJECTIONS, 1997 AND 1998F

	Growth %		*Inflation %*		*Current account %*		*Budget deficit %*		*Output gap %*	
	1997	*1998F*	*1997*	*1998F*	*1997*	*1998F*	*1997*	*1998F*	*1997*	*1998F*
EMU-11	2.4	2.7	1.7	1.7	0.9	0.9	3.7	3.6	-1.7	-1.3
Japan	0.9	0.0	1.7	0.2	2.3	3.2	4.0	4.9	-3.6	-4.6
US	3.8	2.8	2.3	1.4	-2.0	-2.5	0.3	-0.5	1.0	1.0

Note: In this section, EMU-11 includes Austria, Belgium, Finland, France, Germany, Ireland, Italy, Luxembourg, Netherlands, Portugal, and Spain. The figures for current account, budget deficit and output gap are as a percentage of GDP.

Source: Smith Barney Inc/Salomon Brothers Inc.

Exhibit 2: COMPOSITE OF SURVEY MEASURES OF US LONG-TERM INFLATION EXPECTATIONS, 1979–97 (%)

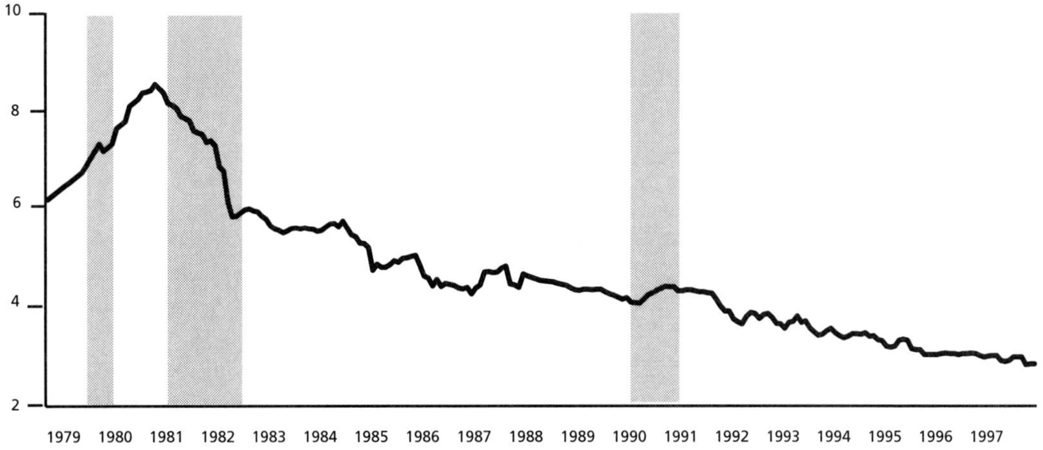

Note: shaded areas represent economic downturns

Sources: Smith Barney Inc/Salomon Brothers Inc, Richard Hoey, Federal Reserve Bank of Philadelphia and University of Michigan.

larger drop to the 5–6% range appears likely, once the Fed has capped inflation risks in the current cycle. This larger drop could occur in 1998 if a continued rise in risk aversion – or risk acknowledgement – prompts a new plunge in global equity markets.

The EMU bloc probably will experience a slight upturn this year that will carry economic growth up to, and possibly above, the pace in the United States. The Asian downturn should undercut export strength from the region, but accommodative monetary conditions and reduced fiscal restraint should buoy both consumption and investment. The persistence of economic slack will keep inflation low for several years. In the near term, EMU bloc bonds probably will perform similarly to Treasuries. Despite Europe's notoriously inflexible labour markets, the presence of some "new age" characteristics in Europe should limit the risks of underperformance as EMU approaches.

The shocks from emerging economies also will moderate the path of interest rates in the industrial economies in 1998. Chances of lower overnight rates in Japan are significant. Despite the tight US labour market, Federal Reserve policy probably will remain on hold as the risks surrounding inflation have become more balanced with the collapse in commodity prices and the spillover from slower Asian demand. Similarly, in Europe, core country rates will remain at the current German level of 3.3%. Considered as a whole, the European zone monetary stance will ease as countries like Italy cut rates sharply in the run-up to EMU.

The yen probably will be the weakest of the major currencies. It could fall substantially versus the dollar if Japan's shift away from massive fiscal restraint in 1997 gives way, as expected, only to modest stimulus in fiscal 1998. By contrast, the US dollar and the Deutschmark now appear to be in a trading range that will persist in 1998. The U-shaped path of US growth in 1998 points to a softer dollar in the short term, and a solid rebound in the second half of the year. Prospective 1998 stability in the short-term interest differential between the US and Germany is at odds with the narrowing that is discounted in forward interest rates.

In coming months, prospects remain for substantial volatility in emerging bond and currency markets that will keep investors cautious. Eventually, however, low yields on benchmark bonds should encourage investors to consider higher-risk assets, at least on a selective basis, in order to outperform over the course of 1998. With respect to local currency instruments, opportunities are likely to develop during 1998, particularly in south-east Asia, as domestic interest rates rise further to steady these currencies and economic policies are strengthened.

POSTPONING THE CYCLICAL CHALLENGE TO THE US NEW AGE

Improved US performance thus far in the 1990s reflects: (1) a technology-induced pick-up of productivity; (2) increased trade and competition; (3) improved government policies, including a prudent fiscal stance; (4) a less cyclical economic structure; and (5) heightened credibility of

Exhibit 3: US UNEMPLOYMENT RATE YEAR-TO-YEAR WAGE GAINS, 1994–97 (%)

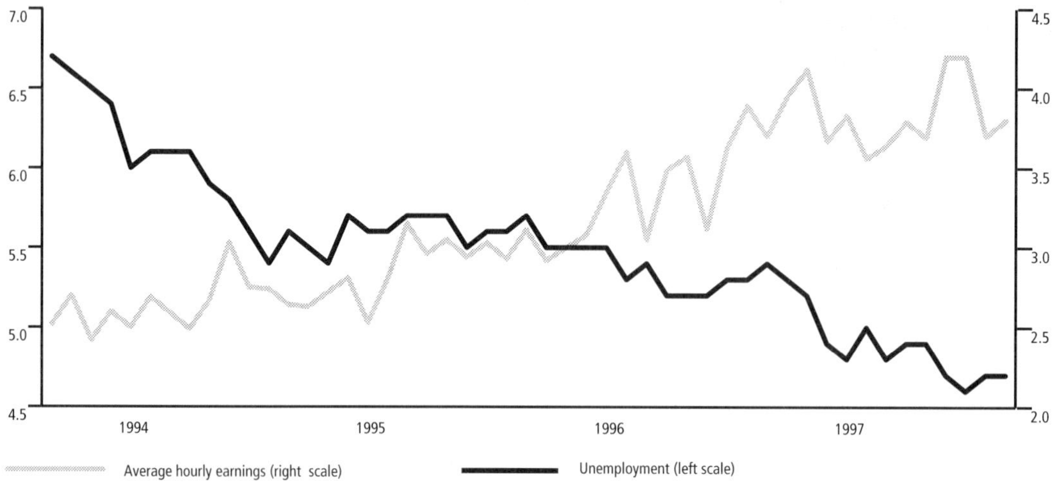

Source: Bureau of Labor Statistics.

monetary policy. If there were reason to expect these long-term sources of improved performance to deteriorate significantly in 1998, the consequences for US asset prices and the dollar would be very unpleasant.

However, that risk appears limited. Rapid investment over the past few years should continue to pay off in 1998 through cost savings. Despite prospective budget surpluses for the first time in more than a generation, it is doubtful that the Republican Congress and the Democratic President will agree on a significant acceleration of discretionary spending. Most important, the Fed remains vigilant about preserving the gains of low inflation. Perhaps the greatest risk would be a shift of the political balance in favour of protectionist forces as the US trade gap widens sharply this year. However, the US administration remains committed to an agenda of free trade and efforts to contain financial instability in emerging economies.

Moreover, US equity market performance thus far does not pose a hazard to the expansion. The S&P 500 is up by roughly 100% over the past three years, adding substantially to wealth. The historically low cost of equity capital remains stimulative. Finally, even large equity market declines have proven misleading in the past: the 30% peak-to-trough plunge in October 1987 was followed by an acceleration of both growth and inflation in 1988.

On balance, the eventual challenge to the United States' improved performance has been and remains the risk that high and rising resource utilisation will boost price pressures. That risk appears low in 1998, but it could revive once external shocks abate. Stimulative financial conditions have driven the US economy at a rapid pace for two years, and probably will trim the unemployment rate in coming months to the lowest level since 1970. Moreover, year-on-year wage gains have picked up to an expansion-high of 4.2%, from only 3.3% in 1996 and 2.9% in 1995 (see Exhibit 3). In addition, in contrast to the past six years, US policymakers cannot count on a large degree of economic slack in all other Group of Seven countries as a buffer against inflation.

In this context, the latest shocks from Asia and Latin America will slow US export demand and lower import prices, helping to contain inflation despite still solid 1998 economic growth. As recently as late 1997, the Fed had appeared poised to tighten again soon in response to strong demand, rising resource utilisation and faster wage gains. As the new external headwinds hit in coming quarters, the Fed will keep policy on hold, while the long bond yield probably will decline further in coming months.

A revival of US growth as 1998 winds down probably will boost long-term yields somewhat above their interim lows. However, with inflation stuck below survey measures of long-term expectations, a further modest decline in these expectations in 1998 should lower the "fair yield" for US bonds, countering cyclical pressures. Improved fiscal performance also will depress the sustainable trading range for the long yield, as net issuance of marketable Treasuries will virtually disappear. If, on top of these developments, investors fear a substantial decline in the US equity market, Treasuries would benefit further.

Exhibit 4:
JAPANESE AND US PRODUCTIVITY GROWTH, BUDGET DEFICITS AS A SHARE OF GDP, AND UNEMPLOYMENT RATES, 1983–97 (PERIOD AVERAGES)

	Productivity growth %				*Budget deficit %*				*Unemployment rate %*			
	1983–87	*1988–92*	*1993–97*	*1997*	*1983–87*	*1988–92*	*1993–97*	*1997*	*1983–87*	*1988–92*	*1993–97*	*1997*
Japan	2.6	2.4	0.9	-0.4	1.4	-2.3	3.2	3.8	2.7	2.2	3.0	3.2
US	1.6	1.0	1.1	1.8	3.3	2.8	2.1	0.4	7.5	6.1	5.8	4.9

Note: Productivity growth is measured as the difference between the growth of real GDP and employment.

Source: OECD.

Exhibit 5:
EU, JAPANESE AND US REGIONAL EXPORT SHARES, 1996 (PERCENTAGE SHARE OF TOTAL)

	To industrial countries				*To developing countries*				
	EU	*US*	*Japan*	*Other*	*Asia*	*Latin America*	*CEEC*	*Other*	*Total*
EU	-	19	6	16	19	7	17	16	100
United States	20	-	11	25	19	18	1	6	100
Japan	15	28	-	4	44	4	1	4	100

CEEC: Central and Eastern European Countries (including former Soviet Union). Other industrial countries include Australia, Canada, Iceland, New Zealand, Norway and Switzerland.

Source: IMF (Direction of Trade Statistics).

EXTENDING JAPAN'S ANTI-NEW AGE

In the 1990s, Japan's productivity growth has slowed, budget deficits have widened, joblessness has risen on a trend basis, the equity market has plunged and the financial sector has weakened sharply – virtually the mirror image of the US "new age" (see Exhibit 4). Thus, Japanese inflation has disappeared largely because the economy has languished since the asset price bubble burst early in this decade.

The latest shocks from abroad appear likely to prolong Japan's "anti-new age" throughout 1998. More than 40% of Japanese exports are bound for Asia – double the US and European proportions – and this region is likely to slow more sharply than any other in 1998 (see Exhibit 5).

Against this background, the Japanese economy will stagnate in 1998. With inflation virtually eliminated, the Bank of Japan probably will focus on supplying liquidity to contain fragility in the financial system. Overnight rates are likely to inch lower, while the yen declines substantially.

Fiscal policymakers appear aimed at shifting to a more stimulative posture in fiscal 1998. With the approach of mid-year Upper House elections, the desire to boost the economy – and to provide support to the financial system – is evident. However, with fiscal consolidation still on the long-term agenda, the chances for a major stimulus appear limited.

MIGHT THE "NEW AGE" SPREAD TO EUROPE?

The suggestion of a "new age" in continental Europe may appear outlandish. The region's average unemployment rate remains close to its post-war high, despite nearly five years of economic recovery. Moreover, labour reforms in many continental European economies – including France and Germany – do not appear sufficient to arrest the trend rise in joblessness since the 1960s. Eventually, in EMU, a continued lack of labour market flexibility would pose critical limits to growth. In the absence of major reforms, Europe could hit this wall in the first few years of the new millennium, triggering the first real test of EMU and risking intense political conflict.

Nonetheless, Europe's achievements in the 1990s of lowering both inflation and fiscal deficits are formidable (see Exhibit 6), while the region's productivity has risen substantially compared with the US in recent decades (see Exhibit 7). In addition, structural changes for the better are in prospect: the advent of the euro and the deregulation of key sectors like telecommunications will trigger a period of intensified cross-border competition that should enhance disinflationary pressures in high-cost countries. The euro also will improve the efficiency of Europe's capital markets, helping to channel savings more effectively to their highest value use. Looking fur-

Exhibit 6: EU INFLATION AND FISCAL DEFICITS AS A SHARE OF GDP, 1970–98F (%)

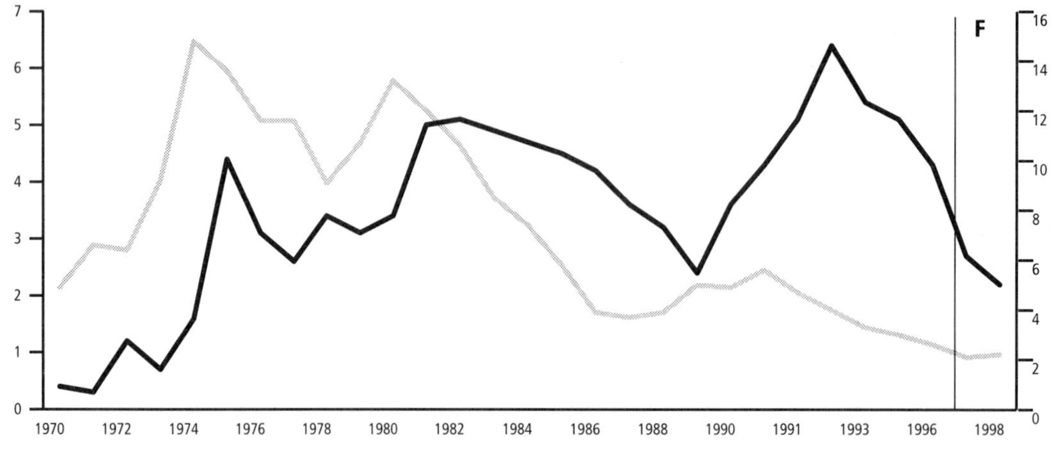

F: European Commission forecast

Source: European Commission.

Exhibit 7: EU AND US REAL GDP PER EMPLOYEE, 1970–97F(%)

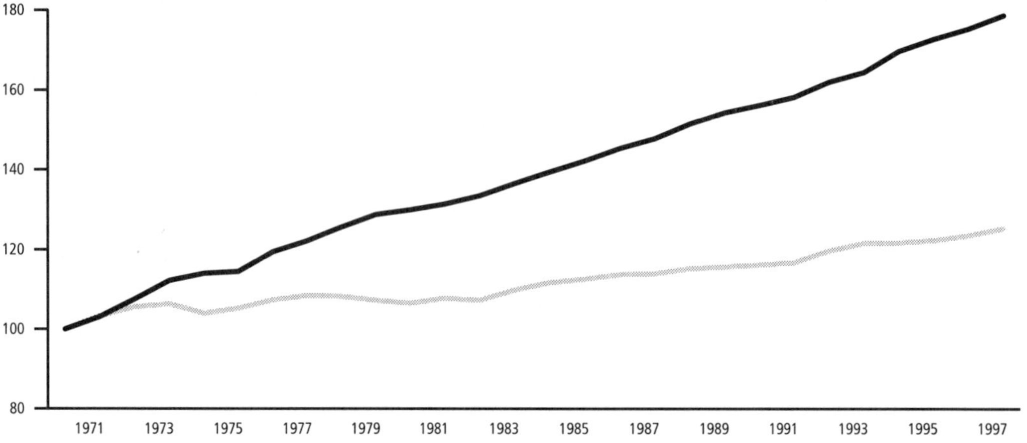

F: European Commission forecast

(1970 = 100)

Source: European Commission.

ther forward, closer integration of eastern European economies with the EU will enhance competition and help contain price pressures, particularly in agriculture and smokestack industries.

Moreover, the next few years are likely to be a period of improved cyclical performance in Europe, with economic growth at or above trend, inflation low and the unemployment rate gradually declining. Compared with Japan and the United States, the EU is somewhat less exposed to the combined shocks from Asia and Latin America because of its smaller trading links. Admittedly, however, EU bank lending exposure to emerging economies (as a share of GDP) exceeds that of US institutions. Moreover, the EU would be comparatively vulnerable to a shock among its eastern neighbours.

At least for some time, it may be difficult to distinguish these favourable cyclical developments from some of the "new age" characteristics widely cited in the United States. European productivity and investment should accelerate modestly as demand picks up. Over the next few years, above-trend economic growth will enhance corporate profitability and reduce budget deficits further, even as Maastricht-induced fiscal restraint fades. To the extent that information technology has accelerated US productivity, this pattern may be reproduceable in coming years in Europe, although it currently lags the US in the introduction of those technologies.

Above all, the European central bank (ECB) should be able to establish a degree of credibility for maintaining price stability without having to match the high real interest rates that were needed in the defence of many European currencies in the 1990s. Certainly, the early management of the euro will be a major challenge, reflecting uncertainty about the signal value of leading indicators – especially the monetary aggregates – and about the response of euro-zone economies to policy changes. Thus, real short-term interest rates after 1999 probably will be higher than might have prevailed in Germany under similar cyclical conditions. However, they should be substantially lower than the high rates that have prevailed thus far in the 1990s on average in the EMU-11, because the risk of intra-European currency crisis will be gone. Ultimately, the real test of ECB credibility will not surface until a meaningful inflation challenge arises, most likely several years after the introduction of the euro.

Kermit L. Schoenholtz
Salomon Smith Barney

Preparing your equity business for the euro

On 4 January 1999 European equity markets will open for business in a new era as a result of moving to euro quotation of shares following a "big bang" during the preceding weekend. This will offer great new opportunities for participants with a strategy, but the ill-prepared may not even open for business. In the remaining few weeks leading up to the deadline all participants must not only consider their own conversion plan but also confirm that their suppliers and customers are equally ready: the financial system is a chain that is only as strong as the proverbial "weakest link".

This event is significant for global equity investors because it is a major step towards the creation of an integrated market equivalent in scale to the Japanese market. If, and when, the UK joins EMU, then the integrated European market would double in size – but still be only half the size of the US market.

This review focuses primarily on the preparations that are necessary and the conversion weekend itself. The final section touches on the strategic impact on businesses that service the equity market.

THE REMAINING WEEKS OF PREPARATION

The equity market can be viewed as a network of businesses supplying each other, and for this network to function efficiently each business – each link in the network – needs to be able to keep up. Some may be so crucial that their failure would imperil the whole system, but others may just cause severe problems to their own business. Exhibit 1 illustrates the range of participants and thus the resources available to your business from the adjacent "link" in the chain.

Exhibit 1: THE CHAIN OF MARKET PARTICIPANTS

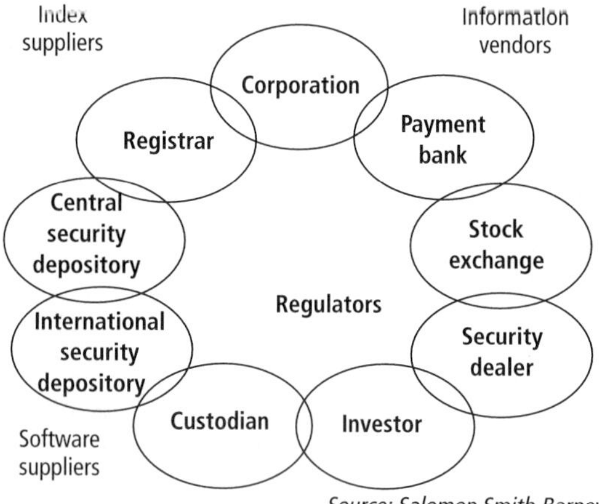

Source: Salomon Smith Barney.

In a national market, it is relatively simple for the authorities to get together with leading market participants in this chain to formulate a national changeover plan, and this has been done in many EU member states. However, the international participant in the EMU changeover faces a vastly more complex challenge in grappling with several uncoordinated, poorly defined and constantly changing national plans. This was the situation that unfolded in the early months of 1998.

Even in today's markets, international trading accounts for a significant proportion of activity and disruption in that segment would have a very serious impact on European equity markets. London-based securities houses have taken a keen interest in the process from the outset because they trade in all European markets and therefore are particularly concerned to promote the smooth emergence of an integrated market for equities throughout the European Union. Accordingly, the London Investment Banking Association (LIBA) held a major workshop in January and identified many issues that needed to be tackled by constituents of the chain.

The need for timely and accurate information on the plans – current and amended – of all the national markets rapidly emerged as critical. That need seems to have prompted a speedy migration of the information flow to web sites as the only practical medium for disseminating the volume of information and enabling original source documents to be available. This flow involved a variety of public entities such as the European Monetary Institute and the Bank of England, as well as commercial news vendors. Exhibit 2 sets out some web-sites that may be useful and the LIBA report (*Trading and Settlement of Equities – post 1 January 1999*, 23 February 1998) lists many useful documents. It will be intriguing to see whether this aspect of EMU serves as a catalyst to even greater use of the Internet in securities trading.

Exhibit 2: USEFUL WEB SITE ADDRESSES

European Community	http://www.europa.eu.int/comm
European Monetary Inst	http://www.ecb.int
Bank of England	http://www.bankofengland.co.uk
Deutsche Bundesbank	http://www.bundesbank.de
Cedel Bank	http://www.cedelgroup.com
Euroclear	http://www.euroclear.com
SWIFT	http://www.swift.com
Deutsche Börse	http://www.exchange.de
London Stock Exchange	http://www.londonstockex.co.uk
ISDA	http://www.isda.org
LIFFE	http://www.liffe.com

The web sites below include general checklists of actions required by a corporation to convert its businesses, rather than specific details for financial market participants:

Fed. of European Accounting Experts	http://www.euro.fee.be
AMUE	http://www.if.net

Source: Salomon Smith Barney.

The LIBA workshop – summarised in the March edition of the Bank of England's *Practical Issues Quarterly* – made several recommendations for action. These covered areas such as:

- the final fixing of exchange rates to the euro;
- the redenomination of shares – avoid methods that change the number of shares in issue and avoid any bunching of "corporate actions";
- ensuring that stock lending is not curtailed;
- avoiding changes to ISIN identifying codes.

Despite the efforts of market participants and officials, not all issues have been resolved. For example, there is as yet no agreement on the correct presentation of historical securities prices. Should they be converted using the official conversion rate or be adjusted to reflect the currency relationship that existed at the time?

THE CONVERSION WEEKEND

But all this is just the run-up to the "conversion weekend" of 31 December 1998 to 4 January 1999 – about 90 hours of frantic activity in the equity, bond, money and foreign exchange market infrastructure. In this short time period it is vital to minimise any unnecessary activity (and hence the clear recommendation not to redenominate share capital in a way that might require a change in the number of shares outstanding).

The starting gun for the weekend will be fired once the Finance Ministers of Euroland meet and formally fix the conversion rates from their national currencies to the euro. The earlier they do this the better because it will give an extra few hours. This may be of little use to organisations that have their processing done outside Europe – in the US, for example. Some banks may find their conversion window even more constrained if they wish to be able to trade as Asian markets open ahead of Europe.

Institutions will have to value their assets in national currency at the year-end and then convert them to euro, using the legally mandated conversion rates and rounding procedures. In the meantime the stock exchanges will have carried out their own conversion and, at some stage, there will have to be a reconciliation to ensure that firms' own prices coincide with the "official" prices. Presumably the normal data vendors will supply this information.

The timetable for processing huge volumes of data would be crowded in any case because of year-end pressures, so conversion procedures are an added burden. At the same time, there will be intense activity in the bond sector because most government bonds will be redenominated over that same weekend. As dawn breaks on 4 January, those institutions that have tested their own systems thoroughly and liaised carefully with their customers and suppliers will be ready to open for business.

THE STRUCTURE OF EURO EQUITY MARKETS

The stock exchanges of Europe face two fundamental changes simultaneously: (a) the euro will sweep away a crucial national distinction; and (b) the technology of the Internet will continue to transform the physical nature of the market-place where shares are bought and sold. The electronic trading infrastructure that already exists is far more advanced technically than investors are aware. EMU may provide the vital psychological stimulus that breaks the logjam. The response of the customers – investors and issuers – will define the future of these markets, but both of these groups are, themselves, also likely to be profoundly influenced by EMU.

Investors will find that some legal constraints on their cross-currency asset diversification may disappear and they will certainly be under even greater pressure to produce high returns (if price stability keeps interest rates around current levels). With a greater array of investment opportunities, the performance benchmark may move swiftly from national indices to broad pan-European indices such as Eurotop 300. Correspondingly, there will be pressure to trade derivatives of such indices, increasing the demand for cheap, interconnected trading systems. Increasingly, portfolios will be built around pan-European sectors rather than along national lines.

Issuers may respond at two levels. First, corporations are likely to reshape their business to extract maximum benefit from this extra dimension of the Single Market. Secondly, there may be micro responses to enhance the attraction of their equity to pan-European investors. Such measures could include redenominating shares to no par value (as in the US), which would eliminate the need for a conversion process as well as removing one of the mysteries of share ownership that might deter broader participation by individuals via electronic trading.

Other barriers to a single European equity market include tax and accounting differences:

- Tax is not likely to be harmonised for very many years, though some slow progress is being made. In December 1997, Finance Ministers debated the report from Commissioner Monti's Taxation Policy Group that included a discussion on the taxation of savings income. The ministers requested the Commission to "make a proposal". That was the first step on a lengthy journey that could still end in deadlock – yet again.
- Accounting standards are being tackled by the International Accounting Standards Committee but the effort to ensure consistency with US GAAP standards is slowing progress. Nonetheless, if companies realise that different accounting techniques are reducing their market rating in comparison with their European peers, then there will be a greater incentive to standardise.

These forces will impact investors and issuers progressively in the years after 1999, but the pressures may be felt by stock exchanges much earlier. The Investment Services Directive – an existing Single Market measure – opens the way to cross-border exchange membership but the rapid rise of electronic trading systems will blur what that means in practice. The technology already exists to access continuous electronic auction systems from virtually anywhere in the world, via the Internet. The only remaining feature of 15 separate national stock exchanges would be the domestic regulatory structure. But investors will soon learn to trade on the system that provides the cheapest execution, consistent with what the users deem to be adequate regulation. That will open a new round of competition to reshape the structure of Europe's equity markets.

CONCLUSION

The advent of a single currency in Europe will act as a catalyst to many profound changes in all businesses associated with trading equities. The preparations in the time remaining to year-end 1998 should include strategic thinking as well as the minimum step of ensuring that the business can function properly in the new currency.

Graham Bishop
Salomon Smith Barney

The Asian effect on Latin American markets

The ripple effects of the Asian crisis began to affect Latin American stock markets in earnest in late October 1997. The aftershocks are likely to continue to impact the region through 1998 and perhaps beyond. Ultimately, we believe that the outcome will be sounder macroeconomic policies that will make Latin America a safer investment, although that result is likely to take months to become apparent.

AN HISTORICAL PERSPECTIVE

The Asian crisis comes relatively quickly on the heels of the Mexican peso devaluation of 20 December 1994. That incident resulted in sounder macroeconomic policies, particularly in Argentina and Mexico, which have resulted in both of those countries being able to better withstand the Asian heat. In Mexico, the devaluation sharply lowered an exchange rate that was widely perceived as overvalued and changed a significant trade deficit into a trade surplus in less than a year. The bottom of the market for Mexico and the rest of Latin America occurred in the first week of March. The bleeding stopped when Mexico introduced a significant, credible economic package that included stringent fiscal measures and aid to banks, coupled with the US-government led US$50 billion backstop. The fact that the government was able to prepay money borrowed from the US is ample testimony to the effectiveness of the administration's policies.

Indeed, Mexico's free floating exchange rate, trade surplus and sound fiscal policies have made that market the safe haven from Asia and have resulted in the best stock market performance in the region since the crisis began. The real hero of the episode for Mexico, Guillermo Ortiz, is now head of the central bank – a role that in our view ensures sound policies.

Argentina's banking system and currency board approach that pegs the peso to the dollar was thoroughly tested in the Mexican devaluation and was proven sound. Thus, the outflow of reserves and flight of bank deposits that some feared in the wake of Asia has simply not happened. We view such outflows as unlikely.

THE CURRENT TEST

The Asian crisis is now testing those markets that have in some way lagged in terms of the critical reforms that have been highlighted as essential – sound currencies and balanced macro policies. Brazil is of course the primary example. The country was running a fiscal deficit of roughly 4% of GDP, a current account deficit in the same neighbourhood, and had a crawling currency band that required intervention by the central bank in the case of capital outflows. Nervousness over whether Brazil would be required by outflows to devalue has continued to plague the stock markets, and a doubling of already steep interest rates in November 1997 has continued the woe of private sector stocks, which were down on aggregate 43% in 1997.

While fears that Brazil will devalue have subsided, the Asian crisis continues to overhang the market. Progress on the fiscal deficit, which requires revision of the constitution in an unwieldy procedure, continues. Although a privatisation process that includes most of the utility sector and the telecom sector continues to hold up public sector stock prices, interest rates have declined only modestly since the big hike. In our view, it will take some stability in Asia, including confidence that neither China nor Hong Kong will devalue, to aid Brazil. Even so, we do not expect a swift reduction of interest rates.

Even before the Asian volatility, real interest rates were extremely high at about 20%. Ultimately, however, the lesson for Brazil is the same as prior to the Asian crisis: in an exchange rate based stabilisation programme, real interest rates can decline only as the market becomes confident that policies are credible. The Asian crisis has turned a bright spotlight on the "credible" in Brazilian policies that continues to give equity investors pause.

The jury is still out on a fiscal tightening package that was introduced at the same time as the interest rate hike. While the package promised savings of slightly over US$50 billion, much of that will be eaten up by the higher cost of servicing internal debt required by the much higher interest rates. The result has been continuing market unease.

Chile has also been affected, primarily because of real economic links, with 37% of the country's exports going to Asia. The country's prime export, copper, has been buffeted by plummeting prices and the result has been extreme (for Chile) peso volatility. That contributed to a 50 basis point hike in interest rates in January 1998 that has put a damper on growth prospects as well as company earnings projections.

In Venezuela, lower oil prices have resulted in a fiscal outlook markedly less robust than prior to the Asian crisis. A US$6 billion current account surplus is threatening to disappear in 1998. The currency is widely viewed as about 35% overvalued and investors remain nervous about a maxi-devaluation despite a recent modest shift in the country's exchange rate band and the 17 months of import coverage on hand in foreign reserves.

Some pressure was felt on the Mexican exchange rate as Asian volatility hit Latin America in late October 1997. The peso, which had been trading at about 8.1 to the dollar, fell at one point to 9.2, but the fall was remarkably short-lived and the peso was at about 8.2 as at the first quarter 1998. That recovery is a testament to the sound policies that have made that market the favourite of Latin American equity investors. Nevertheless, lower projected oil prices have resulted in some fiscal tightening that affects growth prospects marginally and could serve to weaken the peso slightly. Argentina suffered an outflow of reserves that also proved brief. While the stock market continued to trade poorly on fears that a Brazilian devaluation would force the same in Argentina, interest rates have declined and bank deposits have actually grown.

WHAT COMES NEXT?

For the region as a whole, the Asian crisis took some froth off the Latin American stock markets (see Exhibit 1) and that was probably no bad thing. At its peak in July the Brazilian Bovespa was up 93%, Mexico was up 41%, while Chile peaked in June at 35% ahead for the year. The Asian crisis has tempered economic growth prospects for 1998, however. That, combined with our sense that at some point global emerging market investors will shift funds from Latin America to Asia to take advantage of relative bargains, will temper gains in Latin markets, perhaps for the next 12 to 18 months. After the smoke clears, however, a sounder macro environment and stronger company earnings prospects will continue to make the region attractive.

Mexico

Superb economic management makes Mexico a sound equity investment in virtually every scenario except a total Asian meltdown. The question for equity investors over the next year, however, is simply one of valuation. Following the devaluation and subsequent economic recovery, the comparison of company earnings in 1997 with the previous year was impressive, and in most cases suggested earnings growth of over 20%. However, in 1998 over 1997, earnings growth numbers are highly unlikely to be so robust. We envisage an aggregate number somewhere around 10% earnings growth.

Exhibit 1: LATIN AMERICAN STOCK EXCHANGE PERFORMANCE, 1.1.1997 – 27.10.1997 AND 27.10.1997 – 16 .1.1998 (%)

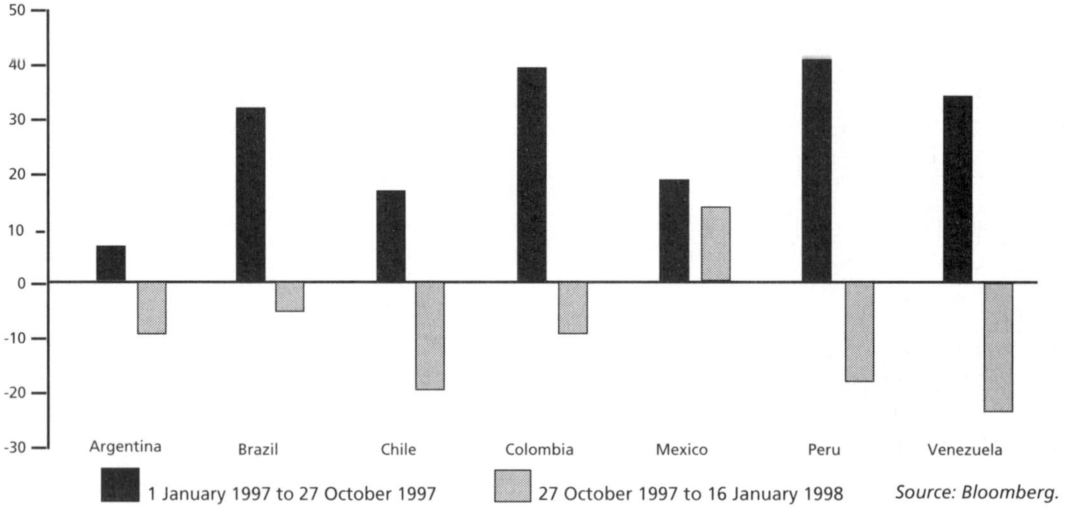

Source: Bloomberg.

It is important for investors to keep in mind that Mexico's recovery came in an atmosphere of virtually no loan growth as the banking system retrenched to absorb post-devaluation pain. Even modest loan growth along with stronger consumer demand suggests that the Mexican recovery is sustainable on a long-term basis. Cyclical sectors like beverages, steel and retail are likely to continue to perform well in such an atmosphere, especially given the sound macro background.

The longer-term question for Mexico is politics: for the first time in the past 70 years or so, the country has an opposition-led Congress that could generate some shifts in fiscal policy. We believe any such moves are likely to be minor, even if accompanied by the shouting and shoving that inaugurated the new Congress' budget discussions in 1997. In the background, the Asian effect here will be to remind the opposition that they do not want to bear the cost of straying from sound economics if they wish to compete for the presidency in 2000.

Venezuela

If Asia continues to cast a pall over oil prices, Venezuelan equities could suffer. In early 1998, the Congress was mulling over fiscal cuts that could restore some confidence. A scheduled increase in oil production of 8% in 1998 will help in any case.

There is a question over how much can be done in response to Asia because of internal politics, however: a presidential election is scheduled for December, and the outlook for major candidates remains extremely uncertain. Significant reforms are not likely, but a shadow IMF deal may be one beneficial side-effect of the Caldera administration's nervousness over falling oil prices.

Argentina

Barring a step-up in Asian pressures, the effect on Argentina is likely in the end to have been only marginally negative. This is because the country had already done so much in response to the Mexican devaluation that there was little more to do, except perhaps for extending some provisions for protecting the banking system in the event of sudden withdrawals. The equity market has suffered and growth prospects have been slashed by most Wall Street analysts from around 7% to about 4% because of lower exports to Brazil.

In our view, however, this effect will be evident but small, because many goods are commodities that are fungible to other markets. The government continues to stick to a 7% growth projection for 1998. If we had to wager on either Wall Street or Buenos Aires here, we would not bet against another upside surprise for Argentina.

Brazil

In the end, the effect of Asia on Brazil is likely to have been salutary. Getting to that point will take some patience, however. The economy is likely to be in recession for at least the first half of 1998 as a consequence of the hike in interest rates. Even assuming modest second half growth, it looks like the best that can be hoped for is about 1% growth in 1998.

The good news, however, is that the slow growth will have a substantially beneficial effect on the current account deficit, which could shrink by about half. The fiscal deficit remains hostage to the interest rate outlook and the chance for reforms. We expect reforms to pass mostly intact, although the effects of lower government spending will not be felt until 1999. Most observers now believe that interest rates will hit pre-crisis levels in June. The Asian effect will also benefit Brazil by keeping the government's feet to the fire in continuing its privatisation programme, and we expect to see the telecom sector substantially privatised in 1998.

At this point it does not look like the Asian crisis and its attendant negative growth effects will derail the reelection of President Cardoso in October. Assuming this, the crisis may provide an added impetus for Cardoso to convene a constitutional convention to pass additional amendments shortly after the election. That would be a definite positive for Brazilian investors.

Chile

The Asian contagion effects on Chile will be felt in the real economy, rather than being strictly of a psychological nature, and those effects will be negative. In order for the government to come close to its 4.5% inflation target for 1998, tight monetary policy will be required because of the higher inflation expected from a weaker peso. That will likely result in a poor environment for equities.

Another negative factor arising from Asia and currency volatility will be a detrimental impact on companies with dollar-denominated debt. Finally, growth for 1998 will not be as robust as originally believed. Forecasts have come down from the area of 7% to 6%. It will take true stability in Asia, and a bottoming of recessions there, before the effects on Chile lift. At that point, a rise in copper prices and a more subdued currency could lead to a reverse in the policy of tighter money and thus a brighter equity picture.

Jim Barrineau
Latin American Equity Strategist
Salomon Smith Barney

Alternative investment strategies: An investor's viewpoint

The US equity market is the most liquid and developed equity market in the world. Although the emphasis of this book is on equity markets, derivatives (principally options and futures and similarly structured products) are integrated instruments within the broad financial market fabric, and the potential they have for fuelling US equity market growth cannot to be understated. While derivatives have expanded equity trading volumes, economic growth and capital market reforms have also fostered enterprise development, and alternative investment sectors such as venture capital, private equity and real estate funds have provided an extra source of new companies and equity securities that have ultimately been listed on US exchanges.

The Nobel laureate economist Merton Miller once told me that he had seen a beggar on a street corner holding a cup to which he had affixed a sign: "Please, no derivatives". Miller is puzzled by the fact that, as he puts it, the term "derivatives" is "the only four-letter word in the English language with 11 letters", because he believes that the derivatives revolution of the past 25 years has been overwhelmingly positive for society. It has made the world a safer place, and allowed institutions and individuals to manage effectively, and at low cost, risks and hazards that had concerned generations of investors.

A few years ago, the representatives of an esteemed Wall Street firm called on me. They told me that they had a new "black box" alternative investment product that would be very effective in mitigating portfolio risk. I listened to their presentation, drew a very different conclusion from theirs and told them that their bit of wizardry would actually have the effect of increasing risk. They were understandably crestfallen, but graciously thanked me for my time before they left. I understand that that was the end of their product.

These two encounters illustrate the different views that people can have about what I call the alternative investment conundrum. The point is that a little scepticism is healthy: there is no such thing as a stupid question when it comes to alternative investments, and it is essential that investors understand what they are buying. One is well advised to perform thorough research, not only on the investment strategy but also on the detailed mechanics of how a contemplated alternative investment is implemented, before making any commitments. We know the results of flawed decision making, which have been all too well publicised.

In any case, whether market players are as hostile as the beggar or as enthusiastic as those Wall Street representatives, it is a safe prediction that the role of alternative investments is only going to increase in importance. We should remember that there was a time when the term "capital markets" referred to trading in bonds, and common stocks were seen as risky. They still are, but now they are at the core of most institutional and individual portfolios. Following a similar trajectory, alternative investments are also gradually becoming mainstream and, as the spotlight shines on them, the attendant risks will be identified, evaluated, managed, monitored and mitigated. Successful, well thought out strategies, effectively marketed to appropriate targets, will flourish, while those that are not will fall by the wayside.

DEFINITIONS AND MODEL SETS

I define "alternative investment strategies" to include:

- private, non-traditional, illiquid investments, such as distressed debt, emerging market equity and debt, international private equity, leveraged buy-out funds, mezzanine financing, oil and gas programmes, real estate, economically targeted investments, timberland and venture capital;

- dynamic, non-traditional, liquid investment strategies involving securities, derivatives or physicals in liquid markets, such as managed futures, commodities, currencies or hedge funds; and
- investments involving longs and shorts and leverage.

One exception might be convertible bonds, which could go either way.

This is obviously a very inclusive definition, but it is not an unusual one. In the 1997 edition of the Goldman Sachs/Frank Russell *Report on Alternative Investing by Tax-Exempt Organisations*, based on a survey of 135 institutions, the asset classes that the survey treats as alternative investments are venture capital, private equity, international private equity, mezzanine financing, oil and gas, and timberland. (It is interesting to note that 52% of the respondents consider real estate to be an alternative asset, while 48% disagree with this.)

Many people may wonder how they can integrate alternative investment strategies into their portfolios. There are two main model sets. The first is very simple: it involves dividing a portfolio into two categories – traditional and non-traditional – and making an allocation based on economic and risk characteristics, as well as on the time and resources needed for effective management and monitoring. One also needs to take into account such factors as liquidity, transaction costs, pricing/valuation and regulatory supervision. This approach allows investors to identify traditional strategies in stocks, bonds and cash, and then add alternatives as a catch-all category for all those strategies that do not fit into the traditional framework and that have potential to add incremental value with an understandable risk that diversifies the overall portfolio. One has to recognise that the investment process is dynamic and evolutionary: new products and strategies are developed on a regular basis. Having a structure that devotes, for example, 80–90% to traditional investments and 10–20% to non-traditional investments gives investment professionals flexibility to add and reduce allocations to alternative investments in a dynamic investment environment.

The second main model set for alternative investors involves developing target allocations, with ranges for each type of traditional and alternative investment. For example, a portfolio framework may be defined that allocates A% to domestic stocks, B% to venture capital, C% to international stocks, D% to emerging equity markets, E% to international private equity, F% to leveraged buyouts, G% to oil and gas, H% to domestic fixed income, I% to international fixed income, J% to distressed debt, K% to commodities, L% to managed futures, M% to longs/shorts, N% to hedge funds, P% to cash, and so on. This model defines each activity and, depending on one's perspective, is either more rigid or more disciplined than the previous model.

These two model sets can be viewed as defining two broad perspectives. They do not prevent investors gauging their own understanding and experience, and then choosing a hybrid approach somewhere between the two.

INVESTORS' RATIONALES AND CHARACTERISTICS

Because of the freshness of the data and the track record of the publication, I would like to return briefly to the 1997 *Report on Alternative Investing by Tax-Exempt Organisations*. One of its most revealing findings shows that, among respondents to the survey, commitments to alternative investments grew by 20% each year between 1986 and 1997, representing an increase in value from US$12 billion to US$91 billion over the period. The report also indicates that over just two years, between 1995 and 1997, the 213 largest pension funds, endowments and foundations in the United States and Canada increased their commitments to alternative investments by 34%, while the average allocation to alternatives increased from 6.2% to 7.6%. It is interesting to note that the only two asset classes to which commitments increased, as proportions of total alternative assets, between 1992 and 1997, were international private equity, which increased by 27%, and leveraged buy-out funds, which increased by 5%.

The report also cites the rationales for alternative investments: 75% of respondents say that the key reason for investing in alternatives is to outperform traditional investments and 83% say that their return expectations for alternatives have been met by actual performance. These greater return expectations for alternative investments are borne out by the "investment staircase": investors whose primary focus is on liquidity and capital preservation are more comfortable with cash, short-term bonds and government bonds; equities and convertible bonds are halfway up the stairs; and those seeking higher returns and who are willing to accept greater risk look for opportunities further up still. This leads them to alternative investments such as venture capital, private equity, distressed debt, currencies or hedge funds. If investors draw a circle around alternative investments, they will find that there are many different segments within the circle.

However, I believe that the key to understanding alternative investments lies in the capacity of institutional investors first to understand themselves and their own characteristics, whether the institution is a pension fund, a foundation or an endowment. The following checklist provides a quick way for institutional investors to begin to contemplate the appropriateness of alternative investments:

- sophistication;
- funding sources;
- expected return;
- asset base;
- pay-out pattern;
- risk tolerance;
- asset classification;
- time horizon;
- benchmarking;
- staff and resources;
- investment process;
- tactical mix;
- legal framework;
- strategic mix; and
- compensation.

One widely held view, which I happen to share, is that alternative investments are very time-intensive. Investors in alternative assets need to have ample staff and/or supporting resources, as well as an adequate level of sophistication in the investment process.

The fit with the overall portfolio is also an important consideration, and this has been one of the principal challenges with alternative investments. There is ample evidence that alternative investments can reduce risk and diversify performance, but many investors face the challenge of building these products into a traditional risk/return framework, such as gauging publicly traded stocks on a total return basis versus measuring private partnerships using internal rate of return. As in the example from my own experience that I cited at the outset, it is not uncommon for providers of these services to announce that they have a great hedge fund or managed futures programme that will really add value, diversify risk and enhance performance. Investors need to ask such people how they have come to that conclusion when they may not know what the portfolio looks like.

Asset base

Another key consideration is the size of an institution's asset base. There is no magic level, but I would suggest that a small (thinly staffed) fund should think twice before making an allocation to alternative investments. Risk is not the only issue here. Given the illiquid nature of private partnerships, for example, investors may be committing themselves to a 10-year programme with little or no opportunity to exit. However, the issue of size can cut both ways, because it raises questions for the largest investors as well as the smallest. I have often had to ask myself whether I should expend the time and effort to understand an alternative investment that might involve a commitment of a few million US dollars to secure a basis point or two against a fund worth billions of dollars, when focusing on a value-added strategy on the corpus of the funds could dwarf the entire commitment to, and the return on, the alternative investment.

Institutional investors need to be aware of their asset base and their asset classifications. Some have just the three traditional asset classes of stocks, bonds and cash. Others have 10 or more classes, including, for example, US large cap, US small cap, Japanese, European and emerging market stocks; high-quality fixed-income securities; high-yield assets; distressed, private and emerging market debt; venture capital; private and special situations equity; convertibles; oil and gas; and real estate. Still others may have allocations along the two models described earlier, or hybrids of them.

Maturity cycle is also important, especially for pension funds, because a young fund may be able to take more risk than a mature fund. One has to ask also about the legal framework: ERISA is one framework for pension funds in the United States, but endowments and foundations have a different framework.

Other questions address funding sources. Where did the money come from? What is its time stream? What is its pay-out pattern? Yet another set of questions concern the investment process. Are meetings quarterly or weekly? Are the development and implementation of the strategy performed internally, or with external managers or outside consultants? What information resources are available? What are the compensation issues for taking on these additional risks?

All of these issues touch on an institution's understanding of itself and the suitability of alternative assets for an investment portfolio. Even benchmarking raises the issue of how to measure the performance of illiquid, long-term investment vehicles, for which comparative performance might often be judged anecdotally.

CHOOSING ALTERNATIVE INVESTMENTS

There is a broad menu of alternative investments and investors should not lump them all together. The best advice is to take a thoughtful, selective approach. For example, I know of a college that made a disproportionately large commitment to one hedge fund, but it knew what it was doing and did it very well.

I tend to take an overall approach that places alternative assets into two investment categories. The first category, comprising more liquid and more volatile assets, includes long and short stocks, bonds, short-term cash, energy derivatives, real estate investment trusts

(REITs), currency overlays and managed futures. The second category, comprising more illiquid and less volatile assets, includes venture capital, distressed debt, long-term arbitrage, oil and gas, and real estate.

There is no one standard investor in alternative assets: endowments, foundations, public funds and private pension funds all have different needs; they are at different points along the evolutionary spectrum; and they are able and willing to participate, to varying degrees, in the complex and ever-changing global investment environment. Over the past few years we have seen the arrival of stocks that look like bonds and bonds that look like stocks, as well as structured products with optionality in them, and, with more money going to emerging markets, we now have emerging market currency issues to deal with.

A final determinant of what an investor ought or ought not to include in its portfolio comprises those considerations that allow it to understand the nature and risk of the investment. I believe in starting with the size of the alternative investment being contemplated and its diversification impact, as well as its correlation with the market, other assets and the investor's style. One strategic reason for using alternative investments is to enhance return and diversification. However, the investor and the provider should both look very closely at whether the proposed investment has an acceptable basis for adding value and whether it really improves diversification. Fortunately, there are ample quantitative tools available with which to compare the expected correlation of one asset class to another. The following are some of the other key considerations on portfolio inclusion:

- leverage;
- concentration;
- performance and experience;
- benchmarks;
- volatility of performance;
- the alpha impact on the total fund;
- people;
- timing and amount of cash flows;
- the investment process;
- liquidity;
- fees;
- tax;
- legal; and
- risk management.

Whether or not the analysis indicates that alternative investments are right for particular investors depends on who and what the investors are, where they are going and what their experience is. Beyond fundamental considerations of risk/return, one quickly gets into a host of secondary but extremely important questions concerning liquidity, tax considerations, legal leverage and benchmarking. Also the people question should not be overlooked; is there a person, internally or externally, who is knowledgeable and experienced in alternative investments, and in a position to lead the effort?

Analysis tools

A full analysis of a potential alternative investment asset or asset class is imperative for a full understanding of the risk/return potential. In this connection, the *Handy Reference for Alternatives*, presented by Gary Cohen (Citibank's senior managing director for alternative investment strategies) at the Global Alternative Investment Management Conference held in Geneva in 1997, is particularly helpful.

Cohen defines common alternative investment categories as real estate, venture capital, direct investment, hedge funds, multi-adviser funds, structured notes, linked deposits, credit notes, asset-backed securities, energy and natural resources. His risk drivers include market, asset, style and strategy correlations; credit diversification, such as through cash flow and default analysis; experience and track record; and consistency of trading strategy. In his view, risk containment involves dynamic capital protection, credit insurance, hedging techniques, use of backstop credit, and use of derivatives and multi-adviser funds.

Gary Cohen also recommends paying attention to such general considerations as an auditable track record; risk-adjusted return versus targeted return versus competition return; the Sharpe ratio; peak-to-trough drawdowns and frequency; volatility against the S&P 500 or similar stock market indices; percentages of winning months and losing months against the benchmark; management action triggers; and stop-loss and close-down limits. Other items to look out for include management fees being less than or equal to 2%; incentive fees being less than or equal to 20%; no general partner perks; no hidden fees; marketing and legal fees agreed beforehand; no excessive commission fees or turnover costs; the track record of, and the agreement on, the trading manager; model validations; reading and understanding the agreements; and the potential for back office errors.

Finally, Cohen presents some thought-provoking maxims for those considering alternative investment strategies:

- diversification is the last free lunch;
- risk drivers equal performance drivers;
- capital protection equals less return;
- investors are risk drivers too;
- performance reverts to the mean;
- beware the mean – distributions are skewed;
- strategy changes equal lack of performance;
- birth-to-death adviser commitment is a must;

- if smart people do it do not discount it; and
- ratios are fine, but do your homework.

SUMMARY

There are few black and white answers to any of the wide range of questions surrounding alternative investments, but one thing is certain – over time, today's alternative investments will come to be viewed more and more as reputable, core investments. The only real problems involve investors' capacity and techniques, both for managing and monitoring these investments, and for truly understanding the risks. If returns from traditional asset classes revert to the mean after several years of outperformance, we may well see greater numbers of institutions delving into alternative investments – but if their expectations are not realistic and the risks are not well managed, they may end up turning their backs on alternative assets for a long period of time. However, there is little question that investors will become much more sophisticated and better able to analyse these products, and to integrate them with their traditional strategies.

William P. Miller II
The Common Fund

Selected issues in cross-border trading

Internationalisation of the equity markets continues to increase, and indeed in some aspects of the equity business and in certain markets is the dominant factor or certainly the dominant growth area.

Considerable publicity has been accorded to privatisations or other primary issuances and listings and to corporate finance activities in the international markets. The engines that foster these activities, however, are cross-border investment activity and cross-border trading, and we therefore propose to survey some legal and regulatory issues with respect to three topics: (a) the rapid growth of electronic trading systems and the regulatory issues that they raise; (b) the evolving regulatory framework for international investments activity in the European Union (EU); and (c) recent US developments under the US Securities and Exchange Commission's Rule 15a-6 with respect to activities of non-US dealers.

ELECTRONIC TRADING SYSTEMS

International markets have seen, and future years will continues to bring, rapid expansion in the use of electronic trading systems, sometimes referred to as "alternative trading systems", to conduct equity and other trading throughout the world. Two basic forces will drive this expansion of electronic trading systems – globalisation and technology:

The term "alternative trading system" comprises a broad range of non-traditional, automated systems that perform some or all of the following functions: centralisation of orders or trading interest; display of orders or trading interest from a variety of sources; matching orders or trading interest; and crossing or otherwise executing transactions. The simplest systems disseminate dealer quotations or indications of trading interest to participants, on the basis of which participants may independently (and "offline") contact a market-maker or dealer to place an order or to negotiate the terms of a transaction (eg, Nasdaq and Easdaq). More advanced systems permit participants to route orders to, or to access and execute trades against quotations entered by, one or more sponsoring dealers, market-makers or exchange specialists. Still others "cross" customer buy and sell orders directly against other customer orders or against exchange or market-maker quotations. A few systems also conduct periodic single-price auctions.

Regulatory environment

Electronic trading systems blur the traditional regulatory dichotomy drawn between exchanges and dealers and other investment firms and raise special issues for regulators that have historically relied on functional regulation to distinguish between exchanges and dealers. Some market participants regard electronic trading systems as competitive service providers, not entities insulated from competition, and therefore believe the systems should not be subjected to the same self-policing duties, disclosure obligations, membership requirements or regulatory environment that apply to traditional exchanges. Other market participants believe that the regulatory regime applicable to dealers and other investment firms is often insufficient to address the regulatory issues (including those relating to competition, access, pricing and transparency, capital adequacy and market and investor protection) raised by electronic trading systems and the increasingly higher trading volumes they enjoy.

Securities regulators worldwide accordingly differ on the appropriate manner in which these systems should be regulated. In the US, the UK and the Canadian provinces of Quebec and Ontario, for example, many electronic trading systems have been registered as investment firms or broker-dealers and compete directly with established securities exchanges and associations (which at least in the US also have regulatory responsibility for such systems in their guise as broker-dealers). In certain other countries, the leading electronic trading systems in practice have been operated by registered exchanges. The expansion of electronic trading systems allowing remote access from around the world creates unique cross-border regulatory issues that securities and futures regulators are seeking to address in a variety of ways.

Regulation as investment firms

Electronic trading systems have been able to offer participants significant advantages over traditional markets in jurisdictions where they are regulated as investment firms (eg, as broker-dealers in the US) rather than as exchanges. Many of these non-exchange systems permit institutional investors to access their trading facilities directly without the intermediation of market-makers (although trades are cleared and settled by clearing brokers that are generally owned and controlled by the system), thereby avoiding costly market-maker spreads. Furthermore, several of these systems (eg, Instinet and Tradebook) offer anonymous trading, which considerably facilitates the purchase and disposition of large quantities of securities in an efficient, liquid market. The significant advantages of these systems have enabled them to claim as much as 20% of trading volume in US over-the-counter equity securities and nearly 5% of trading volume in securities listed on the New York Stock Exchange.

Securities regulatory authorities in these jurisdictions have devoted significant effort to developing rules that attempt to continue to operate on the basis of functional regulation and also balance the regulatory concerns raised by not subjecting trading systems to exchange-type regulation against the importance of encouraging the implementation of efficient, new technologies. For example, in the light of the high volume of trading on "broker-dealer trading systems", the SEC has maintained regulation of such systems as broker-dealers but has adopted special record-keeping and reporting requirements designed to leave an "audit trail" for the investigation of market manipulation and other abuses.

Nonetheless, some of the obligations traditionally imposed on investment firms, again on the basis of functional regulation, may be unnecessary for the proper regulation of electronic trading systems. For example, financial responsibility requirements may be unnecessary for trading systems that do not handle customer funds or securities and that do not include a matching or other execution function or disclaim any principal, settlement, guarantee or enforcement risk with respect to transactions effected on their facilities. On the other hand, financial responsibility requirements are generally thought to be necessary for trading systems that stand behind transactions effected through their facilities, especially when they guarantee anonymity through settlement. In this regard, the UK Securities and Investment Board has established a regulatory regime for "service companies" that generally arrange transactions only among certain classes of professional investors and do not assume any fiduciary, market-making, guarantee or settlement obligations with respect to arranged transactions.

Price transparency remains among the most contentious regulatory issues raised by the increased trading volume enjoyed by non-exchange electronic trading systems. Exchanges in most countries are required to disseminate transaction information to the public (as well as market-maker quotations in quote-driven systems) in order to ensure equal access to price information and trading opportunities. Investment firms and dealers, however, are not subject to such comprehensive dissemination requirements, and accordingly, electronic trading systems regulated as investment firms or dealers have to date generally not needed to maintain the same degree of price transparency as exchanges. While the additional requirements of price dissemination and transparency with respect to exchanges are generally justified on the basis of "functional" regulation, some electronic trading systems raise issues concerning the limits of a distinction in this area based on function.

Side-by-side trading on exchanges and alternative electronic trading systems may therefore result in a "two-tiered" market, where professional and institutional investors with access to trading systems enjoy superior spreads relative to the rest of the market. During its recent investigation of trading on Nasdaq, for example, the SEC determined that bids and offers displayed by market-makers in alternative electronic trading systems were frequently more favourable than those posted publicly on Nasdaq. In response to this concern, the SEC adopted a rule requiring market-makers and specialists to make available publicly (eg, through public quotation displays) any superior prices privately offered through "electronic communications networks" that widely disseminate market-maker orders and permit automatic execution of orders. The London Stock Exchange (LSE) has likewise adopted a rule barring market-makers from displaying quotations on certain price display systems at prices better than quotations on its Stock Exchange Automated Quotation system. The rule does not, however, prohibit market-makers from displaying superior quotations on inter-dealer broker screens, systems operated by a recognised investment exchange or regulated trading systems operated by LSE member firms (eg, Instinet).

Regulation as exchanges

Until now, electronic trading systems regulated as exchanges have, with some important exceptions, generally been operated by established national securities markets. Many securities exchanges have upgraded their trading processes with new technological advances in recent years, either by establishing electronic trading systems alongside traditional exchange facilities or by completely automating their trading facilities. The Frankfurt Stock Exchange, for example, offers members trading both on a traditional "open outcry" trading floor as well as on an independent electronic trading system (Xetra) with remote trading screens located within and outside Germany. The Paris Bourse and the Toronto Stock Exchange, by contrast, have closed their physical trading floors and are completely automated. Similarly, more recently established exchanges, such as Deutsche Terminbörse, the German financial derivatives exchange, have from the outset relied exclusively on automation. The "Second Section" of the Tokyo Stock Exchange is also automated.

In the light of the significant competitive pressures posed by alternative trading systems, registered exchanges and the NASD in the US have also begun to explore automated trading technologies. For example, the Pacific Stock Exchange recently obtained approval from the SEC to establish rules for a proposed computerised, screen-based trading facility for exchange members and their customers implementing the OptiMark System (a sophisticated trade-matching algorithm that enables participants to execute trades anonymously at satisfaction profiles representing each participant's relative willingness to trade at various price and size combinations). More recently, Nasdaq filed a proposed rule change with the SEC that would establish an integrated order delivery and execution service; the service would include a voluntary limit order facility and would permit institutional investors to obtain direct electronic access to trading through sponsoring Nasdaq market-makers. Nasdaq has also entered into an agreement to link its systems and proposed limit order facility to the OptiMark System.

Cross-border regulatory issues

The availability of remote access to international securities and derivatives markets has forced national securities regulators to grapple with the issue of how best to regulate direct access by investors to foreign markets subject to regulation abroad. Electronic trading systems facilitate such remote access and thus increase the urgency of these issues for regulators.

In the US, the SEC has never clarified the regulatory status of foreign entities that provide US persons with the ability to trade directly on foreign markets from the US, although it has given the issue considerable attention in recent years.

In a 1997 concept release, the SEC seemed to recognise the inevitability of automated cross-border trading and sought comment on a number of alternative approaches to regulating access to foreign markets through such systems, including reliance on home country regulation, the imposition of exchange registration requirements, and the regulation of access providers to foreign markets. (While the SEC has not acted on the issues raised in the concept release, the tone and content of the release suggested that the SEC was uncomfortable with relying on home country regulation and was seeking an approach short of full exchange registration and regulation.) The SEC staff also recently withdrew a previous interpretive position and took a no-action stance with respect to screen-based quotation systems that supply US investors with quotations, prices and other trade-reporting information entered by foreign broker-dealers; foreign broker-dealers entering quotations on such systems will not be deemed to have "solicited" US investors, provided that any transactions between a US investor and the foreign broker-dealer resulting from information displayed on a quotation system continue to be duly intermediated by a US broker-dealer pursuant to SEC Rule 15a-6 under the Securities Exchange Act of 1934, discussed below.

Market participants have undertaken various initiatives to advance the liberalisation of cross-border trading further. Some US broker-dealers have established "pass-through" links to trading on foreign markets through intermediation by the facilities of foreign broker-dealers. Tradepoint (a fully automated trading system registered as an exchange in the UK) recently applied to the SEC for a limited volume exemption from the exchange registration requirements of the US securities laws; several foreign exchanges have similarly sought no-action relief from the SEC allowing them to provide US investors with remote access to their trading systems. Meanwhile, Deutsche Terminbörse (DTB) obtained no-action relief from the US Commodity Futures Trading Commission allowing US members to trade certain German index futures through DTB terminals located in the US.

The UK, by contrast, has offered foreign markets and foreign alternative trading systems significantly greater access to UK investors. Instinet, for example, operates in the UK as an investment firm subject to "dealer-style" regulation by the Securities and Futures Authority and the London Stock Exchange. Moreover, a foreign exchange or alternative trading system that is subject to the UK Financial Services Act may seek recognition as a recognised investment exchange or a recognised clearing house if, among other conditions, it is subject to supervision in its home country affording UK investors protection equivalent to that required to be provided by UK-recognised investment exchanges under the Act; it is willing to cooperate, through information sharing arrangements and otherwise, with UK regulatory authorities; and memoranda of understanding or other adequate arrangements exist for cooperation between its home country regulatory authorities and UK regulatory authorities. Nasdaq, for example, is a UK-recognised investment exchange.

In the EU, cross-border trading on exchanges and exchange-based trading systems has been facilitated by the promulgation of the Investment Services Directive (the ISD). Under the ISD, EU investment firms and banks located in one member state (the "home" state) may obtain an EU-wide "passport" allowing them to establish branches or provide cross-border services in another member state (the "host" state), as well as to access the "regulated markets" of the host state, without registering with or obtaining a licence from the host state's securities regulatory authorities (although firms must still comply with host state codes of conduct). Because EU-regulated markets must allow investment firms licensed in every other EU member state to access their facilities, the ISD permits regulated markets to provide terminals and other "appropriate facilities" to firms located in other EU member states without submitting to regulation by such firms' "home" states.

The determination whether a particular market is a "regulated market" for the purposes of the ISD is made by its home state (provided that the market meets certain criteria set out in the ISD). Consequently, the question whether individual alternative trading systems are "regulated markets" for the purposes of the ISD depends on the internal laws of individual EU member states.

Impact of EMU on electronic trading systems

Economic and monetary union (EMU), when it becomes operational, will heighten competition among European exchanges and trading systems, as cross-currency risks are eliminated and market participants become better able to evaluate the relative cost-efficiency of national and supranational markets. The impact of EMU will be particularly pronounced in the fixed-income financial derivatives markets, where a common monetary policy determined by the European central bank will establish euro-denominated interest rates, price sources and interest rate derivative products in place of national interest rates and national derivative products.

The globalisation of the financial markets, as well as the ISD and EMU, has fostered the development of supranational European exchanges that rely heavily on alternative trading technologies to offer equal access to market participants throughout Europe and the rest of the world. For example, Easdaq is a screen-based exchange with multiple market-makers and market participants throughout the world. While Easdaq is regulated as an exchange by the Belgian Commission for Banking and Finance, its EU passport rights and sophisticated electronic trading platform enable it to disseminate price quotations and transaction information to members worldwide. Another approach to creating a Europe-wide stock market is Euro NM, a decentralised market consisting of a network of national markets operated by four EU participating exchanges (the Frankfurt Stock Exchange, the Paris Bourse, the Brussels Stock Exchange and the Amsterdam Stock Exchange) with harmonised listing and code-of-conduct standards and a central order and market-making facility.

In the financial derivatives markets, the proposed merger of the trading facilities of DTB and Soffex, the German and Swiss financial futures and options exchanges, will result in a single, fully automated electronic trading and clearing platform operated by a new European derivative exchange organisation to be called Eurex. As a result of the ISD and its no-action relief from the CFTC, DTB already had 63 remote members by the end of 1997 (up from 35 in 1995) throughout Europe and the US; its merger with Soffex, as well as proposed links with other European futures exchanges, such as Matif, the French futures exchange, would further increase Eurex's pan-European influence.

EU DEVELOPMENTS

As most people are aware, Europe has been moving towards a single economic union which would provide, at least on its face, that entities incorporated within the European Union (EU) and certain other European countries (collectively, the "European Economic Area" or "EEA") will be able to conduct business freely across their borders. The EEA includes the 15 members of the EU, and also includes Iceland, Liechtenstein and Norway. In addition, cross-border business will be able to be conducted in a single currency – the "euro" – in those countries that meet certain economic criteria. In the financial services industry, the European Commission has sought to achieve this with the adoption of several Directives, including the Investment Services Directive (ISD) discussed below. Although a Directive is intended to provide consistency in the application of its terms across EU member countries, in fact, this has often not been the case in the implementation of the ISD.

The ISD was adopted on 10 May 1993 and, although it was required to be implemented by 1 January 1996, it has still not yet been fully implemented by all EEA member countries. The ISD provides a broad outline as to several principles that should apply to cross-border regulation of investment services. It grants a "passport" throughout the countries of the EEA to all investment services firms established or based in an EEA country by authorising such entities to conduct business cross-border, without being required to obtain a licence or establish a branch or affiliate in each country that would be subject to regulation by each country. In particular, the ISD provides that an entity supplying investment services that is located in one country (its "home" country) will be regulated for the most part by the home country, even when doing business in another EEA member country (the "host" country). The adoption of other Directives relating to capital requirements for investment services firms was intended to harmonise regulation across the EEA countries, making the imposition of host country capital requirements unnecessary. However, each host country is required to impose rules, called "Conduct of Business rules", which regulate the way in which an EEA-based entity benefiting from the "passport" may conduct business in that host country.

Although the ISD was intended to liberalise the regulatory scheme for investment firms, in fact in many ways it has produced new barriers to the provision of cross-border investment services, especially for firms that are organised in countries outside the EEA. In the course of implementing ISD, many European countries adopted regulations that appear to impose new or additional restrictions on the ability of investment firms organised under the laws of countries outside the EEA to continue to do business with residents of their countries from outside the EEA. In addition, conduct of business rules adopted by each host country's regulator govern the manner in which a firm based in another EEA country is permitted to carry on business in the host country. These rules in the aggregate impose multiple and potentially conflicting regulation on the way firms conduct business in different countries within the EEA. Moreover, limitations on the types of instruments and services covered by ISD, and therefore eligible for the European passport, create difficulties for firms seeking to provide the full range of services to customers across borders by subjecting the uncovered activities to different licensing and other regulatory requirements imposed by individual countries.

ISD passport

Prior to adoption of the ISD, firms seeking to provide investment services in Europe were subject to the myriad of different licensing and regulatory schemes that existed in each country. Several member countries did not have restrictions on investment activities conducted on a cross-border basis, while others effectively required that firms seeking to provide investment services within their borders establish separately incorporated companies that were subject to their full regulatory regime. The ISD passport, by eliminating separate licensing and incorporation requirements, does provide certain advantages for EEA-based firms. In particular, the passport substantially reduces the cost of doing business by permitting EEA-based firms providing investment services to conduct business throughout the EEA in a single entity subject to home country regulation of capital. However, the new regulations adopted in implementing the ISD have in many cases imposed new requirements or restrictions on non-EEA member firms that had already been providing investment services on a cross-border basis. In other cases, the application of such rules is vague and ambiguous, making an analysis of the developing requirements to non-EEA firms difficult. Although the intermediation of an EEA-based firm in connection with transactions engaged in by a non-EEA firm may be sufficient to permit such firms to continue to engage in their business, this is not entirely clear and may be subject to the interpretation of each host country's regulator. Accordingly, non-EEA firms may need to restructure the way in which they do business in Europe, providing cross-border services and branching from their European affiliates, rather than from the non-EEA firm itself.

Conduct of Business rules

The ISD requires that each member country adopt regulations that relate to the way in which investment firms deal with their residents. Although in adopting these rules each country is to take into account the nature and sophistication of the domestic investors, many countries have provided little or no distinction in the application of these rules. The lack of consistency and guidelines provided for the content of the conduct of business rules means that a firm seeking to provide investment services on a cross-border basis can be subject to 17 different sets of rules, in addition to those imposed by the home country. This can offset much of the benefit that was intended to be achieved from the elimination of requirements to conduct business out of separately incorporated entities, each subject to a different country's regulatory scheme. At the extreme, only issues of incorporation and capital requirements have been made uniform for a given home country's firms. Multiple host country rules can affect most other aspects of cross-border investment business.

Investment activities

The ISD provides a passport to EEA entities only for specifically identified activities and instruments. Those instruments and activities, however, are not necessarily consistent with the scope of activities engaged in by investment firms. Activities that are not covered by the ISD are not subject to the benefit of the passport and regulation of such activities is still subject to the discretion of each country. For example, while transactions in financial futures are covered by the ISD, transactions in commodity futures are not.

Accordingly, a firm can provide services in connection with financial futures cross-border or through branches throughout the EEA, but may be required to obtain a licence or create a separately incorporated entity to engage in commodity futures transactions in the same countries. Other restrictions on passported activities are difficult to apply in practice. For example, foreign exchange transactions are subject to the passport and considered to be investment services, but only where such activities are connected with the provision of investment services. There is no guidance as to how this limitation will be applied and whether it will be applied consistently by each host country.

RECENT DEVELOPMENTS UNDER RULE 15a-6

Background

The US Securities Exchange Act of 1934 makes it unlawful for any "broker" or "dealer" to use any means or instrumentality of interstate commerce to effect any transaction in, or to induce or attempt to induce the purchase or sale of, any security (other than certain exempted securities) unless such broker or dealer is registered with the SEC. This provision could require registration by any non-US broker-dealer (including any non-US bank that falls within the definition of "broker" or "dealer") that, for example, telephones or sends documents into the US to contact US persons with respect to securities transactions.

Beginning in 1964, the SEC staff issued a number of interpretive releases and "no-action" letters intended to limit to some extent the broad extraterritorial application of broker-dealer registration requirements and outline the circumstances in which non-US broker-dealers could participate in US securities activities and engage in certain contacts with US investors without registration. The SEC's efforts to provide guidance with respect to the avoidance of registration by non-US broker-dealers culminated in 1989 with its adoption of Rule 15a-6 under the Securities Exchange Act of 1934, which provides a number of "safe harbour" exemptions from registration for non-US broker-dealers that engage only in certain specified activities with US investors.

Activities permitted by Rule 15a-6

Rule 15a-6 essentially consists of two sets of exemptions: (i) general exemptions, which may be relied on by any non-US broker-dealer; and (ii) conditional exemptions, which may be relied on only if the non-US broker-dealer enters into a "chaperoning" arrangement with an SEC-registered broker-dealer and agrees to certain other specified conditions.

General exemptions

1. Unsolicited transactions. A non-US broker-dealer may effect an unsolicited transaction with any US person. Solicitation, however, is viewed quite broadly by the SEC and will generally include any action intended to induce transactions, develop goodwill or make the broker-dealer known in the US. This exception is thus not extensively relied on.
2. Activities with specified counterparties. The non-US broker-dealer may solicit and engage in securities transactions with specified categories of persons, including broker-dealers and banks acting as principal or agent, certain supranational organisations, non-residents temporarily present in the US, and foreign branches of US entities.
3. Provision of research reports. A non-US broker-dealer may provide research reports to major US institutional investors (as defined below) and effect securities transactions resulting therefrom, subject to certain conditions.

Conditional exemptions

The range of activities in which an unregistered non-US broker-dealer is permitted to engage under the Rule is broadened for those non-US broker-dealers that rely on a "chaperoning" arrangement with an SEC-registered broker-dealer and meet certain other specified conditions. To take advantage of these exemptions, the following requirements must be satisfied:

1. Consent to service of process. A consent to service of process for any civil action brought by, or proceeding before, the SEC or any US self-regulatory organisation must be executed by the non-US broker-dealer and each of its personnel (foreign associated persons) engaged in the solicitation of US investors, and such consents must be held by the chaperoning SEC-registered broker-dealer. With respect to personnel, they can as an alternative be "dual registered" with the SEC and the relevant foreign regulator as applicable (and thus be directly subject to SEC regulation).
2. Provision of information. Each foreign associated person must provide to the chaperoning broker-dealer certain employment and other background information and the non-US broker-dealer must agree to provide to the SEC upon request certain information relating to transactions effected in reliance on the Rule.
3. Responsibilities of the chaperoning broker-dealer. The chaperoning broker-dealer must "effect" all securities transactions entered into between the non-US broker-dealer and the US counterparty. In addition, the chaperoning broker-dealer must take responsibility for, among other things, issuing confirmation statements to the US counterparty, complying with net capital requirements, extending or arranging for extensions of credit, and safeguarding, delivering and receiving funds and securities in connection with such transactions.

If these requirements are satisfied, a foreign associated person of the non-US broker-dealer would be permitted to: (a) contact (eg, by telephone), from outside the US, major

US institutional investors and US institutional investors (as defined below), provided that, in the case of contacts with US institutional investors that are not major US institutional investors, a representative of the chaperoning broker-dealer participates in such contact; and

(b) visit major US institutional investors and US institutional investors in the US, provided that the foreign associated person is accompanied on such visits by a representative of the chaperoning broker-dealer.

Some practical issues regarding Rule 15a-6

Until fairly recently, the utility in relying on the so-called "Conditional Exemptions" of Rule 15a-6 was quite limited. The most obvious and difficult problems were the definitions of "major US institutional investor" and "US institutional investor". The term "major US institutional investor" is defined in Rule 15a-6 as an entity (a) that either is a "US institutional investor" or an SEC-registered investment adviser, and (b) that owns or has under management at least US$100 million. The term "US institutional investor" includes US registered investment companies, banks, savings and loan associations, insurance companies and certain employee benefit plans, charitable organisations and trusts. Neither category includes ordinary corporations, hedge funds, partnerships or individuals. Thus, under the Rule as originally promulgated and until the publication of the April 1997 no-action letter discussed below, even large corporations such as IBM and General Motors – though qualifying as "qualified institutional buyers" under Rule 144A under the US Securities Act of 1933, which was in the process of being drafted at the same time as Rule 15a-6 and was adopted shortly after the adoption of Rule 15a-6 – do not satisfy the definition of "major US institutional investor" under Rule 15a-6 and therefore can not be directly contacted by a non-US broker-dealer seeking to rely on the Rule's safe harbour exemption.

In addition, the requirement that the chaperoning US broker-dealer be responsible for safeguarding, delivering, and receiving funds and securities presented a host of clearance and settlement problems. This provision has generally been viewed as effectively requiring that securities and funds pass through the chaperoning broker-dealer on their way to and from the non-US broker-dealer and the US counterparty, and thus adds time and cost to the process to the detriment of the US investors, particularly those having foreign custodians.

Further, the requirement that the US broker-dealer be responsible for extending or arranging for credit has generally been viewed as making US margin regulations applicable. The recent elimination of "arranging" restrictions in the US margin rules (which in many cases until recently barred a US broker-dealer from arranging for credit to a customer by a third party that it could not extend itself) has lessened the burden of this requirement.

Moreover, the chaperoning provisions effectively required that a representative of the US broker-dealer be available 24 hours a day in order to service US institutional investors that desire to place orders for foreign securities or discuss foreign securities transactions during foreign market hours.

Finally, the SEC staff, in responding to a no-action request in the context of Regulation S under the Securities Act of 1933, cautioned that offers and sales made by non-US broker-dealers to US fiduciaries acting for the account of non-US clients would need to comply with the Conditional Exemptions, despite the fact that such persons are classified as non-US persons (and the transactions constitute "offshore transactions") for the purposes of Regulation S.

Recent developments regarding Rule 15a-6

SEC no-action letters

The SEC staff has responded to many of the practical concerns regarding Rule 15a-6 by issuing two significant no-action letters. The first letter, issued in January 1996, permits (subject to certain conditions specified in the letter) non-US broker-dealers to effect, without registering with the SEC and without complying with Rule 15a-6, transactions in "foreign securities" with US fiduciaries acting for the account of offshore clients.

The second letter, issued in April 1997, significantly expands the definition of "major US institutional investor" and thereby greatly increases the utility of the Conditional Exemptions. Pursuant to the 1997 letter, the term "major US institutional investor" is now deemed to include, in addition to the categories described above, any institutional entity (including a corporation, partnership, unregistered investment adviser or hedge fund) that owns or has under management at least US$100 million in aggregate financial assets. Individuals continue to be excluded.

Pursuant to the 1997 letter, under the Conditional Exemptions a non-US broker-dealer may, in addition to the other activities described above:

(a) permit foreign associated persons to visit, on an unchaperoned basis, major US institutional investors (including US$100 million entities), so long as the number of days on which such unchaperoned visits occur do not exceed 30 per year and the foreign associated person does not accept orders to effect any securities transactions (whether involving US or foreign securities) while in the US;

(b) permit foreign associated persons to engage in oral communications from outside the US with US institutional investors without the participation of a representative of the chaperoning US broker-dealer if (1) such communications occur outside of the trading hours of the New York Stock Exchange, and (2) the foreign associated person does not accept orders to effect transactions in any securities other than those involving "foreign securities";

(c) provide US investors with access to screen-based quotation systems that supply quotations, prices and other trade reporting information input directly by the non-US broker-dealer, so long as any resulting transactions are effected in accordance with the requirements of Rule 15a-6; and

(d) clear and settle directly with major US institutional investors (including US$100 million entities) or US institutional investors (or their custodians) transactions involving "foreign securities" or US government securities, so long as (1) the non-US broker-dealer is not, and will not be, acting as custodian of the funds or securities of such investor, and (2) the non-US broker-dealer is not in default to any counterparty on any material financial market transaction.

Other developments that may impact Rule 15a-6

The SEC staff has long been aware that many securities transactions with US investors are conducted offshore in reliance on Rule 15a-6 and booked by non-US affiliates of SEC-registered broker-dealers due to the onerous net capital and margin requirements (particularly in connection with over-the-counter derivatives) for broker-dealers imposed under US law. To remedy this situation, the SEC has recently (i) proposed the creation of a new, more limited regulatory regime (with an alternative net capital structure permitting the use of statistical models) for a class of broker-dealers (OTC Derivatives Dealers) that engage primarily in over-the-counter derivatives transactions and other non-securities related activities, (ii) proposed amendments to the "haircuts" applicable to certain interest rate products under the Exchange Act's net capital rules, and (iii) issued a concept release regarding whether broker-dealers should generally be permitted to use statistical models to calculate net capital requirements.

The SEC has acknowledged that implementation of these proposals would be intended to bring back to the US certain types of transactions now being booked in offshore affiliates (even when most or all marketing and sales contact with the US investor are conducted from a US entity) and to permit SEC-registered broker-dealers to compete more effectively with banks, unregulated trading vehicles and non-US broker-dealers. Thus, despite indications by the SEC staff that it is considering a more comprehensive review of Rule 15a-6 and may issue a concept release or propose amendments to Rule 15a-6 later this year, these initiatives regarding OTC Derivatives Dealers and the SEC's net capital rules could, if successfully implemented, reduce the importance of US-based investment firms' reliance on Rule 15a-6. The success of these initiatives could also cause the SEC staff in the future to be less willing to liberalise the Rule further or grant additional no-action relief. On the other hand, if the SEC's OTC Derivatives Dealer and net capital initiatives do not produce practical solutions, then increasing globalisation will result in increasing reliance on Rule 15a-6 and further pressure to make adjustments to the Rule to increase its utility.

Alan L. Beller, Cleary Gottlieb and
Marcy Engel*, Salomon Smith Barney

*The authors wish to acknowledge the significant assistance they have received from their colleagues from Cleary Gottlieb, J. Eugene Marans, Dana G. Fleischman and Onnig H. Dombalagian.

Regulation 1998: Focus on the Internet

In the wholesale financial services market, most of the Internet's distinctive features and characteristics have been in use for some time. But in the retail market the impact of the Internet is potentially huge. It offers a distribution channel for standardised products and services, such as primary offerings of securities and sales of collective investment schemes and life products, to private investors around the globe.

The legal and regulatory issues thrown up by the new technology are predictably complex. This chapter reviews some of the steps taken so far by the regulators, and the problems that remain to be addressed.

THE NATURE OF THE INTERNET

The Internet is an informal, worldwide network of computers, operating to a common set of internationally recognised rules known as software protocols.

The project which became the Internet started with the idea of "packet-switching". Traditionally, in order to transfer real-time data electronically between two computers, a direct connection had to be established between them. Packet switching was intended to provide a decentralised network through which US government agencies could communicate with each other after a nuclear attack had wiped out their centralised systems. The computer message would be broken into packets, each of which made its own way to its destination by a variety of routes. Even if some of the messages were lost, the rest would arrive at their intended destination.

This idea was first put forward in 1962, and was taken up as a research project by the US Department of Defence's Advanced Research Projects Agency (ARPA). A live communications network, known as ARPANET, was established by 1969, and began to be used by the military and academics. Other academic networks were set up independently, and then linked up to ARPANET. The Internet has thus been, from its early stages, a network of networks.

Although the US military dropped out in 1982, and ARPANET itself disappeared in 1990, the Internet continued to grow, encouraged by the development of protocols, into a permanent worldwide network of computers, transferring data over the world's telephone systems. By 1989 the number of host computers was over 100,000 and at least 11 foreign countries were connected.

To establish a presence on the Internet, most users will go through an "access provider" – an organisation that operates computers permanently connected to the Internet – offering access through leased lines providing permanent access, or through local dial-up numbers that connect the user to the Internet only for the duration of a telephone call. Leased lines are expensive, and the majority of users with desk-top personal computers connect through a modem and a telephone call. The access provider gives the user an access code, enabling him to log on and be recognised by the access provider, together with a unique electronic address known as an Internet protocol address. The user can then connect through the access provider to the Internet. Where the user connects through a local access provider, the cost of his telephone call is charged at local rates, whether he is communicating with someone next door or on the other side of the world.

The Internet also offers various information retrieval systems, of which the "worldwide web" is easily the most popular. A presence on the web is known as a site. A site is a digital storage place accessible via the Internet. A site can be set up by a direct link from the user's computer to the web, or by renting host space from an access provider.

In commercial terms, both Internet e-mail and web sites offer huge economies by their ability to communicate to a large audience (in the case of e-mail by a direct "postal" mass-mailing exercise) quickly and cheaply. Both can display written and graphic material. Pictures and videos can also be made available on web sites, and audio communications, though generally of poor quality at the moment, will soon also be a viable method of Internet communication.

However, the rapid and anarchic growth of the Internet, with its decentralised approach, and weaving together of so many computers, means that it has no established structure and is difficult to navigate. While various search tools and techniques have been developed to address this, the Internet is still not especially user-friendly.

Different parts of the web can be connected to each other by hypertext mark-up language. This can be used to create special codes, or hyperlinks, which connect directly from one part of a document to another, to a different document on the same site, or to a document on any other site whose address is known or can be identified. The site's e-mail address will typically be included as one of the links, so that by clicking on the link the browser generates an e-mail window in which to write a message. Links can be used to move very rapidly from one document or site to another. There is no limit to the number of hyperlinks that can be carried in a single web document. Some sites are set up as specialist link pages, providing potentially hundreds or thousands of links to other sites dealing with a common topic.

In none of these cases is it necessary for site hosts or operators, who are linked together in this way, to be associated with each other, or to have given their consent to the creation of a link. A link can be created by a completely unconnected third party, and the site operator may never know that the link exists unless he carries out a special search to check the links which have been attached to his site.

Users access the web by means of a software browser. This gives a basic facility to search for information by using links, and connecting the user to various navigation aids, generally described as "search engines". In its most basic form, a search engine comes as a simple word search facility. More sophisticated engines, the most advanced of which are known as "intelligent agents", will search for particular categories of information, help the user to refine the type of information he is looking for, and cross-refer to the preferences of other users with similar interests. They may also deliver the engine's own summary or review of the sites available, encouraging the user to make a decision, based on that summary, as to whether or not to visit a particular site.

A PC user will need to download a web document (ie copy it) into his computer's memory (random access memory) before he can look at it on screen. This is a purely momentary copy, unless the user takes the further step of copying the document on to his hard drive or floppy disc, or prints it out as a hard copy, in which case he may retain the copy indefinitely. The user can view a document comprehensively, by scrolling through it, or selectively, by using a search engine.

THE INTERNET AND FINANCIAL SERVICES

Financial services activity on the Internet is at a relatively early stage of development, but a number of general points can be made.

The greatest potential for Internet commerce is in the retail market. Most of the Internet's distinctive features have been in use in wholesale and business markets for some time. Businesses regularly use direct computer links, such as "Electronic document interchange" to communicate with agents and suppliers, while in the securities and banking markets, computerised international bank payments and clearing house and settlement systems are highly developed and specialised. Sophisticated, bespoke systems, such as these, are tailored to the high net worth businesses and markets concerned, and they are likely to remain of a higher standard and quality than any equivalent on the Internet. This is not surprising considering how much money is spent on developing and maintaining them. Even here, the Internet is a potential competitor which will help to keep the wholesale markets up to the mark. It may also help to improve the efficiency of specific wholesale areas of business, typically information dissemination – eg the distribution of offering circulars and related material, the streamlining of back office operations, and the reduction of trade confirmation and settlement costs. But the Internet's significance is greatest at the retail end of the spectrum, where it can offer advanced international electronic communication facilities, hitherto the prerogative of big business, to private investors around the globe.

The retail market is predominately a mass market, which lends itself to mass sales techniques. Conventional providers of retail financial products and services are banks, life companies, retail fund managers and stockbrokers. Their distribution channels hitherto have been through branch networks and direct sales forces, direct advertising, and sales through networks of freelance agents and intermediaries. More recently, these have extended to include telephone sales services.

A retail market of the size and sophistication of the US can accommodate a relatively high level of specialisation, such as order execution brokers, commodity trade advisers and so on, but there is a big advantage in being able to offer a range of related financial services. Generally speaking, the higher the level of personal contact and trust, the more fruitful and profitable the distribution channel to the provider.

The Internet offers a distribution channel for standardised products and services such as primary offerings of securities, sales of collective investment schemes and life products, and order execution. There is a potential tension here between the pressure towards low-cost standardisation on the one hand and, on the other, the need to devise added-value features that will distinguish the service provider and allow for a more ambitious charging structure. But the Internet is also capable of offering a higher degree of personal service than a retail telephone service or newspaper advertisement, and of doing so more cheaply than a face-to-face selling network or a major advertising campaign. On the other hand, it should be remembered a serious presence on the Internet can be an expensive exercise and, outside the US, the volume of Internet-generated investment business is still fairly low.

Web sites

Internet commerce is predominately based on web sites. Sites are usually owned by a "host", who operates the site directly, or leases it to the actual operator or tenant. A leased site allows the operator to concentrate on his particular marketing or other interests while the host manages the site's infrastructure. Some hosts make a virtue of the number of tenants located on a particular site. In the UK, NatWest's *Buckingham Gate* and Barclays' *Barclay Square* operate as "virtual shopping malls", allowing customers to access and browse through a variety of retail shopping displays. An advantage for financial services (though some financial service providers might see it as a disadvantage) is that a multi-user site of this sort facilitates comparison between different firms offering similar services.

If investors were to make maximum use of such a site, it would ideally need some sort of distinctive reputation or semi-authoritative basis, raising the question of whether the site could be vetted or approved in some way by a regulator or other independent body.

The expectation is that there will be increasing development and use of such sites, and of the link pages and search engines that help to access them. A specialist search engine could help consumers to scour the market for the best saving and lending rates, and so on.

Information and interactivity

Web sites, at their simplest, involve straightforward promotional activity – that is to say a one-way communication by the site operator, which can be accessed by users in their capacity as potential investors, but which does not include a dialogue. This could range from basic information on prices and interest rates, to added-value information in the form of investment analysis or standardised advice. A function of this sort might be provided by a corporate brochure, a newspaper feature or an investment analysis circular. Such sites may also give the user information on how to access further material, by way of links to related pages, or via an e-mail address for enquiries.

The Internet is widely used to supply basic information such as interest rates, stock prices, company analyses, currency rates and so on. Its use on an interactive basis is, however, relatively limited outside the US. There is clearly potential for changing this. The financial industry deals in dematerialised services, most of which can be supplied electronically.

A basic form of interactivity is the exchange of e-mail messages between the site operator and the user to provide some sort of follow-up service, such as the placing of orders or the supply of a credit card number. Another is the provision of transaction backup services in the form of trade reporting and account information, allowing the client, for example, to check the current state of his bank account.

Many US mutual fund companies have established web sites, or sites on proprietary on-line links, providing a range of mutual fund-related services. Their sites allow investors to download the fund's prospectus, complete subscription applications without having to wait for the materials to be posted to them, and give instructions to transfer investments among multiple funds.

A combination of account management and order execution is readily achievable in any moderately sophisticated Internet service. This has been a huge growth area for US retail stockbrokers. In 1994 there were around 400,000 on-line broking accounts, while at the beginning of 1998 some 3 million clients had web-based accounts. In 1997, 17% of US retail share transactions were implemented over the Internet. The cheapness of dealing costs has lead to intensive price competition which, in turn, helped to generate a fall in average dealing commission of 50% in 1997.

In the UK the first Internet dealing service (there are currently five) was launched in 1995 by Charles Schwab. This is, of course, closely tied to the concept of an execution-only service (ie no advice or investment management) where profit margins are particularly thin, and likely to get thinner if Internet trading grows.

True market-wide electronic order execution, of the type available on the Nasdaq market (Small Order Execution Service) or the London Stock Exchange (Stock Exchange Automatic Execution Facility), where one trader enters into a binding contract with another by pressing a button, have yet to become widely available to the retail client. However, interactive facilities are developing that will allow bids and offers to be posted (and ultimately executed) on an Internet bulletin board, or through a central order matching service, at least in relation to a particular stock or limited number of stocks. Spring Street Brewing in the US has been running a bulletin board and related execution facility for trading in its own shares since 1996. The cost of execution on such a system is potentially lower because dealing settlement can be completely automated. There are, however, other issues. How could the integrity of such a market be assessed? How would an investor dealing through a private bulletin board know he was getting the best price? How would the rest of the market know about business being done by such means? A corporate trader who accidentally presses the "execute trade" button on his trading terminal will normally be held to his bargain, but a retail investor in such a position is usually allowed more leeway. The bulletin board operator may be expected to recognise this, and to build appropriate safeguards into any dealing system, such as a warning flash, drawing the investor's attention to the nature of the legal commitment he is about to enter into.

More skilled services, such as personal advice on complicated products or strategies, and discretionary management, are less amenable to standardised distribution. While these services might utilise the Internet, they require a high degree of personal involvement on the part of the financial services firm, which is likely to exceed the capacity of any communication system operating primarily as a data transfer medium. A resolute attempt to cram such a service into an Internet format might lead to unsatisfactory performance by the financial services firm. There is also a practical incentive for firms to distinguish mere information transfer from qualitative advice or discretionary management, because they can generally charge more for the more sophisticated service.

Business done over the Internet is thus likely to gravitate to the lower end of the market in terms of profitability, where standardisation, low overheads, mass-marketing and potentially high volumes of business can offset increased competition and low profit margins. Cost savings come from the ability to cut down on the overheads inherent in branch networks, mailshots and other distribution channels. The marginal cost of additional transactions is potentially very small and some operations, traditionally done in-house, may even be out-sourced by downloading directly on to the client's computer.

An important element in the growth of Internet business will be the development of an efficient e-cash payment system. At the moment most Internet payments are achieved by e-mailing credit card details. But the Internet has the potential for transferring money value from one person to another without reference to a central issuing or accounting authority, such as a bank. It could achieve this on a similar basis to a telephone pay card. The user would obtain cash from his bank account and credit it to a credit account on the Internet, where it would be stored as e-cash. When he wanted to pay for a service he would instruct his computer to transfer e-cash on the Internet from his account to that of the financial services provider.

Disintermediation

Theoretically, the Internet could facilitate the ability of retail investors to deal with each other to such an extent that financial service intermediaries simply disappeared. The idea of disintermediation goes back many years, and is perhaps mostly a question of which service provider can get closest to the customer. There has always been competition between lending banks and securities markets as to which could offer the best source of capital. The growth of the Eurobond market was, in its time, taken as a sign that banks were losing ground as intermediaries between corporate lenders and borrowers, who would now deal with each other directly through international securities offerings. Banks responded by offering fixed-term loans instead of overdrafts, creating a long-term capital facility similar to that provided by the securities debt markets, and becoming involved in the Eurobond market itself as managers and underwriters.

The Internet is capable of providing the investor with all the public information he needs in order to decide whether or not to make an investment in the borrower, without the need for specialist research and advice services. The investor can access all available trading and market data, and instruct an intelligent agent to find the best product to match his needs. He can then send an instruction over the Internet to an execution-only broker to execute the trade directly with the corporate issuer or product provider.

Disintermediation of this sort is already factored into the existing markets for a sophisticated or powerful customer. Such customers usually have their own methods and procedures for making the required decisions, sometimes internally, sometimes by employing external advisers or managers. But if the Internet increases the access of inexperienced clients to vast amounts of information on which their decisions can be based, the need for someone who can interpret it for them, and tell them how to act, should grow rather than diminish, with the financial services firm becoming the client's personal guide to what is on offer on the Internet. This is not hugely different from existing practice, where the financial services adviser collects public information from borrowers and issuers, assesses that information, and makes a recommendation to his clients, based on that assessment, as to whether to buy, sell or hold.

Who will provide the services?

Traditional financial services suppliers, such as banks, life companies and stockbrokers, are likely to continue as major players in Internet financial services. They have established credibility, brand names and experience. However, it is conceivable that the growing role of personal finance software products means that technology companies and the technology interface with the Internet could become the focus of the user's financial affairs. A new generation of investors might emerge whose brand name loyalty was to a specialist Internet access provider, a host or a computer programme, rather than to a traditional financial services firm.

DISTINCTIVE FEATURES OF THE INTERNET

The Internet not only covers (or will shortly cover) all normal forms of communication. It also combines them to produce a number of distinctive characteristics and hybrid features.

Lack of central control

The Internet is not a legal entity. No one controls it and no one has overall responsibility for it. No single legal system applies to it and it is not resident in any particular jurisdiction. Standard protocols and packages are developed with the existing system and its capabilities in mind. The success of particular standard protocols comes from the fact that people adopt them. People adopt them because they facilitate improvements in the exchange and development of other communications and ideas. The system develops further as a result. And so on.

From the point of view of securities regulation, this makes it impossible to lay down any standards as to what appears on the Internet, which the regulator can be certain will be enforceable against all users. It is always possible, of course, for a regulator to say that its particular regulatory approach will or will not apply to any particular part of the Internet, or a particular activity on it. But enforcement of that approach is ultimately only possible in relation to the individual financial service providers or issuers who are, or who at least have substantial assets physically located in, the same jurisdiction as the regulator.

Similar concerns arise regarding the integrity of other aspects of an Internet business system. For instance, there is likely to be considerable demand for an intermediary, such as a bank or similar institution, to guarantee the integrity of an Internet payment system and take on the risk of payment failures. Likewise, customers faced with the prospect of contracting with a counterparty of unknown or indeterminate status or quality, will feel much better if an intermediary is prepared to assume, for a fee, the credit risk of the counterparty failing to perform.

In principle, the desire of the parties for security, measured against the actual risk of default, is likely to leave a gap that will allow such an intermediary to make a profit by contracting to assume these risks. The intermediary would probably need to have its own systems for verifying the identity of the parties to the transaction, obtaining security for any obligation which it guaranteed and authenticating the terms of the sales contract. This resembles existing bank guarantee arrangements as operated in the form of, say, commercial and standby letters of credit and performance bonds. But there is a big difference in scale and in the quality of the parties. How would the intermediary recreate this sort of international guarantee concept at a retail level, between retail counterparties in different jurisdictions?

Lack of permanence and manipulability

Ordinary documents have a permanent tangible identity. They can be readily identified and handled, and once printed are difficult to alter. For this reason, written communications are treated differently from oral communication for a variety of purposes. Electronic documents have no equivalent integrity. The Internet stores and transfers information by reducing it to digital form and while this offers a high degree of accuracy, it is also very easily changed, manipulated or deleted, and the changes are difficult and often impossible to identify retrospectively. This is in stark contrast to normal written forms of communication. Even routine updating of an information document becomes an issue.

Electronic updating of financial services promotional material tends to take place much more frequently than the updating of conventional sales material, because it is so much easier to do. This makes it extremely difficult for anyone to be sure what was being displayed on a particular site at a particular time, and can create significant evidential problems in the event of a dispute, unless the site operator has kept a reliable audit trail of any changes. Regulatory inspection of the site would only be possible on an "as it is" basis, unless site operators were required to keep such an audit trail.

On the other hand, electronic documents do have the potential to be more permanent than, say, a face-to-face conversation or a telephone call. There is a written (or visual) record which, while it does not have an innately permanent tangible form, may be given various degrees of permanence by one or more of the parties involved. Thus, it is up to the individual user whether he chooses to leave his e-mails in his computer memory, delete them, copy them on to hard disc, or print them as a permanent tangible document.

Some of these issues have already had to be looked at in relation to the dematerialisation of securities. Physical share certificates have regularly been dismissed by promotors of new technology as irrelevancies, sustained only by the sentimental attachment of private investors. There is, however, a good deal to be said for not being able to delete the primary evidence of someone's title to a shareholding by the mere flick of a button. In practice, operators of dematerialised systems have had to take extensive steps to replicate the integrity of a physical share certificate. Solutions adopted include the use of a central registrar, the keeping of duplicate records on different systems, regular reconciliations between the records, and the support of a custodian or other institutional backer prepared to compensate the client for any shortfall. In other cases, the original physical certificates, instead of being destroyed, may be stored with a central depository on an immobilised basis, as the ultimate fall-back for an audit check. Such systems tend to be operated on and around exchanges and clearing systems that are centrally controlled and regulated. An equivalent level of control could be achieved on the Internet, but probably only on a partial or decentralised basis. For example, Internet investors could be encouraged to deal through an approved central registry or depository, but could not be made to do so.

Incompleteness/partiality

Documents displayed on a computer screen are accessed and read in a different way from conventional tangible material. Only a very small portion of the text can be displayed in readable form at any one time, and the boundaries of the document may be difficult to identify. The search tools available are designed to compensate for this, making Internet information highly accessible, but in a particular and quite different way from conventional documents.

Electronic search engines, hypertext links and similar devices allow the user to skip through documents looking at particular pre-identified subject matter. The Internet thus lends itself readily to browsing, but makes it difficult for the reader to get a feel for a document of any length, particularly one that is designed to be read in its entirety, unless it is printed out in hard copy form.

The issue becomes more acute where a series of documents or communications are concerned. The browsing technique potentially bypasses information that is of no interest to the user (or to his search engine) or which an opportunistic programmer may wish to steer him away from. An obvious example is investment risk warnings, which may be included in the document but never looked at. In other cases, a search engine may be programmed to provide the investor with its own subjective summary or description of the nature and scope of a site.

The same issue may arise with link pages. Link pages that are maintained as a public service are likely to provide (or at least seek to provide) information on a reasonably objective basis. But link pages that are maintained as a commercial or private enterprise can provide link information that is slanted in whatever way suits the link site operator.

The whole purpose of such devices is to steer the investor towards particular, and therefore limited, categories of information. It is easy enough, whether unintentionally or deliberately, for any or all of them to give the investor a selective view of an investment matter, in a way that is ultimately wrong, misleading or not in his financial interests.

Anonymity and fraud

It is up to the site operator to decide what information he puts on his site. If the information does not make his identity or geographical location clear, the only other source of information on this topic is his electronic address. The basic requirement is that it should be unique. There is no requirement that it should include the operator's full name, or indeed that it should refer to his true name at all. Nor need it identify his actual geographical location. It is also possible to "anonymise" a site or communication or make it look as if it came from or originated in a particular jurisdiction, when it has in fact come from somewhere quite different.

This upsets many of the general assumptions to which investors and regulators have become accustomed. It is, for instance, usually assumed that where an investor does business with a foreign firm, it will be reasonably apparent to the investor that he is dealing with someone outside his own jurisdiction. It is also assumed, in connection with money laundering regulations, that a bank or broker, opening an account for a new customer, will be able to ask the customer for original tangible documents to verify the customer's identity. If all communication is over the Internet, this will become much more difficult.

The potential anonymity of Internet business makes it easier to set up fraudulent or copycat web sites, and more difficult to detect their counterfeit nature. A suspect site can look very authentic and real. It may be a close copy of a genuine site with a familiar or impressive-sounding name. For example, an aspiring fraudster could locate in a jurisdiction without adequate regulation, create a fake site for a non-existent bank with a domain name that looked as if it was in the US and therefore US-regulated. It could then offer high rates of interest for deposits with a 12-month lock-in. Once e-cash is up and running it could collect the deposits directly over the Internet and disappear well before the 12-month lock-in period expired.

Some way of authenticating the identity of financial services providers and counterparties on the Internet is clearly desirable. One possibility is to load existing registers of authorised financial service firms on to the Internet, on a jurisdiction by jurisdiction basis. Another is to set up publicly sponsored sites containing information on the genuineness of specific financial services sites, and notifying investors of scams at the earliest opportunity. In each case, however, it would be necessary for the investor to take the initiative and actively check such sites before doing business.

International scope

Like a telephone call, the Internet is highly international, offering cheap and easy communication across different jurisdictions and national boundaries, without any obvious deterioration in quality or change in presentation. This raises the question of where, in a cross-border transaction, the transaction is deemed to take place for legal and regulatory purposes. The truth is that it is taking place in at least two jurisdictions. This will become more complicated where the access provider or host operating the web site is in one jurisdiction, the site operator in another and the investor in a third.

While these sorts of issues have been around for some time, any problems they have caused have largely been confined to wholesale business professionals and major business entities who understand the risks they are taking. At the retail level – always the most sensitive from the regulatory point of view – direct access by foreign financial service firms has been extremely limited.

There are perhaps two main issues. The first, which has already been touched on, is the danger of a firm located in a lightly regulated foreign jurisdiction selling into, say, Europe or the US in complete disregard of the domestic regulatory requirements. How can the regulators take action against such a practice? The answer is probably a mixture of (a) international cooperation, ensuring that fewer and fewer home jurisdictions are prepared to allow firms to operate on this basis; (b) investor education, warning wherever possible of the effect of dealing with firms who are not subject to any adequate regulatory control in their home jurisdiction; and (c) (hopefully) a certain amount of support from intermediaries such as banks who are prepared to offer a service that minimises risk.

A second major issue is the fact that a financial services firm, which places promotional material on the Internet, is potentially distributing that material throughout every jurisdiction in the world. It seems, therefore, that he will need to comply with the regulations applicable in every jurisdiction. Thus, under the European Union's Investment Services Directive, advertising and marketing are generally the responsibility of the state where the investor is located. As a result, a banker operating a single marketing site in its home state would, under EU law, have to satisfy 17 different sets of EU host state regulations in relation to its advertisements.

A similar issue arises in relation to personal data. The EU's Directive on Data Protection imposes requirements regarding subject access and methods of retention and storage, and prohibits the processing of data without the consent of the subject. Processing includes any operation performed on personal data such as collection, recording, organisation, storage and so on, and would include most forms of communication on the Internet. Data may only be transferred to a non-EU jurisdiction if the subject has given unambiguous consent or the transfer is necessary for the performance of a contract between the data user and the subject. But once data is placed on the Internet, it is impossible to be sure which jurisdictions it may be transferred to.

These problems are somewhat lessened by the difficulties a regulator would have in bringing an enforcement action, as well as, hitherto at least, the reluctance of national regulators to catch each other out in this way.

Reliability

Speed of response on the Internet can be extremely variable, particularly given the huge amount of information that may be moving around. On the other hand, the US experience is that it is much easier to get an order through to a broker via the Internet than by telephone, where long waits in telephone queues are likely when the markets are busy. As with other systems, the need is for a backup system that can take over, if a key service provided through the Internet starts to become unreliable or unavailable.

Security

The Internet operates on open communication lines with a high degree of connectivity. It is vulnerable to the importation of viruses, via floppy discs or downloading. Information on the Internet is also vulnerable to hacking. Unauthorised access to e-mail and web sites is relatively easy to achieve, and the UK Data Protection Registrar has issued a formal warning that Internet e-mail is not a secure medium of communication.

Concerns as to security are most relevant to those who maintain a permanent computer connection to the Internet. A user who merely accesses the Internet on a temporary basis through an access provider, or who rents site space from a host, creates no direct connection between the Internet and his own computer, though of course he will be transferring information backwards and forwards between the two, and confidential or proprietary information once passed to the host or access provider is accessible on the Internet generally.

A user's incoming e-mail, for instance, arrives on the access provider's computer. Before transfer to the user – ie as long as the message remains with the access provider – it remains potentially accessible to anyone who can find the right password. So a hacker who could find a way into the access provider's computer could trawl the material passing through it for, say, credit card numbers. The risk of this happening is sometimes described as no different from the risk that a credit card number will be intercepted over the telephone, but this is an oversimplification. Telephone calls are based on analogue communication, and do not lend themselves to the sophisticated search engines available on the Internet. Nor is there any real equivalent, in a telephone call, of the high "connectivity" of the Internet – ie the huge number of people who are linked up to and potentially have access to each piece of data.

Communications on the Internet are therefore less private than would be the case with a letter, telex, facsimile or telephone call, all of which are inherently structured and operated as communications between two specific and limited persons. This sort of risk can be much reduced by the encrypting of messages and, to a much lesser extent, passwords. The standard of encryption available is, at its best, very good indeed.

One related question is how much access governments should have to encrypted information. A government body that held all the encryption keys could go on fishing expeditions through confidential material without the proprietor ever being aware of this. If, however, public authorities are locked out, this raises the question of who will control the encrypters. If encryption itself is not controlled in some way, governments risk loss of control of major matters such as taxation and monetary policy, as well as the ability to investigate suspected criminal activities. A system could be devised, for example, for buying goods and services on a cross-border basis, through uncrackable encrypted messages, without paying customs duties. The lack of central control over future e-cash systems raises similar concerns. Systems that are not bank account-based can, in combination with encryption, provide absolute secrecy without any regulatory audit trail.

Where encryption is not available, clear notices can be included in documents warning that the information is confidential. This will help to establish the legal basis for action for breach of confidentiality, but seems unlikely to deter someone who still wants to go ahead and access the confidential information. Indeed, in some cases it would probably actively encourage them to do so.

The latest web browsers, such as Internet Explorer and Netscape, include security features that show a warning notice if the user fills in a form on a Web page, is about to send it off, and the information can be read in transit. The user can then choose not to send the information over the Internet, and ask for a fax or telephone number instead.

Promotional activities and advice

Generally, the closer a financial services relationship comes to personal soliciting or advice, the more carefully it needs to be regulated. But at this early stage of Internet commerce, it may be difficult to decide the status of a financial services relationship conducted over the Internet. Is a financial services site operating as an advertisement? If so, at whom is the advertisement directed? Is it providing neutral, factual information, or is it soliciting investment? If it is an interactive site, at what point does it start to provide personal advice to a client on which the client is entitled to rely?

The interactive nature of the Internet, as well as its transitory qualities, means that its written communications have similarities with oral communication. It can replicate some or all of the features of the personal persuasive interaction that takes place between an investor and a potential salesman, without the need for a face-to-face meeting, or indeed without any oral communication at all.

The material available on a web site or on the Internet generally is often described as "information" or "information only", suggesting that the information provided is, of its nature, factual and neutral. Where this is indeed the case the site owner or operator's liability to others is probably limited to the factual accuracy of the information. However, the more persuasive or personalised the material, the more likely it is that it will be treated as personal advice or a recommendation. Insofar as this is not the case, and the sort of personal, tailored advice provided in a conventional advisory relationship is replaced by Internet mass consumption interactive information services, there is liable to be pressure to widen the scope of liability (both regulatory and under the general law) for economic loss caused by incorrect or misleading information provided over the Internet.

Regulatory and legal significance often attaches to the question of who approached whom. Where a broker initiates contact by cold calling a potential investor, particularly a retail investor, any investment decisions that the investor then makes are often much influenced by the advice or sales pitch that he was given by the broker. The broker's resulting duties to the investor are likely to be greater than they would have been if the investor had initiated the contact, with a particular investment objective already in mind. A transaction is typically initiated by the investor where the investor rings up a stockbroker or seeks an appointment at his office to discuss a particular investment matter. It is not at all clear that an investor, browsing through the Internet, who happens to alight on the stockbroker's web site, can be treated as initiating contact in the same way. Web browsing is more akin to leafing through the financial pages of the Sunday newspaper than to walking through the door of the stockbroker's office. If the client wanted to follow up a newspaper advertisement he would have to make a separate conscious decision to write a letter, send a fax or make a telephone call. On a web site, he can achieve this while still reading the advertisement.

THE REGULATORY RESPONSE

The Internet is sufficiently close to other methods of communication for existing regulations to make sense when applied to it. There is, of course, an issue as to exactly how they apply. This sort of problem is not confined to financial services. Storage of a copyright work in digital form in an electronic medium is a reproduction within the meaning of Article 9 of the Berne Convention on copyright. Any distribution of copyright work over an electronic network inevitably results in the creation of at least a transient copy at the receiving end, and possibly further transient copies at points in between. Almost any form of communication on the Internet appears, therefore, to be in breach of the Berne Convention.

The fundamentally decentralised and unregulated nature of the Internet, taken as a whole, is unlikely to change in the foreseeable future. What is possible is that, as the Internet is increasingly used for financial commerce, and as the problems for that commerce become more apparent, there will be shift of business towards parts of the Internet that offer a system of integrity – ie a "flight to quality" – whether in the form of an international standard of approval, or the operation of a particular regulatory regime, or performance guarantees offered by a particular sponsoring intermediary. But all this is some way in the future.

The idea of harmonising national financial service regulations to produce a single international Internet regulatory standard is unrealistic in the short term. Different jurisdictions have fundamentally different attitudes to investor protection, reflecting both high level policy and internal market pressures, although, in the end, internal markets may be dragged into conformity with each other by the inexorable force of international market competition. More practically, a set of international standards could be relatively easily put together to identify the "status" of a site, providing a recognised method for identifying which regulations it conformed with, which jurisdiction it was aimed at, and exactly what services and guarantees it offered – the regulatory equivalent of the Internet's own software protocols.

A further level of international agreement would be useful, regarding the extent to which national regulators would refrain from attempting to impose their requirements on the operators of Internet sites who have no connection with their jurisdictions, other than by accident through the Internet itself. There is, for example, undoubtedly scope for a recognised means of coordinating the many existing regimes for establishing that an advertisement is directed only at certain persons in a given jurisdiction, and that persons in other jurisdictions are not being solicited. An advanced version of this, which is not currently possible technologically, and would probably only be developed if the regulators took a particularly aggressive stance, would be for the financial services firm to identify, via its software, the geographical location of a user who was seeking to access its site, and to block access to persons located in jurisdictions for which the firm did not have regulatory clearance.

Disclaimers are a useful tool in Internet regulation, though they are far from being a panacea for all ills. Two main uses are discussed here. First, they may be used to make it clear that only certain services are being provided. A flat denial by a site operator that it provides investment advice may be enough if it is operating a free site that does not offer financial services. It is of questionable value in other circumstances. A web site disclaimer is unlikely to be read in isolation from the content of the site. If the overall assessment of the site content leads to the conclusion that the operator has, in fact, provided investment advice to the user, the disclaimer will almost certainly be ineffective.

Secondly, the disclaimer may be used to demonstrate that the site operator/financial services firm is only offering its services or products to certain investors, perhaps on a territorial basis, or by reference to their level of sophistication or experience. Where the intention is to impose a territorial limitation, there is obvious difficulty in knowing whether the wording of the disclaimer will be valid worldwide. A statement that services or products are available only to investors located in certain jurisdictions, or only to investors who possess certain other qualifications, may be of doubtful authority unless the firm can demonstrate that it has made some additional effort to verify the investor's status. This might involve a questionnaire to be answered by the investor, a notification to the investor of any detailed conditions that apply, and (depending on the circumstances) controlled access to certain parts of the site, so that an investor would have to be issued with a password before he could access sensitive material, such as prospectuses.

The close connection between access providers, hosts and operators, raises significant issues of liability. While the basic assumption is likely to be that the operator, rather than the access provider or the host, is liable for the material put on to the Internet by the operator, this is capable of abuse, and the host and access provider must ultimately accept some level of responsibility. As "sponsors" they cannot turn a blind eye to something that they know to be in breach of relevant law or regulation. There are no financial services authorities on this issue, but it has been considered in the US in relation to copyright infringement. In *Playboy Enterprises Inc v Frena* 839 F Supp 1552 (MD Fla 1993), the defendant's bulletin board had distributed unauthorised copies of photographs from *Playboy* magazine. The defendant was held to have infringed *Playboy's* copyright, even though he claimed that he did not himself put such material on his board and was unaware that some of his subscribers were doing so. In contrast, in *Villagers Technology Center v Netcom Online Communication Services* 21 November 1995 ND, Cal Netcom, a large Internet access provider, was held not to be liable for copying that it had not initiated because, although breach of copyright was a strict liability, there should still be some element of volitional causation, which is lacking where a system is merely used to create a copy by a third party.

The US regulatory experience

In the US there has been considerable interest, both commercial and regulatory, in the use of the Internet for public offerings and placements. The SEC has proceeded by a series of detailed releases, dealing with both general principles and individual cases.

Delivery of documents

In October 1995, the SEC issued an interpretive release entitled *Use of electronic media for delivery purposes* (Securities Act Release No 33-7233) addressing the electronic delivery of documents such as prospectuses, annual reports to shareholders and proxy solicitation materials by issuers, third parties (such as persons making tender offers or soliciting proxies) and persons acting on their behalf. In that release, the SEC set out its views on the requirements and standards to be met by securities issuers and mutual funds using electronic media to deliver such documents in compliance with the Federal securities laws. Much of the guidance took the form of 51 examples of particular uses of electronic media by securities professionals.

The SEC said that Federal securities laws would be met if such distribution "results in the delivery to the intended recipients of substantially equivalent information as these recipients would have had if the information were delivered to them in paper form". Three factors were cited as relevant in this respect.

1. *Notice of delivery.* Investors should receive the same level of notice as would be required with paper delivery. Sending an e-mail to alert an investor of new information would satisfy the notice requirement, whereas merely posting information on a web site would not.

2. *Document access.* The use of a particular medium should not impede the recipient's ability to access the information, and the recipient should have the opportunity to retain the information or have ongoing access to it equivalent to personal retention. If disclosure is made available by posting a document on the Internet, the document should be accessible as long as required under the applicable delivery requirement. Tangible paper versions must also be available in the event of system failures, or if the investor does not consent to electronic delivery.

3. *Proof of delivery.* Several procedures are required to demonstrate that delivery has taken place. These include obtaining the individual's consent to the receipt of documents by electronic delivery, and a requirement for evidence of actual receipt, such as a return e-mail.

General observations by the NASD

NASD Regulation Inc, the self-regulatory organisation responsible for securities firms and professionals and over-the-counter securities trading, issued a notice to members in July 1996 addressing supervisory and other obligations relating to the use of electronic media. The NASD explained that electronic communications were subject to the same approval, record-keeping and filing requirements as communications by other means, and emphasised that all communications by its members with the public remain subject to the anti-fraud provisions of the Federal securities laws. Members also had to comply with NASD suitability rules, the duty to disclose any material adverse facts to customers and to maintain appropriate supervisory procedures to ensure that the electronic communication systems were not misused.

General observations by the CFTC

The Commodities Futures Trading Commission (CFTC) issued similar guidance in August 1996. This looked at the applicability of the Commodities Exchange Act and the Commission's own regulations to registration duties and other regulatory requirements operating through electronic media. It said, for instance, that if a futures firm operates a site that provides a directory of hyperlinks covering, among other things, futures and options, and receives a fee from commodity trade advisers featured on the site, the site operator would, on the face of it, have to register as a commodity trade adviser. A disclaimer on the web site to the effect that "all materials and information provided with respect to the CTAs are not intended as commodity trading advice and we make no specific recommendations with respect to which CTA best suits your investment needs" would not alter the reasonably anticipatable effects of the information provided or the consequent registration requirements. A commodity trade adviser or pool operator may use electronic delivery for disclosure documents only where the intended recipient provides informed consent to the receipt of the document by means of electronic delivery.

Bulletin boards

The first company to sell securities publicly via the Internet was Spring Street Brewing Co, a New York based microbrewery. Spring Street's initial public offering in 1995 under Regulation A raised US$1.6 million. Investors were solicited through an on-line prospectus. Spring Street subsequently set up Wit-Trade, an on-line bulletin board-based trading system on the Web that allows individuals to buy and sell share in Spring Street over the Internet. Wit-Trade was the subject of an SEC no-action letter in April 1996.

The SEC endorsed the Wit-Trade operation, which it described as an innovative mechanism that had the potential to provide Spring Street shareholders with greater liquidity in their investment. The approval was subject to several conditions, reflecting the fact that Wit-Trade was not a registered broker-dealer. Wit-Trade was required to use an independent agent to handle investor funds, to supplement the information provided about Spring Street on the web in order to highlight the risks inherent in investing in an illiquid and speculative security, and to provide on the web site transaction history, include price and volume data, to facilitate informed investment decisions. Finally, Spring Street was required to maintain and deliver an offering circular in accordance with Regulation A.

In July 1996 the SEC issued a further no-action letter relating to a planned bulletin board service to be established under the name of Iponet. The service separated the process of investor solicitation in a private offering from the conduct of the offering. The SEC addressed two issues. The first was whether an indication of interest in the offering might be accepted electronically. SEC regulations provide for a potential investor to express interest in a prospectus by returning an enclosed or attached coupon or card (Rule 134(d)). The SEC considered that this would be equally applicable to the acceptance of instructions of interest via electronic coupon or card, which a visitor to the bulletin board site would be invited to complete and return via e-mail, or by printing out the card and sending it by conventional post.

The second issue addressed by the SEC was whether the posting of a notice of a private offering in a password-protected page of Iponet (accessible only to Iponet members who had previously qualified as investors) satisfied Regulation D Rule 502(c) of the Securities Act 1933, which limits sales or offers of securities by general solicitation. The site concerned required that those who wished to access the private placement area of the site had to complete an accredited investor questionnaire to identify whether they qualified as an accredited investor under Securities Act Rule 501(a) (by virtue of having a net worth of more than US$1 million or otherwise being a sophisticated investor). Accredited investors would then be permitted to invest in offerings posted on the site but only after a sufficient amount of time had elapsed, so that there could be no implication that the solicitation was in connection with any particular offering. They would be given a password to enter the site, read private offering documents, and indicate their interest by buying securities through the web site, by e-mail or by conventional post. The SEC considered that this arrangement would not involve any form of general solicitation or general advertising in breach of Rule 502(c).

Roadshows

In March 1997, the SEC issued a no-action letter regarding Securities Act restrictions on roadshows for public offerings. Private Finance Network intended to transmit roadshows for public offerings to its subscribers via telephone and satellite. Each transmission would be available only to a restricted audience who would agree not to videotape, copy or further distribute the transmission. Before the show was transmitted, each subscriber would receive a copy of the filed prospectus from the issuer or the underwriter. Subscribers would see the shows in their entirety. The SEC agreed that these transmissions could not be considered to be prospectuses under 2(10) of the Securities Act.

The UK regulatory approach

The various UK regulators all issued guidance on Internet business in the course of 1997.

Overseas firms providing services into the UK

Under UK financial services legislation, broadly speaking, an advertisement issued overseas will be considered to have been issued in the UK and to be subject to UK regulation if it is directed at people in the UK or is made available to them. The inclusion of a disclaimer saying that the message is not directed to persons in the UK is not enough to cure this. Something more, in the form of an actual restriction of access to information, is required. The UK's new Financial Services Authority has said that it will take account of the degree to which someone has taken positive steps towards the material being made available to or received by persons in the UK. This might include requiring pre-registration before access to any potentially offending material to ensure that only those to whom the material was aimed had access.

Procedures for regulated firms

Generally, material held on site will be treated as issued to all persons capable of accessing the site. If certain material is only allowed to be distributed on a restricted basis (for example, private share offers and unregulated collective investment schemes) the firm must be able to demonstrate that only investors falling within the relevant class were able to access the site. Similarly, firms should ensure that a visitor to their site sees any required risk warnings and prescribed statements, preferably on entering the site. Firms must also ensure, in relation to on-line services, that sufficient information is retained to allow them to demonstrate their compliance with the regulatory system. This includes keeping records of electronic advertisements and any changes made to those advertisements. Documents that require an investor's signature must be signed in hard copy form. There is no electronic equivalent of an investor's signature, and the much vaunted concept of the "electronic signature" is, in truth, only an encrypted password, equivalent, as far as an investor is concerned, to a per pro signature.

Prospectuses

The UK's Financial Services Reform Act, due to come into force in 1999 or 2000, is expected to authorise the making of public share offerings by electronic means, subject to certain safeguards. These safeguards are likely to involve:

(a) ensuring that a tangible copy of the prospectus is registered with the Registrar of Companies;

(b) providing a physical, tangible copy of the prospectus to investors on request;

(c) ensuring that the electronic and hard copy versions of the prospectus are identical;

(d) ensuring that, in the electronic format, risk warnings and disclaimers have to be viewed before the investor can access an application form;

(e) taking all reasonable steps to ensure that an investor receives his electronic prospectus at the same time as his electronic application form;

(f) taking all reasonable steps to ensure that the electronic prospectus is in complete format, secure from tampering in transmission, and has been received intact; and

(g) ensuring that the prospectus and related material are made available in such a way that the investor is encouraged to make his decision on the basis of the prospectus, and not solely on the basis of associated promotional material.

Dick Frase
The Personal Investment Authority

Note: The views expressed in this Chapter are the author's own, and should not be taken as representing the views of the Personal Investment Authority.

CHAPTER 1

Argentina

Introduction

The Argentinian equity market has grown substantially since the implementation of the currency convertibility plan in 1991. At the end of 1997 there were 136 companies listed on the Buenos Aires Stock Exchange (BASE). Total share market capitalisation has surged from US$18.4 billion (9.8% of GDP) in 1991 to US$59.2 billion, or 18.6% of GDP at end-1997. It is a fairly developed market, with trading conducted not only through open outcry on the exchange floor but also through a computer-managed matching system (SINAC). Over the first 10 months of 1997, average daily turnover was US$154 million, but this understates trading activity because 10 of the most liquid stocks are also listed as ADRs on the NYSE.

Despite the above-mentioned growth, market capitalisation is still concentrated in a few sectors as a consequence of the aggressive privatisation process implemented by the Menem administration. Energy stocks (oil, gas and electricity) comprise 40% of total market value, while telcos represent 24%. Steel and banks each represent 11% of total market capitalisation, meaning that 86% of the market is concentrated in only four sectors.

The investor profile has changed dramatically since the 1994 launch of the private pension fund system. As at year-end 1997, domestic pension funds' equity portfolios totalled about US$1.8 billion, or 21% of total funds under management (although this only amounts to 3% of market capitalisation).

ECONOMIC AND POLITICAL OVERVIEW

The Republic of Argentina has been governed since 1989 by President Carlos Menem. He won a second presidential term following elections in May 1995, basing the campaign on his identification with the successful convertibility plan – an economic programme that ended hyperinflation by pegging the peso to the US dollar and backing the monetary base with international reserves.

Nevertheless, since then popular support for the plan has diminished as the 1995 recession triggered by the Mexican crisis, the opening of the economy and an ongoing restructuring process in privatised companies caused a sharp increase in unemployment. This discontent was evident in the October 1997 congressional elections, in which the ruling Peronist Party lost its scant majority in the Lower House. The "Alianza" – a new force in Argentinian politics formed by the opposition Radical and Frepaso Parties – seems likely to be the main opponent to Peronism in the 1999 presidential elections.

During 1997, GDP grew an estimated 7.5%, with sales and industrial production maintaining their healthy expansion. The economic cycle was led by fixed investment growth, which reached 21.3% in real terms. There was a sharp increase in imports, which grew 25% versus 1996, while exports increased only 6%. Strong economic activity contributed to improved tax receipts, thus allowing the public sector to meet fiscal deficit goals agreed on with the IMF.

Looking ahead, there are no key political events scheduled before the 1999 presidential elections. Economic performance will continue to be more dependent on the international financial and trade environment than on domestic developments. In this regard, key importance will attach to the evolution of the Asian crisis and its impact on Brazil, Argentina's main trading partner and the most important emerging market in Latin America.

Role of the central bank

Since Menem's rewrite of the charter of the central bank in 1989, the main role of Banco Central de la República (BCRA) has been to defend the currency, taking whatever steps it has thought necessary to maintain peso parity against the dollar. Because, under the convertibility plan, the monetary authority has given up its "lender of last resort" role, it has endeavoured to strengthen the financial

Exhibit 1.1: ARGENTINA MERVAL PRICE INDEX (US$), 1993–97

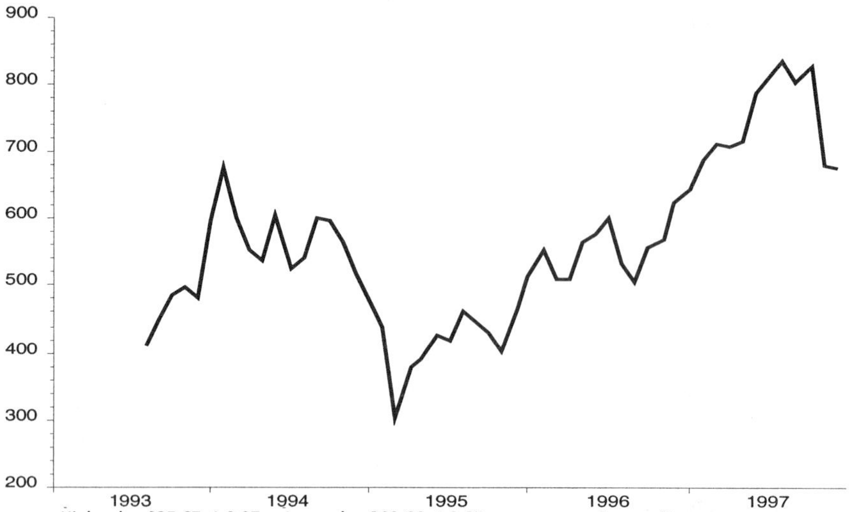

High value 835.67 1.8.97 Low value 302.66 1.3.95 *Source: Datastream*

system through the implementation of several repurchase agreement programmes with international institutions and by requiring high capital ratios, in excess of the Basle Committee's guidelines. As at year-end 1997, about 45% of total banking deposits were "covered" through central bank reserves and other instruments.

MARKET PERFORMANCE

A) In 1997

Market capitalisation increased in 1997 by 32.6% to US$59.2 billion. From a year-end 1996 level of 18,494.87, the BASE General Index reached its all-time high of 25,777.08 (a 39.3% appreciation) on 22 October 1997 on the back of rising corporate earnings and strong economic growth. The market then experienced a significant and rapid correction triggered by the fall in Hong Kong equities that affected most emerging markets. The General Index reached its low for the year on 13 November (18,276.43), 29.1% down from the high point. By the end of December, the market had recovered to 23,071.71, up 24.7% for the year. The popular Merval Index, however, closed 1997 only 5.9% ahead.

Share turnover on the exchange floor amounted to US$9.97 billion in 1997, up from US$7.00 billion in 1996. During 1997, US$1,736.7 million was paid out in cash dividends. This is 6% higher than in 1996 and sets a new record for the Argentinian market. The dividend yield was 2.87%, well above the world average of 1.8% for 1997, as reported by MSCI.

B) Summary information

Global ranking by market value (US$ terms, end-1997): 29
Market capitalisation (end-1997): US$59.2 billion
Growth in market value (local currency terms, 1993–97): 34.7%
Number of domestic/foreign companies listed (end-1997): 136/0
Market value as a % of nominal GDP (end-1997): 18.6%
Market P/E (companies included in Merval and Burcap Indices, end-1997): 16.0
MSCI Index (change in US$ terms, 1997): +21.9%
Short-term (3-month) interest rate (end-1997): 9%
Long-term (30-year) bond yield (end-1997): 10.2%
Budget deficit as a % of nominal GDP (end-1997): 1.7%
Annual increase in broad money (M3) supply (end-1997): 22.3%
Inflation rate (end-1997) : 0.3%
US$ exchange rate (1997): P1.00

C) Year-end share price index and price/earnings ratios

Exhibit 1.2:
YEAR-END SHARE PRICE INDEX AND BASE P/E RATIOS, 1993–97

Year-end	*General Index*	*P/E*
1993	20,607.20	59.9
1994	15,855.62	16.1
1995	16,237.81	14.2

Exhibit 1.2 continued

1996	18,494.87	28.9
1997	23,071.71	16.0

Source: Buenos Aires Stock Exchange.

D) Market indices and their constituents

The BASE General Index (29 December 1977 = 0.00001) comprises all shares listed on the exchange. There are also 15 sectorial price indices.

The Merval Index measures the performance of a portfolio of liquid shares (those which have accounted for 80% of the total traded value in the previous 6 months). Composition of the index is adjusted quarterly.

The Burcap Index is based on a similar portfolio of shares to the Merval, but is weighted according to market capitalisation.

THE STOCK EXCHANGE

A) Brief history and structure

The BASE was founded in 1854 and was the first exchange in Latin America. Activity in the early days centred around the trading of metals, and it was not until 1872 that securities trading began. During the 1930s the market played a significant role in financing public sector investments and mortgages and, in 1937, a Securities Commission was formed in Buenos Aires. Since 1969 this Commission has been an independent government agency which, in accordance with the Stock Exchange Law of 1969, regulates the organisation and operations of Argentina's exchanges.

Argentina's five principal stock exchanges set their own listing requirements and are responsible for corporate disclosure and for the dissemination of trading data. A board of directors oversees the management and operations of each exchange.

Brokers' own self-regulatory organisations, called Mercados de Valores, authorise and are responsible for the activities of brokers and brokerage firms.

B) Different exchanges

There are 11 stock exchanges in Argentina but only five have a Mercado de Valores and can trade independently: these are Buenos Aires, Rosario, Córdoba, the Mercado Regional de Capitales and Mendoza. The BASE is the major market.

C) Opening hours, names and addresses

Floor trading at the BASE takes place from 11.30am to 5.00pm every business day. Trading under the continuous and SINAC systems takes place from 9.30am to 6.00pm.

BOLSA DE COMERCIO DE BUENOS AIRES
(Buenos Aires Stock Exchange)
Sarmiento 299 – 2 piso, 1353 Buenos Aires
Tel: (54) 1 313 7218; Fax: (54) 1 312 6636

BOLSA DE COMERCIO DE ROSARIO
(Rosario Stock Exchange)
2000 Rosario-Pcia Santa Fe, 1402 Córdoba
Tel: (54) 51 24 11 68; Fax: (54) 51 24 10 19

BOLSA DE COMERCIO DE CÓRDOBA
(Córdoba Stock Exchange)
Rosario de Santa Fe 231, 5000 Córdoba
Tel: (54) 51 22 42 30; Fax: (54) 51 22 65 50

MERCADO REGIONAL DE CAPITALES
Calle 48, No 515/7, 1900 La Plata-Pcia, Buenos Aires
Tel: (54) 1 21 47 73; Fax: (54) 1 25 50 33

BOLSA DE COMERCIO DE MENDOZA
(Mendoza Stock Exchange)
Sarmiento Esq España, 5500 Mendoza
Tel: (54) 61 23 12 03/824; Fax: (54) 61 25 85 05/38 04 31

MARKET SIZE

A) Number of listings and market value

Market capitalisation increased by 32.4% to end 1997 at US$59.2 billion. The number of listed companies decreased by 11 to 136.

Exhibit 1.3:
NUMBER OF COMPANIES AND MARKET VALUE OF SHARES LISTED, BASE, 1993–97

Year-end	*No. of listings*	*Market value (US$ million)*
1993	165	44,011.0
1994	156	36,867.2
1995	149	37,779.6
1996	147	44,670.3
1997	136	59,239.9

Source: Buenos Aires Stock Exchange.

Exhibit 1.4:
MARKET VALUE BY SECTOR, BASE, 1996–97

Sector	*1996 (US$ million)*	*1997 (US$ million)*
Raw materials	16,699.0	20,873.9
Utilities	11,134.4	16,746.2
Banks	3,902.4	6,423.0
Metals	4,633.7	6,288.9
Chemicals	2,543.7	2,307.4

Exhibit 1.4 continued

Finance	1,601.2	2,113.7
Trade	1,096.4	1,929.7
Food	1,018.3	744.3
Insurance	102.6	73.0
Construction	648.2	649.3
Paper and printing	371.0	389.7
Other	228.9	258.7
Manufacturing	204.1	158.3
Textiles	253.7	153.4
Beverages	232.9	130.3
Total	44,670.3	59,239.9

Source: Buenos Aires Stock Exchange.

B) Largest quoted companies

The largest quoted company on the BASE at the end of 1997 remained YPF, one of the biggest integrated oil firms in the world. YPF was privatised in 1993, offering 58% of its share capital on the stock market. In terms of market capitalisation, YPF is followed in second place by Telefónica de Argentina, a telecommunications company formed as a result of the privatisation of Empresa Nacional de Telecomunicaciones.

Exhibit 1.5:
THE 20 LARGEST LISTED COMPANIES ON THE BASE, END-1997

Ranking	*Company*	*Market value (US$ million)*
1	YPF	11,896.1
2	Telefónica de Argentina	8,840.7
3	Telecom Argentina	7,087.5
4	Pérez Companc	6,010.5
5	Siderca	2,780.0
6	Banco Galicia y Buenos Aires	2,025.9
7	Banco Rio de la Plata	2,010.0
8	Transportadora Gas del Sur	1,803.5
9	CEI Citicorp Holdings	1,632.2
10	Banco Francés	1,600.4
11	Siderar	1,321.3
12	Astra	1,015.0
13	Aluar Aluminio Argentino	914.8
14	Irsa	718.6
15	Disco	709.6
16	Acindar	550.2
17	Banco Bansud	457.4
18	Massalin Particulares	451.0
19	Molinos Rio de la Plata	420.9
20	Imp. y Exp. de la Patagonia	414.0

Source: Buenos Aires Stock Exchange.

C) Trading volume

Exhibit 1.6:
BASE SHARE TURNOVER BY SECTOR, 1996–97

	Trading value (US$ million)*	
Sector	*1996*	*1997*
Metals	1,291.2	3,133.4
Raw materials	2,069.2	2,787.0
Utilities	1,528.4	987.6
Banks	416.8	682.0
Textiles	186.8	521.9
Chemicals	477.6	414.8
Finance	269.5	397.2
Trade	171.8	381.1
Construction	175.9	299.2
Food	258.5	232.0
Manufacturing	27.2	53.7
Paper and printing	91.2	52.0
Beverages	30.4	19.7
Other	11.9	6.5
Insurance	0.1	0.2
Total	7,006.5	9,968.3

* Floor transactions only.

Source: Buenos Aires Stock Exchange.

Exhibit 1.7:
THE 20 MOST ACTIVELY TRADED BASE SHARES, 1997

Ranking	*Company*	*Trading value* (US$ million)*
1	Telefónica de Argentina	12,994.2
2	YPF	8,405.2
3	Pérez Companc	3,225.7
4	Telecom	2,014.1
5	Acindar	1,121.3
6	CEI Citicorp Holdings	873.8
7	Banco de Galicia	866.4
8	Siderca	814.9
9	Banco Francés	736.0
10	Astra	731.4
11	Siderar	574.4
12	Alpargatas	524.0
13	Comercial del Plata	469.8
14	Renault Argentina	450.0
15	Indupa	399.0
16	Transportadora de Gas del Sur	350.0
17	Banco Rio	341.9
18	Banco Bansud	254.5
19	Irsa	223.7
20	Molinos Rio de la Plata	191.1

*Floor transactions only.

Source: Buenos Aires Stock Exchange.

TYPES OF SHARE

Although preferred shares (*acciones preferidas*) exist in Argentina, most traded equity is in the form of ordinary shares (*acciones ordinarias*). Ordinary shareholders are normally entitled to one vote per share, although some companies have created shares that entitle holders to exercise up to five votes per share.

Preferred shareholders rank above ordinary shareholders in terms of dividend distribution and if the company is liquidated. Preferred shares may be either voting or non-voting.

A significant number of listed stocks are issued through a book entry system, administered by a depository institution called Caja de Valores. The BASE and the Buenos Aires Mercado de Valores own 90% of the Caja's equity.

Under Law No. 24,587 (22 November 1995), all private securities issued in Argentina (including temporary certificates representing them) must be issued to a named beneficiary and cannot be in bearer form. Certified shares may be issued.

DERIVATIVES

Trading in options, stock and bond futures takes place on the BASE. The exchange is organising a joint project with the Chicago Board of Trade to establish a more advanced futures and options market in Buenos Aires. In 1997, the trading of derivatives increased by 52% compared with 1996.

INVESTORS

In 1997, pension fund portfolios continued to grow, with assets amounting to US$8,827 million. Equities account for 21.46% of these portfolios, versus 16.22 % at the end of 1996.

Total funds under management are expected to reach US$20 billion by the year 2000, of which about 40% will be invested in equities. Pension fund activity provides depth to the markets and diminishes the country's dependence on foreign capital inflows.

OPERATIONS

A) Trading system

There are three trading systems operating: (a) a floor-based open outcry auction system; (b) a continuous dealer trading system; and (c) the Computer-Assisted Integrated Negotiation System (SINAC). In 1997, trades executed on SINAC increased significantly.

Since May 1993, it has not been possible to trade shares on the OTC market.

B) List of principal brokers

ABN AMRO Securities
Florida 361 – 1 piso, 1005 Buenos Aires
Tel: (54) 1 320 0711; Fax: (54) 1 325 5291

CASPIAN SECURITIES
25 de Mayo 555 – 11 piso, 1002 Buenos Aires
Tel: (54) 1 313 2554/315 6064; Fax: (54) 1 313 2544

Exhibit 1.8:
COUNTRY FUNDS – ARGENTINA

Fund	*US$ % change 01/01/98 01/01/97*	*US$ % change 01/01/98 01/01/93*	*Fund base currency*	*Fund size (US$ mil)*	*Fund volatility*	*Management group*	*Opal main sector*	*Opal subsector*
Paribas EM Argentina Ptfl	28.32	N/A	US$	N/A	7.717	Paribas Asset Management	Open-End	Equity
Argentina Fund	21.98	88.53	US$	113.16	6.48	Scudder	Closed-End	Equity
Argentinia Inv Co	20.26	44.2	US$	41.1	8.191	Foreign & Col	Open-End	Equity
NatWest/IFC LAIF Argentina Inx	18.28	N/A	US$	5.799	8.026	NatWest Investment Management	Open-End	Equity
Toronto Trust Argentina	9.5	N/A	US$	6.76	7.769	FCMI Group	Open-End	Equity
Argentina Equity Inv II	-31.89	N/A	US$	4.01	6.402	BEA Assoc	Private	Equity
Argentina Equity Invest I	-31.92	N/A	US$	56.989	6.348	BEA Assoc	Private	Equity

Note: details for some funds may not have been included if the data for the US$ % change for 97/98 was not available

Source: Standard & Poor's Micropal.

FRANCÉS VALORES
Tte. Gral. J.D. Perón 362 – 5 piso, 1038 Capital Federal
Tel: (54) 1 342 5390

JP MORGAN
Corrientes 415 – 2 piso, 1043 Capital Federal
Tel: (54) 1 325 8046

MBA (Merchant Bankers Asociados)
140 Alicia M. De Justo, Puerto Madero,
1107 Buenos Aires
Tel: (54) 1 319-5800/5900; Fax: (54) 1 312-6460

MILDESA
25 de Mayo 552 – 8 piso, 1002 Capital Federal
Tel: (54) 1 312 3791; Fax: (54) 1 312 0768

PORTFOLIO INVESTMENT
Lavalle 465 – 2 piso, 1047 Capital Federal
Tel: (54) 1 322 9843; Fax: (54) 1 322 6927

RABELLO Y CÍA
Corrientes 345 – 11 piso, 1043 Capital Federal
Tel: (54) 1 313 2209; Fax: (54) 1 313 2407

SANTANDER
L.N. Alem 356 – 12 piso, 1003 Capital Federal
Tel: (54) 1 319 9180

C) Settlement and transfer

Share transactions are normally settled on T+3. Forward transactions are settled according to the contractual agreement between the parties, but within a maximum of 120 days.

D) Commissions and other costs

All transactions carried out via the open outcry auction are subject to payment of negotiable brokerage commissions. Forward and repo transactions are also subject to negotiable fees. For continuous session and block trading operations, commissions and costs are included in the price. Dealers operating under the SINAC system can either charge negotiable commissions or include them in the transaction price.

TAXATION AND REGULATIONS AFFECTING FOREIGN INVESTORS

Income from the purchase and sale of public or private securities, either Argentinian or foreign, are exempt (for frequent traders) or non-taxable (for infrequent traders) in the case of natural persons residing in Argentina. Losses from the purchase and sale of such securities are not deductible. Income derived from the sale and purchase of shares by a foreign natural person or corporation is tax-free. This exemption also applies to transactions in bonds and other securities.

Under Decree 1,130 dated 4 November 1997, derivatives contracts will be assessable for income tax when the risk is located in Argentina and when the person who obtained the profits is an Argentinian resident. Foreign investors in derivatives are not liable to tax.

There are no limits on the ownership of equity in public companies by foreign investors. Foreign investors can repatriate their investment and remit their profits abroad at any time. The exchange control authority is the Banco Central de la República Argentina (the central bank).

Argentina has signed treaties with various countries for the reciprocal promotion and protection of investments.

Exhibit 1.9:
WITHHOLDING TAXES

Recipient	*Interest %*[1]	*Dividends %*
Resident corporations	6[2]	Nil
Resident individuals	6[2]	Nil
Non-resident corporations and individuals:		
Non-treaty	13.2	Nil
Treaty	10-13.2	Nil

Notes
1. Withholding from payments of interest to non-residents is based on a flat rate of 33% applied to an assumed percentage gross profit margin. This margin is not contestable, but the resultant rate may be limited by bilateral treaty.
2. Resident corporations and individuals who are registered for tax purposes are subject to 6% withholding (25% if not registered), except that banks, financial entities and stock exchange and open market brokers need withhold only 3% from interest (7% if not registered).
3. Gains on the sale of shares are tax-exempt.

Source: Price Waterhouse.

A personal assets tax has been in force since 1991. Individuals resident in Argentina pay the tax on their shareholdings, public bonds, *obligaciones negociables* (corporate bonds) and investment fund units. In the case of individuals resident abroad, no tax is payable on such holdings; however, if the assets are held by corporations, companies and permanent establishments domiciled abroad, they will be assessable to personal assets tax if they are established or domiciled in a country in which there is no registered shares regime. There is, however, an exemption concerning insurance companies, open investment funds, pension funds or banking or financial entities with head offices registered or established in central bank-approved countries.

The personal assets tax to be paid is calculated by applying a rate of 0.5% on the total value of assets subject to tax at 31 December of each year. In the case of individuals resident in Argentina there is an allowance of US$102,300.

LISTING AND REPORTING REQUIREMENTS

A) Listing requirements

Companies are subject to the control of the National Equities Commission (NEC) and the Stock Exchange Association (SEA). Under SEA rules, companies seeking a listing should apply to be quoted on the special board if they have:

a) capital stock in excess of US$60 million;
b) revenue from sales of goods and services that exceeded US$100 million in their latest fiscal year; and
c) enough shareholders to comply with minimum dispersion requirements.

Corporations not qualifying under any of the above categories, or that do not specifically request inclusion, will be traded on the general board.

In September 1997, the BASE board approved a listing fee reform initiative that in 1998 should generate cost savings for listed companies, particularly for those with higher stock trading levels.

B) Reporting requirements

Resolution 290/97 of the NEC and Article 63 of the BASE regulations provide that corporations with shares listed on the stock exchange special board must publish quarterly individual and consolidated financial statements, balance sheet results, complementary notes and any other relevant information. It is not compulsory for companies with shares listed on the general board to submit quarterly financial statements and consolidated information.

Stock exchange rules provide that companies must inform the exchange within five days of the signing of any agreement concerning royalties and franchising, the issue of securities, the mortgaging of a company's property, or the purchase or sale of other companies or shareholdings in other companies.

SHAREHOLDER PROTECTION CODES

Section 300 in Part 2 of the Penal Code provides that a person who makes misrepresentations when offering shares for sale can be sentenced to imprisonment for between six months and two years.

A) Takeovers and mergers

Under both the NEC and BASE regulations, the NEC's and the SEA's approval is required before the merger or takeover of a listed company takes place. Companies must send a letter to the stock exchange setting out the reasons for the proposal, enclosing each corporation's balance sheet and a pro forma consolidated balance sheet. Mergers and takeovers can only take place after the approval of shareholders has been obtained.

B) Directors' dealings

In principle, there are no restrictions on the freedom of directors to deal in their company's shares. However, members of the board of directors cannot take part in any activity that may adversely affect the corporation's interests. If share transactions by directors were to damage the corporation's interests, the member of the board involved would be liable for damages.

C) Compensation fund

There is no stock exchange compensation fund to reimburse investors who may be the victims of fraud or default by a broker or trader.

RESEARCH

Good research on the market is provided by ABN AMRO Securities, JP Morgan and Santander.

The BASE publishes most information in Spanish (eg the *Daily Bulletin*, *Weekly Bulletin* and *Fact Book*), although some information in English is also available, such as the *Quarterly Reports*, a *Fact Book Summary* and an institutional brochure, updated every year.

Information on market performance, listed companies, financial statements and an historical databank of series on trading volume, market capitalisation, stock exchange indices, etc, is available through a computerised system administered by the Caja de Valores. The Instituto Argentino de Mercado de Capitales (IAMC) issues occasional papers on the market.

The Federación Iberoamericana de Bolsas de Valores (FIABV) provides comprehensive information on Latin American stock exchanges and markets. It distributes a *Statistical Year Book*, containing data about its 22 member exchanges.

The Superintendencia de Administradoras de Fondos de Jubilaciones y Pensiones (SAFJP) issues monthly and quarterly statistical reports on the activity of local pension funds, including comprehensive information on equity portfolios and contributions.

FEDERACION IBEROAMERICANA DE BOLSAS DE VALORES
Cerrito 1266 – 5 piso, 1010 Buenos Aires
Tel: (54) 1 392 4401; Tlx: 18510 GALGI AR

INSTITUTO ARGENTINO DE MERCADO DE CAPITALES
25 de Mayo 359 – 8 piso, Buenos Aires
Tel: (54) 1 316 6000; Fax: (54) 1 313 5552

SAFJP
Tucumán 500, 1049 Buenos Aires
Tel: (54) 1 320 5600; Fax: (54) 1 320 5620

Argentina, published by Euromoney Books, provides in-depth information for those wishing to invest or do business in the region. See the order card at the back of the book for details.

CHAPTER

2

Australia

Introduction

Retail investors represented the dominant force in the Australian stock market in 1997, investing a net A$7 billion. This involvement was underpinned by the listing of Telstra, Australia's major telecommunications carrier, and corporate sell-downs of large holdings in ICI and Fosters, offering attractive prices and good yields. The listing of Telstra saw over 1.2 million or almost 1-in-15 Australians take up shares, including a large number of first-time buyers. This consolidated a strong 1990s trend of increasing share ownership by Australians. Well over one-third of Australian adults now have investments (not including company superannuation) in the share market, either directly or indirectly through personal superannuation schemes or managed funds. This compares with 20% in 1994 and 15% in 1991.

Foreign investors have continued to be active in the market (representing about 18% of market activity), while domestic institutions remain net investors in equities, largely driven by compulsory superannuation requirements.

Although Australia is a large producer of raw materials, there is a comparatively low representation of agriculture-oriented companies on the ASX. Mining and energy (termed the resources sector) accounts for a little over one-fifth of total market capitalisation, compared with two-fifths at the end of 1996. This reflects a resources sector facing depressed world demand and falling commodity prices. The remaining four-fifths of capitalisation comprises what is generally referred to as the industrials sector. Among the industrials the principal sub-sectors are banks, building materials, media, retail, transport and "diversified industrials". This last group includes some of Australia's largest multinationals.

ECONOMIC AND POLITICAL OVERVIEW

Australia's political, legal and administrative structures are very stable and are based upon Western democratic principles and systems (particularly, for historic reasons, on those of the United Kingdom).

The new Liberal/National Party coalition government, now in its second year, has confirmed its commitment to financial, industrial and structural reform.

During the 1990s, Australian governments, State and Commonwealth, have privatised a significant portion of the public sector; overall, Australia has had one of the largest programmes among OECD countries (second by value to only the UK). Privatisation has occurred in three main sectors – (a) financial services, (b) electricity and gas, and (c) transport and communication – with proceeds estimated at A$61 billion.

Privatisation proceeds and the government's fiscal consolidation strategy is expected to result in a modest underlying budget surplus in 1998–99 and a decline in total public net debt as a percentage GDP from a recent peak of 36% in 1994–95 to around 19% in 2000–01. This outcome increases the likelihood of a sovereign credit rerating over the medium term.

The release of the Wallis Inquiry Report into the Australian financial system and the subsequent government policy response will result in significant reform within the financial sector. The new legislation, expected in early 1998, effectively allows non-banks to compete with the banking sector thereby improving the competitiveness of the industry.

The Australian economy is now entering its seventh year of expansion and the medium-term outlook appears favourable, with domestic spending supported by low interest rates, improving consumer confidence and a strengthening labour market. GDP growth has increased steadily throughout 1997 and is currently tracking in the 3–4% range, up from 2–2.5% in the latter half of 1996. The pick-up was driven by acceleration in private final

Exhibit 2.1: ASX ALL ORDINARIES PRICE INDEX (A$), 1993–97

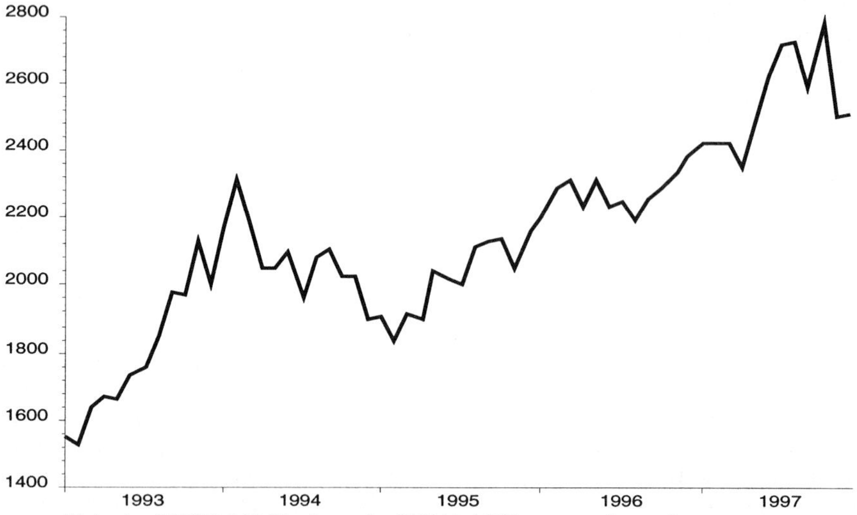

High value 2779.20 1.10.97 Low value 1529.10 1.2.93 *Source: Datastream*

demand, with household spending taking over from business investment as the major source of growth. The strong rise in activity is finally impacting the labour market with recent figures suggesting that an employment recovery, albeit modest, is at last under way.

Weakness in commodity prices, particularly metal prices, coupled with an expected increase in the current account deficit and a decline in interest rate differentials, have placed significant pressure on the Australian dollar. However, the trade-weighted index has not deteriorated due to the large-scale currency depreciation of Australia's major Asian trading partners.

The absence of inflationary pressure throughout the year enabled further easing of monetary policy. With annualised underlying inflation tracking at 1.5%, the Reserve Bank of Australia decided that official interest rates could be reduced. Two reductions of 50 basis points were made in May and July 1997, bringing the official cash rate down to 5.0%.

Role of the central bank

The Reserve Bank of Australia was established in 1959. It has a broad charter whereby its duty is to ensure that its monetary and banking policies best contribute to the stability of the currency, the maintenance of full employment and the economic prosperity and welfare of the Australian people. While the Reserve Bank is operationally independent, it is ultimately subordinate to the government of the day, which can direct the bank to pursue its chosen policies. In practice, however, Australian governments have not sought to challenge its operational independence. The Reserve Bank is overseen by a government-appointed board headed by a full-time Governor.

Mr Ian Macfarlane is the current Governor, appointed in September 1996 for a term of seven years. At the time of his appointment, the coalition government reaffirmed its commitment to the independence of the Reserve Bank and its existing inflationary objectives. Arrangements for additional reporting of the bank's activities were also introduced, including the release of six-monthly statements on monetary policy and inflation, and two appearances per year by the Governor before the House of Representatives to discuss monetary policy.

The policy goals of the Reserve Bank revolve around the maintenance of low inflation over the course of a business cycle, while in the currency market the bank has demonstrated a willingness to intervene (it describes these activities as "smoothing and testing") when it feels that the value of the Australian dollar is not reflecting fundamentals. Over recent years, the bank has also conducted similar operations in the fixed-interest market.

MARKET PERFORMANCE

A) In 1997

During 1997, Australian Stock Exchange (ASX) domestic capitalisation rose by 15.5% to A$453.9 billion (US$335 billion). This represented a good outcome in view of the Asian currency crisis impacting on second-half performance. As a percentage of estimated GDP for 1997, the

ASX domestic market capitalisation is expected to have increased to 81.7% from 71.4% in 1996.

The All-Ordinaries Index recorded a 7.9% increase for the year, driven mainly by a strong performance from the industrials sector, whilst resources stocks were driven down during the second half by lower commodities prices.

During the year, an average of 24,300 equity transactions took place each day, involving an average of 355 million shares worth A$893 million. The average daily value of transactions during 1997 was around 22% higher than the 1996 average. Total ASX turnover for the year came out at A$231.2 billion, almost 25% more than 1996's A$185.8 billion.

Equity raisings largely comprised the Telstra float proceeds, placements of property trusts into the market and issues for specific acquisitions. Of the A$25.3 billion equity raised in 1997, A$12.8 billion was from floats (A$4.28 billion ex Telstra), A$6.9 billion in rights issues/placements, A$1.4 billion in employee options and A$0.9 billion from other sources. Debt financing remained fairly static despite the low interest rate environment, with net debt/equity remaining largely unchanged in 1997 at around 45%. This pattern of equity and debt raisings reflects financing of expansion from internal cash flows and the low level of corporate takeover activity.

The majority of companies in the private sector are listed on the ASX with the top 20 quoted companies accounting for 56% of 1997 domestic market capitalisation. The Australian stock market is also becoming more liquid with market turnover representing 53% of end-1997 total domestic market capitalisation (47% in 1996). Driving this increased liquidity has been the reduction in brokerage rates and stamp duty, the growth of discount brokerage firms, an increase in derivative activity (in particular over-the-counter options and warrants), the growth of quantitative based funds and the large number of floats in recent years.

B) Summary information

Global ranking by market value (US$ terms, end-1997): 14
Market capitalisation (end-1997): US$264 billion
Growth in market value (local currency terms, 1993–97): 62.8%
Market value as a % of nominal GDP (end-1997): 81%
Number of domestic/foreign companies listed (end-1997): 1,157/58
Market P/E (excluding companies reporting losses, end-1997): 18.51
MSCI total returns (with net dividends, US$ terms 1997): -10.4 %
MSCI Index (change in US$ terms, 1997): -12.6%
Short-term (3-month) interest rate (end-1997): 5.07%
Long-term (10-year) bond yield (end-1997): 6.06%
Budget deficit as a % of nominal GDP (1997): 1.49%
Annual increase in broad money (M3) supply (end-1997): 6.6%
Inflation rate (1997): 1.6%
US$ exchange rate (end-1996): A$1.54

C) Year-end share price index, price/earnings ratios and yields

Exhibit 2.2:
YEAR-END ALL-ORDINARIES INDEX, P/E AND GROSS DIVIDEND YIELD, 1993–97

Year-end	*Index*	*P/E**	*Yield (%)*
1993	2,173.6	21.55	3.00
1994	1,912.7	14.79	4.01
1995	2,203.0	16.34	4.00
1996	2,424.6	17.66	3.63
1997	2,615.5	18.51	3.89

* Excluding companies with negative earnings.

Source: Australian Stock Exchange.

D) Market indices and their constituents

The main indicator of the Australian market is the ASX All-Ordinaries Index, which comprises approximately 300 of the most actively traded companies and represents 89% of equity capitalisation (excluding foreign companies listed in Australia). The ASX All-Ordinaries Index was based at 500 on 31 December 1979 and has a complementary index, the ASX All-Ordinaries Accumulation (or total return) Index, which takes into account both movements in share prices and the payment of dividends. Both indices are further broken down into 24 sector indices.

All of the ASX indices are weighted by market capitalisation, with larger companies having proportionally more influence on the indices than smaller companies. As well as sector indices, the ASX compiles indices over mining, resources, industrials and a series of large, medium-sized and small companies, from the ASX 20 Leaders through the Midcap 50 to the ASX Small Ordinaries.

In 1996, in conjunction with the Frank Russell Company, ASX also created new series-style indices across value and growth companies. These indices are known as the ASX/Russell Value and Growth Indices.

THE STOCK MARKET

A) Brief history and structure

Trading in shares has taken place in Australia since 1828, but the real growth of the stock exchange occurred in the latter half of the 19th century when there was strong demand for equity capital to support the growth of mining activities. The forerunners of the present exchange were established in Sydney (1871), Brisbane (1884), Melbourne (1884), Adelaide (1887), Hobart (1882) and Perth (1889).

In 1937, the six capital city stock exchanges established the Australian Associated Stock Exchanges (AASE), a company limited by guarantee, to represent them at national level.

Exhibit 2.3:
NUMBER OF LISTED COMPANIES AND MARKET VALUE OF LISTED SHARES, YEAR-END 1993–97

	1993	*1994*	*1995*	*1996*	*1997*
Companies listed	1,107	1,186	1,178	1,190	1,215
Market capitalisation (A$ million)					
All listed companies	477,247	450,202	546,442	615,368	776,856
Domestic companies	301,235	282,161	329,647	392,784	453,941
All-Ordinaries Index companies	277,879	260,528	310,199	359,259	403,950

Source: Australian Stock Exchange.

Exhibit 2.4:
EQUITY RAISED ON THE ASX MAIN BOARD, 1993–97 (A$ MILLION)

Year	*New floats*	*Rights issues*	*Placements*	*Reinvested dividends*	*Options, calls & staff plans*	*Total*
1993	5,347.7	978.7	5,450.3	2,738.1	1,330.5	15,845.3
1994	4,710.1	3,605.2	3,342.4	3,651.4	1,620.5	16,929.6
1995	4,111.8	2,869.5	2,103.8	3,264.0	1,632.4	13,981.5
1996	3,711.2	1,662.0	5,423.0	3,188.9	1,147.0	15,132.1
1997	12,861.9	4,010.9	2,861.4	3,347.4	2,241.5	25,322.9

Source: Australian Stock Exchange.

Between 1950 and 1970 the stock exchanges introduced many changes in their methods of operation. Most were dictated by the rising volume of business associated with the initial post-war boom in 1950–52, and the discoveries of crude oil in Western Australia in 1953 and nickel in 1963.

The Australian Stock Exchange Limited commenced business in April 1987. It was incorporated under the Australian Stock Exchange and National Guarantee Fund Act 1987. Existing capital city exchanges became wholly owned subsidiaries of the ASX and their members ceased to belong to a particular exchange and became ASX members.

Following the passage of a bill in early 1998 enabling the ASX to proceed with demutualisation, the exchange is well on its way to changing its structure. As well as demutualising, which will ultimately sever the link between membership and ownership of the exchange, the ASX also intends to list on its own exchange once demutualised, at which point the Australian Securities Commission will become its regulator.

B) Opening hours, names and addresses

Trading through the Stock Exchange Automated Trading System (SEATS) takes place on Monday to Friday from 10.00am to 4.05pm (EST). Dealings are permitted outside these hours under the ASX's after-hours dealing rules.

AUSTRALIAN STOCK EXCHANGE LIMITED
20 Bond Street, Sydney, NSW 2000
Postal address: Box H224,
Australia Square 2000
Tel: (61) 2 9227 0000; Fax: (61) 2 9235 0056

Addresses in respective capital cities

Perth
2 The Esplanade, Perth, WA 6000
Postal address: Box D187, GPO Perth 6001
Tel: (61) 9 9224 0000; Fax: (61) 9 9221 2020

Hobart
86 Collins Street, Hobart, Tasmania 7000
Postal address: Box 100A, GPO Hobart 7001
Tel: (61) 3 6234 7333; Fax: (61) 3 6234 3922

Melbourne
530 Collins Street, Melbourne, Vic 3000
Postal address: Box 1784Q, GPO Melbourne 3001
Tel: (61) 3 9617 8611;
Fax: (61) 3 9621 1030

Adelaide
55 Exchange Place, Adelaide, SA 5000
Postal address: Box 547, GPO Adelaide 5001
Tel: (61) 8 8216 5000; Fax: (61) 8 8216 5098

Brisbane
Riverside Centre, 123 Eagle Street, Brisbane, QLD 4000
Postal address: Box 7055, Riverside Centre, Brisbane 4001
Tel: (61) 7 3835 4000; Fax: (61) 7 3835 1004

Sydney
Exchange Centre, 20 Bond Street, Sydney, NSW 2000
Postal address: Box H224, Australia Square 2000
Tel: (61) 2 9227 0000; Fax: (61) 2 9227 0056

MARKET SIZE

A) Number of listings and market value

At 31 December 1997 there were 1,215 listed companies on the ASX, compared with 1,190 at the end of 1996. Domestic market capitalisation rose by 15.6% in 1997 to A$453.9 billion, while total equity capitalisation increased by 26.2% to A$776.9 billion.

B) Largest quoted companies

The National Australia Bank was the largest listed company on the ASX at the end of 1997, with a market value of A$30.3 billion, representing 6.7% of total domestic capitalisation. It was closely followed by News Corporation at A$29.9 billion and The Broken Hill Proprietary Company with a capitalisation of A$29.1 billion.

Exhibit 2.5:
THE 20 LARGEST LISTED COMPANIES ON THE ASX, END-1997

Ranking	*Company*	*Market Value (A$ million)*
1	National Australia Bank	30,267
2	News Corporation*	29,913
3	BHP	29,101
4	Westpac Banking Corp.	18,717
5	Commonwealth Bank	16,729
6	ANZ Banking Corp.	15,285
7	Telstra	13,794
8	Rio Tinto	11,500
9	Coca-Cola Amatil	9,703
10	Coles Myer	8,451
11	Lend Lease Corporation	7,483
12	Woodside Petroleum	7,213
13	Brambles	6,790
14	Western Mining Corp.	6,041
15	Woolworths	5,816
16	CSR	5,242
17	National Mutual	5,063
18	Fosters Brewing Group	5,001
19	Boral	4,467
20	Amcor	4,326

*News Corporation preferred shares included.

Source: Australian Stock Exchange.

C) Trading volume

Exhibit 2.6:
EQUITY TURNOVER ON THE ASX, 1993–97

Year	*Volume (shares million)*	*Turnover (A$ million)*
1993	54,998.6	99,562.5
1994	58,425.0	129,461.6
1995	52,283.4	133,045.0
1996	81,201.0	185,800.0
1997	92,111.0	231,224.0

Source: Australian Stock Exchange.

Exhibit 2.7:
THE 20 MOST ACTIVELY TRADED SHARES ON THE ASX, 1997

Ranking	*Company*	*Turnover value (A$ million)*
1	BHP	21,296
2	National Australia Bank	15,886
3	News Corporation*	12,054
4	ANZ Bank	8,672
5	Westpac Bank	8,658
6	Rio Tinto	7,664
7	Western Mining Corporation	7,417
8	Commonwealth Bank	6,867
9	Telstra	4,601
10	Fosters Brewing	4,435
11	Woodside Petroleum	3,894
12	Brambles Industries	3,410
13	Amcor	3,134
14	Lend Lease Corporation	3,028
15	Coles Myer	3,010
16	CSR	2,792
17	Woolworths	2,769
18	Coca-Cola Amatil	2,511
19	Santos	2,508
20	Pioneer International	2,412

*News Corporation preferred shares included.

Source: Australian Stock Exchange.

TYPES OF SHARE

Ordinary, preferred ordinary, contributing (partly paid), preference, cumulative preference, convertible, redeemable and non-redeemable shares are all traded on the ASX.

Preference shares usually have a fixed dividend rate and rank ahead of ordinary shares for dividend and repayment of capital on the liquidation of a company. Deferred dividend shares, which do not qualify for dividend until a future date, are sometimes issued to raise capital for a project that may not be profitable in the short term.

Exhibit 2.8:
COUNTRY FUNDS – AUSTRALIA

Fund	Class	*US$ % Change* 31/12/96 31/12/97	31/12/92 31/12/97	Currency	*Fund size* (US$ mil)	Volatility	Manager name	Main sector
FP Australian (ex NM)	UK Individual Pensions	-2.38	99.36	£	8.86	4.66	Friends Provident	Equity Growth
Hansard EU Baring Australia	Offshore Territories	-2.61	N/A	US$	N/S	N/A	Hansard Europe	Equity
RSAIFS/Baring Australia	Offshore Territories	-2.74	103.71	US$	2.22	4.99	Royal Life\Baring	Equity
Friends Prov Australian	UK Unit Trusts/OEICs	-2.76	100.41	£	41.33	4.5	Friends Provident Unit Tsts	Equity Growth
Hansard EU JF Australia Trust	Offshore Territories	-3.58	N/A	US$	N/S	N/A	Hansard Europe	Equity
JF Australia	Offshore Territories	-3.87	87.88	US$	25.9	4.49	JF	Equity
KB Lux Key Australia	Luxembourg	-4	N/A	US$	14.53	3.99	Kredietbank Luxembourg	Equity
Baring IUF Australia	Offshore Territories	-4.91	121.42	US$	50.25	4.27	Baring International (Ireland)	Equity
Hansard\JF Australia	Offshore Territories	-5.99	N/A	US$	0.2	5.15	Hansard\Jardine Fleming	Equity
Hansard\Baring Australia	Offshore Territories	-6.63	113.43	US$	1.67	5.18	Hansard\Baring	Equity
Inter Strategie Australie	Luxembourg	-6.67	77.4	US$	16.84	3.98	BNP-Banque Nationale de Paris	Equity
Taiyo Australia Open	Japanese Open Trusts	-7.01	N/A	¥	9.06	3.99	Taiyo ITMCo	Equity Growth
Nomura Aurora Australian	Japanese Open Trusts	-7.06	N/A	¥	28.97	3.51	Nomura ITMCo	Equity Growth
SBC EP - Australia	Luxembourg	-7.19	N/A	A$	68.57	3.23	SBC Mgt Co	Equity
Fidelity Fds Australia	Luxembourg	-7.62	89.91	A$	66.13	3.43	Fidelity Funds (Lux)	Equity
Tokyo Hi Gth Select Austral	Japanese Open Trusts	-8.07	N/A	¥	4.65	3.04	Tokyo ITMCo	Equity Growth
GAM Australia	Offshore Territories	-8.1	96.28	US$	2.2	4.42	GAM Fund Managers IOM	Equity
Nikko Glbl Australia	Japanese Open Trusts	-9.34	N/A	¥	1.99	3.14	Nikko ITMCo	Equity Growth
Daiwa Original Australia Stk	Japanese Open Trusts	-11.01	N/A	¥	4.52	3.51	Daiwa ITMCo	Equity Growth
RG ZelfSelect Australie	Netherlands Unit Trusts	-13.51	N/A	G	9.47	N/A	Robeco Groep	Equity Growth
M&G Australasian	UK Unit Trusts/OEICs	-14.91	118.5	£	49.95	5.27	M&G Group	Equity Growth
GT Australia B	Offshore Territories	-17.93	41.39	US$	3.8	4.16	GT Global	Equity
GT Australia A	Offshore Territories	-18.38	39.24	US$	3.8	4.15	GT Global	Equity
Thornton New Tiger Australia	Offshore Territories	-18.97	N/A	US$	3.24	N/A	Thornton (New Tiger)	Equity
INVESCO Southern Cross Open	Japanese Open Trusts	-24.59	4.73	¥	2.83	3.83	INVESCO ITMCo	Equity Growth
GT Australian Sml Cos B	Offshore Territories	-29.27	44.59	US$	12	5.11	GT Global	Equity
GT Australian Sml Cos A	Offshore Territories	-29.62	42.35	US$	12	5.11	GT Global	Equity
Australian Opportunities	UK Investment Trusts	-33.55	N/A	£	21.52	N/A	Ingot Capital	Equity Growth

Note: details for some funds may not have been included if the data for the US$ % change for 96/97 wasnot available

Source: Standard & Poor's Micropal.

The Listing Rules require that, subject to certain limited exceptions, shares be freely transferable. Each fully paid ordinary share must carry one vote. Preference shares must carry the rights to vote in specified circumstances – namely, on a resolution that affects the rights or privileges of preference shareholders, or that involves capital reduction, liquidation or the sanctioning of a sale of the undertaking of the company, or when the preference dividend is more than six months in arrears.

OTHER MARKETS

There is no over-the-counter market nor any unofficial market in Australia comparable to that operated by the National Association of Securities Dealers in the US.

The ASX derivatives (ASXD) and options market (formerly the Australian Options Market) was established in 1976. It is part of the ASX and is the sixth largest options market in the world. It currently trades options on over 50 of Australia's and New Zealand's leading companies and three indices, including the All-Ordinaries Index. ASXD is now a screen-based, order-driven market, following the successful implementation of the CLICK system at the end of 1997. The CLICK system enables brokers to trade options and other derivative products on screen with firm quotes in a similar fashion to equity trading via the national SEAT system and with access on an equal basis.

The equity warrants market continued to grow strongly in 1997, with more than 100 issues traded at the end of 1997 across 45 different companies. The number of trades in this market increased by 120% to 169,595, with US$1.7 billion of turnover (based on premiums).

INVESTORS

The proportion of Australians with direct exposure to the share market increased from 20.4% in May 1997 to 28.5% by the end of 1997. The 8.1% increase in direct share ownership in the first 9 months of 1997 is more than double the rate of increase between 1994 and 1997. The largest Australian public float, Telstra, was responsible for nearly half of the increase in direct share ownership levels. The planned float in 1998 (by way of a demutualisation) of Australia's largest insurance and superannuation company, AMP Society, is also expected to increase the number of Australians holding shares directly.

OPERATIONS

A) Trading system

Transactions are executed on a broker-to-broker basis by means of Stock Exchange Automated Trading (SEATS) terminals located in brokers' offices.

The SEATS system allows efficient, real-time execution based primarily on priority for best-priced orders. It provides equality of opportunity for participation on the exchange irrespective of the location of stockbroking organisations.

In addition to automatic execution, SEATS has facilities to:

- display the depth of the market;
- print details of each trade as it is executed;
- provide market enquiry for, and monitoring of, selected stocks;
- recall details of bids, offers and trades; and
- maintain and display to the operator a queue of buying and selling orders to be executed in order of priority.

B) List of principal brokers

ANZ McCAUGHAN
Level 10, Stock Exchange Centre
530 Collins Street, Melbourne
Tel: (61) 3 9205 1400

BT SECURITIES
Level 2, Chifley Tower, Chifley Square, Sydney
Tel: (61) 2 259 3322

COUNTY NATWEST
Level 15, Grosvenor Place, 225 George Street, Sydney
Tel: (61) 2 321 4200; Fax: (61) 2 251 2198

MACQUARIE EQUITIES LTD
Level 19, 20 Bond Street, Sydney
PO Box H68, Australia Square, NSW 2000
Tel: (61) 2 9237 3434; Fax: (61) 2 9237 3177 (Research)
Internet: http://www.macquarie.com.au

ORD MINNETT
Level 26, 225 George Street, Sydney
Tel: (61) 2 201 333; Fax: (61) 2 201 318

JB WERE & SON
101 Collins Street, Melbourne, Victoria 3000
Tel: (61) 3 9679 1111; Fax: (61) 3 9679 1498

SALOMON SMITH BARNEY AUSTRALIA PTY LIMITED
Level 14, Grosvenor Place, 225 George Street
Sydney, New South Wales
Tel: (61) 2 9321 4000; Fax: (61) 2 9321 4168

C) Settlement and transfer

There is a fixed settlement regime of T+5, under which settlement is due five business days after the trade date. A T+3 regime is expected to be in place by the end of 1998.

Progress towards a fully electronic settlement system began in 1994 with the introduction of the Clearing House Electronic Sub-register System (CHESS). The second phase of CHESS, which fully automated settlement by providing an electronic match of delivery and payment between brokers, was implemented in August 1996.

D) Commissions and other costs

In April 1984 brokerage rates on share market transactions became negotiable, but many broking organisations still charge the old rates of 2% to 2.5% for private client business of less than about A$10,000. Most brokers have a minimum charge of between A$30 and A$120. For large execution-only transactions, rates fall to as little as 0.2%.

From 1 July 1995 a reduced stamp duty on share transactions came into force in Queensland, New South Wales, South Australia, Tasmania, Victoria and Western Australia. The duty decreased from 0.6% (ie A$6 per A$1,000) to 0.3%. For on-market transactions the duty continues to be split equally between the buyer and the seller (0.15% each). Applicable off-market transactions accrue the duty to the purchaser only.

TAXATION AND REGULATIONS AFFECTING FOREIGN INVESTORS

A) Withholding tax

Fully franked dividends paid to non-resident investors in

Australian resident companies are not subject to dividend withholding tax. Dividends, to the extent they are unfranked, are subject to 30% dividend withholding tax, which is generally reduced to 15% if the investor is resident in a country with which Australia has a double taxation agreement.

Franking credits attached to dividends are really only of advantage to resident shareholders and no refund is available to non-residents. There are dividend streaming rules that prevent companies offering the choice to investors to substitute other dividends for franked dividends. Australian dividend withholding tax and underlying company tax may be creditable against the non-resident's tax liability in its home jurisdiction.

Australia imposes a 10% interest withholding tax on interest paid to non-residents, unless an exemption has been granted by the taxation authorities for interest paid on debentures offered to the public outside Australia to non-residents of Australia. Australia's double tax agreements generally limit the rate of tax on interest to 10% in any case.

Exhibit 2.9:
WITHHOLDING TAX

Recipient	*Interest %*[1]	*Dividends*[2]
Resident corporations or individuals	Nil	Nil
Non-resident corporations or individuals:		
Non-treaty	10	30
Treaty	10–25	15–25

Notes

(1) An exemption from withholding tax can be obtained for interest on certain public issues or widely held issues of debentures. Provisions exist to ensure that discounts and other pecuniary benefits derived by non-residents on various forms of financings are subject to interest withholding tax. Interest paid to non-residents by offshore banking units is exempt from interest withholding tax where offshore borrowings are on-lent only to other non- residents. An offshore borrowing is defined as a borrowing from (i) an unrelated non-resident in any currency, or (ii) a resident in a currency other than Australian currency.

(2) Dividends paid to non-residents are exempt from dividend withholding tax except when paid out of a company that has not borne Australian tax (ie unfranked dividends). Dividends include those stock dividends that are taxable. The rates shown apply to dividends on both portfolio investments and substantial holdings. Unfranked dividends paid to non-residents are exempt from dividend withholding tax to the extent that the dividends are paid out of certain foreign sourced dividend income and the company has specified an "FDA (foreign dividend account) declaration percentage" (ie declared by the company to have been paid out of an account in relation to these dividends).

Source: Price Waterhouse.

B) Gains on disposal of shares

Gains on disposal of shares can be taxed as ordinary income, or under the "capital gains tax" provisions that apply to disposals of shares acquired after 19 September 1985. Provided that the shares are held for more than 12 months, taxable capital gains are calculated after taking account of inflation (otherwise called indexation), and are taxed at personal income tax rates. Capital and income losses on disposal of shares can be offset against realised capital gains.

Gains on disposal of shares can be taxed as ordinary income where they are derived as part of the ordinary conduct of a business or if they are acquired in the course of carrying on business with the purpose of making a profit or gain from disposal. Share market capital gains derived by share traders, banks and insurance companies are treated as income in the ordinary sense and indexation does not apply.

Non-resident investors in Australian non-private companies are only subject to capital gains tax if, at any time during the five years immediately preceding the disposal, the non-resident investor (and/or associates) beneficially owned at least 10% of the issued capital of the company. A similar exemption applies to investments in unit trusts by non-residents.

There is no portfolio exemption from capital gains tax for non-resident investors in unlisted Australian resident companies. Interest expense on borrowed funds for investment in dividend producing shares will usually be tax deductible for Australian purposes, though not for non-residents who would otherwise be subject to dividend withholding tax but for the fact that the dividends are franked.

C) Exchange control and cash transaction reporting

There is no longer any exchange control in Australia. However, significant cash transactions, whether domestic or international, must be reported by financial institutions and other "cash dealers" to a government agency. It is proposed that all significant international wire transfers of funds will also need to be reported. The opening of accounts with financial institutions and other dealers in Australia can only be achieved if the signatory provides appropriate identification.

Payments of dividends and interest to most residents will suffer a withholding by the payer on account of tax if the recipient has not provided its tax file number. The tax file number provisions do not apply to non-residents, but evidence may be required by payers of dividends and interest of the recipient's non-resident status.

D) Foreign Acquisitions and Takeovers Act

Acquisitions of 15% or more of the issued shares or voting power in an Australian company by a single foreign interest and its associates are compulsorily notifiable to the Commonwealth Treasurer and require his approval, unless the total assets of the company are valued at less than A$5 million (A$3 million in the case of companies that have more than 50% of their assets in Australian rural land). Acquisitions with a total value of less than A$50 million will not be examined and will be automatically approved, except in the media, urban real estate, civil aviation and uranium sectors. The Treasurer's approval is required where the total assets of the company are valued at A$50 million or more. Similar rules apply if a number of unassociated foreign persons propose to acquire 40% or more of the voting power or issued shares in an Australian company. The Treasurer is advised by the Foreign Investment Review Board.

Acquisitions of shares are regulated by highly technical and detailed provisions. In broad terms, a person is prohibited from acquiring a *relevant interest* in any shares of an Australian company if the acquisition will result in any person becoming *entitled* to more than 20% of the voting shares in the company. The italicised words are defined in the Act and are subject to a plethora of relevant case law.

There are various exemptions, most notably where the shares are acquired pursuant to a takeover scheme (a formal Part A takeover bid), a takeover announcement (an unconditional on-market Part C bid), a "creeping" takeover (where the offeror acquires not more than 3% of the shares in any 6-month period) or acquisitions made with shareholder approval.

There are deeming provisions that operate to prohibit a downstream acquisition of an Australian company as a result of an upstream acquisition made offshore. Therefore, these laws may be relevant where a non-Australian target holds shares in an Australian company.

REPORTING REQUIREMENTS

Companies listed on the ASX are bound by the ASX Listing Rules, which impose continuous disclosure obligations and require immediate announcement of any information likely to materially affect the price or value of the company's securities. Specific rules require disclosure of events like changes to the nature of the business, certain acquisitions and disposals, dividends, calls and the appointment or dismissal of directors.

Listing Rule 3.1 requires a listed company to disclose immediately any information that a reasonable person would expect to have a material effect on the price or value of the securities of the company. This requirement is reinforced by the continuous disclosure provisions of the Corporations Law that impose civil and criminal liability for failure to disclose material information.

Listed companies must include statements in their annual report detailing the main corporate governance practices in place at the company during the year.

SHAREHOLDER PROTECTION CODES

Legislation prohibits misleading and deceptive conduct in connection with any dealing in securities, market manipulation, false trading and market rigging, fraudulent inducements to deal and insider trading. In addition, the ASX refers to the Australian Securities Commission (ASC) possible serious matters detected by the Surveillance Division relating to insider trading, market manipulation, warehousing, unacceptable conduct and other market abuses that may contravene the law or ASX regulations.

A) Significant shareholdings

A person who becomes entitled to not less than 5% of a listed company's voting shares is required to notify the company within two business days. Subsequent variations of 1% or more must be similarly notified. The company is required to pass this information on to the ASX. There are also provisions that enable a company to trace the beneficial owner of shares where the legal owner has not been required to disclose a substantial shareholding.

B) Insider trading

There are insider trading provisions that broadly prohibit any person in possession of price-sensitive information that is not generally available from dealing, procuring another to deal or communicating the information to another person who he knows or ought to know would be likely to deal in the securities. There is potential civil and criminal liability for breach.

C) Compensation fund

The National Guarantee Fund (NGF) is administered by the Securities Exchanges Guarantee Corporation (SEGC) in accordance with the Corporations Law, and provides investor protection by guaranteeing the performance of all reportable transactions through brokers in securities quoted on the ASX and compensating investors for pecuniary and property loss as a result of unauthorised transfer of securities, cancellation of share certificates in contravention of relevant rules, or the insolvency of a broker member.

RESEARCH

Of the major institutional brokers, J B Were & Son, County Natwest Securities Australia Ltd, Macquarie

Equities Ltd and Ord Minnett Securities Ltd are particularly strong on research.

ASX daily announcements cover the following:

a) company reports;
b) preliminary full-year statements, half-yearly reports and quarterly reports;
c) mining reports;
d) suspension of quotation;
e) dividend and interest payments;
f) new issues;
g) changes in the basis of quotation; and
h) statistics covering the share price index, average yields and stock exchange turnover.

The Dividend List

This is published by the ASX on Fridays and covers all current company dividends, as well as interest payments on debentures, unsecured notes and Australian semi-government and miscellaneous securities.

New Issues and Current Offers and Capital Changes (also published on Fridays) details all current new issues (cash, bonuses and so on, including offers of fixed-interest securities to existing security holders) and takeovers affecting listed securities. It also covers calls outstanding, changes of name and alterations to the Official List.

In addition, the ASX offers a wide range of statistical and research publications, and a catalogue may be obtained from the Information Products Department.

PROSPECTIVE CHANGES

A number of proposals are being considered to simplify the Corporations Law, including provisions relating to:

- share capital rules;
- takeovers;
- fund raising; and
- related party transactions.

The ASX has decided to launch a new internet-based market for small to medium-sized companies seeking to raise venture capital. This new market, to be called the enterprise market (EM), aims to help small to medium-sized unlisted companies to raise debt and equity in a cost-effective way. The launch of this market is planned for March 1998, and more information is available at www.asx.com.au/e.m.

CHAPTER 3

Austria

Introduction

Vienna's stock market failed to reproduce the strong trends of other international exchanges in 1997 and returned a relatively poor index performance (up 13.46%). Domestic turnover reached Sch300.5 billion for the year, an increase of 38.3% over 1996.

In June 1997, Fit, the Vienna Stock Exchange's (VSX) market segment for growth companies was launched with the listing of Hirsch Servo AG.

In terms of structural developments, the registration of Wiener Börse AG in the company register on 18 December 1997 completed the merger of the VSX with ÖTOB, the futures and options exchange. The goal of this merger is to achieve the same dynamic growth on the traditional stock market as on the booming derivatives market.

ECONOMIC AND POLITICAL OVERVIEW

The Austrian economy consolidated its upswing as 1997 progressed. Very low interest rate levels and positive sales and earnings expectations boosted investment which, in turn, stimulated economic growth. GDP is expected to have expanded by 2% in 1997. The US dollar's rise against the schilling and stronger foreign demand increased export sales by more than 10%. Industry output grew by 4%, although construction was weak (+1%). Prices remained stable, and the inflation rate of 1.1% in November was the lowest in the EU. The growth in economic activity halted the increase in the unemployment rate, with employment expanding by 13,000.

The government (a coalition of Social Democrats and the People's Party) holds 67% of the seats in parliament and was able to cut the public budget deficit to 2.6% of GDP in 1997 (from 3.8% in 1996). The medium-term budget programme aims to bring the deficit down to 2.1% of GDP by the year 2000. In order that the Maastricht criteria on aggregate public sector indebtedness may be fulfilled, the government plans privatisations and other measures designed to cut the debt/GDP ratio from 71.7% to 66.1%.

Role of the central bank

The National Bank of Austria is responsible for the regulation of domestic money circulation, the settlement of payments with foreign countries, the stability and purchasing power of the schilling and the printing and issuing of banknotes. The bank is independent of the government.

In order to maintain the schilling's peg to the Deutschmark, Austrian monetary policy is closely linked to that of the German Bundesbank.

MARKET PERFORMANCE

A) In 1997

The Vienna Stock Exchange (WBI) Index improved over the year from 429.20 points to 486.96, representing relatively weak growth by international standards of 13.46%. The ATX, which (like the WBI) began the year close to its low point, rose by 14.1% from 1,134.87 points to 1,294.94. Both indices reached their peaks on 31 July, when the WBI hit 528.47 points and the ATX hit 1,485.69.

Looking at the performance of individual sector indices, chemicals (+50.62%) and energy (+34.07%) recorded the strongest growth. The poorest results were posted by the retail/services sector (-18.85%); foodstuffs, semi-luxury goods and tobacco (-16.60%); and breweries (-7.66%).

Turnover in domestic stocks totalled Sch300.5 billion in 1997, an increase of 38.3% over the previous year's Sch217.3 billion, while market capitalisation of domestic stocks ended the year at Sch451.95 billion, up 26.4% on the end-1996 total of Sch357.5 billion. Issuing activity picked up substantially in 1997 compared with 1996, with an increase in Bank Austria AG preferred stock and flotations of new common shares by Semperit AG and Erste Bank. Last year's big event in Austrian privatisation came in the autumn, when Austria Tabak AG went public.

Exhibit 3.1: WEINER BOERSE (WBI) PRICE INDEX (Sch), 1993–97

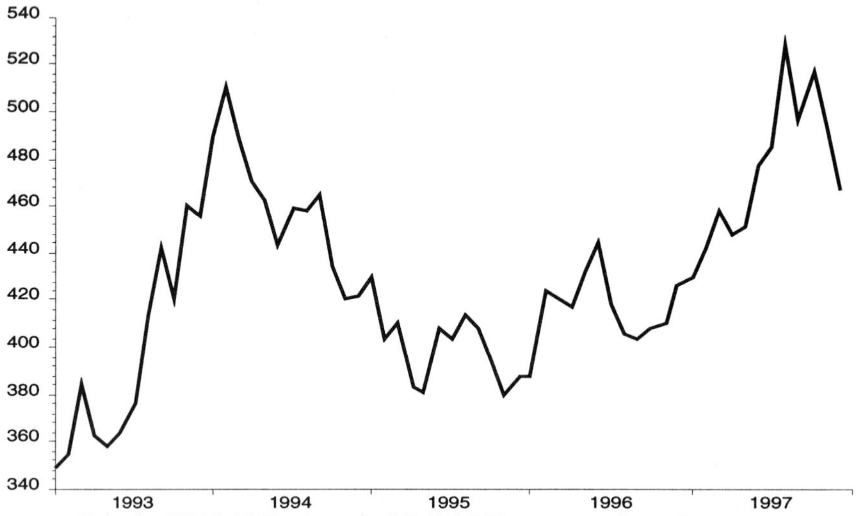

High value 528.29 1.8.97 Low value 348.46 1.1.93 *Source: Datastream*

B) Summary information

Global ranking by market value (US$ terms, end-1997): 34
Market capitalisation (end-1997): US$35.9 billion
Growth in market value (local currency terms, 1993–97): 37.0%
Market value as a % of nominal GDP (end-1997): 18.1%
Number of domestic/foreign companies listed on the official market (end-1997): 100/37
Market P/E (end-1997): 12.2
MSCI total returns (with net dividends, US$ terms, 1997): 1.6%
MSCI Index (change in US$ terms, 1997): +0.3%
Short-term (3-month) interest rate (end-1997): 3.87%
Long-term (10-year) bond yield (end-1997): 5.33%
Budget deficit as a % of nominal GDP (end-1997): 2.6%
Annual increase in broad money (M3) supply (end-1997): 2.5%
Inflation rate (end-1997): 1.1%
US$ exchange rate (1997): Sch12.58

C) Year-end share price index, price/earnings ratios and yields

Exhibit 3.2:
WBI INDEX, P/E RATIOS AND YIELDS, 1993–97

Year-end	*WBI Index*	*P/E*	*Yield (%)*
1993	483.67	24.5	1.35
1994	429.64	20.5	1.46
1995	387.36	18.2	1.90
1996	429.20	15.2	2.00
1997	486.96	12.2	1.90

Sources: Wiener Börse AG and RZB.

D) Market indices and their constituents

The WBI Index is calculated by the Vienna exchange (base date 31 December 1967 = 100) and comprises all domestic shares listed on the official market. The Austrian Traded Index (ATX) is calculated in real time (1991 = 1,000) and is made up of equities dealt in consecutive trading. The WBI30 Index, calculated for 30 selected official market stocks, was introduced in 1995.

The ATX, a measure of the most liquid stocks, tends to be favoured by institutional investors who have used it as a benchmark for their investments in Austrian equities.

ÖTOB (the Austrian futures and options exchange) calculates the ATX50 (used by index trackers), the ATX-MidCap covering the second tier of Austrian equities and the ATP50P performance index.

THE STOCK MARKET

A) Brief history and structure

The VSX was founded in 1771 to provide a market for state-issued bonds, and the first shares issued were those of the Austrian National Bank, set up in 1816.

The Stock Exchange Act 1989 provided for three types

of markets for trading on the VSX – the official market, the semi-official market and the unregulated market.

The merger of the VSX and ÖTOB into the Wiener Börse AG was completed in 1997, with the aim of stimulating the traditional stock market. The organisation of the new Wiener Börse AG is structured around its new corporate identity, and is aimed at transforming the exchange from a national market into an international financial centre in the EU. Of particular significance in the reorganisation is the fully automated market trading system.

At the beginning of 1998 several amendments to Austrian legislation relating to financial markets began to take effect. The Stock Exchange Act is to be amended to open up membership to institutions from outside the European Economic Area. At the same time, several significant sections of the Securities Supervision Act (Wertpapieraufgesichtsgesetz, WAG) came into force, affecting, among other things, disclosure obligations, the full extent of the Austrian Securities Authority's activities and the liabilities of investment advisers.

An amendment to the Investment Fund Act will permit (starting in 1998) holding funds and funds that reinvest interest income, and it should become easier to combine funds. Also, Austrian investment funds will be allowed to take part in OTC options trading.

The Fit market, launched in June 1997 with the listing of Hirsch Servo AG, is the VSX's market segment for growth companies.

The Federal Securities Supervision Authority commenced operations from 1 January 1998 and took over certain market surveillance tasks from the exchange. Its main areas of responsibility are to supervise the activities of market traders and to monitor observance by listed companies of the VSX's disclosure requirements.

B) Different exchanges

The VSX is the only stock exchange in Austria.

C) Opening hours, names and addresses

Official trading hours are Monday to Friday from 8.00am to 3.00pm.

WIENER BÖRSE
Strauchgasse 1–3, 1014 Vienna
Tel: (43) 1 534 990; Fax: (43) 1 535 6857

MARKET SIZE

A) Number of listings and market value

The market capitalisation of all domestic shares listed on the official and semi-official markets was Sch451.95 billion at year-end 1997, up 26.4% compared with the end-1996 total of Sch357.5 billion.

Exhibit 3.3:
NUMBER OF WIENER BÖRSE LISTED SHARES* AND DOMESTIC CAPITALISATION, YEAR-END 1993–97

	1993	*1994*	*1995*	*1996*	*1997*
Domestic	320	180	174	154	117
Foreign	57	53	49	42	40
Total	377	233	223	196	157
Domestic market capitalisation (Sch billion)					
	329.9	312.3	314.4	357.5	451.9

*Includes participation certificates, warrants, investment funds, dividend rights and profit-sharing certificates, but does not include the unregulated market.

Source: Wiener Börse AG.

Exhibit 3.4:
MARKET VALUE OF DOMESTIC LISTED SHARES BY SECTOR, VSX, END-1997

Sector	*Market value (Sch billion)*
Banks	121.6
Energy	91.8
Machines, transport and technology	72.0
Insurance	35.2
Building materials	23.9
Foodstuffs, beverages and tobacco	20.3
Others	18.5
Breweries	14.8
Pulp and paper	14.0
Construction	9.9
Real estate	9.5
Chemicals	6.7
Mining	6.1
Textiles	4.6
Trade and services	1.8
Conglomerates	1.5
Total	451.9

Source: Wiener Börse AG.

B) Largest quoted companies

At the end of 1997, the five largest companies listed on the VSX accounted for 33% of total market capitalisation.

Exhibit 3.5:
THE 20 LARGEST DOMESTIC LISTED COMPANIES BY MARKET VALUE, VSX, END-1997

Ranking	*Company*	*Market value (Sch million)*
1	ÖMV	47,250

Exhibit 3.5 continued

2	VA Technologie	28,770
3	Erste Bank St	27,925
4	CA St	23,247
5	EA-Generali	23,233
6	Weinerberger	21,053
7	Verbund Kat A	20,236
8	Bank Austria	20,210
9	EVN	18,924
10	VA Stahl	16,071
11	Austria Tabak	12,320
12	CA Vz	8,708
13	Mayr-Melnhof	8,161
14	Boehler-Uddeholm	8,145
15	Bank Austria Vz EM	7,983
16	Flughafen Wien	7,793
17	AUA	6,994
18	Bank Austria St EM	6,866
19	Brau Union	6,400
20	Radex-Heraklith	6,055

Source: Wiener Börse AG.

C) Trading volume

Turnover in domestic shares on the official exchange was Sch300.53 billion in 1997 (a rise of 38.33% compared with 1996 levels). Average daily turnover in domestic shares in 1997 was Sch823.3 million.

Exhibit 3.6:
TURNOVER ON THE VSX (SCH BILLION), 1993–97

	1993	*1994*	*1995*	*1996*	*1997*
Domestic	152.6	187.0	259.7	217.3	300.5
Foreign	10.9	6.7	4.9	7.4	7.6
Investment certificates	7.7	N/A	98.1	99.3	61.5

Source: Wiener Börse AG.

Exhibit 3.7:
THE 20 MOST ACTIVELY TRADED DOMESTIC SHARES BY TRADING VALUE, VSX, 1997

Ranking	*Company*	*Turnover (Sch million)*
1	ÖMV	40,311
2	VA Technologie	34,908
3	EVN	26,573
4	Boehler-Uddeholm	17,740
5	VA Stahl	16,918
6	Verbund Kat. A	16,472
7	CA Vz	15,930
8	Wienerberger	15,642

Exhibit 3.7 continued

9	Flughafen Wien	13,500
10	CA St	10,414
11	Radex-Heraklith	7,009
12	Bank Austria Vz	6,924
13	Wolford	6,892
14	AMS	6,850
15	Bank Austria St	6,577
16	Mayr-Melnhof	5,767
17	BWT	3,867
18	EA-Generali St	3,719
19	Bank Austria Vz EM 97	3,659
20	Austria Tabak	3,412

Source: Wiener Börse AG.

TYPES OF SHARE

The majority of shares in Austrian joint stock companies are ordinary shares having voting and dividend rights. Preference shares, with special dividend rights but no voting rights, may also be issued. Ordinary shares may be in either registered or bearer form, although the majority are the latter. Austrian shares usually have par values of Sch100, Sch500 or Sch1,000. A few larger par values in multiples of Sch1,000 exist. On the VSX the majority of shares traded have par values of Sch100.

No more than one-third of the capital of a joint stock company can be issued in the form of preference shares, which may also be in either registered or bearer form. If a company does not pay dividends on preference shares, such shares may acquire voting rights. Since 1986 companies have been able to issue participation certificates, which are similar to preference shares.

The Stock Exchange Act (Börsegesetz) allows the VSX to trade in all kinds of securities, foreign exchange, coins, precious metals, options and financial futures, and to undertake all connected ancillary business.

OTHER MARKETS

The semi-official market on the VSX has grown up alongside the official market and follows the same general rules and listing requirements. It is a regulated free market involving floor trading of securities that have been approved by the VSX but which are not included in the official list.

On the third, so-called "unregulated market" (created by the VSX in 1990), market-makers set binding bid and ask prices for the securities being traded. On the unregulated market, the stringent requirements for the admission to stock exchange listing do not apply.

The Austrian futures and options exchange (ÖTOB)

has now been merged with the VSX and, in June 1997, the VSX opened Fit, its new market for small and medium-sized companies.

INVESTORS

No official breakdown of investors is published. The number of Austrians owning shares is about 4% of the total population. Figures concerning the percentage of foreign investors are not available.

Foreign investors tend to be attracted by Austria's record of high economic growth, opportunities in eastern Europe, a hard currency, social and economic stability, hidden reserves in the property sector and conservative accounting.

OPERATIONS

A) Trading system

All VSX securities are now traded on EQOS (the Electronic Quote and Order-Driven System), which began operations in June 1996. For high turnover shares, the trading session begins at 8.00am with the general order-placing phase. Then, at 9.16am, the opening price is determined during a fully automated auction, followed by consecutive trading under the market-maker system. During the entire trading session, at least three market-makers supply binding quotes (and for shares on which options are written there are at least five market-makers).

EQOS uses an open order book and all orders placed are displayed on screen and can be seen by all market participants, thus improving market transparency.

The introduction of EQOS has brought about the following changes:

1. Dealers are able to communicate directly with each other and to place buy and sell orders into the system. The conclusion of transactions takes place automatically according to a programmed procedure.
2. Banks undertake to make markets in the most liquid equities at all times. Every share has at least three market-makers.
3. EQOS trading sessions begin with an auction where all buy and sell orders are gathered and one price is determined.
4. Stop-loss orders are now prohibited.
5. The limit for price fluctuations has been enlarged from +/-10% to +/-15%.

B) List of principal banks

BANK AUSTRIA
Vordere Zollamtstrasse 13, 1030 Vienna
Tel: (43) 1 711 910; Fax: (43) 1 711 2123

Exhibit 3.8:
COUNTRY FUNDS – AUSTRIA

Fund	*US$% change 31/12/96 31/12/97*	*US$% change 31/12/92 31/12/97*	*Currency*	*Fund size (US$ mil)*	*Volatility*	*Manager name*	*Main sector*	*Class*
ViennaTop	12.84	71.41	Sch	N/A	N/A	Sparinvest Austria KAG	Equity Growth	Austrian Mutuals
Callander Fund Austrian	11.65	51.35	Sch	3.26	4.69	Callander Mgt SA	Equity	Luxembourg
Swiss Life Proteus Aust Share	8.1	97.18	Sch	5.41	4.72	Swiss Life Proteus	Equity	Offshore Territories
Apollo Österreich Gem. MEF	7.01	N/A	Sch	N/A	N/A	Security KAG	Equity Growth	Austrian Mutuals
Vienna Invest	5.95	48.65	Sch	N/A	N/A	Sparinvest Austria KAG	Equity Growth	Austrian Mutuals
Raiffeisen-Österreich-Fonds	5.55	51.92	Sch	N/A	N/A	Raiffeisen KAG	Equity Growth	Austrian Mutuals
EKA-STOCK-AUSTRIA MEF i. WP	4.62	47.96	Sch	N/A	N/A	DIE ERSTE-KAG	Equity Growth	Austrian Mutuals
EQUITY INVEST MEF i. inl. WP	3.48	48.75	Sch	N/A	N/A	Julius Meinl Investment	Equity Growth	Austrian Mutuals
A 5 MEF i. WP	2.22	44.92	Sch	N/A	N/A	Oesterreichische Investment Ges.	Equity Growth	Austrian Mutuals
ViennaStock MEF i. WP	-0.45	N/A	Sch	N/A	N/A	Allgemeine Sparkasse KAG	Equity Growth	Austrian Mutuals
Austrian Index Trust	-2.7	N/A	Sch	N/A	N/A	Carl Spaengler KAG	Equity Growth	Austrian Mutuals
Constantia Austrian Equity MEF	-2.91	47.91	Sch	N/A	N/A	Constantia Privatbank KAG	Equity Growth	Austrian Mutuals
ABI Ostarrichi Fonds MEF	-4.4	N/A	Sch	N/A	N/A	AUSTRO-BAVARIA Investment	Equity Growth	Austrian Mutuals
BBL Invest Austria Cap	-4.47	N/A	Sch	10.9	N/A	BBL-Banque Brussels Lambert	Equity	Belgian Trusts
Aetna MF Austrian Natl Equity	-8.51	-8.03	Sch	0.74	2.8	Aetna Master Fund	Equity	Luxembourg

Note: details for some funds may not have been included if the data for the US$ % change for 96/97 was not available

Source: Standard & Poor's Micropal.

CA IB INVESTMENT BANK
Schottengasse 6-8, 1010 Vienna
Tel: (43) 1 531 310; Fax: (43) 1 531 314 699;
Tlx: 114261

ERSTE BANK
Graben 21, 1010 Vienna
Tel: (43) 1 531 000; Fax: (43) 1 531 003 (112)

RAIFFEISEN ZENTRALBANK ÖSTERREICH
Am Stadtpark 9, 1030 Vienna
Tel: (43) 1 717 070; Fax: (43) 1 717 071 724

C) Settlement and transfer

Deals can be settled for cash or through a weekly clearing system – the so-called "Arrangement". The Arrangement is run by a department of the Österreichische Kontrollbank AG, which is also the central depository for securities. All listed securities are included in the clearing system. The VSX has adopted a rolling settlement, whereby settlement of transactions is now implemented on a daily basis with a three-day fulfilment period (T+3). The settlement date is also considered as the value date. Non-residents may participate in the clearing system by opening a sub-account with an Austrian bank or a foreign depository.

D) Commissions and other costs

For share transactions, the charge to investors is 1.25% of the market value. This includes stock exchange turnover tax, the official broker's fee and the bank's commission.

TAXATION AND REGULATIONS AFFECTING FOREIGN INVESTORS

Under 1993 legislation, non-residents are subject to a 25% withholding tax on interest from bank deposits and on dividends.

Exhibit 3.9:
WITHHOLDING TAX

Recipient	*Dividends %*[1]	*Interest %*[2]
Resident corporations	Nil/25	Nil/25
Resident individuals	25	Nil/25
Non-resident recipients:		
Non-treaty:		
Non-resident corporations and business enterprises	25	Nil
Individuals	25	Nil
Treaty	0-25	0

Notes:
1. In accordance with the Parent/Subsidiary Directive, an exemption from withholding tax is granted for the distribution of profits by an Austrian corporation to an EU parent company if the parent has held a participation of at least 25% during an uninterrupted period of at least 2 years. Under some treaties, the amount of withholding tax is dependent on the proportion of issued share capital held by the recipient.
2. Interest on bank loans in Austrian schillings or foreign currency, on bank accounts and bonds in foreign currency (issued after 31 December 1988) and on bonds denominated in Austrian schillings (issued after 31 December 1983) generally bears a 25% withholding tax. If the recipient is an individual, this withholding tax is final (ie there is no further income taxation and inheritance taxation). Companies receiving interest can secure an exemption from withholding tax through a written declaration from the recipient to the bank or other depository that such interest forms part of the recipient's business income (*Befreiungserklärung*). Interest income received by non-residents without a permanent establishment in Austria is not generally subject to withholding taxation. Interest on convertible bonds is taxed as dividends.

Source: Price Waterhouse.

In 1991 the Austrian National Bank abolished all foreign exchange regulations for both residents and non-residents. Instead of a system of regulation, the Austrian National Bank has introduced extensive reporting requirements in order to monitor the performance of the Austrian currency. The reporting is usually carried out without the involvement of an Austrian bank – ie there can be an obligation on individuals and companies involved in certain transactions to report them to the National Bank. This is in line with the government's policy to harmonise Austria's economy and financial markets with those in other EU member states.

A foreigner wishing to open an account with an Austrian bank or instructing an Austrian bank to acquire securities for that account has to disclose and prove his or her identity to the bank. The bank in turn is bound by the strict Austrian bank secrecy rules not to divulge information provided by the customer to the bank. Violation of the bank secrecy rules is a criminal act. Apart from prosecution and sentencing of bank officials, the bank is also exposed to civil liabilities for damages. Austrian banks must report any suspicious transactions for prior clearance by EDOK – a financial task-force set up within the Ministry of Interior Affairs in order to combat money laundering.

On 1 August 1996 regulations came into force under which securities custody accounts can no longer be operated on an anonymous basis.

LISTING AND REPORTING REQUIREMENTS

A) Listing requirements

The VSX decides on applications for securities to be listed on the exchange. Its rules and regulations are to be adapted to those of the EU.

A listing prospectus must contain details of the person responsible for the prospectus and for auditing the financial data. Particulars must also be included concerning the listing, the shares, the issuer, its capitalisation, the business carried on by the issuer and its assets, financial and profit situations. Details are also required regarding the administration, governance and supervision of the issuer, as well as recent trading and business prospects. For a company to be admitted to listing it must be able to report reasonable profits over the previous three years.

B) Reporting requirements

Once listed, companies are required to publish an annual report and an interim report covering the first six months of the business year. In addition, companies must inform the public immediately of any changes in the rights attached to their shares, changes in ownership of blocks of shares and of any other facts that could affect their share price. The company registry is open to everyone.

Securities listed on the VSX are also subject to conditions imposed by the Wiener Börse Council. There are, for example, guidelines on the printing and format of securities to avoid fraud and to facilitate handling by banks.

SHAREHOLDER PROTECTION CODES

A) Minority rights

Minority shareholders are granted various rights under the Law on Public Companies. For example, the holders of 5% of the shares can demand a special meeting of the shareholders and can also demand that certain matters are put on the agenda of an annual general meeting. The holders of 10% of the share capital can demand a special audit and can apply to the court for auditors to be appointed; they can also file a claim for damages against the members of the board of directors or the supervisory board.

B) Significant shareholdings

Changes in shareholdings have to be reported within seven days if the holding of voting stock reaches, exceeds or falls back below the following limits: 5%, 10%, 25%, 50%, 75% or 90%. The company affected is required to inform the public about changes within nine days of learning of the details.

C) Takeovers and mergers

A legal framework regulating takeovers and mergers is currently being developed by the Ministry of Justice. Takeovers and mergers are subject to anti-trust control under the Cartel Act. A Cartel Act amendment requires pre-merger clearance from the Cartel Court, although, in minor mergers, post-merger notification will suffice.

D) Insider trading

Insider trading has been a criminal offence since 1993. Insiders are defined as executives and employees of public companies, banks, auditors and others, including major shareholders. The crime of insider trading can be committed by using information for the purchase or sale of securities, as a recommendation to sell or to buy, or by providing such information to third parties. Also, non-insiders who intentionally exploit inside information in securities dealing can be prosecuted. Insider dealing can result in a sentence of up to two years imprisonment or large fines.

RESEARCH

Research on the market is produced mainly by the large Austrian banks such as Creditanstalt Investment Bank, RZB, Erste Bank and Bank Austria.

The following publications are available in English from the VSX:

Annual Report, Year Book, Information Folder
Monthly Statistics Report , Stock Exchange Act
Information about EQOS

The *Kursblatt der Wiener Börse* (the official price list of the VSX) provides comprehensive price and other market information for equities traded on all three market segments.

PROSPECTIVE CHANGES

The new integrated Wiener Börse is expected to expand its activities in the areas of IT consulting, as well as consulting relating to the operation of a stock, futures and options exchange.

CHAPTER 4

Bahrain

Introduction

The absence of any organised secondary market in Bahrain during the 1970s and early 1980s encouraged investors to place their funds in the Kuwaiti unofficial market, known as Souq Al Manakh. Following the collapse of that market in 1982, the government of Bahrain established an ad hoc committee to study the crisis and, with the cooperation of the IFC, a feasibility study was prepared showing the importance of establishing an official stock market. The Bahrain Stock Exchange (BSE) commenced operations in 1989. It is a distinct legal entity, chaired by the Minister of Commerce and Agriculture.

Several initiatives have been taken recently in an attempt to attract more liquidity to the BSE, including opening up the stock market to non-resident foreigners, introducing an electronic trading system and establishing a clearing and settlement house. Rules and regulations to allow foreign companies to be listed on the stock exchange are also being studied.

In addition to its prime functions of organising and facilitating share trading, the BSE plays an important role in promoting the establishment of new joint stock companies and in facilitating the flotation of closely held companies.

ECONOMIC AND POLITICAL OVERVIEW

Bahrain is an independent sovereign state ruled by the Al Khalifa family assisted by a Cabinet of appointed ministers.

The 10% drop in average oil prices in 1997 saw the value of oil exports fall, despite higher nominal production due to extra output from Abu Saafa. Non-oil exports increased slightly, largely because of a rise in both aluminium production and prices. In the current invisibles account, increased receipts from tourism were offset somewhat by a rise in payments on import-related services. The EIU estimates real economic growth of some 1.2% for 1997 and 1.7% for 1998.

The government is keen for the private sector to lead the way in the development of the economy, and a gradual privatisation of government agencies is planned, plus the granting of loans to encourage private businesses.

MARKET PERFORMANCE

A) In 1997

Stock prices, as measured by the BSE Index, increased by 49% in 1997, and year-end market capitalisation stood at US$7.1 billion compared with US$5.0 billion at the end of 1996 – an increase of 42%.

Secondary market turnover totalled US$478 million (up 169.8% on 1996). Market trading is dominated by the domestic and offshore investment sectors. In terms of value and volume of shares traded in 1997, the offshore investment sector accounted for 57.6% and 19.5% of total trading respectively, and the domestic banking sector ranked next with 25% and 9.5% respectively.

B) Summary information

Global ranking by market value (US$ terms, end-1997): 51
Market capitalisation (end-1997): US$7.1 billion
Growth in market value (US$ terms, 1993-97): 26.78%
Market value as a % of nominal GDP (end-1997): 76%
Number of domestic/foreign companies listed (end-1997): 37/4
Market P/E (all listed companies, end-1997): 14.4
Short-term (3-month) interest rate (end-1997): 4.25%
Long-term (maturity 2001) interest rate (end-1997): 6.42%
Budget deficit as a % of nominal GDP (1997): 3.9%
Inflation rate (1997): 0.8%
US$ exchange rate (end-1997): BD0.378

C) Year-end share price index and price/earnings ratios

Exhibit 4.1:
YEAR-END SHARE PRICE INDEX AND P/E RATIOS, 1993–97

Year-end	*BSE Index*	*P/E*
1993	1,928.31	12.20
1994	1,518.93	12.55
1995	1,326.56	12.73
1996	1,547.35	14.00
1997	2,310.09	14.40

Source: Bahrain Stock Exchange.

D) Market indices and their constituents

The BSE introduced its arithmetic price average index in 1990. The index covers 25 securities.

THE STOCK MARKET

A) Brief history and structure

The BSE was established in 1987 by an Amiri decree as an independent legal entity responsible for organising the capital market in Bahrain, and trading began in 1989. The exchange is managed by a board chaired by the Minister of Commerce, consisting of eight members representing government and private parties involved in capital market activities.

The exchange also has a full-time director who runs day-to-day operations at the BSE.

B) Different exchanges

There is only one stock exchange in Bahrain.

C) Opening hours, names and addresses

Trading takes place from 10.00am to 11.30am, Sunday to Thursday.

BAHRAIN STOCK EXCHANGE
PO Box 3203, Manama
Tel: (973) 261260 Fax: (973) 256362
E-mail: bse@bahrainstock.com

MARKET SIZE

A) Number of listings and market value

There were 41 companies listed on the BSE at the end of 1997. Market capitalisation was US$7.1 billion compared with US$5.0 billion at the end of 1996, representing an increase of 42%.

Exhibit 4.2:
NUMBER OF COMPANIES LISTED AND MARKET VALUE, BSE, 1993–97

Year-end	*No. of companies listed*	*Market value (BD billion)*	*Market value (US$ billion)*
1993	32	2.1	5.6
1994	35	1.8	4.9
1995	37	1.7	4.7
1996	39	1.9	5.0
1997	41	2.7	7.1

Source: ABC Investment and Services Co.

B) Largest quoted companies

Exhibit 4.3:
TOP 20 COMPANIES LISTED ON THE BSE BY MARKET CAPITALISATION, END-1997

Ranking	*Company*	*Market capitalisation (US$ million)*	*% of market total*
1	Bahrain Telecommunication	1,421.00	20.05
2	Investcorp Bank	1,376.00	19.41
3	Arab Banking Corporation	1,140.00	16.08
4	National Bank of Bahrain	487.00	6.87
5	Bank of Bahrain and Kuwait	449.82	6.34
6	United Gulf Bank	418.04	5.90
7	Bahrain International Bank	385.57	5.44
8	Bahrain Middle East Bank	176.40	2.49
9	Al Ahli Commercial Bank	150.56	2.12
10	National Import and Export Co	149.68	2.11
11	Faisal Islamic Bank of Bahrain	144.20	2.03
12	Bahrain Maritime & Mercantile Int	123.05	1.74
13	Bahrain Saudi Bank	92.84	1.31
14	Taib Bank EC	90.00	1.27
15	Bahrain Islamic Bank	63.45	0.89
16	Bahrain Commercial Facilities	60.48	0.85
17	Bahrain Flour Mills Co	54.01	0.76
18	Arab Insurance Company	51.30	0.72
19	Bahrain Light Industries Co	38.69	0.55
20	United Gulf Industries Corp	35.21	0.50

Source: ABC Investment and Serivces Co.

C) Trading volume

Exhibit 4.4:
TURNOVER ON THE BSE, 1993–97

Year	*Volume (shares million)*	*Value traded (BD million)*	*No. of transactions*
1993	389.6	96.4	8,845

Exhibit 4.4 continued

1994	257.2	60.4	5,986
1995	184.7	40.0	4,174
1996	298.8	66.6	6,681
1997	630.1	180.7	19,087

Source: Bahrain Stock Exchange.

Exhibit 4.5:
SHARES TRADED BY SECTOR ON THE BSE, 1997

Sector	*Value (US$ million)*	*Volume (shares million)*
Investment banking	240.1	360.4
Commercial banking	124.2	166.6
Services	77.1	54.3
Insurance	25.5	22.0
Hotels	10.9	23.5
Industries	1.5	3.2
Total	**479.3**	**630.1**

Source: Bahrain Stock Exchange.

TYPES OF SHARE

Common registered shares are the only type of share traded on the BSE.

INVESTMENT FUNDS

The Bahrain Monetary Agency (BMA) supervises all investment funds (both closed and open-ended) under the Collective Investment Scheme Regulations of 1992.

Given that there is currently no income tax or corporation tax in Bahrain, it has been used as a tax-efficient location to launch a number of funds, some of which have been listed not only in Bahrain but also on foreign stock exchanges. Most domestic funds have been derivative or financial instrument funds as opposed to infrastructure funds.

OPERATIONS

A) Types of trades and spreads

Trade specifications are as follows:

- regular trading, for a minimum value of BD1,500 per transaction;
- block trading, for a minimum value of BD30,000 per transaction;
- odd-lot trading, for a maximum value of less than BD1,500 per transaction.

Exhibit 4.6:
PRICE SPREADS ON THE BSE

Price (BD)	*Price spread (fils)*
Less than 0.100	0.5
0.100 to 0.499	2.0
0.500 to 2.500	5.0
2.500 to 5.000	10.0
Over 5.000	20.0

The maximum ceiling on daily movements of share prices is fixed at 10% for the first 10 minutes of each trading session, and 7% thereafter.

B) Trading system

The trading system adopted by the BSE is known as "written auction". This system applies an auction mechanism in which all bids and offers for shares are written on the board by the responsible broker. Transactions are carried out by the brokers when there are matched orders.

BSE brokers may act as market-makers, dealing in shares for their own account, as well as providing custody, consultancy, advisory and nominee services for their clients. Qualified brokers extending such services must be established as companies with a minimum paid-up capital of BD35,000, and must be backed by a guarantee of BD50,000.

C) Principal brokers

ABC SECURITIES
Tel: (973) 255 087; Fax: (973) 241 179

BBK FINANCIAL SERVICES
Tel: (973) 247 496; Fax: (973) 257 785

GULF SECURITIES
Tel: (973) 272 578; Fax: (973) 258 780

SECURITIES AND INVESTMENT
Tel: (973) 212 141; Fax: (973) 212 140

TAIB SECURITIES
Tel: (973) 212 929; Fax: (973) 212 511

TRUST SECURITIES CO.
Tel: (973) 251 858; Fax: (973) 250 800

D) Settlement and clearing

Settlement is effected by the physical delivery of share certificates through the broker and the receipt of cash or a cheque. Settlement should be completed by the third business day following the date of the transaction. An independent clearing company will soon be established to carry out these tasks.

E) Commission rates

Rates are as follows:

Up to BD10,000:	0.30%
From BD10,000 to BD100,000:	0.20%
Above BD100,000:	0.10%

REGULATIONS AFFECTING FOREIGN INVESTORS

Bahraini individuals and companies are the main investors in the market. There is no restriction on the percentage shareholding in a listed company that may be held by nationals of Bahrain and companies incorporated in Bahrain.

Gulf Cooperation Council member nationals and companies may hold between 25% and 49% of the paid-up capital of any listed company. However, offshore companies can hold up to 100% of the paid-up capital. Shares in Arab Banking Corporation (BSC), Investcorp Bank (EC), Bahrain International Bank (EC) and TAIB Bank may be freely traded. In addition, the BSE has recently been opened to the following categories of investors: (a) non-Bahraini nationals who have been resident in Bahrain for at least one year; (b) licensed investment funds; and (c) foreign companies with branches in Bahrain. However, non-Bahraini residents in Bahrain may not own more than 1% of a listed company's share capital, and the maximum foreign shareholding is 24%.

A company listed on the BSE may not hold more than 10% of its own issued share capital.

TAXATION

Bahrain does not tax capital gains or cash dividends.

LISTING AND REPORTING REQUIREMENTS

A) Listing requirements

A public company wishing to list its shares on the BSE must satisfy the following principal conditions:

- at least two years of audited financial statements;
- paid-up capital of at least BD500,000, and each share at least 50% paid up;
- net sales exceeding 20% of the paid-up capital;
- it should be in sound financial condition; and
- should have realised profits for each of the two previous years.

B) Reporting requirements

Under the BSE internal regulations, all listed companies must supply audited annual financial statements and unaudited semi-annual financial statements. In addition, companies must inform the BSE of the shareholdings of the board of directors, details of dividends, and any financial information and/or factors that could affect the operations of the company.

SHAREHOLDER PROTECTION CODES

All stockbroking companies and market-makers in Bahrain must be capitalised to a minimum of BD350,000 or its equivalent in foreign currencies. Furthermore, they must provide the BSE with a guarantee issued by a local bank of BD50,000 (or its foreign currency equivalent) and the BSE reserves the right to seek a guarantee for a higher sum.

RESEARCH

Prices of shares are quoted and transmitted live from the trading floor via the Reuters Monitor Network worldwide through the codes BSXA, BSXB, BSXC, BSXCD, BSCE and BSXF. The prices of traded shares are also published daily via local newspapers, Bahrain Television and Radio Bahrain.

The BSE publishes (in addition to its annual reports) weekly, monthly, quarterly and semi-annual data on the market, plus a variety of statistics and reports on both market performance and listed companies.

Arab Banking Corporation provides good research on both the market and individual stocks.

CHAPTER

5

Bangladesh

Introduction

Relative to the size of its economy, the Bangladeshi equity market is small compared with the markets of other countries in the region. Market capitalisation as a percentage of GDP stands at just 4.2%. The recent initiative to attract pension and trust funds into the market may lead to improved liquidity.

The retail character of the market is revealed by the fact that, out of the total of 195 brokers on the Dhaka exchange, only five are investment companies or financial institutions. Full membership remains restricted to nationals only.

Recently, the government has tried to hasten the process of structural reform of the market. The drive towards automation has, however, been only partially successful. The Dhaka Stock Exchange (DSE), the main market, has achieved little in this respect, while, on the other hand, the Chittagong Stock Exchange (CSE) has made remarkable progress towards automation since its inception in 1995. Much has been said about installing a central depository system (CDS), but no concrete proposals have yet been made.

ECONOMIC AND POLITICAL OVERVIEW

Political tensions are running high and the absence from parliament of the main opposition party is inhibiting the democratic process.

Fiscal 1997 saw the highest economic growth rate of this decade, but some indicators have worsened since then. In particular, the national inflation rate rose on average by more than 6% in 1997. The rise in fuel prices, the pay hike for government employees and the recent spiralling increases in the price of grain have contributed to this trend. Inflationary pressures led the government to increase the bank interest rate to 8%.

The foreign exchange reserves stood at US$1,670 million on 8 January 1998. A widening food deficit is expected to lead to a deterioration in the balance of payments, and the precarious position of the reserves, sufficient to cover only 2.5 months' of imports, remains a matter of concern. As a result, the government has adopted a policy of gradual taka depreciation, with the currency falling 7.17% against the US dollar in 1997.

Role of the central bank

The Bangladesh Bank operates under the Ministry of Finance and, in the past, most central bank governors have been retired Financial Secretaries. However, the current governor, Mr Lutfar Rahman Sarker, is the second banker to be appointed to the post. Although the Ministry of Finance directs the activities of the Bangladesh Bank, the new governor's appointment has been recognised as a step towards a more autonomous central bank.

The responsibilities of the bank cover setting and implementing monetary policy, including control over the exchange rate and the level and timing of interest rate changes. The Bangladesh Bank is authorised to regulate and supervise the country's banking sector and other financial institutions, and to manage the government's domestic debt. The bank also prepares and publishes regular monetary, financial and exchange rate data.

MARKET PERFORMANCE

A) In 1997

The Dhaka exchange was in the doldrums in 1997. The debâcle of autumn 1997 shattered the confidence of retail investors who predominantly drive the market, and the liquidity crunch in the banking sector further aggravated the situation.

The year began with a continuation of the market correction that had ended the 1996 speculative bull run. In the second week of May, however, the DSE All Share

Index rebounded and moved through 1,200, encouraging some thoughts of a turnaround in sentiment. But the improvement was not sustained and, since the middle of the year, a steady decline in prices has occurred. The market reached its nadir on 2 December 1997, with the index at 711.14 – a level not witnessed since mid-1995.

Volatility in the secondary market tended to attract investors to the primary market. In 1997, 12 companies made IPOs, raising a total of Tk661 million (US$14.5 million).

B) Summary information

Global ranking by market value (US$ terms, end-1997): 69
Market capitalisation (end-1997): US$1,510.53 million
Growth in market value (US$ terms, 1993–97): 237.7%
Market value as a % of nominal GDP (1997, estimate): 4.2%
Number of domestic/foreign companies listed (end-1997): 202/0
Market P/E (end-1997): 14.0
Short-term (3-month Treasury bill) interest rate (end-1997): 8.5-9.5%
Long-term (5-year savings certificate) bond yield (end-1997): 13.5%
Budget deficit as a % of nominal GDP (end-1997, estimate): 5.5%
Annual increase in broad money (M2) supply (end-1997, estimate): 11%
Inflation rate (CPI, 1997): 6%
US$ exchange rate (fiscal year-end 1997): Tk45.45

C) Year-end share price index, price/earnings ratios and yields

Exhibit 5.1:
YEAR-END DSE ALL SHARE INDEX AND P/E, 1994–97

Year-end	*DSE All Share Index*	*P/E*
1994	845.65	na
1995	834,73	24.6
1996	2,300.15	56.1
1997	756.78	14.0

Source: Dhaka Stock Exchange and Union Capital Limited.

THE STOCK MARKET

A) Brief history and structure

The DSE was formed in 1954. Soon after Bangladesh's independence in 1972, a wave of nationalisation brought the exchange to a standstill, but from 1976 onwards the market resumed operations and there are now 195 broker members. The Securities and Exchange Commission (SEC) oversees new listings and is currently developing a regulatory framework for the stock market.

B) Different exchanges

A second exchange, in Chittagong, opened in Bangladesh in October 1995.

C) Opening hours and contact details

Both exchanges trade from Saturday to Thursday between 10.30am and 2.00pm.

DHAKA STOCK EXCHANGE LTD
Stock Exchange Building
9F Motijheel Commercial Area, Dhaka 1000
Tel: (880) 2 956 4601; Fax: (880) 2 956 4727

CHITTAGONG STOCK EXCHANGE
1008 Sheik Mujib Road, Chittagong, 4100
Tel: (880) 31 714 632; Fax: (880) 31 714 101

MARKET SIZE

A) Number of listings and market value

At the end of the 1997 there were 202 companies listed on the DSE and 128 companies listed on the CSE. Total DSE market capitalisation at the end of 1997 was US$1.51 billion.

Exhibit 5.2:
NUMBER OF COMPANIES LISTED AND MARKET VALUE, DSE, 1993–97

Year-end	*No. of companies*	*Market capitalisation (US$ million)*
1993	156	447.31
1994	169	1,025.00
1995	183	1,310.00
1996	186	3,932.17
1997	202	1,510.53

Source: Dhaka Stock Exchange.

Exhibit 5.3:
MARKET VALUE BY SECTOR, END-1997

Sector	*Market value (Tk million)*	*% of total market value*
Engineering	11,465	16.8
Pharmaceuticals	11,059	16.1
Food and Allied	8,692	12.7
Textile	8,659	12.7
Banks	7,296	10.6
Cement	3,809	5.5
Leather	3,806	5.5
Real estate	3,445	5
Insurance	3,178	4.6
Energy	2,673	3.9

Exhibit 5.3 continued

Ceramic	1,225	1.7
Paper and pulp	802	1.1
Other	2,712	3.8
Total	**68,821**	**100.0**

Source: Dhaka Stock Exchange.

Exhibit 5.4:
THE 20 LARGEST LISTED COMPANIES ON THE DSE, MARCH 1997

Ranking	*Company*	*Market capitalisation (Tk million)*
1	Singer Bangladesh	6,244.40
2	BTC Ltd	5,209.20
3	Beximco Pharma	3,550.18
4	Shinepukur	2,549.48
5	Chittagong Cement	2,145.63
6	Square Pharma	2,050.25
7	BOC Ltd	1,780.84
8	Glaxo	1,640.61
9	Padma Oil Co Ltd	1,580.94
10	Bata Shoe	1,490.57
11	Rupali Bank	1,477.75
12	Padma Textile Mill	1,477.11
13	IDLC	1,386.36
14	Monno Fabrics	1,197.27
15	Beximco Textiles	1,175.06
16	United Leasing Co	1,115.33
17	ACI Ltd	1,100.74
18	Bangladesh Lamps	1,070.16
19	Monno Ceramics	865.31
20	Eastern Housing	830.07

Source: Dhaka Stock Exchange.

B) Trading volume

Average daily turnover was US$1.5 million in 1997, compared with US$2 million in 1996.

OPERATIONS

A) Trading system

Both the Dhaka and Chittagong exchanges trade from Saturday to Thursday between 10.30am and 2.00pm, using an open outcry system. On the DSE the name of each stock is read out in a specified order and all business is transacted in that share before moving on to the next. All equity shares are traded in registered form. Short selling is not permitted and no futures or options markets currently exist.

Although the DSE's computerisation of its trading system has ground to a halt, there are moves to restart the process, not least because it represents a precondition of an Asian Development Bank loan. The CSE has already installed a screen-based trading system, which is expected to begin operations in the near future.

B) Principal brokers

UNION CAPITAL LIMITED
Anchor Tower, 7th floor, 1/1/B Free School Street
Sonargaon Road, Dhaka
Tel: (880) 2 966 2888; Fax: (880) 2 865 214

C) Settlement

A bi-weekly netting system operates, with settlement on Tuesdays and Sundays and delivery the day after.

D) Commissions

Brokerage commissions average around 1% of the market value of transactions.

TAXATION AND REGULATIONS AFFECTING FOREIGN INVESTORS

Currently there are no restrictions on foreign ownership of listed stocks, and no prior approval is needed for remittances to, or withdrawals from, non-resident investor taka accounts (NRITAs). However, remittances and withdrawals must be reported to the central bank.

A withholding tax of 25% is deducted at source on dividend payments and interest earnings for non-resident individuals of countries that do not have a double taxation treaty with Bangladesh. For non-resident companies the rate is 15% for dividends and 45% for interest earnings. Capital gains are tax-exempt.

Exhibit 5.5:
COUNTRY FUNDS – BANGLADESH

Fund	*01/01/97 01/01/98*	*01/01/93 01/01/98*	*Fund base currency*	*Fund size*	*Fund volatility*	*Management group*	*Opal main sector*	*Opal subsector*
The Bangladesh Fund	-61.19	N/A	US$	14.4	18.087	Indosuez	Closed-End	Equity

Note: details for some funds may not have been included if the data for the US$ % change for 97/98 was not available

Source: Standard & Poor's Micropal.

REPORTING REQUIREMENTS FOR LISTED COMPANIES

Listed companies must hold their annual general meeting and produce a balance sheet, profit and loss account and cash flow statement within nine months following the close of their financial year. Half-yearly financial statements must be published within one month of the end of the half-year period.

RESEARCH

Union Capital Limited publishes international standard research notes for its clients including a market summary, economic outlook, political summary, sector analysis and company-specific research. A bi-annual country profile is published at the beginning of the year and after the Budget announcement in June. A daily and weekly report is sent out to clients throughout the world.

PROSPECTIVE CHANGES

As part of the agenda to prop up the ailing capital market, the government has recently agreed in principle to amend laws that can facilitate the flow of insurance funds into the capital market. The government has also reportedly prepared legislative changes that will inject pension and trust fund money into the market.

The DSE council, as part of its drive to restore stability in the market, has decided to reintroduce a rolling settlement system (T+4), subject to SEC approval.

The Asian Development bank has also approved a US$80 million loan package for the development of the capital market, the bulk of which has been earmarked for the development of institutional infrastructure.

CHAPTER

6

Belgium

Introduction

The Brussels Stock Exchange (BSE) is representative of the economy, showing a healthy diversity of sectors. There are 133 domestic companies listed, dominated by the banking sector (representing 19.4% of the total). Utilities, chemical companies and insurance companies represent 16%, 12% and 10% respectively, with oil and gas companies accounting for 7%.

End-1997 market capitalisation (at Bfr4,862 billion) expressed as a percentage of GDP (56%) remains well below that of the USA, Japan and the UK. However it is above that of countries where capital democracy is less representative, such as France and Germany. Strong liquidity, with a free float of 47%, is an important characteristic of the Belgian exchange: in the volatile 1997–98 environment, more and more investors are looking for stable and liquid markets. Indeed, the Belgian stock market has proved to be more resilient to the Asian crisis than its European peers.

In 1997 the BEL-20 Price Index (up by a record 28% on the year) was reshuffled following the takeover of one of the most important quoted Belgian banks (BBL) by the Dutch ING. After this successful exchange bid, BBL (Banque Bruxelles Lambert) was replaced by Dexia Belgium. This merger tends to support the view that economic and monetary union (EMU) is well perceived by the local population. The Belgian (and European) markets were characterised by mergers and acquisitions in preparation for EMU, and companies have focused their efforts on finding the best commercial partners; this trend seems set to continue in 1998.

ECONOMIC AND POLITICAL OVERVIEW

The Belgian economy has been growing since early 1996, when the present economic cycle troughed. In the first quarter of 1997 economic activity slowed down, although recent indicators and the overall macroeconomic environment confirm that activity picked up in the second half of the year. On average, the Belgian economy is thought to have grown by 2.5 % in 1997. The CPI for 1997 rose 1.7%, confirming the outlook of growth without inflation.

The most dynamic components of total demand were exports (reinforced by the appreciation of the US dollar) and business investments. The latter have been expanding without interruption since 1995, which contrasts with the lack-lustre performance of this type of expenditure in some neighbouring countries, such as Germany and France.

Satisfactory corporate profitability combined with the high utilisation rate in manufacturing industry has stimulated enterprise investments, albeit at a slightly more moderate pace than in recent years. The strengthening of the US dollar against the Belgian franc (and most other European currencies) has implied upward pressure on import prices, while low interest rates have also supported economic growth.

The government has been granted special powers to approve by decree any discretionary measures necessary to secure the 3% of GDP deficit target. In general, public finances in 1997 were favourably influenced by strengthening economic growth and the low level of interest rates. Indirect taxes (on mineral oils and alcoholic beverages) increased by nearly 5% in 1997 and direct taxes by about 4.5%.

Role of the central bank

The National Bank of Belgium is responsible for the definition and implementation of monetary policy and, since April 1993, has been independent of the government. It manages the foreign exchange reserves of the Belgian–Luxembourg Economic Union and provides clearing system services. The National Bank also maintains links with the Banking and Financial Commission, which is responsible for banking supervision.

The primary objective of monetary policy in Belgium is

Exhibit 6.1: BRUSSELS GENERAL PRICE INDEX (Bfr), 1993–97

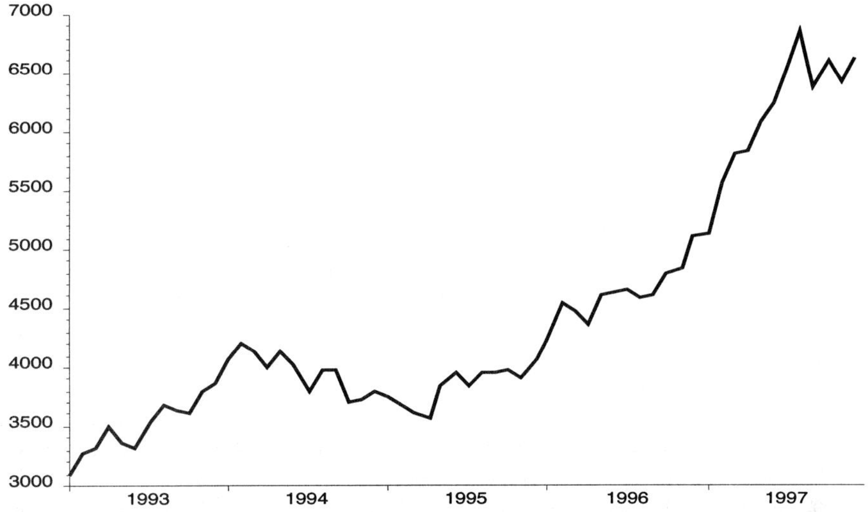

High value 6866.43 1.8.97 Low value 3103.01 1.1.93 *Source: Datastream*

price stability. The intermediate objective is an exchange rate target based on keeping the Belgian franc firmly pegged to the Deutschmark. This is justified by the Belgian economy's high degree of openness and its sensitivity to exchange rate movements, by its close integration with the economies of Germany, France and the Netherlands and by the low rate of inflation. In addition, Belgium has a sizeable current account surplus (almost 5% of GDP since 1993) and has been undergoing a process of fiscal consolidation.

The central bank influences short-term interest rates in order to achieve the exchange rate target, both through the announcement of its own interest rates and through its management of money market liquidity.

MARKET PERFORMANCE

A) In 1997

In 1997, after a bullish first half of the year, the Belgian stock market was hit (although less harshly than the other European stock markets) by the crash in Asia. The BSE achieved a rate of return of 33.9% in nominal terms in 1997 (up by 33% compared with 1996), while the bond market and real estate certificates rose by 9% and 21% respectively. Some growth stocks like Fafer (+204%), Sioen (+148%) and UCO Textile (+111%) boosted the market through their very healthy underlying profitability.

Compared with 1996, the performance of the Belgian market was helped by several elements such as the appreciation of the US dollar (+15%), the lower long bond rate (down from 5.76% to 5.47%), average EPS growth of 16% and the low CPI level.

Market capitalisation at the end of 1997 totalled Bfr4,862 billion, up from Bfr3,806 billion at the end of 1996 (and 56% of current GDP). The BSE All Share Index increased over the year from 10,520.94 to 14,329.21 at end-1997. The best performing sector in 1997 was insurance (up by 58.95%), while banking and chemicals were the next best performers, with increases of 56.2% and 38.9% respectively.

B) Summary information

Global ranking by market value (US$ terms, end-1997): 21
Market capitalisation (end-1997): US$130.7 billion
Growth in market value (local currency terms, 1993-97): 72.4%
Market value as a % of nominal GDP (end-1997): 56%
Number of domestic/foreign companies listed on the official market (end-1997): 133/140
Market P/E (MSCI Perspective companies end-1997): 17
MSCI total returns (with net dividends, US$ terms, 1997): 13.6%
MSCI Index (change in US$ terms, 1997): +10.8%
Short-term (3-month) interest rate (end-1997): 3.2%
Long-term (10-year) bond yield (end-1997): 5.47%
Budget surplus as a % of nominal GDP (end-1997): 2.6%
Annual increase in broad money (M3) supply (end-1997): 7.8%
Inflation rate (end-1997): 1.7%
US$ exchange rate (end-1997): Bfr37.2

C) Year-end share price index, price/earnings ratios and yields

Exhibit 6.2:
YEAR-END SHARE PRICE INDEX, P/E RATIO AND EQUITY YIELDS, 1993-97

Year-end	*Belgian All Shares Index*	*P/E*	*Yield (%)*
1993	7,543.12	17.1	4.0
1994	7,248.67	18.5	4.2
1995	8,401.68	14.3	4.4
1996	10,520.94	15.4	3.7
1997	14,329.21	17.0	2.3

Source: Petercam SA.

D) Market indices and their constituents

The benchmark index of the Brussels exchange is the Bel-20 Price Index (based at 30 December 1990 = 1,000). Futures and options are traded on this index on Belfox, the derivatives market. The index is also often used as a benchmark for the issue of warrants and investment funds. The Bel-20 comprises a basket of 20 Belgian stocks with the highest liquidity and market capitalisation. Two return versions of the index are also calculated, on the basis of both gross and net dividends.

The BSE also calculates the Belgian All Shares Index (previously the Belgian General Return Index). The basis is 1 January 1980 = 1,000 and it is calculated in both a price and return version. The return version is sub-divided into economic sectors for which a sub-return index is calculated.

The Petercam Index, calculated by Petercam SA, also measures performance in terms of return (capital gains and income) on the basis of a representative sample of stocks. It currently comprises five securities. This index is available from the end of 1969 to the end of 1980 as an annual figure, and monthly from January 1981 onwards.

THE STOCK MARKET

A) Brief history and structure

Over the 20 years to 1982, the BSE (founded in 1801) languished even though the economy prospered, particularly in the early years of the period. To rectify this, the de Clercq Laws of 1982 promoted the issuing of new shares by reducing the heavy tax burden on both corporations and shareholders. By giving tax relief on the cost of purchase to shareholders, the law helped to provide the impetus for BSE growth, enabling the market to play a larger role in the provision of capital. It is estimated that in the four years 1982-85, these changes led to approximately Bfr70 billion flowing into the stock market from about 500,000 households. Previously, the annual average new issue volume was only Bfr4.5 billion.

The BSE (established as a limited liability cooperative in 1990) is managed by a board of directors composed of 11 members elected for a 4-year period by the general meeting of all BSE members. The president and the vice-president of the board of directors are nominated by the King for a term of office of four years.

The board of directors is in charge of the general conduct of stock exchange business, defining the general policy of the BSE, supervising the management and determining the amount of annual contributions from members.

The management committee of the BSE acts as an autonomous market authority, responsible for market organisation and operation. Its members are appointed for six years by the Minister of Finance, at the proposal of the board of directors. The committee is responsible for:

- Overall day-to-day management of the stock exchange within the general policy framework defined by the board of directors.
- Acting as market authority in order to decide on the introduction or delisting of securities; to decide whether temporarily to suspend trading; to organise public issues; to decide on membership applications; to suspend or revoke membership; to assure the smooth running of the markets; to develop and organise settlement systems; and to settle professional disputes.
- Announcing all information required to be published by law or exchange regulations.
- Assuring the transparency, integrity and the safety of the markets and, when necessary, imposing disciplinary procedures on members.

The Banking and Finance Commission acts as a second-tier supervisory body.

B) Different exchanges

As of 1 January 1998, there was only one stock exchange in Belgium – the Brussels Stock Exchange. In 1997 the BSE, Belfox and CIK began to discuss closer cooperation which should result by the end of 1999 in "Brussels Exchanges" (a single financial institution trading both stocks and derivatives, and including the Brussels clearing house).

C) Opening hours, names and addresses

Trading on both the cash market and the forward market takes place from Monday to Friday. On the BSE cash market there is a single price fixing (2.00pm) for less liquid stocks and a minimum of two price fixings (11.15am and 3.15pm) for more liquid stocks. On the forward market there is a minimum of two price fixings for less liquid stocks (10.15am and 4.15pm), while the more liquid stocks are traded continuously from 10.02am to 4.30pm.

BOURSE DE BRUXELLES (BEURS VAN BRUSSEL)
Palais de la Bourse, 1000 Brussels
Tel: (32) 2 509 1211 Fax: (32) 2 509 1212

Internet: English: www.stockexchange.be
French: www.bourse.be
Dutch: www.beurs.be

MARKET SIZE

A) Number of listings and market value

At the end of 1997, total market capitalisation of the 133 domestic companies listed on the BSE was Bfr4,862 billion, up 27.7% over the year.

Exhibit 6.3:
NUMBER OF LISTED SHARES AND MARKET VALUE, BSE, 1993-97

Year-end	No. of listed shares Total	Domestic	Foreign	Market value of domestic companies (Bfr billion)
1993	309	159	150	2,818.9
1994	296	155	141	2,677.7
1995	281	143	138	2,984.8
1996	278	139	139	3,806.4
1997	273	133	140	4,862.0

Source: Brussels Stock Exchange and Petercam SA.

Exhibit 6.4:
BREAKDOWN OF MARKET VALUE BY SECTOR, END-1997

Sector	Share of total value (%)
Holding companies	22.2
Banking and financial services	18.1
Electricity and gas	14.6
Chemicals	11.2
Insurance	9.6
Oil	6.3
Retail	4.5
Metal/electronics	3.4
Construction	2.5
Services (miscellaneous)	2.4
Industry (miscellaneous)	1.3
Non-ferrous industries	1.3
Property	0.9
Food	0.8
Steel industries	0.4
Tropicals	0.2

Source: Petercam SA.

B) Largest quoted companies

At end-1997, Electrabel, Fortis AG and Petrofina together accounted for 22.8% of total market capitalisation of domestic companies (Bfr4,862 billion). The top 10 companies' share of total market capitalisation was 54.8% compared with 51.8% in 1996.

Exhibit 6.5:
THE 20 LARGEST LISTED COMPANIES ON THE BSE, END-1997

Ranking	Company	Market value (Bfr billion)
1	Electrabel	466
2	Fortis AG	322
3	Petrofina	320
4	Tractebel	273
5	Générale de Banque	266
6	Générale Belgique	239
7	Kredietbank	202
8	BBL	198
9	Solvay	196
10	Dexia CC	183
11	UCB	178
12	Royale Belge	169
13	Almanij	163
14	GBL	130
15	Electrafina	127
16	Delhaize	97
17	Cobepa	91
18	Barco	83
19	CBR	77
20	Colruyt	74

Sources: Brussels Stock Exchange and Petercam SA.

C) Trading volume

The total value of shares traded in 1997 was Bfr1,229.2 billion, an increase of 51.9% relative to 1996 levels. Domestic companies accounted for Bfr1,064.1 billion of total turnover, or 86.6%.

Exhibit 6.6:
TOTAL TRADING VALUE ON THE BSE, 1993-97 (BFR BILLION)

Year	Domestic companies	Foreign companies	Total
1993	387.4	107.0	494.4
1994	428.9	124.9	553.8
1995	452.9	93.8	546.7
1996	695.3	113.4	808.8
1997	1,064.1	165.1	1,229.2

Sources: Brussels Stock Exchange and Petercam SA.

Exhibit 6.7:
TRADING VALUE BY SECTOR ON THE BSE, 1997

Sector	Trading value (Bfr billion)
Banks and financial services	235.6
Chemicals	135.0

Exhibit 6.7 continued

Holding companies	112.6
Electricity	109.0
Insurance	90.2
Retail	82.4
Oil	79.0
Metal/electronics	63.7
Non-ferrous industries	38.1
Services (miscellaneous)	29.0
Construction	28.5
Industries (miscellaneous)	11.8
Steel	11.7
Property	4.7
Food	3.6
Tropicals	2.0

Sources: Brussels Stock Exchange and Petercam SA.

Exhibit 6.8:
THE 20 MOST ACTIVELY TRADED BSE SHARES, 1997

Ranking	*Company*	*Trading value (Bfr billion)*
1	Petrofina	78.7
2	Fortis AG	66.0
3	Electrabel	64.0
4	BBL	62.8
5	Dexia CC	60.1
6	UCB	55.9
7	Kredietbank	55.2
8	Solvay	54.4
9	Générale de Banque	53.8
10	Delhaize	42.3
11	Union Minière	38.0
12	Barco	35.4
13	Tractebel	33.1
14	Générale de Belgique	25.0
15	Royale Belge	24.1
16	Bekaert	22.3
17	GIB	20.7
18	GBL	20.2
19	Almanij	20.1
20	CBR	19.9

Sources: Brussels Stock Exchange and Petercam SA.

TYPES OF SHARE

The vast majority of listed Belgian equities take the form of ordinary shares, although preferred and founders' shares exist as well.

Since 1991, non-voting shares have been permitted but they cannot represent more than one-third of a company's capital. It is unusual in Belgium to grant different rights to parts of a company's stock. Issuance of non-ordinary stock is always preceded by close scrutiny by the Banking Commission, which imposes extensive requirements on the information to be provided to investors.

Most shares are issued in bearer form. As regards companies that have solicited public savings, shareholders wishing to exercise voting rights relating to bearer shares must deposit such shares at least three days before the general meeting of shareholders. However, the identity of individual shareholders is not published provided that the voting rights relating to the securities deposited represent less than 0.1% of all voting rights.

To permit foreign registered shares to be traded, intermediaries issue bearer certificates that replace the registered shares. The circulation of such bearer certificates is unrestricted.

Since 7 April 1995, companies have been allowed to issue dematerialised stocks. This category ranks alongside registered and bearer shares but has reduced security printing and transaction costs and has tended to improve liquidity.

OTHER MARKETS

In January 1985, a second market (*Second Marché*) was created in Belgium, designed to encourage smaller companies to seek financing through capital issues. There is also a small unlisted securities market (*Marché des Ventes Publiques*).

The Law of 22 July 1991 authorised a market for deposit certificates (*certificats de dépôt*) and commercial paper (*billets de trésorerie*), and the Royal Decree of 29 November 1993 made access to this market easier for private enterprises.

Under the framework of a European Economic Interest Grouping (EEIG) agreement with the stock exchanges of Paris, Frankfurt and Amsterdam, the BSE has introduced a Belgian "New Market" called Euro-NM Belgium for companies with high growth potential. Euro-NM will eventually allow brokers at the four exchanges to trade in each other's stocks.

Easdaq is a pan-European market, located in Brussels. It is designed to become the European version of Nasdaq, the US market for high-growth companies.

A futures and options market (Belfox) was created in 1990, but at present futures and options traded on this market only relate to the securities of a few blue chip companies.

INVESTORS

It is difficult to determine the investor breakdown of the Belgian market because virtually all shares are issued in bearer form.

Banks are active mainly in the bond market and their involvement in the stock market is minor. In fact, there

Exhibit 6.9:
TOP PERFORMING COUNTRY FUNDS – BELGIUM

Fund	US$% change 31/12/96 31/12/97	US$% change 31/12/92 31/12/97	Currency	Fund size (US$ mil)	Volatility	Manager name	Main sector	Class
Top Global Actions Belges	36.5	156.55	Bfr	32.74	N/A	Corluy & Co	Equity	Belgian Trusts
FIB Small Cap Eq-Belgium C	35.81	N/A	Bfr	11.29	N/A	Fortis Investments Belgium	Equity	Belgian Trusts
Paricor Belgian Equities	30	N/A	Bfr	1.05	N/A	Banque Paribas Belgique	Equity	Belgian Trusts
VLAM-21	26.54	N/A	Bfr	57.95	N/A	Corluy & Co	Equity	Belgian Trusts
Zelia Equities	24.85	N/A	Bfr	6.76	N/A	Zelia Assurances	Equity	Belgian Trusts
Citi Belgian Equities	24.42	N/A	Bfr	16.24	N/A	Citibank Belgium	Equity	Belgian Trusts
Cera Invest BEL20-1	22.16	N/A	Bfr	49.12	3.67	Cera Bank	Equity Fixed Term	Luxembourg
Cera Invest BEL20-3	21.2	N/A	Bfr	20.75	N/A	Cera Bank	Equity Fixed Term	Luxembourg
Puilaetco Belgium	21.13	176.15	Bfr	138.17	3.6	Puilaetco	Equity	Belgian Trusts
P.A.M. Belgian Assets Cap	20.93	138.04	Bfr	82.79	3.33	Petercam Asset Management	Equity	Belgian Trusts
KB Equisafe Belgium Invest2	20.34	N/A	Bfr	7.16	N/A	Kredietbank	Equity Fixed Term	Belgian Trusts
Portefeuille BG Act Belgique	20.25	N/A	Bfr	23.04	N/A	BP E. de Rothschild Lux	Equity	Luxembourg
Hermes Belgian Equity	19.17	142	Bfr	138.71	3.41	Delen/Indosuez	Equity	Belgian Trusts
BelEquity Fund	18.77	N/A	Bfr	N/S	N/A	Swiss Life Belgium	Equity	Belgian Trusts
Osiris Strategic Belg Stocks	18.6	N/A	Bfr	63.19	N/A	Banque De Groof	Equity	Belgian Trusts
Belfund	18.54	135.4	Bfr	188.28	3.41	Paribas Belgique-CCB	Equity	Belgian Trusts
BBL Invest High Yield Cap	18.33	162.18	Bfr	64.36	3.37	BBL-Banque Brussels Lambert	Equity	Belgian Trusts
Paribas Invest	18.33	N/A	Bfr	59.2	3.18	Banque Paribas Belgique	Equity	Belgian Trusts
KBP Security Click-Belgium 2	17.98	N/A	Bfr	74.25	3.85	Kredietbank	Equity Fixed Term	Belgian Trusts
RB Belgian Equities	17.92	N/A	Bfr	4.36	N/A	Royale Belge	Equity	Belgian Trusts
ING Intl (B) Belgian Equity	17.85	N/A	Bfr	20.56	N/A	ING - Patriotique	Equity	Belgian Trusts
Osiris H.Yield Belgian Shares	17.53	133.51	Bfr	156.37	N/A	Banque De Groof	Equity	Belgian Trusts
Cera Invest BEL20-4	17.45	N/A	Bfr	64.44	N/A	Cera Bank	Equity Fixed Term	Luxembourg
Cera Invest BEL20-5	17.44	N/A	Bfr	14.45	N/A	Cera Bank	Equity Fixed Term	Luxembourg
Interselex Invest Belga B	17.2	130.22	Bfr	332.3	N/A	Generale de Banque	Equity	Belgian Trusts
BBL Invest Belgium Cap	17.14	143.9	Bfr	291.48	3.39	BBL-Banque Brussels Lambert	Equity	Belgian Trusts
BBL Collect Portfolio Alpha C	17.13	140.32	Bfr	103.42	N/A	BBL-Banque Brussels Lambert	Equity	Belgian Trusts
Cregem Equities B Belg-Index C	16.52	131.13	Bfr	216.73	3.42	Credit Communal de Belgique	Equity	Belgian Trusts
Osiris Belgian Equities	16.13	N/A	Bfr	83.41	N/A	Banque De Groof	Equity	Belgian Trusts
Bacob Belinvest C	16.12	120.5	Bfr	95.14	3.44	Bacob Banque	Equity	Belgian Trusts
KB Belgian Index Fund C	16.06	148.31	Bfr	159.88	3.66	Kredietbank	Equity	Belgian Trusts
KB Instit Fund Belgian Equity	15.82	140.46	Bfr	121.77	3.46	Kredietbank	Equity	Belgian Trusts
Es-Invest Belg Opportunities C	15.6	N/A	Bfr	45.87	N/A	ASLK-CGER Bank	Equity	Belgian Trusts
G-Institutional Belgian Eq B	15.49	142.21	Bfr	190.82	3.47	Generale de Banque	Equity	Belgian Trusts
Parvest Belgium C	15.3	N/A	Bfr	43.16	N/A	Banque Paribas	Equity	Luxembourg
Parvest Belgium D	15.29	N/A	Bfr	4.09	N/A	Banque Paribas	Equity	Luxembourg
Sivek Shares A Cap	15.18	112.16	Bfr	217.62	3.4	Cera Bank	Equity	Belgian Trusts
Maestro Eq Belgium C	15.05	121.53	Bfr	52.03	3.48	Credit a l'Industrie	Equity	Belgian Trusts
KB Equisafe Belgium Invest 1	14.92	N/A	Bfr	9.51	N/A	Kredietbank	Equity Fixed Term	Belgian Trusts
Belginvest Equity Cap	14.91	134.47	Bfr	242.92	3.31	Petercam Asset Management	Equity	Belgian Trusts
Dewaay Belgian Shares C	14.8	114.39	Bfr	51.21	3.3	Banque Dewaay	Equity	Belgian Trusts
FIB Invest Equities Belgium C	14.47	N/A	Bfr	285.95	N/A	Fortis Investments Belgium	Equity	Belgian Trusts
Brivek Aandelen	14.46	N/A	Bfr	21.8	N/A	Banque van Roeselare	Equity	Belgian Trusts
Es Invest Bel-20	14.44	N/A	Bfr	114.03	2.94	ASLK-CGER Bank	Equity Fixed Term	Belgian Trusts

Note: details for some funds may not have been included if the data for the US$ % change for 96/97 was not available

Source: Standard & Poor's Micropal.

are legal requirements to prevent banks from taking stakes in non-banking companies.

Institutional investors dominate activity on the bond market, but are less active in the equity market. They invest well below the legal limit of 25% of their assets in equities.

The Belgian pension fund industry is still young but has grown rapidly over recent years. Although fund managers favour the bond market, equity investments generally account for 35-45% of total exposure.

The level of private investor involvement in the equity market is approximately 20%.

Foreign investors and equity managers (especially those based in London) have been active on the Belgian market since the end of 1981. Their involvement in quantitative terms is difficult to assess, but is probably around 40%.

OPERATIONS

A) Trading system

In April 1996 open outcry for the cash market was replaced by a decentralised, order-driven, transparent trading system called NTS, bought from the SBF-Bourse de Paris. At the end of June 1996 all forward market stocks formerly traded on the CATS system were also transferred to NTS.

Stockbrokers no longer have a sole monopoly on stock exchange transactions; the monopoly has been extended to "authorised intermediaries". The list of such intermediaries includes stockbrokers, banks, savings institutions and, under certain conditions, foreign credit institutions, as well as intermediaries dealing with new financial instruments.

The official market consists of a cash market (*Marché au Comptant*) and a forward market (*Marché Terme*). All officially listed securities are traded either on the cash market or on the forward market. In addition, deals for blocks above Bfr10 million can be broadcast on PDS (Price Display Service) and deals can be made between counterparties outside trading hours.

Cash market

The fully electronic cash equity market is divided into a double fixing (twice a day) and a single fixing (once a day) market.

The cash bond market is regulated by the Fonds des Rentes – a public institution governed by the Ministry of Finance.

Forward market

The forward market is by far the most important in terms of both the size of the companies listed and of share turnover. It is divided into a continuous segment and a semi-continuous segment. The BSE management committee decides which securities are to be traded on the forward market.

Activity on the forward market is dominated by large institutions, professional arbitrage and international trading.

Price regulation

On the forward market, price fluctuations are not limited but the trading system itself provides for short trading halts on every 5% move.

On the narrower cash market, a stock price may not fluctuate with respect to the previous quotation by more than 5% per fixing on the double and single fixing markets.

B) List of principal banks and brokers

Brokers registered as members of the BSE form the Société de la Bourse de Valeurs Mobilières de Bruxelles, which is a legal entity and is represented by the Stock Exchange Commission.

Banks

BANQUE BRUXELLES LAMBERT SA
Avenue Marnix 24, 1050 Brussels
Tel: (32) 2 738 2111; Fax: (32) 2 547 2922

CGER-ASLK
Rue Fossé-aux-Loups 48, 1000 Brussels
Tel: (32) 2 228 2111; Fax: (32) 2 213 9555

DEXIA CC
Boulevard Pachéco 44, 1000 Brussels
Tel: (32) 2 222 1111; Fax: (32) 2 222 5226

GÉNÉRALE DE BANQUE SA
Montagne du Parc 3, 1000 Brussels
Tel: (32) 2 516 2111; Fax: (32) 2 516 2244

KREDIETBANK NV*
Arebergstraat 7, 1000 Brussels
Tel: (32) 2 517 4111; Fax: (32) 2 517 4209
*Not a member of the BSE.

Brokers

DEGROOF SECURITIES SA
Rue Guimard 18, 1040 Brussels
Tel : (32) 2 230 0800; Fax : (32) 2 230 1888

DEWAAY, SERVAIS & CIE
Tour Philips, 2ème étage, Bld Anspach 1, bte 10
1000 Brussels
Tel: (32) 2 227 8711; Fax: (32) 2 227 8899

FORTIS INVESTMENT BELGIUM
Rue du Marais 2, 1000 Brussels
Tel: (32) 2 228 2828; Fax: (32) 2 228 2878

KB-SECURITIES
Vondelstraat 15, 2060 Antwerp
Tel: (32) 3 232 1312; Fax: (32) 3 233 4082

NEDEE & CO
Bellevue 2, 9050 Ghent
Tel: (32) 9 210 2211; Fax: (32) 9 210 2250

PETERCAM SA
Place Ste Gudule 19, 1000 Brussels
Tel: (32) 2 229 6311; Fax: (32) 2 229 6598

VERMEULEN, RAEMDONCK (BBL)
Rue des Princes 8/10, bte 4, 1000 Brussels
Tel: (32) 2 229 2160; Fax: (32) 2 229 2188

C) Settlement and transfer

Settlement on the cash market takes place on the third trading day subsequent to the day of the transaction. On the forward market, payment for securities bought, and delivery of securities sold, takes place according to the BSE's calendar for the settlement of forward transactions. The settlement period for forward transactions is five days and settlement takes place by netting all positions.

In 1967 the CIK (Caisse Interprofessionnelle de Dépôts et de Virements de Titres) was formed to facilitate the settlement and custody of Belgian and foreign securities.

D) Commissions and other costs

(i) *Commissions*. Commissions are negotiable and, if agreed with the client, may be included in the transaction price.

(ii) *Stamp duty*. Share transfers (including depository receipts) attract stamp duty at 0.17%, subject to a limit of Bfr10,000.

(iii) *Transaction costs*. Transaction costs levied by the BSE may be charged to the client.

TAXATION AND REGULATIONS AFFECTING FOREIGN INVESTORS

As a general rule, dividends paid on Belgian ordinary shares are subject to a withholding tax (*précompte mobilier* or *roerende voorheffing*) of 25% and interest to a withholding tax of 15%, unless a lower rate is provided for by a tax treaty between Belgium and the country of the foreign investor. In most treaties the withholding tax rate for dividends is reduced to 15%.

Nevertheless, withholding tax on dividends is reduced to 15% as regards:

a) dividends distributed by listed companies on AFV shares whenever these companies have renounced the tax benefits resulting from the AFV tax regime;
b) dividends distributed by investment companies (UCITS);
c) dividends distributed on shares issued after 1 January 1994 as part of a capital increase implemented after a public issue; or
d) dividends distributed on ordinary shares issued after 1 January 1994 in consideration for cash contributions.

Exhibit 6.10:
WITHHOLDING TAX

Recipient	*Dividends %*[1]	*Interest %*[2]
Resident corporations and branches of foreign corporations	25	Nil, 15
Resident individuals	25	15
Non-resident corporations and individuals:		
Non-treaty	25	15
Treaty	5-20	Nil-15

Notes:
1. Since 1 January 1996, the withholding tax rate levied on dividends derived from contributions to certain capital increases implemented after 1 January 1994 has been reduced from 25% to 15%.
2. No withholding tax is due on (i) interest on commercial debts (including such debts evidenced by commercial documents), and (ii) interest paid by banks established in Belgium to foreign banks or to non-residents if they certify they are the owners or the usufructuary of the funds and that they do not use these funds for professional purposes in Belgium.

Source: Price Waterhouse.

In some cases (provided for by Royal Decree) withholding tax is waived. For instance, it may be waived where it is due from a Belgian subsidiary to an EU parent company, provided that the beneficiary has held 25% or more of the share capital of the subsidiary for an uninterrupted period of one year before such dividend is declared.

There are no restrictions or exchange controls regarding investments in Belgian securities by foreign investors, but controls exist for statistical purposes covering payments remitted from Belgium.

For individuals and foreign companies that have no permanent establishment in Belgium, the tax on stock dividends is generally equal to the withholding tax.

A tax is levied on capital gains realised on investments made by non-resident individuals in shares of a Belgian company if the shares disposed of represent more than 25% of the capital and are sold to a foreign company.

LISTING AND REPORTING REQUIREMENTS

A) Listing requirements

The main market

The listing of securities on the BSE main market is governed by the Royal Decree of 22 December 1995, which implements EU legislation. Requests for listing are examined by the management committee of the BSE, and companies wishing to be listed must also notify the Banking and Finance Commission, which has to assess the appropriateness of such a listing from the viewpoint of protecting the public interest.

Belgium has implemented EC Directive 89/298/EEC of 17 April 1989 regarding coordination of prospectus rules. Under the implementing decree, a company with securities listed in another EU member state may request that the Banking and Finance Commission recognises the prospectus that has been submitted for such prior listing. Additional information is required regarding Belgian market specifics, and the Banking and Finance Commission is required to take a decision within 15 days.

Article 14 of the Royal Decree of 22 December 1995 lays down the conditions for listing ordinary shares on the main BSE market. It is required that:

1. The formalities and conditions set out in the coordinated laws on commercial companies and in the Royal Decree of 22 December 1995 be fulfilled.
2. The legal situation of the issuer complies with the applicable laws and regulations, mainly with respect to its constitution and functioning pursuant to its by-laws and articles of incorporation.
3. The shares comply with all laws and regulations and are freely transferable.
4. The request for listing concerns all shares of the same category, already issued but not yet listed.
5. The expected market capitalisation of the shares to be listed, or, if such market capitalisation cannot be assessed, the own funds of the issuer including the profits of the last financial year, must total at least ECU1 million.
6. The issuer has published or filed, pursuant to applicable laws, its annual accounts for the three financial years preceding the request for listing.
7. The shares are either regularly and continuously traded in one or more member states of the European Union, or are both listed and traded in another state.

Euro-NM Belgium

The conditions for admission to this market have been specifically tailored to the needs of fledgling, rapidly growing companies. The market complies with the conditions of a regulated market in the meaning of the ISD Directive. Admission conditions are, however, less strict than on the main or second markets but continuing information requirements are stricter.

Easdaq

Established by the Royal Decree of 10 June 1996, Easdaq has become a popular screen-based pan-European market focusing on high-growth companies. An interesting aspect of Easdaq is the possibility for an issuer to obtain a dual listing, both on Easdaq and on Nasdaq.

In order to be admitted to trade on Easdaq, a company must appoint a sponsor and show that there are at least two market-makers willing to trade in its securities. A prospectus must be published, which needs to be approved by an EU competent authority. Admission conditions are both quantitative (eg the company's asset value) and qualitative (eg its reputation). There is, however, no requirement as to the length of time a company has to have existed before it can be admitted.

B) Reporting requirements

The following information must be provided regularly by listed companies to their shareholders:

1. Information regarding the rights attached to shares:
   - information concerning any general meeting (date, place and agenda) in order to enable shareholders to exercise their voting rights;
   - information regarding dividends and other rights attached to shares, new issues of stock, stock splits or conversions into stock of other securities; and
   - any amendments to the rights attached to the different types of shares.
2. Information regarding events or decisions likely to have a material effect on the stock price, such as acquisitions, company sales, mergers, takeovers, etc.
3. Annual and half-yearly reports: The half-yearly reports must contain information concerning turnover and profits, but no balance sheet data is required. Annual reports must be published within six months of the close of the financial year and half-yearly reports within four months of the close of the half year.

This information must also be published in the press.

The same reporting obligations apply to Euro-NM Belgium companies as to main market companies, except that Euro-NM Belgium companies must also publish quarterly reports on their activities and results covering the first and third quarters of each financial year. These quarterly reports must be published within two months of the end of the quarter in question.

Easdaq's reporting obligations are drafted such that they supplement the national requirements by imposing certain minimum rules relating to financial reporting. The core of the reporting requirement consists of publishing (in English) all financial audited information annually and all unaudited financial information quarterly. Moreover, issuers must inform Easdaq of certain facts, such as the creation of a stock option plan, and reply to any requests for information by Easdaq.

SHAREHOLDER PROTECTION CODES

A) Significant shareholdings

Where a person or company acquires a 5% interest in the voting rights of a listed company, that person or company is required to announce the fact to the Banking and Finance Commission and the listed company, which in turn must inform the market.

B) Takeovers and mergers

The Banking and Finance Commission ensures that in takeover and merger situations all shareholders and debenture holders are treated equally – ie that they are duly consulted and that they receive equal opportunity to swap, sell or buy new and old instruments. As a general rule, any transaction having as its sole objective the acquisition of a blocking minority is prohibited.

In the event that an individual or a company intends to acquire (by one or several transactions relating to securities issued by a company either listed on a Belgian stock exchange or with shares that are, or were, widely held) the joint or exclusive control of a company, the transferee must notify the Banking and Finance Commission of the fact at least five days before the transaction. If the transfer price includes a control premium, the transferee must offer to minority shareholders the opportunity to sell their shares at the best price obtained during the preceding 12 months, through either a public takeover bid or an undertaking to support the stock price.

C) Insider dealing

Articles 181 to 193 of Book V of the Law of 4 December 1990, as modified by the Laws of 22 March 1993 and 30 January 1996, and as implemented by the Royal Decree of 5 August 1991, specifically regulate insider dealing.

Article 181 of the Law of 4 December 1990 provides that "privileged information" means any information that has not been made public, which is sufficiently clear and which concerns one or more issuers of securities or other financial instruments and which, if made public, could be of a nature to significantly affect the quotation of such securities or financial instruments. Insider dealing attracts penal sanctions only when the securities concerned are listed on a regulated market, supervised by public authorities, open to the general public and located or operating within the EU.

If a complaint is lodged for non-compliance with the insider trading provisions, the courts may request, from the Banking and Finance Commission and from the authorities responsible for the supervision of markets, all information or documents relevant to investigation of the case. Persons dealing on insider information are liable to penalties (imprisonment of between three months and one year and/or fines), to interdiction from business and to treble damages.

D) Compensation fund

Article 60 of the Law of 4 December 1990, as implemented by the Royal Decrees of 2 January 1991, provides for an intervention fund for stock exchange companies (*caisse d'intervention des sociétés de bourse* or *interventiefonds van de beursvennootschappen*). The fund is administered by the Banking and Finance Commission.

Under Article 6 of the Royal Decree of 12 December 1996, indemnification by the intervention fund is limited to Bfr2.5 million per creditor and per bankruptcy or judicial arrangement (*concordat judiciaire* or *gerechtelijk akkoord*). The same decree lays down the conditions to be fulfilled in order to be granted indemnification by the intervention fund.

RESEARCH

Two newspapers specialise in financial topics: *L'Echo* (French) and *De Financieel Ekonomische Tijd* (Dutch). Both newspapers publish the official version of the stock list of the BSE. *Trends-Tendances* (Dutch and French), published weekly, is Belgium's main financial magazine.

Other information and investment advice is available to investors on a weekly basis in papers such as *Swingtrend*, *Budget Hebdo/Week* and *L'Investisseur/De Belegger*, all in Dutch or French.

Major banks and brokerage firms provide their clients with their own bulletins (eg *Bulletin Financier* issued by BBL, *Bulletin Hebdomadaire* from Kredietbank, *Bulletin de la Société Générale de Banque*, and from Paribas, *Notes Outstanding*). All of these are available in either Dutch or French.

The investment research department of Petercam SA maintains close ties with the leading companies in Belgium. In addition to its internal research effort, it publishes a monthly bulletin in three languages, quarterly corporate earnings forecasts, P/E share data and several detailed studies each year. It has a considerable databank and library on all companies followed, and also monitors activity in the equity markets of other countries.

Further information is available from the BSE, including its *Introduction to the Brussels Stock Exchange*, *Annual Report* , the monthly *Statistics Bulletin*, yearly statistics and brochures on the MIM and the Euro-NM Belgium (all in English, French and Dutch).

CHAPTER

7

Bermuda

Introduction

The Bermuda Stock Exchange (BSX) experienced significant growth during 1997. There were 190 securities listed on the BSX as at 31 December 1997, with a total market capitalisation of US$48 billion. This compares with 137 securities listed at end-1996 with a market capitalisation of US$37 billion.

Significant recent events include the signing of an agreement between the BSX and Catex International to establish an electronic risk exchange in Bermuda, and the issue in February 1998 of regulations providing a detailed framework for three classifications of collective investment schemes – a Bermuda Recognised Scheme, a Bermuda Standard Scheme and a Bermuda Institutional Scheme. The Bermuda government is currently contemplating the introduction of investment business licensing regulations that would establish a licensing regime for persons or entities carrying on investment business in Bermuda.

ECONOMIC AND POLITICAL OVERVIEW

In March 1997, Pamela F Gordon succeeded David J Saul as Premier of Bermuda. Premier Gordon will be seeking a mandate at the next general election, which is due to be held in 1998.

Bermuda experienced strong economic growth during the fiscal year ended March 1997. GDP increased by an estimated 5.3% (3.0% adjusted for inflation) to US$2.19 billion. This increase was primarily due to significantly higher foreign currency earnings generated by the international business sector (19.7% up on 1996) and the robust performance of the construction sector. The current account surplus continued to grow in 1997, with preliminary estimates indicating that the annual surplus may exceed US$160 million. Despite the strong growth of the economy, the annual inflation rate fell to 2.1% in 1997.

Role of the central bank

The central bank – the Bermuda Monetary Authority – was established in 1969 as a corporate body and it is operationally independent of government.

The principal objectives of the Authority are to issue and redeem banknotes and coins; to undertake most aspects of the supervision, regulation and inspection of financial institutions; to manage exchange control and regulate transactions in foreign currency and gold on behalf of the government; and to advise and assist the government and public bodies on banking and other financial and monetary matters. The Authority is also responsible for the preparation of monetary, financial and balance of payments statistics, published in its *Quarterly Notice.*

The Authority does not intervene in the foreign exchange markets because the Bermuda dollar is currently pegged one-to-one to the US dollar.

MARKET PERFORMANCE

A) In 1997

The BSX Index closed at 1,400.27 at the end of 1997, up 52% compared with 918.39 at the end of 1996. During the year, domestic market capitalisation rose from US$1.0 billion to US$1.4 billion.

More than 224 million shares worth US$11.2 billion were traded on the BSX in 1997. Of these, 8.0 million shares, valued at US$98.8 million, were those of domestic companies.

B) Summary information

Global ranking by market value (US$ terms, end-1997): 70
Market capitalisation (end-1997): domestic US$1.411 billion; total US$47.870 billion
Growth in market value (domestic companies, 1996–97): 41.1%
Market value as a % of nominal GDP (end-1997): 63.8% (domestic listings only)
Number of domestic/foreign companies listed (end-1997): 33/20
Budget deficit as a % of nominal GDP (1997): 1.6% (including capital spending)

Annual increase in broad money (M3) supply (Sept 1997): 2.4%
Inflation rate (1997): 2.1%
US$ exchange rate (end-1997): Bda$1 (pegged)

C) Year-end share price index

Exhibit 7.1:
YEAR-END SHARE PRICE INDEX, 1993–97

Year-end	*BSX Index*
1993	1,165.65
1994	1,094.28
1995	978.58
1996	918.39
1997	1,400.27

Source: Bermuda Stock Exchange.

D) Market indices and their constituents

The BSX Index is published daily by the BSX. It is capitalisation weighted and based on 20 of the most widely held local securities.

THE STOCK MARKET

A) Brief history and structure

The BSX was first established in 1971 as an unincorporated association. In 1992 the three local commercial banks (Bermuda Commercial Bank, Bank of Bermuda and Bank of NT Butterfield & Son) incorporated the BSX as a limited liability company via a private Act of Parliament. The Act also established the regulatory framework for the exchange.

The ultimate authority of the BSX is its board of directors, called the council. The council comprises representatives of the three banks and public interest representatives of listed issuers, trading members and legal/accounting professionals.

The BSX currently has nine trading members. The exchange created a new membership category – "listing sponsor" – in November 1997. These members can sponsor applications for new listings of mutual funds, Eurobonds, depository receipts and secondary listings. The listing sponsor category is aimed at law firms, accounting firms, fund managers, trust companies and other service providers. Listing sponsors do not have trading privileges on the exchange.

B) Different exchanges

The BSX is currently the only stock exchange in Bermuda.

C) Opening hours and contact details

Trading takes place from Monday to Friday between 9.00am and 10.30am and 3.00pm to 3.30pm.

THE BERMUDA STOCK EXCHANGE
3rd Floor, Phase 1, Washington Mall
22 Church Street, Hamilton HM11, Bermuda
Tel: (1-441) 292 7212; Fax: (1-441) 292 7619
Web site: www.bsx.com

MARKET SIZE

A) Number of listings and market value

The overall market capitalisation of the BSX at year-end 1997 was US$47.87 billion, of which domestic listings accounted for US$1.41 billion.

Exhibit 7.2:
NUMBER OF COMPANIES LISTED, BSX, 1993–97

	No. of companies	
Year-end	*Domestic*	*Foreign*
1993	24	7
1994	27	12
1995	28	12
1996	27	12
1997	33	20

Source: Bermuda Stock Exchange.

B) Largest listed companies

Exhibit 7.3:
THE 20 LARGEST COMPANIES LISTED ON THE BSX, END-1997

Ranking	*Company*	*Market value (Bda$ million)*
1	Bank of Bermuda	571.7
2	Bank of NT Butterfield	329.2
3	Bermuda Electric Light	111.8
4	Argus Insurance	87.6
5	Bermuda Telephone	67.3
6	Bermuda Home	41.9
7	TeleBermuda International	28.7
8	Bermuda Commercial Bank	21.9
9	BF&M	20.9
10	Bermuda Press	15.2
11	Bermuda Container Line	10.5
12	Masters	7.5
13	Watlington Waterworks	6.8
14	Stevedoring Services	5.3
15	Staples	5.2
16	Devonshire Industries	4.8

Exhibit 7.3 continued

17	Bermuda Aviation Services	4.7
18	Millennium International	4.5
19	Bermuda Bakery	4.2
20	Bermuda Computer Services	3.6

Source: Bermuda Stock Exchange.

C) Trading volume

Exhibit 7.4:
TURNOVER OF DOMESTIC SHARES ON THE BSX, 1993-97

	Value traded (Bda$ million)	*Volume traded (shares million)*
1993	60.1	15.3
1994	77.7	15.6
1995	36.0	6.5
1996	36.6	3.6
1997	98.8	8.0

Source: Bermuda Stock Exchange.

Exhibit 7.5:
THE 20 MOST ACTIVELY TRADED SHARES BY VOLUME, END-1997

Ranking	*Company*	*Shares traded ('000)*
1	Bank of NT Butterfield	3,163.1
2	Bank of Bermuda	1,300.5
3	Bermuda Electric Light	253.5
4	Bermuda Commercial Bank	250.8
5	TeleBermuda International	221.7
6	Kentucky Fried Chicken	214.5
7	Bermuda Telephone	212.7
8	Bermuda Home	152.0
9	Argus Insurance	108.1
10	BF&M	97.6
11	Bermuda Press	56.3
12	Bermuda Aviation Services	45.2
13	Bermuda Container Line	39.8
14	Watlington Waterworks	14.7
15	Bermuda Bakery	12.1
16	Bermuda Computer Services	11.8
17	Devonshire Industries	7.9
18	Stevedoring Services	7.6
19	Millennium International	6.4
20	Masters	2.1

Source: Bermuda Stock Exchange.

OPERATIONS

A) Trading system

Trading on the Bermuda exchange takes place using the Bloomberg Financial Networks system on specially designed screens. Real-time quotations can be accessed on any Bloomberg terminal, where a composite page shows the best bid and ask quotes available, the last traded price and daily volume for each listed security. Only authorised dealers at trading members' offices are permitted to enter quotes, which are password protected. Trades are concluded on the telephone in strict price/time priority and then electronically confirmed on the BFMS between the seller and the buyer. The system then updates the ticker and the index automatically and reports the trade details to the BSX and to each side of the trade.

B) List of principal brokers

BCB SECURITIES
Tel: (1-441) 295 5678; Fax: (1-441) 295 4759

BERMUDA INTERNATIONAL SECURITIES
Tel: (1-441) 299 5825; Fax: (1-441) 299 6536

BUTTERFIELD SECURITIES (BERMUDA) LTD
Tel: (1-441) 295 1111; Fax: (1-441) 292 5550

FIRST BERMUDA FINANCIAL SERVICES
Tel: (1-441) 295 1330; Fax: (1-441) 292 9471

LINES OVERSEAS MANAGEMENT
Tel: (1-441) 295 5808; Fax: (1-441) 295 3343

MATHESON INVESTMENT MANAGEMENT
Tel: (1-441) 296 0145; Fax: (1-441) 296 0139

MRM SECURITIES LTD
Tel: (1-441) 295 9166; Fax: (1-441) 295 1607

NOMURA SECURITIES (BERMUDA) LTD
Tel: (1-441) 296 4050; Fax: (1-441) 296 4061

TREMONT CAPITAL LTD
Tel: (1-441) 292 3781; Fax: (1-441) 296 0667

C) Settlement and transfer

Settlement takes place on a rolling T+3 cycle. On T+3 stock certificates and transfer documents are exchanged against payment. The BSX operates a central clearing facility so that all settlement amounts for each buying broker are advised to the clearing banks by the BSX on T+3, with interbank wire transfer of funds on the same day. The BSX then releases the settlement documents to the buying broker, or to the buying broker's order, on confirmation of receipt of funds.

D) Commission and other costs

There are no fixed commissions in Bermuda and the amount charged can range from a flat fee to a graduated percentage based on the size of the trade. There may be a fixed minimum charge but the commission rate is negotiable and may vary between trading members.

TAXATION AND REGULATIONS AFFECTING FOREIGN INVESTORS

A) Taxation

No profits or income tax is payable on securities, or on any capital asset, gain or appreciation. Nor is stamp duty payable on the transfer of securities listed on the BSX. There is, however, a transaction levy payable to the BSX by each trading member based on the value of each trade executed on the BSX.

B) Exchange controls

Foreign investors are free of exchange controls in Bermuda and may deal in any foreign securities without restriction. However, the purchase by foreign investors of securities in companies that are incorporated as "local companies" and that carry on domestic business in Bermuda is limited to a maximum aggregate of 40% of the issued share capital.

LISTING AND REPORTING REQUIREMENTS

The review of all issuers seeking a listing is undertaken by the Listing Committee of the BSX. All listing applications must be sponsored by a trading member or a listing sponsor of the BSX.

The reporting requirements for listed companies are contained in the BSX listing regulations. The exchange has separate regulations for local and international issuers, and it monitors all listed issuers to ensure compliance.

SHAREHOLDER PROTECTION CODES

Policies covering takeovers and mergers and a compensation fund are currently under review by the Bermuda Monetary Authority. Policies regarding insider trading are being developed by the BSX.

RESEARCH

Trading information is distributed by the Bermuda exchange via the BFMS in real-time, and composite trade information is distributed daily by way of a "Daily Trade Report", which is printed the next day in the *Royal Gazette* newspaper in Bermuda.

PROSPECTIVE CHANGES

The BSX has adopted a strategic plan to further develop the exchange, including:

- the introduction of an Index Tracking Fund for local and foreign investors to buy into the Bermuda market through one vehicle;
- continuation of the rapid expansion of mutual fund listings; and
- the introduction of an Asian matching trading facility to enable investors to trade Asian securities in Bermuda when the Asian markets have closed.

CHAPTER

8

Botswana

Introduction

Botswana's equity market (formally established in 1995) is not representative of the economy, which is dominated by the diamond industry. Debswana Diamond Company, for example, one of the country's main producers, is not listed on the Botswana Stock Exchange (BSE). The spread of listed companies is heavily weighted towards the financial services and retail sectors, while the manufacturing sector is not represented.

To a large extent, industry still places reliance on the banks to finance expansion, and privatisation has not yet been undertaken. However, plans to privatise some state-owned assets are beginning to gain momentum. There are also some indications of increasing corporate merger and takeover activity.

Initially, equity trading was dominated by local institutions, but foreign institutions have now become the main force. Also, the number of domestic private investors is increasing following publicity campaigns in Botswana.

ECONOMIC AND POLITICAL OVERVIEW

Botswana gained its independence from Great Britain in 1966. It is a member of the British Commonwealth and a multi-party state, with elections held every five years.

The Botswana Democratic Party has been in power since independence. Legislative power rests with parliament, which consists of a unicameral National Assembly that elects the President. The National Assembly comprises the Speaker, the Attorney-General, 36 members elected by universal suffrage and 4 nominated by the Assembly. A House of Chiefs, made up of 15 members, advises on tribal matters.

The present government is headed by Sir Ketumile Masire, who has announced that he will retire on 31 March 1998. The current Vice-President, the Honourable Festus Mogae, is expected to take over as President. The government actively promotes private sector initiatives and foreign investment in economic diversification and export-oriented domestic industries.

The economy is dominated by diamond mining, which, combined with judicious use of national income, has turned Botswana from one of the least developed economies in Africa to one of the wealthiest in just 30 years. The mining sector (including diamond mining and copper-nickel mining) accounts for 33% of GDP. This means that Botswana's economy is vulnerable to external factors such as diamond sale quotas and world commodity prices. With this is mind, the government has proposed initiatives aimed at diversifying away from minerals by encouraging foreign investment in other sectors of the economy. This support for economic diversification has seen a growth in the non-mining sector in 1997 of 7.6% compared with an average growth of 6.8%.

According to *The Economist, World Figures in 1998*, Botswana had the seventh fastest economic growth rate in the world during the period 1985-95, registering an average annual real GDP increase of 7.1%. GDP grew by an estimated 6% in 1997 compared with 6.9% in 1996; the lower rate was mainly due to minimal growth in the mining sector. GDP per capita (US$2,800) is among the highest in Africa and is higher than that of South Africa.

The inflation rate dropped from almost 10% at the start of 1997 to 7.8% at the year-end. The money market for short-term (3-month to 12-month) paper issued by the central bank is currently offering interest rates between 9% and 11%, continuing the policy of providing a positive real return.

The budget surplus for 1997 was P1,269 million (US$333 million), or 6.9% of GDP. The currency (the pula) was generally stable against the US dollar in 1997, depreciating by 3%. However, the exchange rate appreciated significantly against the Zimbabwean dollar in the wake of that country's economic crisis.

Botswana belongs to the Southern African Customs

Union (SACU) which provides for the free exchange of goods between Botswana, Lesotho, Namibia, South Africa and Swaziland. Around 85% of imports originate from SACU countries. Preliminary estimates indicate an overall balance of payments surplus of P1,785 million (US$464 million) in 1997, compared with P848 million (US$249 million) in 1996. As a percentage of GDP this surplus amounts to 9.6%.

Role of the central bank

The Bank of Botswana, which was established by the Bank of Botswana Act of 1975, is the central bank of the Republic of Botswana. It acts as the banker, fiscal agent and adviser to the government.

In conjunction with the Ministry of Finance and Development Planning, the bank is responsible for the implementation of monetary and exchange rate policies. The bank does not intervene in the foreign exchange markets because the pula is pegged to a basket of currencies comprising the South African rand and the SDR. Although the level and timing of interest rate changes are decided by the bank, the Governor informs the Minister of Finance and Development Planning of impending changes prior to implementation. The Banking Act of 1995 empowers the bank to license and supervise banks as well as to regulate other financial institutions. The Bank of Botswana is also responsible for the preparation of monetary, financial, balance of payments and exchange rate data, which is published in its monthly *Botswana Financial Statistics*.

MARKET PERFORMANCE

A) In 1997

It was a spectacular year for the Botswana Stock Exchange. The Domestic Companies Index rose by 101%, and total capitalisation increased from P1.2 billion to P2.3 billion, making the BSE one of the best performing stock markets in the world in 1997.

Part of the reason for the increase is that foreign investors are becoming more favourably disposed towards the smaller African stock markets. Foreign participation in the BSE has increased dramatically since 1993, when only 3 foreign companies maintained share custody accounts; this figure currently stands at over 50 companies.

With the exception of Sechaba, the largest quoted company, the market is not very liquid. This is generally because stocks have large parent company holdings, leaving only a small free float for investors. However, market liquidity is improving and the total number of shares traded increased from 43 million in 1996 to 61 million in 1997. There were no primary issues of shares in 1997, nor any domestic listings, but eight companies dual listed on the exchange during the year, including De Beers and Morgan Stanley Africa Investment Fund, which is the largest pan-African fund in the world.

The other highlight of the year was the first bond listing on the BSE, which took place in December. The P50 million BDC issue is expected to be the first of several bond issues by parastatals over the next few years.

The structure of the BSE is developing rapidly. Ernst & Young was appointed as secretaries to the exchange in March 1997 with responsibility for compliance issues. A programme is now under way to establish an independent office of the stock exchange which should be in place early in 1998.

B) Summary information

Global ranking by market value (US$ terms, end-1997): 74
Market capitalisation:
domestic US$613 million; foreign US$12,084 million
Growth in market value
(domestic companies, local currency terms, 1993–97): 258%
Market value as a % of GDP (domestic companies, end-1997): 12.6%
Number of domestic/foreign companies listed (end-1997): 12/8
Market P/E (all domestic companies, end-1997): 10.33
Short-term (3-month) interest rate (end-1997): 11.4%
Long-term (1-year) bond yield (end-1997): 12.12%
Budget surplus as a % of nominal GDP (1997): 6.9%
Annual increase in broad money (M3, Sept 1997): 22.4%
Inflation rate (1997): 7.8%
US$ exchange rate (end-1997): P3.81

C) Year-end share price index, price/earnings ratios and yields

Exhibit 8.1:
YEAR-END SHARE PRICE INDEX, P/E RATIOS AND DIVIDEND YIELDS, 1993–97

Year-end	*Domestic Companies Index*	*P/E*	*Dividend yield (%)*
1993	278.72	8.04	na
1994	312.87	9.33	na
1995	332.83	9.97	6.47
1996	352.81	7.28	7.50
1997	708.49	10.33	4.77

Source: Stockbrokers Botswana Ltd.

D) Market indices and their constituents

The liberalisation of exchange controls at the end of 1996 allowed dual listings on the BSE and has resulted in the introduction of three indices. The Domestic Companies

Index (DCI), which replaces the BSE All Share Index, reflects the market movements of the 12 domestic counters. The Foreign Companies Index (FCI) reflects the price movement of the dual listed stocks, while the All Companies Index (ACI) reflects the whole market. All indices are weighted according to market capitalisation.

THE STOCK MARKET

A) Brief history and structure

The Botswana Share Market (BSM), established in 1989, officially became the Botswana Stock Exchange (BSE) on 1 November 1995, heralding the establishment of a new and separate legal entity. The Botswana Stock Exchange Act was passed by parliament in August 1994, and came into force when regulations were published by the government at the end of October 1995. The BSE committee, appointed by the Ministry of Finance and Development Planning, oversees share dealings, listings, takeovers, mergers and suspensions. Ernst & Young, a professional accountancy firm, administers the BSE under the supervision of the stock exchange committee in accordance with internationally accepted standards.

Members of the BSE must be based in Botswana and have minimum net assets in Botswana of P50,000. It is hoped that the stock exchange will launch a central depository in 1999, although at present all transactions are paper-based. The BSE is Botswana's only stock exchange.

B) Opening hours, names and addresses

BSE trading hours are between 9.00am and 4.00pm, Monday to Thursday, and between 9.00am and 12.00 noon on Friday.

BOTSWANA STOCK EXCHANGE
(Post: Private Bag 00417), 4th Floor, Finance House
Khama Crescent, Gabarone
Tel: (267) 374 078; Fax: (267) 374 079

STOCKBROKERS BOTSWANA LTD
(Post: Private Bag 00113)
Ground Floor, Barclays House, Khama Crescent, Gabarone
Tel: (267) 357 900; Fax (267) 357 901

MARKET SIZE

A) Number of listings and market value

The number of domestic companies listed stands at 12, with an end-1997 market capitalisation of P2,335.50 million. Of these companies, five operate in the financial sector (including three banks). In addition, eight foreign companies dual listed in 1997.

Exhibit 8.2:
NUMBER OF COMPANIES LISTED AND MARKET VALUE, BSE, 1993–97

Year-end	*No. of domestic companies listed*		*Market capitalisation*
		(P million)	*(US$ million)*
1993	11	668.80	261
1994	10	1,024.27	377
1995	12	1,120.27	397
1996	12	1,189.80	326
1997	12	2,335.50	613

Source: Stockbrokers Botswana Ltd.

B) Trading volume

Exhibit 8.3:
TURNOVER OF DOMESTIC SHARES ON THE BSE, 1993–97

	Value traded (P million)	*Volume traded (shares)*
1993	48.4	17,684,375
1994	82.1	29,546,245
1995	98.8	44,865,863
1996	103.1	42,784,000
1997	214.8	60,783,802

Source: Stockbrokers Botswana Ltd.

Exhibit 8.4:
THE 10 MOST ACTIVELY TRADED SHARES, BSE, 1997

Ranking	*Company*	*Trading value (US$ '000)*	*Shares ('000)*
1	Sechaba Investment Trust	32,652.5	35,598.3
2	Standard Chartered	7,029.1	2,024.8
3	Barclays Bank of Botswana	6,176.3	2,016.3
4	Sefalana Holding	4,703.9	3,246.1
5	First National Bank of Botswana	1,356.0	634.2
6	Engen Botswana	1,303.3	1,209.5
7	PEP Botswana	1,085.3	1,220.0
8	Metsef	1,054.4	600.0
9	Kgolo Ya Sechaba	977.9	9,524.0
10	Botswana Insurance	744.2	778.9

Source: Stockbrokers Botswana Ltd.

OTHER MARKETS

The BSE is the only equity market in Botswana. The domestic bond market in Botswana at present deals only in three- to nine-month Treasury bills (Bank of Botswana Certificates or BOBCs), which are made available to the public through the BSE. Issued purely as monetary policy instruments to control excess liquidity and maintain interest rates at real levels, they are not for sale to non-residents. The development of the capital market received a major boost towards the end of 1997 with the introduction of the P50 million BDC bond issue.

INVESTORS

Investors holding over 5% of the issued capital of listed companies are classified as "direct investors", while investors holding less than 5% are termed "portfolio investors". Foreign investment on the BSE accounts for 60% of total direct investment and 16% of total portfolio investment. The remaining 24% is held by local institutions and local private investors.

OPERATIONS

A) Settlement and transfer

Settlement of purchases must be made within five working days. Delivery of scrip sold must take place within five working days, against payment within T+5 working days.

B) Commission rates

Brokerage rates on purchases and sales are as follows:

- 2% on amounts up to P50,000;
- 1.5% on P50,000–P100,000;
- 1% on amounts over P100,000.

Commissions on trades generated through registered foreign brokers are as above, and shared between the Botswanan broker and the foreign broker.

A handling fee is charged of P15 on all purchases and P10 on all sales.

TAXATION AND REGULATIONS AFFECTING FOREIGN INVESTORS

Foreign investment is welcomed in Botswana. Non-residents may invest freely on the BSE, and capital and profits are fully remittable.

A) Taxation

All capital gains on listed shares are tax-free. Capital gains for individuals in respect of unlisted shares are calculated on only 50% of the gain, using a sliding scale of P6,500 on the first P45,000 and 40% on the balance. Capital gains for companies in respect of unlisted shares are calculated at a straight 35%.

Withholding tax on dividends is applied at 15% and dividends are paid net of this. Withholding tax and company income tax taken together do not exceed 30% of a listed company's pre-tax profits. Withholding tax on interest is also applied at 15% on amounts paid to non-residents. Company tax is 25%, plus an additional tax at a rate of 10%.

Double taxation agreements exist with South Africa, the UK and Sweden.

B) Exchange controls

The liberalisation of exchange controls announced in the 1995-96 Budget effectively removed all restrictions on genuine current account transactions. Capital account liberalisation represents the next major step towards financial integration with international markets. Phased liberalisation now allows outward investment (subject to central bank approval) for individuals and companies.

There are no prohibitions on foreign ownership of companies in Botswana. For a "direct investor" capital flows in and out of the country require central bank approval. For a "portfolio investor" there are no restrictions on capital and dividend flows. Portfolio investors may not collectively own more than 49% of a listed company's "free" float. Further liberalisation of the exchange control system is likely to result in the central bank playing a more limited role, which should encourage capital flows into and out of Botswana.

RESEARCH AND OTHER INFORMATION

Stockbrokers Botswana Ltd produces regular bulletins on the market's performance and a guide entitled *Investment Opportunities in Botswana.*

Information can also be found on Reuters pages BSTX, BSTY, BSTZ and BSM.BT.

African Equities: A Guide to Markets and Companies, published by Euromoney Books, provides in-depth information for all those wishing to invest and do business in Africa. See the order card at the back of this book for details.

CHAPTER 9

Brazil

Introduction

Politically, 1997 was a fairly positive year for Brazil. In addition to the approval of the re-election amendment, President Cardoso was able to consolidate his leadership in both Houses of Congress, which sanctioned important parts of his political and economic reform project.

In the Brazilian equity market the best performing stocks during the year were those of state or private companies directly or indirectly involved in the privatisation process.

Overall, despite the financial crisis that started in Asia in October and sent a panic wave around world exchanges, the Brazilian stock market was able to overcome the turbulence and, albeit with a high degree of volatility, closed the year with a gain of 44.83% in reals, or an adjusted 34.89% when deflated by the Market General Price Index.

ECONOMIC AND POLITICAL OVERVIEW

During the first half of 1997, the Brazilian economic environment was stable and there was a net foreign investment inflow of over US$4.7 billion, including both portfolio and direct investments.

Internally, the change in command of the central bank, with the former director of the international department, Gustavo Franco, replacing Gustavo Loyola as president, was a clear signal that monetary policy would be maintained without any major surprises. Another important development was the Congressional approval for the General Telecommunications Act, which gave power to the federal government to privatise the whole Telebrás system, comprising 27 state telephone companies.

For the year as a whole, the Brazilian industrial sector recorded a good performance, particularly in capital goods, steel, automotive, electric energy, telecommunications and agro-industry. The automobile industry closed 1997 with all-time records for both production and sales, in spite of the negative effects of the Asian crisis. In the external sector, however, Brazilian economic performance was not as good. The balance of trade recorded a deficit of about US$8.5 billion, with imports totalling US$61.5 billion against exports of around US$53 billion.

Perhaps the most remarkable achievement for the Brazilian economy in 1997 was the lowest rate of inflation recorded in the past 40 years. The IGP-DI (General Price Index) increased just 7.48%, while the National Consumer Price Index (INPC) rose by only 4.34%.

Role of the central bank

Banco do Brasil is not classed as a monetary authority. The real decision-making body in monetary and foreign exchange matters is the National Monetary Council (CMN). It comprises five cabinet ministers, eight federal bank chairmen and a number of private advisers, and is chaired by the Finance Minister. The CMN is in charge of the monetary budget, and in particular the limits applied to aggregate money expansion.

Monetary and credit controls are exercised through reserve requirements in the commercial banking system, bank rediscount policies and open market operations, but interest rate ceilings and mandatory rate reductions have also been used.

MARKET PERFORMANCE

A) In 1997

Through to July, stock market indices were influenced by expectations and government announcements concerning the structuring of companies to be privatised – including the blue chip Companhia Vale do Rio Doce (CVRD) – and also by the increasing volume of domestic capital flowing into mutual funds. These factors fuelled a market gain of over 26% in the first quarter, and took the Bovespa (São Paulo Stock Exchange) Index to an all-time high on 8 July, up 93.4% in just over 6 months.

Things changed, however, following the first shock

Exhibit 9.1: BRAZIL BOVESPA PRICE INDEX (US$), 1993–97

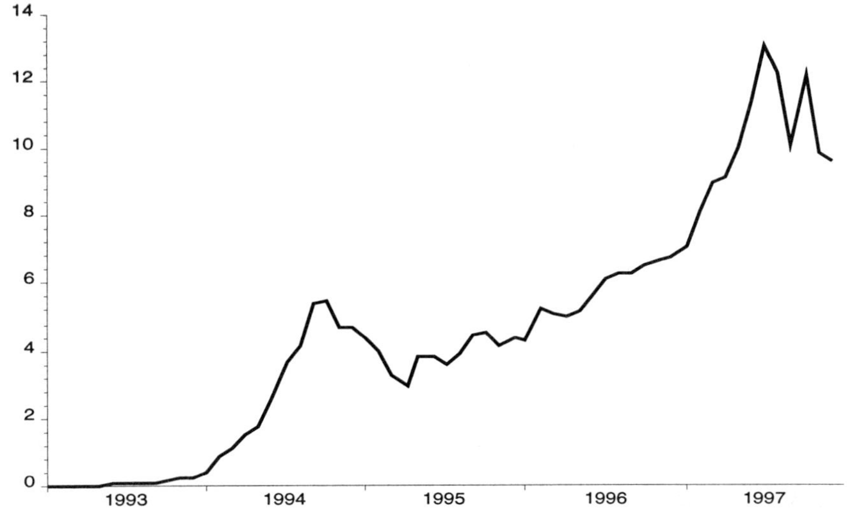

High value 13002.00 1.7.97 Low value 6.78 1.1.93 *Source: Datastream*

waves from a speculative attack on the Thai currency, which provoked a sharp reversal in the Brazilian market, causing the Bovespa Index to decline almost 18% in August. Volatility increased as investors feared a raid on Brazil's own currency, and when this materialised in the fourth quarter, the market plummeted further, although it then recovered part of the loss during November and December.

Brazil's primary market recorded total stock issues in 1997 of R$3,965 million, comprising 23 transactions, including proceeds from the sale of government stakes in privatised energy and transportation companies.

B) Summary information

Global ranking by market value (US$ terms, end-1997): 15
Market capitalisation (end-1997): US$255.4 billion (Bovespa): US$252.8 billion (BVRJ)
Growth in market value (local currency terms, 1993–97): 159.14%
Market value as a % of nominal GDP (end-1997): 31.5%
Number of domestic/foreign companies listed (end-1997): 536/1 (Bovespa); 572/1 (BVRJ)
Market P/E (end-1997): 9.9 (Bovespa); 11.1 (BVRJ)
MSCI Index (change in US$ terms, 1997): +23.4%
Short-term (one-month) interest rate (end-1997): 2.89%
Long bond (one-year) yield (end-1997): 32.15%
Budget deficit as a % of nominal GDP (Oct 1997): 3.2%
Annual increase in broad money (M3) supply (end-1997): 25.62%
Inflation rate (1997): 7.48%
US$ exchange rate (end-1997): R$1.1146

C) Year-end share price indices, price/earnings ratios and yields

Exhibit 9.2:
YEAR-END INDICES (LOCAL CURRENCY TERMS), P/E RATIOS AND GROSS DIVIDEND YIELDS, 1993–97

Year-end	*Bovespa Index*[1]	*IBV Index*	*P/E*	*Yield (%)*
1993	375.5	1,409.3	8.9	0.40
1994	4,353.9	16,466.0	11.5	2.48
1995	4,299.0	16,247.0	*9.4/9.9	3.91
1996	7,040.0	25,953.0	*10.6/9.9	4.08
1997	10,196.5	37,162.0	*9.9/11.1	3.99

*São Paulo/Rio.

Note: [1]Data adjusted according to Bovespa Index divisions. The index was divided by 10 on 26.1.93, 27.8.93, 10.2.94 and 3.3.97.

Source: São Paulo Stock Exchange.

D) Market indices and their constituents

The most widely recognised index of Brazilian share market performance is the Bovespa Index (2 January 1968 = 0.0000000001), calculated by the São Paulo exchange. At four-month intervals (January, May and September) the Bovespa Index notional portfolio is reviewed and changes in the relative participation of each stock in the index are assessed. For the period January-April 1998, the Bovespa Index portfolio comprised 51 stocks issued by 45 listed companies.

The Electric Power Index (IEE) is the first of a series of sectorial indices to be introduced on Bovespa, and it comprises the electric energy sector's most representative companies. All companies are equally weighted in the IEE portfolio, which is rebalanced every four months. At present it comprises 13 companies (the January to April 1998 portfolio).

BVRJ calculates its own index, the IBV index (29 December 1983 = 0.000001). The IBV index covers the most actively traded Rio stocks (31 in December 1997) and is market weighted. IBX-Brazil Index measures the aggregate performance of the 100 most actively traded Brazilian stocks, weighted according to the number of shares outstanding. The index is rebalanced every four months.

THE STOCK MARKET

A) Brief history and structure

The Brazilian stock market dates from the mid-19th century, when a group of brokers organised themselves on the model of the French market of that time. By the early 1960s there was a stock exchange in virtually every state of the nation, although 90% of trading took place on the exchanges of Rio de Janeiro and São Paulo.

Between 1982 and 1985, the Brazilian stock market showed impressive gains following the return to full democracy and civil rule, but 1987 brought a dramatic reduction in turnover and a large fall in the number of issues listed. In 1988, despite rising inflation, inflows of capital to the stock market were stimulated by the liquidity of the economy and the establishment of funds for the conversion of external debt. In 1990 the severe monetary squeeze and fiscal adjustment without an immediate fall in inflation led to a significant drop in the market in real terms. Nevertheless, deregulation, foreign capital inflows and low prices produced a revival in 1991, which despite occasional setbacks, has continued.

The Brazilian stock exchanges' board of directors is composed of six representatives of member firms, from which the chairman and vice-chairman of the board are chosen. The general superintendent, who represents the exchanges' professional management, also has a seat on the board, together with three other members who, respectively, represent public companies, institutional investors and private investors. A further six deputies are selected, three representing brokerage houses and the other three representing listed companies, institutional and private investors.

Brokerage houses are subject to the rules and surveillance of the Conselho Monetário Nacional, as administered by the central bank and the Securities Commission (CVM). They are also subject to monitoring by the exchanges.

B) Different exchanges

There are nine stock exchanges in Brazil, but the São Paulo and Rio de Janeiro exchanges are by far the most important and international.

C) Opening hours, names and addresses

Bovespa's open outcry and electronic trading system sessions are held from 11.00am to 5.00pm each business day. The open outcry session trades stocks and options of the 22 companies that have been the most actively traded in previous months. Other stocks and options are traded on the electronic system.

Floor trading in Rio takes place from 10.30am to 5.00pm. All stocks are traded simultaneously on the floor and through the electronic system. There is a pre-opening period of 30 minutes.

BOLSA DE VALORES DE SÃO PAULO
Rua XV de Novembro 275, 01013 001 São Paulo – SP
Tel: (55) 11 233 2000; Fax: (55) 11 233 2099

in Rio de Janeiro
Rua 7 de Setembro 69/71 – 21/22, 20050-003 – Rio de Janeiro
Tel: (55) 21 532 4616; Fax: (55) 21 532 4715

representative in New York
AIM Brazil Corporation, 450 Park Avenue,
21st Floor, Suite 2101, New York, USA
Tel: (1) 212 750 4197; Fax: (1) 212 750 4198

BOLSA DE VALORES DO RIO DE JANEIRO
Pça XV Novembro 20, 20010 – 010 Rio de Janeiro/RJ
Tel: (55) 21 514 1001; Fax: (55) 21 514 1193
Internet: www.bvrj.com.br

BOLSA DE VALORES BAHIA-SERGIPE-ALAGOAS
Rua Pedro Rolim Bandeira, 143, 3rd Floor, 40015070 – Salvador/BA
Tel: (55) 71 242 3844; Fax: (55) 71 242 5753

BOLSA DE VALORES DO EXTREMO SUL
Rue dos Andradas 1234, 8th Floor
90020 008 – Porto Alegre/RS
Tel: (55) 51 224 2600; Fax: (55) 51 227 4359/226 6996

BOLSA DE VALORES DO PARANÁ
Rua Marechal Deodoro 344, 5th and 7th Floors
80010 010 – Curitiba/PR
Tel: (55) 41 222 5191; Fax: (55) 41 223 6203

BOLSA DE VALORES DE PERNAMBUCO E PARAÍBA
Av Alfredo Lisboa 505, 50030 150 – Recife/PE
Tel: (55) 81 224 8277; Fax: (55) 81 224 8412

BOLSA DE VALORES REGIONAL
Av Com Manoel 1020, 60060 090 – Fortaleza/CE
Tel: (55) 85 231 6466; Fax: (55) 85 231 6888

BOLSA DE VALORES MINAS ESPÍRITO SANTO-BRASÍLIA
Rue dos Carijos 126, 3rd Floor
30120 060 – Belo Horizonte/MG
Tel: (55) 31 219 9005/9501; Fax: (55) 31 273 1202

BOLSA DE VALORES DE SANTOS
Rua XV de Novembro 111/113, 11010-151 – Santos/SP
Tel: (55) 13 219 7800; Fax: (55) 13 219 5119

MARKET SIZE

A) Number of listings and market value

The market capitalisation of shares quoted on Bovespa at the end of 1997 was US$255.4 billion, a 17.7% increase over the year. The Rio de Janeiro market value at the same date totalled US$252.8 billion, up 19% on year-end 1996.

Exhibit 9.3:
NUMBER OF LISTED COMPANIES, BOVESPA AND BVRJ, 1993–97

Year-end	*Bovespa*	*BVRJ*
1993	550	578
1994	544	576
1995	543	570
1996	551	573
1997	537	573

Sources: São Paulo Stock Exchange and Rio de Janeiro Stock Exchange

Exhibit 9.4:
MARKET CAPITALISATION OF LISTED SHARES ON BOVESPA AND BVRJ, 1993–97

	Market value (US$ billion)	
Year-end	*Bovespa*	*BVRJ*
1993	99.43	96.70
1994	189.06	187.35
1995	147.56	147.38
1996	216.93	212.44
1997	255.41	252.80

Sources: São Paulo Stock Exchange and Rio de Janeiro Stock Exchange.

B) Largest quoted companies

Exhibit 9.5:
THE 20 LARGEST LISTED COMPANIES ON BOVESPA, YEAR-END 1997

Ranking	*Company*	*Market value (US$ million)*
1	Telebrás	35,028.98
2	Eletrobrás	26,834.66
3	Petrobrás	21,074.56
4	Telesp	14,106.49
5	Bradesco	9,261.35
6	Vale do Rio Doce	7,511.00
7	Eletropaulo	6,949.92
8	Sabesp	6,604.63
9	Cemig	5,287.68
10	Itaubanco	5,221.15
11	Cesp	5,057.56
12	Brasil	4,885.91
13	Brahma	4,723.86
14	Light	4,327.78
15	Unibanco	3,489.65
16	Copel	3,368.97
17	Lightpar	3,118.00
18	Telerj	2,968.21
19	Telemig	2,754.99
20	Souza Cruz	2,464.36

Source: São Paulo Stock Exchange.

Exhibit 9.6:
THE 20 LARGEST LISTED COMPANIES ON BVRJ, YEAR-END 1997

Ranking	*Company*	*Market value (US$ million)*
1	Telebrás	37,118.75
2	Eletrobrás	26,835.25
3	Petrobrás	21,074.56
4	Telesp	14,106.49
5	Bradesco	9,657.32
6	Vale do Rio Doce	7,511.35
7	Eletropaulo	7,199.57
8	Itaubanco	5,638.86
9	Cemig	5,287.68
10	Cesp	5,057.56
11	Banco do Brasil	4,885.91
12	Brahma	4,723.86
13	Light	4,327.78
14	Copel	3,368.97
15	Brazil Realty	3,184.85
16	Light Participações	3,118.0
17	Telerj	2,968.21
18	Telemig	2,746.04
19	Souza Cruz	2,464.36
20	Paulista de Forca e Luz	2,382.52

Source: Rio de Janeiro Stock Exchange.

C) Trading volume

Total turnover for 1997 on Bovespa was US$191.1 billion, an increase of 95.4% compared with 1996. BVRJ turnover rose by 42% to US$26.8 billion.

Exhibit 9.7:
STOCK EXCHANGE TURNOVER, 1993–97 (US$ MILLION)

Year	*Bovespa*	*BVRJ*	*Total*
1993	38,554	9,116	47,670
1994	88,206	16,019	104,225
1995	69,447	9,914	79,361
1996	97,762	18,805	116,567
1997	191,091	26,779	217,870

Sources: São Paulo Stock Exchange and Rio de Janeiro Stock Exchange.

Exhibit 9.8:
THE 20 MOST ACTIVELY TRADED SHARES ON BOVESPA, 1997

Ranking	*Company*	*Trading value (US$ million)*
1	Telebrás preferred	78,826.49
2	Petrobrás preferred	7,694.17
3	Eletrobrás common	5,741.15
4	Telebrás common	5,432.85
5	Eletrobrás preferred B	5,185.59
6	Telesp preferred	3,400.38
7	Cemig preferred	2,984.41
8	Vale do Rio Doce preferred	2,623.34
9	Brahma preferred	1,792.11
10	Bradesco preferred	1,635.27
11	Cesp preferred	1,247.53
12	Banespa preferred	1,238.02
13	Usiminas preferred	968.76
14	Ericsson preferred	873.10
15	Itaubanco preferred	734.03
16	Light common	711.01
17	Sid. Nacional common	663.65
18	Banco do Brasil preferred	622.80
19	Sid. Tubarão preferred B	554.62
20	Eletropaulo preferred B	481.24

Source: São Paulo Stock Exchange.

Exhibit 9.9:
THE 20 MOST ACTIVELY TRADED SHARES ON BVRJ, 1997

Ranking	*Company*	*Trading value (US$ million)*
1	Telebrás preferred	1,899.36
2	Petrobrás preferred	1,263.13
3	Eletrobrás common	1,031.39
4	Copel preferred B	529.83
5	Vale do Rio Doce preferred	509.60
6	Light common	480.88
7	Telebrás common	373.77
8	Eletrobrás preferred B	342.75
9	Cesp preferred	257.01
10	Cemig preferred	247.65
11	Telesp preferred	188.03
12	Cesp common	179.75
13	Escelsa common	161.80
14	Coelba common	153.71
15	Vale do Rio Doce common	128.84
16	Brahma preferred	126.69
17	Coelce preferred A	109.90
18	CEB preferred	83.50
19	Petrobrás common	72.97
20	Celesc preferred B	71.58

Source: Rio de Janeiro Stock Exchange.

TYPES OF SHARE

Equities issued in Brazil take the form of common and preferred shares. Rights to subscribe to securities, subscription receipts, subscription bonuses and debentures are also traded on the market.

All shares issued in Brazil are in registered form: bearer shares are illegal. Preferred shares (non-voting) rank above common shares for the distribution of dividends and reimbursement of capital on liquidation of the company. Generally, preferred shares are entitled to a specific minimum or fixed dividend. Preferred shareholders may also be entitled to elect separately one or more administrators of the company, in addition to at least one member of the audit committee. Certain amendments to the by-laws may require the prior approval of preferred shareholders.

Brazilian corporations may also issue book shares, which are registered shares kept on deposit at a financial establishment and for which no share certificates are issued.

OTHER MARKETS

Bovespa's Mercantile and Futures Exchange (BM&F) opened on 31 January 1986 and there is a stock options market on BVRJ.

On Bovespa, the most liquid derivative market consists of call and put options on stocks, which accounted for 8.8% of turnover in 1997. Call options are American style, but put options can only be exercised on the expiration date.

Exhibit 9.10:
TOP PERFORMING COUNTRY FUNDS – BRAZIL

Fund	US$% change 01/01/98 01/01/97	US$% change 01/01/98 01/01/93	Fund base currency	Fund size (US$ mil)	Fund volatility	Management group	Opal main sector	Opal subsector
Opportunity Brazil Value	116.1	N/A	US$	1.4	13.187	Opportunity A	Open-End	Equity
Vertice de Investi Cap Estrang	57.88	931.06	US$	0.379	8.506	Vertice	Open-End	Equity
BBM Fund Eq IBOV Shares	45.7	N/A	US$	0.555	-1	BBM Bank Ltd	Open-End	Equity
Sinopia EMF Brazil Indx Plus C	43.43	N/A	US$	0.1	-1	CCF Sam	Open-End	Equity
Inter American Exp Pegasus	43.31	N/A	US$	2.5	-1	SRL Bank International	Open-End	Equity
Matrix Geo Summit B	37.84	N/A	US$	3.04	-1	Banco Matrix	Open-End	Equity
CCF Premium Fund Ltd B	37.17	N/A	US$	16.206	9.505	Banco CCF Brasil	Open-End	Equity
Vista Hedge	36.6	N/A	US$	15.7	-1	Banco Boavista	Open-End	Equity
Lloyds Brazil Equity	32.25	N/A	US$	25.07	-1		Open-End	Equity
UAM Columbus Index	31.86	N/A	US$	36.8	-1	UniBanco	Open-End	Equity
Paribas EM Brazil Ptfl	31.56	N/A	US$	N/A	6.941	Paribas Asset Management	Open-End	Equity
Patrimonio Energy	30.17	N/A	US$	9.8	-1	Banco Patrimoni	Open-End	Equity
Brazvest	30.13	N/A	US$	63.2	9.815	Globalvest Management	Private	Equity
Fonte Cindam Select	28.43	N/A	US$	7.3	-1	Banco Cindam	Open-End	Equity
BBM Fund Equity Shares	24.14	N/A	US$	1.606	-1	BBM Bank Ltd	Open-End	Equity
Patrimonio Privitisation	24.05	N/A	US$	7.2	-1	Banco Patrimoni	Open-End	Equity
NatWest/IFC LAIF Brazil Index	22.1	N/A	US$	16.362	8.962	NatWest Investment Management	Open-End	Equity
GAM Brasilia	22.07	N/A	US$	21.7	7.437	GAM	Open-End	Equity
Vista Equity	21.29	N/A	US$	1.6	-1	Banco Boavista	Open-End	Equity
Patrimonio New Fund Equity	20.43	771.75	US$	14.9	6.886	Banco Patrimoni	Open-End	Equity
Matrix Geo Summit Equity	20.21	N/A	US$	58.73	-1	Banco Matrix	Open-End	Equity
Patrimonio Telecom	19.6	N/A	US$	4.3	-1	Banco Patrimoni	Open-End	Equity
BR Equity Fund	18.59	N/A	US$	1.979	8.152	Primus	Open-End	Equity
The Eagle Fund	18.05	N/A	US$	0.7	8.558	Banco Boavista	Open-End	Equity
Brazil Fund	17.39	147.34	US$	411.65	8.335	Scudder	Closed-End	Equity
Schroder Brazil	17.18	N/A	US$	51.9	-1	Schroders	Open-End	Equity
Opportunity Brazil Strategy	17.01	N/A	US$	2	10.158	Opportunity A	Open-End	Equity
Jupiter Tyndall SF Brazil	16.95	N/A	US$	0.8	6.971	Tyndall	Open-End	Equity
Garantia Equity Fund (No.1)	16.6	N/A	US$	151.82	11.029	Garantia	Open-End	Equity
IB Brazilian Equities	13.58	N/A	US$	6.9	6.795	Bank Icatu	Open-End	Equity
Brazilian Balanced (Arbitral)	11.84	N/A	US$	4.3	4.317	Arbitral Fina	Open-End	Equity
Brazilian Equity Fund	11.66	155.57	US$	99.253	7.687	BEA Assoc	Open-End	Equity
Opportunity Brazil Equities	10.79	N/A	US$	66.1	10.903	Opportunity A	Open-End	Equity
Unifund A	10.5	N/A	US$	11.8	9.16	UniBanco	Open-End	Equity
Opportunity Brazil Balanced	9.54	N/A	US$	2.2	4.233	Opportunity A	Open-End	Equity
Vertice III de Inv Cap Estrang	9.5	231.29	US$	0.255	9.902	Vertice	Open-End	Equity
Patrimonio Cyclical	8.55	N/A	US$	0.8	-1	Banco Patrimoni	Open-End	Equity
Brazilian Inv Co	6.67	120.33	US$	44.1	7.902	Foreign & Col	Open-End	Equity
Brazilian Investments SA	5.98	266.61	US$	38.166	8.081	Banco Bozano Simonsen	Open-End	Equity
Scudder GOF Brazil Equity A-2	5.58	N/A	US$	8.4	7.873	Scudder	Open-End	Equity
Pactual Eternity	5.47	273.67	US$	41.9	8.446	Banco Pactual	Open-End	Equity
IB Brazilian Leveraged Eq	5.25	N/A	US$	1.9	-1	Bank Icatu	Open-End	Equity
Opportunity Brazil Aggressive	4.73	N/A	US$	32.3	14.2	Opportunity A	Open-End	Equity
Evolution Fund Ltd.	4.54	N/A	US$	12.723	7.093	Banco Marka SA	Open-End	Equity

Note: details for some funds may not have been included if the data for the US$ % change for 97/98 was not available

Source: Standard & Poor's Micropal.

Bovespa Index options are traded on the São Paulo exchange and 1997 turnover totalled R$ 9.3 million.

INVESTORS

Financial institutions dominate Brazil's markets, and accounted for close to 40.1% of Bovespa's turnover in 1997. Foreign investors are in second place (accounting for 25.9%) and institutional investors are in third place (19.6%).

OPERATIONS

A) Trading system

Trading on the Brazilian exchanges is conducted at trading posts, around which the floor brokers gather and announce their offers and bids continuously through open outcry. Offers and bids can also be entered into the exchange computer and are displayed on monitors at the trading posts. Trades may be executed on a cash or forward basis.

Block transactions are displayed and can be challenged by other brokers and cancelled by exchange officials at the end of the trading day in favour of more competitive offers or bids.

Computerisation is quite sophisticated. Executed transactions are signed by the selling and buying brokers, entered into the computer and immediately displayed on monitors on the trading floor and at brokerage houses in the main Brazilian cities. The exchanges also maintain a computerised database of transactions and technical and fundamental data on listed stocks.

The majority of trades are made through an automatic trading system called Teletrading, which covers brokers located all over the country in a real-time matching process. However, in 1997, Bovespa implemented the Mega Bolsa trading system, which integrates open outcry and electronic trading; it has the potential to expand market capacity significantly.

B) List of principal brokers

There are 74 member brokerage houses and 10 non-member brokerage houses that trade on the Rio de Janeiro market. On Bovespa there are 76 member brokerage houses and 45 non-member licensees.

Bovespa

BANCO PATRIMONIO DE INVESTIMENTO S.A.
Av. Brigadeiro Faria Lima, No. 1485-4 andar
01480-900 Sao Paulo - SP
Tel: (55) 11 3039 1800; Fax: (55) 11 3039 1900

BOZANO SIMONSEN S/A CCV
Av. Paulista, 1500, Sobreloja, 01310-100 São Paulo
Tel: (55) 11 245 8000; Fax: (55) 11 245 8423

CCF BRASIL CTVM S/A
Av. Brigadeiro Faria Lima, 3064, 1st and 4th Floors
01451-000 São Paulo
Tel: (55) 11 827 5000; Fax: (55) 11 827 5187/5116

COMERCIAL S/A CVC
Av. Paulista, 1439, 3rd Floor – cjs 33 e 34
01311-200 São Paulo
Tel: (55) 11 25 2600/289 5011; Fax: (55) 11 287 6600

GARANTIA S/A CTVM
R. Jorge Coelho 16, 13th Floor, 01451-020 São Paulo
Tel: (55) 11 821 6600; Fax: (55) 11 821 6900

ITAU CV S/A
Rua Boa Vista 185, 4th Floor, 01014-001 São Paulo
Tel: (55) 11 237 5880; Fax: (55) 11 232 9840

BVRJ

AGENDA LTDA
Avenida Rio Branco, 116-11° andar
20040-001 Rio de Janeiro
Tel: (55) 21 221 1122; Fax: (55) 21 231 0085

ÁGORA LTDA
Rua Professor Artur Ramos, 140 – Leblon
2241-110 Rio de Janeiro
Tel: (55) 21 512 6000; Fax: (55) 21 512 7767

LIBERAL CCVM LTDA
Rua do Carmo 7-7, 8 e 10° andares, 20011-020 – Rio de Janeiro
Tel: (55) 21 212 4000; Fax: (55) 21 212 4111

OMEGA CCVM SA
Praça Pio X, 55-4° andar, 20040-020 Rio do Janeiro
Tel: (55) 21 296 4466; Fax: (55) 21 233 4470

NORSUL CCVM S/A
Rua 1° de Março, 23-7°, 20010-000 Rio de Janeiro
Tel: (55) 21 292 6617; Fax: (55) 21 221 2072

C) Settlement and transfer

Physical settlement takes place on the second business day after the execution of the trade, and financial settlement on the third business day. Bovespa operations are settled at CALISPA, the exchange's wholly owned subsidiary, while BVRJ's operations are settled at CLC, an independent clearing house that settles trades entered under the national trading system. The CLC is recognised by the SEC as a depository for US institutional investors.

D) Commissions and other costs

Transaction costs on Brazilian stock exchanges comprise brokerage commissions, trading charges and registration fees for derivatives. Brokerage commissions are negotiable and range from 0.5% to 2% depending on the value of the transaction. Trading charges range from 0.01% to 0.035% depending on the type of transaction. Registration fees in derivative markets vary according to the type of contract, ranging from 0.005% to 0.1%.

Exhibit 9.11:
WITHHOLDING TAX

Recipient	*Interest %*
Non-resident corporations and individuals:	
Non-treaty	15
Treaty	10–25

Source: Price Waterhouse.

TAXATION AND REGULATIONS AFFECTING FOREIGN INVESTORS

Foreign investors may invest directly in shares of Brazilian companies and such investments are treated in the same way as domestic capital in Brazil. Foreign investments must be registered with the Brazilian central bank, which issues a certificate of foreign investment registration. Following implementation of Resolution No. 2,337 issued by the central bank on 28 November 1996, all foreign portfolio investment in Brazil (as described below) is registered electronically with the central bank.

Under Decree No. 1,071 of 2 March 1994, foreign investments in Brazilian stock exchanges became subject to the IOF tax (the "Tax on Credit, Exchange, Insurance or Securities Transactions") levied on the amount of foreign capital inflows. Tax rates may vary from zero to 25% and the Ministry of Finance is empowered to change the rates at any time by way of ordinances. The current IOF rate applying to direct investment in equities through foreign capital investment companies, foreign capital investment funds, foreign capital securities portfolios and foreign institutional investment portfolios (vehicles Annex I to IV) is zero (Decree No 2,219 of 2 May 1997, article 14, § 2, 'e'). Direct investment in equity securities outside these vehicles is not currently subject to IOF.

Capital gains are subject to taxation on nominal gains. From January 1998, capital gains on the disposition of fixed and variable-income securities are generally taxed at 20% and 10% respectively. As a general rule, capital gains on the disposition of non-listed equity securities are subject to withholding income tax at 15%, charged at the time of payment, credit or remittance abroad. Capital gains are exempt from taxation if they relate to investment in Annex I to Annex V vehicles as described below.

From 1 January 1996, dividends on equity securities are not subject to Brazilian taxation.

Foreign investment vehicles

Under current Brazilian regulations there are 11 vehicles through which foreign portfolio investment can be made:

- listed foreign capital investment companies (formerly designated "1404 Companies"), Annex I;
- foreign capital investment funds, Annex II;
- foreign capital securities portfolios, Annex III;
- debt-equity conversion funds;
- venture capital companies;
- foreign institutional investor portfolios ("managed portfolios"), Annex IV;
- American depository receipts and international depository receipts (ADRs and IDRs), Annex V;
- mutual privatisation funds;
- fixed-yield investment funds;
- real estate investment funds; and
- emerging companies investment funds.

Foreign capital investment companies

The foreign capital investment company is a Brazilian-incorporated corporation organised for the purpose of investing in securities, under Annex I to Resolution No. 1,289 issued by the central bank on 20 March 1987. As a corporation, it is managed by an administrative council with functions similar to those of an American board of directors, and by a *diretoria*, which corresponds to a board of executives, headed by a chief executive officer.

The incorporation of an investment company depends on prior authorisation from the Securities Commission (CVM). Its initial capital is subscribed and paid up by an investment bank, brokerage house or securities dealership. After this subscription, the shares have to be sold abroad to foreign investors within 180 days. Any and all future capital increases must be funded only by foreign investors.

The company's portfolio is managed under a contract with a Brazilian financial institution (usually an investment bank, a securities dealership or a brokerage house), which establishes the guidelines and services to be provided and the fees to be paid for the management of the portfolio. The investment company also enters into an agreement with subscription agents for the offering of its shares to foreign investors.

Investment companies are exempt from corporate tax and capital gains tax. All other income paid to the investment company by issuers of securities held by the company is subject to a 15% withholding, except where a lower tax rate is assessed under a treaty to avoid double taxation. Following income distributions and/or total or partial liquidation of investments, the amount attributed to foreign investors, including capital gains and income, can be remitted abroad tax-free.

In addition, certain rules established by the CVM regarding the composition of the company's portfolio must be observed. The major requirement is that 50% of the aggregate value of investments must be represented by shares issued by publicly listed companies controlled by private Brazilian capital.

Foreign capital investment funds

Foreign capital investment funds are open condominium funds, organised under Annex II to Resolution 1,289 issued by the central bank on 20 March 1987. Condominiums are defined as organisations, without legal identity, in which two or more persons hold joint title to certain assets, each title holder (or co-owner) being attributed a part or a fraction of those assets. It is thus a form of joint or common ownership of assets.

The establishment of a fund depends on the prior approval of the CVM. The management of a fund must be exercised exclusively by a Brazilian financial institution (investment banks, securities dealerships and brokerage houses are, again, the authorised managers). The managing powers are exercised through a proxy (contained in the rules of the fund) which all investors must sign.

The rights of investors in the fund are represented by quotas or units, which correspond to a fraction of the assets held in joint ownership. The number of units held by each investor will depend on the amount invested in the fund. In general terms, such units can be redeemed by the fund or sold to a third party. Fund shares can only be placed with foreign investors, the minimum amount per investor being US$5,000.

The local managing institution may enter into agreements with intermediaries abroad for placing the units and for other promotional and representation services. These placing agents must be qualified to operate and/or act as fiduciary agents in the financial or capital markets of the country in which they have their head offices.

The tax rules applicable to foreign capital investment companies also apply to investment funds.

Funds may not invest in shares representing more than 5% of the voting capital or 20% of the total capital of any single company. Also, the total value of the investments of the fund in securities issued by any single company may not exceed 10% of the total investments of the fund.

Foreign capital securities portfolios

Investment in foreign capital securities portfolios, which are governed by Annex III to Resolution No. 1,289 issued by the central bank on 20 March 1987, is limited to foreign-incorporated entities that are listed on a stock exchange in the country of incorporation, and that have a corporate objective which includes investment in Brazilian securities. The securities portfolio shall be managed by: (a) an investment bank, a brokerage house or a securities dealership with its head office in Brazil, duly authorised by the CVM to perform its activities; along with (b) a foreign institution. The formation of the portfolio in Brazil depends on the prior authorisation of the CVM and is subject to a minimum capital requirement of US$100 million.

The tax rules applicable to foreign capital investment companies and investment funds also apply to foreign capital securities portfolios. On redemption of the investment, repatriation of the original investment and capital gains are tax-free.

The main investment restriction is that at least 70% of the portfolio must consist of shares issued by publicly listed companies.

Conversion funds

In February 1988 the central bank issued Resolution No. 1,460, amending the previous regulations on debt-equity swaps. Accordingly, funds originating from conversions can be invested in the Brazilian securities market through foreign capital conversion funds. Conversion funds must be organised under the same rules applicable to foreign capital investment funds, except that an investment in a conversion fund must be kept in Brazil for a minimum period of 12 years from the date of capitalisation of the fund.

The withholding income tax rate on earnings and capital gains distributed by conversion funds paid in through the conversion of credits and Brazilian debt instruments is 20% if at least 67% of the fund's equity is invested in fixed-income assets; it is 10% if at least 67% of the fund's equity is invested in variable-income assets. Receipt of earnings and capital gains by such funds is tax-exempt.

Conversion of debt into portfolio investment can occur with either future maturities or with amounts deposited with the central bank under rescheduling agreements. In the case of amounts deposited with the central bank, an auction system exists so that the bank can benefit from part of the discount applied in the acquisition of the deposit. In the case of future maturities of private sector debt, no auction procedure exists and the formation of a conversion fund is subject only to CVM approval of the fund's regulations.

It should be noted, however, that under current Brazilian regulations the debt-equity conversion programme is suspended for a yet to be determined period of time. The only exceptions are conversions under the Brazilian Privatisation Programme (PND) regulated by central bank Resolutions 1,810, 1,850 and 1,894.

Foreign institutional investor portfolios

On 31 May 1991, the central bank issued Resolution No. 1,832 allowing foreign institutional investors to invest in the Brazilian securities market through a managed portfolio. These regulations constitute Annex IV to central bank Resolution No. 1,289. Of all existing vehicles suitable for foreign investors, this is the one most commonly used.

Non-Brazilian pension funds, insurance companies, mutual funds, financial institutions (through their own funds) and non-profit institutions comprise *inter alia* the "institutional investors" covered by these regulations. Other entities registered with their country's equivalent to the Brazilian Securities Commission (eg the SEC in the United States) are also authorised to take advantage of Resolution No. 1,832.

The management of the portfolio must be undertaken by a Brazilian institution authorised to manage securities portfolios within Brazil. This manager must accept full responsibility for the acts it performs on behalf of the foreign investor and is solely responsible for the registration of the foreign funds entering Brazil as well as for the remittance of income, capital gains and repatriation of the original investment. It also performs the administrative work and makes reports to the Brazilian authorities. As well as equity investments, funds entering Brazil through Annex IV regulations may only be invested in securities issued by public companies.

The taxation rules that apply to a foreign institutional investor portfolios are similar to those applicable to foreign capital investment companies.

ADRs and IDRs

Resolution No. 1,927 issued by the central bank on 18 May 1992 authorises investment of foreign capital in shares of Brazilian companies through the mechanisms of American depository receipts or international depository receipts. These regulations constitute regulatory Annex V to central bank Resolution No. 1,289. The Brazilian authorities refer to the depository institution of the American or international depository receipts as the issuing bank of the ADR/IDR. The Brazilian custodian bank is an institution within the Brazilian financial system and accredited by the CVM to provide share custody services for the purpose of the programmes.

The basic tax rules are that dividends and profits distributed out of income generated as from 1 January 1996 are not subject to withholding income tax. In general terms, capital gains are exempt from taxation provided that (a) the foreign holders of ADRs and IDRs are entities with corporate objectives that include investing funds in the securities markets, and (b) the participants in those entities are natural persons or legal entities resident, domiciled or headquartered outside Brazil.

Mutual privatisation funds

Foreign investment in mutual privatisation funds is regulated by CVM Instruction No. 157 of 21 August 1991 as amended. "Mutual privatisation fund" is defined as a condominium in which individuals or legal entities that are resident, domiciled or headquartered outside Brazil, funds or other entities of foreign collective investment, participate. Such funds constitute a pool of assets to be used to acquire securities issued by companies that may be privatised under the National Privatisation Programme (PND).

The establishment of such a fund is conditional on the prior approval of the CVM, after notifying the central bank. The fund must be organised as a condominium, and the by-laws must regulate the investors' standing in relation to the operation and management of the fund. The fund must be managed solely by a multi-service bank with an investment department, an investment bank, brokerage firm, securities dealership or similar entity that is authorised to manage securities portfolios in Brazil.

The managing institution may accredit intermediary agents, by agreement, for the purpose of taking action abroad to obtain credits for subscription or purchase of quotas, and for promotional services, disclosure and representation of the fund, as well as to act as a fiduciary agent.

The assets of the fund may only be invested in: (i) securities issued by privatised companies; (ii) TDAs; (iii) OFNDs; (iv) debentures issued by Siderbrás; (v) privatisation certificates; and (vi) other credits, assets and bonds that represent federal government debt, and qualify for use under the privatisation programme.

Foreign capital is registered in the name of the foreign investor. The investment recipient will be the fund for foreign capital registration purposes.

Investors can redeem all or part of their monies in cash or in shares or investments in the portfolio, but investments made with monies from the conversion of Brazilian foreign debt instruments and credits must remain in Brazil for at least six years. This six-year lock-in period does not apply to funds paid in as fresh investment.

Income received and capital gains earned by the fund are not subject to Brazilian income tax. However, income distributed and capital gains earned by the condominium member on redemption of its shares in the fund are subject to withholding income tax at 20% if at least 67% of the fund's equity is invested in fixed-income assets; the tax is 10% if at least 67% of the fund's equity is invested in variable-income assets. As of the issuance of Decree No. 2,219/97, the rate of the IOF tax levied on foreign investments in privatisation funds was reduced to zero. This tax is assessed on the amount corresponding to the foreign capital inflow on settlement of the corresponding foreign exchange transaction.

Fixed-yield investment funds

The fixed-yield investment fund is an open condominium fund and follows the same rules as apply to foreign capital investment funds, conversion funds and mutual privatisation funds. The quotas in fixed-yield funds may be acquired by any legal entity domiciled or headquartered abroad. The investors, therefore, do not necessarily have to be institutional investors. The fixed-yield fund may be managed by a multi-service bank with an investment department, by an investment bank, securities dealership or brokerage company organised in Brazil. The IOF rate applicable to exchange transactions arising from transfers for fixed-yield investment funds is 2%.

Under central bank Circular No. 2,388 of 17 December 1993, as amended, fixed-yield investment funds shall include (i) at least 35% in national Treasury and/or central bank bonds; (ii) a maximum 20% in fixed-income securities or acceptance bills from financial institutions; (iii) other fixed-income securities; and (iv) shares in "financial investment funds" (FAFs). All fixed-income securities must be registered with the Central Agency for Custody and Financial Settlement of Bills (CETIP).

Real estate investment funds

Real estate investment funds were created by Law No. 8,668 of 25 June 1993. These funds are constituted as closed condominium funds, and the redemption of quotas is forbidden. Investors can include any legal entities or natural persons resident or domiciled abroad, funds and other collective foreign investment entities.

Emerging companies investment funds – foreign capital

The formation, operation and management of emerging companies investment mutual funds are regulated by the CVM Instruction No. 209 of 25 March 1994 as amended. These funds are designed to invest in diversified portfolios of securities issued by small, emerging companies, as defined in the legislation. The funds are constituted as closed condominium funds, and the redemption of quotas is forbidden. Investors can include any legal entities or natural persons resident or domiciled abroad, funds and other collective foreign investment entities.

LISTING AND REPORTING REQUIREMENTS

In addition to being registered with the CVM, listed companies must provide documents and information, including their by-laws, financial statements, minutes of shareholders' meetings and a complete set of forms describing the company, its history, capital structure, administrative, commercial and production data, accounting procedures and information relating to administrators, investments, and any other relevant facts. This information must be periodically updated and disclosed to both the CVM and the stock exchanges.

"Any other relevant facts" are considered to be any decisions or actions taken by the company that may have a substantial impact on its share price or on the decisions of investors regarding trading in the company's securities.

SHAREHOLDER PROTECTION CODES

A) Significant shareholdings

Any person or group of persons who directly or indirectly acquire shares amounting initially to 10% or more of a kind (common or preferred) or class of outstanding voting shares must provide the CVM with a public declaration stating the purpose of the acquisition and the quantity of shares bought. If participation increases by 5% or more, the same information must be disclosed.

Managers and directors of publicly held corporations must declare their investments in securities issued by that corporation or its affiliated companies. At the annual shareholders' meeting, shareholders representing at least 5% of the capital may demand additional disclosure from the directors as to securities held by them, their employment contracts and benefits.

B) Takeovers and mergers

The acquisition of control of a publicly held company by public offer is regulated by the Brazilian Corporation Law and is subject to CVM authorisation. Public offers must be made through a bank that will guarantee fulfilment of the obligations and commitments assumed by the offeror. The terms and conditions of the offer must be set out in an offer document signed by the offeror and its financial adviser.

Mergers and sales of assets and subsidiaries of Brazilian corporations are also governed by the Corporation Law. All shareholders are assured of the same rights in these transactions, although there are exceptions in relation to the transfer of control in publicly held companies. Any change in the characteristics of preferred shares must be justified and approved at a shareholders' meeting. Dissenting shareholders may withdraw from the company by requesting realisation of their shares.

C) Insider trading

Securities trading is prohibited when carried out by anyone who, by virtue of their office, title or position, gains knowledge of a relevant fact before it is disclosed to the public. This includes anyone in possession of information that they know is privileged and that has not yet been communicated to the market.

Subject to these rules, directors of publicly traded companies may deal freely in the shares of such companies at all times, provided they comply with reporting requirements.

RESEARCH

Research on the Brazilian market is available from a variety or organisations, including: Garantia, Bozano Simonsen, ICATÚ, Patrimonio, Pactual, ING Barings, Merrill Lynch, JP Morgan, Deutsche Morgan Grenfell and from both the São Paulo and Rio de Janeiro exchanges. Among other publications, Bovespa produces a daily bulletin, *BDI Bovespa*, a weekly report, and a monthly magazine, *Revista Bovespa*, which includes a technical report.

Bolsa Hoje (Today's Market) is the daily bulletin issued by BVRJ and distributed by the newspaper publishers of *O GLOBO*. Data include prices (opening, high, low, average and last) as well as volume traded, the value of turnover, indices and open interest in the options market.

BVRJ produces the *Quarterly Financial Report for Brazilian Companies*, issued in English, covering the financial statements of the 100 most traded companies.

IMF Editora (Tel: (55) 21 240 4347) publishes the *Brazil Company Handbook*, and is able to provide high-quality information on the stock market.

Brazil , published by Euromoney books, provides in-depth information for those wishing to invest and do business in the country. For details, see the order form at the back of this book.

CHAPTER

10

Bulgaria

Introduction

Despite six years of attempting to move towards a market-driven economy, foreign investment in Bulgaria remains low in comparison with other central and eastern European countries. After a 12-month trading suspension, the Bulgarian Stock Exchange-Sofia (BSE) received a licence to trade from the Securities and Stock Exchanges Commission on 21 October 1997. Other important developments have included the establishment of the Central Depository and requirements for a relatively high minimum capital (Lv100 million) and a minimum of 20 members to establish a stock exchange.

The BSE-Sofia now has 39 members, among which are the biggest Bulgarian banks and financial houses, as well as three foreign banks – Société Générale, ING Barings and the National Bank of Greece.

Since its revival, the Bulgarian stock market has been dominated by block trades, which represent registration of the forward contracts on the purchase of shares held by privatisation funds. Auction trading on the free market segment began on 24 November 1997.

ECONOMIC AND POLITICAL OVERVIEW

After the economic decline in Bulgaria in 1996, the Currency Board was set up in 1997 and the Deutschmark was chosen as reserve currency, with the Bulgarian lev pegged to the Deutschmark at Lv1,000 = DM1. This helped stabilise the financial system and dampened inflationary trends. A stabilisation programme was signed with the IMF and the World Bank and a set of austere and radical new measures for reforming the economy were adopted by the Bulgarian government. Foreign exchange reserves of the Bulgarian National Bank at the end of 1997 amounted to DM4,217 million, up from DM550 million the previous year.

In 1998 the government envisages 4% GDP growth, based on higher than expected FDI for 1997, which is expected to accelerate the inward capital investment process. The completion of several large privatisation deals and the speeding up of privatisation in all sectors of the economy are expected to further contribute to GDP growth. According to government forecasts, drastic cuts in government spending, higher tax collection and tighter financial control, plus a restrictive incomes policy, will allow Bulgaria to target a zero state budget deficit in 1999.

MARKET PERFORMANCE

A) In 1997

So far, only so-called block trading has taken place on the BSE. Block trades represent registration of the forward contracts on the purchase of shares held by privatisation funds, which were arranged prior to the re-opening of the exchange. Prices are negotiated in advance between buyer and seller and no third party can bid for the same deal. Thus, although the whole process is called "stock exchange trading", foreign investors cannot bid for any announced offer and prices are somewhat artificial. Similarly, market indicators such as capitalisation, yield and P/E ratios cannot be calculated for analytical purposes.

B) Summary information

Turnover (US$ terms, 1997): US$43.69 million

Number of shares traded (1997): 8,325,033

Number of domestic/foreign companies listed on the official market (end-1997): 0/0

Number of domestic/foreign companies registered on the free market (end-1997): 123/0

Short-term (3-month) interest rate (end-1997): 5.8%

Long-term (1-year) bond yield (end-1997): 9.12%

Budget deficit as a % of nominal GDP (end-1997): 3.09%

Annual increase in broad money (M2) supply (end-1997): 570%
Inflation rate (1997): 578.6%
US$ exchange rate (end-1997): Lv1,800

THE STOCK MARKET

A) Brief history and structure

The first Bulgarian Stock Exchange was inaugurated on 8 November 1991 and started trading in May 1992. In the same year another exchange – the Sofia Stock Exchange (SSE) – was established and, during the following two years, a further 20 stock exchanges sprang up across the country, functioning in a completely unregulated environment. The adoption of the Stock Exchanges and Securities Act in July 1995 led to a process of stock exchange consolidation, and five regional stock exchanges were merged into the First Bulgarian Stock Exchange which became the only operational stock exchange in Bulgaria. In December 1995, the First Bulgarian Stock Exchange changed its name and was re-registered as the Bulgarian Stock Exchange (BSE).

In 1996, the newly established Securities and Stock Exchange Commission introduced the requirement that all listed stocks should have their prospectuses approved by the Commission in order to trade on the BSE. Because no company complied with this requirement, trading on the BSE was suspended on 23 October 1996.

The newly elected government decided to set up a national stock exchange and that forced the BSE and the SSE to resume talks on a merger. In July 1997, the shareholders' meetings of the BSE and the SSE approved the merger and decided to rename the BSE the "Bulgarian Stock Exchange-Sofia". The shareholders also approved a capital increase that allowed the state to acquire a 49% stake. The first trading session of the new exchange took place on 10 October 1997. On 12 January 1998 the BSE launched its official floor and began trading in the shares of its first listed company – Elcabel.

The exchange currently has 176 shareholders comprising the Ministry of Finance (49%), banks, brokerage firms, insurance companies and a number of individuals. The BSE has 39 members, among which are banks and brokerage houses. The minimum capital requirement for members has been set at Lv90 million (DM90,000) for brokers acting as agents and Lv250 million (DM250,000) for full licence brokers acting as principals and underwriters.

B) Opening hours, names and addresses

Trading hours on the BSE are between 10.00am and 12.30pm, Monday to Friday.

BULGARIAN STOCK EXCHANGE
1 Macedonia Square, 1040 Sofia
Tel: (359) 2 815 711; Fax: (359) 2 875 566
E-mail: bsebg400.bg Web site: www.online.bg/bse

MARKET SIZE

A) Number of listings and market value

At the end of 1997, there were no officially listed and traded companies on the BSE. The first company to be officially listed was Elcabel, which obtained a quotation in January 1998. All trading to end-1997 was carried out on the free market.

B) Trading volume

Exhibit 10.1:
TURNOVER ON THE BSE, 1997

Year	*Volume (number of shares)*	*Value (Lv million)*
1997	8,325,033	77,335

Source: Bulgarian Stock Exchange.

OPERATIONS

A) Trading system

BSE trading sessions are organised using traditional open outcry (although this is supported by a computerised trading system). Brokers' and clients' buy and sell orders are entered into a computer and shown on large screens. Orders are matched according to their priority (price, time and volume) and the trades are registered by the system after operator confirmation. During the session, details of orders and current trades are broadcast via Reuters in real time.

The BSE is in the process of implementing a real-time electronic trading system designed to integrate the entire trading life-cycle.

B) List of principal brokers

CREDIT BANK
3 Angel Kanchev Str., Sofia
Tel: (359) 2 980 0074; Fax: (359) 2 981 5339

FINANCIAL BROKERAGE HOUSE "ELANA"
4 Kuzman Shapkarev Str., 1000 Sofia
Tel: (359) 2 980 6961; Fax: (359) 2 65 0380

FINANCIAL HOUSE EUROFINANCE
7 Sveta Nedelya Sq., 1000 Sofia
Tel: (359) 2 84 9911; Fax: (359) 2 84 9922

FIRST FINANCIAL BROKERAGE HOUSE
4 Lyuben Karavelov Str., Sofia
Tel: (359) 2 987 7296; Fax: (359) 2 805 689

FIRST INVESTMENT BANK
10 St. Karadja Str., 1000 Sofia
Tel: (359) 2 91 001; Fax: (359) 2 980 5033

ING BANK BRANCH SOFIA
7 Vassil Levski Str., 1000 Sofia
Tel: (359) 2 980 2039; Fax: (359) 2 981 5323

INTERNATIONAL ORTHODOX BANK
"ST. NICOLA"
155 Rakovski Str., 1000 Sofia
Tel: (359) 2 981 8150; Fax: (359) 2 980 7722

SOCIÉTÉ GÉNÉRALE
36 Dragan Tsankov bvd., 1040 Sofia
Tel: (359) 2 91 941, 981 2975; Fax: (359) 2 971 2978

UNITED BULGARIAN BANK
5 Sveta Sofia Str., 1000 Sofia
Tel: (359) 2 84 70 24 21; Fax: (359) 2 84 70 24 09

C) Settlement and transfer

Settlement of trades executed on the BSE is on a gross basis (ie, trades are not netted for each member of the BSE, but are settled on a trade-by-trade basis). The settlement cycle is T+3, with cash being settled first followed by securities. Although settlement is not simultaneous, for participants in the settlement process trades are settled on a delivery versus payment (DVP) basis. Securities settlement takes place via the computerised book entry system at the Central Depository.

All securities to be traded on the BSE must be issued in dematerialised form and be registered with the Central Depository, which was established as a joint stock company in August 1997. The Central Depository performs the following functions:

- the safe-keeping and registration of securities;
- the registration of securities transactions;
- the maintenance of the shareholders' register for all listed companies;
- the settlement of securities transactions;
- the opening and operating of accounts for dematerialised securities.

D) Commissions and other client costs

Commission rates for shares traded on the BSE are set at 0.2% of the nominal transaction value.

TAXATION AND REGULATIONS AFFECTING FOREIGN INVESTORS

A) Taxation

Companies registered (and therefore deemed resident) in Bulgaria are subject to tax on their worldwide income. Foreign-registered entities with headquarters abroad are subject to tax on Bulgarian-source income, but their Bulgarian branches or other permanent establishments are deemed Bulgarian resident companies for tax purposes.

Income derived outside Bulgaria by resident entities and branches of non-resident entities is included in the taxable base for the purpose of corporate income tax.

Profits tax

Basic corporate profits tax is levied at 30%, while a tax rate of 20% is applied to companies where annual profits do not exceed Lv50 million (about US$28,000). The profits tax for commercial banks and other financial institutions is 50%.

Withholding tax

A withholding tax of 15% is payable by non-resident investors on dividends and interest. The rate is reduced under double taxation treaties. Stock dividends are treated in the same way as cash dividends for tax purposes.

Capital gains tax

Realised capital gains are not treated independently and are taxed at the full corporate tax rate.

VAT rates

There is a single rate of 22%.

Stamp duty

No stamp duty is charged on share transfers.

B) Regulations

Trading in foreign currency may only be effected through banks, financial institutions, brokers and exchange offices licensed by the Bulgarian National Bank. Banks, as well as other financial institutions, may trade in foreign currency without limitation.

There are no restrictions on the repatriation of earnings, capital, royalties or interest.

Anyone, local or foreign, may place an unlimited amount of money in an unlimited number of accounts in any bank and any currency in Bulgaria.

LISTING AND REPORTING REQUIREMENTS

A) Listing requirements

In order to be either listed on the listed securities market or admitted to trading on the free market, companies must comply with the following general listing requirements:

- a prospectus, approved by the SSEC, must be submitted to the BSE;
- the shares to be issued must comply with all relevant legislation;
- equal rights must be granted to all shareholders; and
- transferability of shares must be unrestricted.

B) Reporting requirements

All listed companies must publish their interim and annual reports and submit them to the SSEC within 60 and 90 days respectively from the end of the fiscal period. Listed companies are also obliged to inform the BSE, within 10 days of being notified, of a shareholder controlling over 10% of their voting capital or of dealings in the company's shares by insiders.

SHAREHOLDER PROTECTION CODES

BSE members are required to deposit a sum equal to 5% of average daily trading value in the preceding month in a Settlement Guarantee Fund as a guarantee against default.

RESEARCH

The computer system of the BSE is directly connected to the Reuters information system on pages BGBSE1 to BGBSE6. Trading sessions will be reported in real time on pages BGBSE3 and BGBSE4, and members of the BSE will be able to trade through Reuters terminals.

The BSE provides foreign investors with information in English on its activities and members, such as listed companies, traded securities, authorised brokers, statistical data, the rules and regulations of the stock exchange and details of relevant legislation.

Eastern Europe: Investing for the 21st Century, published by Euromoney Books, provides in-depth information for those wishing to invest or do business in the region. See the order card at the back of this book for details.

PROSPECTIVE DEVELOPMENTS

During the course of 1998, the Bulgarian equity market is expected to begin operating to more sophisticated standards. Market prices based on real buy and sell orders will be available and some liquidity is likely to be introduced.

CHAPTER

11

Canada

Introduction

Once again, a heavy resource exposure proved to be a problem for the Canadian stock market in 1997, limiting the market's total return to 15% despite a strong start to the year. By autumn the whole market was drawn into the Asian vortex through the latter's negative impact on the Canadian/US dollar exchange rate and resulting upward pressure on Canadian interest rates. The Toronto Stock Exchange (TSE) 300 composite finished the year down over 7% from its late-September high.

Nevertheless, fallout from Asia was limited by the continuing economic and financial integration of Canada and the US, and the resulting decline in the resource dependence of both the economy and stock market. At year-end 1997, the natural resources sectors accounted for 25.7% of the TSE 300, compared with over 33.2% in 1993. Moreover, Canadian stock market indices exaggerate the importance of resources to the Canadian economy.

In recent years, the floating of control blocks held by family-owned conglomerates, the privatisation of state enterprises, and the easing or elimination of restrictions on foreign investment have enhanced the liquidity of the market. Reflecting healthy turnover, trading value on the Toronto Stock Exchange in 1997 amounted to 52% of the market capitalisation of the Canadian-based companies listed on the exchange.

Thanks to the recent rise in the popularity of mutual funds as a household investment vehicle, direct holdings by institutional investors (including foreigners) have now climbed above 60% of the total value of Canadian equities. Indeed, while households still hold the balance, they have been modest net sellers of equities on a direct basis through most of the 1990s. Rising institutional ownership of equities has also been driven by a shift towards professional management of provincial pension funds. Proposals to move to a market-oriented management of the federal government's universal Canada Pension Plan are now under review.

Capital markets are well developed in Canada, and larger corporations raise funds primarily through stock and bond issuance. Net new equity issues by corporations jumped to a record C$26.2 billion in 1997 from C$15.7 billion in 1996. However, by year-end the pace of new equity issuance had moderated substantially.

ECONOMIC AND POLITICAL OVERVIEW

Canada is a parliamentary democracy with a long history of peaceful coexistence between English, French and aboriginal founding peoples. Nevertheless, demands for additional or complete autonomy for the latter two groups have mounted over the past 25 years. Aided by the popularity of a new leader, Mr Lucien Bouchard, the separatist Parti Quebecois came close to winning a referendum on Quebec independence in 1995. However, polls indicate a significant slippage in support for separatism since that time and this issue appears likely to stay on the back burner through 1998 at least.

Having won a second four-year mandate in 1997 under Prime Minister Jean Chretien, the modestly left-of-centre Liberal Party continues to ride high in the polls. Ottawa has used a restrictive fiscal policy in recent years to achieve a dramatic elimination of its deficit. No sudden reversal to its traditional free spending ways appears imminent; the Liberals have pledged to split any modest surplus evenly between increased social spending, on the one hand, and debt reduction and

Exhibit 11.1: TORONTO SE (300) COMPOSITE PRICE INDEX (C$), 1993–97

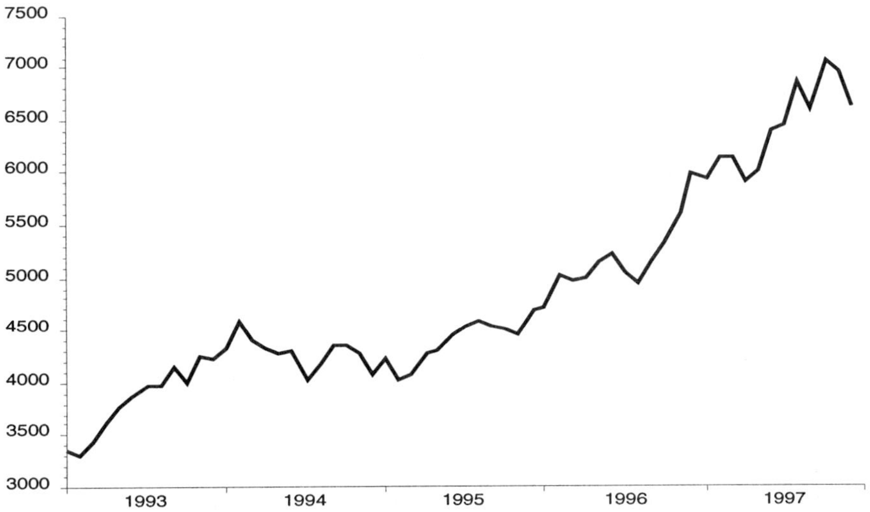

High value 7044.59 1.10.97 Low value 3310.90 1.2.93 *Source: Datastream*

tax cuts on the other. Following the 1997 election, the Reform Party led by Mr Preston Manning took over the role of official opposition from the Bloc Quebecois. While softening its stance recently on the need for tax cuts, Reform continues to make debt reduction a centrepiece of its policy platform.

Canada's economy has continued a gradual integration with that of the US following the further liberalisation of trade under NAFTA. Roughly 80% of Canadian merchandise trade in 1997 was with the US. While more dependent on commodities than other G7 nations, Canada's economy has less exposure than its stock market composition would suggest. Commodities amounted to less than 30% of merchandise exports in 1997, and automobiles and auto parts were the largest export items.

Led by robust growth of 17% in business investment, Canada's real GDP rebounded to 3.8% in 1997 from a meagre 1.2% in 1996. Despite this healthy growth, the unemployment rate declined only modestly through the year from 9.7% to 8.6%. This large pool of unemployed labour, coupled with further corporate and government restructuring and a plunge in commodity prices, sustained an overall trend of disinflation. By year-end 1997, consumer price inflation had declined to 0.8% – below the Bank of Canada's target range of 1–3%.

Role of the central bank

As with the US Federal Reserve Board, the Bank of Canada operates with a degree of autonomy from government that falls midway between the formerly tightly controlled Bank of England model and the independent German Bundesbank. While the Department of Finance appoints the Board of Governors of the bank, Ottawa has generally accepted candidates from within the bank as Governor. Mr Gordon Thiessen, the current Governor, is a career Bank of Canada employee, as were his three predecessors. While the Minister of Finance has ultimate control and responsibility for the broad thrust of monetary policy, in practice the Bank of Canada has free rein for routine operations. Given the mandate to assure price stability, the bank runs the day-to-day setting of short-term interest rates through a 25 basis point target band for the bank rate. Although there is no official target for the Canadian dollar, the Bank of Canada is acknowledged to run a "dirty float" in which it "leans against the wind" of major market pressures on the currency.

MARKET PERFORMANCE

A) In 1997

Following a top quartile performance in 1996, Canada's stock market slipped below the global average in 1997. Commodity price weakness acted as a drag on Canadian performance, both through its influence on resource stock prices and through its undermining of the Canadian dollar, which fell by US$0.03 over the year to close at US$0.699. In local currency terms, the TSE 300 was up by 13.0% in price and provided a 15.0% return including dividends.

After starting 1997 at a level of 5,927, the TSE 300 reached a high of 7,209 before fading to 6,699 by the year-end.

This moderate advance of the overall market index masked an enormous divergence in sector performance. Aided by a decline in Canadian bond yields, interest sensitive stocks achieved exceptional gains. Financial services jumped by 51%, while pipelines rose by 43% and utilities by 37.5%. Sectors linked to the domestic and US economy also scored good gains – notably transportation (31%), communications and media (28%) and merchandising (23%). These sectors benefited from an estimated 4.0% increase in real domestic demand in 1997.

By contrast, the four resource sectors suffered a lamentable year as the collapse of Asian stock markets lowered expectations for global growth. Gold tumbled by 44%, metals and minerals by 28% and forest products by 13%. Oil and gas mustered a slim 3% advance.

Sector price performance correlated broadly with the trends in earnings, where weakness in the resources negated the advance in consumer and interest sensitive earnings. Adjusted for non-recurring items, the TSE 300 earnings index stagnated for the second year in a row at an estimated C$298. Thus the year-end TSE 300 closing price represented a relatively high multiple of around 22.9 times 1997 earnings.

Trading in 1997 was partially fuelled by merger and acquisition activity. Including the value of assumed debt, the dollar value of M&A activity jumped 34% last year to a record C$100.9 billion. The number of transactions was up 7% to 1,274. While consolidation is under way in virtually all industries, the most active sectors in 1997 were communications and media, financial services, and oil and gas.

B) Summary information

Global ranking by market value (US$ terms, end-1997): 7
Market capitalisation (US$ billion, end-1997):
ME: 524.9; TSE: 567.8; VSE: 6.62
Growth in market value (local currency terms, 1993–97):
ME: 65.7%, TSE: -5.8%, VSE: 29.4%
Market value as a % of nominal GDP (end-1997): 94.77%
Number of companies listed (end-1997):
ME: 577; TSE: 1,420; VSE: 1,429
Market P/E (end-1997): ME 19.57; TSE: 22.86; VSE: N/A
MSCI total returns (with net dividends, US$ terms, 1997): 12.8
MSCI Index (change in US$ terms, 1997): +11.2
Short-term (3-month) interest rate (end-1997): 4%
Long-term (30-year government bond) yield (end-1997): 5.96%
Budget surplus as a % of nominal GDP (1997): 0.2%
Annual increase in broad money (M3) supply (Dec 1997): 4.5%
Inflation (1997): 0.8%
US$ exchange rate (end-1997): C$1.4305

C) Year-end share price indices, price/earnings ratios and yields

Exhibit 11.2:
TSE AND ME SHARE PRICE INDICES, P/E AND DIVIDEND YIELDS, 1993–97

Year-end	*Index*	*P/E*	*Yield (%)*
TSE			
1993	4,321.43	99.0	2.26
1994	4,213.61	21.6	2.40
1995	4,713.54	13.8	2.27
1996	5,927.03	24.2	1.83
1997	6,699.44	22.9	1.64
ME			
1993	2,062.71	N/A	0.01
1994	2,045.79	23.2	3.03
1995	2,317.39	13.1	2.81
1996	2,951.66	19.4	2.39
1997	3,404.46	19.6	2.10

Sources: Toronto Stock Exchange and Montreal Exchange.

D) Market indices and their constituents

The TSE Composite Index (usually called the TSE 300), introduced in January 1977, has a 1975 base value of 1,000 and is calculated from the capital-weighted average of its component share prices. The 300 shares included in the index are divided by the base and multiplied by 1,000. Separate indices and sub-indices are calculated daily for individual sectors including metals and minerals, gold and silver, oil and gas, paper and forest products, consumer and industrial products, real estate, transportation, pipelines, utilities, communications, merchandising, financial services and management companies.

The TSE also publishes the Toronto 35 Index for options and futures trading and has recently introduced sub-divisions to the TSE 300 (the Toronto 100 and Toronto 200) and the Montreal Exchange Market Portfolio.

The Canadian Market Portfolio Index (XXM), comprising 25 of the most heavily capitalised stocks listed on at least two Canadian exchanges, is the main index published by the ME. The XXM was introduced in 1986 and has a base value of 1,000 at 4 January 1983. It is a non-weighted price index calculated using the arithmetic average of the prices of its component stocks. The ME also has six sectorial indices covering banking, oil and gas, utilities, forest products, industrial products, and mining and minerals. To obtain a representative cross-section of the Canadian economy, these sectorial indices include some medium-sized firms as well as those that are heavily capitalised.

The VSE Index was originally introduced in 1982 on an arithmetic price-weighted basis to chart the progress of the exchange's junior companies. It was changed to a capital-weighted basis at the beginning of 1986 and three sub-indices were introduced on 1 June 1990. The VSE Index, now referred to as the VSE Composite Index, is a composite of the three sub-indices – commercial/industrial, resource and venture.

THE STOCK MARKET

A) Brief history and structure

The TSE was formed in 1852 as an association of businessmen who met to exchange holdings of securities. They operated as a partnership until 1878 when the exchange was incorporated by a special Act of the Ontario legislature. In 1977, the TSE introduced the computer-assisted trading system (CATS), the world's first truly automated auction system for trading equities in a screen-based environment. All stocks are now traded under the CATS system and, as a result, in April 1997 the trading floor was closed.

The Montreal Exchange is Canada's oldest stock market. While its origins go back to 1817, it was officially incorporated by an Act of the Quebec legislature in 1874. In 1983, the ME became the first Canadian exchange to introduce an automated order-routing and execution system. In September 1990 it implemented an electronic order book for the automated registration, matching and confirmation of market and limit orders for more than 700 stocks inter-listed with the TSE. The electronic book is now accessible from direct access terminals installed in member firms' offices throughout Canada.

The VSE was incorporated in 1907 to serve as a central market-place for raising capital in western Canada. The VSE is widely recognised as one of the major venture capital markets of the world and has become an integral part of the financing process of natural resources and high technology companies in their early stages of development. Since 1990 the VSE has operated a fully automated trading system. In 1996 it launched an evening trading session, VISTA, which corresponds to the beginning of the business day in the Asia Pacific region, thus allowing brokers in Hong Kong or Australia to trade VSE listed stocks in real time.

The Alberta and Winnipeg exchanges specialise in regional stocks and commodities.

Each of the Canadian stock exchanges is a self-regulatory organisation (SRO) with its own by-laws, rules and policies governing members, listed issuers and transactions conducted on or through the exchange and its members. These are broadly similar from exchange to exchange. The stock exchanges are non-profit making organisations, the expenses of which are met by the transaction fees and/or subscriptions paid by members and by companies that are quoted on them, as well as by the sale of electronic and other market data.

The exchanges are each directed by a Governing Committee or Board of Governors comprising members' representatives as well as public governors. These bodies oversee the general business of each exchange, member discipline and the admission of new members.

B) Different exchanges

There are five exchanges in Canada, located in Toronto, Montreal, Vancouver, Alberta and Winnipeg.

C) Opening hours, names and addresses

Trading of stocks on Canadian exchanges takes place during usual North American stock exchange business hours, from 9.30am to 4.00pm (Eastern time), Monday to Friday. The ME offers investors extended trading sessions in both the early morning (8.15am–9.15am) and late afternoon (4.15pm–5.15pm) and the TSE has extended hours in the afternoon (4.15pm–5.00pm). The VSE's evening trading session, VISTA, runs from 5.30pm to 8.30pm.

THE TORONTO STOCK EXCHANGE
The Exchange Tower, PO Box 450, 2 First Canadian Place,
Toronto, Ontario, M5X 1J2
Tel: (1) 416 947 4700; Fax: (1) 416 947 4662

THE MONTREAL EXCHANGE
The Stock Exchange Tower, PO Box 61,
800 Victoria Square, Montreal, Quebec, H4Z 1A9
Tel: (1) 514 871 2424; Fax: (1) 514 871 3553
Internet: www.bdm.org (French) www.me.org (English)

THE VANCOUVER STOCK EXCHANGE
PO Box 10333, 609 Granville Street
Vancouver, BC, V7Y 1H1
Tel: (1) 604 689 3334; Fax: (1) 604 688 6051
E-mail: information.vse.ca Internet: www.vse.ca

THE ALBERTA STOCK EXCHANGE
21st Floor, 300-5th Avenue South West
Calgary, Alberta, T2P 3C4
Tel: (1) 403 262 7791; Fax: (1) 403 237 0450

THE WINNIPEG STOCK EXCHANGE
2901 One Lombard Place, Winnipeg, Manitoba, R3B 0Y2
Tel: (1) 204 942 8431; Fax: (1) 204 947 9536

MARKET SIZE

A) Number of listings and market value

Exhibit 11.3:
STATISTICAL SUMMARY OF LISTINGS ON CANADIAN EXCHANGES, 1996–97

	1996			*1997*		
	ME	*TSE*	*VSE*	*ME*	*TSE*	*VSE*
No. of companies listed	555	1,328	1,495	577	1,420	1,429
No. of issues listed	828	1,626	1,610	852	1,720	1,547
Total quoted market value (C$ billion)	639.0	1,176.7	14.7	750.8	812.3	9.47

Sources: Montreal Exchange, Toronto Stock Exchange and Vancouver Stock Exchange.

B) Largest quoted companies

Exhibit 11.4:
THE 20 LARGEST LISTED COMPANIES ON THE TSE, END-1997

Ranking	*Company*	*Market value (C$ million)*
1	Mobil Corporation	94,873
2	Citicorp	76,172
3	General Motors	65,135
4	Amoco Corporation	60,491
5	Chrysler Corporation	41,096
6	Northern Telecom	33,036
7	BCE Inc	30,288
8	British Gas plc ADS	28,631
9	Thomson Corporation	23,831
10	Royal Bank of Canada	23,302
11	Phillips Petroleum Co	19,305
12	Canadian Imperial Bank of Commerce	18,436
13	Bank of Montreal	16,561
14	Bank of Nova Scotia	16,494
15	Seagram Company Ltd	16,407
16	Toronto Dominion Bank	15,974
17	Imperial Oil Ltd	13,943
18	Occidental Petroleum Group	13,827
19	Canadian Pacific Ltd	13,197
20	Imasco Ltd	11,545

Source: Toronto Stock Exchange.

Exhibit 11.5:
THE 20 LARGEST LISTED COMPANIES ON THE ME, END-1997

Ranking	*Company*	*Market value (C$ million)*
1	Northern Telecom Ltd	33,469
2	BCE Inc	31,473
3	Royal Bank of Canada	25,065
4	Thomson Corporation	23,196
5	Canadian Imperial Bank of Commerce	20,122
6	Bank of Nova Scotia	17,933
7	Bank of Montreal	17,730
8	Seagram Company Ltd	16,627
9	Toronto-Dominion Bank	16,543
10	Imperial Oil Ltd	13,864
11	Canadian Pacific Ltd	13,255
12	Imasco Ltd	11,554
13	Bombardier Inc	10,284
14	Barrick Gold Corporation	9,943
15	Alcan Aluminum Ltd	9,195
16	Power Financial Corporation	9,173
17	Edper Brascan Corporation	7,469
18	Shell Canada Limited	7,437
19	TransCanada Pipelines Limited	7,334
20	Great-West Lifeco Inc	7,116

Source: Montreal Exchange.

Exhibit 11.6:
THE 20 LARGEST LISTED COMPANIES ON THE VSE, END-1997

Ranking	*Company*	*Market value (C$ million)*
1	Mountain Province Mining Inc.	237.2
2	Ultra Petroleum Corp	205.3
3	Francisco Gold Corp	180.1
4	Cambras Comms Corp	140.3
5	GST Global Telecommunications	117.9
6	GenSei Regeneration Sciences Inc	100.7
7	ThrillTime Entertainment	82.7
8	High Desert Mineral resources Inc	79.2
9	Star Choice Communications Inc	78.6
10	Ridgeway Petroleum Corp	73.5
11	Forbes Medi-Tech Inc	72.5
12	Northwest Sports Enterprises Ltd	70.4
13	Arizona Star Resource Corp	70.2
14	Donner Minerals Ltd	65.1
15	Mosaic Oil NL	64.7
16	Datawave Sustem Inc	63.3
17	Metro Resources Company Ltd	60.7
18	First Silver Reserve Inc	56.5
19	Q1 Technologies Corp	54.7
20	First Quantum Mrls Ltd	52.8

Source: Vancouver Stock Exchange.

C) Trading volume

Turnover value on Canada's four main exchanges totalled C$497.6 billion in 1997, up 34.7% on 1996's C$369.4 billion. Total trading volume in 1997 was 40.4 billion shares, up from 39.1 billion in 1996.

Exhibit 11.7:
TRADING VALUE ON CANADIAN EXCHANGES, 1996–97

	1996		*1997*	
	(C$ million)	*%*	*(C$ million)*	*%*
Toronto	301,298.9	81.6	423,169.6	85.0
Montreal	50,166.6	13.6	61,911.7	12.4
Vancouver	12,003.5	3.2	8,670.3	1.8
Alberta	5,971.4	1.6	3,870.7	0.8
Total	369,441.0	100.0	497,622.3	100.0

Source: Toronto Stock Exchange.

Exhibit 11.8:
TRADING VOLUME ON CANADIAN EXCHANGES, 1996–97

	1996		*1997*	
	Volume (million)	*%*	*Volume (million)*	*%*
Toronto	22,341.1	57.2	25,670.2	62.6
Montreal	4,302.0	11.0	4,320.9	10.5
Vancouver	8,322.1	21.3	7,116.0	17.3
Alberta	4,102.2	10.5	3,292.2	4.2
Total	39,067.5	100.0	40,399.3	100.0

Source: Toronto Stock Exchange.

Exhibit 11.9:
THE 20 MOST ACTIVELY TRADED SHARES ON THE TSE, 1997

Ranking	*Company*	*Trading value (C$ million)*
1	Northern Telecom	9,864
2	Newbridge Network	9,835
3	Barrick Gold	8,882
4	Alcan Aluminum	7,206
5	Inco Ltd	6,039
6	Canadian Pacific Ltd	5,754
7	Placer Dome	5,708
8	Petro Canada C/V	5,510
9	Seagram Co	5,490
10	BCE Inc	5,161
11	Bombardier Inc Cl B	5,139
12	Royal Bank of Canada	5,101
13	Renaissance Energy	4,806
14	Canadian Imperial Bank of Commerce	4,085
15	Canadian Occidental Petroleum	3,995
16	Talisman Energy	3,840
17	Canadian Natural Resources	3,652
18	Magna International Cl A	3,662
19	Noranda Inc	3,423
20	Nova Corp	3,343

Exhibit 11.9 continued

Source: Toronto Stock Exchange.

Exhibit 11.10:
THE 20 MOST ACTIVELY TRADED SHARES ON THE ME, 1997

Ranking	*Company*	*Trading value (C$ million)*
1	Bombardier Inc Class B	2,296
2	BCE Inc	2,169
3	Bank of Montreal	2,164
4	Royal Bank of Canada	2,080
5	Biochem Pharma Inc	1,643
6	Canadian Imperial Bank of Commerce	1,568
7	Bank of Nova Scotia	1,441
8	National Bank of Canada	1,341
9	Toronto Dominion Bank	1,316
10	Alcan Aluminum Ltd	1,171
11	Inco Ltd	891
12	Canadian Pacific Ltd	804
13	Imperial Oil Ltd	774
14	Nova Corporation	757
15	Northern Telecom Ltd	756
16	Air Canada	740
17	Seagram Company Ltd	713
18	TransCanada Pipelines Ltd	676
19	Telus Corporation	633
20	Moore Corporation	591

Source: Montreal Exchange.

Exhibit 11.11:
THE 10 MOST ACTIVELY TRADED SHARES ON THE VSE, 1997

Ranking	*Company*	*Trading value (C$ million)*
1	Francisco Gold Corp	342.3
2	Cross Lake Minerals Ltd	312.3
3	Ultra Petroleum Corp	283.2
4	Arizona Star Resource Corp	282.3
5	Forecross Corp US$	221.2
6	Hixon Gold Res Inc	167.2
7	Winspear Resources Ltd	135.7
8	Net Nanny Software International Inc	110.2
9	Pacific Rim Mining Corp	99.5
10	Sutton Resources Ltd	89.1

Source: Vancouver Stock Exchange.

TYPES OF SHARE

There are three principal categories of equity or quasi-equity securities traded on Canadian stock markets: common shares, preferred shares and restricted shares.

Under the corporate laws of most of the principal Canadian jurisdictions, it is possible to create classes of shares having a wide variety of rights, privileges, restrictions and conditions. Where an Ontario or federally incorporated company has only one class of share, the rights of holders must be equal in all respects and must include the rights (a) to vote at any meeting of shareholders of the corporation; (b) to receive any dividend declared by the corporation; and (c) to receive the remaining property of the corporation on dissolution. If there is more than one class of share, these rights must be attached to at least one class, but all such rights are not required to be attached to the same class. Accordingly, it is possible to create various types of "uncommon" equity such as non-voting participating shares, multiple voting shares and preferred shares.

Common shares

Under the TSE and OSC (Ontario Securities Commision) policies, shares cannot be designated as common shares unless the votes attached to them are exercisable regardless of the number of shares owned and unless the voting rights are, on a per share basis, not less than those attached to any other class of the issuer's shares. Participating shares that do not meet these criteria may be classified as "restricted shares" for TSE and OSC purposes, and become subject to the special rules discussed below.

Preferred shares

For shares to be designated as preferred shares they must have attached a preference over the shares of another class of the issuer's securities. Typical preferences are the rights to priority in payment of dividends and in the repayment of capital on dissolution.

Restricted shares

Restricted shares encompass various forms of equity and, as defined by the TSE and the OSC, include any fully participating shares that are not common shares (see above). Restricted shares include non-voting shares, restricted voting shares and subordinate voting shares, but do not include non-participating preferred shares.

Although it was decided in 1984 that restricted shares should not be banned from trading on the TSE, such shares are subject to additional rules requiring, among other things, that:

a) The shares should not be described as "common" or "preferred" but be designated with an appropriate restricted share term such as "non-voting", "subordinate voting" or "restricted voting" shares.
b) Additional disclosure should be made of the restrictions attached to the shares in a prospectus for a public issue of restricted shares and in other shareholder material such as proxy statements.
c) All stock quotations, such as those listed in newspapers and dealer confirmations, should include a code identifying the shares as restricted shares.
d) Holders of restricted shares should be sent all material, such as proxy circulars and annual reports, required by law to be sent to holders of the issuer's voting securities, and should be permitted to attend and speak at shareholders' meetings.

Other types of securities

In addition to the three principal categories of listed equity securities, Canadian stock exchanges also list and post for trading, rights and warrants to purchase securities, depository and instalment receipts for securities, real estate limited partnership units and closed-end investment trust units. Depository receipts represent fully paid underlying shares, the certificates for which are held by a custodian (usually a bank or trust company). Holders of depository receipts have the same rights as holders of the underlying shares. Instalment receipts represent the right of the registered holder to acquire the specified shares on payment in full of the final instalment of the purchase price. Upon such payment and presentation and surrender of the instalment receipt, the shares represented will be registered in the name of the registered holder of the instalment receipt.

OTHER MARKETS

Over-the-counter (OTC) business in Canada accounts for less than 4% of total equity trading each year. Most issues are resource-oriented.

INVESTORS

A 1997 survey conducted by the TSE found that among the adult population:

- 24% own stocks directly;
- 43% own mutual funds;
- 35% own GICS and term deposits of some sort.

Institutional investors (including foreigners) own over 60% of the Canadian equity market, driven by the rise in popularity of mutual funds as an investment vehicle and the shift toward professional management of provisional pension funds.

Exhibit 11.12:
TOP PERFORMING COUNTRY FUNDS – CANADA

Fund	US$ % change 31/12/96 31/12/97	US$ % change 31/12/92 31/12/97	Currency	Fund size (US$ mil)	Volatility	Manager name	Main sector	Class
Acuity Pooled Canadian Equity	40.64	N/A	C$	0.12	N/A	Acuity Investment Management (Pooled)	Equities	Canadian Mutuals
CDA Special Equity Fund (KBSH)	39.98	N/A	C$	13.96	N/A	Canadian Dental Association	Equities	Canadian Mutuals
Phillips, Hager & N Div Inc	38.4	150.85	C$	355.54	2.74	Phillips, Hager & North Investment Management Ltd.	Equities	Canadian Mutuals
REA Inc. d'Invissement IDEM	37.63	47.84	C$	43.07	3.1	REA Inc. (Fonds d'investissement)	Equities	Canadian Mutuals
AIC Advantage Fund	37.22	300.14	C$	1,520.77	5.04	AIC Advantage Fund Series	Equities	Canadian Mutuals
The Pharmaceutical Trust C$	35.74	N/A	C$	19.42	N/A	First Trust Canadian Trust, Series 1	Equities	Canadian Mutuals
AIC Advantage Fund II	35.34	N/A	C$	2,513.11	N/A	AIC Advantage Fund Series	Equities	Canadian Mutuals
The Goodwood Fund	35.13	N/A	C$	1.02	N/A	The Goodwood Fund	Equities	Canadian Mutuals
Standard Life Canadian Div Mtl	34.88	N/A	C$	23.07	2.99	Standard Life Mutual Funds Limited	Equities	Canadian Mutuals
Scudder Canadian Equity Fund	34.32	N/A	C$	164.68	N/A	Scudder Funds of Canada	Equities	Canadian Mutuals
Quebec Growth Fund Inc.	34.28	96.1	C$	13.87	3.56	Montrusco Associates Inc.	Equities	Canadian Mutuals
McLean Budden Amr Eq – Pool	33.09	124.3	C$	119.8	N/A	McLean Budden Ltd.	Equities	Canadian Mutuals
Talvest/Hyperion Sm Cap CD Eq	31.78	N/A	C$	175.9	4.21	Talvest Hyperion Funds	Equities	Canadian Mutuals
National Trust Dividend Fund	31.75	95.11	C$	88.53	2.48	National Trust Mutual Funds	Equities	Canadian Mutuals
Rothschild American Equity	31.34	N/A	C$	33.47	N/A	Investors Group/Rothschild Select	Equities	Canadian Mutuals
CIBC U.S. Index RRSP Fund	31.07	N/A	C$	126.96	N/A	CIBC Securities Inc.	Equities	Canadian Mutuals
Glb Strat Dvrs Latin America	30.92	N/A	C$	13.26	6.37	Global Strategy – Diversified Funds	Equities	Canadian Mutuals
McLean Budden American Growth	30.7	102.54	C$	14.04	N/A	McLean Budden Ltd.	Equities	Canadian Mutuals
Associate Investors Limited	30.15	110.71	C$	9.8	2.66	Leon Frazer, Black & Associates Limited	Equities	Canadian Mutuals
Royal Dividend Fund	29.67	N/A	C$	1,346.94	2.89	Royal Mutual Funds	Equities	Canadian Mutuals
First Canadian Dividend Inc	29.48	N/A	C$	719.59	2.68	Bank of Montreal Investment Mgmt. Ltd.	Equities	Canadian Mutuals
Clean Environment Intl Equity	29.36	N/A	C$	14.73	3.9	Clean Environment Mutual Funds Ltd.	Equities	Canadian Mutuals
Growsafe US 500 Index Fund	28.85	N/A	C$	45.15	N/A	Transamerica Life Insurance Co. of Canada	Equities	Canadian Mutuals
Clean Environment Equity Fund	28.68	130.51	C$	135.42	3.47	Clean Environment Mutual Funds Ltd.	Equities	Canadian Mutuals
Green Line Dividend Fund	27.56	83.81	C$	292.74	2.68	TD Asset Management Inc.	Equities	Canadian Mutuals
NN Can-Euro Fund	27.09	N/A	C$	85.72	N/A	NN Financial Services Ltd.	Equities	Canadian Mutuals
AIC Diversified Canada Fund	26.48	N/A	C$	956.13	3.58	AIC Diversified Fund Series	Equities	Canadian Mutuals
Bissett Canadian Equity Fund	25.96	141.05	C$	212.15	3.37	Bissett & Associates Investment Mgmt. Lt	Equities	Canadian Mutuals
Optima Str : Canadian Eq Sect	25.6	N/A	C$	396.62	3.34	Optima Strategy Funds	Equities	Canadian Mutuals
Phillips, Hager & N US Pl Pen	25.27	129.09	C$	447.62	2.99	Phillips, Hager & North Investment Mgmt Ltd.	Equities	Canadian Mutuals
Growsafe European 100 Index	24.53	N/A	C$	22.13	N/A	Transamerica Life Insurance Co. of Canada	Equities	Canadian Mutuals
CMI GNF Canadian Equity	24.16	94.86	C$	4.02	2.82	CMI Global Network Fund	Equity Growth	Hong Kong SFC Authorised
CMI GNF Canadian Equity	24.16	94.86	C$	3.96	2.75	CMI Global Network Fund	Equity	Luxembourg
CMI GNF Canadian Equity	24.16	94.86	C$	4.02	2.82	CMI Global Network Fund (LUX)	Equity Growth	UK FSA Recognised
CMI GNF Canadian Equity	24.16	94.86	C$	4.02	4.74	CMI Global Network Fund (LUX)	Equity Growth	Investmentfds Deutschland
Millennium Next Genr MWIML	23.73	N/A	C$	23.91	5.12	Morrison Williams Investment Mgmt. Ltd.	Equities	Canadian Mutuals
Investors Canadian Small Cap	23.7	N/A	C$	526.91	N/A	Investors Group	Equities	Canadian Mutuals
Saxon Small Cap	22.68	108.28	C$	14.9	3.17	Saxon Group of Funds	Equities	Canadian Mutuals
CMI Passport Canadian Equity	22.55	N/A	C$	0.07	N/A	CMI Passport	Equity	Offshore Territories
Strat Value Canadian Eq Value	22.26	N/A	C$	12.89	N/A	Strategic Value Funds Management Inc.	Equities	Canadian Mutuals

Note: details for some funds may not have been included if the data for the US$ % change for 96/97 was not available

Source: Standard & Poor's Micropal.

OPERATIONS

A) Trading system

The way in which equities are traded varies between the different exchanges.

Toronto Stock Exchange

The TSE trading floor closed in April 1997 and all listed stocks are now traded under the CATS system, pending the launch of the new trading engine, TOREX.

Montreal Stock Exchange

The Montreal Direct Access system provides the trading desks of member firms with access to the Electronic Order Book, through existing terminals. In addition to this rapid, flexible and low-cost screen trading function, the Montreal Direct Access system provides member firms with extensive market information and internal order management features.

Vancouver Stock Exchange

The VSE, using its Vancouver Computerised Trading (VCT) system, has been fully automated since 1990. In July 1995 the VSE launched a trading interface called VITAL (Vancouver Interface for Trading Access Links). VITAL provides a gateway for order management systems to access VCT. Many brokerage firms use order management systems services to route orders to various stock exchanges. Three such systems providers currently access VCT through VITAL.

B) List of principal brokers

The following list includes members of the TSE, ME and VSE.

BUNTING WARBURG INC
Suite 4100, 161 Bay Street, Toronto, Ontario, M5J 2S1
Tel: (1) 416 364 3293; Fax: (1) 416 364 1976

CIBC WOOD GUNDY
161 Bay Street, PO Box 500, Toronto, Ontario M5J 2S8
Tel: (1) 416 594 7000

FIRST MARATHON SECURITIES
Suite 3200, 2 First Canadian Place,
Toronto, Ontario, M5X 1J9
Tel: (1) 416 869 3707 Fax: (1) 416 869 0089

GOEPEL SHIELDS
701 W Georges Street, Suite 1100, Vancouver,
BC V7Y 1C6
Tel: (1) 604 61 1777

GORDON CAPITAL CORP
Box 67, Suite 5300, Toronto Dominion Center,
Toronto, Ontario, M5K 1E7
Tel: (1) 416 868 7800

LÉVESQUE BEAUBIEN GEOFFRION
Edifice Sun Life, 1155, rue Metcalfe, 5e étage
Montreal, Quebec, H3B 4S9
Tel: (1) 514 879 2222

LOEWEN, ONDAATJE, McCUTCHEON LTD
Suite 2250, 55 Avenue Road, Toronto, Ontario, M5R 3L2
Tel: (1) 416 964 4455; Fax: (1) 416 964 4490

MAISON PLACEMENTS CANADA INC
Place du Canada, Bureau 2230, Montreal,
Quebec, H3B 2N2
Tel: (1) 514 879 1662

MIDLAND WALWYN CAPITAL
BCE Place, Suite 400 – 181 Bay Street
Toronto, Ontario, M5J 2V8
Tel: (1) 416 369 7400; Fax: (1) 416 369 7680

NESBITT BURNS LIMITED
1 First Canadian Place, Suite 5000, PO Box 150
Toronto, Ontario, M5X 1H3
Tel: (1) 416 365 4000; Fax: (1) 416 359 4311

RBC DOMINION SECURITIES
200 Bay Street, PO Box 500, Royal Bank Plaza
3rd Floor, South Tower, Toronto, Ontario M5J 2W7

SCOTIA McLEOD INC
40 King Street West, Box 4085, Station A
Scotia Plaza, Suite 6600, Toronto, Ontario, M5W 2X6
Tel: (1) 416 863 7411; Fax: (1) 416 863 7751

YORKTON SECURITIES INC
Suite 3100, 181 Bay Street, Toronto, Ontario, M5J 2T3
Tel: (1) 416 864 3500; Fax: (1) 416 864 9134

C) Settlement and transfer

The settlement date for trading on Canadian stock exchanges is the third trading day after the transaction date, unless otherwise provided by the exchange or agreed between the parties. The Canadian Depository for Securities (CDS) provides automated facilities for the clearing and custody of securities traded on all Canadian exchanges. Increasingly, the bulk of trades are settled in the CDS's book-based system via a continuous net settlement process.

Options and futures contracts traded at the ME are

cleared by Canadian Derivatives Clearing Corporation (CDCC), which is jointly owned by the major Canadian exchanges. The settlement date for options trades is the day after a transaction via direct debit payment to CDCC, which subsequently pays the premium to the receiving party.

D) Commissions and other costs

In April 1983, the fixed commission rate structure for exchange members on the ME and TSE was abolished in favour of negotiated commission rates. The VSE followed suit in 1988. A number of discount brokerage firms began operating after deregulation. Similar to US discount brokers, these firms charge lower commission rates but they generally do not provide research or investment advice.

TAXATION AND REGULATIONS AFFECTING FOREIGN INVESTORS

Over the past 15 years, Ottawa has relaxed most of the restrictions on foreign investment. The role of the Foreign Investment Review Agency in screening foreign takeovers has been minimised, and the burden of proof has shifted from making the positive case for foreign capital to demonstrating a detrimental impact. Restrictions remain in place in the so-called 'cultural' industries, such as cable companies, publishers, airlines and banks.

A) Investment restrictions

Foreign equity investors are generally subject to the same regulations as domestic equity investors when they purchase equity shares through a Canadian stock exchange. However, foreign investors may be restricted from buying or holding equity shares of companies subject to Canadian ownership requirements. Certain financial institutions such as banks, some Canadian oil and gas companies, broadcasting companies and publicly held Ontario investment dealers are subject to limitations on the percentage of their equity shares that may be held by non-residents of Canada.

In addition, a transaction that will result in the acquisition of control of a corporation or other entity that carries on, directly or indirectly, a "Canadian business", may require prior ministerial approval under the Investment Canada Act (ICA). The acquisition of one-third or more of the voting shares of a corporation is presumed, in the absence of evidence to the contrary, to be an acquisition of control for ICA purposes.

Approval under the ICA is not required (although notice of the acquisition may have to be given) for a direct acquisition of control of a foreign corporation which carries on the "Canadian business" directly as a branch or division of the foreign corporation, or for a direct acquisition of control of a "Canadian business" having assets of less than C$5 million, or an indirect acquisition of control of a "Canadian business" having assets of less than C$50 million. However, these exemptions do not apply if the "Canadian business" is related to Canada's cultural heritage or national identity (as prescribed by ICA regulations). Nor do they apply in the case of an indirect acquisition of a "Canadian business" having assets of between C$5 million and C$50 million, if such assets represent more than 50% of the assets acquired as part of a larger transaction or the acquisition is not effected through the acquisition of control of a foreign corporation. The threshold limits are higher in the case of acquisitions from or by Americans.

B) Taxation

Under Canadian tax law, a non-resident of Canada who disposes of shares of a Canadian public corporation that are listed on a prescribed stock exchange is generally not subject to Canadian capital gains tax unless the non-resident (together with any non-arm's length persons) has held 25% or more of any class or series of shares of the particular corporation at any time during the five-year period immediately before the disposition. This general rule is subject to a number of specific exceptions. Canada's ability to tax capital gains may also be restricted if the non-resident is a resident of a jurisdiction that has a bilateral tax treaty with Canada.

Dividends paid by a Canadian public corporation to a non-resident of Canada are subject to Canadian withholding tax at source. The general withholding tax rate is 25% of the gross amount of the dividend, subject to reduction if the dividend recipient is a resident of a jurisdiction that has a bilateral tax treaty with Canada.

Exhibit 11.13:
WITHHOLDING TAX

Recipient	*Dividends %*	*Interest %*
Resident corporations and individuals	Nil	Nil
Non-resident corporations and individuals:		
Non-treaty	25	25
Treaty	5–25	10–25

Source: Price Waterhouse.

C) Exchange controls

Canada has no system of exchange controls and, subject to the restrictions already discussed, foreign investment has traditionally been welcomed in Canada and has played a significant role in the growth of the Canadian economy. It is estimated that approximately 56% of

Canada's manufacturing industry and over 60% of the petroleum industry is foreign controlled. A major portion of foreign control (approximately 75%) is by US residents.

LISTING AND REPORTING REQUIREMENTS

In 1991, the Canadian Securities Administrators and the US Securities and Exchange Commission adopted a multi-jurisdictional disclosure system (MJDS) intended to facilitate cross-border securities offerings, issuer bids, takeover bids, rights offerings, business combinations and continuous disclosure filings. This policy permits substantial Canadian and US issuers to satisfy certain offering and reporting requirements by submitting disclosure documents that comply only with the requirements of the home country of the issuer. The underlying objective of the policy is to encourage the fair treatment of Canadian and US investors who have been excluded from rights offerings, takeover bids, and business combinations in the past because of the extra costs of complying with the rules of more than one country.

The System for Electronic Data Analysis and Retrieval (SEDAR) was implemented in 1997 and, as a result, all public issuers (other than "foreign issuers" as defined below) are now required to file prescribed disclosure documents electronically. Issuers not incorporated or organised under Canadian laws will not be required to file under SEDAR unless more than 50% of their voting securities are registered in the names of Canadian residents and either:

(a) (i) the majority of the senior officers or directors of the issuer are citizens or residents of Canada, or (ii) more than 50% of the value of the issuer's assets are located in Canada, or (iii) the business of the issuer is administered principally in Canada; or

(b) the issuer has a class of securities listed and posted for trading on a Canadian stock exchange and is not inter-listed on an exchange in any other country.

"Foreign issuers" may elect to make electronic filings even where they are not required to do so. However, once they elect to file electronically, they must continue to do so for at least two years.

A) Listing requirements

In order to become listed on the TSE, or on any of the other Canadian stock exchanges, the issuer must enter into a listing agreement. In the case of the TSE, the agreement requires payment of an initial fee based on the number of shares to be listed and an annual sustaining fee. By becoming listed an issuer is, in effect, bound by the following provisions:

1. To comply with all rules of the TSE.
2. Not to undergo a material change in its business or affairs without the prior consent of the TSE, unless the issuer is exempted from this requirement by the TSE.
3. To make timely disclosure of all material changes and of certain other specified events.
4. Not to issue any securities (other than debt securities that cannot be converted into equity securities) without the prior consent of the TSE.
5. To maintain transfer and registration facilities in Toronto where all listed securities shall be directly transferable and registerable.
6. To notify the TSE at least seven trading days in advance of each dividend record date.
7. To file with the TSE copies of all financial statements required by law or by the TSE to be published or filed for inspection.
8. To file with the TSE copies of all notices, reports or other written correspondence sent by the issuer to holders of its listed securities.
9. To notify the TSE on a monthly basis of any changes to the number of issued securities of any listed class.
10. Not to change the provisions attaching to warrants, rights or other securities outstanding from time to time (other than debt securities that cannot be converted into equity securities) without the prior consent of the TSE.
11. To pay, when due, any applicable fees or charges established by the TSE from time to time.
12. To furnish to the TSE, at any time upon demand, such other information or documentation concerning the issuer as the TSE may reasonably require.

The TSE has published the following minimum listing requirements for foreign companies seeking to list shares on the TSE:

1. Net tangible assets of at least C$10 million.
2. Average pre-tax earnings for the past three financial years of C$2 million.
3. A minimum of one million issued shares held by a minimum of 3,000 public shareholders.
4. The number of issued shares held by the public should have a market value of at least C$10 million.
5. If the applicant company is not listed on a major stock exchange recognised by the TSE for this purpose, there should be 300 public shareholders each holding one board lot or more who are residents of Canada; if the applicant company is listed on a major stock exchange recognised by the TSE for this purpose, there is no requirement to have a Canadian shareholder distribution.
6. Shares of the applicant company must be issued in registered form.
7. All reports to shareholders, notices of meetings and

information circulars must be issued to Canadian security holders in English.

8. All financial information distributed to shareholders should include a conversion rate of the currency in which the financial information is provided into Canadian dollars as of the effective date of the financial information.
9. The applicant company must make arrangements satisfactory to the TSE regarding the expediting of releases in compliance with timely disclosure requirements.
10. If the applicant company is listed on a major stock exchange recognised by the TSE for this purpose, the company may enter into a modified form of listing agreement with the TSE which provides for certain exemptions from requirements of the TSE for so long as the company is listed on such major stock exchange.

The foregoing requirements are guidelines to applicant companies and the TSE maintains a discretion to consider modifications in appropriate cases.

In mid-December 1997, the TSE announced that it will require more detailed information from mining and oil and gas companies on new listing applications. These new requirements are in part, a response to the Bre-X Minerals scandal and parallel changes made by other Canadian stock exchanges.

B) Reporting requirements

In addition to the timely disclosure rules under applicable securities legislation, Canadian stock exchanges apply their own disclosure policies to listed issuers. With respect to the timely disclosure of material events, the policy of the TSE is substantially the same as National Policy 40, which has been adopted by the Canadian Securities Administrators, and is applicable in all the provinces of Canada. For TSE listed issuers, prompt public disclosure is required to be made of all material information and developments that would be likely to result in a change in the price of the issuer's securities. Examples of material developments or changes include, but are not limited to:

1. Actual or proposed changes in the control of the issuer.
2. Actual or proposed acquisitions or dispositions of a significant part of the issuer's assets.
3. Proposed takeovers, mergers, consolidations, amalgamations or reorganisations.
4. Any discoveries, changes or developments in the issuer's resources, technology, products or contracts which could materially affect the earnings of the issuer upward or downward.
5. Proposed changes in capital structure including stock splits or stock dividends.
6. Indicated significant changes in earnings prospects, upward or downward.
7. Changes in dividends.

Favourable and unfavourable facts are required to be disclosed promptly, fully and plainly and in a manner that provides for wide dissemination. The TSE maintains a stock watch programme and monitors and investigates unusual market activity in the securities of listed companies.

New rules integrating the disclosure requirements for primary distributions (ie new issues) and continuous disclosure requirements in the secondary market are anticipated in 1998. These new rules are expected to adopt recommendations made in March 1997 by a committee of the TSE advocating enhanced civil liability for press releases and other public disclosures made in the secondary markets by TSE listed companies.

All TSE listed companies incorporated in Canada must disclose on an annual basis, their approach to corporate governance. This disclosure must be made in the company's annual report or information circular. Guidelines published by the TSE provide, among other things, that the board of directors of every company should explicitly assume responsibility for the stewardship of the corporation.

SHAREHOLDER PROTECTION CODES

A) Insider dealing

The securities statutes of most Canadian provinces contain rules governing insider dealing, as does the Canada Business Corporations Act (CBCA). These rules require timely reporting of insider holdings and changes therein, and prohibit trading in securities by insiders who are in possession of material undisclosed information. Materiality is judged by whether the information could reasonably be expected to have a significant effect on the market price of the relevant securities.

Under the Ontario Securities Act, the scope of the insider trading prohibition is broad and extends beyond the usual range of corporate insiders. A person in a "special relationship" with an issuer is prohibited from trading in its securities where such person has material information relating to the issuer that has not been generally disclosed. A special relationship person is also barred from informing others of such information before it is generally disclosed, other than in the "necessary course of business". Special relationship persons include insiders and affiliates of the issuer, directors, officers and employees of the issuer and of any of the issuer's insiders or affiliates and any of their respective associates. Also included are persons who have, or may have, business or professional dealings with the issuer and thereby have acquired knowledge of the undisclosed material information. Insiders of an issuer include those who hold

10% or more of its voting securities, any of the issuer's directors and senior officers and those of its insiders and subsidiaries. The insider trading prohibition extends to professional advisers such as lawyers and accountants.

Amendments to the Ontario Securities Act in 1987 further expanded the classes of persons in a "special relationship" with an issuer to include persons or companies proposing to make a takeover bid for, or to enter into an amalgamation or other form of business combination with, a reporting issuer; extended insider trading liability to, among others, "tippees"; limited previously available defences to insider trading liability; and significantly increased statutory penalties and fines for violations of the insider trading rules.

Under the Ontario Securities Act, civil liability and quasi-criminal liability are prescribed for breaches of the insider trading rules. Where a special relationship person buys or sells securities or "tips" another in contravention of the insider trading prohibitions, such person is liable to compensate the purchaser or vendor, or the tipper's vendor or purchaser, as the case may be, for damages suffered as a result of the trade. If the person is an insider, associate or affiliate of the issuer, such person may also be accountable to the issuer for any benefit or advantage received as a result of his improper trade.

Defences

Under the 1987 amendments to the insider trading provisions, and later amendments to the regulations under the Ontario Securities Act, liability may be avoided if it can be proved that (i) the person reasonably believed that the material information had been generally disclosed; or (ii) in the case of companies or other unincorporated entities, no director, officer, partner, employee or agent of the company or other entity who made or participated in the decision to trade in securities had actual knowledge of the material information in question and no advice regarding such trade was given by any other person within the company or other entity who had actual knowledge of such material information (the so-called "Chinese wall" defence). Further limited exemptions from liability for insider trading are also provided, for example, in respect of trades in securities pursuant to automatic dividend reinvestment plans.

The reporting obligations of insiders under the securities statutes of British Columbia, Alberta, Saskatchewan, Manitoba and Quebec are similar to those currently in force in Ontario. A common form of insider report has been adopted under provincial securities legislation, the Bank Act and the CBCA.

The TSE has also enacted a by-law prohibiting specified types of activities known as "frontrunning". Generally, frontrunning involves situations where a dealer has specific knowledge of an imminent material trade (ie one that would reasonably be expected to move the market), there is no public knowledge in the market of such trade, the dealer makes a trade before the execution of the material trade for the purpose of profiting from or otherwise taking advantage of its knowledge of the execution of that material trade, and the dealer's trade is not for the benefit of the client for whom the material trade is to be made or for the purpose of hedging a position assumed from a client account.

Apart from the insider trading prohibitions described above and subject to their fiduciary duties at law, directors of a public company are not restricted in their ability to deal in the shares of their own companies. Under Canadian laws, there is no "short swing" trading liability as there is under United States securities laws.

B) Takeover bids

The securities laws of most Canadian provinces prescribe rules governing takeover bids. Provincial securities legislation will apply if a takeover bid is made to shareholders resident within the province. In addition, the corporate laws of the jurisdiction in which the target company is incorporated may also prescribe takeover bid rules. In the case of a federally incorporated company, the CBCA contains a takeover bid code that will apply where the target is incorporated under that statute.

Under the securities laws of most provinces, a takeover bid is triggered only when an offer is made for more than 20% of the voting or equity securities of the target (including those already held by the offeror and its affiliates and associates). Equity securities are generally defined as securities that carry a residual right to participate in the earnings of the issuer and, upon the liquidation or winding-up of the issuer, in its assets, but which do not necessarily carry voting rights. Under the CBCA, the takeover bid rules are triggered whenever 10% or more of the voting securities of a public corporation are to be acquired.

The takeover bid rules in the provincial jurisdictions have undergone substantial revision in recent years. Generally, provincial and federal takeover bid codes currently require that:

1. The takeover bid together with a disclosure document (a "takeover bid circular") must be mailed to all holders of the target's shares in the jurisdiction.
2. The bid must be open for a minimum period of 21 days.
3. Shareholders are entitled to withdraw shares for a specified period after the date of the bid (21 days from the date of the bid under the Ontario Securities Act).
4. The offeror must take up and pay for deposited shares within a specified period.
5. All holders of the same class of securities must be offered the same consideration, and no collateral

agreement with any such holders may offer a greater consideration than that offered to other holders of the same class.

6. In the takeover bid circular, the offeror must state, among other things, its intention to purchase the target's shares in the open market or otherwise during the course of the takeover bid and, if the takeover bid is for cash, its source of funding.

Canadian provincial and federal takeover bid codes prescribe exemptions and, in addition, the local authority has the power to grant exemption orders on a case-by-case basis.

A number of significant changes to the Ontario takeover and issuer bid rules were made in 1987, including the following:

1. The establishment of an "early warning" system which requires public disclosure upon acquiring 10% of any class of equity shares of an issuer (see below).
2. The removal of restrictions on the type of conditions that may be imposed under a bid.
3. The "integration" of share purchases made by way of private agreements within a 90-day period preceding a bid for the same class of equity shares such that offerees under the bid would have to be offered a consideration for their shares at least equal to the highest consideration paid under any of the private agreements.
4. The application of the statutory and issuer bid codes to voluntary acquisitions of non-voting participating shares.
5. The restriction of an offeror's right to purchase shares which were the subject of its bid, during a period of 20 business days following the bid.
6. The exemption from Ontario takeover and issuer bid rules made in compliance with the laws of jurisdictions recognised by the OSC, where the number of Ontario offerees is less than 50, and less than 2% of the target class of securities are registered in the names of Ontario holders.

In 1996 the IDA Committee to Review Takeover Bid Time Limits reported on the adequacy of the time limits established for takeover bids under applicable Canadian securities laws. Among other things, the Committee recommended that:

1. The minimum deposit period for formal takeover bids and the prohibition against taking up shares deposited under a formal bid should be extended from 21 to 35 days.
2. Shareholders' withdrawal rights should be extended to permit shareholders to withdraw shares at any time up to the time when shares are taken up by the offeror.
3. The time period for delivery of a directors' circular should be extended from 10 to 15 days after mailing of the takeover bid.
4. Bidders should have the option of commencing a takeover bid by advertisement with an appropriate summary of its offering circular in wide-circulation financial newspapers, provided that the takeover bid is contemporaneously delivered to the target company; the minimum deposit period and related time limits would commence to run from the date of delivery of the bid circular to the target company.

The Committee expressly stated that their recommendation in favour of a 35-day minimum deposit period was dependent upon implementing the recommendation that bidders be allowed to expeditiously launch bids by publication in the financial press without having to wait a further 10 days to obtain a shareholder list.

Legislation to implement the IDA Committee's recommendations is anticipated in 1998.

C) Compensation funds

It is a condition of registration under the Ontario Securities Act that every dealer participates in a compensation fund or contingency trust fund approved by the OSC and established by a recognised stock exchange or a trust company. One such approved fund is the Canadian Investor Protection Fund (CIPF), which is financed by the country's stock exchanges and the IDA for their respective members. The CIPF is available for claims against dealers and the amount contributed by each dealer may be varied at the discretion of the OSC. Since 1995, all members of the Alberta, Montreal, Toronto, and Vancouver exchanges, the Toronto Futures Exchange and the IDA, have been required to make disclosure to their customers of CIPF protection in accordance with the by-laws of their respective regulatory bodies.

RESEARCH

The exchanges provide information booklets and fact sheets on several aspects of trading in securities and other exchange-traded instruments. The VSE and ME both have internet information sites and there are a number of other sites specifically related to the Canadian equities market. Periodic reports on the market are also available in daily, weekly and monthly publications.

Major newspapers in Canada provide a daily list of high, low and closing prices, volume of trading and dividend payments for all shares listed on the TSE, ME, VSE, ASE and the Ontario OTC markets. These publications also print charts of the TSE and ME indices, closing and percentage change of all sectorial indices and a list of most securities, both by volume of trading and value of trades. Also, the research departments of numerous stockbroking firms publish reports on listed companies and economic matters.

A) Newspapers and periodicals

The Financial Post (daily and weekly), *The Globe and Mail, Report on Business* (daily), *The Montreal Gazette* (daily), *The Vancouver Sun* (daily), *The Edmonton Journal* (daily), *The Calgary Herald* (daily), *The Winnipeg Free Press* (daily), *The Halifax Chronicle-Herald* (daily), *Les Affaires* (weekly), *La Presse* (daily), *Le Devoir* (daily), *Le Journal de Montréal* (daily), *Le Soleil* (daily), *Le Droit* (daily).

B) Other information

The Consolidated Canadian Market Data Feed (CCDF), compiled and broadcast by the TSE, provides customers in Canada, the US and Europe with instantaneous trade and quotation information for all stocks, options and futures traded on the Montreal, Toronto, Alberta and Vancouver exchanges. International information vendors, such as Reuters, Dow Jones and Telekurs, also carry data on the various Canadian markets.

Canada: Business and Finance, published by Euromoney Books, provides in-depth information for those wishing to invest or do business in the country. See the order form at the back of this book for details.

CHAPTER

12

Chile

Introduction

For the Chilean stock market, the past two years have been difficult as a result of monetary tightening in 1996 and the Asian crisis in 1997. In 1997 the IGPA Index fell 2.2% in nominal terms. Market capitalisation of the Bolsa de Comercio de Santiago (SSE), which had risen consistently from US$14.7 billion at the end of 1990 to US$73.1 billion at the close of 1995, declined to US$65.6 billion in 1996 and ended 1997 at US$71.9 billion. One of the problems for Chile is the lack of representation of some important sectors, such as mining and construction, on the stock market. This characteristic inhibits the potential growth of the equity market. The main sectors represented on the SSE are electric utilities, banking, retail, telecommunications and beverages.

Foreign investment in the Chilean market has been tightly regulated by the central bank. The monetary authorities actively discriminate between productive and speculative capital, clearly favouring the former because of worries about the potential destabilising effects of large short-term capital flows in and out of Chile's relatively small economy. Further regulations to discourage short-term speculative investment were introduced in 1996 and 1997.

In general, the investment climate in Chile has become less attractive in recent months as a result of growing concerns regarding the impact of the Asian crisis on the local economy. Also, the gradual depreciation of the peso since the end of October 1997 and high interest rates are shifting investor preferences to fixed-income instruments, which have become more attractive. Nevertheless, restrictions on short-term capital flows, a strong and clean banking system and a deep local capital market guarantee the health of the domestic economy, even in times of crisis.

Advances are being made in many aspects of Chile's capital market system: a new centralised electronic depository has replaced the antiquated safe-keeping services offered by local banks; investment research from local and international firms is increasing as brokers compete for a limited amount of investment capital; and capital market legislation has been continually reviewed and modernised, most recently in 1996 and 1997. The Chilean market is driven mainly by foreign demand through ADRs because very few international investors are registered to trade locally. Also, the derivatives market is very thin even though all the required legislation is in place. However, as the country keeps its economic development moving ahead, further progress should be made in achieving greater market depth and more sophistication.

ECONOMIC AND POLITICAL OVERVIEW

Chile saw a trade deficit of approximately US$1.3 billion for 1997. Although export volume grew during the year, revenues were down mainly because of worsening terms of trade due largely to the Asian crisis. However, the country was able to achieve excellent economic growth estimated at between 6.0% and 6.4%, which continues to be one of the highest growth rates in Latin America. The central bank maintained its tighter monetary policy and, as a result, inflation continued to decrease, reaching about 6.0% at the end of 1997, versus 6.6% for 1996. External national debt stood at approximately US$26.6 billion and international reserves at around US$17.8 billion as at 31 December 1997. Unemployment, at 6.2% nationally, continued its downward trend.

In 1997 President Eduardo Frei began the fourth year of his six-year term. The main goal of government policy has been to improve Chile's international image. The government remains committed to a free market economy and to modernising the state. Further privatisations of state enterprises took place during 1997 and more issues are expected in 1998.

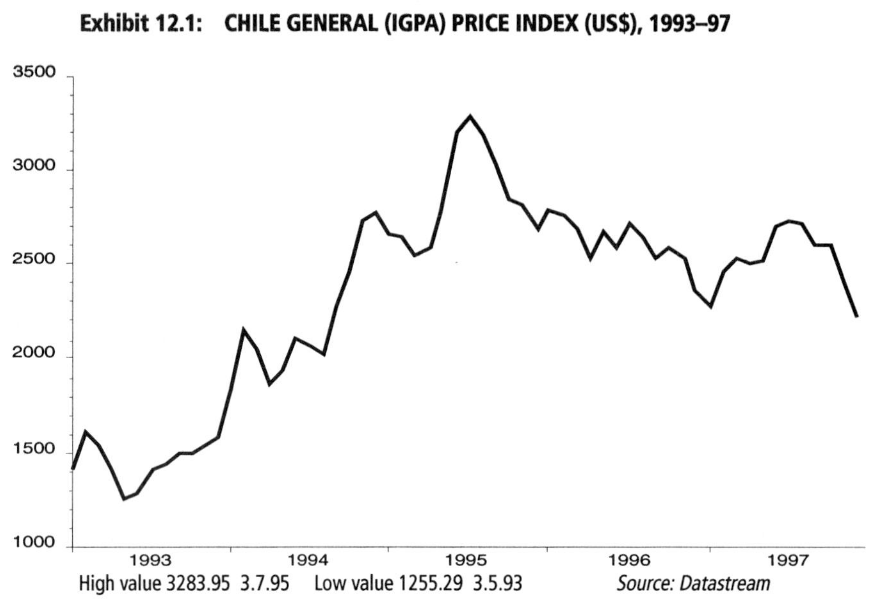

Congressional elections took place in December 1997, highlighting the fact that although the government (the coalition of centre-left parties known as the "Concertación") has held on to its majority in the Representatives' Chamber, its overall political support is dwindling. In the Senate, for example, any amendment to the constitution or any relevant statute will now require negotiations between the government and the opposition. The centre-right opposition parties are becoming stronger and, for the first time, there is a feeling that an opposition candidate has a real chance of winning the 1999 presidential election.

As regards NAFTA, the government is still trying to obtain the "fast track" authorisation from the US authorities that Chile has requested prior to starting negotiations. In spite of President Clinton's personal support for the "fast track" during 1997, the US Congress has once again blocked this possibility. However, entry to NAFTA will continue to be a government priority. Chile already has free trade agreements with Mexico and Canada, has joined Mercosur as an associate member and is negotiating a free trade agreement with the EU. In addition, it has negotiated tax treaties with Argentina and Canada, although the latter is awaiting legislative approval.

Role of the central bank

Established in 1925, the Banco Central de Chile's current structure is regulated by a law passed on 10 October 1989, under which the central bank is a constitutionally autonomous entity. Its primary responsibility is to safeguard the stability of the currency and to ensure the normal flow of internal and external payments. The bank is prohibited from indirectly or directly financing spending by, or loans to, the government or government institutions; its financing operations are restricted to banking institutions.

The central bank plays a key role in short-term macroeconomic management. Since 1985, monetary policy has been geared to regulating real interest rates, and through them to controlling aggregate demand and inflation. To achieve this, the bank issues 90-day inflation-indexed bonds at a fixed interest rate. The central bank also operates in the medium- and long-term markets by auctioning a fixed quantity of bonds. With the objective of maintaining a stable real exchange rate, the bank attempts to closely co-ordinate monetary policy with fiscal policy, which can be difficult because the government and the central bank often have different priorities.

MARKET PERFORMANCE

A) In 1997

Several factors served to depress the stock market in 1997: the most important were relative economic contraction due to rising interest rates as a result of the uncertainty brought about by weak copper prices and the Asian crisis; a decline in international pulp and steel prices; and uncertainties about Brazilian and Argentinian growth prospects because of the problems in Asia. These factors combined to produce a fall of 15% in the value of shares traded, and the IGPA Index (which groups the majority of shares on the Santiago market) fell 2.2% in nominal terms. The IPSA Index ended the year up 12.9% in local currency terms and 9.4% in US dollar terms.

In spite of the lack-lustre performance of the market, two major new companies joined the SSE in 1997, and Chilean companies also increased their participation in the privatisation of Latin American state-owned organisations.

B) Summary information

Global ranking by market value (US$ terms, end-1997): 27
Market capitalisation (end-1997): US$71.9 billion
Growth in market value (US$ terms 1993–97): 60.2%
Market value as a % of nominal GNP (1997): 91.6%
Number of domestic/foreign companies listed (end-1997): 294/0
Market P/E (IPSA Index companies, end-1997): 13.6
MSCI Index (change in US$ terms, 1997): +2.0%
Short-term (3-month) interest rate (end-1997): 6.59%
Long-term (15-year) bond yield (end-1997): 7.41%
Budget surplus as a % of nominal GDP (1997): 0.9%
Annual increase in broad money (M3) supply (end-1997): 20.9%
Inflation rate (1997): 6.0%
US$ exchange rate (end-1997): P439.70

C) Year-end share price index, price/earnings ratios and yields

Exhibit 12.2:
YEAR-END IGPA INDEX, P/E RATIOS AND YIELDS, 1993–97

Year-end	*IGPA Index*	*P/E*	*Yield (%)*
1993	3,915.49	21.58	5.20
1994	5,425.17	20.53	2.63
1995	5,739.97	19.05	3.44
1996	4,902.59	13.35	3.98
1997	4,794.41	14.33	3.84

Source: Santiago Stock Exchange.

D) Market indices and their constituents

The SSE publishes three stock market indices – the General Price Index (IGPA), the Selective Price Index (IPSA) and the Inter-10 Index. The IGPA Index is a market capitalisation-weighted index that is rebalanced at the beginning of each year and currently has 182 constituent companies. The IPSA is a volume-weighted index which is rebalanced quarterly and comprises the 40 stocks most heavily traded during the preceding 12 months. The Inter-10 Index is volume-weighted, revised quarterly and comprises the 10 largest companies with ADRs. Of the three indices, the IPSA is considered by most investors to be the benchmark index for the Chilean stock market.

THE STOCK MARKET

A) Brief history and structure

Chile's first stock exchange, the Bolsa de Corredores, was established in the port of Valparaíso in 1892. By the turn of the century it had been eclipsed by the Bolsa de Comercio (SSE), established in 1893 in the capital city of Santiago. The SSE, a private limited company, has remained the dominant exchange since that time.

In 1989, the Bolsa Electrónica, a screen-based electronic stock exchange was founded and has subsequently gained significant market share. In 1997, a total of US$2.4 billion worth of shares changed hands on the Bolsa Electrónica, accounting for approximately 24.1% of total equity trading in Chile. During 1997, discussions commenced regarding the possibility of merging the Bolsa Electrónica with the SSE.

There are 41 brokerage companies (*Corredores de Bolsa*) operating on the SSE, which is administered by 11 stockbrokers appointed as directors at the annual shareholders' meeting. One of these is elected as president for the year.

The securities markets are principally regulated by the Superintendencia de Valores y Seguros (SVS) and the Superintendencia de Bancos e Instituciones Financieras (SBIF). The SBIF is charged with the overall supervision of credit, budgetary, monetary and public debt policies. It directly supervises all domestic banks, branches of foreign banks operating in Chile and consumer credit companies.

The SVS has wide-ranging powers and responsibilities for the supervision of *sociedades anónimas abiertas* ("open corporations"), stock exchanges, stockbrokers, over-the-counter securities broker dealers (*Agentes de Valores*), insurance companies, open-ended mutual funds, mutual fund and pension fund managers that are open corporations, closed-end investment funds, external auditors, foreign capital investment funds and any entity offering securities publicly. The SVS registers all offerings of debt and equity securities of open corporations in the National Securities Registry. It is also responsible for establishing accounting and disclosure rules for all the entities it supervises.

B) Different exchanges

Chile has three exchanges: the Santiago Stock Exchange, the Bolsa Electrónica and the Valparaíso Stock Exchange. The SSE is by far the largest, handling nearly 75% of total trading, followed by the Bolsa Electrónica.

C) Opening hours, names and addresses

Trading by open outcry on the SSE takes place in three sessions: 10.30am to 11.20am; 12.30pm to 1.20pm; and

4.00pm to 4.30pm. For less active shares, or where no buyer or seller can be found by open outcry, a computer-based bid and offer system is in use. Low volume shares trade by this system between 9.30am and 4.30pm. Once a day, shares are traded by auction – generally for securities with restricted marketability or for very large blocks. There are no market-makers but most brokers trade for their own account. Brokers are allowed to trade off the exchange, provided that the transaction is reported.

BOLSA DE COMERCIO DE SANTIAGO
Mailing address: Casilla 123-D, Santiago
Tel: (56) 2 698 2001; Fax: (56) 2 672 8046

BOLSA ELECTRÓNICA
Huérfanos 770, Piso 14, Santiago
Tel: (56) 2 639 4699; Fax: (56) 2 639 9015

BOLSA DE VALPARAÍSO
Prat 798, Valparaíso
Tel: (56) 3 225 6955; Fax: (56) 3 221 2764

MARKET SIZE

A) Number of listings and market value

At end-1997 the market capitalisation of the SSE totalled US$71.9 billion, 9.7% up on 1996's year-end figure.

Exhibit 12.3:
SSE LISTED COMPANIES AND MARKET CAPITALISATION, 1993–97

Year-end	*No. of companies*	*Market value (US$ million)*
1993	262	44,900.0
1994	279	64,952.0
1995	284	73,087.2
1996	290	65,601.0
1997	294	71,934.6

Source: Santiago Stock Exchange.

B) Largest quoted companies

Exhibit 12.4:
THE 20 LARGEST LISTED COMPANIES ON THE SSE, END-1997

Ranking	*Company*	*Market value (US$ million)*
1	CTC-A	5,770.60
2	Endesa	4,706.14
3	Copec	4,410.00
4	Enersis	3,762.47
5	Chilectra	2,266.30
6	Falabella	2,153.38
7	Chilgener	1,971.76
8	Chile	1,943.90
9	Santiago	1,866.48
10	Cervezas	1,769.37
11	CMPC	1,684.96
12	D&S	1,663.27
13	Santander	1,548.55
14	Andina A	1,268.05
15	Andina B	1, 211.79
16	Emos	1,187.24
17	Quinenco	1,180.10
18	CGE	1,100.45
19	Santangrup	800.24
20	Lan	788.65

Source: Santiago Stock Exchange.

C) Trading volume

US$7.4 billion worth of shares changed hands in 1997, a decrease of 14.9% from 1996. Average daily turnover was US$29.9 million.

Exhibit 12.5:
SHARE TURNOVER, SSE, 1993–97

Year	*Turnover (US$ million)*
1993	3,450.6
1994	6,048.6
1995	11,132.9
1996	8,728.7
1997	7,429.5

Source: Santiago Stock Exchange.

Exhibit 12.6:
THE 20 MOST ACTIVELY TRADED SHARES, SSE, 1997

Ranking	*Company/share*	*Trading value (US$ '000)*
1	Endesa	1,116,590
2	Chilgener	864,616
3	CTC-A	623,514
4	Enersis	617,467
5	Copec	260,669
6	Labchile	158,780
7	Chilectra	145,723
8	Soquimich B	131,009
9	Sta Isabel	114,506
10	D&S	113,601
11	Cervezas	106,191
12	Santander	90,582
13	Entel	85,252

Exhibit 12.6 continued

14	CMPC	80,036
15	Chilquinta	73,343
16	Masisa	63,204
17	Colbun	61,642
18	Edwards A	60,884
19	Andina A	60,823
20	CAP	55,720

Source: Santiago Stock Exchange.

TYPES OF SHARE

Shares of open corporations (those which offer their shares to the public, those with 500 or more shareholders and those with at least 10% of subscribed capital belonging to a minimum of 100 shareholders), long and short-term government bonds, mortgage bonds, corporate bonds and commercial paper, debentures, bank certificates of deposit and state debt are all traded on all three stock exchanges in Chile. In addition, stock index futures, US dollars, US dollar exchange rate futures, real estate investment funds and gold are traded on the SSE. Also, shares of closed corporations (any not defined as open) may be traded twice a month through an auction system. The shares of all open corporations are automatically listed on all three stock exchanges.

All equity securities in Chile are in registered form. Corporate articles may establish non-voting shares or shares with limited voting rights, although Chilean law prohibits the creation of shares with multiple voting rights. Preferred shares can be issued which may or may not have voting rights; they must also have a limited life. Under Chilean company law, shareholders have pre-emption rights, and in 1986 the SSE established a rights market where these entitlements can be traded. Companies may also issue convertibles or other types of bonds.

INVESTORS

As is typical of emerging stock markets, much of the Chilean market equity is firmly held by controlling families and their associates. Unlike many emerging markets, however, Chile also has a relatively well-developed institutional investor base.

A) Pension funds

The social security system was reformed in 1981, and privately administered, individually capitalised pension funds were created, representing a far-reaching change in the securities markets. Individuals are free to choose their pension fund independently of the company for which they work, and the company is obliged to deposit a set percentage of that person's salary into the assigned pension fund. Pension funds are managed by private companies called *administradoras de fondos de pensiones* (AFPs). At the end of July 1997 the pension funds had assets of US$32.513 million, 28.77% of which was invested in shares. The funds are growing at the rate of approximately US$2,400 million per annum.

The pension funds are limited in both their total exposure to shares and their exposure to any one company, but as the amount of money under management grows, the number of equity securities in which they are authorised to invest also increases. Recently, the SVS authorised pension funds to make foreign investments through local brokers.

B) Insurance companies

Pension funds must invest a proportion of their funds in insurance policies on behalf of their contributors. In addition, pensioners who choose to take a lump sum pension entitlement on retirement are obliged to take out an annuity plan with an insurance company. Life insurance companies' assets stood at an estimated US$8.1 billion at March 1997. Roughly 6.6% of these assets are invested in shares.

C) Foreign investment funds

In order to reduce its foreign debt, the government authorised the creation of debt conversion funds. Although no information is available on the operation of these funds, it is believed that two of the three funds which invested in Chile via this mechanism, managed by a subsidiary of Midland Bank, have now liquidated their position entirely and have remitted a substantial proportion of the proceeds as dividends. This leaves only one fund in operation, which is believed to have assets of approximately US$60 million.

In addition, in September 1987 a law was passed to provide the legal framework within which foreign investment funds could invest "new money" in the securities market in Chile. Currently there are 22 foreign investment funds. Total funds under management at September 1997 amounted to US$1,686 million (1996, US$1,408 million). Around 96% of these funds are invested in equities, but because the bulk of this investment was in place by the end of 1990, the funds have not been heavy buyers for some time. These funds collectively account for approximately 3% of total market capitalisation.

D) Open-ended mutual funds

At September 1997 there were 92 funds in Chile (1996, 77) and 14 mutual fund managers. Of these funds, 59 are fixed-interest funds and 33 are risk capital funds with balanced portfolios of shares and bonds. The funds have grown in recent years and, as at September 1997, had US$3,782 million under management (December 1996, US$2,804 million). Recently, the SVS abolished restrictions on foreign investment by open-ended mutual funds.

E) Individual investors

There are no statistics kept concerning the importance of individual investors, but it is estimated that they account on average for approximately 40% of turnover.

OPERATIONS

A) Trading system

Transactions involving the sale and purchase of shares and/or payment of stock subscription preferred rights are executed by brokers both through a computer trading system called Telepregón and on the floor of the exchange.

Fixed-rate and short-term securities are traded by means of an auction in which bids are registered through a computer system. There are two kinds of auctions – regular and electronic. For both, bids put up for auction are ordered according to the type of instrument and profitability. The regular auction is executed by an auctioneer who awards stock to the highest bidder (subject to any minimum price requirements imposed by the seller). The electronic auction is a system whereby offers, bids and awards are conducted through terminals connected to the SSE computer network.

Brokers are allowed to deal outside the SSE, but such transactions must be reported to the exchange to provide for an official record.

B) List of banks and brokers

ABN AMRO
Nueva York 33, Santiago, Chile
Tel: (56) 2 671 5776; Fax: (56) 2 672 2696

BANCO DE BOSTON
Moneda 797-799, PO Box 1946, Correo Central, Santiago
Tel: (56) 2 639 3841; Fax: (56) 2 639 1297

BANCO SANTANDER
Bandera 140, Santiago
Tel: (56) 2 320 8000; Fax: (56) 2 696 0622

BANCO SANTIAGO
Bandera 206, Piso 4, Santiago
Tel: (56) 2 696 7458; Fax: (56) 2 699 3374

BANCREDITO
La Bolsa 64, Piso 3, Of. 213, Santiago
Tel: (56) 2 692 8900; Fax: (56) 2 696 5449

BANKERS TRUST
Av El Bosque 130, Piso 5, Las Condes, Santiago
Tel: (56) 2 203 1330; Fax: (56) 2 203 1331

BICE
La Bolsa 64, Piso 3, Of. 206, Santiago
Tel: (56) 2 692 2800/2801; Fax: (56) 2 698 3118

CELFIN SERVICIOS FINANCIEROS LIMITADA
Apoquindo 3721, Piso 19, Las Condes, Santiago
Tel: (56) 2 246 2444/(56) 2 207 0775; Fax: (56)- 2 246 2420

CITICORP CHILE
Moneda 970, Piso 6, Santiago, La Bolsa 64, Of. 338
Tel: (56) 2 672 4008; Fax: (56) 2 695 7098

LARRAIN VIAL
La Bolsa 88, Of. 2, Santiago
Tel: (56) 2 672 7222; Fax: (56) 2 698 5116

MERRILL LYNCH CHILE SA
Augustinas 640, Piso 13, Santiago
Tel: (56) 2 639 3130; Fax: (56) 2 638 7092

Exhibit 12.7
COUNTRY FUNDS – CHILE

Fund	*US$ % change* 01/01/97 01/01/98	01/01/93 01/01/98	Currency	Fund size (US$ mil)	Fund volatility	Management group	Opal main sector	Opal subsector
Paribas EM Chile Ptfl	15.83	N/A	US$	N/A	7.605	Paribas Asset Management	Open-End	Equity
Chile Fund Inc.	15.42	89.41	US$	363.63	5.823	BEA Assoc	Closed-End	Equity
Genesis Chile	10.07	119.35	US$	471.08	-1	Genesis	Closed-End	Equity
NatWest/IFC LAIF Chile Index	9.66	N/A	US$	8.086	6.213	NatWest Investment Management	Open-End	Equity
Moneda Chile Fund	-0.69	N/A	US$	17.55	-1	Moneda Asset Management	Closed-End	Equity
Five Arrows Chile Fund	-0.91	72.07	US$	247.87	6.349	Five Arrows R	Closed-End	Equity
GT Chile Growth	-1.55	61.81	US$	51.2	6.072	LGT Asset Management	Closed-End	Equity
Pionero	-3.2	N/A	US$	119.98	5.244	Moneda Asset Management	Closed-End	Equity

Note: details for some funds may not have been included if the data for the US$ % change for 97/98 was not available

Source: Standard & Poor's Micropal.

C) Settlement and transfer

Settlement generally takes place two days after a transaction, although transactions can also be settled earlier if an investor wishes, or by deferred payment on the last Wednesday of every month. Deferred transactions are only permitted in the shares of 124 companies and must be accompanied by a deposit.

There is no centralised settlement system. The seller signs a stock transfer form which is taken by his broker to the purchaser's broker for counter-signature by the purchaser. The transfer is then sent to the company for registration. Registration of the new shareholder must take place within five business days from the time the company receives notification of the transaction. A centralised custody system is currently being established.

D) Commissions and other costs

Commissions are paid to the stock exchange and to the broker and are based on the value of the transaction, expressed in inflation-indexed units called *unidades de fomento* (UF).

Brokerage commissions are negotiable and range from a maximum of 1.0% for individual investors to around 0.35% for large institutional transactions.

Exchange fees are calculated on the amount of the transaction and are payable by the broker. They are established by the exchange and vary according to the instrument being traded. For shares, CFI (investment fund units) and share rights, the monthly rates range from 0% (for transactions of UF60,000 or more) up to 0.5% for transactions below UF10,000. Alternatively, investors can elect to agree a single fixed fee of UF582 + 18% VAT for six months, or UF1,017 + 18% VAT for one year.

Value added tax of 18% is payable on both brokerage and stock exchange commissions.

TAXATION AND REGULATIONS AFFECTING FOREIGN INVESTORS

A) Investment registration

Chile has exchange controls, and, to secure the remittance of income and capital, an investment must be registered. There are two principal channels for registration – Decree Law 600, which contains the Foreign Investment Statute, and secondly Law 18,840 (further regulated in Chapter XIV of the Compendium of Foreign Exchange Regulations issued by the central bank).

Under Decree Law 600, a formal agreement is entered into between the Republic of Chile and the investor, guaranteeing the remittance of income and of invested capital. The period for non-allowance of capital repatriation of foreign investments stands at one year under Decree Law 600, which is also applicable to investments under Chapter XIV of the Compendium. One important difference between the two systems is that under Decree Law 600 foreign investors have the right to fix (for 10 years) the overall income tax payable in Chile at an effective rate of 42%. This fixed income tax rate includes corporate taxes payable by the company as well as those payable by foreign investors. At any point during the 10-year period, foreign investors may waive their rights to the fixed rate and become subject to the normal taxation applicable to Chilean companies (15%) and foreign investors (35%, less the 15% tax credit for the tax paid by companies). Under Chapter XIV of the Compendium, foreign investors are directly subject to the normal taxation system.

In 1997, the Foreign Investment Committee changed its policy regarding minimum investments made under Decree Law 600: the minimum has been raised from US$25,000 to US$1 million (except for investments made in physical assets and technology, for which US$25,000 is still the minimum). Other investments are only permitted under Chapter XIV (for which US$10,000 is still the minimum amount). Any investment under Decree Law 600 of more than US$15 million now requires not only Foreign Investment Committee approval but also special central bank approval as a non-speculative or productive investment.

B) Non-resident bank accounts

Non-resident bank accounts are allowed, but are subject to the general provisions regulating foreign exchange. They can be used to convert foreign currency into local currency or to pay commitments approved by the central bank.

C) Taxation of foreign shareholders

Dividends paid by a Chilean stock corporation to shareholders not domiciled or resident in Chile are subject to 35% withholding tax. This withholding tax is applied on the gross amount of the dividends plus an amount equivalent to the proportional corporate tax (first category tax) paid on the taxable profits being distributed as part of the dividends. The amount of corporate tax so added is then deducted as a credit against the withholding tax. Thus, if all of the dividends correspond to taxable profits that have been subject to first category tax (currently 15%), the effective withholding tax rate after deducting the credit would be 20%.

Foreign investment funds (country funds) and institutional investors that bring their investments into Chile under Law 18,657, are subject to a one-off tax of 10% on any profit distribution.

There are no income tax treaties, except with Argentina.

LISTING AND REPORTING REQUIREMENTS

The SVS requires registration of all new issues on the basis of substantive disclosure of information; obliges listed companies to publish quarterly reports as well as audited annual reports incorporating detailed accounting standards; supervises the exchanges, brokers and transactions by insiders; and publishes up-to-date information on listed companies collected in a computerised database from company reports submitted.

SHAREHOLDER PROTECTION CODES

The SSE has its own professional managers who supervise daily operations, maintain an orderly market and take action in cases of price manipulation.

Law 18,046 ("the law") governs the formation of stock corporations, administrative bodies and their authorities, and the distribution of profits, along with division, transformation, mergers, bankruptcy and liquidation. The law defines open stock corporations (OSC) as those that offer their shares to the public at large, those with 500 or more shareholders and those with at least 10% of subscribed capital belonging to a minimum of 100 shareholders. Stock corporations without such characteristics are defined as closed stock corporations (CSC).

A) Takeovers and mergers

The law subjects an OSC to a stricter set of regulations than apply to a CSC. Only OSCs are subject to SVS control. The law is particularly rigorous as regards the information that a bidder for a company must provide to the SVS, investors, shareholders and the general public. Generally, it's required that OSCs and any other company registered in the Securities Registry must divulge all important information regarding the company, its business dealings and its securities. Directors, general managers or persons owning, directly or indirectly, 10% or more of the subscribed capital of a company, must disclose their share dealings within 5 days of the transaction.

The division, transformation or merger of a stock corporation should be agreed to at a shareholders' meeting, and this information must be reported to the SVS and to the SSE. In the event of a stock corporation ceasing payment of one or more of its obligations, a shareholders' meeting must be called within 30 days of the suspension of payment for the purpose of reporting on the legal, economic and financial situation of the company. This information must be reported to the SVS, the SSE and the general public.

The law protects minority shareholders and creditors by establishing that the shareholders' meeting must approve the transfer of all assets or liabilities of the company in relation to takeovers and mergers, with a special quorum of at least two-thirds of the issued shares; shareholders who do not approve a merger may oblige the company to purchase their shares at commercial value (right to withdrawal) and the new company resulting from the takeover or merger is responsible for all obligations of the company or companies absorbed.

B) Insider trading

Directors, administrators and, in general, any person who, by virtue of his position has access to confidential information on the company and its operations, must maintain confidentiality. If they fail to do so and trade on the information, they are required to repay to the company profits obtained from transactions in the company's securities, and any person may demand compensation for damage suffered. Under Law 19,301 enacted on 19 March 1994, criminal sanctions apply for insider trading and other similar offences relating to conflicts of interest.

C) Compensation fund

Chilean law does not provide for any form of stock exchange compensation fund to reimburse shareholders who may be the victims of fraud or default by a market broker or trader. However, brokers must provide a guarantee for a sum equal to UF4,000 (approximately US$100,000) to secure obligations they contract as a result of brokerage operations.

RESEARCH

The SSE provides research information on request, as do some of the larger brokerage companies. Larraín Víal, BICE Chileconsult, Merrill Lynch, ING Barings and HSBC James Capel are some of the best in this respect.

Among the SSE's publications are the following:

Daily Exchange Bulletin
Monthly Report
Quarterly Financial Information Report
Securities Summary

The SSE also provides certain services via its e-mail link.

Chile, published by Euromoney Books, provides in-depth information for those wishing to invest or do business in the country. See the order card at the back of this book for details.

CHAPTER

13

China

Introduction

The introduction of China's economic reform programme in 1978 resulted in the rebirth of the stock market as the government turned to a market-oriented economy, or rather to an economy since described as "socialism with Chinese characteristics". The aim was to provide a solution to the increasingly severe economic problems of poor enterprise efficiency and lack of internationally competitive technology. The Chinese government permitted the issue of a new type of stock available to foreign investors and classified as B shares, to distinguish them from A shares which are reserved for domestic investors. Also introduced were H shares, listed in Hong Kong, and subject to Hong Kong generally accepted accounting principles, and N shares, listed in New York, and subject to that market's accounting standards.

End-1997 total market capitalisation of all listed companies (A, B and H shares) was equal to 25.0% of 1997 GDP. Initially, China listed its heavy industries (steel, shipbuilding and petrochemicals), but recently has allowed a wide range of companies to come to the market, including consumer durables and non-durables' manufacturers, infrastructure companies, light industrial product manufacturers, and base and precious metals companies. Liquidity has been a constant problem for Chinese companies, because typically only 30% of their share capital is listed, with the remainder often held as non-traded shares by the mainland parent company. This has proved to be an investment disincentive for foreign investors, who have become wary of both accumulating and liquidating positions, particularly in the domestic B share markets.

In order to reform its state-owned enterprises (SOEs), China is now encouraging mergers and acquisitions within its industrial sector. However, to date, such activity has been limited either to ministry-led reorganisations that impose new industrial groupings at the operating level (eg China Shipping Development), or industry consolidation that may involve corporate-level vertical integration (eg Yizheng Chemical Fibre). Fiscal policy towards listed enterprises has been favourable and extended tax holidays are common for new listings in China.

Traditionally, China's industries have been almost wholly debt financed, and a large proportion of new issue proceeds are typically used to repay existing debt, often to the parent company. The majority of debt funding is local currency denominated, although certain companies have been allowed to raise foreign debt, occasionally in the form of convertible bonds.

ECONOMIC AND POLITICAL OVERVIEW

Following the 15th Party Congress in September 1997, reform of SOEs was given the highest priority, including turning them into shareholding enterprises. At that Congress, Jiang Zemin cemented his position as the leading figure in the Standing Committee, with Li Peng the number two and, importantly, Zhu Rongji the number three. Zhu became Premier in March 1998 and is continuing with the reform programme.

GDP growth has slowed lately, from 9.7% in 1996 to 8.8% in 1997. China's trade position meanwhile continues to improve. The country registered a trade surplus for 1997of US$40.3 billion, with exports up more than 20% to US$182.7 billion and imports up only about 1% to US$142.4 billion. Foreign direct investment rose 37.7% to US$51.9 billion.

For 1998, the government has set a growth target of 8% (to be achieved in the face of an expected slowdown in export growth) through an increase in infrastructure investment from US$305 billion in 1997 to US$350 billion in 1998. In all, China plans to invest US$750 billion

Exhibit 13.1: SHANGHAI SE COMPOSITE PRICE INDEX (US$), 1993–97

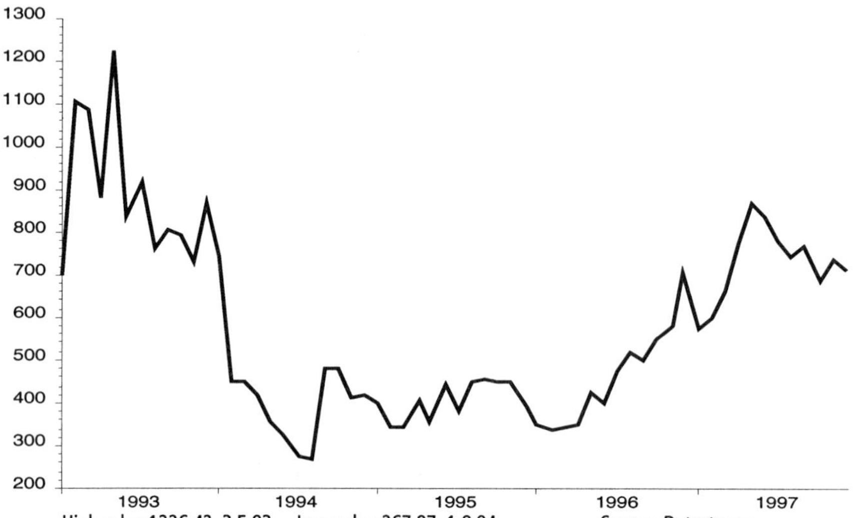

High value 1226.42 3.5.93 Low value 267.97 1.8.94 *Source: Datastream*

in infrastructure-related projects over the remainder of the ninth five-year plan (1998–2000).

MARKET PERFORMANCE

A) In 1997

In 1997, all of China's stock market indices finished the year below the level at which they began it. The best performer was the "red chip" Hang Seng Affiliated Corporations Index, which registered a 7% decline over the year. At the other end of the scale were the Shenzhen B Share Index and the Hong Kong H Share Index, both of which fell 30%. The Shanghai B Share Index fell 15% over the 12 months. Each of these indices followed a similar course, buoyed from the second quarter of 1997 by intense speculative buying, in which retail investors played a large role, followed by a peak in September and then a heavy sell off from October onwards.

The most significant listing of 1997 was that of heavy-weight China Telecom, which raised US$4.02 billion and now accounts for 6.9% of the Hang Seng Index, although it is still very much a "China share". The H share market was dominated by new toll road infrastructure company issues, including Jiangsu Expressway (which raised US$472 million), Zhejiang Expressway (US$441 million) and Sichuan Expressway (US$180 million).

B) Summary information

Global ranking by market value (US$ terms, end-1997): 17
Market capitalisation (end-1997): SHSE (B shares) US$2.20 billion; SZSE (B shares) US$2.07 billion.
Growth in market value (US$ terms, 1993–97): SHSE (A) 304.5%; (B) 57.1%; SZSE (A) 506.3%; (B) 111.8%
Market value (A and B shares) as a % of nominal GDP (end-1997): 21.7%
Number of companies listed (end-1997): SHSE 383; SZSE 362; H shares 39
Market P/E (SHSE B shares, end-1997): 14.1
Market P/E (SZSE B shares, end-1997): 7.7
MSCI Index (change in US$ terms, 1997): -26.4%
Short-term (3-month) interest rate (end-1997): 8.82%
Long-bond yield (10 year) (end-1997): 9.78%
Budget deficit as a % of nominal GDP (1997): 0.77%
Annual increase in money (M2) supply (end-1997): 25.8%
Inflation rate (1997): 5.0%
US$ exchange rate (end-1997): Rmb8.3

C) Year-end share price indices, price/earnings ratios and yields

Exhibit 13.2:
INDICES, P/E RATIOS AND DIVIDEND YIELDS, 1993–97

Year-end	*Share price index*	*P/E*	*Yield (%)*
Shanghai Securities Exchange B Share Index			
1993	103.15	18.2	1.1
1994	62.80	11.3	2.2
1995	47.69	8.61	3.2

Exhibit 13.2 continued

1996	67.03	14.8	2.9
1997	55.88	14.1	2.1
Shenzhen Stock Exchange B Share Index			
1993	141.44	13.9	1.7
1994	86.66	7.7	3.6
1995	59.48	6.0	4.5
1996	151.88	17.5	2.6
1997	98.97	7.7	3.0
Hang Seng China Enterprises Index (H shares)			
1993	1,941.12	19.4	1.0
1994	1,069.67	10.6	1.9
1995	757.12	20.5	3.8
1996	980.55	18.2	1.7
1997	722.99	11.6	1.2
Hang Seng China Affiliated Corporations Index ("red chips")			
1996	1,836.85	29.6	1.2
1997	1,745.62	28.1	1.3

Source: Daiwa Securities (HK) Ltd.

THE STOCK MARKET

A) Brief history and structure

The first stock market in China was informally set up in Shanghai in 1914, though it was not officially opened until 1920. The market's focus was on the trading of government bonds. Thereafter, stock markets were also opened in Beijing and Tianjin. In 1949 when the Chinese Communist Party came to power, the stock exchanges were closed and all securities were abolished. However, the Chinese securities market re-emerged in the early 1980s following the introduction of China's economic reform programmes.

The Shanghai Securities Exchange (SHSE) was established on 26 November 1990 as a non-profit organisation. It is regulated by the China Securities Regulatory Commission. The Shenzhen Stock Exchange (SZSE) started trial operations in December 1990 and officially opened on 3 July 1991. The organisation and structure closely resemble its Shanghai counterpart, except for a percentage fee levied on new listings and set aside in a fund for use by exchange officials to even out price fluctuations.

B) Different exchanges

Trading takes place in two mainland cities – Shanghai and Shenzhen. In addition, the H shares of 39 Chinese enterprises are listed on the Hong Kong Stock Exchange (HKSE) and eight companies have listed their shares on the NYSE.

C) Opening hours, names and addresses

Trading hours for both SHSE and SZSE B shares are Monday to Friday from 9.30am to 11.30am and 1.00pm to 3.00pm.

SHANGHAI SECURITIES EXCHANGE
528 Pudong Nan Road, Shanghai 200210
Tel: (86) 21 6880 8888; Fax: (86) 21 6880 0006
Internet: www.sse.com.cn

SHENZHEN STOCK EXCHANGE
203 Honglixi Road, Shenzhen 518028
Tel: (86) 755 320 3431; Fax: (86) 755 320 3505

MARKET SIZE

A) Number of listings and market value

Market capitalisation on SHSE at year-end 1997 of A and B shares was US$109 billion and US$2.20 billion respectively. Market capitalisation on SZSE at year-end 1997 of A and B shares was US$100 billion and US$2.07 billion respectively.

Exhibit 13.3:
NUMBER OF LISTED SHARES, SHSE AND SZSE, 1993–97

	No. of listed shares			
Year-end	*SHSE*		*SZSE*	
1993	A shares	101	A shares	75
	B shares	22	B shares	19
1994	A shares	169	A shares	118
	B shares	34	B shares	24
1995	A shares	184	A shares	88
	B shares	36	B shares	34
1996	A shares	287	A shares	267
	B shares	43	B shares	42
1997	A shares	372	A shares	348
	B shares	50	B shares	51

Source: Daiwa Securities (HK) Ltd.

Exhibit 13.4:
MARKET CAPITALISATION, H AND B SHARES, 1993–97

	Market capitalisation (US$ billion)			
	H shares	*"Red chips"*	*SHSE B shares*	*SZSE B shares*
1993	2.35	9.85	1.40	0.98
1994	2.59	5.79	1.40	0.69
1995	2.13	7.26	1.14	0.79
1996	3.92	19.31	2.00	2.71
1997	6.19	24.72	2.20	2.07

Source: Daiwa Securities (HK) Ltd.

B) Largest quoted companies

Exhibit 13.5:
THE 20 LARGEST H SHARES, END-1997

Ranking	*Issuer*	*Market value (US$ million)*
1	Beijing Datang Power	655.39
2	Qingling Motors	480.55
3	Guangdong Kelon	392.91
4	Guangshen Railway	378.63
5	Shanghai Petrochem	363.81
6	China Southern.Airlines	303.04
7	Zhenhai Ref and Chem	299.02
8	Zhejiang Expressway	290.49
9	China Shipping Dev	275.94
10	Yizheng Chem Fibre	252.92
11	China Eastern Airlines	252.75
12	Jiangsu Expressway	252.30
13	First Tractor	202.10
14	Beijing Yanhua	195.89
15	Maanshan Iron and Steel	192.31
16	Shenzhen Expressway	144.69
17	Angang New Steel	132.07
18	Jiangxi Copper	128.34
19	Beijing North Star	117.69
20	Sichuan Express	114.38

Source: Daiwa Securities (HK) Ltd.

Exhibit 13.6:
THE 20 LARGEST RED CHIP SHARES, END 1997

Ranking	*Issuer*	*Market value (US$ million)*
1	China Res Entrep	3,458.26
2	Shanghai Industrial	3,111.83
3	Cosco Pacific	1,666.58
4	Guangdong Inv	1,583.79
5	China Os Land and Inv	1,569.37
6	China Mrch Holdings	1,536.11
7	Ka Wah Bank	1,378.15
8	Cnpc Hong Kong	1,310.93
9	Ng Fung Hong	1,071.44
10	China Travel International	993.26
11	China Everbright	985.85
12	Guangzhou Inv	672.36
13	Guangnan Holdings	628.04
14	China Everbright International	530.35
15	Top Glory International	511.15
16	China Aerospace	433.22
17	Founder Hong Kong	409.67
18	Union Bank Of Hong Kong	367.91
19	China Everbright Tech	291.87
20	Cont Mariner	258.42

Source: Daiwa Securities (HK) Ltd.

Exhibit 13.7:
THE 20 LARGEST SHSE B SHARES, END-1997

Ranking	*Issuer*	*Market value (US$ million)*
1	Shanghai Lujiazui Dev B	283.92
2	Zhejing Electricity Power B	222.18
3	Eastern Communications B	181.80
4	Shanghai Dazhong Taxi B	151.69
5	Heilongjiang Electricity B	137.88
6	Shanghai Jinqiao B	72.50
7	Erdos Cashmere B (Inner Mongolia)	71.40
8	Jinan Qingqi Motorcycle B	70.84
9	Shanghai Zhenhua Port B	68.80
10	Shanghai Outer Gaoqiao B	65.31
11	Yitai Coal B	64.74
12	Shanghai Chlor Chemicals B	63.57
13	Huangshan Tourism B	60.00
14	Shanghai World's Best B	58.19
15	Shanghai Tyre and Rubber B	55.25
16	Shanghai Refrigerator Compr B	49.87
17	Tien Tsin Marine B	42.66
18	Js Wuling Diesel B	33.60
19	Shanghai Haixin B	33.03
20	Hainan Airlines B	32.66

Source: Daiwa Securities (HK) Ltd.

Exhibit 13.8:
THE 20 LARGEST SZSE B SHARES, END-1997

Ranking	*Issuer*	*Market value (US$ million)*
1	Shanghai Konka Electric B	166.09
2	Guangdong Electric B	151.53
3	Hainan Donghai Tour B	146.87
4	China International Marine B	142.11
5	Shenzhen Fandga B	115.07
6	Chong Qing Changan B	100.52
7	Bengang Steel Plates B	88.95
8	China Southern Glass B	84.29
9	Guangdong Prvl Expr B	83.26
10	Shandong Chenming B	81.33
11	Wuxi Little Swan B	72.95
12	Jiangling Motor B	65.69
13	Changchai Co B	64.90
14	Shenzhen Seg B	64.27
15	Anhui Gujing B	64.00
16	Tsann Kuen B	62.09
17	China Vanke Co B	58.54
18	Wafangdian Bearing B	52.10
19	Hefei Meiling B	49.72
20	Shanghai China Bicycles B	47.79

Source: Daiwa Securities (HK) Ltd.

C) Trading volume

Total turnover of A and B shares on SHSE in 1997 was US$163 billion and US$2.56 billion respectively. Gross turnover of trading equities and mutual funds on SZSE was US$21 billion.

Exhibit 13.9:
AVERAGE DAILY SHARE TURNOVER, 1997 (US$ MILLION)

	H shares	*"Red chip" shares*	*SHSE B shares*	*SZSE B shares*
1997	164.47	377.40	12.24	11.00

Source: Daiwa Securities (HK) Ltd.

Exhibit 13.10:
THE 20 MOST ACTIVELY TRADED H SHARES, 1997

Ranking	*Issuer*	*Turnoer (US$ million)*
1	China Shipping Development	21.77
2	Beijing Yanhua	18.23
3	China Eastern Airlines	13.96
4	Yizheng Chemical Fibre	13.07
5	Angang New Steel	10.39
6	Zhejiang Expressway Co	9.22
7	Shanghai Petrochem	8.95
8	Jilin Chemical Industries	7.74
9	Beijing Datang Power	6.44
10	China Southern Airlines	6.16
11	Beijing North Star Co	5.35
12	Jiangxi Copper	4.07
13	Maanshan Iron and Steel	4.00
14	First Tractor	3.64
15	Shenzhen Expressway	3.25
16	Sichuan Express	2.82
17	Tianjin Bohai Chemical	2.65
18	Qingling Motors	2.53
19	Jiangsu Expressway	2.19
20	Guangdong Kelon	2.13

Source: Daiwa Securities (HK) Ltd.

Exhibit 13.11:
THE 20 MOST ACTIVELY TRADED "RED CHIP" SHARES, 1997

Ranking	*Issuer*	*Turnover (US$ million)*
1	Cnpc Hong Kong	42.70
2	China Mrch Holdings	40.18
3	China Res Entrep	27.72
4	China Everbright	25.49
5	China Os Land and Inv	19.71

Exhibit 13.11 continued

6	Shanghai Industrial	19.48
7	Guangdong Inv	18.13
8	Ka Wah Bank	16.53
9	Cosco Pacific	16.00
10	China Everbright International	15.36
11	China Travel International	15.29
12	Guangzhou Inv	12.54
13	Shenzhen International Holding	11.91
14	Top Glory International	11.58
15	China Aerospace	10.15
16	China Everbright Tech	9.35
17	Poly Investment Holding	8.58
18	Cont Mariner	7.94
19	Ng Fung Hong	6.59
20	Shougang Ccrd International Enterprises	5.24

Source: Daiwa Securities (HK) Ltd.

Exhibit 13.12:
THE 20 MOST ACTIVELY TRADED SHSE B SHARES, 1997

Ranking	*Issuer*	*Turnover (US$ million)*
1	Shanghai Lujiazui Dev B	1.45
2	Zhejing Electric Power B	1.36
3	Eastern Communications B	0.70
4	Erdos Cashmere B (Inner Mongolia)	0.59
5	Shai Dazhong Taxi B	0.53
6	Yitai Coal B	0.50
7	Sh Zhenhua Port B	0.49
8	Heilongjiang Electric B	0.48
9	Jinan Qingqi Motorcycle B	0.44
10	Shanghai World's Best B	0.42
11	Tien Tsin Marine B	0.36
12	Hainan Airlines B	0.35
13	Shanghai Jinqiao B	0.34
14	Shanghai Refrig Compr B	0.32
15	Js Wuling Diesel B	0.31
16	Shanghai Haixin B	0.26
17	Shanghai Chlor Chemical B	0.26
18	Shanghai Kaikai B	0.26
19	Shanghai Outer Gaoqiao B	0.26
20	Shanghai Diesel Engine B	0.25

Source: Daiwa Securities (HK) Ltd.

Exhibit 13.13:
THE 20 MOST ACTIVELY TRADED SZSE B SHARES, 1997

Ranking	*Issuer*	*Turnover (US$ million)*
1	Bengang Steel Plates B	1.07
2	Shandong Chenming B	0.85

Exhibit 13.13 continued

3	Guangdong Electric B	0.75
4	Changchai Co B	0.48
5	Hefei Meiling B	0.40
6	Anhui Gujing B	0.37
7	Beijing Orient Electric B	0.36
8	China International Marine B	0.35
9	Chong Qing Changan B	0.35
10	China Southern Glass B	0.29
11	Hubei Sanonda B	0.21
12	Foshan Electric and Lighting B	0.19
13	Guangdong Prvl Expr B	0.16
14	Hainan Donghai Tour B	0.15
15	Lizhu Pharmaceutical B	0.14
16	China Mer Shekou Port B	0.13
17	China Vanke Co B	0.13
18	Jiangling Motor B	0.07
19	Health Mineral B	0.04
20	Shn Benelux Enter B	0.01

Source: Daiwa Securities (HK) Ltd.

TYPES OF SHARES

At present, foreign investors can invest directly in the shares of Chinese enterprises through B shares listed on the SHSE or the SZSE, H shares listed on the HKSE and N shares, listed on the NYSE. Foreign investors may invest in so-called "red chips", which are Chinese controlled companies registered in Hong Kong with operational and financial autonomy. In addition, some Chinese shares are listed in Singapore and London, and there are plans for some to list on the Tokyo exchange. It is also possible to obtain exposure to the Chinese economy by investing in foreign companies with substantial investments in China that are listed on the exchanges of other countries, such as Hong Kong, Taiwan and Korea, and through various investment funds targeted at the China market. Convertible bonds issued by Chinese enterprises are the newest instrument that enable foreign investors to invest directly in Chinese enterprises.

As described, listed Chinese companies' share capital comprises two kinds of equity – local shares (A shares) and foreign shares (B or other shares listed in Hong Kong or elsewhere). Local shares are restricted to Chinese nationals, while foreign shares are restricted to foreign investors. Subscriptions for foreign shares, dividends and cash distributions to foreign shareholders are all paid in foreign currencies based on the latest exchange rates quoted by the People's Bank of China. With the exception of the restriction on the status of shareholders, foreign shares have the same rights and obligations as local shares.

Exhibit 13.14:
COUNTRY FUNDS – CHINA

	US$ % change					
	01/01/97	*01/01/93*	*Fund base*	*Fund*	*Fund*	*Management*
Fund	*01/01/98*	*01/01/98*	*currency*	*size (US$ mil)*	*volatility*	*group*
China Fund	32.06	98.16	US$	26.6	12.354	Morgan Grenfell
GT PRC B	15.84	36.2	US$	55	11.123	LGT
GT PRC A	15.31	37.22	US$	55	11.093	LGT
Yamaichi Pure China Fund	15.2	N/A	US$	13	10.04	Yamiachi Euro
Barclays ASF China (PRC)	-0.17	26.27	US$	27.3	11.091	Barclays
Sogelux Fd Equities China	-1.7	N/A	US$	13.8	-1	Sogenal
Guinness Flight China	-4.11	N/A	US$	28.2	-1	Guinness Flight
Thornton New Tiger China	-8.3	53.29	US$	12.2	11.455	Thornton
CH China Investments Ltd	-9.59	N/A	A$	21.192	8.27	CH Investment Management
ABN AMRO China Equity Fund	-12.4	N/A	US$	95.1	-1	ABN AMRO
Fleming FF China	-13.18	N/A	US$	174.5	11.557	Jardine Fleming
Dres Thornton ASF China	-14.12	N/A	US$	56.5	11.658	Thornton
Partner Chine	-17.25	N/A	Ffr	87	11.614	Mondiale/LGM
Jupiter Tyndall GF China	-21.83	7.77	US$	2.2	12.955	Tyndall
Equity Fund of China	-21.89	-12.7	US$	26.291	8.273	Batterymarch
China Investment Trust	-27.62	N/A	£	N/A	12.261	Tyndall
Atlas Chine Investissement	-29.63	N/A	Ffr	46	-1	Fin Atlas
Capital Chine	-33.15	N/A	Ffr	18	-1	Paluel Marmon

Note: details for some funds may not have been included if the data for the US$ % change for 97/98 was not available

Source: Standard & Poor's Micropal.

OPERATIONS

A) Trading system

Trading of B shares is only allowed on the SHSE and SZSE. All B shares are traded in a scripless form using an automatic transfer and computerised system. Buy/sell orders are matched automatically by computer based on price priority followed by time priority, and confirmation is relayed to investors on the same day. Price fluctuations are limited to 10% below or above the previous closing price. Note that foreign brokers with special exchange seats are permitted to execute their orders directly, without passing through local brokers.

B) Settlement and transfer

Settlement time on both domestic exchanges is three days. Turnaround trading time is on the same day. Stock transfer is T+1.

C) Commissions and other costs

SHSE trading costs comprise a brokerage fee of 0.7% of the gross consideration (minimum Rmb5), a transfer fee of 0.1% of par value (minimum US$1), stamp duty of 0.3% of the gross consideration and a clearing fee of US$4 per execution for individuals and corporations (US$8 for custodians). There is no registration fee.

SZSE trading costs comprise a brokerage commission of 0.43%, stamp duty of 0.3%, a stock exchange charge of 0.03%, a clearing charge of 0.0046% and a settlement fee of 0.05%, with a maximum of HK$500 and no minimum charge.

Non-Chinese investors resident outside China are normally exempt from stamp duty on share transactions.

TAXATION AND REGULATIONS AFFECTING FOREIGN INVESTORS

A) Taxation

Tax on dividends

Under 1991–92 legislation, dividends from Chinese companies paid to all shareholders, whether enterprises or individuals, were subject to a 20% withholding tax payable in China. In July 1993, however, the Chinese State Tax Bureau issued a Tax Notice to the effect that dividends paid by a Chinese company to a foreign enterprise with no establishment in China, or to an individual not resident in China, are not subject to withholding tax.

Dividends paid by Chinese companies which are foreign investment enterprises (FIEs) are exempt from income tax. For a company to be treated as an FIE, non-Chinese investors must hold at least 25% of its equity and the company must have applied for and been granted FIE status by the Ministry of Foreign Trade and Economic Cooperation.

Capital gains tax

When a foreign enterprise with no establishment in China, or a foreign individual not resident in China, obtains a gain from the sale of shares in a Chinese company, he may be subject to a Chinese withholding tax levied at a flat rate of 20%. Based on the Tax Notice, however, for the time being such gains will not be taxed. The Ministry of Finance and the State Tax Bureau issued a second notice stipulating that individual income tax will not be charged on gains from the sale of shares by non-resident individuals: this notice had not been withdrawn at the time of going to press.

Double tax treaties

If the withholding tax exemption is terminated, foreign enterprises and individuals resident in countries that have entered into double taxation treaties with China may be entitled to a reduction in the withholding tax imposed on the payment of dividends to foreign investors. China has double taxation treaties with a number of countries, including Australia, Canada, France, Germany, Japan, Malaysia, the Netherlands, Singapore, the United Kingdom and the United States.

Stamp duty

Chinese stamp tax, imposed on the transfer of shares of Chinese publicly traded companies, should not apply to transactions by non-Chinese investors outside China. It is imposed on documents executed or received within China or which should be used within China.

B) Regulations

The main regulatory development during 1997 was the promulgation of the Notice on Strengthening Controls over Overseas Share Issues. This aims to submit the majority of corporate restructurings by Chinese-controlled companies incorporated outside the PRC or Hong Kong to approval from the China Securities Regulatory Commission (CSRC) and, in certain circumstances, the State Council Securities Commission.

Foreign exchange control

The renminbi is not freely convertible into foreign currencies. With effect from 1 January 1994, there has been a unified exchange rate system under which the People's Bank of China publishes a daily exchange rate for the renminbi against the US dollar, based on the previous day's dealings in the interbank foreign exchange market.

In 1994, the China Foreign Exchange Trading Centre (CFETC) began operations. CFETC has set up a computerised network with sub-centres in several major cities, forming an interbank market in which designated foreign exchange banks can trade and settle their foreign currencies. Swap centres, which were supposed to have been abolished, have been retained as an interim measure. Under regulations introduced in 1996, Chinese companies now have access to designated foreign exchange banks in respect of current account items and so, indirectly, to the interbank market.

B share trading is conducted, and dividends on B shares paid, in foreign currencies. On the SHSE this is the US dollar and on the SZSE the Hong Kong dollar.

LISTING AND REPORTING REQUIREMENTS

On both the Shenzhen and Shanghai markets, issuers of new shares must provide a prospectus with accurate and complete information about the company.

As regards reporting requirements, companies listed on China's two exchanges must file interim reports and audited annual reports with the responsible authorities within 60 and 120 days after the first six months and fiscal year-end respectively. Both reports are subsequently made available to the public. Companies that have issued B shares may prepare accounts adjusted to international accounting standards.

Listed companies are required to report material events to the relevant authorities promptly. These events include: agreements with third parties that have a material impact on the company's assets or liabilities; significant changes to the company's business operations; substantial or long-term investments; material losses or the assumption of substantial liabilities; changes to shareholdings of more than 5% of total share capital by at least 2%; engagement in any litigation of material importance; bankruptcy and liquidation; important changes in the production or business environment; new laws or policies that have a marked effect on operations; and significant management changes. The event should also be publicised, unless the authorities agree that publication would harm the company's interests.

SHAREHOLDER PROTECTION

Insider trading and market manipulation are prohibited.

RESEARCH

Comprehensive information and research on the Chinese equity market is provided by Salomon Brothers, Daiwa, SBC Warburg, Peregrine and HG Asia.

CHAPTER

14

Colombia

Introduction

Colombia has three securities exchanges – the Bogotá exchange, the Medellín exchange and the Occidente exchange (in Cali), which were established in 1928, 1961 and 1981, respectively. The most dynamic exchange is Bogotá, which accounted for 55.5% of total volume traded in Colombia in 1997, followed by Medellín with 40.9%.

Since 1991 the government has authorised foreign portfolio investment and removed many of the structural obstacles hindering companies from using equity as a source of finance. These reforms have also eliminated double taxation, exempted dividend income from tax and abolished capital gains tax on the sale of exchange-traded stocks. However, the number of companies financing expansion through equity offerings remains small.

The exchanges have direct electronic trading, which has been modernised and improved, in particular with the development of the Winset trading system.

ECONOMIC AND POLITICAL OVERVIEW

In 1997 the threat of economic sanctions against Colombia remained, because the United States again refused to certify the Colombian government's efforts to fight drug trafficking. During the year the political crisis brought about by the accusation that President Samper had used drug money to support his presidential campaign was eclipsed by other corruption scandals involving the resignation of five government ministers.

Congressional and presidential elections will take place in the first semester of 1998. The former Minister of Internal Affairs, Horacio Serpa, is, according to the polls, the candidate with the greatest chance of becoming president; he is the official candidate of the Liberal Party, currently in power. Congressional elections will be held in March and presidential elections in May (first round) and June (second round).

According to preliminary estimates from the National Planning Department (NPD), GDP grew by 3.2% during 1997, up one percentage point compared with 1996. The unemployment rate rose to 12%, also one percentage point higher than the 1996 level. Inflation, as calculated by the Consumer Price Index, reached 17.68%, down 4% on the 1996 figure.

The current account deficit on the balance of payments increased slightly to around 5.5% of GDP, while net international reserves stood at US$9,881 million at 31 December 1997, unchanged on a year earlier.

During 1997, foreign investment reached an estimated US$6,850 million, 60% higher than 1996 levels. Direct investment totalled US$5,400 million. Extra investment in the financial and petroleum sectors primarily explains this increase. Portfolio investment grew by 36%, from US$1,135 million in 1996 to US$1,547 million in 1997.

During 1998, it is estimated that foreign investment flows will drop to US$2,500 million because of fewer privatisations and a decline in resource sector investment.

Role of the central bank

The Banco de la República is independent of the government and has the following responsibilities:

- to regulate and issue currency (the peso), and implement monetary policy;
- to regulate international exchange and credit markets;
- to administer Colombia's international reserves; and
- to act as lender of last resort to the Colombian banking system.

The Banco de la República is also responsible for preserving the purchasing power of the currency, which is often a difficult goal to achieve in co-ordination with other economic and social objectives, such as low unemployment and a competitive exchange rate. Some

Exhibit 14.1: BOGOTA GENERAL PRICE INDEX (US$), 1993–97

High value 15172.68 1.8.94 Low value 6364.76 3.5.93 *Source: Datastream*

members of the government have argued that the bank's independence should be reduced, but so far there have been no moves in that direction.

MARKET PERFORMANCE

A) In 1997

At the end of the year there were 207 companies listed on Colombia's exchanges, with the top 10 companies accounting for 49% of total market capitalisation. During 1997 market capitalisation increased by 21.9%, mainly due to higher prices rather than an increase in the total shares outstanding. In the same period, share trades as a percentage of total securities traded increased from 3.24% to 6.48%.

In 1997, Bogatá's IBB Index rose by 69.6%, while Medellín's IBOMED picked up 51.1%. Total volume traded on the three exchanges, including auctions, increased by 74%.

This encouraging performance was fuelled by an increase in money market liquidity, a drop of more than 10 points in interest rates and the switching of positions from fixed-income stocks to equities. The latter might have been induced by new taxes imposed on yields and discount gains on fixed-income securities. The ratio of turnover to total market capitalisation remains moderate at 0.6%, indicating that the market is not very liquid.

To date, privatisation has not played as important a role in the Colombian stock market as in other Latin American countries. In 1997, however, Empresa de Energía de Bogotá (EEB – Bogotá's electricity utility) and Gas Natural (the gas distributor in Bogotá) were the subject of foreign investment, while privatisations are also planned in the financial sector. In addition, there has been a high level of takeover activity in the past few years as foreign organisations have taken control of such important institutions as Banco Ganadero (by Spain's Banco Bilbao Viscaya) and Banco Comercial Antioqueño (by Banco Santander).

The Asian crisis has so far had little effect on the Colombian equity market, mainly because Colombian equities represent only around 2-3% of the portfolios of foreign funds.

B) Summary information

Global ranking by market value (US$ terms, end-1997): 42
Market capitalisation (end-1997): US$20.03 billion
Growth in market value (US$ terms, 1993–97): 39.1%
Market value as a % of GDP (end-1997): 22.78%
Number of domestic/foreign companies listed (end-1997): 207/0
Market P/E (end-1997): 15.9
MSCI Index (change in US$ terms, 1997): +37.8%
Short-term (DTF* 90-day) interest rate (end-1997): 21.16%
Long-term (TES public 5-year) bond yield (end-1997): 24.46%
Budget deficit as a % of nominal GNP (end-1997): 4.35%
Annual increase in broad money (M3) supply (end-1997): 25.80%
Inflation rate (1997): 17.68%
US$ exchange rate (end-1997): Ps1,293.58
*Average deposit rate.

C) Year-end share price index, P/E ratios and yields

Exhibit 14.2:
SHARE INDICES, P/E RATIOS AND YIELDS, 1993-97

	1993	*1994*	*1995*	*1996*	*1997*
IBB Index change	+50%	+19%	-15.7%	+11.8%	+69.6%
IBOMED Index change	+30%	+24%	-16.4%	-3.12%	+51.1%
Market P/E ratio	21.7	19.2	9.1	10.7	15.9
Yield (%)	2.1	2.1	3.8	4.6	2.9

Source: Bolsa de Bogotá.

D) Market indices and their constituents

Colombia has two main share price indices: the Bolsa de Bogotá Index (IBB) and the Bolsa de Medellín Index (IBOMED). The IBB and IBOMED indices include the top shares by turnover. The IBB base is 100 at 2 January 1991 and the IBOMED's base is 1,000 at 29 December 1987.

THE STOCK MARKET

A) Brief history and structure

The Bogotá Stock Exchange (BSE), established in 1928, is a company owned by the member brokerage houses and is the country's principal exchange, accounting for nearly 70% of all share transactions.

The Bolsa de Medellín (MSE), also a limited company owned by member brokerage houses, was established in 1961. Both the BSE and MSE are supervised by the National Securities Commission Superintendency (SNV).

B) Different exchanges

There are three exchanges in Colombia located in Bogotá, Medellín and Cali (Occidente).

C) Names and addresses

BOLSA DE BOGOTÁ
Carrera 8, #13-82, 2nd-9th Floors
Apdo. Aereo 3584, Santafé de Bogotá, D.C.
Tel: (57) 1 243 6501; Fax: (57) 1 281 3170
Website: www.bolsaBogotá.com.co

BOLSA DE MEDELLÍN
Carrera 50, #50-48, 2nd Floor
Apdo. Aereo 3535, Medellín
Tel: (57) 4 260 3000; Fax: (57) 4 251 1981
Website: www.bolsaMedellín.com.co

BOLSA DE OCCIDENTE
Calle 8, #3-14, 17th Floor, Cali
Tel: (57) 2 381 7022; Fax: (57) 2 381 6720

MARKET SIZE

A) Number of listings and market value

At the end of 1997 there were 207 companies listed on Colombia's exchanges, of which 128 were registered on the BSE. Total market capitalisation was US$20.03 billion.

Exhibit 14.3:
NUMBER OF LISTINGS AND MARKET VALUE, COLOMBIAN EXCHANGES, 1993–97

Year-end	*No. of listed companies*	*Market value (US$ million)*
1993	176	14,400
1994	198	18,495
1995	193	14,833
1996	208	16,436
1997	207	20,034

Source: Corredores Asociados SA.

B) Largest quoted companies

Exhibit 14.4:
THE 10 LARGEST LISTED COMPANIES, COLOMBIAN EXCHANGES, END-1997

Ranking	*Company*	*Market value (US$ million)*
1	Bavaria	2,888.18
2	Banco Ganadero	1,369.61
3	Suramericana	1,157.22
4	Cementos Argos	957.56
5	Banco de Bogotá	902.59
6	Nacional de Chocolates	596.99
7	Banco de Occidente	540.45
8	Cementos Caribe	533.16
9	Banco Industrial Colombiano	440.41
10	Banco Popular	425.55

Source: Corredores Asociados SA.

C) Trading volume

Total equity turnover in 1997 amounted to US$3,005.2 million, an increase of 74.0% compared with 1996. The increase on the BSE was 212.4%, with trading value rising to US$1,231.8 million. Average daily turnover was US$5.74 million.

Exhibit 14.5:
THE 10 MOST ACTIVELY TRADED SHARES, COLOMBIAN EXCHANGES, 1997

Ranking	*Company/share*	*Traded shares (million)*
1	Banco de Colombia	277.7
2	Banco Ganadero	249.6
3	Cadenalco	79.7
4	Bavaria	44.3
5	Cementos Argos	26.5
6	Banco Industrial Colombiano	21.0
7	Banco de Bogotá	15.2
8	Coltabaco	12.4
9	Banco Santander	9.2
10	Cementos Caribe	8.4

Source: Corredores Asociados SA.

TYPES OF SHARE

Both ordinary shares and dividend preferred shares are traded in the Colombian equity market. Under Colombian law (and Rule 144A), ordinary shares or non-voting dividend preferred registered shares, such as those of Banco Ganadero and Corfivalle, can be represented by ADRs. Listed companies have also issued convertible bonds. The issue of privileged shares is permitted, but such issues are not publicly traded in Colombia.

Fixed-income instruments still represent the overwhelming majority of securities traded on the Colombian exchanges.

INVESTORS

In 1997 institutional investors (such as private pension funds) comprised the most important investor group, accounting for 46.3% of total turnover. This figure includes foreign funds, which accounted for 38.1%. The corporate sector was responsible for 29.5% of market trading, financial institutions for 17.48% and individuals for 6.7%.

OPERATIONS

A) Trading system

In 1996 BSE operations formally transferred from open outcry to an electronic system. Nevertheless, some special operations such as privatisations and public sales are still carried out by open outcry. The BSE electronic system comprises two major modules – Winset Shares for cash or forward share trading between 10.00am and 12.00 noon, and Winset Fixed for all non-share trading between 8.00am and 4.20pm.

B) Principal brokers

BERMUDEZ Y VALENZUELA SA
Cr. 7 No. 32-93, piso 7, Santafé de Bogotá
Tel: (57) 1 288 3677; Fax: (57) 1 285 9318

CASA DE BOLSA SA
Cr.7, No. 33-42, piso 14, Santafé de Bogotá
Tel: (57) 1 287 9600; Fax: (57) 1 287 3046

CO DE BOLSA DEL COMERCIO SA
Cl. 72 No. 13-33, piso 1, Santafé de Bogotá
Tel: (57) 1 255 3280; Fax: (57) 1 235 4029

COMISIONISTAS COLOMBIANOS
DE BOLSA COLBOLSA SA
Cr. 11 No. 82-01, Of. 302, Santafé de Bogotá
Tel: (57) 1 621 2811; Fax: (57) 1 621 4614

COMPANIA GENERAL DE INTERCAMBIO S.A.
Diagonal 74 No. 6-51, Bogota
Tel: (57) 1 210 2774/2936; Fax: (57) 1 210 3071

CONSORCIO BURSATIL SA
Cl. 72, No. 10-07, Of. 1002, Santafé de Bogotá
Tel: (57) 1 346 0600; Fax: (57) 1 210 4384

Exhibit 14.6:
COUNTRY FUNDS – COLOMBIA

Fund	*US$ % change 01/01/97 01/01/98*	*US$ % change 01/01/93 01/01/98*	*Currency*	*Fund size (US$ mil)*	*Fund volatility*	*Management group*	*Opal Main sector*	*Opal subsector*
Colombian Inv Co	11.24	20.85	U.S$	14	6.847	Foreign & Colonial	Open-End	Equity

Note: details for some funds may not have been included if the data for the US$ % change for 97/98 was not available

Source Standard & Poor's Micropal.

CORREDORES ASOCIADOS SA
Cr. 7, No. 71-52, Torre B, piso 16, Santafé de Bogotá
Tel: (57) 1 312 3100; Fax: (57) 1 312 2788

CORREDOR Y ALBAN SA
Cr. 10 No.28-49 Torre A, piso 25, Santafé de Bogotá
Tel: (57) 1 286 9355; Fax: (57) 1 282 1601

CORRETAJE DE VALORES SA
Cr. 7 No. 33-42, piso 11, Santafé de Bogotá
Tel: (57) 1 288 6311

SARMIENTO LOZANO SA
Bogotá: Cr. 7 No. 73-55, piso 8, Santafé de Bogotá
Tel: (57) 1 312 1251; Fax: (57) 1 312 1543
Cali: Cl.8 No.1-16 Of. 201, Cali
Tel: (57) 2 889 1600; Fax: (57) 2 883 6919

C) Settlement and transfer

The Deposito Centralizado de Valores de Colombia (DECEVAL) is authorised by the SNV to operate as a securities depository. It is owned by (among others) the three stock exchanges and the Colombian Banking Association. DECEVAL provides custody services and electronically registers stock transfers.

Inter-broker settlements are handled by the BSE, which calculates the net balance of all payments to be received or paid by each broker. The relevant amount is credited or debited to the broker on the same day the securities are transferred.

There are no special settlement provisions for foreign investors.

D) Commissions and other costs

Commission rates range from 1.0% down to 0.3% depending on the size of the transaction.

TAXATION AND REGULATIONS AFFECTING FOREIGN INVESTORS

Foreign investment in the Colombian equity market is typically effected through foreign portfolio investment funds. Such funds must have as their sole purpose the purchase and sale of securities in the public market. Foreign portfolio investment funds are classified into individual (formed by a single individual or company) and institutional (constituted in any acceptable form by more than one individual or company). Omnibus accounts (foreign investment funds comprising a number of sub-accounts, each one belonging to a single institutional investor) are classed as institutional funds.

Foreign investment funds may invest in all kinds of securities registered with the National Registry of Securities and Intermediaries, including shares, bonds, convertible bonds, and fixed-income securities, with the exception of those guaranteed by the central bank or those issued for monetary policy purposes. Not more than 20% of a foreign investment fund's portfolio may be represented by fixed-income securities with a maturity term shorter than three years.

Portfolio investments must be registered with the central bank within 30 working days after conversion of the foreign exchange to make the investments. Registration is in the name of the investor for individual funds, and in the name of the fund itself for institutional funds. After obtaining initial registration, foreign investment funds need only register additional foreign exchange amounts brought into Colombia for investment in securities, and the total or partial repatriation of money. Foreign investors operating directly in the stock market must register their initial investment within three months of converting the relevant foreign exchange, and must amend the registration every time securities are bought or sold.

The SNV must approve institutional funds before they start operating in the Colombian securities market. The amount each fund plans to invest in the local market must be disclosed to the SNV. Individual funds do not require SNV authorisation to operate. A foreign investment fund may not hold 10% or more of the voting stock of a given company. An omnibus account, including all its sub-accounts, may not hold 40% or more of the voting stock of a given company, and each individual account may not include 10% or more of the voting stock of a given company. A foreign investor requires the authorisation of the Superintendent of Banks in order to acquire 10% or more of the voting stock of a bank or financial sector company.

The administration of foreign portfolio funds is carried out by trust companies or stockbrokers. Such administrators represent the fund and are jointly responsible for any breach of legal provisions.

All members of institutional funds are protected by Colombian law, which gives them certain rights, including the right to receive dividends, the right to examine documents concerning the investments of the fund and the right to repatriate their investments.

Capital gains on equities are not taxable for foreign investment funds. Foreign investors operating directly in the stock market are subject to dividend remittance tax of 7% on the dividend amount to be remitted, but foreign investment funds are expressly exempt from this remittance tax.

LISTING REQUIREMENTS

Companies with publicly traded stock are subject to the supervision and control of the SNV. As a minimum they are required to publish their financial statements annually in the bulletin of their local chamber of commerce.

SHAREHOLDER PROTECTION CODES

Colombian legislation provides for the protection of shareholders by regulating the exercise of shareholders' rights. For example, there must be advance notice of shareholders' meetings, and shareholders are permitted to examine the company's books and records during the 15 working days prior to a meeting called to approve its financial statements.

Legislation applicable to non-voting dividend preferred shares sets out a number of circumstances in which holders of such shares become entitled to vote.

The SNV imposes sanctions on entities subject to its inspection and monitoring that disobey its decisions or violate insider trading rules or other regulations.

RESEARCH

The BSE publishes information on the stock market, the economic and financial position of issuers and on the economy in general. The exchange also publishes a capital market review and statistical data in its daily, weekly, monthly and annual bulletins. The MSE publishes a daily report of the stock market and a monthly summary of the market.

The SNV has an economic research department that studies the market and publishes weekly, monthly and annual reports.

National newspapers also publish economic and financial information.

Colombia, published by Euromoney Books, provides in-depth information for those wishing to invest and do business in the country. See the order card at the back of this book for details.

PROSPECTIVE CHANGES

In 1998 the BSE plans to implement electronic trading for national Treasury bonds issued by the central bank, for OTC deals in association with the Medellín and Occidente exchanges, and for interest rate and currency futures and options.

CHAPTER 15

Costa Rica

Introduction

During 1997, the Costa Rican economy showed signs of a slow recovery. Tax policies aimed at stabilising public finances over the medium term allowed a less restrictive monetary policy compared with 1995 and 1996.

Aggregate demand underwent an important increase, due mainly to greater income from external capital, better coffee prices, lower interest rates and the relaxation of monetary policy.

ECONOMIC AND POLITICAL OVERVIEW

The Monthly Indicator of Economic Activity (IMAE) showed a slow but stable pattern of growth during 1997, totalling around 3.5% for the year as a whole. Cumulative CPI inflation for 1997 was 11.2%, compared with 13.9% in 1996.

Interest rates trended downwards, while plans for the placement of US$200 million in foreign debt bonds freed up the financial pressure that always tends to appear towards the end of the year. The Basic Rate, a weighted average of pubic- and private- sector six-month interest rates stood at 18.5% at end-1997, down 6.1% compared with the end of 1996.

Government revenues expanded by 20% in 1997, helping to underpin some improvement in the public finances generally. Preliminary data reveals that the central government reduced its deficit from 5.3% of GDP in 1996 to 4.2% in 1997.

As regards foreign trade, revenues from tourism grew by around 1.5%, but Costa Rica's cumulative trade deficit from December 1996 through September 1997 was US$576.2 million, an increase of 74% compared with the same period in the previous year. In 1998, however, exports by Intel, the US microprocessor manufacturer that has an assembly plant in Costa Rica, are expected to be worth US$700 million and to produce more income than traditional products such as coffee and bananas. The company is investing between US$300 million and US$500 million in Costa Rica.

During 1997 the strength of capital investment offset the commercial deficit and helped to support a higher level of monetary reserves. As at 31 December 1997, hard currency reserves totalled US$1.107 billion.

Role of the central bank

The central bank is the government's main vehicle for the control of monetary policy, currency and credit. It sets reference rates for time deposits and establishes minimum reserve requirements.

The bank concentrates its efforts on reducing inflation, building up reserves and stabilising the foreign exchange market, and it is hoping to reduce the government's influence over its decisions.

MARKET PERFORMANCE

A) In 1997

Turnover on the Costa Rican stock exchange increased by 38% to US$17.05 million in 1997 and market capitalisation at the end of the year stood at US$810.5 million, an increase of 16.8% compared with end-1996. At 31 December 1997 there were 114 companies listed on the Bolsa Nacional de Valores (112 domestic and 2 foreign), the same as at December 1996.

B) Summary information

Global ranking by market value (US$ terms, end-1997): 71
Market capitalisation (end-1997): US$810.5 million
Growth in market value (local currency terms, 1994–97): 117%
Market value as a % of nominal GDP (end-1997): 9.2%
Number of domestic/foreign companies listed (end-1997): 112/2
Market P/E (end-1997): N/A
Short-term (28-day) interest rate (end-1997): 14.5%
Long term (1-year) interest rate (end-1997): 17.8%
Budget deficit as a% of nominal GDP (1997): 4.2%
Inflation rate (1997): 11.2%
US$ exchange rate (end-1997): C246.4

THE STOCK MARKET

A) Brief history and structure

The Bolsa Nacional de Valores (BNV) began operating in August 1976. It is a self-regulating corporation and is 85% owned by its brokerage firms. The BNV is administered by a board of directors, which is elected by the general assembly. The general manager and a group of executives are accountable for the operation, administration and management of the BNV.

The BNV is regulated by the Comisión Nacional de Valores (National Securities Commission), which is in charge of promoting, regulating and controlling the securities market, including promoters, issuers, brokers and dealers.

The financial markets are regulated by the *Ley Reguladora del Mercado de Valores* (Stock Market Regulation Act), which includes several amendments to the Costa Rican Commercial Code and sets out rules and regulations for the control of stock market operations. It also authorises institutions to provide services regarding the custody of securities, bonds and shares and compensation. In addition, the Superintendencia de Entidades Financieras (SUGEF) is in charge of supervising financial activity in Costa Rica. All financial institutions are regulated by SUGEF.

B) Opening hours, names and addresses

Trading hours on the BNV are Monday to Friday, from 9.00am to 1.30pm.

BOLSA NACIONAL DE VALORES
PO Box 1736-1000, San José
Tel: (506) 256 1180; Fax: (506) 255 0131
E-mail: bnvinternet.bnv.co.cr

MARKET SIZE

A) Number of listings and market value

There are currently 114 companies listed, two of which are foreign. Total market value at the end of 1997 was US$810.54 million.

B) Trading volume

Trading turnover on the exchange for 1997 was US$17.05 million, an increase of 38% over end-1996.

OPERATIONS

A) Trading system

In 1991 the BNV abandoned the open outcry system and switched to an electronic format with brokers connected through terminals in their respective offices.

B) Settlement and transfer

For most transactions, payment must be made by 2.00pm on the day of the transaction. Spot price transactions, however, require that payment be made 24 hours after the transaction.

Since 1983 the exchange has run a specialised depository department, Central de Valores (CEVAL). Under an agreement between the BNV and Cedel, CEVAL is able to offer access to the international bond and equity markets. Negotiations are under way with Euroclear to extend CEVAL's services.

C) Commissions and other costs

In the primary market no commissions are charged, while in the secondary market commissions charged by brokerage firms are negotiable.

TAXATION AND REGULATIONS AFFECTING FOREIGN INVESTORS

There are no investment restrictions on foreign investors in Costa Rica, nor are there any restrictions on repatriation of capital. However, a company may restrict the participation of foreign shareholders under the terms of its articles of association.

A 5% withholding tax is applied to dividends of BNV-registered and traded shares. There is no capital gains tax. The general rate for corporate income tax is 30%.

CHAPTER

16

Croatia

Introduction

Turnover on the Croatian capital markets continued to grow in 1997, albeit at a slower rate (74%) than in 1996, to DM598.0 million. Despite this growth, however, the Zagreb Stock Exchange (ZSE) is not yet representative of the broader Croatian economy. Many important Croatian firms are listed on the ZSE (eg, Pliva and Podravka), but many others are still state property (eg, the Croatian post and telecommunications firm, HPT, and the oil company, INA) or are simply not listed (eg, Agrokor). The capital markets are not yet viewed by companies as a source of finance, although the ZSE and the Varazdin over-the-counter market (VTV) are doing their best to change this situation.

The Croatian Pension Fund and Croatia's Bank Rehabilitation Agency are gradually selling off interests in companies large and small, listed and, primarily, unlisted. In addition, a large number of shares in a wide variety of companies are to be disposed of by the state in a voucher privatisation programme launched at the beginning of 1998.

ECONOMIC AND POLITICAL OVERVIEW

Croatia is a democratic state with a strong presidential form of government somewhat similar to that of France. Croatia's main political party is the Croatian Democratic Union (HDZ). In addition to holding the presidency, it holds 42 seats in the 63-seat House of Counties and 75 seats in the 127-seat House of Representatives. The two largest opposition parties are the Croatian Social Liberal Party and the Social Democratic Party (the former Communist Party). The most recent presidential election took place in June 1997. Incumbent President Franjo Tuđman was returned for an additional five-year term with 61% of the vote.

Since declaring its independence in 1991, Croatia has had close ties with Germany, Austria and, to a lesser extent, the United States. Relations with these countries and with the EU improved in late 1997 after a frosty period in the middle of the year that led to, among other things, the suspension of World Bank lending to Croatia and the rejection by Croatia of a proposed IMF facility. This improvement facilitated the full reincorporation of East Slavonia into the Croatian administrative structure in January 1998 and, with this, Croatia regained full control over the territory within its borders.

Inflation has been kept to less than 4% since 1994 (although the actual rate is difficult to assess because the index's market basket has not changed since 1987), and the kuna has held steady against the Deutschmark during that period. Ministry of Finance estimates for 1997 have growth at 6% plus, government deficits running at less than 2% of GDP and external debt at less than 30% of GDP. Estimated GDP for 1997 totals US$19.2 billion.

The Asian crisis hit Croatia hard, driving share prices down by 20–30% and widening the spread on its foreign debt to more than 300 basis points. Although they have yet to approach pre-crisis levels, both equity and debt have recovered in early 1998 as investors begin to differentiate between Croatia and other emerging markets.

Croatia is rated investment grade for external debt, with BBB- and Baa3 ratings from Standard & Poor's and Moody's, respectively.

Role of the central bank

The monetary independence of Croatia has been established and Croatia's own central monetary institution – the National Bank of Croatia – has been modelled on central banks in developed countries. The bank is responsible for maintaining the stability of the kuna, managing domestic and external liquidity, implementing foreign exchange and monetary policies, issuing banknotes, approving and issuing banking licences and supervising the banking sector.

The bank is not completely independent of the government and is directly responsible to parliament.

MARKET PERFORMANCE

A) In 1997

Market performance in 1997 in Croatia was disappointing. Although turnover was well ahead at DM598 million, the wave of new issues that had been anticipated did not materialise. While two new shares were added to the ZSE's first list, for a total of four (a fifth was added in early January 1998), no major new GDRs were launched. In fact, the ZSE was compelled to delist 31 companies from its TN quotation because they either traded too infrequently or refused to supply the information required of a listed company.

In addition, many of the country's shares trended downwards. In some cases this reflected disappointment that anticipated GDR issues had not materialised, but it also indicated dissatisfaction with internal corporate restructuring, worries over Croatian relations with the West and concern over lack of progress in rebuilding the broader Croatian economy. The Asian crisis inflicted a heavy blow as foreign investors, somewhat surprisingly, sold Croatian shares heavily in response to developments in Asia.

At end-1997, Croatian market capitalisation stood at approximately US$4.25 billion, or about 22% of GDP. Because many issues are traded rarely, perhaps not for months, and their prices are accordingly stale, total market capitalisation is not as helpful a statistic as it is in more developed markets. Figures for 1998 should prove more useful, now that the ZSE has dropped the least-traded shares from its official list.

B) Summary information

Global ranking by market value (US$ terms, end-1997): 54
Market capitalisation (end-1997): US$4.25 billion
Growth in market value (DM terms, 1994–97): 860.16%
Market value as % of GDP (US$ terms, end-1997): 22%
Number of domestic/foreign companies listed (end-1997): 48/0
Market P/E (end-1997): 23.6
Short-term (90-day) interest rate (end-1997): 9.9%
Long bond yield (end-1997): 11.1%
Budget deficit as a % of nominal GNP (Oct 1997): 1.49%
Annual increase in broad money (M4) supply (end-1997): 26%
Inflation rate (to Nov 1997): 3.10%
US$ exchange rate (end-1997): K6.3

MARKET SIZE

A) Number of listings and market value

There were 48 companies listed on the ZSE at end-1997, and market capitalisation stood at about DM6,850 billion.

Exhibit 16.1:
NUMBER OF COMPANIES LISTED AND MARKET VALUE, ZSE, 1994–97

Year-end	*No. of companies listed*	*Market capitalisation (DM million)*
1994	38	796.3
1995	68	580.8
1996	64	5,500.0
1997	48	6,850

Source: Zagreb Stock Exchange.

B) Trading volume

Until 1996, the ZSE derived most of its turnover from the auction sale of shares offered by the Croatian Privatisation Fund. Figures in the exhibit show how low secondary trading was when auction sales figures are removed. However, in 1996 the total value of turnover on the ZSE leaped to DM344 million. Turnover for 1997 totalled DM598.0 million.

Zagrebacka Banka, Pliva, Podravka, Plava Laguna and Varazdinska Banka were the most active shares in ordinary trading in 1997, with Zagrebacka Banka representing over 40% of the total.

Exhibit 16.2:
TOTAL VALUE OF SECURITIES TRADED ON THE ZSE, 1994–97

Year	**Trading value (DM million)*
1994	3.4
1995	4.5
1996	343.7
1997	598.0

*Excluding privatisation auction figures

Source: Zagreb Stock Exchange.

THE STOCK MARKET

A) Brief history and structure

The history of organised capital and commodities markets in Croatia goes back to at least 1918 when the Zagreb Stock and Commodities Exchange was established. The current stock market dates from 1991, when 25 banks from throughout the Republic of Croatia gathered to revive the market, and the present Zagreb Stock Exchange was incorporated as a joint stock company. The much smaller VTV was established in Croatia in 1993.

From the initial 25, the number of members of the ZSE

had increased to 48 at the end of September 1997. Members include both Croatian banks and private brokerage houses. Today, the exchange has 50 members, of which six are 100% owned by foreigners. Management and administration of the stock exchange are the responsibility of the board of directors, consisting of six members chosen by the general assembly of stockholders.

To become a ZSE member and operate on the exchange, banks or brokerage firms must buy a seat, meet certain competency requirements and receive approval from the board of directors. Costs of trading are high: the exchange charges from 0.30% to 0.44% of the value of each trade for its services.

Foreigners are permitted to hold seats on the ZSE, although the number of seats is fixed so they must be purchased from current holders. Substantial foreign pressure is being brought on the exchange to expand the number of seats available to enable more foreigners to join.

B) Different exchanges

The ZSE is the only stock exchange in Croatia.

C) Opening hours, name and address

Trading on the ZSE takes place between 9.00am and 2.00pm from Tuesday to Friday.

ZAGREBACKA BURZA
Ksaver 208, 1000 Zagreb
Tel: (385) 1 4677 925; Fax: (385) 1 4677 680

TYPES OF SHARE

Shares and bonds are traded (generally in registered form) as defined by the Company Act, and short-term securities (up to 365 days) as defined by the Money Market Law.

Securities were redefined by the 1995 Securities Act, which provides for dematerialised securities for public companies that are registered with CROSEC (the Croatian Securities and Exchange Commission).

OTHER MARKETS

There are two organised OTC markets – one in Varazdin (VTV) and one in Osijek. Volumes on the OTC markets are much lower than those on the ZSE. In 1997 the turnover on the VTV averaged around US$160,000 a day and totalled over US$40 million. The VTV market trades from 9.00am to 2.00pm, Monday to Friday. While a number of issues are cross-listed on the ZSE and the VTV, certain shares, most notably Ericsson-Nikola Tesla, are listed only on the VTV. The VTV also uses a real-time trading system, although a different one from the ZSE's.

Trades are executed by manual matching of telephone orders and are notified the next morning. Settlement is formally T+5 but actual settlement times can be much longer because there are no sanctions for failing to comply. Both the ZSE and the VTV compute indices – the CROBEX and VIN, respectively. The IFC is planning to introduce a Croatian index in early 1998.

INVESTORS

Although a sprinkling of high net worth local individuals and some local companies participate as speculators, the Croatian stock market is now dominated by foreign investors. Small shareholders, which because of Croatia's privatisation process constitute a large portion of the population (12.5%), are net sellers.

In 1997, however, acquisitions by foreigner investors were rare. This seems set to change in 1998 as the government grows more serious about divestment (in part because of a need to close the budget deficit), local entrepreneurs become more desperate for cash and foreign investors become more comfortable with Croatian risk.

OPERATIONS

A) Trading system

The current version of the trading system, introduced in April 1996, enables real-time, on-line access for brokers from remote terminals. A completely new, Windows-based trading system is planned to become operational in the first half of 1998. New features will include automated matching (with price and time priority) and improved connectivity with other applications.

As part of the privatisation process, the Croatian Privatisation Fund sells shares from its portfolio through public auction at the ZSE. Payment is made in local currency.

B) Principal Brokers

AUCTOR SECURITIES
Palmoticeva 2, 10000 Zagreb
Tel: (385) 1 481 4139; Fax: (385) 1 481 4143

FIMA
Trg Bana Jelacica 4, 42000 Varazdin
Tel: (385) 42 109 900; Fax: (385) 42 109 990

INVESTCO
Investco, Bo_koviceva 3, 10000 Zagreb
Tel: (385) 1 432 971; Fax: (385) 1 431 478

KARLOVACKA BANKA
Vladka Maceka 8, 47000 Karlovac
Tel: (385) 47 222 049; Fax: (385) 47 224 157

PRIVREDNA BANKA ZAGREB
Savska 28, 10000 Zagreb
Tel: (385) 1 333 895; Fax: (385) 1 333 912

ZAGREBACKA BANKA
Paromlinska 2, 10000 Zagreb
Tel: (385) 1 6104 084; Fax: (385) 1 533 462

TAXATION AND REGULATIONS AFFECTING FOREIGN INVESTORS

A) Taxation

There is no tax on dividends, no capital gains tax and no stamp duty imposed on investors. Income from capital investments and dividends is not taxable and thus losses are not deductible.

B) Foreign investment

Croatian government treatment of foreign investors is, in general, quite favourable, although the recent imposition of a capital gains tax on local securities houses does bring into question the administration's commitment to maintain the tax-free status of foreigners' capital gains over the medium term. There are no restrictions on foreign investment other than in a limited number of strategic industries (eg, arms manufacture) and in the case of certain short-term securities issued by the central bank. Further, there are three main guarantees for foreign investors under the Croatian constitution and laws:

- rights gained by investment of capital cannot be reduced either by laws or by other legal acts;
- transfer of profits is unrestricted; and
- repatriation of capital invested in Croatia is unrestricted.

RESEARCH

High quality research is generally unavailable locally. What is available is usually reserved for preferred clients.

Eastern Europe: Investing for the 21st Century, published by Euromoney Books, provides in-depth information for those wishing to invest or do business in the region. See the order card at the end of this book for details.

PROSPECTIVE CHANGES

KonCar and Varazdinska Banka are scheduled to issue GDRs early in 1998, while the Croatian PTT and other parastatals are due to be privatised during the year. Other positive developments include the implementation of a requirement that brokers maintain a client funds account (from which funds can be removed only to effect client-ordered transactions), progress on the Central Share Depository (which will eliminate delays in re-registration of securities), the Croatian government's new push for economic reform and the emergence of a sizeable number of local investors whose trades seem likely to increase ZSE liquidity.

Croatian securities market legislation is expected to be revised in 1998 for the first time since its introduction in 1995.

CHAPTER 17

Czech Republic

Introduction

After short-lived interest at the beginning of the year, investors by and large abandoned the Prague Stock Exchange (PSE) in 1997. The main market index, the PX50, ended the year at 495, down 8.2% from its end-1996 close and down 21% from its high for the year of 629. Average daily turnover of US$45 million at the beginning of 1997 declined to around US$10 million by the year-end. The loss of investor confidence was prompted by a slowdown in the economy, the devaluation of the crown, and a failure to move forward on key issues such as the formation of a Securities Exchange Commission, new legislation on investment funds and privatisation of the banks.

Politics remains key to the market's regaining investor interest. The collapse of the ruling coalition over a party financing scandal has prompted a split between the two main right-wing parties, the ODA and the ODS. This increases the likelihood that the Social Democrats, along with the Christian Democrats, will prevail in early elections expected to take place in June 1998. Investors are probably going to await the outcome of the elections before re-entering the market.

ECONOMIC AND POLITICAL OVERVIEW

The current state of the Czech economy is characterised by a slowdown in economic growth and stagnant manufacturing output. The central bank's restrictive monetary policy and tight fiscal policy have been oriented towards slowing down inflation and restoring the external balance at the expense of economic growth.

Since the demise of communism in 1989, former Czechoslovakia, currently the Czech Republic, was ruled by centre-right government coalitions until the end of November 1997 when the Prime Minister, Vaclav Klaus, resigned. The apparent reason for his departure centred on revelations about improper political financing but, in fact, signs of a crisis could be seen at the start of the year as a reaction to the sluggish development of the Czech economy during the first quarter of 1997. In response, the government decided to prepare a package of measures, aimed mainly at improving the current account deficit and narrowing the widening gap between productivity and wage growth by limiting aggregate demand. Thus, two austerity programmes were approved – one in April and the other in May 1997. Despite the unstable political situation, in the second half of 1997 these economic measures started bearing fruit. By the end of the year, real wage growth had slowed down to almost zero, the trade balance deficit totalled Kc140.8 billion (around 11% lower than the previous year) and the state budget deficit totalled Kc15.7 billion (about 1% of GDP). In addition, approval was given for a balanced 1998 budget. However, there still remains an urgent need for reforms on a micro level in order to sustain a successful macroeconomic performance.

As of 27 May 1997, following almost two weeks of intervention, the Czech central bank decided to abandon the +/-7.5% fluctuation band for the crown and introduced a free-floating regime. In addition it announced that its monetary policy would be based on the Deutschmark/crown exchange rate, rather than on the previous basket composition (65% Deutschmark and 35% US dollar).

The lack of popular support for belt-tightening, the crown's devaluation in May and the tension within the ruling coalition, led to a weakening of trust in the government. On 10 June the cabinet survived a vote of confidence by just one vote. On 15 December, after the resignation of Klaus's government, President Vaclav Havel named the governor of the Czech National Bank, Josef Tosovsky, as the new Prime Minister. On 28 January 1998, parliamentary backing was secured for the new government, which will stay in power until early elections, expected to take place in June.

Role of the central bank

The Czech National Bank (CNB) was created by legislation in 1992 to be the guarantor of currency stability and the controller of monetary policy. The CNB is legally and

Exhibit 17.1: PRAGUE ZB FREE MARKET PRICE INDEX (US$), 1993–97

High value 870.68 2.5.94 Low value 471.34 1.12.97 *Source: Datastream*

operationally independent of the government. Although the central bank does not formally publish any monetary targets, its main objective is price stability and controlling inflation, which subsequently determines its monetary policies. Other responsibilities include banking sector supervision, management of money circulation and preparation of semi-annual reports to parliament on monetary developments.

The central bank intervenes in the foreign exchange market via daily currency fixings, although in the past the CNB has generally fixed the crown in step with the interbank market.

The CNB controls the development of domestic interest rates by setting the level of its main lending rates (the discount, Lombard and repo rates) and indirectly through stipulating minimum reserve requirements.

MARKET PERFORMANCE

A) In 1997

The year started with a significant rally, as investors expected continued strong economic growth, better capital market regulation and further privatisation. Price increases in blue chips and engineering stocks, such as Skoda Plzen and CKD, drove the rally, and daily turnover averaged a healthy US$45.6 million. After peaking in late February, however, the market began to slide as investors became disillusioned at the pace of reform and indications that the economy was slowing.

The second quarter was characterised by disappointment with first quarter results, a rapid deterioration in the trade deficit and the May currency crisis, all of which prompted a heavy sell-off in Czech equities. Average daily turnover of US$28.1 million was almost 40% down on the first quarter. High interest rates in the wake of the currency crisis put further pressure on the market as investors switched to money market securities.

The stock market posted a short-lived recovery in the third quarter as the shocks of the currency devaluation wore off and investors reacted positively to an austerity package. This pushed up the PX50 from its second-quarter low of 476.7 to 561 by 15 October 1997, an increase of 18%.

In the wake of the Asian crisis, political uncertainty at home, and continued poor corporate results, the fourth quarter saw a return to pessimism, especially as regards banking stocks. Volumes, which were weak during the mini-rally after the devaluation, dropped even further, and the index ended the year at 495.3.

B) Summary information

Global ranking by market value (US$ terms end-1997): 49
Market capitalisation (main and secondary market, end-1997): US$11.73 billion
Growth in market value (local currency terms, 1993–97): -35%
Market value as a % of nominal GDP (end-1997): 22.6%
Number of domestic/foreign companies listed (end-1997): 101/0
Market P/E (main and secondary market companies, end-1997): 13.7
MSCI Index (change in US$ terms, 1997): -24.2%
Prime (3-month Pribor) interest rate (end-1997): 17.1%

Long-term (3-year) bond yield (end-1997): 14.8%
Budget deficit as a % of nominal GDP (1997): 1.3%
Annual increase in money (M2) supply (end-1997): 10.1%
Inflation rate (1997): 10%
US$ exchange rate (end-1997): Kc34.636

C) Year-end share price index, price/earnings ratios and yields

Exhibit 17.2:
SHARE-PRICE INDEX, P/E RATIOS AND YIELDS, 1993–97

Year	*PX50 Index*	*P/E*	*Yield (%)*
1993	705.2	N/A	N/A
1994	557.2	12.5	1.62
1995	425.9	10.4	1.88
1996	539.6	12.7	1.43
1997	495.3	13.7	1.51

Source: Prague Stock Exchange.

THE STOCK MARKET

A) Brief history and structure

The Stock Exchange Law was approved in December 1992 and the PSE started trading on 6 April 1993. The exchange is based on electronic trading and members are connected through an on-line communication system.

Securities on the PSE are traded in either the main or secondary (parallel) market, or they are registered in the free market. Securities, except those traded in the continual system, are traded through a central automated trading system where buy and sell orders are matched once a day using an algorithmic equation. At the determined price, trading can continue as long as matching positions are available. Block trading between parties who have pre-negotiated prices for large blocks of shares can also be settled through the PSE.

Over-the-counter (OTC) pre-negotiated trades are settled directly at the Securities Registration Centre.

An off-exchange trading vehicle called the RM system operates primarily for the millions of individual shareholders created through voucher privatisation. Investors can buy and sell shares at over 350 outlets throughout the Czech Republic, which are connected to a central computer and pricing mechanism. Volumes are substantially lower than on the PSE.

B) Different exchanges

The PSE is the only stock exchange in the Czech Republic. Trading sessions take place on Monday to Friday from 7.30am to 2.00pm.

PRAGUE STOCK EXCHANGE
Rybná 14, 110 00 Prague 1
Tel: (420) 2 2183 2126; Fax: (420) 2 2183 3031

MARKET SIZE

A) Number of listings and market value

Market capitalisation of listed companies on the PSE at year-end 1997 was Kc406.4 billion, down from Kc420.2 billion at the end of 1996. All of the 101 companies listed on the main and secondary markets were domestic.

During 1997 the PSE reduced the number of securities registered in the free market from 1,670 issues to 320 issues because of low liquidity.

Exhibit 17.3:
NUMBER OF COMPANIES LISTED AND MARKET VALUE, PSE, 1993–97

Year-end	*No. of companies*	*Combined main and secondary market capitalisation (Kc billion)*
1993	3	625.37
1994	34	182.18
1995	62	268.45
1996	93	420.20
1997	101	406.40

Source: Prague Stock Exchange.

B) Largest listed companies

Exhibit 17.4:
MARKET CAPITALISATION OF THE 20 LARGEST LISTED COMPANIES, PSE, END-1997

Ranking	*Company*	*Market capitalisation (Kc million)*
1	SPT Telecom	86,996.5
2	CEZ	58,714.9
3	Komercni Banka	24,801.4
4	Unipetrol	18,039.2
5	Tabak	15,118.2
6	Ceska Sporitelna	14,836.6
7	Cokoladovny	12,772.9
8	IPB	11,078.9
9	C Radiokomunikace	9,818.0
10	SPIF Cesky	7,619.4
11	RIF	6,861.4
12	Severoc Doly	6,555.2
13	Komercni Banka IF	6,380.9
14	Skoda Plzen	5,801.6
15	Semor Energetika	5,735.4
16	Prazka Teplaren	5,715.8
17	Vertex	5,503.2

Exhibit 17.4 continued

18	CKD Praha Holding	5,448.2
19	Nova Hut	4,907.7
20	Ceska Pojistovna	4,755.7

Source: Prague Stock Exchange.

C) Trading volume

Exhibit 17.5:
TRADING VOLUME AND VALUE ON THE PSE, 1993–97

Year	*Volume (shares million)*	*Value (Kc million)*
1993	0.41	2,267.55
1994	15.46	27,851.69
1995	82.89	78,928.88
1996	339.19	393,199.58
1997	353.21	679,537.49

Source: Prague Stock Exchange.

Exhibit 17.6:
THE 20 MOST ACTIVELY TRADED SHARES ON THE PSE, 1997

Ranking	*Company/share*	*Turnover (Kc million)*
1	SPT Telecom	52,405
2	Komercni Banka	40,570
3	CEZ	32,877
4	Vertex	7,143
5	Skoda Plzen	6,554
6	Elektrarny Opatov	6,344
7	RIF	5,868
8	Ceska Sporitelna	4,756
9	C Radiokomunikace	4,147
10	Chemopetrol Group	3,793
11	Unipetrol	3,095
12	Komercni Banka IF	3,085
13	SPIF Cesky	3,069
14	Tabak	2,708
15	CKD Praha Holding	2,641
16	CEZ 2	2,524
17	OKD	2,456
18	Prazke Pivovary	2,326
19	Pivov Radegast	2,305
20	IPS Praha	2,236

Source: Prague Stock Exchange.

TYPES OF SHARE

The Securities Law permits a variety of shares, including bearer and restricted-name shares. Shares arising from voucher privatisation and those where issuers so select are issued in dematerialised form, with a central registry handling all the accounts of individual shareholders as well as investment funds.

INVESTORS

The shareholder structure of companies making up the PX50, which represents 80% of total market capitalisation, is dominated by the state and state institutions, representing 44% of the market capitalisation of the index, followed by local investment funds with a 20% stake. Foreign strategic investors hold about 19% of the value of the PX50, while the portion held by foreign portfolio investors (emerging market and regional funds) and individual shareholders continues to decline (each roughly 8% of the index in 1997).

OPERATIONS

A) Trading system

PSE trading is based on an order-driven system, and the market price of all securities is formed once a day (fixing). As well as this basic system, three other trading segments are used at the PSE: continuous trading in selected shares; direct trades in blocks of securities; and automated trades in blocks of securities.

Direct trades are concluded between members, recorded in the automated trading system and settled through the exchange register of securities. Price fluctuations of direct trades are not limited.

Only PSE members are permitted to participate in direct automated trades in blocks of securities. Data on direct trades in blocks of securities is periodically made public, including the minimum and maximum prices attained.

The RM system is designed for smaller investors who may contact any of the 430 centres throughout the country to place an order to buy or sell securities. The RM system operates an on-line trading service that enables users to execute and settle transactions within two minutes.

A third method of trading is via the over-the-counter market, which operates by directly accessing the Central Securities Register. Estimates for OTC trading range as high as 45% of all capital market activity.

B) List of principal brokers

AGROBANKA
Hybernska 18, 110 00 Prague 1
Tel: (420) 2 2444 2127; Fax: (420) 2 2444 6156

CESKÁ SPORITELNA
Na Prikope 28, 110 03 Prague 1
Tel: (420) 2 2421 5639; Fax: (420) 2 2421 4528

Exhibit 17.7:
COUNTRY FUNDS – CZECH AND SLOVAK REPUBLICS

Fund	US$ % change 01/01/97 01/01/98	01/01/93 01/01/98	Currency	Fund size (US$ mil)	Fund volatility	Management group	Opal main sector	Opal subsector
Czech Republic Fund Inc	-3.35	N/A	US$	95.107	4.477	Advantage Adv	Closed-End	Equity
Czech & Slovak Invest Corp	-8.22	-17.6	US$	N/A	3.648	Fleming	Closed-End	Equity
Czech Value Fund	-18.66	N/A	US$	41.501	-1	Regent Pacific	Closed-End	Equity
BB Tschechien Invest	-25.35	N/A	DM	31.5	-1	BB-Invest	Open-End	Equity
Bohemia Investment Company	-25.81	N/A	Sfr	N/A	-1	MC Trustee SA	Closed-End	Equity
ACM/IBA Czech Equity Ptf	-27.83	N/A	Sch	50.5	5.598	East Fund Mgt	Open-End	Equity
F.I.T Czeck Investment	-28.28	N/A	Sfr	N/A	5.87	FIT Inv Mgt	Open-End	Equity
CF Czech Fund	-39.39	N/A	DM	3.3	5.651	CRM Asst Mgt	Open-End	Equity

Note: details for some funds may not have been included if the data for the US$ % change for 97/98 was not available

Source: Standard & Poor's Micropal.

CA IB SECURITIES
Pravaznicka 11, 110 00 Prague 1
Tel: (420) 2 2423 1626; Fax: (420) 2 2423 1635

CITICORP SECURITIES
Evropska 178, 166 50 Prague 6
Tel: (420) 2 2430 4111; Fax: (420) 2 2430 4613

CREDIT SUISSE FIRST BOSTON
Staromestke nam 15, 110 00 Prague 1
Tel: (420) 2 2481 0937; Fax: (420) 2 2481 0996

KOMERCNI BANKA
Balzanova 3, 114 07 Prague 2
Tel: (420) 2 2421 4096; Fax: (420) 2 2421 3428

WOOD & COMPANY
Martinsku 4, 110 00 Prague 1
Tel: (420) 2 2422 7731; Fax: (420) 2 2422 7759

C) Settlement and transfer

Clearing and settlement of stock exchange transactions are carried out by UNIVYC (formerly known as the Stock Exchange Securities Register) according to a "delivery against payment" system on the third day following the day of the trade. Cash settlement is via the clearing centre of the Czech National Bank on the accounts of exchange members.

TAXATION AND REGULATIONS AFFECTING FOREIGN INVESTORS

A) Regulation

The most important legal regulations governing the securities markets are the following:

- Securities Act No. 591/1992 Coll., as amended (which came into effect in January 1993);
- Stock Exchange Act No. 214/1992 Coll., as amended (which came into effect on 15 May 1992);
- Investment Companies and Investment Funds Act No. 248/1992 Coll., as amended (which came into effect on 29 May 1992); and
- Act No. 513/1991 Coll., the Commercial Code, as amended.

Perhaps of greatest direct significance to foreign investors is the Commercial Code which governs contractual relationships. It guarantees equal treatment under the law for foreign investors.

B) Taxation

As of 1 January 1998, the corporate income tax rate was lowered to 35%. This applies to the profits of all companies, including trading branches of foreign companies. Corporate partners in general partnerships and corporate general partners in a limited partnership are subject to corporate income tax on their share of profits in the partnership.

Capital gains are taxable, while capital losses on the sale of fixed assets are tax deductible. Capital losses on the sale of shares are tax deductible only against profits from the sale of shares. Capital losses from the sale of ownership interests in limited liability companies are not tax deductible. Czech companies are required to withhold tax on payments of dividends, interest and royalties. As of 1998, income tax withheld on interest payments is credited against the regular corporate income tax liability.

Exhibit 17.8:
WITHHOLDING TAXES

Recipient	*Dividends (%)*	*Interest (%)*
Resident corporations	25	25
Resident individuals	25	[1]15/20/25
Non-resident corporations and individuals:		
Non-treaty	25	[1]15/25
Treaty	0-25	0-15

Note:
1. The lower rate applies to interest paid to individuals on savings deposits, savings certificates and similar savings accounts with Czech banks.

Source: Price Waterhouse.

LISTING AND REPORTING REQUIREMENTS

A) Listing requirements

The basic conditions for admission of securities to the main market are:

- a minimum public issue of Kc200 million;
- a minimum of 20% of the overall issue to be issued via a public offer; and
- existence of the company for at least two years.

Basic conditions for admission of securities to the secondary (or parallel) market are:

- a minimum issued amount of Kc100 million;
- a minimum of 15% of the shares made available via a public offer; and
- existence of the company for at least two years.

Decisions regarding the registration of securities in the free market are made by the Stock Exchange Quotation Committee.

B) Reporting requirements

Under PSE regulations, companies listed on the main and secondary markets must provide the PSE periodically with economic and financial data (including a quarterly profit and loss statement; an audited financial statement; an annual report; and any other information that may be required by the PSE).

SHAREHOLDER PROTECTION CODES

Investment protection is provided through legislative provisions and international agreements.

Key measures were introduced in 1996 in an amendment to the Commercial Code under which, among other things (a) holders of publicly tradable shares must disclose ownership of 10% or more of the share capital of a company, and (b) holders of publicly tradable shares acquiring in excess of 50% of the share capital of a company must make a general offer to shareholders at a price at least equal to the average stock exchange price prevailing in the previous six months.

In addition to the promotion and protection of foreign capital investments in the Czech Republic guaranteed under the Commercial Code, the Czech government has entered into agreements with a number of states covering both foreign capital investment in the Czech Republic and Czech investment in foreign countries.

Coverage of the risks and obligations arising from exchange transactions is provided by the PSE guarantee fund.

RESEARCH

Trading reports are available through BBS, teletext, videotex and the internet. The daily Czech language newsletter, *Burza*, is published after each trading session and the Friday issue carries additional comment and analysis. An English version of the newsletter, *Prague Stock Exchange*, is published monthly.

Many banks now provide excellent research on the Czech Republic, including Citicorp Securities, CA IB Securities, CS First Boston, Raiffeisen Bank, Wood Securities and Société Générale European Emerging Markets (London).

Eastern Europe: Investing for the 21st Century, published by Euromoney Books, provides in-depth information for those wishing to invest or do business in the region. See the order card at the back of this book for details.

PROSPECTIVE CHANGES

Derivative trading is expected to start from around the third quarter of 1998.

Establishment of the Security Exchange Commission has been approved and it is expected to start functioning during 1998.

A new trading system, Maus, has recently started operating, which for the time being will exist alongside with the old order-driven system. A gradual transfer will be effected between the two and, by the second quarter of 1998, PSE operations are expected to be based fully on Maus and its module Spad, a price-driven system.

CHAPTER 18

Denmark

Introduction

A strong domestic economy, low interest rates, falling unemployment and no problems meeting the Maastricht criteria have combined to create an attractive environment for the stock market in Denmark. Also, foreign ownership of Danish stocks has been rising dramatically over the past five years – up from an estimated 5–6% to around 21%. This increased foreign influence has tended to change the behaviour of listed companies, which are becoming more focused on shareholder value and rights. For example, all five domestic companies that obtained a listing accompanied by a new issue during 1997 had just one class of share and no voting limitations – a significant change when compared with the bulk of existing listed companies. Similarly, more and more companies are granting options to management and starting to use buy-backs as a tool to create shareholder value.

Although one of Europe's smaller equity markets, Denmark's Copenhagen Stock Exchange (CSE) is efficient, stable and underpinned by the participation of large institutional investors. Pension funds and life insurance companies own around 25% of equities, with banks and financials holding a further 15%.

At the end of 1997, the equity market had a total capitalisation (excluding foreign shares) of Dkr642 billion (US$94.1 billion). The market is diversified across a broad range of sectors. Industry accounts for 42% of domestic market capitalisation, and the other leading sectors are banks, commerce and shipping.

Trading is conducted via the CSE's electronic system to which all Danish stockbroking houses are connected. The largest stockbrokers are market-makers in the most liquid equities, while the rest of the market is order-driven. The Danish market also offers futures and options based on Danish equities traded on the CSE; derivative trading is organised and supervised by the Guarantee Fund for Danish Options and Futures.

ECONOMIC AND POLITICAL OVERVIEW

The Social Democrats have been Denmark's largest political party for more than 50 years. They usually dominate the 179-seat Folketing (the single-chamber parliament) and, at parliamentary elections in March 1998, they were returned to power in a coalition with the Radical Liberals. The government is led by Social Democrat Prime Minister, Poul Nyrup Rasmussen, and policy is focused on seeking consensus for a steady economic policy and a cautious approach to relations with the EU. Denmark is one of the more "Euro-sceptic" of EU member states in political terms, but one of the most robust in fundamental economic terms.

Denmark is heavily dependent on foreign trade, with exports and imports accounting for about 30% of GDP. Food, drinks and agricultural products account for around 25% of total exports, with the largest share (about 21%) going to Germany. The 1990s have continued to see the Danish economy in its best shape for a very long time. In 1990 there was a surplus on the current account of the balance of payments for the first time in 27 years, and in 1997 this surplus stood at Dkr7.1 billion, while average inflation in 1997 was estimated at 2.2%.

The central bank raised interest rates slightly during 1997, and the rate for repo transactions and CDs stood at 3.75% at the end of the year. The Danish krone weakened against the US dollar during 1997, falling from Dkr5.89 in January to Dkr6.83 in December.

Exhibit 18.1: COPENHAGEN SE GENERAL PRICE INDEX (Dkr), 1993–97

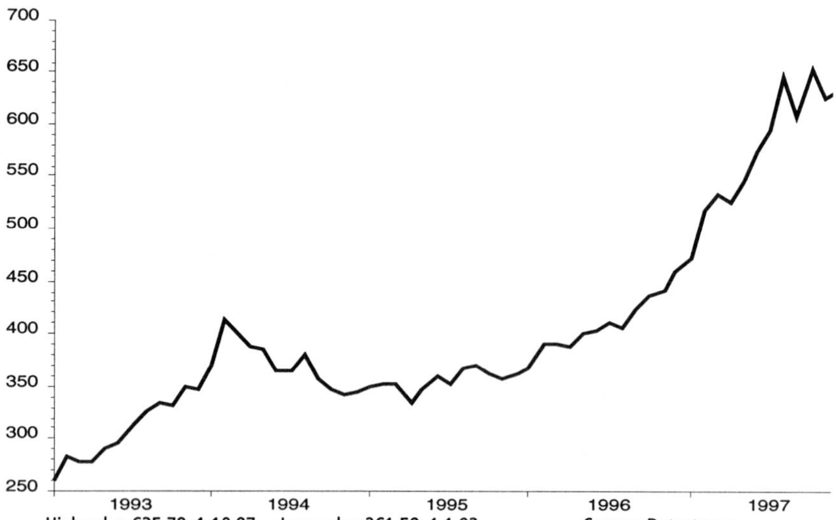

High value 635.78 1.10.97 Low value 261.59 1.1.93 *Source: Datastream*

Government net borrowing in 1997 is estimated at a surplus of Dkr5.2 billion. The forecast for 1998 is a surplus of Dkr25 billion, including a gain of Dkr21 billion from the privatisation of Tele Danmark, equal to 2.4% of GDP.

Role of the central bank

Monetary policy is administered by the central bank (Danmarks Nationalbank), which decides on current interest rate adjustments and the choice of monetary policy instruments. The government is responsible for fiscal and exchange rate policy. The central bank governor is appointed for life. The bank controls the money market through instruments such as CDs, repo against government paper and Treasury bills.

MARKET PERFORMANCE

A) In 1997

The Copenhagen exchange set its second consecutive share trading volume record in 1997. At the same time, share prices rocketed and the KFX Index reached no less than 56 all-time highs before closing the year at 210.55, a 55% increase on end-1996. The All-Share Index jumped 43% and closed 1997 at a record-breaking 675.98.

Share trading totalled Dkr309.5 billion, exceeding the 1996 record-breaking turnover of Dkr216.8 billion by 43% and 1995 turnover by 97%. Average daily turnover amounted to Dkr1.2 billion compared with Dkr867 million in 1996. Repo trading totalled Dkr28.2 billion, a 21% increase on 1996.

Listed companies raised a total of Dkr5.3 billion through new issues in 1997, up from Dkr4.2 billion in 1996. Five Danish companies joined the market, raising Dkr937.5 million – Dkr298 million from the sale of new shares and Dkr639 million from the sale of existing shares.

B) Summary information

Global ranking by market value (US$ terms, end-1997): 24
Market capitalisation (domestic, end-1997): US$94.1 billion
Growth in market value (domestic companies, local currency terms, 1993–97): 112.4%
Market value as a % of nominal GDP (end-1997): 60%
Number of domestic/foreign companies listed (end-1997): 237/12
Market P/E (excluding financials, end-1997): 27.0
MSCI total returns (with net dividends, US$ terms, 1997): 34.5%
MSCI Index (change in US$ terms, 1997): +33%
Short-term (3-month) interest rate (end-1997): 3.93%
Long-term (10-year) bond yield (end-1997): 5.63%
Budget surplus as a % of nominal GDP (1997): 0.5%
Annual increase in broad money (M3) supply (end-1997): 5.2%
Inflation rate (1997): 2.1%
US$ exchange rate (end-1997): Dkr6.826

C) Year-end share price index, price earnings ratios and yields

Exhibit 18.2:
YEAR-END CSE ALL-SHARE INDEX, P/E AND GROSS DIVIDEND YIELDS, 1993–97

Year-end	*CSE All-Share Index*	*P/E**	*Yield (%)*
1993	365.64	19.0	1.4
1994	349.10	19.2	1.8
1995	366.33	20.4	1.7
1996	471.95	19.0	1.8
1997	675.98	27.0	1.5

*Excluding financials.

Source: Alfred Berg – ABN AMRO.

D) Market indices and their constituents

The CSE All-Share Index (January 1983 = 100) has been calculated and published daily since March 1968. It has sub-indices covering the banks, insurance, commerce and service, shipping, industry and investment trusts sectors. The values of all CSE-listed shares (apart from foreign stocks) are used to calculate the indices.

The KFX Index has been calculated and published daily since December 1989. It comprises the 20 largest and most liquid companies on the CSE.

THE STOCK MARKET

A) Brief history and structure

Dealing in securities in Denmark goes back to the late 17th century when merchants acted as both brokers and bankers, but it was not until the 19th century that trading in securities became more formalised.

The CSE changed from a non-profit organisation to a limited company on 1 January 1996, and shares in the exchange are held thus: 60% members, 20% share issuers and 20% bond issuers.

The CSE conducts stock exchange business in compliance with the Danish Securities Trading Act.

B) Different exchanges

The CSE is the only stock exchange in Denmark.

C) Opening hours, name and address

The CSE trading system, ELECTRA, is open on Monday to Friday from 9.00am to 5.00pm.

KØBENHAVNS FONDSBØRS
Nikolaj Plads 2, PO Box 1040, 1007 Copenhagen K
Tel: (45) 33 93 33 66; Fax: (45) 33 12 86 13
E-mail: kfpost.xcse Web site: www.xcse.dk

MARKET SIZE

A) Number of listings and market value

At the end of December 1997, 249 companies were listed on the CSE, including 12 foreign firms. Total market capitalisation amounted to Dkr752 billion, a 55% increase compared with end-1996. Capitalisation excluding foreign shares totalled Dkr642.3 billion.

Exhibit 18.3:
MARKET VALUE OF DOMESTIC SHARES, CSE, 1993–97

Year-end	*Market value (Dkr billion)*
1993	302.3
1994	296.9
1995	333.7
1996	439.6
1997	642.3

Source: Alfred Berg – ABN AMRO.

Exhibit 18.4:
MARKET VALUE OF SHARES BY SECTOR, CSE, 1996–97

	Market value (Dkr million)	
Sector	*1996*	*1997*
Banks	63,858	111,985
Insurance	16,781	23,366
Commerce/service	81,749	131,573
Shipping	72,185	141,409
Industry	181,054	225,586
Investment trusts	7,252	8,138
Unit trusts	16,698	23,484
Domestic total	**439,577**	**642,327**
Foreign companies	59,698	109,858
Overall total	**499,275**	**752,185**

Source: Alfred Berg ABN AMRO.

B) Largest quoted companies

Exhibit 18.5:
THE 20 LARGEST QUOTED COMPANIES ON THE CSE, END-1997

Ranking	*Company*	*Market value (Dkr million)*
1	Novo Nordisk B	63,252
2	Den Danske Bank	48,373
3	D/S 1912 B	34,236
4	D/S Svendborg B	33,720
5	Tele Danmark B	26,999
6	Unidanmark A	23,783
7	Danisco	23,383

Exhibit 18.5 continued

8	Sophus Berendsen B	22,487
9	BG Bank	13,702
10	Carlsberg B	10,629
11	Jyske Bank	7,677
12	Københavns Lufthavne	7,457
13	ISS-Int Service System B	6,507
14	FLS Industries B	6,340
15	Coloplast B	5,883
16	Superfos	5,406
17	Bang & Olufsen Holding B	4,973
18	SAS Danmark	4,794
19	GN Store Nord	4,250
20	Falck	3,792

Source: Alfred Berg – ABN AMRO.

C) Trading volume

Total share turnover in 1997 was Dkr309.5 billion, a 43% increase compared with 1996. Average daily turnover totalled Dkr1,200 million compared with Dkr867 million in 1996.

Exhibit 18.6:
SHARE TURNOVER (DOMESTIC AND FOREIGN SHARES), CSE, 1993–97

	Market turnover (Dkr billion)
1993*	136.1
1994	*176.4*
1995	*160.2*
1996	*216.8*
1997	*309.5*

**Domestic shares only.*

Source: Alfred Berg – ABN AMRO.

Exhibit 18.7:
THE 20 MOST ACTIVELY TRADED SHARES, CSE, 1997

Ranking	*Company*	*Trading value (Dkr million)*
1	Novo Nordisk B	28,623
2	Tele Danmark B	20,920
3	Den Danske Bank	18,813
4	Unidanmark A	18,513
5	Sophus Berendsen B	18,160
6	Danisco	15,523
7	BG Bank	10,825
8	D/S 1912 B	6,359
9	ISS International B	5,870
10	SAS Danmark	5,404
11	D/S Svendborg B	4,813
12	Københavns Lufthavne	4,700
13	Østaslatiske Kompagni	4,523
14	Jyske Bank	4,475
15	Falck	4,200
16	Carlsberg B	3,917
17	Bang & Olufsen Holdings B	3,841
18	Sydbank	3,519
19	GN Store Nord	3,226
20	NeuroSearch	3,012

Source: Copenhagen Stock Exchange.

TYPES OF SHARE

Generally speaking, there are two types of share traded in Denmark – ordinary and preference shares. Danish companies do not, however, necessarily classify their equity as such; instead, they tend to divide it into A and B shares. The A shares typically confer enhanced voting rights on shareholders, usually on a 10:1 basis. In addition, A shareholders may have rights to appoint one or two members to the board of the company. B shares are usually ordinary negotiable instruments with ordinary voting rights.

In some companies, especially banks, there is a limitation on the maximum voting power that can be exercised by a single shareholder. A limitation to 2% of all votes irrespective of the nominal capital that a shareholder owns is not uncommon for banks and insurance companies.

Danish law permits both bearer and registered shares. Shares are issued in bearer form on the CSE but shareholders retain the right to have ownership entered in the share register in their own name.

Existing shareholders have the preferential right (in the form of a tradable option) to purchase new issues by listed companies. Shareholders not wishing to exercise the option may sell it in the market.

Companies may also issue convertible bonds. Convertible bonds are traded on the stock exchange and are listed together with ordinary bonds.

INVESTORS

Share ownership is not statistically recorded in Denmark, but it is estimated that pension funds and life insurance companies own around 25% of equities, private investors 25%, family foundations and trusts 16%, banks and financials 7%, and strategic stakeholders 6%. Non-residents account for the remaining 21% of the market.

OPERATIONS

A) Trading system

Share dealing by open outcry was replaced in September

Exhibit 18.8:
COUNTRY FUNDS – DENMARK

Fund	US$ % change 31/12/96 31/12/97	US$ % change 31/12/92 31/12/97	Currency	Latest fund size ($)	Volatility	Manager name	Main sector	Class
Danske Danish Eq Mngd	19.54	129.31	Dkr	20	3.27	Danske Fund Management Co SA	Equity	Luxembourg
Frontrunner Danish Eq DKK	N/A	N/A	Dkr	3.61	N/A	Frontrunner	Equity	Luxembourg

Note: details for some funds may not have been included if the data for the US$ % change for 96/97 was not available

Source: Standard & Poor's Micropal.

1988 by an electronic trading system called ELECTRA. It combines trading, reporting and information systems, and is in continuous operation during trading hours (9.00am to 5.00pm). Futures and options are also traded through the system.

While authorised trading companies are not obliged to deal through ELECTRA and can trade on the telephone market, they are legally obliged to report transactions in listed securities within 90 seconds. In this way, ELECTRA ensures all market operators act on real-time information from a transparent securities market.

B) List of principal brokers

ALFRED BERG
Amaliegade 35, Postboks 2198, 1017 Copenhagen K
Tel: (45) 33 96 1000; Fax: (45) 33 96 1100

BIKUBEN
Højbro Plads 10, 1200 Copenhagen K
Tel: (45) 43 30 30 30; Fax: (45) 33 15 90 33

CARNEGIE KREDITINSTITUT
Overgaden neden Vandet 9b, 1414 Copenhagen K
Tel: (45) 32 88 0200; Fax: (45) 32 96 1022

DEN DANSKE BANK
Holmens Kanal 2, 1092 Copenhagen K
Tel: (45) 33 44 33 44; Fax: (45) 33 15 36 86

NYKREDIT BANK
Bredgade 40, 1021 Copenhagen K
Tel: (45) 33 42 18 00; Fax: (45) 33 42 18 08

UNIBANK
Torvegade 2, 1786 Copenhagen V
Tel: (45) 33 33 33 33; Fax: (45) 31 57 60 55

C) Settlement and transfer

Transactions in Danish shares are settled three business days after trading. Payment is due on delivery of share certificates.

D) Commissions and other costs

Brokerage is calculated as a percentage of market value except where the share price is below par, in which case the commission is calculated as a percentage of the nominal value.

Stamp duty on shares amounts to 0.5% of the share value, provided the seller is a Danish resident and not a stockbroking company.

TAXATION AND REGULATIONS AFFECTING FOREIGN INVESTORS

A) Taxation of foreign shareholders

Cash dividends paid by Danish companies to foreign shareholders are subject to a Danish tax of 25% withheld at source, or to a lower rate if a double taxation treaty exists between Denmark and the country of the recipient. Where a tax treaty provides for a lower percentage, an application for a refund of the difference between the amount withheld and the amount stipulated in the relevant treaty must be filed with the tax authorities. With respect to certain shares owned by certain non-residents the withholding tax rate is automatically reduced to the applicable rate under the relevant treaty – ie, in order to avoid delay, it may be possible to obtain permission for only the percentage provided for in the treaty to be withheld. No tax is withheld if the Danish dividend-paying company is owned by a foreign company that qualifies under the Parent-Subsidiary Directive.

Exhibit 18.9:
WITHHOLDING TAX

Recipient	Dividend tax limited to: Qualifying companies [1] %	Others %
Resident corporations	[1b]0	25
Resident individuals	[1a]25	25
Non-resident corporations and individuals		
Non-treaty	[1a]25	25

Exhibit 18.9 continued

Treaty	Nil-25	Nil-25
Parent-Subsidiary Directive	Nil	

Notes:
(1) A qualifying company is one with the following shareholding in the Danish subsidiary:
a) no minimum shareholding required;
b) at least 25%.

Source: Price Waterhouse.

B) Non-resident bank accounts
Non-resident persons and companies may, without any prior permission, open bank accounts in Denmark. Deposits can be made in any currency.

C) Exchange control regulations
Exchange control regulations come under the jurisdiction of the Ministry of Industry, but the administration of these regulations is handled by the Danish National Bank.

The currency regulations impose no responsibilities, limitations or restrictions on non-residents' investments, borrowing, lending, or other transfers in, from or to Denmark. Non-residents can therefore freely make direct investments in Denmark, remit profits and dividends and repatriate capital. Direct outward investments and portfolio investments, including domestic investments by non-residents, can freely be made.

There is no maximum on sums that can be transferred to or from Denmark. However, single cross-border transactions in excess of Dkr60,000 must, for statistical purposes, be reported to the central bank.

LISTING AND REPORTING REQUIREMENTS

The rules on prospectuses required for public subscriptions and the reporting requirements for listed companies generally reflect existing EU regulations, perhaps with tighter requirements as to the content of annual and semi-annual financial accounts.

A) Listing requirements
Included in the many conditions necessary to gain a listing on the CSE are (a) that the committee of the exchange must deem listing of the security to be in the public interest, and (b) that volume must be sufficiently large to permit regular turnover.

B) Reporting requirements
Public limited companies must file preliminary accounts with the CSE once the board has decided to recommend the annual accounts to the annual general meeting. This announcement must give various details from the accounts, including profit and loss statements and dividend proposals. In addition, it must contain comparative figures from earlier years, as well as company expectations about the future. It must also state any proposals for increases in the share capital or capital base, or any other important proposals to be put before the general meeting.

Listed companies must also file interim reports and balance sheets with the stock exchange authorities.

Finally, the CSE may require disclosure of any other information it deems necessary or advisable in order to supervise trading. In general terms, this means that listed companies must make available to the public (through the stock exchange) all information that may affect the value of their securities.

SHAREHOLDER PROTECTION CODES

A) Significant shareholdings
Stock exchange regulations require that information immediately be given by shareholders to the company in which they are shareholders and the CSE when: (a) their voting power amounts to at least 5% of the total voting power, or the nominal value they own amounts to at least 5% of the total share capital; or (b) changes of holdings occur to the extent that additional 5% holdings are acquired or disposed of. Shareholders can be fined if they do not provide such information.

Under the Danish Companies Act, a shareholder who owns 90% or more of the shares and the voting rights in a company can demand that the minority be bought out. The minority, for its part, can require that the majority shareholder buy them out. If majority shareholders exploit minority shareholders, the latter may seek remedies available under the Companies Act, such as demanding compensation and seeking to make board members and directors personally liable.

B) Insider trading
Purchase and sale of listed securities cannot be effected by anybody who has knowledge of unpublished information concerning a particular security, provided that such information has or may have a bearing on the price of that security. Violation of this rule is a criminal offence.

Market manipulation is banned. Such manipulation includes acts that have or might have a bearing on stock prices by way of, for example, circulating misinformation about the issue of securities. Violation of this rule is a criminal offence.

The Companies Act provides that members of the board and management shall, when they join the company, inform the board of their shareholding in the company, and subsequently inform it of any acquisition or sale of shares. Board members and managers may not participate in speculative transactions in shares in the company or in companies within the same group.

C) Compensation fund

There is no stock exchange compensation fund. Investors who have been victims of fraud are, therefore, without recourse unless the stockbroker, the company, or the company's officers are personally liable for the fraud. Stockbrokers may have damages covered by liability insurance.

RESEARCH

The CSE publishes the daily *Official List* which gives particulars of each security, including turnover, highest and lowest trading price, closing price and change from the previous day's quotation. More detailed information, including changes in capital, is available in the monthly and annual reports of the CSE.

The majority of stock market research is carried out by the larger banks, such as Den Danske Bank, Unibank and BG Bank, along with some private analysis agencies such as the Danish Stock Survey A/S. Brokers like Alfred Berg and Carnegie Kreditinstitut have well-established research departments. Enskilda, with a local office in Denmark, has recently begun to produce both macroeconomic and company research.

CHAPTER 19

Ecuador

Introduction

Following the liquidation of SATI (Cuenca's stock exchange) in February 1997, Ecuador currently has two stock exchanges – at Quito and Guayaquil. Fixed-income securities continued to account for the vast majority of trading on Ecuador's exchanges in 1997 (97.4% on the QSE and 94.1% on the GSE).

The cautious monetary and exchange policies of Alarcon's interim administration (established in February 1997) has resulted in the achievement of the government's stated economic objectives for 1997 and in the stability of the currency (the sucre) during the year.

ECONOMIC AND POLITICAL OVERVIEW

Following the fall of Bucaram's government early in 1997 (hastened by the attempted implementation of a strong economic policy along the lines of Argentina's Convertibility Plan), the Ecuadorean Congress elected a new President, Dr Fabian Alarcon, who is to hold office until August 1998.

As soon as the new government was established, Alarcon abandoned the idea of convertibility and fiscal adjustment and designed an alternative economic policy, adopting administrative measures to balance the public finances.

According to figures from Ecuador's central bank, GNP growth is estimated at 3.3% for 1997, which can be largely explained by good results in agriculture (especially traditional export products such as bananas and shrimps), as well as in investments in areas like telecommunications and energy.

Annual inflation for 1997 was 30.6% and the sucre was stable against the US dollar. Interest rates trended downwards, especially the active rate. Exports grew by 5.1%, in spite of a cut in oil prices, but imports increased by 22%.

During 1997 the privatisation programme did not yield satisfactory results. In September it was expected that 35% of the assets of Ecuador's communications company (EMETEL) would be privatised through an auction. However, none of the companies qualified to participate in the auction produced an offer by the 19 November deadline.

Role of the central bank

Ecuador's central bank was founded in 1927 and implements the policies of the Monetary Board. It is the government's financial agent and is administered under the Ley de Regimen Monetario. The bank controls import licensing, export approval and foreign loans, and regulates capital repatriation and profit remittance. It does not supervise or regulate the financial sector, which is the job of the Superintendency of Banks.

The bank is largely, but not fully, independent of the government. Only when liquidity problems or withdrawals of deposits affect the stability of the banking system can the Monetary Board authorise the bank to grant loans for a maximum of 60 days. The central bank can only lend to the government when a state of national emergency has been declared. However, the Monetary Board, a technical body, is not really independent because its membership (largely part-time) changes with each new government.

The central bank is no longer the deposit-taking institution for the state's funds. This function is carried out by the Banco del Estado, and the change has introduced a third element into the difficult task of co-ordinating fiscal and monetary policy.

MARKET PERFORMANCE

A) In 1997

The Interinvest Index ended 1997 at 2,248.2 points, an increase of 16.7% on the year. The total return in US dollar terms, however, was -4.1%.

The total value of securities traded on both stock exchanges was US$4.45 billion, an increase of 8.3% compared with 1996. Of the total volume traded, 95.87% was fixed income and only 4.13% equity. Volume traded as a percentage of GDP increased from 23.8% to 25.4%.

Total equity traded in 1997 was US$184.8 million, up 79.9% compared with 1996. The financial sector was the most active, accounting for 62.4% (US$115 million) of turnover. Around 64% (US$118 million) of total turnover took place in just four stocks: Banco del Pacífico (17.3%); La Cemento Nacional (14.3%); Cementos Selva Alegre (14.1%); and Banco La Previsora (18.1%). As regards liquidity, only six stocks traded on more than 50% of the available trading days.

B) Summary information

Global ranking by market value (US$ terms, end-1997): 65
Market capitalisation (QSE, end-1997): US$2,021.34 million
Growth in market value (QSE, US$ terms, 1993-97): 37%
Market value as a % of nominal GDP (end-1997): 10.15%
Number of domestic/foreign companies (QSE, end-1997): 126/2
Market P/E (end-1997): 11.6
Short-term (30-day) interest rate (end-1997): 27.86%
Long-term (5-year) bond yield (end-1997): 31.69%
Budget deficit as a % of nominal GDP (end-1997): 2%
Annual increase in money (M2) supply (end-1997): 27.5%
Inflation rate (1997): 30.6%
US$ exchange rate (end-1997): Su4,422

C) Year-end share price indices and returns

Exhibit 19.1:
YEAR-END SHARE PRICE INDICES AND RETURNS, 1994–97

Year-end	*Interinvest Index*	*Annual return (Su/US$)*	*ECU Index*
1994	1,707.65	70.8/51.10%	N/A
1995	1,515.27	-29.9/-11.27%	3,023.02
1996	1,925.21	30.0/4.42%	3,117.43
1997	2,248.21	16.78/-4.1%	3,121.6

Source: Quito Stock Exchange.

D) Market indices and their constituents

The Interinvest Index tracks the seven largest and most actively traded companies on the exchanges.

In 1997 a new nationwide index of prices and quotations was introduced. Known as the ECU Index, it replaces the previous IAQ Index. The new index, which is based at August 1993 = 1,000, is made up of 10 equity stocks selected each semester.

THE STOCK MARKET

The Quito and Guayaquil exchanges were both established by Corporación Financiera Nacional (CFN) in 1969 and were privatised in 1993. SATI started operating in 1995 but was liquidated in February 1997.

GUAYAGUIL STOCK EXCHANGE
Baquerizo Moreno 1112, Guayaquil
Tel: (593) 5 307 710; Fax: (593) 5 561 871

QUITO STOCK EXCHANGE
Av. Rio Amazonas 540 y Jeronimo Carrion, Quito
Tel: (593) 2 526 805; Fax: (593) 2 500 942

MARKET SIZE

A) Market capitalisation

Exhibit 19.2:
QUITO STOCK EXCHANGE MARKET CAPITALISATION, 1993–97

Year end	*Market value (US$ millions)*
1993	1,474.9
1994	2,692.1
1995	2,565.6
1996	2,224.4
1997	2,021.3

Source: Quito Stock Exchange.

B) Largest quoted companies

Exhibit 19.3:
THE 20 LARGEST COMPANIES LISTED ON THE QSE, END-1997

Ranking	*Company*	*Market value (US$ million)*
1	La Cemento Nacional	289.10
2	Cervecerias Nacionales	223.47
3	La Favorita	184.38
4	Banco del Progreso	134.06
5	Banco Popular	125.48
6	Banco del Pacífico	123.78
7	Banco del Pichincha	121.43
8	Produbanco	81.33
9	Banco Amazonas	60.01
10	Banco de Prestamos	58..31
11	Banco de Guayaquil	56.11
12	Cemento Selva Alegre	53.75
13	Hotel Colon Internacional	49.33
14	Banco La Previsora	47.78
15	Cemento Chimborazo	40.93
16	Ecuatoriana de Aviacion	38.52
17	Banco Bolivariano	36.06
18	Cerveceria Andina	34.31
19	Solbanco	31.18
20	Ingenio San Carlos	28.09

Source: Quito Stock Exchange.

C) Trading volume

The total value of equity traded in 1997 amounted to US$184.8 million, an increase of 79.9% over 1996. Equity trading accounted for only 4.13% of total securities trading value.

Exhibit 19.4:
TOTAL TRADING VALUE (US$ MILLION), 1993-97

Year	Exchange	Equity	Fixed income	Other	Total	No. of companies listed
1993	Guayaquil	97.18	43.61	0.5	141.30	83
1993	Quito	39.95	69.2	-	109.22	34
1994	Guayaquil	408.54	164.16	0.610	573.32	82
1994	Quito	70.43	131.79	-	202.22	35
1995	Guayaquil	231.82	774.6	-	1,006.46	N/A
1995	Quito	130.00	761.60	-	891.60	115
1996	Guayaquil	56.84	1,799.38	-	1,856.22	N/A
1996	Quito	75.28	2,175.75	-	2,251.03	N/A
1997	Guayaquil	122.23	1,937.91	-	2,060.14	N/A
1997	Quito	62.60	2,327.20	-	2,389.80	128

Source: Quito Stock Exchange.

Exhibit 19.5:
THE 10 MOST ACTIVELY TRADED QSE COMPANIES BY TURNOVER VALUE, 1997

Ranking	Company	Trading value (US$ million)
1	La Favorita	11.14
2	Produbanco	11.06
3	Cemento Nacional	10.25
4	Banco del Pacífico	7.38
5	Banco Bolivariano	5.59
6	Banco Popular	4.44
7	Banco La Previsora	3.91
8	Banco Solidario	1.16
9	Banco de Prestamos	0.95
10	Banco de Guayaquil	0.93

Source: Quito Stock Exchange.

OPERATIONS

A) Trading and settlement

Trading takes place from 11.00am to 1.00pm, Monday to Friday. Most transactions are conducted via open outcry. There are also special trading sessions for public offerings.

Cash transactions are settled in T+2 for fixed income, and T+3 for equities.

B) Commissions and other costs

Commissions are negotiable. The exchanges charge an average total commission of 0.1%.

REGULATIONS AFFECTING FOREIGN INVESTORS

A) Investment regulations

Foreign investment is permitted without any restrictions or limitations with respect to remittance of profits, repatriation of capital or mandatory local participation. Legislation provides for the equal treatment of local and foreign investors. Accordingly, foreign investors may establish wholly owned subsidiaries or branches in Ecuador, or acquire total control of companies previously owned by other foreign or local investors. Foreign investments and credits must be registered with the Central Bank of Ecuador, but only for statistical purposes.

Since Ecuador became a member of the World Trade Organisation (WTO) in January 1996, it has executed several bilateral agreements for mutual investment protection and guarantees with the USA and certain European countries.

Following on from the February 1997 political changes, a Constitutional Assembly is considering amending the present constitution, which has been in effect since 1979. It is expected that the amendments will allow private sector participation, both national or foreign, in the oil and electricity sectors, which are currently government-owned. The sale of 35% of the two state-owned telephone companies is scheduled for early 1998.

B) Tax and convertibility considerations

A free currency market exists in Ecuador, operated by the banks and specialised currency exchange firms. Convertibility to US dollars or other hard currencies is unrestricted. The currency market operates on same-day settlement and there are no taxes on currency transactions or remissions.

Income tax for both Ecuadoreans and foreigners is 25% of taxable income. There are no further taxes on dividends, profits or occasional capital gains on equity.

RESEARCH

Very few of the 60 plus local brokerage houses research the equity market. The exceptions are Interinvest (which provides daily and weekly national equity reports, company and economic reports and compiles the Interinvest Index), Valpacifico, Cofivalores, Combursatil and Produvalores.

Ecuador, published by Euromoney Books, provides in-depth information for those wishing to invest or do business in the country. See the order card at the back of this book for further details.

CHAPTER 20

Egypt

Introduction

The continuation of ambitious economic reforms in 1997 had a direct, positive impact on the development of Egypt's capital market, including the sale of shares of many privatised companies. The government recognises the importance of an efficient capital market and is continuing with development plans first introduced in 1992. The regulations provide for unlimited market access to foreign investors and no taxes are levied on capital gains, dividends or repatriation of capital. Total market capitalisation (US$20.8 billion) jumped by 47% in 1997, and now amounts to 29% of GDP.

It is important to note that only 70 of the 650 companies currently listed on the Egyptian exchange are actively traded. However, these companies represent the majority of market capitalisation, and liquidity in them is quite high, with monthly turnover ratios averaging 3.2%. The sectoral distribution of companies on the exchange continues to be oriented towards basic industries because many of these were among the first companies the government privatised. Most of the traded companies are concentrated in cement, metals, construction, chemicals, flour milling, textiles, pharmaceuticals and banking. This is changing, however, as the government continues to privatise companies in more diverse areas and as private companies have begun to join the market in order to raise equity.

Foreign investment continues to be an important driving force. The number of investors has risen significantly in the past five years, with foreigners now accounting for 30% of trading activity and institutional investors representing 80% of funds in the market. The growth of investor interest has resulted in greater competitiveness in the brokerage industry while the entry of foreign institutional investors into the market has spawned a growing pool of reliable research.

ECONOMIC AND POLITICAL OVERVIEW

The November 1997 attack on tourists in Luxor has tended to shore-up support for President Hosni Mubarak's government. The brutal attack was denounced vehemently by the vast majority of Egyptians and also drew condemnation from within Islamic opposition groups.

Economic reforms initiated by Mubarak in 1992 have gained momentum under Prime Minister Dr Kamel El-Ganzouri, and the economy has started to reap benefits from the initial years of austerity. At the end of 1997, real GDP growth was 5.3%, inflation had fallen to 4.5%, the budget deficit was 0.8% of GDP and foreign reserves were in excess of US$20.5 billion. Interest rates on Treasury bills eased during the year to 8.8% and are expected to remain stable for the foreseeable future.

Egypt received international investment assurance through the assignment of ratings in 1997, including the Standard & Poor's and IBCA awards of BBB- investment grade ratings in January and August, respectively.

Role of the central bank

The Central Bank of Egypt is a constitutionally and operationally independent entity that acts as an agent of the Ministry of Finance and as banker to the government.

It sets and implements monetary policy and, through open market operations, intervenes in foreign exchange markets and controls interest rate changes. It supervises the banking sector and regulates certain other financial institutions. The bank also prepares and publishes monetary, financial and foreign exchange data.

The main objectives of the central bank include issuing and maintaining the integrity of the currency, securing financial stability and controlling inflation. With

Exhibit 20.1: EGYPT HERMES FINANCIAL PRICE INDEX (US$), 1993–97

High value 15426.68 3.3.97 Low value 6592.48 1.7.96 *Source: Datastream*

privatisation in the financial sector, the bank is also taking steps to ensure transparency of financial operations and adherence to prudential banking practices.

MARKET PERFORMANCE

A) In 1997

Despite a long correction, which was viewed as both inevitable and necessary given the pace of market growth at the beginning of the year, Egypt's stock exchange continued to experience steady growth in both the volume and value of transactions. The number of listed shares on the exchange grew by 34% and market capitalisation ended the year up 47% at E£71 billion. The CMA Price Index rose by 21% to close at 359.85. Of the 650 companies listed, 198 (or 30%) were traded in 1997. The 48 listed privatised companies represented 24% of the traded companies and 62% of total trading value.

The equity market was largely driven by the manufacturing and finance sectors which together comprised about 91% of total trading value and about 48% and 38% respectively of total market capitalisation. Average daily turnover in the fourth quarter of 1997 had reached US$26.7 million as opposed to US$15.5 million for the same period in 1996, with total market turnover for the year nearly doubling to reach US$5,931 million. Monthly turnover ratios in the most liquid stocks currently average 3.2%.

Privatisation continues to be an important catalyst for trading. However, in the past year, six major private sector IPOs have highlighted internal market energy. New equity issues dominated the primary market as equities issued in 1997 totalled E£18.3 billion, almost 18% up on the 1996 total of E£15.5 billion.

In December, the largest single managed fund in Egypt was launched by the state pension fund, insurance companies and banks, with an authorised capital of E£1 billion, half of which is paid up. The state pension fund, active in the capital market for the first time, is now the leading stockholder.

Egyptian companies continued to enter the international capital markets, issuing five GDRs, all of which are currently traded in London.

B) Summary information

Global ranking by market value (US$ terms, end-1997): 41
Market capitalisation (end-1997): US$20.8 billion
Growth in market value (local currency terms, 1993–97): 453%
Market value as a % of nominal GDP (end-1997): 29%
Number of domestic/foreign companies listed (end-1997): 650/1
Market P/E (end-1997): 12.8
MSCI Index (change in US$ terms, 1997): +25.1%
Short-term (3-month) interest rate (end-1997): 12.75%
Long-term (10-year) bond yield (end-1997): 10.8%
Budget deficit as a % of nominal GDP (1997): 0.8%
Annual increase in broad money (M3) supply (fiscal 1997): 15.7%

Inflation rate (1997): 4.5%
US$ exchange rate (end-1997): E£3.39

C) Market indices and their constituents

The Egyptian stock exchange has a General Index, a Public Subscription Index and a Closed Subscription Index. There are also several sectoral sub-indices covering the following industries: agriculture; mining; construction; manufacturing; transportation; trade; finance; and services. EFG and Hermes indices are also quoted.

THE STOCK MARKET

A) Brief history and structure

The Cairo Stock Exchange was founded in 1883 and as early as 1906 there were 328 joint stock companies traded with a total capital of E£91 million. Activity on the Cairo and Alexandria exchanges was quite brisk until 1958 when trading reached a peak of E£110.7 million.

With President Nasser's nationalisation programme in the early 1960s, trading volumes fell to only E£3-7 million per year and just 32 companies remained listed. The exchanges were never closed, however, and as the market shrank the Egyptian government subsidised the remaining brokers whose commissions had dwindled to almost nothing.

In the mid-1970s the exchanges received support as part of President Sadat's "open-door" economic policy and the implementation of laws encouraging foreign investment and private sector development.

In 1994 the two stock exchanges in Cairo and Alexandria were unified into a single market and are now electronically linked for real-time trading. The link is through a computer-based screen trading system. To help keep pace with the recent marked increase in trading volumes, computerised clearance, settlement and transfer of ownership systems has been installed. The central depository system established in late 1996 has overcome its start-up difficulties and now manages transactions for the majority of the actively traded companies.

B) Different exchanges

There are two linked exchanges in Egypt – the Cairo Stock Exchange and the Alexandria Stock Exchange.

CAIRO STOCK EXCHANGE
4a Sherifen Street, Cairo
Tel: (20) 2 392 1447/8968; Fax: (20) 2 392 8526

ALEXANDRIA STOCK EXCHANGE
11 Talat Harb Street, Menshia, Alexandria
Tel: (20) 3 483 5432

MARKET SIZE

A) Number of listings and market value

Exhibit 20.2:
NUMBER OF COMPANIES LISTED AND MARKET VALUE, 1993–97

Year-end	*No. of companies listed*	*Market value (E£ million)*	*Market value (US$ million)*
1993	674	12,807	N/A
1994	700	14,480	N/A
1995	746	27,420	8,065
1996	646	48,086	14,14
1997	650	70,873	20,845

Source: Capital Market Authority.

Exhibit 20.3:
THE 20 LARGEST LISTED COMPANIES BY MARKET CAPITALISATION, END-1997

Ranking	*Company*	*Market value (E£ million)*	*Trading value (E£ million)*
1	Misr Romania Bank	3,814	56.2
2	Comm Int Bank	3,351	1,082.5
3	Suez Cement	3,088	612.4
4	Abu Qir Fertilizer	3,006	335.5
5	MIBank	2,284	876.9
6	Misr Elededa for Housing and Reconstruction	2,255	303.6
7	Eastern Tobacco Co	1,918	52.2
8	Nasr City for Housing and Urbanisation	1,703	804.0
9	Canal Shipping Agencies	1,695	54.0
10	National Cement	1,578	4.9
11	Al Amria Cement	1,480	887.5
12	Misr Exterior Bank	1,211	58.2
13	Egyptian American Bank	1,195	395.5
14	Alexandria National Iron & Steel	1,099	200.3
15	Paints & Chemical Industries	1,035	847.0
16	National Société Générale Bank	970	165.5
17	Helwan Portland Cement	860	700.6
18	El-Ahram Beverages	855	725.9
19	Golden Pyramids Plaza	828	3.1
20	Egyptian Int'l Pharm Ind	796	483.0

Source: Capital Market Authority.

B) Trading volume

Turnover increased by 121% in 1997 to E£24.2 billion, while the total volume of 373 million shares traded during the year was a 79% increase over 1996. Average monthly trading volume was 31 million shares, up 82% on the monthly average in 1996.

Exhibit 20.4:
EXCHANGE TURNOVER, 1993–97

Year	*Volume (million)*	*Turnover value (E£ million)*
1993	17.7	568.5
1994	59.8	2,557.2
1995	72.2	3,849.4
1996	207.8	10,967.5
1997	372.5	24,219.8

Source: Capital Market Authority.

INVESTORS

Investors are local and foreign in nearly equal proportion, with local individuals and mutual funds, along with foreign portfolio companies active in the market. Institutional investors account for approximately 80% of market activity.

The value of foreign investment constituted about 33% of total trading value in 1997, and net foreign portfolio investment totalled about E£1.9 billion.

OPERATIONS

A) Trading system

The Cairo and Alexandria exchanges are integrated and participants have reciprocal membership with real-time access to all listed stocks. Trading takes place through a computerised order-driven trading system. All trades are matched and confirmed electronically and manually at the end of each trading day.

B) Principal brokers

EFG-HERMES
55 Charles de Gaulle (Giza) Street, Giza, Cairo
Tel: (20) 2 571 7846-48; Fax: (20) 2 571 6121
E-mail: efmglink.com.eg

C) Commissions

In October 1994, brokerage commissions were liberalised and became negotiable. However, they are subject to a minimum of E£2 per transaction and there is still a stipulation that, for transactions not exceeding E£10,000, the commission may not exceed 0.5% for stocks and 0.2% for bonds.

D) Settlement and transfer

The central clearing, settlement and depository system (MCSD) became operational in October 1996. It is a book entry system that allows for real-time electronic confirmation and transfer of title in an immobilised environment. For transactions involving physical shares, the clearing and settlement process typically occurs on a T+4 basis. Where the securities are immobilised at the MCSD, settlement can occur on T+3.

In case of non-delivery of a security or non-payment, the MCSD completes a transaction at T+6 and charges the defaulting broker associated costs plus a fee. As the ultimate counterparty to member trades, the MCSD mitigates settlement risk and allows the settlement system to function efficiently by protecting against failures and delays.

Exhibit 20.5:
COUNTRY FUNDS – EGYPT

Fund	*US$ % change 01/01/97 01/01/98*	*01/01/93 01/01/98*	*Currency*	*Fund size (US$ mil)*	*Fund volatility*	*Management group*	*Opal main sector*	*Opal subsector*
Cairo Bank Mutual Fund	40.11	N/A	E£	N/A	-1		Open-End	Equity
Hermes Egypt Fund Limited	35.97	N/A	US$	N/A	-1	Hermes (Bermu	Open-End	Equity
Egypt Investment Co	29.9	N/A	US$	92.6	-1	Concord Natio	Open-End	Equity
SAIB Growth Fund 1/97	21.38	N/A	E£	N/A	-1	Prime Investm	Open-End	Equity
Delta Mutual Fund	19.8	N/A	E£	N/A	-1		Closed-End	Equity
Bank of Alexandria Fund One	-0.04	N/A	E£	129.49	4.246	Egyptian Fd M	Open-End	Equity
Egyptian American Bk Mutual Fd	-5.65	N/A	E£	N/A	4.649	Egyptian Fd M	Open-End	Equity

Note: details for some funds may not have been included if the data for the US$ % change for 97/98 was not available

Source: Standard & Poor's Micropal.

TAXATION AND REGULATIONS AFFECTING FOREIGN INVESTORS

A) Taxation

Foreign financial institutions operate in the market under the same conditions and restrictions as domestic companies. Shares are free of stamp duty and all dividends are tax-exempt.

There is no capital gains tax and, in 1996, the 40% income tax on mutual funds' profits was abolished.

B) Securities legislation

A company that carries out securities activities must apply to the CMA for a licence and register with the stock exchange, which sets a minimum capital requirement. Management of investment funds may be carried out by foreign companies provided CMA approval is obtained.

LISTING AND REPORTING REQUIREMENTS

A) Listing requirements

Joint stock companies may list securities on the stock exchange under one of two registers – the official or unofficial register. If shares representing not less than 30% of the company's nominal shares are in public hands (held by no less than 150 shareholders) then the stock qualifies to be listed in the official register, as do public issues of securities issued by the government or state-owned companies. All other securities that do not meet the criteria for listing in the official register, as well as foreign securities, must be listed in the unofficial register.

For a public offering, disclosure begins with the publication of a prospectus in two nationwide Egyptian newspapers, of which at least one must be an Arabic language newspaper. The prospectus must contain, among other things, the following information:

i) the objectives of the company, its name, duration and legal form;
ii) the issued and paid-in capital of the company;
iii) information about the offered stocks, the nominal value and class of each stock, its advantages and terms of offer;
iv) the names of the founders, the value of their participation and information about the capital in kind if any;
v) the investment policy of the company with respect to the proceeds of the public offering, and its expectations as to the prospects of such policy;
vi) the amount required to be paid up at subscription, which may not be less than 25% of the nominal value of the stock;
vii) the auditors of the company;
viii) an estimate of the incorporation costs:
ix) details of dividends;
x) any contracts concluded by the founders within the five years preceding incorporation, which the founders intend to assign to the company; and
xi) the names of the chairman, directors and managers.

B) Reporting requirements

A public issuer is obliged to file quarterly reports of its activities with the CMA and to disclose its financial position. The CMA must also receive a copy of the full-year financial statements and the reports of the board and the auditor at least one month before the date set for the general meeting. The issuer must also publish a summary of such reports in two Egyptian national newspapers.

Issuers are also under an obligation to disclose immediately any circumstances that might affect their activities or financial position. Such disclosure must be published in two Egyptian national newspapers.

SHAREHOLDER PROTECTION CODES

Sentences of up to five years' imprisonment in addition to fines of at least E£50,000 may be imposed on anyone convicted of, among other things: (i) carrying out securities activities subject to the Capital Market Law without obtaining a licence; (ii) recording or reporting incorrect data; (iii) attempting to influence market prices; or (iv) breaching a provision of the Capital Market Law or its regulations.

The Capital Market Law also includes provisions that aim to make market dealing in securities transparent and to protect the public from fraud. As an example, companies dealing in securities may not deal on behalf of the company's board members, directors or employees.

The Capital Market Law further provides that an investment fund must not act in a manner that jeopardises the interests of its investors. The investment fund must maintain sufficient liquidity to cover any demands by investors for redemption. Fund managers are required to exert due care to ensure that the fund has a diversified investment portfolio and must otherwise minimise the risk of loss to investors. Fund managers are also obliged to avoid any conflict of interest that may arise between the investor, the fund's shareholders and those dealing in the fund's securities.

From 1 January 1997, any person or entity planning to

enter into a transaction that would result in the acquisition of more than 10% of the shares of a listed company must inform the company at least two weeks in advance of the proposed transaction. If such notification is not made, the transaction shall be null and void.

RESEARCH

EFG-Hermes provides well-regarded research on all active companies and sectors of the economy, as well as quarterly macroeconomic reports and privatisation reviews. CIIC produces reports on Egyptian stocks, as well as macroeconomic reviews.

Egypt: Privatisation and Beyond, published by Euromoney Books, provides in-depth information for those wishing to invest or do business in the country. See the order card at the back of this book for details.

CHAPTER 21

Finland

Introduction

Interest in Finnish equities has revived in the 1990s, boosted not only by liberalised foreign ownership regulations and fiscal changes but also by the growth of Finland's export and manufacturing output, steep falls in interest rates and the floating of the Finnish markka, which has improved companies' competitiveness. In recent times, this optimistic environment has been reflected in the new issues market in particular, with indebted companies improving their balance sheets and seeking stock exchange listings, and the state arranging privatisation projects. In 1997, 10 new companies were listed on the Helsinki Stock Exchange (HEX) – eight on the official list, one on the OTC and one on the brokers' list.

As measured by the HEX Index, shares on the Helsinki exchange ended 1997 32.2% higher than at end-1996. Official list market capitalisation amounted to FM389 billion, an increase of 36.7% on 1996, while total equity trading value reached FM182 billion in 1997, an increase of 80% on the preceding year.

ECONOMIC AND POLITICAL OVERVIEW

Finland's commitment to membership of EMU firmed during 1997. The Finnish parliament votes on the issue on 14 April 1998. All the government parties are now supporting membership and, because the convergence requirements have been fulfilled, Finland is expected to join EMU in the "first wave".

Legislative power in Finland is exercised by a 200-member parliament and by the President of the Republic. In the most recent elections, held in 1995, the seats were distributed between 10 political parties. The three largest parties are the Social Democrat Party (63 seats), the Centre Party (44) and the National Coalition Conservatives (39). Currently the President is Mr Martti Ahtisaari, whose term lasts until 1 March 2000.

The present government, consisting of five parties, was appointed in April 1995. The Social Democrat Party has seven ministerial posts, the Conservatives five, the Left Wing Alliance two, the Green League one and the Swedish People's Party one. There is also one independent expert minister. The Prime Minister is Mr Paavo Lipponen, a Social Democrat.

The Finnish economy has shown brisk growth over the past couple of years. In 1996 total production increased by 3.6% and in 1997 growth is estimated to have picked up further to 5.4% as both domestic demand and exports gained momentum. Robust domestic demand is expected to keep economic activity strong in 1998 as well, even though exports are expected to suffer from problems in Asia.

Helped by moderate pay rises, consumer prices rose by just 1.2% in 1997. The current account on the balance of payments, which showed a surplus of FM22 billion in 1996, stood at FM30 billion for the period January-November 1997. The employment situation has also improved: unemployment was 14.5% in 1997, down from 17.8% in 1994.

The present government has ensured that Finland will meet the Maastricht requirements for EMU: the markka has been in the ERM since October 1995; the inflation rate in 1997 was among the lowest in the EU; the public sector deficit is 3.5% of GDP; and public sector debt is less than 60% of GDP.

Role of the central bank

The Bank of Finland enjoys a relatively independent position in relation to the government and parliament. It operates under the supervision of the parliamentary Supervisory Board.

The bank's monetary policy is based on a 2% inflation target. The indicator monitored for this purpose is "underlying inflation", which is the Consumer Price Index excluding taxes, housing prices and home mortgage interest payments.

Exhibit 21.1: HEX GENERAL PRICE INDEX (FM), 1993–97

High value 3753.94 1.10.97 Low value 829.00 1.1.93 *Source: Datastream*

MARKET PERFORMANCE

A) In 1997

During the first three-quarters of 1997, the HEX Index rose sharply; by 21 October 1997 it was up by 56%. Then the Asian crisis hit and, in seven days, the index lost some 15% of its value. For 1997 as a whole, the HEX Index rose by 32.3%. The biggest gains were posted by the banks and finance sector (+97.7%) and the insurance sector (+93.7%). The metal and engineering sector (+5.4%) and the construction sector (+5.7%) showed the most modest increases in 1997. Total equity trading value in 1997 was FM182 billion, an increase of 80% on the preceding year.

Key factors behind the strong performance were low interest rates and good profit expectations for 1998 and 1999. These factors attracted both domestic and foreign equity investors. In 1997, foreign ownership of Finnish equities increased from 26.9% to 31.5%.

Throughout the year, Nokia shares had a big impact on the HEX Index because the company's market capitalisation is around one-third of the total market capitalisation of the exchange's official list.

B) Summary information

Global ranking by market value (US$ terms, end-1997): 26
Market capitalisation (end-1997): US$74.2 billion
Growth in market value (local currency terms, 1993–97): 185.7%
Market value as a % of nominal GDP (end-1997): 63.7%
Number of domestic/foreign companies listed (end-1997): 124/2
Market P/E (all companies on HEX official list, end-1997): 14.8
MSCI total returns (with net dividends, US$ terms, 1997): 17.3%
MSCI Index (change in US$ terms, 1997): +16.0%
Short-term (3-month) interest rate (end-1997): 3.58%
Long-term (10-year) bond yield (end-1997): 5.48%
Budget deficit as a % of nominal GDP (1997): 1.3%
Annual increase in broad money (M3) supply (end-1997): 5.8%
Inflation rate (1997): 1.2%
US$ exchange rate (end-1997): FM5.4207

C) Year-end share price index, price/earnings ratios and yields

Exhibit 21.2:
YEAR-END HEX INDEX, HEX OFFICIAL LIST P/E AND DIVIDEND YIELDS, 1993–97

Year-end	*HEX Index*	*P/E*	*Yield (%)*
1993	1,582.00	na	0.7
1994	1,846.68	8.9	0.8
1995	1,704.20	20.0	3.1
1996	2,495.93	18.7	2.0
1997	3,302.26	14.8	2.3

Source: HEX Ltd.

D) Market indices and their constituents

The HEX Index is calculated at two-minute intervals during trading and includes all share series quoted on the exchange. Share price indices are also calculated for the 20 most-traded share series (in value terms) and, separately, for each business sector.

In addition, the HEX Index is calculated in the form of daily yield indices and indices for each share series. Share price indices have been retrospectively calculated from the beginning of 1987. Yield index history is from the beginning of 1991.

The HEX Portfolio Index, based on restricted weights, was launched on 1 December 1995. The maximum weight of any single company in this index is 10%. The HEX Portfolio Index, which is updated at 10-minute intervals during trading, is backdated to the beginning of 1991.

The HEX indices are based on Paasche's index formula. The base number is 1,000 on 28 December 1990. The share prices used in the compilation are primarily transaction prices registered at the time of calculation.

The Finnish Traded Stock Index (FOX) is a capitalisation-weighted share price index. It is calculated on a continuous basis from the most recent prices of the 25 most traded HEX shares.

THE STOCK MARKET

A) Brief history and structure

The Helsinki Stock Exchange operated as a free-form association from its establishment in 1912 up to 1984, when it was turned into a non-profit cooperative. In 1995, the cooperative was converted into a limited company.

On 29 December 1997, the Helsinki Stock Exchange and SOM Ltd, the Finnish Securities and Derivatives Exchange Clearing House, merged to form HEX Ltd, Helsinki Securities and Derivatives Exchange Clearing House. This merger has provided clients with one-point access to a comprehensive range of investment instruments, including shares, bonds, and equity and fixed-income derivatives. The five major shareholders of HEX Ltd are Merita Group, OM Gruppen, OKOBANK, Postipankki Ltd and Evli Group. Issuers of listed securities hold 19.9% of HEX Ltd and the brokerage houses hold 17.5%.

The highest decision-making powers lie with the AGM of shareholders, which appoints the board of directors. The board supervises observance of the rules and regulations. It grants and cancels the rights of trading members and other parties operating on the stock exchange, decides on the admission to listing and de-listing of securities, and draws up the rules and regulations of the HEX. The managing director appointed by the board of directors is responsible for the direct management of the affairs of the HEX in accordance with the decisions of the board.

B) Different exchanges

Virtually all trading in Finnish equities takes place on the HEX.

C) Opening hours, names and addresses

Trading hours are from 9.30am to 6.00pm, Monday to Friday. The stock exchange office is open from 8.00am to 5.00pm.

HELSINGIN ARVOPAPERIPÖRSSI OY
(Postal address) PO Box 361, FIN-00131 Helsinki
(Street address) Fabianinkatu 14, World Trade Center Plaza, Keskuskatu 7, Helsinki
Tel: (358) 9 616 671; Fax: (358) 9 6166 7366
Internet: www.hex.fi

MARKET SIZE

A) Number of listings and market value

A total of 126 companies with 152 share series are listed on three parallel lists: 80 companies on the official list; 32 companies on the OTC list; and 15 companies (two of which are foreign) on the brokers' list.

At the end of December 1997, the market capitalisation of all listed shares was FM402 billion (compared with FM292billion in 1996). The market capitalisation of the official list shares was FM389 billion (1996, FM285 billion), of the OTC list shares FM5 billion (1996, FM3 billion) and of the brokers' list shares FM7 billion (1996, FM4 billion).

Exhibit 21.3:
NUMBER OF LISTED COMPANIES AND MARKET VALUE OF LISTED SHARES, HEX OFFICIAL LIST, 1993–97

Year	*Companies listed*	*Market value (FM million)*
1993	58	136,293
1994	65	181,559
1995	73	191,654
1996	71	284,898
1997	80	389,414

Source: HEX Ltd.

Exhibit 21.4:
MARKET VALUE BY SECTOR, HEX OFFICIAL LIST, END-1997

Sector	*Market value (FM million)*
Services	
Banking and finance	26,464
Insurance	19,024
Transport	11,236

Exhibit 21.4 continued

Investment	1,147
Other services	7,001
Services total	**64,872**
Industry	
Telecoms and electronics	121,035
Metals and engineering	50,120
Chemicals	33,137
Food	26,868
Forestry industries	48,519
Multi-business industry	9,657
Other industry	
Industry total	**307,768**
Trade	**16,775**
Market capitalisation total	**389,414**

Source: HEX Ltd.

Exhibit 21.5:
NUMBER OF LISTED SECURITIES BY SECTOR, HEX OFFICIAL LIST, 1996–97

Sector	*End-1996*	*End-1997*
Services		
Banking and finance	5	7
Insurance and investment	8	9
Other services	14	17
Services total	**27**	**33**
Industry		
Metals and engineering	11	16
Forestry industries	4	6
Multi-business industry	7	10
Other industries	22	36
Industry total	**44**	**68**
Bonds and debentures	320	308
Total listed securities	**391**	**409**

Source: HEX Ltd.

B) Largest quoted companies

Exhibit 21.6:
THE 20 LARGEST LISTED COMPANIES ON THE HEX OFFICIAL LIST, END-1997

Ranking	*Company*	*Market capitalisation (FM million)*
1	Nokia Oyj	116,265
2	UPM-Kymmene Oyj	29,472
3	Merita Oyj	24,673
4	Enso Oyj	13,163
5	Neste Oy	13,005
6	Vakuutusosakeyhtiö Sampo	10,719
7	Orion-yhtymä Oyj	10,076

Exhibit 21.7 continued

8	Vakuutusosakeyhtiö Pohjola	8,305
9	Outokumpu Oyj	8,281
10	Raisio Yhtymä Oyj	7,783
11	Metra Oy Ab	6,913
12	Cultor Oyj	6,881
13	Kemira Oyj	6,633
14	Huhtamäki Oy	6,625
15	Valmet Oyj	5,873
16	Rautaruukki Oy	5,862
17	Metsä-Serla Oyj	5,853
18	TT Tieto Oy	5,394
19	OY Stockmann AB	5,036
20	Kesko Oyj	5,007

Source: HEX Ltd.

C) Trading volume

Exhibit 21.7:
TRADING VALUE BY BUSINESS SECTOR, HEX OFFICIAL LIST, 1997

Sector	*Trading value (FM '000)*
Services	
Banking and finance	9,488,109
Insurance and investment	8,206,373
Other services	9,540,404
Services total	**27,234,886**
Industry	
Metals and engineering	24,199,005
Forestry industries	27,212,530
Multi-business industry	3,230,126
Other industries	100,496,297
Industry total	**155,137,958**
Overall total	**182,372,844**

Source: HEX Ltd.

Exhibit 21.8:
THE 20 MOST ACTIVELY TRADED SHARES, HEX OFFICIAL LIST, 1997

Ranking	*Share series*	*Turnover (FM '000)*
1	Nokia Oyj A	69,148,339
2	UPM-Kymmene Oyj	18,581,699
3	Nokia Oyj K	8,712,239
4	Merita Oy A	8,416,760
5	Enso Oyj R	5,197,736
6	Valmet Oyj	4,639,696
7	Raisio Yhtymä Oyj (Free share)	4,373,518
8	Rauma Oy	4,227,171
9	Outokumpu Oyj A	3,952,781

Exhibit 21.8 continued

10	Vakuutusosakeyhtiö Sampo A	3,930,593
11	Vakuutusosakeyhtiö Pohjola B	2,908,235
12	Rautaruukki Oy K	2,792,120
13	Metsä-Serla Oyj B	2,547,413
14	Asko Oyj	2,514,689
15	Kesko Oyj (Free share)	2,466,545
16	Metra Oy Ab B	2,398,511
17	Orion-Yhtymä Oyj B	2,326,662
18	Huhtamäki Oy I	1,869,413
19	Finnlines Oy	1,801,786
20	Kemira Oyj	1,780,788

Source: HEX Ltd.

Exhibit 21.9:
THE MOST ACTIVELY TRADED SHARES, OTC LIST, 1997

Ranking	*Company*	*Turnover (FM '000)*
1	Rakentajain Konevuokraamo Oy	154,675
2	Incap Oy	140,297
3	Efore Oy	136,511
4	Oy Talentum Ab	134,665
5	Sentra Oyj A	128,364

Source: HEX Ltd.

Exhibit 21.10:
THE MOST ACTIVELY TRADED SHARES, BROKERS' LIST, 1997

Ranking	*Company*	*Turnover (FM '000)*
1	Benefon Oy S	336,628
2	Raisio Yhtymä Oyj K	287,963
3	Hansapank AS 1	245,239
4	Turkistuottajat Oy C	155,193
5	AS Eesti Uhispank	151,100

Source: HEX Ltd.

TYPES OF SHARE

New equity issues listed by Finnish companies usually take the form of rights or bonus issues. In both cases, existing shareholders have preferential rights over other subscribers. A share certificate may comprise one or more shares.

INVESTORS

Institutional investors made up around 84% of the French equity market as at end–1997. Foreign ownership accounted for around 43% of shares.

OPERATIONS

A) Trading system

Trading on the HEX is fully computerised and conducted from trading members' offices. The HEX has been working to improve the HETI trading system. The existing workstation software of the windows-based HETI system was renewed during 1997, and trading members can now integrate their own systems directly with the stock exchange trading system.

Australia's Computershare Systems Pty Ltd is currently constructing a new trading system for the HEX, which is expected to go on line in early 1998. The trading systems for equities and derivatives will remain separate for the time being.

Trading on the HEX starts at 9.30am with a pre-trading session during which the brokers enter their bids and offers into the system, without viewing those of other brokers. From 10.20am to 10.30am the computer automatically matches into deals the bids and offers entered during pre-trading. The bids and offers that have not resulted in deals are transferred into free trading.

At 10.30am the free trading phase starts, during which prices can vary. The brokers continue to feed in their bids and offers which the HETI system compares and auto-

Exhibit 21.11:
COUNTRY FUNDS – FINLAND

Fund	*US$ % change 31/12/96 31/12/97*	*US$ % change 31/12/92 31/12/97*	*Currency*	*Fund size (US$ mil)*	*Volatility*	*Manager name*	*Main sector*	*Class*
Merita Private Fund	3.94	151.6	Fmk	120.65	4.57	Merita Bank Luxembourg SA	Equity	Luxembourg
Carlson Eq Finland	N/A	N/A	Fmk	31.1	N/A	Carlson	Equity	Luxembourg
SK OFLIN Evli Select	N/A	N/A		N/A	N/A	Unknown Sector Name SKOLFI.OS	Equity	Offshore Territories
SK OLFIN Gyllenberg Finlandia	N/A	N/A	Fmk	N/A	N/A	Unknown Sector Name SKOLFI.OS	Equity	Offshore Territories

Note: details for some funds may not have been included if the data for the US$ % change for 96/97 is not available

Source: Standard & Poor's Micropal.

matically matches into deals. As well as this automated matching, an agreement procedure is also used.

At the close of free trading at 5.30pm, the daily price for all listed securities is fixed and this corresponds to the closing price for each share. Free trading is followed by after-market trading from 5.35pm to 5.55pm and after-market trading II (on the next day) from 9.00am to 9.25am (official list only), during which bids and offers can no longer be changed, but brokers conclude deals among themselves within the price limits determined during free trading.

B) List of principal brokerage firms

Finnish and foreign banks and companies offering investment services can act as trading members on the HEX. The total number of banks and brokerage houses currently authorised to trade on the HEX is 26.

AG PANKKIIRILIIKE OY
Aleksanterinkatu 44, FIN-00100 Helsinki
Tel: (358) 9 131 551; Fax: (358) 9 1315 5255

ALFRED BERG Finland Oy Ab
Kluuvikatu 3, 7th Floor, FIN-00100 Helsinki
Tel: (358) 9 228 321; Fax: (358) 9 2283 2790

AROS SECURITIES OY
PL 786, FIN-00101 Helsinki
Tel: (358) 9 173 371; Fax: (358) 9 0 622 1511

D. CARNEGIE AB, FINLAND BRANCH
PL 36, FIN-00131 Helsinki
Tel: (358) 9 618 711; Fax: (358) 9 6187 1345

DEN DANSKE BANK
PL 993, 00101 Helsinki
Tel (45) 9 3344 0921; Fax (45) 9 3344 0940

MERITA PANKKIIRILIIKE OY
Fabiankatu 29B, 00100 Merita
Tel: (358) 9 12 341; Fax: (358) 9 612 1145

OY UNITED BANKERS PANKKIIRILIIKE
Aleksanterinkaut 21 A, FIN-00100 Helsinki
Tel: (358) 9 0171 466; Fax: (358) 9 0657 857

PANKKIIRILIIKE ARCTOS SECURITIES OY
Aleksanterinkaut 44, 2nd Floor, FIN-00100 Helsinki
Tel: (358) 9 549 9300; Fax: (358) 9 5499 3333

PANKKIIRILIIKE EVLI OY
PL 1081, FIN-00101 Helsinki
Tel: (358) 9 476 690; Fax: (358) 9 634 382

SKANDINAVISKA ENSKILDA BANKEN
PL 630, FIN-00101 Helsinki
Tel: (358) 9 6162 8000; Fax: (358) 9 171 056

C) Clearing and settlement

All trades concluded on the HEX are cleared and settled by the Central Securities Depository Ltd.

The HETI system transfers book entry trades automatically to the KATI clearing system at the Finnish Central Securities Depository Ltd. Paper-free clearing of book entry securities is performed daily on the delivery-versus-payment principle. The clearing period for trades conducted on the HEX is three banking days. Trades conducted outside the HEX can also be cleared in the KATI system if the traded security is included in the book entry system.

Currently, 99% of all trades on the HEX are concluded using the book entry system. All official list companies must transfer their shares to the book entry system by the end of 1998.

D) Custodian and nominee services

Banks and authorised brokerage firms hold securities in safe custody on an individual basis in segregated portfolios. Settlement and securities administration services provided are based on agreement between the parties.

E) Commissions and other costs

A negotiable commission is charged to both buyer and seller in share transactions and amounts, on average, to 1% of the market value.

TAXATION AND REGULATIONS AFFECTING FOREIGN INVESTORS

Under the Finnish tax system, capital income and earned income are taxed separately. Both individuals and companies pay a tax of 28% on interest income, dividends, rents and sales profits (with some exceptions, such as the sale of one's own residence). Interest income from bank deposits and bonds is taxed at source at 28%.

Transfers of shares are exempt from capital transfer tax if the transfer takes place on the HEX. The rate of capital transfer tax payable on deals done outside the HEX is 1.6%. Deals between non-residents are, however, exempt from capital transfer tax, even if they take place outside the HEX.

For non-resident investors, withholding tax on dividend income of 28% is, in most cases, reduced by the bilateral tax conventions signed by Finland. At present, conventions with almost 60 countries provide for lower tax rates, ranging from nil to 25%. If the state of residence of a non-resident beneficiary of a dividend is not known, tax is withheld at 28%.

From the point of view of foreign investors, for all relevant purposes exchange controls have been abolished since October 1991, although the obligation to report capital transactions to the Bank of Finland remains.

Exhibit 21.12:
WITHHOLDING TAXES

Recipient	*Portfolio**[1]	*Dividends* *Substantial***	*Interest*[1]
Resident corporation	0	0	0
Resident individual	0	0	28
Non-resident corporation or individual:			
Non-treaty	28	28	28
Treaty	0-28	0-20	0-25

* Individuals and corporations.
** Qualifying corporations[2].
Notes:
1. The withholding tax rate on dividends paid to resident individuals is 0%. For resident individuals, the withholding tax rate on interest is generally 28%. As regards non-residents, generally no tax is withheld for interest in Finland. The tax rates given apply only in the case of interest paid for a permanent loan in lieu of contribution of capital.
2. Generally, corporations with a holding of at least 25% of outstanding shares qualify; however, in some cases a holding of 10%, 20% or 50% is required.

Source: Procopé & Hornborg.

LISTING AND REPORTING REQUIREMENTS

A) Listing requirements

The HEX rules contain detailed requirements and procedures for listing. These include provisions covering such matters as specified minimum amounts of share capital and equity capital, the ability to distribute dividends, the provision of audited accounts, the level of public share ownership and the transferability of the shares. The requirements differ slightly for listings on the official list, the OTC list and the brokers' list. The new Companies Act, which became effective on 1 September 1997, requires all listed companies to amend the form of their company to that of a public limited company.

B) Reporting requirements

Under the Securities Market Act, a listed company is required to publish either one interim report of its operations, covering the first six months of a fiscal year, or two reports covering the first four and eight months of each fiscal year. An interim report must be published within three months of the end of the period covered by the report, although, according to current HEX rules, this period is reduced to two months. Annual accounts have to be published not later than one week before the annual general meeting of the company. The Securities Market Act provides that a financial statement bulletin on the annual accounts must be published immediately after their preparation.

A listed company is required to release separate announcements on: the company's future outlook; dividends; changes in share capital; information on subscription of shares; market-making agreements; business acquisitions; agreements on joint ventures; shareholder agreements; mergers and liquidation; changes in the articles of association; changes in the company's management; quotation on another stock exchange; decisions and measures of the authorities; invitations to the general meetings of shareholders and decisions of the general meetings; plus all significant decisions of the company and circumstances that are liable to affect substantially the value of the listed company's shares. When launching an offering, a listed company is required to publish a prospectus.

SHAREHOLDER PROTECTION CODES

A) Significant shareholdings

A shareholder is obliged to disclose details to the company and to the Financial Supervision Office when its shareholding reaches, exceeds or falls below one-tenth, one-fifth, one-third, one-half or two-thirds of the voting rights or share capital of a publicly traded Finnish company.

B) Takeovers and mergers

Offers must be made to minority holders when ownership in a takeover reaches two-thirds of the share capital.

C) Insider trading

The Securities Market Act has been harmonised with EU regulations and directives. The Act defines the status and obligations of listed companies and their managements, and the concept of insider dealing. The Financial Supervision Office is responsible for the application of this law.

RESEARCH

Analysts at Merita Securities monitor companies listed on the HEX and other investment opportunities, produce analyses of companies and trends in the Finnish securities market and prepare forecasts.

Economists at Merita Bank monitor developments in the Finnish economy, and the overall outlook is presented in the monthly *Economic View*, which also includes articles on current topics. Monthly indicators on the Finnish economy are presented on the KANI page on Reuters, with comments on page KANJ.

Both Alfred Berg and Evli Securities also have reputations for good research.

The HETI system provides subscribers with real-time data on trading and HEX indices throughout the trading day. Trade-by-trade information on prices, volumes, and parties is transmitted, together with the best bids and offers and index movements. Company disclosure and newsletters are available via the HETI system in text format and as published by listed companies. The HEX also has a home page on the Internet, containing up-to-date information about Finnish securities, equities and fixed-income derivatives, listed companies, mutual funds and trading members.

Several daily newspapers (eg, *Kauppalehti* and *Helsingin Sanomat*) publish an exchange list that gives, for example, official buying and selling prices, closing prices, the number of shares constituting a round lot, the nominal value of each share and the amount of the most recent dividend paid.

Daily HEX quotations and other information on the Finnish stock market are also available on the Reuters monitor on pages KOPA–KOPM.

Finland, published by Euromoney Books, provides in-depth information for those wishing to invest or do business in the country. See the order card at the back of this book for details.

CHAPTER

22

France

Introduction

At the end of 1997 there were 717 French and 183 non-French companies listed on the Paris Bourse, and total market capitalisation stood at around 49% of GNP. While the majority of the very large companies are quoted, with an average bid-offer spread of around 1.5%, there are still some significant state and private sector companies not listed. Nevertheless, there were 86 new listings on the Paris Bourse in 1997, including that of France Télécom, whose Ffr41.6 billion flotation was the largest ever in France. This offering was the first state sale by the new socialist government.

As with other European telecoms offerings, the France Télécom transaction both reflected and promoted the development of an equity culture in France. There was a record 3.9 million retail (including employee) subscriptions for the offering. Retail ownership currently represents around 20% of the French market, although only some 9% of the population own shares.

The French equity market enjoyed an exceptional year in 1997. Turnover, which has increased by more than 250% since 1992, reached its highest ever level (Ffr2.37 trillion or around 60% of the French market). The headline French index, the CAC 40, rose by nearly 30%, and the broader SBF 120, by 27%.

The market has become sectorally more diverse, with banks and other finance-related stocks representing just over 15% of total market capitalisation in 1997, compared with around 25% in 1996. After the flotation of France Télécom, the telecoms sector now represents approximately 7% of the French market, while the oil sector accounts for about 10%.

Major M&A transactions in 1997 included the formal merger (in May) of AXA and UAP, the merger of Compagnie de Suez and Lyonnaise des Eaux, the absorption of Saint-Louis by Worms et Cie and that of Péchiney International into the Péchiney Group.

Bourse membership increased to almost 140 in 1997, including a significant number of non-French members. In order to ensure a large, diverse membership, the SBF has taken advantage of the 1996 Investment Services Directive to allow non-shareholder membership of the SBF. In 1997 the Paris Bourse also developed a "remote trading" facility for firms located outside Paris.

ECONOMIC AND POLITICAL OVERVIEW

The decision in April by France's President Jacques Chirac to call a snap general election, nearly a year before it was due, turned French politics upside down. Instead of securing a centre-right parliamentary majority (previously 84% of the seats) for the remainder of his presidential term, he handed power to Lionel Jospin's Socialist Party. Jospin did not win enough seats for an overall majority, but, with the support of Communist and Green Party coalition partners, he managed to gain control. This has resulted in a "cohabitation" between a president and a parliament of differing political stances.

This may well be a more stable political situation than at first sight. The threat of parliament being dissolved by President Chirac and the government being ousted by the French public for failing to carry out its election promises (as was the case with the Juppé government), has resulted in a new government that is "forced to succeed".

France's new administration has reinforced its predecessor's commitment to join the single European currency and, indeed, France has met all the EMU convergence criteria.

Role of the central bank

The chief responsibility of the Banque de France is to formulate and implement monetary policy with the aim of ensuring price stability. It carries out this task within the framework of the government's overall economic policy.

Exhibit 22.1: CAC 40 PRICE INDEX (Ffr), 1993–97

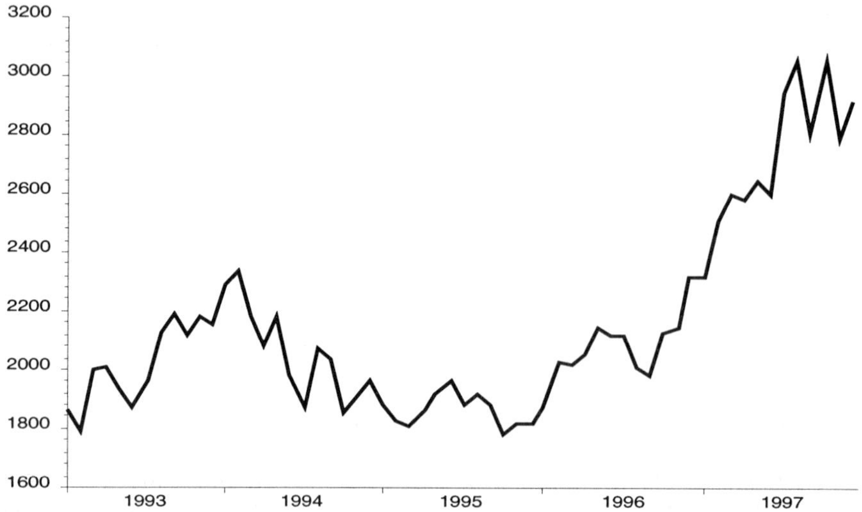

High value 3054.93 1.10.95 Low value 1780.71 2.10.95 *Source: Datastream*

Its duties include formulating monetary policy, interest rate policy and foreign exchange policy, and the gathering and interpreting of monetary policy data.

In addition, the bank issues banknotes and coins, manages cashless means of payment and supervises payment systems.

The Banque de France traditionally functioned as the government's bank. Since its independence in 1993, however, it may no longer grant overdrafts or any other type of credit facility to the Treasury, other public bodies or state-owned corporations, nor may it directly purchase their debt securities.

MARKET PERFORMANCE

A) In 1997

It proved to be another excellent year for French equities. The CAC 40, the headline French equity index, closed at 2,999 – an increase of 29.5% for the year and the best performance since 1988 – and the SBF 120 closed at 1,618 (an increase of 26.9% for the year). On 28 October the CAC 40 reached its low of 2,475.0 due to the crash in Asia, but this was still 7% higher than the 1 January opening level.

During 1997, 86 companies listed their shares on the Paris Bourse – 67 on the regulated markets (Premier Marché, Second Marché and Nouveau Marché), and 19 on the free (unregulated) market. This represented the highest rate of new listings for a decade. At the end of 1997, there were 717 French companies and 183 non-French companies listed on the Paris Bourse.

During the past five years, the average daily number of trades has risen from 58,400 to 148,278 (up 250%) and the average daily turnover has risen from Ffr26 billion to Ffr95 billion (up 350%). In 1997 the total trading value of French equities rose 67.2% from Ffr1.42 trillion to Ffr2.37 trillion, while total trading in non-French equities rose 99.6% from Ffr31 billion to Ffr60 billion. The liquidity of the Paris Bourse (measured as total equity market turnover divided by total equity market capitalisation) was 60%, representing an increase of 27% on 1996 levels.

The equity market capitalisation of the Paris Bourse stood at Ffr4,067 billion at the end of 1997, compared with Ffr3,078 billion for 1996 – an increase of around Ffr1 trillion, or 32%.

B) Summary information

Global ranking by market value (US$ terms, end-1997): 5
Market capitalisation (end-1997): US$678.96 billion
Growth in market value (local currency terms, 1993–97): 51%
Market value as a % of nominal GDP (end-1997): 49%
Number of domestic/foreign companies listed (end-1997): 717/183
Market P/E (end 1997): 19.4
MSCI total returns (with net dividends, US$ terms, 1997): 11.9%
MSCI Index (change in US$ terms, 1997): +10.6%
Short-term (3-month) interest rate (end-1997): 3.63%
Long-term (10-year) bond yield (end-1997): 5.33%
Budget deficit as a % of nominal GDP (1997): 3%
Annual increase in broad money (M3) supply (end-1997): 0.9%
Inflation rate (1997): 1.1%
US$ exchange rate (end-1997): Ffr5.99

C) Year-end share price indices, price/earnings ratios and yields

Exhibit 22.2:
SHARE INDICES, P/E RATIOS AND DIVIDEND YIELDS, 1993–97

Year-end	*CAC 40 Index*	*SBF 250*	*P/E*	*Yield (%)*
1993	2,268.20	1,506.09	27.5	2.7
1994	1,881.15	1,250.66	24.5	3.3
1995	1,871.90	1,232.80	23.8	3.3
1996	2,315.76	1,561.66	38.3	2.7
1997	2,998.90	1,944.90	19.4	2.2

Sources: Paris Bourse and Paribas.

D) Market indices and their constituents

The CAC 40 Index, the main real-time indicator of the Paris Bourse, was developed in 1988 to serve as an underlying index for derivative products. It is based on 40 blue chip stocks chosen from among the 100 largest companies listed on the monthly settlement market, and has a base of 1,000 as at 31 December 1987.

The SBF 250 Index comprises 250 stocks that together give an accurate indication of the performance of the wider French economy. The SBF 120 is made up of the market's top 120 stocks in terms of liquidity and capitalisation, and is designed to serve as a benchmark for indexed funds. The SBF 250 and SBF 120 have a base of 1,000 as at the end of December 1990.

The Mid-CAC, based on mid-cap stocks listed on the Paris Bourse, was launched in May 1995.

Two new indices were created in 1997: the SBF 80, which comprises the stocks included in the SBF 250 index but not included in the CAC 40 index; and the computer industry index (*indice sectoriel spécialisé informatique*), comprising SBF250 stocks specialising in this area.

There is also a Second Marché Index, which is a benchmark for young, mid-cap stocks.

THE STOCK MARKET

A) Brief history and structure

The institutional framework in which financial activities are carried out on the Paris market has been redefined by the incorporation into French law of the EU Investment Services Directive (ISD). The new system is based on the concept of "regulated markets", each managed by a private market company responsible for access, membership and listing rules. Four markets in France are recognised as regulated markets: the stock market, Monep, Matif and the Nouveau Marché. Procedures for membership, prudential control, a code of professional ethics and sanctions to be applied have been unified under new legislation.

The regulatory authorities in charge of supervising the orderly operations of the stock market are:

- the Commission des Opérations de Bourse (COB);
- the Conseil des Marchés Financiers (CMF); and
- the Conseil des Etablissements de Crédits et des Entreprises d'Investissement (CECEI).

The COB, established in 1967, is an autonomous state agency, originally modelled on the US SEC, which acts as stock market watchdog. The COB has strong regulatory powers over the market, issuing regulations covering, for example, insider trading and takeover bids. It is also responsible for policing disclosure requirements and for investigating any violations of securities law, and may impose fines in certain cases.

The CMF oversees (in co-ordination with the CECEI) the accreditation and activities of investment firms. The CMF defines, implements and monitors observance of an investment firm code of conduct.

The CECEI is the regulatory authority responsible for licensing new investment firms and for monitoring adherence to prudential rules, while the Banking Commission checks on solvency.

The implementation of the ISD means that all EU entities authorised to provide investment services in their home territories can have direct access to French regulated markets without a licence. French subsidiaries of credit institutions incorporated abroad now have the same rights as French-owned establishments, although they still have to seek a licence. New French branch offices of non-EEA organisations have to request licences to provide banking services or intermediary financial services.

B) Different exchanges

The national market, the Paris Bourse, is the only stock exchange in France. All securities previously listed on the Paris and regional stock exchanges have been transferred to a single electronic trading system that allows securities houses to trade all securities listed in France.

The Nouveau Marché, France's "junior market" for high-growth stocks, is not, strictly speaking, a section of the Paris Bourse but a separate new exchange that is a 100% subsidiary of the Paris Bourse.

C) Opening hours, names and addresses

The electronic trading system of the Paris Bourse is open from 10.00am to 5.00pm Monday to Friday, with a pre-opening session lasting from 8.30am to 10.00am.

SBF – PARIS BOURSE
39 rue Cambon, 75001 Paris
Tel: (33) 1 49 27 10 00; Fax: (33) 1 49 27 11 71
Telex: 215 561 F; Internet: www.bourse-de-Paris.fr

MARKET SIZE

A) Number of listings and market value

At the end of 1997, market capitalisation of domestic equity securities listed on the Paris Bourse totalled Ffr4,067 billion, up 32.1% compared with the end-1996 market value.

Exhibit 22.3:
LISTED COMPANIES, PARIS BOURSE AND NOUVEAU MARCHÉ, 1993–97

Companies	*1993*	*1994*	*1995*	*1996*	*1997*
Domestic	726	724	710	702	717
Foreign	208	198	194	189	183
Total	934	922	904	891	900

Source: Paris Bourse.

Exhibit 22.4:
DOMESTIC MARKET CAPITALISATION, PARIS BOURSE AND NOUVEAU MARCHÉ, 1993–97 (FFR BILLION)

	1993	*1994*	*1995*	*1996*	*1997*
Shares	2,689	2,415	2,444	3,078	4,067
Bonds	3,877	3,692	4,132	4,531	4,678
Total	6,566	6,107	6,576	7,609	8,745

Source: Paris Bourse.

B) Largest quoted companies

Exhibit 22.5:
MARKET CAPITALISATION OF THE 10 LARGEST COMPANIES ON THE PARIS BOURSE, END-1997

Ranking	*Company*	*Market value (Ffr billion)*
1	France Télécom	218.3
2	Elf Aquitaine	192.6
3	Total	159.5
4	Oréal (L')	159.2
5	Axa	154.3
6	Alcatel Alsthom	124.5
7	Carrefour	120.8
8	Eaux (Cie Gle des)	112.6
9	Rhône-Poulenc	97.2
10	LVMH	87.5

Source: Paris Bourse.

C) Trading volume

Domestic company share turnover in 1997 totalled Ffr2,373.9 billion, an increase of 67% on the 1996 equivalent.

Exhibit 22.6:
SHARE TURNOVER ON THE PARIS BOURSE AND NOUVEAU MARCHÉ, 1993–97 (FFR BILLION)

Year	*Domestic companies*	*Foreign companies*	*Total trading value*
1993	959.7	27.4	987.1
1994	1,101.0	21.0	1,122.0
1995	1,034.6	18.3	1,052.9
1996	1,419.3	31.0	1,450.3
1997	2,373.9	60.6	2,434.5

Source: Paris Bourse.

Exhibit 22.7:
THE 10 MOST ACTIVELY TRADED PARIS BOURSE SHARES, 1997

Ranking	*Company*	*Average daily turnover (Ffr million)*
1	Elf Aquitaine	599.1
2	Alcatel Altsthom	502.5
3	Axa	407.4
4	Total	386.9
5	Carrefour	360.2
6	Eaux (Cie Gle des)	356.8
7	LVMH	323.1
8	Société Générale	319.8
9	Rhône-Poulenc	267.6
10	Oréal (L')	256.1

Source: Paris Bourse.

TYPES OF SHARE

Equity securities traded consist of ordinary or preferred shares, voting and non-voting shares, and shares with single or double voting rights.

Preferred shares with voting rights

The preference might consist of the distribution of a proportionate share of earnings greater than to holders of other types of shares, or a priority in the distribution of earnings up to a certain percentage. These two preferences can be cumulative or non-cumulative. In addition, the articles of incorporation of the company may provide that some shares benefit from double voting rights.

Shares with increased dividend (dividende majoré)

Under the Law of 12 July 1994, listed companies may decide through an extraordinary general meeting of their shareholders to modify their articles of association in order to permit an additional dividend to be paid to shareholders who have held registered shares for a minimum period of two years. The number of qualifying shares per shareholder may not exceed 0.5% of the capital stock of the company.

Non-voting preference shares (ADP)

A specific class of non-voting shares with priority over dividends was created in 1978. Holders of such shares, known as *actions à dividendes prioritaires d'ADP*, have priority over other shareholders to receive payment of a dividend of an amount not less than 7.5% of the paid-in share capital represented by these shares. ADP cannot represent more than 25% of the issued share capital of the company. This first dividend is partially cumulative, as it may draw on the earnings of the three subsequent financial years when earnings from the year of issue are insufficient.

The non-voting status of such shares is contingent upon the payment of the preference dividend. If, for three years, dividends are not paid in full, these shares have regular voting rights until the total is paid.

Investment certificates

To encourage private investment in state-owned French companies, investment certificates (CI) and privileged investment certificates (CIP), were created in 1983. As for ADP, CI or CIP cannot represent more than 25% of the issued share capital of the company.

CI originate from a division of the pecuniary rights and voting rights of shares of a company. The main issuers of CI or CIP include state-owned companies or banks like Rhône-Poulenc, Crédit Lyonnais and Paribas, but also family-owned companies such as L'Oréal or Taittinger which have used CI and CIP to raise capital without diluting control.

Since the Law of 5 January 1988, voting right certificates may be freely transferred to owners of CI. When both certificates are held by the same owner, they are automatically converted into full shares. To avoid losing voting rights, the owner must inform the company of the conversion within 15 days.

Equity-linked instruments

Equity-linked bonds can be repaid in the form of shares representing the capital of the issuing company, or through conversion, exchange or reimbursement of the bond concerned. They may be convertible bonds, or bonds redeemable in shares (ORA) or in investment certificates (ORCI), or bonds with warrants to subscribe for shares (OBSA). Covered warrants on existing shares are also issued both on the domestic market and on the Euromarket by French issuers.

Since the Law of 14 December 1985, it has also been possible to issue "other securities giving a right to allocation of equities representing a share in the capital", which, in practice, offers many possibilities to French companies.

Collective investment schemes (OPCVM, SGP and pension funds)

Collective investment remains extremely popular in France, which ranks second in the world for the volume of assets in collective investment schemes. Their popularity is partly due to special tax incentives for both the funds and their shareholders. They have an important impact on the domestic market by increasing demand and adding significantly to liquidity.

There are four types of OPCVM: SICAVs (mutual funds), FCPs (open-ended common funds), FCPRs (more risky open-ended common funds) and FCPEs (the equivalent of ESOPs). The ISD has created multi-purpose portfolio management companies with a unified charter (SGP) that can now manage collective schemes as well as individual portfolios.

Under the law of 25 March 1997, French employees can participate in private pension funds (*fonds d'épargne*). The legislation aims to create a source of income to supplement the pension paid by the compulsory state scheme organised in the form of a pay-as-you-go system. Moreover, these savings will be invested in the stock market. Further details concerning specific aspects of the legislation (such as the tax benefits and treatment) are expected to be announced during 1998.

Derivatives

Since its 1987 launch, the Monep Paris Traded Options Market has seen sustained growth in turnover for stock and index options. Two index classes and 50 stock classes are traded. The most actively traded equity options are traded continuously from 10.00am to 5.00pm.

Futures are traded on the Matif, which is now a 100% subsidiary of the Paris Bourse.

OTHER MARKETS

There are three markets within the Paris Bourse:

1. The main listing market is the Premier Marché, which has a cash market (*marché au comptant*) where trading in securities is settled for cash within three days, and a *marché à règlement mensuel* (monthly settlement market) for the most active stocks, where settlement is effected at the end of the month.
2. The second market (Second Marché) was launched in February 1983. This market is more flexible and is designed to accommodate medium-sized companies; it

Exhibit 22.8:
QUOTATION GROUPS

	Continu A	*Continu B*	*Fixing A*	*Fixing B*
Securities concerned	Most actively traded securities	Actively traded securities	Less actively traded securities	All securities traded on the unregulated market
Trading hours	10.00am to 5.00pm	10.00am to 5.00pm	11.30am then 4.00pm	3.00pm

requires candidates only to float 10% of their total equity (compared with 25% on the main market).

3. A new stock market, the Nouveau Marché, dedicated to innovative, high-growth companies, was launched on 14 February 1996. In 1998 this will be linked with similar markets in Amsterdam, Frankfurt and Brussels to form Euro NM, and brokers at the four exchanges will be able to trade in each other's stocks.

INVESTORS

In the past few years in France there have been an increasing number of private investors taking an interest in the stock market as a result of the government's privatisation programme. About 12 million French people own shares traded on the Paris Bourse or units in mutual funds, compared with 1.7 million in 1978. Most shares are owned directly, although significant buying and selling takes place through the SICAVs.

OPERATIONS

A) Trading system

The Paris Bourse trading system (NSC-Super CAC) is also the designated trading system of the Brussels, Toronto, São Paulo and Chicago Mercantile exchanges.

Paris Bourse member firms, acting on behalf of clients or for their own account, enter all orders into the Super CAC system. Orders are automatically ranked by price limit, and are queued within each limit to reflect time of arrival. From 8.30am to 10.00am the market is in its pre-opening phase and orders are fed into the centralised order book without any transactions taking place. Each time a new order is entered into the system a "theoretical" price is automatically calculated by the computer. At 10.00am the market opens. Depending on the limit orders received, the central computer automatically calculates the opening price at which the largest number of bids and asks can be matched.

At the same time, the system transforms orders at market price into limit orders at the opening price, with the result that all limit buy orders at higher prices, and all limit sell orders at lower prices are executed in full. Limit orders at the opening price are executed to the extent that matches are available. Orders that are not executed at the opening price remain registered in the computerised order books.

From 10.00am to 5.00pm trading takes place on a continuous basis, and the arrival of a new order immediately triggers transactions if a matching order (or orders) exists on the centralised book. The execution price is the price limit placed on the matching order. Assuming identical price limits, orders are executed as they arrive – first entered, first matched.

Securities are divided into four quotation groups (*groupes de cotation*): *continu* A; *continu* B; fixing A for the regulated market; and fixing B for securities traded on the unregulated market. The classification of securities by quotation group is made by the Paris Bourse according to the volume of trading. Each quotation group has its own rules of quotation and rules as to maximum daily price fluctuations and halts in trading (see Exhibit 22.8).

Data dissemination

Super CAC automatically feeds information into the system's electronic data dissemination network. As a result, client subscribers to the network receive in real time the five most recent transactions completed (time, price, number of shares traded), along with the five best bids and asks in price and quantity, as they appear on traders' screens at Paris Bourse member firms.

Surveillance and control

The Paris Bourse monitors all operations closely, and is empowered to suspend trading temporarily in any security or set a limit on price fluctuations, should it feel this is in the interests of the market.

Block trading

Block trading is subject to the following conditions:

- The shares involved must be among those approved for block trading by the Paris Bourse, which makes approval conditional on high trading volumes. Among such stocks are those underlying options included in an index or underlying options on futures contracts.
- The Paris Bourse establishes a separate minimum volume for trades in each approved stock.

Exhibit 22.9:
TOP PERFORMING COUNTRY FUNDS – FRANCE

Fund	US$ % change 31/12/96 31/12/97	US$ % change 31/12/92 31/12/97	Currency	Fund size (US$ mil)	Volatility	Manager name	Main sector	Class
Declic Actions Francaises	22.9	N/A	Ffr	8.35	N/A	Société Genéralé	Equity	French FCPs
Swissca Cntries Eq France	21.92	N/A	Ffr	67.74	N/A	Swissca Fondsleitung AG	Equity	Swiss Mutual Funds
State Street Actions France C	19.78	89.8	Ffr	23.9	5.42	State Street	Equity Growth	Investmentfds Deutschland
Baring CF French Growth	19.13	N/A	Ffr	6.22	3.79	Baring International (Ireland)	Equity	Offshore Territories
EMIF France Index Plus B	16.31	50.83	Ffr	45.23	5.35	CCF/BHF/HS/KB/BBV	Equity Growth	Investmentfds Deutschland
Tricolore	15.6	88.02	Ffr	60.41	N/A	Cie Fin. Rothschild	Equity	French FCPs
DVG Fonds France	15.31	64.17	DM	70.56	5.15	DVG	Equity Growth	Investmentfds Deutschland
France Valeur	15.17	N/A	Ffr	4.75	N/A	Deutsche Bank	Equity	French FCPs
Hansard EU Fidelity France	15.15	N/A	Ffr	N/S	N/A	Hansard Europe	Equity	Offshore Territories
OASI PARIGI	15.09	N/A	L	N/S	N/A	Deutsche Bank Fondi	Equity Growth	Italian Mutuals
Entrindice France	15.03	N/A	Ffr	15.55	N/A	Dresdner Kleinwort Benson	Equity	French FCPs
Digit CAC 40 C	14.65	N/A	Ffr	29.79	N/A	Sinopia Asset Mngt.	Equity	French FCPs
Fidelity France Fund	14.46	N/A	US$	5.7	N/A	Fidelity Funds	Equity Growth	US Mutuals
G-Equity Fund G-French Eq B	14.42	N/A	Ffr	64.28	5	Generale de Banque (Lux)	Equity Growth	Investmentfds Deutschland
Haussmann Index France	14.22	60.18	Ffr	46.17	N/A	Banque Worms	Equity	French SICAVs
Nomura Aurora France	14.19	39.12	¥	1.55	4.99	Nomura ITMCo	Equity Growth	Japanese Open Trusts
Horizon Index France	14.01	N/A	Ffr	0.98	N/A	Rothschild Banque	Equity	French FCPs
Actiperformance	13.99	N/A	Ffr	30.78	N/A	GMF Vie	Equity	French FCPs
France CAC 40 Invest.	13.98	60.08	Ffr	2.29	N/A	BFT	Equity	French FCPs
Top Indice 40	13.71	N/A	Ffr	8.68	N/A	CPR Gestion	Equity	French FCPs
AGF Opti Index	13.67	N/A	Ffr	20.95	N/A	AGF	Equity	French SICAVs
MDM Opportunites	13.67	N/A	Ffr	65.97	N/A	Mutuel du Mans	Equity	French FCPs
Fima Indice Premiere	13.58	59.16	Ffr	33.23	N/A	Fimagest	Equity	French SICAVs
Fidelity Fds France	13.56	80.98	Ffr	59.75	4.59	Fidelity Funds	Equity Growth	Investmentfds Deutschland
Balzac France Index	13.4	N/A	Ffr	15.55	N/A	State Street Bq	Equity	French FCPs
Virtuose 40	13.39	N/A	Ffr	14.73	N/A	UFG	Equity	French FCPs
CICM CB France Basket	13.04	63.57	Ffr	107.91	4.85	CICM Fund Mgmt Ltd	Equity	Offshore Territories
Centrale Indice Actions	12.88	N/A	Ffr	7.04	N/A	CC Reescompte	Equity	French FCPs
Groupama Actions France	12.87	N/A	Ffr	231.97	N/A	Groupama	Equity	French FCPs
Actip Indice 40	12.63	59.06	Ffr	15.55	N/A	Dresdner Kleinwort Benson	Equity	French SICAVs
Efi Quant	12.62	N/A	Ffr	7.37	N/A	Credit Cooperatif	Equity	French FCPs
BFT Valor France	12.61	N/A	Ffr	18.83	N/A	BFT	Equity	French FCPs
SBC Eq Fd France	12.5	76.64	Ffr	647.76	N/A	Swiss Bank Corporation	Equity	Swiss Mutual Funds
Indice Cac	11.2	N/A	Ffr	0.65	N/A	Gerer Conseil	Equity	French FCPs
Hansard\Fidelity France	11.02	78.61	Ffr	0.36	4.17	Hansard\Fidelity	Equity	Offshore Territories
ADIG Aktien Frankreich	10.94	N/A	DM	20.03	5	Adig Investment	Equity Growth	Investmentfds Deutschland
France 40	10.93	47.46	Ffr	44.69	N/A	Bq Cortal	Equity	French SICAVs
Primerus Actions France C	10.84	N/A	Ffr	2.62	N/A	CCF Capital Management	Equity	French FCPs
Citi PF French Equity	10.83	64.99	Ffr	30.18	4.33	Citiportfolios SA	Equity Growth	Investmentfds Deutschland
AGF 5000	10.77	73.29	Ffr	524.84	N/A	AGF	Equity	French SICAVs
DWS Frankreich Fonds	10.77	N/A	DM	93.58	4.53	DWS	Equity Growth	Investmentfds Deutschland
DIT Fonds Frankreich	10.3	63.36	DM	150.08	4.92	DIT	Equity Growth	Investmentfds Deutschland
CFG France	10.29	54.37	Ffr	6.55	N/A	Cyril Finance	Equity	French FCPs
UBS Eqty Inv France	10.03	66.14	Ffr	393.55	N/A	UBS	Equity	Swiss Mutual Antares

Note: details for some funds may not have been included if the data for the US$ % change for 96/97 was not available

Source: Standard & Poor's Micropal.

Lending of securities (prêt de titres) and repos (pensions)

Legislation passed in December 1987 provides a legal framework for the lending of securities between brokerage firms – ie, to allow due delivery when a seller does not own the securities.

B) List of principal member firms

At present there are 99 member firms active on the Paris Bourse. The principal Parisian firms include the following:

BANQUE PARIBAS
3 rue d'Antin, 75002 Paris
Tel: (33) 1 42 98 12 34; Fax: (33) 1 42 98 09 94

DU BOUZET SA
15 boulevard Poissonnière, 75002 Paris
Tel: (33) 1 55 34 19 92; Fax: (33) 1 55 34 17 90

CCF ELYSEES BOURSE SA
103 avenue des Champs-Elysées, 75419 Paris
Tel: (33) 1 40 70 33 49; Fax: (33) 1 40 70 35 54

CHEUVREUX de VIRIEU SA
46 rue de Courcelles, 75008 Paris
Tel: (33) 1 44 95 24 24; Fax: (33) 1 45 63 23 65

COURCOUX, BOUVET SNC
32 avenue de l'Opera, 75002 Paris
Tel: (33) 1 40 17 50 00; Fax: (33) 1 47 42 56 79

DEUTSCHE MORGAN GRENFELL SC
3 avenue de Friedland, 75008 Paris
Tel: (33) 1 44 95 64 00; Fax: (33) 1 53 75 07 09

EXANE SA
16 avenue Matignon, 75008 Paris
Tel: (33) 1 44 95 40 00; Fax: (33) 1 44 95 40 01

FERRI SA
53 rue Vivienne, 75002 Paris
Tel: (33) 1 40 41 42 43; Fax: (33) 1 40 41 50 99

KLEINWORT BENSON FRANCE SA
11 avenue Myron Herrick, 75008 Paris
Tel: (33) 1 44 95 05 05; Fax: (33) 1 45 63 98 27

MASSONAUD, FONTENAY, KERVERN SA
3 avenue Hoche, 75008 Paris
Tel: (33) 1 44 29 44 00; Fax: (33)1 44 29 44 04

ODDO & CIE
12 boulevard de la Madeleine, 75009 Paris
Tel: (33) 1 44 51 85 00; Fax: (33) 1 44 51 85 10

PINATTON SA
69 boulevard Haussmann, 75008 Paris
Tel: (33) 1 40 17 52 00; Fax: (33) 1 40 17 90 60

SALOMON BROTHERS SA
7 rue de Tilsitt, 75017 Paris
Tel: (33) 1 4055 8420; Fax: (33)1 4055 8460

SBC WARBURG DILLON READ SA
65 rue de Courcelles, 75008 Paris
Tel: (33) 1 48 88 30 30; Fax: (33) 1 40 53 07 07

SGE DELAHAYE SA
17 cours Valmy, 92987 Paris
Tel: (33) 1 42 13 45 45; Fax: (33) 1 42 13 46 15

SMITH BARNEY SA
112 Avenue Kleber, 75016 Paris Cedex 16
Tel: (33) 1 5370 2800; Fax: (33) 1 5370 8734

UBS SA
69 boulevard Haussmann, 75008 Paris
Tel: (33) 1 44 56 45 45; Fax: (33) 1 44 56 45 54

C) Settlement and transfer

Securities have been dematerialised and are represented by computerised holdings with authorised intermediaries (banks, stock exchange member firms, etc) that have an account with the central depository authority, SICOVAM.

There is a computerised settlement system, RELIT, which is based on two G30-recommended principles: (a) delivery versus payment, or the simultaneous exchange of securities and cash on the same day; and (b) a standard timeframe for trade comparisons and settlement. The clearing house operated by the Paris Bourse is integrated in the RELIT system.

As orders are matched automatically on the Super CAC system, trades between member firms need no further confirmation. Automatic delivery and payment takes place at T+3 (or at the end of the month for securities traded on the monthly settlement market). RELIT settles all transactions.

D) Commissions and other costs

In July 1989, fixed commissions were abolished in France. Brokerage fees (*courtage*) are now negotiated freely between clients and member firms.

Transactions in equities on the French market for residents are subject to a stamp duty tax (*impôt de bourse*) amounting to 0.03% of transactions up to Ffr1 million and 0.15% thereafter, payable by both buyer and seller. However, there is an allowance on stamp duty of Ffr150 for each transaction, which means that transactions of less than Ffr50,000 are exempt. In addition there is a ceiling of Ffr4,000 on stamp duty. Non-residents are not subject to stamp duty when trading on the Paris Bourse.

TAXATION AND REGULATIONS AFFECTING FOREIGN INVESTORS

A) Withholding tax

Unless otherwise provided by a double tax treaty, dividends on French shares are subject to a withholding tax of 25%.

Under Section 119 of the French General Tax Code, withholding taxes have been eliminated under certain conditions on dividends paid by a French resident company to another company which holds 25% or more of its shares and is registered in another EU state.

Dividends are paid out of after-tax income. French residents are entitled to a tax credit, known as the *avoir fiscal*, equal to one-half of the dividend paid. Corporate bodies and institutions are usually granted the *avoir fiscal* unless the percentage of the capital which they hold in a French company is higher than or equal to a certain percentage: 5% (Netherlands); 10% (Austria, Finland, India, Ireland, Israel, Korea, Malaysia, Malta, Mauritius, Mexico, New Zealand, Norway, Pakistan, Germany, Singapore, South Korea, Sweden, Turkey, United Kingdom, United States, Venezuela); 15% (Japan); 20% (Switzerland); or 25% (Luxembourg, Spain).

Under 1994 tax regulations, dividends of French origin paid to non-French residents who are entitled to the transfer of the *avoir fiscal* pursuant to a tax treaty are eligible, at the time of payment of the dividend, to withholding tax at the reduced rate provided by such treaty.

Under the US-French tax treaty, US pension funds pay withholding tax at the reduced rate of 15% on dividends of French origin. In addition, these pension funds are entitled to a partial refund of the *avoir fiscal*, equal to the 15% withholding tax.

Amounts distributed as dividends by French companies out of profits that have not been taxed at the ordinary corporate rate or which have been earned and taxed more than five years before the distribution, are subject to a prepayment by such companies equal to one-half of the net amount distributed. When a tax treaty does not provide for a refund of the *avoir fiscal* or when the investor is not entitled to such refund, non-residents may usually obtain directly from the French tax authorities a refund of the net amount of the pre-payment, if any (net of the applicable withholding tax).

Withholding taxes exempt non-residents from any further income tax if they have no other tax liability in France.

Exhibit 22.10:
WITHHOLDING TAX

Recipient	*Rate of dividend withholding tax (minority holdings) %*
Non-treaty countries	25
Tax treaty countries	0-25

Source: Price Waterhouse.

B) Exchange control

As a result of the EU Directive on the liberalisation of capital movements, exchange control regulations have been gradually abolished in France.

Individuals and companies can now open bank accounts abroad as well as foreign currency accounts within France. Restrictions on foreign exchange no longer exist and bank loans (including loans in foreign currencies) can be made to non-residents in France.

REPORTING REQUIREMENTS

The Paris Bourse must be notified of all factors having an effect on the price of shares, such as takeovers, mergers and increases in share capital.

The COB regulates information given to securities holders and to the public by companies, and the issue of securities by such companies. Consequently, the COB exercises continual supervision, ensures that companies publish regular information and verifies the truthfulness of all information given.

Under COB regulation 88-04, companies listed on the Paris Bourse are required to provide the public with the following:

- information relating to any general meeting to be held in order to enable shareholders to exercise their voting rights;
- information regarding the allocation and payment of dividends, new issues of shares, subscription rights, waivers of shareholders' rights to subscribe and the exercise of conversion rights;
- information about any proposed material amendment to the *status* (articles of association) of the company and rights in respect of each type of share;
- information about any change in the share ownership of the company subsequent to the latest published information;
- published newspaper advertisements no later than six months after the fiscal year-end containing the financial statements for the relevant year, the proposed allocation of profits and losses and the report to the shareholders' meeting; and

- published newspaper advertisements within four months of the end of the first six-month period of each fiscal year, containing a report on the company's activities and on its net turnover and profit or loss before tax.

The COB has also adopted regulation 90-02 on disclosure requirements, which sets out three principles:

1. The information given to the public must be true, complete and sincere.
2. Any information which might have an impact on a share price should be published by the relevant company or the relevant investor as soon as possible (subject to certain exceptions).
3. Foreign companies listed on the Paris Bourse should provide the public in France with information as detailed as it provides to the public in its home jurisdiction.

SHAREHOLDER PROTECTION CODES

A) Significant shareholdings

Individuals or companies acting alone or in concert are required, when their voting rights in a quoted company cross the thresholds of 5%, 10%, 20%, 33.3%, 50%, and 66.6% as a result of acquisitions or disposals of shares or securities carrying voting rights on the main or the second market, to notify the CMF within five dealing days from the date of the transaction and to notify the company itself within 15 days of such date. In this notification, buyers must state their intentions for the next 12 months concerning the target company. The CMF then informs the public of such threshold-crossings by publishing a notice in its *Bulletin*. The articles of association of a company may provide for lower thresholds.

Failure to disclose relevant holdings entails automatic suspension for a two-year period of voting rights attached to the shares in respect of which disclosure was not made. Furthermore, the commercial court may cancel all or part of the voting rights of a shareholder in breach of this provision for up to five years, upon application by the chairman of the company, another shareholder or the COB itself.

B) Takeover bids

The procedure for takeover bids was laid down by the Law of 2 August 1989. These provisions introduced the obligation to make a takeover bid when a shareholder of a French listed company becomes the direct or indirect holder of one-third of the issued share capital of the company. In addition, in order to protect minority shareholders, any takeover bid has to be for all of the share capital of the target company, including securities that give the right to purchase or to subscribe for equity securities (eg, convertibles).

The offer must be filed with the CMF and an offer document must be published by the bidder.

Increases in share capital during a bid are generally prohibited and French companies are prohibited from purchasing their own share capital as a way of blocking takeover bids.

Under a procedure known as *offre publique de retrait*, the shares of a French company may be withdrawn from listing in specific situations. These include when a shareholder or shareholders hold more than 95% of the issued share capital, in which case remaining holders can request (or the majority holders can insist) that their shares be bought by the majority shareholders.

In a purchase of a block of shares resulting in the buyer holding more than 50% of the voting rights or the capital, the buyer may apply to CMF to be authorised to carry out a standing offer to purchase all shares owned by any other shareholders. The purchase price shall be the same as that paid for the block (unless otherwise authorised by the CMF).

C) Insider trading

Insider trading is a criminal offence. Inside information is defined as any material, specific, non-public information which, if made public, would have an impact on the price of the relevant share, contract or financial product.

Legal corporate representatives, persons who obtain the information in the course of the preparation or performance of a financial transaction or in the course of their professional activity and, more generally, anyone who receives the information from a professional and would know of the breach of fiduciary duty, would generally be regarded as insiders.

Insider trading is a criminal offence punishable by a fine of up to Ffr10 million (or 10 times the profit resulting from the transaction) and/or imprisonment for up to two years.

D) Investors' and shareholders' associations

The Law of 8 August 1994 allows registered shareholders of at least two years' standing who together hold 5% of the voting rights to join together to form an association. These associations are able to exercise the various rights normally reserved to shareholders owning at least 10% of the capital stock.

E) Member firm guarantees

Each Paris Bourse member firm is responsible to its clients for completing their transactions. In addition, CMF regulations define minimum capital bases for member firms and set prudential ratios for risk cover, risk spread and liquidity.

The same regulations require member firms to maintain strictly separate accounts for clients' funds, to ensure that these are not used for business carried out on the firm's own account (ie, when acting as principals).

The Paris Bourse acts as a clearing house to guarantee final settlement of trades between member firms, thus eliminating the risk of a chain reaction triggered by a default at any level – ie, by a member firm itself, or by one of its clients.

RESEARCH

Caisse des Dépots et Consignations, Société Générale, Crédit Commercial de France, Banque Paribas and Banque Indosuez have extensive research departments. Member firms such as Cheuvreux de Virieu, Cholet Dupont and Ferri also provide useful information on the market.

Financial publications

The annual report of the COB (*Rapport de la Commission des Opérations de Bourse*) contains useful information, as does the *Année Boursière*, which has been published since 1962 and includes figures, statistics and graphs covering market activity for the year.

Financial newspapers include:
AGEFI
Les Echos
Le Journal des Finances Investor
La Synthese Financière
La Tribune Desfossés.

Financial magazines include:
L'Expansion
Le Nouvel Economiste
Option Finance
La Vie Française.

CHAPTER 23

Germany

Introduction

Germany has the largest economy in the EU, contributing 30% to combined GDP. Around 57% of its exports are to EU member states, underlining the high level of economic integration. Opportunities in eastern Europe and in the Asian region are being explored by Germany's export-oriented industries, but still count small in the overall economy.

The German equity market is highly liquid, with turnover reaching 3.4 times average market capitalisation. Foreign investors, enjoying unrestricted access to the German capital market, contribute significantly to this liquidity. Helped by the strong equity performance in recent years, attractive IPOs and publicity for shareholder value concepts, German individual investors have increased their involvement in equity trading, although the market remains highly institutionalised.

Equity trading is concentrated in Frankfurt where floor trading and electronic trading co-exist for cash transactions. However, Deutsche Börse AG (the Frankfurt Stock Exchange operator) has introduced a new electronic platform, Xetra, which ultimately has the capacity to replace floor trading.

ECONOMIC AND POLITICAL OVERVIEW

Since 1983 Germany has been governed by a conservative/liberal government creating a stable environment for industry. The next general election is due in September 1998. With fiscal policy in 1997 focusing on EMU, there was little room for much-demanded tax reforms, although a VAT hike from 15% to 16% will come into effect on 1 April 1998. Throughout 1997 unemployment increased and reached critical levels in eastern Germany.

The election campaign is likely to concentrate on subjects like employment, purchasing power, Europe and EMU, and the outcome is difficult to predict because there is little in the way of new thinking emerging from the CDU or the SPD. Irrespective of the outcome, therefore, no political or economic U-turns are to be expected, and the impact of the result on the stock market will probably be neutral.

While exports remained strong in 1997, private consumption was predictably weak, reflecting labour market trends. A major cause for concern was the growing realisation that Germany cannot afford the current level of social security provision. Economic fundamentals are unlikely to change in 1998, and cost restructuring and a stable to weaker Deutschmark will help the country regain competitiveness and maintain its export success. The crisis in Asia is a concern for the major corporations but will have limited effect overall.

German industry continues to prepare for the single European currency. Aside from organisational and technical concerns, many medium-sized companies feel some unease about the macro consequences. Also, large companies will be confronted with harmonisation of prices for specific products that tend to be at the upper end of the spectrum in Germany (eg cars and pharmaceuticals).

Role of the central bank

The Deutsche Bundesbank, Germany's central bank created in 1957, is responsible for formulating and implementing monetary policy. It does this in the light of the government's general economic policy but fully independent of any instructions from politicians. The bank has gained a reputation for using its instruments effectively to maintain price stability. Key decisions focus on short-term interest rates and the liquidity of the banking system. The bank once again asserted its independence in 1997 by rejecting political demands for either sales or revaluation of Germany's gold reserves.

The role of the Bundesbank will change fundamentally from 1999 onwards as key responsibilities are transferred to the European Central Bank. Targets and instruments will, however, stay very close to the German system, signalling continuity in this important area.

Exhibit 23.1: DAX 30 PERFORMANCE PRICE INDEX (DM), 1993–97

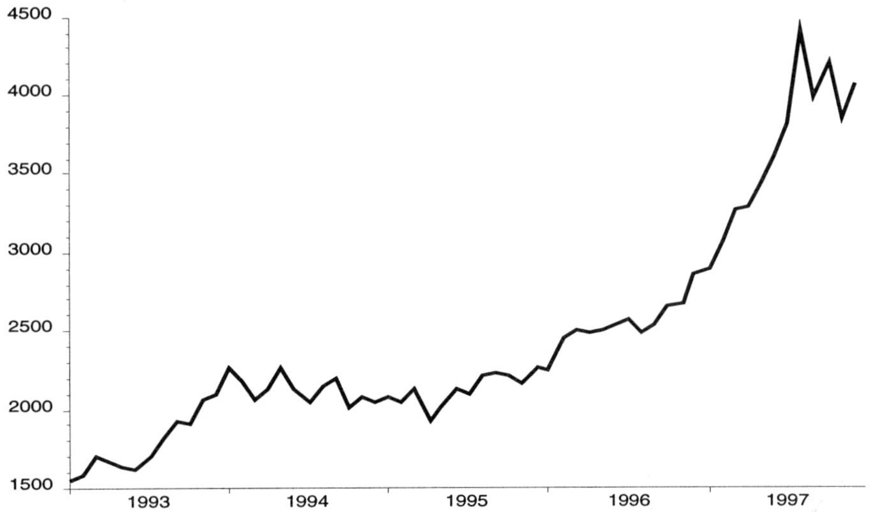

High value 4438.93 31.7.97 Low value 1545.05 1.1.93 *Source: Datastream*

MARKET PERFORMANCE

A) In 1997

During 1997 the DAX Index rose by 47%, closing at 4,249.69. The low for the year was recorded on 2 January at 2,848.77, and the peak on 31 July 1997 at 4,438.93.

Stock turnover on German exchanges in 1997 amounted to DM3,717.5 billion, a 52.2% increase compared with 1996. Of this total, domestic shares accounted for DM3,410.1 billion. The end-1997 market capitalisation of domestic listed companies was DM1,483.85 billion as against DM1,034.07 billion in 1996.

A total of 700 domestic and 1,996 foreign companies were listed on the German stock exchanges at the close of 1997.

Against a background of limited takeover activity among listed companies, the surprise in 1997 was the merger of two Bavaria-based banks (Bayerische Hypotheken and Bayerische Vereinsbank). Rumours about more mergers/takeovers in the banking sector continue to circulate and are boosting share prices accordingly.

B) Summary information

Global ranking by market value (US$ terms, end-1997): 4
Market capitalisation (end-1997): US$824.36 billion
Growth in market value (local currency terms, 1993–97): 85.5%
Market value as a % of nominal GDP (end-1997): 30%
Number of domestic/foreign companies listed (end-1997): 700/1,996
Market P/E (end-1997): 27.7
MSCI total returns (with net dividends, US$ terms, 1997): 24.6%
MSCI Index (change in US$ terms, 1997): +23.3%
Short-term (3-month) interest rate (end-1997): 3.65%
Long-term (10-year) bond yield (end-1997): 5.35%
Budget deficit as a % of nominal GDP (1997): 3.0%
Inflation rate (1997): 1.8%
US$ exchange rate (end-1997): DM1.80

C) Year-end share price index, price/earnings ratios and yields

Exhibit 23.2:
YEAR-END DAX INDEX, P/E RATIOS AND GROSS DIVIDEND YIELDS, 1993–97

Year-end	*Index*	*P/E*	*Yield (%)*
1993	2,266.68	27.5	2.70
1994	2,106.58	28.6	2.50
1995	2,253.88	25.5	2.70
1996	2,888.69	27.6	2.34
1997	4,249.69	27.7	1.82

Source: Deutsche Börse AG.

D) Market indices and their constituents

The German stock index – the DAX – is the most widely observed indicator of trends on the German securities market. The index comprises 30 selected German blue chips. Allianz has the largest weighting on the DAX, with a 9.8% share of the index.

The broader market is measured by the DAX 100 Index (including sub-indices exist for individual industries), while the MDAX (Mid-Cap DAX) represents the German mid-capitalisation sector.

THE STOCK MARKET

A) Brief history and structure

The Frankfurt Stock Exchange (FSE) was one of the first German exchanges to reopen after World War II, but it did not regain its importance until after stabilisation of the currency and the recovery of the German economy.

Since 1991 the FSE, though a public body, has been operated by Frankfurter Wertpapierbörsen AG, a stock corporation controlled by both domestic and foreign market participants. In late 1992 the company was renamed Deutsche Börse AG, and this company now operates both the FSE and the German futures exchange (DTB), and is responsible for the settlement of all exchange transactions in securities and futures in Germany.

There are three types of members of the German stock exchanges: credit institutions, official brokers and free brokers. The official brokers (*Kursmakler*) are appointed to serve as ministerial officers by the provincial governments. Their role is to intermediate in stock transactions and to set official quotations based on buy and sell orders for listed securities that they have executed. The *Kursmaklerkammer* is a public body and represents the official brokers. In particular, it is responsible for their supervision, for the allocation of securities to each of them and for the publication of the official list. The free brokers (*Freimakler*) also act as intermediaries between credit institutions. Alone, or with partners, they intervene as brokers in stock exchange dealings.

B) Different exchanges

There are eight technically independent stock exchanges – in Frankfurt, Düsseldorf, Munich, Hamburg, Berlin, Stuttgart, Hanover and Bremen – but they actually cooperate closely. Recently the stock exchanges of Frankfurt, Düsseldorf and Munich decided to extend their cooperation in order to establish uniform pricing mechanisms for the DAX 100 securities. Each exchange operates three market segments: the official market (*Amtlicher Handel*), the regulated market (*Geregelter Markt*) and a largely unregulated over-the-counter market, the so-called free market (*Freiverkehr*), which is now integrated in the trading of the Deutsche Börse.

C) Opening hours, names and addresses

Official trading hours at the eight exchanges differ. Trading hours at the Deutsche Börse are from 10.30am to 1.30pm, Monday to Friday. The computer system, Xetra, runs from 8.30am to 5.00pm.

DEUTSCHE BÖRSE
Börsenplatz 7-11, 60313 Frankfurt/Main
Tel: (49) 69 2101 5371; Fax: (49) 69 2101 1501

FRANKFURTER WERTPAPIERBÖRSE
Börsenplatz 7-11, D-60284 Frankfurt 4
Tel: (49) 69 2101-0; Fax: (49) 69 2101-2005

RHEINISCH-WESTFALISCHE BÖRSE ZU DÜSSELDORF
Ernst-Schneider-Platz 1, Postfach 104262
D-40033 Düsseldorf
Tel: (49) 211 1389-0; Fax: (49) 211 133287; Tlx: 8582600

HANSEATISCHE WERTPAPIERBÖRSE HAMBURG
Schauenburgerstrasse 47
PO Box 111509, 20415 Hamburg
Tel: (49) 40 36 1302-0; Fax: (49) 40 36 1302-23

BAYERISCHE BÖRSE
Lenbachplatz 2a, D-80333 Munich
Tel: (49) 89 5990-0; Fax: (49) 89 599 032; Tlx: 523515

BERLINER BÖRSE
Fasanenstrasse 3, D-10623 Berlin
Tel: (49) 30 31 1091-0; Fax: (49) 30 311091-79

BREMEN WERTPAPIERBÖRSE
Obernstrasse 2-12, Postfach 10 07 26, D-28007 Bremen
Tel: (49) 421 32 1282; Fax: (49) 421 323123; Tlx: 245948

NIEDERSACHSISCHE BÖRSE ZU HANNOVER
Rathenaustrasse 2, Postfach 4427, D-30044 Hanover
Tel: (49) 511 32 76 61; Fax: (49) 511 32 49 15

BADEN-WÜRTTEMBERGISCHE WERTPAPIERBÖRSE ZU STUTTGART
Konigstrasse 28, Postfach 100441, D-70003 Stuttgart
Tel: (49) 711 29 01 83; Fax: (49) 711 226 8119

MARKET SIZE

A) Number of listings and market value

There were 700 domestic companies listed on the German stock exchanges at the end of 1997, with a combined market capitalisation of DM1,483.9 billion, an increase of 43.5% from the previous year's figure of DM1,034.1 billion.

Exhibit 23.3:
NUMBER OF COMPANIES LISTED AND MARKET VALUE, GERMAN STOCK EXCHANGES, 1993–97

Year-end	*No. of companies* Domestic	*Foreign*	*Domestic market value (DM billion)*
1993	664	633	800.0
1994	666	801	773.9
1995	678	944	826.4
1996	681	1,290	1,034.1
1997	700	1,996	1,483.9

Sources: LGT Bank in Lichtenstein & Co (Deutschland) and Deutsche Börse AG.

B) Largest quoted companies

Exhibit 23.4:
THE 20 LARGEST DOMESTIC LISTED COMPANIES, END-1997

Ranking	*Company*	*Market value (DM billion)*
1	Allianz Holding AG	118.44
2	Deutsche Telekom AG	87.45
3	Daimler Benz AG	69.23
4	Siemens AG	63.92
5	VEBA AG	59.06
6	Bayer AG	51.06
7	Dresdner Bank AG	42.98
8	BASF AG	40.73
9	Hoechst AG	40.19
10	RWE AG	34.01
11	SAP AG	33.65
12	Bay. Vereinsbank AG	33.11
13	Commerzbank AG	31.88
14	Bay. Hypotheken- u. Wechselbank AG	23.70
15	Metro Holding AG	15.01
16	Lufthansa AG	13.62
17	Schering AG	12.04
18	Adidas-Salomon AG	10.59
19	Merck AG	10.32
20	FMC AG	9.16

Sources: LGT Bank in Liechtenstein & Co (Deutschland) and Deutsche Börse AG.

C) Trading volume

Stock trading value for 1997 totalled DM3,717.5 billion, a 52.2% increase over 1996's DM2,441.8 billion.

Exhibit 23.5:
THE 20 MOST ACTIVELY TRADED DOMESTIC SHARES, 1997

Ranking	*Company*	*Trading value (DM billion)*	*Shares (million)*
1	Deutsche Bank AG	254.80	2,500.85
2	Daimler Benz AG	233.76	1,782.66
3	Siemens AG	224.71	2,254.44
4	Volkswagen AG	192.03	183.03
5	Bayer AG	145.10	2,137.42
6	VEBA AG	142.88	1,441.77
7	Allianz Holding AG	142.44	275.56
8	BASF AG	135.04	2,121.98
9	Hoechst AG	116.95	1,642.36
10	Commerzbank AG	109.68	1,983.78
11	Deutsche Telekom AG	102.29	2,811.97
12	Mannesmann AG	96.16	128.35
13	SAP AG	95.22	255.06
14	Dresdner Bank AG	86.40	1,292.62
15	Thyssen AG	69.84	183.92
16	RWE AG	63.79	813.58
17	BMW AG	60.80	46.31
18	Bay. Vereinsbank AG	57.95	673.29
19	Muenchener Rück Vers. AG	53.67	47.61
20	Bay. Hypo- u. Wechselbank AG	52.58	833.65

Sources: LGT Bank in Liechtenstein & Co (Deutschland) and Deutsche Börse AG.

Exhibit 23.6:
TRADING VALUE BY SECTOR, GERMAN EXCHANGES, 1997

Sector	*Trading value (DM billion)*
Chemicals	508.30
Banks	461.97
Automobiles	431.65
Utilities	313.94
Electrical/electronics	284.95
Insurance	195.44
Machinery	173.21
Iron and steel	116.54
Retail	92.95
Textiles	38.52
Construction	31.10
Transport	28.69
Holdings	7.99
Mortgage banks	6.69
Paper	3.39
Breweries	2.36

Source: LGT Bank in Liechtenstein & Co (Deutschland).

Exhibit 23.7:
TOP PERFORMING COUNTRY FUNDS – GERMANY

Fund	*US$ % change* 31/12/96 31/12/97	31/12/92 31/12/97	Currency	*Fund size* (US$ mil)	Volatility	*Manager name*	*Main sector*	*Class*
Glbl Mgr German Geared	72	N/A	US$	1.5	8.62	BIIML	Equity	Offshore Territories
Multiscor Demshares	49.77	139.63	Dm	62.54	5.08	Scor	Equity	Luxembourg
Nürnberger ADIG A	36.89	164.42	Dm	27.81	5.12	Adig Investment	Equity Growth	Investmentfds Deutschland
DIT Wachstumfonds	34.2	163.68	Dm	210.11	5.17	DIT	Equity Growth	Investmentfds Deutschland
Nestor Deutschland	32.93	N/A	Dm	24.26	N/A	Nestor Investment Mgt SA	Equity	Luxembourg
Nestor Deutschland	32.93	N/A	Dm	N/A	N/A	Nestor Investment Mgt SA	Equity Growth	Investmentfds Deutschland
ABN AMRO Germany Equity	32.1	N/A	Dm	N/A	N/A	ABN AMRO Investment Mgt	Equity	Luxembourg
ABN AMRO Germany Equity	32.1	N/A	Dm	N/A	4.82	ABN AMRO Investment Mgt	Equity Growth	Investmentfds Deutschland
Allemagne Opportunite	31.91	141.63	Ffr	60.57	N/A	Deutsche Bank	Equity	French SICAVs
MMWI PROGRESS Fonds	28.89	170.56	Dm	41.25	5.25	MM Warburg Invest	Equity Growth	Investmentfds Deutschland
BBV Invest Union	28.45	115.11	Dm	54.15	4.58	Union	Equity Growth	Investmentfds Deutschland
Taiyo Glbl Germany	28.21	95.54	¥	0.79	4.32	Taiyo ITMCo	Equity Growth	Japanese Open Trusts
Lux Linea	28.18	170.82	Dm	46.79	5.56	MM Warburg Luxinvest SA	Equity	Luxembourg
Lux Linea	28.18	170.82	Dm	37.8	5.56	MM Warburg Luxinvest SA	Equity Growth	Investmentfds Deutschland
Swissca Cntries Eq Germany	27.91	N/A	Dm	229.78	N/A	Swissca Fondsleitung AG	Equity	Swiss Mutual Funds
CAMCO Fonds DM-Aktien	27.68	N/A	Dm	18.93	N/A	CAMCO Inv Mgmt SA	Equity	Luxembourg
CAMCO Fonds DM-Aktien	27.68	N/A	Dm	16.14	N/A	CAMCO Inv Mgmt.SA	Equity Growth	Investmentfds Deutschland
MAT Deutschland Fonds	27.57	104.25	Dm	6.91	5.02	Main Anlage Trust	Equity Growth	Investmentfds Deutschland
Incofonds	27.55	173.86	Dm	N/A	4.78	Commerzinvest	Equity Growth	Investmentfds Deutschland
HMT Proinvest	27.14	127.54	Dm	118.02	5.25	Hamburg-Mannheimer Inv Trust	Equity Growth	Investmentfds Deutschland
MK Alfakapital	27.07	139.32	Dm	305.72	5.69	Munchner Kapitalanlagen	Equity Growth	Investmentfds Deutschland
ADIG Aktien Deutschland	27	N/A	Dm	792.94	5.38	Adig Investment	Equity Growth	Investmentfds Deutschland
Oppenheim DAX Werte	26.79	147.29	Dm	97.25	5.41	Oppenheim KAG	Equity Growth	Investmentfds Deutschland
Privatfonds	26.38	138.2	Dm	5.46	5.48	Metzler Investment	Equity Growth	Investmentfds Deutschland
Plusfonds	26.29	133.22	Dm	213.69	5.2	Adig Investment	Equity Growth	Investmentfds Deutschland
UniDeutschland	26.28	N/A	Dm	441.94	5.39	Union	Equity Growth	Investmentfds Deutschland
Concentra	26.24	139.24	Dm	1,721.38	5.38	DIT	Equity Growth	Investmentfds Deutschland
Glbl Mgr German Index	26.18	N/A	US$	2.7	4.12	BIIML	Equity	Offshore Territories
SBC German Equity Fund UI	26.12	133.36	Dm	33.67	5.46	Universal	Equity Growth	Investmentfds Deutschland
VERI VALEUR Fonds	26.04	175.47	Dm	205.95	4.8	Veritas	Equity Growth	Investmentfds Deutschland
FT Deutschland Dynamik Fonds	25.77	139.08	Dm	45.28	5.06	Frankfurt Trust	Equity Growth	Investmentfds Deutschland
DWS Deutsche Aktien Typ O	25.7	N/A	Dm	154.95	5.37	DWS	Equity Growth	Investmentfds Deutschland
MI Aktien Privatfonds D	25.55	140.37	Dm	26.16	5.22	Metzler Investment	Equity Growth	Investmentfds Deutschland
Hypo Invest Kapital	25.33	137.72	Dm	327.79	5.11	Hypo Capital Mgnt Munich	Equity Growth	Investmentfds Deutschland
Adifonds	25.2	142.25	Dm	731.7	5.76	Adig Investment	Equity Growth	Investmentfds Deutschland
Schmidtbank Aktien Dt FI	25.02	N/A	Dm	23.38	5.06	Franken Invest - Schmidtbank	Equity Growth	Investmentfds Deutschland
Köln Aktienfonds DEKA	24.97	130.15	Dm	217.87	5.12	Deka	Equity Growth	Investmentfds Deutschland
Vereins Lux Portf DM Aktien	24.54	N/A	Dm	57.44	5.02	ADIG Investment Lux SA (ALSA)	Equity	Luxembourg
Vereins Lux Portf DM Aktien	24.54	N/A	Dm	49.48	5.02	ADIG Investment Lux SA	Equity Growth	Investmentfds Deutschland
Allianz Aktienfonds	24.5	N/A	Dm	164.64	5.26	Allianz KAG	Equity Growth	Investmentfds Deutschland
CB Lux Portfolio DM Aktien	24.49	N/A	Dm	25.56	5.03	ADIG Investment Lux SA (ALSA)	Equity	Luxembourg
CB Lux Portfolio DM Aktien	24.49	N/A	Dm	25.63	5.03	ADIG Investment Lux SA	Equity Growth	Investmentfds Deutschland
CMI GNF German Equity	24.4	111.9	Dm	34.91	5.28	CMI Global Network Fund	Equity	Luxembourg
CMI GNF German Equity	24.4	111.9	Dm	33.94	5.26	CMI Global Network Fund (LUX)	Equity Growth	Investmentfds Deutschland

Note: details for some funds may not have been included if the data for the US$ % change for 96/97 was not available

Source: Standard & Poor's Micropal.

TYPES OF SHARE

Two types of equity are commonly issued by German joint stock companies – ordinary shares (*Stammaktien*) and preferred shares (*Vorzugsaktien*). German law permits preferred shares to be issued either with or without voting rights, but they must carry a preferential right to cumulative dividends when profits are distributed. Preferred shares without voting rights may be issued up to a total nominal amount equal to the total nominal amount of all other classes of shares.

The vast majority of German shares are issued in bearer form (*Inhaberaktien*). Registered shares (*Namensaktien*) are relatively rare in Germany, with the exception of insurance company shares. However, the law prescribes that shares must be registered in the owner's name when they are not fully paid up.

OTHER MARKETS

Since the start of operations on the German Financial Futures and Options Exchange (DTB) in January 1990, fully computerised trading in equity options and futures has been available.

In March 1997 Deutsche Börse introduced a new exchange for growth companies, called Neuer Markt. At the end of the year, market capitalisation stood at just over DM9 billion.

INVESTORS

The most recent studies undertaken in Germany by the Deutsche Bundesbank show that around 19% of listed stocks are held by private individuals. Miscellaneous companies account for about 40%, while insurance companies and banks, including investment funds, account for approximately 3% and 12% respectively. The state claims around 7% and foreigners hold 20%.

AVAILABILITY OF COUNTRY FUNDS

Public investment funds are managed by both domestic and international managers. There are a wide range of public funds with an investment focus on the domestic market. Banks and insurance companies currently offer about 65 different "German equity funds" and international asset management groups also offer funds investing in German securities.

OPERATIONS

A) Trading system

In November 1997, the exchange introduced a new electronic trading system, Xetra. It is an order-driven trading system with automatic matching, which brings together wholesale and retail trading in a central order book. Limit and market orders can be entered with various validity constraints and trading limits or conditions for execution, and can be kept in the order book for up to one year. The order book, which is basically transparent, is designed to give all market participants the opportunity to react quickly to changes in the market while preserving their anonymity. In the event of sharp price swings, the system reacts with volatility interruptions to support price continuity.

Xetra is being introduced in stages. By the end of November 1997, the technical infrastructure for the system had been set up. When the third stage ("Release 3") is introduced at the end of 1998, all the main functions required for trading on the exchange will be available, including retail trading. Xetra Release 4 will provide full coverage for the market and complete the implementation of the market model for OTC trading in the form of a search and intermediary market for larger volumes.

At present the DAX 100 equities and selected common and preferred shares that were listed on the (now discontinued) IBIS system are tradable on Xetra. This list will be expanded in Release 3. Trading takes place between 8.30am and 5.00pm.

Members of the stock exchanges comprise banks and the official and unofficial (or free) brokers. Official brokers are appointed by their respective federal state governments. Within the floor trading system (which is an auction system) of the official market (*Amtlicher Handel*) they are responsible for fixing the official daily price – the so-called single price (*Einheitskurs*) determined for all listed securities once on every trading day. This is the price at which most orders could be executed. Brokers are allowed, within certain limits, to effect a balance between supply and demand and, for this purpose, they can trade on their own account.

Free brokers are responsible for fixing the price in both the regulated market and the free market. The procedure is identical to that followed in official trading. Moreover, the free brokers can trade in any security on their own account, although they are only allowed to deal with other stock exchange members.

Highly liquid securities can be continuously traded throughout the official trading session. Orders for these shares are traded in lots of 50 shares or multiples thereof.

Exchange quotations are published in the Official Daily Stock Exchange Quotation List (*Amtliches*

Kursblatt) on every stock exchange business day, while the daily press, as a rule, only publishes the prices of selected securities.

B) List of principal banks and brokers

BAYERISCHE VEREINSBANK AG
Am Eisbach 3, 80311 Munich
Tel: (49) 89 3780; Fax: (49) 3781 7302

COMMERZBANK AG
Kaiserplatz, D-60311 Frankfurt 1
Tel: (49) 69 13620; Fax: (49) 69 28 5389

DEUTSCHE BANK AG
Taunusanlage 12, D-60325 Frankfurt 1
Tel: (49) 69 9103 8439; Fax: (49) 69 9103 4227

DRESDNER BANK AG
Jürgen-Ponto-Platz 1, D-60301 Frankfurt 1
Tel: (49) 69 2630; Fax: (49) 69 263 4831

LGT BANK IN LIECHTENSTEIN & CO (DEUTSCHLAND)
Bleichstrasse 60-62, D-60325 Frankfurt
Tel: (49) 69 298070; Fax: (49) 69 29807 159

METZLER & CO
Grosse Gallusstrasse 18, D-60311 Frankfurt
Postfach: 101548, 60015 Frankfurt
Tel: (49) 69 210 4591; Fax: (49) 69 281429

SAL OPPENHEIM JR & CIE
Unter Sachsenhausen 4, D-50667 Cologne 1
Tel: (49) 221 14501; Fax: (49) 221 145 1512

SALOMON BROTHERS AG
Eurotower
Kaiserstrasse 29
60311 Frankfurt am Main
Tel: (49) 69 260 7450; Fax: (49) 69 232 2570

TRINKHAUS & BURKHARDT KG
Niederlassung Frankfurt, Guiollettstrasse 24
D-6000 Frankfurt 1
Tel: (49) 69 719030; Fax: (49) 69 719 0327

WESTDEUTSCHE LANDESBANK-GIROZENTRALE
Taunusanlage 3, D-6000 Frankfurt 1
Tel: (49) 69 25791; Tlx: 411020

C) Settlement and transfer

Since 1970, the settlement system of the German exchanges has been computerised.

Most securities traded on the exchanges are held in Deutsche Börse Clearing (DBC, the central depository) and cover the security accounts of stock exchange members. Delivery of securities takes place by bookkeeping entries from one security account to another, and payment is made by simply debiting and crediting these accounts.

Standard settlement takes place on the second business day after the bargain. DBC, however, is able to offer any settlement period between real-time settlement and T+40.

If the bargain has been handled by a *Makler*, the *Makler* enters the relevant information into the computer. In all other cases this is done by the seller. The relevant information for the settlement process is taken automatically from Xetra or from the floor trading order-routing system called BOSS. In the case of off-exchange transactions, the seller enters the necessary data into the computer.

D) Commissions and other costs

Share transactions on the German stock exchanges are subject to a commission charge payable to the bank, as well as a brokerage fee payable to the official floor broker. The brokerage fee is eliminated if shares change hands over-the-counter and no floor broker is used.

Bank commissions amount to 1% of the market value of share transactions, with a minimum charge. The brokerage fee, payable to the official broker, is 0.04% for DAX shares and 0.08% for all other shares.

E) Custodian and nominee services

Custodian services are offered by Deutsche Börse and by all the leading banks. Most securities are in bearer form, and DBC provides the network for this service. The few remaining registered issues are delivered with pre-signed transfer deeds. Many banks already operate as sub-custodians in connection with one of the global custodians or offer such worldwide service themselves.

TAXATION AND REGULATIONS AFFECTING FOREIGN INVESTORS

Dividends paid to shareholders are subject to 25% withholding tax.

Under the terms of the EU parent company directive, no German withholding tax is levied on dividends distributed to an EU company holding at least 25% of the voting shares in a corporation. Foreign shareholders resident in tax treaty countries are usually entitled to a refund of a portion of taxes withheld. With many treaty countries the rate is reduced to 15% for holdings of at least 10% or 25% in a German corporation. The USA-Germany double taxation treaty (subject to certain exceptions) reduces the withholding rate to 10% and further to 5% if the shareholder is a company directly holding at least 10% of the voting shares of a corporation.

Withholding taxes levied on dividends paid to foreign shareholders normally settle their respective German income tax obligations. In addition to dividend distributions, foreign shareholders can also be taxed on hidden distributions made by the corporation and on earnings from the sale of dividend coupons and other rights attaching to their shareholdings.

Foreign shareholders are generally not subject to German taxes on capital gains derived from the sale of German stocks, but foreign shareholders who directly or indirectly have held (within a five-year period prior to the sale) more than 25% of a German corporation are subject to income tax on gains realised on a sale of the shareholding or parts thereof. This capital gains tax is often modified or waived when a double taxation treaty applies. The transfer of shares issued by a corporate owner of property located in Germany can be subject to real-estate transfer tax (*Grunderwerbsteuer*).

For the calendar year 1998, a surtax of 5.5% is levied on individual and corporate income taxes and withholding taxes (other than the reduced withholding tax rates referred to above).

The acquisition of substantial shareholdings can be subject to merger control. In addition, registered stock with restricted transfer (some insurance companies have issued this type of share) cannot be transferred without the specific approval of the respective company. Except for certain notification and clearance procedures in sensitive industries (eg, banking and insurance), there are no additional restrictions or regulations affecting foreign minority equity investments in Germany.

Exhibit 23.8:
WITHHOLDING TAXES

Recipient	*Dividends %*
Resident corporations	25
Resident individuals	25
Non-resident corporations and individuals:	
Non-treaty	25
Treaty	5-30

Source: Price Waterhouse.

LISTING AND REPORTING REQUIREMENTS

A) Listing requirements

The most important requirements for admission to the official market (first segment) are as follows:

- Filing of an application together with a bank.
- Publication of a prospectus in the statutory journal.
- Publication of a mandatory interim report.
- A prospective minimum market value of DM2.5 million.
- A spread of at least 25%.
- Establishment for a minimum of three years.

Listing requirements for the regulated market are less strict.

B) Reporting requirements

All German public corporations (ie, joint stock companies, limited liability companies and partnerships partly limited by shares), must publish an annual report containing a statement of the year's profits and losses, a balance sheet, a description of business developments and prospects, a report from the competent statutory body and a profit distribution proposal. Balance sheets and profit and loss statements, as well as comments and explanations relating to them, must be checked by an independent auditor elected by the shareholders. Listed corporations must also publish interim half-yearly reports.

In recent years, German companies (in particular joint stock companies) have made considerable efforts to increase the amount of information available to stockholders. A growing number now also publish quarterly reports. Some issuers with multiple listings also publish financial reports in accordance with US GAAP or IAS standards.

German public corporations have to prepare financial statements on a worldwide consolidated basis for their subsidiaries unless certain exemptions apply.

Under the Stock Corporation Act, a German joint stock company is obliged to publish certain company announcements in the *Federal Gazette* and in one other newspaper. The most important publications concern:

a) annual financial statements;
b) notice of shareholders' meetings;
c) agenda of shareholders' meetings;
d) applications by shareholders for special topics to be included on the agenda;
e) changes to the board of directors and the supervisory board;
f) invitations to exercise pre-emptive rights in the event of capital increases; and
g) invitations to exchange shares – eg, if the company name is changed.

Listed companies are obliged to report immediately any information that may have an impact on the price of their securities (not only shares) to the Federal Securities Trading Supervisory Office and to the stock exchanges, and they must also publish the information immediately, either through electronic wire services or through one of the official stock exchange newspapers.

SHAREHOLDER PROTECTION CODES

A) Significant shareholdings

Shareholders must notify listed companies (and the companies must publish such notifications) of significant holdings (5%, 10%, 25%, 50% or 75%) in that company.

B) Minority rights

Minority shareholders have special rights. Holders of 5% of the share capital can demand:

- an extraordinary shareholders' meeting;
- further topics on the agenda of shareholders' meetings;
- the appointment of a special auditor if there is reason to assume that items in the financial statements have been undervalued or that the notes do not contain obligatory information (also available as a special right to holders of at least DM1 million of share capital).

Holders of 10% or DM2 million of share capital can further:

- demand that the company does not waive its right to compensation claims against directors and members of the supervisory board;
- demand a vote on members of the supervisory board nominated by shareholders prior to the vote on members nominated by the supervisory board;
- file a court motion to remove a member of the supervisory board for a cause relating to the person, if such member has been appointed pursuant to the statutes.

Holders of 25% of the share capital can prevent changes in the statutes or increases of capital and any other decisions that require a 75% majority. A person or company holding 25% of the share capital has to notify the corporation in order to be allowed to exercise these voting rights.

In general, stock corporations are not allowed to acquire their own equity. However, this restriction is currently under review and may be liberalised in the near future.

C) Insider trading

Insider trading legislation under the Securities Trading Act 1994 applies to all market segments and to off-exchange trades. It is a criminal offence (punishable by up to five years in prison) to buy or sell securities on the basis of inside information (primary insiders), to convey or make available to another person inside information, to recommend the purchase or sale of insider securities contrary to the Act (tipping) or to trade on the basis of inside information received from an insider (secondary insiders).

The Federal Securities Trading Supervisory Authority is in charge of supervising transactions on and off the exchanges. Provision has been made for the Authority to co-operate internationally with the competent authorities in other countries.

RESEARCH

Research and information on the German stock market is excellent. Along with the bigger commercial banks (eg, Bayerische Vereinsbank, Commerzbank, Deutsche Bank, Dresdner Bank and Hypobank), the Deutsche Bundesbank provides comprehensive statistical data on the eight exchanges. Deutsche Gesellschaft für Anlageberatung is also an important source.

WestLB offers an investment counselling service, providing foreign investors with basic financial and economic information, as well as individual company research. The bank's most important publications on capital investment in securities and on economic developments are also published in English.

In *Wertpapier*'s 1996 survey of the accuracy of published corporate earnings forecasts, the top six rankings went to LGT Bank in Liechtenstein, Deutsche Bank, Dresdner Bank, Trinkhaus & Burkhardt, Commerzbank and Metzler & Co.

There are four newspapers that provide information on the market. The daily *Frankfurter Allgemeine Zeitung* reports on economic events both in Germany and abroad. More specific reporting on the market is available from the local dailies, *Handelsblatt* and *Börsen Zeitung*. Finally, *Wirtschaftswoche* is published every Friday and covers general economic topics and price reporting.

The most relevant financial magazines for foreign investors are *Capital* and *Manager Magazine*, both published monthly.

Finanzplatz Deutschland: German Capital Markets and Financial System, published by Euromoney Books, provides in-depth information on the country's capital markets. See the order card at the back of this book for details.

CHAPTER 24

Ghana

Introduction

The Ghana Stock Exchange (GSE) began operations in November 1990 and now has 21 quoted companies. The companies listed typically have a multinational partner and tend to be leaders in their sector.

The Ghanaian exchange has been used for corporate restructuring and fund-raising by local companies. A driving force in the development of the stock market has also been the government's desire to privatise its equity holdings.

ECONOMIC AND POLITICAL OVERVIEW

On 7 January 1998, Ghana celebrated the fifth anniversary of its fourth Republic and the first anniversary of its second Parliament. This tends to support the view that constitutional multi-party democracy is now being entrenched in the country and that it will underpin Ghana's political orientation for the foreseeable future.

During 1997, the liberalisation of the economy continued with the government divesting itself of state-owned companies.

Agriculture continues to dominate the economy, accounting for about 43% of GDP. Cocoa is the most important cash crop and plays a key role in the economy, contributing 6% of GDP and about 25% of export earnings.

The local currency, the cedi, continued to depreciate against the major trading currencies, falling from C1,740 to the US dollar at the end of 1996 to C2,249 at 31 December 1997. This depreciation has encouraged businesses to price their goods and services in US dollars, and the government has responded by initiating moves to halt the "dollarisation" of the economy.

Role of the central bank

The Bank of Ghana implements government monetary policies using open market operations and interest rate adjustments.

Throughout 1997, the central bank attempted to bring inflation down by restraining the growth of reserve money, which fell from C902 billion in December 1996 to C867 billion by the end of June 1997. This reflected an 8% drop in non-bank public currency holdings and a fall in commercial bank reserves of C40 billion.

In addition, the bank pursued revenue-enhancing policies while cutting government borrowing and non-concessional loans.

MARKET PERFORMANCE

A) In 1997

The GSE All-Share Index rose by 41.8% in 1997, despite high Treasury bill rates (approaching 50%) encouraging investors to switch to the money market.

Stock market capitalisation declined by 11%, ending the year at C2,552.78 billion, down from C2,863 billion at the end of 1996. The general fall in world gold prices led to a dive in AGC shares, which account for 72% of GSE market capitalisation.

However, both the value and volume of shares traded rose: turnover was up by 235% (to C93,355 million) and volume was up by 251% (to 125,629,140 shares).

B) Summary information

Global ranking by market value (US$ terms, end-1997): 76
Market capitalisation (end-1997): US$1.13 million
Growth in market value (local currency terms, 1993–97): 2,545%
Market value as a % of nominal GDP (end-1997): 17.8%
Number of domestic/foreign companies listed (end-1997): 21/0
Market P/E (all listed companies,end-1997): 5.8
Short-term (3-month) interest rate (end-1997): 44.23%
Long-term (5-year) bond yield (end-1997): 7%
Budget deficit as a % of nominal GDP (end-1997): 8.6%
Annual increase in broad (M2+) money (end-1997): 39.5%
Inflation rate (1997): 20.8%
US$ exchange rate (end-1997): C2,248.91

C) Year-end share price index, price/earnings ratio and yields

Exhibit 24.1:
YEAR-END SHARE PRICE INDEX, P/E AND EQUITY YIELDS, 1993–97

Year-end	*GSE All-Share Index*	*P/E*	*Yield (%)*
1993	132.88	6.7	6.5
1994	298.10	11.7	3.9
1995	316.97	8.1	5.0
1996	360.76	7.6	7.0
1997	511.74	6.4	6.7

Sources: Ghana Stock Exchange and National Trust Holding Co.

D) Market indices and their constituents

Ghana's main index is the GSE All-Share, which is a market capitalisation index of all equity shares listed on the exchange. In view of the disproportionately large capitalisation of Ashanti Goldfields and the fact that some shares are not trading in Ghana, the index includes only AGC shares that are potentially tradable on the GSE – ie, currently 9.8 million shares on the Ghana register.

The Databank Stock Index (DSI) is a composite index of all equity shares listed on the GSE and measures changes in aggregate value.

THE STOCK MARKET

A) Brief history and structure

The Ghana Stock Exchange (GSE) was incorporated in July 1989 as a private company limited by guarantee. The exchange was given recognition as an authorised stock exchange under the Stock Exchange Act 1971 and trading commenced in November 1990. Its status was changed to public company limited by guarantee in 1994.

The GSE is a private sector initiative and is not funded by the government. It is governed by a council of 13 members representing licensed dealing members, listed companies, banks, insurance companies, the money market and the general public. The council sets out the policies of the exchange and its functions include preventing fraud and malpractice, maintaining good order among members, regulating stock market business and deciding on listing applications.

The GSE has two categories of membership – associate membership and licensed dealing membership. The former is open to any individual or group that meets the membership requirements of the GSE; the latter is open only to companies incorporated under the Companies Code of Ghana 1963 and partnerships incorporated under the Incorporated Partnerships Act of 1963. Currently, the GSE has 41 associate members and 11 licensed dealing members.

B) Different exchanges

There is only one stock exchange in Ghana, located in Accra. OTC trading is allowed in Ashanti Goldfields' shares.

C) Opening hours, names and addresses

Trading takes place on the GSE trading floor three times a week on Mondays, Wednesdays and Fridays from 10.00am to 12.00 noon.

GHANA STOCK EXCHANGE
5th Floor, Cedi House, Liberia Road
PO Box 1849, Accra-North
Tel: (233) 21 669 908/669 914; Fax: (233) 21 669 913
E-mail: stockexncs.com.gh

MARKET SIZE

A) Number of listings and market value

There are currently 21 companies listed on the GSE. Market capitalisation at the end of 1997 was C2,552.78 million.

Exhibit 24.2:
NUMBER OF LISTED COMPANIES AND MARKET VALUE, GSE, 1993–97

Year-end	*No. of listed companies*	*Market value (C million)*
1993	15	96.51
1994	17	1,968.43
1995	19	2,399.02
1996	21	2,862.72
1997	21	2,552.78

Source: Ghana Stock Exchange.

B) Largest quoted companies

The market is dominated by Ashanti Goldfields which, with an end-1997 value of C1,853.29 million, accounted for 72.6% of total market capitalisation.

Exhibit 24.3:
THE 10 LARGEST LISTED COMPANIES ON THE GSE, END-1997

Ranking	*Company*	*Market value (C million)*
1	Ashanti Goldfields .(AGC)	1,853.29

Exhibit 24.3 continued

2	Ghana Commercial Bank (GCB)	132.00
3	Standard Chartered Bank (SCB)	128.30
4	Social Security Bank (SSB)	121.13
5	Guiness Ghana (GGL)	76.36
6	Unilever Ghana (UNIL)	68.75
7	Mobil Oil Ghana (MOGL)	33.33
8	Aluworks Limited (ALW)	32.58
9	Accra Brewery (ABL)	22.35
10	Pioneer Tobacco. (PTC)	21.84

Source: Ghana Stock Exchange.

C) Trading volume

GSE turnover totalled C93,355 million (US$41.5 million) in 1997, up 235% in comparison with 1996 levels. Average daily turnover was C606.20 million in 1997.

Exhibit 24.4:
TRADING ON THE GSE, 1993–97

Year	*Turnover (C million)*
1993	3,177.94
1994	73,088.18
1995	27,085.31
1996	27,878.56
1997	93,355.00

Source: Ghana Stock Exchange.

Exhibit 24.5:
THE 10 MOST ACTIVELY TRADED GSE SHARES, 1997

Ranking	*Company*	*Trading value (C million)*
1	Social Security Bank Ltd (SSB)	61,232.55
2	Aluworks Ltd (ALW)	11,519.70
3	Ghana Commercial Bank (GCB)	5,320.40
4	UTC Estates Ltd (UTC-E)	4,563.56
5	Standard Chartered Bank (SCB)	4,425.59
6	Ashanti Goldfields (AGC)	1,441.08
7	Pioneer Tobacco (PTC)	1,407.68
8	Guiness Ghana (GGL)	711.99
9	Unilever Ghana (UNIL)	598.17
10	Enterprise Insurance (EIC)	395.17

Source: Ghana Stock Exchange.

TYPES OF SHARE

Ordinary shares and government bonds are traded on the GSE.

OPERATIONS

A) Trading system

Trading takes place on the floor of the exchange using a call-over system. The authorised dealing officers, who are representatives of stockbroking firms, assemble on trading days on the floor and a designated official of the exchange presides over transactions and directs the conduct of business. Trading is in lots of 100 shares (except for Ashanti Goldfields which trades in round lots of 10 shares).

B) List of brokers

CAL BROKERS
45 Independence Avenue, PO Box 14596, Accra
Tel: (233) 21 221 056; Fax: (233) 21 668 657

DATABANK BROKERAGE
5th Floor, Tower Block, SSNIT Pension House, Accra
Tel: (233) 21 669 110; Fax: (233) 21 669 100

EBG STOCKBROKERS
19 Seventh Avenue, Ridge West, PO Box 16746
Accra-North
Tel: (233) 21 667 109; Fax: (233) 21 775 406

GOLD COAST SECURITIES
350 Nima Avenue, North Ridge, PO Box 17187, Accra
Tel: (233) 21 225 155; Fax: (233) 21 777 380

NATIONAL TRUST HOLDING CO LTD
44 Dyson House, PO Box 9563, Airport, Accra
Tel: (233) 21 229 644; Fax: (233) 21 229 975

STRATEGIC AFRICAN SECURITIES
59 Ring Road Central, PO Box 16446, Airport, Accra
Tel: (233) 21 231 386; Fax: (233) 21 229 816

C) Settlement and transfer

The GSE established manual centralised clearing and settlement procedures in April 1996 as a prelude to the introduction of a computerised system (due to be operational by mid-1999). The manual system operates within a set of rules approved by the exchange council and the Securities Regulatory Commissioner. The settlement period is T+5.

D) Commission and other costs

Brokerage charges are fixed and are based on a declining scale rate from 2.5% to 1% depending on the value of the transaction.

TAXATION AND REGULATIONS AFFECTING FOREIGN INVESTORS

There is a 10% withholding tax on dividend income for all investors, both local and foreign, although capital gains are exempt from tax. The original capital invested, capital gains, dividends or interest earned and related earnings and refunds are fully and freely remittable.

Foreigners (both individual and institutional investors) face restrictions on investing in listed securities. Under the Exchange Control Act 1961, the total holding of all non-resident foreigners in any one listed company shall not exceed 74%. It is also provided that holdings by each non-resident individual or institutional investor shall not exceed 10%. Ghanaians (both resident and non-resident) as well as resident foreigners can, however, hold any percentage of a listed company's shares without limit.

There is no stamp duty on transfers of securities to non-Ghanaian citizens.

LISTING AND REPORTING REQUIREMENTS

A) Listing requirements

Applications for listing must be sponsored by a licensed dealing member of the GSE. The company must comply with the provisions of the Companies Code 1963, and must also meet certain requirements contained in the listing regulations of the GSE. There are three lists available on the GSE – the first, second and third. A company must have a minimum stated capital of C100 million to be on the first list, C50 million to qualify for the second and C20 million for the third. For a company to be eligible for the first list the market value of its floated shares must be at least C30 million, for the second C15 million, and for the third C5 million. In addition, a company must have filed audited accounts for at least five years for a listing on the first list, three years for the second list and one year (which may be waived) for the third list.

B) Reporting requirements

Reporting requirements for listed companies are set out in the Listing Regulations 1990. Companies listed on the exchange must notify the GSE of:

- any recommendation or declaration of dividends or bonuses;
- any meeting at least 21 days before such meeting is held;
- any call to be made on the partly paid share capital of the company;
- any change in the directors, company secretary or auditors of the company;
- any proposed alteration to the regulations of the company;
- any acquisition of shares of another company or any transaction resulting in such company becoming a subsidiary of the company;
- any acquisition of shares resulting in the holding of 10% or more of the stated capital of another listed company;
- the submission of half- and full-year financial statements.

SHAREHOLDER PROTECTION CODES

The exchange has various regulations designed to protect investors, including:

- *Membership regulations.* These stipulate criteria for membership of the exchange, regulations to be complied with by licensed dealing members, codes of conduct and ethical standards for members.
- *Listing regulations.* These prescribe, among other things, the criteria for listing securities, application procedures, the contents of applications and prospectuses, and continued obligations of listed companies.

Under the Securities Act Law (1993) the principal regulatory body in the securities market is the Securities Industries Commission. Its functions include maintaining surveillance of securities to ensure orderly, fair and equitable dealings, as well as registering, licensing, authorising and regulating the stock exchange, investment advisers and securities dealers.

The GSE council also has a supervisory role in order to prevent fraud and malpractice, and it has the power to suspend or expel any member who contravenes any of the regulations of the exchange.

Insider trading carries a fine of C5 million or a jail term of three years.

RESEARCH

Financial reporting in Ghana, which is above average for sub-Saharan Africa, is comparable with Zimbabwe and better than Kenya. Press releases and corporate results contain more than summary information, consolidated financial statements are the norm and accounting policies are disclosed.

Local brokers producing good-quality research include Databank Brokerage Services and Strategic African Securities Limited.

The Marketing and Research Department at the GSE can also provide information on the market.

African Equities: A Guide to Markets and Companies, published by Euromoney Books, provides in-depth information for those wishing to invest in Africa. See the order card at the back of this book for details.

PROSPECTIVE CHANGES

Developments in 1998 are expected to include:

(i) sales of state-owned enterprises, including banks;
(ii) more listings from the private sector;
(iii) the establishment of an automated trading and clearing system;
(iv) development of new financial products such as collective investment schemes, mutual funds and municipal bonds;
(v) improved efficiency through technological upgrading; and
(vi) the listing of more government bonds.

CHAPTER

25

Greece

Introduction

Moody's upgrade of Greece's sovereign debt rating to Baa1 at the end of 1996, coupled with a sharp improvement in macroeconomic indicators throughout 1997, set the background for what proved to be a remarkable year for the Athens Stock Exchange (ASE). Declining interest rates throughout 1997 encouraged many local investors to move into the stock market, while at the same time there was an influx of foreign capital attracted by EU-backed structural and economic reforms.

By international standards, the Greek equity market is still small, with market value representing approximately one-third of GDP at the end of 1997. However, a revitalised economy and productivity gains have improved the prospects for many listed firms. Consolidation in many sectors of the economy, especially in banking and financial services, is expected to increase competitiveness and fuel broad-based economic growth.

Privatisation is part of the convergence programme, but apart from the partial sale of Hellenic Telecommunication (OTE) mainly to institutional investors, no other company was floated in 1997. Nevertheless, the success of the OTE offer has revived hopes that the government will proceed with the sale of other state companies such as the Public Power Corporation, the Public Petroleum Corporation and Hellenic Duty Free Shops.

Along with the development of an improved legal framework for the ASE, a derivatives market is expected to be operational by the end of 1998.

ECONOMIC AND POLITICAL OVERVIEW

Following his election in September 1996, Prime Minister Costas Simitis of the ruling Panhellenic Socialist Movement (PASOK), embarked on a tough economic reform programme that proved fruitful in 1997. Determined to proceed with public sector structural reforms, the former technocrat confronted labour unions head on and slashed welfare benefits. The budget deficit almost halved in 1997, dropping to 4.2% of GDP from 7.5% in 1996, while the PSBR also experienced a steep decline, and is expected to fall to 6.2% of GDP from 10.3% in 1996. As well as significant improvements in economic performance in 1997, budget targets were bolstered by an upward revision of GDP.

A hard drachma was the cornerstone of the government's monetary policy in 1997, leading CPI inflation downward with interest rates following suit. The side effects of stiff monetary policy were seen in the widening current account deficit (4% of GDP in 1997) and the minimal decline in public debt as a percentage of GDP (109.3%, down from 112.6% in 1996).

Role of the central bank

The central bank – the Bank of Greece – is responsible for implementing monetary policy, including interest rates, credit and foreign exchange policies. It is also the main adviser to the government on all general economic policy matters. In recent years, as the banking system has been deregulated, the central bank has tended to shift away from direct controls in favour of indirect measures and thus more into line with European and US practice.

The bank operates as a société anonyme (SA), although the governor and deputy governors are appointed by the state. Consequently, the bank is not politically autonomous despite being among the most independent in Europe from a legal and economic perspective. There is, however, widespread support for new legislation that aims to enhance the bank's independence, and in 1997 the government proceeded to draft legislation that is due to be examined by parliament in 1998.

MARKET PERFORMANCE

A) In 1997

The Athens Stock Exchange (ASE) faired exceptionally

Exhibit 25.1: ATHENS SE GENERAL PRICE INDEX (US$), 1993–97

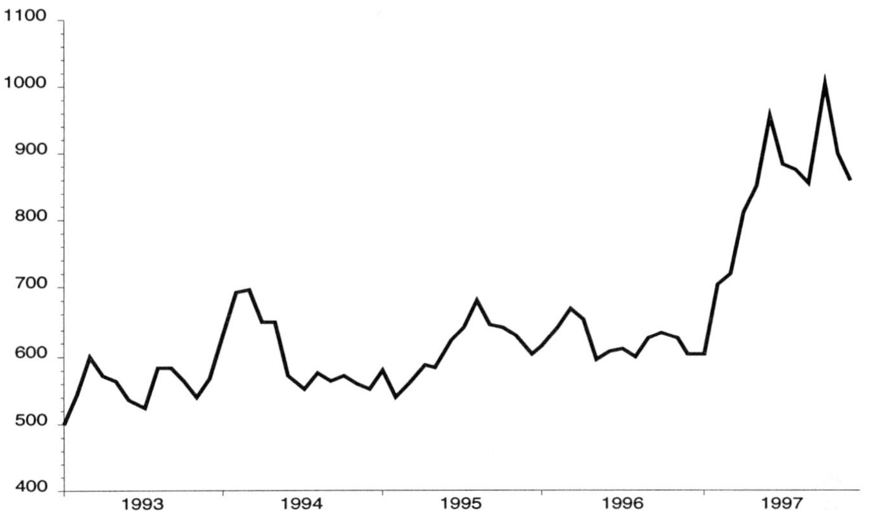

High value 1005.29 1.10.97 Low value 498.18 1.1.93 *Source: Datastream*

well in 1997, with the General Index soaring to an all-time high in October. Perceived political stability under Prime Minister Costas Simitis, coupled with bold monetary and fiscal policies aimed at EMU convergence, strengthened Greece's investment outlook resulting in large foreign inflows to the ASE. There was a second public offering by the government of a 12% stake (following the initial 8%) in Hellenic Telecommunications (OTE) in June 1997.

The ASE General Index rose to an all-time high of 1,809 (up 94%) in October after Greece was chosen to host the 2004 Olympic Games. At a sub-sector level, all indices posted gains, with the best performances in insurance, which rose 130% for the year, and holding companies, which gained 91%. The banking and industrial sectors (in which most of the blue chips are concentrated) both gained approximately 62%. The General Index ended the year up 59% at 1,480.

B) Summary information

Global ranking by market value (US$ terms, end-1997): 33
Market capitalisation (end-1997): US$36.1 billion
Growth in market value (local currency terms, 1993-97): 230.3%
Market value as a % of nominal GDP (end-1997): 30.9%
Number of domestic/foreign companies listed on the official market (end-1997): 227/0
Market P/E (end-1997): 18.4
MSCI Index (change in US$ terms, 1997): +32.6%
Short-term (3-month) interest rate (end-1997): 12.55%
Long-term (7-year) bond yield (end-1997): 10.3%
Budget deficit as a % of nominal GDP (end-1997): 4.2%
Annual increase in broad money (M3) supply (end-1997): 9.5%
Inflation rate (1997): 4.7%
US$ exchange rate (end-1997): Dr282.61

C) Year-end share price index, price/earnings ratios and yields

Exhibit 25.2:
ASE GENERAL INDEX (DRACHMA TERMS), P/E AND AVERAGE DIVIDEND YIELDS, 1993–97

Year-end	*General Index*	*P/E*	*Yield (%)*
1993	958.66	16.7	3.6
1994	868.91	13.1	4.7
1995	914.15	11.1	4.9
1996	933.48	11.9	4.1
1997	1,479.63	18.4	3.8

Source: Athens Stock Exchange and Egnatia Securities.

D) Market indices and their constituents

The ASE General Index, last revised in 1996, comprises 60 companies.

The Parallel Market Index was introduced on 28 August 1995 and has been calculated retrospectively from January 1995.

A new FTSE-ASE Index, created jointly by the *Financial Times* and the Athens Stock Exchange, was launched in September 1997.

THE STOCK MARKET

A) Brief history and structure

Under Law 2,324/95, the Athens exchange was transformed in 1995 from a public institution into a limited company. It is chiefly financed by annual listing fees paid by both equity and fixed-income issuers. A levy of Dr20 per order is also paid by authorised brokers for the system's maintenance.

The ASE board of directors comprises nine members appointed for a three-year period. Three members are nominated by the Minister of National Economy, one member is nominated by the Bank of Greece, two members are nominated by members of the ASE, and the other three are nominated by the Athens Chamber of Commerce and Industry, the employees of the ASE and by institutional investors.

Law 1806/88 allowed for the first time the establishment and operation of stock exchange companies as full members of the ASE. Such companies must have a fully paid registered share capital of at least Dr200 million, and up to Dr1 billion, depending on the services they provide. For holders of more than 10% of the share capital, any transfer of shares requires the permission of the board of directors.

Licences for the establishment of a stock exchange company are granted by the board of directors only after close scrutiny of the company's organisation and financial means, and vetting of all shareholders holding more than 10% of the equity. A bank is not permitted to be a shareholder in more than one brokerage company. As regards foreign companies obtaining membership, the implementation of the Investment Services Directive has given free access to the market to all entities licensed in other regulated markets within the EU.

The Capital Market Committee, established in 1991, is an autonomous supervisory body.

B) Different exchanges

There are two exchanges in Greece: the ASE and the Thessaloniki Stock Exchange Centre (TSEC), which was officially inaugurated in March 1996. The ASE holds a 34% participation in the TSEC, which aims to promote listings on the ASE parallel market of companies operating in northern Greece.

C) Opening hours, names and addresses

The ASE official and parallel markets are open for trading from 10.45am to 1.30pm, Monday to Friday, except for official holidays. There is a half-hour pre-trading session from 10.15am to 10.45am.

ATHENS STOCK EXCHANGE
10 Sophocleous Street, Athens 10559
Tel: (30) 1 321 1301; Fax: (30) 1 321 3938

MARKET SIZE

A) Number of listings and market value

At the end of 1997, the 184 companies listed on the official market and 43 companies on the parallel market of the ASE had a combined market capitalisation of Dr10,294 billion, up 73% on the end-1996 total.

Exhibit 25.3:
NUMBER OF ASE COMPANIES AND MARKET CAPITALISATION, 1993-97

Year-end	*No. of companies*	*Market value (Dr billion)*
1993	150	3,117.1
1994	196	3,628.7
1995	204	4,028.5
1996	218	5,944.8
1997	227	10,294

Source: Athens Stock Exchange and Egnatia Securities.

Exhibit 25.4:
MARKET VALUE OF ASE LISTED SHARES BY SECTOR, END-1997

Sector	*Market value (Dr billion)*
Telecommunications	2,640.2
Banks	2,601.2
Food	1,077.8
Metallurgical	730.2
Building materials	595.8
Construction	304.3
Holding companies	278.5
Investment	226.5
Insurance	182.1
Miscellaneous	171.4
Tobacco	117.6
Containers and paper mills	81.6
Textiles	72.6
Informatics	69.7
Pharmaceuticals and cosmetics	59.6
Leasing	48.7
Mines	45.9
Chemical products	31.9
Mass media	31.5
Flour mills	25.8
Passenger shipping	25.1
Wood products	23.6

Exhibit 25.4 continued

Hotels	22.5
Printed information	14.8
Cold storage	4.0
Total main market	**9,483.2**
Total parallel market	328.1
Grand total	**9,811.3**

Source: Athens Stock Exchange.

B) Largest quoted companies

The two largest companies in terms of capitalisation at the end of 1997 were Hellenic Telecommunications and Hellenic Bottling Company, which together accounted for 32% of total market value.

Exhibit 25.5:
THE 20 LARGEST LISTED COMPANIES ON THE ASE, 1997

Ranking	*Company*	*Market value (Dr million)*
1	Hellenic Telecommunications	2,640,236
2	Hellenic Bottling Company	686,423
3	Alpha Credit Bank	656,370
4	National Bank of Greece	564,420
5	Ergo Bank	372,285
6	Heracles Cement	297,644
7	Titan Cement Co	268,217
8	Commercial Bank	238,221
9	National Mortgage Bank	208,802
10	Intracom	197,910
11	Viohalco	151,871
12	Ionian Bank	138,616
13	Aluminium of Greece	112,799
14	Papastratos	102,989
15	Sidenor	101,677
16	Attica Enterprises	99,969
17	Elval	76,387
18	Bank of Greece	74,096
19	Aspis Pronoia Gen Insurances	73,755
20	Delta Dairy	72,365

Source: Athens Stock Exchange.

C) Trading volume

Exhibit 25.6:
TURNOVER ON THE ASE, 1993-97

Year	*Trading value (Dr billion)*
1993	637.1
1994	1,262.1
1995	1,408.5
1996	1,990.0
1997	5,802.0

Source: Athens Stock Exchange.

Exhibit 25.7:
THE 20 MOST ACTIVELY TRADED SHARES, ASE, 1997

Ranking	*Company*	*Trading value (Dr million)*
1	Hellenic Telecommunications	1,007,357
2	National Bank of Greece	437,462
3	Alpha Credit Bank	425,846
4	Ergo Bank	238,870
5	National Mortgage Bank	221,612
6	Commercial Bank of Greece	208,715
7	Hellenic Bottling Co	137,446
8	Heracles Cement	134,560
9	Titan Cement	134,187
10	Intracom (CR)	125,153
11	Intracom (PR)	84,127
12	Viohalco (CB)	81,931
13	Bank of Piraeus	81,557
14	Ethiki General Insurances	76,769
15	Hellenic Sugar Industry	67,800
16	NIBID	63,711
17	Ionian Bank of Greece	61,097
18	Elval	56,136
19	Mytilineos Holdings	55,984
20	Intrasoft (CR)	55,057

Source: Athens Stock Exchange.

TYPES OF SHARE

Ordinary shares are by far the most common form of equity traded in Greece, comprising over 94% of all shares issued and traded. Preference shares and preferred ordinary shares also exist in the Greek market and account for the remaining 6%. Preference shares have a prior claim to dividend distribution and may be either voting or non-voting. Preferred ordinary shares carry voting rights and a fixed dividend. Convertible bonds are also traded.

The shares of banks, insurance companies, some investment companies, newspaper-owning companies, radio and television stations, property companies and companies involved in public works and public procurements are, by law, registered. Shares in other companies may be registered or bearer.

OTHER MARKETS

A parallel market for medium-sized companies began operating on 30 May 1990. To qualify, companies must

Exhibit 25.8:
COUNTRY FUNDS – GREECE

Fund	US$ % change 01.01.97 01.01.98	US$ % change 01.01.93 01.01.98	Currency	Fund size (US$ mil)	volatility	Management group	Opal main sector	Opal subsector
Dorian Greek Equity	36.63	8.34	Dr	3394.9	7.039	Dorian Asst M	Open-End	Equity
Greek Progress Fund	16.17	15.81	Dr	17462	4.849	Ergobank (Bar)	Closed-End	Equity

Note: details for some funds may not have been included if the data for the US$ % change for 97/98 was not available

Source: Standard & Poor's Micropal.

show satisfactory profits for the past three years, and there is also a minimum capitalisation requirement.

In November 1997, the government created the framework for a derivatives market. The Derivatives Stock Exchange of Athens (DSEA) is an SA with capital of Dr3 billion. Trading is expected to begin at the end of 1998.

INVESTORS

Most investors in the Greek equity market are domestic, private and institutional. Foreign institutional investors, however, are playing an increasing role in the market.

OPERATIONS

A) Trading system

Purchases and sales of equities on the ASE take place using an automatic trading system, called XTS, which covers all listed companies. All securities are traded simultaneously during the session.

In 1996 the ASE launched an international open competition for the procurement and development of an integrated automated trading system (OASIS).

B) Principal brokers

ALPHA BROKERAGE AE
6 Dratsaniou Street, GR-105 59, Athens
Tel: (30) 1 323 4691; Fax: (30) 1 322 2224

BZW HELLAS
1 Kolokotroni St, GR-105 62, Athens
Tel: (30) 1 324 5464; Fax: (30) 1 324 6033

NATIONAL SECURITIES
Melas Mansion, 93 Eolou-Sophocleous St,
GR-105 51, Athens
Tel: (30) 1 325 4973; Fax: (30) 1 325 1072

NICOLAS D DEVLETOGLOU SECURITIES SA
4 Dragatsaniou St, GR-105 59, Athens
Tel: (30) 1 324 4615; Fax: (30) 1 323 3175

SIGMA SECURITIES
10 Stadiou Street, GR-105 64, Athens
Tel: (30) 1 331 1456; Fax: (30) 1 325 2241

C) Settlement and transfer

Equities may be traded on account or for cash. Settlement time is set at T+3.

In 1997 the ASE created a fund to cover the obligations of member firms arising from transactions that have not been cleared on time because of non-delivery of shares or non-payment of money due.

D) Commissions and other costs

Commissions were deregulated in 1995 and are now negotiable. A transfer charge for registered shares of 0.09% of the value of the transaction is also payable. The cost of clearing trades in bearer shares or bearer depository receipts is set at 0.011%.

TAXATION AND REGULATIONS AFFECTING FOREIGN INVESTORS

A) Withholding tax

The profits of all companies, whether distributed or not, are taxed at 35%. This tax is deducted at source and no further tax is charged on dividends. The only exception is for bearer shares of SAs not listed on the stock exchange, where the tax is 40%. Foreign organisations established in Greece pay tax at 40%. In general, capital gains are not taxed.

Exhibit 25.9:
WITHHOLDING TAX

Recipient	Dividends %	Interest %
Resident corporations	1	20, 15[2]
Resident individuals	1	20, 15[2]
Non-resident corporations:		
Non-treaty	1	40, 15[2]
Treaty	25-47	nil-40

Notes:

1. A corporation is taxed on its total annual profits before distributions. Consequently, the profits are taxed only at the company level, and there is no withholding tax on dividends and profits otherwise distributed.
2. Interest earned on deposits with banks operating in Greece, as well as on any kind of bonds and other interest-bearing securities issued by private enterprises, is subject to income tax at the rate of 15% withheld at source.

Source: Price Waterhouse.

B) Exchange controls, repatriation of capital gains and earnings

Non-resident foreign companies and individuals may open current accounts and commercial bank deposit accounts, or hold time deposits in Greek and foreign currencies without restriction. In keeping with its earlier announcements, in 1997 the Bank of Greece lifted all remaining restrictions relating to exchange control. Everybody, including permanent residents, may now freely convert drachmas into foreign currency and keep foreign currency accounts. The interest on foreign currency bank accounts of permanent residents continues to be taxed at 15% per annum; the accounts of non-residents are not taxed.

Foreign investors may invest in Greek securities listed on the ASE and they are allowed to export the proceeds of sale of such securities, including capital gains, dividends and other benefits. Furthermore, foreign investors may invest freely in Greek companies including banks and insurance companies. However, in the case of shipping, the majority of shares in a Greek ship must belong to Greek nationals.

LISTING AND REPORTING REQUIREMENTS

A) Listing requirements

Greek law now complies fully with EU Directives on the harmonisation of stock exchange listing conditions and on the coordination of prospectus conditions. Law 1,914/1990 introduced the following listing rules:

1) *Method of introducing shares*: a company that wishes to be quoted on the ASE and that is not listed on the stock exchange of another country, is obliged to offer for public subscription shares that derive from an increase of capital and that represent in nominal value at least 25% of the total capital.
2) *Offers to subscribe for the shares may be made only by banks or stock exchange companies*: these organisations underwrite the issue and guarantee full coverage of the offer. The subscription price of the shares is fixed by the underwriters.
3) *Minimum subscribers*: at least 100 natural or legal persons.
4) *Minimum capital*: Dr1 billion (own capital, including the most recent financial results).

Additional listing rules apply to construction, shipping, holding and insurance companies.

Listing requirements on the parallel market are as follows:

- own capital of at least Dr250 million;
- satisfactory operating profits for the past three years;
- at least a 15% increase of capital prior to listing, and the new shares offered to the public;
- published prospectus; and
- new issue placed in the market through an underwriter, who guarantees full coverage of the offer.

B) Reporting requirements

Corporations listed on the exchange are required to report three times a year on their finances. All accounts are published in the *Government Gazette*, a daily national newspaper, and in a financial newspaper.

The dismissal of directors need not be announced, but the appointment of directors of all corporations (whether listed or not) must be published in the *Government Gazette*.

SHAREHOLDER PROTECTION CODES

A) Purchase of own shares

Under Law 2 190/1920, an SA that is quoted on the Athens exchange may purchase 10% of its own shares for the purpose of boosting its exchange value. It may do this where it is thought that the quoted price does not reflect the true financial condition and prospects of the company. The acquisition should not result in a reduction of net assets below the amount set out in Articles 15 and 16 of Directive 77/91/EEC.

B) Insider trading

Under Law 1 806/88, insider trading is a criminal offence punishable by imprisonment, unless it is proved that profit was not realised through the use of confidential information obtained by virtue of an office or position in the corporation. The publication or spreading of false information that may affect the price of one or more securities quoted on the ASE is subject to a fine and imprisonment.

C) Market manipulation

A member of the stock exchange who uses misleading or false methods, such as trying to influence the price of a share, is guilty of an offence and is liable to imprisonment and a fine of up to Dr500 million.

RESEARCH

Firms providing research on the Greek market include Sigma Securities, Schroders, BZW Hellas, N. Devletoglou and Egnatia Securities.

The ASE publishes data on prices and trading volume of all listed stocks through the *Daily Official List, Monthly Statistical Bulletin*, a *Fact Book* and the *Annual Bulletin*. Financial statements are summarised in the *Stock Market Yearbook*.

Greece, published by Euromoney Books, provides in-depth information for those wishing to invest or do business in the country. See the order card at the back of this book for details.

CHAPTER

26

Hong Kong

Introduction

The Hong Kong market moved ahead strongly in the first seven months of 1997 in the lead up to, and aftermath of, the handover of sovereignty to China. In the period January-July 1997 the Hang Seng Index rose 21%, to 16,366. However, the latter part of the year was characterised by falling equity prices as the Asian currency crisis began to affect the Hong Kong economy. The Hang Seng fell 34% from its end-July level to close 1997 at 10,723, 20% down for the year as a whole.

The average Hang Seng Index price/earnings ratio fell from 16.7 at the end of 1996 to 12.1 at the end of 1997, and this was accompanied by a rise in the divided yield from 2.9% at end-1996 to 3.9% at end-1997. Market capitalisation fell 8% during the year to HK$3,202.6 billion. There were 658 companies listed on the Stock Exchange of Hong Kong (SEHK) as of 31 December 1997, 75 more than at the end of 1996.

ECONOMIC AND POLITICAL OVERVIEW

On 1 July 1997 China assumed sovereignty over Hong Kong. Many believed that this would ultimately mean an end to *laissez-faire* economics and personal freedoms in the territory, but this now seems very unlikely, and so far it has been "business as usual".

Most commentators in Hong Kong have focused on the likelihood of continuity and prosperity after the handover. They argue that the overriding attitude among China's leaders is more pragmatic than perhaps at any time in China's modern history, and that China needs the vibrant, modern, service-oriented Hong Kong as a blueprint for a market economy. Whereas Shenzhen and other special administrative regions of China are the drawing boards for Chinese capitalism, Hong Kong is a working model. As such it will be an indispensable tool in China's future economic development.

Rather than being a negative factor for the Hong Kong economy and stock market, therefore, the 1997 handover could turn out to be a major positive. The territory is likely to attract large capital inflows from the mainland in search of well-run companies, possibly driving the Hong Kong market to new highs in the future.

Although 1997 will primarily be remembered as the year of the handover of Hong Kong from Britain to China, it will also be remembered for the October stock market crash. A speculative attack on the Hong Kong dollar in October provoked a global sell-off in equities. From peak to trough, Hong Kong stocks fell by 40% in October, precipitating selling in both emerging and developed markets around the world. Such a dramatic drop in a market regarded as a safe-haven was surprising.

In the aftermath of the attack on the currency – which sent overnight interbank rates soaring – the Hong Kong government faces a dilemma. If it continues its US dollar peg policy it risks further speculative attacks and possible upward pressure on interest rates. This could result in continued weakness in the stock market and further price falls in the property sector, and this would have knock-on implications for the banking sector, which is heavily geared to the property sector. As a result, the rating agency Moody's downgraded the outlook for Hong Kong banks from positive to negative soon after the crash. However, if the government floats the Hong Kong dollar, it risks spiralling inflation and pushing the economy into recession. This is a difficult choice but, given the underlying health of the economy, the decision to stick to the US dollar peg is widely believed to be correct. In the long run, however, it implies that inflation in Hong Kong will have to come down to a rate below that in the US. Another consideration is the eventual merger of the Hong Kong dollar with the Chinese renminbi, but this will not take place until the Chinese economy is completely liberalised.

The higher interest rate environment in Hong Kong has also had a negative impact on the retail sector, which

Exhibit 26.1: HANG SENG PRICE INDEX (US$), 1993–97

High value 14567.47 1.8.97 Low value 4900.65 1.1.93 *Source: Datastream*

had already been hit by a downturn in tourism following the handover. The economy is thus likely to face slower growth in 1998.

Role of the central bank

The Hong Kong Monetary Authority (HKMA) came into existence in 1993. Its principal function is to foster monetary and banking stability, and to maintain the currency within its US dollar-linked exchange rate system.

The HKMA is also responsible for supervising the banking system. However, it does not undertake the standard central bank functions of issuing banknotes, acting as a clearing house or providing banking services to the government.

Ultimately reporting to the Financial Secretary of Hong Kong, the HKMA is an independent but integral branch of the government.

MARKET PERFORMANCE

A) In 1997

The Hong Kong market rallied strongly in the first seven months of 1997, particularly in June and July around the time of the handover to China. Subsequently, however, performance was adversely affected by the Asian currency crisis. For Hong Kong, the crisis peaked in October with a sharp fall in equity prices that wiped out the gains from earlier in the year. Over 1997 as a whole, the Hang Seng Index fell by 20%.

B) Summary information

Global ranking by market value (US$ terms, end-1997): 9
Market capitalisation (end-1997): US$413.32 billion
Growth in market value (local currency terms, 1993-97): 7.6%
Market value as a % of nominal GDP (end-1997): 232%
Number of domestic/foreign companies listed (end-1997): 638/20
Market P/E (All Ordinaries Index constituents, end-1997): 12.1
MSCI total returns (with net dividends, 1997): -23.3%
MSCI Index (change in US$ terms, 1997): -25.8%
Short-term (1-month interbank) interest rate (end-1997): 7.23%
Long-term (5-year Exchange Fund Bills) bond yield (end-1997): 9.25%
Budget deficit as a % of nominal GDP (1997): 1.1%
Annual increase in broad (M3) money supply (end-1997): 15.0%
Inflation rate (1997): 5.9%
US$ exchange rate (end-1997): HK$7.7485

C) Year-end share price index, price/earnings ratios and yields

Exhibit 26.2:
SEHK INDEX, P/E AND DIVIDEND YIELDS, 1993-97

Year-end	*Hang Seng Index*	*P/E*	*Yield (%)*
1993	11,888.39	22.60	2.28
1994	8,191.04	10.73	4.13
1995	10,073.39	11.44	3.62
1996	13,451.45	16.69	2.89
1997	10,722.76	12.10	3.90

Source: Stock Exchange of Hong Kong.

D) Market indices and their constituents

The Hang Seng Index is the most widely observed indicator of stock market performance in Hong Kong. The index is computed on an arithmetic basis, weighted by market capitalisation, and is thus strongly influenced by large capitalisation stocks such as HSBC, Hang Seng Bank and Cheung Kong. The index comprises 33 companies, which are divided into four sub-indices – financial (3), property (12), utilities (5), and commerce and industry (13).

The SEHK calculates an All Ordinaries Index (AOI), based at 2 April 1986 = 1,000, along with AOI sectoral indices (base date 2 January 1995 = 2,333.77). The AOI and the sectoral indices are updated once a minute and disseminated to the public through Teletext.

THE STOCK MARKET

A) Brief history and structure

Although formal share trading did not begin in Hong Kong until 1891, exchange records show that stockbrokers were operating in Hong Kong as early as 1866 – the year after Hong Kong's first Companies Ordinance was passed.

The SEHK existed as the only exchange until 1969 when, to counter its reluctance to admit new members, the Far East Stock Exchange was set up by a group of Chinese businessmen. This stimulated business and attracted new money to the colony, and it also inspired the establishment of two other exchanges – Kam Ngan and Kowloon. From 2 April 1986, however, the four exchanges merged to form the Stock Exchange of Hong Kong Ltd.

The SEHK has two types of membership – corporate and individual. At the end of 1997, there were 382 corporate members and 173 individual members.

B) Different exchanges

The SEHK is the only stock exchange in Hong Kong.

C) Opening hours, names and addresses

Trading sessions are from Monday to Friday (except public holidays) between 10.00am and 12.30pm and 2.30pm and 3.55pm. There is no afternoon trading session on Christmas Eve, New Year's Eve and Lunar New Year's Eve.

THE STOCK EXCHANGE OF HONG KONG LTD
1st Floor, 1&2 Exchange Square, PO Box 8888
Tel: (852) 2522 1122; Fax: (852) 2810 4475
Internet: www.sehk.com.hk

MARKET SIZE

A) Number of listings and market value

The total number of securities listed on the exchange at the end of 1997 was 1,533 (658 companies) with a capitalisation of HK$3,203 billion (down 8% over the year).

Exhibit 26.3:
NUMBER OF LISTED SECURITIES, LISTED COMPANIES AND MARKET VALUE, SEHK, 1993-97

Year-end	*Listed securities*	*Listed companies*	*Market value (HK$ billion)*
1993	891	477	2,975.38
1994	1,006	529	2,085.18
1995	1,033	542	2,348.31
1996	1,272	583	3,475.97
1997	1,533	658	3,202.63

Source: Stock Exchange of Hong Kong.

Exhibit 26.4:
MARKET CAPITALISATION OF LISTED COMPANIES BY SECTOR, SEHK, END-1997

Sector	*Market value (HK$ billion)*	*% of total*
Finance	864.01	26.98
Properties	679.29	21.21
Consolidated enterprises	674.29	21.07
Utilities	598.86	18.70
Industrials	320.04	9.99
Hotels	48.23	1.51
Others	17.42	054
Total	**3,202.63**	**100.00**

Source: Stock Exchange of Hong Kong.

Exhibit 26.5:
NEW ISSUES ON THE SEHK, 1993-97

	*New flotations**		*Rights issues*	
Year	*No. of newly listed companies*	*Amount (HK$ million)*	*No of issues*	*Amount (HK$ million)*
1993	68	27,980.69	23	9,226.07
1994	53	17,051.24	19	5,643.12
1995	26	7,641.87	10	1,289.73
1996	49	25,511.72	22	4,653.02
1997	82	81,653.62	49	16,241.59

**For IPOs only.* *Source: Stock Exchange of Hong Kong.*

B) Largest quoted companies

The 20 largest listed companies at end-1997 accounted for 67.5% of market capitalisation.

Exhibit 26.6:
THE 20 LARGEST LISTED COMPANIES ON THE SEHK, END-1997

Ranking	*Company*	*Market value (HK$ billion)*
1	HSBC Holdings	582.32
2	HK Telecommunications	189.59
3	Hutchison Whampoa	188.27
4	China Telecom (HK)	156.68
5	Hang Seng Bank	143.65
6	Sun Hung Kai Properties	129.03
7	Cheung Kong (Holdings)	116.60
8	China Light & Power Co	106.99
9	CITIC Pacific	65.52
10	Swire Pacific	63.97
11	Henderson Land Development Co	63.22
12	Hong Kong Electric Holdings	59.49
13	Hong Kong and China Gas	59.06
14	New World Development Co	51.28
15	Cheung Kong Infrastructure	49.36
16	Wharf (Holdings)	39.01
17	China Resources Enterprise	26.79
18	Bank of East Asia	24.39
19	Shanghai Industrial Holdings	24.11
20	Cathay Pacific Airways	21.34

Source: Stock Exchange of Hong Kong.

C) Trading volume

The total volume of shares traded during 1997 was 1,767.9 billion (1996, 587.3 billion), and turnover value was HK$3,789 billion (1996, HK$1,412.2 billion).

Exhibit 26.7:
THE 20 MOST ACTIVELY TRADED SHARES ON THE SEHK, 1997

Ranking	*Company*	*Trading value (HK$ billion)*
1	HSBC Holdings	268.65
2	Cheung Kong (Holdings)	126.42
3	CNPC (Hong Kong)	94.71
4	Sun Hung Kai Properties	93.72
5	Hutchison Whampoa	93.34
6	Hong Kong Telecom	92.58
7	CITIC Pacific	84.91
8	China Merchants Holdings	72.95
9	Hang Seng Bank	66.54
10	Henderson Land Development	57.33
11	Swire Pacific A	52.33
12	New World Development	51.13
13	Shanghai Hai Xing H	51.00
14	China Resources Enterprise	50.59
15	China Light	48.65
16	Ka Wah Bank	44.95
17	China Telecom (HK)	44.09
18	China Everbright	43.40
19	China Overseas Land	39.83
20	Yizheng Chemical H	39.25

Source: Stock Exchange of Hong Kong.

Exhibit 26.8:
TURNOVER BY SECTOR, SEHK, 1997

Sector	*Turnover* (HK$ billion)*	*% of total*
Consolidated enterprises	943.19	26.85
Properties	842.86	23.99
Industrials	751.50	12.68
Finance	530.90	15.11
Utilities	252.23	7.18
Miscellaneous	168.64	4.80
Hotels	23.52	0.67
Total	**3,512.84**	**100.00**

*Warrant, debt security and unit trust turnover excluded.

Source: Stock Exchange of Hong Kong.

TYPES OF SHARE

Ordinary, preference and preferred ordinary shares, convertible bonds and unit trusts are all traded in the Hong Kong market. Rights and restrictions are the same as in the UK stock market. A number of companies also issue warrants to purchase ordinary shares in connection with the offering of debt or equity securities.

Companies incorporated under Hong Kong's Companies Ordinance may issue preferred, deferred or other shares with special rights or restrictions as the company determines. In practice, however, virtually all shares listed on the SEHK are ordinary shares.

During the 1970s, a number of companies established two classes of ordinary share in order to permit controlling shareholders to reduce their equity investment while retaining voting control. A second class of ordinary share was established with a stated value equal to a fraction (one-fifth or one-tenth) of the company's ordinary shares. While the share has a lower dividend, it carries equal voting rights. Although a small number of companies maintain this structure, the SEHK no longer recognises such shares on new listings.

Derivatives traded on the stock exchange are warrants, convertible bonds and stock options.

During 1993, for the first time, PRC companies directly entered the market by offering H shares listed on

Exhibit 26.9:
TOP PERFORMING COUNTRY FUNDS – HONG KONG

	US$ % change 01/01/97 01/01/98	01/01/93 01/01/98	Currency	Fund size (US$ mil)	Fund volatility	Management group	Opal main sector	Opal subsector
Glbl Mgr HK Bear	16.13	N/A	US$	0.7	8.38	Bermuda Intl	Open-End	Equity
Barclays ASF Hong Kong	2.24	167.47	US$	17.5	9.42	Barclays	Open-End	Equity
Govett Hong Kong Safeguard A	-1.1	N/A	US$	3.2	-1	Govett & Co	Open-End	Equit
Nomura Bull/Bear S HK Bear	-4.5	N/A	¥	1012	-1	Nomura ITMCo	Open-End	Equity
Nikko HK Trend S HK Reverse	-5.62	N/A	¥	653	-1	Nikko	Open-End	Equity
GT Hong Kong B	-6.33	109.74	US$	67.2	9.368	LGT	Open-End	Equity
GT Hong Kong A	-6.81	106.54	US$	67.2	9.361	LGT	Open-End	Equity
Daiwa Power S Bear HK	-7.11	N/A	¥	445	-1	Daiwa	Open-End	Equity
INVESCO Hong Kong & China Gth	-8.85	108.58	£	24.9	9.378	Invesco Intl	Open-End	Equity
INVESCO HK Bear Open	-8.97	N/A	¥	250	-1	Invesco Intl	Open-End	Equity
Yamaichi HK Bull Bear S Bear	-9.19	N/A	¥	899	-1	Yamaichi Japan	Open-End	Equity
HSBC Guaranteed	-9.62	N/A	HK$	77.8	-1	HSBC Asst Mgt	Open-End	Equity
HSBC GIF Hong Kong Equity	-9.78	195.34	US$	151.2	9.844	HSBC Asst Mgt	Open-End	Equity
Jupiter Tyndall GF Hong Kong	-11.68	N/A	US$	1.6	11.029	Tyndall	Open-End	Equity
HSBC Hong Kong Growth	-12.07	176.22	£	27.3	9.661	James Capel F	Open-End	Equity
Shinwako HK Bear Open	-13.92	N/A	¥	22	-1	Shinwako	Open-End	Equity
OMHK HK Stkmkt	-15.33	N/A	US$	1.1	-1	Old Mutual	Open-End	Equity
GAM Hong Kong	-16.2	N/A	US$	1.2	-1	GAM	Open-End	Equity
Baring IUF Hong Kong	-16.38	113.4	US$	38	10.339	Barings	Open-End	Equity
Hang Seng Index Fund	-18.72	N/A	HK$	1049.3	-1	Hang Seng IML	Open-End	Equity
Glbl Mgr HK Index	-19.14	N/A	US$	0.7	8.642	Bermuda Intl	Open-End	Equity
Guinness Flight Hong Kong	-19.98	115.58	US$	20.6	8.544	Guinness Flig	Open-End	Equity
Citi Hong Kong Equity	-20.11	N/A	US$	11	8.756	Citibank	Open-End	Equity
Old Mutual Hong Kong	-21.06	101.03	£	17.5	9.946	Old Mutual	Open-End	Equity
Dao Heng Hong Kong	-22.63	34.09	HK$	23.7	10.815	Daoh Heng Asi	Open-End	Equity
SHK Middle Kingdom	-22.71	120.36	HK$	9.2	9.417	SHK Fd Mgt	Open-End	Equity
OMI Galileo HK Stockmarket	-22.88	N/A	US$	5.3	-1	Old Mutual	Open-End	Equity
Dres Thornton ASF Hong Kong	-23.11	N/A	US$	3	10.505	Thornton	Open-End	Equity
Aetna MF Hong Kong Natl Eqty	-23.3	20.79	HK$	8	8.587	Wright Invest	Open-End	Equity
Colonial Securities Hong Kong	-24.46	119.97	US$	5.2	9.665	Panurgy	Open-End	Equity
Nomura Aurora Hong Kong	-25.03	4.78	¥	7907	9.381	Nomura ITMCo	Open-End	Equity
Nomura SF Hong Kong	-25.27	48.98	US$	0.5	10.01	Nomura Intl	Open-End	Equity
Taiyo Hong Kong Open	-25.31	-9.8	¥	1194	8.883	Taiyo	Open-End	Equity
Schroder Asia Hong Kong	-25.59	102.69	HK$	350.2	11.353	Schroders	Open-End	Equity
Nomura World Index HK B	-25.63	N/A	¥	1673	9.132	Nomura Intl	Open-End	Equity
Mansion House Hong Kong	-25.91	84.89	HK$	49	10.722	Mansion House	Open-End	Equity
Gartmore Hong Kong	-26.73	71.51	£	15.3	9.553	Gartmore	Open-End	Equity
Schroder Asia Hong Kong Sm Co	-26.98	57.16	HK$	18.5	11.754	Schroders	Open-End	Equity
Daiichi Hong Kong Open	-27.08	N/A	¥	121	-1	Daiichi ITMCo	Open-End	Equity
Wright Equi:Hong Kong	-27.2	1.96	US$	7.3	8.651	Wright Invest	Open-End	Equity
Mercury Hong Kong Open	-27.28	N/A	¥	819	8.749	Warburg (Japan)	Open-End	Equity
Manulife GF Index Hong Kong	-27.43	N/A	US$	6.2	-1	Manulife Glob	Open-End	Equity
INVESCO Hong Kong Open	-27.8	N/A	¥	1552	10.067	Invesco Intl	Open-End	Equity
RG ZelfSelect Hongkong	-28.04	N/A	G	23	-1	Robeco	Open-End	Equity

Note: details for some funds may not have been included if the data for the US$ % change for 97/98 was not available

Source: Standard & Poor's Micropal.

the SEHK. At the end of 1997, 39 H shares were listed on the exchange.

INVESTORS

The 1996 SEHK *Members Transaction Survey* showed that individual trading had increased from 31% to 36% over the year and institutional trading had fallen from 61% to 56% in the same period. Principal trading made up the remaining 8%. Local individuals contributed 34% of total market turnover in value terms and local institutions 26%. Overseas trading accounted for the remaining turnover, with the UK and US contributing 32% and 30% of this amount, respectively.

Many regional mutual funds are quoted locally and invest mostly in Hong Kong, with smaller investments in Singapore, Malaysia and, very occasionally, the Philippines and Thailand. There are 46 regional and international funds quoted in Hong Kong.

OPERATIONS

A) Trading system

The SEHK operates an order-driven trading system whereby trades originate from a client order (either a market order or a limit order). Typically, a client places an order with his or her account executive/dealer at the broker's office and the account executive/dealer then calls up a floor trader at the trading hall. The floor trader inputs the order into the computer system through the terminal in his booth.

In November 1993, a computerised trading system called Automatic Order Matching and Execution System (AMS) was introduced. AMS is able to support both automatic order matching and the previous semi-automatic trading system. Under this dual operational mode, all stocks are traded through AMS and are divided into two categories – automatch stocks and non-automatch stocks. The order and trade information for both types of stocks is disseminated to the market and investors through the enhanced Teletext system.

From January 1994, the SEHK relaxed certain provisions relating to short selling of stocks – previously illegal in Hong Kong. The change was designed to enable institutional investors to hedge their positions without breaking the law or infringing local tax regulations. At first, 17 designated securities became eligible to be sold short. The regulations were further liberalised in March 1996 when the number of designated stocks was increased to 241 from 1 May 1997 and again to 310 from 12 January 1998 and the "tick rule", which had prohibited short selling except when the specified stock was on an uptick, was also abolished. "Naked" short selling (ie, the sale of stocks where the seller has not borrowed or made arrangements to borrow in sufficient quantity) remains an offence under the Securities Ordinance.

B) List of principal brokers

BZW (ASIA) LTD
16th Floor, 2 Pacific Place, 88 Queensway
Tel: (852) 2841 5148; Fax: (852) 2868 0092

JAMES CAPEL ASIA LTD
5th Floor, Hutchinson House, 10 Harcourt Road, Central
Tel: (852) 2843 9111

W I CARR (FAR EAST) LTD
43rd Floor, 1 Exchange Square, 8 Connaught Place, Central
Tel: (852) 2820 7373; Fax: (852) 2868 1524

CROSBY SECURITIES LTD
27th Floor, 2 Pacific Place, 88 Queensway
Tel: (852) 2844 4988; Fax: (852) 2845 5154

HG ASIA LTD
30th Floor, Edinburgh Tower, The Landmark, Central
Tel: (852) 2868 0368

JARDINE FLEMING SECURITIES LTD
45th Floor, Jardine House, 1 Connaught Place, Central
Tel: (852) 2843 8888; Fax: (852) 2810 6558

SALOMON BROTHERS HONG KONG LIMITED
Three Exchange Square, 20/F, 8 Connaught Place
Tel: (852) 2501 2000; Fax: (852) 2501-8146

SMITH BARNEY (ASIA) LIMITED
Suites 1001-1006, Two Pacific Place, 88 Queensway
Tel: 852 2844 6688; Fax: 852 2844 6764

SBCI
21st Floor, One Exchange Square, 8 Connaught Place
Tel: (852) 2842 1222

SUN HUNG KAI SECURITIES
Level 12, 1 Pacific Place, 88 Queensway
Tel: (852) 2822 5678; Fax: (852) 2822 5664

WARBURG SECURITIES (FAR EAST)
20th Floor, Alexandra House, 16-20 Chater Road, Central
Tel: (852) 2524 6113

C) Settlement and transfer

The settlement period for members of the SEHK is T+2. The Hong Kong Securities Clearing Company (HKSCC) acts as a medium through which brokers, custodian banks and other financial institutions account for their transactions with each other and through which settlement takes place. CCASS is a computerised book entry clearing and settlement system, under which there are plans for share certificates to become immobilised and for receipt and delivery of shares to be electronically recorded as movements between stock accounts held at the HKSCC.

Most trades in Hong Kong settle against physical broker cheques. Banks may also use an electronic funds transfer system – the Clearing House Automated Transfers System (CHATS).

D) Commissions and other costs

Buyers and sellers of shares and bonds are charged a brokerage fee of not less than 0.25% of the value of the transaction. The minimum charge for brokerage is HK$50. An ad valorem stamp duty is also payable by both the purchaser and the vendor, at a rate of 0.15% (although stock lending and borrowing transactions are exempt). In addition, instruments of transfer must bear a HK$5 embossed stamp before being signed. Overseas institutions are advised to maintain a securities account with a local bank for safe custody. The exchange charges a transaction levy of 0.011% of the amount of the consideration for each purchase or sale of securities, payable by both buyer and seller. A trading tariff of HK$0.50 must be paid to the exchange on each and every purchase or sale transaction.

Nominee companies

A 0.5% commission is deducted from each dividend paid on scrip registered in the name of a nominee company, with a minimum charge of HK$10 and a maximum of HK$2,500.

Registration of shares

A fee of HK$2.50 per scrip is payable to the registrar. The transfer deeds must be completed and signed by the buyer or his nominees and the signature duly witnessed. Given that registration takes place within four to six weeks, there is a period after purchase when the stock cannot be sold.

TAXATION AND REGULATIONS AFFECTING FOREIGN INVESTORS

A) Taxation

Dividends are not taxable, either by way of withholding or otherwise. There is no tax on capital gains.

Hong Kong has not entered into any comprehensive double tax agreements with other countries. It has a territorial system of taxation, and generally only profits derived from a trade or business in Hong Kong or arising from Hong Kong services are subject to tax.

There is no provision for double tax relief for certain types of income earned and taxed in another country. Relief is generally limited to deductions for foreign withholding taxes, as well as net profit taxes on interest income and gains from the sale of certificates of deposit and bills of exchange. No other relief is given for net income taxes paid.

B) Exchange control and repatriation of funds

There are no exchange control regulations operating in Hong Kong and investors have total flexibility in the movement of capital and the repatriation of profits. Funds invested in Hong Kong can be repatriated at will and dividends and interest are freely remittable.

There are no restrictions on foreign portfolio investment in Hong Kong, nor are there limitations regarding ownership of domestic securities by foreigners.

C) Non-resident bank accounts

There are no regulations restricting the freedom of overseas companies or individuals to maintain bank accounts in Hong Kong.

LISTING AND REPORTING REQUIREMENTS

A) Listing requirements

All companies must satisfy the rules governing the listing of securities on the SEHK (the "Listing Rules") before listing of and permission to deal in shares can be granted. These rules cover the size of the company, the amount of capital that must be offered to the public and the disclosure of comprehensive details regarding the company's assets, liabilities, three-year trading record and future prospects.

All new applicants must meet profit record requirements for the three financial years immediately before the application for listing: specifically, profit attributable to shareholders must not be less than HK$20 million in the most recent year, and an aggregate of HK$30 million for the preceding two years. Extensive financial disclosure and reporting requirements are also imposed in relation to annual accounts and listing documents.

B) Reporting requirements

Compulsory undertakings given to the SEHK by listed companies cover, for example, the following matters:

1) *General obligation*: the company must keep the SEHK and shareholders informed as soon as reasonably prac-

ticable of any information relating to the company and its subsidiaries necessary to enable shareholders and the public to appraise the position of the company.

2) *Accounts*: the periods within which listed issuers must prepare and make available to their shareholders their interim and final accounts are three months after the period-end for interim results and five months after the year-end for final results. All issuers are required to include in their accounts a statement of reserves available for distribution to shareholders as at each financial year-end. A statement showing the interest of each director and chief executive and of substantial shareholders in the share capital of the company and, in the case of directors and chief executives, the associated corporations of the company must be included. Disclosures regarding bank loans, overdrafts and other borrowings by the company and its directors are also required.
3) *Dividends*: the company must inform the SEHK immediately after approval by its board of directors of any decision to recommend or not to recommend a dividend, and of any preliminary announcement of profits or losses for any year or other period.
4) *Code of best practice*: listed issuers are required to include in all annual reports and interim reports a statement of compliance with respect to the guidelines set out in Appendix 14 of the Listing Rules. These guidelines are intended to form the skeleton of a code of best practice for directors of listed companies.

SHAREHOLDER PROTECTION CODES

A) Significant shareholdings

The Securities (Disclosure of Interests) Ordinance (Cap. 396) requires disclosure of beneficial interests of directors and chief executives in securities of a listed company and its associated corporations as well as those of persons holding over 10% of the voting share capital of a listed company. A "listed company" in this context includes foreign companies with securities listed on the SEHK. An associated corporation of a listed company includes its holding company and subsidiaries.

B) Takeovers and mergers

The Code on Takeovers and Mergers (the "Takeovers Code") which affects all public listed companies in Hong Kong is administered by the Executive Director of the Corporate Finance Division of the SFC. The Takeovers Code aims to provide for the following:

- all shareholders must be afforded fair treatment, with all shareholders of the same class to be treated on the same basis;
- shareholders must be enabled to make an informed decision as to the merits of an offer by mandatory disclosure of timely and adequate information;
- if any person (or group of persons acting "in concert") acquires shares which carry 35% or more of the voting rights of a company, or any person (or concert group) holding 35-50% acquires an additional 5% of the voting rights, in the 12-month period prior to such additional acquisition, a general offer must be made.

Holders of 10-35% of the voting rights are obliged to report transactions that result in their holding more or less than the 10% lower threshold, and dealings that result in an adjustment to their holdings above or below any whole percentage figure within the range of 10-35%.

In recommending the acceptance or rejection of any offer, directors must have regard to the interests of the shareholders as a whole. If any of the company's directors is faced with a conflict of interest, the company should establish an independent board committee. Restrictions on dealings by the offeror in shares of the offeree are imposed during the offer period.

C) Insider trading

In essence, the Securities (Insider Dealing) Ordinance provides that a person who is connected with a listed company and is in possession of price-sensitive information not available to the general public may not deal in the securities of that company, or any affiliated company.

Although offences can be committed under the Ordinance (for example where a person refuses to co-operate with an enquiry or to tell the truth at an enquiry), insider dealing in itself is still not a crime. However, the Insider Dealing Tribunal has extensive powers to impose penalties on insider dealers. The Tribunal must publish its findings and it may then also make orders to:

a) disqualify a director from being a director, liquidator or manager of (or otherwise involved in the management of) a listed company or any other specified company for a specified period up to five years;
b) make an insider dealer pay the government an amount calculated as the value of the profits made or loss avoided;
c) fine an insider dealer an additional amount up to a maximum of three times the amount of the profit made or loss avoided; and
d) require an insider dealer to contribute to the expenses of conducting the investigation.

D) Compensation fund

Up to HK$8 million (per stockbroker involved) is payable out of the United Exchange Compensation Fund to any person who suffers loss through the default of a stockbroker.

E) Buy-back and financial assistance

A listed company may conduct share repurchases on the SEHK provided that it has obtained a mandate from its shareholders to do so. At present, the Listing Rules provide that a maximum of up to 10% of the issued share capital of a listed company may be repurchased during a prescribed period (generally within a financial year).

In the case of a Hong Kong incorporated company, in order for a buy-back to occur, the purchase price must be financed out of distributable profits or the proceeds of a new issue of shares. Shares that are bought back are treated as cancelled.

It is generally unlawful for a company or any of its subsidiaries to give financial assistance directly or indirectly for the purpose of acquiring shares in that company before, at the same time as or after the acquisition takes place.

RESEARCH

Most of the larger stockbroking firms have a research capability and publish regular reports for distribution to clients. Some of the best research is provided by Sassoon, Merrill Lynch, Asia Equity, Jardine Fleming, Morgan Stanley, Goldman Sachs, Schroders, Lehman Brothers, Bear Stearns, SB Corp, BZW, HG Asia, James Capel Asia and SBC Warburg.

The major banks, including Hongkong and Shanghai Bank, Hang Seng Bank and Standard Chartered Bank, also produce research on the local economy.

Daily newspapers providing information on the stock market include the *South China Morning Post, China Daily,* the *Hong Kong Standard* and *Asian Wall Street Journal* (in English) and the *Hong Kong Economic Journal* and *Financial Daily* (in Chinese). A weekly magazine, the *Far East Economic Review,* contains useful political, economic and business articles.

CHAPTER

27

Hungary

Introduction

Hungary's stock market reopened in 1990, having been closed for the previous 45 years, and 1997 proved to be another successful year after the record-breaking 1996, which saw 136% growth in US dollar terms. The market rose by 56.6% in US dollar terms, and end-1997 market capitalisation as a percentage of GDP rose from about 12% to 34%. Outperformers included the Hungarian blue chips Richter (pharmaceuticals), OTP (banking) and MOL (oil and gas).

Unlike other eastern European countries, Hungary has privatised most of its medium-sized and large companies through strategic sales rather than voucher schemes, and this has deprived the market of some of its best listing prospects. However, the amended Securities Act should result in several new listings (eg, of electricity distributors and banks), while various small and medium-sized private companies are expected to come to the market for fresh capital during 1998-99.

The BSE has become a little more representative of the economy, with 1997 listings for three companies (Mezőgép, NABI and Rába) from the automotive sector (representing 10% of total exports) and Matáv from the telecoms sector. Some important sectors are still under-represented, however, such as financial services (especially insurance) and heavy industry.

Trading is still concentrated in the largest 10 companies, which represent 20% of listings on the exchange but 87.6% of free float and 89.3% of turnover. Following the listing of Matáv in late November, the concentration has become even greater.

ECONOMIC AND POLITICAL OVERVIEW

Recent opinion polls indicate that the governing Hungarian Socialist Party (or MSZP) will win more seats than its rivals at the forthcoming parliamentary elections in May 1998. Approximately 37% of decided voters favour MSZP. A coalition with its current junior partners, the Free Democrats (SZDSZ), looks most likely, although an alliance with the third-placed party, the Young Democrats (FIDESZ), cannot be ruled out. A new socialist-led coalition would almost certainly continue current economic policies.

Real GDP grew by 3.9% during the first three-quarters of 1997, and the ratio of current account deficit to GDP fell year-on-year from 3.8% to 2.3%. The trade deficit has declined substantially, due to a rapidly narrowing gap between exports (38.5% year-on-year growth) and imports (27.1%). Industrial output increased by 16.1% year-on-year in December 1997.

In May 1997 Hungary received encouragement from the EU country studies, and accession negotiations are due to start in April 1998. Hungary could join to the EU in 2002. In November 1997, 85% of voters registered approval for membership of NATO, and negotiations are underway on this front also.

Role of the central bank

Following the creation of a two-tier banking system, the National Bank of Hungary (NBH) has evolved into a more traditional type of central bank, with responsibility for monetary policy and with virtually complete autonomy. Until recently the NBH also managed the country's external debt, but this function was taken over by the state Treasury in early 1997.

Currency reserves in 1997 were adequate to cover approximately six months of imports, and are therefore comfortably above the levels thought necessary to push for complete currency convertibility. Nevertheless, the Hungarian forint remains subject to some capital controls and the currency is on a crawling peg introduced in March 1995. The current rate of devaluation is 0.9% per month, but this may be reduced to 0.8% by the second half of 1998.

NBH President, Gyorgy Surányi, who is thought of as a monetarist and an inflation hawk, has a six-year term of office.

Exhibit 27.1: BUDAPEST (BUX) PRICE INDEX (US$), 1993–97

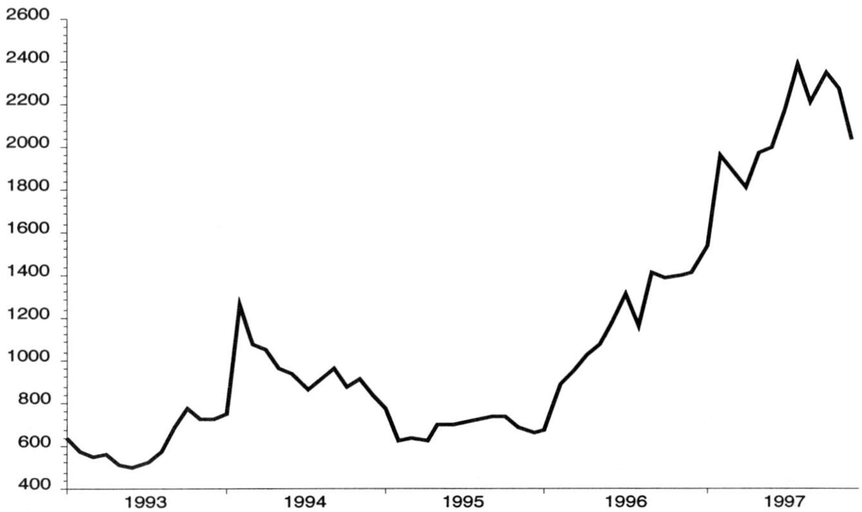

High value 2386.4 1.8.97 Low value 504.7 1.6.93 *Source: Datastream*

MARKET PERFORMANCE

A) In 1997

In a year of records for the Budapest exchange, turnover, at Ft27.3 billion (US$134 million), was higher than the total turnover of the preceding six years (and was almost six times that of 1996).

Total market capitalisation more than doubled during the year, including a capitalisation increase of 259% in the equity market. There were spectacular volume increases on the futures market as well, with 1997 turnover up 600% at Ft1,415.9 billion.

Having reached an all-time high at the beginning of August 1997 (8,483.79 points), the BUX Index ended the year at 7,999.1, up 93.4% on the end-1996 figure.

B) Summary information

Global ranking by market value (US$ terms, end-1997): 44
Market capitalisation (end-1997): US$15.03 billion
Growth in market value (local currency terms, 1993–97): 3,643.5%
Market value as a % of nominal GDP (end-1997): 34.44%
Number of domestic/foreign companies listed (end-1997): 47/2
Market P/E (end-1997): 25.4
MSCI Index (change in US$ terms, 1997): +93.4%
Short-term (3-month) interest rate (end-1997): 19.34%
Long-term (5-year) bond yield (end-1997): 17.29%
Budget deficit as a % of nominal GDP (1997): 4.6%
Annual increase in broad money (M3) supply (end-1997): 12%
Inflation rate (1997): 18.4%
US$ exchange rate (end-1997): Ft203.5

C) Year-end share price index, price/earnings ratios and yields

Exhibit 27.2:
YEAR-END SHARE PRICE INDEX, P/E RATIOS AND GROSS DIVIDEND YIELDS, 1993–97

Year-end	*BUX Index*	*P/E*	*Yield (%)*
1993	1,229	19.1	4.3
1994	1,470	10.5	2.8
1995	1,529	10.9	1.9
1996	4,134	16.5	1.4
1997	7,999	25.4	0.8

Source: Budapest Stock Exchange.

D) Market indices and their constituents

The Budapest Stock Index (the BUX, based at 1,000 on 2 January 1991) comprises the 24 most liquid stocks on the BSE. Calculation of the index is modelled on the German DAX.

In 1995, a new index was introduced – the Central European Stock Index (CESI) – with a base of 1,000 points at 30 June 1995. The CESI measures the price performance of 64 companies (selected by specified criteria) on five central European securities exchanges – in Bratislava, Budapest, Ljubljana, Prague and Warsaw.

THE STOCK MARKET

A) Brief history and structure

The Budapest Stock Exchange was established in June 1990 as a self-governing, non-profit exchange owned by its members.

There are 62 corporate members of the BSE, many of them owned by foreign banks and brokerage houses. Brokerage firms are allowed to execute transactions for both their own and clients' accounts. There are several foreign brokerage firms active on the BSE.

The Hungarian Banking and Capital Market Supervision (HBCMS) is the supervisory authority of the Hungarian securities market, while the legal framework of the stock exchange is laid down in the Securities Act of 1996/CXI. The by-laws of the BSE contain detailed rules covering the operation of the market, and the conditions applying to market traders. The general meeting of the BSE decides on modifications to its charter, while the BSE council is entrusted with the approval and amendment of the rest of the rules. The HBCMS has final approval for all BSE rules and regulations.

B) Different exchanges

The BSE is the only securities exchange in Hungary.

C) Opening hours and address

Official trading hours are 10.15am to 1.15pm, Monday to Friday. Futures trading takes place between 10.30am and 12.30pm, also from Monday to Friday.

THE BUDAPEST STOCK EXCHANGE
Deák Ferenc u. 5
Postal Address: H-1364 Bp., Pf.24, H-1052 Budapest
Tel: (36) 1 117 5226; Fax: (36) 1 118 1737

MARKET SIZE

A) Number of listings and market value

BSE share market capitalisation rose by 259% during 1997 and ended the year at Ft3,058.4 billion. Capitalisation of all securities traded on the exchange increased from Ft2,392.9 billion to Ft5,144.59 billion over the same period. Government bonds and Treasury bills accounted for 36% of total capitalisation.

Exhibit 27.3:
NUMBER OF COMPANIES LISTED AND MARKET VALUE OF SHARES, BSE, 1993–97

Year-end	*No. of companies*	*Equity market value (Ft billion)*
1993	28	81.7

Exhibit 24.7 continued

1994	40	181.5
1995	42	328.8
1996	45	852.5
1997	49	3,058.4

Source: Budapest Stock Exchange.

B) Largest quoted companies

Exhibit 27.4:
THE 10 LARGEST COMPANIES LISTED ON THE BSE, END-1997

Ranking	*Company*	*Total capitalisation (Ft billion)*
1	Matáv Rt	1,124.41
2	MOL	487.08
3	Richter	431.05
4	OTP	207.82
5	Egis	99.66
6	TVK	82.32
7	BorsodChem	75.11
8	Graboplast	56.28
9	Rába Rt	50.97
10	Danubius	49.60

Source: Budapest Stock Exchange.

C) Trading volume

Equity turnover amounted to Ft2,872.71 billion in 1997, an almost six-fold increase on 1996.

Exhibit 27.5:
BSE TURNOVER DATA, 1993–97

Year-end	*Equity turnover (Ft billion)*	*Total turnover (Ft billion)*	*Average daily turnover (Ft million)*
1993	18.24	185.69	736.90
1994	52.00	224.57	891.20
1995	87.27	253.18	1,016.79
1996	490.53	1,145.44	4,618.70
1997	2,872.71	6,736.31	27,272.5

Source: Budapest Stock Exchange.

TYPES OF SECURITIES

In addition to shares, T-bills, government bonds, investment notes and compensation notes are also traded. Compensation notes have been issued by the government as partial recompense for unjust damage to property caused by the previous regime, and can be exchanged for shares or traded for cash on the BSE.

The majority of BSE trading continues to be in bonds and short-term, fixed-rate instruments – mainly government debt securities, such as Treasury bills.

OTHER MARKETS

A BSE derivatives market opened in 1995. Futures traded include the BUX Index, Treasury bills, one-month and three-month Bibor (the Budapest interbank offered rate, published since August 1996) and currency contracts. Foreigners are authorised to trade in BUX futures contracts.

INVESTORS

About 60% of the market's free float is held by foreign investors, which fall into two groups – dedicated regional funds and global funds. Domestic institutions, with the recent advent of private pension funds, have developed a presence in the market and should grow strongly in the next five to ten years. Over the past two years they have increased their assets from zero to Ft57 billion. Mutual funds and insurance companies each had about Ft250 billion (US$1.2 billion) under management in 1997. Thus, including other funds (companies and municipalities), the total amount managed by domestic institutional investors stands at about US$3.0 billion, although the proportion of these assets invested in the local equity market remains low (on average, under 10%).

OPERATIONS

A) Trading system

The VAX-based Central Market Support System (CMSS) began operations in 1993, and BSE member firms have their own workstations. This system was backed up in 1996 by the introduction of the "Prompt Market", which facilitated automated continuous trading.

CMSS is planned to be replaced by the MMTS (Multi Market Trading System) by the summer of 1998. This change is considered as Budapest's "Big Bang" because remote trading will be introduced. All equity, fixed-income (including primary auctions) and derivatives trading will be carried out via MMTS, which will also allow more flexible trading involving, for example, stop-loss orders and negotiated deals.

B) List of principal members

Membership of the BSE is open only to companies, both local and foreign-owned, whose sole activity is dealing in securities. Since 1993, banks have been allowed to operate on the exchange only through single-purpose subsidiaries. From January 1997, the new Securities Act has allowed investment banks to engage in securities dealing.

There are three types of members: (i) agents, with a minimum Ft20 million of registered capital, which can only trade on behalf of their clients; (ii) broker-dealers, with basic capital of at least Ft100 million, which can trade for clients and on their own account; and (iii) investment banks, with a minimum registered capital of Ft1 billion, which can also introduce and underwrite new issues to the BSE and offer margin purchase facilities for their customers. At the end of 1997, 62 firms were members of the exchange.

CA IB SECURITIES
Nagysándor J. utca 10, 1051 Budapest V
Tel: (36) 1 269 0711; Fax: (36) 1 269 0699

CREDIT SUISSE FIRST BOSTON BUDAPEST
Nagyjeno u 12, H-1126, Budapest
Tel: (36) 1 202 2188; Fax: (36) 1 201 9196

DAIWA-MKB
Rakoczi utca 1-3, 1088 Budapest
Tel: (36) 1 266 0364/266 0367; Fax: (36) 1 266 4762

WOOD & COMPANY
Szechenyi Rkt 8, Budapest 8-1054
Tel: (36) 1 268 1525; Fax: (36) 1 268 1529

Exhibit 27.6:
COUNTRY FUNDS – HUNGARY

Fund	*US$ % change* 01/01/97 01/01/98	01/01/93 01/01/98	Fund base currency	Fund size (US$ mil)	Fund volatility	Management group	Opal main sector	Opal subsector
Hungarian Investment Co Ltd	35.02	74.13	US$	N/A	7.221	Govett & Co	Open-End	Equity
First Hungary Fund Ltd	32.75	63.83	US$	122	4.706	First Hungarian	Private	Equity
CA Growth Fund	17.64	N/A	Ft	622.18	4.756	CA IB	Closed-End	Equity

Note: details for some funds may not have been included if the data for the US$ % change for 97/98 was not available

Source: Standard & Poor's Micropal.

C) Settlement

Transactions carried out on the BSE are settled on a T+5 basis by the Central Clearing House and Depository (Budapest) Ltd (KELER).

The money and security positions of every broker are multilaterally netted on a delivery versus payment (DVP) basis, although KELER plans to introduce a system of real-time gross settlement (RTGS).

The amended Securities Act has also introduced dematerialisation, whereby physical securities are replaced by an electronic signal on a securities account and change hands by transfer between accounts held at a depository. At the moment it is not a compulsory system, however, and issuers may opt to keep printed physical securities.

D) Commissions

Brokerage fees vary depending upon the level of service provided and the type of security traded. Typically, fees for dealing in shares are below 0.5% for institutional clients and in the range of 0.8-1.0% for retail clients.

TAXATION AND REGULATIONS AFFECTING FOREIGN INVESTORS

A) Investment regulations

Foreign direct investment may be made in Hungary through the establishment of a wholly owned limited liability company, through establishing a limited liability company or joint stock company that raises capital via a public subscription for shares, or by purchasing shares or an ownership interest in an existing limited liability or a listed or unlisted joint stock company.

There is no general restriction under Hungarian law regarding foreign business participation and investment in Hungary, but foreign participation in certain strategic activities (eg, defence and energy) is limited.

Foreign contributions or foreign purchases of shares inHungarian companies are required to be made in convertible currency or from a convertible forint account. Foreign shareholders are also required to hold registered shares as opposed to bearer shares. If bearer shares are acquired by a foreigner, such shares must be converted into registered shares within three months (or one year if acquired through inheritance).

B) Taxation

Business organisations formed in Hungary, or foreign entrepreneurs carrying on a business in Hungary through a permanent establishment, are subject to a corporate tax on profits earned in Hungary. The corporate tax rate is 18%. In addition, a 20% withholding tax on distributed cash dividends must be withheld and paid by the entity distributing the dividend. The withholding tax may be wholly or partly reclaimed by a foreign recipient if an applicable tax treaty concluded with Hungary provides for a reduced or zero rate. No branch remittance or withholding tax is levied on the repatriation of profits to the head office.

Foreign organisations that do not have a permanent establishment (premises) in Hungary but which receive certain Hungarian-source income (eg, interest and royalties) are subject to a withholding tax of 18%, which must be deducted and remitted by the Hungarian payer of this income. If this withholding tax is reduced under one of the tax treaties concluded with Hungary, the foreign organisation may reclaim the difference between the tax remitted by the Hungarian payer and the tax due under the applicable treaty by submitting a residence certificate (issued by the home tax authorities) and a reclaim form to the Hungarian tax authorities. A refund will be granted in Hungarian forints. In order to convert this into foreign currency, a convertible forint account should be opened by the foreign recipient of the income.

Tax holidays and partial exemptions and credits have been gradually abolished or reduced in recent years. Only a limited number of tax incentives are available in connection with special activities.

Unless reduced by a double tax treaty, withholding taxes are levied on certain payments to individuals: on dividend payments a 20% or 27% tax must be withheld. Capital gains derived from the sale of securities are subject to a 20% tax (although capital losses derived from the sale of securities quoted on the BSE are deductible from capital gains). Hungary has concluded tax treaties with over 40 countries, including all of its major western European partners, Japan and the USA. In general those treaties reduce or eliminate withholding taxes.

C) Foreign exchange

Although the Hungarian forint is not a fully convertible currency, there are certain protections available to investors in Hungary concerning foreign exchange. Dividends and proceeds received on the sale of an investment or on liquidation may be converted into the currency of original investment. In addition, a foreign investor may face business risks due to possible devaluations of the forint.

LISTING AND REPORTING REQUIREMENTS

Public offers of securities within Hungary may be made pursuant to approval of a prospectus by the HBCMS. Before a Hungarian company can issue shares abroad, the permission of the HBCMS must be sought.

There are two listing categories on the BSE – Category A and Category B. The principal requirements for a full listing on the BSE are that: the market value of the securities is at least Ft5 billion (Ft100 million for Category B securities); the minimum number of holders is 1,000 (36 for Category B securities); and at least 25% or Ft5 billion (10% or Ft200 million for category B securities) of the securities are in public hands.

Once listed, a company must conform to certain continuous disclosure requirements. Companies must publish and file with the BSE quarterly reports (Category A) or semi-annual reports (Category B) within 45 days of the end of each period. In addition, an annual report must be filed by each listed company (by 30 April) containing the company's audited annual statements.

Investment funds must file a semi-annual report as described in the Hungarian Investment Funds Act of 1991.

SHAREHOLDER PROTECTION CODES

The Foreign Investment Act (1988) provides full protection for foreign investors against nationalisation, and allows profits, dividends and capital to be remitted overseas. The Hungarian Companies Law establishes a limited right of minority security holders to bring an action against a company. However, the concept of derivative shareholder suits is far from fully developed in Hungary.

The Securities Act provides that the issuer and the underwriter are jointly and severally responsible for any damage incurred by an owner of shares as a result of any misleading information given in the prospectus. In such a case, the public prosecutor and the HBCMS may institute legal proceedings against the issuer and underwriter to render contracts null and void.

The Hungarian Securities Act also provides for the offence of insider dealing.

Hungary has signed bilateral investment protection treaties with most western European countries, and is a member of ICSID (the International Centre for Settlement of Investment Disputes) and MIGA (the Multilateral Investment Guarantee Agency). Investment protection treaties require that compensation with interest be paid in foreign currency for the nationalisation or expropriation of property, including shares, dividends and distributions on the winding-up of a company.

RESEARCH

Thorough research materials are available in both Hungarian and English. BSE stocks are researched by several major brokers, including CS First Boston in Hungary, CA IB Securities, Wood Securities and Société Générale European Emerging Markets (London).

In addition to brokers' reports, Reuters pages BUAA–BUAF provide a daily market report, a listing of new issues, and securities prices in real time.

CHAPTER 28

India

Introduction

Market capitalisation at the Mumbai (Bombay) Stock Exchange (BSE) increased from Rs4,392.3 billion at end-1996 to Rs5,037.2 billion at the end of 1997. Turnover was Rs1,959.53 billion (up from Rs940.72 billion in 1996), representing 39% of market capitalisation. The BSE, with 5,842 quoted companies, is the most important of the Indian stock exchanges.

At the end of 1997, BOLT (the BSE on-line trading system) had been extended to roughly 200 cities, with 400 V-Sat installations. Broker connectivity also increased to 1,753 stations, including 328 through V-Sat lines.

The National Securities Depository received a boost during the year after the Securities and Exchange Board of India (SEBI) set a deadline of 15 January 1998 for institutional investors to convert their shares in eight top companies into dematerialised holdings.

The government has upped the limit for aggregate Foreign Institutional Investor (FII) holdings in a single company to 30% of the equity, and has upped the limit for a single FII's holding in a single company to 10%. The Budget and Finance Bill in February 1997 drastically reduced corporate and individual tax rates, and as from 1998 income from dividends has been exempted from tax.

ECONOMIC AND POLITICAL OVERVIEW

In 1997 the United Front–Congress Party coalition lost office, as did the United Front administration under I.K. Gujral that succeeded it. In the first half of 1998 the country therefore faces yet another election. At present in India the political position of the BJP Party and its allies looks stronger than that of either the Congress Party (despite Sonia Gandhi – the widow of the late Prime Minister Rajiv Gandhi – having entered politics) or the United Front. The BJP has emphasised the need to fund infrastructure through internal savings, which is likely to help pacify Indian industrialists who, worried about the influence of multinational companies, are demanding a level playing field.

The success of the Voluntary Disclosure of Income Scheme, which was introduced in 1997, is expected to make up for the lower indirect tax collected during the year due to a slowdown in the Indian economy. In February 1997, the government reduced both customs and excise duties on a number of items, while introducing a 2% special import duty across the board. Poor tax collection, however, and additional payments to government employees forced the Finance Ministry to increase this duty by another 3% in September 1997 as a mid-term correction. In addition, the government decided to cut 5% off its expenditure, imposed a 10% countervailing duty on EPCG imports, hiked foreign travel tax by over 100% and cleared a fresh tranche of Public Sectur Unit (PSU) disinvestment. Nevertheless, the targeted fiscal deficit for fiscal year 1997–98 of 4.5% of GDP still looks unlikely.

The Indian rupee took a beating in 1997 as a result of the crisis in Asia. The central bank had to intervene, raising lending rates by as much as 2%, and the rupee ended 1997 at Rs39.28 to the US dollar compared with Rs33.03 at the start of the year.

The role of the central bank

The Reserve Bank of India (RBI) was established in Mumbai in April 1935 as a private bank with a paid-up capital of Rs50 million; it was nationalised on 1 January 1949. The executive head of the RBI is the governor, who is assisted in the administration of the bank by the deputy governor and other executive officers. The bank has a central board of directors supplemented by four local boards at Delhi, Calcutta, Chennai and Mumbai, each covering a regional area – northern, eastern, southern and western India respectively.

Exhibit 28.1: INDIA BSE PRICE INDEX (US$), 1993–97

High value 886.04 1.9.94 Low value 391.69 3.5.93 *Source: Datastream*

The RBI is responsible for issuing currency (other than Rs1 notes and coins, which are issued by the Indian government). It is banker to the central government and state governments. The central government is empowered to borrow any amount it likes from the bank, and hence can influence money supply; state government borrowing, on the other hand, is subject to prescribed limits.

The RBI is also responsible for managing public debt – for example, new issues of government loans and the servicing of outstanding public debt. To this end, the bank administers statutory requirements for financial institutions and commercial banks to invest a minimum proportion of their assets in government (and other approved) securities.

The RBI acts as adviser to the government on banking and financial matters and also:

- keeps the interest cost of government debt as low as is consistent with the financial health and reasonable profitability of financial institutions;
- acts as the bankers' bank, holding cash reserves of banks, lending funds for short periods and providing centralised clearing and remittance facilities;
- requires scheduled commercial banks to deposit with it a portion of their demand and time liabilities in the form of cash reserves as a tool for monetary credit control;
- enjoys extensive powers of supervision, regulation and control over commercial and cooperative banks;
- is responsible for foreign exchange management and control; and
- publishes monetary and banking data required for economic planning.

MARKET PERFORMANCE

A) In 1997

The BSE Sensitive Index, which ended 1996 at 3,085.20, rose during 1997 to close the year at 3,658.98 (up 18.6%). The BSE National Index showed a similar trend, rising from 1,363.38 at year-end 1996 to 1,586.60 at the end of 1997. The BSE-200 opened at 305.68 and closed at 354.45 and the Dollex, which takes into account the dollar/rupee exchange rate, began the year at 142.08 and closed at 150.23.

The early weeks of 1997 saw front-running by local operators in anticipation of strong foreign inflows to the Indian markets. This was further aided by the watershed budget announced by the UF government at the end of February. However, the sudden withdrawal of Congress Party support for the UF government on 31 March pulled the Sensitive Index sharply downwards. With the change of Prime Minister and the acceptance of the Finance Bill 1997 without any significant amendments, the market once again began to move ahead. After peaking in August, however, the Sensitive Index started falling again, partly due to the absence of any signs of economic recovery, deteriorating currencies and stock markets in Asia, and leakage of the Jain Commission Report (investigating Rajiv Gandhi's assassination), which ultimately led to the fall of the UF government and the dissolution of the 11th Lok Sabha. In November and December, FIIs were net sellers for the first time since their entry to the stock market in 1992–93.

B) Summary information

Global ranking by market value (US$ terms, end-1997): 20
Market capitalisation (end-1997): BSE US$128.27 billion; All India US$139.42 billion
Growth in BSE market value (local currency terms, 1993–97): 125%
Market value as a % of nominal GDP (end-Nov 1997): 42.2%
Number of companies domestic/foreign listed (end-1997): 5,842/0
Market P/E (BSE National Index, end-1997): 12.08
MSCI Index (change in US$ terms, 1997): +9.6%
Short-term (3-month) interest rate (end-1997): 7.2%
Long-term (10-year) bond yield (end-1997): 11.32%
Budget deficit as a % of nominal GDP (1997): 5%
Annual increase in broad money (M3) supply (end-1997): 15.9%
Inflation rate (1997): 8.7%
US$ exchange rate (end-1997): Rs39.28

C) Year-end share price index, price/earnings ratios and yields

Exhibit 28.2:
YEAR-END SHARE INDEX, P/E AND AVERAGE GROSS YIELD, 1993–97

Year-end	*BSE National Index*	*P/E*	*Yield (%)*
1993	1,613.64	38.6	0.82
1994	1,863.76	38.6	0.82
1995	1,430.75	22.1	1.57
1996	1,363.38	11.78	1.95
1997	1,586.60	12.08	2.06

Source: The Stock Exchange, Mumbai.

D) Market indices and their constituents

The BSE Sensitive Index (base 1978–79 = 100) comprises 30 leading share issues. It is calculated at 30-second intervals during trading hours and is displayed on the PTI Stockscan Network.

The BSE National Index (base 1983–84 = 100) comprises 100 leading scrips quoted on the major exchanges of Mumbai, Calcutta, Delhi, Chennai and Ahmedabad. It is also displayed on the PTI Stockscan Network.

With the divestment of PSU equity by the government and a sharp increase in the number of companies listed over recent years, it was felt that a new, more representative index was necessary. The BSE-200 (base 1989–90 = 100) was therefore introduced in May 1994. It consists of the equity shares of 200 companies, selected on the basis of market capitalisation, turnover and company fundamentals.

The Dollex tracks market movement in US dollar terms.

THE STOCK MARKET

A) Brief history and structure

The BSE (established on 9 July 1875) is the premier Indian exchange, accounting for more than one-third of trading volume, over 70% of listed capital and over 90% of market capitalisation.

The BSE is a voluntary non-profit association of brokers. The governing board of the exchange is the highest decision-making authority and has wide administrative powers. It has a total strength of 19 directors, nine elected by the members, three government nominees, one Reserve Bank of India nominee, five public representatives, and the executive director who is the chief executive of the exchange. The day-to-day administrative work is carried out by various departments under the supervision and control of the executive director.

Individuals as well as corporate bodies who meet the stipulated eligibility criteria can become members of the BSE. Similarly, designated financial corporations on the recommendation of the government can also become members. At present, there are 638 members, including 306 corporate members.

B) Different exchanges

There are 23 recognised stock exchanges in India. The four largest in terms of market value and listings are Mumbai, the National Stock Exchange, Calcutta and Delhi.

C) Opening hours, names and addresses

Trading hours are 9.30am to 4.00pm Monday to Friday, and 10.00am to 12.00 noon on Saturdays (exclusively for carry-forward sessions).

THE STOCK EXCHANGE, MUMBAI
25th Floor, Phiroze Jeejeebhoy Towers, Dalal Street
Mumbai 400 001
Tel: (91) 22 265 5581; Fax: (91) 22 265 8121
Tlx: 011-85925 STEX IN

CALCUTTA STOCK EXCHANGE
7 Lyons Range, Calcutta 700
Tel: (91) 33 22 93 66; Fax: (91) 33 28 37 24

DELHI STOCK EXCHANGE
3 & 4/4B Asaf Ali Rd, New Delhi 110 002
Tel: (91) 11 27 13 02; Fax: (91) 11 32 67 112

NATIONAL STOCK EXCHANGE
Mahindra Towers, 1st Floor, A-Wing, RBC, Worli
Mumbai 400 018
Tel: (91) 22 496 1525; Fax: (91) 22 493 5631

OVER-THE-COUNTER EXCHANGE OF INDIA
Sir Vithaldas Thackersey Marg., New Marine Lines
Mumbai 400 020
Tel: (91) 22 218 8164; Fax: (91) 22 218 8503

MARKET SIZE

A) Number of listings and market value

As at end-1997 there were 5,842 listed companies on the BSE, with a total market capitalisation of Rs5,037.2 billion.

Exhibit 28.3:
NUMBER OF COMPANIES LISTED AND MARKET CAPITALISATION, BSE, 1993–97

Year-end	*No. of companies*	*Market value (Rs billion)*
1993	3,263	2,235.5
1994	4,413	4,000.0
1995	5,399	4,472.9
1996	5,999	4,392.3
1997	5,842	5,037.2

Source: The Stock Exchange, Mumbai.

B) Largest quoted companies

Exhibit 28.4:
THE 20 LARGEST LISTED COMPANIES ON THE BSE, END-1997

Ranking	*Company*	*Market value (Rs billion)*
1	Oil & Natural Gas Commission	406.39
2	Hindustan Levers	275.55
3	Indian Oil Corporation	270.20
4	Mahanagar Telephone Nigam	154.80
5	ITC	151.79
6	State Bank Of India	128.03
7	Gas Authority Of India	103.80
8	Hindustan Petroleum Corp	102.22
9	Videsh Sanchar Nigam	85.10
10	Bharat Heavy Electricals	84.93
11	Reliance Industries	78.79
12	Tata Engineering & Loco	75.82
13	Bajaj Auto	72.23
14	Bharat Petroleum Corp	62.44
15	Industrial Dev Bank Of India	62.26
16	Idbi Grow I-Nit	59.38
17	Hindalco Industries	55.33
18	Uti-Mastergain92	51.02
19	Larsen And Toubro	50.48
20	Tata Iron & Steel Co	49.43

Source: The Stock Exchange, Mumbai.

C) Trading volume

Turnover on the BSE increased by 108% in 1997, to Rs1,959.53 from Rs940.72 in 1996.

Exhibit 28.5:
TURNOVER ON THE BSE, 1993–97

Year	*Total (Rs billion)*	*Daily average (Rs billion)*
1993	675.20	3.16
1994	851.36	4.23
1995	445.76	2.39
1996	940.72	3.95
1997	1,959.53	7.97

Source: The Stock Exchange, Mumbai.

Exhibit 28.6:
THE 20 MOST ACTIVELY TRADED SHARES ON THE BSE, 1997

Ranking	*Company*	*Turnover (Rs billion)*
1	ITC	433.95
2	Reliance Industries	414.04
3	State Bank (N)	352.32
4	Tata Iron & Steel	111.43
5	Tata Tea	80.03
6	Tata Engineering & Loco	66.94
7	Castrol Industries	43.13
8	Mahanagar Telephone Nigam	37.95
9	Associated Cement Companies	36.67
10	Larsen And Toubro	25.24
11	Bajaj Auto	20.28
12	Hindustan Lever	18.22
13	Bses	17.90
14	Bharat Heavy Electricals	17.33
15	Colgate Palmolive (India)	16.66
16	Gujarat Ambuja Cement	11.03
17	Housing Devlop Fin Corp	10.56
18	Ind Cred & Inv Corp India	10.30
19	Hindustan Petro Corp	8.88
20	Indian Petrochem Corp	8.16

Source: The Stock Exchange, Mumbai.

TYPES OF SHARE

Equity shares of companies are the most actively traded instruments. Preference shares are also traded though the volumes are extremely low.

Companies can issue debentures with detachable warrants and convertible debentures. Participatory investment instruments of closed-end and open-end mutual funds are also traded.

An informal secondary market for units of the Unit

Trust of India (UTI) 1964 Scheme (an open-end mutual fund) has also developed, though these units are not listed on any exchange.

INVESTORS

The total number of shareholders in India today is estimated at more than 25 million (excluding investors in UTI 64 and mutual funds generally). Individual investors are the largest holders of equities. Financial institutions and mutual funds are the second biggest group, followed by joint stock companies, government bodies and others. The bulk of buying and selling orders emanate from individual investors but, in terms of volume of business, the market is dominated by the institutions and mutual funds.

Unit Trust of India (UTI) controls the largest single block of investible funds, but its dominance is gradually being eroded by the entry of other mutual funds.

Commercial banks do not generally invest in shares. They do, however, underwrite new issues and sometimes may acquire shares as a result.

OPERATIONS

A) Trading system

Trading is carried out by members and their authorised assistants from trader workstations (TWS) in their offices, via the BSE on-line trading (BOLT) system. BOLT has replaced the open outcry method of trading. BOLT accepts two-way quotations from members, plus market and limit orders, and matches them according to the matching logic specified in the business requirement specifications (BRS) for this system.

B) List of principal brokers

CFL SECURITIES
Regent Chambers, 2nd Floor, Nariman Point,
Mumbai – 400 021
Tel: (91) 22 285 5163/4; Fax: (91) 22 204 9859

ENAM SECURITIES PVT
24, BD Rajabahadur Compound, Ambalal Doshi Marg,
Mumbai – 400 023
Tel: (91) 22 265 3191; Fax: (91) 22 265 3193

M/S RAJARAM BHASIN & CO
Jeevan Mansion Building, 8/4 Deshbandhu Gupta Road,
New Delhi – 110 055
Tel: (91) 11 572 7359; Fax: (91) 11 572 7361

M/S S RAMDAS
Bhupen Chambers, Dalal Street, Fort, Mumbai – 400 023
Tel: (91) 22 267 4689/267 2676; Fax: (91) 22 262 3400

SALOMON BROTHERS ASIA PACIFIC LIMITED
c/o Suite 501, The Oberoi, Dr. Zakir Hussain Marg
New Delhi 110 601
Tel: 91-11-436-5055; Fax: 91-11-436-5019

ZEN SECURITIES LTD
101, Vijayshree Apartments, Nagarjuna Nagar Colony,
Hyderabad – 500 873
Tel: (91) 40 394 506/7; Fax: (91) 40 374 4506/7

C) Settlement and transfer

For settlement purposes, securities traded on the exchange are classified into three groups: specified shares or "A" group; and non-specified securities, which are sub-divided into "B1" and "B2" groups. Currently, equity shares of the 100 top companies are classified as specified shares. Contracts in this group are allowed to be carried over to subsequent settlements up to a maximum permissible period of 75 days. The B1 group contains 800 relatively liquid securities and the B2 group contains all remaining securities (about 5,968 as at 31 December 1997).

Settlement of transactions takes place on an "account period" basis. The account period is a calendar week.

From September 1997, provided shares are registered in the name of an Indian financial institution, a mutual fund registered with SEBI, an FII registered with SEBI or a scheduled commercial bank, a special no carry-forward rolling settlement (T+5) regime applies.

On 15 October 1997, SEBI made the dematerialisation of equities mandatory for financial institutions, FIIs, banks and mutual funds, and set a deadline of 15 January 1998 for eight shares (Reliance Industries, State Bank of India, Tisco, L&T, ICICI, IDBI, IPCL and Bank of India). This will help solve the problem of bad delivery and ensure timely and faster settlement.

D) Commissions and other costs

Brokerage commission is subject to a ceiling of Rs0.25 per share or 2.5% of the contract value, whichever is higher. There is a minimum charge of Rs25 per contract.

Stamp duty is paid by the buyer at a rate of Rs0.50 for every Rs100 of consideration or part thereof.

TAXATION AND REGULATIONS AFFECTING FOREIGN INVESTORS

A) Income tax

Under the Finance Act 1997, no tax is payable on dividends declared by a company and consequently there is no withholding tax on dividends paid by a company to its shareholders. However, a company declaring a dividend is required to pay income tax at the rate of 10% on the amount of dividend distributed. The rates of tax pre-

Exhibit 28.7:
TOP PERFORMING COUNTRY FUNDS – INDIA

Fund	*US$ % change* 01/01/97 01/01/98	01/01/93 01/01/98	Fund Base Currency	Fund size (US$ mil)	Fund volatility	Management group	Opal main sector	Opal subsector
India Performance Fund	25.22	N/A	US$	N/A	-1	Alpha Global	Open-End	Equity
India Advantage Fund Ltd	24.2	N/A	US$	N/A	-1	Birla Capital	Open-End	Equity
Taj Performance	19.76	N/A	US$	16.93	5.73	Chemical Bank	Closed-End	Equity
Fleming Indian Investmt Trust	15.81	N/A	£	N/A	7.666	Fleming	Closed-End	Equity
India Liberalisation A	15.26	N/A	US$	7	7.226	Alliance Cap	Open-End	Equity
Morgan Grenfell India	15.08	N/A	US$	28.3	-1	Morgan Grenfell	Open-End	Equity
Henderson HF India	14.35	N/A	US$	7.8	7.254	Henderson Tou	Open-End	Equity
India Focus Fund	13.9	N/A	US$	8.6	7.667	Citibank	Open-End	Equity
JF India	12.81	75.23	US$	86.1	8.346	Jardine Fleming	Open-End	Equity
India Investment AG	12.56	N/A	Sfr	18.38	6.831	J Baer/M Stan	Open-End	Equity
Fleming FF India	12.36	N/A	US$	108.8	-1	Fleming	Open-End	Equity
Lazard Birla India IT	12.15	N/A	US$	N/A	13.137	Lazard/Birla	Closed-End	Equity
JF India Fund Inc	12	N/A	US$	94.83	9.168	Jardine Fleming	Closed-End	Equity
Five Arrows GF India	11.2	N/A	US$	6.4	-1	Five Arrows R	Open-End	Equity
Indian Inv Co	10.36	N/A	US$	132.6	7.362	Foreign & Col	Open-End	Equity
India Fund Inc	8.86	N/A	US$	289.11	7.019	Advantage Adv	Closed-End	Equity
Indian Opportunities Fund Ltd	5.43	N/A	US$	138.7	7.506	Martin Currie	Open-End	Equity
Bombay Fund	5.24	N/A	US$	90.28	8.475	Barclays	Open-End	Equity
Invesco India Growth	4.26	N/A	US$	24.1	-1	Invesco Intl	Closed-End	Equity
India Fund B	3.79	N/A	£	102.89	7.778	UTI	Open-End	Equity
India Fund A	3.41	-20.65	£	55.014	7.601	UTI	Closed-End	Equity
CS Equity Trust (Lux) India	3.23	N/A	US$	28.1	-1	Credis Equity	Open-End	Equity
India Growth Fund Inc.	2.34	-17.82	US$	121.2	7.037	UTI	Closed-End	Equity
Schroder India	2.03	N/A	US$	257.4	-1	Schroders	Open-End	Equity
HSBC GIF Indian Equity	1.03	N/A	US$	9	-1	HSBC Asst Mgt	Open-End	Equity
KB India Eq Gth	0.33	N/A	US$	11.6	-1	Kleinwort Bensort	Open-End	Equity
MS India Investment Fund	0.23	N/A	US$	347.99	9.663	Morgan Stanley	Closed-End	Equity
20/20 India Fund	-0.21	N/A	C$	31.5	6.361	20/20 Fund Mgt	Open-End	Equity
Schroder India 21st Century	-0.43	N/A	US$	12.1	-1	Schroders	Open-End	Equity
Guinness Flight Madras Indian	-1.2	N/A	US$	15.6	-1	Guinness Flig	Open-End	Equity
India Magnum Fund	-1.73	7.21	US$	N/A	6.257	Morgan Stanley	Closed-End	Equity
Thornton New Tiger India	-2.02	N/A	US$	3.1	-1	Thornton	Open-End	Equity
Aberdeen Prolific IF Ind Opps	-3.55	N/A	US$	9.9	-1	Prolific Intl	Open-End	Equity
Baring Peacock Fund Ltd	-3.61	N/A	US$	50	7.394	Barings	Closed-End	Equity
Taib Everest	-3.79	N/A	US$	N/A	-1	N/A	Open-End	Equity
Pictet C.F. Indiaval	-4.42	N/A	US$	45.6	-1	Pictet	Open-End	Equity
Dresdner Thornton India	-4.74	N/A	US$	3.5	6.856	Thornton	Open-End	Equity
GT Indian Small Cos B	-4.82	N/A	US$	15.5	6.964	LGT	Open-End	Equity
GT Indian Small Cos A	-5.3	N/A	US$	15.5	6.95	LGT	Open-End	Equity
Pioneer India/A	-7.49	N/A	US$	6.9	7.196	Pioneer	Open-End	Equity
Govett India	-7.94	N/A	US$	10.3	8.028	Govett & Co	Open-End	Equity
Pioneer India/C	-7.97	N/A	US$	0.7	-1	Pioneer	Open-End	Equity
Pioneer India/B	-8.22	N/A	US$	7.5	7.16	Pioneer	Open-End	Equity
Oryx (India) Fund Ltd	-8.52	N/A	US$	12.613	-1	Chescor	Closed-End	Equity

Note: details for some funds may not have been included if the data for the US$ % change for 97/98 was not available

Source: Standard & Poor's Micropal

scribed under the 1997 Finance Act for non-corporate (ie, individual) taxpayers are shown in the exhibit.

Exhibit 28.8:
INCOME TAX RATES FOR NON-CORPORATE ASSESSMENTS

Amount	*Rate*
Below Rs40,000	Nil
Rs40,001 to Rs60,000	15% of the amount by which the total income exceeds Rs40,000
Rs60,001 to Rs150,000	Rs2,000 plus 20% of the amount by which the total income exceeds Rs60,000
Rs150,001 and above	Rs20,000 plus 30% of the amount by which the total income exceeds Rs150,000

Source: Dave & Girish & Co.

B) Capital gains tax

Long-term capital gains (ie, capital gains arising on a sale of shares or any other securities listed on a recognised stock exchange in India, or units of the Unit Trust of India or a mutual fund held for more than one year) are taxed at 20% in the case of individuals (both resident and non-resident) and domestic companies.

Capital gains to a non-resident assessee from the transfer of shares in, or debentures of, an Indian company are computed by converting the cost of acquisition, expenditure incurred for such transfer and the full value of the consideration received or accruing as a result of the transfer into the same foreign currency used in the initial purchase.

Income from units acquired in foreign currency by any offshore fund (approved by the Indian government) and long-term gains made by such funds on the transfer of those units are taxed at a flat rate of 10%. However, no other deductions are allowed. The same tax treatment is given to any income and capital gains from any bonds or shares acquired under any scheme approved by the government.

Interest income of FIIs registered with SEBI is also taxed at 20%. Short-term capital gains arising to an FII are taxed at 30%, while long-term capital gains are taxed at 10%.

Non-resident Indians may, however, opt for a flat rate of tax on dividends and long-term capital gains at 20% without deductions.

Exhibit 28.9:
WITHHOLDING TAX

Residents:

Interest payable is subject to withholding tax at 20%. No tax is withheld on payment of royalties or technical service fees between resident companies. For other residents, interest is subject to withholding tax at a rate of 10%.

Non-resident companies:

Type of transfer	*Withholding %*
Income by way of interest on loans or debts, and income from units not falling in any category mentioned below	20%
Income by way of dividends	Nil
Income on monies borrowed or debts incurred in foreign currencies	20%
Income from Indian mutual funds or unit trusts	20%
Income of approved offshore funds on units purchased in foreign currency and long-term capital gains (ie, on sale or redemption after three years) on transfer of units	10%
Interest income on bonds comprised in foreign currency convertible bonds (FCCBs) or dividends on shares of Indian companies comprising GDRs issued outside India	10%
Income by way of long-term capital gains (ie, one year after conversion of GDRs/FCCBs to shares)	10%
Income of FIIs	
- income from securities (other than units)	20%
- short-term capital gains	30%
- long-term capital gains	10%

Other non-residents:

Any income is subject to a 30% rate, or tax at rates applicable to individuals, whichever is higher (or lower treaty rates); however, in the case of non-resident Indians, the rate is 20% on investment income and long-term capital gains.

Treaty rates	*Rate of interest withholding tax %*	*Rate of dividend withholding tax %*
	0–25	7.5–25

Sources: Price Waterhouse and Dave & Girish & Co.

C) Investment through GDRs

In 1993, the government introduced a scheme by which Indian companies with a consistently good track record of three years or more, can issue FCCBs and ordinary shares through global depository receipts (GDRs). The issuers need the prior permission of the Indian government. A non-resident holder of a GDR may transfer it or may ask the overseas depositary appointed by the Indian issuer company to redeem it. Dividends on GDR shares are taxed at 10% and then paid to the depository. GDR transactions outside India between non-residents are income tax free in India. GDR holders are entitled to a credit for tax deducted, on the basis of certification by the depository.

If the shares are held by a non-resident investor for more than 12 months, the resulting capital gains will be treated as long-term capital gains, and therefore taxed at 10%; if the shares are sold within one year then the capital gains will be considered as short-term gains. No wealth or gift tax is payable on holdings of GDRs. If a non-resident investor opts to convert GDRs into the underlying shares, dividends will be taxed at 10%, in addition to any taxation of long-term capital gains.

D) Exchange regulations

Under the Foreign Exchange Regulation Act 1973 (FERA) as amended, investment is now permitted without any restriction through country funds floated outside India for the purpose of investing in units issued by Indian mutual funds. Foreign investors can also invest freely in shares (including GDRs) and bonds issued by Indian companies under a scheme approved by the government. FIIs are allowed to invest in private placements and through the secondary market subject to a ceiling of 24% of their non-resident investments (including investments of overseas corporate bodies, defined as entities owned by non-resident Indians to the extent of 60%), and subject to such investments not exceeding 10% in each company. FIIs are required to register with SEBI, but they do not need any further approval to buy or sell securities.

LISTING AND REPORTING REQUIREMENTS

A) Listing requirements

Companies can only make a public offering with government permission. The government also controls the premium that a company may charge on its shares for both equity and convertible debenture issues. Under guidelines for merchant bankers issued in 1990, managers to the issue have been made responsible for the reasonableness of claims in the prospectus. They have also to ensure completion of all issue formalities. The minimum subscription for all public/rights issues is set at 90% of the issue amount.

B) Reporting requirements

Listed companies are required to keep the stock exchange informed of any important developments likely to affect the market quotation of their securities. They are required to provide all financial data, balance sheets and analysis of shareholdings to the particular stock exchange where their shares are listed. They must report the dates of meetings of directors when the agenda includes consideration of a dividend, a bonus issue or a closure of books.

Yearly accounts must be made available to shareholders and presented to the stock exchange. Any changes in management plans, takeover bids, etc, must also be reported. In addition, half-yearly unaudited financial results are required to be sent to the exchange within two months of the end of the relevant period, and announcements must be made in the press.

SHAREHOLDER PROTECTION CODES

A) Takeovers

The main points of the new takeover code of 30 January 1997 are as follows:

(1) A mandatory public offer is triggered when either the threshold limit of 10% is crossed or there is a change in management control.

(2) For the purpose of consolidation of holdings, acquirers holding not less than 10% but not more than 51% are allowed "creeping acquisition" (ie, without triggering an offer) up to 2% in any period of 12 months. Any purchase by a person holding more than 51% has to be in a transparent manner through a public tender offer.

(3) An acquirer, including persons currently in control of the company, should make a public offer to acquire a minimum of 20% in cases where the conditions for mandatory public offer mentioned earlier apply.

(4) SEBI is not to be involved in the pricing of an offer, which is essentially a market function. Pricing will be based on parameters such as negotiated price, average of the high and low price for the 26-week period prior to the public announcement and the highest price paid by the acquirer for any acquisition in the same period.

(5) The concept of the "chain period" has been introduced, requiring public offers to be made to each shareholder when several companies are acquired through the acquisition of one company.

(6) An escrow deposit of 10% for offers up to Rs1 million and 25% for offers exceeding Rs1 million shall be made.

(7) The target company shall not strip itself of assets or induct any person onto its board during the period of the open offer.

(8) A conditional offer is allowed subject either to minimum mandatory acceptance of 20% with differential pricing, or to a deposit of 50% of the value of the offer placed in escrow in cases where the bidder does not want to be saddled with the 20% acquisition.

B) Insider trading

An "insider" is a person who is connected with a company or deemed to have been connected with a company, and who may reasonably be expected to have access to unpublished price-sensitive information in respect of securities of that company or any other company, and any other person who has received or has had access to such unpublished price-sensitive information.

Unpublished price-sensitive information is defined as "any information which relates to specific matters relating to or of concern directly or indirectly to a company and which is not generally known or published by such company for general information, but which would if it were so published or generally known, be likely to materially affect the price of securities of that company or any other company in the market."

An offence of insider trading is committed if an insider deals in the securities of a company, either on his own behalf or on behalf of any other person, on the basis of any unpublished price-sensitive information; or communicates such information to any other person, with or without his request for such information; or counsels or procures any other person to deal in securities of any company on the basis of such information.

C) Compensation fund

The BSE has a Customers' Protection Fund. The fund is administered by the exchange and financed by contributions from the stock exchange and brokers. It is used to settle claims from customers against defaulting member brokers. It provides compensation of up to Rs225,000 per single customer.

In addition, a trade guarantee fund (TGF) was established in May 1997. It was created to ensure that market equilibrium is not disturbed in the event of payment crises faced by members.

RESEARCH

Larger stock market participants are increasingly resorting to the use of detailed research as a basis for their trading decisions, and this has led to the creation of a number of stock market databases. Most large stockbrokers and merchant bankers have in-house research teams.

Merchant banks are either subsidiaries/divisions of public sector banks (eg, State Bank of India (SBI) Capital Markets Ltd and Canbank Financial Services Ltd), divisions of foreign banks (like ANZ Grindlays Bank, Standard Chartered Bank, Citibank and Merrill Lynch) or associates of large brokerage houses (eg, Champaklal Investment & Financial Consultancy Ltd, J.M. Financial & Investment Consultancy Services Ltd and DSP Financial Consultants Ltd). These merchant banks do not act as banks or handle funds themselves but undertake the management of public issues for companies and also manage portfolios for clients.

The stock exchanges themselves publish a daily list of quotations that is made available to brokers, investors and others on a subscription basis. Some magazines also specialise in analysing and reporting on equity market trends.

India, published by Euromoney Books, provides in-depth information for those wishing to invest or do business in the country. See the order card at the back of this book for details.

CHAPTER

29

Indonesia

Introduction

There are two stock markets in Indonesia – the Jakarta Stock Exchange (JSX) and the Surabaya Stock Exchange (SSX) – although the main focus is on the JSX, which is more liquid than its rival. Despite 1997's events, market development across the past decade has been impressive. The JSX's market capitalisation has grown from Rp4.3 trillion in 1989 to Rp159.9 trillion (US$28.8 billion) at the end of 1997. The number of listed companies has risen from 56 to 282 across the same period, and annual share turnover has risen from Rp964.3 billion to Rp120.36 trillion (US$21.7 billion). The introduction of the Automated Trading System in April 1995 gave a major boost to liquidity.

Trading by domestic investors has been increasing – they accounted for 48% of 1997 turnover, compared with 29.8% in 1994. This trend is likely to continue with the establishment of new open-ended mutual funds and the increased availability of margin financing.

The stock market is dominated by five main industries. As at the end 1997, the telecommunications sector (which consists of Telkom and Indosat) accounted for 24.4% of market capitalisation, followed by cigarettes at 13.9%. The other large sectors are banking (6.7%), forestry (6.4%) and property (5.8%).

Several Indonesian companies (mostly as a result of privatisation) are cross-listed on overseas exchanges such as Indosat on the NYSE, Telkom on the NYSE and LSE, Tambang Timah on the LSE, and Tripolyta on the NYSE. Indonesia's privatisation programme is expected to continue as the main source of primary market deals for the foreseeable future.

ECONOMIC AND POLITICAL OVERVIEW

Following a speculative attack on the rupiah that brought the currency down from Rp2,400 to the US dollar to Rp3,000, in August 1997 Indonesia adopted a tight money policy. Aiming to limit the rupiah's depreciation, the government restricted market liquidity, which had the effect of increasing interest rates and undermining domestic investor sentiment. The monetary crisis then began.

On 8 October, Indonesia asked for IMF assistance to help restore confidence in the Indonesian economy. On 1 November the IMF agreed to a US$23 billion loan, consisting of US$4.5 billion from the World Bank, US$3.5 billion from the ADB, US$10 billion from the IMF and the balance from Indonesia's substantial external assets. In addition, bilateral donors (Australia, China, the Hong Kong Administrative District, Japan, Malaysia, Singapore and the US) agreed to provide extra finance when necessary. The IMF set some macroeconomic targets to be achieved by Indonesia, including a budget surplus of 1% of GDP starting 1998–99, a current account deficit of less than 3% of GDP within two years and inflation within single figures. Following agreement on the IMF package, the government liquidated 16 banks and, on 3 November, announced a deregulatory package including tariff reductions on certain imported commodities and policy measures to promote exports.

Amidst the crisis, Indonesia is projected to achieve economic growth of 6.3% in 1997, with a possible recession occurring in 1998 that could cut growth to 4.2%. The inflation rate is projected to stabilise at 9.8%, down from 11.05% in 1997. In contrast with the current restrictive monetary policy, the 1998–99 fiscal budget looks expansive, partly due to rupiah depreciation. The budget assumed a clearly unrealistic US dollar exchange rate of Rp4,000. Meanwhile, deposit rates will probably remain above 20%, because any reduction below this is felt likely to engender capital flight that would place further pressure on the rupiah.

Aside from the gloomy economic outlook, the political situation is also giving cause for concern: a new President and Cabinet ministers are due to be appointed in March 1998.

Exhibit 29.1: JAKARTA SE COMPOSITE PRICE INDEX (US$), 1993–97

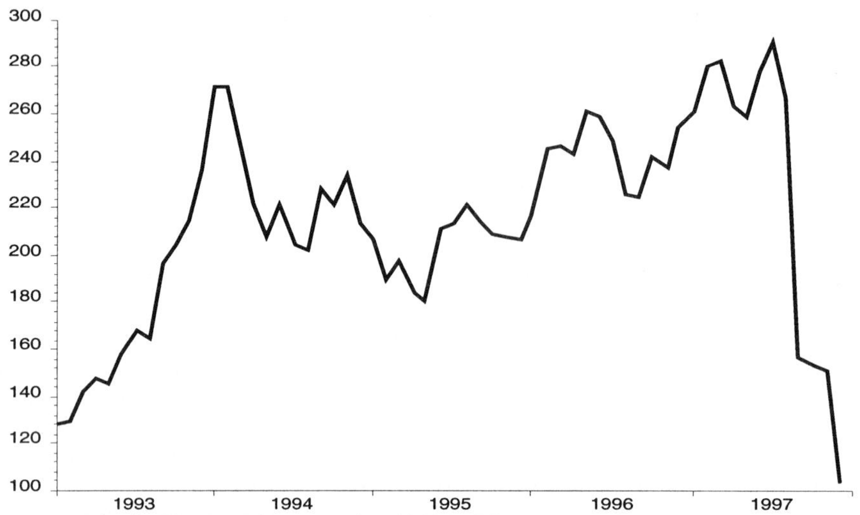

High value 291.17 1.7.97 Low value 103.28 1.12.97 *Source: Datastream*

Role of the central bank

Monetary policy is controlled by the central bank, Bank Indonesia, using a variety of instruments. To control domestic money supply as well as interest rates, Bank Indonesia uses open market operations, buying or selling SBI (Sertifikat Bank Indonesia) and SBPU (Surat Berharga Pasar Uang). It also imposes reserve requirements (which currently stand at 5%), controls the level of domestic credit via lending limits, and monitors capital adequacy ratios.

MARKET PERFORMANCE

A) In 1997

The Indonesian stock market started the year with a continuation of the rally that had begun in the fourth quarter of 1996. The Jakarta Composite Index (JCI) reached a high of 712 in late February. A reversal then brought the index back to 631 by mid-April. Several factors caused this correction, including a hike in US interest rates, lack-lustre calendar 1996 trading results announced by several blue chip companies, and an outbreak of rioting as the general election approached.

In the event, the May general election proceeded smoothly and this boosted confidence in the market, which maintained its bullish trend, leading to a record index high of 741 in July. Robust first quarter corporate results also helped.

By August, the plunging Thai baht had started to destabilise the rupiah. Various central bank initiatives, including doubling the SBI interest rate in order to tighten rupiah liquidity, failed to halt the currency's depreciation. In the stock market it was judged that these measures would have a significant detrimental effect on corporate earnings, and the JCI fell from 721.8 on 1 August to 485.9 on 1 September – down 33% in one month. The market rebounded to around 600 in the first week of September as a result of the government announcement of a wide-ranging economic reform package accompanied by a cut in the one-month SBI rate to 3%. Also, the 49% foreign ownership limit on non-bank shares was abolished.

However, the euphoria was short-lived. The market quickly reversed and continued to decline due to the persistent weakness of the rupiah, despite the IMF assistance package. The Indonesian market received further blows as other Asian economies faltered and as a result of renewed concern about President Soeharto's health. These factors sent the JCI to a new four-year record low of 335 and, by mid-December, the rupiah to an all-time low against the US dollar of Rp6,000.

B) Summary information

Global ranking by market value (US$ terms, end-1997): 38
Market capitalisation (end-1997): US$28.8 billion
Growth in market value (local currency terms, 1993–97): 130.8%
Market value as a % of nominal GDP (end-1997): 13.9%
Number of domestic/foreign companies listed (end-1997): 282/0
Market P/E (all listed companies, end-1997): 11.9
MSCI "Indonesia Free" Index (change in US$ terms, 1997): -74.5%
Short-term (3-month) interest rate (end-1997): 22%

Long-term (5-year) bond yield (end-1997): 30.75%
Budget deficit as a % of nominal GDP (1997E): 3.2%
Annual increase in M2 (end-1997): 16.6%
Inflation rate (1997): 11.05%
US$ exchange rate (end-1997): Rp5,550

C) Year-end share price index and price/earnings ratios

Exhibit 29.2:
JSX COMPOSITE INDEX (Rp TERMS) AND P/E RATIOS, 1993–97

Year-end	*Composite Index*	*P/E*
1993	588.77	28.9
1994	469.64	15.1
1995	513.85	22.7
1996	637.43	17.5
1997	401.71	11.9

Source: Jakarta Stock Exchange.

D) Market indices and their constituents

Share price indices are calculated each day based on regular market closing prices. The main market indicator is the Jakarta Composite Share Price Index, which reflects movements in the market as a whole using stock prices on 10 August 1982 as its base.

The JSX publishes sectoral indices covering 10 industrial sectors and based at 28 December 1995 = 100.

A new index was introduced in February 1997 covering stocks that are of high liquidity and market value. It is called the LQ45 Index and is based at 13 July 1994 = 100.

THE STOCK MARKET

A) Brief history and structure

A stock market has existed in Indonesia since 1912. It was originally established to meet the needs of the Dutch business community and individual Dutch investors. The Jakarta exchange was closed during World War II and remained shut until 1952. Six years later it was closed again when Dutch businesses were nationalised. The re-opening of the exchange by President Soeharto in 1977 was in part the culmination of monetary policies instituted by the government in 1967 to remedy an unfavourable economic environment.

In December 1991, PT Bursa Efek Jakarta, a private company, was established to manage and operate the JSX, taking over from Bapepam (the Capital Market Executive Agency). This was consistent with changes made in 1990 to the role of Bapepam, away from administration and in favour of regulatory supervision. Bapepam therefore now has three principal responsibilities: evaluating and approving new listings; supervising the efficient operation of the capital market; and monitoring the status of listed companies. This supervisory role is given legislative basis in Law No. 8 of 1995 Concerning Capital Markets, the principal source of Indonesia's securities laws.

The JSX has 197 securities houses as exchange members and shareholders. JSX member securities houses consist of underwriters, broker-dealers and investment management companies.

B) Different exchanges

The principal Indonesian stock exchange is in Jakarta. However, in 1989 a second exchange was opened in Surabaya. Shares listed on the SSX are also traded on the JSX and vice versa, although there is no obligation to list shares on both exchanges. The requirements for listing on the JSX are stricter than for the SSX.

C) Opening hours, names and addresses

The JSX and SSX are open Monday to Thursday from 9.30am to 12.00 noon, and from 1.30pm to 4.00pm. On Fridays the exchanges are open from 9.30am to 11.30am and 2.00pm to 4.00pm.

JAKARTA STOCK EXCHANGE
Jakarta Stock Exchange Building
Jl Jendral Sudirman Kav. 52-53, Jakarta 12190
Tel: (62) 21 515 0515; Fax: (62) 21 515 0220
Web site: www.jsx.co.id
E-mail: webmaster@jsx.co.id

SURABAYA STOCK EXCHANGE
Head office
Gedung Medan Pemuda, Jalan Pemuda 2731, Surabaya
Tel: (62) 31 510 646; 512 716; 512 472
Tlx: (62) 31 510 823

Operations office
Plaza Bapindo – Menara 1, 20/F
Jl. Jandral Sudirman Kav. 54-55
Jakarta 12190
Tel: (62) 21 526 6210; Fax: (62) 21 526 6241-3
Web site: www.bes.co.id

MARKET SIZE

A) Number of listings and market value

At the end of 1997, the total market capitalisation of listed shares was Rp159.93 trillion (US$29 billion), a decrease of 68% compared with end-1996.

Exhibit 29.3:
NUMBER OF LISTED COMPANIES AND MARKET VALUE OF LISTED SHARES, JSX, 1993–97

Year-end	*No. of listed companies*	*Market value (Rp billion)*
1993	172	69,299.60
1994	217	103,835.24
1995	238	152,246.46
1996	253	215,026.10
1997	282	159,929.86

Source: Jakarta Stock Exchange.

Exhibit 29.4:
THE 20 LARGEST JSX COMPANIES, END-1997

Ranking	*Company*	*Market value (Rp billion)*
1	HM Sampoerna	38,733.3
2	Indosat Tbk	27,601.1
3	Gudang Garam	24,076.3
4	Telekomunikasi Indonesia	12,694.9
5	Schering Plough Indonesia	10,111.5
6	Tigaraksa Satria	6,783.0
7	Semen Gresik	6,205.2
8	Aneka Kimia Raya	5,272.7
9	Unilever Indonesia	5,250.0
10	Astra International Tbk	4,609.0
11	Daya Guna Samudra Tbk	3,577.9
12	Kalbe Farma	3,088.8
13	Tambang Timah (Persero)	2,492.7
14	Medco Energi Corporation	2,487.7
15	Indofood Sukses Makmur Tbk	2,381.4
16	Lippo Enterprises Tbk	1,822.5
17	Bank Danamon	1,620.3
18	Kawasan Industri Jababeka	1,571.5
19	Hanson Ind Utama Tbk	1,522.5
20	Petrosea	1,520.0

Source: Jakarta Stock Exchange.

B) Trading volume

The value of shares traded rose by 59% in 1997 to Rp120.4 trillion.

Exhibit 29.5:
VALUE OF SHARES TRADED, JSX, 1993–97

Year	*Turnover (Rp billion)*
1993	19,086.24
1994	25,482.80
1995	32,357.50
1996	75,729.89
1997	120,385.17

Source: Jakarta Stock Exchange.

Exhibit 29.6:
THE 20 MOST ACTIVELY TRADED SHARES, JSX, 1997

Ranking	*Company*	*Trading value (Rp billion)*	*Volume (million shares)*
1	Telekomunikasi Indonesia	10,479.21	3,098.29
2	Astra International Tbk	5,950.01	1,980.64
3	Bank Negara Indonesia Tbk	5,115.32	4,328.89
4	Bank International Indonesia	4,661.16	4,482.43
5	HM Sampoerna	3,615.55	433.80
6	Matahari Putra Prima Tbk	2,695.24	1,598.76
7	Bakrieland Development Tbk	2,641.27	1,995.72
8	Putra Surya Multidana Tbk	2,588.37	2,043.05
9	Gudang Garam	2,563.49	268.97
10	Bimantara Citra	2,512.57	1,000.09
11	Lippo Securities	2,276.02	2,496.95
12	Indah Kiat Pulp and Paper	2,236.41	1,761.56
13	Multipolar	2,195.37	2,593.86
14	Asuransi Lippo Life Tbk	2,102.61	1,597.05
15	Citra Marga Nushapala Persada	2,001.33	1,771.36
16	Lippo Bank	1,889.46	1,109.37
17	Semen Gresik	1,825.93	414.06
18	Daya Guna Samudra Tbk	1,787.01	451.52
19	Bank Danamon	1,729.88	2,121.43
20	BDNI	1,727.94	2,104.59

Source: Jakarta Stock Exchange.

TYPES OF SHARE

Instruments traded on the JSX include shares, rights certificates, warrants and bonds.

The principal distinction between shares tends to relate to dividends: preferred shareholders are entitled to priority in payment of accumulated but unpaid dividends. Shares with a fixed return are not allowed.

Listed shares traded on the JSX are in registered form.

OTHER MARKETS

The purpose of the OTC market is primarily to serve as a springboard for smaller, less well-established firms to move across to the JSX. Since its establishment in 1989, the number of companies listed has increased from four to 12, of which five have listed shares and seven bonds. Two firms have made the transition to the JSX.

INVESTORS

Foreign ownership of Indonesian securities used to be restricted to 49% of listed companies. In 1997, the Finance Minister removed this restriction (except in the case of listed Indonesian banks), so that in theory foreign investors may acquire 100% of the listed shares of an Indonesian public company.

The JSX has undertaken active campaigns to increase domestic investors' participation in the capital market, taking roadshows to several Indonesian cities in order to stimulate the population's awareness and interest. Greater levels of domestic investment would add to market liquidity, and provide an incentive for other domestic and foreign investors to tap into the Indonesian market. Despite these efforts, the evidence shows that less than 1% of Indonesian individuals with savings accounts own shares listed on the JSX.

OPERATIONS

A) Trading system

In May 1995, the Jakarta Automated Trading System (JATS) replaced the old manual system. JATS serves as an integrated system connecting trading, clearing and settlement, depository and broker accounting functions.

JATS can accommodate 70,000 transactions daily, and this capacity could be increased to 500,000 transactions a day. The JSX also plans to launch a remote trading mechanism accessible through JATS, which will give brokers access to clients in all 27 provinces of Indonesia.

At present, JATS remains a share certificate-based system, but it is expected that scripless trading and settlement will be introduced in the near future.

Shares can be traded in round or odd lots. On the "regular market" trading is carried out in round lots of 500 shares on the basis of a continuous auction market mechanism with regulated permitted price movements. A round lot for trading in a listed investment fund is 100 shares or units.

Separate from the regular market, there is a "negotiated market" covering:

Exhibit 29.7:
COUNTRY FUNDS – INDONESIA

Fund	*US$ % change* 01/01/97 01/01/98	01/01/93 01/.01/98	Fund base currency	Fund size (US$ mil)	Fund volatility	Management group	Opal main sector	Opal subsector
IndoValue A	18.71	N/A	US$	18.7	-1	IndoValue Cap	Open-End	Equity
SHK Indonesia Fund	-20.33	-22.09	US$	20.16	4.889	SHK Fund Mgt	Closed-End	Equity
Nikko GIUF Indonesia Fund	-50.71	N/A	US$	0.3	9.458	Nikko	Open-End	Equity
Nomura Aurora II Indonesia	-58.88	N/A	¥	300	-1	Nomura ITMCo	Open-End	Equity
JF Indonesia Trust	-60.09	N/A	US$	5.6	13.671	Jardine Fleming	Open-End	Equity
Fidelity Fds Indonesia	-60.93	N/A	US$	15.7	13.625	Fidelity	Open-End	Equity
IAP Indonesia A	-61.07	N/A	US$	2.7	-1	Indosuez	Open-End	Equity
Dres Thornton ASF Indonesia	-63.59	N/A	US$	3.5	15.084	Thornton	Open-End	Equity
JF Indonesia	-63.69	-47.22	US$	29.8	14.439	Jardine Fleming	Closed-End	Equity
Indonesia Equity Fund	-65.65	-56.2	US$	16.818	12.829	Daiwa	Closed-End	Equity
Indonesia Development Fund	-65.68	-59.78	US$	64.13	16.051	Templeton	Closed-End	Equity
MBf Indonesian Growth	-65.89	-70.2	US$	0.2	10.75	MBf	Open-End	Equity
Indonesia Fund	-66.57	-53.21	US$	40.327	13.644	BEA Assoc	Closed-End	Equity
Batavia Fund	-66.77	-33.87	US$	14.764	14.867	Darier Hentsc	Closed-End	Equity
Malacca Fund (Cayman) Ltd	-67.61	-43.67	US$	7.7	13.041	Indosuez	Open-End	Equity
NM ASF Indonesian	-68.22	N/A	US$	2.1	-1	National Mutual	Open-End	Equity
Jakarta Growth Fund	-70.11	-53.61	US$	41.453	14.567	Nomura Intl	Closed-End	Equity
Thornton New Tiger Indonesia	-70.37	-58.82	US$	1.9	21.931	Thornton	Open-End	Equity
Edinburgh Java Trust	-70.5	-63.83	£	N/A	13.931	Edinburgh Funds	Closed-End	Equity
N.Applegate Indonesian Gth	-70.74	-49.21	US$	0.6	14.967	Credit Lyonnais	Open-End	Equity
Lippo Indonesian Growth	-72.61	15.49	US$	16.6	20.463	Lippo Global	Open-End	Equity
Barclays ASF Indonesia	-72.91	-54.08	US$	5.9	17.807	Barclays	Open-End	Equity
Paribas EM Indonesia Ptfl	-73.49	N/A	US$	N/A	15.037	Paribas Asset	Open-End	Equity
Java Fund (Cayman) Ltd.	-75.03	-63.75	US$	19.92	19.868	Lippo Global	Closed-End	Equity
ImPac AP Indonesia	-77.46	N/A	US$	0.5	-1	Impac Asset M	Open-End	Equity
Nomura Jakarta Fund	-79.39	-67.84	US$	8.215	16.62	Morgan Grenfell	Private	Equity

Note: details for some funds may not have been included if the data for the US$ % change for 97/98 was not available

Source: Standard & Poor's Micropal.

- block trading (single trades of at least 200,000 shares);
- odd-lot trading (single trades of less than 500 shares); and
- cross-trading (in circumstances where there is a matching sale order and purchase order for the same stock by the same broker acting for different customers, or a matching sale order and purchase order from brokers at the same price and in the same quantities).

B) List of principal brokers

BARING SECURITIES INDONESIA
11th Floor, Jl. MH Thamrin Kav. 9, Jakarta 10350
Tel: (62) 21 420 7146; Fax: (62) 21 420 7145

BZW NIAGA SECURITIES
21st Floor Graha Niaga, Jl. Jend Sudirman Kav. 58, Jakarta
Tel: (62) 21 523 2221; Fax: (62) 21 523 2269

CREDIT LYONNAIS CAPITAL INDONESIA
1203 Plaza 89, 6, Jl. Raslina Said Kav. X-7,
Jakarta 12940
Tel: (62) 21 850 4549; Fax: (62) 21 850 4514

JARDINE FLEMING NUSANTARA
17th Floor World Trade Center
Jl. Jend. Sudirman Kav. 29-31, Jakarta 12190
Tel: (62) 21 515 1880; Fax: (62) 21 515 1883

LIPPO SECURITIES
8th Floor Lippo Centre
Jl. Gatot Subroto Kav. 35-36, Jakarta 12950
Tel: (62) 21 520 5671; Fax: (62) 21 520 5596

MAKINDO
BNI Building, 27th Floor
Jl. Jend Sudirman Kav. 1, Jakarta 10200
Tel: (62) 21 570 2665

PEREGRINE SEWU SECURITIES
19th Floor, Chase Plaza Tower
Jl Jend Sudirman Kav 21, Jakarta 1290
Tel: (62) 21 250 5410; Fax: (62) 21 250 5417

PT SALOMON BROTHERS NUSA SECURITIES
Gedung GKBI #25-02, JI. Jend. Sudirman No. 28
Jakarta 10210
Tel: (62) 21 574 0955; Fax: (62) 21 574 0981

SIGMA BATARA
Lippo Plaza, 4th/5th Floor
Jl Jend Sudiman Kav 25, Jakarta 12920
Tel: (61) 21 250 3910; Fax: (61) 21 520 3918

WI CARR INDONESIA
Niaga Tower Lt. 20
Jl. Jend. Sudirman Kav. 58, Jakarta 12190
Tel: (62) 21 522 6008; Fax: (62) 21 250 5530

C) Settlement and transfer

Most transactions on the exchange are for regular rather than cash settlement. The basic system is that share certificates and payment must be settled through the exchange clearing and depository companies by T+4.

D) Commissions and other costs

Exchange members charge a negotiable fee for their services of up to 1%.

A securities transaction tax on the sale of listed securities is levied at a rate of 0.1% of the transaction value. In addition, VAT is payable at the rate of 10% on commission fees.

JSX members are required to pay a securities transaction fee of 0.04% of each month's cumulative transaction value for stocks and other registered securities.

TAXATION AND REGULATIONS AFFECTING FOREIGN INVESTORS

Generally, dividends paid by Indonesian corporations to foreign shareholders in approved projects are subject to a withholding tax of 20%, unless a reduced rate has been established by a tax treaty between Indonesia and the country of the foreign investor. Tax treaties have been signed with Australia, Austria, Belgium, Bulgaria, Canada, Denmark, Finland, France, Germany, Hungary, India, Italy, Japan, Republic of Korea, Luxembourg, Malaysia, the Netherlands, New Zealand, Norway, Pakistan, the Philippines, Poland, Singapore, Sweden, Switzerland, Sri Lanka, Taiwan, Thailand, Tunisia, the UK and the US.

Exhibit 29.8:
WITHHOLDING TAX

	Dividends		
	Portfolio %	*Substantial holdings %*	*Interest %*
Resident corporations	0	0	15
Resident individuals	15	15	15
Non-resident corporations and individuals:			
Non-treaty	20	20	20
Treaty	10–20	10–15	10–15

Source: Price Waterhouse and Sigma Batara.

In general, there are no restrictions on the movement of funds into and out of Indonesia. Repatriation of profits by foreign investors in a foreign investment company is permitted at any time, while repatriation of capital is permitted only after any tax concessions given to the foreign investment company have expired, unless the funds remitted are derived from a sale of shares to an Indonesian citizen. The ability of foreign investors to repatriate both capital and profits is guaranteed by the Foreign Capital Investment Law of 1967, as amended.

LISTING AND REPORTING REQUIREMENTS

A) Listing requirements

In order for companies to be listed on the JSX, they must be founded and domiciled in Indonesia and must:

- provide a registration statement as a public company declared effective by Bapepam for a public offering;
- provide a financial statement audited by a public accountant registered with Bapepam, with an unqualified opinion for the most recent fiscal year;
- have a minimum of 200 shareholders, whether individual or institutional;
- have listed all fully paid shares;
- have been founded and in operation for a minimum of three years;
- have operational income and net profits for the past two fiscal years; and
- have minimum total assets of Rp20 billion, minimum stockholders' equity of Rp7.5 billion and minimum paid-up capital of Rp2 billion.

B) Reporting requirements

Public companies are required to submit routine reports and reports on important events to both Bapepam and the JSX. All reports delivered by listed companies to the stock exchange are immediately published for investors through announcements on the exchange floor. Investors can obtain this information directly from the JSX or from brokerage companies.

SHAREHOLDER PROTECTION CODES

The principal regulatory organisation relevant to publicly listed companies is Bapepam. The agency has the power to suspend trading in stocks of companies quoted on the exchange and/or to delist companies in order to protect the interests of public investors.

There are regulations which, among other things, provide protection against fraud in securities trading, market manipulation and false or misleading statements. In addition to the suspension of trading licences, the chairman of Bapepam may impose fines for failure to submit required reports. There is also the possibility of administrative sanctions and criminal prosecution, but no prosecutions of this type have been brought to date.

A) Substantial shareholdings

An individual or company who acquires 5% or more of a listed company must disclose the shareholding and any subsequent changes. Disclosure must be made within 10 days of the relevant transaction date.

B) Mergers and takeovers

Under Bapepam regulations, where a party wishes to acquire 20% or more of a listed Indonesian company, the offeror must make a general "tender offer" to all shareholders. An offer for control of a listed company must be announced in the Indonesian press and an offer statement must be cleared by Bapepam.

Generally, a tender offer must be made where a party acquires, through the stock exchange, shares in a listed company, resulting in the offeror holding 20% or more of such shares, where the acquisition is made for the purpose of "controlling" the target company. Control is defined as the power to influence the company, other than by reason of holding an official position in the company. The target company has the opportunity to submit a statement to Bapepam endorsing or disputing the tender offer. All shareholders in the company may accept the offer in accordance with the terms of the offer document.

Agreed corporate acquisitions, consolidations or mergers are regulated by Indonesia's Law on Limited Companies. The transaction must be approved by three-quarters of the votes validly cast at a general meeting of the shareholders of both companies, at which a minimum of three-quarters of the issued voting shares are represented. In such circumstances, minority shareholders' rights, as well as the best interests of the company and its employees and the interests of the public and healthy business competition, must be taken into account.

C) Insider trading

There are restrictions on insider trading in securities with respect to trading on the JSX and the OTC market. There are no other specific legal provisions with respect to insider trading in other situations (ie, trading in unlisted securities) but the general criminal and civil statutes covering fraud could apply in certain cases.

D) Compensation fund

There is no compensation fund for reimbursement of shareholders who may be the victims of fraud or default by a market broker or trader.

RESEARCH

The JSX produces various publications, including the *Annual Fact Book*, periodical statistics (annual, quarterly, monthly, weekly) and the *Indonesian Capital Market Journal* (in cooperation with ECFIN).

Both international securities firms active in Asia and local brokers are now able to provide analysis and advice on the equity market. Firms in Jakarta include Schroders, PT Sassoon Securities, PT Sigma Batara, PT Makindo, Jarding Fleming Nusantara, BZW and Peregrine.

A useful source of information on the Indonesian economy is the World Bank, JL H.R. Rasuna Said Kav. B-10, PO Box 1324, Jakarta; telephone (62) 21 252 0316.

Indonesia, published by Euromoney Books, provides in-depth information for those wishing to invest or do business in the country. See the order card at the back of this book for details.

CHAPTER 30

Ireland

Introduction

Between 1973 and 1995 the Irish Stock Exchange (ISE) was a constituent unit of the International Stock Exchange of the United Kingdom and Ireland. In December 1995, in response to the EU Directive on investment services, responsibility for regulation of the market was transferred from the London exchange to the Irish central bank, and a separate Board of Exchange was established. However, many of the administrative links with London remain, and Irish companies previously quoted in London are now entitled to "dual primary" listing status.

The Irish market is relatively small; total capitalisation stood at IR£37.1billion at the end of 1997, representing about 54% of GDP. The market is concentrated, with the 15 leading companies accounting for 75% of total market value. As a result, certain sectors are over-represented: financials account for around 40% of market capitalisation, pharmaceuticals 11%, foods 10%, construction 11%, and paper and packaging stocks 8%.

There are three securities markets: the official list (main market), an Exploration Securities Market (ESM) and a Developing Companies Market (DCM). Although the dominant investors in Irish equities have traditionally been the domestic long-term savings institutions, international investors have become more prevalent in recent years, and now hold in excess of 30% of the market.

There was a resurgence of flotations and new equity issues generally in 1997, reflecting the overall buoyancy and optimism in the economy.

ECONOMIC AND POLITICAL OVERVIEW

The Republic of Ireland is a sovereign independent state. It has been a member of the EU since 1973 and in 1979 joined the European Monetary System. The President is the head of state, while legislative power resides with parliament. The two largest political parties are Fianna Fail and Fianna Gael, which are centrist in ideology and attract support from a wide spectrum of society.

The most recent general election was in June 1997, following which a coalition government was formed between Fianna Fail, the Progressive Democrats and a number of independents. The maximum term of a government is five years, although in the past a general election has usually been called before that period expires.

Ireland is currently experiencing a period of strong economic growth that combines both a high level of economic expansion and subdued inflation. GNP growth was an estimated 8.8% in 1997, while inflation averaged just 1.5%. Irish inflation has in fact been extremely low in recent times and one has to go back as far as 1985 to find a level exceeding 4%. Ireland has run a surplus on the balance of payments for a number of years and in 1997 this represented 0.7% of GNP.

The Irish pound or punt, has been a member of the ERM since its foundation in 1979 but has effectively been floating since the introduction of the wider 15% ERM bands in August 1993. In recent times, movements in the currency have been influenced by Ireland's proposed membership of the European single currency. For example, having trended up against the Deutschmark early in 1997, the punt weakened sharply in the second half of the year as the perception grew that the currency would enter EMU at its central parity rate (DM2.41). The punt also lost ground against both the US dollar and sterling during the year, to the tune of 16% and 13% respectively.

Irish fiscal policy has been conducted within strict parameters over the past few years, with government borrowing kept well below the Maastricht criterion of 3% of GNP. Rapid economic growth since 1993 has helped in this respect. The borrowing requirement was just 0.6% of GNP in 1997, while general government debt as a percentage of GDP was an estimated 67%. These are levels that should guarantee Ireland's membership of EMU when it starts in 1999.

Exhibit 30.1: IRELAND SE GENERAL (ISEQ) PRICE INDEX (US$), 1993–97

High value 3402.91 1.10.97 Low value 1191.19 1.1.93 *Source: Datastream*

Role of the central bank

Until EMU is launched at the start of 1999, monetary policy will continue to be conducted by the Irish central bank, which sees price stability as its primary objective. Because Ireland is a small, open economy, the level of the exchange rate is of critical importance to the achievement of this aim, and the bank has occasionally intervened in the foreign exchange market to manipulate the value of the punt.

However, in recent times the bank has been heavily influenced by the government's political commitment to ensuring that Ireland is among the founding members of the single currency. During the latter half of 1997, for example, the bank did not raise interest rates when Irish economic conditions undoubtedly warranted such a move. More recently it failed to enter the foreign exchange market to support the Irish pound when it fell significantly against both sterling and the German mark in response to the growing perception that the punt would joint EMU at its central ERM rate.

When the bank wishes to influence short-term interest rates it generally does so by means of gilt repurchase agreements with the commercial banks. A short-term facility (STF) – a penal lending rate similar to the German Lombard – is also used.

MARKET PERFORMANCE

A) In 1997

It proved to be another excellent year for the Irish equity market with the ISEQ Index rising 48.7%. Taking account of dividends, the total return on the index was 52.7%.

Financial stocks and, in particular, the banks, were the best performers in 1997, recording gains of 76% and 78.6% respectively. Non-financial stocks underperformed, gaining 37.1%, while the food sector rose 19.7%.

ISE turnover trebled in 1997, from IR£7.3 billion to IR£23.0 billion. The vast majority of business was concentrated in the 10 leading stocks as ranked by market capitalisation, with Bank of Ireland and AIB the two most traded stocks. Total funds raised through equity issues on the ISE rose from IR£923 million in 1996 to IR£1,753 million in 1997, with a net 15 new companies admitted to the market.

B) Summary Information

Global ranking by market value (US$ terms, end-1997): 39
Market capitalisation (domestic end-1997): US$25.9 billion
Growth in market value (local currency terms, 1993–97): 200.8%
Market value as a % of nominal GDP (end-1997): 54%
Number of domestic/foreign companies listed (end-1997): 83/19
Market P/E (main 55 companies in the ISEQ Index, end-1997): 19.1
MSCI total returns (with net dividends, US$ terms, 1997): 15.8%
MSCI Index (change in US$ terms, 1997): +13.3%
Short-term (3-month) interest rate (end-1997): 6.19%
Long-term (10-year) bond yield (end-1997): 5.55%
Budget deficit as a % of nominal GDP (1997): 0.6%
Annual increase in broad money (M3) supply (end-1997): 18.4%
Inflation rate (1997): 1.5%
US$ exchange rate (end-1997): IR£1.4301

C) Year-end share price index, price/earnings ratios and yields

Exhibit 30.2:
ISE YEAR-END SHARE PRICE INDEX, P/E AND GROSS DIVIDEND YIELDS, 1993–97

Year-end	*ISEQ Index*	*P/E*	*Yield (%)*
1993	1,888.94	18.2	2.0
1994	1,850.76	13.7	2.9
1995	2,232.45	13.6	2.8
1996	2,725.63	12.8	2.7
1997	4,053.80	19.1	2.0

Source: Davy Stockbrokers.

D) Market indices and their constituents

The ISE's own share price performance index, the ISEQ Overall Index, covers the performance of all Irish listed ordinary shares and the ordinary shares of companies on the DCM, and has two sub-indices covering financial sector shares and general shares respectively. As of 31 December 1997, the index also includes 10 Northern Ireland companies that are officially listed in Dublin, one of which (BCO) is on the DCM. The index is calculated each minute during trading hours.

The ISE introduced total return indices on 1 June 1993. The ISEQ Total Return Index has the same constituents and base (1,000 on 4 January 1988) as the ISEQ Overall Index. Also like the ISEQ Overall, it has two sub-indices – the ISEQ Financial Total Return and the ISEQ General Total Return. The total returns index series is calculated on the basis of reinvested gross dividends on the ex-dividend date.

Individual brokers also produce their own indices, and the most widely used is published by Davy Stockbrokers. The Davy indices give market performance as well as a more detailed sectoral breakdown. P/Es and dividend yields are also produced at a sectoral level.

THE STOCK MARKET

A) Brief history and structure

Dating back to the 1790s, the ISE is one of the oldest exchanges in the world. In 1799 the Irish parliament introduced legislation regulating the sale of government securities and providing for the licensing of stockbrokers. The procedures introduced by this Act are still in use today.

Dublin and Cork joined the Federation of Stock Exchanges of Great Britain and Ireland in 1965 and the ISE was formed in 1971. (The Cork exchange ceased operating in the mid-1980s, although brokers still have offices in the city.) In 1973 the ISE was amalgamated with London to form the International Stock Exchange of the United Kingdom and the Republic of Ireland Ltd, with Irish members assuming full membership of the International Stock Exchange. However, the link was discontinued in response to the EC Directive on investment services and, from December 1995, responsibility for the regulation of the market was transferred to the Irish central bank and a separately established Board of Exchange.

B) Different exchanges

The ISE is the only stock exchange in Ireland. It is located in Dublin.

C) Opening hours, names and addresses

Official trading hours are between 8.30am and 5.30pm. Market floor sessions take place from 9.30am and 2.15pm for about one hour each time.

THE IRISH STOCK EXCHANGE
28 Anglesea Street, Dublin 2
Tel: (353) 1 677 8808; Tlx: 93437; Fax: (353) 1 77 6045
E-mail: info@ise.ie Web site: www.@ise.ie

MARKET SIZE

A) Number of listings and market value

Excluding UCITS, there were 102 companies listed on the ISE at the end of 1997 (83 domestic and 19 foreign). End-1997 market capitalisation (domestic and foreign equities, including DCM and ESM) stood at IR£37.1 billion, representing an increase of 79% on the end-1996 figure.

Exhibit 30.3:
NUMBER OF COMPANIES LISTED AND MARKET CAPITALISATION, ISE, 1993–97

Year-end	*Number of domestic companies listed*	*Value of listed shares (IR£ billion)*
1993	80	12.33
1994	80	13.00
1995	80	16.11
1996	76	20.72
1997	83	37.09

Source: Irish Stock Exchange.

Exhibit 30.4:
ISE MARKET CAPITALISATION – ANALYSIS BY SECTOR, 1996–97

	Year-end capitalisation (%)	
Sector	*1996*	*1997*
Financials	37.1	40.4
Food	13.6	9.5
Building and construction	13.5	11.1

Exhibit 30.5 continued

Paper and packaging	10.5	7.5
Pharmaceuticals	9.3	11.0
Other industrial	10.2	9.7
Other	3.1	8.0
Resource	2.7	2.8
Total	**100.0**	**100.0**

Source: Davy Stockbrokers.

B) Largest quoted companies

The Irish market is unusually concentrated with the five largest stocks at the end of 1997 accounting for 55% of total market value. The top 10 stocks accounted for 69% of market value.

Exhibit 30.5:
THE 20 LARGEST LISTED COMPANIES ON THE ISE, END-1997

Ranking	*Company*	*Market value (IR£ million)*
1	AIB	5,790
2	Bank of Ireland	5,544
3	Elan Corporation	3,558
4	CRH	3,154
5	Smurfit	2,155
6	Irish Life	1,271
7	Kerry Group	1,231
8	Independent Newspapers	955
9	NIE	861
10	Avonmore	752
11	Waterford Wedgwood	700
12	Powerscreen	657
13	Greencore Group	645
14	Irish Permanent	643
15	Woodchester	556
16	Ryanair Holdings	527
17	Galen Holdings	480
18	Kingspan Group	391
19	DCC	387
20	Tullow Oil	371

Sources: Irish Stock Exchange and Davy Stockbrokers.

C) Trading volume

Turnover in official list, ESM and DCM stocks totalled IR£23.02 billion in 1997, representing an increase of 214% on 1996. Turnover in the 10 largest stocks on the market accounted for 77% of this total.

Exhibit 30.6:
TURNOVER ON THE ISE OFFICIAL LIST, ESM AND DCM, 1993–97

Year	*Turnover (IR£ million)*
1993	6,012
1994	6,440
1995	8,256
1996	7,318
1997	23,017

Source: Irish Stock Exchange.

Exhibit 30.7:
THE 20 MOST ACTIVELY TRADED ISE SHARES, 1997

Ranking	*Company*	*Turnover (IR£ million)*
1	Bank of Ireland	4,178.66
2	AIB	3,977.82
3	CRH	2,455.35
4	Smurfit	1,965.33
5	Irish Life	1,278.96
6	Tullow Oil	1,153.83
7	Greencore	1,095.34
8	Dana Petroleum	670.27
9	Independent Newspapers	515.27
10	Irish Permanent	450.10
11	Waterford Wedgwood	443.66
12	Anglo Irish Bank	431.93
13	Kerry Group	334.26
14	Kingspan	261.00
15	Dragon Oil	239.83
16	Fyffes	237.64
17	DCC	235.11
18	Avonmore Foods	221.41
19	Crean (James)	194.25
20	Ryanair Holdings	153.45

Source: Irish Stock Exchange.

TYPES OF SHARE

The ISE trades ordinary shares, preference shares, warrants, convertible loan and debenture stocks, government securities and approved unlisted securities.

OTHER MARKETS

The Unlisted Securities Market (USM) and Smaller Companies Market (SCM) were both closed at the end of 1996. The Developing Companies Market (DCM) was launched in 1997 and is designed to cater for the needs of smaller and medium-sized developing companies. Four companies had been admitted to the DCM by 31 December 1997. The Exploration Securities Market (ESM) continues to operate and is targeted specifically at companies in hydrocarbon and mineral exploration and development. At end-1997 it consisted of 11 companies.

Exhibit 30.8:
TOP PERFORMING COUNTRY FUNDS – IRELAND

Fund	*US$ % change* 31/12/96 31/12/97	31/12/92 31/12/96	Currency	*Fund size* (US$ mil)	Volatility	Manager name	Main sector	Class
Gartmore Irish Smaller Cos Wts	110.38	N/A	£	7.38	N/A	Gartmore Investment Ltd	Equity Growth	UK Investment Trusts
Standard Life Pen Irish Eqty	31.71	237.47	IR£	6.26	3.9	Standard Life	Equity Growth	Irish Group Pensions
Standard Life Pen Irish Eqty 2	31.71	N/A	IR£	N/A	N/A	Standard Life	Equity Growth	Irish Individual Pensions
Standard Life Pen Irish Eqty	31.24	230.99	IR£	1.16	3.83	Standard Life	Equity Growth	Irish Individual Pensions
Gartmore Irish Smaller Cos	31.15	N/A	£	51.71	N/A	Gartmore Investment Ltd	Equity Growth	UK Investment Trusts
AIPUT Smaller Companies (m)	30.88	222.95	IR£	120.55	4.46	AIB Investment Managers	Equity Growth	Irish Group Pensions
AIPUT Irish Equity (m)	30.6	237.63	IR£	42.83	4.1	AIB Investment Managers	Equity Growth	Irish Group Pensions
Friends Prov Pen Irish Eq (m)	27.25	231.85	IR£	119.07	3.72	Friends Provident	Equity Growth	Irish Group Pensions
UBIM Pension Irish Equity	26.87	226.11	IR£	2.47	3.59	Ulster Bank Investment Mgrs	Equity Growth	Irish Group Pensions
Friends Prov Pen Irl Eqty	26.86	214.9	IR£	22.55	3.59	Friends Provident	Equity Growth	Irish Individual Pensions
New Ireland Pension Irish Eqty	26.45	226.03	IR£	142.87	3.7	New Ireland	Equity Growth	Irish Group Pensions
Irish Life Pen Irish Eq (m)	25.56	205.67	IR£	379.94	3.83	Irish Life	Equity Growth	Irish Group Pensions
AIB Invest. Man. Charifund	25.24	178.9	IR£	38.11	4	AIB Investment Managers	Equity Growth	Irish Charities
Scot Prov Pen Irish StockMkt	24.12	232.45	IR£	3.2	3.37	Scottish Provident	Equity Growth	Irish Individual Pensions
Irish Life Irl Eq Special Inv	22.43	N/A	IR£	8.88	3.47	Irish Life	Equity Growth	Irish Unit Linked Funds
Bk of Ireland Small Irl Eq (m)	22.23	155.51	IR£	198.53	3.73	Bank of Ireland Asset Mgmt	Equity Growth	Irish Group Pensions
NU Irish	20.12	176.95	IR£	0.68	3.24	Norwich Union	Equity Growth	Irish Unit Linked Funds
Hibernian Life Hi-Irish Cos.	19.93	158.4	IR£	48.48	3.01	Hibernian Life	Equity Growth	Irish Unit Linked Funds
Irish Progressive Irish Eqty 4	19.52	N/A	IR£	N/A	2.89	Irish Progressive Life	Equity Growth	Irish Unit Linked Funds
Irish Progressive Irish Eqty 1	18.6	147.8	IR£	N/A	2.88	Irish Progressive Life	Equity Growth	Irish Unit Linked Funds
Irish Life Charite Irl Eq	18.24	177.07	IR£	1.02	3.43	Irish Life	Equity Growth	Irish Charities
Irish Life Irish Equity 4	17.95	155.17	IR£	10.77	3.27	Irish Life	Equity Growth	Irish Unit Linked Funds
Ulster Bank Irish Equity	17.77	N/A	IR£	2.94	3.34	Ulster Bank Investment Mgrs	Equity Growth	Irish Unit Trusts
Norwich Union Special Invest.	17.6	N/A	IR£	1.33	3.13	Norwich Union	Equity Growth	Irish Unit Linked Funds
CMI GNF Irish Equity	17.44	132.74	IR£	0.6	2.75	CMI Global Network Fund (LUX)	Equity Growth	UK FSA Recognised
CMI GNF Irish Equity	17.44	132.74	IR£	0.76	2.78	CMI Global Network Fund	Equity	Luxembourg
Irish Life Irish Equity 5	17.08	145.83	IR£	8.73	3.27	Irish Life	Equity Growth	Irish Unit Linked Funds
Irish Life Irish Equity 6	16.85	143.3	IR£	5.39	3.27	Irish Life	Equity Growth	Irish Unit Linked Funds
New Ireland Irish Equity 1 & 2	16.51	160.69	IR£	41.46	3.16	New Ireland	Equity Growth	Irish Unit Linked Funds
New Ireland Irish Equity 5	16.48	158.07	IR£	27.07	3.16	New Ireland	Equity Growth	Irish Unit Linked Funds
New Ireland Emerging Cos 5	16.46	121.72	IR£	0.1	3.16	New Ireland	Equity Growth	Irish Unit Linked Funds
New Ireland Irish Equity 6	16.25	N/A	IR£	14.01	3.16	New Ireland	Equity Growth	Irish Unit Linked Funds
Standard Life Irish Equity	16.13	140.72	IR£	13.54	2.91	Standard Life	Equity Growth	Irish Unit Linked Funds
CMI Passport Irish Equity	16.03	N/A	IR£	0.14	N/A	CMI Passport	Equity	Offshore Territories
New Ireland Charities Equity	15.75	132.43	IR£	N/A	3.82	New Ireland	Equity Growth	Irish Charities
Canada Life Irish Equity	14.9	130.55	IR£	180.51	3.18	Canada Life	Equity Growth	Irish Unit Linked Funds
Norwich Union Equity 1(i)	14.31	116.27	IR£	79.77	3.12	Norwich Union	Equity Growth	Irish Unit Linked Funds
Norwich Union Equity 2	14.03	113.36	IR£	0.15	3.31	Norwich Union	Equity Growth	Irish Unit Linked Funds
AIB Inv. Mgrs. Irish Equity	14.02	143.34	IR£	3.83	3.41	AIB Investment Managers	Equity Growth	Irish Unit Trusts
GRE Life Equity	13.28	127.54	IR£	9.17	2.9	GRE Life	Equity Growth	Irish Unit Linked Funds
Scottish Provident Irish Eqty	11.97	151.46	IR£	7.94	2.62	Scottish Provident	Equity Growth	Irish Unit Linked Funds
New Ireland Equity 1 & 2	11.05	115.65	IR£	6.19	3.1	New Ireland	Equity Growth	Irish Unit Linked Funds
New Ireland Equity 5	11	113.35	IR£	4.62	3.1	New Ireland	Equity Growth	Irish Unit Linked Funds
B/I Lifetime Equity	10.88	113.99	IR£	10.92	3.02	BIAM/Lifetime	Equity Growth	Irish Unit Linked Funds

Note: details for some funds may not have been included if the data for the US$ % change for 96/97 was not available

Source: Standard & Poor's Micropal.

OPERATIONS

A) Trading system

Equity trading on the ISE takes the form of order-driven broker-to-broker dealing.

Under the stock exchange dealing rules, all trades must be reported within five minutes to the ISE through the Stock Exchange Automatic Quotation System (SEAQ), in order to provide a record of the time of execution and price.

B) List of principal brokers

AIB CAPITAL MARKETS PLC
AIB International Centre, PO Box 2750, IFSC, Dublin 1
Tel: (353) 1 874 0222; Fax: (353) 1 605 4067

BCP STOCKBROKERS
72 Upper Leeson Street, Dublin 4
Tel: (353) 1 668 4688; Fax: (353) 1 668 4246

BLOXHAM STOCKBROKERS
9-12 Fleet Street, Dublin 2
Tel: (353) 1 677 6653; Fax: (353) 1 677 6901

BUTLER & BRISCOE
3 College Green, Dublin 2
Tel: (353) 1 677 7348; Fax: (353) 1 677 7044

CAMPBELL O'CONNOR & CO
8 Cope Street, Dublin 2
Tel: (353) 1 677 1773; Fax: (353) 1 679 1969

DAVY STOCKBROKERS
Davy House, 49 Dawson Street, Dublin 2
Tel: (353) 1 679 7788; Fax: (353) 1 671 2704

GARBAN BUTLER
3 College Green, Dublin 2
Tel: (353) 1 670 7067; Fax: (353) 1 670 7377

GOODBODY STOCKBROKERS
122 Pembroke Road, Dublin 2
Tel: (353) 1 667 0400; Fax: (353) 1 667 0280

MONEY MARKETS INTERNATIONAL
26 Lower Baggot Street, Dublin 2
Tel: (353) 1 676 6277; Fax: (353) 1 676 5250

W&R MORROGH
74 South Mall, Cork
Tel: (353) 21 270 647; Fax: (353) 21 277 581

NCB STOCKBROKERS
Ferry House 48/53, Lower Mount Street, Dublin 2
Tel: (353) 1 661 4977; Fax: (353) 1 661 0860

RIADA STOCKBROKERS
1 College Green, Dublin 2
Tel: (353) 1 679 1441; Fax: (353) 1 679 1430

TIR SECURITIES IRELAND LTD
2/F Seagrave House,
19-20 Earlsford Terrace, Dublin 2
Tel: (353) 1 662 1500; Fax: (353) 1 661 9962

C) Settlement and transfer

Settlement and transfer arrangements are the same as in the United Kingdom (see Chapter 72).

D) Commissions and other costs

Commission rates on equity dealing are by negotiation and vary with the size of transaction.

Transfers on the register of Irish quoted companies involve the payment of a stamp duty of 1% of the market value of the purchase or the consideration, whichever is the higher. A purchase and sale of a security within an account period will not incur stamp duty as no transfer on the register occurs. Capital duty at the rate of 1% of the amount contributed to the capital of the company is also payable in respect of allotments of shares in limited liability companies.

TAXATION AND REGULATIONS AFFECTING FOREIGN INVESTORS

Distributions received from an Irish resident company by an investor who is neither a resident nor ordinarily residing in Ireland are relieved from income or corporation tax in Ireland and there is no withholding tax on dividends paid by Irish resident companies, whether payable to an Irish resident or a non-Irish resident investor. However, the company paying the dividend may be liable to pay advance corporation tax (ACT) on payments of dividends. The amount of ACT payable is, subject to the offsetting of tax credits on distributions received by the paying company, equal to the tax credit attaching to the dividend paid.

Exhibit 30.9:
WITHHOLDING TAXES

Recipient	*Dividends %*	*Interest %*
Resident corporations	Nil	26
Resident individuals	Nil	26
Non-resident corporations and individuals:		
Non-treaty	Nil	26
Treaty	Nil	Nil–26

Source: Price Waterhouse.

The standard rate of corporate tax is 32%. Manufacturing companies (which include financial services and other companies operating in the International Financial Services Centre in Dublin and the Shannon Airport Zone) pay tax at a reduced rate of 10%. The tax credit which attaches to a dividend will depend upon whether or not the profits out of which the dividend is paid are liable to tax at the standard 32% rate or the reduced 10% rate. The tax credit for a dividend paid wholly out of profits subject to Irish corporation tax at the rate of 32% is 11/89ths, whereas the tax credit for a dividend paid wholly out of profits subject to Irish corporation tax at the rate of 10% is 1/18th. Dividends paid out of profits of a company that have been taxed at both rates will carry a tax credit between 1/18th and 11/89ths.

A) Tax treaties

Ireland has negotiated double tax treaties with 30 countries. Relief from double taxation may be provided by way of credit for and/or repayment in whole or in part of Irish tax. Many of the modern treaties (eg, with the UK) entitle a resident of the other contracting state to a repayment from the Irish Revenue of an amount equal to the excess of the Irish tax credit attaching to a dividend from an Irish resident company over a stated percentage (limited to 15% by many of the treaties). In order for the resident of the other contracting state to be entitled to this payment, he must be the beneficial owner of the dividend and not a corporate investor controlling more than a stated percentage (determined by the terms of the particular treaty). Depending on the terms of the particular treaty and the domestic law in the country in which the foreign investor is resident, the recipient of the dividend may be entitled to a credit for Irish tax (including underlying tax paid by the company) against his domestic tax liability in his country of residence.

B) Exchange controls

In keeping with its policy of liberalising exchange controls, the Irish government allowed all existing exchange controls to lapse on 31 December 1992. Legislation was introduced in the form of the Financial Transfers Act 1992, allowing the Minister for Finance to impose, from time to time, restrictions on the movement of capital or payments between Ireland and other countries. The current restrictions apply to Iraq and Libya.

LISTING AND REPORTING REQUIREMENTS

At present, the listing and reporting requirements are practically identical to those in the UK, save that applications for new listings are made to the Committee of the Irish Unit of The Stock Exchange and applications are governed by the European Communities (Stock Exchange) Regulations 1994 (as amended). The basic *UK Listing Rules* manual is used, as modified by the *Irish Supplement* issued by the Committee.

Under the Stock Exchange Act 1995, the Central Bank of Ireland is responsible for regulating the stock exchange and member firms in Ireland. This Act implemented the EU Investment Services Directive and resulted in the splitting up of the UK and Irish exchanges, effective from 8 December 1995. Listing and reporting requirements thus require Central Bank of Ireland approval.

The Irish Companies Act 1963 contains a detailed code on prospectuses designed to protect the investing public. Full disclosure of all material facts is required and there are both civil and criminal sanctions for breach of the code. This code has been supplemented by the implementation in Ireland of the EU Directive on Prospectuses (Council Directive 89/298/EEC).

SHAREHOLDER PROTECTION CODES

A) Substantial shareholdings

The Companies Act 1990 requires disclosure to a public limited company (plc) of the acquisition of an interest in shares which represents 5% or more of any class of voting rights in the company. A notification to the company is also required on the disposal of such shareholding. Once a shareholder holds an interest in shares that represents 5% or more of any class of voting shares in a plc, any change (by way of acquisition or disposal) of 1% or more must also be notified to the company. The concept of an interest in shares is broadly defined. In certain circumstances the legislation also requires notification to the ISE of any acquisition or disposal of an interest in shares of a listed Irish plc. Notification by the shareholder will be necessary where such transaction results in a percentage of share capital in which the person involved has an interest crossing thresholds (on the way up or down) of 10%, 25%, 50% or 75%.

The ISE's substantial acquisition rules require that a shareholder must make a notification to the company and the Stock Exchange Announcements Office of any acquisitions resulting in the shareholder holding 15% or more (beyond any whole percentage figure) of the voting rights in a company.

B) Directors' dealings

The Companies Act 1990 requires disclosure of transactions entered into between a company and its directors. It provides for the making of disqualification and restriction orders against directors and requires disclosure to the company of dealings in the company's shares by directors. A common theme of these and other provisions in the Act is that they embrace the concept of a shadow director – ie, a person in accordance with whose directions or instructions the directors are accustomed to act. Shadow directors and directors are treated alike for the purposes of the legislation.

C) Mergers and takeovers

The Irish Takeover Panel Act, 1997, and *Takeover Rules and Substantial Acquisition Rules* (the "Green Book") apply to all offers for the acquisition of companies whose shares are listed on the Irish official list. Under the Green Book, a purchaser of shares in a company is obliged to make a "mandatory offer" for the equity capital of a company where it acquires shares which, when added to the shares held or acquired by persons acting in concert with it, give it or them 30% or more of the voting rights in the company.

The Irish Takeover Panel Act 1996 established an Irish Panel to regulate M&A activity. The Panel began operating on 1 July 1997.

D) Insider trading

The Companies Act 1990 (the "Act") makes insider dealing a criminal offence. The offence is very broadly defined and the ISE is given extensive powers to carry out investigations and to require information from people. As well as severe criminal sanctions, a person engaged in unlawful insider trading may also be liable under civil law to compensate parties sustaining loss due to the unlawful activity and to account to the company concerned for any profit arising out of the unlawful dealing.

E) Compensation fund

An Investor Compensation Bill is expected to be published in early 1998. This will establish a compensation fund to recompense private investors who are the victims of fraud.

RESEARCH

The following publications are available from the ISE:
Daily Official List – Irish
The Stock Exchange in Ireland – A Brief History
The Stock Exchange
The Rules and Regulations of the Stock Exchange
Admission of Securities to Listing (with Irish Supplement)
Stock Exchange Fact Book (quarterly)
Stock Exchange Fact Sheet (monthly)
Equity Actuary List (annually)

There is no specific financial newspaper covering the securities markets, but the *Sunday Business Post* is a weekly financial paper and the *Irish Times* business section is a good daily publication for Irish financial news. Other publications include *Business and Finance* (weekly) and *Irish Business* (monthly).

The equities division of Davy Stockbrokers offers a technology-based dealing service in equities and is regarded as a leading source of continuous information on the state of the market. In addition to equity and fixed-interest analysis, the research division also operates a specialised consultancy service providing economic forecasts and analysis to large industrial and commercial companies, as well as carrying out consultancy projects for public and private sector clients.

In addition, NCB Stockbrokers and Goodbody Stockbrokers provide a comprehensive range of services to the investment community.

CHAPTER

31

Israel

Introduction

The Tel Aviv Stock Exchange (TASE) is the Middle East's largest and most advanced capital market. At the end of 1997 there were 659 companies listed on TASE, and 1,046 shares and convertibles were traded. Shares made up 51% of total market capitalisation, government bonds 44%, other bonds 3% and convertibles 2%. Shares represented 17.6% of total financial assets held by the public at the end of 1997, an increase of 22% compared with the end of 1996. Equity market capitalisation amounted to US$46.3 billion (up around 29% on end-1996) and was the equivalent of 48% of Israel's GDP.

After a three-year bear market, stocks rebounded in 1997. The turnaround had started in the second half of 1996 and continued for most of 1997, driven mainly by declining inflation, lower interest rates (for the first seven months), a fall in the government and current account deficits, and effects from world stock exchanges (mainly the New York exchange, where Israeli companies are traded OTC). However, towards the end of the year interest rates (both nominal and real) began to rise and data about a slowing economy accumulated, and these factors, combined with the crisis in Asia, saw stock prices in retreat.

ECONOMIC AND POLITICAL OVERVIEW

Control of the occupied territories dominated Israel's relations with the rest of the world and the domestic political scene. The right-wing Likud Party, returned to power in May 1996, is headed by Prime Minister Benjamin Netanyahu, who is viewed as generally hostile to further concessions on Israel's part. Thus a relatively cold relationship with the Palestinian Authority drew political pressure from Europe and the US.

On the economic front, 1997 was a "mixed bag". The high levels of economic growth over the past seven years (5.8% per annum on average in real terms) slowed down and real GDP grew by just 1.9% in 1997. The slowing economy, declining investment and high wages saw unemployment rise to 7.7% (compared with 6.5% in 1996).

On the other hand, the government's budget deficit fell to 3.0% of GDP, and fiscal restraint coupled with monetary tightening brought inflation down to 7% (the lowest level in 28 years). The current account deficit declined as well, to 3.7% of GDP (US$3.6 billion, compared with US$5.3 billion in the previous year). Privatisation and the buoyant stock market attracted foreign investment, which, on a net basis, rose from US$5.6 billion in 1996 to US$8.6 billion in 1997.

Forecasts for 1998 indicate that the economy will grow at a slower rate than in 1997. The Bank of Israel is likely to ease monetary restraint, and inflation in 1998 is expected to come out below the lower end of the 7–10% target range.

Role of the central bank

The Bank of Israel's (BOI) functions are to administer and regulate the currency system, and to regulate the credit and banking system in accordance with government economic policy. Its aim is to promote (via monetary measures) price and currency stability, along with high levels of production, employment, national income and capital investment.

Foreign currency policy is managed via a foreign currency basket, composed of five major world currencies. The shekel can move relative to the basket within a sloping band that is usually derived from the expected inflation gap (the difference between Israel's inflationary target and inflation abroad).

MARKET PERFORMANCE

A) In 1997

During the first seven months of 1997, TASE share prices rose sharply. Over this period, the TA-100 Index rose by 46.8%. The TA-25 (Maof) was up 44.8%, and the Karam

Exhibit 31.1: TEL AVIV SE MISHTANIM 100 PRICE INDEX (US$), 1993–97

High value 9.26 1.8.97 Low value 5.19 1.3.95 *Source: Datastream*

54.6%. Moderate price declines and shrinking trading volume set in from August onwards, and share indices fell by between 4.3% and 17%. For the year as a whole the TA-100 was up 37.9%, the TA-25 (Maof) by 38.7% and the Karam by 28.25%.

Turnover of shares and convertibles totalled US$14.2 billion in 1997, compared with US$8 billion in 1996. Average daily share turnover was 80% higher in 1997 than in 1996.

The US dollar yield on shares and convertibles in the commercial bank sector was 32.7% in 1997. For the industrial sector it was 24.6% and for the insurance sector it was 24.2%.

B) Summary information

Global ranking by market value (US$ terms, end-1997): 30
Market capitalisation (end-1997): US$46.35 billion
Growth in market value (US$ terms 1993–97): -10%
Market value as a % of nominal GDP (end-1997): 48.3%
Number of domestic/foreign companies listed on the official market (end-1997): 657/2
Market P/E (end-1997): 13.6
MSCI Index (change in US$ terms, 1997): +22.9%
Short-term (3-month) interest rate (end-1997): 14.0%
Long-term (5-year) bond yield (end-1997): 4.3%
Budget deficit as a % of nominal GDP (end-1997): 3%
Annual increase in broad money (M2) supply (end-1997): 24%
Inflation rate (1997): 7%
US$ exchange rate (end-1997): Shk3.536

C) Five-year performance

Exhibit 31.2:
YEAR-END GENERAL SHARES AND CONVERTIBLES INDEX (IN SHK TERMS), 1993–97

1993	*1994*	*1995*	*1996*	*1997*
270.15	163.77	186.66	184.84	249.87

Source: Bank Leumi.

D) Market indices and their constituents

TASE compiles a variety of indices reflecting share price movement. Among them are the General Shares and Convertibles Index, which includes all shares, derivatives (except Maof options) and convertible bonds traded on TASE; the TA-100 (Mishtanim) Index, which comprises the equivalent of blue chip companies in Israel; the TA-25 (Maof) Index, which includes the 25 TA-100 shares with the highest market value; and the Karam Index, which covers smaller company shares.

THE STOCK MARKET

A) Brief history and structure

The trading of securities in Israel pre-dates the establishment of the country and began in 1935 when the Anglo-Palestine Bank, together with the country's leading banks and brokerage firms, founded the Exchange Bureau for Securities, an unofficial stock exchange operating according to criteria stipulated by the banks. The founding of Israel, together with a marked increase in transaction volume and the number of listed securities, necessitated an official facility for securities trading.

The Tel Aviv Stock Exchange (TASE) was incorporated as a public company and began operations in 1953. Membership of TASE is reserved for commercial banks and brokerage firms that meet admission criteria relating to reputation, financial standing, integrity and experience. There are 27 members, of which 13 are banks (including the central bank) and 14 are brokerage firms.

In order to make stock market trading more understandable to international investors, from 1 January 1997 share prices have been denominated in agorot (100 agorot = Shk1) rather than as a percentage of their nominal value.

In August 1997 the exchange introduced a fully computerised, continuous and simultaneous trading system called TACT (Tel Aviv Continuous Trading).

B) Different exchanges

The TASE is the only exchange in Israel.

C) Opening hours, names and addresses

Transaction days are Sunday to Thursday (excluding holidays) and trading takes place between 10.00am and 3.30pm for shares, warrants and convertible bonds. Trading of TA-25 (Maof) options takes place between 10.00am and 5.00pm.

THE TEL AVIV STOCK EXCHANGE
54 Ahad Ha'am Street, Tel Aviv 65202
Tel: (972) 3 567 7411; Fax: (972) 3 510 5379
Web site: www.tase.co.il Tlx: 341762 TASE IL

MARKET SIZE

A) Number of listings and market value

At the end of 1997 there were 659 companies listed on TASE, and equity capitalisation totalled US$46.3 billion, up 29.1% on end-1996.

Exhibit 31.3:
NUMBER OF COMPANIES LISTED AND EQUITY MARKET CAPITALISATION, TASE, 1993–97

Year-end	*No. of companies listed*	*Market value (US$ million)*
1993	558	57,800
1994	638	32,704
1995	654	36,820
1996	655	35,900
1997	659	46,346

Sources: Tel Aviv Stock Exchange and Bank Leumi.

Exhibit 31.4:
MARKET VALUE BY SECTOR, TASE, 1997

Sector	*Market value (US$ million)*
Commercial banks	7,546
Mortgage and finance banks	1,072
Insurance companies	1,798
Commerce and services	6,671
Real estate, construction and agriculture	4,719
Industrial companies	17,777
Investment and holding companies	6,677
Oil and gas exploration companies	85
Total	**46,346**

Sources: Tel Aviv Stock Exchange and Bank Leumi.

B) Largest quoted companies

The largest five companies accounted for 26.2% of total market capitalisation at the end of 1997.

Exhibit 31.5:
THE 20 LARGEST LISTED COMPANIES ON TASE, END-1997

Ranking	*Company*	*Market value (US$ million)*
1	Bank Hapoalim	2,958
2	Teva	2,951
3	Bank Leumi	2,376
4	Bezek	2,023
5	Koor Industries	1,762
6	Israel Chemicals	1,625
7	IDB Development	1,103
8	Bank Discount	972
9	Clal Israel	914
10	IDB Holdings	903
11	Dead Sea Works	871
12	Discount Investment	788
13	Clal Industries	781
14	The First Int'l Bank	713
15	Tadiran	700
16	Leumi Insurance	671
17	Makhtesim	644
18	Bromine	622
19	Super-sol	592
20	Clal Electronics	536

Source: Tel Aviv Stock Exchange.

C) Trading volume

Total turnover of stocks and convertibles was US$14.2 billion in 1997, compared with US$8 billion in 1996. The 20 most actively traded shares accounted for 45.7% of daily average share turnover in 1997, compared with 43.3% in 1996.

Exhibit 31.6:
THE 20 MOST ACTIVELY TRADED SHARES, TASE, 1997

Ranking	*Company*	*Trading value (US$ million)*
1	Bank Leumi	674.28
2	Koor Industries	575.47
3	Teva	571.29
4	Bank Hapoalim	539.28
5	Israel Chemicals	366.01
6	Bezek	352.79
7	Bank Discount	327.05
8	Discount Investment	279.73
9	Formula	231.71
10	Super-sol	221.28
11	Makhteshim	188.57
12	Clal Electronics	180.92
13	Tadiran	178.83
14	Clal Israel 10	175.35
15	Clal Industries	170.48
16	IDB Holdings	167.70
17	IDB Development	166.30
18	Agis	159.35
19	Industrial Building Co	156.56
20	Agan	144.04

Source: Tel Aviv Stock Exchange.

TYPES OF SHARE

Ordinary shares constitute the bulk of equity-related trading in Israel. The remainder comprises warrants and convertible capital notes, cumulative preference shares, cumulative and participating preference shares and redeemable preference shares.

Most companies quoted on TASE are closely held and, as a result, the acquisition of control of companies through stock exchange purchases is a rare phenomenon. Many of these closely held companies have a special class of share (sometimes known as "founder" shares) and, although the holders are in a minority, they maintain effective voting control. In the past few years, the TASE and the Securities Authority have addressed the issue of companies that give preferential voting rights to certain classes of shares, and have ruled that:

(a) If it is the first listing of a company's shares, the company's capital may consist of only one kind of share, granting equal voting rights (subject to some exceptions).

(b) If securities of the company are already listed, any further listing must be of the shares that have the most preferred voting rights. It is still permitted to issue new shares that have preferential rights to dividends (but not voting rights).

As a result of this provision, listed companies with more than one class of share wishing to make further offerings of non-preferred shares, first go through a process of "equalisation of rights" among all shareholders, including the grant of "compensation" to shareholders holding shares with preferred voting rights. This is followed by a consolidation of the company's share capital into one class of share. Companies with shares already listed and which do not wish to make further offerings are not required to equalise voting rights and may maintain their existing capital structure.

Equity derivatives on the exchange include warrants and convertible bonds, and options on the Maof Index are also traded.

INVESTORS

The main shareholder categories at the end of 1997 were domestic individuals (accounting for 71.2% of market

Exhibit 31.7:
COUNTRY FUNDS – ISRAEL

Fund	*US$ % change 01/01/97 01/01/98*	*01/01/93 01/01/98*	*Fund base currency*	*Fund size (US$ mil)*	*Fund volatility*	*Management group*	*Opal main sector*	*Opal subsector*
Israel Fund	31.84	N/A	US$	N/A	5.726	BZW Inv Mgt	Closed-End	Equity
State Street Actions Israel	23.66	N/A	Ffr	5	5.689	State Street	Open-End	Equity
First Israel Fund	20.8	N/A	US$	64.6	5.898	BEA Assoc	Closed-End	Equity
Israel 2000	15.33	N/A	US$	6.6	5.545	Rothschild As	Open-End	Equity
Horizon Emergence Etoile	9.98	N/A	Ffr	18	-1	Rothschild As	Open-End	Equity
Scontinvest Mid East Israval	8.33	N/A	US$	12.3	5.802	Scontinvest	Open-End	Equity
France Israel Croissance	0.28	N/A	Ffr	62	-1	Abeille CF	Open-End	Equity

Note: details for some funds may not have been included if the data for the US$ % change for 97/98 is not available

Source:Standard & Poor's Micropal.

value), foreign investors (13.2%), provident funds (9.7%) and mutual funds (5.1%).

Most shares traded on TASE are held by "interested parties", defined as institutional bodies or individuals holding over 5% of a firm's equity. In 1997, they owned 71.5% of total equity capitalisation.

Funds specialising in Israeli securities now operate abroad. The First Israel Fund and the Israel Growth Fund (IGF) were floated in the US in the early 1990s. In April 1998, Horizons, a new Israeli fund for foreign investors was launched.

OPERATIONS

A) Trading system

Up until August 1997, the TASE had two methods of trading. The first was trading in shares on the two-sided list and this took place in two stages. The first stage, known as the "Meretz", was a computerised multilateral trading session, during which all orders were batched and a single price was set for all securities for which orders were matched. The second stage, or "Mishtanim", was a continuous bilateral session conducted in several cycles in which differently priced transactions could be executed for the same shares. There was no limit on the number of transactions per cycle.

The second trading method was the computerised call system (Karam), under which the prices of securities were set only once a day.

In August 1997 the exchange introduced a fully computerised, continuous and simultaneous trading system called TACT (Tel Aviv Continuous Trading). Orders are routed from bank branches and institutional investors to the trading engine at TASE. The system combines many functions, including sending buy and sell orders, price discovery, real-time reaction and trade confirmation. When TACT commenced operations, it held the shares of the 100 most active companies. By the end of 1997, 131 shares and convertibles were traded through the TACT system. The Karam is still used for the less active and "heavy" securities.

Short selling of securities is not common on the TASE. This is due to the fact that it is only allowed against borrowing, and because of tax considerations.

B) List of principal banks and brokers

Banks and banking institutions

BANK LEUMI LE-ISRAEL
32, Yehuda Halevy St, Tel Aviv
Tel: (972) 3 514 8111

BATUCHA, SECURITIES & INVESTMENT
9, Karl Neter St, Tel Aviv
Tel: (972) 3 564 3232

FIRST INTERNATIONAL BANK OF ISRAEL
9, Ahad Ha'am St, Tel Aviv
Tel: (972) 3 519 6111

HAPOALIM BANK
50, Rothschild Blvd, Tel Aviv
Tel: (972) 3 567 3333

ISRAEL BROKERAGE AND INVESTMENT
9, Ahad Ha'am St, 26th Floor, Tel Aviv
Tel: (972) 3 519 3444

ISRAEL DISCOUNT BANK
38, Yehuda Halevy St, Tel Aviv
Tel: (972) 3 514 5000

ISRAEL GENERAL BANK
38, Rothschild Blvd, Tel Aviv
Tel: (972) 3 564 5645

MERCANTILE DISCOUNT BANK
103, Alenby St, Tel Aviv
Tel: (972) 3 564 7333

UNION BANK OF ISRAEL
6, Ahuzat Bayit St, Tel Aviv
Tel: (972) 3 519 1631

UNITED MIZRAHI BANK
48, Lilienblum St, Tel Aviv
Tel: (972) 3 567 9211

C) Settlement and transfer

The Stock Exchange Clearing House acts as the members' depository for securities listed on TASE. It handles the stock and cash settlement of all stock market deals and also acts as intermediary for the servicing of deposited securities.

Trades are settled by the clearing house on the day after the transaction. Bank members credit and debit their customers' accounts on the same day, while non-bank members make cash debits and credits on the following day. The clearing system is computerised.

Because most traded securities are registered with nominee companies, settlements and transfers are effected to a large extent through the clearing house and the nominees' books.

D) Commissions and other costs

Commissions are charged on all securities transactions. Fees charged by banks depend mostly on the volume of the transaction. They range between 0.8% and 1% of the trade value for transactions up to US$3,000, and are around 0.5% for transactions of over US$7,000. The minimum commission fee is US$6.10. A bank's customer who has a securities account is charged a quarterly management fee of 0.125% (but not less than US$5.30) of the portfolio's value. Investors with accounts at brokerage companies pay commissions ranging between 1% on relatively small transactions and 0.25% on large amounts.

TAXATION AND REGULATIONS AFFECTING FOREIGN INVESTORS

A) Capital gains

Gains on the sale of securities listed on TASE, or of securities of Israeli companies listed on recognised foreign exchanges are exempt from capital gains tax in Israel unless sold by a person trading in securities as a business.

B) Withholding tax

In the absence of a treaty authorising a lower withholding rate, income tax on interest and dividends paid to a non-resident is deducted at source at a rate of 25%. A foreign resident wishing to obtain a reduction or exemption from the deduction of tax at source must now provide the tax authorities with a letter from its local tax officer regarding, among other things, the "fiscal residence" of the foreign resident.

The withholding tax on dividends in the UK treaty is 15%, and in the US treaty it is between 12.5% and 17.5%.

Exhibit 31.8:
WITHHOLDING TAXES

Recipient	*Dividends[1] %*	*Interest %*
Resident corporations	0/25	0–45
Resident individuals	25	0–45
Non-resident corporations and individuals:		
Non-treaty	25	25
Treaty	0–25	0–25

Notes:
1. Dividends out of the profits of approved enterprises are liable to 15% withholding tax, subject to treaty provisions.

Source: Price Waterhouse.

C) Regulations

Foreign investors may buy and sell listed and unlisted Israeli securities provided that all payments are made through an account opened in the name of the foreign resident at a local bank or other institution designated as an "authorised dealer". Interest and dividends paid on investments made in foreign currency through an authorised dealer may be repatriated in free foreign currency at the current exchange rate.

D) Exchange controls

Under laws enacted to liberalise foreign currency markets, foreign investors may invest in interest-bearing shekel or foreign currency denominated loans. All such transactions must be executed through authorised dealers and, if originally purchased in foreign currency, all proceeds of sale can be repatriated in free foreign currency.

REPORTING REQUIREMENTS

The reporting requirements for listed Israeli companies are set out in the Securities (Periodical and Immediate Reports) Regulations 5730-1970. All reports must be sent simultaneously to the Securities Authority, TASE and the Companies Registry. The regulations provide that all relevant companies must:

1) Issue a periodical (annual) report including details of the company's investments, its subsidiaries, and its directors, and a review of certain "special events" occurring during the previous tax year, including material agreements and other events that materially affect the company's business, assets or liabilities.
2) As part of the periodical report, publish annual financial statements and a directors' report at least 14 days prior to the annual general meeting of the company, and no later than the earlier of four months from the end of the company's fiscal year or 14 days after their signature by the company's auditors.
3) Publish unaudited reviewed accounts on a quarterly basis (including unaudited financial statements and a profit and loss account), as well as an abridged directors' report. These must be published no later than two months after the end of the relevant quarter.
4) Report any changes in the board of directors, the senior officers or the holdings of any "interested party" (a holder of more than 5% of the company's share capital or the holder of a right to elect a director, or an affiliate of either of the above or any member of the board of directors).
5) Report the sale or disposal, or negotiations regarding the sale or disposal of, a substantial portion of its assets and the commencement or cessation of a business activity in which a substantial portion of its assets have been, or are to be, invested.
6) Report any resolution of the board of directors relating to a recommendation to a general meeting of the company for the payment of a dividend, the issue of bonus shares, an alteration in the paid-up share capital, the premature redemption of debentures, the issue of debentures or the cancellation of any securities.
7) Report on the date, place and agenda of any general meeting at least seven days prior to the meeting.
8) Report on any transaction with an interested party or any negotiations in respect of such a transaction.

9) Report any event not within the usual course of business of the company that substantially affects or is likely to affect the profits, property or liabilities of the company.

All reports referred to in numbers (3) to (9) above (except (6)) are defined as "immediate reports" and must be made on the same day as the relevant information is known to the company or, if the information is only made known to the company after 10.00am, on the following day.

SHAREHOLDER PROTECTION CODES

The function of the Securities Authority is to protect the interests of the public investing in securities, and all prospectuses require its approval. The Securities Authority may also demand that a company provide certain reports and further information in respect of a report. In the event that a company does not meet the Securities Authority's demands, it may order the suspension of trading of the company's securities, and, in such cases, officers of the company are liable to criminal proceedings.

Additional protections for shareholders are provided for in the Securities Law and the Companies Ordinance, as detailed in the following sub-sections.

A) Directors

A listed company must elect two public directors who are unconnected with the management or control of the company. The appointment and the dismissal of a public director needs to be approved by a special governmental committee. A public director is entitled to demand information from the company and his remuneration is fixed by law. A public director must also sit on each committee of the board of directors.

A listed company must also appoint an audit committee consisting of at least three members, all of whom must be unconnected with the management or control of the company. Both the public directors should be members of the audit committee.

Any member of the board of directors or senior officer of a listed company who, directly or indirectly, has an interest in a contract or a proposed contract of the company must declare the nature of the interest and such contracts must be approved by the board of directors, the control committee and even, in some cases, a general meeting of the company.

General company law also provides protection to shareholders in an Israeli company in respect of transactions or proposed transactions concerning the company in which the company's directors, officers or interested parties have a direct or indirect interest. Such transactions require various approvals, including in some cases the approval of disinterested shareholders in a general meeting.

Directors are, in the ordinary course of affairs, entitled to acquire and dispose of shares in the company in which they are directors, although any such acquisition or disposal must be immediately reported to the relevant authorities.

B) Insider trading

Insider dealing is a criminal offence and a civil tort. The Securities Law 5728-1968 imposes *prima facie* liability upon "key insiders" – directors, general managers, financial officers and so forth – in respect of dealing in the company's securities, and such people must prove, if they hold securities for a period of less than three months, that such dealings were not made on the basis of insider information in order to rebut the presumption of liability.

C) Lock-up provisions

The TASE has issued regulations concerning lock-up provisions in respect of shares held prior to an offering. Broadly speaking, persons holding more than 5% of the shares of the company prior to an offering may not effect any transaction or action in respect of these shares prior to the offering or for three months after the offering, and may only trade 2.5% of their holdings in each of the 14 months thereafter. Persons holding less than 5% may not effect transactions three months after the offering and may only trade 12.5% of their holdings in each of the five months thereafter. In a recent change, the regulations have been expanded so that they now apply to bonus shares issued during the lock-up period.

D) Market manipulation

The Securities Law provides that any person who induces or attempts to induce another to acquire or sell securities based upon false or misleading statements or by concealing material facts, or who fraudulently manipulates the price of securities is committing a criminal offence and is liable to imprisonment for up to five years or a fine.

RESEARCH

On each trading day the TASE publishes an official list of prices for every security traded on the exchange (in both Hebrew and English). This list includes prices, exchange turnover, turnover outside the exchange and outstanding positions. Attached to this official list is a "blue list" containing unit trust prices and prices of securities not listed on the exchange but traded on the official market.

The TASE also publishes several pamphlets giving information on securities law, trading procedures, rules, guides about convertible debentures and warrants, stocks, bonds, regulations for listing companies and voting rights, and various lists showing daily, monthly and annual prices and trading volumes for the market.

The Bank of Israel (BOI), the country's central bank, publishes a periodical entitled *Capital Market Developments.* This includes a comprehensive survey of events in the capital market in the period under review.

There are also Internet sites for the BOI, the Central Bureau of Statistics (CBS), the TASE and some of the major newspapers.

Bank/broker publications

Through their research departments, the main commercial banks publish material on the securities market. For the most part, these publications take the form of reports rather than in-depth research, and they are distributed in bank branches as a customer service. Monthly and quarterly bulletins, in Hebrew and English, surveying recent capital market developments are also published.

National Consultants' publications

National Consultants provides research and consultancy services on the capital markets. Its publications are produced in Hebrew and in English and provide data on companies traded on the TASE and in New York.

Newspapers and periodicals

Topical reports on exchange events and investment data can be obtained from a number of financial newspapers like *Globus, Shaar, Telegraph* and *Mabat,* as well as from the financial sections of the daily newspapers, such as *Yediot Aharonot, Maariv, Haaretz, Hadashot Davar,* the *Jerusalem Post* (published in English) and the English weekly business news update, *Israel Business Today.*

Additional sources of information for investors are various economic journals published in Israel. These include *The Economic Quarterly, The Banking Quarterly* and the *Bank of Israel Survey.*

PROSPECTIVE CHANGES

A draft bill is being considered by the Knesset to replace the existing Companies Ordinance. Certain key changes concern the election of independent public directors and the drawing up of a takeover code.

The authorities have been considering whether to allow the opening of a new stock exchange, although little progress is being made at the moment.

TASE is examining draft proposals for the following: allowing corporate reorganisations to be performed with greater ease; preventing large swings in the Maof Index; and allowing parallel registration of shares on TASE and on foreign stock exchanges.

CHAPTER 32

Italy

Introduction

Italian financial markets prospered in 1997, despite modest GDP growth of about 1.4%. Helped by falling long-term interest rates, the BCI All-Share Index, which had begun the year at 666.40, stood at 1,053.18 on 31 December 1997, a rise of 58% (or in excess of 60% if dividends are taken into account).

In 1997, the Italian government completed a L26,000 billion flotation of Telecom Italia, its biggest ever privatisation. It also privatised Banco di Roma and sold a third tranche in the Eni group. It has promised to continue its programme of privatisation in 1998.

Despite a degree of political instability (as demonstrated by the draft budget crisis in September 1997) and continued concerns regarding corruption, the centre-left government under Romano Prodi has put paid to many of Italy's political and economic problems, and has transformed the country's prospects of joining EMU. Calculations of the probability that Italy will join EMU on 1 January 1999 peaked close to 100% at the end of 1997.

ECONOMIC AND POLITICAL OVERVIEW

Italy's EMU convergence problems have centred on public finance, because, as recently as 1996, the government deficit was 6.7% of GDP and public debt exceeded 120% of GDP. The other convergence parameters were not expected to cause problems, and this indeed proved to be the case. As regards public finance, a mixture of tough policy and sheer luck managed to squeeze the deficit below 3% of GDP and to keep the still high debt/GDP ratio on a falling path for the third consecutive year. In addition, the support of the French socialist government for a wide EMU and the flexible attitude adopted to measuring fiscal parameters in the Maastricht criteria, both served to increase the likelihood of Italy's inclusion in the first round of EMU.

Although some of the measures keeping the deficit below 3% of GDP were temporary (such as the Euro Tax), the massive prospective deficit impact of falling short-term interest rates boosts the likelihood of fiscal stability (Italian debt is low duration and thus more sensitive to short than long rates). Given that short rates at end-1997, after a two-point fall, were still 250 basis points higher than German equivalents, there is a large potential for interest expense to fall further, both as a result of inertia and upon more short-rate convergence. So, the deficit will stay below 3% of GDP unless strong measures reducing the primary surplus are taken (which is not a risk specific to Italy).

Despite a VAT hike in late 1997, year-on-year Italian inflation fell from 2.6% in December 1996 to 1.5% in December 1997, thanks to subdued domestic demand, very low import price growth (notwithstanding the strength of the dollar) and manageable increases in the unit cost of labour. Despite this, and modest growth (with low investment), monetary policy remained fairly restrictive. The Bank of Italy cut official rates three times in January, June and December 1997, amounting to a 200 basis point decrease, but for most of the year the monetary conditions index – reflecting the impact of both interest and exchange rates – remained flat in real terms, keeping the restrictive tilt of policy inherited from 1996. Only at the end of the year did policy become neutral. Prospects for 1998 are for a substantial relaxation, as convergence in short rates, minor movements in foreign exchange rates and possibly a small upturn in inflation combine to move real monetary conditions towards expansion.

Role of the central bank

The Bank of Italy is responsible for monetary policy (except as regards foreign exchange matters, which are the Treasury's province) and for the supervision of banks and other financial intermediaries. The bank's monetary policy is set by a Directorate, including the governor, appointed by the Bank's Council under government approval. The bank has authority to set monetary policy independently of Treasury needs or other political pres-

Exhibit 32.1: MILAN MIBTEL PRICE INDEX (L), 1993–97

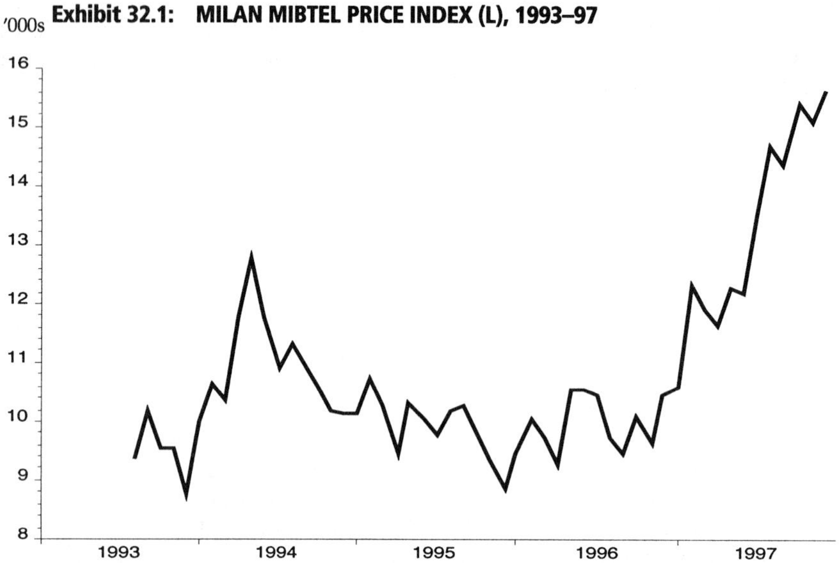

High value 15,612.0 1.12.97 Low value 8,778.6 1.12.93 *Source: Datastream*

sure; its charter does not single out a precise objective, but bank officials have made clear that their primary concern is with price stability. At various times, intermediate targets have changed, from M2 (or domestic credit) to the exchange rate to CPI inflation.

Monetary policy is operated through official rates (discount and fixed-term advances, both of which define bank policy but do not determine market rates), reserve requirements (due to be lowered in the transition process to EMU) and repos, which acquired increasing importance in tuning short-term liquidity and are currently the main conduit for controlling base money. Interbank rates – the short-run operational target – are determined via an efficient on-screen market known as MID.

MARKET PERFORMANCE

A) In 1997

At the end of 1997 the Historical Index closed at 16,341, up 58% over the year. The shares of 213 companies (including four foreign firms) were listed on the Italian Stock Exchange (ISE). Year-end total market capitalisation was L600 trillion (up by 55.4% on the end-1996 figure) or about 31% of GDP. Market turnover for 1997 totalled L338 trillion, representing 69% of average market capitalisation.

B) Summary information

Global ranking by market value (US$ terms, end-1997): 10
Market capitalisation (end-1997): US$340 billion
Growth in market value (local currency terms, 1993–97): 156%
Market value as a % of nominal GDP (end-1997): 30.8%
Number of domestic/foreign companies listed (end-1997): 209/4
Market P/E (MSCI data, 117 companies, end-1997): 24.7
MSCI total returns (with net dividends, US$ terms, 1997): 35.5%
MSCI Index (change in US$ terms, 1997): +33.6%
Short-term (3-month) interest rate (end-1997): 4.9%
Long-term (10-year) bond yield (end-1997): 5.5%
PSBR as a % of nominal GDP (1997): 2.7%
Annual increase in broad money (M3) supply (Oct 1997): 6.9%
Inflation rate (1997): 1.5%
US$ exchange rate (end-1997): L1,760

C) Year-end share price index, price/earnings ratios and yields

Exhibit 32.2:
YEAR-END SHARE PRICE INDEX, AVERAGE P/E AND DIVIDEND YIELDS, 1993–97

Year-end	*Historical Index*	*P/E*	*Yield (%)*
1993	9,500	24.0	1.8
1994	9,813	41.0	1.7
1995	9,138	30.2	1.7
1996	10,332	18.9	2.4
1997	16,341	24.7	2.3

Source: Italian Stock Exchange.

D) Market indices and their constituents

The most widely recognised stock exchange price indices are the MIB, the MIBTEL and the MIB 30. The MIB and MIBTEL indices are based on the prices of all listed shares, while the MIB 30 Index is computed on a sample of the 30 most liquid and highly capitalised shares. All these indices are capitalisation-weighted. The MIB Index (comprising the general index, three macro indices and 20 sector indices) is computed daily using official prices of each share, and it is disseminated in current value (end of previous year = 1,000) and in historical value (2 January 1975 = 1,000). The MIBTEL Index (base 3 January 1994 = 10,000) and the MIB 30 Index (base 31 December 1992 = 10,000) are disseminated once a minute using the most recent available price of each share in the index.

The Banca Commerciale Italiana (BCI) calculates the Comit Index each day. Its methodology is similar to the MIB indices and it includes all ISE listed shares (base average 1972 = 100).

On 3 November 1997 the ISE launched MIDEX, a capitalisation-weighted index comprising 25 medium-sized stocks. The composition of MIDEX is updated twice a year (March and September), its base is 30 December 1994 = 10,000 and it is disseminated once every minute.

THE STOCK MARKET

A) Brief history and structure

The Milan Stock Exchange, the main Italian market prior to recent reforms, was established in 1808. Up until 1991 trading took place by means of an open outcry auction system on 10 regional stock exchanges, although Milan accounted for 99% of all trading in the 1980s. Following a programme of major reforms affecting both the stock market and the role of intermediaries, a national computerised order-driven trading system was introduced in November 1991 and all securities, listed in Milan and on the other stock exchanges, were gradually transferred to the new system. Since April 1994 (shares) and July 1994 (warrants, convertible bonds and bonds), all listed securities have been traded electronically.

The legal framework for capital markets and intermediaries was amended by Legislative Decree 415/96 implementing the European Investment Services Directive. Under the Decree, the Italian Stock Exchange became a private limited company (majority owned by authorised intermediaries) responsible for the regulation, promotion and management of exchange trading, the unlisted securities market and the Italian Derivatives Market (IDEM).

Under its regulatory powers, the ISE is responsible for:
1. The organisation and functioning of the markets, the admission of intermediaries, market surveillance and the management of critical situations.
2. The requirements and procedures for the admission of securities and the ongoing regulation of listed companies.
3. Stock exchange management and the enforcement of a code of behaviour for all market operators.

B) Different exchanges

There is one nationwide exchange trading equities on a computerised system, based in Milan.

C) Opening hours, names and addresses

Equity trading hours are as follows:
Main market: opening auction, 8.00am–9.30am; continuous trading, 10.00am–5.00pm.
Second market: electronic auction, 3.00pm–5.00pm.

ITALIAN STOCK EXCHANGE
Piazza Degli Affari 6, 20123 Milan
Tel: (39) 2 853 44636; Fax: (39) 2 853 44638
Tlx: 321430 MICOMB I

MARKET SIZE

A) Number of listings and market value

There were 213 companies listed on the ISE at the end of 1997, and total equity market capitalisation was L600,042 billion, an increase of 55.4% over the year.

Exhibit 32.3:
NUMBER OF LISTED COMPANIES, SHARE ISSUES LISTED AND MARKET VALUE, ISE, 1993–97

	1993	*1994*	*1995*	*1996*	*1997*
Number of companies listed	222	223	221	217	213
Number of share issues listed	329	324	316	307	301
Market value (L billion)	234,256	293,566	325,568	386,157	600,042

Note: 1993 figures are for the Milan Stock Exchange.

Source: Italian Stock Exchange.

Exhibit 32.4:
MARKET VALUE BY SECTOR, ISE, END-1997

Sector	*Number of companies*	*Capitalisation (L billion)*
Industrial		
Minerals, metals, petroleum	6	83,543
Automotive	13	28,246
Chemicals	24	14,417
Textiles, clothing	24	13,995

Exhibit 32.4 continued

Food	7	13,175
Electronics	29	13,045
Construction	16	5,969
Machinery	10	5,856
Paper	7	1,887
Miscellaneous	2	156
Services		
Public utilities	12	151,115
Media	8	17,076
Transportation/tourism	20	11,654
Distribution	6	4,066
Financial		
Banking	37	124,390
Insurance	22	91,755
Holding companies	33	17,094
Real estate/construction	14	1,792
Financial services	3	598
Miscellaneous	4	215

Source: Italian Stock Exchange.

B) Largest quoted companies

Exhibit 32.5:
THE TOP 20 SHARES ON THE ISE BY CAPITALISATION, END-1997

Ranking	*Company*	*Market value (L billion)*
1	Eni	80,904.0
2	Telecom Italia	75,548.2
3	Telecom Italia Mobile	62,231.2
4	Generali	38,339.2
5	Fiat	24,054.2
6	Credito Italiano	15,794.8
7	INA	14,472.0
8	San Paolo Torino	13,849.8
9	Banco Ambrosiano Veneto	12,621.5
10	IMI	12,585.0
11	Alleanza Assicurazioni	12,331.7
12	Rolo Banca 1473	10,968.6
13	Banca Commerciale Italiana	10,921.0
14	Mediaset	10,253.3
15	Banca di Roma	9,319.7
16	Montedison	8,739.4
17	Pirelli SpA	8,064.8
18	Ras	7,268.2
19	Banca Fideuram	7,144.0
20	Edison	6,727.5

Source: Italian Stock Exchange.

C) Trading volume

The value of equity trading in 1997 totalled L337,548 billion, up from L156,521 billion in 1996.

Exhibit 32.6:
SHARE TURNOVER, ISE, 1993–97

Year	*Trading value (L billion)*
1993	103,501
1994	190,093
1995	140,341
1996	156,521
1997	337,548

Source: Italian Stock Exchange.

Exhibit 32.7:
THE 20 MOST ACTIVELY TRADED SHARES, ISE, 1997

Ranking	*Company*	*Trading value (L billion)*
1	Eni	38,261.8
2	Telecom Italia	36,255.2
3	Generali	22,263.5
4	Telecom Italia Mobile	19,734.5
5	Fiat	17,570.4
6	Credito Italiano	12,839.1
7	Telecom Italia Rsp	11,373.0
8	Banca Commerciale Italiana	10,185.0
9	Telecom Italia	9,844.6
10	Montedison	8,709.1
11	Ina	8,249.1
12	San Paolo di Torino	7,690.5
13	Imi	6,888.9
14	Pirelli SpA	6,410.5
15	Mediaset	5,329.7
16	Mediobanca	4,874.7
17	Edison	4,786.7
18	Alleanza Assicurazioni	4,783.8
19	Olivetti	4,313.9
20	Italgas	4,226.8

Source: Italian Stock Exchange.

TYPES OF SHARE

There are three types of listed shares on the Italian market: ordinary, preference and saving. Saving shares are usually in bearer form and have a right to a fixed dividend of 5% of the par value. They also have a preference over other categories of shares in the liquidation of assets, but have no voting rights. In some cases they are convertible into ordinary shares. Such shares may only be issued by companies that have their ordinary shares already officially listed. Shares with no voting rights cannot be issued in respect of more than 50% of the capital.

Exhibit 32.8:
TOP PERFORMING COUNTRY FUNDS – ITALY

Fund	*US$ % change* 31/12/96 31/12/97	31/12/92 31/12/97	Currency	*Fund size* (US$ mil)	Volatility	Manager name	Main sector	Class
Hansard EU Fidelity Italy	43.71	N/A	L	N/A	N/A	Hansard Europe	Equity	Offshore Territories
EMIF Italy Index Plus B	43.55	N/A	L	4.11	7.9	CCF/BHF/HS/KB/BBV	Equity	Luxembourg
EMIF Italy Index Plus B	43.55	N/A	L	5.61	8.88	CCF/BHF/HS/KB/BBV	Equity Growth	Investmentfds Deutschland
EMIF Italy Index Plus A	43.49	N/A	L	1.71	7.9	CCF/BHF/HS/KB/BBV	Equity	Luxembourg
Sogitalia	40.7	142.18	Ffr	92.99	N/A	Société Générale	Equity	French FCPs
Deka Italien	40.69	N/A	DM	13.19	7.25	Deka	Equity Growth	Investmentfds Deutschland
Groupe Indosuez Italy	39.75	N/A	L	21.49	N/A	Groupe Indosuez Fd Mgt Co	Equity	Luxembourg
Groupe Indosuez Italy	39.75	N/A	L	14.72	N/A	Groupe Indosuez Fd Mgt Co	Equity Growth	Investmentfds Deutschland
DWS Italien	39.55	N/A	DM	58.18	N/A	DWS	Equity Growth	Investmentfds Deutschland
Fidelity Fds Italy	38.89	152.2	L	192.08	5.85	Fidelity Funds (Lux)	Equity	Luxembourg
Fidelity Fds Italy	38.89	152.2	L	159.37	7.1	Fidelity Funds	Equity Growth	Investmentfds Deutschland
Mosais Actions Italiennes	38.45	92.9	L	17.62	6.08	Credit Agricole	Equity	Luxembourg
DVG Fonds Italia	38.21	103.52	DM	86.7	7.15	DVG	Equity Growth	Investmentfds Deutschland
Hansard\Fidelity Italy	37.99	36.2	L	0.18	5.8	Hansard\Fidelity	Equity	Offshore Territories
Sogelux Fd Equities Italy	37.93	N/A	L	47.92	N/A	Société Générale Bank & Trust	Equity	Luxembourg
Mida Azionario	37.67	N/A	L	N/A	N/A	Fidagest	Equity Growth	Italian Mutuals
BBL Invest Italy Cap	37.51	N/A	L	24.24	6.52	BBL-Banque Brussels Lambert	Equity	Belgian Trusts
Schroder Intl Sel Italian Eq	37.33	N/A	L	25.85	N/A	Schroder Intl Sel	Equity	Luxembourg
Schroder Intl Sel Italian Eq	37.33	N/A	L	20.44	N/A	Schroder Intl Sel	Equity Growth	Investmentfds Deutschland
CU PP Italian Growth	37.15	97.75	L	5.64	6.73	CU Privilege Portfolio	Equity	Luxembourg
Pictet C.F. Valitalia	37.06	136.72	L	8.01	6.89	Pictet and Cie	Equity	Luxembourg
SBC Eq Fd Italy	36.57	100.37	L	259.39	N/A	Swiss Bank Corporation	Equity	Swiss Mutual Funds
G-Equity Fund G-Italian Eq B	36.45	N/A	L	30.36	6.63	Generale de Banque	Equity	Luxembourg
G-Equity Fund G-Italian Eq B	36.45	N/A	L	28.9	7.78	Generale de Banque (Lux)	Equity Growth	Investmentfds Deutschland
G-Equity Fund G-Italian Eq A	36.4	N/A	L	9.23	6.63	Generale de Banque	Equity	Luxembourg
Fondersel Italia	36.21	N/A	L	N/A	N/A	Sogersei	Equity Growth	Italian Mutuals
Sanpaolo Azioni	34.29	N/A	L	N/A	N/A	Sanpaolo Fondi	Equity Growth	Italian Mutuals
DIT Fonds Italien	33.55	69.56	DM	152.89	7.64	DIT	Equity Growth	Investmentfds Deutschland
CS EF (Lux) Italy	33.53	83.57	L	11.95	5.87	Credit Suisse AM Funds	Equity	Luxembourg
CS EF (Lux) Italy B	33.53	83.57	L	91.69	5.87	Credit Suisse AM Funds	Equity Growth	Investmentfds Deutschland
CICM CB Italy Basket	33.38	N/A	L	7.56	6.4	CICM Fund Mgmt Ltd	Equity	Offshore Territories
Parvest Italy C	33.18	N/A	L	135.58	6.38	Banque Paribas	Equity	Luxembourg
Parvest Italy C	33.18	N/A	L	104.39	7.58	Banque Paribas	Equity Growth	Investmentfds Deutschland
Parvest Italy D	33.13	N/A	L	0.86	6.38	Banque Paribas	Equity	Luxembourg
Citi PF Italian Equity	32.5	N/A	L	59.89	N/A	Citiportfolios	Equity	Luxembourg
Citi PF Italian Equity	32.5	N/A	L	39.53	N/A	Citiportfolios SA	Equity Growth	Investmentfds Deutschland
Centrale Italia	29.81	N/A	L	N/A	N/A	La Centrale Fondi	Equity Growth	Italian Mutuals
Gestifondiaz. Italia	29.79	N/A	L	N/A	N/A	Gestifondi	Equity Growth	Italian Mutuals
CMI Passport Italian Equity	29.14	N/A	L	0.01	N/A	CMI Passport	Equity	Offshore Territories
Ducato Azionario Italia	29.05	N/A	L	N/A	N/A	Synergest	Equity Growth	Italian Mutuals
CMI Ins Co Italian Equity	28.96	19.32	£	0.67	6.97	CMI Insurance Company (IOM)	Equity	Offshore Territories
IMI-Italy	28.54	89.36	L	N/A	N/A	Imigest	Equity Growth	Italian Mutuals
Oyster Italian Opportunities	28.53	N/A	L	18.65	N/A	Global Investment Selection	Equity	Luxembourg
The Sailor's-Italian Equity	28.38	N/A	L	13.2	N/A	Banca Brignone/Ceresole&C.Sim	Equity	Luxembourg

Note: details for some funds may not have been included if the data for the US$ % change for 96/97 was not available

Source: Standard & Poor's Micropal.

OTHER MARKETS

From 2 January 1998, new requirements for admission to Italy's parallel market, the Mercato Ristretto, came into force. These are as follows:

- estimated market capitalisation of L1 billion;
- ownership by the public of at least 20% of the category of shares for which listing is requested;
- audited certification by official accountants.

The issuer must also provide Consob (Italy's highest regulatory authority) with a prospectus meeting the same requirements as for the ISE.

An equity derivatives market began operations in November 1994. It trades MIB 30 Index futures (FIB 30), MIB 30 Index options and stock options on the 18 most liquid and largest capitalised shares listed on the ISE. Contract settlement takes place daily through a centralised clearing house.

INVESTORS

The main categories of Italian equity investors are private individuals, insurance companies, investment funds, investment companies, overseas investors, a few pension funds and banks.

OPERATIONS

A) Trading system

The electronic trading system is managed by the ISE and is run by CED Borsa, a private company, which manages all the exchange data processing facilities. The system is supported by a network that connects all authorised securities firms throughout Italy. It enables trading in real time of all securities, independent of physical location.

There are two trading systems: *servizio Affari* for shares, warrants and convertible bonds; and *servizio Mot-Spe* for bonds and odd-lots.

Continuous equity trading is organised in five phases. During the pre-opening phase (8.00am–9.30am) authorised intermediaries can insert buy and sell orders, but no contracts are matched. In real time the system calculates and disseminates the theoretical opening price at the level capable of maximising the quantity of securities traded. Validation starts at 9.30am; in 10 minutes the system checks all listed securities that meet the regulation conditions. During this phase, compatible orders (for price and quantity) are matched at the same opening price, according to price-time priority rules. Orders only partially satisfied or not satisfied are transferred to the negotiation phase book, in which authorised intermediaries may place buy and sell orders that are automatically matched according to usual time and price priority rules. At 5.00pm the closing phase begins; no new orders may be inserted and the system computes official prices as the weighted average of prices of all contracts.

Price variation parameters have been set and are managed by the market department of the ISE. Securities are subject to five minutes of suspension every time the new price varies by more than 10% against the reference price or by more than 5% against the previous price in the same session.

Block trading is allowed for orders above the minimum block lot fixed by the ISE, which varies (according to the average trading volume) between L500 million to L5 billion. Authorised intermediaries must report all trades to the authorities within 90 seconds. They are disclosed to the public after 30 minutes.

B) List of principal brokers

Legislative Decree 415 of July 1996, which incorporated the European Union Investment Services Directive into Italian law, authorised investment firms and banks of EU countries to trade directly on the ISE.

AKROS
Corsa Italia 3, 20122 Milan
Tel: (39) 2 802 51

BANCO NAPOLI FUMAGALLI & SOLDAN
Via Meravigli 16, 20123 Milan
Tel: (39) 2 724 381

CIMO
Piazza Missori 3, 20123 Milan
Tel: (39) 2 724 001

DEUTSCHE BANK
Via del Gallo 6, 20122 Milan
Tel: (39) 2 863 79894

EUROMOBILIARE
Via Turati 9, 20122 Milan
Tel: (39) 2 62041

GIUBERGIA WARBURG DILLON READ
Via Santa Maria Segreta 6, 20123 Milan
Tel: (39) 2 721 001

IMI SIGECO
Corso Mateotti 4/6, 20121 Milan
Tel: (39) 2 775 133

INTERMOBILIARE
Piazza Lagrange 2, 10123 Turin
Tel: (39) 11 516 2411

INTERSIM
Corsa di Porta Nuova 1, 20121 Milan
Tel: (39) 2 290 9966

SALOMON BROTHERS AG
Via San Paolo 10, 20121 Milan
Tel: (39) 2 777 3500; Fax: (39) 2 777 3535

SIMCREDIT
Via Broletto 16, 20121 Milan
Tel: (39) 2 722 79734

C) Settlement and clearing

All share transactions are settled on a T+5 rolling settlement basis.

Clearing procedures are managed by the Bank of Italy through its clearing and payments system (*stanze di compensazione*), to which all intermediaries (SIMs, individual stockbrokers and banks) belong. The settlement system performs all matching and netting procedures centrally.

D) Commissions and other costs

Commission fees are negotiable.

TAXATION AND REGULATIONS AFFECTING FOREIGN INVESTORS

A) Capital gains

Currently, institutions and companies pay capital gains tax at the normal corporate rate. From 1 July 1998, however, new rules for the taxation of investment income and capital gains will take effect. Under the new system there will be two levels of taxation, depending upon whether or not an investment is classified as a substantial holding. For listed companies a substantial holding is more than 2% of the voting rights or more than 5% of the capital, and for unlisted companies more than either 20% of the voting rights or 25% of the capital. Capital gains of private resident investors from substantial holdings will be taxed at a rate of 27%. All other equity holdings will be taxed at 12.5%.

However, non-resident investors will be exempt from capital gains taxation on non-substantial holdings and other income that would normally be subject to the 12.5% rate if they are resident in a country that has a tax treaty containing an exchange of information clause and which is not considered a tax haven.

B) Withholding tax

Dividends are subject to an initial withholding tax of 10% and are included in personal/corporate tax returns, with a tax rebate of nine-sixteenths of the amount of the dividend. Private investors may choose to pay a definitive withholding tax of 12.5%, while remaining anonymous. The withholding tax on dividends for foreign private investors is 32.4%. Under double taxation agreements, in many cases this rate is lower.

From 1 July 1998, dividends from a non-substantial participation distributed by a resident corporation to a private resident investor will be subject to a definitive 12.5% withholding tax. The 58.73% imputation credit will not be granted. However, with respect to dividends paid on listed securities, the investor may opt for the ordinary method of taxation.

Dividends distributed to non-resident investors will be subject to a definitive 27% withholding unless a treaty provides for a lower rate. If the investor can show that tax was paid on the dividends in his country of residence, a refund may be claimed, depending on the amount of tax paid abroad. However, the refund will not exceed four-ninths of the Italian withholding tax.

Exhibit 32.8:
WITHHOLDING TAX

Recipient	*Dividends[1] %*	*Interest[2] %*
Resident corporations	10, 12.5	12.5, 15, 27
Resident individuals	10, 12.5	12.5, 15, 27
Non-resident corporations and individuals:		
Non-treaty	32.4[3]	12.5, 15, 27
Treaty	5-32.4	Nil-25

Notes:
1. The relevant treaty should be consulted to see if a reduced rate for dividends is applicable in the case of payments to corporations having requisite control.
2. Different rates on interest are applicable according to the source.
3. Non-residents have the right to be reimbursed for up to two-thirds of the withholding effected, on provision of a certificate from the appropriate foreign tax office declaring they have definitely paid abroad a tax on the same profits.

Source: Price Waterhouse.

C) Stamp duty

Resident investors engaging in securities transactions on regulated markets no longer have to pay stamp duty. However, a stamp duty of L140 on every L100,000 or fraction of the transaction value will continue to be due on securities transactions concluded directly between resident investors.

D) Investment restrictions

Generally, there are no restrictions on foreign investments in Italy. Foreign individuals and companies may freely purchase and sell listed Italian stocks. Under a law on money laundering, financial transactions of L20 million or more are subject to reporting by banks and financial intermediaries.

E) Non-resident bank accounts

Non-residents may freely open bank accounts, either in lire or foreign currency, with an authorised bank. The former, known as an external lire account, is the standard account used for all kinds of transactions, either commercial or financial. This account can be credited with the proceeds of the conversion of foreign currency into lire, or with remittances made by Italian residents in connection with imports or other commercial or financial transactions. Cash withdrawals exceeding L20 million must be declared to the Italian exchange control authorities.

F) Repatriation

Italian law guarantees the repatriation of capital and profits. At present, profits and dividends may be remitted abroad without limitation.

G) Exchange controls

At the end of the 1980s, Italy abolished all foreign exchange regulations, adopting the general principle that all transactions are free unless specifically prohibited.

LISTING AND REPORTING REQUIREMENTS

A) Listing requirements

From 2 January 1998, the ISE imposes the following requirements on companies seeking an exchange listing:

a) An estimated market capitalisation of L10 billion.
b) Ownership by the public of at least 25% of the category of shares for which listing is requested.
c) The submission of three annual reports, of which the last must include financial statements audited by official accountants. (In exceptional cases one annual report may be accepted.)
d) The appointment (for at least one year) of a financial intermediary to act as sponsor.

Foreign issuers must demonstrate that there are neither legal obstacles to their compliance with Italian provisions on information requirements nor impediments of any kind to the exercise of all rights attaching to securities to be listed on the ISE. Prior to listing, the issuer must prepare a prospectus.

B) Reporting requirements

Reporting requirements for listed companies include the following:

a) *Periodical information*: on the occasion of board meetings and shareholders' meetings approving the annual report, dividends and half-yearly statements, a press release must be issued to the authorities and to two press agencies; the annual report and the half-yearly report shall be sent to Consob 20 days before the meetings, and the meeting resolutions together with the approved reports must be sent to Consob within 30 days after the meetings.
b) *Price-sensitive information*: for major corporate events or information that might have a bearing on the market price of securities, a press release must be sent to Consob and the ISE 15 minutes before its issue to the public.
c) *Corporate control*: Consob must be advised of any shareholder that purchases more than 2% of the shares of a listed company within 48 hours of the transaction.

SHAREHOLDER PROTECTION CODES

A) Minority rights

Shareholders are protected by the reporting requirements described in the previous section and by minority shareholders' rights set out in the Civil Code and applicable to all companies. For example, any shareholder who believes that a resolution passed at a shareholders' meeting violates Italian law and/or the articles of the company is entitled to request the court to examine the resolution. Also, several types of action may be brought against the directors:

i) Shareholders may require the corporation to bring an action against its directors to recover damages for injuries suffered by the corporation as a consequence of the directors' fraudulent or negligent acts. Such an action must be authorised by a resolution duly passed by an ordinary shareholders' meeting.
ii) Any shareholder may sue the directors directly for damages if they have personally suffered a loss as a consequence of the fraud or negligence of the directors.
iii) Shareholders representing not less than 10% of the corporate capital may request a court investigation of a corporation's affairs if there are grounds for believing that the directors or auditors are guilty of a breach of duty to the corporation.
iv) Any shareholders who believe that actions taken by the directors are not consistent with the articles or the corporation's best interests may notify the board of statutory auditors to this effect, and the board must submit a report on the matter to an ordinary shareholders' meeting. If the holders of not less than 5% of the share capital so request, the auditors must investigate any particular action taken by the board of

directors, and if they find that the directors have acted in violation of the laws or the corporate charter, they must immediately report to an extraordinary shareholders' meeting.

B) Substantial shareholdings

Consob must be informed within 48 hours of the acquisition of 2% or more of a listed company.

C) Insider trading

In May 1991, Italy adopted an insider trading law forbidding purchases, sales or other transactions involving transferable securities, by persons possessing non-public information obtained through capital holdings or the exercise of their employment, profession or duties. The insider trading law also forbids revealing such information to a third party. Violators of these provisions are subject to criminal sanctions with penalties including imprisonment of up to one year and fines from L10 million to L300 million, with the possibility that a judge may increase the fine up to three times this amount for serious violations.

Persons spreading false or exaggerated information, or employing any device, scheme, or artifice to materially influence the price of transferable securities, are subject to imprisonment for up to six months and fines from L1 million to L30 million. These sanctions are doubled if the persons disseminating the information are controlling shareholders or hold similar, privileged positions.

The insider trading law applies not only to transferable securities in regulated Italian markets, but also to such securities on any other regulated market in the EU.

D) Compensation fund

In 1992, as part of the reform of the Italian financial market, the Cassa di Compensazione e Garanzia was established in the form of a joint stock company, to ensure the proper settlement of trading on the stock exchange, to protect investors in the case of insolvency of intermediaries and to act as the clearing house for derivatives trading.

RESEARCH

The largest securities firms, such as Intermobiliare and Warburg, provide good information on the Italian stock market. According to the insider trading law, all research carried out by authorised intermediaries must be reported to Consob and, after a short delay, to the public. Analitica, Databank and Mediobanca collect and disseminate publications about listed companies' balance sheets. More general information about market structure and performance are published in the Italian Stock Exchange Council publications:

Italian Stock Exchange Official List (daily)
La Borsa Valori (monthly)
Facts and Figures (annual report)
Financial daily newspapers: *Il Sole 24 Ore; MF*
Financial weekly publications: *Il Mondo; Mondo Economico; Milano Finanza.*

CHAPTER

33

Jamaica

Introduction

The Jamaica Stock Exchange (JSE) is one of the most antiquated stock markets in the world. A key objective for 1997 was to modernise the operations of the exchange and make it a more efficient and more transparent market-place for investors. To this end, a Central Securities Depository was established and the experimental stages of electronic trading were introduced. By the middle of 1998, the electronic trading software should be installed and active.

Of the 50 stocks listed on the exchange, approximately 30% are actively traded. The relationship of turnover to total value is 6.54%, which indicates that the market is not very liquid.

Jamaican companies have tended to prefer debt financing to equity in order to fund expansion. However, very high interest rates have led several listed companies to accept financial assistance from the government in the form of injections of equity financing. This has tended to increase activity in the market – a trend that is expected to continue in 1998. The downside to this is that some listed companies that are in dire straits have not received any assistance, and their continued existence is in doubt, while for certain of the firms that have received assistance in the form of equity, the government now has a controlling interest.

ECONOMIC AND POLITICAL OVERVIEW

In the December 1997 general election the People's National Party (PNP) secured a resounding victory, winning 50 out of the 60 available seats. This victory is the PNP's third consecutive win, and makes national history because the PNP is the first political party to achieve this.

The dual focus of government policies during 1997 was to stabilise the Jamaican dollar and to reduce the level of inflation. Both objectives were met via "money market operations". There was a small decline in the value of the Jamaican dollar, which ended the year at J$36.59 to the US dollar (down J$1.56). This relative stability was maintained using money market instruments to attract investors to high interest rate securities and away from the US dollar. Outstanding domestic debt stood at J$11.05 billion at the end of 1997, while the local Treasury bill rate closed the year at 28.08% (despite staying below 20.00% for most of 1997). Keeping money supply growth to a minimum, the government was able to reduce inflation from 25.4% in September 1996 to 9.2% in December 1997.

Role of the central bank

The Bank of Jamaica has a board of directors (appointed by the Minister of Finance) which is responsible for the policy and general administration of the bank.

The main objectives of the bank are to maintain price and currency stability and its key responsibilities are as follows:

- to issue and redeem banknotes and coins;
- to keep and administer Jamaica's reserves;
- to influence the volume and conditions of the supply of credit in order to foster production, trade and employment, consistent with the maintenance of monetary stability in Jamaica and the external value of the currency;
- to encourage the development of money and capital markets in Jamaica; and
- to act as banker to the government.

Fiscal and monetary policies continue to be formulated by the Minister of Finance, with the Bank of Jamaica being delegated responsibility for implementing monetary policy.

MARKET PERFORMANCE

A) In 1997

The JSE continued its 1996 bull run and, in 1997, the market index gained a total of 3,230.68 points (19.4%) to close at 19,846.67. The market peaked on 11 December

1997 at 20,569.81, while its low point was on 5 May at 14,799.46. Despite rising interest rates towards the end of the year, the market gathered momentum, indicating increased interest in the JSE on the part of individual and institutional investors.

The majority of listed companies are seen as undervalued – the average price to book ratio is 0.63 – and this led to increased takeover activity during the year. The first half saw the successful takeover of one of the country's blue chip manufacturing firms by a foreign company at a price widely regarded as too cheap. Later in the year, similar comments were made following the bid by a local listed company for one of its subsidiaries, which is also listed, and this bid did not succeed.

B) Summary information

Global ranking by market value (US$ terms, end-1997): 63
Market capitalisation (end-1997): US$2.17 billion
Growth in market value (local currency terms, 1993–97): 90.1%
Market value as a % of nominal GDP (end-1997): 31.9%
Number of domestic/foreign companies listed (end-1997): 49/1
Market P/E (all listed companies, end-1997): 8.63
Short-term (182-day T-Bill) interest rate (end-1997): 28.08%
Long-term bond yield (end-1997): 29.64%
Budget deficit as a % of nominal GDP (1997): 7.2%
Annual increase in broad money (M3) supply (end-1997): 11%
Inflation rate (1997): 9.2%
US$ exchange rate (end-1997): J$36.59

C) Year-end share price index

Exhibit 33.1:
YEAR-END SHARE PRICE INDEX, 1993–97

Year-end	*JSE Index*
1993	13,099.68
1994	16,676.74
1995	14,266.99
1996	16,615.99
1997	19,846.67

Sources: Jamaica Stock Exchange and Mayberry Investments.

D) Market indices and their constituents

The JSE Index is a market-weighted index comprising ordinary shares of all listed companies. A one cent movement in the share price of each of the included companies has a weighted point impact on the stock market index.

THE STOCK MARKET

A) Brief history and structure

In order to coordinate and organise the growing level of trading activity in government and corporate bonds and equities, the Kingston Stock Market Committee was established in 1961 under the auspices of the Bank of Jamaica. The Committee consisted of stockbrokers and the investment officers of the commercial banks. From these origins the JSE evolved, and it was incorporated with limited liability under the Companies Act of Jamaica in September 1968, commencing operations in February 1969.

Trading is restricted to broker-members who trade both as agents and as principals, although there is provision for associate non-trading membership for financial institutions such as trust companies.

The broker-members are directors of the exchange, with the right to exercise all the powers of directors under the Companies Act of Jamaica. The exchange is governed by a council to which broker-members delegate their powers.

In December 1993 a Securities Commission was established to regulate the securities industry, including the JSE. The exchange has continued to set rules of conduct for members and market operations, although in late 1996 the Securities Commission took over responsibility for setting standards for, and granting licences to, brokerage houses, institutional investors and advisers.

B) Different exchanges

The JSE is the only stock exchange operating in Jamaica.

C) Opening hours, names and addresses

The JSE is open for trading on Monday to Thursday from 9.30am to 2.00pm and, for settlement, on Friday from 10.00am to 11.00am. Regular office hours are Monday to Friday, 8.30am to 4.30pm.

THE JAMAICA STOCK EXCHANGE
40 Harbour Street, PO Box 1084, Kingston
Tel: (876) 922 0806 / 967 3271-4; Fax: (876) 922 6966
Tlx: 2165/2167
E-mail: jse@infochan.com
Web site: www.jamstockex.com

MARKET SIZE

A) Number of listings and market value

There were 49 domestic companies listed on the JSE at the end of 1997, and market capitalisation totalled J$79.62 billion, up 20.4% on the end-1996 total.

Exhibit 33.2:
NUMBER OF COMPANIES LISTED AND MARKET VALUE, JSE, 1993–97

Year-end	*No. of companies*	*Market value (J$ billion)*
1993	45	41.88
1994	47	58.02
1995	48	50.76
1996	50	66.12
1997	49	79.62

Sources: Jamaica Stock Exchange and Mayberry Investments.

B) Largest quoted companies

The two largest quoted companies, Telecommunications of Jamaica and CIBC Holdings, together accounted for 45.1% of total market value.

Exhibit 33.3:
THE 20 LARGEST COMPANIES LISTED ON THE JSE, END-1997

Ranking	*Company*	*Market value (J$ million)*
1	Telecommunications of Jamaica	18,927.41
2	CIBC Holdings	16,951.92
3	Bank of Nova Scotia	12,879.82
4	Carreras Group	7,281.60
5	Grace Kennedy	2,957.78
6	Desnoes and Geddes	2,427.68
7	Lascelles	2,256.00
8	NCB Group	2,121.52
9	CIBC (Jamaica)	1,546.67
10	Jamaica Flour Mills	1,536.00
11	Kingston Wharves	1,406.87
12	Caribbean Cement	1,308.33
13	Jamaica Producers' Group	1,061.46
14	Courts (Jamaica)	958.85
15	Seprod Group	757.38
16	Jamaica Broilers' Group	607.13
17	Life of Jamaica	516.75
18	Caldon Finance Group	427.50
19	Pegasus Hotels	377.67
20	First Life Insurance	315.00

Sources: Jamaica Stock Exchange and Mayberry Investments.

C) Trading volume

The value of turnover (including block transactions) on the JSE in 1997 was J$4.59 billion, a 0.86% decline relative to 1996.

Total volume traded in 1997 was 905.42 million shares, a 62% increase on the 1996 total of 560.53 million shares.

Exhibit 33.4:
TRADING VOLUME AND VALUE (INCLUSIVE OF BLOCK TRANSACTIONS), JSE, 1993–97

	1993	*1994*	*1995*	*1996*	*1997*
Volume (shares '000)					
	567,454	741,754	3,565,607	560,528	905,419
Value (J$ million)					
	8,346	5,155	11,560	4,629	4,594

Source: Jamaica Stock Exchange.

Exhibit 33.5:
THE 20 MOST ACTIVELY TRADED ISSUES, JSE, 1997

Ranking	*Company*	*Trading value (J$ million)*
1	Jamaica Flour Mills	1,561.33
2	CIBC (Jamaica)	526.24
3	Bank of Nova Scotia	426.84
4	Telecommunications of Jamaica	331.29
5	Carreras	292.87
6	Kingston Wharves	267.39
7	Grace Kennedy	257.86
8	Citizens Bank	196.11
9	Lascelles	138.55
10	Pegasus Hotels	94.18
11	Jamaica Broilers	88.69
12	Caribbean Cement	83.63
13	NCB Group	58.15
14	Jamaica Producers	55.91
15	Desnoes & Geddes	38.86
16	Hardware & Lumber	29.07
17	Gleaner Company	23.35
18	Trafalgar Development Bank	18.37
19	Courts (Jamaica)	13.67
20	Goodyear (Jamaica)	11.43

Source: Jamaica Stock Exchange.

TYPES OF SHARE

The ordinary shares of 45 listed companies are listed on the exchange. The preference shares of four companies, as well as the corporate bonds of one company, are also listed. In addition, one company lists a preference security that is US dollar-denominated and another company has promissory notes that are US dollar-denominated. Approximately 17.27 billion ordinary shares are listed on the exchange.

The majority of trading activity takes place in ordinary shares with very little trading in either bonds or preference shares. Government securities are not listed but are traded on an over-the-counter market regulated by the central bank.

INVESTORS

Financial institutions are the most significant investors in the market, although in terms of the number of share dealing accounts, the majority of investors are individuals.

OPERATIONS

A) Trading system

Securities are traded at an open session where the presiding officer recognises calls from the floor to sell to a bid, buy from an offer or enter into a cross transaction. Securities are traded in the sequence in which they appear on the board, with a time limit allocated for the trading of each security. Board lots range from 500 to 2,000 stock units, depending on price.

In 1996 the exchange introduced a second call-over session at which the 15 most liquid stocks are traded. Also, trading in individual stocks can now be halted if the price moves by between 10% and 15% during a trading day.

Principal transactions between a broker-member and his own client are disclosed and may take place only in the absence of interest by other broker-members. Provision exists to facilitate off-the-board block transactions involving a consideration in excess of J$50,000.

B) List of principal brokers

ALPHA FINANCIAL SERVICES
11 Trinidad Terrace, Kingston 5
Tel: (876) 960 5000; Fax: (876) 960 4972

BARITA INVESTMENTS
15 St Lucia Way, Kingston 5
Tel: (876) 926 2686; Fax: (876) 929 8432

BUCK SECURITY BROKERS LTD
2 Holborn Road, Kingston 5
Tel: (876) 929 2654; Fax: (876) 929 4337

EDWARD GAYLE & CO
18 Trafalgar Road, Kingston 5
Tel: (876) 927 3022; Fax: (876) 927 3026

MAYBERRY INVESTMENTS
11/2 Oxford Road, Kingston 5
Tel: (876) 929 1908; Fax: (876) 929 1501

M/VL STOCKBROKERS
17 Knutsford Boulevard, Kingston 5
Tel: (876) 960 1570; Fax: (876) 960 1571

PAUL CHEN YOUNG & CO
2-6 Granada Crescent, Kingston 5
Tel: (876) 929 3261; Fax: (876) 929 3264

PRUDENTIAL STOCKBROKERS LTD
2 St Lucia Avenue, Kingston 5
Tel: (876) 926 1877; Fax: (876) 929 2819

C) Settlement and transfer

Settlement takes place between brokers on a trade-by-trade basis. All trades between Monday and Thursday of one week are subject to inter-broker settlement on the following Friday. Brokers and their clients settle in seven days.

The Jamaica Central Securities Depository (JCSD) opened in 1997 in order to facilitate book-entry settlement.

D) Commissions and other costs

Commission rates for equity transactions are negotiable.

REGULATIONS AFFECTING FOREIGN INVESTORS

The securities market is regulated by the Securities Commission and the Stock Exchange Council.

Investment inflows (including portfolio investment) and outflows are free of any exchange control restrictions, and there is no capital gains tax in Jamaica.

There is no stamp duty on equity transactions, and a guaranteed tax credit attaches to dividends paid by financial institutions.

LISTING AND REPORTING REQUIREMENTS

A) Listing requirements

The listing of securities on the JSE is at the absolute discretion of the Stock Exchange Council. The minimum requirements for the listing of a company's securities are:

- Total issued share and loan capital of J$200,000 or more (the share capital portion being not less than J$100,000).
- In the case of ordinary shares/stock, a minimum of 100 shareholders holding in their own right not less than 20% of the issued ordinary capital (such percentage being not less than J$50,000 in nominal value), excluding the holding(s) of one or more controlling shareholder(s).

Companies incorporated in Jamaica may be listed via a prospectus issue, an offer for sale, an offer by tender or a placing.

B) Reporting requirements

Listed companies are required to conform to the provisions of the Companies Act of Jamaica and to provide the exchange with unaudited quarterly and audited annual financial statements containing certain minimum information and within specific time periods.

Under the Stock Exchange Rules, listed companies must provide the JSE with copies of all public announcements regarding "dividends, profits, issues, expansion programmes and any other changes including any information necessary to enable share/stockholders to appraise the position of the company and to avoid the establishment of a false market in the company's securities". Companies are specifically required to give the exchange notice of profit figures and also any decisions of their board of directors to recommend or declare dividends, make a rights issue, or increase the authorised share capital. More generally, "material information" is required to be disclosed on a timely basis.

SHAREHOLDER PROTECTION CODES

Under the Securities Act 1993, a Securities Commission was set up charged with the regulation of the securities industry. It can undertake investigations and, in certain circumstances, take over the management of the stock exchange or a dealer for a period of up to 90 days. The Securities Act governs the activities of securities dealers. Thus, for example, securities dealers must maintain trust accounts for their clients, and provide them with contract notes confirming a sale or purchase order. Dealers are prohibited from selling securities short.

Under the Securities Act, a company that issues securities to the public must maintain a record of the interests of directors, controlling shareholders and shareholders owning 10% or more of the company's voting stock. Such holdings, and any changes in them, must be reported to the JSE.

The Act also contains a number of provisions to prevent stock manipulation, fraud and insider trading. Under Section 44, a person is prohibited from creating or doing anything that is likely to create a "false or misleading appearance of active trading in any securities", or from otherwise manipulating the price of securities. A person convicted of a trading offence is liable to pay compensation to anyone who suffers loss as a result of a false security price or a price otherwise affected by a violation of the Act.

Two substantial changes to the Securities Act were introduced in April 1996. The first gave JPs wider powers to deal with unlicensed dealers, and the second imposed tighter controls on the creation of mutual funds.

In 1996 the JSE issued a new set of "General Principles and Rules" on takeovers and mergers.

A compensation fund has been established to indemnify losses to clients of broker-members (in defined circumstances) up to a maximum amount of J$1 million. Contributions are made by broker-members at the rate of 0.1% of consideration for equity transactions.

RESEARCH

Information on the Jamaican market can be obtained from the JSE's web site at www.jamstockex.com and from the JSE library. Some of the larger brokers, for example Mayberry Investments, also provide research.

PROSPECTIVE CHANGES

Currently, settlement of equity transactions in Jamaica can take up to nine business days. Plans are in hand to introduce a shorter, rolling settlement cycle based on delivery versus payment. In due course, the JSE expects to move towards a T+3 settlement cycle.

Automated trading is expected to begin during the second quarter of 1998.

CHAPTER 34

Japan

Introduction

Post-war stock market history in Japan has been characterised by several underlying trends – institutionalisation, strong economic growth, liberalisation and deregulation, as well as changes in the philosophy of stock investment. In the 1980s, in particular, the Japanese securities markets changed substantially, with rapid deregulation and globalisation. In the second half of the 1980s and through into the 1990s the capital markets have continued to expand as instruments have proliferated and new derivative markets have been created.

The Japanese stock market tumbled to a two-and-a-half year low in 1997 as the market succumbed to the twin blows of a sharply decelerating domestic economy and a financial system in distress. The end result was a dreadful year for the equity market, but a year in which bond prices soared to new highs as the yen fell to a five-year low against the US dollar.

In June 1997 the Securities and Exchange Council proposed a comprehensive and drastic set of securities market reforms specifically timed to coincide with the Japanese "Big Bang". In the meantime, several securities companies, including Yamaichi, one of the "Big Four", collapsed during the year.

ECONOMIC AND POLITICAL OVERVIEW

Although not yet officially recognised, the expansion in 1996, which had been supported by a series of massive fiscal injections, probably came to an end sometime in the second half of 1997, as the economy contracted 1.4% in the six months to September. Much of the blame is attributable to the policymakers' mistaken belief that the economy was on a sufficiently strong self-sustaining recovery path to withstand a tightening of fiscal policy. Notwithstanding the fragile state of consumer confidence, the government cut back public spending, while simultaneously raising consumption tax and withdrawing a ¥2 trillion tax rebate. This switch to fiscal austerity, in line with the Prime Minister's pledge to meet the targets set out by the Ministry of Finance of reducing the government deficit to 3% by 2002, has been the biggest factor tipping the economy into a cyclical recession.

The subsequent collapse in consumer spending has been one of the steepest in Japan's post-war history, and has fed through to rising inventories, lower output and slowing capital spending. Moreover, the construction sector, the most important employer in the economy, has been hardest hit by government spending cuts, and, with the government allowing a string of failures among major banks and brokers, uncertainty over future employment prospects has become acute: unemployment is currently at 3.5%. As corporate bankruptcies accelerate towards fiscal year-end, consumer confidence is expected to remain depressed, suppressing consumption well into 1998.

The credit crunch has been a crucial factor underlying the rising tide of corporate bankruptcies. Under the strain of bad debts, banks have been struggling to meet capital adequacy requirements, and have been restructuring their balance sheets by sharply curtailing their commercial loans. As the cyclical downturn accelerates, an increase in the exposure to sub-standard loans is inevitable, putting further downward pressure on the economy. Although the injection of public funds (¥13 trillion) into the system via the Financial Stabilisation Programme should help to partially restore capital adequacy and confidence in the system, the near-term prospects remain dire.

On the fiscal front, the government's response to the slowing economy has so far been ineffective. Despite its commitment to fiscal retrenchment, it looks inevitable that some form of fiscal injection, whether it be a tax cut or increased public works spending, needs to be implemented. The issue revolves around the timing and the magnitude of the injection. In contrast, the Bank of Japan

Exhibit 34.1: NIKKEI 225 STOCK AVERAGE PRICE INDEX (¥), 1993–97

High value 22455.49 1.7.96 Low value 14485.41 3.7.95 *Source: Datastream*

has been pursuing a policy of monetary ease given the problems facing the banking system. More importantly, subsequent to the events of November, it acted as a "lender of last resort" by supplying ample liquidity to the system, standing ready to halt a run out of real or illiquid assets into money by making more money available. In the face of falling asset prices, the absence of inflationary pressures and the onset of a cyclical downturn, central bank policy is expected to remain directed towards the problems of the banking system, and there is little pressure for an interest rate hike.

Role of the central bank

The Bank of Japan was reformed in 1997, making its operations more transparent. Continued accountability to the Ministry of Finance is not likely to compromise the bank's independence. The Bank of Japan's main policy aims are to maintain price stability and to promote growth. In addition, it is required to regulate the currency and to control the credit markets in order to promote the smooth functioning of general economic activity.

MARKET PERFORMANCE

A) In 1997

The Japanese equity market managed to flirt with the 21,000 resistance level on the Nikkei 225 Index in June, recovering from 17,000 in January, but the gains represented an extension of the two-tier market that had emerged in late 1996. The advance was narrow, and never broadly based. International blue chips, characterised by their strong earnings momentum and visibility, and backed by a clear management focus and strategy across the entire group, continued to be aggressively marked up, while companies lacking these qualities were severely penalised. The polarisation in favour of companies seen as able to enhance shareholder value continued to dominate the market.

Despite this backdrop, signs of a cyclical slowdown were growing stronger as the effects of fiscal tightening began to feed through. Notwithstanding the fact that the recovery was being underpinned by strong public spending and that confidence was still fragile, the government took the decisive step towards fiscal rectitude in the budget in order to meet the targets set out under the Fiscal Reform Programme. It eliminated the ¥2 trillion special income rebate, hiked the consumption tax from 3% to 5% and cut public spending severely. This triggered a record post-war plunge in consumption as consumer confidence collapsed. The economy had entered a cyclical recession by the second half of the year, which was compounded by the threat of a potential financial meltdown in the south-east Asian economies and, with it, Japan's export markets. Reflecting these developments, both at home and abroad, and signs of further problems of asset quality at major banks, the market quickly began to lose ground, and by the end of the third quarter, the Nikkei 225 stood at 17,887.71, down 7.61% on the year.

Investor confidence was dealt another blow by a string of bankruptcies at major financial institutions, sending shock waves reverberating through the markets. In November, the collapse of Sanyo Securities (a top ten broker) and Hokkaido Takushoku Bank (a city bank) was followed by that of Tokuyo City Bank and Japan's oldest broker, Yamaichi Securities, which filed for bankruptcy under the strain of illegal trading losses of US$2 billion that it had incurred compensating favoured clients. These bankruptcies served to reinforce the view that the true scale of Japan's bad debt problems far exceeded the officially publicised figures, due to poor disclosure and lax regulation: each failure revealed that the true size of the problem was far worse than expected. The integrity of Japan's financial system was called into question, and concerns over the banking system's capital adequacy mounted as the capital base became eroded not only by increasing non-performing loans but also by the slumping stock market. The Bank of Japan and the Ministry of Finance responded promptly and successfully "to provide liquidity in a sufficient and decisive manner in order to prevent any delay in payments of deposits and other liabilities of financial institutions" and to avert a run on the financial system by stepping in as the lender of last resort. An emergency financial stabilisation programme worth ¥30 trillion was drawn up by the government, with ¥17 trillion earmarked to protect depositors and the rest to recapitalise the banks.

However, these developments within the financial sector only served to exacerbate the economic downturn. As banks responded by cutting back on loans to shore up their balance sheets and restore their capital adequacy, it brought on a credit crunch, which has led to rising bankruptcies increasing further their bad debts and perpetuating a downward spiral. Notwithstanding the government's attempt to kick-start the economy through two packages, the Nikkei 225 tumbled to a two-and-a-half year low of 14,488.21 in December, and finished the year down 21% at 15,259.

B) Summary information

Global ranking by market value (US$ terms, end-1997): 2
Market capitalisation (end-1997): US$2,162 billion
Growth in market value (domestic companies, local currency terms, 1993–97): -13.4%
Market value (domestic shares only) as a % of nominal GDP (end-1997): 55.4%
Number of domestic/foreign companies listed (TSE, end-1997): 1,805/60
Market P/E (end-1997): TSE 1st, 37.6; TSE 2nd, 28.5
MSCI total returns (with net dividends, US$ terms, 1997): -23.7%
MSCI Index (change in US$ terms, 1997): -24.2%
Short-term (3-month) interest rate (end-1997): 0.5%
Long-term (10-year) bond yield (end-1997): 1.655%
Budget deficit as a % of nominal GDP (1997): 3.8%
Annual increase in broad money (M3) supply (end-1997): 3.5%
Inflation rate (1997): 1.3%
US$ exchange rate (end-1997): ¥129.92

C) Year-end share price index, price/earnings ratios and yields

Exhibit 34.2:
NIKKEI AVERAGE, P/E AND AVERAGE YIELDS, 1993–97

Year-end	*Nikkei Average*	*Tokyo Stock Price Index*	*TSE 1st section P/E*	*TSE 1st section Yield (%)*	*TSE 2nd section P/E*	*TSE 2nd section Yield (%)*
1993	17,417.24	1,307.66	64.9	0.79	92.1	0.71
1994	19,723.06	1,439.31	79.5	0.71	149.3	0.60
1995	19,868.15	1,577.70	86.5	0.85	82.0	0.77
1996	20,147.27	1,470.90	79.3	0.79	55.2	0.76
1997	15,258.74	1,175.03	37.6	0.92	28.5	0.98

Source: Tokyo Stock Exchange.

D) Market indices and their constituents

The Tokyo Stock Price Index (TOPIX) is a composite index of all common shares listed on the first section of the TSE. It is supplemented by sub-indices for each of 33 industry groups and three size groups (large, medium and small) into which companies listed on the first section are classified. To maintain the continuity of the indices, the base market value is adjusted from time to time in order to reflect only price movements resulting from auction market activity and to eliminate the effect of other factors, such as new listings, delistings and new share issues.

The Nikkei Stock Average, or Nikkei 225, and the Nikkei 500 are calculated as simple averages of the component stock prices, adjusted by a divisor to account for non-market factors, rights and changes to the constituent issues.

The Osaka Securities Exchange (OSE) introduced the Nikkei 300 in 1994. It includes 300 issues listed on the first section of the TSE, and is weighted by market capitalisation. The index base is 1 October 1982, and its composition is reviewed every October.

THE STOCK MARKET

A) Brief history and structure

The Japanese stock market has a history of over 100 years, beginning with the establishment of the Tokyo Stock Exchange in 1878.

Securities listed on the TSE are classified into either the first or second sections depending principally upon size, turnover and share ownership.

Japan's stock exchanges and the over-the-counter market are governed by the Securities and Exchange Law administered by the Minister of Finance. There is strong reliance on self-regulation.

B) Different exchanges

There are eight stock exchanges in Japan, located in Tokyo, Osaka, Nagoya, Kyoto, Hiroshima, Fukuoka, Niigata and Sapporo.

C) Opening hours, names and addresses

Cash market trading hours on full business days are as follows:

- Tokyo: 9.00am to 11.00am and 12.30pm to 3.00pm;
- Kyoto: 9.00am to 11.00am and 12.30pm to 3.30pm;
- Niigata, Sapporo and Fukuoka: 9.00am to 11.30am and 12.30pm to 3.30pm;
- Osaka: 9.00am to 11.00am and 12.30pm to 3.10pm;
- Hiroshima: 9.00am to 11.30am and 12.30pm to 4.00pm;
- Nagoya: 9.00am to 11.00am and 12.30pm to 3.15pm.

Trading hours on the TSE derivatives market are from 9.00am to 11.00am and 12.30pm to 3.10pm for TOPIX futures and options and equity options; from 9.00am to 11.00am and 12.30pm to 3.00pm for Nikkei 225 futures and options; and from 9.00am to 11.00am and 12.30pm to 3.15pm for Nikkei 300 futures and options.

TOKYO STOCK EXCHANGE
2-1, Nihombashi-Kabuto, Chuo-ku, Tokyo 103
Tel: (81) 3 3666 0141; Fax: (81) 3 3663 0625

KYOTO STOCK EXCHANGE
66, Tachiurinishi-machi Higashinotoin-higashiiru
Shijo-dori Shimogyo-ku, Kyoto 600
Tel: (81) 75 221 1171; Fax: (81) 75 541 1128

NIIGATA STOCK EXCHANGE
1245, Hachiban-cho, Kamiohkawamae-dori, Niigata 951
Tel: (81) 25 222 4181; Fax: (81) 25 222 4551

OSAKA SECURITIES EXCHANGE
8-16, Kitahama 1-Chome, Chuo-ku, Osaka 541
Tel: (81) 6 229 8607; Fax: (81) 6 227 5272

HIROSHIMA STOCK EXCHANGE
14-18, Kanayama-cho, Naka-ku, Hiroshima 730
Tel: (81) 82 541 1121; Fax: (81) 82 541 1128

SAPPORO STOCK EXCHANGE
14-1, Nishi 5-chome, Minami 1-jo, Chuo-ku,
Sapporo 060
Tel: (81) 11 241 6171; Fax: (81) 11 251 0840

NAGOYA STOCK EXCHANGE
3-17, Sakae 3-chome, Naka-ku, Nagoya 460
Tel: (81) 52 262 3171; Fax: (81) 52 241 1527

FUKUOKA STOCK EXCHANGE
14-2, Tenjin 2-chome, Chuo-ku, Fukuoka 810
Tel: (81) 92 741 8231; Fax: (81) 92 713 1540

MARKET SIZE

A) Number of listings and market value

At the end of 1997 there were 1,805 domestic companies listed on the TSE, of which 1,327 were listed on the first section. Total market value was ¥280.9 trillion, a decrease of 19.2% on 1996. Following the listing of one company and the delisting of eight during 1997, the number of foreign companies listed in Tokyo at the year-end was down from 67 to 60.

Exhibit 34.3:
NUMBER OF LISTED COMPANIES, LISTED ISSUES AND MARKET VALUE, TSE, 1993–97

	1993	*1994*	*1995*	*1996*	*1997*
Number of listed companies					
1st section	1,234	1,235	1,253	1,293	1,327
2nd section	433	454	461	473	478
Total	1,667	1,689	1,714	1,766	1,805
Number of listed issues					
1st section	1,234	1,236	1,255	1,297	1,327
2nd section	433	455	461	473	479
Total	1,667	1,791	1,716	1,770	1,806
Market value (¥ billion)					
1st section	313,563.3	342,140.9	350,237.5	336,385.1	273,908.0
2nd section	10,794.1	16,251.5	15,478.5	11,193.2	7,022.1
Total	324,357.4	358,392.4	365,716.0	347,578.3	280,930.0

Source: Tokyo Stock Exchange.

Exhibit 34.4:
FINANCING BY LISTED COMPANIES, 1993–97

Year	*Equity issues (¥ million)*	*Overseas issues of Japanese equities (¥ million)*	*Total (¥ million)*
1993	822,791	0	822,791
1994	935,742	0	935,742
1995	584,409	54,006	638,415
1996	1,453,999	619,970	2,073,969
1997	1,099,576	62,795	1,162,371

Source: Tokyo Stock Exchange.

Banks, electric appliances and transportation equipment were by far the major sectors, accounting for 15.46%, 14.89% and 10.80% of total market capitalisation respectively at the end of 1997.

Exhibit 34.5:
MARKET VALUE OF DOMESTIC COMPANIES BY SECTOR, TSE, END-1997

Sector	*Market value (¥ million)*
Banks	43,435,666
Electric appliances	41,818,934
Transportation equipment	30,331,262
Retail trade	13,305,697
Land transportation	13,068,668
Chemicals	12,878,774
Electric power and gas	12,653,683
Pharmaceutical	10,679,677
Machinery	8,835,287
Wholesale trade	8,200,347
Foods	8,171,235
Services	8,096,076
Communication	7,735,658
Construction	6,127,743
Other financing business	5,380,270
Insurance	5,185,869
Securities	5,181,462
Iron and steel	4,444,146
Non-ferrous metals	3,847,878
Real estate	3,802,870
Textiles	3,386,109
Rubber products	2,894,312
Glass and ceramics products	2,811,902
Precision instruments	2,294,399
Oil and coal products	1,754,438
Metal products	1,707,123
Pulp and paper	1,668,062
Air transportation	1,413,867
Marine transportation	894,348

Exhibit 34.5 continued

Warehousing and harbour transportation	637,399
Mining	312,334
Fishery and forestry	247,288
Total	280,930,040

Source: Tokyo Stock Exchange.

B) Largest quoted companies

Exhibit 34.6:
THE 20 LARGEST DOMESTIC COMPANIES LISTED ON THE TSE, END-1997

Ranking	*Company*	*Market value (¥ billion)*
1	Toyota Motor	14,219
2	Tokyo-Mitsubishi Bank	8,412
3	Nippon Telegraph & Telephone	6,168
4	Sumitomo Bank	4,680
5	Honda Motors	4,667
6	Sony	4,665
7	Matsushita Electric Industrial	4,034
8	Seven-Eleven Japan	3,847
9	Sanwa Bank	3,830
10	Nomura Securities	3,415
11	Takeda Chemical Industries	3,267
12	Tokyo Electric Power	3,219
13	Hitachi	3,104
14	Ito-Yokado	2,762
15	Canon	2,634
16	Fujitsu	2,605
17	Fuji Photo Film	2,573
18	Seibu Railway	2,469
19	Dai-Ichi Kangyo Bank	2,403
20	Industrial Bank of Japan	2,361

Source: Tokyo Stock Exchange.

C) Trading volume

Share trading value for domestic stocks during 1997 totalled ¥108.5 trillion, an increase of 6.5% compared with 1996.

Exhibit 34.7:
TRADING OF DOMESTIC SHARES, VOLUME AND VALUE, 1993–97

Year	*Volume (shares million)*	*Value (¥ billion)*
1993	86,934	86,889.1
1994	84,514	87,355.6
1995	92,033	83,563.9
1996	100,171	101,892.6
1997	107,567	108,500.2

Source: Tokyo Stock Exchange.

Exhibit 34.8:
THE 20 MOST ACTIVELY TRADED DOMESTIC SHARES ON THE TSE, 1997

Ranking	*Company*	*Trading value (¥ billion)*
1	Sony	3,251
2	Toyota Motor	2,693
3	Nippon Telegraph and Telephone	2,438
4	Bank of Tokyo Mitsubishi	2,060
5	Honda Motors	1,932
6	Fujitsu	1,736
7	Canon	1,603
8	Matsushita Heavy Industries	1,550
9	Tokyo Electron	1,507
10	Matsushita Electric Industrial	1,431
11	Sumitomo Bank	1,415
12	Advantest	1,354
13	NEC	1,304
14	Hitachi	1,243
15	Fuji Bank	1,142
16	Fuji Photo Film	1,136
17	Seven-Eleven Japan	1,121
18	Takeda Chemical Industries	1,011
19	Sakura Bank	983
20	Sanwa Bank	955

Source: Tokyo Stock Exchange.

TYPES OF SHARE

The following categories of securities may be traded on the Japanese stock exchanges: ordinary shares, preferred shares, deferred shares, shares to be retired with profits, shares without voting rights, convertible shares, straight bonds, convertible debentures, debentures with pre-emptive rights to new shares and separable warrant debenture bonds.

Preferred and deferred shares take a preferred or deferred position with respect to distributions of profits or surplus assets on liquidation. Shares to be retired with profits are intended to be issued by a company that is scheduled to be dissolved at a given future date (for example, on completion of a project for the purposes of which the company was incorporated). Japanese companies' use of preferred shares, deferred shares and shares to be retired with profits increased during 1997.

Convertible debentures carry conversion rights at a conversion price determined on the basis of the market price of the shares on a certain day prior to the date of issue of such convertible debentures. Separable warrant debenture bonds allow transactions in two forms - as one unit or in separated segments of warrant and bond. The Japanese Ministry of Finance taxes the warrant segment on the same basis as shares, while the bond element is taxed as if it were a regular bond. Warrant rights are currently restricted to new shares.

Nikkei 225 futures contracts are traded on the Osaka Securities Exchange (OSE), while broader TOPIX index futures contracts are traded on the TSE. Options on the Nikkei 225 stock index are traded on the OSE and options on the TOPIX are traded on the TSE. In 1994 the OSE introduced a new stock index, the Nikkei 300, and respective futures and options contracts began trading the same day. In addition, in December 1997 the TSE introduced sector index futures. Equity options on certain specified stocks are traded on the TSE and OSE.

All financial derivatives markets in Japan are regulated by the Ministry of Finance.

OTHER MARKETS

Unlisted shares may be traded on the over-the-counter (OTC) market and the Japan OTC Securities Company acts as the intermediary between securities companies for OTC issues. The main role of the OTC market is to facilitate the raising of funds from the investing public by unlisted, small and medium-sized companies. Equity issues tradable over-the-counter must be registered with the Japan Securities Dealers' Association.

INVESTORS

Exhibit 34.9:
SHARE OWNERSHIP BY INVESTOR TYPE (PERCENTAGE OF ALL LISTED COMPANIES)

	1950	*1970*	*1986*	*1996*
Financial institutions	9.9	30.7	40.9	39.3
Non-financial corporations	5.6	22.0	24.1	23.8
Investment trusts	n/a	1.2	1.3	2.0
Securities companies	12.6	1.4	2.0	1.1
Individuals (Japanese)	69.1	41.1	25.2	23.6
Foreign investors	n/a	3.3	5.7	9.8
Others	2.8	0.3	0.8	0.5

Source: Tokyo Stock Exchange.

OPERATIONS

A) Trading system

All securities, whether money market or capital market issues, must be traded through an authorised securities dealer who is a member of the Japan Securities Dealers'

Exhibit 34.10:
TOP PERFORMING COUNTRY FUNDS – JAPAN

FUND	US$ % change 31/12/96 31/12/97	31/12/92 31/12/97	Currency	Fund size (US$ mil)	Volatility	Manager name	Main sector	Class
The Sakura Japan Fund	58.23	N/A	US$	1.2	N/A	Ardent Investment Mgmt Ltd	Equity	Offshore Territories
Heisei Japan	22.02	-11.9	¥	8.06	8.13	Alpha Global	Equity	Offshore Territories
Gartmore Select Japanese Wts	7.33	N/A	£	0.74	N/A	Gartmore Investment Ltd	Equity Growth	UK Investment Trusts
Glbl Mgr Japan Bear	6.62	N/A	US$	0.24	7.08	BIIML	Equity	Offshore Territories
Schroder Japan Growth Fund Wt	6.27	N/A	£	5.35	15.09	Schroder Inv Mgmt Ltd	Equity Growth	UK Investment Trusts
CIBC Japanese Equity Fund	5.13	N/A	C$	18.31	N/A	CIBC Securities Inc.	Equities	Canadian Mutuals
AGF Japan Class	4.11	16.17	C$	77.46	4.78	AGF Group of Funds	Equities	Canadian Mutuals
Vista:Japan/A	1.63	N/A	US$	3.9	N/A	Vista Funds	Equity Growth	US Mutuals
Warburg Japan Growth/Cm	1.52	N/A	US$	37.1	N/A	Warburg Funds	Equity Growth	US Mutuals
Chase Vista Japan Eq	1.44	11.52	US$	76.55	4.64	Chase Vista Family of UT Fds	Equity Growth	Hong Kong SFC Authorised
Chase Vista Japan Eq	1.44	11.52	US$	45.18	4.59	Chase Vista Family of UT Fds	Equity	Luxembourg
Chase Vista Japan Eq	1.44	11.52	US$	76.55	6.12	Chase Vista Family of UT Fds	Equity Growth	Investmentfds Deutschland
Nochu N Max	1.21	N/A	¥	75.12	N/A	Nochu ITMCo	Equity Growth	Japanese Open Trusts
Vista:Japan/B	0.94	N/A	US$	0.6	N/A	Vista Funds	Equity Growth	US Mutuals
Warburg Japan Growth/Adv	0.85	N/A	US$	N/A	N/A	Warburg Funds	Equity Growth	US Mutuals
Nomura Rainbow Info Electron	-0.22	43.96	¥	148.97	5.49	Nomura ITMCo	Equity Growth	Japanese Open Trusts
GAM Japan	-0.36	63.54	US$	924.9	4.22	GAM Fund Managers IOM	Equity	Offshore Territories
GAM Japan	-0.36	63.54	US$	"1,165.00"	4.15	GAM Fund Managers IOM	Equity Growth	Hong Kong SFC Authorised
Taiheiyo Active Open	-0.43	N/A	¥	3.53	N/A	Taiheiyo ITMCo	Equity Growth	Japanese Open Trusts
Universal Network Active Open	-0.89	N/A	¥	3.74	N/A	Universal ITMCo	Equity Growth	Japanese Open Trusts
Baer Multistock Japan Stock A	-0.92	N/A	¥	214.3	4.81	Julius Baer	Equity	Luxembourg
Baer Multistock Japan Stock A	-0.92	N/A	¥	285.7	4.81	Julius Baer	Equity Growth	Investmentfds Deutschland
Baer Multistock Japan Stock D	-0.93	N/A	¥	19.19	4.81	Julius Baer	Equity	Luxembourg
JRIA Japan	-2.31	N/A	US$	2.29	4.3	J Rothschild Intl Assurance	Equity	Offshore Territories
GAM Japan Capital Fund	-2.47	N/A	US$	35.4	4.02	GAM Funds	Equity Growth	US Mutuals
Colonial Newpt Jpn Opp/Z	-2.89	N/A	US$	1.6	N/A	Colonial Newport Funds	Equity Growth	US Mutuals
Universal New Stock Open	-2.95	N/A	¥	2.44	N/A	Universal ITMCo	Equity Growth	Japanese Open Trusts
UBS Tokyo-Hedged	-2.97	N/A	Sfr	N/S	N/A	UBS	Equity Growth	Swiss Foundation Funds
Colonial Newpt Jpn Opp/A	-3.22	N/A	US$	4.4	N/A	Colonial Newport Funds	Equity Growth	US Mutuals
Tokyo Hi Power S Multi-Media	-3.75	N/A	¥	2.58	5.04	Tokyo ITMCo	Equity Growth	Japanese Open Trusts
Colonial Newpt Jpn Opp/B	-3.88	N/A	US$	6.5	N/A	Colonial Newport Funds	Equity Growth	US Mutuals
Colonial Newpt Jpn Opp/C	-3.88	N/A	US$	2.7	N/A	Colonial Newport Funds	Equity Growth	US Mutuals
Taiyo New Horizon Open	-4.08	N/A	¥	16.31	N/A	Taiyo ITMCo	Equity Growth	Japanese Open Trusts
Yamaichi Sel Hi Technology	-4.12	-2.21	¥	14.53	5.13	Yamaichi ITMCo	Equity Growth	Japanese Open Trusts
Govett Japan Safeguard A	-4.27	N/A	US$	2.68	N/A	Govett Safeguard Funds Ltd	Equity	Offshore Territories
Govett Japan Safeguard A	-4.27	N/A	US$	3.3	N/A	Govett Safeguard Funds Ltd	Equity Growth	Hong Kong SFC Authorised
Tokyo Best Open	-4.36	9.87	¥	16.9	3.48	Tokyo ITMCo	Equity Growth	Japanese Open Trusts
Manulife GF Japanese Gth	-4.4	-8.55	US$	8.09	5.47	Manulife Global Fund Ltd	Equity	Luxembourg
Manulife GF Japanese Gth	-4.4	-8.55	US$	9.78	5.54	Manulife Global Fund Ltd	Equity Growth	Hong Kong SFC Authorised
Chase Vista Japan Sm Cap Eq	-4.42	N/A	US$	11.14	N/A	Chase Vista Family of UT Fds	Equity Growth	Hong Kong SFC Authorised
Chase Vista Japan Sm Cap Eq	-4.42	N/A	US$	9.16	N/A	Chase Vista Family of UT Fds	Equity	Luxembourg
Chase Vista Japan Sm Cap Eq	-4.42	N/A	US$	11.14	N/A	Chase Vista Family of UT Fds	Equity Growth	Investmentfds Deutschland
Asahi New Sel MultiMedia	-4.61	N/A	¥	28.82	4.73	Asahi ITMCo	Equity Growth	Japanese Open Trusts
Oasi Tokyo	-4.64	N/A	L	N/S	N/A	Deutsche Bank Fondi	Equity Growth	Italian Mutuals

Note: details for some funds may not have been included if the data for the US$ % change for 96/97 is not available

Source: Standard & Poor's Micropal.

Association. The three main dealers are Nomura, Nikko and Daiwa, which collectively handle around 50% of all transactions in shares by domestic securities companies.

The TSE market is a continuous auction market where buy and sell orders directly interact with one another. The trading of shares is carried out under the *zaraba* method, which is similar to an open outcry system. Prices are first established at the beginning of the trading session, based on orders placed by regular members before the start of trading. The central book is kept by Saitori members who function solely as intermediaries between the regular members; they are not allowed to trade any listed stock for their own account, or to accept orders from the investing public. After the opening price is established, Saitori members match orders in accordance with price priority and time precedence.

The 150 most active domestic stocks are traded on the trading floor, and there is an electronic system in respect of these stocks called the Floor Order-Routing and Execution System (FORES). The FORES is designed (i) to automate the order-routing process for small orders (up to 300,000 shares), (ii) to replace manual order books with electronic order books having order execution capability, and (iii) to computerise reporting-back and trade confirmation processes. Transactions in less actively traded shares take place under the Computer-assisted Order-routing and Execution System (CORES).

In addition to CORES, the TSE has developed CORES-F and CORES-O for futures and options trading.

B) List of principal brokers

DAIWA SECURITIES
6-4, Ohtemachi 2-chome, Chiyoda-ku, Tokyo 100
Tel: (81) 3 243 2111

KANKAKU SECURITIES
13-16, Nihombashi-Kayaba-cho 1-chome, Chuo-ku
Tokyo 103
Tel: (81) 3 5640 7805

KOKUSAI SECURITIES
27-1, Shinkawa 2-chome, Chuo-ku, Tokyo 104
Tel: (81) 3 348 7211

NEW JAPAN SECURITIES
11, Kanda-Surugadai 3-chome, Chiyoda-ku, Tokyo 101
Tel: (81) 3 3219 1111

NIKKO SECURITIES
3-1, Marunouchi 3-chome, Chiyoda-ku, Tokyo 100
Tel: (81) 3 283 2211

NOMURA SECURITIES
9-1, Nihombashi 1-chome, Chuo-ku, Tokyo 103
Tel: (81) 3 211 1811

SALOMON BROTHERS ASIA LIMITED
Akasaka Park Building, 2-20, Akasaka 5-chome
Minato-ku, Tokyo 107
Tel: (81) 3 5574 4111; Fax: (81)3 5574 5551

SMITH BARNEY ASSET MANAGEMENT CO, LTD.
Yebisu Garden Place Tower, 28th Floor
4-20-3, Ebisu, Shibuya-ku, Tokyo
Tel: (81) 3 5424 6100; Fax: (81) 3 5424 6023

WAKO SECURITIES
6-1, Nihombashi-Koami-cho, Chuo-ku, Tokyo 103
Tel: (81) 3 667 8111

C) Settlement and transfer

Almost all TSE share transactions are settled on the third business day following the day of the trade (T+3). The clearing and settlement procedure for share trading includes trade comparison, trade netting, settlement of book-entry transfers and money settlement. While settlement of book-entry transfers takes place through the Japan Securities Depository Centre (JASDEC), with the Japanese Securities Clearing Corporation (JSCC) acting as agent for JASDEC, money settlement is effected through the TSE with same-day funds availability.

D) Commissions and other costs

Brokerage commissions are negotiable for that portion of trade value in excess of ¥1 billion. For lesser amounts there is a fixed scale of charges. (From 1 April 1998 the negotiable portion will be increased to the excess over ¥50 million, and by end-1999 brokerage commissions are due to become fully negotiable.)

Exhibit 34.11:
COMMISSION RATES FOR TRADING IN SHARES (EXCLUDING 3% CONSUMPTION TAX)

Trading value (¥ million)	*Rate*
1–5	0.900% + ¥2,500
5–10	0.700% + ¥12,500
10–30	0.575% + ¥25,000
30–50	0.375% + ¥85,000
50–100	0.225% + ¥160,000
100–300	0.200% + ¥185,000
300–500	0.125% + ¥410,000
500–1,000	0.100% + ¥535,000
Over 1,000	Negotiable

TAXATION AND REGULATIONS AFFECTING FOREIGN INVESTORS

A) Dividends

Japanese corporation dividends paid to foreign shareholders are subject to Japanese withholding tax at 20% of their gross amount. Reduced tax treaty rates may apply if the shareholder is a resident of a country with which Japan has such a treaty. These rates range from nil to 20%, depending on the country, legal status of the shareholder and requisite ownership requirements for each tax treaty. The shareholder must submit, through the payer of the dividend, an application in advance to the tax authorities.

Stock dividends and the distribution of retained earnings by issuing new shares are treated for withholding tax purposes in the same way as distributions of cash dividends, and, as in the case of distribution of remaining assets (in excess of the paid-in capital and capital reserve) on liquidation of a company, are subject to withholding tax as described.

In 1995, a special tax exemption on imputed dividends arising out of share redemptions took effect in respect of listed and publicly quoted shares. This exemption is a temporary measure applicable from 1995 to 1999.

Exhibit 34.12:
WITHHOLDING TAX

Recipient	*Dividends (portfolio) %*	*Dividends (substantial holdings) %*	*Interest %*
Japanese corporations	20	20	20
Resident individuals	20 or 35[1]	20	Nil or 20[2]
Foreign corporations and non-resident individuals:			
Non-treaty	20	20	Nil, 15 or 20[3]
Treaty	Nil-20	Nil-20	Nil-20

Notes:

1. The 35% rate would apply if the taxpayer elects not to aggregate portfolio dividend income with other income.
2. Interest on bank deposits and/or certain designated financial instruments is subject to a 15% national withholding tax and a 5% local inhabitants withholding tax (20% combined). Taxation of such interest is fully realised by tax withholding so that resident individuals are not required to aggregate such interest income with other income. Interest on loans made by resident individuals is not subject to withholding tax; instead, it is taxed in the aggregate with other income.
3. Dividends and interest earned by non-resident individuals and/or foreign corporations are subject to a 20% national withholding tax under Japanese domestic tax laws. An exceptional rate of 15% is applied to interest on bank deposits and/or certain designated financial instruments accruing on or after 1 April 1988. Interest on loans, however, is taxed at a 20% rate even after 31 March 1988.

Source: Price Waterhouse.

B) Capital gains

For non-resident investors having no permanent establishment in Japan, capital gains from the sale of shares in a Japanese corporation are taxed under national income tax at 20% and under local tax at 6%. Some tax treaties, including those with the US, Germany, the Netherlands and Switzerland, provide exemptions from Japanese taxes on capital gains arising from transfers of shares in Japanese corporations.

C) Exchange controls

Under the Foreign Exchange and Foreign Trade Control Law there are no limitations on the repatriation of capital and earnings, provided that the underlying transactions are proper and legal.

Direct inward investment (ie, the acquisition of shares in any non-listed corporation or the acquisition of shares in a listed corporation which, when aggregated with those already owned by the foreign investor and related parties, represent 10% or more of the total shares issued by the corporation) requires only a report to be filed with the Ministry of Finance and other ministries within 15 days of the transaction date, except in respect of the acquisition of shares in any company in the business of aircraft, arms, atomic energy and other industries relating to national security, and agriculture, forestry, fisheries, mining, oil and the manufacture of leather and leather products. In respect of such excepted industries, prior reports must be filed with the ministries and there is a 30-day suspension period during which the government investigates the report.

When an acquisition of shares in a listed corporation is made through an authorised securities company in Japan and the acquisition represents less than 10% of the corporation's issued capital when aggregated with the existing holdings of the investor and its related parties, formalities are minimal.

D) Non-resident bank accounts

The Foreign Exchange and Foreign Trade Control Law governs non-resident bank accounts. As a general rule, foreigners can freely open a non-resident bank account (either yen-denominated or foreign currency-denominated) with an authorised foreign exchange bank in Japan. Authorised foreign exchange banks are required to maintain records of yen-denominated deposits made by exchange non-residents separately from other deposits.

Deposits by an exchange non-resident with a bank other than an authorised foreign exchange bank require prior Ministry of Finance permission.

LISTING AND REPORTING REQUIREMENTS

The basic disclosure and listing requirements are governed by the Securities and Exchange Law (SEL), while listing eligibility criteria and reporting procedures form part of the listing regulations of the exchanges.

A) Listing requirements

A company wishing to have equity listed on the TSE is required to file an application for listing with the TSE, which is examined by the exchange, placing emphasis on the public interest and investor protection. The application must include basic information and details concerning the company's shares and their ownership, as well as a securities report in two sections, providing more detailed information on the company, its financial condition and the issue. The first section is made available for public inspection. If the TSE considers a listing to be appropriate, it may authorise quotation subject to Ministry of Finance (MOF) approval.

Having obtained MOF approval, the company is required to enter into a listing agreement with the TSE, whereby the company agrees that it shall abide by the SEL and the TSE rules and regulations, including Business Regulations, Listing Regulations and Regulations for the Supervision of Listed Securities.

B) Reporting requirements

As well as yearly, half-yearly and extraordinary reports, listed companies must give prompt notice to the exchange of matters such as the dishonouring of any bill or cheque drawn by it; material changes in, or suspension of, any of its businesses; and any other fact having a material impact on its business. Notice must also be given of various corporate decisions or resolutions such as the issuing of new shares, capital reduction, mergers, dividends, stock splits, variations of class rights and any other matters of importance with regard to the rights or privileges attached to its securities. To protect investors, the SEL requires a substantial level of disclosure in proposed takeovers and notification is required to be filed with the MOF.

C) Foreign companies

The TSE established a foreign stock section in 1973 in order to facilitate cross-border capital flows and internationalisation of the Japanese securities market. The exchange has modified its disclosure requirements for foreign companies so that the documents to be submitted by a foreign company to the exchange, both in initially applying for listing and afterwards, have been reduced in number and simplified. In order to maintain a fair and orderly market, listed foreign stocks are traded within a limited time span (9.00am to 11.00am and 12.30pm to 3.00pm). A comprehensive breakdown of the rules and regulations and listing requirements necessary for foreign companies seeking a quotation on the Japanese market is given in a booklet published by the TSE entitled *A Listing Guide for Foreign Companies.*

SHAREHOLDER PROTECTION CODES

The TSE regulations attempt to ensure fair and orderly transactions in listed securities and the protection of investors. The exchange takes steps to ensure full disclosure of financial statements of listed companies and publicises business activities of these companies so as to provide data to help public investors. Also, in 1992 the Securities and Exchange Surveillance Commission was created as the Japanese equivalent of the US SEC.

A) Significant shareholdings

Any shareholder owning in excess of 5% of a company's total issued shares is required to file a report with the MOF.

B) Insider trading

In order to prevent any officer or major shareholder of a company using sensitive information obtained through his office or position, the SEL provides that if a company officer or its major shareholder (holding 10% or more of the total issued shares) makes a profit from a sale or purchase of the company's shares and certain other securities within six months of such purchase or sale, the company may, within two years of such a person making a profit from this information, require him to account to the company for the profit. The SEL contains further provisions with regard to the unjust use of confidential information or fraudulent action for the purpose of inducing securities transactions.

In addition, insider trading is barred under a more general provision in the SEL prohibiting unfair dealings. This expressly prohibits dealing in stocks and other specified securities by company officers and other specified persons if they become aware of certain material facts concerning the business operations of an issuer company. This prohibition does not apply if such a fact is made known to the general public by specified methods.

C) Investment advisers and securities companies

In view of misconduct by some investment advisers, the MOF has issued legislation imposing restrictions on excessive publicity and solicitation by investment advisers.

The law also restricts or prohibits cash and securities being kept in custody by advisers, and loans to customers by advisers. All investment advisers have to be registered with the MOF. If any adviser wishes to conduct a discretionary investment management service, it must obtain a licence from the MOF, which requires a specified level of paid-in capital and net assets, good organisation and sound financial background.

It is unlawful for a securities company to compensate customers' losses arising from securities transactions and to undertake investment for a customer's account on a discretionary basis. It is also unlawful for a customer to insist a securities company agree to compensate the customer's losses.

D) Company law

A number of amendments were made to company law during 1997:

- Stock options may be granted to company directors in the form of subscription rights to new shares or rights to buy treasury stock from the company.
- The redemption of shares with distributable profits may be authorised by board resolution.
- Merger procedures have been rationalised.
- Holding companies can now own Japanese companies.
- Criminal sanctions for corporate crimes have been made more severe.

Further amendments envisaged include dealing on the Internet and strengthening the authority of directors and auditors.

E) Compensation fund

In 1969 the Securities Deposit Compensation Fund Foundation was established with the aim of promoting investor protection. It may compensate all or part of any losses incurred by investors as a result of a securities company collapsing. During Japan's "Big Bang" process, this compensation fund scheme will be enlarged and strengthened by making the foundation a judicial body under the Securities and Exchange Law.

RESEARCH

The "Big Three" – Nomura, Daiwa and Nikko – together with Wako and Yamatane, all produce respected research.

Publications issued by the TSE:

Fact Book
Constitution of the TSE
Listing Regulations of the TSE
Annual Securities Statistics
TSE Monthly Statistics Report
Business Regulations of the TSE
Brokerage Agreement Standards
A Listing Guide for Foreign Companies
TOPIX Data Book

Newspapers and magazines:

Oriental Economist (weekly)
Japan Economic Journal (daily)
Asian Wall Street Journal (daily)
Far Eastern Economic Review (weekly)
Global Investor (monthly)
Nikkei Weekly (weekly)

Japan's Financial Systems, published by Euromoney Books, provides in-depth information for those wishing to invest or do business in the country. See the order card at the back of this book for details.

CHAPTER 35

Jordan

Introduction

The Amman Financial Market (AFM) is a government-mandated vehicle for both the regulation and institutionalisation of the securities market in Jordan. A wide range of companies are listed on the exchange, from family-run businesses to large-scale firms that are partially state-owned. Total market capitalisation stood at US$5.45 billion at the end of 1997, representing 67.6% of estimated nominal GDP for 1997.

Stock market liquidity is sensitive to Jordanian monetary policy; and the turnover ratio dropped from 26% in 1994 to 15.4% in 1996. Other factors behind this reduction, however, included an increase in the number of subscribed shares and a general decline in price levels.

Under the Securities Law No. 23 of 1997, the AFM is being restructured to create three different entities – the Jordan Securities Commission, the Amman Stock Exchange and a central depository for clearing and settlement.

The effect of major tax cuts implemented in 1997, coupled with the removal of the 15% capitalisation tax and the 50% foreign-ownership ceiling, created further incentives for foreign direct and indirect investment. As a result, investment in the AFM by global and regional emerging markets funds is on the rise, and a number of international firms are assessing joint ventures and investment opportunities with many of Jordan's manufacturing and mining concerns.

ECONOMIC AND POLITICAL OVERVIEW

The Hashemite Kingdom of Jordan came into existence in 1928 and became independent in 1946. The country is governed under a constitutional monarchy headed by King Hussein Ibn Talal, who came to power in 1952. Executive powers are vested in the Council of Ministers headed by a Prime Minister appointed by the King. The legislative body is the parliament, made up of the upper house, appointed by the King, and the house of deputies, elected by the people. Since 1989, there have been significant democratic reforms, including liberalisation of the press and the legalisation of political parties.

Consecutive governments in Jordan have maintained an economic strategy that tries to build on the Economic Adjustment Programme first agreed with international agencies in 1989. The focus has been to reduce current account spending, decrease public expenditure by cancelling food and energy subsidies, and increase public revenues through the gradual imposition of taxes on consumption as a preliminary step towards introducing value-added tax. The government, under Prime Minister Dr Abdel Salam Majali, is also trying to reduce its international borrowing and to convert loans into investment.

A major overhaul of economic laws is underway, with the objective of improving the general business and investment environment in the country. A new Securities Law and a reformed Companies Act were enacted in 1997, with the aim of implementing major upgrades in Jordan's capital market and introducing legal frameworks to allow for the creation of various investment vehicles such as investment funds.

The government is also active in its privatisation programme. It has demonstrated its commitment to the process by creating a specialised privatisation unit within the Prime Minister's Office; liquidating holdings in listed companies if they are worth less than 5% of its overall market value; offering major holdings for sale to international buyers; and commercialising state-run businesses like Jordan's national carrier and telecommunications companies.

Real GDP growth for 1997 was expected to reach 5.3% compared with 5.2% in 1996. Control of government expenditure and stabilisation of the dinar over the past two years have contributed to reducing the rate of inflation during 1997 to 3.0% against 6.5% in 1996.

Exhibit 35.1: AMMAN SE FINANCIAL MARKET PRICE INDEX (US$), 1993–97

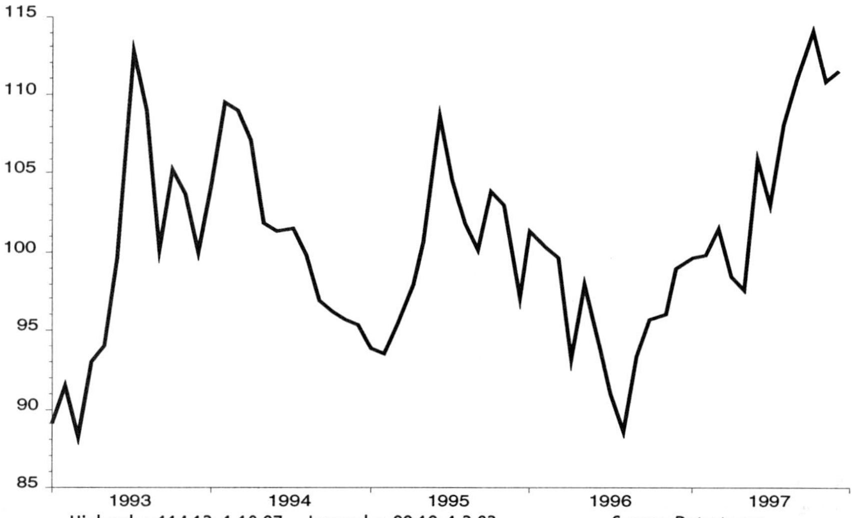

High value 114.13 1.10.97 Low value 88.18 1.3.93 *Source: Datastream*

The Jordanian government has forecast a budget deficit of US$52.2 million in 1998, compared with US$92 million in 1997.

Role of the central bank

The central bank co-ordinates monetary policy and works in conjunction with the Ministry of Finance: its main aim is to ensure the strength of the dinar. The bank has tended to move away from tight monetary policy and high interest rates, and it has also removed the remaining restrictions on foreign currency flows, anticipating the abolition of the dinar peg to the US dollar as confidence is boosted and foreign reserves reach higher levels.

The board of the central bank is made up of a governor, appointed by royal decree, and two deputy governors, as well as nominees from the government and several heads of the major banks.

MARKET PERFORMANCE

A) In 1997

At the end of 1997 there were a total of 139 listed companies on the AFM, comprising 97 on the main market (called the "Organised Market") and 42 on the Parallel Market. Overall market turnover jumped to JD424.9 million (US$599.3 million), an increase of 50.4% compared with 1996's JD282.6 million. The AFM Price Index of the 60 most actively traded shares weighted by market capitalisation reached 169.2 at year-end 1997, an increase of 10.3% on year-end 1996.

Total market capitalisation at the end of 1997 stood at JD3.86 billion (US$5.45 billion) compared with JD3.46 billion at the end of 1996. The Organised Market price/earnings ratio was 14.7 as opposed to 13.5 in 1996, giving Jordan an attractive regional comparative advantage. Banks (mainly Arab Bank and Housing Bank) currently make up 51.8% of market capitalisation, while industrials (primarily cement, phosphate and potash companies) represent 36.0%. The remaining 12.2% consists of service and insurance companies.

During 1997, for the first time, a Jordanian company – Arab Potash – issued a global depository receipt (GDR), which amounted to US$50 million. Also, Jordan Phosphate Mines issued the first Jordanian Eurobond (US$100 million).

B) Summary information

Global ranking by market value (US$ terms, end-1997): 53
Market capitalisation (AFM Organised Market, end-1997): US$5.1 billion
Growth in market value (local currency terms, 1993–97): 11.5%
Market value as a % of nominal GDP (end-1997): 68%
Number of domestic/foreign companies listed (end-1997): 139/0
Market P/E (end-1997): 14.7
MSCI Index (change in US$ terms, 1997): -1.8%
Short-term (3-month) interest rate (end-1997): 8.5%
Long-term (9-year) bond yield (end-1997): 9.5%
Budget deficit as a % of nominal GDP (end-1997): 3.6%
Annual increase in broad money supply (Sept 1997): 6.8%
Inflation rate (1997): 3.0%
US$ exchange rate (end-1996): JD0.709

C) Year-end share price index and P/E ratios

Exhibit 35.2:
YEAR-END SHARE PRICE INDEX AND P/E RATIOS, 1993–97

Year-end	*AFM Price Index*	*Organised Market P/E*	*Dividend (%) yield ratio*
1993	158.5	23.2	2.16
1994	143.6	18.1	2.30
1995	159.2	17.4	2.32
1996	153.5	13.5	2.54
1997	169.2	14.7	2.31

Source: Amman Financial Market.

THE STOCK MARKET

A) Brief history and structure

The AFM opened in 1978 following an initiative by the Central Bank of Jordan and the IFC. The latter continues to be closely involved in AFM operations. The AFM is one of the most developed stock markets in the region and it is included in indices prepared by the IFC and Morgan Stanley.

B) Opening hours, name and address

The AFM is closed on Thursdays and Fridays. Trading hours on Saturday to Wednesday are as follows: 9.00am–9.30am Parallel Market; 9.45am–10.00am Bond Market; 10.00am–12.00 noon Organised Market.

AMMAN FINANCIAL MARKET
PO Box 8802, Housing Bank Centre, 6th Floor, Amman
Tel: (962) 6 607 171; Fax: (962) 6 686 830
E-mail: afm@go.com.jo

MARKET SIZE

A) Market value

Total market capitalisation was JD3.86 billion at the end of 1997, compared with JD3.46 billion at the end 1996. Organised Market capitalisation increased from JD3.2 billion to JD3.6 billion.

Exhibit 35.3:
NUMBER OF COMPANIES LISTED AND MARKET VALUE, AFM ORGANISED AND PARALLEL MARKET, 1993–97

Year-end	*No. of companies listed*	*Market value (JD billion)*
1993	101/13	3.36/0.10
1994	95/21	3.23/0.18
1995	97/29	3.31/0.19
1996	97/35	3.23/0.23
1997	97/42	3.60/0.26

Source: Amman Financial Market.

B) Largest quoted companies

The 10 largest quoted companies accounted for 69.6% of total market capitalisation at the end of 1997.

Exhibit 35.4:
THE 20 LARGEST COMPANIES BY MARKET CAPITALISATION, AFM, END-1997

Ranking	*Company*	*Market value (JD million)*
1	Arab Bank	1,430.0
2	Arab Potash	517.4
3	Jordan Cement Factories	182.5
4	Jordan Phosphate Mines	136.2
5	The Housing Bank	130.0
6	Jordan National Bank	74.8
7	Jordan Petroleum Refinery	66.8
8	Cairo Amman Bank	54.8
9	Zara For Investment	52.0
10	Arab International Hotels	44.5
11	Arab Jordan Investment Bank	44.4
12	Arab Banking Corporation/Jordan	44.1
13	Jordan Hotel and Tourism	44.0
14	Jordan Islamic Bank	42.8
15	Arab Inter for Investment & Education	38.9
16	Arab Pharmaceutical Manufacturing	37.4
17	Dar Al Dawa Dev & Invest	34.1
18	Jordan Investment & Finance Bank	33.3
19	Jordan Kuwait Bank	32.1
20	Industrial Development Bank	30.0

Source: Amman Financial Market.

C) Trading volume

Total trading value on the secondary market rose to JD424.9 million in 1997, a 50.4% increase compared with 1996. Trading value on the Organised Market increased 44.3% to JD304.1 million.

Exhibit 35.5:
TRADING VALUE ON THE ORGANISED MARKET, 1993–97

Year	*Trading value (JD million)*	*% change*
1993	933.4	6.2
1994	430.3	-53.9
1995	362.1	-15.8
1996	210.7	-41.8
1997	304.1	44.3

Source: Amman Financial Market.

Exhibit 35.6:
THE 20 MOST ACTIVELY TRADED SHARES, AFM, 1997

Ranking	*Company*	*Value traded (JD million)*	*Shares traded (million)*
1	Arab Bank	69.1	0.2
2	The Jordan Cement Factories	35.3	9.5
3	Jordan Kuwait Bank	26.3	8.3
4	The Housing Bank	18.8	3.8
5	Jordan National Bank	16.7	8.4
6	Jordan Electric Power	8.7	4.8
7	Arab Pharmaceutical Manufacturing	8.6	2.1
8	Jordan Phosphate Mines	8.1	2.2
9	Bank of Jordan	7.8	2.9
10	Arab Potash	7.8	1.2
11	ME Complex For Eng, Electronic & Heavy Ind	7.7	10.9
12	Industrial Development Bank	7.2	3.2
13	Jordan Islamic Bank	6.4	1.8
14	Dar al Dawa Dev & Investment	5.5	1.0
15	Jordan Petroleum Refinery	4.1	0.4
16	National Portfolio Securities	4.0	3.1
17	Arab Inter For Investment & Education	3.9	1.1
18	Jordan Investment & Finance Bank	3.8	1.2
19	International Tobacco & Cigarettes	3.3	2.8
20	Universal Modern Industries	3.0	2.5

Source: Amman Financial Market.

TYPES OF SHARE

Shares traded in Jordan are regulated by the AFM Act. Two types of shares are traded on the stock market – common/ordinary and preferred shares. (In addition, there are development bonds, corporate bonds and Treasury bills and bonds.)

INVESTORS

Individual shareholders are the main investors in the market. They own around 50% of total shares, and there is limited participation by institutional investors. In Jordan the latter consist of the Social Security Corporation, insurance companies, savings funds and various employees' savings and investment funds. Non-Jordanian institutional shareholders increased their interest in 1997 and their proportion of total market capitalisation rose from 35.9% to 38.3%.

OPERATIONS

A) Trading system

The market currently operates under an open outcry system, but in October 1996 the AFM signed an agreement with the Paris Bourse and SICOVAM to obtain technical assistance to modernise the stock exchange in accordance with international standards of trading, clearing and settlement. Work on the project is scheduled to be completed by the end of 1998. Plans are also underway to build a new AFM complex.

B) List of principal brokers

ARAB JORDAN INVESTMENT BANK
PO Box 8797, Amman
Tel: (962) 6 671 578; Fax: (962) 6 671 578

INDUSTRIAL DEVELOPMENT BANK
PO Box 1982, Amman
Tel: (962) 6 642 216; Fax: (962) 6 647 821

JORDAN INVESTMENT AND FINANCE BANK
PO Box 950 601, Amman
Tel: (962) 6 665 145; Fax: (962) 6 681 410

MIDDLE EAST BANK
PO Box 560, Amman
Tel: (962) 6 663 160; Fax: (962) 6 688 573

NATIONAL SECURITIES COMPANY
PO Box 7711, Amman 11118
Tel: (962) 6 562 4361; Fax: (962) 6 562 4362

PHILADELPHIA INVESTMENT BANK
PO Box 925993, Amman
Tel: (962) 6 663 172; Fax: (962) 6 683 247

UNION BANK FOR SAVING AND INVESTMENT
PO Box 35104, Amman
Tel: (962) 6 675 558; Fax: (962) 6 666 149

C) Settlement

In accordance with the AFM Act, inter-broker settlement on the exchange occurs on T+1, whereas client settlement as well as share registration must take effect by T+3.

D) Commissions and other costs

The rate of commission charged by brokers to their clients is fixed by a scale tariff with rates determined by the size of the order.

Exhibit 35.7:
COMMISSION ON SHARE AND BOND TRANSACTIONS

Transaction size	*Broker/dealer charges (%)*
Shares	
From JD1–20,000	0.65
From JD20,001–No limit	0.50
Bonds	
From JD1–No limit	0.10

The AFM charges brokers 20% of the commission rates.

Stamp duty of 0.15% of the nominal value of each share transferred is charged to the buyer.

TAXATION AND REGULATIONS AFFECTING FOREIGN INVESTORS

In the second half of 1995, several amendments were made to the regulations governing non-Jordanian investors. These amendments include a 10% tax on dividends in order to encourage capital accumulation: there is no withholding tax on capital gains.

The Investment Promotion Law, passed on 16 October 1995, removed some of the hurdles and obstacles to foreign investment. The Cabinet's prior investment approval is no longer needed, and foreign investors are able to invest on the same terms as local investors.

The Promotion of Non-Jordanian Investments No. 39 of 1997 abolished the non-Jordanian equity ownership ceiling of 50% in respect of the transportation, banking, telecommunications and agriculture sectors. However, the limit still applies in the construction, trade services and mining sectors.

Repatriation of investment capital and income (in any convertible currency) by non-Jordanians is free of restrictions.

REPORTING REQUIREMENTS

Under the AFM regulations, all listed companies must comply with certain reporting requirements. In addition to presenting financial statements, companies must inform the AFM of the shareholdings of the board of directors, dividends and any financial information and/or factors that could affect the operation of the company.

RESEARCH

Share prices are transmitted live from the trading floor via both Reuters Monitor Network and ACCESS Arabia, and are published in local newspapers and broadcast on Jordanian television. Also, the AFM web site can be accessed at www.accessme.com/AFM.

In addition to its annual report, the AFM publishes monthly bulletins that provide comprehensive data on the market, and the *Jordanian Shareholding Companies Guide* which includes data and financial ratios for listed companies.

International securities houses such as ING Barings, Nomura and HSBC, as well as local brokers National Securities, provide good coverage and detailed company analysis.

FUTURE DEVELOPMENTS

The Jordan Securities Commission (JSC), the regulatory body appointed in September 1997 in accordance with the new Securities Law, is currently engaged in drafting a new set of rules and guidelines regulating the capital market and its participants. Regulations expected to be issued in 1998 will relate to public offerings, mutual funds, disclosure and reporting requirements, as well as the qualification and licensing of market intermediaries. The JSC will also oversee the creation of an independent stock exchange owned by its members, as well as the establishment of a central depository for clearing and settlement, both of which are expected to be operational before the end of 1998.

CHAPTER 36

Kenya

Introduction

The Nairobi Stock Exchange (NSE) is one of the oldest in Africa. Currently, it has 58 quoted companies, and more listings are expected in 1998. Between 1992 and 1997, market capitalisation rose by 396% and the value of shares traded increased 15-fold from Ksh384.6 million to Ksh6,148 million (US$106 million).

The equity market is used as a source of funds for industry through new issues and rights issues. It is also a major forum for the implementation of the Kenyan government's privatisation programme, facilitating the sale of its investment stakes directly to the public. In 1997 the government sale of its 33.3% stake in a premier hotel chain, Serena, was heavily oversubscribed. Another successful issue was the November 1997 rights offering by Africa's second largest brewery, Kenya Breweries, which raised Ksh1.5 billion for the construction of a new brewery in neighbouring Tanzania.

ECONOMIC AND POLITICAL OVERVIEW

Kenya continues to enjoy relative political stability and peace. The country held its second multi-party elections in 1997, which maintained the ruling Kanu Party's dominance of the country's politics.

GDP growth fell to 2.9% in 1997 from 4.6% in 1996, partly due to the drought in the first half of the year which was followed by devastating floods occasioned by El Nino rains, both of which badly disrupted farming activities. The situation was further compounded by an outbreak of violence in the coastal region that disrupted the US$300 million-a-year tourism industry, the economy's single largest foreign exchange earner.

The Kenyan economy is dominated by agriculture, which contributes 30% of GDP. International coffee and tea prices have recently been on the increase, boosting foreign exchange inflows. The manufacturing sector accounts for 16% of GDP and the emphasis here is on achieving export-led growth.

Annual average consumer price inflation rose from 4.5% in 1996 to 11.2% in 1997, while bank interest rates remained high at between 25% and 32%. The Kenyan shilling exchange rate, which had remained stable from 1995 until mid-1997, recorded dramatic losses of about 10% in July as a consequence of the IMF's refusal to renew the country's ESAF facility due to the government's tardiness in privatising the power and telecoms sectors, and concerns about high levels of corruption. During 1997, the exchange rate fluctuated between Ksh53 and Ksh72 to the US dollar.

The government deficit stood at 0.1% of GDP in 1997 due to improved revenue collection and strict controls on expenditure.

Role of the central bank

The Central Bank of Kenya is the government's banker. Over recent years its main aim has been to curb inflation and money supply through open market operations, and it is currently working on bringing down bank interest rates in order to encourage investment and GDP growth. The bank has also overseen the dismantling of foreign exchange controls.

The Act governing the operations of the bank was amended in 1997 to give it more powers to regulate monetary policy. The governor of the bank is to enjoy security of tenure and the government will not be allowed to run an overdraft in excess of 5% of current revenue.

MARKET PERFORMANCE

A) In 1997

The NSE 20 Share Index stood at 3,115.14 at the end of the year, more or less unchanged on its 1996 close, although overall market capitalisation rose by 15.5% in 1997 to Ksh114 billion (US$1.94 billion). Turnover was up 55% in local currency terms at Ksh6.15 billion, and volume rose by 27% to 144 million shares.

Exhibit 36.1: NAIROBI STOCK EXCHANGE PRICE INDEX (US$), 1993–97

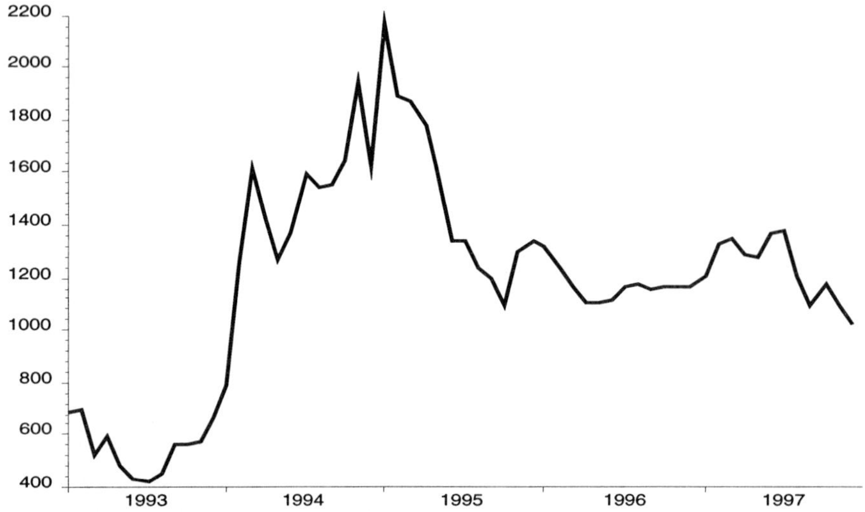

High value 2165.65 2.1.95 Low value 421.15 1.7.93 *Source: Datastream*

B) Summary information

Global ranking by market value (US$ terms, end-1997): 66
Market capitalisation (end-1997): US$1.94 billion
Growth in market value (local currency terms, 1993–97): 17.6%
Market value as a % of nominal GNP (end-1997): 24.55%
Number of domestic/foreign companies listed (end-1997): 42/16
Market P/E (NSE 20 Index, end-1997): 11.1
Short-term (3-month deposit) interest rate (end-1997): 20%
Long-term (5-year) bond yield (end-1997): 17.5%
Budget deficit as a % of nominal GDP (1997): 1.0%
Annual increase in broad money (M3) supply (end-1997): 8.98%
Inflation rate (1997 average): 11.2%
US$ exchange rate (end-1997): Ksh58.80

C) Year-end share price index, price/earnings ratios and yields

Exhibit 36.2:
YEAR-END NSE 20 SHARE INDEX, P/E AND DIVIDEND YIELDS, 1993–97

Year-end	*Index*	*P/E*	*Yield (%)*
1993	2,513.74	9.4	6.0
1994	4,559.40	9.8	4.2
1995	3,468.88	12.4	4.3
1996	3,114.11	27.8	4.4
1997	3115.14	11.1	6.3

Source: Nairobi Stock Exchange.

THE STOCK MARKET

A) Brief history and structure

The Kenyan stock market began operations in the 1960s, and an open outcry, floor-based, continuous auction trading system has been in use since 1991. In 1995 the NSE became a company limited by guarantee. The regulatory body, the Capital Markets Authority (CMA), was established in 1990.

The NSE is mainly financed by listing fees and clearing levies charged on all transactions carried out by member firms (of which there are currently 20). In addition, a network of securities representatives, investment advisers and investors' agents spread the operations of the exchange countrywide.

The delivery and settlement system was computerised during 1995 and a central depository system is expected to become operational in 1998.

B) Different exchanges

The NSE is the only exchange in Kenya.

C) Opening hours, names and addresses

NSE trading takes place via open outcry on the floor of the exchange on Monday to Friday from 10.00am to 12.00 noon.

NAIROBI STOCK EXCHANGE LTD
Nation Centre, 1/F Kimanthi St
PO Box 43633, Nairobi
Tel: (254) 2 230 692; Fax: (254) 2 224 200

MARKET SIZE

A) Number of listings and market value

At the end of 1997, there were 58 companies listed on the NSE, of which 16 were foreign. Total market capitalisation stood at US$1.94 billion.

Exhibit 36.3:
NUMBER OF COMPANIES LISTED AND MARKET VALUE OF LISTED SHARES, NSE, 1993–97

	1993	*1994*	*1995*	*1996*	*1997*
Companies listed	54	56	56	58	58
Market value (Ksh billion)	96.9	136.8	112.9	99.9	114.0
Market value (US$ billion)	1.42	3.10	1.87	1.79	1.94

Source: Nairobi Stock Exchange.

Exhibit 36.4:
MARKET VALUE BY SECTOR ON THE NSE, END-1997

Sector	*% of market value*
Agricultural	10.26
Commercial and services	12.11
Finance and investment	38.51
Industrial and allied	39.30

Source: Nairobi Stock Exchange.

Exhibit 36.5:
THE 20 LARGEST COMPANIES LISTED ON THE NSE, END-1997

Ranking	*Company*	*Market value (US$ million)*
1	Barclays Bank	251.5
2	Bamburi Cement	223.7
3	Kenya Power & Lighting	161.5
4	Kenya Commercial Bank	146.9
5	Standard Chartered Bank	128.9
6	Brooke Bond Kenya	91.4
7	Firestone East Africa	74.2
8	BAT Kenya	63.8
9	Kenya Airways	58.9
10	Kenya Breweries	54.0
11	Total Kenya	50.0
12	National Bank of Kenya	42.5
13	Lonrho Motors (EA)	42.3
14	Sasini Tea and Coffee	40.5
15	Uchumi Supermarkets	39.8
16	Nation Publishers and Printers	39.7
17	NIC Bank	37.4
18	Kakuzi	32.0
19	EA Portland	30.6
20	CFC Bank	30.0

Source: Nairobi Stock Exchange.

B) Trading volume

The value of shares traded in 1997 totalled US$106 million, up 49% from US$71 million the previous year.

Exhibit 36.6:
STOCK TRADING VOLUME AND VALUE, 1993–97

Year	*Volume (shares million)*	*Value (Ksh million)*	*Value (US$ million)*
1993	27	825	14
1994	42	3,076	69
1995	62	3,345	60
1996	113	3,962	71
1997	144	6,148	106

Source: Nairobi Stock Exchange.

Exhibit 36.7:
THE 20 MOST ACTIVELY TRADED NSE SHARES, 1997

Ranking	*Company*	*Trading value (US$ million)*
1	Kenya Power & Lighting	15.64
2	Kenya Commercial Bank	14.94
3	Barclays Bank	8.80
4	Kenya Airways	5.85
5	Sasini	5.82
6	NIC Bank	5.39
7	Firestone	5.04
8	Uchumi	4.92
9	Kenya Breweries	4.47
10	Bamburi	3.42
11	ICDC	3.27
12	Standard Chartered Bank	2.98
13	National Bank	2.53
14	Nation Printers	2.38
15	Diamond Trust	2.20
16	Kakuzi	1.81
17	EA Portland	1.37
18	BAT Kenya	1.35
19	HFCK	1.32
20	Brooke Bond	0.95

Source: Nairobi Stock Exchange.

TYPES OF SHARE

There are two types of share traded on the NSE – ordinary and preference. In addition, corporate and government bonds are also traded.

INVESTORS

There are an estimated 700,000 investors in Kenya.

OPERATIONS

A) Trading system

Floor trading takes place for two hours a day on all working days. It is conducted using the continuous auction, open outcry method. Data is captured in a tailor-made computer system that facilitates the exchange's role as a clearing house.

B) Principal brokers

Most activities of the merchant banks are outside the securities market, but the banks are involved as investment advisers and also underwrite new issues. The main firms are as follows:

DYER & BLAIR LTD
Reinsurance Plaza, 9th Floor, Taifa Road
PO Box 45396, Nairobi
Tel: (254) 2 227 803; Fax: (254) 2 218 633

EQUITY STOCKBROKERS LTD
Queensway House, 3rd Floor, PO Box 47198 Nairobi
Tel: (254) 2 221 452; Fax: (254) 2 221 672
E-mail: equity@form_net.com
Web site: www/Kenyaweb.com.equity

KESTREL CAPITAL (EA) LTD
Lonhro Building, 7th Floor, PO Box 40005, Nairobi
Tel: (254) 2 251 893; Fax: (254) 2 243 264

NGENYE KARIUKI & CO LTD
Travel (UTC) House, 5th Floor, PO Box 12185, Nairobi
Tel: (254) 2 224 333; Fax: (254) 2 217 199

SHAH MUNGE & PARTNERS LTD
Nation Centre, 12th Floor, Kimathi Street
PO Box 14686, Nairobi
Tel: (254) 2 227 300; Fax: (254) 2 213 024

STANDARD STOCKS LTD
Hazina Towers, 11th Floor, PO Box 13714, Nairobi
Tel: (254) 2 220 225; Fax: (254) 2 240 297

SUNTRA STOCKS LTD
Commonwealth House, 2nd Floor, Moi Avenue
PO Box 74016, Nairobi
Tel: (254) 2 337 220/223 294; Fax: (254) 2 224 327

C) Settlement and transfer

Physical settlement takes place with the NSE acting as a clearing house. There is currently no netting of trades. Delivery takes place on T+7 and settlement on D+7. There are penalties for non-delivery or late deliveries with the NSE instituting buy-in procedures against defaulting brokers.

D) Commissions and other costs

Transaction charges as stipulated by the Capital Markets Authority (CMA) are summarised in Exhibit 36.8.

TAXATION AND REGULATIONS AFFECTING FOREIGN INVESTORS

A) Tax treaties

Kenya has double taxation treaties with the following countries: Belgium, Canada, Denmark, Germany, India, Italy, Norway, Sweden, the UK and Zambia.

Exhibit 36.8:
COMMISSIONS AND OTHER CHARGES ON NSE TRADES

Consideration (Ksh million)	*Brokerage commission (%)*	*Transaction fee(%)*		*Compensation fund fee (%)**		*Total cost to investor (%)*
		To CMA	*To NSE*	*To CMA*	*To NSE*	
On the first 10	1.70	0.14	0.14	0.01	0.01	2.00
On the next 40	1.50	0.14	0.14	0.01	0.01	1.80
Over 50	0.80	0.14	0.14	0.01	0.01	1.10

*The compensation fund fee payable to the CMA is charged on the broker's commission and does not increase the cost to the investor.

Source: Nairobi Stock Exchange.

B) Exchange controls and restrictions on foreign share ownership

Most exchange control provisions were suspended in May 1995. The Exchange Control Act was repealed with effect from 27 December 1995, but the Central Bank of Kenya retains the power to regulate the movement of currency under the Central Bank (Amendment) Act of 1995.

Foreign currency may be purchased and remitted freely through the commercial banks. Forex bureaux have been licensed to engage in the buying and selling of foreign exchange, cash or travellers' cheques, bank drafts and other transfers only in internationally convertible currencies. The commercial banks and bureaux are free to set exchange rates competitively in all transactions with customers, and these rates normally fluctuate daily according to demand and supply. However, the central bank does have a reporting requirement for large capital transfers.

C) Investment restrictions

It is no longer necessary for foreign investors to obtain government approval to make loans and equity investments in Kenya. Nevertheless, except with the sanction of the Capital Markets Authority, foreign investors may neither hold in aggregate more than 40% of the issued share capital of any Kenyan listed company, nor individually purchase more than 5% of the shares of any such company. In the case of a public offering, the limits apply to the shares on offer. Existing holdings in excess of the limit are not affected nor are pre-emption rights. Once the aggregate 40% foreign shareholding is reached, further purchases may only be made from other foreign shareholders, and for this purpose an informal foreign board has been established at the NSE.

D) Income tax

All income accrued in or derived from Kenya by any person is potentially subject to income tax, regardless of that person's residency, although the rate is determined by residency. From 1998 the corporate tax rate on Kenyan resident companies is 32.5% and on non-resident foreign branches 40%. Non-residents are taxed at source on dividend and interest income at 10% and 12.5% respectively.

E) Capital gains

Tax on capital gains has been suspended. There is, however, a divided compensating tax, applicable only to companies that pay dividends effectively out of untaxed profits. The effective rate is 48% of the dividend and is payable by the company. With effect from 1998, gains derived from trading in quoted securities by insurance companies are exempt from tax.

F) Withholding tax

Withholding tax is deductible from certain payments to non-residents as set out in the exhibit.

Exhibit 36.9:
WITHHOLDING TAX

Recipient	*Dividends %*	*Interest %*
Foreign corporations and non-resident individuals:		
Non-treaty	10	12.5
Oil industry	Nil	10
Treaty	10	12.5

Notes:

1. The withholding rate on rents paid to foreign corporations and non-resident individuals is 30%.

Source: Price Waterhouse.

LISTING AND REPORTING REQUIREMENTS

A) Listing requirements

An applicant for listing on the NSE must:

- Appoint a member of the exchange to sponsor its application. The sponsor is responsible for ensuring compliance with NSE listing requirements.
- Submit to the NSE its memorandum and articles of association; a prospectus or offer for sale document approved by the CMA; and the Companies Act and other supporting documents.
- Seek the agreement of the NSE Committee and the approval of the CMA for the issue.
- Publish any prospectus at a time and for a period specified by the CMA.

B) Reporting requirements

The NSE requires that listed companies make prompt and full public disclosure of material developments in their affairs. The following information must be given to the exchange not later than 24 hours after a decision has been made on:

- A proposed distribution of dividends, a change in capital structure or any moves that could affect the market price of the company's shares.
- Any proposed alteration to the memorandum and articles of association of the company.
- Details received by the company concerning any changes to substantial shareholdings.
- Any application filed with a court to wind up the company or any of its subsidiaries or associated companies.
- Any acquisition of shares of another company or any transaction resulting in such a company becoming a subsidiary or associated company.

• Any major change of business policy or operations.

Listed companies are also required to make periodic reports: (i) half-yearly results, not later than three months after the end of the first half of the year; and (ii) annual results, not later than three months after the end of the financial year. Printed annual reports must be submitted to the exchange and stockholders not later than six months after the year-end. The contents of the annual report are specified in the regulations.

SHAREHOLDER PROTECTION CODES

All trading in listed securities must take place through the NSE and be recorded on the NSE board. No off-board trading is permitted except in very limited circumstances.

There is no comprehensive code of practice governing shareholder protection. While the CMA regulations and the Companies Act of Kenya do provide for full disclosure on the making of a public offer of shares, minority shareholders are essentially dependent on the articles of association of the individual companies and various remedies under the Companies Act, including petitioning for a winding up order.

A) Takeovers and mergers

There are various reporting and disclosure requirements under the Capital Markets Authority Act in the event of a "takeover", which is deemed to occur when 25% voting control is acquired in a listed company, whether directly or indirectly. The NSE is in the process of preparing a compulsory code to regulate takeovers and mergers, which is expected to include a requirement for compulsory offers to be made following acquisitions over certain thresholds.

B) Insider trading

Under the CMA Act, insiders connected with a corporate body are not permitted to deal in any securities of that body if they have acquired information that is not generally available to the public and which would be likely to materially affect the prices of those securities. There are stringent penalties for breaches. Further, under NSE regulations, insiders should refrain from trading, even after the material information has been released to the press and other media, for a period of at least 14 days to permit thorough public dissemination and evaluation of the information.

C) Compensation fund

There are two compensation funds supervised by the NSE and the CMA. The funds are financed through a levy on all commissions charged by brokers. Although there are strict membership rules, particularly on the financial discipline of brokers, the compensation funds are intended to indemnify investors from losses resulting from default or fraud.

RESEARCH

Reliable information on the market can be obtained from the NSE, which keeps annual reports for all companies at its information/resource centre.

The NSE publishes a quarterly handbook on listed companies, general brochures, a monthly bulletin and a daily price list detailing exchange transactions. The latter is widely disseminated by both print and electronic media, including Reuters.

Few brokers have research departments (although Kestrel Capital and Dyer & Blair are exceptions) but most publish either weekly, bi-monthly or monthly market newsletters. A number of investment advisers also carry out research on the market and make reports available either free or by subscription.

African Equities: A Guide to Markets and Companies, published by Euromoney Books, provides in-depth information for those wishing to invest or do business in Africa. See the order card at the back of this book for details.

PROSPECTIVE CHANGES

The central depository system is expected to become operational in 1998.

OTHER INFORMATION

There is an Investment Promotion Centre to assist and facilitate investments in Kenya by local and foreign enterprises (Tel: (254) 2 221 401-4).

CHAPTER 37

Korea

Introduction

The Korean Composite Stock Price Index plunged 42% in 1997 to end the year at 376.31, the lowest year-end level since 1986. This comes after significant declines in both 1996 (-18%) and 1995 (-38%). The collapse was a direct result of the Asian currency crisis, which resulted in the devaluation of the Korean won against the US dollar and the failure of numerous Korean corporations.

Faced with a near-complete financial sector meltdown, the Korean government was forced to seek a bailout package orchestrated by the IMF, and to accept the conditions attached to that package, including drastic amendments to foreign ownership restrictions. By the end of the year the foreign ownership limit had been increased to 55% for all listed stocks except Kepco (25%), Posco (25%), SK Telecom (33%) and Dacom (33%). Although the Asian currency crisis has had a dramatic effect on the stock market and the fortunes of Korea's corporate sector in 1997, the removal of onerous foreign ownership restrictions is likely to be viewed in hindsight as a major positive step towards liberalisation of the Korean market.

Korean Stock Exchange (KSE) market capitalisation plummeted in 1997, ending the year at US$41.88 billion, down from US$139 billion at the end of 1996. There were 726 companies listed on the KSE at December 1997 – 34 less than at the end of 1996.

ECONOMIC AND POLITICAL OVERVIEW

The second half of 1997 saw weakness in the Korean market develop into a full-blown emergency as the Asian currency crisis embraced Korea leading to a collapse in the currency and a credit squeeze on the banking sector. Soaring costs of foreign currency and local debt led to an increase in corporate bankruptcies and debt default. The situation became so bad that the government was forced to approach the IMF, which organised an enormous bailout package for the country. The package is accompanied by austerity measures designed to reduce economic growth and tackle Korea's many structural problems.

The economy continued to slow in 1997, posting a real GDP growth rate of 5.6%, down from 6.8% in 1996, but the slowdown was not enough to avoid the fallout from the Asian currency crisis. With a current account deficit of 5.2% of GDP, Korea proved a prime target for currency speculators. During 1997 the Korean won lost half its value against the US dollar, falling from W840.9 at the end of 1996 to W1,695 at the end of 1997. Most of this deterioration occurred in the fourth quarter of 1997, and such a sudden and large decline in the currency was enough to push many companies to the verge of bankruptcy and beyond. The economy is expected to slow drastically in 1998 and there is a possibility that we will see negative real economic growth for the first time in many years.

Role of the central bank

The Bank of Korea was established in June 1950. Its capital was originally W1.5 billion, but under an amendment to the Bank of Korea Act in 1962, the bank was reconstituted as a special juridical entity with no capital. The profits of the bank, after depreciation and crediting authorised reserve funds, are paid into the government's general revenue account.

The bank's supreme policy-making body is the Monetary Board which is responsible for monetary policy and banking supervision. The board comprises nine members appointed by the president, and is chaired by the Minister of Finance or, in his absence, the governor of the bank.

The bank's main function is to control the nation's money supply and it is legally obliged to do all it can to fight inflation and preserve the value of the currency. It is the issuer of banknotes and coins in Korea and acts as banker to the banking sector and the government.

Since the 1980s the central bank has followed a policy of open market operations. It sells monetary stabilisation bonds (MSBs) direct to the public and also to non-bank fi-

Exhibit 37.1: KOREA SE COMPOSITE PRICE INDEX (KOSPI) (US$), 1993–97

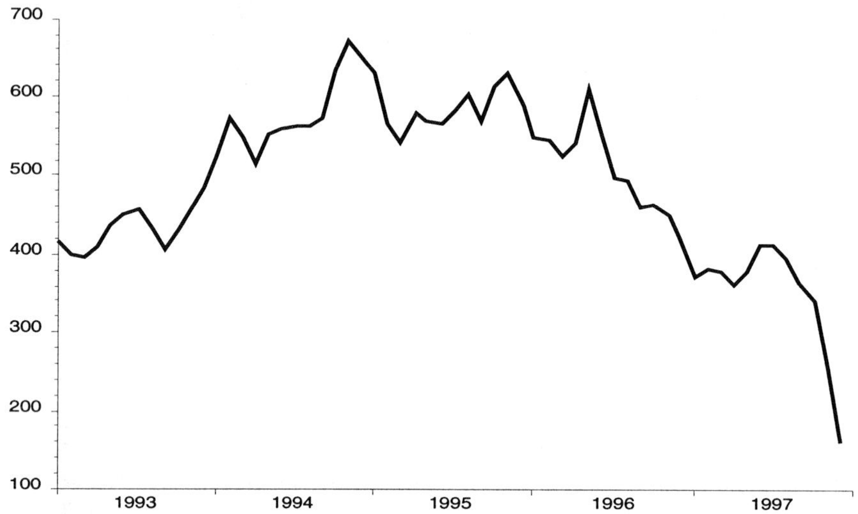

High value 672.76 1.11.94 Low value 160.47 1.12.97 *Source: Datastream*

nancial intermediaries, and the government relies increasingly on bond issuance rather than direct borrowing from the bank. The central bank is also responsible for some aspects of foreign exchange control but this role is expected to diminish as further foreign exchange deregulation is planned.

MARKET PERFORMANCE

A) In 1997

The Korean stock market – which had shown some signs of strength in the first half of 1997 – went into free fall in July as the Thai baht was devalued and the Asian currency crisis began to gather momentum. In local currency terms, the Korea Composite Index fell by more than 50% from peak to trough in 1997. Although there is the possibility of a rebound in the first few months of 1998, this is likely to be short-lived. The major structural problems inherent in both the economy and the corporate sector need to be addressed before a long-term recovery can be achieved.

B) Summary information

Global ranking by market value (US$ terms, end-1997): 31
Market capitalisation (end-1997): US$41.88 billion
Growth in market value (local currency terms, 1993–97): -36.99%
Market value as a % of nominal GNP (end-1997): 9.1%
Number of domestic/foreign companies listed (end-1997): 726/0
Market P/E (end-1997): 19.3
MSCI Index (change in US$ terms, 1997): -67.3%
Short-term (90-day) interest rate (end-1997): 15.5%
Long-term (5-year) bond yield (end-1997): 24.6%
Budget deficit as a % of nominal GDP (1997): 0.83%
Annual increase in broad (M3) money supply (end-1997): 15.3%
Inflation rate (1997): 4.5%
US$ exchange rate (end-1997): W1,695

C) Year-end share price index, price/earnings ratios and yields

Exhibit 37.2:
KSE INDEX, P/E AND AVERAGE YIELDS, 1993–97

Year-end	*Composite Index*	*P/E*	*Yield (%)*
1993	866.18	14.1	1.4
1994	1,027.37	21.8	1.2
1995	882.94	17.9	1.1
1996	651.22	19.4	1.5
1997	376.31	17.9	1.9

Source: Korean Stock Exchange.

D) Market indices and their constituents

The main index is the Korea Composite Stock Price Index (KOSPI) published by the KSE. The Composite Index is supplemented by section indices, industrial sector indices and indices by capital size.

The KOSPI 200 was introduced in May 1994 as a base index for the futures and options markets.

THE STOCK MARKET

A) Brief history and structure

The KSE was established on 11 February 1956 and began trading on 3 March 1956. In 1988 the exchange was reorganised, and its status was changed from a state-run organisation to the present non-profit membership organisation.

In 1991 the KSE opened its membership to foreign securities companies and, beginning in 1992, foreign investors were allowed to directly invest in the Korean stock market. The KSE closed its trading floor on 1 September 1997 when the market became fully automated.

The board of directors (comprising a chairman, a senior executive director, four executive directors, two member directors and three public directors) is responsible for the administration of the exchange.

B) Different exchanges

The KSE in Seoul is the only stock exchange in Korea.

C) Opening hours, names and addresses

From Monday to Friday, trading hours are from 9.30am to 11.30am during the morning session and from 1.00pm to 3.00pm during the afternoon session. On Saturdays, there is a morning session followed by an "after-hours" session (from 11.40am to 12.10pm).

KOREA STOCK EXCHANGE
33 Yoido-dong, Youngdungpo-ku, Seoul 150-010
Tel: (82) 2 3774 9000; Fax: (82) 2 786 0263 / 782 0417

MARKET SIZE

A) Number of listings and market value

There was a drop in total share market value from W117.4 trillion at the end of 1996 to W70.9 trillion at the end of 1997. The dominant sector in 1997 was machinery and electronics, which, with a year-end capitalisation of W19.4 trillion, accounted for 27.3% of the total.

Exhibit 37.3:
NUMBER OF LISTED COMPANIES AND MARKET VALUE, 1993–97

Year-end	*No. of listed companies*	*Total market value (W billion)*
1993	693	112,665.3
1994	699	151,217.2
1995	721	141,151.4
1996	760	117,369.9
1997	726	70,988.9

Source: Korean Stock Exchange.

Exhibit 37.4:
MARKET VALUE BY SECTOR, KSE, END-1997

Industry	*Market capitalisation (W billion)*	*% of total*
Machinery and electronics	19,396.60	27.3
Banking (including securities)	11,318.70	15.9
Utilities	10,710.78	15.0
Chemicals	6,495.35	9.1
Base metals	5,893.90	8.3
Telecommunications	3,918.67	5.5
General construction	2,234.18	3.1
Wholesaling	2,177.68	3.0
Foods and beverages	1,743.67	2.4
Textiles and apparels	1,699.43	2.3
Insurance	1,166.45	1.6
Transport and storage	893.69	1.2
Non-metallic minerals	887.66	1.2
Paper and paper products	864.52	1.2
Real estate	599.29	0.8
Retailing	346.54	0.4
Other manufacturing	166.67	0.2
Leather	114.1	0.1
Mining	88.86	0.1
Wood and wood products	77.83	0.1
Printing	68.33	0.0
Hotels	65.93	0.0
Fisheries	55.06	0.0
Service	5.02	0.0
Total	**70,988.90**	**100.0**

Source: Korean Stock Exchange.

Exhibit 37.5:
20 LARGEST COMPANIES LISTED ON THE KSE, END-1997

Ranking	*Company*	*Market value (W million)*
1	Korea Electric Power Corporation	9,863,011
2	Pohang Iron & Steel	4,310,093
3	Samsung Electronics	3,996,910
4	SK Telecom	2,767,439
5	Daewoo Heavy Industry	1,761,991
6	Hyundai Electronics	1,204,000
7	LG Electronics	1,188,142
8	Dacom Corporation	1,151,228
9	LG Semiconductor	1,149,390
10	Yukong	992,112
11	Kookmin Bank	936,530
12	Shinhan Bank	930,160
13	Samsung Display Device	881,621
14	Hyundai Motor	850,135
15	LG Information & Communications	802,750

Exhibit 37.5 continued

16	Korea Exchange Bank	651,750
17	Cho-Hung Bank	643,857
18	Korea Long-Term Credit Bank	642,653
19	LG Chemical	630,469
20	Housing & Commercial Bank	622,645

Source: Korean Stock Exchange.

B) Trading volume

The value of shares traded in 1997 totalled W162.3 trillion, an increase of 13.8% on the previous year. The most active sector in terms of trading volume was banking, which accounted for 24.7% of the total.

Exhibit 37.6:
STOCK TRADING VOLUME AND VALUE, 1993–97

Year	*Volume shares (million)*	*Value (W billion)*
1993	10,398	169,918
1994	10,911	229,772
1995	7,656	142,914
1996	7,785	142,642
1997	12,125	162,282

Source: Korean Stock Exchange.

Exhibit 37.7:
TRADING VOLUME BY SECTOR, KSE, 1997

Sector	*Total trading volume (shares million)*	*Average daily volume (shares '000)*	*% of total*
Banking (incl securities)	2,995.7	10,259.1	24.7
Machinery & electronics	2,756.5	9,440.1	22.7
Chemicals	1,271.6	4,354.9	10.5
General construction	1,034.6	3,543.2	8.5
Wholesaling	794.1	2,719.4	6.5
Textiles and apparel	669.2	2,291.9	5.5
Basic metals	553.8	1,896.5	4.6
Paper and paper products	381.3	1,306.0	3.1
Foods and beverages	352.6	1,207.5	2.9
Leather	248.8	852.1	2.1
Utilities	232.5	796.3	1.9
Non-metallic minerals	222.4	761.5	1.8
Retailing	143.9	492.9	1.2
Transport and storage	129.7	444.1	1.1
Insurance	106.70	365.6	0.9
Other manufacturing	93.60	320.4	0.8
Mining	26.6	91.0	0.2
Wood and wood products	24.0	82.3	0.2
Printing	22.8	78.2	0.2
Fisheries	21.1	72.1	0.2

Exhibit 37.6 continued

Real estate	20.2	69.3	0.2
Hotels	14.7	50.2	0.1
Telecommunication	8.9	30.5	0.1
Service	0.0	0.0	0.0
Total	12,125.30	41,525.10	100.0

Source: Korean Stock Exchange.

Exhibit 37.8:
THE 20 MOST ACTIVELY TRADED KSE SHARES, 1997

Ranking	*Company*	*Total value (W billion)*	*% of market total*
1	Korea Electric Power Corporation	3,924.33	2.4
2	Pohang Iron & Steel	3,784.24	2.3
3	Samsung Electronics	3,536.63	2.2
4	LG Electronics	1,543.26	1.0
5	LG Semicon	1,511.72	0.9
6	Daewoo Securities	1,501.77	0.9
7	LG Information & Communications	1,491.86	0.9
8	Kookmin Bank	1,481.59	0.9
9	Hyundai Electronics	1,466.94	0.9
10	SK Telecom	1,429.20	0.9
11	Hyundai Engineering & Construction	1,394.77	0.9
12	Taeheung Leather	1,331.88	0.8
13	LG Chemical	1,177.94	0.7
14	Daewoo Heavy Industry	1,118.00	0.7
15	Cho Hung Bank	1,040.97	0.6
16	Shinhwa	1,031.01	0.6
17	Yukong	1,017.81	0.6
18	Korea Exchange Bank	984.59	0.6
19	Samsung Heavy Industry	936.81	0.6
20	LG Securities	882.82	0.5

Source: Korean Stock Exchange.

TYPES OF SHARE

All Korean shares have a nominal value, and may be either bearer or registered. The equity instruments most commonly traded are common shares and non-cumulative and participating preferred shares. Convertible bonds and bonds with warrants may also be listed on the KSE. Although legally recognised, deferred shares are not available on the Korean market. Common shares are entitled to normal voting rights of one vote per share.

Listed preferred shares are mainly non-cumulative, participating, non-voting and non-redeemable, with preferred status in the distribution of dividends. Non-voting preferred shares may acquire a vote if the preferential dividend is not declared. Preferred shares with preferential rights to

Exhibit 37.9:
TOP PERFORMING COUNTRY FUNDS – KOREA

FUND	*US$ % change* 01/01/97 01/01/98	01/01/93 01/01/98	Fund base currency	Fund size (US$ mil)	Fund volatility	Management group	Opal main sector	Opal subsector
Daehan Synthetic Trust	17.11	N/A	US$	75.41	12.685	Daehan	Closed-End	Equity
Daehan Win Trust	-20.68	N/A	US$	63.59	8.532	Daehan	Open-End	Equity
CITC Balanced Fund plc	-25.48	N/A	US$	51.049	-1	Citizen	Open-End	Equity
Bordier Korea	-29.19	-29.99	US$	15	8.81	Bordier & Co	Open-End	Equity
Daehan Blue Chip Trust II	-31.65	N/A	US$	50.04	-1	Daehan	Open-End	Equity
Seoul Trust	-34.36	-43.77	US$	N/A	7.705	Daehan	Open-End	Equity
Daehan Index Trust	-35.54	N/A	US$	78.44	7.527	Daehan	Open-End	Equity
Hambros Asian Korea Advantage	-36.17	N/A	US$	2.2	-1	Hambros	Open-End	Equity
Korea Trust	-38.81	-38.73	US$	0	7.914	Daehan	Open-End	Equity
Korea Equity Select (L) Ltd	-40.85	N/A	US$	44.145	-1	Pacific Gemin	Open-End	Equity
CITC Seoul Legend Trust	-41.82	N/A	US$	50.748	-1	Citizen	Open-End	Equity
Schroder Korea	-44.32	-42.68	US$	N/A	10.524	Schroders	Closed-End	Equity
Korea Investment Fund Inc	-44.82	-57.6	US$	58.11	9.655	Alliance Cap	Closed-End	Equity
JF Korea	-44.89	-59.4	US$	60.2	10.156	Jardine Fleming	Open-End	Equity
CITC Seoul Select Trust	-44.99	N/A	US$	46.272	8.236	Citizen	Open-End	Equity
New Korea Trust	-45.3	-36.31	US$	202.52	8.565	Daehan	Open-End	Equity
CITC Seoul Prosperity	-46.18	N/A	US$	73.006	11.023	Citizen	Open-End	Equity
Daehan Korea Emerging Growth	-46.51	-43.58	US$	59.53	9.12	Daehan	Closed-End	Equity
CITC Seoul Century Trust	-46.54	N/A	US$	52.239	-1	Citizen	Open-End	Equity
CITC Seoul Optima Trust	-46.75	N/A	US$	52.663	-1	Citizen	Open-End	Equity
CS Equity Fund Korea	-48.66	N/A	US$	N/A	8.489	Credit Suisse	Open-End	Equity
Daehan Intl Investment Trust	-48.79	-3.25	US$	94.76	12.275	Daehan	Closed-End	Equity
Citi Korea Equity	-49.5	N/A	US$	2.1	10.209	Citibank	Open-End	Equity
Korea Special Opportunities	-50	N/A	US$	51.8	-1	Oreins Capital	Open-End	Equity
Daehan Prime Equity Trust	-50.16	N/A	US$	52.72	-1	Daehan	Open-End	Equity
Korea 1990 Trust	-50.8	-48.41	US$	41.84	9.444	Citizen	Closed-End	Equity
Korea Capital Fund	-51.46	-73.33	US$	2.3	8.72	Daehan	Open-End	Equity
The Yellow Sea Inv Co	-52.02	N/A	US$	7	9.447	Chemical Bank	Open-End	Equity
Greater Korea Trust	-52.61	N/A	US$	27.1	10.728	Korea Inv Trust	Open-End	Equity
Korea Intl Investment Fund Ltd	-53.12	-21.16	US$	90	11.071	Intl Inv Advi	Open-End	Equity
NICAM Asia Pacific UF Korea	-54.97	N/A	US$	3.4	10.504	Nikko	Open-End	Equity
NM First Korean	-55.52	N/A	US$	3.3	-1	National Mut	Open-End	Equity
Indosuez Korea	-55.56	-61.19	US$	8.5	9.013	Indosuez	Open-End	Equity
Regent New Korea Gth	-55.84	N/A	US$	5	8.709	Regent Fd Mgr	Open-End	Equity
Daehan Selective Eqt Tst	-56.04	N/A	US$	44.19	9.91	Daehan	Open-End	Equity
Korea Golden Opp Inv (L) Ltd	-56.92	N/A	US$	N/A	-1	Pacific Gemin	Open-End	Equity
CITC Seoul Excel Trust	-57.31	N/A	US$	38.81	10.163	Citizen	Closed-End	Equity
Daehan Blue Chip Index Trust	-58.32	N/A	US$	111.32	13.152	Daehan	Closed-End	Equity
Seoul Horizon Trust	-58.35	-45.65	US$	71.45	9.617	Citizen	Open-End	Equity
Daehan Korea Trust	-58.72	-55.63	US$	38.33	11.008	Daehan	Closed-End	Equity
CITC Seoul Access Trust	-59.41	N/A	US$	64.23	10.424	Citizen	Open-End	Equity
Jupiter Tyndall GF Korea Vis	-60.12	-67.91	US$	0.7	10.785	Tyndall	Open-End	Equity
Baring Korea Feeder Fund	-60.99	-61.63	US$	16.3	11.896	Barings	Open-End	Equity
Baring Korea Trust	-61.33	-57.38	£	21.9	13.894	Barings	Open-End	Equity

Note: details for some funds may not have been included if the data for the US$ % change for 97/98 is not available

Source: Standard & Poor's Micropal.

dividends may also be issued as redeemable shares and may be redeemed only from the company's net profits.

The 1984 amendments to the Commercial Code permit issuance of transferable warrants evidencing pre-emptive rights to acquire shares at specified prices for a stipulated period. Warrants with long-term options to buy shares at specified prices are not available.

OTHER MARKETS

There is an organised OTC market called Kosdaq. It is a floorless, computerised stock market where transactions are carried out through an electronic network. Since December 1997, foreigners have been allowed to invest in venture capital and other companies listed on the Kosdaq market. Furthermore, companies listed on Kosdaq are now allowed to issue securities in overseas markets.

On 7 July 1997, the KSE launched a stock index options market. (A successful stock index futures market has been operating for some years.) The KOSPI 200, which is composed of 200 leading companies listed on the KSE and representing about 70% of its total market capitalisation, is the underlying index. The options are European-style and trading is fully computerised.

INVESTORS

Individuals comprise by far the largest group of shareholders. They were responsible for 70% of total trading in 1996, institutions for 23.9% and foreign investors for 6.0%.

OPERATIONS

A) Trading system

The KSE is a typical order-driven market where buying and selling orders compete for the best price. Throughout the trading session, customers' orders are continuously matched according to price and time priority. There is a daily price change limit of 8% above and below the previous day's closing price.

On 1 September 1997, the KSE switched to a fully automated trading system and, in November, a new computer system called KATS (KSE Automated Trading System) was launched. It can handle up to a million orders or 150 million shares a day, completing the trading process from order placement to trade confirmation within 30 seconds.

B) List of principal securities companies

DAEWOO
34-3, Yoido-dong, Youngdeungpo-ku, Seoul 150-010
Tel: (82) 2 768 3355

DAISHIN
34-8, Yoido-dong, Youngdeungpo-ku, Seoul 150-010
Tel: (82) 2 769 2000

DONGWON
34-7, Yoido-dong, Youngdeungpo-ku, Seoul 150-010
Tel: (82) 2 768 5000

HYUNDAI
34-4, Yoido-dong, Youngdeungpo-ku, Seoul 150-010
Tel: (82) 2 768 0011

KEB SMITH BARNEY SECURITIES CO. LTD.
13th Floor, Dong-Ah Life Insurance Building
33, Da-Dong, Chung-ku, Seoul 100-180
Tel: (82) 2 3705 0921; Fax: (82) 2 3705 0991

LG
34-6, Yoido-dong, Youngdeungpo-ku, Seoul 150-010
Tel: (82) 2 768 7000

SHINYOUNG
34-8, Yoido-dong, Youngdeungpo-ku, Seoul 150-010
Tel: (82) 2 780 7000

SK
23-10, Yoido-dong, Youngdeungpo-ku, Seoul 150-010
Tel: (82) 2 3773 8245

SSANGYONG
23-2 Yoido-dong Youngdeungpo-ku, Seoul 150-010
Tel: (82) 2 3772 1000

C) Settlement and transfer

Transactions on the KSE are classified into regular way transactions and cash transactions. Settlement of regular way transactions is due on the second business day following the trading day. Cash transactions are due on the trading day.

Shares and investment trust certificates are traded as regular way transactions, while bonds may be traded as either regular way or cash transactions.

The securities company must pay money and/or deliver securities on the basis of the net balance between purchases and sales to the Korea Securities Depository (KSD), the clearing agent of the exchange. The KSD pays money and/or delivers securities to the securities company according to the time limit for settlement. As with the delivery of securities, a book entry clearing system is employed. Listed companies (with some exceptions) must have a transfer agent. At present there are three transfer agents (the KSD and two banks).

The transfer of shares requires the actual delivery of certificates, but entry of a transaction in the broker's books and in the KSD's books is deemed to be actual delivery of share certificates for the purpose of a transfer. The name of the new owner is registered in the company's books only upon request.

D) Commissions and other costs

Brokerage commission is negotiable. Currently, securities companies charge commission of around 0.3%.

Securities transaction tax is levied on the seller at a rate of 0.3% of trading value, and this includes the agricultural and fishery tax of 0.15%.

TAXATION AND REGULATIONS AFFECTING FOREIGN INVESTORS

The taxation of non-residents and foreign corporations depends on whether they have a permanent establishment in Korea. Non-residents without a permanent establishment in Korea are subject to 27.5% withholding tax on dividends and interest income.

Effective from 25 October 1997, a non-resident individual or non-Korean corporation is not subject to Korean taxation on capital gains realised on a sale of shares unless the non-resident shareholder:

- has a permanent establishment in Korea (whether or not such capital gains are attributable to such permanent establishment); or
- has, together with shares owned by any entity in certain special relationships with such a non-resident holder, owned 25% or more of the total issued and outstanding shares at any time in the calendar year of the sale date and during the five calendar years before the calendar year of the sale date; provided that the country or the region where the non-resident holder resides also exempts from capital gains tax gains made on the sale of shares or similar securities owned by a Korean resident. Where a non-resident holder is subject to Korean tax on capital gains, the lesser of 27.5% of the gain or 11% of the gross proceeds realised from the sale is taxed unless reduced rates are available under double tax treaty conditions.

Foreign investors wishing to make a portfolio investment in the Korean stock market are required to register with the SEC. All stock transactions by foreign investors should be made through the KSE. Unless there is an emergency, there is no restriction on repatriation of investment capital and interest.

As of December 1997, the aggregate foreign investment ceiling is 50% of a listed company's shares. A single investor is allowed to hold up to 5%. By way of exception, aggregate foreign shareholding limits in four particular companies have been set at lower levels – namely Kepco (25%), Posco (25%), SK Telecom (33%) and Dacom (33%) – and an individual ceiling applies of 1%.

LISTING AND REPORTING REQUIREMENTS

A) Listing requirements

The KSE is divided into two sections. After the shares of a company have been listed for at least one year in the second section, the listing may be moved to the first section if the company meets a number of more stringent requirements. To be listed on the first section, among other conditions, companies must have declared a dividend of 6% or more for minority stockholders on at least two occasions during the past three fiscal years, and the ratio of after-tax profit to paid-in capital must be 10% or more during the past three fiscal years. The total number of shares held by minority stockholders must be 40% or more of the floating shares, and the number of minority stockholders must be 1,000 or more. Companies that do not satisfy these criteria are traded on the second section.

A company wishing to have its securities listed on the KSE must enter into a listing agreement with the exchange whereby the company agrees to observe various stock exchange regulations.

Foreign companies have been allowed to list on the KSE from May 1996.

B) Reporting requirements

Under the Securities and Exchange Law, a listed company is required to file yearly and half-yearly financial reports with the Securities and Exchange Commission and the KSE, and to report any of the following occurrences to both bodies:

a) the suspension of banking transactions;
b) the cessation of all or part of its business activities;
c) the filing of an application for the commencement of reorganisation proceedings or for the commencement of *de facto* reorganisation;
d) the decision to change its stated business purposes;
e) the occurrence of any catastrophe;
f) the initiation of a suit that may materially affect its business or the value of its listed securities;
g) the initiation of a takeover of, or merger with, another company;
h) the transfer of all or a substantial part of its business, the lease of its entire business, or its taking over of another company;
i) the merger or consolidation with another company;
j) the occurrence of any event that is a statutory basis for its dissolution;

k) a resolution by its board of directors approving an increase or decrease in its capital;
l) the suspension or cessation of operations due to any extraordinary circumstance;
m) the assumption of management control by its trading bank;
n) any other event that may materially affect the management of the company.

In addition, the regulations of the SEC and the KSE require a listed company to file a report with respect to certain other events. These include, for example, investment in another company in excess of 10% of the company's paid-up capital; the board resolution regarding the execution of a technology inducement agreement or a joint venture agreement; a decision to issue convertible bonds or bonds with warrants; or a decision to revalue its assets.

SHAREHOLDER PROTECTION CODES

Securities transactions in Korea are regulated by the Securities and Exchange Law, plus decrees and regulations made under the Act.

A) Mergers and takeovers

In order to merge with or take over the business of another company, a special resolution of the shareholders must be obtained. This must be adopted by a majority of at least two-thirds of the votes of the shareholders present, representing at least half the issued shares.

In addition, if a shareholder has notified the listed company in writing before the general shareholders' meeting of his opposition to the company's merger or takeover plans, he may demand that the company repurchase his stock at a negotiated price.

Until recently, 50% plus one share of the total outstanding shares must be purchased through a tender offer when a company or an individual acquires more than 25% of the outstanding shares of a company. However, this threshold was reduced to 40% plus one share with effect from January 1998. There are also plans to revise the regulations concerning mandatory tender offers.

B) Insider trading

Any person who has obtained non-public information concerning a particular security, either in the performance of his duty or by reason of his relationship to the corporation, or any other persons to whom such information is transferred, may not use such information or let any other person use it in connection with a purchase, sale, or any other transaction in the security. Any person who violates the insider trading regulations is subject to criminal sanctions and is liable to the injured parties for damages in connection with the transaction.

An officer, employee or principal shareholder (one who owns 10% or more of the total number of the company's shares or who otherwise exercises control over the company) who realises a profit from a sale or purchase within six months, may be compelled to return this profit to the company. Furthermore, it is a criminal offence for such persons to sell short shares of the corporation. Such officers and principal shareholders are required to report the following to the Securities and Exchange Commission and the KSE: (a) the status of shares owned by them within 10 days after they become officers or principal shareholders; and (b) changes in share status by the tenth day of the following month.

With certain exceptions, employees and officers of securities companies, the KSE and its regulatory agencies, are barred from trading listed securities whether in their own name or in the name of any third party for their own account.

C) Compensation funds

Investors who suffer losses because of fraud or default by brokers or traders have second preferential rights (first preferential rights being held by the exchange itself) to the security deposits of such brokers or traders deposited with the KSE. In addition, the KSE manages a fund to compensate losses arising from a breach by a trader or securities company with respect to buying and selling transactions in the securities market. Each securities company must make contributions to the compensation fund equivalent to 1/100,000 of the amount of each buying and selling transaction on the exchange.

A Securities Investor Protection Fund was set up in April 1997 in order to guarantee repayment of deposits made by investors to securities companies. Every securities company is required to make a basic contribution (1% of their shareholders' equity) and annual contributions (0.1% of the average annual deposit amounts) to the fund.

RESEARCH

The KSE publishes a *Fact Book* containing detailed statistics plus historical data, and the *Korea Stock Exchange*, designed to provide foreign investors with an overview of how the exchange operates. *Securities Markets in Korea*, published by the Korea Securities Dealers' Association (KSDA), contains comprehensive information on the structure and administration of the securities market. The address of the KSDA is: 34 Yoido-dong, Youngdeungpo-ku, Seoul 150-010.

The *Korea Company Handbook*, a comprehensive

English language directory of corporate statistics and company news, is published bi-annually by Asia Pacific Infoserv, Inc.

Of the major brokers, research by Daewoo and Ssangyong is particularly highly regarded.

Korea, published by Euromoney Books, provides in-depth information for those wishing to invest or do business in the country. See the order card at the back of this book for details.

PROSPECTIVE CHANGES

The Korean government is expected to introduce new regulations covering the consolidation of financial statements, the easing of requirements for capital increases by financial institutions and the introduction of an interim dividend system.

CHAPTER

38

Lebanon

Introduction

By international standards, the Lebanese equity market is still considered as a pre-emerging market in terms of its size, its number of listed firms, and the economic sectors reflected on the Beirut Stock Exchange (BSE). Unlike the Egyptian and Moroccan stock markets, which have greatly benefited from large-scale privatisation programmes, the growth of the Lebanese market remains in the hands of private sector issuers.

Although BSE liquidity has improved markedly in 1997 compared with 1996, turnover as a percentage of total market capitalisation (21.7%) remains low in relation to the region's other equity markets. The anticipated switch to a continuous trading system on the BSE should, however, serve to improve liquidity. Despite the lack of an investing culture, both in Lebanon and the Middle-East generally, there is evidence of growing interest in the Lebanese stock market, and this should help underpin trading and listing activity on the BSE in 1998.

In 1997, the Lebanese Cabinet approved a law allowing direct foreign portfolio investment in the shares of Solidere, the BSE's largest listed company with a market capitalisation of over US$2 billion. This has led to a diversification of the firm's shareholder base, albeit with increased volatility in its stock price.

ECONOMIC AND POLITICAL OVERVIEW

Lebanon is slowly recovering from its devastating 15-year civil war (1975–1990), though many of the political issues that gave rise to the conflict have yet to be resolved. Politically, Lebanon is still considered a high-risk country, and the continued fighting between Hizbollah guerillas and Israel in the southern region undermines stability. Although pressure from the political opposition is rising, the current government (led since October 1992 by Rafik Hariri) is still backed by a parliamentary majority and by the Lebanese people.

There are around 35,000 Syrian troops stationed in Lebanon, and all security issues, foreign policy, Lebanon's position in the Middle East peace talks, and the domestic status quo are overseen by the Syrian government. Most Lebanese accept the Syrian presence as necessary to bolster political stability.

Lebanon's political structures are based on a confessional system laid down by the French in 1943 (the year of independence and the end of the French mandate on the country), as modified by the 1989 Taif Agreement. The agreement stipulates that positions of public office and the 128-seat parliament are divided equally between Muslims and Christians.

During 1997, the Lebanese economy grew by 3.5–4% in real terms. For the past five years, growth has averaged 5%, fuelled by public spending (mainly on infrastructure projects) and by domestic business investment. Slower growth in 1997 was mainly due to the sharp slowdown in the real estate sector, although this was partly offset by increased tourism. Already there are signs of a pick-up in the commercial real estate sector.

Lebanon still suffers from a large current account deficit, which is the result of a recurring trade deficit. The trade deficit reached US$6.165 billion in November 1997, but this was offset by large capital inflows in the form of remittances and investments denominated in Lebanese pounds. The balance of payments registered a US$419.9 million surplus – the fifth consecutive annual surplus. This led to a 0.8% increase in central bank gross foreign currency reserves, which reached US$5.932 billion at the end of 1997. Meanwhile, inflation remains on a downward trend, and consumer prices rose only 8% in 1997, compared with 8.9% in 1996.

Despite a recurring budget deficit, the Lebanese pound continued its appreciation against the US dollar, rising 1.62% in 1997. The currency was not affected by the drop in interest rates on Treasuries as demand for deposits and investments denominated in Lebanese pounds remained firm. The central bank has successfully implemented a

Exhibit 38.1: LEBANON BLOM PRICE INDEX (US$), 1993–97

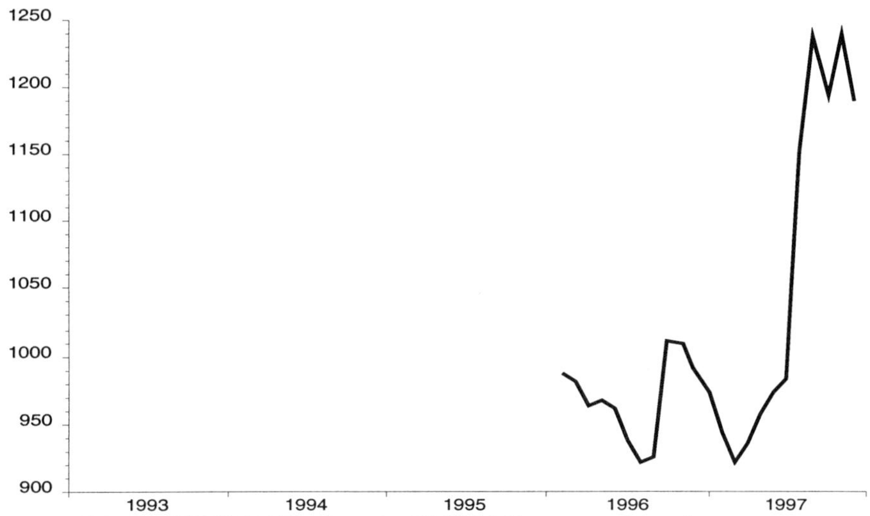

High value 1239.63 3.11.97 Low value 921.08 3.3.97 *Source: Datastream*

monetary policy based on stabilising the domestic currency's exchange rate while containing inflation. Monetary stability should be maintained if the Lebanese government succeeds in containing the budget deficit to a planned 37.4% of revenues in 1998.

Role of the central bank

The Lebanese central bank enjoys complete political autonomy. It is responsible for issuing the national currency, keeping government accounts, advising the Cabinet and auctioning debt securities on behalf of the Lebanese Treasury. For the past five years the central bank has concentrated on monetary stability as the prerequisite for sustained economic growth. In addition, it has played a major role in restoring confidence in the Lebanese pound, resulting in a significant reduction in the dollarisation of the Lebanese economy.

The central bank has also sought to develop the Lebanese capital market and strengthen the banking sector. In 1997, it introduced major legislation regulating mutual funds and finance companies.

MARKET PERFORMANCE

A) In 1997

In its second year of operations, the Beirut exchange witnessed a considerable increase in activity, both in terms of number of listings and level of trading activity. At the end of December 1997, a total of eight companies were listed on the BSE, compared with six at the end of 1996. The newcomers were both banking stocks and the listings served to boost investor interest in publicly traded equities.

The volume and value of shares traded on the BSE in 1997 amounted to 59,173,871 and US$639,827,188, respectively. The daily average number of shares traded was 241,526 shares with a value of US$2,611,540 – a significant increase over 1996 levels. Furthermore, the Lebanese stock market returned 21.75% in 1997 (excluding dividends) boosted by banking stocks, which more than doubled. Stock market capitalisation reached US$2.94 billion, or 20% of GDP, versus US$2.2 billion and 18% of GDP in 1996. Growth in the Lebanese equity market in 1998 should be fuelled by additional share listings of firms in the trade and insurance sectors.

B) Summary information

Global ranking by market value (US$ terms, end-1997): 57
Market capitalisation (end-1997): US$2.9 billion
Growth in market value (US$ terms, 1996–97): 44.53%
Market value as a % of nominal GDP (end-1997): 20%
Number of domestic/foreign companies listed on the official market (end-1997): 8/0
Market P/E (banking sector end-1997, estimate): 16.1
Short-term (3-month) interest rate (end-1997): 13%
Long-term (2-year) bond yield (end-1997): 16.73%
Budget deficit as a % of nominal GDP (end-1997): 23.7%
Annual increase in broad money (M3) supply (end-1997):18.5%
Inflation rate (1997): 8%
US$ exchange rate (end-1997): L£1,527

C) Market indices and their constituents

An index measuring both BSE and parallel market share prices is compiled by Lebanon Invest. The Lebanon Invest Stock Price Index (LISPI) is based at 22 January 1996 = 100. The LISPI is an equal-weighted price index, which neutralises the predominance of Solidere, the BSE's largest listed company. As more companies list shares and as market depth improves, the weights of the various stocks will be factored into the index.

In March 1996, Banque Du Liban et D'Outre-Mer introduced the BLOM Stock Index, which tracks the performance of listed equities as well as Solidere A and B shares. The index is based at 22 January 1996 = 100 and gives Solidere a 90% weighting.

Due to the increasing interest in banking shares, Lebanon Invest recently introduced a banking index based at 7 January 1997 = 100. The LIBX is an equal-weighted price index of listed and OTC bank shares. At the end of 1997, the LIBX stood at 211.98, reflecting the substantial price appreciation of banking stocks during the year.

THE STOCK MARKET

A) Brief history and structure

The Beirut Stock Exchange was originally set up in the 1920s, and was one of the first stock markets in the region. It was supervised by the French colonial administration and traded in joint-venture stocks listed on both the BSE and the Paris Bourse. By the 1970s the BSE listed 45 companies, but in 1983, at the height of the civil war, it was forced to close.

In July 1994, the government appointed a new Beirut Stock Exchange Commission to re-open the dormant exchange. The BSE was officially reopened on 22 January 1996. It is hoped that the exchange will provide an important vehicle for Lebanese companies to raise capital for expansion.

B) Opening hours and address

Share prices are established on each business day at 10.00am and 11.00am.

BOURSE DE BEYROUTH
Sadat Tower, 2nd Floor, Sadat Street, Beirut
Tel: (961) 1 807 552; Fax: (961) 1 807 331
E-mail: bse@bse.com.lb
Web site: www.bse.com.lb

TYPES OF SHARE

Shares are available in bearer and nominal form.

OTHER MARKETS

There is an unregulated over-the-counter equity market, where shares of firms in economic sectors not represented on Lebanon's official stock market are traded.

In addition, a parallel market has been established by Société Financière du Liban, a company jointly owned by 45 Lebanese commercial banks.

INVESTORS

Lebanese individual investors continue to dominate share trading on the BSE. Nonetheless, 1997 saw increased participation on the part of institutional Lebanese investors (mostly banks and market-makers), actively trading shares for their own account. Also, a number of Arab individual and institutional investors have recently entered the Lebanese equity market.

OPERATIONS

A) Trading system

Trading is via open outcry, with price fixing of shares taking place at 10.00am. A further fixing takes place at 11.00am after brokers have responded to the initial fixing. (The BSE has announced plans to introduce an electronic continuous auction system during 1998.)

B) Principal brokers

Share trading on the official market is limited to BSE members, of which there are currently 13. To become a member, brokers must pay an initial exchange fee of US$10,000, plus US$2,000 per annum thereafter to renew membership status.

AUDI INVESTMENT BANK SAL
Charles Malek Avenue, Achrafieh, Beirut
Tel: (961) 1 200 951; Fax: (961) 1 602 746

BANQUE D'AFFAIRES DU LIBAN ET D'OUTRE MER
El Daher Building, Abd El-aziz Street, Hamra, Beirut
Tel: (961) 1 346 290; Fax: (961) 1 602 248

FIDUS
Sami 50th Street, UCA Building, 7th Floor
PO Box 116-5188, Beirut
Tel: (961) 1 381 267/8; Fax: (961) 1 425 115

LEBANON INVEST
Gefinor Center, Suite 1101, Clemenceau Street
Ras, Beirut
Tel: (961) 1 340 812; Fax: (916) 1 340 813

MEDITERRANEE INVESTMENT
Rachid Karame Street, Verdun, Beirut
Tel: (961) 1 866 925/7/8; Fax: (961) 1 869 263

C) Settlement and clearing

Settlement takes place on a T+3 basis. Clearing operations are regulated by Midclear, an independent clearing house under the supervision of the BSE's committee.

D) Commission and other costs

Commission charges range from 0.4% to 0.01%, depending on the size of the deal.

TAXATION AND REGULATIONS AFFECTING FOREIGN INVESTORS

A) Exchange controls

There are no foreign exchange controls in Lebanon.

B) Income tax

A 10% flat rate of income tax is payable.

C) Capital gains

Capital gains on the transfer of companies' shares are tax-free. Dividend distributions are subject to 5% withholding tax.

LISTING REQUIREMENTS AND SUPERVISION

A) Listing requirements

The main market is open to companies with a minimum capital of US$3 million, while the BSE's parallel market is targeted at companies with capital of at least US$1 million.

Companies listing on the BSE are required to offer at least 25% of their capital to the investing public.

B) Exchange supervision

The Financial Market Council (FMC) is responsible for the organisation, regulation and supervision of market participants and market securities. The FMC is an independent body with a large degree of autonomy from the government.

RESEARCH

The improved level of trading in Lebanese equities has prompted several local and international investment firms to increase their coverage of the BSE. Firms such as Merrill Lynch, ING Barings, Paribas Capital Markets, HSBC James Capel, Lebanon Invest and Bank Audi now offer periodic research reports, both on the country and on traded stocks.

The Lebanese Banking Association issues quarterly macroeconomic reports and the Banque du Liban issues reports periodically on various sectors.

Lebanon: A New Era, published by Euromoney Books, provides in-depth information for those wishing to invest or do business in the country. See the order card at the back of this book for details.

CHAPTER 39

Lithuania

Introduction

In 1991 Lithuania was among the first states in central and eastern Europe to start mass voucher scheme privatisation of state property. During the initial stage of the programme, which continued until 1994, over 5,700 state enterprises went public and about 1.5 million Lithuanian residents became shareholders. The most pressing task of the time was to establish a reliable and transparent securities market.

The Lithuanian Securities Commission, a regulatory body, was established in September 1992, and the National Stock Exchange of Lithuania (NSEL) opened on 14 September 1993. The NSEL is modelled on the French system and trading is centralised, dematerialised, screen-based and order-driven.

A total of 607 companies were listed on the NSEL at the end of 1997, compared with 460 at the end of 1996, and market capitalisation ended the year 67% up at US$2,551 million.

Major capital market developments in 1997 included the launch of the blue chip LITIN Index, a letter of agreement with USAID regarding its financial assistance in the acquisition of a new NSEL trading system, and the introduction of reduced transaction commissions.

ECONOMIC AND POLITICAL OVERVIEW

Lithuania is a republic with a parliament comprising 137 deputies elected for four years. The current parliament was elected in November 1996.

Executive power belongs to the President, who is elected for five years. The present incumbent, Valdas Adamkus, was elected on 4 January 1998, having received 50.31% vote in the second ballot. The main political parties are the Homeland Union (a right-of-centre party that holds 51% of the votes in the parliament), the Social Democrats, the Christian Democrats, the Central Union, the Lithuanian Democratic Workers' Party and the Democratic Party.

Lithuania has signed free trade agreements with all the EU countries, EFTA, Poland, Slovakia, the Czech Republic, Slovenia, Latvia and Estonia. Agreements with Hungary, Romania and Bulgaria are expected to be signed soon. Lithuania has formed a strategic partnership with Poland, establishing a Consultative Committee of Presidents as well as a joint Lithuanian-Polish parliament. In addition, the government plans to sign two agreements with Russia in mid-1998 concerning investment and taxation issues.

Under the government's 1997–2000 programme, a strict fiscal policy was implemented in 1997. In consequence, the ratio of government debt to GDP decreased by 5% over the year and the state budget deficit ended the year at US$174.5 million.

In December 1997 the average one-month interest rate for commercial bank loans exceeded the interest rate for local currency (litas) term deposits by 2.29%, and fell short of the interest rate on litas loans by 4.58%.

Role of the central bank

The litas is pegged to the US dollar at a fixed exchange rate of 4:1 and, under an April 1994 law a modified currency board arrangement was established. Under the legislation:

- commercial banks are required to keep a specified level
- of reserves at the Bank of Lithuania;
- to a limited extent the Bank of Lithuania can extend loans to commercial banks while acting as lender of last resort;
- the Bank of Lithuania remains responsible for banking supervision.

After the introduction of the currency board, the government took over the function of regulating market interest rates by offering its bills at auction.

The currency board provides for automatic money issuance, which requires the full backing of the national currency by gold and convertible foreign currencies.

The 1997-2000 plan provides for the phasing out of the currency board arrangement and for the development of the central bank's monetary policy functions. The first steps were taken in 1997, with the Bank of Lithuania implementing repo transactions and establishing term deposit auctions.

MARKET PERFORMANCE

A) In 1997

Over the 12-month period to end-1997 the LITIN-A Index fell by 21.1% from 1,660.68 to 1,327.47. Total NSEL equity turnover increased three-fold to US$365 million, while trading value per session averaged US$1.4 million (versus US$0.5 million in 1996). Total executed transactions increased six-fold to 71,118, and market capitalisation moved ahead by 67% from US$1,525 million in December 1996 to US$2,551 million at the end of 1997.

B) Summary information

Global ranking by market value (US$ terms, end-1997): 58
Market capitalisation (end-1997): US$2.55 billion
Growth in market value (US$ terms, 1993–97): 14,272%
Market value as a % of nominal GDP (end-1997): 27.36%
Number of domestic/foreign companies listed (end-1997): 607/0
Market P/E (top 52 companies, end-1997): 9.2
Short-term (3-month) interest rate (end-1997): 9.46%
Long-term (1-year) bond yield (end-1997): 10.97%
Budget deficit as a % of nominal GDP (end-1997): 1.55%
Annual increase in money (M2) supply (end-1997): 33.8%
Inflation rate (1997): 8.4%
US$ exchange rate (end-1997): L4.0

C) Year-end share price indices

Exhibit 39.1:
YEAR-END SHARE PRICE INDICES, 1995–97

Year-end	*LITIN-A*	*LITIN-G*
1995	1000.00	1000.00
1996	1660.68	1930.85
1997	1327.47	1862.90

Source: National Stock Exchange of Lithuania.

D) Market indices and their constituents

All NSEL price indices are weighted by company market capitalisation. The LITIN-A Index comprises shares of all the companies listed on the upper tier Group-A (48 shares at the end of 1997). It was introduced on 1 January 1996 with an initial value of 1,000.

The LITIN-G Index is a global market index that includes all shares quoted on the NSEL. It was launched at the same time as the LITIN-A, and is also based at 1 January 1996 = 1,000.

In April 1997 the LITIN Index was launched to monitor the performance of selected "blue chips". It currently contains the five best-performing companies.

THE STOCK MARKET

A) Brief history and structure

The first exchange in Lithuania was opened in Klaipeda in 1775 and traded in export goods (eg, wood, linen and grain) until 1945. Kaunas Stock Exchange traded in foreign currency and state securities from 1923 until 1940, while Vilnius Stock Exchange was in operation between 1926 and 1936. After World War II the Lithuanian financial market was moribund for half a century. The National Stock Exchange of Lithuania was established in September 1992 and held its first trading session a year later. It is a non-profit joint stock company, controlled by the Ministry of Finance (44%), brokerage houses and banks.

Trading rules, listing requirements and membership procedures are set out in NSEL regulations, instructions and enforcement notes. The NSEL focuses on the harmonisation of its rules with EU Directives, G30 recommendations and international standards.

B) Opening hours, names and addresses

Trading sessions are held on Monday to Friday from 11.00am to 2.00pm.

NATIONAL STOCK EXCHANGE OF LITHUANIA
41 Ukmerges St, 2600 Vilnius
Tel: (370) 2 72 38 71; Fax: (370) 2 72 48 94
E-mail: nse@nse.lt Web site: www.nse.lt

MARKET SIZE

A) Number of listings and market value

By the end of 1997, the number of companies listed on the NSEL (including banks and investment companies) had risen by 32% to 607. Market capitalisation at end-1997 stood at US$2.6 billion.

Exhibit 39.2:
NUMBER OF COMPANIES LISTED AND MARKET VALUE, NSEL, 1996–97

Year-end	*No. of listed companies*	*Market value (US$ million)*
1996	460	1,525
1997	607	2,551

Source: National Stock Exchange of Lithuania.

B) Largest quoted companies

Exhibit 39.3:
THE 20 LARGEST LISTED COMPANIES ON THE NSEL, END-1997

Ranking	*Company*	*Sector*	*Market value (US$ million)*
1	Mazeikiu nafta	Oil refinery	248.32
2	Lietuvos energija	Electricity and heating	144.60
3	Vilniaus bankas	Banking	116.68
4	Lietuvos dujos	Gas	106.61
5	Naftotiekis	Oil distribution	70.22
6	Lietuvos juru laivininkyste	Shipping	62.22
7	Kalnapilis	Brewery	60.00
8	Bankas Hermis	Banking	51.65
9	Lietuvos kuras	Petroleum and fuel	44.66
10	Klaipedos juru kroviniu kompanija	Stevedoring	38.70
11	Lietuvos zemes ukio bankas	Banking	32.01
12	Kedainiu cukrus	Sugar	25.15
13	Dirbtinis pluostas	Artificial fibre	23.89
14	Lietuvos Taupomasis bankas	Banking	23.25
15	Ekranas	Electronics	22.61
16	Lietuvos draudimas	Insurance	21.83
17	Statybos apdailos masinos	Machinery	21.37
18	Akmenes cementas	Building materials	21.18
19	Anyksciu vynas	Wine, soft drinks	20.25
20	Rokiskio suris	Dairy	19.62

Source: National Stock Exchange of Lithuania.

C) Trading volume

In 1997, an average of 844,000 shares were traded at each session, and an overall total of 215 million shares changed hands during the year. Total turnover value in equity securities for 1997 was US$365 million, which translates to average turnover per session of US$1.4 million.

Exhibit 39.4:
THE 20 MOST ACTIVELY TRADED NSEL SHARES, 1997

Ranking	*Company*	*Turnover (US$ million)*
1	Bankas Hermis	47.20
2	Sanitas	16.90
3	Rokiskio suris	16.65
4	Vilniaus bankas	11.16
5	Akmenes cementas	8.99
6	Baltijos laivu statykla	7.99
7	Utenos gerimai	7.87
8	Vilniaus Vingis	7.63
9	Ukio bankas	6.44
10	Lietuvos juru laivininkyste	6.29
11	Siauliu bankas	6.29
12	Lietuvos dujos	5.84
13	Lietuvos Taupomasis bankas	5.83
14	Klaipedos nafta	5.82
15	Lietuvos energija	4.96
16	Lietuvos zemëes ukio bankas	3.93
17	Birzu akcine pieno bendrove	3.51
18	Baltik vairas	3.37
19	Lietuvos draudimas	3.14
20	Ekranas	2.91

Source: National Stock Exchange of Lithuania.

TYPES OF SHARE

The securities market is entirely dematerialised. Ordinary registered shares and preferred stocks of domestic companies, subscription rights and Treasury bills are traded on the NSEL.

Options and futures are not traded on the NSEL.

INVESTORS

The Central Securities Depository of Lithuania collects data on securities held in the accounts of brokerage firms. At end-1997 the value of shares totalled L1.88 billion. Foreign investment accounted for 48.9% of all the holdings, compared with 34% at the beginning of 1997 – 18.5% of foreign investment in equities originated from the US, 8% from Estonia, 6.7% from the UK and 2.4% from Sweden.

OPERATIONS

A) Trading system

Trading on the NSEL is order-driven, screen-based, centralised and dematerialised. For shares, the exchange uses a single-price auction system (an electronic call auction). It was installed with the assistance of SBF-Bourse de Paris and SICOVAM in 1993, and since then has undergone a number of modifications. The main feature of the system is that order-matching produces a single price per security.

Price fluctuations of official list and Group A shares are limited to 10%, while the price of Group B stocks may not vary by more than 20% between sessions. Blocks of securities can be traded off-exchange without influencing prices on the main market.

In 1998 the NSEL intends to introduce continuous trading on the existing system platform, and then to acquire, adapt and implement a new trading system that will include market data dissemination, surveillance, risk management and other important tools.

B) List of principal brokers

At the end of 1997, 49 brokers were members of the NSEL. All brokerage companies must be registered in Lithuania.

ALTERNA INVEST
Suite 507, 41 Ukmerges, 2600 Vilnius
Tel: (370) 72 47 74; Fax: (370) 2 72 52 54

BANK VILNIAUS BANKAS
41 Ukmerges, 2600 Vilnius
Tel: (370) 2 72 15 59; Fax: (370) 2 72 15 51

FINASTA
Suite 510, 41 Ukmerges, 2600 Vilnius
Tel: (370) 2 72 34 63; Fax: (370) 2 72 34 91

MENDES PRIOR EUROPE
Suite 506, 41 Ukmerges, 2600 Vilnius
Tel: (370) 2 72 24 95; Fax: (370) 2 72 39 93

SUPREMA
Suite 605, 41 Ukmerges, 2600 Vilnius
Tel: (370) 2 72 37 97; Fax: (370) 2 72 60 49

VILFIMA
Suite 602, 41 Ukmerges, 2600 Vilnius
Tel: (370) 2 72 42 59; Fax: (370) 2 72 42 79

C) Settlement and transfer

The exchange settles most securities trades on a T+3 rolling settlement schedule. Settlement is executed by the Bank of Lithuania (the central bank), the Central Securities Depository of Lithuania and the NSEL.

The depository system is fully centralised, and securities movements are recorded by relevant book entries in the securities accounts. Each issue is granted an ID code according to ISIN standards, and clearing and settlement procedures in general comply with G30 recommendations.

A guarantee fund has been established in order to ensure settlement of central market trades.

D) Commissions and other costs

There are no fixed commissions imposed by law or regulations. The rates charged by brokers generally range from 0.5% for large transactions to 2% for single small trades.

Stock exchange fees vary from 0.01% to 0.15% of transaction value, depending on the type of security and the list it is quoted on.

TAXATION AND REGULATIONS AFFECTING FOREIGN INVESTORS

Under the 13 June 1995 Law No. I-938 "On Foreign Capital Investment in the Republic of Lithuania", foreign investment is permitted in all spheres of economic and commercial activity with the exception of the following sectors:

- security and defence;
- manufacture or sale of narcotic substances, and other non-medicinal, poisonous substances;
- growing, processing and sale of cultures that contain narcotic and poisonous substances; and
- organising lotteries.

There are no other restrictions on foreign investments, nor are there foreign exchange control restrictions on inward investment or on the repatriation of capital and earnings.

Dividend payments by Lithuanian companies to resident and non-resident corporations, as well as to individuals, are free of taxes. Interest payments by Lithuanian companies to non-resident corporations (excluding offshore companies) are also free of taxes. A 10% withholding tax is imposed on payments by Lithuanian companies to non-resident companies in respect of the use of trademarks, licences and business names (royalties), unless a double taxation agreement specifies a lower rate. A 29% withholding tax is imposed on interest and royalties paid by Lithuanian companies to offshore companies registered in tax haven zones or countries. A list of such zones and countries is drawn up by the Lithuanian government.

Lithuanian companies are required to withhold 20% tax on interest payments made to all individuals, whether resident or non-resident.

Exhibit 39.5:
WITHHOLDING TAX

Recipient	*Dividends %*	*Interest %*
Resident corporations	Nil	Nil
Resident individuals	Nil	Nil
Non-resident corporations and individuals:		
Non-treaty	Nil	Nil
Treaty	0-15	0-10

Source: Price Waterhouse.

Capital gains are subject to taxation under the standard rules. This means that income earned by resident companies from the disposal of shares is subject to 29% profit tax for registered corporations and 24% income tax for other enterprises. Income earned from the disposal of shares by foreign non-resident corporations, is not subject to taxation in Lithuania. Income earned from the disposal of shares by individuals, whether resident or non-resident, is exempt from taxation.

LISTING AND REPORTING REQUIREMENTS

A) Listing requirements

Issuers must register their securities with the Securities Commission (SC) if:

- the issuer is a public limited company;
- there were more than 50 holders of at least one class of securities at the most recent financial year-end;
- they intend to issue securities for public trading.

SC registration procedures require the preparation of a prospectus (or, if the securities are intended for private placement, an abridged prospectus), containing key information about the issuer and the securities offered, along with audited financial statements.

B) Reporting requirements

Listed companies are responsible for:

- filing annual (audited), semi-annual and quarterly reports with the SC and the NSEL;
- disclosing information concerning shareholders with interests of 5% or more in the company's voting stock;
- disclosing (within five days) details of any "material event" that could influence investors' decisions to buy or sell the company's securities or that could affect the market price of those securities.

SHAREHOLDER PROTECTION CODES

A fine of up to L10,000 (US$2,500) and/or imprisonment for up to five years may be imposed for failure to provide information, or for providing false information, in a prospectus or periodic reports. A fine of up to L100,000 (US$25,000) and/or up to five years' imprisonment may be imposed on a person who withholds information on material events.

Anyone who, acting alone or in concert, acquires or disposes of 10%, 20% 33%, 50% or 66% of a company's voting stock must inform the company and the SC. Also, if a person acquires more than 50% of a company's voting stock he must submit a tender offer to buy the remaining shares of the issuer at a price not less than the weighted average share price paid in acquiring the 50% holding.

RESEARCH

The NSEL publishes weekly and quarterly bulletins and annual reports. The exchange also maintains an electronic database that includes the financial statements of listed companies. Market data is available through information vendors, including Reuters and Dow Jones Telerate, and quotes are e-mailed to domestic news agencies, a list of subscribers and other interested parties. In addition, information is displayed on the NSEL web site at www.nse.lt.

CHAPTER

40

Luxembourg

Introduction

The growth of the Luxembourg Stock Exchange (LSE) has been closely associated with the growth of Luxembourg as a financial centre. European Union pressure is increasing for Luxembourg to harmonise its low-tax regime with those of its partners. Its neighbours, notably Belgium and Germany, resent the outflow of capital into the Grand-Duchy, lured by zero withholding tax on non-residents, together with banking secrecy laws.

The stock exchange is very concentrated, with the five largest domestic companies accounting for over 57% of domestic market capitalisation and the largest 20 for almost 95%. The dominance of foreign shares and the relatively small domestic capitalisation mean that the exchange is not representative of Luxembourg's economy.

Following a review of the legal and regulatory framework of the Luxembourg capital market, the LSE's rules and regulations were updated with effect from 2 January 1997.

ECONOMIC AND POLITICAL OVERVIEW

Luxembourg's Prime Minister, Jean-Claude Juncker, is the leader of the Christian Social Party (CSV), which is the senior partner in a two-party ruling coalition.

The country enjoys the highest per capita income in the EU. Dependent on the economic performance of its neighbours, Luxembourg nonetheless outperforms them consistently. Yet, despite real GDP growth rates remaining positive in 1997 (an increase of 3.6% compared with 3.0% in 1996), unemployment rose steadily to 3.8% (although this is still only about a third of the EU average).

Luxembourg has traditionally followed a conservative fiscal policy, with expenditure plans based on the expected increase in real GDP and projected inflation. Although expenditure growth has generally exceeded these guidelines in the past, the increase in revenue has also been higher than forecast. Luxembourg maintains the lowest level of public debt in the EU (below 5% of GDP in 1997), and its budget deficit is well within the Maastricht Treaty reference levels.

Role of the central bank

The Luxembourg Monetary Institute (LMI), a public institution, controls banking and other financial operations in Luxembourg. It also ensures the enforcement of international conventions and EU Directives applicable to its sphere of duties. The LMI will be the Luxembourg central bank within the European System of Central Banks (ESCB).

The LMI is responsible for enforcing compliance with banking regulations. In agreement with the Minister of the Treasury, the LMI issues regulations governing the periodic reporting requirements of credit institutions and other matters, such as supervision on a consolidated basis, loan loss provisioning and balance sheet items.

The LMI also fulfils informational and statistical roles.

MARKET PERFORMANCE

A) In 1997

Both the main LSE indices (the Luxembourg Share Index and the Luxembourg Share Return Index) closed the year around 25% ahead. In addition, the exchange recorded substantial growth in its trading activity in 1997, which totalled Lfr89.7 billion. In part, the increased turnover was attributable to the implementation of the Automated Trading System, SAM, the MultiFixing Market (MFX) version of which has been in operation since 2 January 1996.

B) Summary information

Global ranking by market value (US$ terms, end-1997): 35
Market capitalisation (domestic, end-1997): US$33.38 billion
Growth in market value (local currency terms, 1993–97): 59.9%
Market value (domestic companies only) as a % of nominal GDP (end-1997): 223.3%
Number of domestic/foreign companies listed (end-1997): 56/228
MSCI Index (increase in US$ terms, 1997): -4.1%

Exhibit 40.1: LUXEMBOURG PRICE INDEX (LFR), 1993–97

High value 6804.01 1.10.97 Low value 2140.68 1.1.93 *Source: Datastream*

Short-term (3-month) interest rate (end-1997): 3.5%
Long-term (10-year) bond yield (end-1997): 5.41%
Budget surplus as a % of nominal GDP (1997): 0.9%
Inflation rate (1997): 1.2%
US$ exchange rate (end-1997): Lfr36.72

C) Year-end share price index and yields

Exhibit 40.1:
YEAR-END SHARE PRICE INDEX AND AVERAGE EQUITY YIELDS, 1993–97

Year-end	*Index*	*Yield (%)*
1993	4,733.47	1.98
1994	4,301.38	2.64
1995	4,309.88	2.70
1996	5,622.99	2.43
1997	7,009.24	2.21

Source: Luxembourg Stock Exchange.

D) Market indices and their constituents

The Luxembourg Share Index, published by the LSE, comprises 13 domestic stocks and is based at 2 January 1985 = 1,000. The LSE also calculates the Luxembourg Share Return Index, incorporating dividend payments, which also has a base of 1,000 on 2 January 1985.

THE STOCK MARKET

A) Brief history and structure

The LSE opened for trading on 6 May 1929. A Grand Ducal Decree vested the operation, administration and management of the exchange in a joint stock company. The Société Anonyme de la Bourse de Luxembourg, is owned 80% by the state savings bank and 20% by private citizens.

The real upsurge for the exchange came in 1963 after the introduction by the US authorities of a withholding tax, leading to a growth in the Eurodollar bond market.

Under the Law on Exchanges of 21 September 1990, responsibility for the LSE was vested in the Exchange Supervisory Authority, which replaced the former Government Commissioner.

The exchange establishes its own rules and regulations that are subject to approval by the Ministry of Finance. The LSE has a monopoly on quoting and publishing the prices of securities, but securities trading is not exclusive to exchange members.

The LSE is managed by its own board of directors, which consists of at least nine members elected by the general meeting of shareholders. The board nominates a number of committees, the most important being the Stock Exchange Committee, which is responsible for the day-to-day running of the exchange.

B) Different exchanges

The LSE is the only stock exchange in Luxembourg.

C) Opening hours, names and addresses

Formal trading begins at 10.45am and ends at 1.15pm, Monday to Friday. Almost all bond trading and most of the trading in shares takes place off the exchange.

SOCIÉTÉ DE LA BOURSE DE LUXEMBOURG SA
Avenue de la Porte-Neuve,
BP 165, L-2011 Luxembourg
Tel: (352) 47 79 36-1; Fax: (352) 47 32 98
Web site: www.bourse.lu

MARKET SIZE

A) Number of listings and market value

Exhibit 40.3:
NUMBER OF COMPANIES LISTED AND MARKET VALUE, LSE, 1993–97

	No. of companies		*Market capitalisation*
Year-end	*Domestic*	*Foreign*	*(Lfr billion)*
1993	62	204	11,113.09
1994	66	267	9,000.93
1995	67	289	11,101.90
1996	54	224	13,756.07
1997	56	228	17,772.52

Source: Luxembourg Stock Exchange.

Exhibit 40.4:
MARKET VALUE BY SECTOR, LSE, 1996–97

	Market value (Lfr billion)	
Sector	*1996*	*1997*
Domestic	1,038.43	1,255.74
Foreign	12,717.64	16,516.78
Total	**13,756.07**	**17,772.52**

Source: Luxembourg Stock Exchange.

B) Largest quoted companies

Exhibit 40.5:
THE 20 LARGEST DOMESTIC COMPANIES LISTED ON THE LSE, END-1997

Ranking	*Company*	*Market value (Lfr million)*
1	Vendôme Luxury Group	203,700.0
2	Safra Republic Holdings	141,063.9
3	Minorco	139,866.7
4	Audiofina	92,175.4
5	Banque Générale du Luxembourg	77,207.5
6	Exor Group	69,470.3
7	Kredietbank SA Luxembourg	66,622.2
8	Millicom International Cellular	63,874.3
9	Banque Internationale à Luxembourg	62,491.0
10	Quinsa	45,314.2
11	Bolton Group International	43,080.5
12	Arbed	36,994.4
13	Espirito Santo Financial Holding	29,219.2
14	Dinvest	27,690.2
15	Luxempart	19,789.5
16	Cegedel	16,483.5
17	Gefinor	16,358.3
18	Socfinasia	12,479.6
19	Insinger	10,772.5
20	Deya	10,642.3

Exhibit 40.5 continued

Source: Luxembourg Stock Exchange.

C) Trading volume

Exhibit 40.6:
THE 15 MOST ACTIVELY TRADED DOMESTIC SHARES, LSE, 1997

Ranking	*Company*	*Number of trades*	*Trading value (Lfr million)*
1	Banque Internationale à Luxembourg	2,948	3,315.00
2	Banque Générale de Luxembourg	1,370	2,506.08
3	Arbed	2,258	1,527.69
4	Audiofina	1,633	1,270.61
5	Kredietbank SA Luxembourg (priv)	1,460	1,250.15
6	Socfinasia	2,511	1,228.47
7	Luxempart	1,440	1,219.41
8	Quinsa (ord)	846	1,176.48
9	Intercultures	4,166	1,077.32
10	Kredietbank SA Luxembourg (ord)	698	1,072.36
11	Exor Group (ord)	341	804.78
12	Selangor	2,399	632.54
13	Cegedel	739	565.20
14	Exor Group (priv)	223	541.23
15	Safra Republic	118	418.56

Source: Luxembourg Stock Exchange.

Exhibit 40.7:
THE 15 MOST ACTIVELY TRADED UCITS, 1997

Ranking	*Fund*	*Turnover (Lfr million)*
1	Mercury Selected Eastern European	2,213.27
2	Fleming Flagship Latin American Fund	582.64
3	Fleming Flagship China Fund	471.08
4	Templeton Global Emerging Fund	348.24
5	Fleming Flagship Eastern European	337.57
6	Fidelity European Growth	303.35

Exhibit 40.7 continued

7	Vontobel Eastern European Equity	272.13
8	Fidelity Asean Fund	267.97
9	Fleming Flagship American Fund	260.36
10	Immo-Croissance (Cap)	253.45
11	Alfred Berg Norden Aktier	238.01
12	Crédit Suisse Money Market DEM Fund	236.11
13	Morgan Stanley Emerging Market Debt Fund	232.30
14	Dewaplus	223.79
15	PharmaWealth	215.38

Source: Luxembourg Stock Exchange.

TYPES OF SHARE

A) Shares of Luxembourg companies

Under Luxembourg company law, shares are issued in bearer form or in registered form. With bearer shares, all the shareholders' rights are vested in the share certificate. For registered shares, these rights are evidenced by an entry in the share register. The holder of a bearer share may at all times demand conversion into a registered share. A conversion of registered shares into bearer shares may be requested, unless prohibited by the articles of incorporation. Such conversion pre-supposes that the shares are fully paid up. Registered shares must have a minimum of one-quarter of their face value paid up.

B) Shares with restricted negotiability

All shares listed on the LSE must be freely negotiable. Shares, the acquisition of which is subject to the consent of the other shareholders, may be listed only if the market is not disrupted by the restriction. Shares that are not fully paid up may be listed if their negotiability is not restricted and only after due publication of their status.

OTHER MARKETS

LSE rules allow trading in unlisted securities using a public auction procedure. However, volume is not significant and auctions occur only a few times a year. Several banks have important trading commitments in over-the-counter (OTC) foreign stocks and bonds, which are not listed on the exchange. Some firms have become substantial market-makers in such securities.

There are also several dozen domestic issues that are regularly traded OTC. The majority of orders for these issues come through branches of the three major domestic banks.

OPERATIONS

A) Trading system

An automatic trading system, Système Automatique de Marché (SAM), was launched on 2 January 1996 and replaced the open outcry method of trading that had, since

Exhibit 40.8:
COUNTRY FUNDS – LUXEMBOURG

Fund	US$ % change 31/12/96 31/12/97	US$ % change 31/12/92 31/12/97	Currency	Fund size (US$ mil)	Volatility	Manager name	Main sector	Class
Deka Benelux	19.84	N/A	DM	14.27	4.76	Deka	Equity Growth	Investmentfds Deutschland
Aetna MF Belgian/Lux Natl Eq	13.49	123.84	Bfr	1.03	3.63	Aetna Master Fund	Equity	Belgian Auslands
Aetna MF Belgian/Lux Natl Eq	13.49	123.84	Bfr	1.09	3.68	Aetna Master Fund	Equity	Luxembourg
Wright Equi: Belgium/Lux	11.43	N/A	US$	1.7	3.02	Wright Equity Funds	Equity Growth	US Mutuals
Lux Avantage1 A Cap	1.88	N/A	Lfr	133.55	N/A	Caisse D'Epargne de L'Etat	Equity	Luxembourg
Lux Avantage1 B Dis	1.86	N/A	Lfr	124.49	N/A	Caisse D'Epargne de L'Etat	Equity	Luxembourg
Generalpart B	1.59	196.38	Lfr	106.51	2.94	BGL-Banque Generale Du Luxembourg	Equity	Luxembourg
Generalpart A	1.58	196.46	Lfr	27.09	2.94	BGL-Banque Generale Du Luxembourg	Equity	Luxembourg
KB Lux Luxinvest C	1.24	N/A	Lfr	19.07	N/A	Kredietbank Luxembourg	Equity	Luxembourg
KB Lux Luxinvest D	1.24	N/A	Lfr	4.78	N/A	Kredietbank Luxembourg	Equity	Luxembourg
BIL Luxpart C	0.94	N/A	Lfr	122.7	N/A	BIL-Banque Internationale a Luxembourg	Equity	Luxembourg
BIL Luxpart D	0.92	N/A	Lfr	117.23	N/A	BIL-Banque Internationale a Luxembourg	Equity	Luxembourg
LuxiPrivilege B	0.51	N/A	Lfr	13.2	2.39	Soc Europ Bqe-Dewaay-Le Foyer	Equity	Luxembourg
LuxiPrivilege A	0.45	N/A	Lfr	6.01	2.39	Soc Europ Bqe-Dewaay-Le Foyer	Equity	Luxembourg

Note: details for some funds may not have been included if the data for the US$ % change for 96/97 is not available

Source: Standard & Poor's Micropal.

1929, required the physical attendance of traders on the trading floor.

All securities are traded on trading screens connected to the SAM system according to the so-called Multi Quote Trading (MFX) system. The MFX market is a decentralised market operating between the stock exchange's member firms via a network of screens. Operation of the market is supervised through screens installed at the LSE.

On 8 December 1997, the LSE launched a second market segment, the On-Demand Continuous Market, or MCD, which operates alongside MFX. It is a quote-driven market designed for institutional investors.

On 30 May 1997, the Amsterdam, Brussels and Luxembourg exchanges signed a Memorandum of Cooperation and Understanding on cross-membership and electronic links. The Memorandum aims primarily at facilitating the access of all members of the three Benelux exchanges to each others' trading systems.

B) List of principal banks and brokers

BANQUE DELEN LUXEMBOURG
287 Route Darlon, 1150 Luxembourg
Tel: (352) 445 0601; Fax: (352) 445080

BANQUE DE LUXEMBOURG
14 Boulevard Royal, L-2449 Luxembourg
Tel: (352) 49 9241; Fax: (352) 47 2665

BANQUE ET CAISSE D'EPARGNE DE L'ETAT
1 Place de Metz, L-1930 Luxembourg
Tel: (352) 4015-1; Fax: (352) 227 687

BANQUE GÉNÉRALE DU LUXEMBOURG
27 Avenue Monterey, L-2163 Luxembourg
Tel: (352) 47 991; Fax: (352) 47 992 579

BANQUE INTERNATIONALE À LUXEMBOURG
2 Boulevard Royal, L-2449 Luxembourg
Tel: (352) 45 901; Fax: (352) 45 90 2010

CIM SOCIÉTÉ DE BOURSE SA
10 Avenue de la Liberté
L-1930, Luxembourg
Tel: (352) 474470-1; Fax: (352) 487693

COFIBOL
Bp 1634, 16 D'Epernay
1490 Luxembourg Gare, Luxembourg
Tel: (352) 484401; Fax: (352) 400648

CRÉDIT SUISSE (LUXEMBOURG)
56 Grand-rue, L-1660 Luxembourg
Tel: (352) 460 011-1; Fax: (352) 47 5541

PUILAETCO (LUXEMBOURG)
3 Place Clairefontaine, L-1341 Luxembourg
Tel: (352) 47 3025; Fax: (352) 47 1570

VAN MOER, SANTERRE LUXEMBOURG SA
Rue Charles Partel, 2134 Luxembourg
Tel: (352) 454 5221; Fax: (352) 449880

C) Settlement and transfer

LSE transactions are settled through a recognised clearing system and settlement takes place on the third calendar day following the trade day (T+3).

D) Commissions and other costs

Commission rates on all securities transactions are negotiable.

TAXATION AND REGULATIONS AFFECTING FOREIGN INVESTORS

The Institut Belge-Luxembourgeois du Change (IBLC) exercises control over exchange transactions in the Belgian-Luxembourg Economic Union. In practice, however, there is complete freedom of trade and exchange for all purposes and the IBLC merely compiles statistics. Non-residents may open a bank account in Luxembourg without governmental authorisation.

The legal and regulatory provisions basically impose no restrictions on investments made by foreign natural persons or corporate entities in the private sector. Equity shares may be purchased by non-residents and proceeds may be freely repatriated. There is no withholding tax on dividends distributed by holding companies, but dividends of commercial companies are generally subject to withholding tax, as mitigated by double tax treaties. Subject to various other conditions, there is no corporate tax on commercial company dividends.

Exhibit 40.9: WITHHOLDING TAX

Recipient	*Dividends (portfolio)* [1, 2] %	*Dividends (substantial holdings)* [3] %
Resident corporations	25	–[4]
Resident individuals	25	25
Non-resident corporations and individuals:		
Non-treaty	25	25/0[5]
Treaty[6]	7.5–25	0–15

Notes

1. Dividends and interest that represent a right to profit participa-

tion paid by Luxembourg holding companies or investment funds are exempt from withholding taxes.
2. A tax of 25% is withheld on dividend payments by Luxembourg companies. 50% of the dividend payments received by Luxembourg residents are tax-exempt; this tax exemption applies also to non-residents filing for a tax refund with the Luxembourg authorities.
3. As per the double tax treaties, a substantial holding is considered to arise:
(a) For Austria, Bulgaria, China, the Czech Republic, Denmark, Germany, Hungary, Indonesia, Ireland, Japan, the Republic of Korea, Malta, Morocco, the Netherlands, Norway, Poland, Romania, the Slovak Republic, Spain, Sweden, Switzerland and the UK, where the recipient company holds at least 25% of the Luxembourg company's shares or voting power.
(b) For Belgium, where the recipient owns a 25% investment or an investment of Lfr250 million at cost. Such investment may be held by several Belgian companies, provided one owns at least 50% of the shares of each of the others.
(c) For Brazil and Mauritius, where the recipient holds at least 10% of the Luxembourg company's shares.
(d) For Finland and France, where the recipient owns a 25% investment. Several Finnish or French companies may together own 25%, as long as one of the companies owns more than 50% in each of the others.
(e) For the US, where the recipient US company has held during the entire year (alone or with up to three other US companies each holding at least 10% of the shares) 50% of the Luxembourg company's shares, and a maximum of 25% of the gross income of the Luxembourg company originates from interest and dividends from non-group companies.
(f) For Singapore, where the recipient company holds at least 25% of the Luxembourg company's shares; dividends paid to the government of Singapore are exempt.
4. A resident parent company fully liable to income tax, or a Luxembourg branch of an EU-resident company or of a company resident in a double taxation treaty country, has a substantial holding when the direct participation in a qualifying resident or non-resident subsidiary amounts to at least 10% or to a purchase price of Lfr50 million. The same applies when the cumulative participation of several resident corporations reaches at least 10% of the capital of a non-resident company or a minimum of Lfr50 million and when one of the resident companies owns a participation of more than 50% in each of the others. Dividends paid to a holding company or to an investment fund do not benefit from this exemption.
5. No withholding tax is levied on dividend distributions paid by a Luxembourg subsidiary to an EU parent company that can prove at the moment of distribution that it held a direct participation of at least 25% for an uninterrupted period of at least two years. The exemption applies only to dividends from those shares that have been held uninterruptedly during the two-year period.
6. A double taxation treaty with Russia has been approved by the Luxembourg parliament; double tax avoidance treaties are under negotiation with Argentina, Portugal, South Africa, Tunisia, Thailand and Vietnam.

Source: Price Waterhouse.

LISTING AND REPORTING REQUIREMENTS

A) Prospectus requirements for a new listing

Both domestic and foreign companies must publish a prospectus outlining the terms and conditions of the issue and giving information on the financial status of the issuer. The exact content of the prospectus to be filed is laid down in the schedules to the Grand Ducal Decree of 28 December 1990. Applications for listing must be submitted on behalf of the issuer by a member of the LSE and are then transmitted to the Stock Exchange Commission.

An applicant must also file its statutory documents, annual reports for the past three years and latest interim accounts. A *notice légale*, containing facts about the issuer and the securities issued, must be filed with the chief registrar of the District Court in Luxembourg.

In the past, the LSE only accepted applications from companies that had been in existence for at least three years. This restriction has now been lifted. The Rules and Regulations of the LSE now state that "if the listing of shares is sought by a recently incorporated company which has not published its annual accounts for the three years preceding the application, the listing shall be supported by the following documents: (a) a curriculum vitae, evidencing the professional experience and knowledge necessary for the performance of the company's activities, and a judicial record and banking references concerning the persons responsible for the company's management; and (b) three-year financial estimates compiled or approved by independent auditors."

Where securities have been listed on a stock exchange of another member state of the European Economic Area for at least three years, the applicant is exempted from publishing a full prospectus when providing a certificate from the relevant authorities that it has duly complied with all EU regulations regarding information and admission to the exchanges.

For a foreign company's shares to be listed on the LSE, the company must be of good standing and the shares must have been validly issued under the laws of its country of incorporation. The aggregate net value of the shares listed, or the net asset value of the issuer, must generally amount to a minimum of Lfr50 million or its equivalent.

B) Disclosure requirements for listed companies

The issuer must publish annual and semi-annual reports containing both a balance sheet and a profit and loss account. The publication shall be made in one or several newspapers throughout Luxembourg, or shall be made available to the public either in written form at places in Luxembourg indicated by announcement or through wide circulation by other means approved by the Stock Exchange Committee.

Companies must disclose to the LSE any information that is believed to be useful for investor protection, and the LSE may compel such disclosure if necessary.

Undertakings for collective investment (UCITS) are supervised by the Luxembourg Monetary Institute, and must submit monthly financial statements including information on the portfolio held, changes in net assets and changes in the number of shares outstanding.

A company must inform the public of any event in its sphere of activity that is not publicly known and that may have a significant impact on the price of its shares. The LSE may waive this obligation if the disclosure would have an adverse effect on the company's legitimate interests.

Issuers that have securities simultaneously listed on other EU exchanges must provide the LSE with the same information as it makes available to such other markets.

SHAREHOLDER PROTECTION CODES

A) Disclosure of significant shareholdings

The law of 4 December 1992 on the information to be published where a significant shareholding in a listed company is acquired or transferred implemented Council Directive 89/592/EEC. The law came into force on 1 March 1993.

Any natural person or corporate entity that acquires or sells a significant shareholding in a Luxembourg company which is listed on a stock exchange in an EU member state must inform the company and the Stock Exchange Commissioner. The law is not applicable to undertakings for collective investment. A shareholding is deemed to be significant if the shareholder reaches, directly or indirectly, 10%, 20%, 33.3%, 50% or 66.6% of the voting rights in the company. Acquisitions whereby a shareholder reaches or exceeds the above ownership levels must be notified to the company and to the Stock Exchange Commissioner within seven days from the shareholder's actual or constructive knowledge of the shareholding.

A company so notified must in turn issue a notice concerning the shareholding, although the Stock Exchange Commissioner may waive this disclosure requirement if he believes such a waiver to be in the interests of the public or of the company.

In Luxembourg, disclosure is made public via the official LSE price list.

B) Insider trading

Insider trading is a criminal offence. Brokers, or any persons under their authority, who acquire privileged information may neither, directly or indirectly, buy or sell securities listed on the LSE. Privileged information is defined as precise information, unknown to the public, about issuers of securities that would, if publicised, be likely to have a significant influence on the price of such securities. Any transaction concluded with a Luxembourg resident on the LSE or over-the-counter by a member of the LSE in possession of privileged information is considered unlawful. It is also prohibited to transmit privileged information to third parties or to give advice to third parties on the basis of such privileged information concerning transactions in the relevant securities. Penalties include imprisonment for up to five years and a fine of up to Lfr1 million.

RESEARCH

The larger banks and brokers are good sources of information on the market, especially Banque Internationale à Luxembourg, Kredietbank SA Luxembourgeoise and Banque Générale du Luxembourg.

Four local newspapers – the *Luxemburger Wort, Tageblatt, Journal* and *Républicain Lorrain* – print daily prices of some 120 issues and investment funds, and several foreign newspapers print selected prices.

The LSE publishes a comprehensive range of periodicals and brochures on the stock market. These include:

Annual Report (French and English);
Facts and Figures (French and English);
Facts Book (French and English);
Stock Exchange Statistics (French and English);
Activity Report (French).

The LSE also transmits on-line information to teletransmission systems such as Reuters, Telekurs, Dafsa and AP-Dow Jones. In April 1997 the LSE launched a web site targeted initially at professionals, such as issuers, lead managers, lawyers and other advisers.

PROSPECTIVE CHANGES

A key area for the LSE in 1998 will be preparatory work for the introduction of the single currency, in line with the recommendations of the Luxembourg Transition Plan and the Federation of European Stock Exchanges.

CHAPTER

41

Malaysia

Introduction

At the end of 1997, the Kuala Lumpur Stock Exchange (KLSE) listed 444 companies on the main board and 264 on the second board. Year-end market capitalisation stood at RM375.8 billion, 53% below the previous year's close. In US dollar terms the decline was even more marked. Turnover for calendar 1997 was RM408.6 billion, or 109% of closing market capitalisation.

A key event in 1997 for the stock market was the exchange's end-August "designation" of KLSE Composite Index (KLCI) component stocks. By declaring the 100 index stocks "designated", share sales could only be executed after stocks had been lodged with local brokers – something that many foreign investors were unable to do. The move was an attempt to stop short selling, but the result was that the KLCI dropped 14% over a five-day period before the trading restrictions were relaxed.

ECONOMIC AND POLITICAL OVERVIEW

The cooling of the Malaysian economy, on a trend that started in 1996 when real GDP growth fell to 8.2% from the previous year's 9.5%, continued into 1997. GDP growth was 7.4% in 1997, with exports staying flat and structural monetary tightening dampening domestic consumer spending. On 28 March the central bank announced steps to curb increases in asset prices. Lending limits were imposed on property (20% of total bank loans) and share financing (15%), effective from 1 April.

In late May, and once again in July (after the Thai baht had been allowed to float), the Malaysian ringgit came under severe pressure. Bank Negara, the Malaysian central bank, tried to defend the currency on each occasion, and the resulting spikes in interbank rates marked the start of a period of escalating interest rates. For example, the three-month interbank rate, which had started 1997 at 7.3%, ended the year at 9.2%. On the other hand inflation, stable at 3.5% during 1996, eased to 2.7% in 1997, as the impact of economic slowdown and rising interest rates took effect. The weakening currency did not, as had been expected, manifest itself as imported inflation during 1997.

Once the central bank had ceased using foreign exchange reserves to try to slow the ringgit's depreciation in the region-wide currency slide, the Malaysian currency quickly weakened below the long-term RM2.50 to the US dollar resistance level. By the end of December it had reached RM3.875, down 35% for the year. The current account deficit, running at 9% of nominal GNP in 1995 and 5% in 1996, narrowed to 3.5% in 1997, as imports moderated in response to the now more expensive ringgit prices.

On the political front, Malaysia's reputation for stability remained intact. The National Front coalition, controlled by UMNO, continued in office. A new body linking economics and politics was established in November 1997. The National Economic Action Council (NEAC) – with Daim Zainuddin, former Finance Minister and currently Special Economic Adviser to the government, as the Executive Director – aims to identify and implement the actions necessary to arrest Malaysia's economic slowdown.

Role of the central bank

Bank Negara Malaysia's principal tasks and objectives are to issue currency; to maintain reserves at levels sufficient to safeguard the value of the currency; to act as banker and financial adviser/agent to the government; to promote monetary stability and a sound financial structure; and to influence the credit situation to the country's advantage.

In the context of formulation and implementation of monetary policy, the central bank is independent within the government, but not of the government.

MARKET PERFORMANCE

A) In 1997

The year started on a volatile note as price upturns on the KLSE were capped by bouts of profit-taking. A weaker trend emerged in March as investors reacted adversely to central bank credit tightening measures on the purchase of property and stocks.

Exhibit 41.1: KUALA LUMPUR COMPOSITE PRICE INDEX (US$), 1993–97

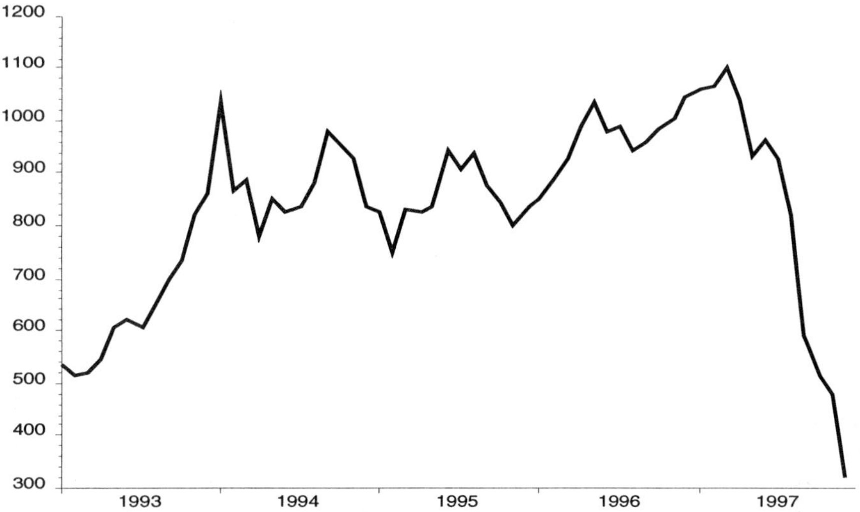

High value 1101.02 3.3.97 Low value 320.80 1.12.97 *Source: Datastream*

Prices continued to head downwards over the next two months due to heavy selling by foreign funds concerned about a possible devaluation of the Thai baht. Buying support surfaced occasionally, but profit-taking erased most gains.

On 2 July the baht was floated from its 25-year-old fixed exchange rate regime. Subsequently, currency speculators raided the ringgit and Malaysia found itself enveloped in the crisis. Malaysia's economy, and others in the region, were perceived to be in the same boat as that of Thailand, and would thus suffer a similar fate. In the ensuing months, stock market performance deteriorated steadily and a relentless downtrend emerged.

For the year as a whole, the benchmark Composite Index closed down 51.9% at 594.44. The broad-based EMAS Index lost 56.5% to end the year at 151.21. Market capitalisation was slashed by RM430.97 billion (US$111.2 billion), or 53.4%, ending the year at RM375.8 billion.

B) Summary information

Global ranking by market value (US$ terms, end-1997): 23
Market capitalisation (end-1997): US$96.98 billion
Growth in market value (local currency terms, 1993–97): -39.4%
Market value as a % of nominal GDP (end-1997): 135%
Number of domestic/foreign companies listed (end-1997): 705/3
Market P/E (end-1997): 10.31
MSCI Index (change in US$ terms, 1997): -68.8%
Short-term (3-month) interest rate (end-1997): 9.09%
Long-term (10-year) bond yield (end-1997): 7.84%
Budget surplus as a % of nominal GDP (end-1997): 1.80%
Annual increase in broad money (M3) supply (end-1997): 18.5%
Inflation rate (1997): 2.7%
US$ exchange rate (end-1997): RM3.875

C) Year-end share price index, price/earnings ratios and yields

Exhibit 41.2:
YEAR-END SHARE PRICE INDEX, KLSE P/E AND AVERAGE YIELDS, 1993–97

Year-end	*Composite Index*	*P/E*	*Yield (%)*
1993	1,275.36	40.2	1.0
1994	971.24	28.5	1.6
1995	995.17	24.5	1.8
1996	1,237.96	28.6	1.3
1997	594.44	10.3	3.3

Source: Kuala Lumpur Stock Exchange.

D) Market indices and their constituents

The principal official index is the KLSE Composite Index. The exchange also computes 11 other indices (Emas, Infrastructure, Consumer Products, Industrial Products, Construction, Trading/Services, Finance, Property, Hotels, Mining, Plantations and the Second Board Index).

THE STOCK MARKET

A) Brief history and structure

The KLSE, established in 1930, originates from the Singapore Stockbrokers' Association. In May 1938, the KLSE was registered as the Malaya Share Brokers' Association, but business was disrupted by World War II and the Association was not re-established until 1946. It then continued in existence until 1960 when the Malayan Stock Exchange was instituted.

In June 1964, the trading floors in Singapore and Malaysia were reconstituted to form a joint exchange – the Stock Exchange of Malaysia and Singapore (SEMS). However, in an effort to further the growth of Kuala Lumpur as a major financial centre, the Malaysian government terminated currency arrangements with Singapore in 1973 and, in turn, the formal linkage of the two exchanges. Consequently, in July 1973, The Kuala Lumpur Stock Exchange Berhad was incorporated under the Companies Act of 1965.

The KLSE is self-regulating. A committee of five elected members and four government-appointed members and full-time staff monitor trading operations and stockbroker behaviour and establish listing requirements. Besides the KLSE itself, principal regulatory authorities include the Securities Commission (SC), which is responsible for both the equities and futures markets, and the Foreign Investment Committee (FIC), which is concerned with distribution of equity ownership. The SC began operations in March 1993, and has absorbed the functions of the Capital Issues Committee and the Panel of Takeovers and Mergers. The Registrar of Companies, the Ministry of Finance and the central bank, Bank Negara, also monitor securities market developments.

B) Opening hours, names and addresses

Trading on the exchange takes place on Monday to Friday from 9.00am to 12.30pm and 2.30pm to 5.00pm.

KUALA LUMPUR STOCK EXCHANGE
Exchange Square, Bukit Kewangan
50200 Kuala Lumpur
Tel: (60) 3 206 7099; Fax: (60) 3 206 3699
Web site: www.klse.com.my

MARKET SIZE

A) Number of listings and market value

At 31 December 1997, 708 companies were listed on the KLSE (705 domestic and 3 foreign) with a market capitalisation of RM375.8 billion.

Trading/services represented the most important sector in terms of market capitalisation. At end-1997 companies quoted in this sector were valued at RM131.66 billion (35% of the total).

Exhibit 41.3:
NUMBER OF LISTED COMPANIES AND MARKET VALUE, KLSE, 1993–97

	No. of companies			*Market value*
Year-end	*Domestic*	*Foreign*	*Total*	*(RM billion)*
1993	410	3	413	619.64
1994	475	3	478	508.85
1995	526	3	529	565.63
1996	618	3	621	806.77
1997	705	3	708	375.80

Source: Kuala Lumpur Stock Exchange.

Exhibit 41.4:
MARKET CAPITALISATION BY SECTOR, KLSE, END-1997

	Sector	*Market capitalisation (RM billion)*
Main board	Consumer products	37.08
	Industrial products	48.08
	Construction	17.73
	Trading/services	131.66
	Infrastructure project companies	10.06
	Finance	49.98
	Hotels	1.09
	Properties	19.43
	Plantations	27.02
	Mining	1.85
	Trusts	0.26
	Closed/fund	0.21
	Loans	7.07
	Warrants/TSR	2.65
Second board		21.63
Total		375.80

Source: Kuala Lumpur Stock Exchange.

B) Largest quoted companies

The two largest quoted companies at the end of 1997 were once again Telekom and TNB. Together they accounted for 16% of total market capitalisation.

Exhibit 41.5:
LARGEST LISTED COMPANIES ON THE KLSE, END-1997

Ranking	*Company*	*Market value (RM million)*
1	Telekom	34,484.19
2	TNB	25,729.84
3	PGas	15,959.36
4	Maybank	12,920.57
5	Sime Darby	8,698.78

Exhibit 41.5 continued

6	Rothmans	8,637.28
7	Resorts	7,151.57
8	Genting	6,846.42
9	YTL	6,376.06
10	KLK	5,951.89
11	YTL Power	5,702.59
12	B-Toto	5,692.09
13	MISC	4,980.00
14	G Hope	4,518.92
15	Nestlé	4,221.00
16	Renong	3,999.22
17	Magnum	3,511.56
18	RHB	3,135.71
19	KYB	2,834.77
20	UE (M)	2,565.36

Source: Kuala Lumpur Stock Exchange.

C) Trading volume

Average daily volume of trading was up 9.10% to 292.4 million shares in 1997, compared to 268.0 million shares in 1996. However, the total value of trading in 1997 fell to RM408.6 billion, a 12% decrease on the 1996 figure of RM463.3 billion.

Exhibit 41.6:
SHARE TURNOVER, KLSE, 1993–97

Year	*Trading value (RM billion)*
1993	387.3
1994	316.1
1995	178.6
1996	463.3
1997	408.6

Exhibit 41.7:
THE 20 MOST ACTIVELY TRADED KLSE SHARES, 1997

Ranking	*Company*	*Volume ('000)*	*Value (RM '000)*
1	MBF Capital	1,671,767	6,981,789
2	Renong	1,443,985	4,944,100
3	KLIH	1,344,037	6,399,519
4	Rekapac	1,221,921	3,404,581
5	Suria	995,110	2,762,808
6	Sime Darby	966,665	6,511,042
7	Aokam	884,004	3,876,153
8	Anson	786,729	3,907,042
9	CP Bhd	775,012	9,487,659
10	Tai Ping	749,611	1,887,575
11	Magnum	730,824	2,494,977
12	Econs	723,717	2,556,518
13	Sinora	688,131	8,073,215
14	TNB	672,586	6,362,505
15	B-Group	666,598	1,662,505
16	RHB	602,739	3,240,814
17	Sriwani	588,868	3,554,159
18	MRCB	587,166	2,394,560
19	UE (M)	571,373	6,654,157
20	Commerz	538,569	2,669,157

Source: Kuala Lumpur Stock Exchange.

TYPES OF SHARE

Malaysian securities laws allow considerable flexibility in designing different classes of share and packages of share rights. In practice, most publicly listed companies issue ordinary shares. Preference shares, loan securities, real property trust units, warrants and call warrants are also traded on the exchange. Preference shares can have cumulative or non-cumulative dividends, and can be redeemable and/or participating.

OTHER MARKETS

On 15 December 1995 the Kuala Lumpur Options and Financial Futures Exchange Berhad (KLOFFE) began operating. It trades a futures contract on the KLSE Composite Index.

On 6 October 1997, the Securities Commission of Malaysia announced plans for the establishment of a new exchange to be known as the Malaysian Exchange of Securities Dealing and Automated Quotation ((Mesdaq) Mesdaq will initially trade high-tech companies and is expected to commence operations in 1998.

INVESTORS

In 1997, 81% of the Malaysian equity market was held by domestic investors, while 19% was held by foreigners. Individuals accounted for 13% of the market, while institutional investors represented around 87%.

OPERATIONS

A) Trading system

SCORE (System for Computerised Order-Routing and Execution), the exchange's semi-automated trading system, was introduced in 1989, leading to the phasing out of the traditional open outcry method of trading. The conversion to automatic matching was completed in November 1992.

Exhibit 41.8:
COUNTRY FUNDS – MALAYSIA

Fund	US$ % change 01/01/97 01/01/98	01/01/93 01/01/98	Fund base durrency	Fund size (US$ mil)	Fund volatility	Management group	Opal main sector	Opal subsector
JF Malaysia	-33.81	116.09	US$	33.9	7.942	Jardine Fleming	Open-End	Equity
Daiwa Original Malaysia	-50.7	N/A	¥	339	8.052	Daiwa	Open-End	Equity
Nikko Glbl Malaysia	-52.42	N/A	¥	3986	8.053	Nikko	Open-End	Equity
Nomura Aurora Malaysia	-54.44	N/A	¥	1808	8.695	Nomura ITMCo	Open-End	Equity
Fidelity Fds Malaysia	-60.82	3.03	US$	29.9	9.68	Fidelity	Open-End	Equity
HSBC GIF Malaysian Equity	-61.46	-11.2	US$	3.7	11.309	HSBC Asst Mgt	Open-End	Equity
Barclays ASF Malaysia	-61.67	-5.48	US$	3	11.782	Barclays	Open-End	Equity
Yamaichi World Sel Malaysia	-64.19	N/A	¥	229	9.051	Yamaichi Japan	Open-End	Equity
Genesis Malaysia Maju	-64.99	19.46	US$	29.9	12.69	Genesis	Closed-End	Equity
Malaysia Equity	-66.9	-35.88	US$	11.9	12.749	Daiwa Intl Ca	Closed-End	Equity
Paribas EM Malaysia Ptfl	-67.42	N/A	US$	N/A	12.397	Paribas Asset	Open-End	Equity
ImPac AP Malaysia	-68.13	N/A	US$	0.8	-1	Impac Asset M	Open-End	Equity
Nikko GlUF Malaysia Fund	-69.31	N/A	US$	0.1	10.544	Nikko	Open-End	Equity
RG ZelfSelect Maleisie	-69.34	N/A	G	53.2	-1	Robeco	Open-End	Equity
Thornton New Tiger Malaysia	-72.09	-37.62	US$	1.9	13.794	Thornton	Open-End	Equity
Malaysia Fund Inc.	-72.57	-44.71	US$	205.53	12.275	Morgan Stanley	Closed-End	Equity
Malaysia Capital Fund	-73.25	-51.95	US$	21.8	11.752	MeesPierson M	Closed-End	Equity
MBf Malaysian	-80.14	-67.44	US$	N/A	16.935	MBf	Open-End	Equity

Note: details for some funds may not have been included if the data for the US$ % change for 97/98 was not available

Source: Standard & Poor's Micropal.

B) List of principal brokers

The business of dealing in securities is carried out by either publicly or privately owned member companies. They must have a minimum paid-up capital of RM20 million. Foreigners are allowed to participate in the equity of a member company but their interest is limited to 30% (although this may be increased to 49% with Ministry of Finance approval).

BOTLY SECURITIES
1/F Plaza Teh Teng Seng, No. 227, Jalan Kampar
35250 Ipoh, Perak Darul Ridzuan
Tel: (60) 5 253 1313; Fax: (60) 5 253 6785

HWANG-DBS SECURITIES
Levels 2, 3, 4, 7, 8 Wisma Sri Pinang
60 Green Hall, 10200 Penang
Tel: (60) 3 263 6996; Fax: (60) 3 263 9597

INTER-PACIFIC SECURITIES
Level 7, Shahzan-Prudential Tower
30 Jalan Sultan Ismail, 50250 Kuala Lumpur
Tel: (60) 3 244 1888; Fax: (60) 3 244 1686

OSK SECURITIES
10/F Plaza MBF
Jalan Ampang, 50450 Kuala Lumpur
Tel: (60) 3 262 4388; Fax: (60) 3 261 8254

TA SECURITIES
Menara TA One
22, Jalan P. Ramlee, 50250 Kuala Lumpur
Tel: (60) 3 232 1277; Fax: (60) 3 232 2369

C) Settlement and transfer

Exchange trading is scripless and all KLSE securities transactions are settled through the Central Depository System (CDS).

Settlement is by book entry. Investors have CDS accounts recording deposits and withdrawals of scrip, inter-account share transfers and trade settlements, although cash settlement arrangements for both buyers and sellers continue to be valid. Foreigners, including broker-dealers, fund managers and custody organisations, may open CDS accounts directly through any authorised depository agent (ADA).

Trade settlement procedures include:

(a) A buyer of CDS prescribed securities has his CDS account credited on the fifth market day, but stock is held under lien until payment is made by the seventh market day. If an investor fails to make payment by the seventh market day, the shares are transferred into a stock clearing account and the broker will sell out on the eighth market day.

(b) A seller's CDS account is debited on the fifth market day. If the shares are not in the seller's account by the fifth market day, a buy-in against him will be instituted by the KLSE (through his broker) on the sixth market day.

(c) As the system carries out trade settlement in a batch run at the end of the day, both the seller's and the buyer's CDS accounts are debited and credited on the night of the fifth market day.

D) Commissions and other costs

Brokerage is charged to both buyer and seller and the minimum brokerage commission is RM5 on equity transactions. For shares denominated in Malaysian ringgit and priced under 50 sen, the commission is 0.5 sen per share; for shares with a price of 50–99sen, the commission is 1 sen per share; and for shares priced at RM1 and above, the commission is 1% on the first RM500,000 and 0.75% on the next RM500,000 to RM2 million. On amounts exceeding RM2 million the rate is 0.5%. Commissions for shares quoted in another currency are 1% of the value for ready contracts and 1.5% for other contracts.

Stamp duty on share certificates was abolished in January 1994.

In addition to the clearing fee of 0.05%, fees arising from the use of the CDS are of five types:

1. a deposit fee of RM10 per scrip;
2. a withdrawal fee of RM15 per 1,000 shares or part thereof;
3. a transfer fee of RM10 per transfer;
4. an account opening fee of RM10 per account; and
5. a requested statement fee of RM1 per page for the first 100 pages and RM0.30 per page thereafter.

One significant area of saving to investors as a result of the establishment of the CDS is registration. Under the system, a depositor becomes a beneficial shareholder, with legal status as a registered shareholder, when the shares he deposits are confirmed by the registrar. As no registration procedure is necessary, no registration fees are payable.

TAXATION AND REGULATIONS AFFECTING FOREIGN INVESTORS

There is no withholding tax on dividends in Malaysia. However, dividends are franked (ie, paid net) with the 28% income tax paid by distributing corporations deducted from the gross dividend. The 28% tax deducted is credited to the shareholder's tax account for set-off against its Malaysian tax liability due. A non-resident investor (an individual or a corporation) is subject to income tax at 28% on the amount of gross dividend income received from Malaysia. Therefore, as far as the foreign investor is concerned, the effect of these provisions is that there is no further tax on Malaysian dividends. There is no tax on capital gains.

Foreign acquisition of investments exceeding RM5 million in value or the equivalent of 15% or more of voting power in a Malaysian company requires the prior approval of the Foreign Investment Committee. However, it should be noted that there is no law restricting the percentage of foreign ownership in Malaysian corporations. The Foreign Investment Committee is a government policy-making committee. Although guidelines issued by it are not law they are invariably adhered to.

Malaysian exchange control regulations are liberal. The relevant authority is Bank Negara, the governor of which is also the Controller of Foreign Exchange who administers controls on behalf of the government.

There are no restrictions on a non-resident undertaking direct or portfolio investment in Malaysia. A non-resident may freely open an external account in ringgit. There are no restrictions on debits to external accounts. Credits in excess of RM100,000, or its equivalent in foreign currency, from residents require the completion of an exchange control form that can be approved by an authorised bank. An external account may be overdrawn up to RM100,000. A non-resident may also maintain current or time deposit accounts in foreign currency with a commercial bank.

Profits, dividends and principal resulting from the liquidation of securities may be freely repatriated, subject to the completion of exchange control forms for transactions in excess of RM100,000.

LISTING AND REPORTING REQUIREMENTS

A) Listing requirements

The KLSE listing manual sets out in detail the various procedures to be followed by companies seeking a listing on the KLSE (see Exhibit 41.9) and their responsibilities and continuing obligations after being listed.

B) Reporting requirements

Ongoing reporting requirements include the timely disclosure of all material information affecting the affairs and business of the company and its subsidiaries, financial results and dividend declarations; information to be

Exhibit 41.9:
REQUIREMENTS FOR NEW LISTINGS ON THE KLSE

	Main board	*Second board*
Issued and paid-up share capital	Minimum capital requirement of RM50 million with no maximum specified.	Minimum capital of RM10 million and a maximum of RM40 million.
Shareholding spread	At least 25% of the issued and paid-up capital is in the hands of the public and a minimum percentage or minimum amount (depending upon the size of the paid-up capital) of the issued and paid-up capital should be in the hands of at least 500 shareholders holding 500 to 10,000 shares each.	At least 25% but not more than 50% of the issued and paid-up capital must be in the hands of the public. Regardless of the size of the paid-up capital, at least 15% should be in the hands of at least 500 shareholders holding 500 to 10,000 shares each.
Track record	Track record of 3 financial years with an average after-tax profit of RM4 million per annum and an aggregate minimum after-tax profit of not less than RM25 million over the 3 financial years; or a track record of 5 financial years, with an average after-tax profit of not less than RM2 million per annum and an aggregate after-tax profit of not less than RM25 million over the 5 financial years.	Track record of 3 financial years, with an after-tax profit of not less than RM1 million per annum and an average after-tax profit of not less than RM2 million per annum over the 3 financial years.
Advertising of prospectus	Full advertisement of the prospectus.	Not required to advertise the full prospectus. Only a summary of the relevant details.
Independent directors	Every listed company should have at least 2 independent directors.	Every listed company should have at least 2 independent directors.
Major shareholdings	In respect of companies involved in construction, services or specialised activities a moratorium of 1 year, from the date of admission to the main board, may be imposed on the sale of substantial shareholdings. Thereafter divestment of up to a maximum of 20% per annum is allowed. In lieu, substantial shareholders may provide a profit guarantee of the performance of the company over the next 2 years.	A moratorium of 1 year from the date of admission to the second board may be imposed on the sale of substantial shareholdings. Thereafter divestment of up to a maximum of 15% per annum is allowed. In lieu, substantial shareholders may provide a profit guarantee of the performance of the company over the next 2 years.
Listing fees – Initial and additional listing fees	RM500 per million ringgit or part thereof of issued capital, with a minimum of RM2,000 and a maximum of RM50,000.	RM250 per million ringgit or part thereof of issued capital, with a minimum of RM1,000 and a maximum of RM5,000.
– Annual listing fees	Paid-up capital — Monthly fee Not exceeding RM2 million — RM100 Not exceeding RM50 million — RM250 Not exceeding RM100 million — RM500 Above RM100 million — RM750	RM200 per million ringgit or part thereof with a minimum of RM500 and a maximum of RM2,000.
Transition to the main board	Not applicable.	Main board (MB) requirements regarding track record, and issued and paid-up capital must be complied with. The company must have been listed for 3 years. Flexibility is applied as to the share spread requirement – at least 50% of normal MB requirements. A short advertisement must be inserted in a newspaper in the event that the transition is approved by the SC and the KLSE.

set out in annual reports; and the annual submission of an equity analysis to ensure compliance with share spread requirements. The manual also touches on the contents of prospectuses for the issue of shares, abridged prospectuses in connection with rights issues, trust deeds for loan securities and property trusts, and the memorandaand articles of association of companies. In addition, there are sections on takeovers, acquisitions and realisations. Penalties for errant listed companies are wide ranging and clearly spelt out.

The KLSE listing manual includes a comprehensive corporate disclosure policy to ensure that all investors enjoy equal access to information.

SHAREHOLDER PROTECTION CODES

A) Significant shareholdings

The Companies Act 1965 requires those with substantial interests to reveal them to the company concerned and to the KLSE.

B) Takeovers and mergers

The Code on Takeovers and Mergers came into force in Malaysia on 1 April 1987. The Code is given legislative effect because it constitutes subsidiary legislation under the Securities Commission Act 1993, unlike the British approach which is self-regulatory. Its provisions, however, are very similar to both the London and Singapore codes. The Code has the basic rationale of restricting or directing company directors and their advisers in the exercise of their powers to ensure that the interests of the respective shareholders are fairly and equally protected in a takeover.

The acquirer should be prepared to wait and to pay a fair and, if necessary, a full price for the acquisition and privilege of control. Shareholders are to be given all necessary facts in relation to an offer and should be given sufficient time to consider it. Any mode of acquiring more than 33% of the voting rights of a public company, whether listed or otherwise, is considered as a takeover and is liable to regulation under the Code. In the case of an acquisition of shares of companies listed on the stock exchange, once the takeover point is triggered the purchaser is required to make an immediate announcement to the KLSE. In cases of acquisitions other than on the stock exchange, the purchaser need only make an announcement when he fulfils the conditions of the sale and purchase agreement. The Code requires that the offer shall in the first instance be put to the board of directors of the offeree company or its advisers. Further procedures for a takeover and/or merger are spelt out in the Code and practice notes issued by the Securities Commission (SC).

Breaches of the Code are criminal offences and may render the persons responsible for the breach liable to a fine or imprisonment. In addition, the SC may impose other sanctions such as reprimand, public censure and, as in the UK model, temporary or permanent deprivation of stock exchange facilities.

The SC has also established criteria for reverse takeovers and back-door listings. A reverse takeover is defined by the SC as a situation whereby a listed public company acquires other assets/businesses for an issue of new shares and as a result there is a change in control of the listed public company. A back-door listing also relates to an acquisition of new assets/businesses either for cash or an issue of new shares, without a change in the dominant shareholder or group of shareholders but with a very significant change in the business direction of the public listed company. Reverse takeovers and back-door listings require the approval of the SC unless they are cash acquisitions and certain other conditions are met, one of which is that there is no disposal of the existing core business of the listed public company. Only companies that have been listed on the KLSE for at least two years are permitted to undertake reverse takeovers or back-door listings.

C) Insider trading

Both the Securities Industry Act 1983 and the Companies Act 1965 address the issue of insider trading. Under these laws, officers, agents and employees of a company and officers of the KLSE have a duty not to make improper use of information acquired by virtue of their positions to gain an advantage for themselves or for others, or to damage the company. The term "agent" is defined very broadly and includes bankers, solicitors, auditors, accountants, stockbrokers and professional advisers. There are severe criminal penalties for violating these provisions and, in 1997, civil liability was also introduced, enabling the SC to claim the gains made by an insider and also to have punitive damages imposed.

D) Due diligence

Under 1996 amendments to the Securities Commission Act, it is an offence to submit in any proposal to the SC any information or statement that is false or misleading or from which there is a material omission. The SC has also introduced due diligence practices and requirements to ensure that submissions contain greater disclosure of information than was previously required. In particular, where a securities offering is proposed, the draft form of the prospectus to be issued is required to be part of the submission and must contain a disclosure of relevant risk factors and an industry overview relevant to the company proposing the securities offering.

E) Compensation fund

On becoming a member, and annually thereafter, each member of the KLSE is required to contribute to a compensation fund held in trust by the KLSE. The fund is intended to be used to compensate victims of default or fraud by a stockbroking company or any of its directors.

RESEARCH

Comprehensive market research is carried out by foreign brokers specialising in south-east Asian markets, and is published in regular newsletters and reports. Most of the local stockbroking companies have their own research units reviewing macroeconomic and market trends, and providing detailed sectoral studies. Internationally, Hoare Govett, Merril Lynch, Deutsche Morgan Grenfell and ING Barings cover Malaysia in depth, while information can also be obtained from Singapore brokers and from the KLSE.

The main local financial newspaper is the *Business Times*. The business pages of local newspapers (such as the *New Straits Times*) also provide economic and financial information. The main business magazines are the monthly *Investor's Digest* published by the KLSE, the bi-monthly *Malaysian Business*, *Far Eastern Economic Review* and *Asiaweek*.

Malaysia 2020, published by Euromoney Books, provides in-depth information for those wishing to invest or do business in the country. See the order card at the back of this book for details.

CHAPTER

42

Mauritius

Introduction

The Stock Exchange of Mauritius (SEM) has achieved a number of objectives under its reform and modernisation programme. A depository system has been put in place to ensure that the clearing and settlement of securities transactions is up to international standards and, as from November 1997, trading has taken place on a daily basis, as compared with three sessions per week previously. The exchange is also considering installing a computerised trading system in 1998. On the regulatory front, the SEM is expected to publish a new set of listing rules and disclosure requirements soon.

At 31 December 1997, total market capitalisation was Rs36.9 billion (US$1.65 billion) giving a market capitalisation to GDP ratio of 43.5%. Turnover in 1997 rose by about 19% to Rs1.9 billion (or Rs2.9 billion if the Nedcor deal in which the South African banking group took a 20% strategic stake in a local bank is included). Over the past year liquidity has been improving (5.1%) due to the establishment of a large mutual fund and new foreign investment inflows (US$29.4 million in 1997). There were no new equity offerings in 1997 but the corporate debenture market witnessed phenomenal growth with over Rs2.5 billion raised. This proliferation of debenture issues was due to favourable fiscal treatment (interest earned being exempt from tax) and a very liquid banking sector.

ECONOMIC AND POLITICAL OVERVIEW

There was a split in the Labour Party (LP)/MMM coalition government in 1997, after months of political wrangling. The split left the LP (under Prime Minister Dr N. Ramgoolam) firmly in power with a comfortable majority in parliament, with MMM MPs forming the bulk of the opposition. The new Finance Minister, Dr Bunwaree, presented his first budget, confirming the major policies set out in the December 1996 "New Economic Agenda". This focused on promoting renewed business confidence and increasing investment to maintain the economy on its current growth rate of 5–6% per annum. The budget also reaffirmed the government's commitment to further privatisation in its bid to modernise the economy: Mauritius Telecom, the local and international telecoms operator, was earmarked as the next state-controlled company to be privatised. Overall, although new economic initiatives have yet to emerge, the government appears more determined to initiate much-needed reforms in various sectors such as health and education.

In 1997, most sectors of the economy fared relatively well with an overall 5% real GDP growth rate. Tourism and services performed especially well, growing by 14% and 6% respectively. The savings rate is expected to increase marginally to 24.1% from 23.9% in 1996, while the investment rate is likely to improve from 26.1% to 27.2%. The annual rate of inflation remained almost unchanged at 6.6% in 1997, despite a hike in sales tax from 5% to 8%. The trade deficit for the year was around Rs8.7 billion (excluding the import of aircraft), but this deficit is largely mitigated by strong gross tourism revenues, leaving a small and manageable current account deficit. The overall balance of payments is still expected to post a surplus, while foreign reserves stood at Rs15.3 billion at December 1997 – representing 20 weeks of import cover.

Role of the central bank

The Bank of Mauritius (BOM) oversees both domestic and offshore banking activities. It also implements government monetary policy. The BOM is ultimately accountable to the government and therefore falls short of being truly independent.

The main monetary policy objectives in recent times have been the achievement of price stability and a stable exchange rate for the rupee. The control of inflation is exercised through liquidity management of commercial banks by weekly auctions of Treasury bills.

Exhibit 42.1: MAUTITIUS SE SEMDEX PRICE INDEX (US$), 1993–97

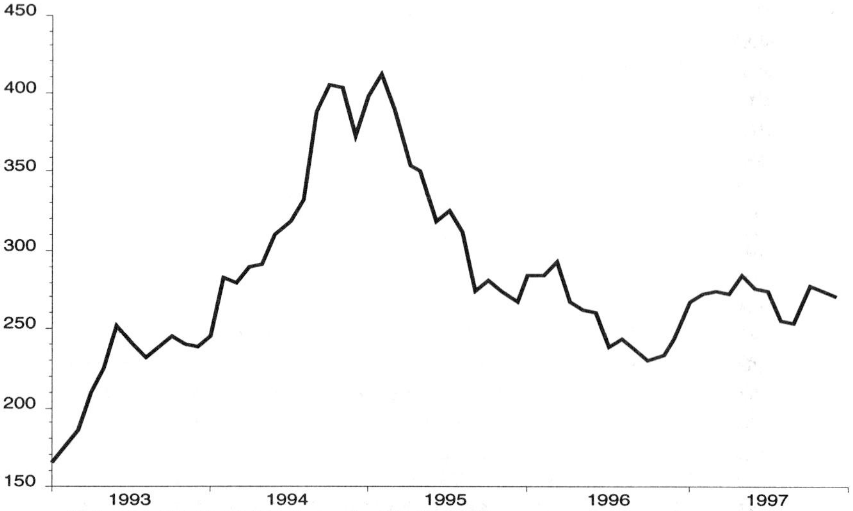

High value 411.15 1.2.95 Low value 164.61 1.1.93 *Source: Datastream*

MARKET PERFORMANCE

A) In 1997

The Semdex posted a modest 10.5% rise in 1997 in local currency terms (as against a rise of 5.5% last year), but this represented a fall of 1.0% in US dollar terms. Transactions were concentrated on just a couple of counters, while most other stocks remained thinly traded. Of note is the continued impact of foreign institutional investors on the market. Stocks that were the subject of foreign interest tended to record robust gains (in US dollar terms), ranging from 21% for New Mauritius Hotels to 14% for Mauritius Commercial Bank.

B) Summary information

Global ranking by market value (US$ terms, end-1997): 68
Market capitalisation (end-1997): US$1.65 billion
Growth in market value (local currency terms, 1993–97): 150.1%
Market value as a % of nominal GDP (end-1997): 43.5%
Number of domestic/foreign companies listed (end-1997): 44/2
Market P/E (all listed companies, end-1997): 14.1
Short term (3-month) interest rate (end-1997): 8.94%
Long bond (1-year) yield (end-1997): 8.96%
Budget deficit as a % of nominal GDP (1997): 4.6%
Annual increase in broad money (end-1997): 11.8%
Inflation rate (1997): 6.6%
US$ exchange rate (end-1997): Rs22.397

C) Year-end share price index, price/earnings ratios and yields

Exhibit 42.2:
YEAR-END SHARE PRICE INDEX (RS TERMS), P/E RATIOS AND GROSS DIVIDEND YIELDS, 1993–97

Year-end	*Semdex*	*P/E*	*Yield (%)*
1993	302.63	12.0	4.2
1994	473.67	16.5	3.3
1995	344.44	11.1	5.1
1996	353.46	11.4	4.0
1997	391.12	14.1	4.3

Source: Stock Exchange of Mauritius.

D) Market indices and their constituents

The Semdex price index comprises all listed shares.

THE STOCK MARKET

A) Brief history and structure

The Stock Exchange of Mauritius (SEM) is a private company incorporated in 1989, and is responsible for operating the stock exchange and providing facilities for dealing in securities. The SEM's shareholders comprise 11 stockbroking companies, each holding one share of Rs300,000, so that the exchange's total issued share capital is Rs3.3 million. Stockbroking companies are required to have at least two licensed stockbrokers, each furnishing a guarantee for Rs250,000 as capital for the company.

The SEM is governed by the Stock Exchange Act 1988 and the Companies Act. It operates under the control and supervision of the Stock Exchange Commission, the stock market's regulatory authority. The exchange is managed by an executive committee of 13 members, comprising nine members elected by the stockbroking companies, three appointed by the Minister of Finance to represent listed companies and investors, and one representing the Chambre des Courtiers. The chairman and deputy chairman are elected annually by the executive committee.

B) Opening hours, names and addresses

The official market operates daily from 10.00am. OTC market trading takes place on Tuesdays and Thursdays from 2.00pm. Trading sessions normally last about one hour.

THE STOCK EXCHANGE OF MAURITIUS LTD
2nd Floor, Les Cascades
33 Bis Edith Cavell Street, Port Louis
Tel: (230) 212 9541; Fax: (230) 208 8409
E-mail: stockexbow.intnet.mu

MARKET SIZE

A) Number of listings and market value

Total market capitalisation at the end of 1997 was Rs36.9 billion (US$1.6 billion), an increase of 10.5% compared with end-1996.

Exhibit 42.3:
NUMBER OF COMPANIES LISTED AND MARKET VALUE, SEM, 1993–97

Year-end	*No. of companies listed*	*Market value (Rs million)*
1993	30	14,768.15
1994	35	28,536.06
1995	41	27,817.76
1996	45	33,376.74
1997	46	36,934.88

Source: Stock Exchange of Mauritius.

B) Largest quoted companies

Exhibit 42.4:
THE 10 LARGEST COMPANIES LISTED ON THE SEM, END-1997

Ranking	*Company*	*Market value (Rs million)*
1	Mauritius Commercial Bank	5,621.87
2	State Bank of Mauritius	4,857.75
3	New Mauritius Hotels	4,240.00
4	Sun Resorts	4,058.28
5	Rogers & Co	2,646.48
6	Air Mauritius	1,534.58
7	Ireland Blyth	1,350.18
8	Mon Tresor Mon Desert	1,135.49
9	Grand Baie Hotel	1,111.00
10	Mauritius Breweries	776.62

Source: Stock Exchange of Mauritius.

C) Trading volume

Turnover on the official list in 1997 amounted to Rs2.97 billion (US$132.5 million) and the total number of shares traded was 164 million. Average turnover per trading session was Rs18.7 million (US$0.83 million).

Exhibit 42.5:
VALUE OF TRANSACTIONS ON THE OFFICIAL LIST AND OTC MARKETS, 1993–97

Year-end	*Official list turnover (Rs million)*	*OTC market turnover (Rs million)*
1993	691.6	128.2
1994	1,517.7	423.2
1995	1,220.5	232.5
1996	1,601.7	175.8
1997	2,967.0	366.9

Source: Stock Exchange of Mauritius.

Exhibit 42.6:
THE 10 MOST ACTIVELY TRADED SECURITIES ON THE SEM, 1997

Ranking	*Company*	*Turnover (Rs million)*
1	State Bank of Mauritius	1,319
2	Mauritius Commercial Bank	395
3	New Mauritius Hotel	265
4	Sun Resorts	162
5	Rogers & Co	141
6	Air Mauritius	53
7	Happy World Foods	45
8	Finlease 12%	43
9	Grand Baie Hotel	41
10	Mon Tresor Mon Desert	34

Source: Stock Exchange of Mauritius.

TYPES OF SHARE

There are two types of share on the SEM – ordinary and preference.

OTHER MARKETS

The SEM operates two markets: the official market for dealing in listed securities and the OTC market for unlisted securities. The OTC market began operations in April 1990 and, at the end of 1997, the shares of 62 companies were traded.

INVESTMENT FUNDS

A) Investment trusts

Four investment trusts are currently quoted on the SEM official list with a combined capitalisation of Rs1,234 billion, representing 3.3% of overall market capitalisation. The trusts cater for investors seeking a well-diversified portfolio of both local and international securities.

The following restrictions apply to investment trusts. They may not:

- invest more than 20% of the value of their assets in any single investment and must hold shares in at least 10 separate companies;
- invest more than 10% of their assets in unit trusts or approved investment institutions;
- hold more than 20% of the voting rights of a company.

B) Unit trusts

There are three authorised unit trusts operating in Mauritius: the National Mutual Fund (operating a General Fund and a Property Trust) and the Multipliant Trust.

OPERATIONS

A) Trading system

Since January 1994, trading has been carried out by open outcry for spot transactions on both the official and OTC markets. When a quotation cannot be reached by open outcry, buy and sell orders are matched by computer to determine the quoted price.

B) Principal brokers

ASMO SECURITIES & INVESTMENTS
43 Sir William Newton Street, Port Louis
Tel: (230) 212 1269; Fax: (230) 208 8508
E-mail: asmobow.intnet.mu

COMPAGNIE DES AGENTS DE CHANGE
9th Floor, Stratton Court, Poudriere Street, Port Louis
Tel: (230) 212 2578; Fax: (230) 208 3455; E-mail: cacintnet.mu

GENERAL BROKERAGE
8th Floor, Les Cascades Building
33 Bis, Edith Cavell Street, Port Louis
Tel: (230) 212 9863; Fax: (230) 212 9867: E-mail: gblintnet.mu

MCB STOCKBROKERS
MCB Head Office, Raymond Lamusse Bldg
Sir William Newton Street, Port Louis
Tel: (230) 208 2801; Fax: (230) 208 9210
E-mail: mcb.sbintnet.mu

C) Settlement and transfer

The central depository system (CDS), now fully operational, is based on a five-day clearing and settlement period. Assisted by the Bank of Mauritius, which acts as a clearing bank, CDS ensures strict delivery versus payment.

To date, 16,000 securities accounts have been opened with CDS.

D) Commission and other costs

Exhibit 42.7:
BROKERAGE CHARGES

Value of transaction (Rs)	*Total fee*
Less than Rs3 million	1.25%
More than Rs3 million, but less than Rs6 million	1.15%
More than Rs6 million but less than Rs10 million	1.05%
More than Rs10 million	0.90%

TAXATION AND REGULATIONS AFFECTING FOREIGN INVESTORS

There is no capital gains tax or withholding tax and exchange control has been suspended. No stamp duty or registration duty is payable on dealings in securities listed on the stock exchange.

Tax treaties have been signed with France, Germany, the UK, Italy, Sweden, India, Zimbabwe, Malaysia, Swaziland, Pakistan, China and Madagascar. Ratification of treaties is expected soon with the following countries: South Africa, Luxembourg, Russia, Namibia, Belgium, Singapore and Botswana. Treaties with other countries are being negotiated.

LISTING AND REPORTING REQUIREMENTS

A) Listing requirements

In addition to having an adequate trading record with published or filed accounts for the three years preceding the request for listing, there are two conditions to be satisfied for admission to the official list:

1. market capitalisation of at least Rs20 million; and
2. a public shareholding of at least 25% (although this

Exhibit 42.8:
COUNTRY FUNDS – MAURITIUS

	US$ % change 01/01/97 01/01/98	01/01/93 01/01/98	*Fund base currency*	*Fund size (US$ mil)*	*Fund volatility*	*Management group*	*Opal Main sector*	*Opal subsector*
Mauritius Ltd	-4.75	N/A	US$	24.938	4.065	Lloyds GSY	Closed-End	Equity

Note: details for some funds may not have been included if the data for the US$ % change for 97/98 is not available *Source: Standard & Poor's Micropal.*

can be reduced at the SEM's discretion) with a minimum of 200 shareholders, unless listing application relates to shares with a minimum nominal value of Rs2 million.

The listing of foreign companies is being encouraged by a relaxation of the above requirements and a reduction of the fees payable.

B) Reporting requirements

Companies must notify the SEM of any major developments in their sphere of activity, including:

1. any decision to pay a dividend or other distribution on listed securities, or to fail to make a dividend or interest payment;
2. the announcement of profits or losses on a half-yearly basis, (copies of the half-yearly interim report must also be provided);
3. any proposed change in capital structure, issues or redemptions of securities;
4. a change in the rights attached to any class of listed security;
5. details of major acquisitions or realisations of assets;
6. any change in the directorate or of senior executive officers;
7. any proposed alteration of the memorandum and articles of association of the company;
8. the publication of audited annual accounts, and the source and application of funds statement;
9. any notice of changes to substantial shareholdings and details thereof;
10. any acquisition of shares of another company, or a transaction resulting in such a company becoming a subsidiary of the listed company.

Provisional financial statements must be made public within three months of the financial year-end.

SHAREHOLDER PROTECTION CODES

The Stock Exchange Act prohibits insider dealing, any fraudulent inducement to invest, the issue of false statements and misleading documents, and stock market manipulation.

The SEM maintains a fund for the compensation of persons who may suffer pecuniary losses through the default of any member company.

RESEARCH

African Equities: A Guide to Markets and Companies, published by Euromoney Books, provides in-depth information for those wishing to invest or do business in Africa. See the order card at the back of this book for details.

CHAPTER 43

Mexico

Introduction

The Mexican equity market turned in a remarkably strong performance during 1997, with its principal index, the IPC, gaining 55.6% in nominal terms to close the year at 5,229. Thanks to the fact that the peso barely moved during the year, the return in US dollars terms was almost the same at 52.2%. The market's advance was supported by strong economic growth (around 7.25%), the successful completion of the July elections and the positive outcome of the Zedillo administration's negotiations with Congress concerning the 1998 Budget. However, towards the end of the year clouds began to appear on the horizon as the crisis in Asia threatened to cause problems for Mexico's trade balance and raised questions concerning the sustainability of economic growth.

The Mexican Stock Exchange (MSE) increasingly represents the activities of the country's most important companies, and the ratio of market capitalisation (US$156 billion at the end of 1997) to GDP is 39%. Nevertheless, some key sectors are not listed: perhaps the most important "absentees" are the two state-run enterprises, Pemex, the national oil monopoly, and the CFE or Federal Electricity Commission, which operates the electric power grid.

The International Quotations Section (SIC) of the Mexican exchange began operations in 1997 with the listing of four Argentinian stocks.

ECONOMIC AND POLITICAL OVERVIEW

Mexico made significant strides toward democracy during 1997 with the successful completion of the all-important July elections. The voters of Mexico City elected a mayor for the first time in decades and, at the same time, elections were held to the Chamber of Deputies where the long-time dominant party, the PRI, lost its majority to a coalition led by the centre-left PRD and the centre-right PAN. Still, despite his lack of a majority in the Chamber of Deputies, President Zedillo was able to persuade the Mexican Congress to approve the bulk of his proposed 1998 Budget. Most notably, he was able to resist pressure to reduce value-added tax, which would have hurt government revenues and widened the deficit.

The Mexican economy saw remarkable growth during 1997, significantly beyond the expectations of most analysts at the beginning of the year. It is estimated that GDP grew by almost 7.3%, with consumer spending and investment leading the way. Although exports remained robust, the growth of imports was greater such that on a net basis, the impact of the external sector on growth was negative.

A major positive factor supporting growth during 1997 was the strength of the peso, which closed the year at N$8.06 to the US dollar, little changed (despite inflation of 15.7%) from the 1996 year-end level of N$7.9. This was the second year of peso revaluation in real terms and was important in helping to reduce inflationary pressures. The 1997 inflation rate represented the second straight year of improvement after the 27.7% rise in 1996 which, in turn, followed a 52% increase in 1995.

The combination of the firm peso and strong economic growth inevitably produced a deterioration in the trade balance and the current account. Still, the deficit on current account was small compared with the amount of direct foreign investment, with the result that gross international reserves were up substantially. The trade balance ended 1997 with a US$1,165 million surplus versus the 1996 surplus of US$6,531 million.

Another important factor behind Mexico's economic success was the strength of the public sector fiscal accounts. The government estimates that the public sector deficit was just 0.6% of GDP in 1997.

Role of the central bank

The Banco de Mexico is an autonomous institution, independent from the government. Its only objective is to achieve price stability through monetary policy and, to this end, every January it publishes a "Monetary

Exhibit 43.1: MEXICO IPC (BOLSA) PRICE INDEX (US$), 1993–97

High value 5354.40 1.10.97 Low value 1517.96 1.3.95 *Source: Datastream*

Programme" in which it specifies the net domestic credit ceiling and the minimum international reserves expected to accumulate during the year, as well as the expected changes to the monetary base. The central bank also participates in the formulation of exchange rate policy, established by a joint central bank/Treasury committee, with the latter having a decisive vote. The exchange rate is free floating. The bank manages the level of liquidity in the economy to match the demand for money but does not set the level of interest rates.

MARKET PERFORMANCE

A) In 1997

The IPC Index ended the year at 5,229.35, up 55.6% on the 1996 close of 3,361.03. In 1997, the MSE saw equity turnover of US$53 billion, which represented approximately 33% of the year-end market capitalisation (US$156 billion). This compares with 40% and 38% for 1996 and 1995. The Mexican exchange estimates that at the end of 1997, 35% of its capitalisation was in the hands of foreigners. Of this total, some 80% was in the form of ADRs, another 19% was held through free subscription ordinaries and the remaining 1% was held via the NAFINSA trust.

During 1997 there was substantial M&A activity and some privatisation (although not as much of the latter as many had hoped for). As regards M&A, the market saw the sale of strategic interests in Mexico's cigarette industry, which came under the control of foreign interests as a result of divestitures by Cigatam, a subsidiary of Grupo Carso, and by Empresas La Moderna. There was also the sale to Wal-Mart of a controlling interest in Cifra, Mexico's largest retail chain. Finally, the privatisation of Mexico's railroad industry continued with the sale of the Pacifico-Norte line to a Mexican consortium led by Grupo Mexico, with participation by ICA and the Union Pacific Company. What did not take place was the planned privatisation of 49% of the oil monopoly's secondary petrochemical industry.

B) Summary information

Global ranking by market value (US$ terms, end-1997): 19
Market capitalisation (end-1997): US$156 billion
Growth in market value (local currency terms, 1993–97): 102%
Number of domestic/foreign companies listed (end-1997): 194/4
Market value as a % of nominal GDP (end-1997): 39.82%
Market P/E (end-1997): 17.9
MSCI Mexico Free Index (change in US$ terms, 1997): +51.6%
Short-term (28-day) interest rate (end-1997): 18.75%
Long-term (1-year) bond yield (end-1997): 19.85%
Budget deficit as a % of GDP (1997): 0.59%
Annual increase in broad money (M3) supply (end-1997): 28.92%
Inflation rate (1997):15.7%
US$ exchange rate (end-1997): N$8.06

C) Year-end share price index, price/earnings ratios and yields

Exhibit 43.2:
MSE SHARE PRICE INDEX (N$ TERMS), P/E AND GROSS DIVIDEND YIELDS, 1993–97

Year-end	*IPC Index*	*P/E*	*Yield (%)*
1993	2,602.63	18.8	1.2
1994	2,375.66	18.9	1.5
1995	2,778.47	20.5	1.1
1996	3,361.03	13.5	1.5
1997	5,229.35	17.9	1.5

Source: Mexican Stock Exchange.

D) Market indices and their constituents

The IPC Index comprises the 35 most representative stocks traded. These stocks are chosen every two months depending on factors such as trading value and trading volume. As of 31 December 1997, Telmex accounted for 18.86% of the index.

The INMEX Index was developed late in 1992 as an underlying index for derivative products. Unlike the IPC, it is based on 20 companies, is reviewed every six months, and no single issuer can account for more than 10% of the index. Companies in the index must have either medium or high marketability.

THE STOCK MARKET

A) Brief history and structure

The MSE was established in 1894 and is located in Mexico City. Founded as a private institution, the exchange was very much overlooked as a means of raising capital until the mid-1970s. The few shares listed in the early years of the market were those of banks, industrials and mining companies.

Traditionally, the Mexican financial system and market trading have been dominated by banks, family groups and other insiders. By 1975 there were fewer than 5,000 active investors and daily trading rarely exceeded US$1 million.

In 1975 a number of significant events took place. New securities legislation strengthened the regulatory powers of the Mexican Banking and Securities Commission (MBSC). Regulations were issued requiring banks to invest 8% of their savings deposits in shares or mortgage bonds and permitting them to lend to brokerage firms. A new, private-sector orientated government came to power, and a liquidity crisis following a major devaluation (after 22 years of currency stability) convinced the government that a viable securities market had to be created. Another relevant factor was the discovery of substantial oil reserves, which created a mood of optimism about Mexico's future. In the years that followed, the MSE was buoyant. A massive publicity campaign by the exchange brought some 25,000 new investors into the market, which in turn stimulated a new issue boom.

Significant reforms were made to the Mexican Securities Market Law in 1993, mainly directed at increasing investment opportunities through a wider self-regulatory scheme and the quotation of foreign instruments on the MSE. The collapse of the Mexican market in 1994–95 triggered the "Tequila effect", which hit emerging markets globally.

The MSE is currently owned by 33 brokerage firms (*casas de bolsa*), six of which are foreign. The Mexican Securities Market Law sets standards for registration of brokers in the National Registry of Securities and Brokers, a prerequisite to becoming a member of the exchange. The activities of the exchange are subject to the supervision of the Ministry of Finance and Public Credit through the MBSC.

The MBSC is responsible for monitoring the registration of all new issues of shares, bonds and commercial paper, establishing disclosure and subsequent reporting standards and regulating the activities of the stock exchange and the brokers.

B) Opening hours and addresses

The MSE's opening hours are Monday to Friday from 8.30am to 3.00pm.

BOLSA MEXICANA DE VALORES
Paseo de la Reforma 255, Col Cuauhtémoc
06500, México D.F.
Tel: (52) 5 726 6600; Fax: (52) 5 726 6836
Website: www.bmv.com.mx

MARKET SIZE

A) Number of listings and market value

Total market capitalisation at end-1997 was N$1,262.47 billion, an increase of 50.53% on the previous year.

Exhibit 43.3:
NUMBER OF LISTED COMPANIES AND EQUITY MARKET CAPITALISATION, 1993–97

Year-end	*Number of listed companies*	*Market value (N$ million)*
1993	190	623,843
1994	206	641,461
1995	186	699,776
1996	193	838,682
1997	194	1,262,468

Sources: Mexico Stock Exchange, ING Barings México.

Exhibit 43.4:
MARKET VALUE SECTOR, END-1997

Sector	*Market value (US$ billion)*
Communications and transportation	32.86
Services	19.17
Holding companies	20.62
Commerce	24.71
Construction	15.54
Industrials	38.86
Mining	4.46
Total	156.22

Source: ING Barings México..

B) Largest quoted companies

Telmex remains Mexico's largest quoted company in market value terms, accounting for 11.74% of total market capitalisation.

Exhibit 43.5:
THE 20 LARGEST COMPANIES LISTED ON THE MSE, END-1997

Ranking	*Company*	*Market value (US$ billion)*
1	Telmex	18.34
2	Cifra	11.66
3	Cemex	6.75
4	Kimber	6.44
5	GCarso	6.10
6	Banacci	4.74
7	GModelo	4.42
8	Televisa	4.41
9	Femsa	4.31
10	Alfa	4.06
11	GFinbur	3.93
12	Telecom	3.84
13	Bimbo	3.23
14	GFB	3.04
15	Desc	2.78
16	Soriana	2.63
17	Moderna	2.49
18	GMexico	2.49
19	Tvaztca	2.44
20	Livepol	2.28

Source: Mexican Stock Exchange.

C) Trading volume

Exhibit 43.6:
MSE EQUITY VOLUME AND TRADING VALUE, 1993–97

Year	*Trading volume (shares million)*	*Trading value (US$ million)*
1993	28,144	62,357.82
1994	23,843	84,101.49
1995	26,186	35,492.35
1996	24,463	45,557.00
1997	24,714	52,795.50

Source: Mexican Stock Exchange.

Exhibit 43.7:
THE 20 MOST ACTIVELY TRADED ISSUES ON THE MSE, RANKED BY VALUE, 1997

Ranking	*Issuer and series*	*Stock volume (shares million)*	*Trading value (US$ million)*
1	Telmex L	3,030.8	6,736.4
2	Alfa A	388.4	2,720.8
3	Femsa B	411.2	2,522.1
4	GCarso A1	356.3	2,382.9
5	Cemex B	429.3	2,040.5
6	Cemex Cpo	428.4	1,831.9
7	Cifra V	915.0	1,689.3
8	Kimber A	325.3	1,644.2
9	Banacci B	639.4	1,618.2
10	Cifra C	754.5	1,269.2
11	GFB B	2,442.5	1,266.2
12	Cifra A	667.1	1,253.6
13	Tamsa	54.5	1,074.3
14	Televisa Cpo	67.4	1,063.8
15	Vitro	260.3	974.4
16	Moderna A	182.8	965.9
17	Apasco	130.6	906.9
18	GModelo C	116.6	876.8
19	ICA	192.4	875.6
20	Desc B	103.1	824.1

Source: Mexican Stock Exchange.

TYPES OF SHARE

All shares of Mexican companies must be registered. Typically, a Mexican company issues three different series of shares. The first (usually Series A) may legally be held only by Mexican nationals, while the second (usually designated as Series B) may also be owned by foreign investors. The third series (usually Series C) carries all corporate rights (except voting rights). Finally, free sub-

Exhibit 43.8:
COUNTRY FUNDS – MEXICO

Fund	US$ % change 01/01/97 01/01/98	US$ % change 01/01/93 01/01/98	Fund base currency	Fund size (US$ mil)	Fund volatility	Management group	Opal main sector	Opal subsector
Mexico Equity & Income	59.03	70.82	US$	141.44	7.871	Advantage Adv	Closed-End	Equity
Emerging Mexico Fund Inc	53.84	4.96	US$	70.53	8.324	Santander Mgt	Closed-End	Equity
Paribas EM Mexico Ptfl	51.14	N/A	US$	N/A	9.138	Paribas Asset	Open-End	Equity
NatWest/IFC LAIF Mexico Index	49.28	N/A	US$	13.633	9.085	NatWest Inv M	Open-End	Equity
Mexico Fund Inc.	47.94	14.63	US$	927.37	8.963	Impulsora del	Closed-End	Equity
Wright Equi:Mexico	42.38	N/A	US$	18.8	9.05	Wright Invest	Open-End	Equity
RG ZelfSelect Mexico	41.83	N/A	G	28.7	-1	Robeco	Open-End	Equity
Mexican Inv Co	39.98	6.06	US$	23.8	9.644	Foreign & Col	Open-End	Equity
Acciones E Inversiones Comunes	28.91	3.24	N$	N/A	6.155	BBV Probursa	Open-End	Equity
Nikko Glbl Mexico	22.92	N/A	¥	1202	6.868	Nikko	Open-End	Equity
Profin SA De CV	16.53	-29.42	N$	N/A	7.662	BBV Probursa	Open-End	Equity
Promotora De Analisis Fdmental	15.7	2.18	N$	N/A	8.121	BBV Probursa	Open-End	Equity
Jupiter Tyndall SF Mexico	13.74	N/A	US$	0.4	7.689	Tyndall	Open-End	Equity
Promercado SA De CV	6.83	-40.08	N$	N/A	8.124	BBV Probursa	Open-End	Equity
KOKUSAI Gth Sel Mexico	6.32	N/A	¥	19	4.907	Kokusai	Open-End	Equity

Note: details for some funds may not have been included if the data for the US$ % change for 97/98 was not available

Source: Standard & Poor's Micropal.

scription shares (Series L) have no voting rights. Registration is usually handled by the broker and no special authorisation is needed to acquire shares not restricted to Mexican nationals.

Although Series A shares can only be held by Mexican nationals, foreign investors may acquire these shares through a trust called a "neutral fund" managed by the Mexican development bank, NAFINSA. Series A shares bought by foreign investors have to be committed to this trust in order to be registered: NAFINSA will then issue participation certificates (CPOs) corresponding to the shares in the trust. Such certificates carry economic but not voting rights, and they must be reissued for placing on foreign exchanges.

OTHER MARKETS

In July 1993, the MBSC approved the introduction of a second-tier market on the MSE. This parallel market aims to attract medium-sized companies to the Mexican stock market.

The establishment of an options and futures exchange has been approved by the authorities and it is due to begin operations in the second quarter of 1998. Trading will be automated and the central securities depository for the stock market (SD Indeval) will function as the central clearing organisation. Initially, options and futures on indices and highly liquid stocks will be traded, but other kinds of derivatives will be added as the market develops.

INVESTORS

Information on the holdings of different categories of shareholder is not available for the Mexican stock market. However, the Mexican exchange estimates that about 35% of the market is owned by foreign investors.

OPERATIONS

A) Trading system

IPC Index constituent stocks are traded via open outcry, and trading in all other stocks is conducted under the BMV-SENTRA automated system.

Trading in stocks can be suspended for 30 minutes if the price change exceeds 5% of the previous close. (Stocks that have an ADR programme traded on a foreign public exchange are not subject to the 5% rule.)

B) List of principal brokers

ABACO CASA DE BOLSA
José Ma. Ibarrarán No 84 – 4° piso, Col. San José Insurgentes
Delegación Benito Juárez, 03900 México DF
Tel: (52) 5 326 8000; Fax: (52) 5 326 8077

ACCIONES Y VALORES DE MEXICO
Av. Paseo de la Reforma No. 398 – 6° Piso
Col. Juárez, Delegación Cuauhtémoc, 06600 México DF
Tel: (52) 5 326 4848; Fax: (52) 5 326 4836

CASA DE BOLSA BANCOMER
Av Universidad No 1200 – 2° Piso
Col. Xoco, Delegación Benito Juárez, 03339 México DF
Tel: (52) 5 238 7700; Fax: (52) 5 621 3932

CASA DE BOLSA BITAL
Av. Paseo de la Reforma No 156 – Piso 18
Col Juárez, Delegación Cuauhtemóc, 06600 México DF
Tel: (52) 5 721 2222; Fax: (52) 5 721 2749

CASA DE BOLSA INVERLAT
Bosques de Ciruleos No 120 – Piso 12
Col Bosques de las Lamas, Delegación Miguel Hidalgo, 11700 México DF
Tel: (52) 5 325 3000; Fax: (52) 5 325 3699

INTERACCIONES CASA DE BOLSA
Av Paseo de la Reforma No 383 – Piso 14
Col Cuauhtemóc, Delegación Cuauhtemóc, 06500 México DF
Tel: (52) 5 264 1800; Fax: (52) 5 326 8600

IXE CASA DE BOLSA
Periféricp Sur No 314, San Angel Tlacopac, 01049 Mexico DF
Tel: (52) 5 481 7777; Fax: (52) 5 481 7682

MEXIVAL BANPAÍS CASA DE BOLSA
Av Paseo de la Reforma No 359 – 4° Piso
Col Cuauhtemóc, Delegación Cuauhtemóc, 06500 México DF
Tel: (52) 5 208 2044; Fax: (52) 5 525 6490

VALORES FINAMEX
Río Amazonas No 91 – 3° Piso,
Col Cuauhtemóc, Delegación Cuauhtemóc, 06500 México DF
Tel: (52) 5 227 5100; Fax: (52) 5 209 2322

OPERADORA DE BOLSA SERFIN
Ave. Prolongación Paseo de la Reforma No. 500 PB
Col. Lomas de Santa Fe, Delegación Alvaro Obregón, 01219 México DF
Tel: (52) 5 257 8000; Fax: (52) 5 257 8302

SALOMON BROTHERS INC.
Ruben Dario No. 281, Piso 14
Office 1402, Mexico D.F., C.P. 11580
Tel: 525 281 2222; Fax: 525 281 2222

C) Settlement and transfer

In the case of spot transactions, normal settlement is on the second business day following the trade.

The Institute for the Deposit of Securities (SD Indeval) functions as a clearing house and depository for securities listed in Mexico, eliminating the need for physical transfer. Over 75% of shares traded are held by Indeval.

D) Commissions and other costs

Brokerage commissions are freely negotiable, although banks and institutional investors usually pay a commission of 0.8% regardless of the value of the transaction.

TAXATION AND REGULATIONS AFFECTING FOREIGN INVESTORS

Treaties to avoid double taxation have been signed with Belgium, Canada, France, Germany, Italy, Japan, Korea, the Netherlands, Norway, Singapore, Spain, Sweden, Switzerland, the United Kingdom and the United States. A treaty with Ecuador is awaiting ratification.

The following tax rules apply to investments in equity securities through the MSE by non-residents:

a) Capital gains on transactions carried out through the stock exchange are exempt from tax.

b) Non-resident shareholders are subject to a tax of 34% on dividends, but this is paid by the company declaring the dividend, which means that no withholding is applicable. However, if the dividends are paid out of profits on which the company has already paid the relevant corporate tax, such dividends are tax-free. For this purpose, companies are entitled to create an "after-tax profits account".

Exhibit 43.9:
WITHHOLDING TAXES

Recipient	*Dividends %[1]*	*Interest %*
Resident corporations	Nil	2
Non-resident corporations and individuals:		
Non-treaty[1]	Nil	4.9–35

Notes: 1. Th3 statutory withholding rates mentioned above may be reduced by treaty. In the past few years Mexico has embarked on a policy of negotiating a network of tax treaties with its principal trading and investment partners.

Source: Price Waterhouse.

Under the Foreign Investment Law of 28 December 1993, foreign investors may hold up to 100% of the capital stock of Mexican corporations or partnerships, but foreign investment in certain sectors (eg the oil industry, the basic petrochemical industry and national air transportation) is restricted. It is possible, however, for foreign investors to acquire MSE-listed equity securities of restricted corporations through the acquisition of limited voting stock (typically Series C or L), or through government investment trusts.

Foreign investors may now hold up to 49% of the capital stock of financial institutions (eg holding companies of financial groups, multiple banking credit institutions, brokerage firms, securities specialists and insurance institutions). In addition, new regulations for the establishment of affiliates of foreign financial institutions in Mexico were included in the Banking Law in order to comply with NAFTA.

LISTING AND REPORTING REQUIREMENTS

A) Offering and listing requirements

All public offerings of securities must be previously approved by the MBSC, and the underlying securities must be registered at the National Registry of Securities and Securities Dealers. Generally, the MBSC will want to establish that the issuer is, and will be solvent, and that the characteristics of the securities and the terms and conditions of the offering will permit a good spread of the securities in the market.

The procedures and requirements for listing equity securities are set out in the internal regulations of the MSE. Only securities previously registered at the National Registry may be listed on the MSE.

Companies seeking a listing for securities on the Mexican exchange must file with the General Director's Office of the MSE a listing application, accompanied by the official authorisation issued by the MBSC evidencing registration of the securities. The company must also file standard corporate documentation, such as amended bylaws and minutes of shareholders' and board meetings, along with certified financial statements.

B) Reporting requirement

Listed companies are required to publish annual audited financial statements, unaudited quarterly financial statements, plus other financial and operating information that might affect their share price.

SHAREHOLDER PROTECTION

The Securities Market Support Fund protects the clients of securities intermediaries and is funded by all MSE brokerage firms.

RESEARCH

Investors can obtain information from the MSE and the principal brokers listed above. The MSE publishes various annual and monthly financial reports, statistics, monthly market indicators and other bulletins. Also, the major newspapers in Mexico carry a financial section with information on the stock market.

Most of the brokerage houses (and the Mexican Brokerage Houses' Association) publish information that is available on request. Internationally, information on the Mexican market is available from Merrill Lynch, Banco Santander, BBV, Goldman Sachs and Salomon Brothers.

Stock exchange publications include the following: *Stock Exchange Daily Money and Capital Markets Bulletins; Monthly Market Indicators; Monthly Trading Reports; Annual Financial Statistics Report; Monthly Trading Summary by Brokerage Firms; Monthly Financial Information Report* (only in Spanish); and *Quarterly Financial Information Report* (only in Spanish).

Mexico: The Next Step, published by Euromoney Books, provides in-depth information for those wishing to invest or do business in the country. For further details, see the order card at the back of this book.

CHAPTER 44

Morocco

Introduction

Total market capitalisation of the Casablanca Stock Exchange (CSE) at the end of 1997 stood at DH118.6 billion (US$13.2 billion), up from DH75.6 billion in 1996. There are 49 listed companies, the largest being ONA (valued at DH14.5 billion) and the smallest Lecarton (DH15.2 million). Even though total market value represents only 37.8% of GDP, most important sectors of the Moroccan economy are represented on the exchange. For example, there are seven listed banks out of a total of 13, accounting for more than 70% of the sector's assets and 31.6% of overall market value. In addition, some of the largest Moroccan industrial companies are listed on the CSE, including SAMIR (oil refinery); SONASID (steel mill); Brasseries du Maroc (beverages producer); Cosumar and Lesieur (consumer goods); and Société Métallurgique d'Imiter (mining).

Morocco's privatisation programme has encouraged individual investor interest and this has helped local mutual funds attract more than DH9 billion (US$1 billion) in the past two years.

ECONOMIC AND POLITICAL OVERVIEW

Morocco is a constitutional monarchy and King Hassan II has been Head of State since 1961. Following the November 1997 election, the government has not yet been nominated, but it is expected that a left-of-centre coalition will take power after 40 years of domination by the right.

The first macroeconomic figures published for 1997 indicate that real GDP growth was -2.2% (nominal GDP = -1.2%) against +12.0% in 1996 (nominal = +14.1%). Even though agricultural GDP accounts for only 10–20% of total GDP, the volatility of the sector once again had a significant impact on Moroccan economic growth. Agricultural GDP fell by 26% in 1997 as against +79% in 1996. Non-agricultural GDP rose by 3.1%.

There was a record low inflation rate of 1% in 1997 due to falling food prices. Excluding food, the CPI inflation rate for 1997 was 2.9%.

The recovery in public finances begun in 1996 continued in 1997, when the deficit fell to 1.9% of GDP (vs 3.0% in 1996), due mainly to increased privatisation revenues and substantial extra indirect tax revenues.

Role of the central bank

The main function of the central bank – Bank Al Maghrib – is to manage money circulation and to foster Morocco's economic development in line with government economic and financial objectives. Maintaining price stability is therefore paramount.

To fulfil its role, the bank can issue money and intervene in the foreign exchange markets. It also acts as a financial adviser and banker to the state, grants loans to the banking system and regulates all aspects of banking. The decrease in Treasury bond interest rates in 1997 indicates that current monetary policy is to force lending rates down in order to stimulate the economy.

Bank Al Maghrib is headed by a governor appointed by the King. The governor's role is to oversee the bank's activities and to act as spokesperson.

MARKET PERFORMANCE

A) In 1997

The Casablanca stock market soared 49.3% as measured by the CSE General Index (47% as measured by the CFG25 Index). The market surge began in February and continued until the end of April, following which there was a downwards adjustment (-10%) in May. The second half of 1997 saw the market stabilise at the new higher level. In US dollar terms, the performance of the CFG25 Index over the year was +32%.

Exhibit 44.1: MOROCCO SE CFG25 PRICE INDEX (US$), 1993–97

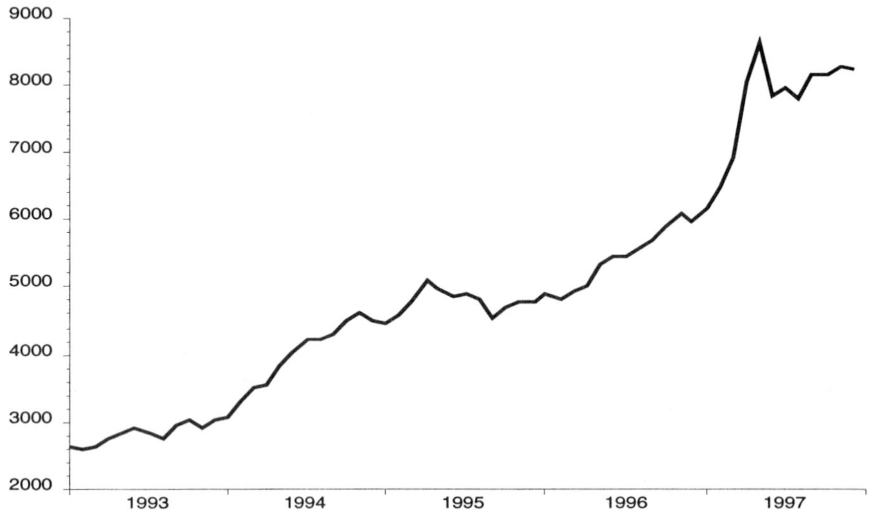

High value 8652.22 1.5.97 Low value 2596.01 1.2.93 *Source: Datastream*

B) Summary information

Global ranking by market value (US$ terms, end-1997): 47
Market capitalisation (end-1997): US$13.2 billion
Growth in market value (local currency terms, 1993–97): 273.6%
Market value as a % of nominal GDP (end-1997): 37.8%
Number of domestic/foreign companies listed (end-1997): 49/0
Market P/E (all listed companies, end-1997): 18.6
MSCI Index (change in US$ terms, 1997): +32.6%
Short-term (3-month) interest rate (end-1997): 6.75%
Long-term (5-year) bond yield (end-1997): 8.40%
Budget deficit as a % of nominal GDP (1997): 1.9%
Annual increase in broad money supply (1997): 8.1%
Inflation rate (1997): 1%
US$ exchange rate (end-1997): DH9.0

C) Year-end share price index, P/E ratio and yields

Exhibit 44.2:
YEAR-END SHARE PRICE INDEX, P/E RATIOS AND GROSS DIVIDEND YIELDS, 1993–97

Year-end	*CSE General Index*	*P/E*	*Yield (%)*
1993	259.78	14.02	3.87
1994	342.33	21.50	3.00
1995	342.39	19.26	2.65
1996	447.13	16.48	2.52
1997	667.52	18.60	2.01

Source: Casablanca Stock Exchange.

D) Market indices and their constituents

The General Index (IGB) included all local companies listed on the CSE. It has been calculated by the exchange on a daily basis since 1993.

The CFG25 Index was introduced in December 1993 by the Casablanca Finance Group. The CFG25 has been computed and maintained retrospectively on a monthly basis since December 1987. The 25 constituent companies (chosen on the basis of size and liquidity) represent 85% of total market capitalisation.

The Upline Securities Index ("US 10") is calculated by Upline Securities and measures price performance of the top 10 listed companies by market capitalisation and value traded.

THE STOCK MARKET

A) History and structure

The CSE was originally established as a private stock exchange in 1929. In 1948, the government took control of the exchange and set up an open outcry trading system. This structure was maintained more or less unchanged until 1993, when a major CSE restructuring took place involving the creation of a regulatory body, CDVM (Conseil Deontologique en Valeurs Mobiliere), dedicated to ensuring investor protection and the fulfilment of listing requirements.

Recent developments have included the privatisation of the stock exchange in 1995 and the approval, at the end of 1996, of a law establishing a central depository, which is expected to become operational in May 1998.

B) Opening hours, names and addresses

Trading on the official market takes place on Monday to Friday from 8.30am to 12.45pm.

CASABLANCA STOCK EXCHANGE
Avenue de L'Armée Royale, Casablanca
Tel: (212) 2 45 2626; Fax: (212) 2 45 2625

MARKET SIZE

A) Number of listings and market value

Over the past five years, market value has increased by 273%. At the end of 1997, CSE market capitalisation totalled DH118.6 billion (US$13.2 billion), a 57% increase on the end-1996 total of DH75.6 billion. During 1997, three companies were delisted (one for non-compliance with reporting requirements and two because they were taken over) and five companies were listed.

Exhibit 44.3:
NUMBER OF COMPANIES LISTED AND MARKET VALUE, CSE, 1993–97

Year-end	*No. of companies listed*	*Market value (DH million)*
1993	65	31,754
1994	61	48,463
1995	44	50,827
1996	47	75,583
1997	49	118,621

Source: Casablanca Finance Group.

Exhibit 44.4:
THE 20 LARGEST COMPANIES ON THE CSE, END-1997

Ranking	*Company*	*Market capitalisation (DH million)*
1	ONA	14,500
2	BCM	11,726
3	BMCE	8,356
4	SNI	8,267
5	Lafarge Ciments	6,622
6	Samir	6,605
7	Société Brasseries du Maroc	6,076
8	Lesieur	5,620
9	Wafabank	5,464
10	Crédit du Maroc	3,419
11	Ciments du Maroc	3,386
12	CIOR	3,326
13	BMCI	3,020
14	Centrale Laitière	2,955
15	Cosumar	2,929
16	CIH	2,700
17	BNDE	2,685
18	Financière Diwan	2,661
19	Asmar	2,134
20	Sonasid	2,126

Source: Casablanca Finance Group.

B) Trading volume

Turnover on the exchange reached DH32.33 billion, an increase of 58.8% over the figure for 1996. Average daily trading value increased to DH130.4 million.

Exhibit 44.5:
THE 20 MOST ACTIVELY TRADED COMPANIES ON THE CSE, 1997

Ranking	*Company*	*Turnover value (DH million)*
1	BMCE	5,473
2	ONA	3,819
3	BCM	2,421
4	SNI	2,074
5	Samir	1,740
6	Wafabank	1,553
7	BNDE	981
8	Brasseries du Maroc	917
9	Sonasid	778
10	CIOR	727
11	Eqdom	708
12	BMCI	653
13	Financière Diwan	642
14	Lafarge Ciments	534
15	SMI	439
16	CIH	435
17	Credor	338
18	Centrale Laitière	277
19	Fertima	245
20	Cosumar	242

Source: Casablanca Finance Group.

OPERATIONS

A) Trading system

There are three trading systems: an open outcry market operating from 11.00am to 12.45pm each trading day; electronic quotation, which operates between 8.30am and 10.30am; and an OTC market on which all transactions must be reported to the CSE before 12.45pm. The electronic system was introduced on 4 March 1997, and currently four companies are traded – BMCE, Samir, Sonasid and Fertima. The CSE hopes to include all listed companies in the electronic system in 1998 and then to phase out open outcry. The OTC market will be replaced by block trades on the electronic quotation system.

Exhibit 44.6:
COUNTRY FUNDS – MOROCCO

Fund	US$ % change 01/01/97 01/01/98	01/01/93 01/01/98	Fund base currency	Fund size	Fund volatility	Management Group	Opal main sector	Opal subsector
Framlington Maghreb	28.83	N/A	US$	26.159	4.166	Framlington	Closed-End	Equity
Maroc Croissance	28.22	N/A	Ffr	16	4.359	Bqe Chaabi	Open-End	Equity
Maroc Privatisation	24.16	N/A	Ffr	13	4.044	SMC	Open-End	Equity
Atlas Maroc	20.32	N/A	Ffr	58	37.407	Fin Atlas	Open-End	Equity

Note: details for some funds may not have been included if the data for the US$ % change for 97/98 was not available

Source: Standard & Poor's Micropal.

B) Settlement and transfer

Settlement and transfer for the open outcry market, electronic trading and the OTC market take place on a T+3 basis. A new central depository is due to become operational in May 1998.

C) Commissions and other costs

Stock exchange tax is set by the SBVC at 0.39% for shares. Other commissions (payable to the broker and the custodian) are negotiable.

REGULATIONS AFFECTING FOREIGN INVESTORS

There are no restrictions on foreign investment through the Moroccan stock market, or on repatriating capital or dividends. Foreign holdings in listed companies are not subject to any upper limit, although disclosure rules apply to foreign investors as they do to domestic investors.

There is no capital gains tax for non-Moroccan investors, but a 10% withholding tax applies on dividends.

The independent CDVM watchdog body regulates the activities of brokerage firms and enforces disclosure rules applicable to listed companies.

RESEARCH

Research on the Moroccan market is provided by Casablanca Finance Group, ING Barings, Maroc Inter Titre and Upline Securities.

African Equities: A Guide to Markets and Companies, published by Euromoney Books, provides in-depth information for those wishing to invest or do business in Africa. See the order card at the back of this book for details.

CHAPTER

45

Netherlands

Introduction

Until the 1980s, the Dutch equity market was of little economic importance because companies preferred to rely on their close relationships with the banks for funding rather than to raise equity finance. However, moves in the early 1980s to deregulate the market and reduce corporate taxation increased the popularity of equity issues. In 1996, the Amsterdam Stock Exchange (ASE) and the Europe Options Exchange (EOE) merged to become Amsterdam Exchanges (AEX).

At the end of 1997, market capitalisation totalled G1,071 billion, an increase of 36% on the end-1996 figure of G788 billion. Equity market turnover was G1.10 trillion, up 73% on 1996. Although market capitalisation represents around 146% of Dutch GDP, the market has traditionally been very concentrated. The combined market capitalisation of the five largest companies accounts for 49% of total market capitalisation.

ECONOMIC AND POLITICAL OVERVIEW

The Netherlands is a constitutional monarchy and a member of the EU. It is governed by a coalition of the Labour Party, the Democratic Party and the Liberal Party, headed by Labour Prime Minister, Wim Kok.

The Dutch economy grew by 3.0% in 1997, which is above the average growth rate of its major trading partners. The labour market was very dynamic and 1997 saw the creation of around 150,000 jobs. This strong employment growth was accompanied by a fall in unemployment, which declined by 1% to 5.5% of the labour force. With economic growth likely to remain at around 3.0% in 1998, labour market prospects continue to be favourable.

Inflation was once again very moderate in 1997, averaging 2.2%, although in 1998 it is likely to climb to an average of 2.6%, partly as a consequence of an increase in the level of wage settlements. In 1996 and in 1997 the rise in hourly wages exceeded inflation by around 0.3%, and in 1998 it is expected to do so by 0.9%. Fiscal policy is likely to remain focused on moderating wage costs, although in 1997 priority was given to the reduction of the budget deficit.

The 1997 budget deficit outcome was significantly better than expected, and, at 1.3% of GDP, clearly below the Maastricht criterion of 3% of GDP. The 1998 budget puts the Dutch budget deficit at 1.7%, and a lower result is a distinct possibility because the factors behind the 1997 windfalls – principally higher growth-induced tax revenues – will apply in 1998 and beyond. The national debt, according to the EMU definition, is still well above the reference value of 60% of GDP, but is continuing its downward trend sufficiently quickly to meet the Maastricht criterion. As regards the other criteria, the Netherlands traditionally has had an excellent reputation; in particular, the Dutch guilder has proved to be the most stable currency within the European exchange rate mechanism (ERM).

Role of the central bank

The main task of De Nederlandsche Bank (DNB) is to protect the value of the guilder and to guide the currency in a direction beneficial to the economy. Indeed, exchange rate policy is currently the most important component of monetary policy, the prime objective being to stabilise the guilder against the Deutschmark. A stable guilder is seen as fostering foreign trade and capital transactions, and eventually leading to stable domestic prices.

In anticipation of EMU, DNB has recently adjusted its money market policy to a system likely to be adopted by the European Central Bank. To date, DNB has steered money market rates by means of the conditions on which it lends to domestic banks to cover their shortages. If the money market is not tight enough to give DNB automatic control of market rates, a shortage is created by imposing cash reserve requirements or by issuing Nederlandsche Bank Certificates (NBCs).

Exhibit 45.1: CBS ALL SHARE GENERAL PRICE INDEX (G), 1993–97

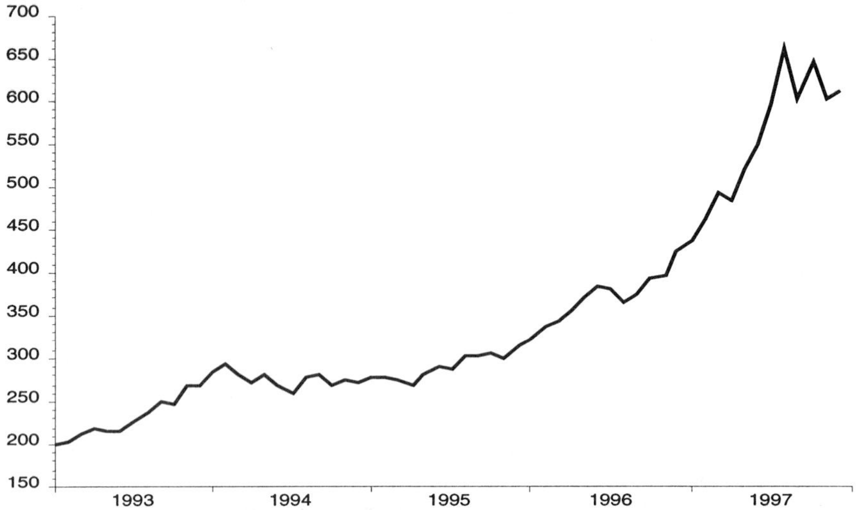

High value 662.00 1.8.97 Low value 198.00 1.1.93 *Source: Datastream*

MARKET PERFORMANCE

A) In 1997

For the second year in a row, the Dutch stock market performed well as indices repeatedly achieved new highs. The CBS All Share Index and the Amsterdam Exchanges Index (AEX) both rose by around 41%. As in 1996, persistent low interest rates helped underpin market buoyancy. After an extremely bullish first half (up 56% by the first week of August), the market slid by 9.6% in the second half of 1997, mainly due to the financial crisis in south-east Asia.

During the year, technology stocks and consumer durables stocks performed particularly well: clear outperformers included Philips (74%), Baan (118%) and ASML (208%). Also, insurance company AEGON (72%) performed strongly. Underperformers in 1997 included Grolsch (-26%), Gucci Group (-30%) and Endemol (-32%).

In 1997, total turnover on the AEX increased by 12.6% to a record level of G2.21 trillion. Turnover in Dutch equities rose by 73% to G1.10 trillion.

B) Summary information

Global ranking by market value (US$ terms, end-1997): 8
Market capitalisation (end-1997): US$525.90 billion
Growth in market value (local currency terms, 1993–97): 138.4%
Market value as a % of nominal GDP (end-1997): 146%
Number of domestic/foreign companies listed (end-1997): 450/213
Market P/E (end-1997): 19.8
MSCI total returns (with net dividends, US$ terms, 1997): 23.8%
MSCI Index (change in US$ terms, 1997): +21.6%
Short-term (3-month) interest rate (end-1997): 3.75%
Long-term (10-year) bond yield (end-1997): 5.32%
PSBR as a % of nominal GDP (1997): 1.5%
Annual increase in broad money (M3, end-1997): 7.4%
Inflation rate (average, 1997): 2.2%
US$ exchange rate (end-1997): G2.0365

C) Year-end share price index, price/earnings ratios and yields

Exhibit 45.2:
YEAR-END SHARE PRICE INDEX, AVERAGE P/E AND DIVIDEND YIELDS, 1993–97

Year-end	*CBS All Share Index*	*P/E*	*Yield (%)*
1993	280.8	14.3	3.9
1994	278.0	13.2	3.7
1995	321.5	13.0	3.7
1996	437.3	18.6	2.6
1997	618.8	19.8	2.3

Sources: MeesPierson and Amsterdam Exchanges.

D) Market indices and their constituents

The Netherlands Central Bureau of Statistics (CBS) has calculated share price indices since 1918. The CBS All Share Index (introduced in 1952) and Total Return

Index are chain indices suitable for long-term analysis. The calculation of these indices includes all ordinary shares of Dutch companies listed on the AEX, except the shares of property funds, investment funds and holding companies.

In January 1994 the AEX Index was established. It comprises a weighted average of the 25 most actively traded Dutch stocks, selected annually based on their turnover in the previous three calendar years.

In October 1995 the Amsterdam Midkap Index (AMX) was introduced with a view to stimulating interest in medium-sized companies.

THE STOCK MARKET

A) Brief history and structure

The Amsterdam stock market is the oldest in the world and has been a major influence in the development of other exchanges. Indeed, the New York Stock Exchange is based on the Dutch system.

Amsterdam started its stockbroking business nearly 400 years ago by offering investors the opportunity to buy a share in the cargoes being transported to and from the East Indies. This method of sharing risk and reward became widely adopted and, as a result, the Amsterdam exchange was instrumental in the formation and development of many of today's Dutch trading companies.

The AEX, formed in 1996 by the merger of the ASE and the EOE, is a private limited company with shareholders.

B) Different exchanges

The AEX is the only recognised stock exchange in the Netherlands.

C) Opening hours, names and addresses

Official exchange hours are from 9.30am to 4.30pm, Monday to Friday. All securities are traded on a continuous basis.

AMSTERDAM EXCHANGES
Beursplein 5, 1012 JW Amsterdam
Tel: (31) 20 550 4444; Fax: (31) 20 550 4960
Web site: www.aex.nl

MARKET SIZE

A) Number of listings and market value

At end-1997 there were 663 companies listed on the AEX and total market capitalisation of listed Dutch shares amounted to G1,071.2 billion, an increase of 36% over 1996.

Exhibit 45.3:
NUMBER OF COMPANIES LISTED AND MARKET VALUE, AEX, 1993–97

Year-end	*No. of companies listed*	*Market value (G billion)*
1993	541	449.4
1994	537	491.0
1995	532	571.0
1996	514	788.0
1997	663	1,071.2

Source: Amsterdam Exchanges.

B) Largest quoted companies

At the end of 1997, Royal Dutch accounted for 22% of total market capitalisation, and the combined market capitalisation of the five largest companies accounted for 49% of the total.

Exhibit 45.4:
THE 20 LARGEST LISTED COMPANIES ON THE AEX, END-1997

Ranking	*Company*	*Market value (G million)*
1	Royal Dutch	238,660
2	Unilever Cert	80,021
3	Dordtsche Petroleum Mij	80,021
4	ING Group Cert	71,510
5	ABN AMRO Holding	56,260
6	AEGON	52,603
7	Philips Electronics	42,155
8	KPN	39,951
9	Ahold	27,628
10	Akzo Nobel	24,923
11	Elsevier	21,859
12	Wolters-Kluwer	18,010
13	Heineken	17,711
14	PolyGram	17,460
15	Fortis AMEV NV	16,571
16	Baan Company	12,798
17	VNU	10,838
18	ASM Lithography	9,177
19	Vendex Int	8,613
20	Hagemeyer	8,347

Source: Amsterdam Exchanges.

C) Trading volume

The value of shares traded in 1997 grew by 73% to G1.10 trillion from G636 billion in 1996. In 1997, 6.43 billion shares were traded on the AEX.

Exhibit 45.5:
COUNTRY FUNDS – NETHERLANDS

Fund	US$ % change 31/12/96 31/12/97	31/12/92 31/12/97	Currency	Fund size (US$ mil)	Volatility	Manager name	Main sector	Class
BBL (L) Invest Equi-Fix Neth.1	29.1	N/A	G	26.92	N/A	BBL-Banque Brussels Lambert	Equity Fixed Term	Luxembourg
Pictet C.F. Nedval	23.21	N/A	G	28.83	4.52	Pictet and Cie	Equity	Luxembourg
Parvest Holland C	21.89	221.16	G	163.4	4.67	Banque Paribas	Equity	Luxembourg
Parvest Holland D	21.85	220.93	G	5.03	4.67	Banque Paribas	Equity	Luxembourg
KBP Security Click-Netherl 1	21.62	N/A	Bfr	36.36	3.84	Kredietbank	Equity Fixed Term	Belgian Trusts
EMIF Netherlands Index Plus B	21.54	188.25	G	124.42	4.72	CCF/BHF/HS/KB/BBV	Equity	Luxembourg
EMIF Netherlands Index Plus A	21.53	188.14	G	7.75	4.72	CCF/BHF/HS/KB/BBV	Equity	Luxembourg
BBL Invest Netherlands Cap	21.37	N/A	G	64.19	N/A	BBL-Banque Brussels Lambert	Equity	Belgian Trusts
UBS Eqty Inv Netherlands	20.49	199.55	G	128.59	N/A	UBS	Equity	Swiss Mutual Funds
ING Intl Dutch Equity Cap	20.29	N/A	G	42.71	N/A	ING Bank	Equity	Luxembourg
ING Intl Dutch Equity Dis	20.27	N/A	G	1.87	N/A	ING Bank	Equity	Luxembourg
MeesPierson UF Dutch Equity	20.2	N/A	G	4.35	N/A	MeesPierson Trust (Lux) SA	Equity	Luxembourg
SBC EP – Nethlands	19.76	N/A	G	245.58	4.36	SBC Mgt Co	Equity	Luxembourg
Cera Invest EOE Click1	19.37	N/A	G	27.76	N/A	Cera Bank	Equity Fixed Term	Luxembourg
Sivek Dutch Eq Index A Cap	18.97	N/A	G	97.65	N/A	Cera Bank	Equity	Belgian Trusts
G-Equity Fund G-Dutch Eq B	18.84	N/A	G	85.43	4.26	Generale de Banque	Equity	Luxembourg
G-Equity Fund G-Dutch Eq A	18.83	N/A	G	17.22	4.26	Generale de Banque	Equity	Luxembourg
Es-Invest Eq Netherlands C	18.39	N/A	G	77.38	N/A	ASLK-CGER Bank	Equity	Belgian Trusts
BIL Equities Pays-Bas D	18.21	N/A	G	108.67	4.43	BIL-Banque Internationale a Lux	Equity	Luxembourg
BIL Equities Pays-Bas C	18.2	N/A	G	115.1	4.43	BIL-Banque Internationale a Lux	Equity	Luxembourg
CU PP Dutch Growth	17.78	199.01	G	16.93	4.35	CU Privilege Portfolio	Equity	Luxembourg
Citi Dutch Equities	17.14	N/A	Bfr	25.16	N/A	Citibank Belgium	Equity	Belgian Trusts
CICM CB Netherlands Basket	16.55	167.96	G	68.91	4.07	CICM Fund Mgmt Ltd	Equity	Offshore Territories
Puilaetco Holland	16.3	N/A	G	2,094.60	N/A	Puilaetco	Equity	Belgian Trusts
CS EF (Lux) Netherlands	16.14	213.96	G	26.58	4.13	Credit Suisse AM Funds	Equity	Luxembourg
Wright Equi Netherlands	15.44	149.49	US$	15.1	3.64	Wright Equity Funds	Equity Growth	US Mutuals
Rabobank Holland Dutch EQ	14.11	N/A	G	33.61	N/A	Rabobank Asset Management	Equity	Luxembourg
Aetna MF Dutch Natl Equity	12.59	169.63	G	10.08	3.61	Aetna Master Fund	Equity	Luxembourg
KBP Security Click-Netherl 2	-3.18	N/A	Bfr	114.39	N/A	Kredietbank	Equity Fixed Term	Belgian Trusts
KBP Security Click-Netherl 3	-4.4	N/A	Bfr	10.2	N/A	Kredietbank	Equity Fixed Term	Belgian Trusts

Note: details for some funds may not have been included if the data for the US$ % change for 96/97 was not available

Source: Standard & Poor's Micropal.

TYPES OF SHARE

The majority of domestic shares in the Netherlands are bearer shares, while foreign equities are generally in registered form.

All types of equity may be traded on the Dutch market. The majority of shares are either ordinary or preferred, although convertibles, depository receipts, profit-sharing certificates and warrants exist as well.

In the Netherlands a share represents a relationship with the company, characterised as a "membership right" rather than as ownership. This relationship gives shareholders certain rights to influence the course of events within the corporation through the use of their voting rights.

Preferred shares entitle the holder to a preferred position in the distribution of corporate profits. Usually such shares carry a fixed distribution rate and are cumulatively preferred. Preferred shares may also be profit sharing so that, in addition to the amount of primary (preferred) dividend, they also share in the remaining profits available for distribution.

Holders of convertible bonds are entitled under the issue conditions to obtain one or more corporate shares by transferring the bond to the corporation. Until the date of conversion, the bondholder has a monetary claim against the corporation payable in accordance with its terms.

OTHER MARKETS

Stock exchange trading in shares may take place on the official market or the much smaller over-the-counter market for domestic unlisted securities. Financial futures, stock options and index options are traded on the AEX-Optiebeurs.

In February 1997 a new market (NMAX) was launched in Amsterdam for high-growth smaller companies. This will eventually be linked to similar markets in Paris, Brussels and Frankfurt to form a pan-European exchange called Euro NM. By January 1998, there were five companies listed on the NMAX.

OPERATIONS

A) Trading system

In September 1994 a new equity trading system was introduced, called Trading System Amsterdam (TSA). It comprises a retail and a wholesale segment. The retail segment is organised as a central market for transactions below the wholesale limit, and is managed by a single *hoekman* (or market-maker specialist) who is obliged to quote fixed bid and offer prices to banks and brokers. The wholesale segment is organised so that banks and brokers can trade directly with one another on screen via AIDA (the Automatic Interprofessional Dealing System Amsterdam), and can announce their bid and offer prices nationally and internationally via the Amsterdam advertisement screen called ASSET.

The quotation officer, an official of the AEX, supervises trading and the observance of trading rules, and may suspend or halt floor trading he deems it necessary.

Amsterdam Exchanges has recently decided to revise the TSA with the aim of strengthening the central market and especially its order-driven character. ASSET will be abolished and AIDA will be integrated in the Limit Order Book. Meanwhile, the privileges granted to *hoekmen* are under revision to ensure that these specialists only participate in trades when there is an actual need for their services.

B) List of principal brokers

ABN AMRO BANK
Foppingadreef 22, Amsterdam 1102 BS
Tel: (31) 20 628 9393

BANK LABOUCHERE
Keizersgracht 617, Amsterdam 1017 DS
Tel: (31) 20 520 9300

BARCLAYS DE ZOETE WEDD NEDERLAND
Weteringschans 109, Amsterdam 1017 SB
Tel: (31) 20 626 8630

CLN OYENS & VAN EEGHEN
Nachtwachtlaan 20, Amsterdam 1058 EA
Tel: (31) 20 514 6000

DEUTSCHE BANK – DE BARY
Herengracht 450, Amsterdam 1017 CA
Tel: (31) 20 555 4911

ING BANK
Foppingadreef 7, Amsterdam 1102 BD
Tel: (31) 20 563 9111

KEMPEN & CO
Herengracht 182, Amsterdam 1016 BR
Tel: (31) 20 557 1571

VAN MEER JAMES CAPEL
Herengracht 466, Amsterdam 1017 CA
Tel: (31) 20 550 2502

MEESPIERSON
Rokin 55, Amsterdam 1012 KK
Tel: (31) 20 521 1188

SMITH BARNEY (NETHERLANDS) INC.
World Trade Center, Schiphol Boulevard 193
1118 BG Schiphol Airport
Tel: (31) 20 316 0800; Fax: (31) 20 653 2662

C) Settlement and transfer

The settlement period for securities transactions is three trading days.

D) Commissions and other costs

Commission rates in the retail market range from 0.012% to 0.05% of the transaction value.

TAXATION AND REGULATIONS AFFECTING FOREIGN INVESTORS

Dividends paid to non-residents are subject to a 25% withholding tax. However, in most cases the rate will be reduced for residents of countries that have entered into a tax treaty with the Netherlands. Provided that a private shareholder does not own 5% or more of the share capital of a company, no capital gains tax will be levied in the Netherlands.

In general, there are no exchange control restrictions on the repatriation of capital and earnings.

Exhibit 45.6:
WITHHOLDING TAX

Recipient	*Dividends %*
Resident corporations	25 or Nil[1]
Resident individuals	25
Non-resident corporations and individuals:	
Non-treaty	
Portugal	25/Nil[2]
Other	25
Treaty	Nil–25[2]

Notes:

1. The nil withholding tax rate applies to payments to a resident corporation when its shareholding qualifies for the participation exemption and the shares form part of an enterprise carried on in the Netherlands.

2. Indicates member states of the EU. The EU Parent/Subsidiary Directive has applied since 1 January 1992. Under the Directive, dividends paid by a Dutch company (BV or NV) to a qualifying parent company resident in another EU member state must be exempted from Dutch withholding tax, provided certain conditions are met. The most important conditions in the Directive are as follows:

a. the EU parent company must have held at least 25% of the Dutch dividend-paying company's capital (or, in certain cases, voting rights) for a continuous period of at least one year prior to the distribution date; and

b. withholding tax exemption will apply only to dividends paid on shares held for at least one year prior to the date of payment.

There are other proposals that relax these holding period requirements significantly.

Source: Price Waterhouse.

REPORTING REQUIREMENTS

The Securities Charter (*Fondsenreglement*) of the AEX sets out reporting requirements. Companies with listed securities are under an obligation to make their annual report and accounts available to the public, and must publish half-yearly figures (in the case of listed shares). In addition, a company should inform the public immediately of any important changes in the way its securities are held or any events that may have a significant influence on the quoted price of its securities.

Half-yearly statements should consist of quantitative information concerning at least net sales and pre-tax or after-tax profits. In addition, a report should be included about the activities and results during the first six months of the fiscal year concerned. Both the quantitative information and the report should be submitted within four months of the end of the half-year period.

SHAREHOLDER PROTECTION CODES

A) Significant shareholdings

Under the Major Holdings Disclosure Act 1996, any person directly or indirectly acquiring or disposing of a capital interest or voting rights must give written notice of such acquisition or disposal if, as a result of such acquisition or disposal, the percentage of capital interest or voting rights they hold falls within another percentage range as compared with the percentage range prior to such acquisition or disposal. The ranges are 0–5%, 5–10%, 10–25%, 25–50%, 50–66.66% and over 66.66%. Notification must be given to the company and the Securities Board of the Netherlands, which will disclose the information to the public.

B) Takeovers and mergers

Public offers for shares traded either on the AEX or on the over-the-counter market are regulated by the Merger Code (*Fusiegedragsregels*). The Merger Code is quasi-legislation promulgated by the Social and Economic Council (SER), a public body consisting of representatives of the employers' organisations, representatives of the trade unions and independent experts appointed by the government.

The Merger Code aims to protect the interests of both shareholders and employees of companies involved in any merger or takeover. The protection of shareholders is effected through procedural rules that prescribe full disclosure of the offer, and regulate contesting the offer by transactions in shares and any trading by the company's directors and officers or their relatives. Also, the rules prescribe that all shareholders shall be treated equally and that the offeror shall not make a more advantageous offer within the next three years unless it obtains consent from the Merger Committee. The rules of the Merger Code set minimum requirements concerning the information to be presented to shareholders and employees and their representatives.

The Merger Code permits tender bids. In the offer document the bidder must state a recommended or base price per share and the total number of shares it is willing to purchase. A bidder may not, on completion of a tender bid, hold in excess of 30% of the target company's issued share capital. Provisions are also included covering partial bids at a fixed price for a maximum of 30% of the shares of the target company.

C) Insider trading

A legally backed Model Code, designed to combat insider trading, has been operating since 1987 and is expected to be fully revised in 1998. The code prohibits members of the board of a listed company from trading in securities issued by their company when they have knowledge of confidential information that could be expected to influence the quoted price of the securities. It also prevents them from disseminating such information or using it to encourage third parties to trade in the securities. It prohibits trading during periods preceding the publication of a prospectus or other relevant financial information or within six months of a previous sale or purchase.

The Act on Insider Trading defines the abuse of inside information as taking advantage of such information. The law penalises the offender with a maximum of two years imprisonment and/or a fine of G100,000 (or, for corporate entities, G1 million). The Act is not applicable to transactions in unlisted stocks, for which legal action may only be based on general legal principles. The major obstacle has been the difficulty in proving that the claimant(s) suffered damage. Amendments to the insider trading rules that would facilitate the prosecution of insider trading cases have been proposed and are expected to become effective in 1998.

If acting in good faith, a *hoekman* in possession of inside information may deal on behalf of his principals.

D) Compensation fund

There is a fund from which victims of fraud or default by a market broker or trader may be reimbursed.

RESEARCH

Research on the stock market and listed companies is supplied by the research departments of the securities divisions of the larger Dutch banks (such as MeesPierson, ABN AMRO and ING) and their subsidiaries. Among brokers, H. Wesselius and Kempen have a strong research reputation.

The *Officiele Prijscourant*, a daily publication issued by the AEX Committee, carries official announcements and all the official prices of traded securities. *Het Financieel Dagblad* is a newspaper published in Dutch with an English summary.

CHAPTER 46

New Zealand

Introduction

Equity capitalisation of the New Zealand Stock Exchange (NZSE) amounts to just over 53% of measured GDP. Of the six largest listed companies by market capitalisation, all except Telecom New Zealand derive a substantial proportion of their revenues from outside the country. Most of New Zealand's larger companies tend to be listed in Australia or elsewhere because this minimises monitoring and transaction costs for foreign investors. In general, it is the smaller corporations that are active in New Zealand's domestic markets. Paradoxically, there is virtually no listed exposure to the primary industries (other than forestry) in which New Zealand has a comparative advantage.

The New Zealand market is characterised by high levels of foreign ownership, with a little over 55% of the equity market and 60% of the bond market held by overseas investors. Futures and options are available but are very illiquid and thus not widely used. Disclosure requirements are not as tight as for many developed stock markets, but the overseas listings of a lot of New Zealand's larger companies has meant that they have had to comply with requirements in those jurisdictions.

Execution has been facilitated by the introduction of screen trading, and settlement systems are now up to international standards.

ECONOMIC AND POLITICAL OVERVIEW

New Zealand is governed by a National Party–NZ First Party coalition, formed in December 1996. At the end of 1997, Jenny Shipley became leader of the National Party and succeeded Jim Bolger as Prime Minister; the leader of the NZ First Party, Winston Peters, is her deputy. The coalition was the first government to be formed under the newly introduced proportional representation ("mixed member proportional", or MMP) electoral system, which is similar to that operating in Germany.

The centre-right coalition holds 61 seats – a majority of one in the 120-seat parliament. This majority is slim, but governments in New Zealand have typically run for the full three-year term. The next election is due in November 1999, but an earlier contest cannot be ruled out. The right-wing party, Act, has eight seats and is not part of the coalition, but it could play a critical role in maintaining the government in office.

The economy has been growing at about 2.5% annually for the past two years. Monetary and fiscal policy have been working against each other for about a year, with the net effect of steady growth. Although New Zealand's fiscal position remains very strong, with recorded operating surpluses over the past four years, those surpluses are diminishing, so fiscal policy is being eased via income tax cuts and increased government spending.

Against that stimulus, monetary policy remains very tight, with short-term interest rates closing 1997 at about 9%. However, on a monetary conditions index (which combines short-term interest rates and the trade-weighted exchange rate index), the monetary situation eased in 1997 due to a 10% fall in the trade-weighted exchange rate during the year.

Prospects for a boost to domestic demand around mid-1998 are good, fuelled by increased government spending, another round of tax cuts and windfalls from insurance companies. The weaker currency is good news for the export sector but New Zealand's exposure to Asian economies is high.

Inflation is close to the middle of the Reserve Bank's 0–3% target and will remain well under control given the current tight monetary regime.

The large current account deficit (6.4% of GDP in the year to September 1997) is worrying. In 1997 the trade surplus improved but the problem lies with the large investment income deficit, which reflects increasing

Exhibit 46.1: NEW ZEALAND SE CAPITAL 40 PRICE INDEX (NZ$), 1993–97

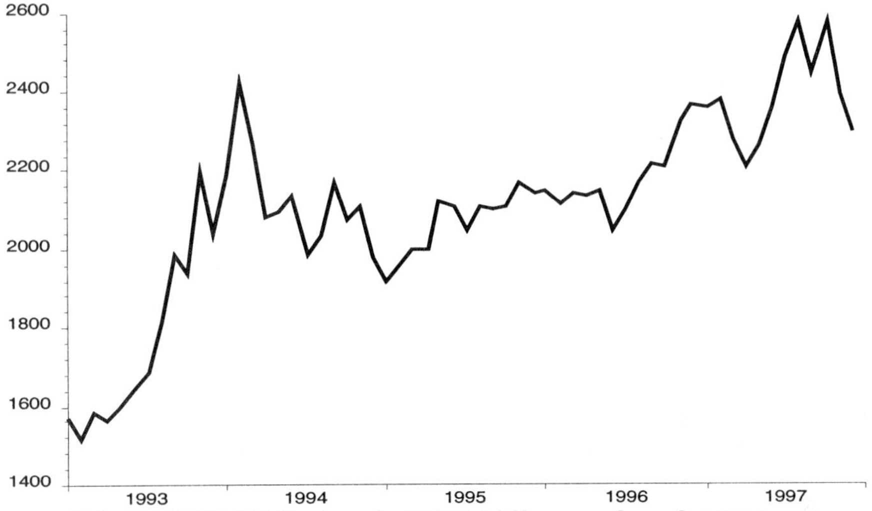

High value 2575.09 1.10.97 Low value 1513.33 1.2.93 *Source: Datastream*

foreign ownership of New Zealand-based assets and poor returns from New Zealand-owned operations offshore. There appears to be little relief in sight and the external deficit will remain uncomfortable for at least the next year or so.

Role of the central bank

The Reserve Bank of New Zealand is operationally independent of the government. Its duty is to formulate and implement monetary policy with the aim of achieving and maintaining price stability. To this end, the Minister of Finance and the Reserve Bank Governor establish and publish precise policy targets. Once a target is set, the central bank is free of government influence in implementing monetary policy in order to achieve the target.

From December 1996 monetary policy has been formulated with the sole objective of maintaining consumer price inflation within a target 0–3% band. Because New Zealand is an open economy, exchange rate movements play a significant role in containing inflation. However, the central bank claims not to intervene in the foreign exchange markets to influence the exchange rate and has not done so since the New Zealand dollar was floated. The bank does not directly set the level of interest rates.

MARKET PERFORMANCE

A) In 1997

New Zealand equities performed well until the mini-crash in October. Up to then, the focus for the market had been on an upswing in earnings as a result of the probable economic recovery and further easing of monetary policy. However, the developing crisis in Asia and investor nervousness had an adverse effect on the market. The focus switched to the impact of the crisis on New Zealand, given its large exposure to Asia, and GDP growth and earnings forecasts were revised downwards.

The NZSE40 Index finished the year down 1.89%. For overseas investors, returns were reduced by the weakness of the New Zealand dollar, which fell by about 17% against the US dollar.

B) Summary information

Global ranking by market value (US$ terms, end-1997): 37
Market capitalisation (end-1997): US$30.5 billion
Growth in market value (local currency terms, 1993–97): 14.7%
Market value as a % of nominal GDP (end-1997): 53%
Number of domestic/foreign companies listed (end-1997): 149/59
Market P/E (end-1997): 15.3
MSCI total returns (with net dividends, US$ terms, 1997): -14.1%
MSCI Index (change in US$ terms, 1997): -16.7%
Short-term (3-month) interest rate (end-1997): 8.9%
Long-term (10-year) bond yield (end-1997): 7.0%
Budget surplus as a % of nominal GDP (1997, forecast): 2.0%
Annual change in broad money (M3) supply (1997): 8.0%
Inflation rate (CPIX, 1997): 1.5%
US$ exchange rate (end-1997): NZ$1.72

C) Year-end share price index, price/earnings ratios and yields

Exhibit 46.2:
SHARE PRICE INDEX, AVERAGE P/E AND DIVIDEND YIELDS, 1993–97

Year-end	*NZSE40 Index*	*P/E*	*Yield (%)*
1993	2,188.07	16.8	4.4
1994	1,914.24	11.8	5.0
1995	2,149.82	11.8	4.8
1996	2,359.64	15.6	4.2
1997	2,314.91	15.3	4.8

Source: Credit Suisse First Boston.

D) Market indices and their constituents

The main public market index is the NZSE40, which is calculated by the exchange. The index covers 40 of the largest and most liquid listed stocks, weighted by the number of securities in issue. Membership of the NZSE 40 Index is reviewed quarterly.

The NZSE30 Selection Index covers the 30 largest and most liquid issuers with equity securities quoted on the NZSE. It is weighted by float capital, and membership is reviewed quarterly. The index has been recalculated back to 1 January 1991.

The NZSE10 Index reflects the movement of prices in selected securities of the top ten listed stocks that account for the majority of turnover on the NZSE. The index is updated on a real-time basis and quoted by all the major electronic media. The NZSE10 was established in 1988 with a base level of 1,000 and it underlies the NZSE10 Futures Contract administered by the New Zealand Futures and Options Exchange. In addition, a Smaller Companies Index (NZSE-CSI) was introduced in 1993.

The exchange also calculates capital, gross and sectoral indices.

THE STOCK MARKET

A) Brief history and structure

In 1915, the Stock Exchange Association of New Zealand, a loose-knit body of regional exchanges and forerunner to the present NZSE, was formed to bring about agreement on common rules. The NZSE today operates under the authority of the Sharebrokers Act Amendment 1981, which came into force in 1983.

During 1989, the exchange undertook a comprehensive review of its management structure and systems. From April 1989 a board of directors was appointed, the separate regional exchanges were abolished and the management of the trading floors became the responsibility of the board of the exchange.

Screen-based trading was introduced in June 1991 and the regional trading floors have now closed.

Membership of the NZSE can be on either an individual or a corporate basis. The rules governing brokers' relationships with each other and with the exchange are set out in the rules and regulations of the exchange. The NZSE is funded from annual fees and charges paid by its members, levies paid by listed public companies and charges for information supplied. Since 1985 the exchange has been a full member of the FIBV (the International Federation of Stock Exchanges) and since 1990 it has been a member of the East Asia & Oceanic Stock Exchange Federation.

B) Different exchanges

The NZSE is the only exchange in New Zealand. It operates its screen-based trading system and associated administrative functions from its offices located in Wellington.

C) Opening hours, names and addresses

Trading hours of the NZSE are 9.30am to 3.30pm, Monday to Friday, with a pre-opening session between 8.30am and 9.30am.

NEW ZEALAND STOCK EXCHANGE
9th Floor, ASB Bank Towers, 2 Hunter Street
PO Box 2959, Wellington
Tel: (64) 4 472 7599; Fax: (64) 4 473 1470
Web site: www.nzse.co.nz

MARKET SIZE

A) Number of listings and market value

NZSE equity market capitalisation at 31 December 1997 was NZ$52.54 billion, down NZ$2.14 billion (3.9%) on the end-1996 figure. There were a total of 224 companies listed – 143 domestic and 81 foreign.

Exhibit 46.3:
NUMBER OF COMPANIES LISTED AND MARKET VALUE, NSE, 1993–97

	No. of companies		*Market capitalisation*
Year-end	*Domestic*	*Foreign*	*(NZ$ million)*
1993	137	52	45,804.9
1994	149	59	42,360.0
1995	145	60	49,021.3
1996	136	65	54,684.6
1997	143	81	52,543.3

Source: New Zealand Stock Exchange.

Exhibit 46.4:
NZSE MARKET VALUE BY SECTOR, END-1997

Sector	*Market value (NZ$ million)*
Media and communications	17,953.30
Forestry	7,311.16
Energy processing distribution and utilities	5,967.27
Investment	3,970.14
Food and beverages	2,826.17
Transport	2,727.03
Property	2,572.31
Building materials and construction	1,800.11
Consumer	1,636.39
Agriculture and fishing	1,422.33
Ports	1,394.36
Leisure and tourism	950.15
Intermediate and durables	857.42
Finance and other services	635.82
Textiles and apparel	270.30
Mining	249.07
Total	**52,543.34**

Source: New Zealand Stock Exchange.

B) Largest quoted companies

Exhibit 46.5:
THE 20 LARGEST LISTED SHARE ISSUES, NZSE, END-1997

Ranking	*Company/issue*	*Market value (NZ$ million)*
1	Telecom Corporation of NZ (ord)	14,634.2
2	Carter Holt Harvey (ord)	4,601.9
3	Brierley Investments (ord)	3,295.4
4	Lion Nathan (ord)	2,114.0
5	Fletcher Challenge (Energy)	2,105.6
6	Fletcher Challenge (Paper)	1,536.8
7	Fletcher Challenge (Building)	1,226.5
8	Fletcher Challenge (Forests)	1,165.3
9	Independent Newspapers (ord)	1,109.7
10	Wilson & Horton (ord)	1,033.1
11	Air New Zealand B (ord)	958.2
12	Sky City (ord)	946.9
13	Power New Zealand (ord)	916.4
14	Ports of Aukland (ord)	841.4
15	Natural Gas Corporation	840.0
16	Tranz Rail Holdings (ord)	823.5
17	Air New Zealand A (ord)	676.4
18	Warehouse Group (ord)	658.4
19	Fernz Corporation (ord)	647.4
20	Fisher & Paykel Industries (ord)	646.5

Source: New Zealand Stock Exchange.

C) Trading volume

NZSE trading volume increased by 22.6% in 1997 to 6,989.9 million shares. The value of shares traded increased by 26.8% to NZ$16,376.5 million.

Exhibit 46.6:
TRADING VOLUME AND VALUE, NZSE, 1993–97

Year	*Volume (shares million)*	*Value (NZ$ million)*
1993	6,362.2	12,548.8
1994	5,615.4	11,852.8
1995	6,233.2	13,027.1
1996	5,702.2	12,910.0
1997	6,989.9	16,376.5

Source: New Zealand Stock Exchange.

Exhibit 46.7:
THE 20 MOST ACTIVELY TRADED SHARES, NZSE, 1997

Ranking	*Company/share*	*Turnover value (NZ$ million)*
1	Telecom Corporation of NZ	3,562.3
2	Fletcher Challenge (Energy)	1,169.3
3	Fletcher Challenge (Paper)	1,117.4
4	Lion Nathan (ord)	1,031.0
5	Carter Holt Harvey (ord)	1,030.7
6	Brierley Investments	1,004.9
7	Air New Zealand B (ord)	798.9
8	Fletcher Challenge (Forests)	633.4
9	Fletcher Challenge (Building)	608.4
10	Telstra Corporation (partly paid)	286.4
11	Deutsche Bank warrants on National Australia Bank	214.9
12	Air New Zealand A (ord)	209.2
13	Tranz Rail Holdings	207.3
14	Fernz Corporation (ord)	202.5
15	Fisher & Paykel Industries (ord)	176.7
16	Independent Newspapers (ord)	175.7
17	Restaurant Brands NZ (ord)	169.8
18	Sky City (ord)	165.1
19	Guinness Peat Group (ord)	164.2
20	Warehouse Group (ord)	160.8

Source: New Zealand Stock Exchange.

TYPES OF SHARE

Fully or partly paid ordinary, specified preference, redeemable specified preference and cumulative preference shares; rights; and equity warrants can be traded on the NZSE, along with convertible notes and company options. The most commonly traded shares are ordinary.

Convertible securities in New Zealand have a unique feature in that the fixed dividend is deductible by the

Exhibit 46.8:
COUNTRY FUNDS – NEW ZEALAND

Fund	US$ % change 31/12/96 31/12/97	31/12/92 31/12/97	Currency	Fund size (US$ mil)	Volatility	Manager name	Main sector	Class
Hansard EU JF New Zealand	-18.25	N/A	US$	N/A	N/A	Hansard Europe	Equity	Offshore Territories
JF New Zealand	-18.63	70.95	US$	3.9	4.23	JF	Equity	Offshore Territories
Hansard/JF New Zealand	-20.27	N/A	US$	0.2	4.52	Hansard/Jardine Fleming	Equity	Offshore Territories
Capstone Intl:New Zealand	-23.13	13.5	US$	5.7	4.23	Capstone Funds	Equity Growth	US Mutuals
New Zealand	-36.51	52.76	£	31.98	5.11	Exeter Asset Mgmt Ltd	Equity Growth	UK Investment Trusts

Note: details for some funds may not have been included if the data for the US$ % change for 96/97 was not available

Source: Standard & Poor's Micropal.

company for taxation purposes, unlike the dividend on ordinary shares.

Convertible notes are strictly debt securities that are convertible into ordinary shares. On conversion, these notes generally participate in bonus issues made during their lifetime.

Convertible preference shares generally carry a fixed dividend rate and the right to convert on a predetermined basis and on a fixed date to ordinary shares and, on conversion, to participate in bonus issues.

Options confer the right to subscribe for ordinary shares, usually at a fixed price and exercise date. In some cases, on conversion, the option holder will participate in bonus issues.

Equity warrants are long-dated institution-issued options over specific securities. The terms may vary from 15 months to five years. Each warrant constitutes a right to one share, unless the terms of the issue allow for adjustments at a contracted price after the initial issue. Warrants may be issued as either call warrants or put warrants. It is the originating institution that maintains the obligations attached to the warrant.

Transferable rights to subscribe to a new or existing security are also traded on the exchange.

OTHER MARKETS

Companies that cannot comply with all the listing requirements of the NZSE may be approved for admission as non-standard listings. Quotations of such companies are indicated with an "NS" tag.

OPERATIONS

A) Trading system

Trading on the NZSE takes place via a national automated, screen-based trading system, which allows brokers to enter bids and offers into a terminal at their individual offices. Bids and offers are captured on a time priority basis at each successive price level. The screen-based trading system is interfaced to the FASTER settlement system. Brokers may communicate inter-office and inter-broker via the screen trading system. All quotations are captured electronically and disseminated by broadcast signal to brokers and other media. The computer system provides a matched sale advice to each party. Matched trades generate automated trade reports at the end of each trading day. Sales data is also disseminated via the broadcast signal.

B) List of principal brokers

ANZ SECURITIES (NZ) LTD
PO Box 6243, Auckland
Tel: (64) 9 308 9867; Fax: (64) 9 309 9410

BT SECURITIES (NZ) LIMITED
PO Box 4145, Wellington
Tel: (64) 4 471 0470; Fax: (64) 471 0439

BZW NEW ZEALAND LTD
PO Box 3464, Auckland
Tel: (64) 9 358 7500; Fax: (64) 9 377 9797

CAVILL WHITE SECURITIES LTD
PO Box 4172, Auckland
Tel: (64) 9 377 1201; Fax: (64) 9 377 1975

COUNTY NATWEST SECURITIES NEW ZEALAND
PO Box 1821, Wellington
Tel: (64) 4 496 9100; Fax: (64) 4 499 9940

CREDIT SUISSE FIRST BOSTON
PO Box 3394, Wellington
Tel: (64) 4 474 4400; Fax: (64) 4 472 3764

MERRILL LYNCH (NEW ZEALAND) LTD
PO Box 817, Auckland
Tel: (64) 9 356 2929; Fax: (64) 9 356 2933

ORD MINNETT SECURITIES NZ LTD
PO Box 290, Wellington
Tel: (64) 4 495 0333; Fax: (64) 4 495 0347

SALOMON SMITH BARNEY NEW ZEALAND LIMITED
Trust Bank Centre, Level 20, 125 The Terrance
Wellington
Tel: (64) 4 496 9100; Fax: (64) 4 499 9940

SBC WARBURG NEW ZEALAND EQUITIES LTD
PO Box 45, Auckland
Tel: (64) 9 913 4800; Fax: (64) 9 913 4888

JB WERE & SON LTD
PO Box 887, Auckland
Tel: (64) 9 309 9800; Fax: (64) 9 309 9861

C) Settlement and transfer

A broker-to-broker accounting system (BBA) provides a centralised accounting and reporting system for all transactions between members, and allows them to monitor their day-to-day obligations to one another.

A fixed settlement period of T+5 applies to all trades of NZ$100,000 or more. Delivery at any time up to a maximum of five business days from the trade applies to all other trades. Notification fees for buy-ins are charged after T+8. The average delivery time for documents is currently 2.5 days.

An electronic registration system has been in operation since 1992. Known as FASTER, it allows for the electronic transfer of securities in the settlement of market transactions between brokers. In February 1997 the FASTER system was amended to enable market participants to settle using simultaneous, final and irrevocable delivery versus payment (SFI DVP), although they can still use the long-standing net cash DVP method should they choose.

D) Commissions and other costs

Commission rates are negotiable. There is currently no stamp duty payable in New Zealand on the transfer of debt or equity securities, and no security transfer tax is payable.

E) Custodian and nominee services

Nominee companies have been established by custodian banks and brokers to facilitate trading in registered securities and to provide custody services as legal owner, principally on behalf of foreign beneficial owners of securities.

TAXATION AND REGULATIONS AFFECTING FOREIGN INVESTORS

A) Non-resident withholding tax

Non-resident withholding tax (NRWT) is currently imposed on New Zealand dividends paid to non-resident shareholders at the rate of 30% of the amount of the dividend. Where the shareholder resides in a country with which New Zealand has a double tax treaty, a lesser rate (usually 15%) is applicable. Interest payments are also subject to NRWT at a rate of 15%, reduced to 10% by most double tax treaties. No NRWT is payable on interest to non-associated lenders where an "approved issuer levy" (of 2%) has been paid by the borrower. There is no formal capital gains tax.

New Zealand has agreements for the relief of double taxation on income with Australia, Belgium, Canada, China, Denmark, Fiji, Finland, France, Germany, India, Indonesia, Ireland, Italy, Japan, the Republic of Korea, Malaysia, the Netherlands, Norway, the Philippines, Singapore, Sweden, Switzerland, the UK and the US.

Dividends paid to New Zealand residents are subject to resident withholding tax (RWT) at the same rate as company tax (currently 33%). RWT also applies to interest payments at the current rate of 24% if the recipient's IRD number is supplied, or 33% otherwise.

Exhibit 46.9:
WITHHOLDING TAX

Recipient	*Dividends %*	*Interest %*
Resident corporations	33[1]	24[2]
Resident individuals	33[2]	24[2]
Non-resident corporations and individuals:		
Non-treaty	30	15[3]
Treaty	15/20	10/15[3]

Notes:

1. Domestic corporations receiving foreign source dividends and taxable bonus shares are required to deduct a withholding payment of 33% of the gross dividend. The amount of the withholding payment may be offset by foreign withholding taxes and tax paid under the "branch equivalent" regime.
2. Domestic withholding taxes apply to both interest and dividends. Unless the recipient holds an exemption certificate, the rate of the interest withholding tax is 24%. The rate of withholding tax on dividends paid to resident individuals is 33% reduced by the aggregate imputation and withholding payment credit attached to the dividend or taxable bonus share.
3. Net interest income is subject to reassessment at the branch tax rate where the payer and the recipient are "associated persons" but withholding tax is the minimum liability. Withholding tax is not imposed where the recipient of the interest has a fixed establishment in New Zealand.

Source: Price Waterhouse.

B) Investments by non-residents

As regards non-land transactions, generally all investments by overseas persons are permitted if they fall below a threshold of NZ$10 million.

The consent of the Treasurer is required for:

- investments resulting in 25% or more of the beneficial interest in specified securities or voting power being vested in overseas persons; and
- investments where the value of the business assets or expenditure incurred in establishing the business or consideration provided exceed NZ$10 million.

Certain land transactions by an overseas person require the consent of the Overseas Investment Commission.

C) Exchange controls

There are no exchange controls in New Zealand.

LISTING AND REPORTING REQUIREMENTS

A) Listing requirements

The Listing Rules of the NZSE contain the terms of a listing contract. Under this contract, companies wishing to have their securities traded through the exchange undertake to abide by the rules imposed in order to facilitate the efficient operation of the market in the interests of securities issuers, buyers, sellers and brokers.

B) Reporting requirements

The NZSE requires listed companies to supply all relevant information promptly to the exchange for immediate dissemination in order to inform both existing shareholders and prospective shareholders who may wish to trade on the market. Preliminary company announcements for the full and half year are required by the exchange within 75 days of the balance date, and annual audited accounts are required within four months of the balance date.

SHAREHOLDER PROTECTION CODES

The Market Surveillance Panel of the NZSE administers the application of the Listing Rules, aimed at ensuring that the conduct of issuers achieves the highest standards of integrity and that trading takes place in an efficient manner with fair information provided. The panel represents the interests of all market participants but is independent of any one sector group.

A) Securities Act provisions

The Securities Act 1978 requires all securities offerings to be accompanied by a registered prospectus containing the information and reports specified in the Securities Regulations 1983. Various exemption notices have been issued by the Securities Commission, the body which administers the Securities Act, the effect of these notices being to exempt companies whose securities are listed on an exchange in Australia, Hong Kong, the US or the UK from compliance with certain provisions of the Securities Act and Securities Regulations. It is necessary for the offering document and any material contracts referred to in that document to be filed with the Registrar of Companies in Wellington.

The Securities Amendment Act 1988 requires the holder of securities in a listed company, whether these securities are held beneficially or non-beneficially, to disclose its shareholding once it exceeds 5%, and to disclose all movements of more than 1% thereafter.

The Securities Amendment Act also regulates insider trading. Rights of action are given to persons who buy the securities of a public issuer from, or sell them to, persons with inside information about the public issuer. The Act is intended to be self-policing. The onus is on the public issuer, its members and the person trading with insiders to initiate legal action.

B) Takeovers

The NZSE has provided a takeover code in its Listing Rules covering the conduct of transactions that have the potential to change the control of a listed company. The exchange's code contains various provisions for shareholder protection, including notice periods, requirements for disclosure, restrictions on defensive tactics, and provisions for compulsory acquisitions.

C) Companies Act provisions

The Companies Act 1993 introduced substantial shareholder protection, including enhanced rights to information, derivative rights and a minority buy-out or appraisal right.

D) Financial reporting

The Financial Reporting Act 1993 established an Accounting Standards Review Board which has as its principal function the approval of accounting standards. Companies are required to prepare financial statements in accordance with standards set down by the Board and, to the extent that there is no applicable standard, in accordance with generally accepted accounting practice.

E) Compensation fund

The NZSE administers a Fidelity Guarantee Fund which was established to meet claims from people who have suffered monetary loss from a sharebroking transaction as a result of a member being unable to meet its financial obligations.

RESEARCH

The quality of stockbroker research is high. Most broking firms with corporate membership provide research on individual listed companies on a regular basis.

Banks operating in New Zealand do not generally provide research on listed companies, only research of an economic nature.

Datex Services Limited provides a similar service to UK Extel and Australian Stock Exchange Research services.

DATEX SERVICES LIMITED
PO Box 30-988, Lower Hutt, Wellington
Tel: (64) 4 5693 293; Fax: (64) 4 5697 997

NZSE publications

Fact Book – annual summary of year-end data
Supplement to Fact Book – summary of end-March data
Weekly Diary – weekly summary of all announcements, plus statistics
Monthly Turnover of Securities Report
Daily Memo – twice daily, contains all company announcements
Quarterly Report – summarises market performance
New Zealand Stock Exchange Rules
New Zealand Stock Exchange Listing Rules

Major newspapers

The New Zealand Herald (daily)
The Dominion (daily)
The Evening Post (daily)
The Christchurch Press (daily)
National Business Review (weekly)
Otago Daily Times (daily)
The Independent (weekly)
Southland Times (daily)

CHAPTER 47

Nigeria

Introduction

The Lagos Stock Exchange (LSE) was established in 1960. As at December 1997, the 264 quoted securities comprised 26 government stocks, 56 industrial loan stocks and 182 equities. Many of the companies listed are small and the largest 50 account for about 90% of market capitalisation.

Developments over the past few years include the opening of the stock market to foreign investors, the abolition of the Nigerian majority ownership requirement, deregulation of interest rates (which boosted the capital market) and the provision of infrastructure through the Petroleum Trust Fund. Both the level of foreign ownership in Nigerian companies and the flow of foreign capital into the country are now unrestricted.

ECONOMIC AND POLITICAL OVERVIEW

The Nigerian economy has considerable potential, thanks to its huge oil and gas reserves, solid mineral resources and responsive agricultural sector. Oil accounts for over 80% of government revenues and 95% of hard currency earnings.

Foreign debt owed to multilateral agencies and the Paris Club amounts to over US$30 billion. Nevertheless, the balance of payments position continues to be favourable, and foreign exchange reserves amounted to over US$7 billion at December 1997. The naira exchange rate strengthened in 1997, ending the year at N75 to the US dollar.

In 1998 the government plans to privatise the telecommunications and power sectors of the economy through a policy of guided deregulation.

The transition to democracy promised by the military administration appears to be on track, and a fully democratic government is expected to be in place by 1 October 1998.

MARKET PERFORMANCE

A) In 1997

It was not a particularly good year for industry, the economy or the stock market. The All Share Index fell by 7.9% during the course of 1997; having opened the year at 6,992.1, it closed at 6,440.5. The decline in equity market capitalisation, however, was less pronounced – it fell about 1.3% to end 1997 at N282 billion. Notable features of the year included a sharp decline in the price levels of the major oil marketing companies such as Unipetrol Nigeria, Total Nigeria and African Petroleum, and the prices of some of the major conglomerates also lost ground, including Lever Brothers Nigeria, PZ industries and Nestlé Nigeria.

B) Summary information

Global ranking by market value (US$ terms, end-1997): 55
Market capitalisation (end-1997): US$3.76 billion
Growth in market value (local currency terms, 1993–97): 584%
Market value as a % of nominal GDP (US$ terms, end-1997): 9%
Number of domestic/foreign companies listed (end-1997): 182/0
Market P/E (all listed companies, end-1997): 11.9
Short-term (3-month) interest rate (end-1997): 21%
Long-term (1 to 5-year) bond yield (end-1997): 15%
Budget deficit as % of GDP (1997): 0.2%
Annual increase in broad money (M3) supply (end-1997): 16.9%
Inflation rate (1997): 8%
US$ exchange rate (end-1997): N75

C) Year-end share price index and price/earnings ratios

Exhibit 47.1:
LSE INDEX (LOCAL CURRENCY TERMS), P/E AND DIVIDEND YIELDS, 1993–97

Year-end	*All Share Index*	*P/E*
1993	1,543.8	5.6
1994	2,205.0	5.5
1995	5,092.2	9.2
1996	6,992.1	11.2
1997	6,440.51	11.9

Source: Lagos Stock Exchange.

D) Market indices and their constituents

The Stock Exchange All Share Index was introduced in 1984 and covers all 182 listed equities.

THE STOCK MARKET

A) Brief history and structure

The Lagos Stock Exchange (LSE) was established in 1960 as a limited liability private company. It represented an attempt by the government to boost the capital market, finance growing budget deficits and mobilise finance from the savings sector of the economy. The LSE Act was passed in 1961, and prohibited all off-exchange stockbroking activities.

In 1977 the LSE was reorganised and renamed the Nigerian Stock Exchange, with trading floors in Lagos, Port Harcourt and Kaduna. In 1979 a Securities and Exchange Commission was established to regulate the market. It is responsible for the registration of all public offerings; determining the price, amount and timing of all new issues; ensuring fair and orderly market trading on the exchanges; and supervising the activities of brokers, underwriters and other market participants.

In 1997 the Nigerian Stock Exchange reverted to its original name of the Lagos Stock Exchange. The exchange currently has six trading floors – the original three, plus Kano, Onitsha and Ibadan. Lagos remains the head office of the exchange. The LSE is mainly financed by listing fees, and its council members are indemnified by the LSE for liability arising out of bona fide transactions by such council members.

A new exchange, the Abuja Stock Exchange located in the new federal capital, is expected to begin trading in mid-1998, and it is anticipated that it will handle the privatisation of utilities as announced by the government in the 1998 budget.

B) Different exchanges

There are six trading floors in Nigeria, located in Lagos, Kaduna, Port Harcourt, Kano, Onitsha and Ibadan.

C) Opening hours and address

Trading takes place every business day from 11.00am onwards.

LAGOS STOCK EXCHANGE
PO Box 2457, 2/4 Customs Street, Lagos
Tel: (234) 1 266 0287; Fax: (234) 1 266 8724
E-mail: nse@linkserve.com.ng

MARKET SIZE

A) Number of listings and market value

At the end of 1997 there were 182 companies listed on the LSE. Total market capitalisation was N282.0 billion, a decrease of 1.3% on the end-1996 figure.

Exhibit 47.2:
NUMBER OF COMPANIES LISTED AND TOTAL MARKET CAPITALISATION, LSE, 1993–97

Year-end	*No. of listed companies*	*Market value (N billion)*	*Market value (US$ billion)*
1993	174	41.2	1.03
1994	177	65.5	0.77
1995	181	71.1	1.74
1996	184	285.6	3.57
1997	182	282	3.76

Source: Lagos Stock Exchange.

B) Trading volume

The volume of shares traded in 1997 was 1,312.5 million shares, valued at N11,072.1 million (up 57% on 1996).

Exhibit 47.3:
TRADING VALUE OF SHARES, LSE, 1993–97

	1993	*1994*	*1995*	*1996*	*1997*
Naira (million)	662	986	1,839	7,058	11,072
US$ (million)	8.3	12.3	22.9	88.2	147.6

Source: Lagos Stock Exchange.

TYPES OF SHARE

There are two types of share on the LSE – ordinary shares and preference shares.

Ordinary shares have no special rights or restrictions attached to them, outside those contained in the Companies and Allied Matters Decree 1990. As in the UK, subject to the rights of other classes of shares, ordinary shares are unlimited in their rights to distributable profits.

Preference shares are also regulated by the Companies and Allied Matters Decree 1990, with special rights as to receipt of dividends in priority to ordinary shares. These rights may be cumulative or non-cumulative. The creation of non-voting preference shares is prohibited.

OTHER MARKETS

Nigeria's second market, called the Second-tier Securities Market (SSM), was launched in April 1985. Its purpose is to encourage speculation in the market, as well as patronage of the equities market by wholly-owned Nigerian companies. The SSM is officially regulated by the Nigerian SEC, in addition to LSE supervision.

The SSM, which is included in the daily official list of the LSE, is subject to normal dealing rules. However, it has less restrictive listing requirements.

There are plans to introduce an over-the-counter (OTC) market where unquoted shares and certain long-term securities can be traded.

OPERATIONS

A) Trading system

The trading system in the equities market is run by stockbrokers and dealers who act as both brokers and market-makers. A call-over system fixes the prices of equities once each day, with members gathering to bid for and offer securities. There is insufficient volume at the moment to create a continuous market.

Brokers have the exclusive licence for brokerage operations, while only merchant banks are allowed to underwrite corporate shares and bonds.

An automated trading system is due to be installed by the second half of 1998, and this is expected to increase market volume and liquidity.

B) List of principal brokers

CSL STOCKBROKERS
Primrose Towers, 17A Tinubu Street, Lagos
Tel: (234) 1 266 5944; Fax: (234) 1 266 5126

ICON STOCKBROKERS
63/71 Broad Street, Lagos
Tel: (234) 1 266 2607; Tlx: 21437

NIGERIAN STOCKBROKERS
Nal Towers, 12th floor
Marina 20, PO Box 4591, Lagos
Tel: (234) 1 264 6837; 263 5539; 260 0420

SECURITIES TRANSACTIONS & TRUST CO
Foreshore Towers, 2A Osborne Road
PO Box 51045, Falomo, Ikoyi, Lagos
Tel: (234) 1 269 3826; Fax: (234) 1 689 038

TRW STOCKBROKERS
47 Cambell Street, Lagos
Tel: (234) 1 264 5363

C) Settlement and transfer

In 1997, an automated clearing, settlement and delivery systems known as the Central Security Clearing System (CSCS) was introduced. A settlement timetable of T+5 was adopted in accordance with international settlement standards for emerging markets. The CSCS also acts as a custodian agency for local and foreign securities.

D) Commissions and other costs

Subject to a minimum commission of N50, brokerage commission chargeable on purchases or sales of equities is between 1% and 2.75% of market value, depending on transaction size.

TAXATION AND REGULATIONS AFFECTING FOREIGN INVESTORS

Withholding tax on rents, dividends, interest and directors' fees remains at 10%. Withholding tax is levied at an equal rate on all shareholders, whether corporate or individual, resident or non-resident. All deductions, computations, payments and receipts of income tax and withholding tax must be in the currency in which the income was received.

Capital gains tax was reduced from 20% to 10% from 1 January 1997.

LISTING AND REPORTING REQUIREMENTS

A) Listing requirements

On the LSE main market a five-year trading record is required for listing, but applicants need only have a three-year record in order to join the SSM.

B) Reporting requirements

LSE reporting requirements are contained in the listing requirements set out in the *Green Book* issued in 1992. Companies listed on the exchange must notify the LSE of:

1) proposed distributions of dividends, changes in capital structure or any moves that could affect the price of the company's shares on the markets;
2) proposed changes in the character or nature of the business of the company or of the group, or any change in voting control or beneficial ownership of securities carrying voting control;
3) the date and time when the board of directors is to meet to discuss dividends (14 days in advance);
4) any proposed alteration to the memorandum or articles of association of the company; or
5) any changes in the directorship of the company.

Listed companies are also required to notify the LSE of any intention to take over other companies or plans to acquire other businesses or parts of other businesses; to furnish the exchange with such information as it requires; and to issue a circular to members of the company according to LSE specifications.

In addition, companies must notify the LSE (immediately after the relevant board meeting) of:

1) intentions to make a drawing or redemption of any securities, disclosing at the same time the date of the

drawing and, in the case of registered securities, the period of closure of the transfer books (or the date of striking the balance) for the drawing;

2) the amount of the security outstanding after any purchase or drawing has been made;
3) preliminary profits for any year, half year or quarter, and comparative figures in respect of profits before taxation and after taxation, even if this calls for qualification that such figures are provisional or subject to audit; or
4) any dividends and other distributions to members recommended or declared to be paid, including approval for the payment of dividends, interest, rights or scrip issues.

SHAREHOLDER PROTECTION CODES

As soon as a shareholding of an individual or corporate body in a quoted company reaches 5% of the equity capital, the beneficial owner must notify the exchange.

There is no code of practice governing takeovers and mergers. Instead, the principal legislation is the Companies and Allied Matters Decree 1990, which stipulates that minority dissenting shareholders must be provided for in a takeover/merger scheme.

To protect minority rights further, the sanction of the Federal High Court is required, as well as the approval of the NEPB and SEC. Takeovers and mergers have to take place by way of a scheme or contract, involving an offer and acceptance, put before the shareholders of both companies and sanctioned by the court.

The SEC is expected, in its overall supervisory role, to deal with insider trading under its umbrella powers of market surveillance, and particularly under its specific power of "protecting the integrity of the securities market from any abuses arising from the practice of insider trading". However, because this power is not yet clearly defined, the SEC's powers have not been employed.

Under the SEC Act 1979, directors cannot deal in the shares of their own company if this would distort the market in a fraudulent manner or constitute insider dealing.

There is no stock exchange compensation fund. However, the LSE has rules that it enforces against dealer members responsible for investor losses as a result of default or fraud. Members are requested to provide security in cash, in stocks or by mortgage. This Members Securities Fund, according to the articles of the LSE, can be retained by the LSE Council, called-in or enforced. All market dealers must be registered with the SEC.

RESEARCH

Information on the market can be obtained from the LSE, the SEC, merchant banks and major stockbrokers – in particular, Icon Stockbrokers Ltd and Nigerian Stockbrokers Ltd. The LSE publishes a *Daily Official List* which provides information on exchange transactions. The LSE's code on the Reuters network is NSXA-B.

African Equities: A Guide to Markets and Companies, published by Euromoney Books, provides in-depth information for those wishing to invest or do business in Africa. See the order card at the back of this book for details.

CHAPTER

48

Norway

Introduction

A strong international market and excellent economic prospects helped boost the Norwegian equity market in 1997. Equity turnover rose 47%, market capitalisation increased by 37% and the All Share Index ended the year 31.5% ahead. New issue volume totalled Nkr21 billion, up by 132% compared with 1996.

At the end of 1997, foreign investors' holdings represented 31.1% of the Norwegian stock market, down from 33.6% the year before.

ECONOMIC AND POLITICAL OVERVIEW

Norway is a constitutional monarchy and the minority coalition government is led by Prime Minister Kjell Magne Bondevik. The next national elections are due in September 2001.

The economic recovery that began in 1993 still continues, with Norway showing the strongest economic growth in the Nordic region. GDP growth (4.2% in 1997) is expected to remain at a healthy 3.9% in 1998, fuelled by strong growth in the oil industry. Unemployment declined from 3.6% in 1996 to 2.6% at year-end 1997. Inflation is expected to remain at 2.3% throughout 1998.

Role of the central bank

Norges Bank is operationally independent, though it responds to guidelines set by the Treasury. Operating within these guidelines, the central bank is in charge of implementing monetary policy and it also intervenes in the foreign exchange market. Its other responsibilities include supervising the banking sector and other financial institutions, and preparing, with the Ministry of Finance, monetary, financial and exchange statistical data.

MARKET PERFORMANCE

A) In 1997

The market capitalisation of listed companies on the Oslo Stock Exchange (OSE) at the end of 1997 was Nkr556 billion, an increase of 37.2% on the year-end 1996 figure. There were a net 45 new listings during the year, bringing the total number of listed companies to 217, and the value of new issues increased by 132% to Nkr20.9 billion. Turnover in 1997 totalled Nkr341.1 billion, up 47.3% on 1996, and the turnover ratio was 68.7%. The All Share Index rose 31.5% in 1997, closing at 1,273.6. For the second year in a row, the financial sector was the best performing sector, and the Finance Index rose by 53.8%.

B) Summary information

Global ranking by market value (US$ terms, end-1996): 25
Market capitalisation (end-1997): US$75.54 billion
Growth in market value (local currency terms, 1993–97): 170%
Market value as a % of nominal GNP (end-1997): 52%
Number of domestic/foreign companies listed (end-1997): 196/21
Market P/E (end-1997): 14.3
MSCI total returns (with net dividends, US$ terms, 1997): 6.2%
MSCI Index (change in US$ terms, 1997): +4.8%
Short-term (3-month) interest rate (end-1997): 3.85%
Long-term (10-year) bond yield (end-1997): 5.49%
Budget surplus as a % of nominal GDP (1997): 7.3%
Annual increase in broad money supply (M2, end-1997): 6.3%
Inflation rate (1997): 2.3%
US$ exchange rate (end-1997): Nkr7.36

C) Year-end share price index, price/earnings ratios and yields

Exhibit 48.1:
YEAR-END SHARE PRICE INDEX (NKR TERMS), OSE P/E AND DIVIDEND YIELDS, 1993–97

Year-end	*All Share Index*	*P/E*	*Yield (%)*
1993	613.08	42.8	1.3
1994	656.78	17.1	1.6
1995	732.96	13.1	2.5

Exhibit 48.2: OSLO SE GENERAL PRICE INDEX (Nkr), 1993–97

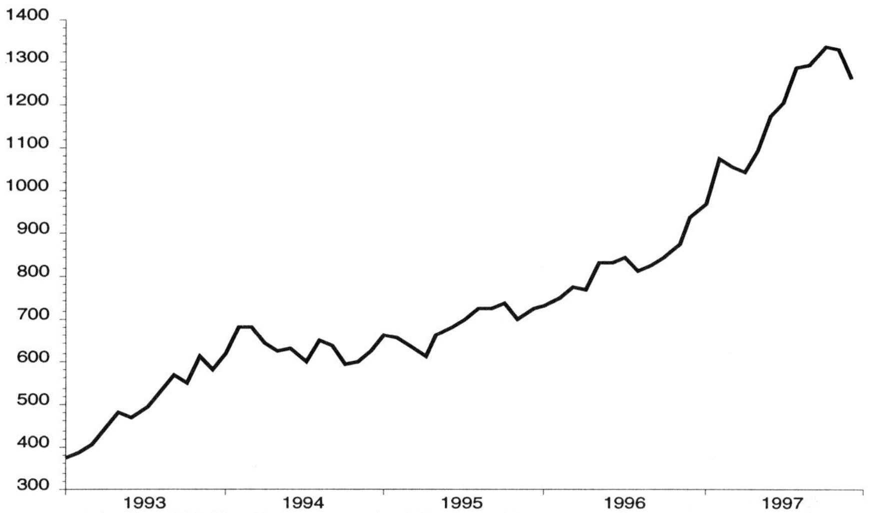

High value 1338.40 1.10.97 Low value 372.12 1.1.93 *Source: Datastream*

Exhibit 48.1 continued

1996	968.37	13.3	2.1
1997	1,273.61	14.3	2.0

Sources: Oslo Stock Exchange and Alfred Berg.

D) Market indices and their constituents

The All Share Index comprises all listed stocks and has a base of 100 as at 1 January 1983.

THE STOCK MARKET

A) Brief history and structure

The OSE was founded in 1819 and operated solely as a foreign exchange market until commodities trading was introduced in 1850. The market for share and bond trading did not begin until 1881. Foreign exchange trading continued at the stock exchange until 1988, when the Norwegian central bank assumed responsibility for this activity. Today the OSE comprises an equity, bond and derivatives market.

The OSE is a non-profit institution, financed through fees from listed companies and broker members. The exchange is supervised by the Norwegian Ministry of Finance, but governed by the Stock Exchange Council (made up of 21–25 members appointed by the Crown). The Council appoints the board of directors (5–7 members), which in turn appoints the president and vice-president of the exchange. Although the president oversees the day-to-day business of the OSE, all major decisions are made by the board of directors.

The OSE is regulated by the Oslo Stock Exchange Regulations, laid down by the Ministry of Finance. The regulations, which were implemented on 17 January 1994, have been revised in connection with the European Economic Area agreement, and harmonised with those that apply in other major European markets.

B) Different exchanges

Norway's three stock exchanges (Bergen, Trondheim and Oslo) formally merged on 1 January 1991. From this date, the exchanges in Bergen and Trondheim became branches of the OSE.

C) Opening hours, names and addresses

For stocks and options, pre-trading begins at 9.30am, while continuous trading starts at 10.00am and closes at 5.00pm. Odd lot matching takes place between 5.00pm and 5.30pm.

OSLO BØRS
PO Box 460, Sentrum, 0105 Oslo 1
Tel: (47) 234 1700; Fax: (47) 241 6590; Tlx: 77242

BERGEN BRANCH
Olav Kyrresgt 11, 5000 Bergen
Tel: (47) 5532 3050; Fax: (47) 5531 0397

TRONDHEIM BRANCH
Dronningens gt 12, 7011 Trondheim
Tel: (47) 7388 3115; Fax: (47) 7353 4565

MARKET SIZE

A) Number of listings and market value

At the end of 1997, total market capitalisation stood at Nkr556 billion, up 37.2% on end-1996. The market capitalisation of domestic companies was Nkr490.3 billion, up 33.7% on the end-1996 total.

Exhibit 48.3:
NUMBER OF COMPANIES LISTED AND MARKET VALUE, OSE, 1993–97

Year-end	*Number of companies listed*	*Market capitalisation (Nkr million)*
1993	131	205,844
1994	146	246,622
1995	165	292,322
1996	172	405,284
1997	217	556,001

Source: Oslo Stock Exchange.

Exhibit 48.4:
MARKET VALUE BY SECTOR, END-1997

Sector	*Market value (Nkr billion)*
Domestic companies	490.3
Foreign companies	65.7
Total	**556.0**
Banks	48.5
Insurance	15.5
Industry	337.1
Shipping	99.4
Medium-sized company market (SMB)	41.2
Primary capital certificates	14.3
Total	**556.0**

Source: Oslo Stock Exchange.

B) Largest quoted companies

Norsk Hydro continues to dominate the list of the largest quoted companies. At the end of 1997 it accounted for 16.8% of total domestic market capitalisation.

Exhibit 48.5:
THE 20 LARGEST DOMESTIC COMPANIES ON THE OSE, END-1997

Ranking	*Company*	*Market value (Nkr million)*
1	Norsk Hydro	82,352
2	Orkla	30,726
3	Den norske Bank	22,289

Exhibit 48.6 continued

4	Saga Petroleum	16,893
5	Petrol. Geo-Serv	16,703
6	Chr. Bank & Kr.	16,424
7	Kværner	16,058
8	Storebrand	15,465
9	Bergesen d.y.	13,114
10	Aker RGI	9,989
11	Aker Maritime	8,905
12	Fred. Ol. Energy	8,874
13	Schibsted	8,760
14	NetCom	8,441
15	Norske Skog	8,045
16	Spb NOR	6,810
17	Tomra Systems	6,647
18	Smedvig	6,402
19	Rieber & Søn	5,649
20	NCL Holding	5,477

Source: Oslo Stock Exchange.

C) Trading volume

Turnover in 1997 totalled Nkr341.1 billion, 47.3% higher than 1996's total.

Exhibit 48.6:
EQUITY TURNOVER, 1993–97

Year	*Turnover (Nkr million)*
1993	125,508
1994	124,449
1995	156,744
1996	231,651
1997	341,121

Source: Oslo Stock Exchange.

Exhibit 48.7:
THE 20 MOST ACTIVELY TRADED SHARES ON THE OSE, 1997

Ranking	*Company*	*Trading value (Nkr million)*
1	Norsk Hydro	25,440
2	Nycomed A	17,352
3	Kværner A	12,323
4	Nycomed B	12,014
5	Orkla A	11,081
6	Storebrand ord.	10,456
7	Fokus Bank	10,168
8	Den norske Bank	9,609
9	Petroleum Geo-Services	8,026
10	NCL Holding	7,445
11	Saga Petroleum A	7,330

Exhibit 48.7 continued

12	Nera	6,202
13	Chr. Bank og Kreditkasse	6,177
14	Elkem	5,907
15	Awilco B	5,600
16	Bergesen d.y. A	4,678
17	Norske Skog A	4,274
18	Sævik Supply	4,159
19	ASK	3,976
20	Aker RGI A	3,953

Source: Oslo Stock Exchange.

TYPES OF SHARE

Under Norwegian law, shares can be issued only in registered form. The name and address of the beneficial owner of the shares must be registered on the company's books. Until then, shareholders cannot exercise voting rights or receive dividends. Companies cannot purchase their own shares.

As a result of the European Economic Area agreement, the rules restricting foreigners from acquiring more than one-third of the voting share capital in a Norwegian company (40% for shipping companies) are no longer applicable. In practice, this means that restricted shares have been abolished and all shares are now unrestricted.

Primary capital certificates issued by 12 Norwegian savings banks are listed on the OSE. The certificates are similar to shares in that they carry an entitlement to dividends. However, the dividend is not calculated based on the bank's entire profit, but on a part equivalent to the ratio of primary capital to equity. Holders of primary capital certificates have the same voting rights as people with savings accounts at the bank.

Listed companies may also issue convertible shares, convertible bonds and warrants.

OTHER MARKETS

The OSE list is divided in two sections – the main list and the SMB list (for smaller and medium-sized companies). The OSE is also the centre for options trading in Norway.

INVESTORS

Foreigners own about 31% of market capitalisation (down from 34% in 1996), while private individuals have reduced their holdings from about 20% to less than 10%. As at end-1997, the government and municipalities held around 15% of market capitalisation.

OPERATIONS

A) Trading system

A new automated trading system that will enable brokers to trade from remote locations is due to become operative early in 1998. At present brokers require an office at the exchange.

B) List of principal brokers

ALFRED BERG NORGE A/S
Stortorvet 10, 6 e.t.g, PO Box 483, Sentrum, 0105 Oslo
Tel: (47) 2200 5000; Fax: (47) 2241 7480

CHRISTIANIA BANK
Middelthunsgt 17, PO Box 1166, Sentrum, 0107 Oslo
Tel: (47) 2248 5000; Fax: (47) 2256 8650

DEN NORSKE BANK ASA
Stranden 21, Postboks 1171, Sentrum, 0107 Oslo
Tel: (47) 2248 1050; Fax: (47) 2248 2983

FONDSFINANS
Haakon VII's gt 2, PO Box 1782, Vika, 0122 Oslo
Tel: (47) 2311 3000; Fax: (47) 2311 3003

EXHIBIT 48.8:
COUNTRY FUNDS – NORWAY

Fund	*US$ % change 31/12/96 31/12/97*	*US$ % change 31/12/92 31/12/97*	*Currency*	*Fund size (US$ mil)*	*Volatility*	*Manager name*	*Main sector*	*Class*
Balzac Norway Index	N/A	N/A	Nkr	0.53	N/A	State Street Bq	Equity	French FCPs
Frontrunner Norway Eq NOK	N/A	N/A	Nkr	2.83	N/A	Frontrunner	Equity	Luxembourg
SK Olnor Vesta Green	N/A	N/A	Nkr	N/A	N/A	Unknown Sector Name SKOLNO.OS	Equity	Offshore Territories

Note: details for some funds may not have been included if the data for the US$ % change for 96/97 was not available

Source: Standard & Poor's Micropal.

HANDELSBANKEN MARKETS
Radhusgt 27, PO Box 1342 Vika, 0113 Oslo
Tel: (47) 2294 0900; Fax: (47) 2233 6915

SAGA SECURITIES
Munkedamsvn 45
PO Box 1770, Vika, 0122 Oslo
Tel: (47) 2201 0000; Fax: (47) 2283 0122

SUNDAL COLLIER
Munkedamsvn 45, PO Box 1444, Vika, 0115 Oslo
Tel: (47) 2201 6000; Fax: (47) 2201 6060

A. SUNDVALL AS
Grev Wedels Plass 9, PO Box 657, Sentrum, 0106 Oslo
Tel: (47) 2242 1084; Fax: (47) 2233 7027

C) Settlement and transfer

Settlement takes place at a maximum of T+3 based on payment against delivery.

D) Commissions and other costs

Transaction costs are not fixed, although the typical range for commission fees is 0.3–0.5% of bargain value.

TAXATION AND REGULATIONS AFFECTING FOREIGN INVESTORS

During 1996 and 1997 the regulations governing the Norwegian securities market were revised, primarily to incorporate the principles of the European Economic Area agreement. The most visible change has been the abolition of most restrictions on foreign ownership of Norwegian equities. Foreigners were previously only allowed to purchase one-third of the voting share capital in a Norwegian company (40% in the case of shipping companies), but these restrictions have been removed. However, restrictions remain as regards acquisitions of Norwegian companies. Governmental approval is required to buy more than one-third of the voting share capital where the target company has turnover in excess of Nkr50 million, or employs more than 50 people, or has received state aid of Nkr5 million for at least one specific research and development project in the past eight years.

A) Dividends

Dividends paid to non-resident shareholders in Norwegian companies are subject to a withholding tax of 25%. This rate may be reduced under the terms of a tax treaty between Norway and the shareholder's country of residence.

Exhibit 48.9:
WITHHOLDING TAX

Recipient	*Dividends %* *Regular rate*	*Parent/subsidiary*
Non-treaty	25	25
Treaty	Nil–25	Nil–25

Source: Price Waterhouse.

B) Capital gains

There is a capital gains tax of 28% on the sale of shares. Tax treaties vary in their application of this tax to non-residents.

C) Exchange controls

Almost all exchange controls were abolished in 1990.

D) Non-resident bank accounts

Non-residents are free to open accounts at Norwegian banks, and transfers to or from such accounts are unrestricted. Interest accrued on a bank account can be paid to a non-resident without the deduction of withholding taxes.

LISTING AND REPORTING REQUIREMENTS

A) Prospectus requirements

A prospectus must be prepared for public offerings directed at more than 50 persons, and worth more than Ecu40,000.

B) Listing requirements

To be listed on the main list, a company must have been in operation for at least three years and have an estimated quoted value of at least Nkr10 million. If the company's quoted value cannot be determined, its share capital according to the latest balance must be at least Nkr10 million. The board of the OSE can allow a company that has been in operation for less than three years to be listed if it believes that this is in the interests of both investors and the general public.

There must be at least 500 shareholders, each holding at least one trading block. One trading block on the main list is the number of shares making up a market capitalisation value of approximately Nkr10,000.

To be quoted on the SMB list a company must meet more or less the same requirements as for the main list, except that a share capital of Nkr8 million is sufficient, and smaller companies may be listed if the OSE board believes there will be a market for the shares. To be listed on the SMB the company must have at least 100 shareholders, each holding one trading block.

Companies seeking a listing on the OSE must also sign a listing agreement with the exchange.

C) Reporting requirements

Annual and semi-annual financial statements must be submitted to the exchange, which must further be advised of any tender offer, bid or merger proposals from listed companies, capital increases or decreases or changes to the articles of incorporation. The exchange may fine, suspend or delist a company found to be in breach of its reporting requirements or the Stock Exchange Act.

Any other information likely to materially influence the share price must be submitted immediately to the OSE. Enforcement authority is given to the government Banking Insurance and Securities Commission (BISC) and failure to comply is punishable by law.

Listed companies have a duty to inform the OSE (before or, at the latest, at the same time as the information is released to third parties) of all reports and information sent to shareholders or of any other information that is relevant to the correct pricing of, and the conduct of a fair and orderly market in, their shares. Should a company fail to fulfil these obligations, it may be fined.

Companies must provide the stock exchange with a list of names of the board members, members of the control committee, auditors and others who are obliged to notify the OSE of their trading in the company shares (see "Insider trading" below). Also, companies must provide the stock exchange with a list of people who receive secret information that might have an influence on the price of their shares.

SHAREHOLDER PROTECTION CODES

A) Significant shareholdings

There are rules requiring OSE notification if any shareholder (or group of shareholders acting in concert) acquires more than 10% of the share capital or voting rights of a listed company. Similar notification has to be given if any shareholder acquires 20%, 33.3%, 50%, 66.6% or 90%.

B) Takeovers and mergers

A purchaser acquiring 40% or more of the voting capital in a company must offer to buy the remaining shares in the company. The offer price shall be at least as good as the highest price paid by the purchaser in the six-month period before it reached the 40% limit.

C) Insider trading

Insider trading (and incitement to it) is prohibited and punishable under the Securities Trading Act. Before directors, members of the board (including co-opted members and observers), members of the control committee, and high level executives of a company trade in its securities, they are under a duty to investigate (in order to satisfy themselves) that they do not possess secret information that might have an influence on the company's share price. If they do possess such information they are prohibited from dealing. These rules also apply to the company's auditor.

Directors, members of the board (including co-opted members and observers), members of the control committee, auditors and high level executives are required under the Securities Trading Act to report their trading in the company's securities to the OSE. These same people are not allowed to trade in the company's securities in the two months prior to the issue of the annual report and one month prior to the release of quarterly reports, and they must give to the OSE a list of names of people to whom they are closely related and companies in which they have a dominant position, to the extent that these people and companies have interests in the company's shares.

D) Compensation fund

Stockbrokers are legally required to carry insurance for compensation claims or to provide security for any liability they may incur.

RESEARCH

The best research on the Norwegian stock market is provided by the large Norwegian banks, such as Den norske Bank and Sparebanken NOR (Union Bank of Norway), along with stockbrokers such as Alfred Berg and Saga Securities. Statistical information on market performance is also available through the OSE, which has a web site at www.ose.no.

FUTURE DEVELOPMENTS

The committee working on proposals for a new Stock Exchange Act is expected to present its recommendations during 1998.

CHAPTER

49

Oman

Introduction

In 1997, the opening up of the economy, the granting of permission for foreigners to invest in the capital market and the relaxation of the taxation laws all helped to fuel a spectacular boom on the Muscat Securities Market (MSM). The MSM was one of the best-performing exchanges in the world in 1997, and ranked among the top three emerging markets. The uncertainties of the Asian currency crisis had little impact, primarily due to the stable economic environment in Oman. The market closed the year with the MSM Composite Index at an all-time high and investor sentiment remaining buoyant. Market capitalisation, which stood at 25% of GDP in 1995 and 28% in 1996, rose to an estimated 54% of GDP in 1997.

ECONOMIC AND POLITICAL OVERVIEW

Oman occupies an area of 30,000 square kilometres in the south-eastern part of the Arabian Peninsula. Its neighbours are Yemen in the south-west, Saudi Arabia in the west and the United Arab Emirates in the north. Relations between these countries have always been cordial and any disputes have been settled peacefully at the negotiating table.

On 23 July 1970, His Majesty Sultan Qaboos bin Said succeeded his father as the Sultan of Oman, and since this date the country has been socially and politically stable.

In an effort to sustain historic economic growth levels, the government has embarked on a comprehensive 25-year plan leading up to the year 2020. This is aimed at the diversification of national sources of income away from dependence on oil, and has so far reduced oil's share of GDP to about 41%. As part of its plans to attract foreign investment and technology, the government reformed the tax laws in 1996 and established the Omani Centre for Investment Promotion and Export Development.

GDP growth was an estimated 5.1% in 1997. Inflation is under control and has been growing at less than 1% per annum over the past five years. The Omani rial is pegged to the US dollar.

Role of the central bank

The Central Bank of Oman (CBO) was established by the government in 1974 to regulate banks and companies operating in the financial sector.

The central bank licenses commercial banks, specifies capital adequacy standards (12% by end-1998) and specifies cash reserve and lending ratio requirements. It also imposes an upper limit (currently 20% of the bank's net worth) on investments made by commercial banks in government bonds.

The central bank manages Oman's foreign exchange reserves and is also responsible for issuing government bonds.

MARKET PERFORMANCE

A) In 1997

The MSM Index soared by 141% in 1997, from 199.36 to 480.58. All the sectoral sub-indices rose, with banking/investment companies and insurance firms performing best with growth of 223%. Market capitalisation increased by 170% from US$3.23 billion at end-1996 to US$8.73 billion at end-1997, while trading volume jumped six-fold from US$695 million in 1996 to US$4,188 million in 1997.

The banking and investment sector remained the most heavily capitalised at 56.3% of overall market capitalisation. There were 36 primary market issues in 1997 (compared to 27 in 1996) raising US$955.4 million (US$331.9 million in 1996). Foreign investments in the market stand at about 11.7% of market capitalisation.

B) Summary information

Global ranking by market value (US$ terms, end-1997): 50
Market capitalisation (end-1997): US$8.73 billion
Growth in market value (local currency terms, 1993–97): 442%
Market value as a % of nominal GDP (end-1997): 54%
Number of domestic/foreign companies listed (end-1997): 119/1
Market P/E (all listed companies, end-1997): 25.5

Short-term (up to 1 year) interest rates (end-1997): 8.193%
Long-term (above 1 year) interest rates (end-1997): 10.856%
Budget deficit as a % of nominal GDP (1997): 4.2%
Annual increase in M2 money supply (end-1997): 24%
Inflation rate (end-1997): 0.2%
US$ exchange rate (end-1997): OR0.385

C) Year-end share price index

Exhibit 49.1:
MSM SHARE PRICE INDEX, 1993–97

Year-end	*MSM Index*
1993	113.71
1994	146.16
1995	158.13
1996	199.36
1997	480.58

Source: Muscat Securities Market.

D) Market indices and their constituents

The MSM Index is calculated by dividing the aggregate current market value of selected listed companies by the aggregate base market value (at July 1990 prices) multiplied by 100. Share turnover is used as the basis for selecting companies for inclusion. Sectoral indices are also calculated covering industrials, banking and investment, insurance and services.

THE STOCK MARKET

A) Brief history and structure

The Muscat Securities Market (MSM) was established by Royal Decree 53/88 (the MSM Law) and share trading started in May 1989. The exchange provides a mechanism for the transfer of shares in all joint stock companies established in Oman, whether public or private. An agreement was signed in 1996 providing for cross-listings between Muscat, Bahrain and Kuwait.

For foreign investors, the MSM is one of the most accessible of the Arab markets. There are no taxes on dividends or capital gains, there are no restrictions on foreign investors repatriating their profits, and the Omani currency is freely convertible.

Membership of the MSM is compulsory for:

(i) the central bank, and banks and other financial institutions licensed by the central bank;
(ii) companies with shares listed on the MSM;
(iii) intermediaries authorised under the MSM Law; and
(iv) public authorities with MSM-registered stocks.

The board of directors of the MSM comprises the chairman (the Minister of Commerce and Industry) and the executive president, as well as one representative from the Ministry of Finance, one from the Central Bank of Oman and four others nominated by the Chamber of Commerce and Industry.

At present, the MSM acts as regulator, runs the exchange, and administers a computerised transfer department, but there are plans for these functions to be separated. The MSM will become a private sector institution and a Securities and Exchange Commission will take over regulation, while settlement and depository functions will be spun off to a publicly listed depository.

B) Opening hours, names and addresses

The MSM is open from Saturday to Wednesday. The regular market trades from 10.00am to 11.00am and the parallel market from 11.30am to 12.30pm.

MUSCAT SECURITIES MARKET
PO Box 3265, Ruwi, Postal Code 112
Tel: (968) 702 607; Fax: (968) 702 691

MARKET SIZE

A) Number of listings and market value

The number of domestic companies listed on the MSM has risen from 77 in 1989 to 119 in 1997. Market capitalisation rose by 170% during 1997, from OR1.2 billion to OR3.4 billion.

Exhibit 49.2:
NUMBER AND VALUE OF ISSUES ON THE PRIMARY MARKET, 1993–97

Year	*Number of issues*	*Value (OR million)*
1993	10	40.0
1994	24	107.2
1995	24	47.2
1996	27	127.8
1997	36	367.5

Source: Muscat Securities Market.

Exhibit 49.3:
MARKET CAPITALISATION BY SECTOR, END-1997

Sector	*Market share (%)*
Banking and investment	56.3
Industry	14.5
Services	11.3
Insurance	3.7
Other	14.2

Source: Muscat Securities Market.

Exhibit 49.4:
MARKET CAPITALISATION, MSM, 1993–97

Year-end	*Market capitalisation (OR million)*
1993	620.2
1994	843.1
1995	938.1
1996	1,244.7
1997	3,361.5

Source: Al Ahlia Portfolio Securities Co.

B) Largest quoted companies

Exhibit 49.5:
THE 20 LARGEST LISTED COMPANIES ON THE MSM, END-1997

Ranking	*Company*	*Market value (OR million)*
1	Oman International Bank	277.7
2	National Bank of Oman	180.0
3	Bank Muscat Al Alhi Al Omani	170.6
4	Al Ahlia Portfolio Co	144.9
5	Commercial Bank of Oman	138.2
6	Oman National Holding Co	134.3
7	Oman Cement Co	108.5
8	Ominvest	108.2
9	Dhofar International Development	106.1
10	Oman Flour Mills	90.6
11	Bank of Oman, Bahrain and Kuwait	67.7
12	Oman and Emirates Investment (Oman)	61.1
13	Oman Investment and Finance Co	56.1
14	Raysut Cement Co	40.5
15	Financial Services	38.8
16	Gulf Investment Services	36.0
17	Oman Aviation Services	35.3
18	Oman United Holding Co	34.2
19	Transgulf Indus Inv Co	33.2
20	Dhofar Insurance Co	32.3

Source: Muscat Securities Market.

C) Trading volume

Exhibit 49.6:
TURNOVER ON THE MSM, 1993–97

Year	*Turnover (OR million)*
1993	83.5
1994	126.2
1995	109.2
1996	267.7
1997	1,612.6

Source: Muscat Securities Market.

Exhibit 49.7:
THE 20 MOST ACTIVELY TRADED MSM STOCKS, 1997

Ranking	*Company*	*Turnover (OR million)*
1	Oman International Bank	128.4
2	Al Ahlia Portfolio Services	122.8
3	Dhofar Int'l Development	113.8
4	Oman National Holding Co	108.4
5	National Bank of Oman	107.9
6	Ominvest	94.3
7	Commercial Bank of Oman	88.0
8	Bank Muscat At Ahli Al Omani	74.2
9	Oman & Emirates Investment (Oman)	57.7
10	Bank of Oman, Bahrain & Kuwait	40.3
11	Gulf Investment Services	38.3
12	Oman Securities Portfolio	37.9
13	Oman Savings & Finance Bank	36.0
14	Oryx Joint Investment Fund	27.7
15	Alliance Housing Bank	26.3
16	Oman United Insurance Co	21.7
17	Muscat Insurance Co	21.2
18	Al Anwar Ind & Trading Co	21.1
19	Renaissance Services	18.2
20	Majan Joint Inv Account	18.1

Source: Muscat Securities Market.

TYPES OF SHARE

Both equity and preference shares may be listed on the MSM.

OTHER MARKETS

Equity trading on the MSM takes place on three levels – the regular market, the parallel market and the third market.

The regular market is for established companies with a history of profitability and liquidity. The parallel market is for new companies or for companies that no longer meet the requirements for a full listing on the regular market. The third market is comparatively small and is used for trading shares of privately held joint stock companies.

INVESTORS

Foreign investors owned 11.7% of equity market capitalisation as at end-1997.

OPERATIONS

A) Trading system

In addition to the computerised market network running the depository and transfer system, the trading floor has an electronic trading board where share prices are displayed following each transaction.

Screen-based trading is scheduled to be introduced in 1998. The system will support remote orders, immediate verification of share ownership and on-line cross-listing with other exchanges.

B) List of principal brokers

There are 14 licensed brokerage companies operating on the MSM. Foreign brokerage companies are not allowed to operate on the MSM. The main brokers are as follows:

AL AHLIA PORTFOLIO SECURITIES
PO Box 2232, Postal Code 112
Tel: (968) 771 1325; Fax: (968)790 754

AL SHALMAN SECURITIES
PO Box 577, Postal Code 114
Tel: (968) 771 2713; Fax: (968) 797 331

GULF INVESTMENT SERVICES
PO Box 974, Ruwi, Postal Code 112
Tel: (968) 787 711; Fax: (968) 783 703

NATIONAL BANK OF OMAN
PO Box 751, Ruwi, Postal Code 112
Tel: (968) 787 493; Fax: (968) 787 490

OMAN & EMIRATES INVESTMENT HOLDING CO
PO Box 2205, Postal Code 113
Tel: (968) 796 946; Fax: (968) 797 764

OMAN SECURITIES PORTFOLIO CO
PO Box 3591, Postal Code 112
Tel: (968) 771 2723; Fax: (968) 771 0842

C) Settlement and transfer

Transfer contracts are audited and matched at T+1. On T+3 contracts are registered in the company's books at the MSM depository department. Settlements are confirmed to brokers at T+4.

The MSM depository department is automated and serves as the centre for registration, transfer and settlement functions. A specialist consultancy firm has been commissioned to introduce an electronic system integrating trading, settlement and depository functions in order to ensure that the MSM meets G30 and IOSCO standards.

D) Commissions and other costs

Normal transactions attract brokerage commission at OR7.5 per OR1,000. For orders valued at more than OR100,000, brokerage commission is OR5 per OR1,000. Generally there are no other client costs.

TAXATION AND REGULATIONS AFFECTING FOREIGN INVESTORS

Foreign individuals or organisations wishing to set up a business in Oman require a licence, but no permission is required for foreigners who wish to invest in the shares of listed companies or investment funds (provided this is permitted by the company's articles of association).

A) Taxation

Tax in Oman is governed by the Company Income Tax Law issued under Royal Decree No. 47/81 and various other Royal Decrees and Ministerial Decisions. Tax in Oman is referred to as income tax but relates only to businesses; there is no private direct taxation. Tax is charged on the profits of businesses which have no "permanent establishment" in Oman and the rate varies according to the level of foreign ownership.

A new withholding tax was introduced in Oman during late 1996. The rate of withholding is 10% and applies to royalties, management fees and other similar payments made by Omani businesses that have no permanent establishment in Oman. The withholding tax does not apply to profits (whether capital or income) realised by overseas investors trading through the MSM.

There is no capital gains tax as such but capital gains are treated as part of regular income and taxed under the income tax laws. As a result of Royal Decree 77/89, taxation is not applied to any distribution of profits received by an establishment or company in respect of its shares in the capital of another company provided taxation has already been paid by the distributor. Accordingly, there is no double taxation on distributions of dividends in Oman so long as the distributor has paid its assessed income tax.

Oman does not have a comprehensive system of double taxation treaties (although some are now in place) but deductions in respect of taxes paid in other jurisdictions may be allowed in individual cases. A number of double taxation treaties are under consideration, including one with the UK.

B) Exchange controls

There are no relevant exchange controls currently imposed by the Omani government.

LISTING AND REPORTING REQUIREMENTS

A) Listing requirements

Companies listed on the regular market must fulfil the following terms and conditions:

1. The company shall be an Omani joint stock company.

2. The subscribed capital of the company shall not be less than OR500,000.
3. The company must have been trading for at least one year.
4. The company should have earned a net profit from its business for at least one complete fiscal year prior to its listing.
5. There must be at least 50 shareholders and there must be at least 20 small shareholders who each own between one and 2,000 shares. The percentage of ownership of these small shareholders shall not be less than 5% of the total subscribed shares.
6. At least 2% of the company's shares shall have been circulated for at least one year on the parallel market prior to an application for listing on the regular market.
7. The company shall submit comprehensive financial statements indicating its financial position fairly and clearly for the period immediately prior to the date of the listing application.
8. The company shall publish its final accounts and balance sheet in two daily newspapers if a period of six-months has elapsed since the publication of the last balance sheet and final accounts.
9. At its own discretion, and in certain circumstances, the MSM board of directors may exempt any company from the above terms in the public interest.

New companies, or those that no longer satisfy the conditions for a listing on the regular market, are listed on the parallel market. New companies seeking to join the parallel market must meet the following conditions:

1. The company shall be newly established and should have completed the requirements of its incorporation as a legal entity.
2. The newly established company shall submit a listing application and the following supporting documents: its articles of incorporation and articles of association; a certificate of registration from the relevant authorities; a list of the names of its directors; a sample stock certificate; and a list of people authorised to sign for the company and their specimen signatures.

In relation to offers of securities (whether for public or private subscription) a prospectus must be prepared and approved by the MSM. There is a general requirement to include in any prospectus all information that may assist an investor in making an investment decision, including, but not limited to, such statements of information as the MSM considers necessary.

B) Reporting requirements

Companies are required to submit to the MSM and publish audited financial statements. Quarterly statements must also be submitted and published, but these need not be audited.

There is also an ongoing requirement for companies to notify the MSM of any important information that may affect the market pricing of a company's stock and the MSM is entitled to publish such information, or may require that the company publish it.

Penalties for non-disclosure range from warnings and fines to imprisonment.

SHAREHOLDER PROTECTION CODES

The Commercial Companies Law, No. 4, 1974, establishes the legal framework for all joint stock companies listed in Oman. The law defines the respective rights and responsibilities of companies' shareholders and boards of directors. It expressly forbids insider trading and price manipulation, while giving the company, shareholders and third parties the right to recover damages against directors if the latter are responsible for fraud, negligence or other legal violations.

The MSM Law and Executive Regulations establish the legal framework for the MSM, including the rights and responsibilities of members, listed companies, intermediaries, investors and the MSM. The disciplinary committee of the MSM has broad powers to investigate and settle cases of violation. Insider trading, price manipulation and rumour-spreading are expressly prohibited. In cases of insider trading or manipulation, the affected contracts may be cancelled by the MSM.

Investors have the right to seek recovery of damages through the MSM or through the courts.

RESEARCH

The Research and Studies Department of the MSM publishes a monthly statistical bulletin containing data about the market and listed companies, and also an annual guide providing more in-depth information about MSM-listed companies. Information on daily trading and share prices is fed into the Reuters network.

PROSPECTIVE CHANGES

The current functions of the MSM are to be divided between a restructured MSM, a Securities and Exchange Commission and a central depository which, like the new MSM, will be a private sector institution. It is anticipated that interim regulations will be issued in 1998 prior to more comprehensive legislation.

CHAPTER

50

Pakistan

Introduction

Pakistan has three exchanges – in Karachi, Lahore and Islamabad. Trading on the Karachi Stock Exchange (KSE) is dominant, accounting for approximately 80% of equity transactions in Pakistan. At the end of 1997 there were 781 companies listed on the KSE, and market capitalisation stood at Rs524.1 billion (US$11.9 billion).

During the past five years, Pakistan's economic reform process has opened up the KSE to foreign investors. They are now, for the most part, free to purchase any share with no limit on ownership, and to repatriate capital and profits in full. To increase market transparency, computerised trading has been installed and a central depository system has been established.

ECONOMIC AND POLITICAL OVERVIEW

Despite the constant threat of Pakistan defaulting on loan repayments, political turmoil and the deteriorating situation as regards law and order, the Pakistani market continued its upward trend in 1997, with minor corrections. Enthusiasm among investors was boosted after the victory of the Pakistan Muslim League with a massive mandate in the general election.

Pakistan's economic performance remained depressed. GDP growth decreased from 6.1% in 1995–96 to 3.1% in 1996–97. Most sectors reflected this trend, with agriculture, for example, growing by just 0.7%, compared with 5.27% in the preceding year. The rate of inflation, as measured by the Consumer Price Index, rose to 11.37% from 10.8% in 1995–96, while the budget deficit amounted to 6.2% of GDP in 1996–97. During 1997, the Pakistani rupee depreciated by 9.8% against the US dollar.

Role of the central bank

The State Bank of Pakistan conducts its business through two main branches – the issue department and the banking department. Together these undertake most of the standard functions carried out by a central bank, such as banknote issuance, banking services for the government and foreign exchange control. The bank works with the government to maintain monetary stability. It also has an important regulatory role, controlling scheduled banks' activities and approving bank licences.

The State Bank is a tool of government rather than an independent formulator of policy.

MARKET PERFORMANCE

A) In 1997

The KSE-100 Index rose by almost 31% during the year, but overall market capitalisation increased by a more modest 11.1% from Rs471.7 billion to Rs524.1 billion. In US dollar terms market value remained more or less unchanged at US$11.9 billion, due to depreciation of the rupee.

B) Summary information

Global ranking by market value (US$ terms, end-1997): 48
Market capitalisation (end-1997): US$11.9 billion
Growth in market value (local currency terms, 1993–97): 37.8%
Market value as a % of nominal GDP (end-1997): 19.6%
Number of domestic/foreign companies listed (end-1997): 781/0
Market P/E (KSE-100 Index companies, end-1997): 12.86
MSCI Index (change in US$ terms, 1997): +24.2%
Short-term (3-month) interest rate (end-1997): 13.75%
Long-term (10-year) bond yield (end-1997): 15%
Budget deficit as a % of nominal GDP (end-1997): 6.2%
Annual increase in broad money (M2) supply (June 1997): 14%
Inflation rate (1997):11.37%
US$ exchange rate (end-1997): Rs44.05

Exhibit 50.1: KARACHI STOCK EXCHANGE PRICE INDEX (US$), 1993–97

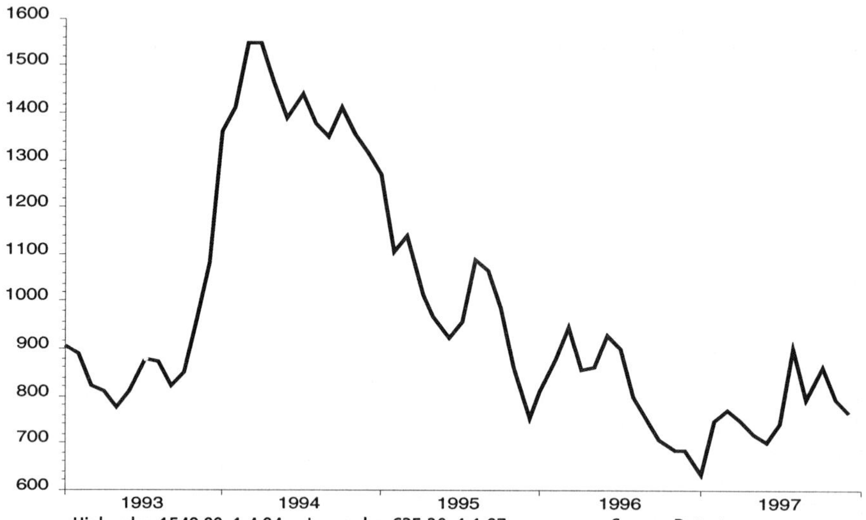

High value 1548.99 1.4.94 Low value 635.20 1.1.97 *Source: Datastream*

C) Year-end share index,P/E and average gross yields

Exhibit 50.2:
YEAR-END SHARE PRICE INDEX (RS TERMS), P/E RATIOS AND GROSS DIVIDEND YIELDS, 1993–97

Year-end	*SBP General Index*	*KSE-100 Index*	*KSE-100 P/E*	*KSE-100 Yield (%)*
1993	234.16	2,164.0	N/A	N/A
1994	232.47	2,049.0	15.0	5.3
1995	190.14	1,498.0	10.8	2.8
1996	136.55	1,340.0	9.7	2.1
1997	137.60	1,753.8	12.9	3.9

Sources: Karachi Stock Exchange and Kausar Abbas Bhayani.

D) Market indices and their constituents

The KSE-100 Index (launched in November 1991) is the most widely followed measure of stock market performance in Pakistan. The KSE-100 is a capital-weighted index and its composition is regularly reviewed and revised.

On 29 August 1995 the KSE All Share Index was introduced, providing, among other things, a basis for index trading.

The State Bank of Pakistan (SBP) General Index was launched in 1980–81and was rebased at June 1992 = 100.

THE STOCK MARKET

A) Brief history and structure

The KSE was set up in September 1947 and registered as a company limited by guarantee in March 1949. In 1954 the Dacca Stock Exchange was established in what was then Eastern Pakistan (now Bangladesh). Just before the 1971-72 war with India began, an exchange started operations in Lahore.

In the 1970s under the nationalisation programme of Zufilkar Ali Bhutto, Pakistan's first elected Premier, market activity declined almost to nothing. However, in 1985, the government decided to introduce incentives designed to boost trading, such as making dealing tax-free and reducing taxes on listed companies. Since then, trading has risen substantially, and a large part of it is attributable to foreign investors.

Membership of the KSE is of two types – active and non-active. Only active members are permitted to trade in the trading hall of the exchange and to appoint authorised agents to act on their behalf. Foreign brokers are not allowed to trade on the exchange.

The management of the KSE is vested in the president and the governing board of directors. The president is elected directly by the general body of members, along with 14 other directors.

B) Different exchanges

There are three stock exchanges in Pakistan, in Karachi,

Islamabad and Lahore. The KSE is the biggest, accounting for over 80% of securities traded.

C) Opening hours, names and addresses

The KSE is open from Monday to Friday. The first trading session, during which trading is conducted both by open outcry and electronically (through KATS), is from 10.00am to 1.00pm. The second session, which is KATS only, takes place from 2.30pm to 5.00pm

THE KARACHI STOCK EXCHANGE
Stock Exchange Building, Stock Exchange Road, Karachi
Tel: (92) 21 242 5502/3/4/8; Fax: (92) 21 241 0825
Web site: www.kse.org

THE LAHORE STOCK EXCHANGE
19 Khayaban-e-Iqbal, Egerton Road, Lahore
Tel: (92) 42 636 8111/8555

THE ISLAMABAD STOCK EXCHANGE
Anees Plaza, Fazal-ul-Haq Road, Islamabad
Tel: (92) 51 216 040/41

MARKET SIZE

A) Number of listings and market value

At the end of 1997 there were 781 companies listed on the KSE with a combined market value of Rs524.1 billion (up 11.1% on end-1996).

Exhibit 50.3:
NUMBER OF COMPANIES LISTED AND KSE MARKET VALUE, 1993–97

Year-end	*No. of companies listed*	*Market value (Rs million)*
1993	653	380,443.2
1994	724	397,778.3
1995	764	326,691.0
1996	782	471,665.5
1997	781	524,149.0

Sources: Karachi Stock Exchange and Kausar Abbas Bhayani.

Exhibit 50.4:
MARKET VALUE BY SECTOR ON THE KSE, END-1997

Sector	*Market value (Rs million)*
Transport and communication	168,519
Fuel and energy	146,803
Chemical and pharmaceutical	71,427
Investment companies/securities/banks	26,300
Food and allied industries	23,133
Textile spinning	11,614
Synthetic and rayon	11,363
Insurance companies	7,286
Textile composite	7,149
Auto and allied engineering	6,245
Mutual funds	4,644
Leasing companies	4,490
Sugar and allied industries	4,487
Miscellaneous	3,942
Paper and board	3,384
Modarabas	3,172
Cables and electrical goods	2,297
Tobacco	1,937
Engineering	1,443
Leather and tanneries	1,307
Textile weaving	1,053
Glass and ceramics	804
Woolen	423
Vanaspati and allied industries	290
Jute	246
Construction	36
Total	**524,149**

Exhibit 50.4 continued

Sources: Karachi Stock Exchange and Kausar Abbas Bhayani.

B) Largest listed companies

The combined market capitalisation of the 20 largest companies at the end of 1997 was Rs375.96 billion, representing 71.7% of the market total.

Exhibit 50.5:
THE 20 LARGEST LISTED COMPANIES, KSE, END-1997

Ranking	*Company*	*Market value (Rs billion)*
1	PTC	164,735.10
2	Hub Power Company	66,304.95
3	Pakistan State Oil Company Limited	30,977.07
4	Fauji Fertilizer Company Limited	22,620.77
5	ICI Pakistan Limited	15,269.69
6	Engro Chemical Pakistan Limited	10,000.64
7	Sui Southern Gas Company Limited	9,889.38
8	Sui Northern Gas Pipelines Limited	7,677.57
9	Muslim Commercial Bank Limited	7,191.14
10	Shell Pak	6,574.84
11	FFC Jordan	6,167.79
12	Karachi Electric Supply Corporation Limited	4,242.26
13	Nestlé Milkpak Limited	3,470.24
14	Dawood Hercules Chemical Limited	3,419.40
15	Dewan Salman Fibre Limited	3,268.28
16	Pakistan Oilfields Limited	3,042.00
17	Faysal Bank Limited	2,897.95
18	BOC Pakistan Limited (formerly Pakistan Oxygen)	2,757.89
19	Askari Commercial Bank Limited	2,747.34
20	Adamjee Insurance Company Limited	2,702.94

Source: Karachi Stock Exchange.

C) Trading volume

Daily volume averaged 55.19 million shares in 1997, an 87.7% increase on 1996's 29.4 million.

Exhibit 50.6:
THE MOST ACTIVELY TRADED SHARES, KSE, 1997

Ranking	*Company*	*Volume (shares million)*
1	Hub Power	3,621.97
2	Pakistan Telecommunication Co	3,531.74
3	ICI Pak	2,716.80
4	Dewan Salman Fibre	674.83
5	FFC Jordan	671.15
6	Japan Power	256.07
7	Dhan Fibre	188.53
8	Southern Electric	133.00
9	Sui Northern Gas Co	105.94
10	Karachi Electric	95.41
11	Fauji Cement	76.38
12	Sui Southern Gas Co	68.46
13	DG Khan Cement	64.56
14	Schon Bank	58.76
15	Muslim Commercial Bank	48.87
16	Fauji Fertilizer	46.13
17	Bank of Punjab	43.10
18	Faysal Bank	36.68
19	Banker Equity	31.14
20	Nishat Mills	30.67

Source: Karachi Stock Exchange.

TYPES OF SHARE

Sections 90 and 91 of the Companies Ordinance 1984 provide that a limited company shall issue only fully paid-up ordinary shares. It is no longer permitted to issue partly paid shares or preference shares, but it is possible to issue shares of different classes whereby voting rights vary proportionately to the paid-up value of the shares. Subject to compliance with the requirements of the Ordinance, a company may issue shares at a premium or at a discount.

INVESTORS

An estimated 70% of shares are owned by private investors, with the balance held by institutional investors. There are fewer than 700,000 investors, and some of the large listed companies have less than 250 shareholders.

Mutual funds play an important role in the securities market. The largest fund is National Investment Trust, followed by The Investment Corporation of Pakistan (ICP), which was originally constituted as a national equity market support mechanism to stabilise the stock market via counter-cyclical action.

OPERATIONS

A) Trading system

Trading on the KSE takes place through open outcry and via the Karachi Automated Trading System (KATS). Of the 781 listed companies, 774 are traded through KATS and the remaining 7 stocks (the most actively traded) are dealt in under the open outcry system. The minimum lot size is 500 for shares having a market value of less than Rs50, and this minimum reduces to 100 where the share value exceeds Rs50.

B) List of principal brokers

JAHANGIR SIDDIQUI & CO LTD
14th Floor, Chapal Plaza,
Hourat Mahani Road, Karachi
Tel: (92) 21 243 1181; Fax: (92) 21 243 1178

Exhibit 50.7:
COUNTRY FUNDS – PAKISTAN

Fund	*US$ % change 01/01/97 01/01/98*	*01/01/93 01/01/98*	*Fund base currency*	*Fund size (US$ mil)*	*Fund volatility*	*Management group*	*Opal main sector*	*Opal subsector*
Paribas EM Pakistan Ptfl	30.84	N/A	US$	N/A	11.461	Paribas Asset	Open-End	Equity
Pakistan Investment Fund Inc	26.29	N/A	US$	68.003	9.119	Morgan Stanley	Closed-End	Equity
JF Pakistan Trust	20.7	N/A	US$	3.8	10.819	Jardine Fleming	Open-End	Equity
Pakistan Fund	18.7	-16.76	US$	12.56	8.979	Morgan Grenfell	Closed-End	Equity
Thornton New Tiger Pakistan	14.55	N/A	US$	0.4	9.522	Thornton	Open-End	Equity
N. Applegate Pakistan Growth	-1.77	-37.22	US$	0.7	8.823	Credit Lyonnais	Open-End	Equity

Note: details for some funds may not have been included if the data for the US$ % change for 97/98 was not available

Source: Standard & Poor's Micropal.

JARDINE FLEMING SECURITIES
2nd Floor, Bahria Complex II,
Mt Khan Road, Karachi 7400
Tel: (92) 21 561 0861–5; Fax: (92) 21 561 0170

UBS SECURITIES
1st Floor, State Life Building,
1–A, II Chundrigar Road, Karachi,
Tel: (92) 21 242 0081; Fax: (92) 21 241 8061

KHADIM ALI SHAH BUKHARI & CO LTD
6th Floor, Trade Centre,
II Chundrigar Road, Karachi, 74200
Tel: (92) 21 263 5501; Fax: (92) 21 263 0202

KAUSAR ABBAS BHAYANI
512–514, 5th Floor Stock Exchange Building,
Stock Exchange Road, Karachi
Tel: (92) 21 241 7675; Fax: (92) 21 242 1755

C) Settlement and transfer

Trading is divided into three distinct segments, each of which has its own settlement procedure: these are (a) ready counter; (b) provisionally listed counter; and (c) spot transactions.

Ready counter

Transactions in this segment are settled through a centralised clearing house. Transactions taking place from Wednesday to the following Tuesday are settled on the Tuesday in the week after, and clearing dates are notified in advance. The KSE Clearing House nets out purchases and sales and the related financial obligations.

"Eligible securities" are settled through the Central Depository System on the same timetable but in book entry form.

Provisionally listed counter

Companies that make a public offering of at least Rs100 million are traded on this segment. During the period of provisional listing, clearing takes place on a daily basis.

Spot transactions

For a minimum of 14 days before closure of a company's share transfer books, transactions are required to be carried out on a spot basis and must be settled within 24 hours directly between the buying and selling members.

D) Commissions and other costs

Exhibit 50.8:
BROKERAGE RATES

Market value	*Rates for institutions (per share)*	*Rates for individual clients (per share)*
Up to Rs4.99	Rs0.05	Rs0.15
Rs5.0 to Rs9.99	Rs0.08	Rs0.15
Rs10.00 to Rs19.99	Rs0.13	Rs0.15
Rs20.00 to Rs39.99	Rs0.20	Rs0.25
Rs40.00 to Rs59.99	Rs0.30	Rs0.35
Rs60.00 to Rs79.99	Rs0.50	Rs0.60
Rs80.00 to Rs99.99	Rs0.60	Rs0.75
Rs100.00 to Rs249.99	Rs1.00	Rs1.25
Rs250.00 to Rs499.99	Rs2.00	Rs2.50
Rs500.00 and above	Rs3.00	Rs3.50

The rate of stamp duty on share transfers is 1.5%, subject to a minimum of Rs1.

TAXATION AND REGULATIONS AFFECTING FOREIGN INVESTORS

Under Section 3 of the Finance Act 1995, foreign investment can be made in any business/commercial activity in Pakistan, except (a) arms and ammunition; (b) security printing, currency and mint; (c) high explosives; (d) radioactive substances; and (e) trading in important goods. Permission for investment in these sectors must be sought from the Board of Investment.

Under the Protection of Economic Reforms Act 1992, safeguards are provided against government acquisition of foreign investments in industrial or commercial enterprises, and in commercial banks or other financial institutions.

LISTING AND REPORTING REQUIREMENTS

The law governing the stock exchange in Pakistan is the Securities and Exchange Ordinance 1969 and the Securities and Exchange Rules 1971.

A) Listing requirements

A company seeking a listing on either the KSE or the Lahore exchange must submit certain documents and particulars of the company as part of a formal application to the exchange, in compliance with the exchange's listing regulations. If it meets these requirements a report is submitted to the company affairs committee. The prospectus of a company making a public offering of shares must be published in a newspaper with a circulation in the province where the shares are to be listed. Exchange listing takes place approximately five weeks after the publication of a prospectus.

Prospectuses must be approved by the relevant stock exchange, the Controller of Capital Issues and the Corporate Law Authority.

B) Reporting requirements

Listed companies are required to keep the exchange informed of any changes in the board of directors or any material change in the nature of the company's business that is likely to affect the market quotation of its securities. They are required to provide all financial data, dates of meetings and information relating to bonus and dividend issues. Yearly and half-yearly accounts must also be submitted to the stock exchange. The quotation department conducts the daily quotation board, maintains a record of all transactions that take place in the trading hall of the exchange and is responsible for all company announcements made during trading hours.

SHAREHOLDER PROTECTION CODES

Investor protection is provided by the Companies Ordinance 1984 and the Securities and Exchange Ordinance 1969. Part X of the Companies Ordinance makes provision for the prevention of oppression and mismanagement of minority shareholders. Under Section 290(1) of the Ordinance, if any member or members holding at least 20% of the issued share capital of a company file a complaint, or if the Registrar of Companies is of the opinion that the affairs of the company are being conducted or are likely to be conducted in an unlawful or fraudulent manner, or in a manner not provided for in the memorandum of association of the company, oppressive to the member or members, or prejudicial to the public interest, then such member or members may file a petition to the court for an order.

Section 222 of the Ordinance requires the filing of a return of beneficial ownership of listed securities by the chief executive, directors, chief accountant and auditors of a listed company, and by a shareholder of such a company beneficially owning 10% or more of the issued shares. Section 223 of the Ordinance prohibits such persons from short selling securities of listed companies and Section 224 requires them to account for gains made upon a sale of the listed security within six months of its acquisition and to pay such gains to the company.

A major issue of concern is insider trading. While the Companies Ordinance provides for disclosure of trading by the directors and principal officers of each company, in practice this is difficult to verify. Nevertheless, the Finance Act 1995 has added a section to the Ordinance prohibiting stock exchange deals by insiders and another prohibiting the making of fictitious and multiple applications for new issues.

The past few years have seen certain significant amendments to the Securities and Exchange Ordinance 1969, covering the regulation of asset management companies, central depository companies and the registration of a credit rating agency.

RESEARCH

Until very recently, all but the large blue chip listings were poorly researched. However, further liberalisation of the market and other measures taken to attract foreign investment have encouraged some of brokers to convert their businesses into brokerage houses with teams of analysts producing detailed information on all listed companies.

Kausar Abbas Bhayani has a consistent record for producing good quality, in-depth research on individual stocks and the market in general.

The KSE research department provides services to the international financial institutions and brokerage house. Its activities includes financial analysis of companies listed on the exchange, soon to be available through the KSE's web site at www.kse.org, and publication of various newsletters and a *KSE Fact Book*.

Pakistan, published by Euromoney Books, provides in-depth information for those wishing to invest or do business in the country. See the order card at the back of this book for details.

PROSPECTIVE CHANGES

A Law Commission inquiry is undertaking a review of statutes on corporate affairs and is expected to make recommendations designed to achieve more effective corporate governance, efficient disclosure mechanisms and a restructuring of the regulatory framework.

The Securities and Exchange Commission Act 1997 will provide for the creation of an SEC for Pakistan.

CHAPTER

51

Panama

Introduction

The Bolsa de Valores de Panama, or Panama Securities Exchange (PSE), started operations on 26 June 1990, and now has 17 national and international members. The board of directors of the exchange includes nine principal members and nine alternates, allowing for broad-based representation. The main goal of the PSE is to create a continuous market for the purchase and sale of securities.

The Comisión Nacional de Valores (CNV), or National Securities Commission, is the market regulator and functions under the Ministry of Commerce and Industries. The CNV has five members: the Minister of Commerce, the General Manager of the National Bank and three representative members from the private sector (banking, commerce and industry). The CNV regulates the public sale of securities and mutual funds, the activities of broker-dealers and stock exchange operations.

The US dollar has been the legal tender currency in Panama since 1904. It circulates freely and is used in all commercial and business dealings. The official currency, the balboa, only exists in the form of coins minted to the same size and value as US coins.

ECONOMIC AND POLITICAL OVERVIEW

Annualised GDP growth for 1997 was an estimated 4.0%, and investment is projected to remain the strongest component of demand, with its share of GDP climbing from about 23% in 1993 to approximately 34% in 1997. Inflation for the 12 months ending in June 1997 hovered around 1.8%, one of the lowest rates in Latin America. The monetary system continues to be based on the US dollar and the exchange rate is fixed at B1 = US$1.

The government of President Ernesto Pérez Balladares introduced an economic reform programme in 1995 and plans to continue deregulating and privatising sectors of the economy in order to boost economic activity. Economic growth in 1998 should remain strong due to high levels of foreign investment in newly privatised industries and in development projects located in the canal and port areas. The canal itself is due to come under Panamanian control in 1999.

An across-the-board reduction in tariffs in 1997 meant that Panama became eligible to join the World Trade Organisation. Meanwhile, the Banking Reform Law should come into effect in 1998 together with prospective Securities Exchange Reforms aimed at developing the local markets to attract the regional registration and trading of securities.

In July 1996 Panama was able to restructure its external debt in a Brady-style agreement that enabled the country to resume payments on its commercial bank debt and normalise its relations with external private creditors. In January 1997, Moody's assigned a Ba1 rating to Panama's government bonds in connection with this restructuring agreement. Standard & Poor's assigned a BB+ to Panama's long-term debt and a B rating to its short-term debt. In February 1997, the government successfully carried out a Brady buy-back programme through a US$500 million Eurobond issue in the international markets.

Role of the central bank

Instead of a formal central bank, Panama's National Banking Commission is responsible for interpreting and applying the legal framework that regulates the banking sector. It supervises the reserve system and interest rates, and acts as the clearing house for government reserves. The Banco Nacional de Panama is the government's fiscal agent and carries out additional central bank functions such as receipt of tax revenue, holding reserves and extending short-term loans to the government.

MARKET PERFORMANCE

A) In 1997

The BVP Index rose by 60.3% in 1997, closing at 445.44 points, making it, according to Bloomberg, the third best performing of the world's major indices. Total equity market (domestic and foreign) capitalisation stood at US$2.25 billion at the end of the year, up 68.4% from 1996's US$1.33 billion.

The equity market average P/E multiple at the end of 1997 was 21.14 compared with 17.79 at year-end 1996. The dividend yield decreased from 3.60% in 1996 to 3.06% in 1997, while the price to book value ratio was 2.22 compared with 1.81 the year before.

B) Summary information

Global ranking by market value (US$ terms, end-1997): 62
Market capitalisation (domestic, end-1997): US$2.18 billion
Growth in market value (US$ terms, 1994–97): 171.6%
Market value as a % of nominal GDP (end-1997): 50%
Number of domestic/foreign companies listed (end-1997): 24/7
Market P/E (end-1997): 21.14
Short-term (3-month) interest rate (end-1997): 7%
Long-term (5-year) bond yield (end-1997): 9.5%
Budget deficit as a % of nominal GDP (1997): 1.5%
Inflation rate (June 1997): 1.8%
US$ exchange rate (end-1997): B1

C) Year-end share price index, price/earnings ratios and yields

Exhibit 51.1:
YEAR-END PRICE INDEX, P/E AND DIVIDEND YIELD, 1993–97

Year-end	*BVP Index*	*P/E*	*Yield (%)*
1993	153.34	6.30	5.56
1994	215.76	11.01	2.80
1995	222.44	9.40	4.00
1996	277.87	17.79	3.60
1997	445.40	21.14	3.06

Source: Panama Securities Exchange.

D) Market indices and their constituents

The BVP Index is a capitalisation-weighted index that measures the performance of 13 listed securities on the PSE. Its base of 100 was set at December 1992.

THE STOCK MARKET

A) Brief history and structure

The PSE started operations on 26 June 1990 and its main goal is to create a continuous market for the purchase and sale of local and foreign securities, both public and private, as well as currencies, futures and options. It has more than 60 stockholders, none of whom owns more than 2.5% of the equity. Other shareholders are national and international banks, broker-dealers, insurance companies, industrial and commercial enterprises and professional and private investors. To own a seat on the exchange, a company must form a Panamanian corporation with no less than US$100,000 of paid-in capital, and purchase 250 shares of the exchange's outstanding stock. The exchange sells seats to the highest bidder through auctions to companies that qualify. To date, 17 companies have become members of the exchange.

B) Different exchanges

The PSE is the only exchange authorised to operate in Panama.

C) Opening hours, names and addresses

Floor trading takes place on every business day from 11.00am to 12.00 noon.

BOLSA DE VALORES DE PANAMA SA
Calle Elvira Mendez y Calle 52
Edif. Vallarino, Planta Baja, Panama City
Tel: (507) 269 1966; Fax: (507) 269 2457

MARKET SIZE

A) Market value

As of 31 December 1997, 24 common stocks from a wide range of industries, including banks, breweries, mining, reforestation, insurance companies, mutual funds and conglomerates were listed for regular trading on the PSE. Domestic equity market capitalisation stood at US$2.18 billion at end-1997, an increase of 70% over the 1996 year-end figure of US$1.28 million. Total equity market capitalisation was US$2.25 billion end-1997, up 68.4% from US$1.33 billion in 1996.

Exhibit 51.2:
YEAR-END MARKET CAPITALISATION (IN US$ MILLION), PSE, 1994–97

	1996	*1997*
Domestic equities	1,279.5	2,175.1
Foreign equities	54.6	71.6
Domestic debt	1,083.0	1,963.3
Foreign debt	56.3	50.0
Other domestic	116.3	180.0
Total capitalisation	2,589.7	4,440.0

Source: Panama Securities Exchange.

B) Largest quoted companies

Exhibit 51.3:
THE 10 LARGEST COMPANIES LISTED ON THE PSE, END-1997

Ranking	*Company*	*Market value (US$ million)*
1	Empresa General de Inversiones	497.22
2	Banco del Istmo	342.00
3	Cervecería Nacional	239.44
4	Grupo Assa	222.00
5	Primer Banco de Ahorros	149.73
6	Capitales Nacionales	142.09
7	Coca Cola de Panama	103.77
8	Banco Disa	44.00
9	Banco Internacional de Panama	66.00
10	Conase	65.04

Source: Panama Securities Exchange.

C) Trading volume

PSE total turnover (including debt securities) in 1997 was US$711.9 million, an increase of 130% compared with US$446.5 million in 1996. Share trading totalled US$55.66 million in 1997, more than double the US$24.2 million traded in 1996.

Exhibit 51.4:
TRADING VOLUME AND VALUE (IN MILLIONS) ON THE PSE, 1995–97

	1995	*1996*	*1997*
Shares (units)	0.77	0.98	2.39
Shares (US$)	8.65	24.25	55.66
Debt (US$)	181.50	305.93	496.13
Other securities (US$)	11.23	116.31	159.17
Total trading (US$)	233.38	446.49	711.96

Source: Panama Securities Exchange.

Exhibit 51.5:
THE 10 MOST ACTIVELY TRADED SHARES, PSE, 1997

Ranking	*Company*	*Turnover (US$ '000)*
1	Interamerica's Fund Ltd	13.356
2	Banco del Istmo	8.231
3	IDS Holding Corp	7.668
4	Cervecería Nacional	6.674
5	Empresa General de Inversiones	5.575
6	Capitales Nacionales	2.093
7	Primer Banco de Ahorros	1.548
8	Unión Nacional de Empresas	1.319
9	Coca-Cola de Panama	1.095
10	Grupo Assa	0.957

Source: Panama Securities Exchange.

TYPES OF SECURITIES TRADED

All forms of stocks, bonds (government and corporate) and commercial paper (known locally as *valores comerciales negociables*) are traded on the floor of the PSE.

OPERATIONS

A) Trading system

The PSE uses an open outcry auction trading system. All trades on the exchange are "lock in" and matching takes place on the trade date. Only PSE members are allowed to participate in the trade comparison and settlement system.

B) List of principal brokers

BANISTMO BROKERS
PO Box 6-3823, El Dorado, Panama 5
Tel: (507) 270 1049; Fax: (507) 270 1717

BANTAL BROKERS
PO Box 135, Panama
Tel: (507) 263 7072; Fax: (507) 264 7106

BG INVESTMENT
PO Box 4592, Panama 5
Tel: (507) 227 3200; Fax: (507) 225 2868

BINCAP BROKERS
PO Box 11181, Panama 6
Tel: (507) 264 6833; Fax: (507) 263 4096

CAPITAL TRADERS OF PANAMA
PO Box 7201, Panama 5
Tel: (507) 264 2044; Fax: (507) 223 5147
E-mail: capitalpanama.phoenix.net
Web site: www.panama.phoenix.net/capital

CITIVALORES
PO Box 555, Panama 9a
Tel: (507) 263 5544; Fax: (507) 264 0659

WALL STREET SECURITIES
PO Box 6-809, Panama 6A
Tel: (507) 227 4577; Fax: (507) 227 4100

C) Settlement and transfer

Central Latinoamericana de Valores SA (LATINCLEAR) provides custody, administration, clearing, settlement and transfer services. It uses a combination of trade-for-trade and daily netting for the settlement of securities transactions. The settlement period is T+2.

Exhibit 51.6:
COUNTRY FUNDS – PANAMA

Fund	US$ % change 01/01/97 01/01/98	01/01/93 01/01/98	Fund base currency	Fund size (US$ mil)	Fund volatility	Management group	Opal main sector	Opal subsector
Panama Balanced Fund	30.89	N/A	US$	8.276	-1	Wall Street S	Open-End	Equity

Note: details for some funds may not have been included if the data for the US$ % change for 97/98 was not available

Source: Standard & Poor's Micropal.

D) Commissions and other costs

Brokers' commissions are negotiable.

TAXATION AND REGULATIONS AFFECTING FOREIGN INVESTORS

Any income produced within the territory of Panama is subject to income tax, while income from investments or operations in a foreign country are explicitly exempt from income tax. The income tax system applies to both nationals and foreigners.

A) Dividend tax

The general rule is that corporations operating in Panama must withhold 10% of amounts they pay out as dividends. However, companies do not have to withhold dividend tax if the relevant income is from a tax-free source, comes from a transaction carried out in a foreign country or is from dividends on which dividend tax has already been paid.

Legislation to abolish this tax is due before the National Assembly in 1998.

B) Capital gains tax

Capital gains from the sale of CNV-authorised securities are exempt from tax.

C) Foreign investment

Foreign investors can purchase 100% of any stock or debt issued in Panama. Also, there are no restrictions on the repatriation of capital and income from dividends, interest and capital gains.

LISTING AND REPORTING REQUIREMENTS

Corporations that wish to sell securities to the public must obtain authorisation from the CNV. The company must submit a prospectus, including information about the business (plus three years audited financial statements), the industry and the securities to be issued.

Registration with the PSE is also required if securities are to be listed on the exchange. Foreign securities may be offered and sold in Panama upon completion of a registration procedure.

RESEARCH

The PSE posts daily trade information on the Reuters, Telerate and Bloomberg networks. The exchange also produces several publications and booklets on market and PSE activities, on a weekly, monthly and yearly basis.

Panama, published by Euromoney Books, provides in-depth information for all those wishing to invest or do business in the country. See the order card at the back of this book for details.

PROSPECTIVE CHANGES

The PSE should move to a fully electronic trading system by the end of 1998. In addition, a group of market traders and the international rating agency Duff & Phelps have plans to establish a regional rating agency in Panama by the end of 1998.

CHAPTER

52

Peru

Introduction

Peru remains stable politically and economically, and the Lima Stock Exchange (LSE) is now one of the most important and potentially profitable emerging markets of Latin America. The absence of capital gains tax on exchange transactions for both locals and foreigners provides an added investment attraction.

Despite a slightly disappointing market performance in 1997 – mainly due to external factors, such as the Asian economic crisis and domestic political events – the LSE still recorded volume growth and expanded its range of investor services.

ECONOMIC AND POLITICAL OVERVIEW

In April 1995, President Fujimori was re-elected, indicating support on the part of the majority of Peruvians for the government's economic policies and measures that have helped bring peace to Peru as well as remarkable economic growth over the past five years. The government's structural reform programme has already modified the nature of the state's historically overbearing role in the economy by privatising state-owned assets, eliminating price controls, deregulating the financial and labour markets, liberalising trade barriers and simplifying domestic and foreign investment regulations.

Since the start of the privatisation programme in June 1991, the state has transferred US$6.8 billion worth of assets, with investment commitments of US$4.6 billion. In 1997, the state transferred US$305 million in assets and shares.

As a result of the structural reform programme, inflation has been reduced from 7,650% in 1990 to 6.46% in 1997. Contributing to this reduction has been the relative stability of the exchange rate. At the end of 1997 the sol stood at S2.74 to the US dollar, with an accumulated devaluation for 1997 of 4.8%. GDP growth in 1997 was 7.2% (compared with 2.8% in 1996), and the main growth sectors were construction and electricity.

Role of the central bank

Reforms of the central bank, introduced during Fujimori's first term, were aimed at institutionalising a new ethos of independence and conservatism in central bank policy. At the beginning of 1993, the various reforms were consolidated in the Ley Orgánica del Banco Central de Reserva del Perú. The main provisions of the law are as follows:

- The central bank's objective is to maintain monetary stability. In doing so, its functions are to regulate the money supply, to administer international reserves, to issue notes and coins and to provide information about the nation's finances; it is independent of government. It is administered by seven directors, four of whom (including the bank president) are appointed by the executive branch of government, and three by Congress.
- The central bank allows interest rates to be determined by a competitive market although it is responsible for the level of reserve requirements set by the commercial banks on their deposits.
- The public sector cannot be financed by the central bank. The bank can only buy Treasury bonds in the secondary market up to a limit calculated as the equivalent of 5% of the previous year's monetary base stock.
- The central bank can participate in the foreign exchange market as both buyer and seller.

Given the history of the bank's role in macroeconomic policy, the law makes its independence explicit and specifies an objective for monetary policy designed to keep inflation in check rather than contributing to it.

The bank has maintained restrictive control of the money supply since August 1990.

MARKET PERFORMANCE

A) In 1997

Following a patchy 1996, the main LSE indices ended the year higher. The General Index and the Selective Index increased in nominal terms by 25.45% and 32.12%

Exhibit 52.1: LIMA SE GENERAL (IGBL) PRICE INDEX (US$), 1993–97

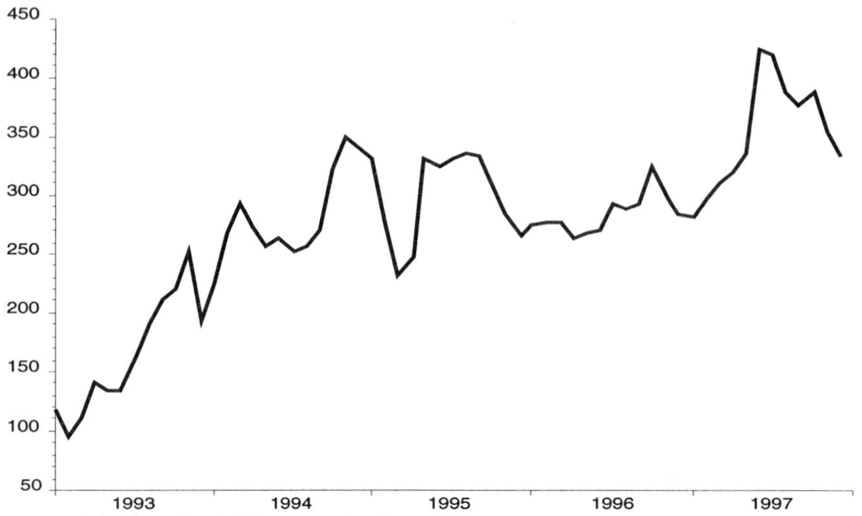

High value 423.5 2.6.97 Low value 95.4 1.2.93 *Source: Datastream*

respectively. Good performances were also recorded at the sectorial level: common mining stocks registered an impressive 79.5% rise, and mining employee stocks ended the year 62.82% ahead.

The value of LSE and OTC securities trading in Peru in 1997 totalled US$12,051.08 million, a 42% increase on the previous year. Trading on the exchange floor amounted to US$6,699.76 million, up 32.28% on 1996. Of this, 74.3% was accounted for by cash transactions, and the balance comprised repo operations. In the cash market, share turnover totalled US$4,295.36 million.

OTC trading rose in 1997 by 56.18% to US$5,351.32 million. OTC turnover as a percentage of total trading increased from 40.5% in 1996 to 45% in 1997.

B) Summary information

Global ranking by market value (US$ terms, end-1997): 43
Market capitalisation (end-1997):US$17,383 million
Growth in market value (US$ terms, 1993–97): 241.9%
Market value as a % of nominal GDP (end-1997): 27.37%
Number of domestic/foreign companies listed (end-1997): 251/3
Market P/E (Selective Index companies, end-1997): 12.24
MSCI Index (change in US$ terms, 1997): +17.7%
Short-term (30-day) interest rate (US$ terms, end-1997): 16.07%
Long-term interest rate: 5.525%
Budget deficit as a % of nominal GDP (end-1997): 0.09%
Inflation rate (1997): 6.46%
US$ exchange rate (end-1997): S2.74

C) Year-end share index, price/earnings ratio and yield

Exhibit 52.2:
YEAR-END INDICES (LOCAL CURRENCY TERMS), PRICE/EARNINGS RATIO AND YIELD, 1993–97

Year-end	*General Index*	*Selective Index*	*Selective index P/E*	*Selective index yield (%)*
1993	930.47	985.86	44.01	0.79
1994	1,414.92	1,678.91	21.00	0.32
1995	1,243.37	1,686.32	13.00	N/A
1996	1,429.02	2,015.34	10.00	2.5
1997	1,792.71	2,662.66	12.24	N/A

Source: Lima Stock Exchange.

D) Market indices and their constituents

Two main indices (both weighted by trading volume) are calculated by the LSE. The General Index (IGBVL, based at 30 December 1991 = 100) covers the 51 most liquid shares and the Selective Index (ISBVL, also based at 30 December 1991 = 100) tracks the performance of the 15 leading blue chips. The LSE calculates eight sectorial indices covering banks, industrials, mining, insurance, utilities, diverse, industrial employee shares and mining employee shares.

THE STOCK MARKET

A) Brief history and structure

The Lima Mercantile Exchange (Bolsa Mercantil de Lima) was established over 140 years ago. In 1898 it was reorganised and in 1949 it was renamed the Bolsa de Comercio de Lima. With the creation of the regulatory commission CONASEV in 1970, the exchange underwent huge changes and, since then, has been known as the Bolsa de Valores de Lima (Lima Stock Exchange). Since December 1995, when the LSE merged with the Arequipa Stock Exchange (founded in 1988), it has been the only stock market in Peru.

All regulations governing the exchange, CONASEV and the brokers are now consolidated in a single piece of legislation – the 1996 Securities Market Law (Legislative Decree no. 861).

B) Opening hours, names and addresses

LSE trading hours are from 9.30am to 2.00pm.

BOLSA DE VALORES DE LIMA
Pasaje Acuña 106, Lima
Tel: (51) 14 26 7939 / 0714; Fax: (51) 14 26 7650

MARKET SIZE

A) Number of listings and market value

At the end of 1997, there were 254 companies listed on the LSE, including three foreign companies – Credicorp, Southern Peru Copper Corporation and (a 1997 listing) Newmont Mining Corporation. During the year, some domestic companies in the electricity sector obtained listings, such as Electro Sur Medio SA and Electro Sur Este SA. LSE market capitalisation has increased every year since 1990, and at end-1997 it stood at US$17.4 billion (up 25.6% compared with end-1996).

Exhibit 52.3:
NUMBER OF LISTED COMPANIES AND MARKET VALUE, LSE, 1993–97

Year-end	*No. of companies*	*Market value (US$ million)*	*Market value (S million)*
1993	235	5,084.44	10,992.57
1994	220	8,162.54	17,835.15
1995	243	11,701.20	27,170.40
1996	239	13,842.19	35,934.22
1997	254	17,383.00	47,629.42

Source: Lima Stock Exchange.

B) Largest quoted companies

Exhibit 52.4:
THE 20 LARGEST LISTED SHARES BY MARKET VALUE, LSE, END-1997

Ranking	*Company/share*	*Market value (US$ million)*	*Market value (S million)*
1	Telefónica del Perú B	3,331.91	9,129.46
2	Credicorp	1,544.43	4,231.74
3	Banco de Crédito	925.55	2,536.00
4	Cementos Lima	638.54	1,749.60
5	Backus	577.95	1,583.58
6	Buenaventura A	491.63	1,347.07
7	Edegel B	354.16	970.40
8	Backus (E)	321.43	880.73
9	Alicorp	251.66	689.54
10	Luz del Sur B	228.24	625.37
11	Pesquera Austral	215.88	591.50
12	Cementos Norte Pacasmayo	207.42	568.32
13	Edelnor	199.08	545.47
14	Southern Perú Copper	181.94	498.53
15	Volcan A	180.47	494.48
16	Egenor B	136.62	374.35
17	Ferreyros	129.73	355.47
18	Graña y Montero	128.81	352.93
19	Minsur (E)	128.77	352.83
20	Buenaventura (E)	116.35	318.81

(E) Employee shares.

Source: Lima Stock Exchange.

C) Trading volume

Exhibit 52.5:
TURNOVER ON THE LSE AND OTC MARKETS, 1993–97

Year	*Trading value (US$ million)*
1993	1,981.55
1994	4,054.60
1995	5,279.72
1996	8,491.60
1997	12,051.08

Source: Lima Stock Exchange.

Exhibit 52.6:
THE 20 MOST ACTIVELY TRADED SHARES BY TURNOVER VALUE, LSE, 1997

Ranking	*Company/share*	*Value (S million)*
1	Telefónica del Perú B	1,998.71
2	Buenaventura A	1,083.15

Exhibit 52.6 continued

3	Credicorp	684.53
4	Backus (E)	615.62
5	Minsur (E)	427.68
6	Cementos Lima	353.95
7	Luz del Sur B	352.25
8	Tele 2000	310.76
9	Volcan (E)	279.47
10	Buenaventura (E)	262.27
11	Buenaventura B	252.97
12	Milpo (E)	250.73
13	Volcan A	243.40
14	Edegel B	243.32
15	Morococha (E)	238.31
16	Atacocha (E)	231.34
17	Southern Perú Copper	226.98
18	Embotelladora Latinoamericana	214.12
19	Pesquera Austral B	213.38
20	Ferreyros	181.81

(E) Employee shares.

Source: Lima Stock Exchange.

TYPES OF SHARE

There are three types of shares in Peru – common, non-voting and employee (E) shares. Common shares grant the right to vote and are freely transferable, while non-voting stock carry rights to a preferred distribution.

Employee shares were issued in the 1970s by industrial, mining and fishing sector companies to their workers, but are not permitted to amount to more than 50% of the company's paid-up capital. Employee shares are a very important part of the total volume of securities traded on the LSE. Unlike common shares, employee shares do not grant their holder the right to vote, but can be freely transferred and are considered as preferred shares. It is no longer legal to issue new employee shares, except in cases of capital increases by companies that already have them in order to maintain the existing balance between common and employee shares. Under the 1996 Securities Market Law, issuers of employee shares can agree terms with holders for the redemption or conversion of their shares into common stock, non-voting stock, bonds or any other security.

Other securities traded on the LSE are preferred subscription certificates and bonds.

INVESTORS

At the end of December 1997 the LSE central depository (CAVALI) held 471,724 accounts worth US$6,247.06 million and 35.9% of market capitalisation. The value of non-resident investor accounts registered at CAVALI represented 49.92% of the total value.

OPERATIONS

A) Trading system

Securities trading is carried out through brokerage houses and transactions are effected under the open outcry trading system (*pregón* or *de viva voz*) or via the electronic trading system (ELEX). The following types of transaction take place:

- cash transactions, settled on T+3;
- term transactions for 30, 60, 90 or a maximum of 180 days;
- report transactions involving two simultaneous operations – one in cash where one party (*reportante*) pays to acquire title from another party (*reportado*), and a second transaction whereby both parties agree to rebuy or resell the same title at a future date at the price and terms agreed upon; and
- cash-term transactions, generally for bills of exchange and promissory notes.

B) List of principal brokers

ARGOS
Miró Quesada 221, Piso 5, Lima
Tel: (51) 1427 6656; Fax: (51) 14 27 5575

Exhibit 52.7:
COUNTRY FUNDS – PERU

Fund	*US$ % change 01/01/97 01/01/98*	*01/01/93 01/01/98*	*Fund base currency*	*Fund size (US$ mil)*	*Fund volatility*	*Management group*	*Opal main sector*	*Opal subsector*
Peruvian Inv Co	11.09	N/A	US$	24	6.019	Foreign & Colonial	Open-End	Equity
Peru 2000	-1.57	N/A	US$	15.312	3.343	Peru Select G	Open-End	Equity

Note: details for some funds may not have been included if the data for the US$ % change for 97/98 was not available

Source: Standard & Poor's Micropal.

CREDIBOLSA
Centenario 156-La Molina, Lima
Tel: (51) 13 49 0500; Fax: (51) 13 49 0796

G&B SAB
Jir. Miró Quesada 260 of. 1002, Lima
Tel: (51) 14 28 0500; Fax: (51) 14 26 9434

PERUVAL
Los Incas 172, Piso 7 – San Isidro
Tel: (51) 1421 4527; Fax: (51) 1421 8824

PRISMA
Republica de Panama 3680 – San Isidro
Tel: (51) 1421 0806; Fax: (51) 1421 0804

SEMINARIO Y CIA
Miro Quesada 247 & 403 – Lima
Tel: (51) 1428 9014; Fax: (51) 1428 4240

C) Settlement and transfer

In May 1997, the LSE department responsible for stock clearing and settlement was hived off to form a new, legally independent institution called CAVALI, which is owned by LSE members. CAVALI acts as a central depository and transactions are settled in a maximum period of 72 hours (T+3).

D) Commissions and other costs

The main transaction costs are brokerage fees, which range from 0.1% to 1% of the amount traded. In addition, investors must pay sales tax (18%) on brokerage fees. The LSE, CAVALI and CONASEV also charge fees for share transactions of (respectively) 0.0825%, 0.06% and 0.05%.

TAXATION AND REGULATIONS AFFECTING FOREIGN INVESTORS

Under Legislative Decree 662 (the Foreign Investment Promotion Law), Legislative Decree 757 (the Framework Law for Private Investment) and their regulations (Supreme Decree 162–92-EF), the government promotes and guarantees foreign investment in Peru. Foreign investors have the following rights:

a) to remit abroad, in freely convertible currency, without prior authorisation of any public authority, the total amount of their capital, dividends and profits;
b) to convert foreign currency to national currency, or vice versa, at the most favourable exchange rates effective at the time of the transaction;
c) to execute stability agreements with the government, which guarantee for 10 years the stability of the tax regime in force at the time of the agreement; free disposal of foreign currency; free remittance of capital and profits abroad; and non-discriminatory treatment with respect to domestic investors; and
d) to acquire shares, participations or rights owned by national or sub-regional investors, without limitation.

With regard to taxation, non-domiciled entities pay taxes only on Peruvian source income. Dividends paid by local corporations are not subject to income tax.

Capital gains on shares and other stock exchange securities, as well as (in defined circumstances) readjustment of capital paid to holders of debt instruments, are exempt from tax until the year 2000.

LISTING AND REPORTING REQUIREMENTS

A) Listing requirements

In order for securities to be quoted and traded on the stock exchange, they must be recorded in the Securities Market Public Registry administered by CONASEV.

In addition, regulations were published in 1995 covering the "Public Offering of Foreign Corporate Shares".

B) Reporting requirements

The recording of securities in the Public Registry binds the issuer to inform CONASEV and the LSE of important facts affecting (or that could affect) the price of a security being traded and to ensure that investors have the necessary information on which to make decisions. The law states that companies must inform CONASEV and the exchange of transformation of the company, merger or dissolution, modifications to the corporate objectives, details of the treatment of profits, distributions, increases or reductions of capital and strikes.

Listed companies must also deliver quarterly financial statements and their annual reports to CONASEV and to the LSE.

SHAREHOLDER PROTECTION CODES

Under the 1996 Securities Market Law (Legislative Decree 861), transactions carried out in the securities market are regulated by the National Supervisory Commission of Companies and Securities (CONASEV) and by the LSE.

A) Insider trading

Directors, managers and auditors of a company and, in general, whoever has access to the company because of their position or job, must keep unpublished information strictly confidential if it might affect the price of securities. Breach of this law can lead to the dismissal of directors and managers, and to fines for auditors. Also, there are civil remedies available for damages. The 1996 Securities Market Law has laid down more stringent penalties for insider trading and share price manipulation, including the amendment of the Penal Code to classify them as criminal offences subject to up to seven years imprisonment.

B) Takeover bids

Regulations have recently been introduced laying down mechanisms and procedures for takeovers.

C) Guarantee fund

Under Article 158 of the Securities Market Law, the LSE must maintain a guarantee fund to reimburse brokerage house clients in the event of fraud. All brokerage houses contribute a given percentage of total traded volume to the fund. The percentage 0.0075% and is set by Supreme Decree.

RESEARCH

In order to distribute stock market information at a local level, the LSE has eight information offices in the country's main cities – Chiclayo, Cusco, Huancayo, Icá, Piura, Tacna, Trujillo, Iquitos, Chimbote and Arequipa.

The LSE publishes a comprehensive range of periodicals and reports on the stock market. These include daily and weekly bulletins; a monthly statistics annex; and quarterly, semi-annual and annual statistical reports. Information can also be obtained electronically (BOLFAX) and is available on Reuters and the Internet.

Internationally, Citicorp, BBV, Banco Santander and BCI are respected for the quality of their research.

Peru, published by Euromoney Books, provides in-depth information for those wishing to invest or do business in the country. See the order card at the back of this book for details.

PROSPECTIVE CHANGES

The LSE is studying the possibility of establishing of a derivatives market to trade options and futures on stock exchange indices. Also, 1998 is expected to see implementation of ADR and GDR trading on the LSE.

CHAPTER

53

Philippines

Introduction

Economic instability in 1997 (which spread on a regional and even global scale) sent warning signals to investors who pulled out of the Philippine Stock Exchange (PSE) in large numbers. The PSE Composite Index hit a four-year low of 1,740.18 in October, just eight months after setting an all-time high of 3,447.60 in February.

The Philippines has one official stock exchange with two computer-linked trading floors located in Pasig and Makati. As of December 1997, there were 221 companies listed with a total market capitalisation of P1,251.3 billion (US$31.30 billion). Market turnover for the year was P586.2 billion (US$19.89 billion).

Foreign investors are generally allowed to acquire 100% of the equity of a Philippine listed company, although there are businesses where foreign ownership is restricted by law. To monitor foreign ownership in these nationally important companies, their common shares are usually classified as "A" shares, which are generally limited to Philippine nationals, and "B" shares, which both Philippine and foreign nationals may buy.

The Philippine exchange is administered by a board of governors chaired by a non-broker president appointed by the board.

ECONOMIC AND POLITICAL OVERVIEW

Backed by generally healthy macroeconomic fundamentals, the Philippine economy remained resilient in 1997 in the face of the destabilising effects of currency turbulence in the Asian region. Overall, the economy posted a respectable GNP growth rate of 5.8%, exceeding revised targets. Prudent monetary and fiscal policies helped hold inflation down to 6.1%.

Externally, the country's overall balance of payments position weakened compared with that of the same period last year owing to region-wide negative sentiment that had adverse repercussions on inflows of service receipts and investments. This translated to an overall deficit of US$1.21 billion for the first nine months of 1997 compared with a US$3.75 billion surplus a year before.

Meanwhile, the central bank's gross international reserves declined from US$11.75 billion at end-December 1996 to US$9.87 billion at end-November 1997. The decline was traced mainly to substantial net foreign exchange sales by the central bank to banks and the national government in an effort to temper sharp fluctuations in the value of the peso. At end-December 1997, the peso was trading at P39.97 to the US dollar.

Role of the central bank

The Bangko Sentral ng Pilipinas (BSP) was established on 3 July 1993 as the Philippines' central monetary authority. BSP enjoys both fiscal and administrative autonomy, although it is still a government-owned corporation. BSP's P50 billion capital is fully subscribed by the government, and P10 billion has been paid up.

The BSP functions and operates as an independent and accountable body in carrying out its primary objective of maintaining price stability conducive to balanced and sustainable economic growth. The BSP is also charged with promoting and maintaining monetary stability and the convertibility of the Philippine peso.

In accordance with its mandate, the BSP (through its policy-making body, the Monetary Board) formulates and implements policies aimed at managing the expansion or contraction of monetary aggregates, mainly through open market operations, and pursues a flexible, market-oriented foreign exchange rate policy where its role is limited to ensuring orderly conditions in the market.

MARKET PERFORMANCE

A) In 1997

The volatility of the stock market in 1997 was alarming.

Exhibit 53.1: PHILIPPINES SE COMMERICIAL/INDUSTRIAL PRICE INDEX (US$), 1993–97

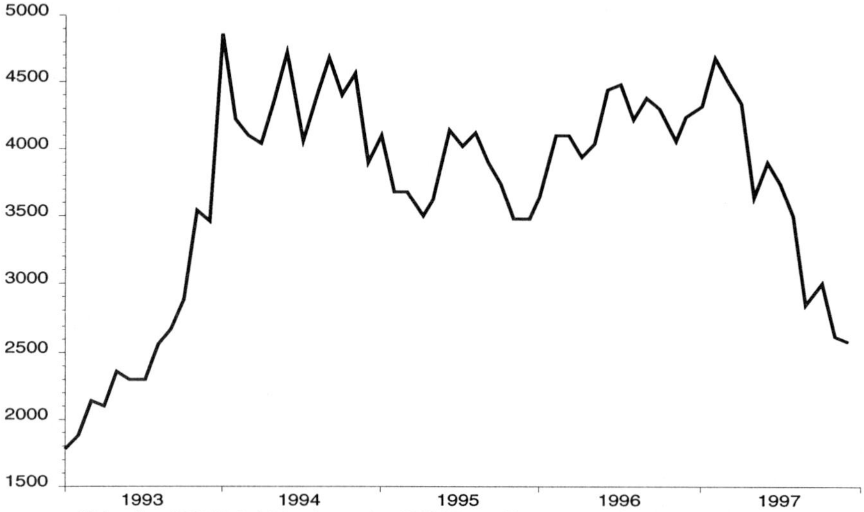

High value 4859.29 3.1.94 Low value 1783.97 1.1.93 *Source: Datastream*

The Composite Index recorded a new high of 3,447.60 in February, with the market spurred on by encouraging macroeconomic fundamentals and positive corporate earnings. However, the run was short-lived as negative factors began to build for both the Philippines and the region. Internal concerns included peso depreciation, high interest rates, fear of a property glut, the widening trade deficit and the loan exposure of banks. Currency turmoil and shooting interest rates depressed earnings of most listed companies and further dampened investor sentiment. As a result, the Composite Index collapsed to its lowest point in four years (1,740.18) in October, closing the year slightly higher at 1,869.23.

B) Summary information

Global ranking by market value (US$ terms, end-1997): 36
Market capitalisation (end-1997): US$31.30 billion
Growth in market value (local currency terms, 1993–97): 14.9%
Market value as a % of nominal GNP (end-1997): 36%
Number of domestic/foreign companies listed (end-1997): 221/0
Market P/E (all Composite Index companies, end-1997): 10.2
MSCI Index ("Philippines Free", change in US$ terms, 1997): -63%
Short-term (91-day T-bill) interest rate (end-1997): 17.7%
Long term (10-year) bond yield (Nov 1997): 21.066%
Budget surplus as a % of nominal GNP (end-1997): 0.06%
Annual increase in broad money (M3) supply (Nov-1997): 23.94%
Inflation rate (1997): 6.1%
US$ exchange rate (end-1997): P39.97

C) Year-end share price index, price/earnings ratios and yields

Exhibit 53.2:
YEAR-END SHARE PRICE INDEX, AVERAGE P/E AND DIVIDEND YIELD, 1993–97

Year-end	*Composite Index*	*P/E*	*Yield*
1993	3,271.51	32.6	0.40
1994	2,785.51	23.6	0.39
1995	2,594.18	19.1	0.57
1996	3,170.56	26.3	0.83
1997	1,869.23	10.2	1.29

Sources: Philippine Stock Exchange.

D) Market indices and their constituents

The PSE Composite Index represents 15 industries and is calculated on the weighted market capitalisation method. The criteria for selecting index stocks are market capitalisation, liquidity, representation, maturity and stock type. Sub-indices include commercial and industrial (50 companies), property (10), mining (7), oil (10) and banking and financial services (10).

THE STOCK MARKET

A) Brief history and structure

The Philippine stock market dates back to 1927 when the Manila Stock Exchange (MSE) was officially incorporated. In 1963, the Makati Stock Exchange (MKSE) was launched. The two exchanges operated as separate entities for the next 30 years, although they were basically trading the same listed issues. On 14 July 1992, a unified Philippine Stock Exchange (PSE) was incorporated, and its two trading floors – the main trading floor in Pasig and the extension in Makati – were linked via computer.

The Philippine stock market is regulated by the Securities and Exchange Commission (SEC), a quasi-judicial government agency under the administrative supervision of the Department of Finance. It is responsible for the registration of securities, the regulation of the securities markets and exchanges, the licensing of brokers and dealers, and the issuance of rulings and opinions on securities trading.

B) Different exchanges

The PSE is the only stock exchange in the Philippines. It has trading floors in Pasig and Makati.

C) Opening hours, names and addresses

Trading hours are from 9.30am to 12.00 noon, with a pre-opening period from 9.00am to 9.30am during which posting takes place. There is a 10-minute extension after 12.00 for executing orders at the last closing prices. Trading days are Monday to Friday, except for holidays and days when the central bank clearing office is closed.

Philippine Stock Exchange Centre
Exchange Road, Ortigas Centre, Pasig City
Tel: (63) 2 636 0122-41; Fax: (63) 2 634 5113/634 5920

Philippine Stock Exchange Plaza
Ayala Triangle, Ayala Avenue, Makati City
Tel: (63) 2 891 9001-03; Fax: (63) 2 891 9004/891 9021

MARKET SIZE

A) Number of listings and market value

Total market capitalisation of the PSE at the end of 1997 was P1,251.29 billion (US$31.30 billion), down 41.03% on year-end 1996. Five new companies came to the market in 1997, bringing the total number of companies listed on the PSE to 221.

Exhibit 53.3:
NUMBER OF COMPANIES LISTED AND MARKET VALUE, PSE, 1993–97

Year-end	*No. of companies listed*	*Market capitalisation (P billion)*
1993	182	1,088.8
1994	189	1,386.5
1995	205	1,543.9
1996	216	2,121.1
1997	221	1,251.3

Source: Philippine Stock Exchange.

Exhibit 53.4:
MARKET CAPITALISATION BY SECTOR, PSE, END-1997

Sector	*Market capitalisation (P billion)*
Commercial and industrial	744.72
Banks and financial services	253.03
Property	230.13
Mining	14.44
Oil	8.97
Total	**1,251.29**

Source: Philippine Stock Exchange.

B) Largest quoted companies

Exhibit 53.5:
THE 20 LARGEST LISTED ISSUES, PSE, END-1997

Ranking	*Company*	*Market value (P billion)*
1	Ayala	129.72
2	Ayala Land	115.93
3	San Miguel	95.97
4	Phil. Long Distance Tel	95.68
5	Manila Electric	86.31
6	Metropolitan Bank and Trust	61.32
7	SM Prime Holdings	59.58
8	Bank of the Phil. Islands	50.01
9	Petron	31.41
10	Benpres Holdings	27.44
11	Far East Bank and Trust	26.46
12	Filinvest Development	20.25
13	Equitable Banking	18.53
14	Phil. Commercial Int'l Bank	17.51
15	Jollibee Foods	14.75
16	ABS-CBN Broadcasting	14.03
17	JG Summit Holdings	13.91
18	Phil. National Bank	12.24
19	C & P Homes	9.83
20	Rizal Commercial Banking	9.70

Source: Philippine Stock Exchange.

C) Trading volume

Turnover for 1997 totalled P586.2 billion (US$19.89 billion). This compares with P668.82 billion in 1996 and P378.98 billion in 1995. Total trading volume for 1997 was 1,924.0 billion shares, down from 2,273.8 billion in 1996.

Exhibit 53.6:
THE 20 MOST ACTIVELY TRADED SHARES, PSE, 1997

Ranking	*Company*	*Turnover value (P million)*
1	Phil. Long Distance Tel	30,388.71
2	Metropolitan Bank and Trust	29,369.54
3	Manila Electric	28,465.59

Exhibit 53.6 continued

4	Belle	24,901.19
5	San Miguel	18,758.09
6	Ayala Land	17,547.78
7	Phil. National Bank	12,844.51
8	Empire East Land Holdings	12,383.29
9	Bank of the Phil. Islands	11,395.18
10	SM Prime Holdings	11,059.52
11	C & P Homes	10,521.94
12	Petron	10,398.05
13	Pilipino Telephone	10,344.67
14	Ayala	10,074.14
15	Music	10,058.46
16	Filinvest Land	9,786.50
17	Metro Pacific	8,484.80
18	Sinophil	8,358.65
19	Greater Asia Resources	7,025.93
20	Equitable Banking	6,474.34

Source: Philippine Stock Exchange.

TYPES OF SHARE

Both preferred and common shares are traded on the PSE. Common shares of companies that are eligible for foreign ownership are classified into "Class A" and "Class B" shares. Class A shares are restricted to Philippine nationals, while Class B shares are open to both Philippine and foreign nationals. There is a 40% limit on the foreign ownership of companies engaged in, for example, operating public utilities, and exploring and developing natural resources. Foreign investors are barred, however, from buying into companies engaged in the mass media, the retail trade and rural banking.

Preferred shares are generally non-voting, but are given preference as regards dividends on a company's liquidation.

OTHER MARKETS

Stocks of corporations not listed on the PSE but registered with and licensed by the SEC for sale to the public may be traded over-the-counter by brokers outside PSE trading hours. OTC transactions are carried out by direct inquiries and negotiations between dealers, who may not act as both principals and agents.

INVESTORS

Individual domestic investors are the majority participants in the Philippine market. Foreign investment is dominated by the Taiwanese, who are closely followed by the Japanese and Hong Kong Chinese.

OPERATIONS

A) Trading system

Investors must place their orders through stockbrokers licensed by the Securities and Exchange Commission. Bid and ask prices are keyed into the Automated Trading System/Maktrade, and prioritising of orders takes place according first to price, then to location (by trading floor), and then to time (first entered equals first done). The minimum board lot varies depending on the market price of the security, as does the minimum price fluctuation for each issue. The price of an issue is automatically frozen if it moves beyond a trading band set at not more than 50% above or 40% below the previous day's closing price. The PSE may lift the freeze after a company has provided an explanation for the sharp movement of its stock.

B) List of principal brokers

ABACUS SECURITIES CORPORATION
Unit E 2904-A Phil. Stock Exchange Centre
Exchange Road, Ortigas Centre, Pasig City
Tel: (63) 2 634 5104-11; Fax: (63) 2 634 2104/634 2108

ABN AMRO HOARE GOVETT SECURITIES (PHILS)
3/F Pacific Star Building
Sen. Gil Puyat Ave. cor. Makati Ave, Makati City
Tel: (63) 2 811 5706; Fax: (63) 2 812 7909/819 5849

ANGPING & ASSOCIATES SECURITIES
Suite 2003–04, The Peak
No. 107 Alfaro St., Salcedo Village, Makati City
Tel: (63) 2 848 5369-76; Fax: (63) 2 848 2572

DEUTSCHE MORGAN GRENFELL (PHILS)
23/F Tower 1 & Exchange Plaza
Ayala Ave. cor Paseo de Roxas, Makati City
Tel: (63) 2 894 6600; Fax: (63) 2 894 6605/894 6622

ING BARING SECURITIES (PHILS)
20/F Tower 1 & Exchange Plaza
Ayala Ave. cor Paseo de Roxas, Makati City
Tel: (63) 2 840 8400; Fax: (63) 2 891 9777/891 9727

JARDINE FLEMING EXCHANGE CAPITAL SECURITIES
22/F Tower 1 & Exchange Plaza
Ayala Ave. cor Paseo de Roxas, Makati City
Tel: (63) 2 841 9800; Fax: (63) 2 841 9802

OCBC SECURITIES PHILS
Unit 3104-C, 31/F PSE Centre
Exchange Road, Ortigas Centre, Pasig City
Tel: (63) 2 635 5765/635 3434-36; Fax: (63) 2 635 5766

PCCI SECURITIES BROKERS
3/F PCCI Corporate Centre
118 Alfaro St., Salcedo Village, Makati City
Tel: (63) 2 893 3920/893 3923-24; Fax: (63) 2 893 4340

Exhibit 53.7:
COUNTRY FUNDS – PHILIPPINES

Fund	US$ % change 01/01/97 01/01/98	US$ % change 01/01/93 01/01/98	Fund base currency	Fund size (US$ mil)	Fund volatility	Management group	Opal main sector	Opal subsector
Jupiter Philippine Inv Co	N/A	N/A	US$	12.8	-1	Jupiter Asset	Open-End	Equity
JF Philippine Fund Inc	-55.92	-6.73	US$	N/A	8.67	Jardine Fleming	Closed-End	Equity
Nomura Aurora II Philippine	-56.3	N/A	¥	1868	-1	Nomura ITMCo	Open-End	Equity
Philippine Strat Inv (Holding)	-58.01	N/A	US$	10.625	11.657	Philippines I	Closed-End	Equity
JF Philippine	-58.94	1.27	US$	10.4	8.432	Jardine Fleming	Open-End	Equity
Nikko GIUF Philippines Fund	-60.44	N/A	US$	0.1	9.245	Nikko	Open-End	Equity
First Philippine Fd	-61.01	-34.66	US$	216.29	10.571	Clemente Cap	Closed-End	Equity
Paribas EM Philippines Ptfl	-63.9	N/A	US$	N/A	10.592	Paribas Asset	Open-End	Equity
Jupiter Tyndall GF Ph'ppines	-64.13	N/A	US$	4.9	10.132	Tyndall	Open-End	Equity
Barclays ASF Philippines	-64.19	-27.67	US$	3.5	9.964	Barclays	Open-End	Equity
Manila Fund (Cayman) Ltd	-67.56	-13.22	US$	9.6	10.926	Indosuez	Closed-End	Equity
Thornton New Tiger Philippine	-68.12	-14.86	US$	2.8	12.042	Thornton	Open-End	Equity

Note: details for some funds may not have been included if the data for the US$ % change for 97/98 is not available

Source: Standard & Poor's Micropal.

PEREGRINE SECURITIES PHILS
17/F Tower 1 & Exchange Plaza
Ayala Ave. cor Paseo de Roxas, Makati City
Tel: (63) 2 848 5298/848 5576; Fax: (63) 2 848 5738

PRYCE SECURITIES
9/F BPI Paseo de Roxas Condominium Centre
8753 Paseo de Roxas, Makati City
Tel: (63) 2 816 2426-27/810 7451-56; Fax: (63) 2 815 0071

C) Settlement and transfer

From December 1997, the transfer of securities has been effected by book entry at the Philippine Central Depository (PCD). Settlement of trades in listed securities takes place four days after the transaction date.

D) Commissions and other costs

Brokerage commission

Commission charges, which are paid by both the buyer and seller, are 1.5% (maximum) of the total transaction value, plus 10% VAT.

Transfer fee

A transfer fee of P100 plus 10% VAT is charged to the buyer by the transfer agent for every certificate traded.

Cancellation fee

Sales transactions and/or direct transfers are subject to a cancellation fee of P20 per stock certificate or stock assignment, plus 10% VAT.

PCD fees

Transactions are subject to an ad valorem rate of 0.0000834%, with no maximum or minimum amount, in lieu of transfer and cancellation fees. VAT of 10% is also added.

TAXATION AND REGULATIONS AFFECTING FOREIGN INVESTORS

The Philippine government has generally welcomed foreign investment, except in industries reserved for Filipinos.

A) Withholding tax

A new tax reform law, Republic Act No. 8424, took effect on 1 January 1998. Under this law, and except in cases where tax treaties are in force, dividends received from domestic corporations are subject to a withholding tax of 25% if the recipient is a non-resident individual not engaged in trade or business in the Philippines, and 34% (33%, effective 1 January 1999, and 32%, effective 1 January 2000) if the recipient is a non-resident foreign corporation. The rates for dividends paid to non-resident foreign corporations may be reduced to a special 15% rate if the country in which the non-resident foreign corporation is domiciled (a) imposes no taxes on foreign-source dividends or (b) allows a credit against the tax due from the foreign non-resident corporation of an amount equal to at least 19% (18% for 1999, and 17% thereafter) of such dividends.

B) Capital gains

The 1996 tax on capital gains realised from shares listed

and traded through the stock exchange has been replaced by a percentage tax on the disposition of such shares (other than their sale by a dealer in securities) at 0.5% of the gross sale proceeds. This is payable by the seller or transferor.

C) Documentary stamp tax

The documentary stamp tax rate on purchase transactions is P1.50 for every P200 par value of the stock being transferred or fraction thereof.

D) Exchange regulations

Registration of foreign investments with the central bank is only required if the foreign exchange needed to repatriate the proceeds from the sale of investments and the remittance of dividends is to be sourced from the banking system. Foreign investments in listed equities, including those traded over-the-counter, may be registered either directly with the central bank or via a designated custodian bank.

LISTING AND REPORTING REQUIREMENTS

A listing agreement is executed by corporations prior to listing on the PSE. The listing agreement provides for the publication of notices and/or the filing of certain documents within a certain number of days. All listed companies must submit an audited financial report within 105 days from the end of their fiscal year. Annual reports must be filed within 15 calendar days after the annual meeting. All corporations are also required to file annual lists of directors and major stockholders.

Under SEC rules, every corporation with securities listed or traded on the PSE must make a reasonably full, fair and accurate disclosure of every material fact relating to or affecting it, which may be of interest to investors. A fact is deemed to be material if it could affect an investor's decision to sell a company's securities – for example, dividend declarations, the sale or acquisition of significant capital assets, the discovery of ores and the execution of a merger, consolidation or joint venture.

SHAREHOLDER PROTECTION CODES

A) Takeovers and mergers

Under the Philippine Corporation Code, a merger requires a vote of the majority of the board of directors and stockholders representing at least two-thirds of the outstanding capital stock. The merger must also be approved by the SEC. In cases of mergers or consolidations of banks or banking institutions, building and loan associations, trust companies, insurance companies, public utilities, educational institutions and corporations governed by special laws, the recommendation of the appropriate government agency is also required before the SEC grants its approval.

A minority stockholder who objects to the merger or consolidation may demand fair payment for his shares.

B) Insider trading

The Philippine Revised Securities Act makes it unlawful (subject to specified exceptions) for an insider to sell or buy a security if he knows of a fact of special significance with respect to the issuer or the security that is not generally available. An "insider" includes the issuer, as well as any of its directors, officers or affiliates. Under SEC rules, a stockbroking firm is not permitted to deal in the shares of a company in which members of the broking firm also hold office. Otherwise, directors are allowed to deal freely in the shares of their companies subject to the insider trading rules.

C) Compensation fund

There is a Securities Industry Protection Fund from which compensation may be paid to investors for losses due to fraud or default by a stockbroker or dealer. The maximum amount payable per investor is currently P10,000 (US$250) but the SEC plans to increase this.

RESEARCH

Most securities and brokerage houses have their own research arms; for example OCBC Securities, Jardine Fleming Capital Securities and ING Baring Securities. The PSE likewise has its own research department which provides a wide variety of data. A further useful source is:

UNIVERSITY OF ASIA AND THE PACIFIC
(formerly Centre for Research and Communication)
Pearl Drive, Ortigas Centre, Pasig, Metro Manila
Tel: (63) 2 631 0935-40

PSE publications include:
Weekly Report
Monthly Report
Annual Factbook
Investments Guide

Philippines, published by Euromoney Books, provides in-depth information for those wishing to invest or do business in the country. See the order card at the back of this book for details.

CHAPTER 54

Poland

Introduction

The Warsaw Stock Exchange (WSE) is the main stock exchange in Poland. It operates alongside a fledgling OTC market that caters for smaller businesses.

Listed companies currently represent the following industry sectors: banking, trade, construction, glass, textiles, brewing, food processing, chemicals, electronics, wood, pharmaceuticals, insurance, printing metallurgy and white goods. Following new issues planned for 1998, software development, telecoms, machinery and advertising will also be represented.

Derivatives trading was introduced on 16 January 1998. Three-month and six-month futures contracts on the WIG-20 blue chip index were the first derivatives traded on the Polish exchange.

Unlike in the early 1990s when retail investors actively participated in trading, the WSE is becoming increasingly dependent on large institutional investors. The estimated total free float held by institutional investors is now 65%.

ECONOMIC AND POLITICAL OVERVIEW

Following parliamentary elections in September 1997, the Solidarity bloc is back in power, and the new coalition government seems to have regained the confidence of the investment community. Leaders of the AWS – the senior coalition party – have supported continued reforms and have not pushed populist election campaign promises. The UW – the junior coalition partner – has changed its image from an ultra liberal, centre-right party to one more friendly to social reforms, but this has not weakened its sound, conservative attitude towards the economy.

The main economic policy difficulty faced by the new government lies in the restructuring of publicly held corporations in the run-up to their privatisation. Painful restructuring measures are needed in large ailing industries like coal mining, shipping and railways. The government must also manage mounting external balances. In 1997, the trade and current account deficits reached 8% and almost 4% of GDP respectively. With US$21 billion in foreign reserves, the deficits remain manageable, but further quick deficit growth could eventually spark devaluation. The political establishment is far from complacent on the issue, having restricted the budget deficit and focused on monitoring the trade deficit.

With a slightly lower deficit at 1.5% of GDP, the budget is due for approval in late February 1998. The new government has increased budgeted expenditures for flood-damage reconstruction while lowering the overall budget. The lower deficit will be achieved through cuts in non-investment spending and higher excise tax revenues. Whether public sector-based AWS supporters will continue to accept restrictive fiscal policy in the coming years remains an open question.

In a bid to slow steep loan growth, the central bank has increased mandatory reserves for commercial banks and has not hesitated to raise interest rates. Yields on Treasury bonds have continued to grow, pushing real interest rates to 8–10%.

Role of the central bank

The primary goal of the National Bank of Poland (NBP) is to curb inflation. It is also responsible for the interbank settlement system; foreign currency reserve management; strengthening banking sector liquidity and solvency; fostering overall development in the banking sector; and reporting on the balance of payments and foreign currency receivables and payables. The NBP is the only body entitled to issue domestic currency.

The president of the NBP is nominated by Poland's President and appointed by parliament for a six-year term. The Monetary Policy Council functions in a similar way to central bank boards in other European countries. The Council is responsible for establishing the principal monetary policy assumptions and presenting these to

Exhibit 54.1: WARSAW GENERAL PRICE INDEX (US$), 1993–97

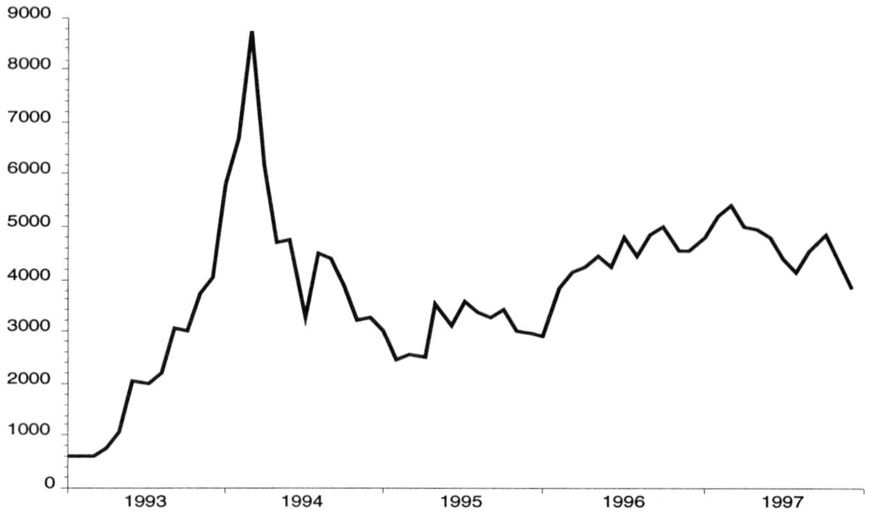

High value 8724.6 1.3.94 Low value 611.2 1.2.93 *Source: Datastream*

parliament, accepting NBP budgets, and setting official interest rates and obligatory reserve requirements.

MARKET PERFORMANCE

A) In 1997

While previously some 20 new companies had been admitted to exchange trading each year, 62 new companies, including 15 National Investment Funds, joined the WSE list in 1997. Market capitalisation increased by 60% during the year, and the value of equity turnover rose by 38% compared with 1996. The WIG Index closed the year 2.3% ahead at 14,668.

B) Summary information

Global ranking by market value (US$ terms, end-1997): 46
Market capitalisation (end-1997): US$13.34 billion
Growth in market value (US$ terms, 1993–97): 421%
Market value as a % of nominal GDP (end-1997): 8%
Number of domestic/foreign companies listed (end-1997): 143/0
Market P/E (WIG Index companies, end-1997): 12.6
MSCI Index (change in US$ terms, 1997): -23.6%
Short-term (3-months) interest rate (end-1997): 26.09%
Long-term (1-year) bond yield (end-1997): 24.02%
Budget deficit as a % of nominal GDP (1997): 1.9%
Annual increase in broad money (M3) supply (end-1997): 28.8%
Inflation rate (1997): 13.2%
US$ exchange rate (end-1997): Z3.5180

C) Year-end share price index, price/earnings ratios and yields

Exhibit: 54.2:
YEAR-END SHARE PRICE INDEX (Z TERMS), P/E RATIOS AND GROSS DIVIDEND YIELDS, 1993–97

Year-end	*WIG Index*	*P/E*	*Yield (%)*
1993	12,439	23.9	0.4
1994	7,473	16.4	0.4
1995	7,589	7.8	2.3
1996	14,342	14.8	1.2
1997	14,668	12.6	1.4

Source: Warsaw Stock Exchange.

D) Market indices and their constituents

The WSE main market index, the WIG, is a total return index weighted by market capitalisation. The base date for the index is 16 April 1991, and its base value is 1,000. The WIRR is a total return index, introduced on 1 January 1995, and it covers companies listed on the WSE parallel market. Its base value is also 1,000. Both the WIG and the WIRR are calculated using IFC methodology.

The WIG-20 Index was introduced on 16 April 1994 (with a base value of 1,000) and it covers the 20 largest and most liquid companies on the WSE main market.

The NIF Index is a portfolio price index, introduced on 12 June 1997, which covers 15 National Investment Funds. The index reflects the market value of NIF shares received on conversion of one privatisation certificate. The index base value is 160 points.

THE STOCK MARKET

A) Brief history and structure

The first stock exchange in Warsaw was opened in 1817 and, prior to 1939, Poland had seven separate exchanges. During half a century of communist rule the Polish financial market was more or less non-existent. The WSE in its current form was established in April 1991: it is a joint stock company, with the State Treasury, banks and brokerage houses as its shareholders.

Listing rules and trading practices, as well as compliance with corporate disclosure standards, are regulated by the Rules of the Warsaw Stock Exchange.

In October 1994 the WSE was admitted as a full member of the International Federation of Stock Exchanges (FIBV).

B) Opening hours, names and addresses

Trading sessions are held daily from Monday to Friday, from 11.00am to 3.00pm.

WARSAW STOCK EXCHANGE
6/12 Nowy Swiat, 00-400 Warsaw
Tel: (48) 22 628 3232; Fax: (48) 22 628 1754
E-mail: gieldaikp.atm.com.pl

MARKET SIZE

A) Number of listings and market value

Exhibit 54.3:
NUMBER OF LISTED COMPANIES AND MARKET CAPITALISATION, WSE, 1993–97

Year-end	*No. of listed companies*	*Market value (US$ million)*
1993	22	2,559
1994	44	3,100
1995	65	4,576
1996	83	8,333
1997	143	13,340

Source: Warsaw Stock Exchange.

B) Largest quoted companies

Exhibit 54.4:
THE 10 LARGEST QUOTED COMPANIES, WSE, END-1997

Ranking	*Company*	*Sector*	*Market value (US$ million)*
1	Handlowy	Banking	832.4
2	KGHM	Heavy industry	739.9
3	Elektrim	conglomerates	649.1
4	BPH	Banking	539.6
5	BSK	Banking	513.9
6	PBK	Banking	454.8
7	BIG-BG	Banking	416.9
8	BRE	Banking	394.7
9	WBK	Banking	346.6
10	Debica	Chemicals	337.8

Source: Warsaw Stock Exchange.

C) Trading volume

A total of 1.25 billion shares were traded in 1997. Total equity turnover for the year was Z14.5 billion, and the average per session was Z60 million.

Exhibit 54.5:
TRADING VOLUME AND VALUE ON THE WSE, 1993–97

Year	*Trading volume (million shares)*	*Trading value (Z billion)*
1993	108	7.75
1994	336	23.42
1995	528	13.27
1996	935	10.50
1997	1,247	14.50

Source: Warsaw Stock Exchange.

Exhibit 54.6:
THE 10 MOST ACTIVELY TRADED SHARES ON THE WSE, 1997

Ranking	*Company*	*Turnover (US$ million)*	*% of total*
1	Elektrim	698.8	5.8
2	Handlowy	570.8	4.8
3	Universal	545.6	4.5
4	KGHM	541.5	4.5
5	Mostostal-Export	488.4	4.1
6	BRE	450.5	3.8
7	BSK	408.1	3.4
8	Optimus	369.9	3.1
9	Budimex	365.3	3.0
10	Okocim	294.2	2.5

Source: Warsaw Stock Exchange.

TYPES OF SHARE

Shares of domestic companies, Treasury bonds and privatisation certificates issued under the National

Exhibit 54.7:
COUNTRY FUNDS – POLAND

Fund	US$ % change 01/01/97 01/01/98	01/01/93 01/01/98	Fund base currency	Fund size (US$ mil)	Fund volatility	Management group	Opal main sector	Opal subsector
Fleming Poland Fund Ltd	-11.56	N/A	US$	31.876	-1	Fleming	Closed-End	Equity
Pioneer First Polish Trust	-14.3	214.89	Z	939.51	4.471	Pioneer	Open-End	Equity
Polish Investment Company	-16.11	N/A	US$	45.691	-1	Foreign & Colonial	Open-End	Equity
Pioneer Agressive Inv Trust Fd	-18.71	N/A	Z	N/A	-1	Pioneer	Open-End	Equity

Note: details for some funds may not have been included if the data for the US$ % change for 97/98 was not available

Source: Standard & Poor's Micropal.

Investment Funds (NIF) programme are traded on the WSE. Also, when a company makes a rights issue, the subscription rights are automatically traded on the WSE during the subscription period.

OTHER MARKETS

In January 1998, the WSE launched a derivatives market. The first derivative instruments traded were three and six-month futures contracts on the WIG-20 Index.

INVESTORS

There were about 1.2 million investment accounts with Polish brokerage houses at the end of 1997. Foreign investment on the exchange was estimated at about 30%.

OPERATIONS

A) Trading system

Trading on the WSE is order-driven, centralised and paperless. The exchange uses two trading systems – single-price auction (electronic call auction) and continuous trading.

The electronic call auction is based on the French model. The main feature of the system is that a single price per security emerges as the result of orders submitted. After the initial call auction, additional trading takes place at the set price during so-called post-auction trading (the balancing and crossing phases).

Continuous trading was introduced on the WSE in 1992 and was fully computerised in 1995. Initially, this method of trading was used only for Treasury bonds. As of July 1996, most liquid stocks have been gradually introduced to continuous trading. By the end of 1997, 46 equities were traded in the continuous quotation system, along with NIF certificates. Futures contracts started trading in this system in January 1998.

Large blocks of securities can be traded off-session, without influencing prices on the retail market.

B) List of principal brokers

In January 1998, the WSE had 36 trading member firms. Exchange member firms include:

ABN AMRO BANK (POLSKA)
ul. Faksal 19, 00-372 Warsaw
Tel: (48) 22 695 4900; Fax: (48) 22 695 4821

CENTRUM OPERACJI KAPITAŁOWYCH
BANK HANDLOWY W WARSZAWIE
ul.Kasprzaka 18/20, 01-211 Warsaw
Tel: (48) 22 661 71 25; Fax: (48) 22 625 69 49

CENTRALNY DOM MAKLERSKI GRUPY PEKAO
ul. Wołoska 18, (Curtis Plaza),
02-675 Warsaw
Tel: (48) 22 640 28 40, 640 28 41;
Fax: (48) 22 640 28 00, 621 26 00

CREDIT SUISSE FIRST BOSTON
Al Jerozolinskie 81, 02 001 Warsaw
Tel: (48) 22 695 0050

DOM MAKLERSKI BIG BG
ul. Jana Pawła II 15, IV floor,
00-828 Warsaw
Tel: (48) 22 697 67 96, 697 67 97; Fax: (48) 22 697 67 67

DOM MAKLERSKI CA IB SECURITIES
Al. Jerozolimskie 56 C, 00-803 Warsaw
Tel: (48) 22 630 62 72/630 61 99; Fax: (48) 22 630 62 68

DOM MAKLERSKI CITIBROKERAGE
ul. Fredry 6, 00-095 Warsaw
Tel: (48) 22 657 78 79; Fax: (48) 22 657 78 80

ING BARINGS WARSAW
ul. Emilii Plater 28, 00950 Warsaw
Tel: (48) 22 630 5691; Fax: (48) 22 630 7267

SOCIÉTÉ GÉNÉRALE
Immeuble Peugrex, 44/46 ul. Zlota, Warsaw
Tel: (48) 22 625 4500; Fax: (48) 22 625 7156

C) Settlement and transfer

The settlement system is based on T+3 and delivery versus payment – ie, a selling broker does not get paid until it delivers securities, and a buying broker does not receive securities until it has paid for them. Accounting, the preparation of data for settlement and registration are computerised.

D) Commissions and other costs

There are no fixed commissions imposed by law or under exchange rules. The rates generally applied by brokers do not include research and range from 0.3% to 1.2% for shares.

TAXATION AND REGULATIONS AFFECTING FOREIGN INVESTORS

There are no restrictions on foreign investments. The rule of free entry and exit applies to all foreign investors.

Dividend payments from Polish companies to resident corporations are subject to a 20% withholding tax, but Polish companies are given a tax credit equal to the amount of the withholding tax, provided they have sufficient taxable profit to utilise the credit. If it is not possible to utilise the tax credit in a fiscal period, it may be carried forward and utilised in the following fiscal period. The net result is that resident corporations with taxable income suffer no tax on dividends received from other resident corporations. Dividend payments by resident corporations to non-resident entities are subject to withholding tax of 20% (unless a double tax treaty specifies a lower rate). Polish corporations are also required to withhold tax of 20% on payments made to non-Polish entities of interest and royalties (unless a double tax agreement specifies a lower rate).

Exhibit 54.8:
WITHHOLDING TAXES

Recipient	*Dividends %*	*Interest %*	*Royalties %*
Resident corporations	20	N/A	N/A
Resident individuals	20	N/A	N/A
Non-resident corporations and individuals:			
Non-treaty	20	20	20
Treaty	0–20	0–20	0–20

Source: Price Waterhouse.

Capital gains are subject to taxation under the standard rules. This means that income earned from the disposal of shares is subject to 38% tax for corporations and up to 44% tax for individuals (the rate depends on the amount of the gain). However, the detailed regulations include many waivers and exemptions.

A number of bilateral tax treaties concluded by Poland provide that income earned by foreign investors on disposals of shares in Polish companies is not subject to taxation in Poland.

On 22 January 1996 the Minister of Finance issued a special waiver of corporate income tax on gains made by foreign companies from the sale of joint stock company shares acquired on the WSE. The waiver is conditional upon similar treatment of this type of income applying to a Polish company in the country of residence of the foreign company.

Income earned by individuals from the sale of Polish Treasury and municipal bonds and shares admitted to public trading, which were purchased on the basis of a public offer or acquired on the stock exchange or OTC market, is exempt from taxation up to 1 January 2000. (This exemption is not applicable if the individual's business involves the purchase and sale of securities.) Income earned by individuals from participation in trust funds is also exempt from taxation until 1 January 2000.

In general, there are no exchange control restrictions on inward investment or on the repatriation of capital and earnings.

REPORTING REQUIREMENTS

Issuers must publish a prospectus designed to enable investors to evaluate the financial condition and prospects of the issuer, as well as the terms and conditions of the securities offered. Before publication the prospectus must be filed with, and cleared by, the Polish Securities Commission (PSC), the central government administrator for the public trading of securities.

The issuer is obliged to notify the PSC, the WSE and the Polish Press Agency (PAP) of any changes in the particulars included in the prospectus and to provide current and periodical information. The disclosure requirements are to submit yearly, half-yearly and quarterly reports, as well as monthly figures on sales and profits. In addition, an issuer must disclose (within 24 hours) any information that could affect the market price of its securities.

SHAREHOLDER PROTECTION CODES

Under the Securities Law, a combined maximum fine of Z5 million and up to five years' imprisonment can now be imposed on a person who, in a prospectus or by means of other information to investors, provides wrongful information or withholds details that could be material. This provision makes the management board of a company, as well as advisers who prepare the prospectus, liable.

The same combined fine and imprisonment can be imposed on a person who, during public trading, makes use of insider information. Insider information is defined as information concerning the issuer or security that has not been made available to the public and disclosure of which could influence in a material way the price of the security. Anyone who, alone or in agreement with others, causes an artificial rise or fall in the price of securities, can be imprisoned for up to three years and fined up to Z5 million.

Anyone who acquires 5% or more of the voting rights of a listed company must inform the PSC, the Consumer and Competition Protection Office and the company. When 10% or more is acquired, every 2% change thereafter must also be reported. Anyone who intends to acquire blocks of shares exceeding the thresholds of 25%, 33% or 50% must inform the PSC, which may, after obtaining the opinion of the Consumer and Competition Protection Office, prohibit the acquisition if it would infringe provisions of the Securities Law or the Law on Counteracting Monopolistic Practices, or if it would threaten national interests or the national economy.

RESEARCH

Real-time WSE data is available through information vendors, including Reuters, Dow Jones Telerate and some domestic providers.

Investment advice and portfolio management are subject to PSC licensing requirements. In order to offer portfolio management services a firm has to employ at least two licensed advisers and obtain a permit from the PSC.

Poland's Financial System, published by Euromoney Books, provides in-depth information for those wishing to invest or do business in the region. See order card at the back of the book for details.

CHAPTER 55

Portugal

Introduction

In 1997 the Lisbon Stock Exchange (LSE) performed well, underpinned by a calm political environment, a credible commitment to join EMU, renewed confidence on the part of non-resident investors and healthy trading results from many listed companies.

The government pursued its privatisation programme energetically, with a record Esc800 billion – worth of shares sold through the market. The three most important privatisation issues (EDP, Portugal Telecom and Brisa) were all heavily oversubscribed.

The inclusion of the Portuguese equity market in Morgan Stanley Capital International's developed market indices was a turning point in non-resident investor perceptions of the LSE, and the market reacted with a very strong rally; the BVL-30 Index ended the year 75% ahead.

ECONOMIC AND POLITICAL OVERVIEW

From March 1997 onwards it was clear that Portugal would have no difficulty in fulfilling the criteria to join EMU, due in particular to the decreasing cost of public debt.

GDP growth of about 3.8% (versus 3% in 1996) exceeded the European average, while year-on-year inflation, helped by moderate wage settlements and limited demand-side pressures, fell from 3.3% in 1996 to 2.1%.

Official estimates are for a public deficit to GDP ratio of 2.7% in 1997 (compared with the budgeted 2.9%), mainly due to extra direct tax proceeds, reduced interest charges and the tight control of current expenses. Public debt, as reduced by privatisation proceeds, is estimated at 64% of GDP, down from 65.4% in 1996.

Long-term interest rate spreads relative to German bunds fell from 110 basis points to just 30 at the end of 1997.

Role of the central bank

The Bank of Portugal plays a vital role in (a) the setting and implementation of monetary and exchange rate policies, (b) the management of Portugal's external liquid assets and (c) intervention in the international financial markets to help maintain the stability of the domestic financial system.

The central bank also supervises the banking system, controls the normal operations of the cheque clearing houses and is responsible for the preparation of monetary, financial and exchange statistical data. The bank also decides on money market intervention rates.

MARKET PERFORMANCE

A) In 1997

The Portuguese equity market rose by 75% in local currency terms in 1997, representing its best performance for many years. Even with a record supply of privatisation offerings (over Esc800 billion, or 20% of market capitalisation at the beginning of 1997), buy-side pressure was maintained.

Retail domestic investors entered the market in force, searching for better returns than the 4% offered on time deposits. In the EDP privatisation alone, some 640,000 investors (around 10% of the adult population) bought shares. Retail investors also boosted unit trust subscriptions: the global value of equity assets under management by investment trusts rose four-fold, which cannot be explained by price appreciation alone. At the same time, pension funds increased their equity market exposure to over 10%, while non-resident investors, who have traditionally accounted for two-thirds of market free float, saw their share decrease to less than 50%.

B) Summary information

Global ranking by market value (US$ terms, end-1997): 32
Market capitalisation (end-1997):US$38.23 billion
Growth in market value (local currency terms, 1993–97): 248%
Market value as a % of nominal GDP (end-1997): 41%
Number of domestic/foreign companies listed (end-1997): 75/0
Market P/E (end-1997): 21.2
MSCI total returns (with net dividends, US$ terms, 1997): 46.7%

Exhibit 55.1: BANCO TOTTA ACORES PRICE INDEX (Esc), 1993–97

High value 4831.5 1.10.97 Low value 1637.9 1.1.93 *Source: Datastream*

MSCI Index (change in US$ terms, 1997): +43.9%
Short-term (90-day) interest rate (end-1997): 5.07%
Long-term (10-year) bond yield (end-1997): 5.6%
Budget deficit as a % of nominal GDP (1997): 2.7%
Annual increase in broad money (M3) supply (end-1997): 6.5%
Inflation rate (1997): 2.1%
US$ exchange rate (end-1997): Esc183.326

Exhibit 55.2:
YEAR-END SHARE PRICE INDEX, 1993–97

	1993	*1994*	*1995*	*1996*	*1997*
BVL-30 Index	1,565.16	1,699.54	1,605.30	2,164.50	3,781.31

C) Market indices and their constituents

The BVL General Index has been the official market index of the Lisbon exchange since February 1991, and has a base of 1,000 at 5 January 1988. It includes all listed shares on the LSE official market, although the exact number of companies in the portfolio of the index can change daily as a result of admissions, exclusions, suspensions and the absence of quotations.

In 1993, the LSE began calculating the BVL-30, which is a total return, value-weighted, blue chip stock index. The companies included in the BVL-30 index account for 80% of total market value. Recently, this index has begun to take over from the General Index as the benchmark reference for the Portuguese stock market.

The Oporto Derivatives Exchange calculates the PSI-20, representing 78% of market capitalisation, to serve as a cash basis for futures contracts. This PSI-20 is a price return, value-weighted index.

THE STOCK MARKET

A) Brief history and structure

The origin of the Lisbon Stock Exchange can be traced back to 1 January 1769, when the Traders' Assembly – as the chamber of brokers was known – began meeting regularly in the eastern tower of the Praça de Comercio to settle their accounts. After 225 years in the old tower, the LSE moved in 1994 to new premises in the modern part of town.

In 1974 domestic stock exchanges were closed as a result of the political and economic changes following the April Revolution. The LSE reopened in 1975 for bonds and in 1977 for shares, while the Oporto exchange restarted operations in January 1981. EU membership marked the start of a period that has seen dramatic growth in the scope and activity of the Portuguese stock market.

The LSE is divided into three markets, each with specific requirements regarding admission to listing and trading:

- In the official market, created on 23 July 1991, securities are traded through a computer-linked system (TRADIS).

- The second market, created in January 1992, is intended for trading securities that do not meet all the requirements for admission to the official market. The main purpose of this market is to allow access to the stock exchange for small and medium-sized companies.
- The unofficial market, created on 22 October 1991, is intended for securities that do not meet the requirements for the other two markets. Securities can be admitted to this market for a limited or unlimited period of time.

In 1992, the LSE was privatised. It is now under the management of the Lisbon Stock Exchange Association.

B) Different exchanges

The stock exchange in Lisbon trades stocks, bonds and unit trusts, while the Oporto exchange trades futures contracts.

C) Opening hours, names and addresses

LSE trading hours are Monday to Friday from 9.00am to 9.30am for pre-opening and 9.30am to 4.30pm for continuous trading. Trading hours for daily calls are Monday to Friday from 9.30am to 4.00pm.

The Oporto Derivatives Exchange is open Monday to Friday from 9.30am to 4.30pm.

BOLSA DE VALORES DE LISBOA
Edificio de Bolsa, Rua Soeiro Pereira Gomes, 1600 Lisboa
Tel: (351) 1 790 0000/795 2031; Fax: (351) 1 795 2021

BOLSA DE DERIVADOS DO OPORTO
Av da Boavista 3433, 4100 Oporto
Tel: (351) 2 618 5858; Fax: (351) 2 618 5566

MARKET SIZE

A) Number of listings and market value

At the end of 1997, there were 75 companies listed on the official market. They were capitalised at Esc7,008 billion, an increase of 95% over the year.

Exhibit 55.3:
NUMBER AND VALUE OF COMPANIES LISTED ON THE OFFICIAL MARKET, 1993–97

Year	*No. of companies*	*Market capitalisation (Esc billion)*
1993	89	2,057.28
1994	83	2,320.65
1995	78	2,499.41
1996	73	3,599.34
1997	75	7,007.98

Source: Banco Cisf.

B) Largest quoted companies

Exhibit 55.4:
THE 20 LARGEST COMPANIES LISTED ON THE OFFICIAL MARKET, END-1997

Ranking	*Company*	*Market value (Esc million)*
1	Portugal Telecom	1,117,636
2	EDP	618,838
3	BCP	564,600
4	BES	478,504
5	Telecel	421,615
6	BPI	348,818
7	Modelo Continente	302,940
8	Sonae Investimentos	297,760
9	BPA	279,400
10	Cimpor	263,390
11	BTA	216,840
12	Soporcel	166,796
13	Mundial Confianca	162,810
14	Jerónimo Martins	160,749
15	BPSM	132,988
16	Semapa	106,144
17	BMC	95,517
18	Tranquilidade	83,980
19	Sonae Imobiliária	83,663
20	Inparsa	66,495

Source: Banco Cisf.

Exhibit 55.5:
VALUE OF COMPANIES BY SECTOR, OFFICIAL MARKET, END-1997

Sector	*Market value (Esc million)*	*% of total market value*
Banks	2,266,017	32.3%
Communications	1,578,833	22.5%
Retail	775,179	11.1%
Electric utilities	618,838	8.8%
Non-metal mining products	419,024	6.0%
Forestry products	344,206	4.9%
Insurance	309,076	4.4%
Real estate	137,490	2.0%
Construction	115,508	1.6%
Motorways	103,447	1.5%
Food and beverages	95,803	1.4%
Holdings	93,105	1.3%
Engineering	89,479	1.3%
Chemicals	53,639	0.8%
Others	8,331	0.1%
Total	**7,007,975**	**100.0%**

Source: Banco Cisf.

C) Trading volume

Official market turnover (including bonds) on the LSE in 1997 was Esc5,850 billion, a 93% increase on 1996.

Exhibit 55.6:
TRADING VALUE ON THE LSE (INCLUDING BONDS AND GOVERNMENT SECURITIES), 1993–97

Year	*Daily average (Esc million)*	*Total turnover (Esc million)*
1993	11,888	2,794,747
1994	14,709	3,633,209
1995	9,257	2,268,169
1996	12,250	3,025,828
1997	23,780	5,849,974

Source: Banco Cisf.

Exhibit 55.7:
EQUITY TURNOVER BY SECTOR, OFFICIAL MARKET, 1997

Sector	*Trading value (Esc million)*	*% of total*
Communications	947,954	26.6%
Banks	934,126	26.2%
Electric utilities	446,148	12.5%
Non-metal mining products	349,922	9.8%
Retail	287,175	8.0%
Forestry products	200,509	5.6%
Insurance	106,554	3.0%
Construction	89,796	2.5%
Holdings	74,253	2.1%
Engineering	38,933	1.1%
Motorways	30,663	0.9%
Food and beverages	23,637	0.7%
Real estate	21,508	0.6%
Chemicals	16,751	0.5%
Others	1,788	0.1%
Total	**3,569,717**	**100.0%**

Source: Banco Cisf.

Exhibit 55.8:
THE 20 MOST ACTIVELY TRADED SHARES ON THE OFFICIAL MARKET, 1997

Ranking	*Company*	*Turnover (Esc million)*
1	Portugal Telecom	692,198
2	EDP	446,148
3	BCP	312,992
4	Cimpor	285,910
5	Telecel	240,688
6	BES	161,935
7	Sonae Investimentos	150,396
8	BPI	124,434
9	BTA	122,265
10	Jerónimo Martins	91,630
11	BPSM	88,35
12	Portucel Industrial	88,214
13	Mundial Confianca	79,855
14	BPA	79,342
15	Inparsa	65,361
16	Semapa	41,549
17	Sonae Industria	41,086
18	Modelo Continente	40,514
19	Inapa	34,734
20	Brisa	30,610

Source: Banco Cisf.

TYPES OF SHARE

The Portuguese Corporation Law provides for all the usual types of shares, which may be traded either directly or on the stock market.

Shares are usually bearer, although many companies have issued registered shares. Banks and other credit institutions may only issue registered shares.

The Securities Code makes provision for shares represented only by data input in the company's computer (ie, dematerialised shares).

OTHER MARKETS

The OTC market includes all purchases and sales of securities that are outside the regular stock exchange and second market mechanisms and carried out by brokers or any other financial intermediaries with legal and statutory authorisation.

The Oporto Derivatives Exchange was established in June 1996. Five futures contracts are traded, including a PSI-20 stock index future and futures contracts on Portugal Telecom stock and EDP stock.

OPERATIONS

A) Trading system

The TRADIS computerised trading system provides automatic execution of orders and continuous trading. At the end of 1997 it included 115 issues (23 bonds or similar, 83 shares and nine participation bonds). All other securities are traded under the traditional roll-call procedure, with three prices set each day.

A new trading system will be launched in 1998. It is based on the *Nouveau Sistème de Cotacions* of the Société des Bourses Françaises, and will be ready to operate in time for the European single currency.

Exhibit 55.9:
COUNTRY FUNDS – PORTUGAL

Fund	US$ % change 01/01/97 01/01/98	01/01/93 01/01/98	Fund base currency	Fund size (US$ mil)	Fund volatility	Management group	Opal main sector	Opal subsector
Paribas EM Portugal Ptfl	53.08	N/A	US$	N/A	4.226	Paribas Asset	Open-End	Equity
Portugal Fund Ltd	41.18	163.7	US$	28.429	4.625	Lloyds GSY	Closed-End	Equity
Portugal Fund Inc	38.74	178.98	US$	84.233	3.917	BEA Assoc	Closed-End	Equity
Portuguese Smaller Cos	36.2	N/A	US$	62.856	3.397	Banco Privado	Closed-End	Equity
Capital Portugal Fund	31.74	140.65	Esc	19903	4.523	Gestfondo	Closed-End	Equity

Note: details for some funds may not have been included if the data for the US$ % change for 97/98 was not available

Source: Standard & Poor's Micropal.

B) List of principal brokers

LJ CARREGOSA
Av da Boavista 1083, 4100 Oporto
Tel: (351) 2 607 9030; Fax: (351) 2 607 7887

CENTRAL INVESTIMENTOS
Rua Castilho 233, 4th Floor, 1070 Lisbon
Tel: (351) 1 381 4000; Fax: (351) 1 387 3793

CFI CO FINANCIERA INTERNACIONAL
Rua Braamcamp 52, 5th Floor, 1200 Lisbon
Tel: (351) 1 386 3730; Fax: (351) 1 386 2037

DB CORRETORA
Rua Castilho 20, 5th Floor, 1250 Lisbon
Tel: (351) 1 311 1204; Fax: (351) 1 352 6490

DOURO
Largo Jean Monnet 1, 5th Floor, 1100 Lisbon
Tel: (351) 1 352 2345; Fax: (351) 1 352 2339

FINANTIA CORRETORA
Rua General Firmino Miguel 5, 6th Floor, 1600 Lisbon
Tel: (351) 1 720 2000; Fax: (351) 1 726 5310

FINCOR
Rua Braamcamp 9, 7th Floor, 1250 Lisbon
Tel: (351) 1 312 7000; Fax: (351) 1 354 4949

PARS
Av de Boavista 3521, 3rd Floor, Room 302, 4150 Oporto
Tel: (351) 2 610 4167; Fax: (351) 2 610 4164

TITULO
Avenida de Berna 10, 5th Floor
Edificio Finibanco, 1050 Lisbon
Tel: (351) 1 790 2945; Fax: (351) 1 793 7267

C) Settlement and transfer

One of the most important aspects of the reform of the Portuguese securities market has been the creation of a national clearing and settlement system and a central securities depository, the Central de Valores Mobiliarios (Central). Central is the clearing organisation responsible for the settlement of fungible securities registered with the central depository. This clearing system also includes Banco de Portugal and the financial intermediaries. In addition, the LSE acts as a clearing organisation for the settlement of non-fungible securities and fungible securities not yet registered with Central.

Physical settlement of transactions involving securities deposited with Central takes place on T+3, while financial settlement is on T+4. Other fungible securities transactions (net) are settled on the 15th and 30th of every month by the stock exchange compensation centre (transactions in individual securities are controlled on T+2). Non-fungible securities are also settled by physical delivery through broker companies on T+3 physical and T+4 financial.

D) Commissions and other costs

Subject to prescribed limits, brokerage commissions became negotiable in May 1996. The limits are that on transactions worth up to Esc1 million, brokerage cannot exceed 0.5%, and that brokers can impose a minimum transaction charge of Esc1,000.

In September 1997 stock exchange transaction fees were reduced from 0.2% to 0.1% on close-end investment trust unit transactions and from 0.5% to 0.4% on rights transactions.

Brokerage commissions and stock market levies are payable by the seller and the buyer. The banks also charge commissions on stock transactions on a fully negotiable basis.

TAXATION AND REGULATIONS AFFECTING FOREIGN INVESTORS

Dividends are subject to a 25% withholding tax. However, in the case of listed companies, the tax rate is only applicable to 50% of the dividend, resulting in an effective rate of 12.5%. Dividends received by residents and non-residents are subject to an additional withholding tax of 5% in respect of inheritance and gift tax.

As a result of the implementation of EU Directive 90/435, an EU company holding at least 25% of the shares of a Portuguese company for at least two years will benefit from a reduced tax rate. This will be 10% until 31 December 1999, and nil thereafter.

LISTING AND REPORTING REQUIREMENTS

A) Listing requirements

To be listed on the LSE, a company must file a prospectus complying with the relevant EU Directives and meeting an extensive list of requirements. Information to be provided includes balance sheets for the past three years; a description of the organisation, its activities, its profitability and its financial structure; and details about the shares to be offered (in particular disclosure of any special rights).

In some cases, the issue of securities requires prior notice to the Minister of Finance.

Certain market capitalisation and distribution requirements must be fulfilled before a company may be listed. For an equity issue, a company must have a potential equity market capitalisation of at least Esc500 million, and a minimum of 25% of the share capital, or 500,000 shares, must be spread among investors.

B) Reporting requirements

Companies with listed securities must publish their annual balance sheets and accounts within 30 days of board approval. Listed companies must also publish half-yearly accounts and quarterly reports within 30 days of the end of the relevant period.

SHAREHOLDER PROTECTION CODES

A) Significant shareholdings

Companies and the authorities must be informed whenever listed shares are acquired or disposed of and, as a result, the percentage of voting rights held by the purchaser or seller exceeds or falls below 10%, 20%, 33.3%, 50% or 66.6% of the total voting rights.

B) Takeovers and mergers

Under the Securities Code, as recently amended, an acquisition or exchange of shares in a company must be carried out by means of a public offer whenever any of the following apply:

- The target company is a "public subscription company", meaning a company with part or the whole of its share capital in public hands by reason of: (i) having been incorporated through public subscription; (ii) having made any share capital increase through public subscription; (iii) its shares being or having been quoted on a stock exchange market; or (iv) its shares having been subject to a public offer of sale or exchange.
- The shares to be acquired by the offeror, either alone or when added to any shares in the target company acquired by the offeror since 1 January of the previous calendar year, carry more than 20% of the voting rights in the target company.
- The offeror already owns more than 50% of the voting rights in the target, but less than two-thirds, and wants to acquire (i) more than 3% in a year; or (ii) shares that, when added to the shares it already owns, will carry two-thirds or more of the voting rights in the target.

If the shareholding that the offeror is seeking to acquire, either alone or when added to the shares in the target company it already owns, will grant it more than 50% of the voting rights in the target company, then the public offer must be a general offer for all the target company's outstanding shares, warrants and convertible bonds.

For the purpose of these rules, shares in the target company (which include shares arising under warrants or convertible bonds) will be considered to be owned by the offeror if they are held by any holding company or subsidiary of the offeror, or any person acting in concert with the offeror.

C) Insider trading

The Securities Code lays down a framework for controlling insider trading, covering officers and staff from issuers and key regulatory agencies.

All officers and personnel of CMVM (the Securities Commission) and any persons or organisations, public or private, rendering services to the Commission are subject to confidentiality in connection with all facts that come to their knowledge in the exercise of their duties. They are not allowed to disclose or use, to their own or other people's advantage, directly or through any third party, their knowledge of such facts either to conduct any transactions on the securities markets or for any other purpose. Breaches can lead not only to disciplinary sanctions but also to civil and criminal liability.

Additionally, anyone who, due to his capacity as officer or shareholder of a securities issuing entity, or by reason of services rendered to such or any other entity, has any privileged information and, knowing that such information is of a privileged nature, (i) tries to take advantage of it by directly or indirectly acquiring or disposing of (on his own account or on behalf of any third party) securities issued by such entity or by any other entities to which such information relates; or (ii) conveys such information to any third party, otherwise than in the performance of the duties of his office, job, service or profession which led to his having access to such information; or (iii) advises or instructs any third party, based on the information, to acquire or dispose of the securities referred to above, will be liable for imprisonment for up to two years and to a fine.

Finally, financial intermediaries are also subject to confidentiality rules.

RESEARCH

All annual reports of Portuguese companies are published in the *Diário da Republica*, and (along with interim reports) can also be obtained from the companies concerned. Most include at least a summary in English. Major companies are audited by international accounting firms.

The stock exchange has a databank (SIIB) containing all listed companies and most unlisted companies, as well as bond and share performance for the past three years.

In 1997 the Lisbon exchange launched a number of new information services, including the *Electronic Quotations Bulletin*, and it continues to issue various regular publications on the stock market, including:

- a monthly analysis of the securities markets containing statistical information on listed securities, turnover, quotations and market indicators;
- an annual report, analysis and statistics book containing statistical information, legislation on capital markets and information on other subjects such as the organisation and functioning of the LSE; and
- periodic information, such as brochures concerning the LSE's national and international activities.

Some "business letters" are now published, and nationwide newspapers have developed economics pages and supplements.

Independent detailed research on companies and the economy can be obtained from major banks and broker-dealers. Those with good reputations include BSN-Dealer, Cisf-Dealer, Gesfinc, BPA, BPI, M-Valores and Midas Corretora.

Portugal, published by Euromoney Books, provides in-depth information for those wishing to invest or do business in the country. See the order card at the back of this book for details.

CHAPTER

56

Romania

Introduction

The first Bucharest Stock Exchange (BSE) opened in 1882, although in subsequent years much of the trading took place off the market. A new exchange was formally established on 21 April 1995, with Canadian and British technical assistance, and opened on 23 July 1995. There are currently 126 broker members of the exchange, which is open daily. The exchange's trading system is order-driven and fully automated, with all trades matched and reported immediately.

Rasdaq, the Romanian OTC market, is based on the US Nasdaq model and came into being in November 1996 as a second-tier market. It is equipped with a Central Depository (SNCDD) and a Central Registry (RRA). Rasdaq has 156 broker members and is driven by market-makers. On both the BSE and Rasdaq markets, trading is centralised, paperless, screen-based and continuous.

All securities trading is regulated by the Romanian National Securities Commission (NSC). In addition, however, the exchange is under the control of the Exchange Committee and Rasdaq under the control of the Stock Dealers' Association.

Major capital market developments in 1997 included central bank cash settlement, first order accounts, custodian allowances for the BSE and automatic multi-custodian settlement for Rasdaq. Also in 1997, the BSE launched an official market index and introduced volatility limitation policies.

ECONOMIC AND POLITICAL OVERVIEW

The new Constantinescu government pushed through nearly 100 ordinances in 1997, aiming (under the guidance of the IMF and World Bank) to provide a genuine framework for a market economy. One of the first and most dramatic pieces of legislation was the liberalisation of all remaining price controls, causing the prices of many basic items to rise by over 100%. It is too early to tell whether the current leadership will hold the new coalition together in the face of opposition from the vested interests of the old regime, but so far popular support remains steady.

The IMF is providing a structural loan of US$430 million in staged payments of US$86 million a month, subject to regular monitoring visits at which officials examine progress on stabilisation, monetary and fiscal discipline, structural reforms and macroeconomic indicators. At the same time, a new batch of privatisation measures was designed to place the vast majority of state assets in private hands by the end of 1998. Unemployment has been forecast to double as a result.

Between 1994 and 1996, the Romanian economy showed artificial growth of between 3.9% and 6.9%, but 1997 was telling, witnessing a 6% decline in GDP. Inflation remains a problem. The government has released nearly all controls, and inflation overcame the currency depreciation to hit a new year-on-year high of 151.4% in 1997.

Role of the central bank

The key objective of the Romanian National Bank (BNR) is to maintain the stability of the currency.

MARKET PERFORMANCE

A) In 1997

The BET Index stood at 757.86 at end-1997, down 24.2% from its 19 September 1997 base of 1,000. Total market capitalisation of the 76 companies listed on the BSE was US$632 million at the end of the year, an increase of more than 950% over the figure for year-end 1996. On Rasdaq there were 2,602 companies traded and their market capitalisation was US$1,505.2 million at the end of 1997, up 385% over end-1996.

Total BSE equity turnover for 1997 was US$262 million and the equivalent Rasdaq figure was US$371 million.

B) Summary information

Global ranking by market value (US$ terms, end-1997): 73
Market capitalisation (end-1997): BSE US$632.4 million; Rasdaq US$1,505.2million
Growth in market value (US$ terms, 1995–97): BSE 532.24%
Market value as a % of nominal GDP (end-1997): 5.6%
Number of domestic/foreign companies listed (end-1997): BSE: 76/0
Market P/E average (end-1997): BSE (first-tier companies) 22.3
Short-term (12-week T-Bill) interest rate (end-1997): 90%
Long-term (1-year) bond yield (end-1997): 75%
Budget deficit as a % of nominal GDP (end-1997): 3.7%
Inflation rate (1997): 151.4%
US$ exchange rate (end-1997): L8.0

C) Year-end share price index, price/earnings ratios and yields

Exhibit 56.1:
YEAR-END SHARE PRICE INDEX AND P/E RATIO, 1997

Year-end	*BET Index*	*P/E*
1997	757.86	22.3

Source: Bucharest Stock Exchange.

D) Market indices and their constituents

On 19 September 1997 the BSE launched the first official index, the BET, with a base of 1,000 points. It is a total return index weighted by company market value and comprises the 10 most liquid companies listed on the first tier of the BSE. The composition of the BET Index is reviewed each quarter by an Index Committee.

THE STOCK MARKET

A) Brief history and structure

The first Bucharest Stock Exchange opened in 1882 and by 1935 a total of 56 companies were listed. But then, during half a century of communist rule, the Romanian capital market was non-existent. A new exchange was established on 21 April 1995, and Rasdaq, the second-tier market, opened in November 1996.

The BSE is a public institution under private management, while Rasdaq is a limited partnership 100% owned by the Stock Dealers' Association. All securities trading is regulated by the Romanian National Securities Commission (NSC). In addition, however, the exchange is under the control of the Exchange Committee and Rasdaq under the control of the Stock Dealers' Association. The two markets have different listing rules, trading practices and corporate disclosure requirements.

B) Opening hours, names and addresses

Trading sessions are held on Monday to Friday from 9.15am to 2.30pm at the BSE and from 10.00am to 2.00pm at Rasdaq.

BUCHAREST STOCK EXCHANGE
8 Doamnei Str., Bucharest 70421
Tel: (40) 1323 0900; Fax: (40) 1 323 5732

RASDAQ SRL
2 Expozitiei Blvd., World Trade Centre D38, Bucharest
Tel: (40) 1 222 4884; Fax: (40) 1 222 4658

MARKET SIZE

A) Number of listings and market value

At the end of 1997, market capitalisation of the 76 companies listed on the BSE was US$632 million. On Rasdaq there were 2,602 companies quoted, with market capitalisation of US$1,505.2 million.

Exhibit 56.2:
NUMBER OF LISTED SHARES AND MARKET VALUE, BSE, 1995–97

Year-end	*No. of listed companies*	*Market value (US$ million)*
1995	9	100
1996	14	60
1997	76	632

Source: Bucharest Stock Exchange.

Exhibit 56.3:
NUMBER OF SHARES TRADED AND MARKET VALUE, RASDAQ, 1996–97

Year-end	*No. of listed companies*	*Market value (US$ million)*
1996	1,615	310.4
1997	2,602	1,505.2

Source: Rasdaq.

B) Largest quoted companies

At end-1997, the BSE's three largest companies – Oltchim, Altro and Terapia – together accounted for 47% of total BSE market capitalisation. Rasdaq's three largest companies – Sidex, Romcim and Petromidia – together accounted for 33% of total Rasdaq market capitalisation.

Exhibit 56.4:
THE 10 LARGEST LISTED COMPANIES ON THE BSE, END-1997

Ranking	*Company*	*Sector*	*Market value (US$ million)*
1	Oltchim	PVC	150.6
2	Alro	Aluminium	72.3

Exhibit 56.4 continued

3	Terapia	Pharmaceutical	72.2
4	Dacia	Car maker	69.9
5	Azomures	Fertilizers	65.6
6	Antibiotice	Pharmaceutical	45.2
7	Policolor	Paints	33.1
8	Arctic	White goods	31.3
9	Otelinox	Stainless steel	18.7
10	Compa	Spare parts	12.6

Source: Bucharest Stock Exchange.

Exhibit 56.5:
THE 10 LARGEST COMPANIES TRADED ON RASDAQ, END-1997

Ranking	*Company*	*Sector*	*Market value (US$ million)*
1	Sidex	Steel	253.78
2	Romcim	Cement	140.27
3	Petromidia	Refinery	100.16
4	COST	Special steels	44.06
5	CNM	Navy fleet	33.73
6	Romcif	Cement	25.94
7	Casial	Cement	18.97
8	Moldocim	Cement	17.24
9	Rolast	Rubber	16.91
10	Sanex	Ceramics	16.57

Note: Trading in COST shares began on 30 January 1998.

Source: Rasdaq.

C) Trading volume

Total BSE equity turnover for 1997 was US$262.4 million (which translates to average turnover per session of US$1.09 million). Total Rasdaq equity turnover for 1997 was US$371 million (which translates to average turnover per session of US$1.5 million).

Exhibit 56.6:
SHARE VOLUME AND TURNOVER ON THE BSE, 1995–97

Year	*Trading volume (shares million)*	*Trading value (US$ million)*
1995	0.04	0.96
1996	1.141	5.27
1997	603.88	262.40

Source: Bucharest Stock Exchange.

Exhibit 56.7:
SHARE VOLUME AND TURNOVER ON RASDAQ, 1997

Year	*Trading volume (shares million)*	*Trading value (US$ million)*
1997	796.45	371.00

Source: Rasdaq.

Exhibit 56.8:
THE 10 MOST ACTIVELY TRADED BSE SHARES, 1997

Ranking	*Company*	*Trading value (US$ million)*	*% of total trading*
1	Oltchim	61.66	23.49
2	Azomures	42.96	16.37
3	Antibiotice	28.42	10.83
4	Terapia	21.93	8.35
5	Alro	18.20	6.93
6	Arctic	16.56	6.31
7	Policolor	14.03	5.34
8	Dacia	11.45	4.36
9	Compa	8.43	3.21
10	Armatura	5.11	1.94

Source: Bucharest Stock Exchange.

Exhibit 56.9:
THE 10 MOST ACTIVELY TRADED RASDAQ SHARES, 1997

Ranking	*Company*	*Trading value (US$ million)*	*% of total trading*
1	Romcim	79.39	25.1
2	Moldocim	18.11	5.7
3	Sidex	14.83	4.7
4	Petromidia	14.23	4.5
5	Casial	12.55	4.0
6	Rolast	12.02	3.8
7	Ductil	9.98	3.2
8	Romcif	8.1	2.6
9	Rulmenti Alexandria	7.58	2.4
10	Victoria Prahova	7.15	2.3

Source Rasdaq.

TYPES OF SHARE

Ordinary shares of domestic companies are traded on the BSE and Rasdaq.

INVESTORS

The shares of some 4,000 companies have been fairly thinly distributed among Romania's citizens, and it is estimated that there are about 12 million individual shareholders.

Foreign investors are estimated to account for around 30% of 1997's BSE and Rasdaq trading.

OPERATIONS

A) Trading system

Trading on the BSE is order-driven, centralised and paperless. At the BSE, a single price auction takes place during the first 15 minutes of trading time; for the remaining five hours, trading is continuous. The trading system is fully computerised. Price variation during one session cannot exceed +/-50%, and large blocks of securities can be traded off-exchange without influencing prices on the retail market.

B) List of principal banks and brokers

ACTIVE INTERNATIONAL
Bd. Unirii, nr. 45, Bl. E3, Sc 2A, Et. 6, Ap. 52
Sector 3, Bucharest
Tel: (40) 1 323 0401

BIG BROKERAGE
Str. Vasile Lascar, nr. 8, Ap 5
Sector 2, Bucharest
Tel: (40) 1 311 2501

CA IB SECURITIES
Union International Centre
Str. Ion Campineanu, nr 11, Bucharest
Tel: (40) 1 312 0413

GENERAL INVESTMENT GROUP
Bd. Nicolae Titulescu, nr 1, Bl. A7, Sc. A, Et. 7, Ap. 21
Sector 1, Bucharest
Tel/Fax: (40) 1 311 3539

VANGUARD
Bd. Unirii, nr. 45
Sector 3, Bucharest
Tel: (40) 1 323 6640

C) Settlement and transfer

BSE

Complying with G30 recommendations, settlement is based on T+3 and delivery versus payment. Accounting, the preparation of data for settlement and registration are fully computerised. Off-exchange deals can be settled by agreement between the parties.

Rasdaq

Settlement on Rasdaq complies with G30 recomendations and is performed by the Central Clearing and Depository on a T+3 basis. Cross and special trades can be settled by agreement. Registration is carried out by brokers or a custodian bank or directly by the Central Registry.

D) Commissions and other costs

Commission rates applied by brokers are negotiable in the range of 0.75%–2% .

TAXATION AND REGULATIONS AFFECTING FOREIGN INVESTORS

There are no legal restrictions on foreign investors. However, there is a 1.5% foreign investment tax on the buy side.

Payments of dividends by Romanian companies to resident entities are subject to a 10% withholding tax.

Dividend payments by resident corporations to non-resident entities or individuals are also subject to a 10% withholding tax unless a double taxation treaty specifies a lower rate. Capital gains are treated as normal profits and taxed at the standard rate of 38%.

Exhibit 56.10:
WITHHOLDING TAXES

Recipient	*Dividends %*	*Interest %*	*Royalties %*
Resident corporation	10	N/A	N/A
Resident individuals	10	N/A	N/A
Non-resident corporations and individuals:			
Non-treaty	10	10	20
Treaty	0–20	1–15	0–20

Source: Coopers & Lybrand.

REPORTING REQUIREMENTS

For a public offer of securities, issuers must prepare an NSC-approved prospectus containing details of the issuer and the securities being offered. Information in the prospectus must be certified by the issuer, which shall be liable for its truth, accuracy and completeness.

BSE-listed companies must publish quarterly reports and notify the exchange of all material events.

SHAREHOLDER PROTECTION CODES

In general, market surveillance mechanisms and enforcement methods are weak and do not match Western standards.

The Securities Law imposes penalties (a maximum fine of 3% of registered capital and/or up to two years' imprisonment) on a person who in a prospectus or by other means provides misleading information or withholds details that could be material. This provision makes the management board of a company, as well as advisers who prepare the prospectus, liable.

The same combined fine and imprisonment can be imposed on a person who, during public trading makes use of insider information. "Insider information" is defined as information concerning an issuer or a security that has not been made available to the public and disclosure of which could influence in a material way the price of the security. Anyone who, alone or in agreement with others, causes an artificial rise or fall in the price of securities, can be imprisoned for up to two years and fined up to the full value of any trade executed.

Anyone who acquires 5% or more of the voting rights of a listed company must inform the market and the market authorities, including the NSC. Anyone who acquires 51% of a listed company's voting stock must make a public takeover offer for the balance.

RESEARCH

Real-time market data distribution is provided by the BSE and Reuters. The Romanian press agency, Mediafax, and other domestic information vendors provide real-time data on Rasdaq transactions.

CHAPTER 57

Russia

Introduction

The Russian stock market is relatively young, but growing rapidly. Almost all the major companies are now quoted on the exchanges or the OTC market, although total market capitalisation at the end of 1997 represented only about 30% of GDP. The turnover to total value ratio (12%) indicates low current liquidity. In 1997 some of the major state-owned companies like Svyazinvest, Norilsk Nikel and Rosneft came up for privatisation at the "loans-for-shares" auctions, and huge financial and industrial conglomerates like Unexim, Yukos-Rosprom, Gazprom and Lukoil fought for control of the newcomers.

The Russian stock market was very active in 1997, gaining 160% by October, and was ahead by around 70% at the year-end. Following the October crisis, the larger foreign investors deserted the market.

There are seven major stock exchanges in Russia, two of which – the Moscow Interbank Currency Exchange (Micex) and the Moscow Stock Exchange (MSE) – account for more than 90% of total exchange turnover. Most corporate stocks (approximately 90%) are traded through the RTS electronic trading system.

Equity market research by the major consulting and data companies continues to be hampered by the poor quality of company information and the lack of consistent reporting standards.

ECONOMIC AND POLITICAL OVERVIEW

The Russian reform programme came under pressure at the beginning of 1997, coinciding with President Boris Yeltsin's protracted recovery from heart surgery. Hopes ran high when Yeltsin announced his return by reshuffling the government in March to include dynamic reformers Boris Nemtsov and Anatoly Chubais, but there was still the pro-communist Duma to reckon with. Yeltsin blustered happily about abolishing it. Meanwhile, the new Tax Code, crucial for attracting foreign investment and streamlining Russia's tax system, was postponed, along with many other reforms.

The 1997 inflation rate fell to 11% from 22% the year before and, for the first time since the beginning of the reform programme, some slight production growth was witnessed. By the end of 1997 GDP was up 0.4% and production had increased by 1.9% compared with 1996. The central bank refinancing rate fell substantially from 48% in February 1997 to 28% by the year-end, while unemployment decreased slightly from 6.6 million to 6.4 million.

Mass privatisation, in particular "loans-for-shares" auctions, have created an economic oligopoly in Russia. The seven major financial industrial groups (FIGs) control over 40% of the economy, helped by the fact that only they can attract the capital needed for industrial restructuring.

Role of the central bank

The primary role of Russia's central bank is to protect the stability of the rouble. It is also the federal government's banker, acting as lender of last resort to Russian credit institutions and holding most of Russia's official reserves. Other responsibilities include issuing banking licences; monitoring bankruptcy and liquidation proceedings involving credit institutions; supervising acquisitions in the banking sector; and overseeing government securities transactions and foreign investments, as well as analysing and forecasting Russian economic developments.

The composition of the central bank's board of directors is approved by the Duma, and the bank is accountable to the Duma to the extent that it is required to present an annual report on its activities and to seek the Duma's comments on monetary policy. The Minister of Finance and the Minister of Economics participate in board meetings and can vote.

Exhibit 57.1: RUSSIA ASP GENERAL PRICE INDEX (US$), 1993–97

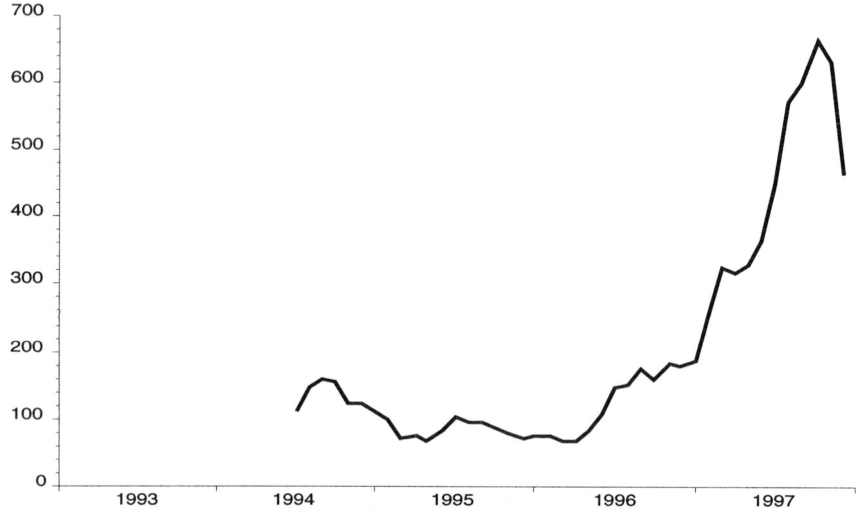

High value 663.84 1.10.97 Low value 66.69 1.4.96 *Source: Datastream*

MARKET PERFORMANCE

A) In 1997

The Russian stock market rose rapidly in the first half of the year, boosted by excellent performances by regional energy, oil and gas and telecommunications companies. The ASP-General Index was around 160% ahead after the first nine months of 1997. This represented significant outperformance relative to most established and emerging markets. However, the October crisis threw the market into turmoil, a rapid correction occurred, and by the year-end the market's rise had been cut back to 70%.

One of the notable events of the year was the government's withdrawal of Gazprom shares from RTS trading. Gazprom shares can now only be traded on the Moscow, St Petersburg, Yekaterinburg and Siberian Stock Exchanges.

B) Summary information

Global ranking by market value (US$ terms end-1997): 22
Market capitalisation (end-1997): US$129 billion
Growth in market value (local currency terms, 1994–97): 470.79%
Market value as a % of nominal GDP (end-1997): 28.7%
Number of domestic/foreign companies listed (AK&M database companies, end-1997): 353/0
Market P/E (end-1997): 7.78
MSCI Index (change in US$ terms, 1997): +111.6%
Short-term (90-day) interest rate (end-1997): 44.33%
Long-term (1-year) bond yield (end-1997): 78.8%
Budget deficit as a % of nominal GDP (US$ terms, end-1997): 7.5%
Annual increase in broad money (M2) supply (end-1997): 25%
Inflation rate (1997): 11%
US$ exchange rate (end-1997): R5,960

C) Market indices and their constituents

ASP-General Index

The ASP-General Index, based at September 1992 = 100, is a market capitalisation-weighted index calculated in both rouble and US dollar terms for 190 companies. Five sectoral indices have been introduced, covering industrials, extraction, utilities, services and financials.

RTS Index

The RTS Index is the only official RTS market indicator and is calculated every 30 minutes during the trading session. The index includes all RTS traded shares and is based at 31 December 1997 = 396.858. There is also an RTS Technical Index and an RTS-2 Index, which covers 225 non-liquid shares.

AK&M indices

These include the AK&M Composite Index, the Industrial Companies Stock Index and various sectoral indices. All AK&M indices are computed by determining the relative change of listed companies' total market capitalisation. All indices are based at 1 September 1993 = 1.0.

The Moscow Times Index

This index was introduced in September 1994 by Skate Consulting Agency to follow the performance of the most liquid and most highly capitalised Russian stocks. It is a daily average of 50 companies. Both the principal and sectoral indices have a base value of 100.

Micex Composite Index

The Micex Composite Index has been calculated since September 1997, and tracks the share prices of five leading Russian companies traded on Micex.

THE STOCK MARKET

A) Brief history and structure

The securities market in Russia was established in 1990 with the privatisation of Kamaz, the world's largest manufacturer of heavy-duty trucks. Although Kamaz was taken public prior to any legislation regarding public companies, by June 1990 the Council of Ministers of the USSR had passed regulation No. 590 establishing the legal requirements for setting up joint stock companies. With the dissolution of the USSR in December 1990, the Russian Federation introduced its own legislation regulating public companies and the securities market. In 1990 and 1991, numerous Russian commercial banks, trading companies and financial institutions registered as joint stock companies and sold their shares to the public.

The first exchanges were established in 1990, initially to trade commodities, such as oil, grain, lumber and currencies. The exchanges were set up by capital-rich organisations such as banks and trading companies. Later, brokerage firms developed and began trading in both securities and commodities. By the middle of 1992, the Ministry of Finance passed a regulation requiring brokerage firms to specialise in either commodities or securities, and brokers and financial institutions trading securities needed to be licensed for such activities.

In addition to universal exchanges with commodity and equity trading, several exchanges specialised in stock trading. The Central Stock Exchange in Moscow was founded on 14 November 1990; the Leningrad Stock Exchange, which was later renamed the St Petersburg Stock Exchange, was founded on 28 February 1991. Currently, there are 60 officially registered stock and commodity exchanges with licences to trade securities, 50 of which began their activities in 1992. During the 1992–94 voucher privatisation programme, several of these exchanges succeeded in attracting a significant portion of voucher trading, but since the conclusion of the programme in July 1994, stock and commodity exchanges in Russia have played a minimal role in the securities market. The majority of Russian equities are traded on the OTC market, in an informal dealer-to-dealer trading system.

B) Opening hours, names and addresses

Trading hours differ across the exchanges (although all use Moscow time):

- Micex trades from Monday to Friday, 10.00am to 6.00pm;
- MCSE trades Monday to Thursday, 10.30am to 6.30pm and 7.30pm to 10.00pm, and on Friday, 10.30am to 6.30pm;
- RSE trades Monday to Friday, 11.00am to 6.15pm and 8.00pm to 12 midnight; and
- RTS trades Monday to Friday, 11.00am to 6.00pm.

MOSCOW INTERBANK CURRENCY EXCHANGE (MICEX)
119021 Moscow, 4 Zubovsky Blvd.
Tel: (7) 095 201 2817; Fax: (7) 095 201 2723

MOSCOW STOCK EXCHANGE (MSE)
125047 Moscow, Miusskaya Pl. 2, bld.2
Tel: (7) 095 250 3332; Fax: (7) 095 250 1734

MOSCOW CENTRAL STOCK EXCHANGE (MCSE)
Moscow, 9 "B", Bolshaya Maryinskaya Str.,
Tel: (7) 095 215 7542; Fax: (7) 095 215 2008

RUSSIAN STOCK EXCHANGE (RSE)
101000 Moscow, 26 Myasnitskaya Str.
Tel: (7) 095 262 2352; Fax: (7) 095 262 5757

RUSSIAN TRADING SYSTEM (RTS)
Moscow, korp.5 Chayanova Ul.
Tel: (7) 095 705 9031; Fax: (7) 095 973 4236

SIBIRSKAYA STOCK EXCHANGE (SSE)
630194 Novosibirsk, 5 Frounze Str.
Tel: (7) 3832 216 951; Fax: (7) 3832 210 619

ST PETERSBURG STOCK EXCHANGE (SPSE)
St Petersburg, 274 Ligovsky Prosp.
Tel. (7) 812 296 0523; Fax: (7) 812 296 1080

YEKATERINBURG STOCK EXCHANGE (YSE)
620 Yekaterinburg, 109 Furmanova Str.
Tel: (7) 3432 221 225; Fax: (7) 3432 294 941

VLADIVOSTOK STOCK EXCHANGE (VSE)
Vladivostok, 62a Partizansky Prosp.
Tel: (7) 4232 228 009; Fax: (7) 4232 261 922

MARKET SIZE

A) Market value

End-1997 total capitalisation was estimated to amount to US$129 billion, an increase of 135 % from 1996. However, the top 20 companies accounted for more than 80% of this total, with oil and gas companies accounting for more than 60% and energy companies accounting for 12%.

Exhibit 57.2:
THE 20 LARGEST LISTED COMPANIES BY MARKET CAPITALISATION, END-1997

Ranking	*Company*	*Capitalisation (US$ million)*
1	Gazprom	28,598.87
2	Lukoil	15,466.64
3	Unified Energy System	12,312.53
4	Yukos	7,493.92
5	Sidanko Oil Company	5,810.38
6	Surgutneftegaz Oil Company	4,640.41
7	Surgutneftegaz	4,565.41
8	Sibneft	3,274.39
9	Mosenergo	3,248.64
10	Slavneft	3,161.57
11	Tatneft	3,159.10
12	Eastern Oil Company	2,876.61
13	Rostelecom	2,486.11
14	Sberbank of Russia	2,412.00
15	Onaco	1,562.99
16	Moscow Telephone	1 305.21
17	Irkutskenergo	941.44
18	Vimpelcom	857.96
19	Noyabrskneftegaz	709.80
20	Purneftegaz	661.51

Source: Skate.

B) Trading volume

Daily turnover in 1997 amounted to US$62.4 million, a more than four-fold increase over 1996. Total 1997 RTS turnover stood at US$15.6 billion, or 5.3 times more than in 1996.

Exhibit 57.3:
THE MOST ACTIVELY TRADED SHARES, RTS, 1997

Ranking	*Company*	*Trading value (US$ million)*	*% of total*
Common shares			
1	Unified Energy System	3,441.37	22.0%
2	Lukoil	2,996.20	19.1%
3	Mosenergo	1,694.39	10.8%
4	Rostelecom	946.42	6.0%
5	Surgutneftegaz	901.45	5.8%
6	Gazprom*	472.94	3.0%
7	Sberbank of Russia	394.14	2.5%
8	Norilsk Nikel	375.24	2.4%
9	Tatneft	373.09	2.4%
10	Irkutskenergo	357.60	2.3%
Preferred shares			
1	Unified Energy System	424.32	2,7%
2	Surgutneftgaz	400.18	2,6%
3	Lukoil	369.23	2,4%

Exhibit 57.3 continued

*Gazprom shares were withdrawn from RTS trading in July, and are currently traded on the MSE, SPSE, YSE and SSE.

Source: RTS.

TYPES OF SHARE

A) Registered shares

Registered stocks may be common or preferred. Under Russian law, common stocks differ in voting rights (ordinary and cumulative), and also in dividend payment schedules. Preferred shares are divided into type A and B. Type A were sold to workers' collectives on favourable terms, while B shares are held by property funds (the government). Preferred stocks have a fixed dividend rate of A = 10% and B = 5% of the issuer's net income. They can be converted into common shares or exchanged for the bonds of the same issuer. The amount of preferred shares must not exceed 25% of the issuer's authorised capital.

B) Bearer shares

Bearer shares were widely issued by a number of investment companies in 1994, but issues and turnover of such securities decreased significantly during 1995 following a number of financial scandals.

C) Convertible bonds

In 1995, convertible bonds of Lukoil became the first such issue by a Russian company to trade on international markets. The issue size was US$321 million.

D) American depositary receipts

In 1995–96 a number of Russian companies issued equity in ADR form through the Bank of New York. ADR-1 programmes were launched by 22 companies.

INVESTORS

The majority of investors in Russian equities are small and medium-sized US hedge funds. Several country-specific funds have been established to make direct and portfolio investments in Russian companies. By the end of 1997, foreign investors represented approximately 60% of the Russian equity market.

Exhibit 57.4:
COUNTRY FUNDS – CIS/RUSSIA (EX BALTICS)

Fund	US$ % change 01/01/97 01/01/98	01/01/93 01/01/98	Fund base currency	Fund size (US$ mil)	Fund volatility	Management group
Signet New Capital Markets C	273.15	N/A	US$	5	-1	New Cap Mgt
The Hermitage	234.75	N/A	US$	526.4	-1	Hermitage Cap
Firebird Fund LP	141.18	N/A	US$	63.5	18.284	Firebird Advr
Firebird New Russia Fund Ltd	137.9	N/A	US$	29.2	-1	Firebird Advr
Russian Prosperity	119.48	N/A	US$	168.4	-1	Westman Leand
Clariden Russia Eqty	116.71	N/A	US$	47.8	18.914	Clariden
Croesus-UFG Russia Fund Ltd	104.69	N/A	US$	100	-1	UFG-Croesus M
Fleming Russia Securities	96.41	N/A	US$	43.63	14.999	Fleming
FP Russian Equity	95.16	N/A	US$	7.3	-1	FP Consult SA
MC Russian Mkt Fund	94.17	N/A	US$	10.6	-1	MC Securities
Optima Opportunity Fund Ltd(e)	93.95	N/A	US$	23.863	12.538	Optima Mgt LP
Fleming Frontier Russia	90.91	N/A	US$	13.4	-1	Fleming
Russian Investment Co	89.79	N/A	US$	11.929	-1	Foreign & Colonial
Oracle Eastern European	74.64	N/A	US$	14.8	13.989	Oracle Mgt Lt
Golden Tiger Inv Co (FKI)	72.07	N/A	US$	11.834	-1	Regent Pacific
Eastern Capital	69.77	N/A	US$	10	15.975	Connor Asst M
Brunswick Russian Growth	67.38	N/A	US$	105.5	-1	Brunswick Cap
UAF Russia Fund	65.45	N/A	US$	N/A	-1	Regent Pacific
Rurik Investment	59.79	N/A	US$	80.3	-1	Alfred Berg
Lexington Troika Dialog	55.69	N/A	US$	110.2	-1	Lexington Mgt
Regent White Tiger	54.98	N/A	US$	153.7	16.261	Regent Pacific
Red Horizon Partners Ltd	54.59	N/A	US$	0.739	-1	Broadway Capital
Regent Red Tiger	50.12	N/A	US$	79.8	16.59	Regent Pacific
Magnum Russia Equity	48.7	N/A	US$	4.1	-1	Magnum Fund Mgt
Alpha Eastern Europe F Ltd	46.67	N/A	US$	6.509	15.404	Alpha Global
Templeton Russia Fund Inc	44.49	N/A	US$	107.55	-1	Templeton
Gems Russia Fd Ltd A	43.06	N/A	US$	6.22	9.652	Kenmar Gems
Regent Blue Tiger Inv Co	41.29	N/A	US$	67.9	-1	Regent Pacific
Russia Value Fund LP	29.68	N/A	US$	60.8	8.651	San Antonio C
Russian Opportunities	16.54	N/A	US$	N/A	-1	N/A

Note: details for some funds may not have been included if the data for the US$ % change for 97/98 was not available

Source: Standard & Poor's Micropal.

Among Russian investors, the most prominent are large commercial banks or their subsidiary investment companies trying to establish control over the most attractive and liquid companies. The most recent market entrants in Russia are unit trusts and, by the end of 1997, 20 of these had been established.

OPERATIONS

A) Trading system

Since the middle of 1995, regular trading of stocks on the over-the-counter market has been carried out through the electronic Russian Trading System (RTS). Only members of the National Association of Securities Market Participants (Naufor) are allowed to trade through RTS, which is designed along similar lines to the US Nasdaq system.

RTS functions in real time and forms a unified trading network, operational between 11.00am and 6.00pm local time. Transactions concluded through RTS require official registration by traditional means.

At the end of 1997, RTS-1 quoted 107 share prices of 64 issuers, while RTS-2, which quotes less liquid stocks, quoted 225 shares of 154 issuers. Liquidity is maintained by the rule that all RTS market-makers must support two-way quotes for at least three stocks, while other participants must support one-way quotes for at least three stocks.

B) Principal brokers

ALFA CAPITAL BROKERAGE
12, Akademik Sakharov Prosp., Moscow
Tel: (7) 095 928 9494; Fax: (7) 095 208 0863

BRANSWCK VARBURG BROKERAGE
52/1, Kosmodaminskaya Nab., Moscow
Tel: (7) 095 258 5200; Fax: (7) 095 258 5201

CA & CO INVESTMENT GROUP
22, Olkhovskaya Str., Moscow
Tel: (7) 095 971 5401; Fax: (7) 095 264 5545

CS FIRST BOSTON
5, Nikitsky Per., Moscow
Tel: (7) 095 967 8200; Fax: (7) 095 967 8710

EASTERN INVESTMENT COMPANY
15, Kamenskaya Naberezhnaya, Moscow
Tel (7) 095 258 7708; Fax: (7) 095 258 7778

ING BANK EURASIA
21, Krasnopresnenskaya Ul., Moscow
Tel: (7) 095 755 54 55; Fax: (7) 095 755 54 99

JS BANK METALLINVESTBANK
2, Slavyanskaya Pl., Moscow
Tel: (7) 095 220 7932; Fax: (7) 095 220 7988

REAGENT EUROPEAN SECURITIES
20, bld. 7, Chaplygina Str., Moscow
Tel: (7) 095 967 3132; Fax: (7) 095 967 3121

RINAKO PLUS
17/23 Taganskaya Str., Moscow
Tel: (7) 095 258 5656; Fax: (7) 095 258 5657

AO SALOMON BROTHERS
Mosenka Plaza, 24/27 Sadovaya-Samotechnaya
103051 Moscow
Tel: (7) 501 258 5150; Fax: (7) 501 258 5149

TROYKA DIALOG
6, bld.3, 1-st Kolobovsky per., Moscow
Tel: (7) 095 258 0500; Fax: (7) 095 258 0547

C) Settlement and transfer

As a rule, when transactions are executed between Russian brokers, re-registration of shares into the buyer's name is the responsibility of the seller or its nominee. For transactions with foreign investors, Russian brokers take responsibility for re-registration, which usually takes about five days.

D) Commissions and other costs

Commissions in the Russian market are negotiable and usually range between 0.3% and 1.5% (plus 20% VAT). Buyers are also charged a registration fee of up to 1% by the company's registrar for transferring share ownership.

TAXATION AND REGULATIONS AFFECTING FOREIGN INVESTORS

A) Regulations

Investment activity of foreign legal entities and individuals is regulated by the law of the Russian Federation "On Foreign Investment in RSFSR" of 4 July 1991 as amended (the "Foreign Investment Law"), which defines foreign investment as "all types of material assets and intellectual property invested by foreign investors into objects of entrepreneurial and other types of activity with the aim of making an income (profit)".

Three principal forms of state guarantees are provided to foreign investors by the Foreign Investment Law, namely that:

- Foreign investments will not be subject to less favourable treatment than other investments (Article 6).
- No nationalisation, requisition or confiscation of foreign investments is to be effected except in "exceptional instances provided for by legislative acts, when such measures are adopted in social interests", and then only with full compensation (Articles 7 and 8).
- Foreign investors shall have the unrestricted right of remittance abroad of the foreign currency proceeds of investments and revenues received in respect of such investments (Article 10).

The participation by foreign investors in securities transactions is at present the most common form of foreign investment. The main legislation on this is the "Law on the Securities Market" No. 39-FZ of 22 April 1996 (the "Securities Law"). Foreign investors in the Russian securities market are also subject to central bank regulations.

Acquisition of Russian securities by foreign investors may be subject to certain restrictions. The Securities Law specifically provides that Russian issuers may restrict the acquisition of their mass-issued securities by foreign entities. These restrictions are reflected in the charters of Russian companies and usually apply to shares. Additional restrictions are contained in separate pieces of Russian legislation: for example, there is Presidential Decree No. 529 establishing a 9% limit for foreign ownership in the charter capital of Gazprom. There are also restrictions on the shares of certain types of companies, such as banks.

B) Taxation

The issue of ordinary shares (common stock) and other securities by a Russian joint stock company is subject to a securities tax of 0.8% of the nominal value. The tax does not apply to the initial issue on formation of a company or to an increase in charter capital upon statutory revaluation of assets.

Trading in Russian stocks offshore by foreign holders is generally exempt from Russian taxation. However, on a sale of stock (or other assets) by a foreign legal entity to a Russian entity, the Russian purchaser is required to withhold 20% tax on the gain, which may be recoverable depending on the availability of exemption under a double tax treaty.

In the absence of specific legislation or clear guidance on the taxation of onshore discretionary management or execution services that may involve entering into contracts by an onshore nominee or agent, considerable uncertainty exists about possible tax consequences.

Dividend payments by a Russian company are subject to a 15% withholding where the recipient is a legal entity. Foreign shareholders may be able to obtain a reduction or elimination of such withholding under an applicable tax treaty, but it should be noted that procedures for applying treaty benefits are cumbersome and expensive. Given the additional procedural burdens of paying dividends in hard currency and the widespread practice of onshore custodians being treated effectively as domestic recipients, portfolio investors, including mutual funds, are likely to experience difficulty in repatriating gross dividends.

REPORTING REQUIREMENTS

All Russian joint stock companies must present statutory accounts to tax inspectors on a quarterly basis, and these accounts are available to shareholders at annual shareholders' meetings. In addition, many of the largest joint stock companies publish financial statements in local Russian-language newspapers. Several of the Russian blue chip companies have hired Western auditors to prepare their financial statements to GAAP standards.

Public companies must publish and distribute information on the financial condition and business activities of their enterprise. Any open joint stock company with more than 5,000 shareholders must publish, on a quarterly basis, a balance sheet and profit and loss statement in a generally accessible publication with a minimum circulation of 50,000 copies.

SHAREHOLDER PROTECTION CODES

A Presidential Decree of 16 July 1997 established a Commission for the Protection of Investors' Rights in the Financial and Stock markets of Russia. All holders of common shares in a Russian company enjoy the following general rights:

- to receive notice of a general meeting of shareholders at least 30 days in advance;
- to participate in the general meeting of shareholders of the company either personally or by proxy, to vote on all questions within its competence, and to receive dividends and a share of the property of the company in the event of its liquidation;
- to obtain an extract from the company's register of shareholders;
- to receive a copy of the company's charter, including all amendments and additions thereto; and
- to receive and to accept an offer to purchase their shares in the company from any party who acquires 30% or more of the shares of the company.

RESEARCH

A number of specialised information and consulting agencies are providing stock market research and research on companies, industries and markets. The most reliable of them are AK&M, Skate Press, Interfax, Ros Business Consulting, Prime-TASS, Sobolev and Expert. Specific market and company research is also provided by the major Russian and foreign brokerage houses, investment companies and banks.

Reuters, Bloomberg and Tenfore distribute information about the Russian securities market worldwide, and information is also available on the Internet. An all-Russian telecommunications system is currently being developed for the securities markets.

The Currency Market in Russia, published by Euromoney Books, provides in-depth information for those wishing to invest in the country. It is also available in Russian. See the order card at the back of this book for details.

CHAPTER 58

Singapore

Introduction

The Singapore stock market does not accurately represent the economy. The economy is driven by the manufacture of electronics components, yet manufacturing companies are grossly under-represented on the Stock Exchange of Singapore (SES). Though the Second Board (Sesdaq) has seen a proliferation of new issues over the past few years, most of these are very small companies, especially contract manufacturers. Also, a significant proportion of the large manufacturing companies in Singapore (eg, Seagate, Motorola and Sony) are foreign-owned and are not listed on the Singapore exchange. Thus, while the manufacturing sector accounts for around 30% of GDP, manufacturing stocks make up only about 10% of SES market capitalisation. Aside from the manufacturing sector, important utility/services companies such as Singapore Power and the Port of Singapore Authority are also not listed.

Being an island state with a small economy, market concentration is another characteristic of the SES. The big four banks and big three property companies account for 22% of the entire market capitalisation. Together with Singapore Telecom, SIA and Keppel Corporation, these 10 companies make up 47% of the Singapore market.

Due to a lack of quality stocks on the SES, and a proliferation of financial institutions, the market is well researched. Foreign investors are welcomed and there is a trend towards opening up the market to even greater foreign participation. Some companies (the latest being Singapore Press Holdings) have merged their foreign and local share tranches to create a more level playing field for foreign investors. In the past, foreigners have often complained about having to pay hefty premiums for foreign tranche stocks.

ECONOMIC AND POLITICAL OVERVIEW

Following a bitterly fought campaign in the run-up to the general election on 2 January 1997, the People's Action Party (PAP) managed to raise its share of the popular vote to 65% and won all but two seats in the 83-seat parliament. Significantly, the main opposition party, the Singapore Democratic Party, was trounced and did not win a single seat in the new parliament.

The Singapore economy started 1997 on a weak note – dragged down by the global electronics industry downturn – but it ended the year on a firmer footing. Real GDP growth rose from 4.1% in the first quarter of 1997 to an estimated 6–8% by the fourth quarter. As well as a rebound in the manufacturing sector, GDP growth was boosted in the second half of 1997 as a result of a strong performance by the finance industry. Ironically, the Asian currency and stock market meltdown has led to a surge in financial trading activities, and Singapore counts among the top five foreign exchange trading centres in the world.

But the two major pillars of the economy – manufacturing and financial services – are unlikely to sustain growth into 1998. Recent indications point to continued excess capacity in the computer electronics industry, especially hard disk drives and semiconductors, with the excess capacity problem made worse by a shift in consumer demand towards low-margin budget PCs, and the continued economic collapse in Asia. Current estimates are for a fall in real GDP growth in 1998 to no more than 3%.

Along with a slowdown in the economy and a depressed property and stock market, analysts believe there is considerable downside risk for the Singapore dollar exchange rate. Between 1986 and 1996, the currency rose 34% against the US dollar, but it has depreciated by 20% over the past two years.

Role of the central bank

The Monetary Authority of Singapore (MAS) is a quasi-central bank that performs all the normal functions of a central bank except it does not issue currency notes and coins. The MAS is a statutory board, created by an act of parliament.

Exhibit 58.1: SINGAPORE STRAITS TIMES INDUSTRIAL PRICE INDEX (US$), 1993–97

High value 5322.16 1.2.96 Low value 2862.31 1.1.93 *Source: Datastream*

As its chairman is also the Minister of Finance, its operations are not entirely independent of the government.

The MAS has an enviable track record of maintaining low inflation and currency stability. The Authority acts as an agent bank for the government and is primarily responsible for the implementation of monetary policy. However, following the creation of the Government of Singapore Investment Corporation, the management of the country's massive external assets has been hived off to the newer entity.

More so than in most other countries, the MAS specifically targets the Singapore dollar against a basket of currencies, the major components being the US dollar, the Malaysian ringgit, the yen and the Deutschmark. Given its small size and heavy dependence on external trade, the external value of the currency is of great importance to Singapore. The MAS actively manages the Singapore dollar via both the foreign exchange and money markets. In the forex market, the MAS intervenes mainly by buying/selling Singapore dollars against US dollars. However, more often than not, it achieves its exchange rate targets by raising or lowering interest rates.

The main objectives of the MAS are to maintain price stability, to foster non-inflationary economic growth and to promote the development of the financial sector.

MARKET PERFORMANCE

A) In 1997

The Singapore market performed poorly in 1997, dragged down by the Asian financial turmoil in the second half of the year. The key market barometer, the Straits Times Industrial Index, started the year at 2,216.8 and was hovering around the 2,000 level when the Thai baht was floated on 2 July 1997. Thereafter, the STI Index quickly lost ground and sank to 1,529.8 by the year-end. The market was pummelled further in early 1998 on concerns that even Singapore's strong financial position will not be able to shield the economy from the ill-effects of the regional meltdown.

Apart from the regional currency crisis, the Singapore stock market was depressed by continued concerns about the health of the property market as the oversupply situation intensified. New residential units are being constructed even as the stock of unsold units continues to rise. In the commercial and industrial segments the oversupply situation is far less pronounced, but demand is likely to be very weak in the face of the current Asian economic turmoil.

Stocks in the high-tech electronics sector were the star performers in the first nine months of 1997 on confidence of an impending recovery in that sector. Electronics stocks, led by Creative Technology, rose an average of 72% in the first nine months before giving up all their gains by the year-end as sentiment turned bearish on oversupply concerns as well as fast-falling Asian demand. Singapore companies are particularly exposed to the disk drive and semiconductor industries, both of which were hit by excess capacity and plunging prices.

B) Summary information

Global ranking by market value (US$ terms, end-1997): 18
Market capitalisation (end-1997): US$196.29 billion
Growth in market value (local currency terms, 1993–97): 41%
Market value as a % of nominal GNP (end-1997): 149%
Number of domestic/foreign companies listed, main board (end-1997): 241/53
Market P/E (end-1997): 15.2
MSCI total returns (with net dividends, US$ terms, 1997): -30%
MSCI Index ("Singapore Free", change in US$ terms, 1997): -41.2%
Short-term (3-month interbank) interest rate (end-1997): 6.7%
Budget surplus as a % of nominal GNP (1997): 3.2%
Annual increase in broad money (M3) supply (end-1997): 10%
Inflation rate (1997): 2.1%
US$ exchange rate (end-1997): S$1.6775

C) Year-end share price index, price/earnings ratios and yields

Exhibit 58.2:
MARKET INDEX, P/E AND DIVIDEND YIELDS, 1993–97

Year-end	*Straits Times Industrial Index*	*P/E*	*Yield (%)*
1993	2,425.68	25.8	1.1
1994	2,239.56	21.0	1.7
1995	2,266.54	24.0	1.5
1996	2,216.79	21.7	1.7
1997	1,529.84	15.2	2.0

Sources: JM Sassoon & Co Limited and Stock Exchange of Singapore.

D) Market indices and their constituents

The most widely observed indicators of share performance on the SES are the Straits Times Industrial (STI) Index, published by the Straits Times newspaper group, and the SES share indices, calculated by the exchange. The STI Index has 30 constituents and is computed on a real-time basis. As well as the SES All Singapore Index, sectoral indices are calculated by the exchange for industrials, financials, hotels and properties.

In addition, the Oversea-Chinese Banking Corporation (OCBC) calculates its own share price index, the OCBC 30 Index, which has 30 constituents, including bank shares, and is weighted by market capitalisation.

The *Business Times* Singapore Regional Index tracks the performance of stocks with substantial exposure to the Asian region.

THE STOCK MARKET

A) Brief history and structure

The Stock Exchange of Singapore Ltd was incorporated on 24 May 1973. Its origins can be traced back to 1930 when the Singapore Stockbrokers' Association was established.

The SES has 33 member companies, comprising 122 stockbroking members, 867 dealers and 2,323 dealers' representatives. The exchange is regulated by the Securities Industry Act of 1986 and supervised through a set of rules and regulations enforced by the elected Stock Exchange of Singapore Committee.

In March 1989, trading in all stocks was brought under the Central Limit Order Book (Clob) system – a fully computerised trading system with no trading floor.

B) Different exchanges

The SES is the only stock exchange in Singapore.

C) Opening hours, names and addresses

Trading sessions are held daily, Monday to Friday, from 9.00am to 12.30pm and 2.00pm to 5.00pm.

STOCK EXCHANGE OF SINGAPORE LTD
20 Cecil Street #26-01/08, The Exchange
Singapore 049705
Tel: (65) 535 3788; Fax: (65) 535 3544; Tlx: RS21853

MARKET SIZE

A) Number of listings and market value

Main board market capitalisation at the end of 1997 totalled S$329.27 billion, up 28.7% on end-1996. The number of listed securities on the main board at the same date was 294, up from 266 at the end of 1996.

Exhibit 58.3:
NUMBER OF SES LISTED COMPANIES BY SECTOR AND MARKET CAPITALISATION, YEAR-END 1993–97

Sector	*1993*	*1994*	*1995*	*1996*	*1997*
Industrial and commercial	138	157	180	197	225
Finance	29	33	30	30	30
Hotels	18	18	18	18	18
Property	20	-	19	19	20
Plantations	1	1	1	1	1
Total companies listed	205	229	248	266	294
Market value (S$ billion)	233.5	256.1	282.6	255.9	329.27

Source: Stock Exchange of Singapore.

B) Largest quoted companies

At the end of 1997, the top five companies accounted for over 37% of market capitalisation.

Exhibit 58.4:
THE 20 LARGEST LISTED COMPANIES ON THE SES, END-1997

Ranking	*Company*	*Market Value (S$ billion)*
1	Singapore Telecom	47.88
2	Daimler Benz	46.18
3	SIA	10.39
4	OCBC	9.70
5	Hong Kong Land	8.40
6	UOB	8.30
7	DBS	7.23
8	Jardine Matheson	6.45
9	City Developments	6.19
10	SPH	5.83
11	Jardine Strategic	5.37
12	OUB	4.53
13	FAI Insurances	4.04
14	Keppel Corporation	3.68
15	ST Engineering	3.57
16	Dairy Farm	3.37
17	Creative Ltd	3.04
18	DBS Land	2.61
19	Guangzhou Investment	2.50
20	Fraser & Neave	2.18

Source: Stock Exchange of Singapore.

C) Trading volume

Exhibit 58.5:
SHARE TRADING VOLUME, SES MAIN BOARD AND CLOB INTERNATIONAL, 1995–97

Year	*Volume (billion shares)*
1995	37.69
1996	30.51
1997	47.14

Exhibit 58.6:
THE 20 MOST ACTIVELY TRADED SHARES, SES, 1997

Ranking	*Company*	*Volume (million shares)*
1	Hong Kong Land	1,168.12
2	Singapore Telecom	960.55
3	DBS Land	722.04
4	Hotung	684.25
5	IPC Corporation	637.53

Exhibit 58.6 continued

6	AFP	626.98
7	Tianjin Zhong Xin	477.61
8	FHTK Holding	458.18
9	Keppel Corporation	448.58
10	NatSteel Ltd	401.28
11	Wing Tai Holdings	401.01
12	UOB Foreign	393.50
13	SMB United	362.06
14	UIC	359.13
15	OCBC Foreign	343.34
16	City Developments	340.31
17	SIA Foreign	338.08
18	CM Telecom	332.51
19	DBS Foreign	326.60
20	OUB Foreign	323.95

Source: Stock Exchange of Singapore.

TYPES OF SHARE

Most domestic listings on the SES are for ordinary shares. The other issues quoted are a small number of bonds, loans and warrants.

OTHER MARKETS

Sesdaq

The SES dealing and automated quotation system (Sesdaq) is the second securities market in Singapore, designed to provide an alternative for growing small and medium-sized, Singapore-incorporated companies to raise funds for expansion. As of 31 December 1997, 62 companies were quoted with a market capitalisation of S$3.17 billion.

Options

Equity options trading began in 1993. Currently call and put options on seven underlying stocks are traded on the options market. These are Keppel Corporation, Singapore Airlines, NatSteel, City Developments, Creative Technology, DBS and UOB.

Clob

On 2 January 1990 the exchange introduced an OTC market, known as Clob International, to allow investors to trade in a number of international securities listed on foreign exchanges. As at 31 December 1997, 112 Malaysian stocks, nine Hong Kong stocks and seven other international stocks were quoted on Clob International. Companies quoted on Clob do not have to adhere to the corporate disclosure policy rules that apply to companies listed on the main board or Sesdaq.

Exhibit 58.7:
COUNTRY FUNDS – SINGAPORE

Fund	US$ % change 01/01/97 01/01/98	01/01/93 01/01/98	Fund base currency	Fund size (US$ mil)	Fund volatility	Management group	Opal main sector	Opal subsector
Nikko Singapore Active Open	-31.34	N/A	¥	468	-1	Nikko	Open-End	Equity
Thornton New Tiger Singapore	-33.2	33.88	US$	5.8	9.747	Thornton	Open-End	Equity
Dres Thornton ASF Singapore	-35.33	N/A	US$	8.7	8.199	Thornton	Open-End	Equity
Singapore Sesdaq Ltd	-39.4	70.07	US$	N/A	11.835	Govett & Co	Closed-End	Equity
HSBC GIF Singaporean Equity	-41.81	6.54	US$	4.4	11.038	HSBC Asset Mgmt	Open-End	Equity
RG ZelfSelect Singapore	-43.8	N/A	G	13	-1	Robeco	Open-End	Equity
Fidelity Fds Singapore	-44.09	14.85	US$	24.6	9.107	Fidelity	Open-End	Equity
Singapore Fund Inc	-44.85	-7.1	US$	115.63	7.14	DBS Asst Mgt	Closed-End	Equity
Nikko GIUF Singapore Fund	-45.01	N/A	US$	0.1	7.639	Nikko	Open-End	Equity
Barclays ASF Singapore	-47.03	23.62	US$	3	9.737	Barclays	Open-End	Equity

Note: details for some funds may not have been included if the data for the US$ % change for 97/98 is not available

Source: Standard & Poor's Micropal.

However, corporate announcements of companies quoted on Clob are disseminated as quickly as possible to investors.

INVESTORS

Most SES investors are private individuals, with this category comprising 98.6% of shareholders in 1995, as against 91.5% in 1975. However, over the same period the value of their stake declined from 28.9% to 19.2%, while that of corporate and institutional investors grew from 40.7% to 75.4%. Nevertheless, individuals do contribute significantly to market liquidity. There has been a marked swing towards local share ownership since independence in 1965, boosted by the change of regulations to allow savings to be invested in equities.

All the major domestic banks have well-developed and growing investment departments, and a number of merchant banks also manage funds. There are several local unit trusts, such as the Singapore Growth Fund, and a number of regional investment organisations investing a substantial portion of their assets in Singapore.

OPERATIONS

A) Trading system

Under the fully computerised Clob trading system, the trading workstations installed at brokers' offices are linked directly to the SES's computer system. Investors' orders are keyed in and matched in the Clob system and confirmations are sent to brokers automatically. The Clob system maintains an order book for every traded security and matches buy and sell orders. Each order in the order book has a limit price. This is the highest price (for a buy order) or the lowest price (for a sell order) at which the order can be executed. Orders in the system are held according to price, then time priority.

B) List of principal brokers

GK GOH STOCKBROKERS
50 Raffles Place, No. 33-00 Shell Tower, Singapore 0104
Tel: (65) 225 1228

KEPPEL SECURITIES
10 Hoe Chiang Road No. 08-01, Keppel Towers
Singapore 089315
Tel: (65) 221 5688; Fax: (65) 226 1543

KIM ENG SECURITIES
UIC Building, 5 Shenton Way No. 13-00, Singapore 0106
Tel: (65) 220 9090; Fax: (65) 225 8746

OCBC SECURITIES
18 Church Street, No. 06-00 OCBC Centre South
Singapore 0104
Tel: (65) 535 2882; Fax: (65) 532 2768

ONG & CO
76 Shenton Way No. 06-00, Ong Building,
Singapore 079119
Tel: (65) 223 9466; Fax: (65) 224 0075

JM SASSOON & CO
1 Raffles Place, UOB Centre No. 44-00,
Singapore 0104
Tel: (65) 535 2888; Fax: (65) 533 7956

SALOMON BROTHERS SINGAPORE PTE. LIMITED
1 Temasek Avenue, #39-02, Millenia Tower
Singapore 039192
Tel: (65) 432-1230; Fax: (65)-432-1239

SMITH BARNEY (SINGAPORE) PTE. LTD.
20 Collier Quay, #18-00 Tung Centre
Singapore 049319
Tel: (65) 538-1233; Fax: (65) 538-3511

TAT LEE SECURITIES
63 Market Street No. 12-06/07, Tat Lee Bank Building
Singapore 048942
Tel: (65) 533 9666; Fax: (65) 533 6989

VICKERS BALLAS & CO
30 Raffles Place No. 07-00, Caltex House, Singapore 048622
Tel: (65) 535 8111; Fax: (65) 532 2331

C) Settlement and transfer

All shares are dealt on a ready basis for seven-day settlement. Since July 1994, all trades of Singapore listed companies have been cleared through the computerised book entry system.

There is a book-based settlement system for main board securities. Share ownership and changes in ownership of immobilised securities are effected by book entries in the securities accounts of depositors. Immobilised scrips are registered in the name of the Central Depository Pte Ltd (CDP), a central nominee that holds securities on behalf of depositors.

D) Commissions and other costs

Exhibit 58.8:
SES BROKERAGE CHARGES

Consideration	*Rate*
On the first S$250,000	1.0%
On the next S$250,000	0.9%
On the next S$250,000	0.8%
On the next S$250,000	0.7%
On the next S$500,000	0.5%
On amounts exceeding S$1.5 million	Negotiable, subject to a minimum of 0.3% Minimum brokerage is S$2 per contract.

In addition to brokerage, the following charges are payable: a clearing fee of 0.05% on the value of the contract, subject to a maximum of S$100; a contract stamp duty of 0.05% on the value of the contract; a transfer stamp duty of 0.2% on the value of the contract when shares are sent for registration (not payable on securities settled on a book entry basis); and a goods and services tax (GST) of 3% on brokerage and clearing fees.

TAXATION AND REGULATIONS AFFECTING FOREIGN INVESTORS

Singapore does not levy dividend tax or withholding tax on dividends paid to non-residents. However, tax at the corporate tax rate of 26% is deducted from gross dividends payable, representing the corporate tax on the listed company's profits out of which dividends are franked.

There are no foreign exchange controls or capital gains tax on the trading of securities by non-residents. Purchases and sales of securities are not subject to any restrictions except for those of banking stocks and stocks in certain strategic companies. There are no foreign exchange controls or limitations on the repatriation of income, capital gains and capital.

LISTING AND REPORTING REQUIREMENTS

A) Listing requirements

Applications for new listings of securities have to be submitted to the SES for approval. The SES listing manual (November 1993, as amended) sets out the listing application procedures for the different types of securities that may be listed on the exchange, as well as the listing requirements.

The SES listing rules are not exhaustive and the exchange retains the right to make listing subject to special conditions or to waive compliance. Suitability for listing depends on a number of factors including a minimum size and an adequate trading record under present management. Other factors include the integrity of the management and controlling shareholders, the company's market position and relative stability and whether there are any material conflicts of interest.

A Singapore incorporated company applying for a primary listing should have a paid-up capital of at least S$15 million, and at least S$4 million or 25% of its issued and paid-up capital (whichever is greater) should be in the hands of not less than 1,000 shareholders. The company should have an operating record of at least five years with a cumulative consolidated pre-tax profit of at least S$7.5 million for the past three years and a minimum pre-tax profit of S$1 million for each of those three years.

Foreign companies may also seek an SES listing where certain requirements are met. Listing may either take the form of a primary listing, where the foreign corporation's equity securities are not listed on the foreign corporation's home exchange, or a secondary listing where equity securities are already listed on a foreign exchange.

Once approval for listing has been given by the SES, an offer of shares in the relevant company to the public in Singapore (if any) must be accompanied by a prospectus that has been registered with the Registrar of Companies. The contents of the prospectus must comply with the detailed rules contained in the SES listing manual and the provisions of the Companies Act, Chapter 50, of Singapore.

B) Reporting requirements

The SES listing manual establishes the corporate disclosure policy to which listed companies are required to adhere. To achieve a fair and orderly market, the SES requires each listed company to make available to the public any information known to the listed company necessary to avoid the establishment of a false market or which would be likely to materially affect the price of its securities, and to take reasonable steps to ensure that all who invest in its securities have equal access to that information. The listing manual also sets out the criteria that the SES will apply in approving applications from Singapore-listed companies to make rights issues, bonus issues or stock splits.

Section 203A of the Companies Act permits listed companies, subject to certain conditions, to provide shareholders with a summary financial statement instead of a full annual report. The listing manual was amended in February 1996 to cater for this, although the SES retains discretion to require a listed company to disclose additional information in the summary financial statement.

SHAREHOLDER PROTECTION CODES

The Securities Industry Council was established in January 1978 as an advisory body to provide guidance to the SES and to coordinate its activities with the needs of the investing public and the business community and also with government policies. The Securities Industry Council acts as an advisory body to the Minister of Finance and also advises the SES on matters referred to it by the exchange. Members of the Securities Industry Council are drawn from the public and private sectors, with the majority coming from the latter.

A) Significant shareholdings

A shareholder is required to inform a listed company if he or she acquires a shareholding in that company of 5% or more, and to inform it of any subsequent changes to the shareholding. The company in turn is required to disclose such information to the SES.

B) Insider trading

Under the Securities Industry Act, insider dealing, market manipulation, share rigging and fraudulent behaviour are criminal offences carrying a maximum fine of S$50,000 or seven years' imprisonment for an individual, and a maximum fine of S$100,000 for a company.

Among other things, the Securities Industry Act provides for the licensing and conduct of dealers, investment advisers and their representatives. It also introduced more detailed regulations concerning the conduct of securities business. The Securities Industry Regulations, Regulation 37A, exempts stabilisation actions by a manager of an initial public offering from Section 98(3) of the Securities Industry Act, which prohibits any form of participation in securities transactions that would have the effect of maintaining or stabilising the price of the securities on the SES.

C) Takeovers and mergers

The procedures for takeover bids are covered by the Companies Act, the SES listing manual and the Singapore Code on Takeovers and Mergers, which is modelled on the City of London Code and administered by the Securities Industry Council. While the Code does not have the force of law, violation can lead to reprimand or censure and a possible suspension of trading.

RESEARCH

Various brokerage firms offer detailed market and stock reports. JM Sassoon is one of the best local brokers in this respect. Of the foreign brokers, Hoare Govett, WI Carr, Salomon Smith Barney and SG Warburg provide well-regarded research.

The following information is available from the SES: *Company Statex Service* – a weekly updating service designed to provide investors with the latest financial reports of listed companies – and *Investment Management in Singapore*, which provides a comprehensive account of the securities market in Singapore.

Singapore, published by Euromoney Books, provides in-depth information for those wishing to invest or do business in the country. See the order card at the back of this book for details.

CHAPTER 59

Slovakia

Introduction

Equity trading in Slovakia takes place either on the Bratislava Stock Exchange (BSE) or through the RM System (RMS). Under Slovak law, all publicly traded securities (with the exception of some government securities) must be dematerialised (book-entered) and must be registered at the Securities Centre of the Slovak Republic. The majority of trading takes place on the BSE, where the electronic trading system is currently being upgraded.

Because the Securities Act requires that all shares in privatised companies must be publicly traded, the vast majority of companies are quoted on the BSE. However, liquidity is low and market capitalisation at the end of 1997 was just 9.8% of GDP.

Slovak companies tend to prefer using bank loans to finance expansion, and Slovakofarma was the only important company that raised its share capital during 1997. However, it's likely that companies will soon start to look for fresh equity from the market due to their substantial indebtedness and the prevailing high interest rates.

ECONOMIC AND POLITICAL OVERVIEW

Since the 1994 elections, the Slovak ruling coalition has comprised the centrist Movement for a Democratic Slovakia (the largest political party), the ultra-left Workers Party and the ultra-right Slovak National Party. Despite some disagreements, it is very likely that the coalition will survive until the next parliamentary elections, due to be held on 25 and 26 September 1998. The long-running row between the Prime Minister, Vladimir Meciar, and the Slovak President, Michal Kovac, has had a deleterious effect on the image of country abroad, and was one of the main reasons for Slovakia's exclusion from the first round of Nato and EU enlargement.

In spite of the negative political background, the economy is still doing quite well. GDP growth has slowed down but preliminary figures show that it reached some 5% in 1997, after 6.9% growth in 1996. The lower growth was in part a result of high interest rates imposed by the National Bank of Slovakia (NBS) in a campaign to protect the currency against devaluation. NBS efforts have so far proved successful and the exchange rate of the Slovak koruna, which is calculated relative to a 60% Deutschmark and 40% US dollar basket, has been relatively stable. Inflation stood at 6.4% year-on-year in December 1997, as against 5.4% in December 1996, mainly due to administrative measures like the import surcharge.

The budget deficit is under control at only 1.8% of GDP, while the current account deficit has decreased and at the end of 1997 should be below 8% of GDP.

Role of the central bank

The National Bank of Slovakia (NBS) is operationally independent of the government. The National Bank of Slovakia Act No. (566/1992) defines the powers of the NBS, which include enforcing banking regulations, injecting liquidity into the banking system and overseeing bank supervision. At the end of 1997 the government proposed that half of the NBS board members should be appointed by the government; however, final approval of an amendment to the NBS Act to that effect will be subject to parliamentary approval in 1998.

MARKET PERFORMANCE

A) In 1997

The SAX Index rose 1.4% during the year, from 178. 98 to 182.48. This increase was mainly due to price rises for the two biggest companies on the market, and the generally weak market is reflected in the fact that BSE market capitalisation fell by 15% to end the year at SKK64 billion (US$1.8 billion).

Exhibit 59.1: SLOVAKIA SAX 16 PRICE INDEX (US$), 1993–97

High value 384.38 1.3.94 Low value 101.12 1.11.93 *Source: Datastream*

B) Summary information

Global ranking by market value (US$ terms, end-1997): 67
Market capitalisation (end-1997): US$1.8 billion
Growth in market value (local currency terms, 1993–97): 59.2%
Market value as a % of nominal GDP (end-1997): 9.8%
Number of domestic/foreign companies listed (end-1997): 9/0
Market P/E (all listed companies, end-1997): 11.1
Short-term (30-day) interest rate (end-1997): 26.5%
Long-term (3-year) bond yield (end-1997): 13.5%
Budget deficit as a % of nominal GDP (1997): 1.8%
Annual increase in M2 supply (end-1997): 8.9%
Inflation rate (end-1997): 6.4%
US$ exchange rate (end-1997): SKK34.8

C) Year-end share price index, price/earnings ratios and yields

Exhibit 59.2:
YEAR-END SHARE PRICE INDEX, P/E RATIOS AND GROSS DIVIDEND YIELDS, 1993–97

Year-end	*SAX Index*	*P/E*	*Yield (%)*
1993	109.58	4.7	4.0
1994	214.27	9.5	2.8
1995	157.80	6.7	3.5
1996	178.98	10.4	3.2
1997	182.48	11.1	3.1

Source: CA IB Securities.

D) Market indices and their constituents

The SAX Index was introduced in September 1993 with a base value of 100 points. It comprises the 16 most liquid BSE shares.

THE STOCK MARKET

A) Brief history and structure

The Bratislava Stock Exchange was opened in 1993 under the voucher privatisation programme initiated by the government. Shares in more than 500 companies and 500 investment funds became publicly traded. Since then, private banks, brokerage houses and investment funds have been established to service the market, which is split into two parts – the official BSE and the over-the-counter RMS. In July 1995 the Ministry of Finance took steps to enhance market transparency, while regulations passed recently ban off-exchange transactions and move them to the BSE and the RMS as direct trades.

With effect from 1 August 1997, the BSE implemented a reconstruction programme to divide floor trading into three distinct markets as follows: (a) the listed securities market (initially with 13 shares traded); (b) the registered securities market (initially 44 shares); and (c) the free market (890 shares). These three markets differ from each other according to the stringency of admission requirements and the level of subsequent disclosure required.

B) Different exchanges

There is only one exchange, which is located in Bratislava.

C) Opening hours, name and address

BSE trading takes place on Monday to Friday from 11.00am to 2.00pm.

BRATISLAVA STOCK EXCHANGE
Vyosoka 17, PO Box 151, SK 814 99 Bratislava
Tel: (421) 7 5036 111/102; Fax: (421) 7 5036 103

MARKET SIZE

A) Number of listings and market value

The division of the BSE markets in August 1997 led to a decrease in the number of companies traded on the listed securities market; at the end of 1997, nine companies were listed and market capitalisation stood at SKK64 billion.

Exhibit 59.3:
NUMBER OF COMPANIES LISTED AND MARKET VALUE, BSE, 1993–97

Year-end	*No. of companies listed*	*Market capitalisation (SKK billion)*
1993	7	40.2
1994	13	54.6
1995	19	55.5
1996	19	75.0
1997	9	64.0

Source: CA IB Securities.

B) Largest quoted companies

The 10 largest quoted companies represented some 75% of total market capitalisation at end-1997.

Exhibit 59.4:
THE 10 LARGEST COMPANIES LISTED ON THE BSE, END-1997

Ranking	*Company*	*Sector*	*Market value (US$ million)*
1	Slovnaft	Refinery	419
2	VSZ	Steel	324
3	Slovakofarma	Pharmaceuticals	233
4	VUB	Banking	150
5	Nafta	Energy	124
6	Slovenska poistovna	Insurance	49
7	ZSNP	Aluminium	36
8	Vahostav	Construction	19
9	Povazske strojarne	Engineering	19
10	Chemolak	Chemical	13

Source: CA IB Securities.

C) Trading volume

Total BSE turnover in 1997 was SKK161 billion (US$4.6 billion), a 41% increase on 1996.

Exhibit 59.5:
TURNOVER ON THE BSE, 1993–97

Year	*Value traded (SKK million)*	*Volume traded (shares million)*
1993	166	0.12
1994	6,284	8.59
1995	40,069	45.16
1996	114,116	131.24
1997	161,154	140.22

Source: CA IB Securities.

Exhibit 59.6:
THE 10 MOST ACTIVELY TRADED DOMESTIC SHARES, 1997

Ranking	*Company*	*Trading value (SKK million)*	*Shares (million)*
1	VSZ	11,776	17.7
2	VUB	8,814	5.0
3	Slovnaft	8,226	8.4
4	Nafta	4,180	52.7
5	Slovakofarma	3,609	0.8
6	Drotovna	2,229	3.0
7	Slovenska poistovna	1,920	1.3
8	JCaP	1,458	1.7
9	Chemolak	816	0.6
10	ISK	694	0.6

Source: CA IB Securities.

TYPES OF SHARE

Only common shares are traded.

OTHER MARKETS

The RM System (RMS) operates as an OTC market. It was established in May 1993 and trading hours are from 10.00am to 3.00pm. There are approximately 150 offices nationwide, mainly serving small retail investors. Prices are set by "matching" buy and sell orders, and price volatility for each stock is limited in the range +/-10% from the weighted average price of the previous trading day.

OPERATIONS

A) Trading system

All traded shares are issued in book entry form, records are kept by the Securities Centre (a company 100%

Exhibit 59.7:
COUNTRY FUNDS – CZECH AND SLOVAK REPUBLICS

Fund	US$ % change 01/01/97 01/01/98	01/01/93 01/01/98	Currency	Fund size (US$ mil)	Fund volatility	Management group	Opal main sector	Opal subsector
Czech Republic Fund Inc	-3.35	N/A	US$	95.107	4.477	Advantage Adv	Closed-End	Equity
Czech & Slovak Invest Corp	-8.22	-17.6	US$	N/A	3.648	Fleming	Closed-End	Equity
Czech Value Fund	-18.66	N/A	US$	41.501	-1	Regent Pacific	Closed-End	Equity
BB Tschechien Invest	-25.35	N/A	DM	31.5	-1	BB-Invest	Open-End	Equity
Bohemia Investment Company	-25.81	N/A	Sfr	N/A	-1	MC Trustee SA	Closed-End	Equity
ACM/IBA Czech Equity Ptf	-27.83	N/A	Sch	50.5	5.598	East Fund Mgt	Open-End	Equity
F.I.T Czeck Investment	-28.28	N/A	Sfr	N/A	5.87	FIT Inv Mgt	Open-End	Equity
CF Czech Fund	-39.39	N/A	DM	3.3	5.651	CRM Asst Mgt	Open-End	Equity

Note: details for some funds may not have been included if the data for the US$ % change for 97/98 was not available

Source: Standard & Poor's Micropal.

owned and supervised by the Ministry of Finance) and shares are registered in the name of the owner of the account. Physical securities are held at a custodian bank.

B) Settlement and transfer

Settlement of stock exchange trades takes place on T+3 on a delivery versus payment basis. Sale proceeds are credited to the client's account on T+5.

C) Commissions and other costs

Brokerage fees vary from 0.6% to 1% depending on the size of transaction. Transaction fees levied by the Securities Centre range from SKK25 to SKK4,449, plus SKK0.06 per share for any additional volume above 50,000 shares.

RMS commissions range from a minimum SKK25 to SKK38,500 plus 0.1% for any additional trade volume above SKK10 million.

TAXATION AND REGULATIONS AFFECTING FOREIGN INVESTORS

A) Taxation

There is a 15% withholding tax on dividends and interest on debt securities. The withholding tax rate on dividends is usually lower – owing to a number of double taxation treaties – if a foreign investor holds a significant stake in a company. There is no capital gains tax for non-residents.

B) Exchange controls and regulations

Slovakian korunas are not freely convertible. Most foreign currency transactions must take place at specific offices (*devízové miesto*) as defined in the Foreign Exchange Act (usually a local bank). However, any foreigner is free to purchase or sell local shares with any type of counterparty. There is some uncertainty about whether non-residents can freely purchase foreign currency with Slovakian korunas. Accordingly, keeping a record of investment transactions is advisable. However, investment protection treaties exist with various countries and investors from those countries can freely repatriate all dividends, interest and earnings from the sale of investments, under applicable provisions of the relevant treaty.

Domestic and foreign investors are prohibited from acquiring more than 15% and 3% (respectively) of bank shares unless they have obtained prior authorisation from the National Bank of Slovakia.

LISTING AND REPORTING REQUIREMENTS

A) Listing requirements

Exhibit 59.8:
THE MAIN REQUIREMENTS FOR ADMISSION TO THE LISTED SECURITIES MARKET

Registered securities market	*Free market*
Minimum share capital (SKK million)	500
Market capitalisation of shares (SKK million)	100
Market capitalisation of shares (publicly held)	100
Involvement period in business	3 years
Financial information in prospectus	3 years

Source: Cernejová & Hrbek.

Shares of both domestic and foreign companies (subject to obtaining the appropriate approval from the Ministry of Finance and, in the case of foreign issuers, also from the National Bank of Slovakia) can be listed on the BSE, subject to the requirements set out in Exhibit 59.8. In addition, the listed securities market is open only to issuers that are at least 25% publicly held, unless the BSE determines that there is sufficient liquidity despite a lesser percentage in public hands.

Entry requirements for the registered securities market and the free market of the BSE are not as stringent as for the listed securities market. No specific conditions are required to be fulfilled by an issuer apart from the need to obtain the approval of the Ministry of Finance.

A detailed prospectus (including financial data compiled in accordance with IAS) must accompany all applications to join the listed securities market. A short-form, less detailed prospects is required for admission of securities to the registered securities market or the free market.

B) Reporting requirements

Companies on the listed securities market must provide annual financial statements (consolidated, if applicable), audited by a member of the Slovakian Chamber of Auditors, along with regular quarterly financial statements. Additionally, issuers of shares traded on the listed securities market must give notification of facts or circumstances that could have an effect on the price of their shares.

The registered securities market requires the semi-annual filing of financial statements and an announcement on the outcome of general meetings. For free market, as the lowest-tier market, only statutory minimum disclosure is required.

SHAREHOLDER PROTECTION CODES

A) Significant shareholdings

The Securities Act requires disclosure of ownership at, or passing through 5%, 10%, 20%, 30%, 50% or 65% of any publicly traded issues. A disclosure report from the Securities Centre is published and includes the issuer's name, the type of security, the ISIN number, the name of the shareholder, and that shareholder's previous and new stakes.

B) Takeover regulations

Under the Securities Act, no single person, or persons acting jointly, can acquire a stake of more than 30% in the publicly tradable shares of a company without extending a public offer. A public offer may not be valid for less than 30 days or more than 60 days and the purchase price may not be lower than the average price in the past six months.

Unsuccessful bidders cannot reintroduce a public offer until at least one year after the expiry of the offer period.

C) Insider trading

Insider trading is prohibited. Any non-publicly available information regarding an issuer that might affect the price of its securities is regarded as insider information. Any person who becomes aware of insider information is prohibited from dealing in the relevant securities or otherwise using such information for his own or a third party's benefit, until such information has become public.

RESEARCH

CA IB Securities offers comprehensive research on both the Slovakian equity market and individual stocks.

CA IB SECURITIES
Dubravska cesta 2, SK-81703 Bratislava
Tel: (421) 74341 111; Fax: (421) 7 4341 120

CHAPTER

60

Slovenia

Introduction

Ljubljana Stock Exchange (LSE), the only Slovenian exchange, was badly affected by the February 1997 central bank introduction of custody accounts for foreign investors, which substantially increased transaction costs. The SBI Index fell by 22% in three days and there was a mass exodus of foreign investors from the Slovene equity market. The Bank of Slovenia eased the regulations in June, but foreign investors are not allowed to sell shares to domestic investors for a period of seven years.

The number of companies on the main market (tiers A and B) of the LSE increased from 20 at the end of 1996 to 26 at the end of 1997, and on the OTC (tier C) 53 companies were quoted at the end of 1997 (compared with 25 in 1996). Most turnover is concentrated in a few major companies, which are also of interest to foreign investors. The increased number of quoted companies boosted end-1997 market capitalisation by 125% to T399 billion, representing 11.2% of GDP.

A new law on mergers and acquisitions was adopted by parliament in 1997. It regulates M&A transactions and makes a full takeover offer mandatory when any listed company acquires 25% or more of the shares of another listed company.

ECONOMIC AND POLITICAL OVERVIEW

Slovenia is strategically positioned at some of Europe's most important crossroads, including the main road and rail links between Greece and the rest of Europe, and the southern route between western and eastern Europe. Following a referendum, the country declared itself independent on 25 June 1991, and, since 8 October 1991, the Republic of Slovenia has been an autonomous, independent and sovereign state. It is the most developed of the six former Yugoslav republics, and the most prosperous of any of the states to emerge from former communist central and eastern Europe.

After the general election in November 1996, a centrist coalition of Liberal Democrats, the People's Party and the Pensioners' Party was formed in early 1997, with Janez Drnovsek, a Liberal Democrat, as the Prime Minister. The main objectives of the new government focused on Slovenia's negotiations to join Nato and the EU, reform of the pension system and the introduction of new fiscal, banking and labour legislation. In the second half of the year, Slovenia was invited by the EU to join the first round of countries signing the Association Agreement, but, despite an intensive diplomatic effort, the country was not included into the first round of Nato expansion. In November 1997 presidential elections were held and Milan Kucan was re-elected for a new five-year term.

GDP grew by an estimated 2.9% in 1997 and the inflation rate was 9.5%. The current account deficit is estimated to have been US$35 million in 1997, while foreign exchange reserves increased to US$4,425 million from US$4,130 million in 1996. External debt totalled US$4,253 million. The budget deficit is estimated at 1.2% of GDP, up from 0.8% in 1996.

Role of the central bank

The Bank of Slovenia is autonomous and is responsible for managing monetary policy and the exchange rate, and for supervising the commercial banking network.

MARKET PERFORMANCE

A) In 1997

Market capitalisation totalled T399 billion (US$2.4 billion) at 31 December 1997, up from T177 billion (US$1,047 billion) at the end of 1996. Equities represented 79% of total market capitalisation. LSE turnover in 1997 amounted to T108.3 billion (US$0.6 billion), of which 80.8% was in equities. The SBI Index increased by 18.7% in 1997.

Exhibit 60.1: SLOVENIAN SE (SBI) PRICE INDEX (US$), 1993–97

High value 1630.12 2.5.94 Low value 935.96 1.8.96 *Source: Datastream*

B) Summary information

Global ranking by market value (US$ terms, end-1997): 59
Market capitalisation (end-1997): US$2.4 billion
Growth in market value (local currency terms, 1993–97): 477.3%
Market value as a % of nominal GDP (end-1997): 11.2%
Number of domestic/foreign companies listed (end-1997): 26/0
Market P/E (all tier A and B companies, end-1997): 14.63
Short term (3-month) interest rate (end-1997): 21.1%
Long term (5-year) yield (end-1997): 6.2%
Budget deficit as a % of nominal GDP (1997): 1.2%
Annual increase in broad money (M3) supply (Nov 1997): 3.25%
Inflation rate (1997): 9.5%
US$ exchange rate (end-1997): T167.7

THE STOCK MARKET

A) Brief history and structure

The Ljubljana Stock, Commodities and Foreign Exchange was established in 1924, mainly to trade government bonds and corporate debentures. The LSE was closed in 1941 due to World War II, and was abolished in 1953. It re-opened in December 1989 and was renamed the Ljubljanska Borza following Slovenia's declaration of independence on 25 June 1991.

The LSE consists of the main market (tiers A and B) and the open market (tier C). The exchange is a legal entity and is funded out of membership fees (initial and annual) and commission fees charged on the volume of trading. It is a self-governing and self-regulating organisation.

The Securities and Exchange Commission (SEC) monitors the operation of the entire securities market.

B) Opening hours, name and address

There is only one stock exchange in Slovenia. Trading takes place every day from 9.30am to 1.00pm via the LSE electronic trading system, BIS.

LJUBLJANA STOCK EXCHANGE
Slovenska 56, 1000 Ljubljana
Tel: (386) 61 171 02 11; Fax: (386) 61 171 02 13

MARKET SIZE

A) Number of listings and market value

At the end of 1997 there were 26 companies listed on the LSE main market (tiers A and B) with a further 53 trading on tier C.

Exhibit 60.2:
NUMBER OF COMPANIES LISTED AND MARKET VALUE, LSE, 1993–97

Year-end	*No. of companies listed*	*Market capitalisation (DM million)*
1993	16	579.7
1994	11	326.0
1995	12	445.7

Exhibit 60.2 continued

1996	20	1,373.4
1997	26	3,346.7

Source: Ljubljana Stock Exchange.

Exhibit 60.3:
THE 10 LARGEST COMPANIES LISTED ON THE LSE BY MARKET CAPITALISATION, END-1997

Ranking	*Company*	*Market value (US$ million)*
1	Krka	385.6
2	Lek	325.4
3	Petrol	200.0
4	Mercator	84.1
5	Istrabenz	80.6
6	Luka Koper	79.2
7	SKB Bank	73.9
8	BTC	61.3
9	Radenska	45.1
10	Droga	44.0

Source: Ljubljana Stock Exchange.

B) Trading volume

Equity turnover on the LSE totalled T87.6 billion (US$517.5 million) in 1997, accounting for 80.8% of total trading value.

Exhibit 60.4:
THE 10 MOST ACTIVELY TRADED SHARES, LSE, 1997

Ranking	*Company*	*Turnover (T million)*	*% of total turnover*
1	Krka	17,567	32.8
2	Lek	17,443	32.6
3	Mercator	9,636	18.0
4	SKB Bank	7,480	14.0
5	Petrol	6,809	12.7
6	Kolinska	2,980	5.6
7	Luka Koper	2,092	3.9
8	Terme Èate	2,042	3.8
9	Istrabenz	1,718	3.2
10	Droga	1,709	3.2

Source: Ljubljana Stock Exchange.

TYPES OF SECURITIES

The following securities may be traded on the exchange:
- shares;
- corporate and other legal entity bonds;
- government bonds; and
- other securities as provided by law.

OPERATIONS

A) Trading system

Electronic trading of all listed securities via the BIS system started on 21 January 1994. Software for the system is based on that used on the Alberta Stock Exchange. It is designed for smaller exchanges and has the flexibility to support the automation of all stock exchange activities.

B) List of principal brokers

ABH
Slovenska 50, 1000 Ljubljana
Tel: (386) 61 133 3121; Fax: (386) 61 310 985

BANKA CA IB
Kotnikova 5, 1000 Ljubljana
Tel: (386) 61 132 1174; Fax: (386) 61 132 9186

BPH
Tomsiceva 1, 1000 Ljubljana
Tel: (386) 61 125 6145; Fax: (386) 61 125 7053

MEDVESEK PUSNIK
Gradnikove brigade 11, 1000 Ljubljana
Tel: (386) 61 141 4 078; Fax: (386) 61 141 4105

NIKA BDP
Dunajska 20, 1116 Ljubljana
Tel: (386) 61 133 155; Fax: (386) 61 133 1347

NOVA LB
Subiceva 2, 1000 Ljubljana
Tel: (386) 61 125 5333; Fax: (386) 61 222 518

PUBLIKUM BP
Miklosiceva 38, 1000 Ljubljana
Tel: (386) 61 131 8193; Fax: (386) 61 133 1050

TMB
Strossmaerjeva 13, 2000 Maribor
Tel: (386) 62 224 756; Fax: (386) 62 223 188

SAVINJSKA BP
Savinjska c. 21, 3310 Zalec
Tel: (386) 63 715 573; Fax: (386) 63 715 574

SKB BANKA
Ajkovscina 4, 1000 Ljubljana
Tel: (386) 62 133 2132; Fax: (386) 6 328 267

C) Members

At the end of 1997 there were 46 members of the LSE. The annual membership fee is DM10,000 with an initial fee of DM3,000.

D) Settlement

Under the electronic BIS system, all trades are cleared on a T+2 rolling settlement basis and delivery is against payment. Clearing and settlement takes place via the Central Securities Clearing Corporation (KDD).

E) Commissions

The total cost of transactions, inclusive of brokerage fees and the stock exchange levy of 0.113%, is usually in the range of 1–1.5% of the trade value.

TAXATION AND REGULATIONS AFFECTING FOREIGN INVESTORS

The Stock Exchange Act restricts membership of the exchange to domestic subjects and legal entities. A foreign broker may become a member only if it establishes a branch office or a joint venture company in Slovenia. This regulation is expected to change in 1998.

In February 1997, in order to defend the currency, the central bank introduced custody accounts for foreign portfolio investors, effectively halting the flow of portfolio investment into Slovenia. Under the regulation, the domestic custody bank must deposit at a foreign bank the same amount of foreign currency as was brought into the country by the foreign portfolio investor. High transaction costs for trading via these custody accounts more or less put a stop to foreign portfolio investment. The regulation was eased in June 1997, and foreign investors can now buy shares without additional cost, but they are not allowed to sell them to domestic buyers until seven years have elapsed from the date of purchase. Though this regulation is not expected to last seven years, neither is it likely to be removed in 1998.

Repatriation of profits, interest and invested capital is guaranteed by legislation. Dividends paid to foreign investors are taxed at 15%, while dividends paid to domestic investors are subject to a 25% withholding tax.

As of 1 January 1994, legal entities with capital gains deriving from trading in securities are taxed through corporation tax (at a basic rate of 25%). For individuals, under legislation that came into force on 1 January 1997, capital gains are taxed at 30% on average, although the tax does not apply if securities are held by the same investor for more than three years.

LISTING AND REPORTING REQUIREMENTS

A) Listing requirements

In order for a company's securities to be listed on the LSE appropriate information must be disclosed. A prospectus must include information on a company's legal status, its main activities, its revised business results for the past three years and its future business prospects. The capital requirement for companies listing on the LSE was lowered in 1997 to T1 billion (from T1.2 billion previously) on the main market and to T500 million (from T600 million previously) on tier C.

B) Reporting requirements

Continuing disclosure is prescribed by law. This disclosure consists of audited financial statements for the year, semi-annual financial statements (in both cases including management discussion and analysis), all information regarding corporate actions (shareholders' meetings, dividends and interest payments), new securities issues, the appointment and removal of directors, changes in substantial shareholder holdings (at 10%, 25%, 50% and 75% of the voting rights) and any other material changes.

SHAREHOLDER PROTECTION CODES

The "Law on Takeovers" came into force on 16 August 1997. The law applies to all publicly traded shares and stipulates that a person (acting alone or in concert) who acquires 25% or more of a company's voting shares (including any shares already owned) must submit a public offer for the company. The law also requires that a person acquiring directly or indirectly 5% of the voting shares in a company is obliged to notify the company and the Securities Market Agency within three days of the acquisition. The company concerned must publicly announce details of any notifications it receives, also within three days.

RESEARCH

Reliable and detailed research on the Slovenian market is produced by Banka CA IB in Ljubljana.

Eastern Europe: investing for the 21st Century, published by Euromoney Books, provides in-depth information for those wishing to invest or do business in the region. See the order card at the back of the book for details.

CHAPTER 61

South Africa

Introduction

The Johannesburg Stock Exchange (JSE) is the largest in Africa and has a capitalisation of more than 10 times that of all the other African markets combined. The role of the JSE was originally to raise finance for the expansion of the mining industry. Listings soon broadened to include industrial companies and these accounted for the majority of the 615 domestic companies quoted at the end of 1997.

South Africa's exclusion from the international financial system and the operation of tight exchange controls long contributed to a "hot-house effect", trapping capital within the country and forcibly channelling investment into the equity market. Intense competition for shares pushed up prices and the absence of state pensions also meant substantial inflows of funds into the contractual savings industry. Due to a lack of alternative investments, institutional investors tended to hold on to stock, reducing liquidity and adding to the upward price pressure.

In 1995, however, the JSE opened its doors to foreign and corporate members and set about trying to end its reputation as one of the world's most illiquid markets. The move – part of a broader deregulation package – paralleled the London stock market's "Big Bang" of 1986, although changes have been phased in over time. Automated trading began in March 1996 and, during 1998, a central securities scrip depository will be introduced, accompanied by an electronic settlement system for equity transactions.

ECONOMIC AND POLITICAL OVERVIEW

South Africa established a fully representative democratic government in May 1994. For the period 1994 to 1999, a government of national unity is in operation, with a multi-party Cabinet exercising executive powers of government under the leadership of President Nelson Mandela. Regional elections were successfully held for provincial and municipal levels of government in a number of provinces in 1995 and 1996. This second tier of government is now in place.

The culmination of many years of intense negotiation resulted in South Africa's adoption of a new constitution, which took effect on 4 February 1997. The bill of rights included in the constitution is one of the most extensive in the world. Although the interim constitution which preceded it was generally vertically based (ie it governed the relationship between the state and similar public authorities on the one hand and the individual on the other), the final constitution has a much wider ambit in that it is likely to have an extensive horizontal effect as well. This could have profound repercussions as regards contractual relations and in the commercial sphere generally.

The government has implemented a programme of economic restructuring, including fiscal reform, monetary stabilisation, tariff and protection reductions to create a more competitive economy, and to promote the development of social infrastructure.

The government has appointed advisers to look at the privatisation of, among other things, the airports company, state-owned airlines, some resource companies in mining and forestry and sections of the power utility. Sale of some of these assets could take place in 1998. A National Framework agreement was also concluded between government and labour relating to the restructuring of state assets.

The first of the state development initiatives in infrastructural development, "The Maputo Corridor", will commence in 1998. The private sector will develop road, rail and port facilities under tender from the South African and Mozambican governments. Further such "Spatial Development Initiatives" (SDIs) are in the advanced planning stage.

The South African economy has been in a recovery phase

Exhibit 61.1: JOHANNESBURG SE INDUSTRIALS PRICE INDEX (R), 1993–97

High value 9145.5 1.8.97 Low value 4363.00 1.1.93 *Source: Datastream*

since 1993, but real GDP growth has been modest, remaining between 2% and 3% per annum. The sharp fall during 1996, required a tightening of monetary and fiscal policy, and conditions during 1997 were such that there was limited scope for any relaxation in this policy stance. The Asian economic crisis and slowing demand in world markets will dampen any recovery in the economy during 1998, and another year of 2% real GDP growth is anticipated.

Role of the central bank

The South African Reserve Bank (SARB) is an independent statutory body established and regulated by an Act of Parliament, and its role is entrenched in the constitution. The primary objective of SARB is to "protect the internal and external value of the currency in the interest of balanced and sustainable economic growth in the Republic".

The bank has four main functions: to formulate and implement monetary policy; to manage the money and banking system of the country; to provide economic and financial services to the government; and to publish economic and statistical information and data.

In order to carry out its functions, SARB regulates interest rates through setting the bank rate and engages in open market and discounting operations with the banking system. It utilises money supply targets as a guideline to policy, but interest rates are the operational variable.

SARB is also responsible for bank supervision and financial regulation in South Africa through its Bank Supervisory Department.

MARKET PERFORMANCE

A) In 1997

Market capitalisation of the JSE at the end of 1997 totalled R1,329.5 billion, compared with R1,135.1 billion at the end of 1996 (an increase of 17%). Turnover on the JSE also rose in 1997, to R206.5 billion, up 76% on the previous year.

The JSE All Share Index fell by 6.8% between end-1996 and end-1997. This mainly reflected weaker commodity price trends, the impact of the Asian crisis and the pedestrian performance of the South African economy.

B) Summary information

Global ranking by market value (US$ terms, end-1997): 16
Market capitalisation (domestic companies, end-1997): US$232.78 billion
Growth in market value (local currency terms, 1993–97): 53.1%
Market value as a % of nominal GDP (end-1997): 215%
Number of domestic/foreign companies listed (end-1997): 615/27
Market P/E (all listed companies, end-1997): 16.9
MSCI Index (change in US$ terms, 1997): -10.6%
Short-term (3-month) interest rate (end-1997): 14.5%
Long-term (10-year) bond yield (end-1997): 13.5%
Budget deficit as a % of nominal GDP (1997): 4.2%
Annual increase in broad money (M3) supply (end-1997): 17.2%
Inflation rate (CPI, 1997): 6.1%
US$ exchange rate (end-1997): R4.85

C) Year-end share-price index, price/earnings ratios and yields

Exhibit 61.2:
JSE YEAR-END SHARE PRICE INDICES, P/E AND DIVIDEND YIELDS, 1993–97

Year-end	*JSE All Share Index*	*Gold Index*	*Industrial Index*	*Yield P/E*	*(%)*
1993	4,892.99	2,164	5,573	18.2	2.4
1994	5,866.91	2,023	6,984	18.9	2.1
1995	6,228.42	1,343	7,987	16.6	2.3
1996	6,658.00	1,506	7,922	15.0	2.7
1997	6,202.31	801.76	7,426	16.9	2.7

Source: Johannesburg Stock Exchange.

D) Market indices and their constituents

As well as the overall ordinary share market (tracked by the JSE All Share Index), the JSE actuaries indices cover individual sectors or groups of shares considered to be affected by similar broad economic developments. Shares listed on the exchange are categorised into five groups, for which separate indices are compiled: overall; mining producers; mining finance; financial; and industrial.

The JSE actuaries indices are market capitalisation-weighted – ie the proportion assumed to be invested in each index counter is the ratio of its market capitalisation to the total market capitalisation of all shares included in that index. The index weights are therefore the number of shares in issue for each of the index constituents. The JSE actuaries indices are calculated regularly throughout the trading day.

THE STOCK MARKET

A) Brief history and structure

The JSE was established to provide a market-place for the shares of the many mining and financial companies formed shortly after the Witwatersrand goldfields were discovered in 1886. The exchange dates from 8 November 1887.

The JSE is the sole licensed equity market in South Africa. It is owned by its member firms and directed by a committee of stockbrokers elected annually by the membership. The committee in turn elects a chairman and not more than two deputy chairmen, and may additionally appoint an executive president and five non-stockbrokers. The term of the committee is three years, and one-third of the members must retire annually.

B) Different exchanges

The only stock exchange in South Africa is located in Johannesburg.

C) Opening hours, names and addresses

The JET trading system operates from 8.45am to 6.00pm Mondays to Fridays (excluding public holidays), and includes the following sessions:

- pre-opening: 8.45am to 9.30am;
- opening: 9.30am;
- continuous trading: 9.30am to 4.00pm;
- run-off: 4.00pm to 6.00pm.

THE JOHANNESBURG STOCK EXCHANGE
17 Diagonal Street, PO Box 1174, 2000 Johannesburg
Tel: (27) 11 377 2200; Fax: (27) 11 834 3937

MARKET SIZE

A) Number of listings and market value

At 31 December 1997, the market value of listed equities was R1,330 billion. There were 642 companies (615 domestic and 27 foreign) and 759 securities listed.

Exhibit 61.3:
NUMBER OF COMPANIES LISTED AND MARKET VALUE, JSE, 1993–97

	No. of companies		*Market capitalisation*
Year-end	*Foreign*	*Domestic*	*(R million)*
1993	32	615	737,632
1994	26	614	919,803
1995	26	613	1,022,656
1996	27	599	1,135,100
1997	27	615	1,329,500

Source: Johannesburg Stock Exchange.

Exhibit 61.4:
CAPITAL RAISED ON THE JSE, 1997

Issue type	*Amount raised (R million)*
Rights issues	9,671
New listings (54)	2,739
Other (bonus shares, debentures, etc)	37,908
Total	**50,318**

Source: Johannesburg Stock Exchange.

B) Largest quoted companies

Exhibit 61.5:
THE 20 LARGEST COMPANIES BY MARKET CAPITALISATION, JSE, END-1997

Ranking	*Company*	*Market value (R million)*
1	Anglo Am Corp SA Ord	45,989

Exhibit 61.5 continued

2	S A Breweries Ltd Ord	41,877
3	De Beers Consol Mines	37,640
4	Liberty Life Ass Ord	32,939
5	Sasol	30,799
6	Richemont Securities Dr	27,666
7	Billiton	26,725
8	Standard Bnk Invcorp Ord	25,785
9	Nedcor	24,805
10	First Nat Bank Hldgs	18,828
11	Minorco SA	18,609
12	Rembrandt Group	18,531
13	Absa Group	17,720
14	Liberty Holdings Ord	16,417
15	Orion Selections	15,424
16	Nbs Boland Group	14,806
17	Anglo American Platinum	13,922
18	Investec Group	13,393
19	Beverage & Con Ind Hldgs	12,604
20	Dimension Data Hldgs	11,636

Source: Johannesburg Stock Exchange.

C) Trading volume

Equity turnover increased by just over 76% from R117.4 billion in 1996 to R206.5 billion in 1997.

Exhibit 61.6:
SHARE TURNOVER, JSE, 1993–97

Year	*Trading value (R million)*
1993	34,127
1994	62,542
1995	63,247
1996	117,357
1997	206,542

Source: Johannesburg Stock Exchange.

Exhibit 61.7:
THE 20 MOST ACTIVELY TRADED SHARES, JSE, 1997

Ranking	*Company*	*Trading value (R million)*
1	De Beers Consol Mines	10,092
2	Sasol	9,319
3	SA Breweries Ord	7,814
4	Richemont Securities Dr	6,867
5	Anglo Am Corp SA Ord	6,442
6	Liberty Life Ass Ord	4,990
7	Barlow Ord	4,805
8	Gencor	3,616
9	Rembrandt Group	3,456
10	First Nat Bank Hldgs	3,396

Exhibit 61.7 continued

11	Persetel Q Data Holdings	3,201
12	Anglo American Platinum	3,109
13	Orion Selections	2,962
14	Nedcor	2,923
15	Billiton	2,738
16	Iscor	2,701
17	Dimension Data Hldgs	2,613
18	Absa Group	2,612
19	Standard Bnk Invcorp Ord	2,380
20	Investec Group	2,319

Source: Johannesburg Stock Exchange.

TYPES OF SHARE

Shares traded on the JSE are registered securities comprising ordinary shares and preference shares, which can be cumulative, participating, redeemable and/or convertible. Convertible and non-convertible debentures are also listed.

Ordinary shares have dividend rights and a right to participate in the capital of the company on winding up, subject to prior claims by creditors, debenture holders and preference shareholders. While non-voting shares may not be listed, high or low voting shares may be listed.

Preference shares are a hybrid, having some characteristics of equity and some of debt. They normally promise a dividend that is either fixed or variable, or a combination of both. Sometimes they participate over and above their fixed rate of dividend in some proportion of the dividends paid on the ordinary shares. They may be redeemed either at the option of the company or at a fixed or determinable future date. Sometimes they are convertible into ordinary shares or other securities.

All securities listed on the JSE must be fully paid up and freely transferable.

Equity warrants were introduced on to the JSE in 1997. The warrants may be either call or put instruments, and may be either covered or uncovered. In the case of covered warrants, the underlying securities must be held by a custodian throughout the duration of the warrant issue for the benefit of the warrant holders. To date all warrants listed have been uncovered call warrants.

INVESTORS

The type and number of shareholders on the JSE is difficult to ascertain and analyse because of the widespread use of nominee names. Nevertheless, there are figures evidencing increased interest on the part of non-resident investors. Net purchases by non-residents in 1997 totalled R26.2 billion, almost five times greater than the 1996 amount.

Exhibit 61.8:
COUNTRY FUNDS – SOUTH AFRICA

Fund	*US$ % change* 01/01/97 01/01/98	01/01/93 01/01/98	Fund base currency	Fund size US$ mil)	Fund volatility	Management group	Opal main sector	Opal subsector
Old Mutual South Africa	15.25	N/A	£	N/A	5.601	Old Mutual	Closed-End	Equity
Intrust	9.17	146.34	R	725.32	6.334	Investec	Closed-End	Equity
Genbel South Africa Ltd	1.89	121.47	R	5458.3	7.035	Genbel/Unisen	Closed-End	Equity
Spes Bona Investment Co	1.7	N/A	US$	58.379	8.411	Rosenwald Rod	Open-End	Equity
Syfrets Gl South Africa Mgd	1.12	N/A	US$	0.7	5.995	Syfrets Mgt	Open-End	Equity
OMI Galileo South African Eq	-0.73	N/A	US$	N/A	-1	Old Mutual	Open-End	Equity
SAGA	-5.84	N/A	US$	81.06	-1	Old Mutual	Open-End	Equity
Southern Africa Fund Inc	-8.38	N/A	US$	117.99	5.5	Alliance Cap	Closed-End	Equity
S&P Southern Africa	-9.13	N/A	£	5.9	5.111	Save & Prosper	Open-End	Equity
Credit Suisse South Africa	-9.24	N/A	£	3.7	5.094	Credit Suisse	Open-End	Equity
New South Africa Fund	-10.99	N/A	US$	89.77	5.648	Fleming	Closed-End	Equity
UBS Eqty Inv South Africa	-15.65	91.72	US$	19631	4.972	UBS (Intrag)	Open-End	Equity
ASA Limited (est.)	-39.71	-27.28	US$	434.46	7.424	ASA Ltd	Closed-End	Equity

Note: details for some funds may not have been included if the data for the US$ % change for 97/98 was not available

Source: Standard & Poor's Micropal.

OTHER MARKETS

A) Development and venture capital markets

Junior to the main board of the JSE is the development capital market (DCM). The JSE established the DCM in 1984 with the primary objective of giving smaller, growing companies the opportunity to raise capital. Similarly, a second subsidiary sector of the JSE, the venture capital market (VCM), was established in 1989 to facilitate the listing of venture capital companies.

B) South African Futures Exchange

The South African Futures Exchange (SAFEX) is regulated by the Financial Markets Control Act of 1989. Currently, SAFEX is the only licensed derivatives exchange in South Africa. Futures contracts are traded on the All Share, All Gold and Industrial indices.

C) Traded options on individual shares

The Traded Options market was set up by SAFEX as a joint initiative with the JSE.

Trading takes place in option contracts covering six underlying shares – Anglo American, De Beers, Liberty Life, Richemont, SA Breweries and Sasol. In the period September to end-December 1997, 75,360 contracts were traded.

OPERATIONS

A) Trading system

The JSE operates an order-driven, centralised trading system called Johannesburg Equity Trading System (JET) with dual trading capacity and voluntary market-makers. A specialist manages an electronic order book for odd lots against which incoming orders automatically trade. Market-makers voluntarily quote prices, and a book for trading orders with special terms is provided.

B) List of principal brokers

BARNARD, JACOBS, MELLET & CO
PO Box 62200, Marshalltown, 2107
Tel: (27) 11 283 0300; Fax: (27) 11 283 0392

DEUTSCHE MORGAN GRENFELL
Private Bag X9933, Sandton, 2146
Tel: (27) 11 322 6700; Fax: (27) 11 322 6899

FLEMING MARTIN SECURITIES
PO Box 934, Johannesburg, 2000
Tel: (27) 11 240 2400; Fax: (27) 11 838 2344

HSBC SIMPSON McKIE
PO Box 951, Houghton, 2041
Tel: (27) 11 481 4200; Fax: (27) 11 646 8383

ING BARINGS SOUTHERN AFRICA
PO Box 782080, Sandton, 2146
Tel: (27) 11 302 3000; Fax: (27) 11 302 3131

INVESTEC SECURITIES
PO Box 691, Johannesburg, 2000
Tel: (27) 286 4700; Fax: (27) 286 9923

MERRILL LYNCH SMITH BORKUM HARE
PO Box 5591, Johannesburg, 2000
Tel: (27) 11 498 6000; Fax: (27) 11 833 1968

SBC WARBURG DILLON READ SECURITIES (SOUTH AFRICA)
PO Box 652863, Benmore, 2010
Tel: (27) 11 322 7000; Fax: (27) 11 784 8260

SMK SECURITIES
PO Box 61346, Marshalltown, 2107
Tel: (27) 11 833 8110; Fax: (27) 11 836 9118

SOCIÉTÉ GÉNÉRALE FRANKEL POLLAK
PI Box 6872, Johannesburg 2000
Tel: (27) 11 488 1400; Fax: (27) 11 488 1414

C) Settlement and transfer

Buying and selling orders are electronically matched in the JET system. The trade information is transferred electronically to the Equity Clearing House (ECH), a department within the JSE.

Trades in equities are concluded for settlement in 52 weekly accounts each year. The norm is to trade for settlement in the account immediately following the trade date.

Clients, excluding financial institutions, are required to settle their trades with member firms within seven business days by payment for purchases (irrespective of the non-availability of shares) and by delivery of shares sold. Cash for deliveries by member firms through the ECH is settled on a net basis at the end of the day via cheque payment.

The net positions due for settlement in each account by member firms are prepared on Friday night and are marked to market. The margin between the contract value of the trades and the marked-to-market value are settled on Monday before deliveries commence on Tuesday.

The JSE is working with the banking industry and company registrars towards the establishment of a central depository.

In 1998 an electronic settlement system for equity transactions (Strate) will be introduced. The system includes the following:

- Contractual settlement, which means that settlement has to take place on the agreed settlement day.
- Rolling settlement, where transactions (securities and funds) become due for settlement a set number of business days after the trade date.
- Gross settlement, which is the settlement of transactions on a trade-by-trade basis, without aggregation or netting.
- The introduction of simultaneous, final and irrevocable delivery versus payment (SFIDvP) at the client level. SFIDvP entails the secure transfer of ownership with secure transfer of value.

A first batch of shares is expected to be designated for electronic settlement in the last quarter of 1998.

D) Commissions and other costs

All commissions are fully negotiable.

TAXATION AND REGULATIONS AFFECTING FOREIGN INVESTORS

South Africa's tax system is source based and so only taxes income the source of which is, or is deemed to be, South African. The definition of "gross income" excludes income not derived from a source within South Africa unless such income is deemed to have been earned or accrued within South Africa. Where income is deemed to be from a South African source but the real source is in another country, relief from double taxation may be claimed under a double taxation treaty, where applicable, or by way of a credit for foreign tax payable, at the option of the taxpayer. The credit may not exceed the South African tax liability on the same income and may not be carried forward or backward to another tax year.

South Africa has double taxation treaties with many countries, including most industrialised countries. The treaty with the USA will come into force in 1998. It is a standard provision of such agreements that a state may not impose any tax in such a way that it has a more burdensome effect on nationals of the other state than on its own. The double tax treaties generally provide that taxes are not imposed unless there is some form of permanent residence in South Africa.

If a company pays dividends, including dividends derived from capital profits (except if they are liquidation dividends or distributions arising from capital profits on a deregistration), to any of its shareholders, the company itself is obliged to pay an amount of tax based on the amount of the dividend declared. The dividends are not taxed in the hands of the recipients. This secondary tax (STC) is currently levied at 12.5%. Certain countries (such as the United Kingdom) have decided to allow STC as a credit against their local taxes. The government has indicated that in due course it intends to remove the STC charge and replace it with some other form of taxation on dividends. Because foreign companies operating through branches in South Africa would earn the profits of the South African operation themselves (without the need to declare dividends), their tax rate on South African sourced income is 40%, rather than the 35% charged to South African companies (which in addition, if they declare dividends, would pay STC).

Any interest accruing on or after 3 June 1992 to individuals who are not ordinarily resident in the Republic of South Africa and who do not carry on business in South Africa, and to companies which are neither managed nor controlled in the Republic of South Africa and which do not carry on business in South Africa, is exempt from tax in South Africa. For these purposes, the Republic of South Africa includes its neighbouring countries within the common monetary area. This applies even if, on ordinary source principles, the interest would otherwise have been taxable in the Republic of South Africa.

Although there is no capital gains tax at present in South Africa, this is a matter that is being considered by the authorities, particularly in the context of trusts.

LISTING AND REPORTING REQUIREMENTS

South African securities legislation in general is based on regulation by disclosure rather than by prohibition. Where shares or debentures are offered to the public, the Companies Act requires the disclosure of reliable information sufficient to enable investors to value the shares or debentures and assess the merits of the investment.

A) Listing requirements

Where application is made for shares of a company to be listed on the JSE, a pre-listing statement (or prospectus), a formal application for listing and a general undertaking by the company (to fulfil the JSE's requirements) in the form of a resolution of the board of directors must be lodged with the exchange, along with certain other documents.

The JSE's procedures and requirements for listing are consolidated in a single manual.

B) Reporting requirements

The Fourth Schedule to the Companies Act sets out the information that must be disclosed and taken into account in preparing interim reports and also annual financial statements and provisional annual financial statements of all companies, whether listed or unlisted. Comprehensive minimum disclosure requirements are now stipulated for interim reports and provisional annual financial statements. Furthermore, annual financial statements must now include a detailed cash flow statement.

Income statements and balance sheets must be included in the interim report that all listed companies (other than gold and coal-mining companies) are required to issue in respect of the first six months of their financial year. In both interim reports and annual financial statements, every listed company must make timely and full disclosure of all interest-bearing borrowings and off balance sheet finance. Also, all listed company announcements, other than dividend announcements and interim reports, must be submitted to the Stock Exchange News Office Service for verification and distribution.

SHAREHOLDER PROTECTION CODES

During 1997 the disciplinary rules were rewritten to enable better self-regulation by the JSE of its members and the market generally. A new development has been the ability of the surveillance department to investigate abnormal price movements in shares on an intra-day basis.

A) Takeovers and mergers

The Securities Regulation Code on Takeovers and Mergers of the Security Regulation Panel (SRP) governs all public companies and private companies (where (i) shareholders' interests exceed R5 million and (ii) there are more than 10 shareholders) involved in mergers and acquisitions in which control of 35% or more of the securities will pass or if there are acquisitions of 5% or more to a holding exceeding 35% but not 50% in a 12-month period. Once such a transaction takes place the remaining shareholders of the company concerned are entitled to sell their shares on the same terms and conditions as the majority. Sufficient information (prepared with the highest standards of care and accuracy) must be given to the holders of securities, in good time, to enable them to reach a properly informed decision.

In the case of takeovers and mergers, the JSE will not readily agree to a suspension. Companies are expected to issue cautionary announcements at regular intervals.

B) Insider trading

The SRP currently exercises control over insider trading, although the King Commission, which issued a report during 1997 on insider trading, has recommended that this function should be moved to the FSB. The Commission has also recommended wide-ranging changes to the legislation to make it more effective.

An insider is a person who makes deals based on information obtained through a relationship of trust or a contractual relationship, regardless of whether or not the person concerned is directly a party to that relationship. A breach of the insider trading provisions exposes the offender to a fine not exceeding R500,000, or to imprisonment for a period not exceeding 10 years, or to both.

There still has not been a single conviction for insider trading, and new legislation significantly enhancing the powers of the SRP is awaited.

C) Compensation funds

The fidelity insurance policy, underwritten by Lloyd's of London, provides protection for member firms against, among other things, criminal acts by employees, and receipt of forged, lost or stolen securities. The extent of the cover is R100 million.

The JSE Guarantee Fund has assets of R90.8 million available to reimburse, in whole or in part, clients and other market participants who sustain losses as a consequence of the default of a JSE member.

RESEARCH

The bulk of research on JSE listed companies is provided by the leading firms of stockbrokers. Good quality information on the South African equity market is produced by Société Générale Frankel Pollak (Pty) Ltd, a member of the JSE. The major life assurers and certain merchant banks and mining houses also have substantial in-house research facilities.

Financial publications include:
The Business Day (daily)
The Financial Mail (daily)
Finance Week

JSE publications include:
Annual Report (annual financial statements and Executive President's review);
Monthly Bulletin (containing monthly trading statistics and company notes about rights and capitalisation issues, name changes, capital repayments and reductions, mergers and takeovers);
Facts at your Fingertips (statistical information of particular interest to local and foreign investors);
Understanding the JSE-Actuaries Indices; and
The Mechanics of Investment on the JSE for Foreign Investors.

Investing in South Africa: A Market Profile, published by Euromoney Books, provides in-depth information for those wishing to invest or do business in the country. See the order card at the back of this book for details.

CHAPTER 62

Spain

Introduction

In 1997 the Spanish stock market played an increasingly important role in the country's economy. The Madrid General Index rose by 42.2%, following a rise of 38.9% in 1996. Falling interest rates and the growth in company profits generated a bullish market, and the volume of shares traded on the Madrid Stock Exchange (MSE) doubled compared with 1996.

Company profits, the main pillar of support, grew by 18% in 1997, and this trend was combined with a fall in interest rates. The gap between Spain's long-term interest rates and the EU's lowest rate narrowed (less than 50 basis points at the year-end), with the 10-year government bond yield at below 6%. At the same time, there was a larger flow of funds into shares, via both direct investment from individuals and collective investment through mutual and pension funds.

ECONOMIC AND POLITICAL OVERVIEW

Spain's centre-right government under José María Aznar, elected 18 months ago, is reliant on the support of Catalan nationalists to maintain its hold on power. The Catalan party has so far backed the government's economic policy and its drive towards EMU membership but Aznar now faces a series of important regional elections, beginning in 1998. Spain witnessed an economic recovery in 1997, and GDP growth of 3.3% was more than a point higher than in 1996. There was also a sharp cut in both short and long-term interest rates, which ended 1997 at an all-time low. Official rates were cut on six occasions (from 6.25% to 4.75%), initially in response to the slowdown in inflation to around 2%, and subsequently to the efforts made to secure EU converge once Spain's qualification for EMU was beyond all doubt.

In addition to pursuing the low inflation requirement, Spain also met other Maastricht criteria, often more comfortably than core countries (eg a 2.8% public deficit in 1997 and a reduction in the debt/GDP ratio from 68.9% to 68.0%).

As regards the crisis in Asia, after having dropped 21% in only 15 days in October, in the following two months the stock market recovered the ground lost and reached its highest level for the year. Although the Asian crisis has not yet been resolved, Spain's relatively weak links with the area mean that no serious repercussions are expected on corporate results.

Role of the central bank

European Union-based legislation was passed in 1995 to increase the independence of the Bank of Spain. The law grants the central bank full powers to establish and execute monetary policy, with the ultimate objective of securing price stability. The Bank of Spain has also been given a key consultative and executive role in the implementation of government exchange rate policy, which needs to be compatible with the Bank of Spain's monetary and inflation rate objectives.

Since Spain joined the EMS, Bank of Spain monetary control has focused in particular on the exchange rate and on the M4 monetary aggregate.

MARKET PERFORMANCE

A) In 1997

The Madrid General Index rose 42.2% in local currency terms, fuelled by falling interest rates, 3.3% GDP growth and an inflation rate down to 2%. The IBEX ended 1997 up 40.8% at 7,255 – practically an all-time high. This spectacular rise, added to 1996's equally outstanding performance, has doubled market capitalisation in just two years.

The fiscal attractions of investment funds and low yields on risk-free investments (FIAMM and deposits) prompted a steady flow of funds into the stock market. For

Exhibit 62.1: MADRID STOCK EXCHANGE GENERAL PRICE INDEX, (Pta) 1993–97

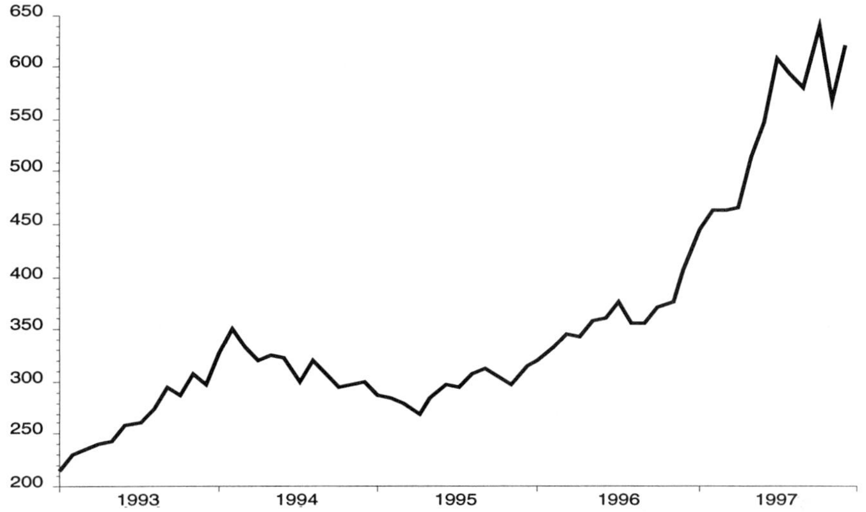

High value 640.20 1.1.97 Low value 214.25 1.1.93 *Source: Datastream*

the second year running (and despite the hefty volume of privatisations), demand for equities far exceeded supply.

The best performing sectors were those most closely related to economic activity, such as banks (particularly BCH, BBV and Santander) and construction companies (ACS and Acciona), whereas electrical utilities, which have been penalised by regulatory changes, did not enjoy such a good year.

B) Summary information

Global ranking by market value (US$ terms, end-1997): 11
Market capitalisation: US$292.61 billion (MSE); US$281.73 billion (BSE)
Growth in market value (local currency terms, 1993–97):
112.4% (MSE); 255.3% (BSE)
Market value as a % of nominal GDP (end-1997):
57.1% (MSE); 55.0% (BSE)
Number of domestic/foreign companies listed (end-1997):
381/4 (MSE); 316/4 (BSE)
Market P/E (end-1997):
19.1 (MSE General Index companies); 17.8 (BSE)
MSCI total returns (with net dividends, US$ terms, 1997): 25.4%
MSCI Index (change in US$ terms, 1997): +23.1%
Short-term (3-month) interest rate (end-1997): 4.58%
Long-term (10-year) bond yield (end-1997): 5.54%
Budget deficit as a % of nominal GDP (1997): 2.8%
Annual increase in broad money (M4) supply (end-1997): 3.6%
Inflation rate (1997): 2.1%
US$ exchange rate (end-1996): Pta151.26

C) Year-end share price index, price/earnings ratios and yields

Exhibit 62.2:
YEAR-END MSE SHARE PRICE INDEX, P/E AND AVERAGE YIELDS, 1993–97

Year-end	*Madrid General Index*	*P/E*	*Yield (%)*
1993	322.77	14.7	3.42
1994	285.01	12.2	3.95
1995	320.07	12.0	3.80
1996	444.77	15.1	2.80
1997	632.55	19.1	3.14

Source: Madrid Stock Exchange.

D) Market indices and their constituents

The MSE General Index comprises 122 stocks and represents 93% of total market capitalisation (excluding foreign stocks). The criteria used to include stocks in the index are trading frequency, capitalisation and liquidity. The index is dominated by banks, utilities and communication companies, which together account for 74% of index capitalisation.

The IBEX-35 is a more restricted index, oriented to derivatives trading. The IBEX is the official index of the continuous market of the Spanish Sociedad de Bolsas (owned by the four exchanges). It comprises the 35 most liquid stocks traded on the SIBE electronic trading system, which account for 79% of total market capitalisation (excluding foreign stocks).

The BSE has its own index – the BCN Global 100. It comprises 100 companies and the sectorial breakdown differs from that of Madrid.

THE STOCK MARKET

A) Brief history and structure

Although the first attempts at establishing a stock exchange in Madrid date back to 1796, it was not until 1831 that the MSE was actually founded. Since that time other exchanges have been established in Barcelona, Bilbao and Valencia. Historically, Madrid has been by far the most active and the most international of the exchanges in Spain, followed by the Barcelona Stock Exchange (BSE), founded in 1915.

In July 1989 the Spanish Securities Market Act took effect, entailing a major change not only in regulations governing the securities markets but also their overall structure. A basic element of the reform was the setting up of a National Stock Market Commission, similar to agencies in other countries such as the SEC in the USA, the COB in France and the SIB in the UK. A second significant change was that the individual broker members of the exchange were replaced by securities companies and brokerage firms.

B) Different exchanges

There are four stock exchanges in Spain: Madrid, Barcelona, Bilbao and Valencia. In October 1995 the Spanish Stock Market Interconnection System (SIBE) was established. It has almost replaced the traditional open outcry floor trading system and allows the four stock markets to place their orders through terminals connected to the mainframe.

C) Opening hours, names and addresses

The continuous market operates from Monday to Friday from 10.00am to 5.00pm. Pre-opening trading takes place from 9.00am to 10.00am. Some traditional floor trading still takes place from 9.00am to 12.15pm, five days a week.

BOLSA DE MADRID
Plaza de la Lealtad 1, 28014 Madrid
Tel: (34) 1 589 2600; Fax: (34) 1 531 2290
Web site: http://www.bolsamadrid.es

BOLSA DE BARCELONA
Paseo Isabel II, 1, 08003 Barcelona
Tel: (34) 3 401 3555; Fax: (34) 3 401 3859

BOLSA DE BILBAO
Olavarri 1, 48001 Bilbao (Vizcaya)
Tel: (34) 4 423 6818; Fax: (34) 4 424 4620

BOLSA DE VALENCIA
San Vincente 23, 46002 Valencia
Tel: (34) 6 387 0100; Fax: (34) 6 387 0133

MARKET SIZE

A) Number of listings and market value

MSE market capitalisation at the end of 1997 was Pta44,260 billion, 40% up on the end-1996 figure (Pta31,631 billion). There were 320 companies listed on the BSE at the end of 1997, with a total market capitalisation of Pta42,615billion.

Exhibit 62.3:
NUMBER OF LISTED COMPANIES, TOTAL MARKET VALUE AND NEW LISTINGS, MSE, 1993–97

Year	*No. of companies*	*Market value (Pta billion)*	*New listings (Pta billion)*
1993	376	20,833	714.3
1994	379	20,401	1,334.0
1995	373	22,899	527.2
1996	361	31,631	578.6
1997	385	44,260	224.0

Source: Madrid Stock Exchange.

Exhibit 62.4:
MARKET VALUE BY SECTOR, MSE, END-1997

Sector	*Market value (Pta billion)*
Banks	12,172
Foreign stocks	8,643
Electricity, water and gas	8,029
Communications	4,985
Oil and chemicals	2,835
Construction	2,174
Miscellaneous (industries and services)	2,168
Metal working	1,285
Food, drink and tobacco	1,103
Portfolio investment	867
Total	**44,260**

Source: Madrid Stock Exchange.

Exhibit 62.5:
MARKET VALUE BY SECTOR, BSE, END-1997

Sector	*Market value (Pta billion)*
Banks	13,466
Services and various	7,734
Electrical industries	6,569
Chemical industries	6,014
Iron and steel industry and mining	3,203

Exhibit 62.5 continued

Cement and building	2,710
Trade and finance	1,384
Foodstuffs, agriculture and forestry	578
Real estate	512
Transferable securities	325
Textile and paper industries	120
Total	**42,615**

Source: Barcelona Stock Exchange.

B) Largest quoted companies

Exhibit 62.6:
THE 20 LARGEST LISTED COMPANIES ON THE MSE, END-1997

Ranking	*Company*	*Market value (Pta billion)*
1	Telefónica	4,086.7
2	BBV	3,334.4
3	Endesa	2,813.3
4	Santander	2,438.9
5	Repsol	1,950.0
6	Iberdrola	1,807.6
7	BCH	1,215.5
8	Popular	1,179.8
9	Gas Natural	1,179.1
10	Argentaria	1,135.6
11	Banesto	919.0
12	Acesa	491.5
13	Tabacalera	454.8
14	Fenosa	444.8
15	Pryca	429.6
16	Sevillana	425.3
17	Valenciana de Cementos	411.2
18	Cepsa	410.3
19	Bankinter	357.6
20	FCC	348.3

Source: Madrid Stock Exchange.

Exhibit 62.7:
THE 20 LARGEST COMPANIES ON THE BSE, END-1997

Ranking	*Company*	*Market value (Pta billion)*
1	Telefónica	4,086.7
2	BBV	3,334.4
3	Endesa	2,813.3
4	Santander	2,438.9
5	Repsol	1,950.0
6	Iberdrola	1,807.6
7	BCH	1,215.5
8	Popular	1,179.8

Exhibit 62.7 continued

9	Gas Natural	1,179.1
10	Argentaria	1,135.6
11	Banesto	919.0
12	Acesa	491.5
13	Tabacalera	454.8
14	Fenosa	444.8
15	Pryca	429.6
16	Sevillana	425.3
17	Valenciana de Cementos	411.2
18	Cepsa	410.3
19	Bankinter	357.6
20	FCC	348.3

Source: Barcelona Stock Exchange.

C) Trading volume

Compared with 1996, the value of share turnover on the MSE increased by 103% in 1997 to Pta20,484.6 billion. On the BSE, share trading in 1997 was Pta3,298.3 billion, a 164% increase on the previous year.

Exhibit 62.8:
SHARE TURNOVER (PTA MILLION) ON THE MSE AND BSE, 1993–97

Year	*BSE*	*MSE*
1993	415,864	5,528,838
1994	834,756	7,310,260
1995	684,398	6,672,482
1996	1,248,398	10,099,780
1997	3,298,301	20,484,629

Sources: Madrid Stock Exchange and Barcelona Stock Exchange.

Exhibit 62.9:
THE 20 MOST ACTIVELY TRADED SHARES, MSE, 1997

Ranking	*Company*	*Trading value (Pta million)*
1	Telefónica	4,018,019
2	Endesa	2,265,572
3	Repsol	1,873,936
4	BBV	1,391,861
5	Iberdrola	1,358,929
6	Santander	1,261,417
7	Argentaria	763,974
8	Popular	669,918
9	BCH	519,036
10	Banesto	381,918
11	Gas Natural	331,649
12	Fenosa	327,258
13	Tabacalera	262,360
14	Acerinox	261,244

Exhibit 62.9 continued

15	Bankinter	237,948
16	Asturiana Zinc	229,660
17	Pryca	169,561
18	Acesa	163,765
19	Dragados	137,791
20	Mapfre	128,137

Source: Madrid Stock Exchange.

Exhibit 62.10:
THE 20 MOST ACTIVELY TRADED SHARES, BSE, 1997

Ranking	*Company*	*Trading value (Pta million)*
1	Telefónica	592,924
2	Repsol	384,365
3	Endesa	340,322
4	Santander	268,876
5	Argentaria	183,214
6	BBV	169,266
7	Banesto	113,828
8	Iberdrola	104,968
9	Popular	98,961
10	BCH	95,940
11	Gas Natural	57,160
12	Fenosa	55,699
13	Tabacalera	54,691
14	Acerinox	45,409
15	Asturiana Zinc	36,573
16	Tubacex	34,673
17	Acesa	29,967
18	Catalana Occidente	29,477
19	Aceralia	29,423
20	Cementos Molins	24,305

Source: Barcelona Stock Exchange.

TYPES OF SHARE

Virtually all shares traded in Spain are ordinary shares (*ordinarias*), although preference shares (*preferentes*) and convertible debentures exist as well. All bank shares are required to be registered (*nominativas*), while most other shares are bearer (*al portador*).

In addition, a book entry form (*anotaciones en cuenta*) for the representation of securities has been introduced in order to simplify trading operations.

OTHER MARKETS

The futures and options markets, Meff, began operating in 1992. Meff Renta Variable offers futures and options on the IBEX-35 Index and options on selected stocks.

MEFF RENTA VARIABLE
Torre Picasso pl 26, 28020 Madrid
Tel: (34) 1 585 0800; Fax: (34) 1 571 9542

INVESTORS

The growth in individual and institutional investment was impressive during 1997. As well as privatisations, there were public offerings by a large number of private companies and these changed the face of share ownership in Spain, increasing the role of individuals and collective investment institutions.

The public sector's weight in shares has been losing importance, largely due to privatisations over the past few years, and this trend looks set to continue.

OPERATIONS

A) Trading system

The SIBE trading system was launched in October 1995, replacing the CATS system that had been in operation since 1989. It is an electronic system that trades shares listed on Spain's four stock exchanges under the principle of "multilateral trading". SIBE has almost replaced traditional open outcry.

Under SIBE, operators can view on-screen data on 72 different shares simultaneously, and can trade any of them without interrupting the flow of information about the others. Fixed-income securities and shares can be traded from the same terminal.

B) List of principal brokers

AB ASESORES
Plaza de la Lealtad 3, 4th Floor, 28014 Madrid
Tel: (34) 1 580 1100; Fax: (34) 1 521 8884

BBV
Clara del Rey, 26, 28002 Madrid
Tel: (34) 1 374 6000; Fax: (34) 1 374 6202

BENITO & MONJARDIN
Alfonso XII 26, 28014 Madrid
Tel: (34) 1 531 4499; Fax: (34) 1 523 1731

DEUTSCHE MORGAN GRENFELL
Paseo de la Castellana, 18, Sociedad de Valores, 28046 Madrid
Tel: (34) 1333 5544; Fax: (34) 1 335 5593

MERRILL LYNCH
Ed. Torre Picasso 40, Plaza Ring Picasso, 28020 Madrid
Tel: (34) 1 514 3000; Fax: (34) 1 514 3001

Exhibit 62.11:
COUNTRY FUNDS – SPAIN

Fund	US$ % change 31/12/96 31/12/97	31/12/92 31/12/97	Currency	Fund size (US$ mil)	Volatility	Manager name	Main sector	Class
DWS Iberiafonds	31.85	212.09	Dm	40.54	4.8	DWS	Equity Growth	Investmentfds Deutschland
Spanish Smaller Companies	30.72	109.25	US$	29.32	4.01	ACM Offshore Funds	Equity	Luxembourg
DVG Fonds Espana	28.96	174.94	Dm	37.47	5.47	DVG	Equity Growth	Investmentfds Deutschland
Sogiberia	28.07	164.11	Ffr	94.79	N/A	Societe Generale	Equity	French FCPs
DIT Fonds Iberia	26.13	220.86	Dm	41.17	5.25	DIT	Equity Growth	Investmentfds Deutschland
Nikko Glbl Spain	25.19	134.83	¥	4.02	3.63	Nikko ITMCo	Equity Growth	Japanese Open Trusts
SBC Eq Fd Spain	24.67	158.86	Pta	85.55	N/A	Swiss Bank Corporation	Equity	Swiss Mutual Funds
Sogelux Fd Equities Spain	24.27	N/A	Pta	34.91	N/A	Societe Generale Bank & Trust	Equity	Luxembourg
Thornton Dres ES Spain	23.73	183.69	Dm	3.29	5.21	Thornton Dresdner	Equity	Offshore Territories
Balzac Spain Index	23.5	N/A	Pta	0.07	N/A	State Street Bq	Equity	French FCPs
CU PP Spanish Growth	23.35	127.28	Pta	23.21	4.81	CU Privilege Portfolio	Equity	Luxembourg
CICM CB Spain Basket	22.01	N/A	Pta	7.64	N/A	CICM Fund Mgmt Ltd	Equity	Offshore Territories
CS EF (Lux) Spain B	21.83	146.01	Pta	53.6	4.59	Credit Suisse AM Funds	Equity Growth	Investmentfds Deutschland
BBL Invest Spain Cap	21.16	N/A	Pta	21.33	N/A	BBL-Banque Brussels Lambert	Equity	Belgian Trusts
Caixa Funds Spanish Shares	18.94	118.14	Pta	13.97	4.98	Societe Monegasque de Bq Privee	Equity	Luxembourg
G-Equity Fund G-Spanish Eq B	18.8	N/A	Pta	21.61	4.93	Generale de Banque	Equity	Luxembourg
G-Equity Fund G-Spanish Eq B	18.8	N/A	Pta	18.46	5.8	Generale de Banque (Lux)	Equity Growth	Investmentfds Deutschland
G-Equity Fund G-Spanish Eq A	18.78	N/A	Pta	3.35	4.93	Generale de Banque	Equity	Luxembourg
Callander Fund Spanish	17.54	75.46	Pta	3.01	5.07	Callander Mgt SA	Equity	Luxembourg
Bacob Espana	17.19	119.78	Bfr	14.68	4.47	Bacob Banque	Equity	Belgian Trusts
Groupe Indosuez Spain	17.06	N/A	Pta	17.87	N/A	Groupe Indosuez Fd Mgt Co	Equity	Luxembourg
Groupe Indosuez Spain	17.06	N/A	Pta	17.35	N/A	Groupe Indosuez Fd Mgt Co	Equity Growth	Investmentfds Deutschland
Aetna MF Spanish National Equity	16.84	76.06	Pta	0.19	4.08	Aetna Master Fund	Equity	Luxembourg
Aetna MF Spanish National Equity	16.84	76.06	Pta	0.43	4.79	Aetna Master Fund	Equity Growth	Investmentfds Deutschland
EMIF Spain Index Plus A	16.49	131.23	Pta	1.84	4.82	CCF/BHF/HS/KB/BBV	Equity	Luxembourg
EMIF Spain Index Plus B	16.34	131.08	Pta	60.58	4.84	CCF/BHF/HS/KB/BBV	Equity	Luxembourg
EMIF Spain Index Plus B	16.34	131.08	Pta	23.3	5.72	CCF/BHF/HS/KB/BBV	Equity Growth	Investmentfds Deutschland
JPM Peseta Spain	2.27	N/A	Pta	N/A	1.95	JP Morgan Investment GmbH	Equity Growth	Investmentfds Deutschland

Note: details for some funds may not have been included if the data for the US$ % change for 96/97 is not available

Source: Standard & Poor's Micropal.

SALOMON BROTHERS INTERNATIONAL LIMITED
C – General Castanos, 4, Segundo,
Madrid 28004
Tel: (34) 1 391 5330; Fax: (34) 1 310 2054/308 1344

SANTANDER INVESTMENT
Paseo de la Castellana 32, 28046 Madrid
Tel: (34) 1 520 9000; Fax: (34) 1 575 4463

SBC WARBURG
C/Fortuny 18–2°, 28010 Madrid
Tel: (34) 1 436 9000; Fax: (34) 1 36 9040

C) Settlement and transfer

A clearing and settlement house owned by the four exchanges and the banks and brokers began operations at the end of 1992. Meanwhile, a new book entry system has reduced the settlement period to T+3.

D) Commissions and other costs

Commissions are fully negotiable, but maximum commissions must be reported to the National Stock Market Commission.

The requirements for margin buying and short selling are fixed and published by brokerage firms.

TAXATION AND REGULATIONS AFFECTING FOREIGN INVESTORS

A) Taxation

For tax purposes a distinction is made between resident and non-resident shareholders. Non-resident entities (without a permanent establishment in Spain) obtaining Spanish source income are subject to a withholding tax at 25% on dividends and interest, except for payments arising from government debt, which are free of withholding tax.

A distinction is also made between EU and non-EU resident and non-resident companies. In order to avoid double taxation, dividends distributed by a subsidiary to its parent company are not taxed in the country of the subsidiary company if both are EU companies. A parent company is defined as one that holds 5% or more of the total capital.

Spanish legislation provides for capital gains taxes on investors from countries that do not have a double taxation agreement, although in practice this is seldom levied. Double taxation agreements also provide for reimbursement of the difference between withholding tax and the tax specified in the agreement, but in practice this is extremely difficult to obtain.

Spain has tax treaties based on the OECD model. The reduced treaty rates range from 5% to 18%.

Exhibit 62.12: WITHHOLDING TAX

Recipient	*Dividend %*	*Interest %*
Resident corporations and individuals	25	25[1]
Non-resident corporations and individuals:		
Non-treaty	25	25
Treaty	5–18	Nil–15

Note:

1. Does not apply if recipient is a resident bank, savings association or other financial institution subject to corporate tax, provided such income does not represent portfolio income.

Source: Price Waterhouse.

B) Investment regulations

There is freedom for foreign investment in Spain except for:

(a) Non-EU investments in sectors that have their own regulations – eg gambling, television, radio, air transport and defence-related activities – which require the Cabinet's prior approval.

(b) Investments made by public authorities other than EU states require the Cabinet's prior authorisation, except for those that have been liberalised under international agreements ratified by Spain.

(c) Investments from non-EU countries that could harm the Spanish state's interests require the Cabinet's prior authorisation when the amount involved is more than Pta5,000 million. If the investment is less, the Ministry of the Economy grants the approval.

Foreign investment in Spain and settlement of operations must be declared to the Investment Registry at the Ministry of the Economy. The holders of the investment, and the public notaries, broker-dealers and brokers involved all have to declare details. There are no limits governing the length of time investments can or must be held.

Prior administrative verification (not the same as authorisation) is required for direct investments when the foreign shareholding is more than 50% of the capital stock (either before or after the operation) and the following conditions exist: (a) the investment is more than Pta500 million; (b) the foreign holding plus reserves amounts to more than Pta500 million; and (c) the foreign investor is an individual or entity resident in a country regarded as a tax haven.

Foreign investors acting in accordance with the regulations enjoy the right to transfer abroad funds from the sale of their investment and any legally obtained profits, freely making payments from them.

C) Resident bank accounts

Spanish residents can open foreign currency accounts at branches of entities that carry out their activities abroad.

D) Non-resident bank accounts

Non-residents may hold all types of bank account. The peseta is fully convertible.

REPORTING REQUIREMENTS

The information that listed companies are required to supply is grouped into two categories – periodic and non-periodic.

(i) *Periodic information.* Annual financial statements, a management report and auditor's report must be published by Spanish entities before the publication in the *Borme* (the official bulletin) of the notice calling the annual shareholders' meeting, and by foreign entities no later than two months after the documents have been approved by the relevant body. Both parent company and consolidated statements must be presented. Entities must publish preliminary results and other information quarterly and full financial statements must be made public half-yearly in a form similar to that for annual statements. Statements must be presented in line with the format set out by the Spanish Securities Market Commission and supplied on diskette.

(ii) *Non-periodic information.* All relevant economic and legal matters that affect listed securities must be made public and presented on diskette. Foreign companies should publish in Spain all information made public in their home country or in other countries where the securities are traded. Companies requesting a listing for the first time must declare holdings of more than 5% as well as those of directors and management.

SHAREHOLDER PROTECTION CODES

A) Significant shareholdings

Investors must inform the MSE, the BSE, the Spanish Securities Market Commission and the company concerned of significant holdings, understood to be 5% of the capital or successive multiples of 5%.

B) Takeovers and mergers

Takeover bids are obligatory when an investor acquires a stake in a listed company representing 25% or more of the issued capital. Stakes held or acquired by the investor or by entities belonging to the same group or by others acting in concert with the investor, are regarded as belonging to the same individual or entity.

The following are excluded from the mandatory takeover regulations: (a) acquisitions made by the Deposit Guarantee Fund; (b) acquisitions made pursuant to the Law on Enforced Expropriation; (c) cases where all the shareholders of the affected company agree to sell or exchange their shares; and (d) acquisitions occurring as a consequence of the reorganisation or restructuring of economic sectors (as determined by the relevant government committee).

As soon as a takeover bid is launched, share trading is suspended until the necessary documents are delivered to the Securities Market Commission setting out the identity of the investors making the bid, the type and number of shares affected, consideration, timescale, etc. On the basis of these documents and the type of takeover bid, the Commission authorises it and/or insists on changes being made to the conditions in order to guarantee equal treatment for all shareholders.

C) Insider trading

Under the revised penal code that came into force in May 1996, the scope of the prohibition on insider trading in Spain (previously only applicable to civil servants and exchange personnel) was extended to any person who uses or provides others with sensitive inside information (obtained by virtue of that person's professional or business activity) that may affect the price of quoted securities.

A person committing such an offence is liable to imprisonment for up to four years when the losses or gains generated by such information exceed Pta75 million. Also, the Spanish Capital Market Act envisages withdrawal of administrative authorisation in respect of brokerage companies or agencies and portfolio management companies found guilty of breaching the insider trading provisions.

D) Investor representatives

The MSE and the BSE both have an Investors' Ombudsman.

RESEARCH

In London, some of the best research on Spain is provided by the stockbroking firms Merrill Lynch and SBC Warburg Dillon Read. In Madrid, extensive economic and company research is provided by most of the intermediaries.

The MSE publishes comprehensive market data, including information on prices, trading volume, dividends declared and new issues. In particular, there is a daily share price bulletin, a CD-Rom of the whole year's daily bulletins, the MSE magazine (monthly), periodic information on listed companies (on disk), an annual report and a fact book.

Similar publications are available through the Barcelona exchange, including a fact sheet, an exchange yearbook, quarterly information on listed companies and an official price bulletin.

In Madrid, the Stock Exchange Information System (SIB) provides data on statistical series and the financial situation of listed companies, and an on-line electronic information system (InfoBolsa).

Information on the BSE and on other national and international stock markets is available through Databolsa SA.

CHAPTER

63

Sri Lanka

Introduction

The Colombo Stock Exchange (CSE) was one of the best performing markets in Asia in 1997. Market capitalisation at the end of the year stood at US$2.08 billion, a rise of 13% over 1996, and participation in the market by local investors showed encouraging growth. Also in 1997, second board listings and over-the-counter (OTC) trading were introduced for companies that do not meet the criteria for a main board listing.

The Securities and Exchange Commission (SEC) is the watchdog body in Sri Lanka that regulates markets and market-related activities.

ECONOMIC AND POLITICAL OVERVIEW

The People's Alliance government and the main opposition group, the United National Party, are both firmly committed to the establishment of a free market economy. Meanwhile, however, it is hoped that the implementation of the government's proposal for the devolution of power to enable a degree of self-rule in areas inhabited mainly by ethnic minorities will bring about a political solution to the protracted ethnic crisis crippling the economy. Most of the areas previously held by the rebel Liberation Tigers of Tamil Eelam (LTTE) are now in government hands and the administration is optimistic that the war in the north and east of the country will be over this year.

Economic growth picked up sharply in 1997 to an impressive 6.4% and, despite a predicted long dry spell attributed to the "El Niño" phenomenon in the initial part of 1998, the growth rate is expected to remain at around 6% for the coming year. Even in the event of a prolonged drought, the nation's power supply will not be affected as the government has taken steps to expand the non-hydro based power generation capacity to tide over any shortfall in hydro power output. The reduction in the bank reserve requirement to 12% and wide-ranging tax and tariff concessions given in the 1998–99 Budget should help boost corporate profits in the coming year.

Improving tea prices, a marked increase in tourist arrivals and a sharp rise in garment exports made 1997 a very good year for businesses in Sri Lanka. Impressive third quarter results point towards very encouraging bottom lines in the financial statements for the year to 31 March 1998. The inflation rate was 9.6% for the 12-month period ending on 31 December 1997 compared with 16% for 1996, and the rate is expected to fall further to 8% in 1998. Interest rates fell in 1997, with Treasury bill yields coming down to 10% from 17% in 1996 and prime lending rates falling to 12% against 18% in 1996.

With inflation easing further and the PSBR coming down sharply (to 7.6% of GDP) as a consequence of the accelerated privatisation programme, interest rates are expected to continue downwards in the coming year. Unemployment fell to 10% in 1997 and investment rose to 26% of GDP. Exports climbed 14% and the current account deficit declined to just 4% of GDP as the balance of payments recorded a surplus of US$400 million. Gross external assets at US$2.5 billion was equivalent to over five months' imports.

The Sri Lankan rupee fell 7% against the US dollar in 1997. In view of the sharp decline in other Asian currencies in the second half of 1997, the central bank could be tempted to devalue the rupee at a faster rate in 1998 to maintain the competitiveness of the country's exports.

Role of the central bank

The Central Bank of Sri Lanka (CBSL), established in 1949, is the monetary authority in Sri Lanka. As well as acting as banker to the government and the commercial banks, CBSL implements government monetary policy. It is also responsible for regulating and controlling banking activities and exchange control in the island.

The Monetary Board of the CBSL, consisting of the governor of the Central Bank, the permanent secretary of the Ministry of Finance and another member nominated by the President (who is also the Minister of Finance), is responsible for the issue and regulation of currency notes and coins in circulation.

Exhibit 63.1: COLOMBO SE ALL SHARE PRICE INDEX (US$), 1993–97

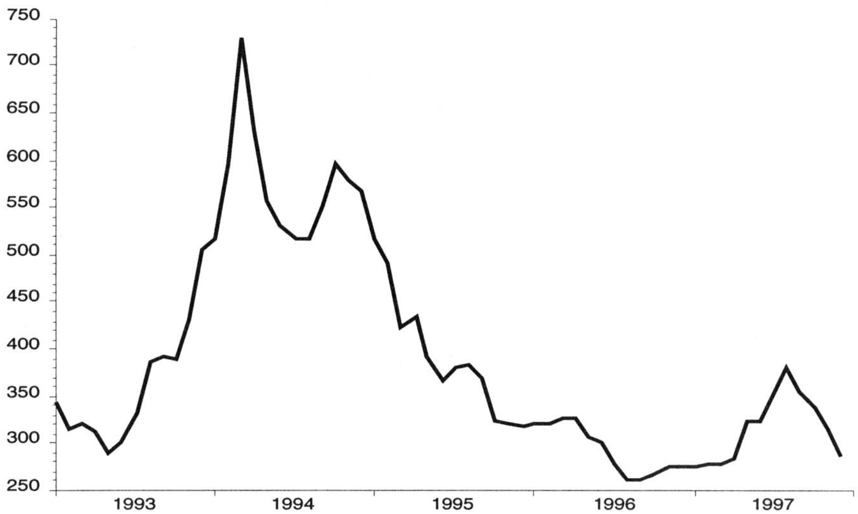

High value 729.08 1.3.94 Low value 259.85 2.9.96 *Source: Datastream*

The Sri Lankan rupee is convertible for current account transactions but capital account transactions are still regulated by the Controller of Exchange at the CBSL. The rupee is pegged to a basket of hard currencies dominated by US dollars, and the exchange rate is determined by the CBSL announcing buying and selling rates for foreign currencies each day. The central bank regulates the money supply by issuing short-term Treasury bills and longer-term Treasury bonds. Interest rates are determined by the CBSL setting the statutory reserve ratio (SRR) for commercial banks and by fixing repo and base rates.

MARKET PERFORMANCE

A) In 1997

The All Share Index rose 16% (in local currency terms) from 603 to 702.2 during 1997, while the blue chip Sensitive Index appreciated 19%, climbing from 897.7 to 1,068.0. Market capitalisation increased 13% from US$1.84 billion at the end of 1996 to US$2.08 billion at end-1997. Transactions involving foreign investors continued to play an important role in the stock market, and in 1997 foreigners accounted for over 43% of turnover.

B) Summary information

Global ranking by market value (US$ terms, end-1997): 64
Market capitalisation (end-1997): US$2.08 billion
Growth in market value (local currency terms, 1993–97): 4.5%
Market value as a % of nominal GDP (end-1997): 15%
Number of domestic/foreign companies listed on the main and second board (end-1997): 239/0
Market P/E (all companies, end-1997): 12.4
MSCI Index (change in US$ terms, end-1997): +11.5%
Short-term (3-month) interest rate (end-1997): 11.27%
Long term (1-year) Treasury bill rate (end-1997): 11.36%
Budget deficit as a % of nominal GDP (1997): 7.6%
Annual increase in broad money (M2) supply (end-1997): 13.8%
Inflation rate (average 1997): 9.6%
US$ exchange rate (end-1997): Rs62.0

C) Year-end share index, price/earnings ratios and yields

Exhibit 63.2:
CSE INDICES, P/E RATIOS AND AVERAGE YIELDS, 1993–1997

	1993	*1994*	*1995*	*1996*	*1997*
P/E ratio	24.6	16.3	11.2	10.7	12.4
Dividend yield	1.2	1.6	4.3	4.1	3.2
CSE All Share Index	978.97	986.7	663.7	603.0	702.2
CSE Sensitive Index	1,442.44	1,438.8	990.5	897.7	1,068

Source: CDIC Sassoon Cumberbatch.

D) Market indices and their constituents

Performance of the CSE is measured using two indices – the All Share Index (ASI) consisting of all stocks on the market, and the Sensitive Index (SI), which includes 25 selected blue chip stocks.

THE STOCK EXCHANGE

A) Brief history and structure

The Colombo stock market has been in existence since 1896. First formed to finance the plantation sector, it functioned under the aegis of the Colombo Share Brokers' Association and trading (using a call-over system) continued until June 1984. The re-emergence in the 1970s of the private sector as a dominant force in the economy resulted in the restructuring of the stock market, and the trading floor was opened to the investing public from 2 July 1984.

The introduction of the central depository system in 1992 facilitated a streamlined settlement process. In 1997, a second board was opened for companies that do not meet the criteria set for a main board listing.

The CSE is organised in the form of a company limited by guarantee. The board of directors is the main policy-making body of the exchange and consists of five directors appointed by, and four directors nominated by, the Finance Ministry on the recommendation of the Securities and Exchange Commission of Sri Lanka, the statutory body responsible for the regulation of the capital market. Sub-committees are appointed by the board as required.

Membership of the CSE is restricted to stockbrokers who are permitted to act as intermediaries or agents of buyers and sellers. At present there are 15 member firms.

B) Opening hours, name and address

The Colombo Stock Exchange (CSE) opens for trading daily (except for Saturdays, Sundays and mercantile holidays) from 9.30am to 12.30pm.

COLOMBO STOCK EXCHANGE
#04-01 West Block, World Trade Centre
Echelon Square, Colombo 1
Tel: (94) 1 448 937; Fax: (94) 1 445 279

MARKET SIZE

A) Number of listings and market value

At the end of 1997, there were 239 companies listed on the CSE , and their combined market capitalisation was Rs129.4 billion (US$2.08 billion).

Exhibit 63.3:
NUMBER OF COMPANIES LISTED AND MARKET CAPITALISATION, CSE, 1993–97

Year-end	*No. of companies listed*	*Market value (Rs billion)*
1993	201	123.8
1994	215	143.2
1995	226	106.9
1996	235	104.2
1997	239	129.4

Sources: CDIC Sassoon Cumberbatch and Colombo Stock Exchange.

B) Largest quoted companies

Exhibit 63.4:
THE 20 LARGEST COMPANIES BY MARKET CAPITALISATION, CSE, END-1997

Ranking	*Company*	*Market value (Rs million)*
1	John Keells Holding	11,192
2	National Development Bank	7,704
3	DFCC Bank	6,407
4	Hatton National Bank	5,600
5	Hayleys	5,280
6	Ceylon Tobacco	4,616
7	Commercial Bank	4,125
8	Sampath Bank	2,668
9	Lion Brewery	2,500
10	Aitken Spence	2,355
11	Grain Elevators	2,055
12	Nestlé	2,015
13	Richard Pieris	1,867
14	Distilleries Co. of Sri Lanka	1,800
15	Ceylon Cold Stores	1,760
16	Trans Asia	1,750
17	Lanka Lubricants	1,560
18	Asian Hotels	1,550
19	Colombo Dockyard	1,520
20	Dipped Products	1,450

Source: CDIC Sassoon Cumberbatch.

C) Trading volume

Exhibit 63.5:
CSE SHARE TURNOVER DATA, 1996–97

	1996	*1997*
Total turnover (Rs million)	7,403	18,200
Domestic	3,354	10,400
Foreign	4,048	7,800
Average daily turnover	31.0	75.9
Total number of trades	98,191	206,312
Domestic	87,782	189,772
Foreign	10,409	16,540
Total number of shares traded (million)	227	515.4
Domestic	133	336.8
Foreign	94	178.3

Source: CDIC Sassoon Cumberbatch.

Exhibit 63.6:
THE 20 MOST ACTIVELY TRADED SHARES, CSE, 1997

Ranking	*Company*	*Turnover value (Rs million)*	*% of total*
1	DFCC	1,993	10.3
2	John Keells Holdings	1,660	9.1
3	NDB	1,622	8.8
4	Sampath Bank	1,290	7.1
5	Hayleys Limited	721	3.9
6	Asia Capital	673	3.7
7	Commercial Bank	524	2.9
8	Ceylon Brewery	461	2.5
9	Ceylon Grain Elevators	433	2.4
10	Aitken Spence	371	2.0
11	Asian Hotels	364	2.0
12	Lion Brewery	353	1.9
13	Kegalle Plantations	322	1.8
14	Lanka Ceramics	321	1.8
15	Forbes Ceylon	312	1.7
16	Vanik Incorporated	282	1.5
17	Bogawantalawa Plantations	256	1.4
18	Dipped Products	244	1.3
19	Kotagala Plantations	240	1.3
20	Colombo Dockyard	238	1.3

Sources: CDIC Sassoon Cumberbatch and Colombo Stock Exchange.

TYPES OF SHARE

Securities traded at the CSE are mainly ordinary shares with a par value of Rs10. Preference shares, unsecured debentures and share warrants are also traded. Debt securities, however, may not be sold to foreigners. Shares, both ordinary and preference, and share warrants can be sold to locals or foreigners.

INVESTORS

Foreign investors accounted for around 43% of trading activity in the market in 1997. Local interest is increasing as a result of a series of extremely successful plantation company initial public offerings (IPOs).

OPERATIONS

A) Trading system

A state-of-the-art automated trading system was introduced in 1997, since when trading has been fully computerised and the trading floor has ceased to be used.

B) Settlement and transfer

The CSE operates a two-tiered settlement cycle: buyer-to-broker settlement takes place on T+5 and broker-to-seller and inter-company settlement takes place on T+6. Brokers charge 0.1% per day interest for settlements after T+5. The forced sale date is T+15.

Trading is on a non-scrip basis and securities must be deposited at the Central Depository System (CDS) before they can be sold. The transfer of securities is effected immediately on conclusion of a sale. The following commercial banks operating in Sri Lanka provide custodial services: American Express Bank, ANZ Grindlays Bank, Bank of Ceylon, Citibank, Deutsche Bank and Standard Chartered Bank.

C) Commissions and other costs

Transactions of up to Rs1 million attract a commission of 1.4% subject to a minimum of Rs10 per transaction. Commission charged on transactions exceeding Rs1 million is 1.15%. There are no other charges.

TAXATION AND REGULATIONS AFFECTING FOREIGN INVESTORS

Bilateral investment agreements, backed by constitutional guarantee, provide protection for foreign investments in Sri Lanka. These agreements provide for:

- protection against nationalisation;
- prompt payment and adequate compensation;
- remittance of capital and income;
- dispute resolution under the international conventions for the settlement of investment disputes.

Bilateral agreements have been signed with Egypt, China, Denmark, Belgium, France, Germany, Italy, Japan, Korea, Luxembourg, Malaysia, The Netherlands, Norway, Romania, Singapore Sweden, Switzerland, Thailand, the United Kingdom and the USA.

A) Withholding tax

A listed public company is entitled to deduct from any dividend payable to a non-resident shareholder income tax equal to 15% of such dividend. The tax so deducted can be claimed as a deduction from the tax payable by the shareholder (other than a company) provided the dividend forms part of his assessable income.

In addition to withholding tax, resident companies are required to pay advance company tax (ACT) on every qualifying distribution, for which resident shareholders are given credit. Non-resident shareholders, however, are excluded from the imputation credit.

Foreign investors who are resident in the countries with which Sri Lanka has concluded double taxation treaties can claim credit in their own countries for the amount of tax paid by them in Sri Lanka. Ratified double tax treaties have been signed with the following countries: India, Germany, Norway, Japan, Pakistan, Malaysia, the Czech

Exhibit 63.7:
COUNTRY FUNDS – SRI LANKA

Fund	US$ % change 01/01/97 01/01/98	01/01/93 01/01/98	Fund base currency	Fund size (US$ mil)	Fund volatility	Management group	Opal main sector	Opal subsector
Sri Lanka Growth	15.04	N/A	US$	26.7	6.7	Carlson	Closed-End	Equity
Regent Sri Lanka	12.88	N/A	US$	8.1	6.161	Regent Pacific	Closed-End	Equity
Thornton New Tiger Sri Lanka	1.54	N/A	US$	0.5	8.178	Thornton	Open-End	Equity

Note: details for some funds may not have been included if the data for the US$ % change for 97/98 was not available

Source: Standard & Poor's Micropal.

Republic, the UK, Singapore, France, Denmark, Poland, the Netherlands, Finland, Sweden, Switzerland, Belgium, Romania, Canada, Korea, Yugoslavia, Bangladesh, Thailand, Italy, Australia, Indonesia, United Arab Emirates and Mauritius. Most of the treaties provide for tax on dividends at 15%.

B) Capital gains tax and stamp duty

Capital gains arising from transactions in listed securities are tax-exempt. Transfers of shares in listed companies are exempt from stamp duty.

C) Exchange control

Share investment in Sri Lanka and repatriation of proceeds must take place through Share Investment External Rupee Accounts (SIERA) opened with commercial banks. Individuals and regional funds as well as companies incorporated outside Sri Lanka are permitted to open SIERA accounts. The repatriation of proceeds arising out of investments made after 5 June 1990 are not subject to exchange control regulations.

LISTING AND REPORTING REQUIREMENTS

A) Listing requirements

CSE listings currently fall into three categories – the main board, second board and OTC.

Main board

Qualifications for a main board listing are as follows:

- The company must have either minimum issued and paid-up share capital or market capitalisation of Rs75 million.
- At least 25% of the company's shares must be in the hands of the public. (The definition of "public" as used here excludes holdings by parent, subsidiary, associate company, directors, the family members of directors and their nominees.)
- At least 10% of the company's issued and paid-up share capital must be in the hands of 300 or more shareholders who hold between 100 and 10,000 shares each.
- The company must be able to show a satisfactory three-year operating record.

Second board

Qualifications for a second board listing are as follows:

- The company must have either issued and paid-up capital or market capitalisation of Rs5 million.
- At least 10% of the company's shares must be in the hands of the public (with "public" defined as for main board listings above).
- The company must have at least 50 shareholders.

OTC

Qualifications for joining the OTC trading register are as follows:

- The company must be a public company registered in Sri Lanka.
- The company must be registered with the CSE for OTC trading.

B) Reporting requirements

Listed companies in Sri Lanka are required to submit quarterly profit statements to shareholders and the CSE within two months of the end of each quarter, and audited accounts to shareholders and the CSE within six months of the end of each financial year.

Corporate disclosure policy is based on immediate public disclosure and dissemination of material information, denial or confirmation of rumours and reports, quick response to unusual market action and preventing insider trading.

SHAREHOLDER PROTECTION CODES

Trading of listed securities by persons having access to unpublished price sensitive information in relation to such securities by virtue of their being connected with the company is illegal in Sri Lanka.

The introduction of a Mergers and Takeovers Code during 1995 has succeeded in preventing back-door takeovers by increasing disclosure and transparency.

The Sri Lankan Companies Act contains provisions for the protection of minority shareholders' rights. In the event of oppression or mismanagement of a company, any shareholder is entitled to make an application to the District Court.

The Securities and Exchange Commission of Sri Lanka has established a fund to compensate investors who suffer financial loss arising from the failure of a licensed stockbroker or licensed stock dealer to meet its contractual obligations.

RESEARCH

Daily, weekly and fortnightly publications are issued by most of the broking firms. The CSE itself publishers daily, weekly, monthly and quarterly releases on the stock market and also publishes an *Annual Report*, a *Fact Sheet* and an annual *Handbook of Listed Companies*.

PROSPECTIVE CHANGES

Market-making, share lending and short selling are planned to be introduced in order to improve liquidity and turnover.

CHAPTER

64

Sweden

Introduction

The Swedish market soared to an all-time high in early August, 38% above the end-1996 level, although this was followed by an 11% decline due to the Asian crisis. At the year-end, the All Share Index was up 23.8%. A stronger US dollar reduced these returns for US investors, while European investors were only marginally affected by currency factors.

Share trading increased by 47% to Skr1,346 billion (US$171 billion) from Skr918 billion in 1996. The turnover rate remained at 66%, and firmly above 60% for the fourth year in a row. Year-end market capitalisation reached Skr2,164 billion (US$273 billion). Sweden is among the few OECD countries where market value exceeds GNP (123%), while equity turnover amounts to 77% of GNP.

Following 54 admissions and 22 delistings (primarily due to acquisitions) in 1997, at the year-end there were 245 domestic and 16 foreign companies traded in the automated execution system in Stockholm, 100 of them on the main market and 161 on the parallel markets for small or young companies. In the absence of blue chip new issues or major privatisations, the amount raised in new issues and IPOs declined to Skr17 billion (1996: Skr24 billion).

Foreign investors accounted for 29% of total equity turnover in 1997, and they are estimated to hold 32% of market capitalisation (or some Skr700 billion).

ECONOMIC AND POLITICAL OVERVIEW

The Swedish battle against budget deficits and high inflation has been successful. At 1.9%, consumer price increases during 1997 were well within the Riksbank's target range of 1–3%. This could leave some room for programmes that would boost capacity utilisation, provided the budget remains close to balance. So far, efforts to significantly reduce unemployment have amounted to little more than window-dressing; open unemployment remains at 8% of the labour force and an almost equal number of people are "occupied" in public works or educational programmes. After a year with only 2% real GNP growth, domestic demand is projected to pick up during 1998. However, as a result of the impact on export demand of the turbulence in Asia, real GNP growth could well be confined to around 2.5% in 1998.

During 1997 the Swedish parliament unilaterally decided not to join European Monetary Union from the start in 1999. However, many of Sweden's major companies have declared their intention to introduce the new euro currency at the first opportunity. Current plans are also that the Stockholm Stock Exchange (SSE) will commence euro-denominated trading of the most active securities very early in 1999.

Role of the central bank

The Riksbank is formally independent but the board is elected by parliament. The governor has a longer mandate, however, which does not coincide with the general election cycle. Monetary policy is conducted by alterations in repo rates.

The Swedish Financial Supervisory Authority assumes the role of "competent authority", as defined by the EU, and also supervises all types of authorised financial activities in Sweden. Financial statistics are compiled by the Riksbank, Statistics Sweden (SCB) and the Financial Supervisory Authority.

MARKET PERFORMANCE

A) In 1997

The Stockholm All Share Index (SX-GX), having begun the year at 2,371, advanced by 16.0% during the first quarter and by 13.5% in the second quarter. A new all-time high was achieved in August, but then prices began to slide due to the problems in south-east Asia, and the index ended the year 23.8% ahead at 2,936. Variations between sectors were quite marked. Banking and insurance was up 43.1%, and the engineering sector by 30%, whereas chemicals and pharmaceuticals, along with real

Exhibit 64.1: SWEDISH OMX PRICE INDEX (Skr), 1993–97

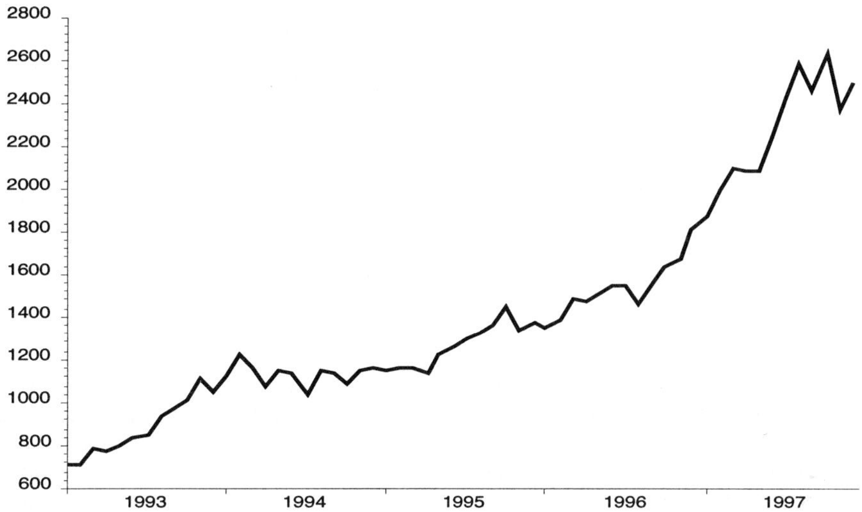

High value 2636 25 1.1.97 Low value 711.60 1.2.93 *Source: Datastream*

estate and construction, underperformed, posting rises of 7.7% and 5.4%, respectively. The best performing stocks on the main market were Segerström & Svensson (+192%), Elektronikgruppen (+173.8), HL Display (+167%) and Eldon (+124%).

Companies on the parallel markets performed well, with index gains of 32.3% for the small company market OTC list and 25.7% for the unlisted market (O-list).

B) Summary information

Global ranking by market value (US$ terms, end-1997): 13
Market capitalisation (end-1997): US$273 billion
Growth in market value (local currency terms, 1993–97): 142.7%
Market value as a % of nominal GNP (end-1997): 123%
Number of domestic/foreign companies listed (including OTC and O-list, end-1997): 245/16
Market P/E (all listed companies, capital-weighted, end-1997): 22.0
MSCI total returns (with net dividends, US$ terms, 1997): 12.9%
MSCI Index (change in US$ terms, 1997): +11.6%
Short-term (3-month) interest rate (end-1997): 4.34%
Long-term (10-year) bond yield (end-1997): 5.97%
Budget deficit as a % of nominal GNP (1997): 1.4%
Annual change in broad money (M3) supply (end-1997): -91.28%
Inflation rate (1997): 1.9%
US$ exchange rate (end-1997): Skr7.94

C) Year-end share price index, price/earnings ratios and yields

Exhibit 64.2:
YEAR-END SHARE PRICE INDEX, AVERAGE P/E AND DIVIDEND YIELDS, 1993–97

Year-end	*SSE All Share Index*	*P/E*	*Yield (%)*
1993	1,338	31.0	1.5
1994	1,451	14.0	2.0
1995	1,716	11.0	2.8
1996	2,371	17.0	2.4
1997	2,936	22.0	2.1

Source: Stockholm Stock Exchange.

D) Market indices and their constituents

The SSE All Share Index (SX-GX), comprises all A-list shares and is weighted for the market value of each company. The Affärsvälden General Index is also widely followed. In addition, there are nine business sector indices, of which engineering is the largest sector, followed by chemicals and pharmaceuticals.

The Swedish OMX index is a traded index based on the 30 most actively traded companies on the SSE. Representing about 75% of market capitalisation and market turnover, it is regarded as a leading market indicator.

Performance of the parallel markets for smaller companies and unlisted securities is measured by the SX-OTC and SX-O indices.

THE STOCK MARKET

A) Brief history and structure

Organised trading on the Stockholm exchange can be traced back to 1776. For the first 90 years it was basically a commodity exchange until securities exchange legislation was enacted in 1862. Initially, trading was sporadic until the formal establishment of a stock exchange in an international sense took place in 1901.

In the past few years, Sweden has modernised its securities market legislation to make it compatible with EU directives. The Act on Stock Exchanges and Clearing Operations, effective from 1993, transformed the SSE into a limited company with the exchange members and issuers as shareholders. On the supervisory side, the former agencies for control of banks and insurance companies respectively have been merged into the Financial Supervisory Authority, performing the duties of an EU-defined "competent authority".

Stockholm has been the first exchange to implement fully the EU option of remote membership with direct access to the decentralised automated trading system, SAX. By the end of 1997, 15 out of 48 member firms were remote – ie trading direct from their offices in London, Zürich and the Scandinavian capitals. Another eight members are majority owned by foreign interests.

There are three different markets for trading shares in Sweden (with transactions all executed through the SSE's automated SAX trading system). The market for officially listed shares (the A-list) accounts for over 90% of trading volume. The parallel market consists of the OTC list which caters for small and medium-sized companies and, finally, there is the O-list or unlisted securities market. The latter market has less formal requirements and will sometimes be used as an intermediate step for companies that may, for example, lack the required track record for a full listing. The same legislation applies to all three lists, applicants sign materially the same contract concerning information obligations and the stock exchange has the same judicial power over each of the markets.

In July 1997 the Stockholm Stock Exchange and the Copenhagen Stock Exchange signed a letter of intent concerning a common trading system. Beginning in 1998–99 the two countries' equity markets will share the same trading system, SAX 2000. Members of both exchanges will have a full overview of the respective order books, but only those with dual memberships can directly execute trades on both sides. Swedish shares will be traded in Swedish kronor and cleared via the Swedish Central Securities Depository, while Danish shares will be traded in Danish kroner and cleared via the Danish VP.

B) Different exchanges

The Stockholm exchange is the only authorised cash market for the trading of equities.

C) Opening hours, names and addresses

Trading on the exchange is from 10.00am to 5.00pm, Monday to Friday except for holidays. On the day preceding a holiday, trading usually closes at 1.00pm. Swedish intermediaries are, however, allowed to trade off-exchange.

STOCKHOLMS FONDÖRS AB
PO Box 1256, SE-111 82 Stockholm
Tel: (46) 8 613 8800; Fax: (46) 8 243 488

MARKET SIZE

A) Number of listings and market value

At the end of 1997 a total of 261 companies were listed on the SSE, including 16 foreign stocks. The official A-list included 100 companies, while 59 were traded on the smaller company OTC list and 102 on the O-list for unlisted securities. Total market capitalisation at year-end 1997 was Skr2,164 billion, up 28.2% from a year earlier.

Exhibit 64.3:
MARKET VALUE OF EQUITY SHARES OF DOMESTIC COMPANIES (ALL LISTS), 1993–97

Year-end	*Market value (Skr billion)*
1993	891.6
1994	977.0
1995	1,143.6
1996	1,687.7
1997	2,164.0

Source: Stockholm Stock Exchange.

Exhibit 64.4:
MARKET VALUE BY SECTOR, SSE A-LIST, END-1997

Sector	*No. of listed companies*	*Market value (Skr billion)*
Engineering	26	819
Banking and finance	7	299
Chemicals and pharmaceuticals	6	280
Other industry	18	115
Forestry	5	113
Investment companies	5	109
Real estate and construction	13	60
Services	14	29
Wholesale and retail trade	6	15
Total	**100**	**1,838**

Source: Stockholm Stock Exchange.

Exhibit 64.5:
NUMBER OF NEW LISTINGS, 1993–97

	1993	*1994*	*1995*	*1996*	*1997*
Domestic	21	39	16	17	51
Foreign	0	1	1	1	3
Total	21	40	17	18	54

Source: Stockholm Stock Exchange.

B) Largest quoted companies

Exhibit 64.6:
THE 20 LARGEST LISTED COMPANIES ON THE SSE, END-1997

Ranking	*Company*	*Market value (Skr billion)*
1	Ericsson	292.2
2	Astra AB	224.7
3	Volvo	93.9
4	ABB AB	88.0
5	Investor AB	73.8
6	Svenska Handelsbanken	65.3
7	Hennes & Mauritz	63.9
8	FöreningsSparbanken	63.5
9	Skandinaviska Enskilda Banken	58.9
10	Sandvik AB	58.5
11	Nordbanken Holding AB	57.1
12	Incentive AB	48.9
13	Atlas Copco AB	43.5
14	Electrolux AB	40.3
15	Sydkraft AB	39.5
16	Skandia	38.3
17	Scania AB	35.7
18	SCA AB	35.3
19	Skanska AB	34.1
20	Stora AB	32.1

Source: Stockholm Stock Exchange.

C) Trading volume

Turnover increased by 46.6% to Skr1,345.6 billion in 1997.

Exhibit 64.7:
TOTAL SHARE TURNOVER, 1993–97 (SKR BILLION)

	1993	*1994*	*1995*	*1996*	*1997*
Domestic	339.2	657.7	658.2	876.1	1,211.7
Foreign	0.2	1.1	6.6	42.0	133.9
Total	339.4	658.8	664.8	918.1	1,345.6

Source: Stockholm Stock Exchange.

Exhibit 64.8:
THE 20 MOST ACTIVELY TRADED SHARES, SSE, 1997

Ranking	*Company*	*Trading value (Skr billion)*
1	Ericsson	226.2
2	Astra	160.6
3	Volvo AB	73.1
4	ABB AB	58.0
5	Nokia AB Oy	55.7
6	Autoliv Inc	42.4
7	Skandinaviska Enskilda Banken	38.2
8	Pharmacia & Upjohn Inc	37.6
9	Electrolux AB	32.5
10	Hennes & Mauritz AB	25.7
11	Investor AB	25.5
12	Svenska Handelsbanken	25.1
13	Sandvik AB	25.0
14	Skandia	24.4
15	Scania AB	23.9
16	Stora AB	23.4
17	FöreningsSparbanken	21.1
18	Nordbanken Holding AB	19.0
19	Trelleborg AB	17.8
20	Incentive AB	16.9

Source: Stockholm Stock Exchange.

TYPES OF SHARE

Swedish companies may issue ordinary or preference shares, although most trading on the stock exchange is in ordinary shares. Shares are held in a computerised book entry system with shareholders normally registered in their own name via an account-holding bank or independent broker. Investors may choose to keep their shares in a bank nominee account and most foreign investors use this option.

Shares in Swedish companies are frequently divided into A shares and B shares. A shares carry normal or full voting rights (generally one vote per share), while B shares carry reduced voting rights (usually one share entitles the owner to one-tenth of a vote). However, some older companies – for example SKF, Ericsson and Electrolux – retain differentials of up to 1:1,000. Swedish law prohibits non-voting shares.

OTHER MARKETS

As well as the main (A-list) market, the SSE operates two parallel markets for equity shares. The small company market, the OTC, was created in the early 1980s to promote risk capital formation for small enterprises, while the O-list was established in the second half of the 1980s in order to bring unlisted securities under the same rules and regulations as officially listed companies.

Exhibit 64.9:
COUNTRY FUNDS – SWEDEN

Fund	US$ % change 31/12/96 31/12/97	US$ % change 31/12/92 31/12/97	Currency	Fund size (US$ mil)	Volatility	Manager name	Main sector	Class
Balzac Sweden Index	N/A	N/A	Skr	1.11	N/A	State Street Bq	Equity	French FCPs
Frontrunner Swedish Eq SEK	N/A	N/A	Skr	2.96	N/A	Frontrunner	Equity	Luxembourg
Aragon Sv Swedish Eq	18.48	N/A	Skr	13.53	3.88	Aragon Fondkommission AB	Equity	Luxembourg
S-E-Banken Fund Sverige	12.86	N/A	Skr	157.98	3.76	S-E-Banken	Equity	Luxembourg
Carlson Sweden	5.52	206.55	Skr	10.77	4.85	Carlson	Equity	Luxembourg
SSF Swedish Shares	0.09	N/A	Skr	29.54	N/A	Svenska Handelsbanken	Equity	Luxembourg

Note: details for some funds may not have been included if the data for the US$ % change for 96/97 was not available *Source: Standard & Poor's Micropal.*

Established in 1985, the Swedish Options Market (OM Stockholm) serves as an exchange and clearing house for derivative instruments. At present, OM Stockholm offers futures and options on individual Swedish stocks and on the Swedish OMX equity index, plus a standardised interest rate swap and interest rate options.

OM GROUP
Information Department
PO Box 16305, S-103 26 Stockholm
Tel: (46) 8 700 0600; Fax: (46) 8 723 1092

INVESTORS

The Swedish stock market has traditionally been dominated by institutional investors, such as assurance and investment companies, mutual funds and foundations.

Foreign interest in the Swedish market has been growing since the early 1980s, fostered by the removal of foreign exchange controls. In 1997 foreign investors were responsible for 29% of SSE equity trading and, at the end of the year, they were estimated to hold 32% of all Swedish shares.

OPERATIONS

A) Trading system

The SSE introduced screen-based and decentralised automated trading for shares in 1989. Trading members, who no longer operate on the exchange floor, may use either ordinary PCs as workstations or connect their mainframe computers to the SAX trading system. They may also be located outside Sweden.

Shares are normally traded in round lots of 50, 100, 500, 1,000 or 2,000; the size of the round lot is determined by the convention of trading in lots with a market value of approximately Skr18,000 on the A-list and Skr9,000 on the parallel markets. There is an automated sub-system for trading small orders below one round lot. However, to improve efficiency, shares can be lumped together from this small order market for execution in the round lot market, or vice versa. During 1997 an average of 19,400 transactions a day were processed by the SAX automated system, some 10% of these in the small order market.

The SSE plans to introduce a new generation of automated trading system, SAX 2000, during 1998. This system will have a significantly improved capacity and will be prepared for multi-currency trading, clearing via different institutions, plus the handling of derivatives and combination trades. The new system will be the trading platform for the new OM Group, comprising both cash market and equity derivative trading, as well as serving the Stockholm and Copenhagen markets.

B) List of principal banks and brokers

ABB AROS FONDKOMMISSION
SE-113 96 Stockholm
Tel: (46) 8 458 5600; Fax: (46) 8 457 1875

ALFRED BERG FONDKOMMISSION
PO Box 70447, SE-107 25 Stockholm
Tel: (46) 8 723 5800; Fax: (46) 8 611 1681

CARNEGIE FONDKOMMISSION
SE-103 38 Stockholm
Tel: (46) 8 676 8800; Fax: (46) 8 676 8895

ERIK PENSER FONDKOMMISSION
PO Box 7405, SE-103 91 Stockholm
Tel: (46) 8 463 8000; Fax: (46) 8 611 2705

HAGSTRÖMER & QVIBERG FONDKOMMISSION
SE-103 71 Stockholm
Tel: (46) 8 696 1700; Fax: (46) 8 696 1701

E. ÖHMAN J:OR FONDKOMMISSION
Box 7415, 103 91 Stockholm
Tel: (46) 8 402 5000; Fax: (46) 8 200 075

SBC ARBITECH
PO Box 1722, SE-111 87 Stockholm
Tel: (46) 8 453 7300; Fax: (46) 8 24 9 130

SKANDINAVISKA ENSKILDA BANKEN
SE-106 40 Stockholm
Tel: (46) 8 763 8000; Fax: (46) 8 676 9019

SPARBANKEN SVERIGE
SE-105 34 Stockholm
Tel: (46) 8 790 1000; Fax: (46) 8 790 2899

SVENSKA HANDELSBANKEN
SE-106 70 Stockholm
Tel: (46) 8 701 1000; Fax: (46) 8 701 2103

Discount broker

AKTIESPARARNAS INVESTERINGS
Norrtullsgatan 6, 4tr, SE-113 89 Stockholm
Tel: (46) 8 457 1700; Fax: (46) 8 457 1875

C) Settlement and transfer

Clearing and settlement takes place on a continuous T+3 working-day cycle. Thus, payment for purchased shares is made on the third business day following the transaction, unless other terms have been explicitly agreed. At the time of purchase, notification is given of the delivery date of the shares. The seller must deliver the shares no later than one day after the transaction date.

Share prices are always quoted in Swedish kronor, but settlement can normally be made in any predetermined convertible currency.

Almost all documentation for companies listed on the exchange, including foreign companies, is handled through the Värdepapperscentralen (VPC). The VPC operates a computer system that maintains lists of shareholders of each company, registers voting rights and handles the distribution of shares and dividends. Foreign investors therefore need to register with the VPC through their Swedish bank or broker.

D) Commissions and other costs

Brokerage commissions are not subject to approval by the supervisory authority, Finansinspektionen. For shares on the A-list, brokers typically charge 0.45% for the first Skr500,000 of any contract note and 0.3% for the amount above this level. OTC and O-list transactions have traditionally attracted commission at 0.65% of the consideration, but because they are handled using the same routines as A-list shares some brokers have started to charge the standard 0.45%. The minimum commission is about Skr200 per contract, although a cross-border trade commands a higher minimum.

Recently, commission rate competition among intermediaries has become more visible. Some have specialised in execution only of larger trades, charging commission of 0.15–0.20% of the consideration. Also, a few members have opened Internet trading services, charging about 0.25%.

TAXATION AND REGULATIONS AFFECTING FOREIGN INVESTORS

Unless there is a double taxation treaty between Sweden and the foreign investor's country of residence, a withholding tax of 30% is levied on dividends paid to non-residents. (Sweden has entered into double taxation agreements with about 70 countries.) Sweden has implemented the Parent/Subsidiary Directive, which means that if the shareholder is a legal entity domiciled in another EU country and (a) holds at least 25% of the capital and (b) meets the conditions set out in Article 2 of the Directive, dividends are tax-free.

There is no capital gains or wealth tax levied by Sweden for non-residents.

Foreign investors must register with the VPC in order to receive dividends, and this can be done through a Swedish or foreign broker or bank that is itself registered by the VPC as an account-operating institution. When dividends are paid, the VPC withholds the relevant taxes.

Exhibit 64.10:
WITHHOLDING TAX

Recipient	*Dividends %*
Resident corporations	Nil
Resident individuals	30
Non-resident corporations and individuals:	
Non-treaty	30
Treaty	0–30

Source: Price Waterhouse.

For most Swedish companies, all restrictions on foreign ownership of shares were abolished on 1 January 1993.

As of 1 July 1990, Swedish exchange control regulations were essentially abolished. The remaining controls are aimed only at providing the central bank and the national tax board with sufficient data to maintain statistics on the balance of payments and for tax control purposes.

LISTING AND REPORTING REQUIREMENTS

A) Listing requirements

To be officially listed on the SSE's A-list a company must have at least a three-year track record, and not less than 25% of its share capital must be in the hands of a minimum of 2,000 investors.

Under the Act on Exchange and Clearing Activities, applications for new listings of securities must be submitted to the stock exchange for approval. Applications must be accompanied by listing particulars containing information necessary to enable investors to make an informed assessment of the business and financial position of the issuer and of the rights attached to the securities. The Swedish Financial Supervisory Authority (FSA) has issued detailed regulations regarding the contents of particulars, which generally correspond to the requirements set out in EU Directive 89/390/EEC. Publication of the full listing particulars or a notice giving details, among other things, of where to obtain copies of the full particulars, must take place in at least one national newspaper.

Listing particulars do not have to be submitted if the listing relates to securities issued by an EEA state or if the securities constitute shares in a securities fund or in a foreign investment fund situated in a country within the EEA area. In addition, following the EEA Treaty, the exchange shall not check and approve listing particulars if the issuer, at the time of the application to the SSE, has already received the approval of the particulars in another state within the EEA area.

Another situation where the exchange does not check and approve the listing particulars is where a public offer prospectus has been drawn up in accordance with the requirements for listing particulars and the prospectus has been approved of by either the FSA or the equivalent foreign authority in a state within the EEA area. In such cases the exchange accepts the prospectus as listing particulars.

In fact, based on a supplement to the EU listing directive, the SSE can waive almost all listing requirements if the company is seeking a parallel listing on another recognised exchange. However, it is not obliged to do so.

The SSE may request that foreign listing particulars be translated into Swedish and be supplemented with information specific to the Swedish market.

B) Reporting requirements

Once listed, companies must observe continuing information and reporting obligations. The basic rules are found in the Act on Exchange and Clearing Activities, which stipulates that a listed company shall keep the exchange informed of its business, publish such information regarding its activities and shares that may be of importance for the valuation of the shares, and otherwise provide the exchange with such information as is necessary for the exchange's performance of its duties.

This information includes both regularly recurring matters (eg dividends and interim figures) and exceptional matters. Among other things, a listed company must notify the exchange of any major new developments in its operations and of changes in its capital structure, financial condition or of any board decisions to change the general character or nature of its business. The listing rules contain detailed provisions as to the issuing of the annual report and accounts, half-yearly reports and preliminary profits statements for the full year.

Changes to the board personnel and executive officers, must be notified immediately and copies of directors' service contracts of more than one year's duration must be available for inspection. Listed companies must also adopt and secure compliance with rules governing the conduct and disclosure of dealings by directors and their families in the listed securities of the company in terms no less exacting than those of a model code issued by the stock exchange.

SHAREHOLDER PROTECTION CODES

The Swedish Companies Act contains provisions designed to protect minority shareholders, such as the principle of equal treatment of shareholders, voting rules for amendment of the articles of association and for reduction of the share capital, and rules regarding the right/obligation to buy out a minority.

A) Significant shareholdings

Immediately after an acquisition or sale of shares, the purchaser or seller shall notify the company and the exchange where the shares are quoted if the transaction results in the number of votes held reaching, exceeding or falling below 5% of votes in the company. Notification is also required where holdings reach, exceed or fall below 10%, 15%, 20% and so on.

B) Financial intermediaries

The Securities Business Act lays down a framework of rules governing the securities business. The Act encompasses the following services:

- Trade in financial instruments for someone else's account.
- Intermediation between buyers and sellers of financial instruments or taking part in some other way in transactions with respect to such instruments.
- Trade in financial instruments for one's own account.

- Administration of financial instruments belonging to someone else.
- Underwriting and other services in connection with new issues or public offers to buy or sell financial instruments.

In order to provide any of these services, a Swedish investment firm must obtain authorisation from the FSA. However, under the Investment Services Directive (93/22/EEC), investment firms established in another country within the EEA area may conduct business through a branch in Sweden or carry on cross-border activities into Sweden after notifying the FSA. The business which the foreign investment firm may conduct in Sweden is limited to what is covered by the firm's authorisation in its home state.

C) Insider trading

The Insider Act came into force on 1 February 1991. Individuals found guilty of insider trading are liable to fines or imprisonment for up to four years. As of 1 January 1997, the Insider Act has been extended to impose a prohibition on engaging in short-term dealing by persons having a leading position in, or being close to, a stock market company. As of the same date, "undue price influence" is a criminal offence under the Financial Instruments Trading Act, directed towards market manipulation operations.

D) Compensation fund

There is no stock exchange compensation fund to reimburse shareholders who may be victims of fraud or default by a market broker or trader. However, all financial institutions in Sweden are under the supervision of the FSA. If problems occur in a securities transaction, the investor should first approach his intermediary. Should he remain dissatisfied, he may ultimately lodge his complaint with the FSA. The VPC has strict liability for damages arising from incorrect or misleading information in a share register.

An investor protection scheme based on an EU Directive is expected to be in place in late 1998. Under this programme, investors may be compensated up to the equivalent of ECU20,000 per institution in the case of default.

RESEARCH

Research on the Swedish market is extensive and thorough, especially as far as the heavily traded multinational companies are concerned. Foreign investors may obtain research and market information from major banks and brokers, as well as from newspapers and magazines, both in Sweden and abroad.

Some of the best research is conducted by Alfred Berg, Handelsbanken, Carnegie International and Enskilda Securities. Handelsbanken's London branch provides a comprehensive range of services to foreign investors. These include weekly and monthly market reports, investment strategies and regular company updates.

The Stockholm daily newspaper, *Svenska Dagbladet* and the business newspapers, *Dagens Industri* and *Finanstidningen,* publish English language issues on Swedish business topics, obtainable from their international advertising departments. The weekly business magazine, *Affärsvärlden,* publishes a business report, in English, 22 times a year. Another weekly publication is *Veckans Affärer.*

CHAPTER

65

Switzerland

Introduction

The fully automated Swiss Exchange (SWX) recorded total turnover of over Sfr1 trillion for the first time in 1997; the new record was Sfr1,018 billion (US$697 billion), representing a 26% increase compared with 1996. Swiss equity turnover grew by 48% to Sfr714.9 billion. The success of electronic trading was highlighted in the warrant market, where premiums grew by 124% in 1997.

At the end of 1997 there were 216 domestic companies listed on the SWX with a total market capitalisation equivalent to 220% of GNP. The market is, however, extremely concentrated. The 10 largest quoted companies on the SWX accounted for more than 69% of total market capitalisation at the end of 1997, while Novartis alone represented more than 19%. Chemicals and pharmaceuticals constitute 40.7% of the market, and banks and insurance companies together account for 31.5%.

Ahead of EMU, the SWX took some far-reaching strategic decisions in 1997. It decided to merge its subsidiary Soffex, the electronic exchange for standardised derivatives, with its German counterpart DTB. The SWX and Deutsche Börse AG both hold a 50% stake in this new derivatives exchange, which is called Eurex. As a result, 210 members of Soffex and DTB will be able to trade Swiss and German products on a single electronic platform. Eurex is expected to open during 1998.

The SWX also initiated a joint venture with Deutsche Börse in Germany, SBF Paris Bourse in France and Dow Jones Corporation in the US, aiming to launch new pan-European stock indices in February 1998.

ECONOMIC AND POLITICAL OVERVIEW

In view of the improving prospects for the Swiss economy and the uncertainties surrounding EMU, the Swiss National Bank maintained a relatively generous monetary policy in 1997. During the year, signs of a gradual economic recovery began to emerge, and real GDP rose in the second and third quarters. On an annual basis, the growth rate is expected to be 0.5% in 1997, compared with a 0.5% contraction in 1996. The inflation rate is currently also 0.5%.

The 1996 depreciation of the Swiss franc relative to the US dollar continued: the rate at 31 December 1997 was Sfr1.46 to US$1.00, versus Sfr1.33 a year earlier.

Role of the central bank

The Swiss National Bank (SNB) is independent of the federal government and has a tradition of keeping inflation low and pursuing a philosophy of pragmatic monetarism.

Assuming a direct link between monetary growth and inflation, the SNB has been able to maintain price stability by keeping a tight rein on the money supply. Positive current account surpluses and the gold backing of the Swiss franc have helped to stabilise prices and strengthen the domestic currency, but the key to the Swiss franc's strength is the central bank's conservative financial policies.

MARKET PERFORMANCE

A) In 1997

The Swiss Performance Index increased by just over 55% in local currency terms during the year, and market capitalisation grew by the same percentage amount, from Sfr539.9 billion at end-1996 to Sfr839.2 billion at end-1997.

Turnover in domestic shares on the Swiss stock market was valued at Sfr714.9 billion in 1997, 48% up on the 1996 figure of Sfr481.7 billion. The number of domestic companies listed grew by three during the year to 216, and the number of foreign companies listed fell by 11 to 212.

B) Summary information

Global ranking by market value (US$ terms, end-1997): 6
Market capitalisation (end-1997): US$574.16 billion

Exhibit 65.1: SWISS MARKET PRICE INDEX (Sfr), 1993–97

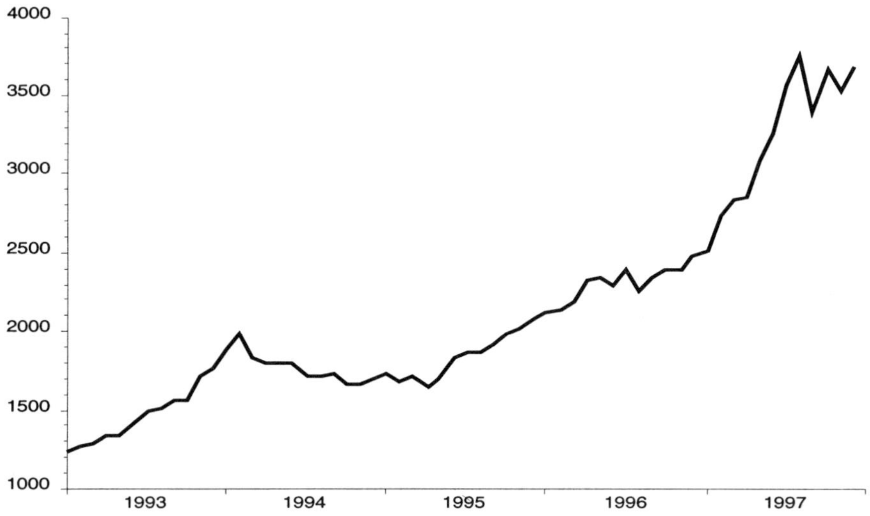

High value 3752.66 1.8.97 Low value 1238.57 1.1.93 *Source: Datastream*

Growth in market value (local currency terms, 1993–97): 108.61%
Market value as a % of nominal GDP (end-1997): 264%
Number of domestic/foreign companies listed (end-1997): 216/212
Market P/E (all Swiss shares, end-1997): 20.8
MSCI total returns (with net dividends, US$ terms, 1997): 44.2%
MSCI Index (US$ terms, 1997): +43.2%
Short-term (3-month Euromarket) interest rate (end-1997): 1.92%
Long-term (over 7-year) bond yield (end-1997): 3.33%
Budget deficit as a % of nominal GDP (1997): 2.4%
Annual change in broad money (M3) supply (Oct 1997): -5.6%
Inflation rate (1997): 0.5%
US$ exchange rate (end-1997): Sfr1.4616

C) Year-end share price index, price/earnings ratios and yields

Exhibit 65.2:
YEAR-END SHARE PRICE INDICES, P/E AND GROSS DIVIDEND YIELDS, 1993–97

Year-end	*SPI Index*	*SBC All Share Index*	*P/E*	*Yield (%)*
1993	1,867.8	1,012.6	20.5	1.5
1994	1,725.5	1,928.3	15.1	2.2
1995	2,123.4	1,132.0	16.8	1.5
1996	2,511.9	1,321.2	38.2	1.4
1997	3,898.2	2,033.9	20.8	N/A

Source: Swiss Exchange.

D) Market indices and their constituents

The Swiss Performance Index (SPI) has been published by the SWX since 1987. It is computed in real time throughout the stock exchange session on the basis of all stock prices posted on the Swiss market. It covers 323 shares.

The Swiss Market Index (SMI) was introduced on 30 June 1988. Also calculated by the SWX, it includes the 22 largest stocks by capitalisation (about 70% of total market capitalisation) and constitutes a basis for Soffex index options and futures. SMI and SPI are computed by the SWX.

THE STOCK MARKET

A) Brief history and structure

The Geneva exchange was formally established in 1850. The stock exchange in Basle followed in 1876 and the Zürich exchange was founded one year later.

Since 1996, however, all Swiss and foreign shares have been traded electronically on the SWX. The changes were confirmed by a new Federal Stock Exchange Act, which came into force in February 1997.

B) Different exchanges

Trading now takes place on the SWX's electronic system and , as a result, the trading floors in Zürich, Geneva and Basle have been closed.

C) Opening hours, names and addresses

SWX trading takes place between 9.30am and 4.30pm, although the system is available for order entry from 6.00am to 9.30am and from 4.30pm to 10.00pm.

SWISS EXCHANGE AND SOFFEX
Selnaustrasse 32, CH-8021 Zürich
Tel: (41) 1 229 2111; Fax: (41) 1 229 2233

SWISS EXCHANGE GENEVA
8, rue de la Confédération, CH-1204 Geneva 11
Tel: (41) 22 818 5830; Fax: (41) 22 818 5840
Web site: http://www.swx.ch

MARKET SIZE

A) Number of listings and market value

At the end of 1997 there were 428 companies listed on the SWX (of which 212 were foreign and 216 domestic). Total market capitalisation amounted to Sfr839.2 billion.

Exhibit 65.3:
NUMBER OF COMPANIES LISTED AND MARKET VALUE, SWX, 1993–97

	No. of companies		*Market capitalisation*
Year-end	*Domestic*	*Foreign*	*(Sfr billion)*
1993	261	258	402.26
1994	215	242	372.58
1995	216	233	458.10
1996	213	223	539.94
1997	216	212	839.19

Source: Swiss Exchange.

B) Largest quoted companies

The 10 largest quoted companies on the Swiss stock market accounted for 69% of total market capitalisation. Novartis registered shares alone represented 19% of total market value.

Exhibit 65.4:
THE 20 LARGEST SWX SHARES BY MARKET VALUE, END-1997

Ranking	*Company/category of share*	*Market value (Sfr million)*
1	Novartis N	147,697.52
2	Roche GS	101,906.72
3	Nestlé N	86,297.08
4	CS Group N	59,675.95
5	UBS I	44,836.24
6	Rueckv N	39,942.28
7	SBV N	35,541.22
8	Zuerich N	32,644.72
9	Novartis I	15,568.48
10	ABB Ag I	14,972.63
11	Ciba Sc N	11,981.13
12	UBS N	9,294.44
13	Clariant N	8,871.84
14	Holderbk I	6,106.69
15	Alusuisse N	5,753.90
16	Baloise N	5,468.47
17	Elektrowatt I	4,621.45
18	Sulzer N	3,365.37
19	SGS Surveillance I	3,238.94
20	SMH N N10	2,960.91

I = *Inhaberaktie* (bearer shares); N = *Namenaktie* (registered shares).

Source: Swiss Exchange.

C) Trading volume

Turnover in domestic shares on the Swiss stock market was valued at Sfr714.9 billion in 1997, 48% up on the 1996 figure of Sfr511.8 billion. Total equity turnover (including foreign stocks and warrants) in 1997 amounted to Sfr823.1 billion, of which 95% represented Swiss shares and warrants.

Exhibit 65.5:
THE 20 MOST ACTIVELY TRADED SWX SHARES, 1997

Ranking	*Company/category of share*	*Trading value (Sfr million)*
1	Novartis N	103,976,426
2	Roche GS	81,067,827
3	UBS I	80,850,856
4	CS Group N	63,447,179
5	Nestlé N	56,573,807
6	Rueckv N	32,883,438
7	SBV N	30,020,362
8	Zuerich N	30,262,776
9	ABB Ag I	15,070,794
10	Alusuisse N	13,208,027
11	Ciba Sc N	12,857,688
12	UBS N	10,936,449
13	Novartis I	8,901,330
14	Holderbk I	7,049,000
15	Clariant N	7,022,553
16	Sulzer N	6,615,839
17	SMH N N10	3,683,869
18	SGS Surveillance I	3,450,216
19	Elektrowatt I	3,042,864
20	Baloise N	2,318,541

I = *Inhaberaktie* (bearer shares); N = *Namenaktie* (registered shares).

Source: Swiss Exchange.

TYPES OF SHARE

After the historic decision by Nestlé in November 1988 to make its registered shares freely available to international investors, the significance of the distinction between registered and bearer shares has changed profoundly. Previously, registered stock was generally available only to Swiss nationals, which led over a period of years to the establishment of a wide discrepancy in the price of registered and bearer shares in the same company, with the former trading at a considerable premium. This became a long-standing source of irritation to foreign investors, forced to pay more to participate in Swiss equities than their domestic counterparts. The Nestlé decision led to a sharp narrowing of the price differential between the two types of security.

Participation certificates are also traded on the SWX.

OTHER MARKETS

In 1988 an options market in Swiss shares (Soffex) was established, but trading is limited to put and call options on a small number of equities and the market index. Futures on the SMI Index and options on futures have also been available since November 1990. Soffex has been owned and operated by the SWX since 1993.

In September 1997 the SWX and Deutsche Börse AG of Germany announced they would merge their derivative markets. DTB and Soffex would thus disappear and be replaced by a new exchange, named Eurex, owned jointly by the two exchanges. Trading on Eurex is due to start in 1998.

INVESTORS

Because of banking secrecy rules, it is extremely difficult to make an assessment of the breakdown of investors. However, according to most estimates, about 50% of Swiss securities transaction volume originates from institutional investors.

OPERATIONS

A) Trading system

All securities listed on the SWX are traded via the exchange's electronic trading system.

Transactions in the cash or spot market are the most common, although forward transactions of up to nine months are possible through the off-exchange functions of the trading system.

The electronic trading system fully integrates trading and settlement and is available to all members. It provides permanent access to the central order book over the course of the trading day, and trades are generated according to matching rules on the basis of supply and demand. The system also provides OTC trading functions between members as well as reporting facilities for non-exchange transactions.

The trading day is made up of three periods, each of which is assigned specific functions that determine the way in which orders are processed:

(a) In the pre-opening period, orders are held in the book without being matched. The theoretical opening price is displayed continuously.
(b) During the opening period, as many as possible of the orders in the order book are executed at the opening price. This forms the first official price of the trading day. After this, continuous trading begins.
(c) During continuous trading, orders are executed against the order book or integrated into the order book according to their price and arrival time.

B) List of principal banks

Zürich

BANK JULIUS BAER
Bahnhofstrasse 36, 8010 Zürich
Tel: (41) 1 228 5111; Fax: (41) 1 211 2560

BANK LEU
Bahnhofstrasse 32, 8022 Zürich
Tel: (41) 1 219 1111; Fax: (41) 1 219 3197

BANK OPPENHEIM PIERSON
Uraniastrasse 28, 8022 Zürich
Tel: (41) 1 214 2214; Fax: (41) 1 214 2222

BANK SARASIN
Zweigniederlassung Zürich,
Talstrasse 66, 8022 Zürich
Tel: (41) 1 213 9191; Fax: (41) 1 221 0454

BANK J VONTOBEL
Bahnhofstrasse 3, 8022 Zürich
Tel: (41) 1 283 7111; Fax: (41) 1 283 7650

CREDIT SUISSE
Paradeplatz 8, 8070 Zürich
Tel: (41) 1 333 1111; Fax: (41) 1 332 5555

WARBURG DILLON READ
Swiss Bank Centre, Europastrasse, 1
CH-8152 Opfikon, Zürich
Tel: (41) 1 238 1111; Fax: (41) 1 238 7606

Geneva

BANQUE PARIBAS (SUISSE)
Place de Hollande 2, 1211 Geneva
Tel: (41) 22 787 7111; Fax: (41) 22 787 8000

Exhibit 65.6:
TOP PERFORMING COUNTRY FUNDS – SWITZERLAND

Fund	*US$ % change* 31/12/96 31/12/97	31/12/92 31/12/97	Currency	*Fund size* (US$mil)	Volatility	Manager name	Main sector	Class
Swiss Mkt Index Quant Lvrgd	72.73	N/A	Sfr	5.58	N/A	Millenium Asset Mgmt (ire)	Equity	Offshore Territories
BBL Invest Switzerland Cap	47.28	N/A	Sfr	44.37	N/A	BBL-Banque Brussels Lambert	Equity	Belgian Trusts
MOSAIS Actions Suisses	47.12	N/A	Sfr	16.9	N/A	Credit Agricole	Equity	Luxembourg
CS Equity Fd Swiss Blue Chips	46.94	198.17	Sfr	633.54	4.54	Credit Suisse AM Funds	Equity	Swiss Mutual Funds
CS Equity Fd Swiss Blue Chips	46.94	198.17	Sfr	633.54	4.54	Credit Suisse	Equity Growth	Investmentfds Deutschland
DVG Fonds Helvetia	45.72	221.58	DM	99.75	4.6	DVG	Equity Growth	Investmentfds Deutschland
EMIF Switzerland Index Plus A	45.09	N/A	Sfr	74.78	4.84	CCF/BHF/HS/KB/BBV	Equity	Luxembourg
Parvest Switzerland C	44.89	N/A	Sfr	195.51	N/A	Banque Paribas	Equity	Luxembourg
Parvest Switzerland C	44.89	N/A	Sfr	195.51	4.37	Banque Paribas	Equity Growth	Investmentfds Deutschland
EMIF Switzerland Index Plus B	44.88	N/A	Sfr	74.78	4.83	CCF/BHF/HS/KB/BBV	Equity	Luxembourg
EMIF Switzerland Index Plus B	44.88	N/A	Sfr	74.78	4.91	CCF/BHF/HS/KB/BBV	Equity Growth	Investmentfds Deutschland
Parvest Switzerland D	44.88	N/A	Sfr	195.51	N/A	Banque Paribas	Equity	Luxembourg
Swissbar	44.58	216.01	Sfr	77.31	4.46	Bank Julius Baer	Equity	Swiss Mutual Funds
SaraSwiss	44.23	N/A	Sfr	131.39	4.28	Banque Sarasin Basel	Equity	Swiss Mutual Funds
Groupe Indosuez Switzerland	43.89	179.13	Sfr	25.25	5.21	Groupe Indosuez Fd Mgt Co	Equity	Luxembourg
Groupe Indosuez Switzerland	43.89	179.13	Sfr	25.25	5.33	Groupe Indosuez Fd Mgt Co	Equity Growth	Investmentfds Deutschland
Swiss Mkt Index Quant UnLvrgd	43.84	N/A	Sfr	1.96	N/A	Millenium Asset Mgmt (ire)	Equity	Offshore Territories
FL Trust Switzerland	43.75	149.23	Sfr	32.94	3.87	Banque Ferrier Lullin	Equity	Luxembourg
UBS Eqty Inv Switzerland	43.74	200.76	Sfr	2,360.98	4.43	UBS	Equity	Swiss Mutual Funds
UBS Eqty Inv Switzerland	43.74	200.76	Sfr	2,360.98	4.43	UBS	Equity Growth	Investmentfds Deutschland
SBC 100 Index-Fund Switzerland	43.62	219.26	Sfr	1,270.53	4.15	Swiss Bank Corporation	Equity	Swiss Mutual Funds
SBC Eq Fd Switzerland	43.41	205.63	Sfr	593.96	4.25	Swiss Bank Corporation	Equity	Swiss Mutual Funds
Pictet Valsuisse	43.31	196.44	Sfr	177.66	4.52	Pictet & Cie	Equity	Swiss Mutual Funds
Deka Schweiz	43.2	N/A	DM	48.62	4.66	Deka	Equity Growth	Investmentfds Deutschland
Leu Swiss Equities	42.8	N/A	Sfr	78.6	N/A	Swiss Investment Company	Equity	Swiss Mutual Funds
UBZ Swiss Equity Fund	42.72	N/A	Sfr	54.05	4.52	UeberseeBank AG	Equity	Swiss Mutual Funds
UBZ Swiss Equity Fund	42.72	N/A	Sfr	54.05	4.52	UBZ	Equity Growth	Investmentfds Deutschland
CS Equity Fund Swissac	42.65	221.69	Sfr	143.77	4.55	Credit Suisse AM Funds	Equity	Swiss Mutual Funds
Prevista Actions Suisses	42.07	226.99	Sfr	N/S	N/A	Prevista	Equity Growth	Swiss Foundation Funds
BEC Swissfund	42.01	211.81	Sfr	N/S	4.23	BEC Fund Administration	Equity	Swiss Mutual Funds
UAP Swiss Securities	40.78	189.92	Sfr	28.99	4.24	Union Assurances Paris	Equity	Luxembourg
Synchrony Swiss Stocks	40.4	N/A	Sfr	42.03	N/A	Synchrony SA	Equity	Swiss Mutual Funds
ONDA SVIZZERA	40.06	182.64	Sfr	32.31	4.3	Banca del Gottardo	Equity	Swiss Mutual Funds
Multihelvetia	39.86	190.76	Sfr	169.54	4.3	Banca della Svizzera Italiana	Equity	Swiss Mutual Funds
CMI GNF Swiss Equity	39.5	154.32	Sfr	10.76	4.65	CMI Global Network Fund	Equity	Luxembourg
CMI GNF Swiss Equity	39.5	154.32	Sfr	10.76	4.75	CMI Global Network Fund (LUX)	Equity Growth	Investmentfds Deutschland
AAA Actions Suisse Multi	39.48	N/A	Sfr	N/S	N/A	E.I.M. S.A.	Equity Growth	Swiss Foundation Funds
Coutts GF Swiss Equity	39.42	N/A	Sfr	18.45	N/A	Coutts & Co – Global Fd	Equity	Offshore Territories
Coutts GF Swiss Equity	39.42	N/A	Sfr	18.45	N/A	Coutts & Co – Global Fd	Equity Growth	Investmentfds Deutschland
DIT Fonds Schweiz	39.05	199.59	DM	111.67	4.52	DIT	Equity Growth	Investmentfds Deutschland
CICM CB Switzerland Basket	38.47	207.83	Sfr	134.2	4	CICM Fund Mgmt Ltd	Equity	Offshore Territories
CICM CB Switzerland Basket	38.47	207.83	Sfr	134.2	4	CICM Fund Mgmt Ltd	Equity Growth	Investmentfds Deutschland
RG ZelfSelect Zwitserland	38.46	N/A	G	3.87	N/A	Robeco Groep	Equity Growth	Netherlands Unit Trusts
RBZ Swiss Equity	38.31	178.74	Sfr	13.55	4.19	Rothschild Fund Management AG	Equity	Swiss Mutual Funds

Note: details for some funds may not have been included if the data for the US$ % change for 97/98 is not available

Source: Standard & Poor's Micropal.

BANQUE CANTONALE DE GENEVE
Quai de l'Ile 17, 1211 Geneva 2
Tel: (41) 22 317 2727; Fax: (41) 22 793 5960

CREDIT SUISSE
Place Bel-Air 2, 1211 Geneva
Tel: (41) 22 391 2111; Fax: (41) 22 391 2591

LOMBARD ODIER
11 Rue de la Corraterie, 1211 Geneva 11
Tel: (41) 22 709 2111; Fax: (41) 22 709 2911

PICTET & CIE
29 Boulevard Georges-Favon, 1211 Geneva 11
Tel: (41) 22 705 2211; Fax: (41) 22 781 3131

SALOMON BROTHERS FINANZ AG
Schipfe 2, 8022 Zurich
Tel: (41) 1 215 4500; Fax: (41) 1 215 4590

SMITH BARNEY INTERNATIONAL INC.
6-8 rue de Candolle, 1205 Geneva
Tel: (41) 22 708 0321; Fax: (41) 22 329 1289

UNION DE BANQUES SUISSES
8, Rue du Rhône, 1211 Geneva 2
Tel: (41) 22 388 6111; Fax: (41) 22 388 9652

C) Settlement and transfer

Securities that are the subject of cash deals must be delivered and paid for on the third business day (*Valutatag*) after the trade date. Settlement (DVP) is carried out by SEGA, the Swiss depository and clearing organisation.

D) Commissions and other costs

Brokerage fees are negotiable. In addition, a stock exchange fee of Sfr0.10 per Sfr1,000 is levied.

TAXATION AND REGULATIONS AFFECTING FOREIGN INVESTORS

A) Taxation

Dividends paid by Swiss companies, as well as interest paid on bonds issued by Swiss companies and on Swiss bank accounts, are subject to a 35% Swiss withholding tax. Whereas Swiss investors can fully reclaim such withholding tax, foreign resident shareholders can obtain relief only if they are domiciled in a country that has concluded a double tax treaty with Switzerland. In addition, any interest earned on bank accounts is subject to 35% Swiss withholding tax, although relief under double taxation treaties also applies here.

Exhibit 65.7:
WITHHOLDING TAX

	Dividends %		
Recipient	*Portfolio*	*Substantial holdings*[1]	*Interest %*[2]
Resident corporations and individuals	Nil[3]	Nil[3]	Nil[3]
Non-resident corporations and individuals:			
Non-treaty	35	35	35
Treaty	0–35	0–35	0–35

Notes:
1. A substantial holding arises where the recipient company holds at least the following percentages in the Swiss company's voting power or shares: Trinidad and Tobago, Thailand and Jamaica, 10%; Finland, France and Germany, 20%; Belgium, Bulgaria, Egypt, Greece, Iceland, Indonesia, Ireland, Japan, Korea, Luxembourg, Malaysia, Mexico, Morocco, the Netherlands, Norway, Poland, Portugal, Singapore, Spain, Sri Lanka, Sweden and the UK, 25%; Pakistan, 33.33%; and the US (with some other requirements), 95%.
2. Withholding tax is levied only on interest on bonds, bond-like loans and interest paid by banking institutions.
3. The statutory rate of 35% is levied but refunded, provided the respective earnings are declared as income for tax purposes.

Source: Price Waterhouse.

Stamp tax of 2% is levied on share issues. Such tax is charged either on the nominal value of the newly issued shares or on the price paid by the investor for the new shares, whichever is higher. Exempt from such stamp tax are shares issued on the formation of companies with a capital below Sfr250,000, shares issued in a merger or demerger of companies, and fund certificate issues.

A transfer tax is levied on the transfer of securities if a professional securities dealer participates in such a transaction as a party or as an intermediary. The tax rate is 0.15% for Swiss securities and 0.3% for foreign securities. Money market instruments, Eurobond and foreign share issues, and the underwriting and sale of bonds to investors are, however, exempt from the transfer tax. Trades executed by security dealers for their own trading portfolios are partially (50%) exempt from the tax.

VAT is charged at a rate of 6.5% on the sale of goods and services within Switzerland, but as services rendered to foreign investors are regarded as a tax-exempt export, no VAT is charged on most services (including share transacting and asset management) rendered to foreign investors.

B) Regulations

No exchange controls exist in Switzerland and the Swiss franc is freely convertible into any other currency.

Foreign investors may at any time repatriate their funds deposited in Switzerland as well as any earnings and gains realised on such funds. Foreign investors are generally also free in the choice of their investments.

There are no special regulations on bank deposits held by foreigners in Switzerland. Banks, however, under banking and criminal law must identify the legal owner of any funds deposited with them and, if a trustee or a legal entity appears as the legal owner, must also identify the ultimate beneficial owner of such funds. As banks, financial institutions and other financial intermediaries may not assist in the laundering of funds from criminal origins, they must examine the source of the funds if a criminal origin is suspected. In certain types of "suspicious" transactions, banks will, therefore, demand that the investor explains the source of the funds.

If a bank suspects that a customer's funds stem from criminal origins, and the customer cannot offer a satisfactory explanation, the bank may notify the authorities of its suspicion and, in any event, has to block the funds concerned. Also, under a revision of the Swiss Rules on Money Laundering that will come into force on 1 April 1998, banks, financial institutions and other financial intermediaries will have an obligation to notify the criminal investigation authorities. Any bank that fails to identify the legal or beneficial owner of funds or assists in money laundering activities is itself subject to criminal sanctions.

LISTING AND REPORTING REQUIREMENTS

A) Listing requirements

Companies seeking a listing on the SWX must publish a prospectus. The prospectus must include, among other things, the company's date of incorporation, name and registered domicile; the composition of the share capital; the names of the directors and auditors; the most recent audited financial accounts (and unaudited interim accounts if the most recent audited accounts are older than nine months); details of the dividends paid during the preceding five years; and the names of affiliated or subsidiary companies with a description of their capital. The prospectus must also describe the company's operations and any special risk associated with its business or the securities to be listed. The information in the prospectus must be presented in such a manner that it is not misleading for the average investor.

If investors suffer losses because of an incorrect, incomplete or misleading prospectus, they have a legal claim for damages against any parties (including banks, auditors and attorneys) who have contributed to the publication of the deficient prospectus.

B) Reporting requirements

Listed companies and companies that have issued bonds must publish their accounts in the *Swiss Official Journal of Commerce* or provide, free of charge, copies of such accounts to interested parties. According to listing regulations, listed companies must also disclose unaudited six-monthly accounts and reports to the stock exchange and to the public, and announce any developments that substantially affect the financial situation of the company.

In preparing their accounts, listed companies must apply either FER standards (accounting standards developed by the Swiss Board for Accounting Standards) or internationally accepted standards such as IAS or US GAAP.

SHAREHOLDER PROTECTION CODES

The Federal Stock Exchange Act came into effect in February 1997 and authorises the Federal Banking Commission to supervise all stock market trading and all security dealers operating in Switzerland. The Swiss Exchange acts as central reporting agency on behalf of the Federal Banking Commission.

A) Minority rights

Swiss corporate law does not afford extensive protection to minority shareholders; in principle, the majority shareholders, through their voting power in the shareholders' meeting, can control the board of directors and thereby also the company's business policy. Minority shareholders have the right neither to representation on the company's board nor to any specific share of the company's earnings. Minority shareholders may, however, sue the directors if the directors have wilfully or negligently violated their duties. To gather information on such acts they may ask for special information at the shareholders' meeting and, if the meeting rejects their demand, request a special audit of the company. Such requests may, however, only be filed by shareholders representing 10% of the company's share capital or shares with a nominal value of at least Sfr1 million. The courts will grant a special audit if the shareholders concerned can show that there are reasonable grounds for suspicion that the directors have violated their duties.

B) Significant shareholdings

The new Stock Exchange Act requires shareholders who hold more than 5% of a company's shares, or by acquisitions exceed 5%, 10%, 20%, 33.3%, 50% or 66.6% holding levels in a company's shares, to inform the company and the stock exchange about their holdings.

C) Takeovers and mergers

The new Stock Exchange Act contains rules on tender offers that will enter into force early in 1998. They are designed to ensure that minority shareholders are adequately informed about an offer and are not put under undue pressure to accept it. The Act does not define any standard for the tender price.

In addition, the Act requires any person who has purchased more than 33.3% of a listed company's shares to extend an offer to all shareholders. In such cases, the tender price may not be more than 25% below the price paid by the tenderor for shares of the target company in the preceding 12 months. Companies, however, may exclude the application of the mandatory purchase rule in their articles of incorporation (and several companies have introduced such provisions).

D) Insider trading

Under Article 161 of the Swiss Criminal Code insiders are prohibited from trading on the basis of confidential information. The notion of "confidential information" is, however, severely restricted; the Criminal Code mentions as examples the acquisition of a company, the merger of two companies and the issuance of securities. Courts therefore have decided that information on changes in a company's earnings is not confidential information for the purpose of Article 161.

The SWX surveillance department may forward the results of any investigation to the Federal Banking Commission, which can then forward them to a criminal court.

RESEARCH

Most of the major Swiss banks produce high quality research on the Swiss market, including Bank Julius Baer, Pictet & Cie, Bank Sarasin, Bank J Vontobel, Union Bank of Switzerland, SBC and Credit Suisse.

The following publications are available from the SWX:

Swiss Exchange Monthly Report
Swiss Exchange Annual Report
Listing on the Swiss Exchange
Swiss Exchange Matching Rules
The Federal Act on Stock Exchanges and Securities Trading
The Listing Rules
Swiss Exchange Handbook

Financial newspapers include:

Finanz and Wirtschaft
Finanzmarkt Schweiz
Neue Zurcher Zeitung
Schweizerische Handelszeitung
L'AGEFI
Le Journal de Genève.

Switzerland: A Guide to the Capital and Money Markets, published by Euromoney Books, provides in-depth information for those wishing to invest or do business in the country. See the order card at the back of this book for details.

CHAPTER

66

Taiwan

Introduction

The monetary authorities in Taiwan are slowly but surely liberalising the restrictions on foreign investment. From March 1996 foreign individuals and corporations have been permitted to buy shares directly, up to an annual limit of US$5 million and US$10 million respectively. Foreign institutional investors meeting certain criteria have been able to invest in the market directly since December 1990. The tight regulations on capital inflows and outflows have also been relaxed significantly, and the ceiling on foreign ownership of domestic shares is now 25% of total market capitalisation.

There were 404 companies listed on the Taiwan Stock Exchange (TSE) at the end of 1997, and total market capitalisation stood at NT$9,402.28 billion (US$288.07 billion). Although the listed companies cover a wide range of industries, the market is dominated by the banking and insurance sector and electronics companies, which together accounted for 29.5% and 23.9% of total market capitalisation respectively at the end of 1997. Investors are predominantly individuals, accounting for 90.7% of turnover in listed shares.

ECONOMIC AND POLITICAL OVERVIEW

The political agenda in 1997 was dominated by the local government elections held in November. In a shock result, the ruling Kuomintang Party lost its majority, raising doubts about its political future. The opposition Democratic Progressive Party, which favours Taiwan's independence from the mainland, won more than half of the seats contested. News of the result had a negative impact on the stock market, sending share prices sharply lower as doubts emerged over the future course of economic policy.

Taiwan did not escaped the effects of the Asian currency crisis in the second half of 1997. Interest rates were initially raised to help protect the Taiwanese dollar from speculative attack, though the government subsequently allowed the currency to fall to maintain its competitiveness against its regional neighbours. The currency depreciated by more than 20% between the beginning of July and the end of December 1997. However, the fundamental economic situation in Taiwan remains favourable. The country continues to generate a large current account surplus, inflation is low and corporate balance sheets are in much better shape than elsewhere in the region. Real GDP growth is estimated at 6.4% in 1997, compared with 5.7% in 1996. Interest rates are expected to come down as the regional crisis subsides, and economic growth could pick up further in 1998.

Role of the central bank

The Central Bank of China (CBC) is both the government bank and an agency under the Executive Yuan (parliament). It issues local currency, controls the money supply, credit and public debt via its authority over interest rates and bank reserve requirements, and acts as the government's fiscal agent, overseeing all foreign exchange operations.

The CBC's objectives are to foster a stable CPI level and moderate economic growth, to promote full employment, and contribute to a favourable balance of payments situation. The levers used by the CBC to achieve these targets include money supply management and bank credit control via reserve ratios. The bank works with the Ministry of Finance to oversee the financial markets and financial institutions.

MARKET PERFORMANCE

A) In 1997

From early on in the year it became apparent that the economy was beginning to recover and, during the first

Exhibit 66.1: TAIWAN SE WEIGHTED PRICE INDEX (US$), 1993–97

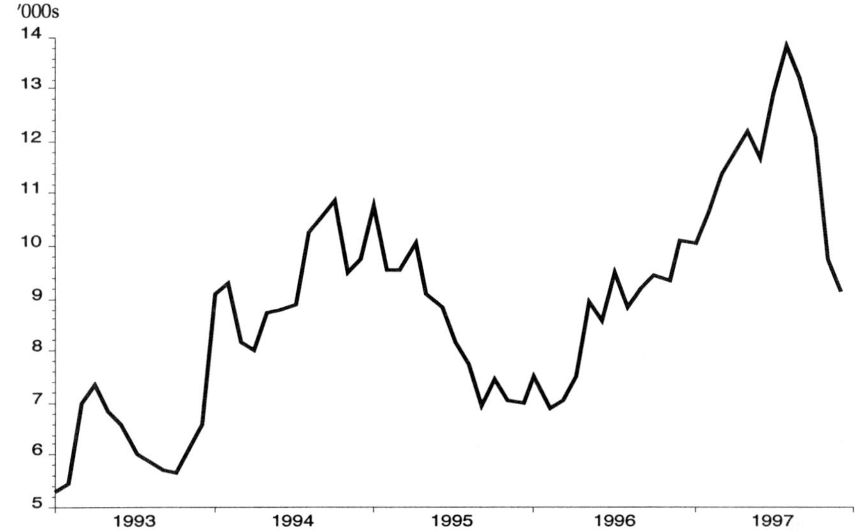

High value 13825.90 1.8.97 Low value 5283.34 1.1.93 *Source: Datastream*

eight months, this helped push the stock market to new highs. The TSE Index shot up from the year's low of 6,820.35 on 4 January, the first trading day, to the year's high of 10,116.84 on 26 August. Daily trading value reached a new record high of NT$297.1 billion on 17 July.

From September, however, the over-bought market started to fall. The crisis in south-east Asia and the depreciation of the Taiwanese dollar contributed to negative sentiment, with the TSE Index moving to a lower trading range of 7,000–8,000. At the year-end the market closed at 8,187.27, up 18% over the 12-month period.

B) Summary information

Global ranking by market value (US$ terms, end-1997): 12
Market capitalisation (end-1997): US$288.07 billion
Growth in market value (local currency terms, 1993–97): 82.7%
Market value as a % of nominal GDP (end-1997): 115.7%
Number of domestic/foreign companies listed (end-1997): 404/0
Market P/E (all listed companies, end-1997): 27.04
MSCI Index (change in US$ terms, 1997): -6.9%
Short-term (3-month) interest rate (end-1997): 7.65%
Long-term (10-year) bond yield (end-1997): 6.45%
Budget deficit as a % of nominal GDP (1997): 7.53%
Annual increase in broad money (M3) supply (end-1997): 10.5%
Inflation rate (1997): 0.8%
US$ exchange rate (end-1997): NT$32.638

C) Year-end share price index, price/earnings ratios and yields

Exhibit 66.2:
YEAR-END TSE INDEX, AVERAGE P/E AND DIVIDEND YIELDS, 1993–97

Year-end	*TSE Index*	*P/E*	*Yield (%)*
1993	6,070.56	34.7	0.8
1994	7,124.66	33.5	2.2
1995	5,158.65	21.3	3.9
1996	6,933.94	29.0	3.4
1997	8,187.27	27.0	2.8

Source: Taiwan Stock Exchange.

D) Market indices and their constituents

There are three popular market indices in Taiwan. The TSE Capitalisation-Weighted Stock Index is the oldest and the most widely quoted. It is a weighted share price index, comparable in construction to the Standard and Poor's 500 Index in the US and the Tokyo Stock Exchange Stock Price Index, where a wide selection of listed shares are weighted according to the number of shares outstanding.

The Economic Daily News Index and the Commercial Times Index are also quoted.

THE STOCK MARKET

A) Brief history and structure

The origin of the securities market in Taiwan is closely

connected with the 1954 land reform: to compensate large landowners for land that was redistributed to farmers, the owners received bonds and shares in four large government-owned enterprises. Economic growth in subsequent years led to the emergence of a new middle class with funds available to support a securities market.

The government set about creating the market with the establishment in 1960 of the Securities and Exchange Commission, renamed in 1997 the Securities and Futures Commission (SFC). The SFC has broad authority to supervise all aspects of securities dealings, including public offerings, the day-to-day operations of trading markets and the business of securities companies. The TSE was incorporated two years later. It is managed by a 15-member board of directors and three supervisors. The SFC appoints five of the directors and one of the supervisors.

During the 1980s, the SFC focused on improving the management of a rapidly growing stock market. Steps were taken to computerise trading, improve accounting standards and procedures, increase the number of qualified certified public accountants and financial analysts, and liberalise and clarify the legal framework for issuing and trading securities. As a result, the TSE has become one of the most technologically advanced markets in Asia.

The Taiwan Securities Central Depository Corporation (TSCD) began operations in January 1990, and provides centralised custodial services.

Regulations have been proposed to authorise the trading of futures and options on the TSE Index.

B) Different exchanges

The TSE in Taipei is the only official stock exchange in Taiwan, although there is also a small OTC market.

C) Opening hours, names and addresses

Trading hours are Monday to Friday from 9.00am to 12.00 noon, and Saturdays from 9.00am to 11.00am.

TAIWAN STOCK EXCHANGE CORPORATION
7–10th Floors, City Building
85 Yen-Ping South Road, Taipei
Tel: (886) 2 2311 4020; Fax: (886) 2 2311 4004

ROC (OTC) SECURITIES EXCHANGE
15F No. 100, Sec 2, Roosevelt Road, Taipei
Tel: (886) 2 2369 9555; Fax: (886) 2 2369 1300

MARKET SIZE

A) Number of listings and market value

At the end of 1997 there were 404 companies listed on the TSE with a market capitalisation of NT$9,402.3 billion (US$288.1 billion), an increase of 24.9% over the year.

Exhibit 66.3:
NUMBER OF COMPANIES LISTED AND MARKET VALUE, TSE, 1993–97

Year-end	*No. of companies*	*Market value (NT$ billion)*
1993	285	5,145.4
1994	313	6,504.3
1995	347	5,108.4
1996	382	7,537.4
1997	404	9,402.3

Source: Taiwan Stock Exchange.

Exhibit 66.4:
MARKET VALUE BY SECTOR, TSE, END-1997

Sector	*Market value (NT$ billion)*	*% of total*
Banking and insurance	2,771.54	29.48
Electronics	2,253.20	23.96
Textiles	602.47	6.41
Construction	495.56	5.27
Plastics	487.92	5.19
Steel	367.73	3.91
Food and feeds	344.43	3.66
Electric and machinery	298.29	3.17
Transportation	274.29	2.92
Others	253.54	2.70
Automobile	234.72	2.50
Wire and cable	199.38	2.12
Cement	185.42	1.97
Department stores	143.77	1.53
Chemicals	141.89	1.51
Rubber	114.48	1.22
Pulp and paper	87.66	0.93
Glass and ceramics	82.05	0.87
Tourism	44.39	0.47
Conglomerates	19.55	0.21
Total	**9,402.28**	**100.00**

Source: Taiwan Stock Exchange.

B) Largest quoted companies

The 20 largest quoted companies accounted for 39.3% of total market capitalisation at the end of 1997.

Exhibit 66.5:
THE 20 LARGEST QUOTED COMPANIES, TSE, END-1997

Ranking	*Company*	*Market value (NT$ billion)*
1	Cathay Life Insurance	506.47
2	TSMC	297.27
3	United Micro Electronics	263.54

Exhibit 66.5 continued

4	First Bank	246.30
5	China Develop	242.83
6	Hua Nan Bank	236.84
7	Chang Hwa Bank	223.10
8	Shin Kong Life Insurance	188.00
9	China Steel	181.75
10	Nan Ya Plastic	170.40
11	Asustek Computer	166.99
12	Formosa Plastic	157.68
13	ICBC	122.57
14	ASE	116.45
15	Chiao Tung Bank	104.81
16	United World Chinese Commercial Bank	102.05
17	ACER	95.21
18	Formosa Chemical & Fiber	93.84
19	China Trust Commercial Bank	92.59
20	Far East Textile	85.92

Source: Taiwan Stock Exchange.

C) Trading volume

Share turnover increased by 188.5% in 1997 to NT$37,241.2 billion.

Exhibit 66.6:
SHARE TURNOVER, TSE, 1993–97

Year	*Share trading value (NT$ billion)*
1993	9,056.7
1994	18,812.1
1995	10,151.5
1996	12,907.5
1997	37,241.2

Source: Taiwan Stock Exchange.

Exhibit 66.7:
THE 20 MOST ACTIVELY TRADED SHARES, TSE, 1997

Ranking	*Company*	*Trading volume (shares million)*
1	United Micro Electronics	20,828
2	TSMC	13,690
3	China Steel	13,669
4	Hualon-Teijran	13,539
5	ACER	12,373
6	Winbond Electronics Corp	12,326
7	Mosel Vitelic	11,179
8	Macronix International	10,981
9	ASE	9,367
10	BES Engineering Corp	7,180
11	China Develop	6,954
12	Mitac International Corp	6,746
13	Pacific Electric Wire & Cable	6,533
14	China Petrochemical	6,528
15	Walsin Lihwa	5,914
16	Compal Electronic	5,822
17	Yageo	5,570
18	Liton Electronic	5,404
19	Chuntex Electronic	5,400
20	Shinkong Synthetic Fibers	5,378

Source: Taiwan Stock Exchange.

TYPES OF SHARE

Most securities listed on the TSE are ordinary shares. A small number of preferred shares and corporate bonds have also been listed on the TSE, but neither type of security is common in Taiwan.

Regulations have been issued to enable foreign companies to list Taiwan Depository Receipts (TDRs) on the TSE or on the over-the-counter market, but no company has yet done so.

Currently the only TSE listed equity derivatives are convertible bonds.

OTHER MARKETS

A few public companies have listed their shares on a small over-the-counter (OTC) market operated by the ROC Over-the-Counter Securities Exchange. However, the OTC market is more active in the trading of government and corporate bonds.

INVESTORS

The Taiwan stock market is dominated by individual investors, who account for 90.7% of total turnover in listed shares. Many local institutions, such as banks, insurance companies or pension funds, are prohibited or restricted from investing in listed shares. Foreign involvement in the market through qualified foreign institutional investors and mutual funds is small but growing.

OPERATIONS

A) Trading system

All shares must be traded through the stock exchange where a fully automated trading system (FAST) is in use for most listed stocks.

The broker or trader enters details of an order through his terminal into the main computer of the exchange, and

Exhibit 66.8:
TOP PERFORMING COUNTRY FUNDS – TAIWAN

Fund	US$ % change 01/01/97 01/01/98	US$ % change 01/01/93 01/01/98	Fund base currency	Fund size (US$ mil)	Fund volatility	Management group	Opal main sector	Opal subsector
Taiwan Arbitrage Co Ltd	31.91	N/A	US$	11.086	-1	Regent Fund Mgr	Open-End	Equity
GT Taiwan	28.51	109.6	US$	34.9	11.91	LGT	Open-End	Equity
Regent Underval Ast Taiwan 3	25.11	N/A	US$	27.6	8.918	Regent Fund Mgr	Closed-End	Equity
JF Taiwan Trust	23.31	N/A	US$	40.6	-1	Jardine Fleming	Open-End	Equity
Formosa Growth Fund	21.33	129.43	US$	361	8.891	Kwang Hua Sec	Closed-End	Equity
New Taipei Fund	13.92	125.03	US$	69.55	9.074	National Inv	Closed-End	Equity
BGI Instit'l Taiwan	13.27	N/A	US$	N/A	-1	Barclays	Open-End	Equity
Taiwan Equity Fund Inc	12.82	N/A	US$	48.73	11.34	Daiwa	Closed-End	Equity
Thornton Taiwan Equity Growth	10.04	103.81	US$	35.1	8.425	Thornton	Open-End	Equity
ImPac AP Taiwan	9.8	N/A	US$	0.7	-1	Impac Asset M	Open-End	Equity
Baring Taiwan Fund Ltd	9.27	N/A	US$	66	10.15	Barings	Closed-End	Equity
Schroder Taiwan	9.06	N/A	US$	168.3	10.774	Schroders	Open-End	Equity
Taiwan Opportunities Fund Ltd	8.88	N/A	US$	191.5	8.56	Martin Currier	Open-End	Equity
Formosa Fund	8.69	74.83	NT$	6417	9.866	Kwang Hua Sec	Closed-End	Equity
NM ASF Taiwan	6.76	N/A	US$	63.2	-1	National Mutual	Open-End	Equity
Taipei Fund NAV	5.16	81.53	NT$	532.3	8.969	National Inv	Closed-End	Equity
Taiwan American Fund	5.15	N/A	US$	31.3	-1	Martin Currier	Closed-End	Equity
Taiwan Investment Trust	4.36	N/A	£	N/A	8.664	Tyndall	Closed-End	Equity
Taiwan Capital	2.81	N/A	US$	45.8	9.977	Govett & Co	Open-End	Equity
Taiwan Investment Company	-1.06	N/A	US$	38.75	-1	Foreign & Col	Open-End	Equity
INVESCO Taiwan Growth	-1.75	52.19	US$	40.1	8.618	Invesco Intl	Open-End	Equity
Taiwan Index Fund	-2.43	68.97	US$	230.64	9.498	Barclays	Closed-End	Equity
GP Taiwan Index Fund Ltd	-2.7	N/A	US$	1729.9	8.63	Grand Pacific	Open-End	Equity
Yamaichi Dynamic Taiwan Fd	-5.73	N/A	US$	11	9.586	Yamiachi Euro	Open-End	Equity
Govett Taiwan OTC	-7.09	N/A	US$	13.1	-1	Govett & Co	Open-End	Equity
Jupiter Tyndall GF Taiwan	-7.47	N/A	US$	3.8	9.492	Tyndall	Open-End	Equity
Paribas EM Taiwan Ptfl	-11.12	N/A	US$	N/A	9.342	Paribas Asset	Open-End	Equity
ROC Taiwan Fund	-11.22	23.83	US$	289.94	-1	Intl Inv Trus	Closed-End	Equity

Note: details for some funds may not have been included if the data for the US$ % change for 97/98 was not available

Source: Standard & Poor's Micropal.

all orders are executed based on TSE trading rules. During trading hours, the basic functions of the FAST trading system are as follows:

- to collect orders from brokers;
- to sort the orders on a price and time priority basis;
- to execute orders;
- to log the market price;
- to send order confirmation reports to brokers;
- to send trade reports to brokers; and
- to send market data to brokers and quote vendors.

The par value of stock has been standardised at NT$10 and the standard board lot is 1,000 shares. All shares now conform to these specifications.

Trading prices are subject to limits of 7% up or down from the previous trading day's closing price. The SFC has stated that these limits will be relaxed, and eventually abolished, but no schedule has been announced.

B) List of principal brokers

CAPITAL SECURITIES
15F, 87 Chung Hsiao E Rd Sec 4, Taipei
Tel: (886) 2 2777 1077; Fax: (886) 2 2751 9281

CORE PACIFIC SECURITIES
2F, 237 Fuhsing S Rd Sec 1, Taipei
Tel: (886) 2 2706 7777; Fax: (886) 2 2708 5393

FUBON SECURITIES
B1F, 237 Chienkuo S Rd Sec 1, Taipei
Tel: (886) 2 2754 2866; Fax: (886) 2 2708 3242

GRAND CATHAY SECURITIES
3F, 17 Hsuchang St, Taipei
Tel: (886) 2 2383 1111; Fax: (886) 2 2314 2206

JIH-SUN SECURITIES
3F, 111 Nanking E Rd Sec 2,Taipei
Tel: (886) 2 2504 8888; Fax: (886) 2 2507 1047

MASTERLINK SECURITIES
1F, 209 Fuhsing S Rd Sec 1, Taipei
Tel: (886) 2 2731 3888; Fax: (886) 2 2731 3350

NATIONAL SECURITIES
7F, 2 Chungking S Rd Sec 1, Taipei
Tel: (886) 2 2349 5123; Fax: (886) 2 2349 5080

POLARIS SECURITIES
3F, 270 Chung Hsiao E Rd Sec 4,Taipei
Tel: (886) 2 2776 6288; Fax: (886) 2 2711 3294

PRESIDENT SECURITIES
1F, 14, Lane 228, Nanking E Rd Sec 5,Taipei
Tel: (886) 2 2747 8266; Fax: (886) 2 2746 3799

SALOMON BROTHERS TAIWAN LIMITED
Walsin Financial Building, 9th Floor
No. 117 Min Sheng East Road, Sec 3, Taipei, 10646
Tel: (886) 2 719 6647; Fax: (886) 2 718 0582

SMITH BARNEY SECURITIES INVESTMENT CONSULTING CO. LTD. – SICE
207, Sec. 2, Tun Hua S. Road, 15th Floor, Taipei
Tel: (886) 2 2 739 1233; Fax: (886) 2 2 739 6161

TAIWAN INTERNATIONAL SECURITIES
31 F, 97 Tunhwa Rd Sec 2, Taipei
Tel: (886) 2 2708 4567; Fax: (886) 2 2326 2828

TAIWAN SECURITIES
1F, 123 Nanking E Rd Sec 2,Taipei
Tel: (886) 2 2507 5000; Fax: (886) 2 2507 1100

YUAN TA SECURITIES
12F, 225 Nanking E Rd Sec 3,Taipei
Tel: (886) 2 2717 7777; Fax: (886) 2 2717 0743

C) Settlement and transfer

Delivery and settlement are handled by the computerised Exchange Clearing Department. Sales of shares by brokers and traders are offset by purchases of the same issue on the same day, so that only net balances of equity are delivered. Similarly, only net balances of cash are computed and paid. Settlement via delivery of stock or payment of cash must be made to the commissioning broker by the next business day.

In 1990, the exchange established the Taiwan Securities Central Depository (TSCD). The settlement of securities transactions in the TSE market is now handled by the TSCD via its book entry system. Settlement takes place on T+2.

D) Commissions and other costs

Brokerage commission rates for stocks, warrants and beneficiary certificates range from 0.1425% to 0.1% depending on the size of the transaction.

E) Custodian and nominee services

In 1990 the TSCD became the centralised custodial service for all listed shares. In general, use of TSCD custody services is not mandatory, but brokers are linked to it by computer and take-up is increasing. Nominee services are not available.

TAXATION AND REGULATIONS AFFECTING FOREIGN INVESTORS

A) Exchange controls

The Republic of China (ROC) government has a comprehensive system of currency controls. A resident individual may convert up to US$5 million per year from foreign currency into Taiwanese dollars, and a resident company or a resident individual may convert up to US$5 million per year from Taiwanese dollars into foreign currency. Trade payments, technology transfer fees, payments to foreign construction companies and certain other similar payments are permitted without limit. In general, any other conversion of currency involving Taiwanese dollars requires central bank approval.

B) Taxation

Capital gains on the sale of ROC shares are not subject to income tax. Transfers of shares and bonds are subject to securities transaction tax at 0.3% and 0.1%, respectively, payable by the seller.

Exhibit 66.9:
WITHHOLDING TAXES

Recipient	*Dividends %*	*Interest %*
Resident corporations	15	10[1]
Resident individuals	15	10[1]
Non-resident corporations and individuals:	35[2], 25[3]	20

Notes:
1. Withholding tax on bank interest is 10%, on transferable certifi-

cates of deposit 20%, and on short-term commercial paper 20%.
2. The withholding rate is 20% for an approved investment project under the Statute for Investment by Overseas Chinese or the Statute for Investment by Foreign Nationals.
3. The withholding tax rate for dividends distributed by a company to an enterprise having no fixed place of business within the ROC is reduced to 25%.

Source: Price Waterhouse.

C) Foreign investment

The monetary authorities are slowly continuing to liberalise regulations restricting foreign investment. The government has announced that individual foreigners and corporations are permitted to buy shares directly up to an annual limit of US$5 million and US$10 million respectively. In addition, foreign institutions with approval from the central bank and securities regulators can now buy listed shares, and the limit on investment by any single institution has been raised from US$400 million to US$600 million. Repatriation of capital is also to be significantly deregulated, scrapping the three-month rule and allowing immediate repatriation. The rule allowing investors to remit earnings only once a year has been abolished.

In the meantime, however, the four specific channels established to encourage limited foreign investment into the TSE continue to operate. First, five securities investment trust enterprises (SITEs) have established a total of nine mutual funds for investment in ROC securities. In general, the SITE purchases the securities and issues its own securities, called "beneficial certificates", to a foreign depository or to a special-purpose foreign investment company. The depository or investment company then issues depository receipts or shares to investors, which are traded on prominent overseas exchanges.

These mutual funds may invest either in listed shares or in government, corporate or financial bonds. In general, dividends are subject to 15% withholding tax when paid to the SITE and an additional 5% withholding tax when paid by the SITE to the foreign investor. Interest is subject to 10% withholding tax when paid to the SITE and an additional 10% withholding tax when paid by the SITE to the foreign investor. If a bond is redeemed by the issuer, the difference between the redemption price and the price paid by the SITE is considered interest, and taxed accordingly.

Secondly, since 1991, more than 233 "qualified foreign institutional investors" (QFIIs) have received permission to invest specified amounts of money on the TSE. A QFII must be a major bank, insurance company, fund manager or foreign brokerage firm that meets the SFC's criteria for total assets, net worth, years of experience and/or amounts of securities holdings.

A QFII may invest in listed shares or government or corporate bonds, beneficiary certificates or money market instruments, but not in convertible bonds. In general, a QFII may hold up to 10% of the shares of a listed company, but all foreigners together may not hold more than 25% of the shares of any listed company. Additional restrictions or prohibitions apply to investment in certain companies involved in businesses in which foreign investment is restricted or prohibited. Margin trading is not permitted. Up to 30% of a QFII's remitted funds may be invested in time deposits of up to three months. Other cash assets must be kept in demand accounts.

Each QFII must appoint a local custodian, a local agent to exercise shareholders' rights and a local broker. Each purchase or sale must be supported by a written order from the QFII and settlement must be confirmed by the custodian and completed by the following trading day. In general, dividends or interest paid to a QFII are subject to 20% withholding tax.

Two other channels exist for foreign investment in certain listed companies. Twenty-six companies have issued global depository receipts (GDRs) and 35 companies have issued "Euro-convertible bonds" – ie bonds that are convertible into the issuer's common stock. Dividends paid on GDRs are subject to a 20% withholding. Interest paid and gains at redemption on Euro-convertible bonds are subject to a 20% withholding.

LISTING AND REPORTING REQUIREMENTS

A) Listing requirements

The TSE is undertaking a large-scale review of its initial listing regulations in an effort to make them less rigorous and more flexible.

When a company applies for initial listing, a portion of its shares, as specified according to the level of its paid-in capital, must be offered publicly. In the case of a listed company applying for an increase of capital for cash, at least 10% of the increased capital must also be publicly offered, and 10–15% of the increased amount must be offered to the issuer's employees.

B) Reporting requirements

All listed companies must submit to the SFC annual, semi-annual and quarterly financial statements and monthly operating reports. The SFC requires that financial reports of listed companies be audited by accounting firms consisting of at least three certified public accountants and be signed by at least two certified public accountants. Criminal liability exists for accountants who are knowingly involved in the preparation of fraudulent financial reports.

In addition, a listed company must report within two days any event that may have a material impact on the market for its shares. In this regard, the SFC has specifically requested listed companies to announce within two days any sale or purchase of assets exceeding 20% of its paid-up capital, or a different amount as prescribed by the SFC.

SHAREHOLDER PROTECTION CODES

A) Significant shareholdings

Listed companies must file with the SFC and announce to the public the class, number and par value of all shares held by any director, supervisor, manager or holder of more than 10% of its total shares. Any transfer by any such person must be reported to the SFC by the issuer and the transferor.

B) Insider trading

Trading by "insiders" based on unannounced material information is prohibited. For this purpose, the term "insider" includes directors, supervisors, managers and shareholders holding 10% of the issuer's equity, plus their spouses, minor children and nominees, any person who has learned such information due to his occupation or controlling relationship with the issuer, and any person who has learned such information from any of the foregoing. The SFC has instituted a system for monitoring stock prices to curb trading abuses. Since the beginning of 1991, several well-publicised insider trading cases have been prosecuted. Investors also have initiated civil actions against company directors and major shareholders for damages. Sanctions, including prison terms and treble damages, have been awarded.

The SFC itself does not have criminal or civil enforcement powers. Criminal actions may be prosecuted only by district attorneys on the recommendation of the SFC. Civil actions may only be brought by investors who assert that they have suffered damage. The SFC is empowered to curb abuses and violations of applicable laws and regulations through administrative measures such as issuing warnings, imposing fines and revoking licences.

RESEARCH

Brokerage firms provide general information and analysis on trends in the market. Many brokerage firms maintain limited research facilities and produce monthly publications in Chinese.

Also, many brokerage firms are affiliated with securities investment consulting enterprises (SICEs) – companies established specifically to provide investment and trading advice.

To facilitate the dissemination of financial and other data, the TSE has developed an investor's information system called the "Stock Market Observation Post". Through the terminals set up in trading halls of securities firms, or through line-feeds provided by information vendors, potential investors can make enquiries about the current financial and operational data of listed companies, and can receive news on material events that might affect the company.

The following publications are available from the TSE:

The Status of Securities Listed on the Taiwan Stock Exchange (monthly)
Taiwan Stock Exchange Monthly Review
Taiwan Stock Exchange Statistical Data (annual)
Charts of Stock Indices, Trading Volume and Value (annual)
Taiwan Stock Exchange Annual Report
Highlights of Taiwan Securities Trading (annual)
Listed Companies and Securities Firm Directory (annual)
Taiwan Stock Exchange Factbook (annual)

CHAPTER

67

Thailand

Introduction

The 35% decline in the Stock Exchange of Thailand (SET) Index in 1996 paled in comparison with the bleak realities of 1997. The index began the year at 832 and, after reaching a high of 859 on 22 January, it plunged 46% to 459 in mid-June. The 2 July decision to float the Thai baht prompted a rally that saw the equity market surge to 682, but this petered out as instability enveloped the whole region, and the index began a long slide on thin volume to eventually close out 1997 at 372.69 – down 55.2% for the year.

The market remains unrepresentative of the real economy due to large private industrial holdings and substantial foreign direct investment. Year-end market capitalisation of US$24.0 billion represented only 15.3% of 1997 GDP. Market value is concentrated in the banking, communication, energy and finance sectors, which accounted for 53% of year-end capitalisation. Financial stocks accounted for 54% of daily trading value and the banking sector alone provides approximately half of the market's profits.

Stockbroking is slowly being liberalised after a painful year for Thai financial institutions, but there have been few concrete changes due to strong opposition from existing brokers. During 1997, the authorities closed down 56 finance companies, 25 of which had broking operations. Some of the closed firms hope to resume operations after recapitalisation, but most are unlikely to survive.

ECONOMIC AND POLITICAL OVERVIEW

In 1997, GDP contracted by approximately 0.3%, compared with 7.0% growth in 1996. The slowdown occurred against a crisis background as Thailand's currency, the baht, was floated on 2 July and halved in value by the end of the year. The main factors behind the GDP turnaround were prime rates of above 15% during the second half, export growth of only 3.8%, manufacturing production falling by 16.4% and private investment falling by 5%. Private consumption also fell by 4.0% as retail sales, automobiles, consumer electronics and VAT receipts all came in short of expectations. In a macro context, the slowdown was attributed to adjustments in the Thai economy after a decade of double-digit growth, fuelled in recent years by easy borrowing and lax central bank controls.

From Bt25.77 to the US dollar at the end June 1997, the currency fell to Bt47.25 at the year-end. The Bank of Thailand had been intervening in both the domestic and overseas foreign exchange markets since July 1996 to prevent "speculative attacks", but by February 1997, the scale of the central bank's intervention efforts had risen dramatically. As the three-month roll for May 1997 came due, it became apparent to speculators that the baht peg was unlikely to be sustained. Despite the central bank implementing a two-tier currency system on 15 May to try to sterilise offshore and onshore baht, by end June, having wiped out US$39 billion in currency reserves, the Bank of Thailand allowed the baht to float. By early August, with the three-month roll again creating pressure, Thailand agreed to a US$17.2 billion IMF programme. With the IMF's assistance, year-end reserves rose to US$27 billion, but the central bank still had US$18 billion of forward positions outstanding. Finally, on 30 January 1998, the Bank of Thailand lifted the constraints of the two-tier system.

The consumer price index was steady in 1997 at 5.6%, with food prices rising by 7.1% and non-food items by 4.4%. The projected inflation rate for 1998 is 16.2%, somewhat subject to currency swings. While core inflation remains manageable, the precarious financial situation has been a concern since early 1997 and the governments efforts to prop up weak financial institutions continues to cause concern.

The estimated 1997 current account deficit of US$3.0 billion represents 1.9% of GDP as against 7.9% in 1996. This persistently high deficit is due mainly to the trade balance,

Exhibit 67.1: BANGKOK SET PRICE INDEX (US$), 1993–97

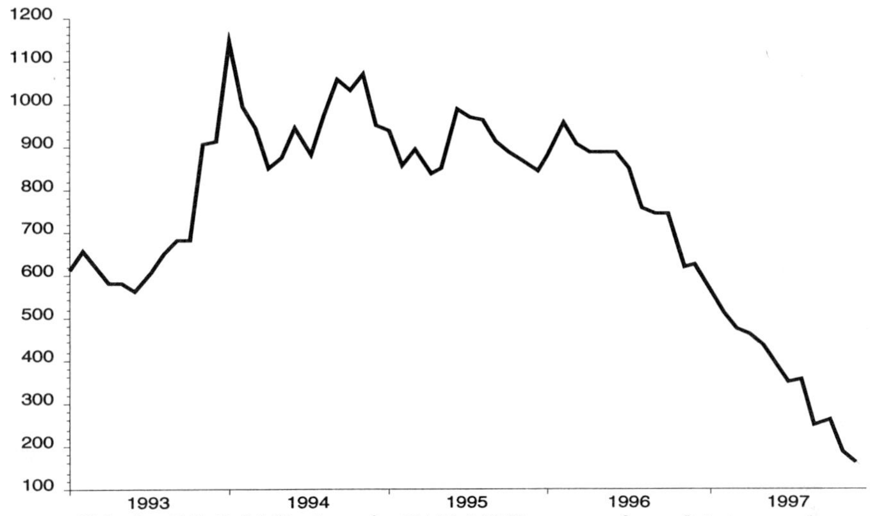

High value 1141.42 3.1.94 Low value 164.34 1.12.97 *Source: Datastream*

which has been exacerbated by over-investment. Following devaluation, it is no surprise that Thailand recorded its first balance of payments deficit (US$10.0 billion) since 1985.

In November 1997, Chuan Leekpai formed a Democrat-led coalition, replacing General Chavalit's bungling administration with well-respected bureaucrats. While Chuan has a thin majority, the opposition is in disarray and the educated urban classes are behind him. His government has deftly handled ongoing negotiations with the IMF, made real progress on the domestic financial crisis and inspired a degree of foreign confidence.

Role of the central bank

The Bank of Thailand (BOT) has traditionally outlined its priorities as establishing an inflation-controlled monetary policy, a stable foreign exchange rate and a tight fiscal policy. However, throughout the 1990s, its foreign exchange policy (based on a basket of currencies) left the bank with little real control over monetary policy, which led to excessive capital inflows and liquidity in the market.

Until 1995, the BOT was held in very high esteem. However, a series of errors of judgement and questionable dealings through 1996–97 have left whole departments within the BOT under threat of disbandment. Beginning with fraud and concealment over the problems at the Bangkok Bank of Commerce in 1996, and the general state of the whole financial system throughout 1997, the BOT has been dealt blow after blow. Its ill-advised handling of the currency reserves and the financial meltdown that occurred from July 1997 onwards also helped undermine the bank's reputation. There were a record number of retirements at the BOT in 1997 and, by the time the Ministry of Finance is through, there may be many more in 1998.

MARKET PERFORMANCE

A) In 1997

It was a year of worsening disappointments for Thai investors. Following a lukewarm January rally, the SET Index rose 3.3% to 859 on 22 January. However, it then began to stumble on rumours about the stability of finance companies. By end-February, when Finance One (once Thailand's largest finance company) went bust, the index had plummeted 17.7%. The market then fell away steadily to 459 in mid-June, before rising 41% to 657 in the post-devaluation rally. As instability hit the whole region in August, however, the SET Index began a long and largely uninterrupted slide of 43% to 372.69 at the year-end. For the 12 months as a whole, the index lost 55.2% in baht terms and 75.7% in US dollar terms.

During 1997 market capitalisation fell 75.0% from US$95.9 billion to US$24.0 billion and average daily turnover fell 68.2% from US$209.6 million to US$66.6 million.

B) Summary information

Global ranking by market value (US$ terms, end-1997): 40
Market capitalisation (end-1997): US$23.99 billion
Growth in market value (US$ terms, 1993–97): -81.96%
Market value as a % of nominal GDP (end-1997): 15.3%

Number of domestic/foreign companies listed (end-1997): 431/0
Market P/E (all common shares, end-1997): 6.59
MSCI Index ("Thailand Free", US$ terms, 1997): -74.3%
Short-term interest rate (end-1997): 19.99%
Long-term bond yield (average 1997): 11.5%
Budget deficit as a % of nominal GDP (1997): 2.31%
Annual change in broad money (M2) supply (US$ terms, Nov 1997): -27.99%
Inflation rate (1997): 5.7%
US$ exchange rate (end-1997): Bt47.25

C) Year-end share price index, price/earnings ratios and yields

Exhibit 67.2:
SET INDEX, P/E AND DIVIDEND YIELDS, 1993–97

Year-end	*SET Index*	*P/E*	*Yield (%)*
1993	1,682.85	26.09	2.01
1994	1,360.09	19.51	1.86
1995	1,280.81	19.75	2.25
1996	831.57	11.97	3.50
1997	372.69	6.59	6.04

Source: Thailand Securities Depository Co.

D) Market indices and their constituents

The two most widely recognised indices of the stock market are the SET Index and the SET 50, both calculated by the exchange. The SET Index includes all corporate securities and mutual funds in its calculation. The SET 50 comprises 50 of the largest capitalisation and most liquid stocks in the market.

The SET Index (base 30 April 1975 = 100) and the SET 50 (base 16 August 1995 = 100) calculate current market value by taking the price of the most recent trade in each stock.

THE STOCK MARKET

A) Brief history and structure

The Bangkok Stock Exchange Company, established as a partnership in 1962, was the first organised stock exchange in Thailand.

In May 1974 the Securities Exchange of Thailand Act was passed, incorporating some of the recommendations of the Robbins Report (sanctioned in 1969). The Act established a new exchange, the Securities Exchange of Thailand (renamed the Stock Exchange of Thailand in January 1991), which began operations on 30 April 1975 with 14 quoted securities.

The SEC Act of 1992 was enacted to provide a regulatory framework for the capital markets. Under the Act the SEC became responsible for the regulation and supervision of the primary market while the secondary market remained the responsibility of the SET.

The SET is operated by an 11-member board of governors. Five members are appointed by the SEC, another five are appointed by the member companies, and a full-time president is an ex-officio member. The board of governors is responsible for the formulation of policy and the control of exchange operations. Rules and regulations prescribed by the board require SEC approval.

Only member companies of the SET are authorised to buy or sell securities on the SET. Membership is limited to securities companies licensed by the SET to engage in securities business as stockbrokers.

B) Different exchanges

The SET is the principal stock exchange in Thailand.

C) Opening hours, names and addresses

SET trading hours are from 10.00am to 12.30pm and 2.00pm to 4.30pm, Monday to Friday.

STOCK EXCHANGE OF THAILAND
132 Sindhorn Building, 2/Floor, Wireless Road, Bangkok 10330
Tel: (66) 2 254 0960; Fax: (66) 2 254 3032
Web site: www.set.or.th

MARKET SIZE

A) Number of listings and market value

The number of companies listed on the SET fell from 454 at the end of 1996 to 431 at end-1997. Due to the sluggish economy and the depreciation of the currency, 1997 year-end market capitalisation fell 75% to US$23.9 billion.

Exhibit 67.3:
NUMBER OF LISTED COMPANIES AND MARKET VALUE, SET, 1993–97

Year-end	*No. of companies listed*	*Market value (US$ million)*
1993	347	133,015.73
1994	389	132,030.18
1995	416	142,582.75
1996	454	95,928.00
1997	431	23,986.11

Source: Stock Exchange of Thailand.

Exhibit 67.4:
SECTOR RANKINGS BY MARKET CAPITALISATION, SET, END-1997

Ranking	*Sector*	*Market capitalisation (US$ million)*
1	Banking	4,953.34
2	Energy	3,851.53

Exhibit 67.4 continued

3	Communications	2,291.83
4	Transportation	2,126.80
5	Entertainment	1,142.58
6	Building and furnishing materials	1,097.35
7	Electronic components	869.44
8	Property development	794.38
9	Chemicals and plastics	713.66
10	Food and beverages	594.01
11	Finance and securities	587.55
12	Pulp and paper	572.33
13	Insurance	570.01
14	Commerce	532.84
15	Agribusiness	522.24
16	Textiles, clothing and footwear	456.87
17	Hotel and travel services	421.55
18	Electrical products and computer	183.50
19	Packaging	167.26
20	Vehicles and parts	146.20
	Other	593.42

Source: Stock Exchange of Thailand.

B) Largest quoted companies

At the end of 1997 the SET's largest company was PTT Exploration and Production, which accounted for 11% of total market value. The top 20 companies represented 60% of SET capitalisation.

Exhibit 67.5:
THE 20 LARGEST LISTED COMPANIES ON THE SET, END-1997

Ranking	*Company*	*Market value (US$ million)*
1	PTT Exploration and Production	2,689.94
2	The Bangkok Bank	1,822.82
3	Thai Airways International	1,585.18
4	Advanced Info Service	1,148.95
5	The Thai Farmers Bank	1,015.87
6	BEC World	812.69
7	Electricity Generating	706
8	Siam Cement	609.52
9	Delta Electronics	507.93
10	Bangkok Expressway	435.92
11	Telecom Asia Corporation	414.01
12	The Bangkok Bank of Commerce*	398.71
13	Siam Commercial Bank	387.14
14	Shinawatra Computer & Communications	369.60
15	Advance Agro	342.78
16	Krung Thai Bank	306.85
17	Siam Makro	292.06
18	Grammy Entertainment	222.22
19	Bank of Ayudhya	211.64
20	First Bangkok City Bank	200.91

*Suspended 15 May 1997.

Source: Stock Exchange of Thailand.

C) Trading volume

In value terms, 1997 turnover decreased 61% to US$19.67 billion, and average daily turnover was down from US$209.6 million to US$79.6 million. Total volume for 1997 rose to 20,902.35 million shares, compared with 1996's 19,359 million.

Exhibit 67.6:
EQUITY TRADING VALUE ON THE SET, 1993–97

Year	*Turnover (US$ million)*
1993	88,045.92
1994	84,554.42
1995	61,398.37
1996	50,934.00
1997	19,674.02

Source: Stock Exchange of Thailand.

Exhibit 67.7:
SET TRADING VALUE BY TYPE OF SECURITY, 1997

Security	*Turnover (US$ million)*
Ordinary shares	17,587.77
Unit trusts	120.97
Warrants	1,965.25
Total	**19,674.02**

Source: Thailand Securities Depository Co.

Exhibit 67.8:
THE 20 MOST ACTIVELY TRADED SHARES BY VALUE, SET, 1997

Ranking	*Company*	*Trading value (US$ million)*
1	Thai Farmers Bank	3,103.46
2	The Bangkok Bank	3,047.10
3	Industrial Finance Corp of Thailand	2,258.02
4	PTT Exploration and Production	774.41
5	Telecom Asia Corporation	752.79
6	Phatra Thanakit	752.34
7	Siam Cement	751.20
8	Safari World	710.25
9	Advanced Info Service	635.26
10	Siam Commercial Bank	600.54
11	BEC World	439.25
12	Bank of Ayudhya	414.84
13	National Finance and Securities	357.25
14	Dhana Siam Finance and Securities	356.58
15	Tipco Asphalt	323.59
16	Krung Thai Bank	313.20
17	Bangkok Expressway	293.94
18	Nava Finance and Securities	280.44
19	Bumrungrad Hospital	243.11
20	Charoen Pokphand	229.14

Source: Stock Exchange of Thailand.

TYPES OF SHARE

Shares, unit trusts, warrants and short-term warrants for shares and convertible debentures are currently traded on the SET.

OTHER MARKETS

An SEC-approved OTC market – the Bangkok Stock Dealing Centre (BSDC) – was set up in November 1995. It is intended to serve the needs of companies not yet qualified for listing on the SET.

A Derivatives Market Act is expected to be passed during 1998. Although over-the-counter derivatives are not treated as "securities", the SEC, with a view to encouraging the development of the OTC market, has resolved to allow securities companies to buy and sell derivatives and conduct limited related activities.

INVESTORS

Since the 1980s, foreign investors have played an increasing role in the Thai market, and there has been significant extra interest over the past three years. Foreign investor transactions on the SET have increased from 26% of total trading value in 1995, to 34% in 1996 and 44% in 1997.

OPERATIONS

A) Trading system

Trading is conducted on three separate boards: the main board is for regular trading; the special board is for big lots, odd lots and bonds; and the foreign board is for trading by foreigners once foreign ownership has reached its specified limit.

All trading in listed securities must take place through member securities companies and, unless they have special permission, members may not trade listed securities outside the SET. In order to trade securities in the OTC market, members must become dealers.

The automated electronic trading system of the SET (Asset) was implemented in June 1991. The system has a capacity of over 400,000 transactions daily and processes in real time, transmitting information to members' offices nationwide. Orders are given priority first according to price and then according to the time they were placed. The two main trading alternatives under the ASSET system are automatic order matching (AOM) and put-through (PT).

The trading system used will depend upon which board the shares are being traded on. On the main board, a minimum transaction must constitute at least one board lot (100 shares if priced below Bt500 each, and 50 shares if priced above Bt500) or a multiple thereof. When a transaction in one single lot exceeds Bt10 million (US$0.4 million) in market value or 10% of the registered paid-up capital (whichever is lower), members must, after obtaining SET approval, conduct the trade on the special board as a big lot transaction.

Short selling will be permitted on the SET from 1 January 1998. Regulations have been formulated concerning short selling and securities lending, under which the SET will decide which shares may be short sold. Brokers must ensure that securities are available within the clearing house deadline, must disclose the risks involved to clients and must require them to open a margin account. Secondly, lending for the purpose of purchasing securities is now a "securities business" and requires a licence. Licences may be issued to banks, finance companies, securities companies and financial institutions. The purpose of the loan must be to settle a short sale or for other defined purposes.

B) List of principal brokers

The SET's membership is limited to securities companies licensed by the Minister of Finance to engage in securities trading and banking. Some of the main brokers are listed below:

ABN AMRO
4th Floor, CP Tower Building, 313 Silom Road
Bangrak, Bangkok 10500
Tel: (66) 2 638 2950; Fax: (66) 2 231 0345

CREDIT LYONNAIS SECURITIES
14th Floor, Maneeya Centre Building, 5 18/5
Ploenchit Road, Pathumwan, Bangkok 10330
Tel: (66) 2 652 0827; Fax: (66) 2 652 0834

DRESDNER KLEINWORT BENSON
26/F, Abdul Rahim Place, 990 Rama IV Road
Bangkok 10500
Tel: (66) 2 636 1880/1; Fax (66) 2 636 1870

JARDINE FLEMING THANAKOM SECURITIES
191 Silom Complex, 29th Floor, Silom Road
Bangrak, Bangkok 10550
Tel: (66) 2 231 3730

MERRILL LYNCH INTERNATIONAL BANK
Suite 303, Tower A, Diethelm Tower, 93/1
Wireless Road, Bangkok 10330
Tel: (66) 2 252 31356; Fax: (66) 2 266 3137

PHATRA THANAKIT
252/6 Samnakyan Muangthai-Phatra 1 Building
5-16th Floor, Rajadapisek, Huaykwang 10310
Tel: (66) 2 256 1503/05

Exhibit 67.9:
COUNTRY FUNDS – THAILAND

Fund	*US$ % change* 01/01/97 01/01/98	01/01/93 01/01/98	Fund base currency	Fund size (US$ mil)	Fund volatility	Management group	Opal main sector	Opal subsector
JF Thailand	-33.55	18.78	US$	117.4	7.429	Jardine Fleming	Open-End	Equity
Thai Development Capital Fund	-35.38	-23.46	US$	27.538	5.279	Crosby Asst M	Closed-End	Equity
Nikko GlUF Thailand Fund	-36.62	N/A	US$	1.1	7.581	Nikko	Open-End	Equity
Dres Thornton ASF Thailand	-49.52	N/A	US$	6.4	10.121	Thornton	Open-End	Equity
Nomura Aurora Tailand	-56.29	N/A	¥	23465	-1	Nomura ITMCo	Open-End	Equity
Thai Rural Equity	-57.17	N/A	Bt	759.67	7.085	Mutl Fd Publi	Private	Equity
MBf Thailand	-57.52	-81.28	US$	0.3	8.52	MBf	Open-End	Equity
HSBC Thai Equity	-60.75	N/A	US$	10.4	-1	HSBC Asst Mgt	Open-End	Equity
Barclays ASF Thailand	-61.88	-52.8	US$	7.6	13.491	Barclays	Open-End	Equity
Siam Fund (Cayman) Ltd	-62.19	-47.22	US$	39	9.768	Indosuez	Closed-End	Equity
Siam Selective Growth	-62.85	-46.66	£	N/A	11.297	Bermuda Intl	Closed-End	Equity
Bangkok Fund	-64.07	-57.41	US$	196.74	7.684	Merrill Lynch	Closed-End	Equity
MFC Invesco Thailand	-65.57	N/A	US$	1.1	-1	Invesco Intl	Open-End	Equity
Fidelity Fds Thailand	-67.48	-48.23	US$	172	13.297	Fidelity	Open-End	Equity
Sinchada Fund	-67.74	N/A	Bt	619.93	10.509	Mutl Fd Publi	Closed-End	Equity
Sinpattana Fund	-68.45	N/A	Bt	406.93	9.367	Mutl Fd Publi	Closed-End	Equity
Thai Prime Fund	-68.47	-64.18	US$	318.42	-1	Nomura Intl	Closed-End	Equity
Sinpinyo Four	-68.94	-79.87	Bt	710.85	9.964	Mutl Fd Publi	Closed-End	Equity
Old Mutual Thailand	-68.97	-51.85	£	4.8	13.589	Old Mutual	Open-End	Equity
Sinpinyo Five	-69.04	-77.81	Bt	2055.8	10.598	Mutl Fd Publi	Closed-End	Equity
Sub Thawee Two	-69.43	-59.85	Bt	1902.8	10.465	Mutl Fd Publi	Closed-End	Equity
Thai Capital Fund Inc.	-70.03	-64.77	US$	81.7	10.816	Daiwa	Closed-End	Equity
Thai-Euro Fund Ltd (Undiluted)	-70.42	-64.95	US$	292.66	11.117	Lloyds GSY	Closed-End	Equity
SCB Prime Fund	-70.76	-71.06	Bt	760.87	14.441	SCB Asst Mgt	Closed-End	Equity
Abtrust New Thai IT	-70.99	-61.15	£	N/A	9.681	ABTRUST	Closed-End	Equity
SCB Munkhong Fund	-71.4	-69.29	Bt	2895.9	12.033	SCB Asst Mgt	Closed-End	Equity
Satang Daeng	-71.56	N/A	Bt	1007.5	11.054	Mutl Fd Publi	Closed-End	Equity
Satang Daeng Two	-71.65	N/A	Bt	594.38	11.065	Mutl Fd Publi	Closed-End	Equity
Sub Anan Fund	-71.75	-72.4	Bt	1537.3	11.177	Mutl Fd Publi	Closed-End	Equity
Adkinson Growth Fund 1/97	-71.83	N/A	Bt	591.53	12.679	Mutl Fd Publi	Closed-End	Equity
Ruam Pattana Two	-72.33	-65.67	Bt	9056.6	11.055	Mutl Fd Publi	Closed-End	Equity
Siam City	-72.65	N/A	Bt	1024.3	10.841	Mutl Fd Publi	Closed-End	Equity
Siam City Two	-72.65	N/A	Bt	719.77	11.457	Mutl Fd Publi	Closed-End	Equity
Roong Roj One	-73.9	N/A	Bt	771.79	11.162	Mutl Fd Publi	Closed-End	Equity
Sinpinyo Seven	-74.55	N/A	Bt	1575.6	12.196	Mutl Fd Publi	Closed-End	Equity
Nakornthon Fund	-74.61	N/A	Bt	798.12	12.317	Mutl Fd Publi	Closed-End	Equity
ImPac AP Thailand	-75.14	N/A	US$	2.1	-1	Impac Asset M	Open-End	Equity
Paribas EM Thailand Ptfl	-75.91	N/A	US$	N/A	14.323	Paribas Asset	Open-End	Equity
Thai Fund Inc.	-76.93	-74.73	US$	281.82	12.913	Morgan Stanley	Closed-End	Equity
Thailand Growth Fund	-66.83	-60.39	US$	118.8	10.529	Nikko	Private	Equity
Thailand International Fund	-71.29	-61.75	US$	291.45	11.044	Fidelity	Closed-End	Equity
Thana Phum	-73.35	-79.01	Bt	1282.9	12.013	Mutl Fd Publi	Closed-End	Equity
Thornton New Tiger Thailand	-48.39	-23.14	US$	12.5	11.493	Thornton	Open-End	Equity
United Fund	-73.34	N/A	Bt	389.26	11.846	Mutl Fd Publi	Closed-End	Equity

Note: details for some funds may not have been included if the data for the US$ % change for 97/98 is not available

Source: Standard & Poor's Micropal.

SALOMON BROTHERS ASIA PACIFIC LTD – BRANCH OFFICE
Sintorn Tower 3, 27th Floor,
130–132 Wireless Road, Pathumwan,
Bangkok 10330
Tel: (66) 2-263-3800; Fax: (66) 2-263-3770

SECURITIES ONE
101/1 SG Tower Mahadlekluang 3
Rajdamri Road, Lumpini, Patumwan,
Bangkok 10330
Tel: (66) 2 652 1234

C) Settlement and transfer

SET trading is cleared and settled by the Thailand Securities Depository Company (TSD), established in November 1994 as a subsidiary of the SET. At the end of the trading day, TSD sends a report of net trading and net cash balances to members via computer, or failing this a written report is sent the following day. Securities must be settled by T+3 in accordance with G30 recommendations.

D) Commissions and other costs

In 1997 the SET revised its brokerage commission rate rules. The old fixed rates, which were applied to all types of investors, remain unchanged as guidelines: 0.5% of the trade value for listed common stocks and warrants on common stocks; and 0.3% of the trade value for unit trusts and warrants on unit trusts. The new rules will have an impact on the inter-broking firms, but retail investors will not be affected. The changes can be summarised as follows:

- Brokers are now free to negotiate commission rates with sub-brokers.
- Brokers can now also negotiate commission rates with foreign brokers, but the minimum charge must not be less than 60% of the fixed rate of 0.5%.

Brokers can negotiate commission rates with foreign investors, but the minimum charge is the fixed rate of 0.5%.

E) Custodian and nominee services

Because most foreign investors do not wish to receive physical delivery of securities, custodian services are widely available. Major banks offering custodian arrangements include Citibank, Deutsche, HSBC and Standard Chartered.

Nominee services are available from most brokers. Foreign brokers and banks tend to base their nominees in Singapore to take advantage of the double taxation treaty and resultant exemption from capital gains tax.

TAXATION AND REGULATIONS AFFECTING FOREIGN INVESTORS

A) Taxation

All Thai companies pay corporate income tax (net profit tax) at the rate of 30%. However, the Board of Investment (BOI) provides waivers for up to eight years for investment promotion and partial waivers (at a 15% rate) for an additional four years to promote investment in certain areas.

There are no withholding taxes levied on payments of interest and royalties to resident corporations, except in the case of interest on deposits or negotiable instruments paid by a bank or finance company, where the withholding tax rate is 1%. Payments of interest, dividends and royalties to resident individuals are subject to withholding tax at personal income tax rates, with the following exceptions:

1. There is a withholding tax at a flat rate of 15% on interest on bank deposits, loans to a finance company and debentures of listed companies.
2. Listed company dividends are subject to withholding taxes of 0–10%.

Withholding tax on interest, dividends and royalties paid to non-resident corporations and individuals is at 0–15%.

Exhibit 67.10:
WITHHOLDING TAX

Recipient	*Dividends %*	*Interest %*
Resident corporations	Nil/10[1]	Nil/1[2]
Resident individuals	10	15
Non-resident corporations and individuals:		
Non-treaty	10	15
Treaty	10	3–15

Notes:
1. The nil rate applies to a recipient company that is listed on the SET, or a company that holds 25% or more of the share capital in the dividend-paying company for at least three months before and after the dividends are earned.
2. The 1% rate is in respect of interest on deposits or negotiable instruments paid by a bank or a finance company.

Source: Price Waterhouse.

B) Non-resident bank accounts

Non-resident accounts can be opened freely by persons who are ordinarily not resident in Thailand. Accounts maintained by non-residents are of two types – transferable or blocked.

Credits to non-resident transferable accounts must emanate from:

- baht derived from the sale to authorised agents of foreign currency remitted from abroad;

- baht transferred from other non-resident transferable accounts (suitable evidence must be produced that the remitter also enjoys non-resident transferable status);
- expense allowances payable to non-residents; or
- baht payments from residents who have received exchange control approval to remit funds abroad or into non-resident transferable accounts.

The funds in non-resident transferable accounts may be used for any purpose, including payment to residents in Thailand and the purchase of foreign exchange to be remitted abroad. No overdraft facilities are permitted on non-resident transferable accounts.

Non-resident blocked accounts can be opened using deposits emanating from local sources and remittances from abroad. This type of account may only be operated in Thailand and remittances from abroad are allowed subject to the prior approval of the exchange control authorities. No overdrafts are permitted on these accounts.

C) Exchange controls

The Bank of Thailand began liberalising corporate exchange controls in 1990, allowing easier conversion and outward remittance of foreign currency. In 1991 it announced that the proceeds of investment in securities comprising capital gains, dividends and share certificates could be freely remitted overseas.

D) Foreign ownership restrictions

Under the Alien Business Act, foreign shareholdings are generally limited to a maximum of 49%. Foreign shareholdings may be further limited by laws governing (a) specific areas of business (eg, banks, finance and insurance companies), (b) investment promotion licences and (c) concession permits, or by a particular company's memorandum or articles of association.

In June 1997, as a result of amendments to the Commercial Banking Act, majority foreign ownership of banks and finance companies will be permitted by the Ministry of Finance on a case-by-case basis, for a maximum period of 10 years. Thereafter, foreign-owned shares in banks and finance companies will not be compulsorily expropriated but foreign owners will suffer gradual dilution of control because future capital issues may only be subscribed for by Thai companies or individuals. This will apply until the foreign-owned shares are reduced to less than 49% of capital.

REPORTING REQUIREMENTS

Companies intending to make public offerings of their shares and those with shares listed on the SET are required by the SEC Act to submit reports on the following events to the SEC and the SET without delay:

- when the company suffers any serious damage;
- when operations are partially or entirely interrupted or suspended;
- when the company's corporate objectives or lines of business are changed;
- when the company's operation or management is partially or wholly surrendered to a third person by contractual arrangements;
- when the company is involved in a takeover bid as defined by Section 247 of the SEC Act;
- when there is an incident of such type and magnitude that it will have a bearing on the rights of securities holders or will affect investment decisions or the prices of securities.

The above reports are additional to regular reports and information that the company must furnish in the form of prospectuses, listing statements and periodical financial statements. Listed companies must submit quarterly and semi-annual unconsolidated, unaudited (but reviewed) financial statements to the SET within 45 days of the end of the period to which they relate. Consolidated statements must follow within 60 days of the period-end.

From 1 January 1999, companies will be required to include comparative cash flow statements in their quarterly, semi-annual and annual reports.

The SET or the SEC, as the case may be, has sole discretion to demand additional information or personal statements from directors or officers of the company.

SHAREHOLDER PROTECTION CODES

A) Significant shareholders

Directors, officers, managers and auditors of a company that has offered shares to the public must report to the SEC the amount of securities they hold in the company in combination with their respective spouses and minor children. They are also required to file reports when there is a change in their holdings.

If an individual's shareholding in a company increases or decreases by an amount equivalent to 5% or more of the total shares issued, the change in holding must be reported to the SEC on the following business day and a copy of the report must be sent to the SET. If warrants or convertible instruments covering 5% or more of the issued share capital are acquired or disposed of, a report must also be submitted on the business day after the transaction.

B) Market manipulation

Chapter 8 of the SEC Act contains broad provisions relating to unfair practices that constitute a violation of the SEC Act. A broker company, an issuing company or such companies' directors, officers or managers are prohibited from disseminating, circulating or giving misleading information about the financial status, results of operations or prices of shares of companies traded on the SET or OTC market. No broker company, management of a broker company or company issuing securities is allowed to give information relating to downward or upward trends of share prices unless the information has been given to the SET. It is unlawful for any person to spread rumours with a view to moving share prices up or down.

Members of the management staff, auditors, SET or SEC officials may be liable for conspiracy to defraud other investors if they or their family members are found soliciting buying or selling shares on the SET or the OTC market by using insider information. It is a violation of the SEC Act for anyone to manipulate share prices or to corner the market.

C) Tender offers

An individual acquiring 5% or more of the shares of a company in a 12-month period and, as a result, taking his total ownership up to 50% from his original holding of 25% or more, is required to make a tender offer to buy shares from the public. The same requirement is imposed upon any individual who wishes to purchase or acquire 25%, 50% or 75% or more of all the issued shares of a company while their current holding is less than 25%, 50% or 75% respectively. Anyone who acquires up to 50% of a target company as a result of a public tender offer may not within a six-month period after the closing date of the tender offer acquire more shares in the company at a higher price or under conditions that are more favourable to potential sellers than those stipulated in the original tender offer.

D) Separation of clients' assets

Regulations were formulated in 1997 covering the separation of clients' assets from brokerage company assets. Such assets must be ring-fenced and maintained in separate accounts; brokers must obtain clients' consent to deal with their assets; errors in postings to accounts must be corrected on the day that they occur; and brokers must send clients an account of transactions at least once a month.

E) Regulatory authority

The supervision of the securities industry is the responsibility of the SEC located at:

14th–16th Floor, Diethelm Tower B93/1 Wireless Road
Lumpini, Patumwan, Bangkok 10330
Tel: (66) 2 252 3223; Fax: (66) 2 256 7737

RESEARCH

Local broker research on the Thai stock market is not extensive and foreign brokers produce the bulk of English language fundamental research on the major Thai companies. Firms with fully staffed teams on the ground who are most highly regarded include ABN Amro/HGA, Crédit Lyonnais, Jardine Fleming, Dresdner Kleinwort Benson, Merrill Lynch and Phatra Thanakit. In addition, the SET produces a fact book and a yearly report, which contain extensive statistical information on market performance.

PROSPECTIVE CHANGES

In December 1997, a comprehensive restructuring project for Thailand's capital markets was announced as part of Thailand's IMF-supervised recovery programme. The planned changes include an improved bankruptcy law requiring finance and securities businesses to separate their business operations; increased disclosure concerning the performance of public companies; increased capital of securities companies in proportion to margin loans extended; the speedy passage of a bill to regulate the derivatives market; the lifting of restrictions on foreign ownership of securities brokerage firms; tax changes to allow equal treatment for investors on the SET and the Bangkok Stock Dealing Centre; and the regular issue of government bonds with a two-year maturity to set a benchmark for medium- and long-term debt instruments.

CHAPTER

68

Trinidad and Tobago

Introduction

Market capitalisation on the Trinidad and Tobago Stock Exchange (TTSE) rose by 122.4% in 1997, ending the year at TT$19.68 billion. There were 26 companies quoted on the exchange, including two foreign listings (Canadian Imperial Bank of Commerce WI Holdings and Life of Barbados Limited), both based in Barbados.

The equity market is open to foreign investors but is concentrated, with the five largest companies accounting for nearly 67% of total capitalisation, and Republic Bank alone accounting for 18.3%. Turnover in the five most actively traded stocks represented almost 62% of the total in 1997.

ECONOMIC AND POLITICAL OVERVIEW

Trinidad and Tobago is an independent republic with a democratically elected parliament. In November 1995 the United National Congress, led by Basdeo Panday, in partnership with the National Alliance for Reconstruction, came to power.

Macroeconomic performance continued to strengthen during 1997 with real output growing by 3.2%. This expansion was achieved against a background of low inflation (3.65%) and a balance of payments surplus for the fifth consecutive year.

The government continued its tax reform programme in 1997 with a view to strengthening the tax base, lowering taxes and making the system more transparent and efficient. Increased revenue (resulting mainly from increases in capital receipts and grants) helped the government to end the year recording a surplus of 1.36% of GDP.

Role of the central bank

The central bank's objectives in 1997 continued to focus on maintaining exchange rate stability, fostering a low inflation environment and facilitating increases in the levels of savings and investment. To this end the monetary authorities made increased use of open market operations as a tool for liquidity management.

The exchange rate of the Trinidad and Tobago dollar relative to the US dollar depreciated by 1.6% during 1997.

MARKET PERFORMANCE

A) In 1997

The TTSE Composite Share Index ended 1997 at 352.30, up 110.4% on the end-1996 figure of 167.41, while market capitalisation increased during the year by 122.4% to TT$19.68 billion. The volume of shares traded in 1997 was 100.7 million, valued at TT$846.1 million.

B) Summary information

Global ranking by market value (US$ terms, end-1997): 56
Market capitalisation (end-1997): US$3.12 billion
Growth in market value (local currency terms, 1993–97): 590.4%
Market value as a % of nominal GDP (end-1997): 45.0%
Number of domestic/foreign companies listed (end-1997): 24/2
Market P/E (top six companies, end-1997): 14.76
Short-term (3-month) interest rate (end-1997): 6.75%
Long term (10-year) bond yield (end-1997): 9.95%
Budget deficit as a % of nominal GDP (1997): 0.44%
Annual increase in broad money (M3) supply (end-1997): 1.6%
Inflation rate (1997): 3.65%
US$ exchange rate (end-1997): TT$6.299

C) Year-end share price index, price/earnings ratios and yields

Exhibit 68.1:
YEAR-END SHARE PRICE INDEX, P/E RATIOS AND GROSS DIVIDEND YIELDS, 1993–97

Year-end	*TTSE Composite Index*	*P/E*	*Yield (%)*
1992	60.2	11.4	7.0
1993	82.5	8.3	7.0
1994	88.6	13.0	6.7
1995	150.2	10.3	5.3

Exhibit 68.1 continued

1996	167.4	10.3	4.6
1997	352.3	14.8	3.8

Source: Trinidad and Tobago Stock Exchange.

D) Market indices and their constituents

The TTSE Composite Index tracks the performance of all shares listed on the exchange and is based at January 1983 = 100.

THE STOCK MARKET

A) Brief history and structure

A securities market existed informally in Trinidad and Tobago for well over 20 years prior to the opening of the Trinidad and Tobago Stock Exchange. The market achieved significance when, in the early 1970s, the government decided as a matter of policy to "localise" the foreign-owned commercial banking and manufacturing sectors of the economy. The thrust of the policy was to encourage such companies to divest and sell a majority of their shares to nationals.

The two bodies chosen to effect this policy were the Capital Issues Committee, set up to direct developments in the primary market, and the Call Exchange (an association of share dealers), established to monitor activities in the secondary market. With this infrastructure in place, the decision was taken to establish rules and regulations to facilitate the orderly development of the domestic capital market.

The TTSE is managed by a board of directors consisting of 11 individuals. The policies of the board and day-to-day operations are administered by a general manager and a deputy general manager. Policy proposals are prepared by management and submitted to the board or its various committees as appropriate. Only when policies are approved by the board are they implemented.

A second-tier market (for public companies with securities that are not fully transferable and, therefore, cannot be granted a full listing) began operating in 1996.

There are six TTSE member firms. The requirements for membership include standards for minimum capital, independence, skill and suitability. The Membership Committee ensures conformity with the rules governing the conduct of members, as well as compliance with capital requirements by member firms. In return for the right to execute transactions on the floor of the exchange, members are charged a monthly fee of 2% of the commission they earn.

B) Opening hours, names and addresses

The exchange hours are Monday to Friday from 8.00am to 4.00pm.

TRINIDAD AND TOBAGO STOCK EXCHANGE
65 Independence Square, Port of Spain, Trinidad, WI
Tel: (1 868) 625 5107; Fax: (1 868) 623 0089

MARKET SIZE

A) Number of listings and market value

At the end of 1997 the 26 companies listed on the exchange had a market capitalisation of TT$19.68 billion. The five largest companies accounted for close on 67% of this total, with Republic Bank accounting for 18.3%.

Exhibit 68.2:
NUMBER OF LISTED COMPANIES AND MARKET VALUE, TTSE, 1993–97

Year-end	*No. of companies*	*Market value (TT$ million)*
1993	26	2,851.0
1994	27	3,873.9
1995	27	6,750.7
1996	27	8,852.2
1997	26	19,684.4

Source: Trinidad and Tobago Stock Exchange.

Exhibit 68.3:
THE FIVE LARGEST LISTED COMPANIES ON THE TTSE, END-1997

Rank	*Name*	*Market capitalisation (TT$ million)*	*% of market*
1	Republic Bank	3,596.9	18.3
2	CIBC(WI) Holdings	3,403.6	17.3
3	Royal Bank	2,720.1	13.8
4	ANSA McAl	1,784.9	9.1
5	Bank of Nova Scotia	1,589.8	8.1

Source: Trinidad and Tobago Stock Exchange.

B) Trading volume

Exhibit 68.4:
TRADING VOLUME AND VALUE, 1993–97

Year	*Volume ('000)*	*Value (TT$ '000)*
1993	77,908.4	300,970.4
1994	67,625.0	300,891.0
1995	131,651.8	812,395.2
1996	121,347.8	645,996.1
1997	100,746.0	846,076.9

Source: Trinidad and Tobago Stock Exchange.

Exhibit 68.5:
THE 20 MOST ACTIVELY TRADES SHARES ON THE TTSE, 1997

Ranking	*Company*	*Trading value (TT$ million)*
1	Royal Bank	145.9
2	Guardian Holdings	115.7
3	Neal & Massy Holdings	92.4
4	Trinidad Cement	86.7
5	Bank of Commerce	84.9
6	Angostura Holdings	84.4
7	Republic Bank	65.2
8	ANSA McAl	53.0
9	National Flour Mills	22.6
10	Caribbean Communications Network	22.3
11	Agostini's	17.7
12	West Indian Tobacco Company	15.7
13	Bank of Nova Scotia	10.7
14	Pt Lisas Industrial Port Dev Corp	6.3
15	L.J. Williams "B"	6.1
16	Readymix (WI)	5.7
17	Lever Brothers (WI)	3.6
18	Life of Barbados	2.5
19	Berger Paints	1.2
20	Flavorite Food	1.0

Source: Trinidad and Tobago Stock Exchange.

INVESTORS

The great majority of shares are held by institutions, with only an estimated 15% owned by individual investors.

OPERATIONS

A) Trading system

Trading takes place on the stock exchange floor on Tuesday, Wednesday and Friday commencing at 9.30am. Securities are traded in alphabetical order, at the conclusion of which a call-over procedure is employed before trading ends.

Members can act both as agents for clients and as principals for their own accounts. However, clients' orders take precedence over brokers' own transactions.

B) List of member companies

BOURSE SECURITIES
86B Independence Square, Port of Spain, Trinidad, WI
Tel/fax: (1 868) 623 0415/6

CARIBBEAN STOCKBROKERS
67 Independence Square, Port of Spain, Trinidad, WI
Tel: (1 868) 624 4415; Fax: (1 868) 624 4416

MONEY MANAGERS
2nd Floor, Union Club Building
65 Independence Square, Port of Spain, Trinidad, WI
Tel: (1 868) 623 1763; Fax: (1 868) 623 7815

RELIANCE STOCKBROKERS
Gordon Grant Building, 10 St Vincent Street
Port of Spain, Trinidad, WI
Tel: (1 868) 623 6945; Fax: (1 868) 623 8241

TRINIDAD & TOBAGO STOCKS & SHARES
29 Chacon Street, Port of Spain, Trinidad, WI
Tel: (1 868) 623 5961; Fax: (1 868) 625 6713

WEST INDIES STOCKBROKERS
23A Chacon Street, Port of Spain, Trinidad, WI
Tel: (1 868) 623 4861; Fax: (1 868) 627 5002

C) Settlement and transfer

The exchange operates on a cash basis. The settlement period is five business days.

D) Commissions and other costs

The commission charged by members is as follows:

- 1.5% on the first TT$50,000 of consideration;
- 1.25% on the next TT$50,000 of consideration; and
- 1% on the excess.

On every transaction, clients are required to pay 0.1% of the transaction cost, or TT$1.00, whichever is higher. There is no stamp duty.

REGULATIONS AFFECTING FOREIGN INVESTORS

A) Direct investment

Changes in the regulatory structure governing foreign involvement in the securities market have reflected the active attitude that the government is now taking towards encouraging foreign investment in general. The regime is now governed by the Foreign Investments Act. Under this Act, there is no restriction on foreign investment shareholdings in private companies, and there is no absolute bar to investment in any sector. Foreign investors face the same requirements as local investors in areas regulated by legislation, such as commercial banking and finance and the formation and operation of companies.

B) Securities investment

Foreign investors in local public companies are allowed up to a total cumulative shareholding of 30% without the need for a licence. The consideration for shares acquired by a foreign investor must be paid in an internationally traded currency through an authorised dealer (commercial banks) except where, in the case of a company incorporated in Trinidad and Tobago, such consideration is financed out of capital reserves or retained earnings generated from its operations in Trinidad and Tobago.

C) Taxation

Capital gains

Gains on the disposal of chargeable assets within 12 months of acquisition are subject to tax at standard corporate rates.

Withholding tax

Exhibit 68.6: WITHHOLDING TAX

Recipient	*Dividends (portfolio) %*	*Dividends (substantial holdings) %*	*Interest %*
Resident corporations and individuals	Nil	Nil	Nil
Non-resident corporations and individuals:			
Non-treaty:			
Individuals	15	15	20
Corporations	10/15	10/15	20
Treaty:	15	10/15	Nil–20

Source: Price Waterhouse.

LISTING AND REPORTING REQUIREMENTS

A) Listing requirements

Any company seeking a listing on the TTSE must submit an application to the exchange. An application will not normally be considered in respect of any security with an initial market capitalisation expected to be below TT$1 million. A sufficient proportion (normally 25%) of any class of issued equity capital is required to be in the hands of the public – that is, persons who are not associated with the directors or major shareholders – but the TTSE can admit a security where a lower proportion is held by the public if it believes an effective and fair market may operate in the security.

B) Reporting requirements

All listed companies enter into a listing agreement with the exchange. Their disclosure and reporting obligations are governed by this agreement. Among the stipulated obligations is the requirement to notify the Board of the Stock Exchange of any important decisions and to prepare a half-yearly or interim report to be sent to the holders of securities or inserted as a paid advertisement in two leading daily newspapers no later than six months from the date of the notice convening the annual general meeting of the company.

SHAREHOLDER PROTECTION CODES

The Securities Act of 1995 lays down various regulations covering insider trading, false market information and market rigging transactions. Penalties for breach are a fine of TT$200,000 and two years' imprisonment. The Act also imposes disclosure requirements for listing shares, and specifies procedures for the suspension of quoted shares under certain circumstances.

RESEARCH

The TTSE publishes a *Daily Trading and Quotation Summary* on each trading day. This shows, for each security, the opening price; the highest, lowest and closing prices; outstanding bids/offers; and the date of the last transaction.

In addition, a *Weekly Official List* is published. This gives issued capital and dividend information on listed companies; the highest, lowest and closing prices; the sectoral indices; the most actively traded stocks; dealing and settlement dates; and any other data available, such as listed company financial results and dates of annual general meetings.

CHAPTER 69

Tunisia

Introduction

Two new companies were listed on the Tunis Stock Exchange (TSE) in 1997 – Arab Tunisian Lease (a leasing company) and Star (an insurance and reinsurance company). This brought the total number of listed companies up to 33, but even with these new listings, TSE market capitalisation fell by 33.4% in 1997 to TD2,632 million (US$2.29 billion).

The stock market is not very representative of the economy, and accounts for only a relatively small percentage of the capital of the leading banks. Moreover, the lack of reliable market information has had an impact on the role of the stock market in the economy. Companies are still owned mainly by important family groups who generally do not feel comfortable publishing their balance sheets and other financial information. The banks, rather than the stock exchange, therefore tend to be the preferred source of finance for expansion and new projects.

Foreign investors and local investors receive identical fiscal treatment, and capital gains and dividends are not taxed; the only tax is a withholding tax on bonds. Mutual funds are also tax-exempt.

ECONOMIC AND POLITICAL OVERVIEW

Tunisia was under French control until 1956, when independence came with the appointment of President Habib Bourguiba, who remained in power until November 1987. He was succeeded by Zine Al-Abidine Ben Ali, under whose rule the political situation has been very stable.

Tunisia is known for its stability and the conservative fiscal management of its government. The authorities have adopted measures to attract foreign investment, including raising the ceiling for foreign investment on the TSE from 10% to 49%. A free-trade zone agreement operates between Tunisia and the EU, and Tunisia's most important trading partners are France, followed by Italy and Germany.

Tunisia's budget deficit represented an estimated 2.8% of GDP in 1997, up from 2% in 1996. GDP growth, which was maintained at around 4.5% between 1992 and 1996, is expected to increase to 6% between 1997 and 2001, while the inflation rate (4.8% between 1992 and 1996) is expected to fall to 3.7% for the period 1997–2001. Interest rates fell from 7.8% in 1996 to 6.9% in 1997, but are expected to increase slightly in 1998. Tunisia recorded a small balance of payments surplus (1.1%) in 1997.

The country has been rated by IBCA at BBB- for unsecured long-term currency debt obligations, A3 for short-term foreign currency issues and A- for local currency issues.

Tourism, as measured by the number of nights spent by foreigners in the country, increased by 19% year-on-year in 1997, with the industry accounting for 7% of GDP. In the agricultural sector, cereal production fell by 50% in 1997, while olive oil production increased five-fold; fruit production remained steady between 1996 and 1997.

Role of the central bank

The Banque Centrale aims to ensure the stability of the Tunisian dinar in international currency markets. The dinar has been convertible for current transactions since 1993.

The central bank is also responsible for supervising the banking system.

MARKET PERFORMANCE

A) In 1997

The TSE Index fell by 20.2% in 1997, closing at 455.64. Even with the new listings during the year, market capitalisation declined by 33.4% to TD2,632 million, compared with TD3,951 million at end-1996.

The Tunisian market is not very liquid, and the volume of transactions has fallen from TD918 million in 1995, to TD625 million in 1996 and TD454 million in 1997.

B) Summary information

Global ranking by market value (US$ terms, end-1997): 61
Market capitalisation (end-1997): US$2.29 billion
Growth in market value (local currency terms, 1993–97): 163.2%
Market value as a % of nominal GDP (end-1997): 18.2%
Number of domestic/foreign companies listed (end-1997): 33/0
Market P/E (end-1997): 12
Short-term (10-day) interest rate (end-1997): 6.31%
Long-term (5 to 10-year) bond yield (end-1997): 10%
Budget deficit as a % of nominal GDP (end-1997): 2.8%
Inflation rate (1997): 4.8%
US$ exchange rate (end-1997): TD1.15

C) Year-end share price index, price/earnings ratios and yields

Exhibit 69.1:
YEAR-END TSE INDEX, P/E RATIOS AND GROSS DIVIDEND YIELDS, 1993–97

Year-end	*Index*	*P/E*	*Yield (%)*
1993	251.02	12	3.9
1994	507.22	25	2.5
1995	634.71	26	2.5
1996	570.64	23	2.9
1997	455.64	12	4.3

Source: Tunis Stock Exchange.

D) Market indices and their constituents

The TSE Index (base 1990 = 100) includes all companies listed on the exchange except for new introductions, which are included after a one-year period.

THE STOCK MARKET

A) Brief history and structure

The Tunis exchange was established in 1969, but was initially unattractive to foreign investors. Since then, however, the TSE has been enlarged and modernised. In particular, in 1996 the exchange introduced the French Super CAC automated trading system, which it is hoped will correct the problems of lack of transparency and illiquidity that have beset the market since 1991.

The Conseil de Marché Financier (the Tunisian Securities and Exchange Commission) was set up in 1995 and is responsible for overseeing the TSE.

B) Different exchanges

The TSE is the only exchange in Tunisia.

C) Opening hours, name and address

The exchange is open Monday to Friday, from 9.00am to 11.00am. From 9.00 am to 10.00 am orders are registered, and from 10.00 am to 11.00 am there is continuous trading. Price fixing occurs at 10.00am and 10.45am.

BOURSE DES VALEURS MOBILIERES DE TUNIS
19 bis, Rue Kamal Ataturk, 1001 Tunis
Tel: (216) 1 259 411; Fax: (216) 1 335 817

MARKET SIZE

A) Number of listings and market value

Exhibit 69.2:
NUMBER OF COMPANIES LISTED AND MARKET CAPITALISATION, TSE, 1993–97

Year-end	*No. of companies listed*	*Market value (TD million)*
1993	19	1,000
1994	21	2,525
1995	25	3,655
1996	31	3,951
1997	33	2,632

Source: Tunis Stock Exchange.

B) Largest quoted companies

Exhibit 69.3:
THE 10 LARGEST COMPANIES LISTED ON THE TSE, END-1997

Ranking	*Company*	*Market value (TD million)*
1	Tunis Air	251.1
2	Union Bancaire pour le Commerce et l'Industrie	228.6
3	Banque du Sud	196.1
4	Société Tunisienne de Banque	192.0
5	Banque de Tunisie	187.8
6	Banque Internationale Arabe de Tunise	186.0
7	Banque Nationale Agricole	168.0
8	ATB	161.0
9	Banque de l'Habitat	139.4
10	Amen Bank	125.9

Source: International Maghreb Merchant Bank.

C) Trading volume

Exhibit 69.4:
THE 10 MOST ACTIVELY TRADED SHARES ON THE TSE, 1997

Ranking	*Company*	*Trading value (TD million)*	*Shares*
1	Banque Internationale Arabe de Tunise	33.1	1,513,443
2	Tunis Air	32.1	1,258,930
3	Banque Nationale Agricole	26.3	1,070,215
4	T. Leasing	17.7	1,026,365
5	Société Tunisienne de Banque	15.9	578,664
6	Banque de Tunisie	12.9	555,995
7	BTEI	8.8	554,222
8	Alkimia	8.3	445,992
9	Banque du Sud	7.6	391,497
10	Banque de l'Habitat	7.1	321,620

Source: International Maghreb Merchant Bank.

TYPES OF SHARE

Most shares on the TSE are common, although some preferred shares (both with and without voting rights) have been issued.

OTHER MARKETS

There are two markets in Tunisia. The main market is for companies able to meet the full listing requirements – ie, that they must be a public shareholding company, be of a minimum size and have an adequate trading record. The second-tier or parallel market is open to smaller companies unable to meet the requirements for a listing on the main market.

INVESTORS

Only local individuals invest in the Tunisian market, with domestic institutions not participating. Foreign investors – generally long-term institutional investors – represent only 5% of trading volume on the TSE.

OPERATIONS

A) Trading system

There are 23 companies currently trading on the Super CAC electronic system. Of these, three (BTEI, Al Kimia and Air Tunis) are traded continuously, subject to a price fluctuation limit of 3–4.5% a day, while the remaining companies trade on the fixed system, subject to a price fluctuation limit of 3% a day. Reuters and Telerate transmit quotations, but not as yet in real time.

B) Principal banks/brokers

Merchant banks

INTERNATIONAL MAGHREB MERCHANT BANK
Boulevard du 7 Novembre 1987
Immeuble Maghrebia Tour A 2035,
Charguia II, Tunis
Tel: (216) 1 708 220; Fax: (216) 1 708 020

Brokers

LE CAPITAL
Mr Slah Laajimi, 4 Rue de Niger,
Tunis 1002
Tel: (216) 1 800 144; Fax: (216) 1 800 786

C) Settlement and transfer

Settlement and transfer are carried out by STICODEVAM, a centralised clearing house.

D) Commissions and other costs

Brokerage commission ranges between 0.6% and 0.8% depending on the broker. Commission rates are negotiated by the Association des Intermediaires en Bourse.

TAXATION AND REGULATIONS AFFECTING FOREIGN INVESTORS

A) Ownership restrictions

Foreigners are not allowed to hold more than 49% of the share capital of listed companies.

B) Taxation

Foreign investors are exempt from dividend and capital gains tax.

The following countries have signed double taxation agreements with Tunisia: Germany, Austria, Belgium, Canada, Korea, Denmark, Egypt, France, Indonesia, Italy, Jordan, Norway, the UK, Sweden and the US as well as several North African countries.

C) Exchange controls

Exchange control in Tunisia is the responsibility of the central bank, which issues permits connected with payments for imports and services not delegated to approved intermediaries. Import and export certificates are issued by the General Directorate of Foreign Trade in conjunction with the Ministry of National Economy and the central bank.

The exchange value of the Tunisian dinar is determined with reference to a basket of currencies. The central bank sets the selling and buying rates of foreign currencies daily for both cash and term transactions.

LISTING AND REPORTING REQUIREMENTS

A) Listing requirements

Companies seeking a listing on the main TSE market must submit an application to the Conseil du Marché Financier for approval. The principal listing requirements for the main market are that a company must:

- be a public shareholding company;
- have capital of at least TD1 million;
- have been established (and actively operating) for at least three years;
- submit annual accounts for the past three years;
- have distributed at least one dividend during the past three years;
- have at least 300 shareholders; and
- have at least 20% of its capital held by shareholders not holding individually more than 5% each.

Companies seeking a listing on the TSE second-tier market must also submit an application to the Conseil du Marché Financier for approval. The principal listing requirements for the second-tier market are that a company must:

- be a public shareholding company;
- have paid-up capital of at least TD500,000;
- have been in existence for at least two years;
- have distributed at least one dividend during the past two years;
- have at least 100 shareholders; and
- have a minimum of 10% of its capital held by shareholders, each holding not more than 5%.

B) Reporting requirements

Companies listed on the TSE must:

- publish net operating results, board meeting reports, general meeting reports and the auditors' report no later than one month after the AGM;
- submit after general meetings a copy of financial statements, a copy of the resolutions approved by the general meeting, a copy of the report of the board meeting and a copy of the certified public accounts.

Listed companies must also submit to the TSE unaudited interim statements no later than two months after the end of the half-year period to which they relate.

Finally, listed companies must publish details of any major changes that could affect the value of their shares.

RESEARCH

Prices of shares are quoted and transmitted through the Reuters and Telerate systems, and are published daily in the local newspapers. In addition, the TSE publishes a bulletin that provides information on prices, new issues and the volume traded in each stock.

IM Bank is the first licensed merchant bank in Tunisia and it offers corporate advisory services for listed and unlisted companies. IM Bank plans to launch an investment fund for the MENA area, including Tunisia, Morocco, Egypt and Jordan.

CHAPTER

70

Turkey

Introduction

Securities trading in Turkey has a long history, but the stock market in its present form, centred around the Istanbul Stock Exchange (ISE), is relatively young. Following extensive restructuring of the Turkish capital markets and the enactment of the Capital Markets Law in 1981, the ISE commenced operations in 1986. Since then, the exchange has grown rapidly. The number of companies traded has more than doubled over the past 12 years of operation, reaching 258 at the end of 1997.

Turkey has pursued a policy of gradual financial and economic deregulation since the early 1980s. The government's desire to develop a deeper capital market stems partly from the need to privatise the large and very inefficient state economic enterprises (SEEs). The privatisation programme is being carried out by the Privatisation Administration and, since the inception of the programme in 1985, the Administration has privatised (in whole or in part) 123 SEEs. Shortcomings in the legal infrastructure have been a major impediment to the successful implementation of the privatisation programme, but the imminent sale of the bigger SEEs like telecoms, iron and steel factories and refineries, will significantly increase ISE market capitalisation.

Since 1989, foreign investors have been permitted to trade in listed securities without restrictions. As a result, foreign institutional investors now account for a substantial proportion of daily trading and own over 48% of publicly held stocks.

ECONOMIC AND POLITICAL OVERVIEW

Constitutionally secular, Turkey is a parliamentary democratic republic. The current coalition government, consisting of the centre-right Motherland Party (ANAP), the Turkish Democratic Party (DTP) and the Republican People's Party (CHP), came into power at the end of June 1997 following the resignation of the Welfare-True Path Party coalition government. In the period leading up to the change of government, political tension had increased significantly, and the Constitutional Court subsequently disbanded the Welfare Party because of its anti-secular political orientation.

Economic activity remained robust in 1997, with year-end GNP growth estimated at 6%, following on from growth rates of 7.1% and 8% in 1996 and 1995, respectively. Consumer price inflation, however, surged to 99.1%, due mainly to government price adjustments in public goods such as fuel products, which then triggered other price increases. As part of its stabilisation programme, the government announced that it would keep prices of public goods static at least for the first six months of 1998, apart from adjusting for exchange rate changes. Depreciation of the Turkish lira against an indicative basket (consisting of US$1 and DM1.5) was 78.5% in 1997.

On the external front, foreign trade figures show the Turkish economy adjusting to the Customs Union with the EU, and the rapid rise in the trade deficit in 1996 decelerated in 1997; the deficit increased by 7.4% in the first nine months of the year, compared with 54.9% in the same period of 1996. The year-end trade deficit is estimated at US$20 billion excluding the so-called trunk trade with former USSR states. Despite political uncertainties, net capital inflows continued in 1997, amounting to US$7.5 billion in the first nine months and more than enough to cover the US$1.1 billion current account deficit. Hence, reserves increased by an ample US$4.9 billion in the January–September period after accounting for net errors and omissions. Foreign exchange reserves increased by 14.9% to US$18.7 billion at the end of 1997, notwithstanding the rush to foreign exchange in the last quarter of the year induced by the international financial crisis.

The allegedly balanced budget of the former govern-

Exhibit 70.1: ISTANBUL SE NATIONAL PRICE INDEX (US$), 1993–97

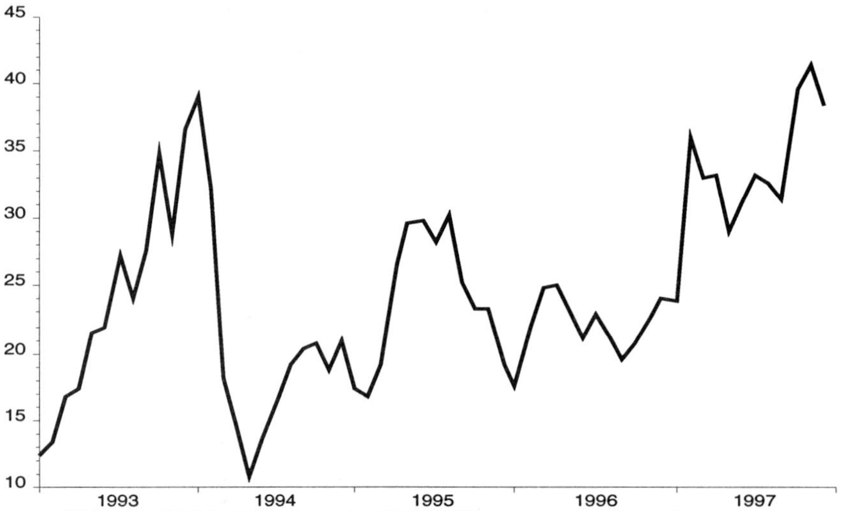

High value 41.37 3.11.97 Low value 10.78 2.5.94 *Source: Datastream*

ment had to be revised by the current government, and a preliminary deficit of TL2,331 trillion (US$15.3 billion) has been recorded for 1997, amounting to 8% of estimated GNP. The primary balance (ie, excluding interest payments) shows an estimated deficit of TL52 trillion (US$341 million), due mainly to a shortfall in privatisation revenue. The 1998 budget is supposed to yield a primary surplus of TL1,907 trillion (US$8 billion), although the budget deficit is still expected to amount to TL4,000 trillion (US$16.7 billion).

Role of the central bank

The main objectives of the Central Bank of the Republic of Turkey (CBRT) include maintaining the value and stability of the Turkish lira, and facilitating credit and finance. The bank sets and implements monetary policy, plays an active role in foreign exchange markets, supervises and regulates the banking sector and other financial institutions, and prepares monetary, financial, and statistical data. It is also active in open market operations and the primary interbank market, with the aim of monitoring liquidity levels and short-term interest rates.

The administrative assembly of the CBRT consists of six members and the bank's governor, who is appointed by the Council of Ministers for a five-year term. The bank is a joint stock company capitalised at TL25 billion, and the Under-Secretary of the Treasury is the majority shareholder.

The CBRT and the Treasury signed a protocol at the end of July 1997 to improve coordination and cooperation between the two institutions in order to promote financial market stability.

MARKET PERFORMANCE

A) In 1997

In local currency terms, the ISE National-100 Index rose by 253.6% in 1997, from 976 to 3,541. In US dollar terms it increased by a more modest 84.5% to close the year at 9.79.

Total ISE market capitalisation soared to TL12,654 trillion from TL3,275 trillion at the end of 1996, up 286.4%. In US dollar terms, there was a rise of 102.4% to US$61,365 million from US$30,327 million. Equity turnover increased by 198.8% and 54.4% in Turkish lire and US dollar terms, respectively, to TL9,048 trillion and US$58,176 million. Average daily turnover was TL35.78 trillion (US$229 million) in 1997.

B) Summary information

Global ranking by market value (US$ terms, end-1997): 28
Market capitalisation (end-1997): US$61.37 billion
Growth in market value (local currency terms, 1993–97): 216.3%
Market value as a % of nominal GNP (end-1997): 32.2%
Number of domestic/foreign companies listed (end-1997): 258/0
Market P/E (all companies, end-1997): 24.4
MSCI Index (change in US$ terms, 1997): +111.4%
Short-term (30-day) interest rate (end-1997): 83.2%
Long-term (1-year) bond yield (end-1997): 95.26%

Budget deficit as a % of nominal GNP (1997): 8%
Annual increase in broad money (M3) supply (end-1997): 102.3%
Inflation rate (CPI, 1997): 99.1%
US$ exchange rate (end-1997): TL205,110

C) Year-end share price index, price/earnings ratios and yields

Exhibit 70.2:
YEAR-END ISE NATIONAL-100 INDEX, P/E AND DIVIDEND YIELDS, 1993–97

Year-end	*ISE National-100*	*P/E*	*Yield (%)*
1993	207	25.75	1.65
1994	272	24.83	2.78
1995	400	9.23	3.56
1996	976	12.15	2.87
1997	3,451	13.33	2.83

Sources: Istanbul Stock Exchange and TEB Research.

D) Market indices and their constituents

The ISE computes the ISE National All Share Index, the ISE National-30, the ISE National-100, various sectoral indices and the ISE Regional New Market Index. All the indices are composed of National Market (as opposed to Regional Market) companies, excluding investment trusts, and are weighted according to the publicly held portion of each constituent company. The stocks are ranked in ascending order according to market capitalisation and turnover, and those stocks that have the highest values are included in the National-30 and National-100 indices.

In 1997 the ISE National-100 Index dropped two zeros for simplification purposes and its base value was changed from 1986 = 100 to 1986 = 1.

THE STOCK MARKET

A) Brief history and structure

The concept and operations of an organised securities market in Turkey have their roots in the second half of the 19th century. Following the proclamation of the Turkish Republic, a law was enacted in 1929 to reorganise the fledgling capital markets under the new name of the Istanbul Securities and Foreign Exchange Bourse. Soon, the bourse became very active and contributed substantially to the funding requirements of new enterprises across the country.

The early 1980s saw a marked improvement in both the legislative and institutional framework of the Turkish capital markets. In 1981, the Capital Market Law was enacted and one year later the main regulatory body responsible for the supervision and regulation of the Turkish securities markets, the Capital Markets Board based in Ankara, was established. The ISE was formally inaugurated at the end of 1985. Under Turkish legislation, the ISE is responsible for developing and maintaining the central securities market of Turkey for the benefit of the national economy in general and the Turkish capital market in particular.

The ISE is governed by a Council, composed of five members. The chairman of the Executive Council, representing the members and acting also as the chief executive officer, is appointed by the government.

Members of the ISE are classified into three groups: the investment and development banks; the commercial banks; and the brokerage houses. All members are incorporated and are under the comprehensive supervision and control of the Capital Markets Board (CMB) and of the ISE.

Foreign investors now account for a substantial proportion of daily trading and hold around 48% of publicly held stocks. The net equity investment in Turkey by foreign portfolio managers has been estimated at US$3.7 billion.

B) Opening hours, names and addresses

The ISE is open from Monday to Friday. Trading on the primary market, wholesale and official auction transactions, takes place between 9.15am and 9.45am. National Market, Regional Market and New Company Market trading takes place between 10.00am and 12.00 noon, and between 2.00pm and 4.00pm. Trading on the Watch List Companies Market takes place between 9.15am and 9.30am.

ISTANBUL MENKUL KIYMETLER BORSASI (IMKB)
(Istanbul Stock Exchange)
Istinye 80860, Istanbul
Tel: (90) 212 298 2100/2371; Fax: (90) 212 298 2500
Web site: www.ise.org Tlx: 27163 IMKB TR

MARKET SIZE

A) Number of listings and market value

At the end of 1997 there were 258 companies listed on the ISE. The market value of ISE shares totalled TL12,654.31 trillion (US$61.36 billion), which represents an increase of 286.4% (102.4% in US dollar terms) over 1996.

Exhibit 70.3:
NUMBER OF LISTED COMPANIES AND MARKET CAPITALISATION, ISE, 1993–97

Year-end	*No. of companies listed*	*Market value (TL trillion)*
1993	160	546.32
1994	176	836.12

Exhibit 70.3 continued

1995	205	1,264.99
1996	228	3,275.04
1997	258	12,654.31

Source: Istanbul Stock Exchange.

B) Largest quoted companies

Exhibit 70.4:
THE 20 LARGEST ISE LISTED COMPANIES, END-1997

Ranking	*Company*	*Market value (TL billion)*
1	T Is Bank	1,898,738
2	Akbank	912,500
3	Koç Holding	777,239
4	Tüpras	702,669
5	Sabanci Holding	637,500
6	Yapy kredi Bankasi	474,525
7	T Garanti Bankasi	410,000
8	Türk Hava Yollari	365,000
9	Petrol Ofisi	346,500
10	Petkim	337,500
11	Çukurova Elektrik	285,000
12	Ford Otosan	240,206
13	Eregli Demir Çelik	202,752
14	Arçelik	197,438
15	Migros	177,188
16	T Sise Cam	170,800
17	Aktas Elektrik	165,000
18	Tofas Fobrika	148,050
19	Trakya Cam	127,560
20	Enka Holding	126,000

Source: TEB Research.

C) Trading volume

Total equity turnover in 1997 was TL9,048 trillion (US$58.1 billion), a rise of 198.5% in local currency terms and 53.97% in US dollar terms. The average daily trading value of stocks was TL35.91 trillion (US$231 million) in 1997.

Exhibit 70.5:
TRADING VALUE BY SECTOR, ISE, 1997

Ranking	*Sector*	*Trading value (TL billion)*
1	Holdings	1,411,532
2	Utilities	915,998
3	Banking	823,494
4	Automotive and parts	734,035
5	Iron, steel and cast	692,882
6	Miscellaneous	598,886
7	Textiles	522,301
8	Electrical/electronics	515,231
9	Energy (petroleum)	513,365
10	Food	359,202
11	Financials	317,756
12	Cement	269,660
13	Chemicals (general)	206,173
14	Media and publishing	159,075
15	Building materials	128,908
16	Pulp/paper	115,176
17	Glass and earthenware	94,163
18	Pharmaceutical	90,111
19	Machinery	88,989
20	Leisure	80,599
21	Fertilizer	78,394
22	Cables	68,730
23	Non-ferrous metals	64,482
24	Beverages	62,375

Source: TEB Research.

Exhibit 70.6:
THE 20 MOST ACTIVELY TRADED SHARES, ISE, 1997

Ranking	*Company*	*Turnover (TL billion)*
1	Eregli Dernir Celik	500,211
2	Çukurova Elektrik	470,397
3	Dogan Holding	441,808
4	Tüpras	321,924
5	T Is Bank	272,192
6	Sabanci Holding	267,242
7	Aktas Elektrik	248,472
8	Tofas Fobrika	225,510
9	Ihlas Holding	192,171
10	Alcatel Teletas	187,649
11	Türk Hava Yollari	182,620
12	Petrol Ofisi	173,962
13	Egs Dis Ticaret	163,147
14	Yapi Kredi Bankasi	160,315
15	Kepez Elektrik	153,182
16	Akbank	151,648
17	Ford Otosan	145,177
18	Koç Holding	136,302
19	Petkim	103,835
20	Anadolu Isuzu	102,583

Source: Istanbul Stock Exchange.

TYPES OF SHARE

The ISE trades equities, non-voting stock, revenue-sharing certificates, depository receipts, foreign securities and real estate certificates.

Under the Turkish Commercial Code, share certificates of joint stock companies may be either bearer or registered, and most of the share certificates traded on the ISE are bearer. However, the Banking Law requires banks to have registered share certificates. For companies with registered shares, the CMB requires a "blank endorsement" to ensure that the shares effectively trade as if they were bearer.

OTHER MARKETS

The main, official market for ISE equity trading is called the "National Market". There is also an ISE "Regional Market", set up with the aim of promoting regulated trading in stocks of small and medium-sized companies incorporated in all parts of the country. The Regional Market also includes companies that do not qualify for the National Market or that have been temporarily or permanently delisted from it.

In July 1996 trading began on the New Companies Market. This was formed in order to enable young companies with growth potential to offer their stocks to the public via an organised ISE market.

The Watch List Companies Market was established to trade stocks of companies under special surveillance or investigation because, for example, they have not made full disclosure of important transactions or have otherwise failed to comply with the listing regulations.

The "wholesale market" is designed for trading National Market, Regional Market and non-ISE listed stocks in large quantities. Block sales of stocks under the privatisation programme take place in this market.

The international market (ISE IM) began trading on 25 February 1997. Stocks of foreign companies and foreign mutual funds are traded in the form of depository receipts. The market is tax-exempt for foreign investors and all trading, settlements and payments take place in US dollars or other convertible currencies approved by the ISE Executive Council.

OPERATIONS

A) Trading system

The computerised trading system of the ISE was completed in mid-November 1994. The software runs on a fault-tolerant central computer system and supports demanding and sophisticated screen-oriented trading. Prices are determined on a "multiple price-continuous auction" method, with buy and sell orders matched automatically on a price and time priority basis. Buyers and sellers enter their orders into the computer system through their workstations located at the ISE. It is a blind order system with counterparties identified upon matching.

From 3 April 1997, the Capital Markets Board has authorised margin trading, short selling, and securities lending and borrowing for the most liquid ISE stocks.

B) Members of the exchange and brokerage regulations

The investing public can deal in listed stocks only through a member of the ISE. All members are incorporated.

All intermediary institutions, including banks, wishing to engage in capital market operations are required to meet specific qualifications laid down in the Capital Markets Law and regulations. Banks wishing to join the ISE must establish a separate department for their capital market operations. To carry out intermediary activities in the capital markets, they may either acquire an existing brokerage house or establish a new one.

C) List of principal brokers

At the end of 1997 the ISE had 142 members (2 commer-

Exhibit 70.7:
COUNTRY FUNDS – TURKEY

Fund	*US$ % change* 01/01/97 01/01/98	01/01/93 01/01/98	Fund base currency	Fund size (US$ mil)	Fund volatility	Management group	Opal main sector	Opal subsector
Nomura Aurora II Turkey	84.4	N/A	¥	1484	-1	Nomura ITMCo	Open-End	Equity
Turkish Investment Fund	65.77	100.89	US$	35.226	12.254	Morgan Stanley	Closed-End	Equity
Turkey Trust	46.8	177.86	£	N/A	12.175	ABTRUST	Closed-End	Equity
Turkish Growth Fund IX	29.69	N/A	US$	1.4	12.932	Alliance Cap	Closed-End	Equity
Alternatif Fon 1	17.28	N/A	TL	N/A	7.883	Alternatifban	Open-End	Equity
Alternatif Fon 3	4.36	N/A	TL	N/A	-1	Alternatifban	Open-End	Equity
Alternatif Fon 2	-11.63	N/A	TL	N/A	-1	Alternatifban	Open-End	Equity

Note: details for some funds may not have been included if the data for the US$ % change for 97/98 was not available

Source: Standard & Poor's Micropal.

cial banks and 140 brokerage houses). Members that handled the most turnover on the stock market in 1997 are listed below:

ALFA MENKUL KIYMETLER AS
Akmerkez E3 Kulesi Kat: 4
Nispetiye Caddesi Ulus
80600 Etiler, Istanbul
Tel: (90) 212 282 1200; Fax: (90) 212 282 1811

ATA MENKUL KIYMETLER AS
Emirhan C, Atakule A Blok No 145
K2-3, 80700 Balmumcu, Istanbul
Tel: (90) 212 258 8525; Fax: (90) 212 258 9949

FINANS YATIRIM AS
Nispetiye Caddesi Akmerkez B Kulesi Kat 2-3
80600 Etiler, Istanbul
Tel: (90) 212 282 1700; Fax: (90) 212 282 2250

GARANTI MENKUL KIYMETLER AS
Mete C.No 38/3, 80090
Sarhan 80090, Taksim, Istanbul
Tel: (90) 212 249 9296; Fax: (90) 212 244 5638

GLOBAL MENKUL DEGERLER AS
Maya Akar Center, Büyükdere C. No: 100-102
80280 Esentepe, Istanbul
Tel: (90) 212 211 4900; Fax: (90) 212 211 4901

INTER YATIRIM MENKUL DEGERLER AS
Muallim Naci Caddesi No 91
80840 Ortaköy, Istanbul
Tel: (90) 212 236 4141; Fax: (90) 212 236 3918

IS YATRIM ve MENKUL KIYMETLER AS
Büyükdere Caddesi Maya Akar Center No. 100-102
Kat 8 Esentepe, Istanbul
Tel: (90) 212 212 0460; Fax: (90) 212 211 0812

KORFEZ YATRIM AS
Bahçeler sokak No. 25
80290 Mecidiyeköy, Istanbul
Tel: (90) 212 267 3819; Fax: (90) 212 266 3720

TACIRLER MENKUL KIYMETLER A.S.
Nispetiye C. Akmerkez B3 Blok, Kat 9 Etiler, Istanbul
Tel: (90) 212 282 1020; Fax: (90) 212 282 0997

YAPI VE KREDI BANKASI A.S.
Büyükdere C. YKB Plaza, A Blok, Kat 6/11
Levent 80620, Istanbul
Tel: (90) 212 280 1688; Fax: (90) 212 268 1902

D) Settlement and transfer

Takasbank-ISE Settlement and Custody Bank Inc is owned by the Istanbul exchange and 103 of its members. Takasbank handles the settlement of transactions conducted on the ISE and also acts as central depository and custodian.

The stock market settlement period is two days (T+2). Multilateral netting is employed for stocks, and payments are cleared by same-day funds under a delivery versus payment system. Book entry settlement is used.

TAXATION AND REGULATIONS AFFECTING FOREIGN INVESTORS

The Capital Markets Board, which governs stock market activities, has set no limit to foreign holdings in listed companies. This also applies to state-owned concerns (SEEs) privatised under the reform programme.

A foreign national may purchase the shares of a Turkish company listed on the ISE and may freely sell those shares and repatriate dividends and proceeds without any governmental approval, provided that it utilises the services of a Turkish Bank or authorised intermediary institution. Foreign shareholders are entitled to exercise voting and management rights associated with their shares, subject to a requirement to register their shareholding with the Foreign Investment General Directorate if the percentage of the shares held equals or exceeds 10% of the issued stock of the company.

Withholding taxes on payments by a domestic corporation to a foreign corporation resident in a non-treaty country vary from 0 to 25%, while withholding taxes on payments to non-resident individuals vary between 5% and 25%. Turkey has tax treaties with 37 countries and the effective tax rate applicable to investors from such countries varies between 7.5% and 15% on dividends and between 10% and 12% on interest.

The agreement between the Turkish government and the US government for the avoidance of double taxation and the prevention of fiscal evasion became effective on 17 December 1997.

LISTING AND REPORTING REQUIREMENTS

A) Listing requirements

A company applying for listing on the ISE must fulfil the following main requirements:

a) The annual and quarterly financial reports of the previous year should have been independently audited and the group companies should have consolidated financial reports.

b) At least three calendar years must have elapsed since its incorporation. This obligation is reduced to two years if at least 25% of the capital is publicly held.

c) The company must have earned profits before taxes in the past two consecutive years. (This obligation is reduced to one year if at least 25% of the capital is publicly held.)

d) The aggregate amount of the paid-in or issued capital must be at least TL100 billion.

e) The company's free float must be 15% if its capital does not exceed TL250 billion; 10% if the capital is between TL250 billion and TL500 billion; and 5% if the capital is in excess of TL500 billion.

f) The financial position of the corporation must be examined and approved by the Executive Council.

B) Reporting requirements

Companies traded on the ISE must submit financial statements to the exchange on a quarterly basis. The annual and semi-annual financial statements are subject to external independent audit requirements according to standards specified by the CMB, and must be submitted to the exchange within 10 weeks and six weeks, respectively, of the end of the period concerned. The semi-annual results of banks must be submitted within eight weeks. The first and third-quarter interim results are not required to be externally audited and they must be presented to the exchange within four weeks (six weeks for banks) following the end of the period concerned.

SHAREHOLDER PROTECTION CODES

All transactions on the ISE are under the control of the ISE management. To prevent unjustified and potentially detrimental price fluctuations, the ISE has authority to suspend trading in any security for a specific time.

The CMB has the right to suspend or ban permanently the brokerage activities of intermediaries, as well as the right to pursue legal action against any intermediary violating CMB regulations. There are also certain cases where the ISE can suspend the trading activities of a member or cancel permanently the membership of an intermediary.

A) Significant shareholdings

Special situations that must be disclosed to the public include:

- When a person or a legal entity (acting alone or in concert) acquires 10% or more of the total stock in issue, or when a holding falls below 10%.
- When the total purchases or sales of shares of an ISE-listed company by its chairman, members of the board of directors, general manager, deputies or shareholders owning 10% or more of the issued stock, amount to at least 1% of the issued stock.

B) Insider trading

The 1992 amendment to the Capital Markets Law penalises insider trading with penalties of one to three years imprisonment and fines of between TL500 million and TL1 billion. Activities such as market manipulation, dissemination of misleading information and engaging in activities outlawed by the CMB are also punishable by the same penalties. The amendment directs that fines imposed as a result of any of these acts will not be less than three times the financial benefit obtained as a result of them.

C) Mandatory tender offers

If a party (acting alone or in concert) acquires, directly or indirectly, 25% or more of the capital or voting rights of a publicity traded company, it must make an offer to buy out the other shareholders. A similar obligation is imposed on parties that already own between 25% and 50% of the capital and voting rights of a publicly traded company, and that increase their holding by 10% or more in any given 12-month period.

D) Compensation fund

There is no fund available to compensate investors who may be the victims of fraud or default by market traders.

RESEARCH

TEB Research in Istanbul provide excellent research on the market, as does the research department at the ISE.

ISE publications

The ISE publishes a daily bulletin in Turkish incorporating, among other items, the previous day's closing and high-low prices, the number and value of shares traded, the weighted average price and the number of contracts. The bulletin also includes information on international market transactions and aggregate totals of off-exchange odd-lot transactions. Such information is consolidated in weekly and monthly bulletins (the monthly bulletin is also published in English).

In addition, the ISE publishes introductory books about the ISE; quarterly bulletins and annual reports; a *Yearbook of Companies*; and monthly newsletters in Turkish and English.

Data dissemination

Trading information, daily market information and statistics are disseminated through international and local data vendors on a real-time basis. Market information is broadcast on a real-time basis via Turkish radio and television, and on teletext during the trading sessions.

Turkey's Financial System: An Engine for Growth, published by Euromoney Books, provides in-depth information for those wishing to invest or do business in the country. See the order card at the back of this book for details.

FUTURE DEVELOPMENTS

The ISE is about to launch a futures and options market. It will be fully automated and fully integrated with the clearing system. Instruments expected to be traded include index futures, index options and stock options.

The Wide Area Network (WAN), a decentralised trading system that will link brokerage houses and foreign investors in Turkey and abroad, is currently being developed.

CHAPTER

71

Ukraine

Introduction

In 1997 the Ukrainian equity market quadrupled in size and established itself as the fifth largest in eastern Europe, with capitalisation estimated at US$5.3 billion, or 11.8% of 1997 GDP. There are 140 companies listed on the electronic trading system (PFTS), though only 30 companies are traded daily. Market capitalisation of the top 30 stocks amounts to US$4 billion. The PFTS accounts for 90% of transactions on regulated markets and approximately 25% of total turnover. The PFTS does not, however, provide clearing or settlement services.

Due to the slow and inefficient privatisation process, only 10–30% of the most interesting companies (from an investor's point of view) have been privatised. As a result, the Ukranian market is illiquid, which is highlighted by the annual turnover to total market capitalisation ratio of 0.013. Currently no derivatives are traded.

In addition to the PFTS, there are four exchanges operating in Ukraine – the Ukrainian Stock Exchange, the Kyiv International Stock Exchange, the Donetsk Stock Exchange and the Ukrainian Interbank Currency Exchange. Volume of trade on these exchanges is very low (approximately 5% of overall equity turnover in Ukraine) because few attractive enterprises are listed.

ECONOMIC AND POLITICAL OVERVIEW

Since independence in 1991, official statistics show Ukraine to have experienced GDP contraction. However, growth in the "real", primarily unmeasured economy is starting to show itself. Growth indicators include increased expenditure on luxury goods and continuing low inflation despite high monetary growth.

After experiencing hyperinflation between 1992 and 1995, monetary stabilisation has been achieved and inflation in 1997 stood at 10.1%. Ukraine's large invisibles surplus (Ukraine is the major gas transit country in Europe) helps counteract its merchandise trade deficit, and resulted in a 1997 current account deficit estimated at 3.7% of GDP. External debt to GDP, traditionally low, is expected to decline further in 1998 (to 15%) as agreements to write off 30% of Russian debt come into force.

The IMF has been working closely with Ukraine, monitoring its progress monthly. Current agreements allow for a second standby facility of approximately US$542 million. Overspending deficit targets landed Ukraine in trouble in the first few months of the facility, but the recent IMF recommendations have released the back tranches. Deficit spending remains a concern, especially in the context of the run-up to the March parliamentary elections.

The main challenges facing Ukraine are to bring the current grey economy into the formal sector and to promote economic growth. In order to achieve these goals, the country needs transparent and fair legislation encouraging competition and reducing barriers to business development.

Ukraine's political system is characterised by strong tensions between the left-wing parliament and President Kuchma. The most influential political groupings are the Communist and Socialist Parties, the centrist People's Democratic Party of Ukraine and the "Gromada" Party, and the democratic-oriented Narodny Ruh. The March 1998 parliamentary elections were expected to help clarify Ukraine's complex political situation.

Role of the central bank

The March 1991 Law on Banks and Banking laid the foundations for a two-tier banking system and changed the role of the National Bank of Ukraine (NBU) from actively directing banks to supervising them. In addition, the NBU controls the following areas:

- regulation of currency issuing and money supply;
- granting banking licences;
- setting criteria for evaluating commercial banks' performance; and
- organising settlement and cash services.

MARKET PERFORMANCE

A) In 1997

Throughout the first nine month of 1997 the Ukrainian market experienced a rapid increase in share prices, outperforming other emerging markets in central and eastern Europe. By September 1997, the Wood-15 stock market index had risen 159% in US dollar terms. The most heavily traded stocks were electricity generating and chemical companies, accounting for 63% and 13% respectively of total turnover. However, investors overestimated the market's potential and this, combined with the Asian financial crisis, resulted in a three-month decline in the Wood-15 Index. Nevertheless, at the year-end the index still showed a gain of 81% in US dollar terms. In 1997 daily liquidity rose five-fold to over US$5 million, with 70% traded OTC.

B) Summary information

Global ranking by market value (US$ terms, end-1997): 52
Market capitalisation (end-1997): US$5.3 billion (PFTS only: US$4.55 billion)
Market value as a % of nominal GDP (end-1997): 11.8%
Number of domestic/foreign companies traded (end-1997): 140/0
Short-term (63-day T-bill) interest rate (end-1997): 43.6%
Long-term (1-year) bond yield (end-1997): 46.37%
Budget deficit as a % of nominal GDP (US$ terms, end-1997): 6.1%
Annual increase in broad money (M3) supply (end-1997): 33.9%
Inflation rate (1997): 10.1%
US$ exchange rate (end-1997): Hr1.899

C) Market indices and their constituents

Introduced in October 1997, the PFTS Index is a capitalisation-weighted index. It is calculated from reported last sale prices. Issues included in the index are selected on the basis of industry sector and liquidity considerations. The first stock market index to be introduced in Ukraine – the Wood-15 Index – was launched by brokers Wood & Company on 13 June 1997.

THE STOCK MARKET

A) Brief history and structure

The Ukrainian OTC Stock Trading System Association (known by its Ukrainian acronym, "PFTS") is a non-governmental, member-administered, association of licensed Ukrainian securities dealers. Registered in March 1996 with 16 founding members, PFTS membership (at December 1997) stood at 213 firms from 10 major Ukrainian cities – Dnipropetrovsk, Donetsk, Kharkiv, Kherson, Kramatorsk, Kyiv, Lviv, Odessa, Sevastopol and Vinnytsa. The PFTS trading system is an electronic "dealer" market system similar to the one used by the Nasdaq market in the United States.

The PFTS consists of an OTC stock trading system and a technical centre. Organised in accordance with internationally recognised principles of self-regulation, PFTS maintains active arbitration, mediation, disciplinary, trading, and clearance and settlement committees. It is regulated directly by the Ukrainian Commission on Securities and Capital Markets (SEC) and is governed by a nine-member board of directors.

B) Different exchanges

In addition to the PFTS, there are four exchanges operating in Ukraine – the Ukrainian Stock Exchange, the Kyiv International Stock Exchange, the Donetsk Stock Exchange and the Ukrainian Interbank Currency Exchange. However, these other stock exchanges account for only about 5% of overall equity turnover.

C) Opening hours, names and addresses

Trading on the PFTS takes place on Monday to Friday from 11.00am to 5.00pm.

PFTS
31 Shorsha, 5th Floor, Kiev, Ukraine 252030
Tel: (380) 44 264 1808; Fax: (380) 44 264 2254
E-mail: pfts@pfts.com

MARKET SIZE

A) Number of listings and market value

At the end of 1997, total market capitalisation of the 140 companies listed on the PFTS was US$5.3 billion, of which the top 30 companies accounted for almost 80%.

Exhibit 71.1:
NUMBER OF LISTED COMPANIES AND MARKET VALUE, PFTS, END-1997

Year-end	*No. of listed companies*	*Market value (US$ billion)*
1997	140	4.6

Source: Wood & Company.

B) Largest quoted companies

At end-1997, Dnyproenergo, Centerenergo and Donbasenergo accounted for 22% of total market capitalisation.

Exhibit 71.2:
THE 15 LARGEST LISTED COMPANIES ON THE PFTS MARKET, END-1997

Ranking	*Company*	*Market value (US$ million)*
1	Dnyproenergo	457.39
2	Centerenergo	354.60
3	Donbasenergo	349.20
4	Zakhidenergo	236.11
5	Dnyprooblenergo	232.94
6	Ukrnafta	227.21
7	Kyivenergo	185.91
8	Rosava	138.60
9	Niznydniprovsky Pipe Rolling Plant	94.25
10	Stirol	86.62
11	Dniproshina	77.43
12	Laza	67.03
13	Galychcyna Oil Refinery	66.05
14	Dnyprovsky Metallurgical Plant	58.58
15	Zaporizhtransformator	53.08

Source: PFTS.

C) Trading volume

The value of shares traded increased steadily during 1997, and totalled US$192 million for the year.

Exhibit 71.3:
TOTAL TRADING VALUE ON THE PFTS MARKET, 1997

Year	*Turnover (US$ million)*
1997	192

Source: PFTS.

Exhibit 71.4:
THE 15 MOST ACTIVELY TRADED PFTS SHARES, 1997

Ranking	*Company*	*Trading value (US$ million)*
1	Centerenergo	13.22
2	Niznydniprovsky Pipe Rolling Plant	13.08
3	Ukrnafta	10.23
4	Dniproshina	9.16
5	Zakhidenergo	8.86
6	Dnyproenergo	7.57
7	Donbasenergo	6.83
8	Kyivenergo	6.32
9	Hartzisk Pipe Rolling Plant	5.79
10	Stirol	5.56
11	Azot	4.93
12	Kyivoblenergo	4.34
13	Dnyprooblenergo	3.64
14	Enakievsky Metallurgical Plant	2.84
15	Ghydachiv Cellulose – Paper Combinat	2.38

Source: PFTS.

TYPES OF SHARE

The PFTS trades common stock, compensation certificates (privatisation vouchers), Ukrainian Treasury bills, municipal bonds and NDCE promissory notes.

INVESTORS

Currently, the main market participants are non-resident investment banks and brokers and Ukraine-specific country funds, which in 1997 raised nearly US300 million. Non-resident investors account for approximately 70% of total turnover.

OPERATIONS

A) Trading system

The PFTS trading system is an electronic dealer or quote-driven market system that uses a derivative of the National Association of Securities Dealers Automated Quotation (Nasdaq) Portal Software. The system permits dealers to display and accept firm and binding securities quotations as to price, quantity and settlement terms.

B) Settlement and transfer

The PFTS recently completed the development of standardised settlement (payment) procedures, and is currently developing pilot programmes with continued USAID assistance to implement an electronic share registry system and to provide rudimentary depository functions for PFTS-traded issues.

TAXATION AND REGULATIONS AFFECTING FOREIGN INVESTORS

A) Foreign investment regulations

There are no restrictions on foreign investments, and the rule of free entry and exit applies to all foreign investors. However, for a foreign investor to enjoy all the privileges and guarantees provided under the new Law On Foreign Investments, such investment must be registered with the state authorities. State registration of foreign investments is carried out by the Department of Foreign Economic Relations of the city and state administration. Holders of state-registered investments enjoy the following guarantees:

- State protection against any changes in relevant legislation. (An investor may, at his request, enjoy the rights and privileges provided for by the previous legislation for a period of 10 years.)
- State guarantees against nationalisation.
- Compensation for moral and material damage caused by unlawful actions of the state authorities (with com-

pensation calculated on the basis of market prices ruling on the date the damage was caused).

- In cases of investment seizure, investors can freely repatriate the invested assets within a six-month period.
- The right to freely repatriate, after payment of all taxes due under Ukrainian tax laws, income from investment activities.

B) Taxation

The 1997 Tax Law provides that all entities (physical persons and legal companies) with Ukrainian source income, including residents and non-residents, are subject to Ukrainian taxation (unless provided otherwise by a relevant double taxation treaty) at a rate of 30% of profits. Note that certain activities carry different tax rates, such as insurance (3% of gross income). The mechanism for calculating "profits" has been streamlined in an effort to tax the actual profit instead of the company's turnover.

Exhibit 71.5:
COMPANY PROFIT TAX RATES

Recipient	*General tax rate*	*Dividends %*	*Interest %*	*Royalties %*
Resident corporations	30	30	30	30
Nonresident corporations:	30	30	15[1]	15
Non-treaty	0–15	0–15	0–15	0–15

Note:

1. Unless the interest is obtained under a securities transaction, in which case such interest is subject to 30% withholding tax.

The new Tax Law categorises Ukrainian non-residents into two groups: those who carry on profit-generating activities in Ukraine (a) through a permanent representative office or (b) without a permanent office.

Reacting to the emergence of a Ukrainian securities market and the circulation of commercial paper, the new Ukrainian Tax Law specifically identifies and subjects certain activities of non-residents to the following taxes:

- 30% on dividends paid by Ukrainian companies;
- 30% on gross profits received in the form of interest on securities paid by entities not subject to profits tax; and
- 10% on profits received as insurance premiums and insurance payments from risk reinsurance in Ukraine.

Note, however, that the new Tax Law does not apply to income earned by physical persons (whether resident or non-resident).

REPORTING REQUIREMENTS

Issuers are required to inform the public about their financial and economic condition and their operating results at least once a year by means of an annual report. The annual report must be published no later than nine months after the financial year-end and must be sent to all shareholders as well as to the registering authorities. The annual report must include trading results of the issuer; information on its financial condition as confirmed by an auditor or inspector; information regarding any new issues of securities; and reasons for any changes in executive personnel.

In addition to the annual reporting requirements, issuers are subject to continuing reporting obligations. Within two days of any changes in the issuer's economic activities that could affect the value of its securities, the issuer must provide details to the registering authorities and the stock exchange, as well as publishing such new information in the official stock exchange newspaper.

SHAREHOLDER PROTECTION CODES

The Securities Law provides that if a party has subscribed for or purchased securities prior to the publication by the issuer of information regarding changes in its circumstances that could affect the value of its securities, that person may unilaterally terminate the purchase agreement within 15 days after the publication of such information. If a purchaser exercises this right and terminates the agreement, the issuer is required to reimburse the purchaser for all expenses and any possible losses resulting from the subscription or purchase of the securities. Moreover, an issuer of securities is required to provide an indemnity for any losses occurring as a result of inadequate information regarding its securities.

Under the Ukrainian anti-monopoly legislation, anyone who intends to acquire 10% or more of the voting rights of a company must inform the Anti-Monopoly Committee. If a person intends to acquire more than 25% of the voting rights (provided such shares are worth more than US$100,000) a special permit from the Anti-Monopoly Committee is required. The Anti-Monopoly Committee may prohibit acquisitions of shares that might result in a commercial monopoly or that could threaten the national interest. In addition, foreign investment cannot exceed 49% of the authorised capital of a company engaged in the communications industry.

Anyone who causes damage to a company by obtaining, using or disclosing confidential information can be fined.

RESEARCH

Financial and other information on the Ukrainian equity market is very difficult to obtain and verify. Currently, none of the Ukrainian issuers makes available financial statements that have been prepared or audited in accordance with generally accepted accounting principles or international accounting standards. Furthermore, many issuers consider financial statements as strictly confidential and do not release them publicly. This situation may improve following the establishment of the Public Information Centre (PIC), supervised by the Ukrainian SEC. The PIC's database contains financial information on over 300 enterprises and details can be obtained on request.

Some of the large stockbroking firms and investment banks operating in Ukraine have research capabilities and publish reports analysing the economy and particular companies. Among them, Wood & Company (see below for contact details) has a consistent record for producing in-depth coverage of key Ukrainian industries and over 40 PFTS-listed companies.

WOOD & COMPANY
Volodymyrska 6, 252025 Kiev
Tel: (380) 44 246 4350; Fax: (380) 44 246 4340

A number of international information agencies provide general information on the stock market and economic developments in Ukraine. The most reliable among them are Reuters and Bloomberg.

CHAPTER

72

United Kingdom

Introduction

The London Stock Exchange (LSE) plays a vital role in maintaining London's position as one of the world's leading financial centres. It is one of the top three exchanges globally and it is also the world's leading international exchange, with more international companies listed and more international equities traded than any other exchange.

The exchange provides comprehensive trading and information services, operating a range of markets and collating and disseminating market information. One of the highlights of 1997 was the introduction in October of the new Stock Exchange Trading Service (SETS), facilitating screen-based order-driven trading in FT-SE 100 equities.

Other major events during the year included the launching of the FT-SE Eurotop 300 Index, which provides a tradable index of Europe's 300 largest companies, the signing of a Memorandum of Understanding with the Korean Stock Exchange, and the completion of the transfers from the LSE's settlement system to the Crest system.

The FT-SE 100 Index closed 1997 at 5,135.5, representing a gain for the year of 25%. End-1997 equity market capitalisation was £3,686.2 billion (up 8.4%), while share turnover for the year totalled £1,012.5 billion (up 36.5%).

ECONOMIC AND POLITICAL OVERVIEW

On the political front, May 1997 saw "New Labour" under Tony Blair sweep into office with a massive majority. Labour was quick to implement change, while the economy moved from a recovery phase to full-blown expansion.

In 1997 the UK entered its sixth year of recovery with GDP growth of 3.5%, the third highest in the EU. The UK, which has historically suffered inflation problems mainly because of rigid labour markets, seemed to have emerged from the turbulent 1980s with a new and flexible labour force. As a result, pay settlements and wages stayed firmly under control despite the unemployment rate falling from 6.5% to 5% by the year-end. The headline inflation measure picked up to 3.1% in 1997 from 2.5% previously, but this was mainly as a result of higher interest rates: the more important core rate of inflation, which excludes mortgage interest payments, actually came down to 2.8% in 1997 from 3.0% in 1996.

The recovery, however, was not as balanced as some observers might have wished. The government, in a pre-election pledge had promised not to raise personal taxes during the course of the current parliament. In Labour's first Budget Statement in July 1997, taxes were indeed left unchanged but the dividend tax credit was abolished hitting the corporate although not the household sector. Meanwhile, consumers found themselves benefiting from the demutualisation of building societies into banks, resulting in windfall gains to the tune of around £33 billion .

With the economy already growing and consumers unrestrained by tax changes but buoyed by windfall gains, consumer spending started to accelerate sharply in 1997. In response, the newly formed Monetary Policy Committee (MPC) was forced to raise base rates. Short-term interest rates rose in five quarter-point moves from 6% to 7.25% by the year-end. As rates rose in the UK, against a benign international interest rate environment, it added fuel to an already robust sterling, which, on the Bank of England's trade-weighted measure, rose 8.6% in 1997 after appreciating by 15.6% in 1996. This proved particularly damaging to the UK manufacturing sector and, although exports held up well during the year, by early 1998 the evidence of a decline was starting to mount.

The unbalanced nature of the economy is indicated by the fact that industrial production rose a mere 1.4% in 1997 compared with 4.5% growth seen in the service sector. The divergence was further highlighted at the end of

Exhibit 72.1: FTSE 100 PRICE INDEX (£), 1993–97

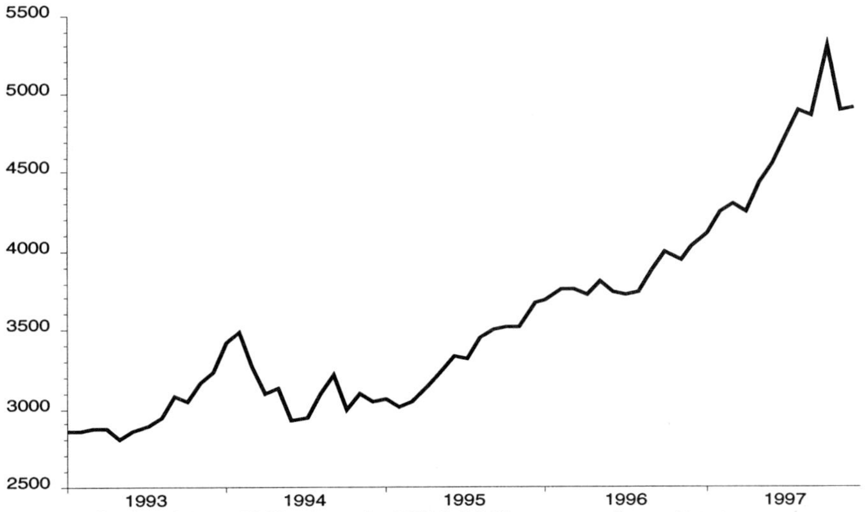

High value 5317.1 1.10.97 Low value 2813.1 3.5.93 *Source: Datastream*

1997 when manufacturing production showed its biggest quarterly fall since the recession in 1991.

In 1998, the big questions facing the markets are when will the slowdown come, and when it does come, how severe will it be? With sterling clearly overvalued at around DM3.00 and interest rates having risen five times in 1997, the MPC is obviously trying to engineer a slowdown before the recovery leads to rising inflation. If growth is stronger for longer than many expect, the MPC will carry on raising rates and a hard landing may be in store for 1999. However, if as some believe, the economy is already slowing, base rates at 7.25% have already peaked and the UK is heading for a soft landing.

Role of the central bank

Founded in 1694, the Bank Of England is one of the oldest central banks. However, 1997 saw some of the bank's functions radically reformed. On 6 May 1997, the Labour Chancellor of the Exchequer, Gordon Brown, announced that the government was giving the Bank of England operational independence in setting interest rates, with the express aim of delivering "price stability" for the UK economy. Previously the Chancellor was responsible for interest rate policy and this role now falls on the newly formed Monetary Policy Committee (MPC). The bank is expected to provide continuing support to the government's economic policy and its objectives for growth and stability, without prejudicing the central aim of price stability. An independent Bank of England is a necessary but not sufficient criterion for UK entry into EMU.

The bank's role in setting monetary policy is to deliver price stability as defined by the government's inflation target, which is announced in every Budget Statement. At present this target is to achieve underlying inflation (RPIX, which is inflation measured by the retail price index excluding mortgage interest payments) of 2.5%. In addition the Bank of England is required to publish a quarterly inflation report in which it accounts for its monetary actions, sets out and justifies its analysis of the economy, and explains how it intends to meet the government's current inflation target.

Operational decisions on interest rate policy are now made at the monthly MPC meetings. The Governor, the two Deputy Governors and six non-bank members attend the meeting and decisions are made by a vote of the committee. Each member has one vote and, if there is no majority, the Governor has a casting vote. The Treasury also has the right to be represented in a non-voting capacity. Two of the MPC non-bank members take management responsibility for monetary policy and market operations respectively. They are appointed by the Governor, and the remaining four non-bank members are appointed by the Chancellor. These six members of the committee are appointed for an initial three-year period, with no limit to the number of terms that can be served.

Other reform proposals made at the same time related to the foreign reserves and the central bank's role in debt management. In addition, on 20 May 1997 in a statement to the House of Commons, the Chancellor announced that responsibility for banking supervision was to be transferred from the Bank of England to a new "Securities and Investments Board", later renamed the "Financial Services Authority".

On a day-to-day basis the central bank is managed by the Governor and two Deputy Governors, one of whom supports the Governor on monetary stability and the other on financial stability. The "court" of the bank, responsible for its management, comprises no more than 19 members consisting of the Governor, his two Deputies and 16 non-executive members.

MARKET PERFORMANCE

A) In 1997

For the third year running, in sterling terms UK equities were the best performing asset class, beating gilts (government stocks), cash and overseas equities on a total return basis. The FT-SE 100 ended the year at 5,136.5, up 25%. This was the result of falling gilt yields, which made equities and in particular financials more attractive, combined with strong earnings and dividend growth. Gilt yields at the long end shrugged off five base rate rises and were driven lower by international bond strength, a new independent Bank of England and Labour's more positive stance on EMU.

"Buying big" was a very successful strategy in 1997. The top 15 stocks outperformed the All-Share Index by around 15%. This effect was magnified by sterling strength as the mid and small cap indices are more sensitive to overseas earnings. This also meant that the general industrials group, which is concentrated in the mid and small cap indices, underperformed the market by 17% over the year.

Bid activity continued apace with the £3 billion takeover of MAM by Merrill Lynch of the US and the French firm Lafarge's £2 billion bid for Redland. The electricity sector lost three companies as US firms again bought UK utilities. Meanwhile, the two largest companies in the alcoholic beverages sector – Grand Met and Guinness – merged to create Diageo, a new £22 billion company.

B) Summary information

Global ranking by market value (US$ terms, end-1997): 3
Market capitalisation (domestic: US$2,073.68 billion
Growth in market value (local currency terms, 1993–7): 34.78%
Market value as a % of nominal GDP (end-1997): 183.2%
Number of domestic/foreign companies listed (end-1997): 2,465/526
Market P/E (All FT-SE 100 companies, end-1997): 19.12
MSCI total returns (with net dividends, US$ terms, 1997): 22.6%
MSCI Index (change in US$ terms, 1997): +19.1%
Short-term (3-month) interest rate (end-1997): 7.5%
Long-term (10-year) bond yield (end-1997): 6.3%
Budget deficit as a % of nominal GDP (1997): 2.1%
Annual increase in broad money (M4) supply (end-1997): 6.9%
Inflation rate (retail price index, 1997): 2.8%
US$ exchange rate (end-1997): US$1.65

C) Year-end share price index, price/earnings ratios and yields

Exhibit 72.2:
YEAR-END SHARE PRICE INDEX, P/E AND DIVIDEND YIELDS, LSE, 1993–97

Year-end	*FT-SE 100 Index*	*P/E*	*Yield (%)*
1993	3,418.4	20.7	3.5
1994	3,065.5	16.3	4.2
1995	3,689.3	15.6	3.9
1996	4,118.5	15.9	3.9
1997	5,135.5	19.2	3.2

Source: London Stock Exchange.

D) Market indices and their constituents

The most widely observed index is the FT-SE 100 Index, based on the 100 largest listed companies by market capitalisation and calculated on a minute-by-minute basis.

The Eurotrack 100 Index uses real-time prices for the top 100 Continental European and Irish shares from the London exchange's SEAQ International and SEAQ services, and is calculated and published once-a-minute in Deutschmarks. The FT-SE Eurotrack 200 was introduced in February 1991 and is also calculated once-a-minute.

Introduced in October 1992, the FT-SE Actuaries Share Indices comprise the FT-SE Mid 250, the FT-SE Actuaries 350 with industry baskets and the FT-SE SmallCap Index. These indices were designed to give greater stock market visibility to the medium and smaller company sectors.

The FT-SE Mid 250 provides a real-time benchmark for medium to large-sized companies falling directly beneath the FT-SE 100 Index. The FT-SE Actuaries 350, which combines the FT-SE 100 with the FT-SE Mid 250, provides a benchmark covering some 90% of the UK equity market by value. Real-time industry sector indices calculated on the 350 (known as industry baskets) provide an instant view of industry performance across the market. The FT-SE SmallCap Index comprises approximately 450 companies with a market capitalisation of between £20 million and £150 million. These companies represent approximately 7% of market turnover.

The FT-SE Actuaries All-Share Index covers the three capital segments (large, medium and small companies) of the market, and combines the FT-SE 100, the FT-SE Mid 250 and the FT-SE SmallCap.

THE STOCK MARKET

A) Brief history and structure

Dealings in stocks and shares began with the merchant venturers in the 17th century and, gradually, an informal market developed around the coffee houses in the City of London. In 1773, New Jonathan's Coffee House became the stock exchange, although it was not formally constituted until 1802, with some 550 subscribers and 100 clerks.

By 1967, local share markets in other parts of the country had grouped themselves into six regional exchanges and in 1973 all seven exchanges in the British Isles amalgamated to form the Stock Exchange of Great Britain and Ireland, with trading floors in London, Birmingham, Manchester, Liverpool, Glasgow and Dublin. Regional trading floors ceased operations in the late 1980s, however, and all trading, even in regional stocks, was routed through the central market. (In December 1995, the Dublin Stock Exchange separated from the UK exchange, which then became formally known as the London Stock Exchange.)

A new regional structure was announced in 1990, following consultation with senior representatives of the regional broking community. The exchange established a representative structure in the regions which has developed its business relationships with all market users, including local stockbroking firms and listed companies. The present market includes not only the ordinary shares of local and foreign companies and fixed-interest securities issued by private borrowers, but also the primary and secondary markets in British government (gilt-edged) securities.

The exchange is self-regulating and operates under its own rules and articles of association. Management is under the control of a board of 19 directors appointed from within the securities industry.

Historically, there had long been a rigid division between stock exchange member firms of brokers and jobbers – ie, between firms acting solely as agents on behalf of investors but not making markets, and the jobbing firms which made markets, quoting two-way prices, but having no direct contact with the public. The introduction of dual capacity in 1986 involved member firms becoming broker-dealers. Trading is now based on a system of committed market-makers who are free to conduct agency business. Equally, broker-dealers executing client orders can take positions but are obliged to state clearly on any given transaction whether they are acting as principal or as agent. Some brokers have elected to conduct agency business only.

B) Different exchanges

The London Stock Exchange is the only exchange in the UK. It has regional offices in Glasgow, Belfast, Manchester, Birmingham and Leeds.

C) Opening hours, names and addresses

Trading hours are Monday to Friday from 8.30am to 4.30pm, although dealing can take place outside these hours.

LONDON STOCK EXCHANGE
Old Broad Street, London EC2N 1HP
Tel: (44) 171 797 1000

MARKET SIZE

A) Number of listings and market value

At the end of 1997 there were 2,465 listed domestic companies and 526 listed overseas companies with a combined market capitalisation of £3,686.2 billion, an increase of 8.4% over 1996.

Exhibit 72.3:
NUMBER OF COMPANIES LISTED AND EQUITY MARKET VALUE, LSE, 1993–97

	No. of companies		*Market capitalisation*
Year-end	*Domestic*	*Foreign*	*(£ billion)*
1993	1,927	485	2,734.9
1994	2,070	464	2,728.8
1995	2,078	525	3,257.3
1996	2,171	533	3,400.0
1997	2,465	526	3,686.2

Source: London Stock Exchange.

Exhibit 72.4:
DOMESTIC EQUITY MARKET CAPITALISATION BY SECTOR, LSE, 1996–97

	Market value (£ million)	
Sector	*End-1996*	*End-1997*
Mineral extraction		
Extractive industries	11,731.3	12,453.8
Oil, integrated	75,381.1	93,229.3
Oil exploration and production	9,053.2	10,103.6
Total	96,165.6	115,786.7
General industrials		
Building and construction	8,876.5	10,299.1
Building materials and merchants	21,792.2	22,619.8
Chemicals	18,769.4	20,519.5
Diversified industrials	28,615.5	20,192.6
Electronic and electrical equipment	21,456.0	18,905.7
Engineering	43,083.9	45,379.1
Engineering, vehicles	11,109.7	11,236.8
Paper, packaging and printing	11,227.3	9,520.9

Exhibit 72.4 continued

Textiles and apparel	3,361.6	3,129.6
Total	168,292.1	161,803.1
Consumer goods		
Alcoholic beverages	24,384.5	28,447.4
Food producers	32,785.7	39,663.8
Household goods	5,097.7	5,835.8
Healthcare	6,580.2	8,921.0
Pharmaceuticals	76,171.9	108,914.2
Tobacco	15,336.1	21,279.1
Total	160,356.1	213,061.2
Services		
Distributors	10,331.0	9,301.0
Leisure and hotels	21,930.4	23,770.3
Media	59,267.3	56,677.3
Retailers, food	26,539.1	33,621.5
Retailers, general	57,326.8	63,589.6
Breweries, pubs and restaurants	23,140.1	25,405.1
Support services	23,651.8	34,090.0
Transport	27,964.5	31,979.7
Total	250,151.0	278,434.4
Utilities		
Electricity	22,816.5	31,411.1
Gas distribution	10,531.7	15,386.9
Telecommunications	49,296.0	66,975.7
Water	14,434.7	19,840.8
Total	97,078.9	133,614.4
Financials		
Banks, retail	110,539.6	189,400.3
Insurance	20,412.2	27,927.7
Life insurance	20,218.7	36,978.2
Other financial	11,310.3	21,617.1
Property	21,319.2	26,870.2
Total	188.175.6	302,793.5
Investment trusts	41,787.5	43,716.0
Other funds		
Offshore investment companies and funds	7,934.8	N/A
Currency funds	465.9	N/A
Other S.842 investment trusts	1,270.9	N/A
Total	9,671.6	N/A
Grand total	**1,011,678.4**	**1,249,209.4**

Source: London Stock Exchange.

B) Largest quoted companies

Exhibit 72.5:
THE 20 LARGEST LISTED UK COMPANIES BY MARKET CAPITALISATION, LSE, END-1997

Ranking	*Company*	*Market value (£ million)*
1	Glaxo Wellcome	51,433.6
2	British Petroleum	47,159.2
3	Shell Transport & Trading	43,751.4
4	HSBC	40,987.5
5	Lloyds TSB	40,556.9
6	SmithKline Beecham	34,415.3
7	British Telecommunications	30,254.0
8	Barclays	24,350.1
9	Diageo	22,011.5
10	Halifax	19,176.4
11	Zeneca	18,851.8
12	Marks & Spencer	17,373.8
13	National Westminster Bank	17,106.6
14	BAT Industries	17,028.2
15	Unilever	16,103.6
16	Abbey National	14,757.7
17	Prudential	13,783.6
18	Vodafone	12,873.1
19	Cable & Wireless	12,156.3
20	BG	11,272.6

Source: London Stock Exchange.

C) Trading volume

Total LSE equity turnover for 1997 was £1,012.5 billion, up 36.5% on the previous year and a new record. Total customer turnover (excluding intra-market business) was £633.9 billion (38.0% ahead of 1996).

Exhibit 72.6:
TURNOVER AND VOLUME OF EQUITIES (UK LISTED ONLY) BY SECTOR, 1997

Sector	*Turnover value (£ million)*	*No. of bargains*
Mineral extraction		
Extractive industries	12,264.6	130,367
Oil, integrated	54,121.4	379,898
Oil exploration and production	11,049.1	160,705
Total	77,435.1	670,970
General industrials		
Building and construction	6,837.6	140,528
Building materials and merchants	22,888.6	326,252
Chemicals	24,752.1	227,848

Exhibit 72.6 continued

Diversified industrials	28,209.8	406,560
Electronic and electrical equipment	16,357.8	345,122
Engineering	44,861.6	534,409
Engineering, vehicles	11,143.3	118,755
Paper, packaging and printing	7,290.1	125,794
Textiles and apparel	2,194.7	69,263
Total	164,535.6	2,294,531
Consumer goods		
Alcoholic beverages	29,811.5	207,059
Food producers	30,088.3	346,442
Household goods	4,640.5	78,319
Healthcare	7,578.1	161,303
Pharmaceuticals	61,138.9	530,115
Tobacco	20,041.7	188,127
Total	153,298.9	1,511,365
Services		
Distributors	7,509.5	133,617
Leisure and hotels	22,475.5	415,793
Media	53,001.6	471,308
Retailers, food	24,922.0	338,047
Retailers, general	50,949.3	675,084
Breweries, pubs and restaurants	19,408.2	231,838
Support services	20,928.0	363,516
Transport	29,693.5	482,810
Total	228,887.8	3,112,013
Utilities		
Electricity	30,281.2	713,197
Gas distribution	13,309.2	319,239
Telecommunications	65,271.1	639,952
Water	16,705.9	236,846
Total	125,567.4	1,909,234
Financials		
Banks, retail	156,692.2	1,747,370
Insurance	24,906.1	224,450
Life assurance	22,091.9	414,083
Other financial	10,645.4	127,605
Property	15,163.8	204,666
Total	229,499.4	2,718,174
Investment trusts		
Investment trusts	20,536.4	741,455
Housing income investment companies	0.0	0
Open-ended investment companies	18.5	14
Split capital investment trusts	1,334.6	62,133
Venture capital investment trusts	1.8	251
Total	21,891.3	803,853

Exhibit 72.6 continued

Other funds		
Offshore investment companies and funds	1,220.4	13,699
Currency funds	0.0	2
Other S.842 investment trusts	1,272.8	25,374
Total	2,493.2	39,075
Grand total	**1,003,608.7**	**13,059,215**

Source: London Stock Exchange.

Exhibit 72.7:
THE 20 MOST ACTIVELY TRADED SHARES, LSE, 1997

Ranking	*Company*	*Turnover value (£ million)*
1	HSBC	48,267.4
2	British Telecommunications	39,977.4
3	Shell Transport and Trading	25,879.0
4	British Petroleum	25,247.0
5	Glaxo Wellcome	24,313.1
6	Lloyds TSB	20,788.2
7	Smithline Beecham	19,761.5
8	Barclays plc	19,462.1
9	National Westminster Bank	15,448.4
10	BAT Industries	14,764.4
11	Halifax	14,409.1
12	Grand Metropolitan	14,380.9
13	Reuters	12,586.0
14	Imperial Chemical Industries	12,505.7
15	Unilever	12,076.8
16	Zeneca	11,568.2
17	Cable & Wireless	10,439.7
18	Vodaphone	10,132.8
19	BTR	10,047.5
20	Abbey National	9,991.9

Source: London Stock Exchange.

TYPES OF SHARE

The share capital of a company may be divided into a number of different classes. UK law does not closely prescribe what rights attach to different classes of share, subject to the general rule that all shares rank equally as to dividend and capital. It is left to the specific terms of the memorandum and articles of association of each company, or the terms of issue of the shares, to modify the general rule and to lay down the particular rights attaching to each class. It is common for a company to issue ordinary or preference shares.

If it is authorised to do so by its articles of association, a company may issue redeemable shares. Redeemable

Exhibit 72.8:
EQUITY TURNOVER (UK AND IRISH EQUITIES), 1993–97

	Customer business		*Intra-market business*		*Total*	
Year	*No. of bargains*	*Value (£ million)*	*No. of bargains*	*Value (£ million)*	*No. of bargains*	*Value (£ million)*
1993	9,179,453	347,365.6	1,164,080	216,601.8	10,343,533	563,967.4
1994	8,100,353	357,760.3	1,285,952	248,242.5	9,386,305	607,649.0
1995	8,642,266	390,078.4	1,174,988	256,253.6	9,817,204	646,332.0
1996	9,622,581	459,428.6	1,339,827	282,190.5	10,962,408	741,614.1
1997	11,195,500	633,904.4	2,150,845	378,630.5	13,346,345	1,012,534.8

shares can only be redeemed by a public company out of its distributable profits or the proceeds of a fresh issue of shares made for the purpose of a redemption.

Companies may split their shares into smaller denominations, issue further bonus shares paid out of the company's reserves to existing shareholders (called scrip or capitalisation issues) or consolidate shares into larger units. Companies sometimes issue separate subscription rights, usually in the form of warrants or options to subscribe, with specified exercise prices and dates. In rare cases the warrants may be perpetual.

All listed shares in UK companies are issued in registered form. For stamp duty reasons bearer shares are not usually issued, although there are bearer receipt arrangements in some internationally traded shares.

A) Ordinary shares

The normal type of share dealt on the London exchange is the ordinary share. It gives the holder, *pro rata*, the right to dividends which are declared by the company in a general meeting and, in the event of a winding-up, the right to the assets after any prior classes have been repaid. Usually, it is the only class of share to carry full voting rights (normally one vote per share). Ordinary shares under UK law must be issued with a par value, which is the minimum amount that must be paid in respect of their issue.

Section 89 (1) of the Companies Act 1985 confers pre-emptive rights upon existing shareholders when further shares are allotted for cash. While private companies may exclude this provision in their articles of association, public companies must rely upon Section 95 of the Companies Act under which the pre-emptive rights may be disapplied or modified by the shareholders passing a special resolution to such effect.

The exchange has its own rules relating to the pre-emptive rights of shareholders of listed companies. It prefers an issue of shares on a pre-emptive basis but does permit a general disapplication of the statutory pre-emption rights provided this is approved annually by special resolution. However, the Investment Committees of the Association of British Insurers and the National Association of Pension Funds (ICs) representing institutional shareholders, will only advise their members to approve a resolution for an annual disapplication, if it is restricted to an amount of shares not exceeding 5% of the issued ordinary share capital shown by the latest published annual accounts. Although the full annual disapplication of entitlements may be sanctioned each year at its annual general meeting, a company should not, without prior consultation with the ICs, make use of more than 7.5% of its issued ordinary share capital (again shown by the latest published annual accounts) by way of non pre-emptive issues for cash in any rolling three-year period.

B) Preference shares

The precise rights attaching to preference shares will be set out in the company's memorandum or articles, or in the resolution that provides for their issue. Preference shares carry the right to a fixed dividend expressed as a fixed percentage of the par value of the share, or to a repayment of capital on a winding-up in priority to ordinary shares, or both.

Preference shares are sometimes issued with the right to convert, without further payment, into ordinary shares at specified conversion prices and dates.

Cumulative preference shares entitle the holder to a cumulative dividend if, as a result of the company having made a loss or insufficient profit in previous years, it is unable to pay the preference dividend during that prior period.

If the shares are participating preference shares they entitle the holder, in addition to the fixed dividend, to an agreed share of the remaining profits once the fixed portion of the preference dividend has been paid, thereby enabling the holder to participate in the growth of the company.

Exhibit 72.9:
TOP PERFORMING COUNTRY FUNDS – UK

Fund	*US$ % change 31/12/95 31/12/97*	*31/12/92 31/12/97*	*Currency*	*Fund size (US$ mil)*	*Volatility*	*Manager name*	*Main sector*	*Class*
Jupiter Extra Inc Wts	393.57	39.49	£	2.52	30.91	Jupiter Asset Mgmt Ltd	Equity	UK Investment Trusts
Second St Davids Cap (2003)	244.11	N/A	£	10.11	N/A	Guildhall Inv Mgmt Ltd	Equity Growth	UK Investment Trusts
Fulcrum - Cap (1999)	229.04	543.8	£	13.73	11.03	Maunby Inv Mgmt Ltd	Equity Growth	UK Investment Trusts
Framlington Dual-Cap (1999)	217.41	477.84	£	12.13	13.25	Framlington Inv Mgmt Ltd	Equity Growth	UK Investment Trusts
ENIC	190.28	N/A	£	235.99	N/A	Henderson Investors	Equity	UK Investment Trusts
City of Oxford Wts	188.45	-34.78	£	0.41	36.51	Hambros	Equity	UK Investment Trusts
Guinness Flight Extra Inc Wts	157.85	N/A	£	1.88	N/A	Guinness Flight Inv Tst Mgrs	Equity	UK Investment Trusts
Schroder Split Cap (2002)	107.73	N/A	£	30.41	9.07	Schroder Investment Mgmt Ltd	Equity Growth	UK Investment Trusts
Gartmore Scotland-Cap (2001)	101.46	312.29	£	37.51	6.53	Gartmore Investment Ltd	Equity Growth	UK Investment Trusts
St Davids-Cap (1998)	101.41	326.91	£	26.16	7.94	Guildhall Investment Mgmt Ltd	Equity Growth	UK Investment Trusts
Perpetual Income & Growth Wts	99.42	N/A	£	25.57	N/A	Perpetual Portfolio Management Ltd	Equity	UK Investment Trusts
Schroder Income Growth Fund Wt	87.66	N/A	£	11.43	N/A	Schroder Investment Mgmt Ltd	Equity Income	UK Investment Trusts
Investors Capitial Wts	82.03	N/A	£	30.48	N/A	Ivory & Sime Plc	Equity Income	UK Investment Trusts
INVESCO Blue Chip-Ord (1998)	74.25	182.71	£	19.97	8.66	INVESCO Asset Mgmt Ltd	Equity	UK Investment Trusts
Framlington I&C Cap (2008)	74.02	197.55	£	51.93	7.94	Framlington Inv Mgmt Ltd	Equity Growth	UK Investment Trusts
For & Col Income Gth Wts	73.07	N/A	£	2.96	11.15	Foreign & Colonial Mgmt Ltd	Equity	UK Investment Trusts
Kleinwort Hi Inc-Ord (1998)	71.59	191.56	£	70.14	6.57	Kleinwort Benson Inv Mgmt Ltd	Equity	UK Investment Trusts
Yeoman - Cap (1998)	69.63	241.28	£	63.67	6.78	Abbey Life Investment Svs Ltd	Equity Growth	UK Investment Trusts
City of Oxford-Ord (1999)	64.6	356.7	£	17.85	8.7	Hambros	Equity	UK Investment Trusts
M&G Income - Cap (2001)	64.51	290.23	£	103.89	5.3	M&G Investments Mgmt Ltd	Equity Growth	UK Investment Trusts
Edinburgh Income-Ord (2000)	60.09	84.66	£	13.72	7.73	Edinburgh Fund Mngrs Plc	Equity	UK Investment Trusts
Murray Split - Cap (1998)	58.79	305.74	£	32.37	6.54	Murray Johnstone Ltd	Equity Growth	UK Investment Trusts
Jove - Cap (2004)	58.65	-18.48	£	8.28	24.03	Aberdeen Fund Managers	Equity Growth	UK Investment Trusts
Aberdeen High Income	53.47	N/A	£	103.33	5.74	Aberdeen Fund Managers	Equity Income	UK Investment Trusts
Gartmore Shd Equity-Ord(2002)	53.22	N/A	£	153.03	6.35	Gartmore Investment Ltd	Equity	UK Investment Trusts
Glbl Mgr UK Geared	49.01	N/A	US$r	0.33	5.69	BIIML	Equity	Offshore Territories
M&G Recovery -Cap (2002)	48.91	35.33	£	104.93	8	M&G Investments Mgmt Ltd	Equity Growth	UK Investment Trusts
Framlington 1000 Sm Cos WTS	45.77	N/A	£	4.2	N/A	Framlington Inv Mgmt Ltd	Equity Growth	UK Investment Trusts
J.Phoenix Ord (2005)(NS 842)	44.6	116.4	£	41.72	2.92	Graham	Equity Income	UK Investment Trusts
Contra-Cyclical Cap (2001)	43.05	107.2	£	8.78	13.04	Rea Bros (Inv Mgmt) Ltd	Equity Growth	UK Investment Trusts
Fleming Geared Growth	41.82	138.25	£	N/A	4.98	Fleming Inv Mgmt Ltd	Equity	UK Investment Trusts
Exeter Capital Growth	41.05	216.49	£	20.16	4.26	Exeter Fund Managers	Equity Growth	UK Unit Trusts/OEICs
Fleming Claverhouse	40.52	165.81	£	374.92	3.82	Fleming Inv Mgmt Ltd	Equity	UK Investment Trusts
Danae-Cap (2002)	39.16	113.5	£	9.94	6.02	Aberdeen Fund Managers	Equity Growth	UK Investment Trusts
Jupiter Extra Ord (2000)	38.15	115.87	£	83.35	4.94	Jupiter Asset Mgmt Ltd	Equity	UK Investment Trusts
Century NEL M'c/Ex Cap Gth **	37.54	175.59	£	0.35	3.59	Century Life - NEL M'choice	Equity Growth	UK Individual Pensions
INVESCO Recovery Ord (1998)	37.02	238.92	£	17.55	5.57	INVESCO Asset Mgmt Ltd	Equity Income	UK Investment Trusts
INVESCO City & Commercial Wts	36.75	N/A	£	1.27	8.05	INVESCO Asset Mgmt Ltd	Equity Growth	UK Investment Trusts
Fleming Inc & Cap-Ord (2002)	36.74	135.92	£	77.83	3.57	Fleming Inv Mgmt Ltd	Equity	UK Investment Trusts
Danae Wts	36.51	89.39	£	0.58	6.28	Aberdeen Fund Managers	Equity	UK Investment Trusts
Jupiter Geared - Cap (1999)	36.47	165.69	£	26.81	4.46	Jupiter Asset Mgmt Ltd	Equity Growth	UK Investment Trusts
Martin Currie Smlr Cos Inc Wts	36.21	-4.01	£	3.49	8.13	Martin Currie Investments Mgmt Ltd	Equity	UK Investment Trusts
M&G Equity - Cap (2011)	36.11	N/A	£	143.41	N/A	M&G Investments Mgmt Ltd	Equity	UK Investment Trusts
Ivory & Sime ISIS Wts	35.68	N/A	£	2.12	9.59	Ivory & Sime Plc	Equity Growth	UK Investment Trusts

Note: details for some funds may not have been included if the data for the US$ % change for 96/97 was not available

Source: Standard & Poor's Micropal.

INVESTORS

There are now over 10 million private shareholders in the UK, a three-fold increase from 1983. However, as the number of private shareholders has increased, the proportion of shares owned by private individuals has fallen. In 1975, 37.5% of UK quoted equities were owned by private individuals, but by 1981 this had fallen to 28.2% and is now about 24%. Of the remaining 80%, most are owned by institutional investors, with some 16% owned by foreigners.

OPERATIONS

A) Trading system

In October 1997, the introduction of the new order book transformed the way that the FT-SE 100 shares are traded. Under the new system (called the Stock Exchange Trading Service, or SETS), when bid and offer prices match, orders automatically execute against one another on screen. There are four types of order:

- *Limit*: which is logged to specify the size and price at which a participant wishes to deal. If matches can be found, the order is immediately executed, in whole or in part. If not, it remains on the order book until a suitable match comes along within the expiry date or the order is deleted.
- *Fill or kill*: these are only executed immediately in full or rejected. They may include a limit price.
- *Execute and eliminate*: these are similar to "at best", but with a specified limit price, so that it is matched immediately at no worse than the specified price.
- *At best*: market users enter their buy or sell orders which are then executed immediately at the best price available in the system.

The order book applies initially to the UK's largest companies that make up the FT-SE 100 Index (and if a company moves out of the FT-SE 100, it remains within SETS). Shares outside the FT-SE 100 continue to be traded under the quote-driven system (SEAQ) with market-makers quoting their best buy and sell prices.

B) List of principal merchant banks and brokers

ABN AMRO EQUITIES (UK) LTD
4 Broadgate, London EC2M 7LE
Tel: (44) 171 601 0101; Fax: (44) 171 374 1134

BT ALEX BROWN
1 Appold Street, Broadgate, London EC2A 2HE
Tel: (44) 171 982 2000; Fax: (44) 171 982 2293

CAZENOVE & CO
12 Tokenhouse Yard, London EC2R 7AN
Tel: (44) 171 588 2828; Fax: (44) 171 606 9205

DEUTSCHE MORGAN GRENFELL
150 Leadenhall Street, London EC2N 4DA
Tel: (44) 171 545 8000; Fax: (44) 171 545 4455

DRESDNER KLEINWORT BENSON SECURITIES
20 Fenchurch Street, London EC3P 3DB
Tel: (44) 171 623 8000; Fax: (44) 171 623 4069

GOLDMAN SACHS SECURITIES
Peterborough Court, 133 Fleet Street, London EC4A 2BB
Tel: (44) 171 774 1000; Fax: (44) 171 774 1510

HSBC JAMES CAPEL
Thames Exchange, 10 Queens Street Place,
London EC4R 1BL
Tel: (44) 171 621 0011; Fax: (44) 171 621 1402

MERRILL LYNCH INTERNATIONAL
PO Box 293, 20 Farringdon Road, London EC1M 3NH
Tel: (44) 171 772 1000; Fax: (44) 171 772 2929

MORGAN STANLEY INTERNATIONAL
25 Cabot Square, London E14 4QA
Tel: (44) 171 513 8000; Fax: (44) 171 513 8990

NOMURA INTERNATIONAL
Nomura House, 1 St Martins-Le-Grand,
London EC1A 4NP
Tel: (44) 171 521 2224; Fax: (44) 171 521 2189

PANMURE GORDON
35 New Broad Street, London EC2M 1NH
Tel: (44) 171 638 4010; Fax: (44) 171 588 5293

ROBERT FLEMING SECURITIES
25 Copthall Avenue, London EC2R 7DR
Tel: (44) 171 638 5858; Fax: (44) 171 628 0683

SALOMON BROTHERS INTERNATIONAL LIMITED
Victoria Plaza, 111 Buckingham Palace Road.
London SW1W OSB
Tel: (44) 171 721 2000; Fax: (44) 171 222 7062

SMITH BARNEY EUROPE, LTD.
3 Lombard Street, London, EC3V 9AA
Tel: (44) 171 398 6000; Fax: (44) 171 398 6050

WARBURG DILLON READ
1 Finsbury Avenue, London EC2M 2PA
Tel: (44) 171 606 1066; Fax: (44) 171 382 4800

C) Settlement and transfer

Settlement takes place on a five-day rolling basis. The full transition to Crest, the electronic share settlement system which first became operational in August 1996, was completed in 1997.

This settlement system is managed entirely by Crest Company and is no longer a function of the London Stock Exchange.

D) Commissions and other costs

Commissions are negotiable. The rate of stamp duty payable on a share transfer is 0.5%.

TAXATION AND REGULATIONS AFFECTING FOREIGN INVESTORS

UK corporations do not have to withhold tax on distributing dividends to shareholders but are normally required to pay advance corporation tax (ACT) on such dividends. Residents of countries having a double taxation treaty with the UK containing relevant credit provisions may claim a tax credit payment up to an amount equivalent to the amount of ACT paid, less a withholding tax. However, a number of changes to the UK tax regime have recently been announced. ACT will be abolished from April 1999 and, while tax credits will remain available on dividends paid by UK corporations, the amount of those credits will be reduced. The effect of these changes will be that, from April 1999 onwards, tax credit payments will no longer be due to non-resident individual investors or non-resident corporate portfolio investors, and the amount of tax credit payments due to non-resident corporate investors with substantial holdings will be significantly reduced.

Exhibit 72.10:
WITHHOLDING TAX

Recipient	*Dividends %*[1]	*Interest %*
Resident corporations	Nil	20
Resident individuals	Nil	20
Non-resident corporations and individuals:		
Non-treaty	Nil	20
Treaty	Nil–25	Nil–20

Note:

1. A tax credit equivalent to the advance corporation tax paid by the corporation is available to UK resident shareholders on dividends received. Some double taxation treaties allow a tax credit (less normally a 15% withholding) also to non-resident individuals and usually to corporate portfolio investors. No credit is available in the case of foreign income dividends or certain other distributions associated with share transactions. (In the case of Belgium, Trinidad and Tobago and Zimbabwe, the 15% withholding tax is increased to 20%, and in the case of the Philippines, it is increased to 25%, thus effectively eliminating the credit at the current rate.)

Source: Price Waterhouse.

Since October 1979, there have been no exchange controls on inward or outward investment, or on the remittance or repatriation of funds from the UK.

There are no specific legal regulations applying solely to foreign equity investors other than the Secretary of State's power under the Industry Act 1975 Part II to prohibit the change of control of important manufacturing undertakings that have special significance to the UK. However, the acquisition of an interest in a listed company may be subject to investigation on competition grounds by either the EU or the UK competition authorities or, where the company operates in a regulated sector such as banking or insurance, may require prior regulatory approvals or may trigger other regulatory consequences.

LISTING AND REPORTING REQUIREMENTS

A) Listing requirements

All applications for new listings of securities must first be submitted to the LSE for approval, and very stringent requirements must be met before a quotation is granted. Applications for listing are governed by Part IV of the Financial Services Act 1986 (as amended by the Public Offers of Securities Regulations 1995), and the procedures necessary to obtain a full listing are set out in the Exchange's Listing Rules, also known as the "Yellow Book".

A company wishing to have its securities listed on the exchange must prepare a prospectus or listing particulars giving details about the company and its business, which must be prepared and then published in accordance with the exchange's requirements. Broadly, a prospectus is required when securities to be listed are offered to the public for the first time prior to admission to listing, whereas listing particulars are generally required where an issuer applies for listing of its securities in other circumstances. Publication of the full prospectus or listing particulars, an abbreviated version, or of a notice giving details of where to obtain copies of the full prospectus or particulars, must take place in at least one national newspaper.

B) Reporting requirements

A listed company must observe disclosure obligations as a condition of the continuation of its listing. It must, in general, notify the exchange of any major new developments in its sphere of activity that are not public knowledge and of changes in its financial condition, in the performance of its businesses and its expectations of its performance, which may lead to substantial movement in the price of its securities. It must also notify such matters as major interests in its shares, the dates on which results and dividends are expected to be announced and changes in capital structure.

There are also detailed provisions in the Listing Rules concerning the annual report and accounts to be issued by a company within six months of its financial year-end. Half-yearly reports on a company's activities and profit or loss for the first six months of each financial year must also be prepared and published. The Listing Rules require that a listed company include in its annual report and accounts statements as to whether or not it has complied with (a) certain parts of the code of best practice published in December 1992 by the Committee on the Financial Aspects of Corporate Governance (the Cadbury Code) and (b) certain of the best practice provisions annexed to the Listing Rules. The latter reflect the requirements relating to remuneration committees from the code of best practice in the report of the Study Group on directors' remuneration published in July 1995 (the Greenbury Code). The Listing Rules also require the annual report and accounts to include a report to shareholders, on behalf of the board, by the company's remuneration committee containing specified information.

Specific obligations relate to company directors. Changes of directors must be notified and copies of directors' service contracts of more than one year's duration must be available for inspection. A director's service contract available for inspection must disclose or have attached to it details of the unexpired term of the contract and details of any notice period, all details of the director's remuneration, including salary and other benefits, any commission or profit-sharing arrangements, any provision for compensation payable upon early termination of the contract and any other matters necessary to enable investors to estimate the possible liability of the company following early termination of the contract. Companies must require directors (and some employees) and their families to comply with internal rules governing dealings by directors and their families as strict as the model set of rules published by the exchange. Directors who wish to buy or sell securities in their own companies must comply with the provisions of the Criminal Justice Act 1993 (discussed in the next section).

Foreign companies are subject to a simplified set of continuing obligations if they are already listed on their domestic stock exchange.

SHAREHOLDER PROTECTION CODES

A) Regulatory framework

The single most important piece of shareholder protection legislation is the Financial Services Act 1986 (FSA). This lays down the framework for the rules under which all investment businesses (including activities relating to the securities markets) must operate. Broadly, investment business may only be carried on by persons who are authorised under the FSA. Currently, overall responsibility for the regulatory framework lies with the Securities and Investments Board (SIB), which supervises the various autonomous self-regulating organisations (SROs) through which the system is administered. Most firms seeking authorisation to carry on investment business do so through application to an SRO. Breach of an SRO's rules by a member can give rise to a civil action by a private investor who suffers loss as a result. SIB has set up a compensation scheme for investors with unsatisfied claims against regulated investment businesses by reason of insolvency.

In May 1997, the government proposed sweeping changes to the UK financial regulatory system. A new super regulator is to be established to bring regulation under a single body. It was announced in November 1997 that the new body will be called the Financial Services Authority. The legislation creating the Financial Services Authority will be enacted in two stages. First, a new Bank of England Act will transfer responsibility for banking supervision to SIB. Royal Assent is expected in Spring 1998. Secondly, a new Financial Services Act is proposed to rationalise the existing legislation and to transfer to the Financial Services Authority the functions of the SROs, together with the responsibilities currently exercised by other regulatory bodies including the Insurance Directorate of the Department of Trade and Industry, the Building Societies Commission and the Securities and Investments Board. Enactment is planned for Autumn 1999 when the Financial Services Authority will become responsible for all regulated activities and new ombudsmen and compensation arrangements will become operational. The SROs will then be wound up.

The aims of the Financial Services Authority will include protecting consumers of financial services, promoting orderly markets and maintaining confidence in the financial system. Its regulatory functions will include policy formation and review, and supervision of authorised firms and individuals, including conducting investigations and taking disciplinary action.

B) Insider trading

The exchange investigates share price movements for signs of insider trading, which first became a criminal offence in 1980. If evidence of an offence is found, the matter is passed to the relevant authorities who may prosecute. The exchange cooperates with the Takeover Panel in the investigation of dealings during contested takeovers in order to improve detection of possible market manipulation.

The Criminal Justice Act 1993 implemented an EU Directive on insider trading and significantly extended the scope of the original law in a number of areas. It is a criminal offence for an individual, who has inside information as an insider, to deal in securities that are "price-affected" securities in relation to that information, or to encourage another person to deal. It is also a criminal offence for such an individual to disclose the information to another person, other than in the proper performance of his employment, office or profession. The dealing in question must either be on a regulated market or must involve a professional intermediary.

One of the most significant changes to the original UK legislation is that there is no longer a requirement for an insider to be "connected" with the issuer to which his information relates. This significantly expanded the number of potential insiders. The territorial scope of the legislation was widened to catch dealings on most EU markets, rather than just UK markets.

C) Takeovers and mergers

The City Code on Takeovers and Mergers, administered by the Takeover Panel, was drawn up in 1968 to regulate the conduct of takeovers in the UK. Since July 1997, the Code no longer applies to offers for Irish incorporated companies that are listed in the UK. These are now regulated by the Irish Takeover Panel.

The Code applies to public companies, both listed and unlisted, and to any private company that has had various kinds of public involvement in the 10 years prior to the acquisition. The Code is not concerned with the commercial advantages or disadvantages of a takeover. The Code lays down general principles of good standards of commercial behaviour to be followed by the parties to a takeover transaction and also contains detailed rules designed to ensure, among other things, that all shareholders of the target company are treated fairly and equally by an offeror and are given sufficient information and advice to enable them to reach a properly informed decision, that all offer documents and other information sent to shareholders are prepared with the highest standards of care and accuracy, and that the board of the target company takes no action to frustrate an offer.

The Code does not carry the force of law, but any person who has breached it may find the facilities of the securities markets withheld. It has been made clear by both the government and other regulatory authorities that anyone wanting to make use of the UK securities markets should conduct matters relating to takeovers in accordance with the Code. Certain aspects of the Financial Services Act and the regulatory regime established under it have also enhanced the effectiveness of the Code; for example, where a person is authorised by a regulatory body to carry on investment business, that regulator may withdraw authorisation if the Code is not followed.

The Takeover Panel is not a statutory body, although its decisions are subject to judicial review. However, the range of circumstances in which judicial review of such decisions will be appropriate is very narrow, and any intervention by the courts is likely to be by way of declaratory orders that would not be retrospective – ie, preventing the Panel from repeating any error, but allowing contemporary decisions to take their course.

The status of the Panel may change if the proposal for a Takeover Directive, adopted by the European Commission in February 1996, is implemented. As the proposed Directive is currently the subject of debate in Europe, it is difficult to predict whether or not it will be adopted. The Industry Council met in December 1997 to consider adopting a revised proposal and to try to reach a common position. If adopted, the Thirteenth Company Law Directive on Takeovers will require statutory regulation of takeovers to be implemented by member states at a domestic level.

RESEARCH

There is a vast array of research information available to investors concerning the UK market.

Stock exchange publications

Stock Exchange Fact Book (quarterly)
Stock Exchange Fact Sheet (monthly)

Financial newspapers

Financial Times (daily)
The Wall Street Journal (Europe) (daily)
Financial News

Financial magazines

Euromoney (monthly)
Investors' Chronicle (weekly)
The Economist (weekly)
Global Investor (monthly)

CHAPTER 73

United States of America

Introduction

There are eight stock markets in the US, and the three national markets – the New York Stock Exchange (NYSE), the Nasdaq Stock Market (Nasdaq) and the American Stock Exchange (AMEX) – are the largest. The principal exchange is still the NYSE, although its share of turnover among the three main markets has fallen from 73% in 1990 to 44% in 1997. The NYSE's market capitalisation, however, is equal to around 116% of GDP, by far the highest of all the exchanges. The second exchange, Nasdaq, tends to list smaller companies and, while it lists almost twice the number of companies, its capitalisation is only 20% of the NYSE total.

The NYSE set records in 1997 for trading volume, non-US listings and market capitalisation. It had its 10 busiest trading days ever in 1997, led by 28 October, when 1.2 billion shares were traded, and 19 December, when 793 million shares were traded.

The Dow Jones Industrial Average of blue chip stocks closed 1997 at 7,908.25, up 1,459.98 points, or 23%, while the more broadly based NYSE Composite Index rose by 181.89 points (30%) and ended the year at 511.19. The combined market capitalisation of the NYSE, Nasdaq and AMEX stood at US$11.41 trillion at end-December 1997, 28% ahead of the end-1996 total. Market value on all three main markets increased in 1997.

ECONOMIC AND POLITICAL OVERVIEW

The US economy began 1997 with considerable momentum following a robust end to 1996. The above-trend pace was spurred by healthy consumer spending, a busy housing sector, strong monetary growth and firm capital investment trends. Against this background, the Federal Reserve changed course and tightened monetary policy in March, lifting the target rate on Fed funds to 5.5% from 5.25% – the first such tightening move since February 1995. With the Fed adopting an asymmetrical bias toward further tightening, long-term interest rates continued to rise through the first quarter of the year, peaking at 7.17% in mid-April.

However, somewhat slower economic activity in the middle quarters of the year, combined with continued better-than-expected news on the inflation front, kept the Fed from adopting a more aggressive policy stance. Moreover, by late summer it had become apparent that the adverse currency developments brewing in south-east Asia were likely to discourage the monetary authorities from tightening monetary policy further despite continued healthy trends in the domestic economy.

Indeed, once the full brunt of the Asian crisis shocked the world's markets in late October, investor expectations began to shift towards the possibility of monetary easing by the G7 authorities in an effort to preclude a potentially adverse deflationary shock from overseas. As a result, long-term bonds in the US rallied sharply, bringing yields down below 5.7% and undercutting the previous cyclical lows achieved in late 1993. At the same time, commodity prices plunged and the dollar, as the safe-haven currency, continued to strengthen.

The Asian crisis notwithstanding, the US economy turned in an impressive performance in 1997. Real GDP expanded close to 4%, its fastest annual increase in 10 years, while the unemployment rate plunged to 4.75%, its lowest sustained level since the late 1960s. Average consumer price inflation declined to just 2.3% in 1997. Meanwhile, faster wage and salary gains fuelled rising real incomes and worker productivity rose smartly.

Congress finally passed the Balanced Budget Act of 1997 and agreed to a cut in the capital gains tax rate from

Exhibit 73.1: DOW JONES INDUSTRIALS PRICE INDEX (US$), 1993–97

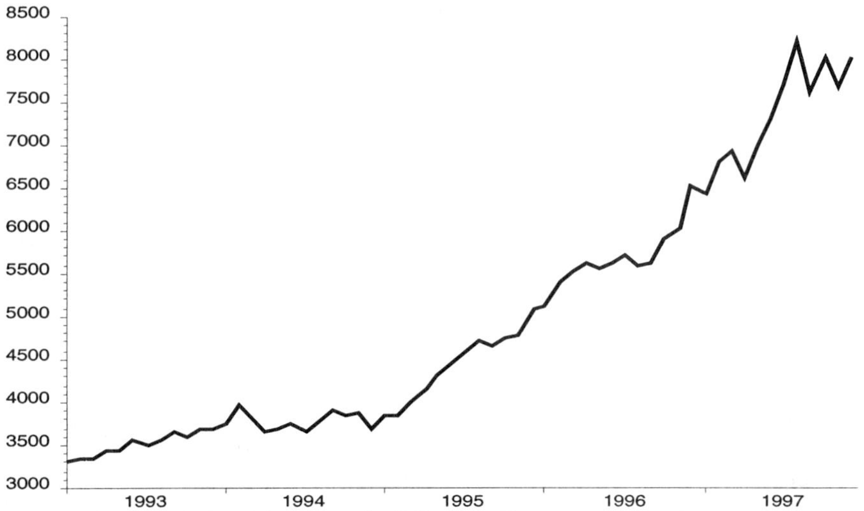

High value 8194.04 1.8.97 Low value 3301.12 1.1.93 *Source: Datastream*

28% to 20%. Impressively, 1997 saw a dramatic decline in the government budget deficit to just 0.11% of GDP and progress toward the administration's first submission of a balanced budget in over 30 years.

On the political front, 1997 will be remembered as a year in which President Clinton continued to ward off accusations of impropriety, and began a serious confrontation with Saddam Hussein over United Nations weapons inspections.

Role of the central bank

The Federal Reserve, created by an Act of Congress in 1913, is the US's central bank. The Federal Reserve System consists of a seven-member board of governors plus a nationwide network of 12 Federal Reserve Banks (FRBs) and 25 Reserve Bank branches. The FRBs were established by Congress as the operating arm of the nation's central banking system, and they have both public and private elements.

In addition to providing a variety of financial services to the US Treasury, financial institutions and the public, the Reserve Banks act as vital sources of information about the economy and financial developments in all parts of the nation.

The US Congress has ultimate authority over the Federal Reserve and oversees it through appropriate committees. The board of governors is required by law to report to Congress annually on the Federal Reserve's activities. As regards monetary policy, the Federal Reserve is required by statute to report to Congress twice a year on its plans and objectives. Members of the board, particularly the chairman, are frequently requested by Congressional committees to testify on financial and economic issues.

MARKET PERFORMANCE

A) In 1997

It turned out to be yet another stellar year for the US financial markets, with all major indices achieving new all-time highs. For the year, the S&P 500 posted a total return (including dividends) of 33.4%, the index's 11th best performance on record. The Dow Jones Industrial Average gained 22.6%, closing at 7,908.25 after peaking at 8,259.31 on 6 August, while the New York Stock Exchange Index rose 30.3% and the Nasdaq Composite Index climbed 21.6%. It was the third consecutive year of 20%+ gains in the equity market – a period of above-average performance unequalled in this century. Once again, stocks significantly outperformed bonds for the fourth straight year, although the bond market still produced a respectable 14.9% total return.

Yet, despite the strong gains in financial markets, the year was characterised by heightened investor anxiety and a notable increase in market volatility. Indeed, 1997 produced three distinct market corrections in March/April (-9.6% on the S&P), August (-6.3%) and October/November (-10.8%), with the latter being the first decline in excess of 10% since the bear market in 1990. Moreover, the NYSE's circuit-breakers were triggered on a record 219 days, more than twice the 101 days in 1996.

It was also a year marked by vigorous rotation between market sectors and segments. The first half of the year was dominated by the outperformance of large capitalisation stocks, which were perceived to be taking market share from their smaller competitors. But with the passage of the capital gains tax reduction and a shift in relative earnings momentum, investors began to move back into small and mid-cap stocks in the summer – a rotation that gained strength during the August correction and persisted into early autumn.

However, the onset of the Asian currency crisis in late October rattled the US equity market, culminating in a 535 point loss on 27 October – the largest point drop on record apart from the crash in 1987. For the remainder of the year, investors embraced the traditionally defensive utilities and non-cyclical sectors, and biased their investment decisions away from those companies perceived to be exposed to the Asian region in favour of domestically oriented stocks, particularly in the consumer sectors.

The market's impressive performance in 1997 was driven largely by the favourable combination of declining long-term interest rates and continued strong corporate earnings growth (+10% vs 1996). However, while corporate profits clearly exceeded investor expectations, they did not keep pace with the sharply rising equity market, and thus valuations were stretched to their highest levels in over 25 years. By mid-summer, the P/E of the S&P 500 had reached 23.2 on a trailing basis while the dividend yield declined to a record low at 1.6%.

Also instrumental in fuelling the market's resilient advance in 1997 was the continued strong flow of funds backdrop. Of particular note was the surge in M&A activity. According to Securities Data Corporation, US companies announced an amazing US$920 billion-worth of mergers and acquisitions, shattering previous records. At the same time, US firms indicated a record US$180 billion of share repurchase intentions and equity mutual funds took in a record US$231 billion of new cash flow.

Finally, a look at the sector composition of stock market performance in 1997 reveals greatest relative strength from the finance sector, which soared 45.4% for the year, followed by healthcare (+41.5%), communication services (+37.2%), consumer cyclicals (+34.4%) and consumer staples (+31.8%). Lagging sectors included basic materials (+7.0%), utilities (+18.6%) and energy (+21.9%).

B) Summary information

Global ranking by market value (US$ terms, end-1997): 1
Short-term (3-month T-bill) interest rate (end-1997): 5.16%
Long-term (30-year) government bond yield (end-1997): 5.95%
MSCI total returns (with net dividends, US$ terms, 1997): 33.4%
MSCI Index (change in US$ terms, 1997): +31.7%
Budget deficit as a % of nominal GDP (end-1997): 0.11%
Annual increase in broad money (M3) supply (end-1997): 8.4%
Inflation rate (1997): 2.3%

NYSE
Market capitalisation (end-1997): US$9,413.1 billion
Growth in market value (local currency terms, 1993–97): 107.09%
Market value as a % of nominal GDP (end-1997): 116.45%
Number of domestic/foreign companies listed (end-1997): 2,691/356
Market P/E (S&P 500 Index companies, end-1997): 23.9

Nasdaq
Market capitalisation (end-1997): US$1,834.8 billion
Growth in market value (local currency terms, 1993–97): 131.9%
Market value as a % of nominal GDP (end-1997): 22.69%
Number of domestic/foreign companies listed (end-1997): 5,032/455
Market P/E (domestic common and beneficial interest stocks, end-1997): 61.8

AMEX
Market capitalisation (end-1997): US$162.16 billion
Growth in market value (local currency terms, 1993–97): 20.03%
Market value as a % of nominal GDP (end-1997): 2%
Number of domestic/foreign companies listed (end-1997): 708/63
Market P/E (all listed companies, end-1997): 21.7

C) Year-end share price indices, price/earnings ratios and yields

Exhibit 73.2:
YEAR-END SHARE PRICE INDICES, 1993–97

	1993	*1994*	*1995*	*1996*	*1997*
Dow Jones Industrial Average	3,754.09	3,834.44	5,117.12	6,448.27	7,908.25
NYSE Composite Index	259.08	250.94	329.51	392.30	511.19
Nasdaq 100 Index	398.28	404.27	576.23	821.36	990.80
S&P 500 Index	466.45	459.27	615.93	740.74	970.43

Sources: New York Stock Exchange and Nasdaq.

Exhibit 73.3:
NYSE AND NASDAQ P/E RATIOS AND NYSE COMMON STOCK INDEX YIELD, 1993–97

Year-end	*NYSE P/E*	*Nasdaq P/E*	*NYSE yield (%)*
1993	23.4	39.8	2.8
1994	19.9	29.7	3.0
1995	18.1	35.3	2.7.5
1996	19.8	50.3	2.3
1997	22.5	61.8	1.8

Sources: New York Stock Exchange and Nasdaq.

D) Market indices and their constituents

Dow Jones averages

There are four Dow Jones averages: the Industrial Average, the Transportation Average, the Utility Average and the Composite Average.

The Dow Jones Industrial Average is one of the most frequently quoted indices, often referred to simply as the Dow. It is the simple arithmetic average of price movements of 30 large manufacturing companies. The Transportation Average is the average of price movements of 20 transport companies, and the Utility Average is the average of price movements of 15 utility companies. The Composite Average is a combination of these three averages.

Standard and Poor's (S&P) 500 Index

The S&P 500 Index is calculated by taking the total market value of the 500 stocks in the index, dividing by their weighted average market value during the period 1941 to 1943 and then multiplying by 10.

NYSE Composite Index

This index covers all common stocks traded on the NYSE. Each is weighted by its market value. In addition, the NYSE publishes specialised indices for industrial, utility, transport and financial companies. The indices are a measure of the changes in aggregate market value of NYSE common stocks, adjusted to eliminate the effects of capitalisation changes, new listings and delistings.

Nasdaq Index

The Nasdaq Composite Index (February 1971 = 100) is the most broadly based of all the major US market indices, measuring the performance of 5,551 securities. It is market value-weighted, as are its sub-indices covering banks, biotechnology, computers, industrials, insurance, other finance, telecommunications and transportation. The Nasdaq National Market (NNM) also compiles the market value-weighted NNM Composite Index (measuring 4,237 issues) and the NNM Index. On 1 February 1985 the Nasdaq 100 and Nasdaq Financial Indices were launched (at 250) to measure some of the 100 largest (by market value) non-financial and financial issues.

AMEX Composite Index

Introduced on 2 January 1997, this is a capitalisation-weighted, price appreciation index (based at 29 December 1995 = 550), which replaces the AMEX Market Value Index (in use since 1973). Components of the index include the common stocks or American depository receipts (ADRs) of all AMEX-listed companies, real estate investment trusts (REITs), master limited partnerships and closed-end investment vehicles. Five sub-indices of the Composite Index track companies in the information technology, financial, healthcare, natural resources and industrial sectors.

THE STOCK MARKET

A) Brief history and structure

New York Stock Exchange

The NYSE is the largest exchange in the world. Its origins date back to 1792 when 24 brokers signed an agreement to trade, principally in the new government's debt, from an outside location on Wall Street. The name "New York Stock Exchange" was adopted in 1863, the year in which the exchange moved to the premises that it still occupies today.

The Nasdaq Stock Market

More than 50% of shares traded in the US are traded on Nasdaq. By using a blend of screen-based trading technology and market-maker competition, Nasdaq has greatly influenced the way stocks are traded around the world. In addition, a variety of new market services have automated many of the order-entry, execution and post-execution stages.

In January 1992, newly installed computer facilities in the UK permitted Nasdaq to commence the operation of the world's first inter-continental stock market during London's trading hours.

The equities traded via Nasdaq include common shares, convertible debentures, regular foreign shares and ADRs, and equity securities listed on US exchanges. More foreign shares trade on Nasdaq than on all the other American markets combined.

American Stock Exchange

An outdoor market-place until 1921, the name American Stock Exchange was adopted in 1953. Through the years, the AMEX has earned a reputation for innovation, opening the industry to new ideas through the introduction of state-of-the-art trading floor technology and new derivative products.

As a primary equities market and a derivative securities market-place, the AMEX provides auction market trading for common and preferred stocks and corporate and government debt securities, as well as options and warrants on equities and stock indices.

Based in New York, the exchange provides a market for stocks and bonds of companies not large enough to qualify for the NYSE. Its listing requirements are less stringent and it encourages the registration of relatively young companies. It also lists a considerable number of foreign stocks.

Exhibit 73.4:
NASDAQ, NYSE AND AMEX LISTINGS AND MARKET VALUE, 1993–97

	No. of companies			*No. of issues*			*Market value (US$ billion)*		
Year-end	*Nasdaq*	*NYSE*	*AMEX*	*Nasdaq*	*NYSE*	*AMEX*	*Nasdaq*	*NYSE*	*AMEX*
1993	4,611	2,362	868	5,393	2,927	1,005	791.2	4,545.4	135.1
1994	4,902	2,570	824	5,761	3,150	981	786.5	4,448.3	113.6
1995	5,122	2,675	791	5,955	3,279	936	1,159.9	6,013.0	137.3
1996	5,556	2,907	751	6,384	3,531	896	1,511.8	7,300.4	126.7
1997	5,487	3,047	771	6,208	3,674	893	1,834.8	9,413.1	162.2

Sources: New York Stock Exchange and Nasdaq.

B) Opening hours, names and addresses

All the US markets are open from 9.30am to 4.00pm, Monday to Friday.

NEW YORK STOCK EXCHANGE
11 Wall Street, New York, NY 10005
Tel: 1 (212) 656 3000
Web site: www.nyse.com

THE NASDAQ STOCK MARKET
1735 K Street, NW, Washington DC 20006
Tel: 1 (202) 728 8000
Web site: www.nasdaq.com

AMERICAN STOCK EXCHANGE
86 Trinity Place, New York, NY 10006
Tel: 1 (212) 306 1000
Web site: www.amex.com

BOSTON STOCK EXCHANGE
One Boston Place, Boston MA 02108
Tel: 1 (617) 723 9500

MIDWEST STOCK EXCHANGE
One Financial Place
440 South LaSalle Street, Chicago, Illinois 60605
Tel: 1 (312) 663 2222

PACIFIC STOCK EXCHANGE
301 Pine Street, San Francisco, CA 94104
Tel: 1 (415) 393 4000

CINCINNATI STOCK EXCHANGE
49 East Fourth Street, Cincinnati, Ohio 45202
Tel: 1 (513) 621 1410

PHILADELPHIA STOCK EXCHANGE
1900 Market Street, Philadelphia, PA 19103
Tel: 1 (215) 496 5000

MARKET SIZE

A) Number of listings and market value

At the end of 1997 there were:

- 3,047 companies listed on the NYSE with a market value of US$9.4 trillion, a capitalisation increase of 29% compared with end-1996;
- 5,487 companies listed on Nasdaq with a market value of US$1,834.8 billion, an increase of 21% over the year; and
- 771 companies listed on AMEX with a total market value of US$162.2 billion, an increase of 28% on end-1996.

B) Largest quoted companies

Exhibit 73.5:
THE 20 LARGEST LISTED COMPANIES ON THE NYSE, END-1997

Ranking	*Company*	*Market value (US$ million)*
1	General Electric	287,823
2	Coca-Cola	222,963
3	Exxon Corporation	176,967
4	Merck & Co	174,002
5	Morris (Philip)	116,447
6	Pfizer	113,018
7	Bristol-Myers Squibb	112,547
8	Johnson & Johnson	102,737
9	International Business Machines	102,416
10	AT&T	101,796
11	Wal-Mart Stores	91,714
12	American International Group	83,738
13	Eli Lilly and Company	75,810
14	Schering-Plough	73,443
15	Bell Atlantic	72,942
16	Walt Disney	72,813
17	SBC Communications	72,342
18	Fannie May	69,721
19	Berkshire Hathaway	68,711
20	American Home Products	67,851

Source: New York Stock Exchange.

Exhibit 73.6:
THE 20 LARGEST LISTED COMPANIES ON NASDAQ, END-1997

Ranking	*Company*	*Market value (US$ million)*
1	Microsoft	156,005
2	Intel	114,830
3	Cisco Systems	56,442
4	Dell Computer	27,972
5	WorldCom	27,442
6	MCI Communications Corporation	23,797
7	Oracle Corporation	21,877
8	Washington Mutual	16,411
9	Sun Microsystems	14,938
10	Amgen	14,246
11	Tele-Communications	13,200
12	Fifth Third Bancorp	12,662
13	3Com Corporation	12,087
14	Applied Materials	11,052
15	LM Ericsson Telephone Company	10,542
16	Comcast	9,734
17	Tellabs	9,595
18	HBO & Company	9,592
19	Costco Companies	9,501
20	PeopleSoft	8,775

Source: Nasdaq.

Exhibit 73.7:
THE 20 LARGEST LISTED COMPANIES ON AMEX, END-1997

Ranking	*Company*	*Market value (US$ million)*
1	BAT Industries	29,122.1
2	Viacom Cl. B	14,596.8
3	Imperial Oil	9,690.0
4	EdperBrascan Corporation	5,062.8
5	Hasbro	4,218.5
6	Thermo Instrument Systems	4,188.4
7	Nabors Industries	3,188.9
8	Canadian Occidental Petroleum	3,090.8
9	First Empire State Corporation	3,068.1
10	Keane	2,675.5
11	Telephone and Data Systems	2,450.8
12	Wesco Financial Corporation	2,136.0
13	Giant Food	2,014.2
14	Forest Laboratories	1,987.4
15	Courtaulds	1,881.0
16	FINA	1,870.1
17	NFC	1,787.2
18	United States Cellular Corporation	1,650.1
19	Tubos de Acero de Mexico	1,508.1
20	Cablevision Systems Corporation	1,333.8

Source: American Stock Exchange.

C) Trading volume

Exhibit 73.8:
VOLUME ON THE NYSE, NASDAQ AND AMEX, 1993–97

Year	*NYSE shares traded (million)*	*Nasdaq shares traded (million)*	*AMEX shares traded (million)*
1993	66,923	66,540	4,582
1994	73,420	74,353	4,522
1995	87,217	101,200	5,072
1996	104,636	138,112	5,628
1997	133,312	163,882	6,170

Sources: Nasdaq and New York Stock Exchange.

Exhibit 73.9:
THE 20 MOST ACTIVELY TRADED SHARES, NYSE, 1997

Ranking	*Company*	*Trading value (US$ million)*
1	International Business Machines	104,348
2	Compaq Computer	92,652
3	Telecomm Brasil	79,465
4	General Electric	64,765
5	Merck	61,813
6	Philip Morris	60,530
7	Citicorp	58,846
8	Chase Manhattan New	58,406
9	Texas Instruments	46,799
10	Coca-Cola	46,459
11	AT&T Corp	43,477
12	Motorola	42,118
13	Boeing	41,521
14	Exxon	41,114
15	Pfizer	38,309
16	Micron Technology	37,947
17	Hewlett-Packard	37,775
18	Bristol-Myers Squibb	36,413
19	du Pont de Nemours	34,673
20	Procter & Gamble	34,650

Source: New York Stock Exchange.

Exhibit 73.10:
THE 20 MOST ACTIVELY TRADED SHARES, NASDAQ, 1997

Ranking	*Company*	*Trading volume (million shares)*
1	Cisco Systems	5,386.6
2	Ascend Communications	3,892.0
3	Intel	3,887.9
4	Dell Computer	3,719.0
5	Tele-Communications	2,456.3

Exhibit 73.10 continued

6	3Com	2,200.4
7	Microsoft	2,097.9
8	Oracle	1,970.2
9	Applied Materials	1,804.2
10	WorldCom	1,784.8
11	FORE Systems	1,519.5
12	Sun Microsystems	1,490.3
13	Pairgain Technologies	1,474.6
14	MCI Communications	1,457.7
15	Altera	1,396.4
16	Atmel	1,321.7
17	Netscape Communications	1,238.7
18	Oxford Health Plans	1,207.2
19	Xilinx	1,200.4
20	Staples	1,144.3

Source: Nasdaq.

Exhibit 73.11:
THE 20 MOST ACTIVELY TRADED SHARES, AMEX, 1997

Ranking	*Company*	*Trading volume (million shares)*
1	Standard & Poor's Depository Receipts (SPDRS)	801.4
2	Viacom (Cl. B)	223.1
3	Trans World Airlines	222.8
4	Harken Energy Corporation	214.5
5	Echo Bay Mines	188.7
6	JTS Corporation	177.0
7	Nabors Industries	172.9
8	Hasbro	159.1
9	Royal Oak Mines	140.9
10	Grey Wolf Industries	132.9
11	IVAX Corporation	132.5
12	Tubos de Acero de Mexico	108.8
13	Pegasus Gold	104.4
14	First Australia Prime Income Fund	99.6
15	Bema Gold Corporation	99.4
16	HEARx	93.0
17	Keane	72.0
18	Metromedia International Group	70.1
19	Greyhound Lines	68.1
20	Ampex Corporation	65.6

Source: American Stock Exchange.

TYPES OF SHARES

A) Common stock

Shares carrying the right both to vote and to participate in a distribution of the net assets of the corporation on dissolution are generally referred to as "common stock", of which there can be more than one class. The general rule is one share/one vote.

B) Preferred stock

The articles of incorporation of a company may authorise one or more classes of preferred shares, which can have different limitations and preferential rights relating to voting, convertibility, redeemability, dividends and liquidation. Combinations of these characteristics create varieties such as cumulative convertible preferred stock, adjustable-rate cumulative preferred stock, exchangeable preferred stock and floating-rate preferred stock.

C) American depository receipts

American depository receipts (ADRs) are negotiable certificates in registered form, issued in the US by a US bank, certifying that a specific number of foreign shares have been deposited with an overseas branch of the bank (or another financial institution), which acts as a custodian in the country of origin.

ADRs provide a practical opportunity for investors who want to invest in the shares of a foreign corporation to buy, hold and sell their interests in these foreign securities without having to take physical possession of the securities, while receiving dividends and exercising voting rights conveniently. A holder of ADRs can, at any time, request the underlying shares. Conversely, ADRs enable foreign corporations with shares that have not been admitted to a US stock exchange to obtain access to US public capital markets. Usually, only shares traded on a recognised foreign stock exchange are represented by ADRs.

D) Trust certificates of beneficial interest

A trust certificate of beneficial interest represents an equity interest in the underlying assets of a trust that holds debt securities or other interests. The certificates represent pro rata ownership of the underlying assets. The holders of the certificates are entitled to receive dividends based on their pro rata ownership but voting power may be limited to the election of trustees.

E) Warrants

Warrants are certificates that, just like an option, give the holder the right to purchase or sell shares at a stipulated price within a determined period. Unlike options, which usually are for a limited duration, warrants can be held for several years and, in some cases, without a time limit. Warrants are often attached to other securities and function as an added purchase inducement. In many cases warrants may be traded separately once issued.

F) Stock index warrants/options

Futures and options tied to the performance of major national and international stock markets have been traded over-the-counter and on the futures and options markets for many years. Recently, stock index derivatives have

Exhibit 73.12:
TOP PERFORMING COUNTRY FUNDS – US

Fund	US$ % change 31/12/96 31/12/97	US$ % change 31/12/92 31/12/97	Currency	Fund size (US$ mil)	Volatility	Manager name	Main sector	Class
Royal US Equity Fund C$	80.53	178.3	C$	348.58	9.38	Royal Mutual Funds	Equities	Canadian Mutuals
American Heritage Fund	75	5.42	US$	16.1	8.64	American Heritage Funds	Equity Growth	US Mutuals
Munder: Micro Cap Equity/Y	71.53	N/A	US$	12.1	N/A	Munder Funds	Equity Growth	US Mutuals
Munder: Micro Cap Equity/K	71.24	N/A	US$	2.7	N/A	Munder Funds	Equity Growth	US Mutuals
Munder: Micro Cap Equity/A	71.23	N/A	US$	7.6	N/A	Munder Funds	Equity Growth	US Mutuals
FMI Focus Fund	69.74	N/A	US$	12.8	N/A	FMI Funds	Equity Growth	US Mutuals
US Financial Equities	62.65	N/A	US$	16.6	3.47	Eldon Financial Cap Mgmt	Equity	Offshore Territories
Fidelity Sel: Brokerage	62.32	246.03	US$	663.6	5.5	Fidelity Select Funds	Equity Growth	US Mutuals
AJR International	61.26	N/A	US$	7.5	6.13	Atlantic Investment Mgmt Inc	Equity	Offshore Territories
FBR Small Cap Financial	58.1	N/A	US$	100.6	N/A	FBR Funds	Equity Growth	US Mutuals
Hartford Capital Apprec/Y	56.01	N/A	US$	33.4	N/A	Hartford Funds	Equity Growth	US Mutuals
Titan Financial Services	55.55	N/A	US$	26.8	N/A	Titan Funds	Equity Growth	US Mutuals
Alpine US Real Est Eq/Y	55.42	N/A	US$	26	4.56	Evergreen Funds	Equity Growth	US Mutuals
Hartford Capital Apprec/A	55.11	N/A	US$	288.5	N/A	Hartford Funds	Equity Growth	US Mutuals
Oakmark Select	55.02	N/A	US$	981.6	N/A	Oakmark Funds	Equity Growth	US Mutuals
Alpine US Real Est Eq/A	55.01	N/A	US$	8.3	4.58	Evergreen Funds	Equity Growth	US Mutuals
Brazos/JMIC Small Cap Gr	54.52	N/A	US$	127.6	N/A	Brazos/JMIC Funds	Equity Growth	US Mutuals
Hartford Capital Apprec/B	54.15	N/A	US$	224.4	N/A	Hartford Funds	Equity Growth	US Mutuals
Alpine US Real Est Eq/C	53.94	N/A	US$	3.3	4.57	Evergreen Funds	Equity Growth	US Mutuals
J Hancock Regional Bank/A	53.92	260.12	US$	1,836.40	3.4	John Hancock Funds	Equity Growth	US Mutuals
Alpine US Real Est Eq/B	53.87	N/A	US$	8.3	4.58	Evergreen Funds	Equity Growth	US Mutuals
J Hancock Regional Bank/B	52.83	248.42	US$	5,500.60	3.4	John Hancock Funds	Equity Growth	US Mutuals
MFS Strategic Growth/I	52.11	N/A	US$	18.7	N/A	MFS Funds	Equity Growth	US Mutuals
MFS Strategic Growth/A	50.4	N/A	US$	91.1	N/A	MFS Funds	Equity Growth	US Mutuals
Century Shares Trust	50.13	127.72	US$	436	3.85	Century Funds	Equity Growth	US Mutuals
SAFECO Growth	49.96	179.22	US$	1,030.50	4.68	SAFECO Funds	Equity Growth	US Mutuals
SAFECO Growth/Adv A	49.61	N/A	US$	5.6	N/A	SAFECO Funds	Equity Growth	US Mutuals
Glbl Mgr US Geared	49.48	N/A	US$	4.4	5.87	BIIML	Equity	Offshore Territories
Gabelli International Ltd	48.74	186.44	US$	25.7	2.91	Gabelli Securities Inc	Equity	Offshore Territories
SAFECO Growth/Adv B	48.7	N/A	US$	3	N/A	SAFECO Funds	Equity Growth	US Mutuals
Cambrian Fund	48.56	406.27	US$	22	6.09	Atlantic Investment Mgmt Inc	Equity	Offshore Territories
Gabelli Value Fund	48.23	175.25	US$	694.6	4.05	Gabelli Funds	Equity Growth	US Mutuals
Mass Inv Growth Stock/A	48.15	149.36	US$	2,258.00	4.36	Mass Investors Funds	Equity Growth	US Mutuals
Delaware Voy Aggr Grth/A	48.08	N/A	US$	16.2	7.85	Delaware Voyageur Funds	Equity Growth	US Mutuals
FBR Financial Services	47.74	N/A	US$	43.6	N/A	FBR Funds	Equity Growth	US Mutuals
For & Col US Smaller Cos Wts	47.62	N/A	£	12.04	9.93	Foreign & Colonial Mgmt Ltd	Equity Growth	UK Investment Trusts
Evergreen Micro Cap/Y	47.59	79.53	US$	53.7	3.93	Evergreen Funds	Equity Growth	US Mutuals
Transamerica Prem Eq/Inv	47.51	N/A	US$	187.2	N/A	Transamerica Funds	Equity Growth	US Mutuals
Mass Inv Growth Stock/B	47.11	N/A	US$	190.2	4.35	Mass Investors Funds	Equity Growth	US Mutuals
Evergreen Micro Cap/A	47.1	N/A	US$	4.9	3.92	Evergreen Funds	Equity Growth	US Mutuals
State St Rsrch: Aurora/S	46.98	N/A	US$	1.2	4.33	State Street Research Funds	Equity Growth	US Mutuals
Delaware Voy Aggr Grth/C	46.72	N/A	US$	2.2	7.85	Delaware Voyageur Funds	Equity Growth	US Mutuals
State St Rsrch: Aurora/A	46.64	N/A	US$	208.1	4.32	State Street Research Funds	Equity Growth	US Mutuals
Regan International Ltd	46.43	N/A	US$	51.79	N/A	Regan Fund Management Ltd	Equity	Offshore Territories

Note: details for some funds may not have been included if the data for the US$ % change for 96/97 was not available

Source: Standard & Poor's Micropal.

begun to be traded on the regular securities exchanges. This rapidly growing market on various exchanges includes options and warrants (but not futures, which, unless the Commodity Futures Trading Commission has granted an exemption from the exchange-trading requirement, are restricted to the futures exchanges). Options and warrants are based on the NYSE Composite Index, the S&P 500, the FT-SE 100, the French CAC 40, the German DAX, and the Japanese Nikkei 225 indices.

G) Stock index participations

Stock index participations are hybrid products involving shares, stock index futures and stock index options. They can be seen as the economic equivalent of trading in a portfolio of securities to which the index is tied. An attempt by the SEC to authorise the trading of stock index participations on securities markets was challenged successfully in court because derivative products "with any element of futurity" fall under the exclusive jurisdiction of the Commodity Futures Trading Commission (CFTC) which oversees the commodities markets.

OTHER MARKETS

A) Chicago Board Options Exchange

In October 1990 the SEC approved a proposal by the CBOE to extend its activities to the trading of stocks.

B) Instinet

Instinet is a computerised execution service (Institutional Networks Corporation), registered with the SEC. The service permits subscribers to search for the opposite side of a trade, without the cost of brokerage. Instinet is used by many mutual funds and other institutional investors.

C) Rule 144A securities

Rule 144A, adopted by the SEC in April 1990, is designed to facilitate secondary market trading in "non-fungible" unregistered securities among "qualified institutional buyers" by providing a safe harbour from the registration requirements of the Securities Act 1933. Qualified institutional buyers (QIBs) are institutions that have US$100 million invested in securities of issuers that are not affiliated with the qualified buyer. Particular rules apply to broker-dealers, banks and thrifts. Nasdaq responded by developing trading systems specifically designed to permit trading under Rule 144A among QIBs.

OPERATIONS

A) Trading system

NYSE

Trading in stocks listed on the NYSE is conducted as a centralised continuous auction at a designated location on the trading floor, with brokers representing their customers' buy and sell orders. An electronic order-routing and reporting system, SuperDot, links member firms all over the world directly to the trading floor of the NYSE. With electronic speed and efficiency, SuperDot can direct market and limit orders to the specialist post where each stock is traded or to the member firm's booth on the trading floor.

The largest membership category is that of the commission broker. A commission broker is an employee in one of about 500 securities houses (stockbrokers) devoted to handling business on the exchange. He executes orders for his firm on behalf of its customers at agreed commission rates. These houses may deal on their own account as well as on behalf of their clients. Banks, however, are not allowed to act as principals and may only deal on their customers' behalf.

Other traders include the following categories:

- *Independent floor brokers* work within the exchange (on the floor) and execute orders for other exchange members who have more than they can handle alone or who require assistance in carrying out large orders. The floor broker takes a share in the commission received by the firm he is assisting.
- *Registered traders* are individual members in their own right who buy and sell on their own account. Alternatively, they may be trustees who maintain membership for the convenience of dealing and to save fees.
- *Specialists* are dealers assigned by the NYSE to conduct the auction and maintain an orderly market in one or more designated stocks. The specialist also acts as both broker and dealer. In his role as a broker or agent, he represents orders in his assigned stocks, arriving at his post electronically or entrusted to him by a floor broker, to be executed if and when a stock reaches a price specified by a customer. As a dealer, he buys and sells shares in his assigned stocks as necessary to maintain an orderly market, usually trading against the prevailing trend. He must always give precedence to public orders.

AMEX

Trading is conducted in an open auction market where free market competition enables buyers and sellers to get the best possible price. All trades are made public immediately over a worldwide consolidated tape network. Under AMEX rules, all public orders receive priority and there is no middleman.

An automated trading system at the AMEX enables brokers to electronically route equity orders directly to the specialist's post. Market orders and eligible limit orders are executed and made public within seconds, giving all investors the same information advantage.

Nasdaq

Nasdaq uses a screen-based system that centralises trading information to enable securities firms, no matter where they are located, to compete openly with one another via the computer. Unlike the exchanges, it has an electronic rather than a physical trading floor.

Another difference relative to the traditional exchanges is that Nasdaq trading is carried out by competing dealers or market-makers (535 in total) rather than by a single specialist. No limits are imposed on the number of market-makers that can compete for business in a security. Very active securities, such as Novell (59), Intel (46), and Apple (48) could have more than 60 market-makers. The typical stock has 11.

Through workstation terminals, market-makers enter the prices at which they are willing to buy and sell securities. They also use these terminals to negotiate trades, execute orders and report transactions. Nasdaq, in turn, sends the trade details to the clearing corporation for clearance and settlement and to information vendors for worldwide dissemination to securities firms, investors and the financial press.

B) List of principal brokers

ALEX BROWN & SONS
1 South Street, Baltimore, MD 21202
Tel: 1 (410) 727 1700

BEAR, STEARNS & CO
245 Park Avenue,
New York, NY 10167
Tel: 1 (212) 272 2000

CITIBANK
399 Park Avenue, New York, NY 10043
Tel: 1 (212) 291 1000

CS FIRST BOSTON
11 Madison Avenue, New York, NY 10010
Tel: 1 (212) 325 2000

DONALDSON, LUFKIN & JENRETTE
SECURITIES CORPORATION
277 Park Avenue, New York, NY 10172
Tel: 1 (212) 504 3000

GOLDMAN, SACHS & CO
85 Broad Street, New York, NY 10004
Tel: 1 (212) 902 1000

HAMBRECHT & QUIST
One Bush Street, San Francisco, CA 94104
Tel: 1 (415) 439 3300

LEHMAN BROTHERS
Three World Financial Center,
200 Vesey Street, American Express Tower
New York, NY 10285
Tel: 1 (212) 526 7000

MERRILL LYNCH CAPITAL MARKETS
World Financial Center, North Tower
250 Vesey Street, New York, NY 10281
Tel: 1 (212) 449 1000

MORGAN STANLEY & CO
1585 Broadway, New York, NY 10036
Tel: 1 (212) 761 4000

NATWEST SECURITIES CORP
175 Water Street, New York, NY 10038
Tel: 1 (212) 602 4776; Fax: 1 (212) 602 5773

PAINE WEBBER
1285 Avenue of the Americas, New York, NY 10019
Tel: 1 (212) 713 2000

PRUDENTIAL SECURITIES
One Seaport Plaza, 199 Water Street, New York, NY 10292
Tel: 1 (212) 214 1000

SALOMON SMITH BARNEY
388 Greenwich Street, New York, NY 10013-2396
Tel: 1 (212) 816 6000

CHARLES SCHWAB & CO
101 Montgomery Street, San Francisco, CA 94104
Tel: 1 (415) 627 7000

SCHRODER & CO
787 Seventh Avenue, New York, NY 10019
Tel: 1 (212) 492 6000

C) Settlement and transfer

From the moment a trade is executed on any major US exchange, a computerised system handles recording, settlement, delivery and safekeeping.

The Intermarket Trading System (ITS) is an electronic communications network that links the participating exchanges and the OTC market, and facilitates the execution of orders in eligible securities at the best ITS quote. ITS is not an automatic order-routing system, as each market-maker is responsible for monitoring and using the system appropriately.

All transactions made on the major exchanges (unless otherwise specified) must be settled within the Three Day Delivery Plan. Under this plan, "regular way" transactions, which constitute most transactions on the exchange, are due for settlement by delivery of the securities against payment on a T+3 basis. The exchange is authorised to impose late fees of up to US$100 a day per account for non-compliance.

The Midwest Clearing Corporation (MCC) provides clearing and settlement services for traders within the securities and banking industries. MCC participants can trade on any exchange or in any market and then settle those trades at a single location. The MCC is electronically linked to other clearing agencies.

D) Commissions and other costs

Fixed rates of commission were abolished in May 1975, and since then commissions have been subject to negotiation between the broker and customer on a competitive basis.

Since the introduction of negotiated commissions, the opportunity has arisen for the development of discount brokers. These brokers charge commission at rates about 60% less than those charged by other brokers, but offer no advice or any other service apart from execution of the transaction.

Stocks traded over-the-counter are sold to the client on a net price basis; the price as quoted by the dealer already takes into account the dealer's commission.

TAXATION AND REGULATIONS AFFECTING FOREIGN INVESTORS

A) Taxation

Dividends are subject to a withholding tax of 30% but tax treaties in most cases reduce the rate to 15% for portfolio investments and 5% or 10% for dividends paid by companies to non-residents having a substantial shareholding in that company. Rents and royalties are also subject to US withholding tax, although many tax treaties provide for exemptions or reduced rates. Interest on deposits with banks and insurance companies is exempt from US withholding tax. "Portfolio interest" is also not subject to US withholding tax. Generally, interest that does not qualify for the portfolio interest exception (including related party interest, certain contingent interest and certain interest received by banks) is subject to US withholding tax unless such tax is reduced or eliminated by a tax treaty.

In general, gains from the disposition of property (other than certain real property), including gains from the sale or exchange of stock or non-contingent debt and gains from options or warrants, are not subject to US withholding tax. Gains from the sale, exchange or retirement of certain contingent payment debt obligations, however, may be treated as interest and, therefore, be subject to the withholding rules described above for interest income. Income other than gains from investments in financial instruments that are neither stock nor debt for US tax purposes may also be subject to a withholding tax of 30% if such income is treated as paid from US sources and if such withholding rate is not reduced or eliminated by a treaty.

Additionally, as of 1997, substitute interest and dividends have been treated as interest and dividends for US withholding tax purposes.

Recent regulations, generally effective for payments after 31 December 1998, adopt more stringent standards for claiming the benefits of reduced withholding tax under tax treaties. In some circumstances, foreign persons who wish to claim the benefits of a treaty will be required to obtain a US taxpayer identification number and a certificate of residence in the foreign country (or other acceptable proof of such residence).

Exhibit 73.13: WITHHOLDING TAX

	Dividends % (portfolio)	*Dividends % (substantial holdings)*[1]	*Interest %*[2]
Resident corporations and individuals	Nil	Nil	
Non-resident corporations and individuals:			
Non-treaty countries	30	30	30
Treaty countries[3]	7.5–30	5–30	0–30

Notes:

1. These rates generally apply where the recipient corporation owns at least 10% of the outstanding voting shares of the payer corporation.
2. Portfolio interest (received on certain debt obligations issued after 18 July 1984) and interest paid by banks and insurance companies to specified foreign taxpayers may be exempt from tax.
3. Special rules may be applicable to payments to non-residents from foreign corporations doing business in the US.

Source: Price Waterhouse.

B) Exchange and investment restrictions

The US does not impose exchange controls and consequently foreign investors are not restricted as to repatriation of share capital, loans and income to their home country. Dividends, interest, royalties and service fees may also be repatriated freely. The US does, however, have certain "earnings stripping" limitations that may restrict the ability of US corporations to claim interest deductions for interest paid to related foreign shareholders.

Restrictions on direct foreign investment do exist in sensitive fields, such as communications, aviation, mining on federal land, energy, banking, insurance, real estate, agricultural land, coastal shipping and defence. Congress is currently considering measures that would tighten the review of proposed acquisitions of US firms by foreign entities.

C) Federal securities regulation

Securities regulations in the US derive from two basic securities laws (the Securities Act 1933 and the Securities Exchange Act 1934) passed during the "New Deal" era after the market crash in 1929. The SEC administers both Acts and has produced an extensive body of rules and regulations under each. The Securities Act 1933 makes it unlawful to offer securities to the public unless a registration statement has been filed with the SEC or an exemption is available. Any written offer must be made through the preliminary prospectus contained in the registration statement. A security may not be traded on a national securities exchange in the US (including the NYSE and AMEX) unless registered under the Securities Exchange Act 1934. Securities not registered and listed on a national securities exchange, but which are sold in the over-the-counter markets (including Nasdaq) or otherwise in the US, may also be required to be registered under the Securities Exchange Act 1934. Any foreign private issuer with total assets exceeding US$10 million and a publicly traded security held by at least 300 persons that are US residents, in each case as of the last day of such issuer's fiscal year, is required to register such security under the Securities Exchange Act 1934. Issuers of securities that are registered under the Securities Exchange Act 1934 automatically become subject to other requirements of the Securities Exchange Act 1934, including those related to periodic reporting, proxy solicitation, tender offers and insider reporting and trading. The Securities Exchange Act 1934 imposes annual (Form 10-K), quarterly (Form 10-Q) and current (Form 8-K) reporting requirements on US issuers, but only imposes an annual (Form 20-F) and a limited current (Form 6-K) reporting requirement on foreign private issuers. Foreign private issuers are exempt from the proxy solicitation, tender offer and insider reporting and trading requirements of the Securities Exchange 1934.

LISTING AND REPORTING REQUIREMENTS

A) Listing requirements for US companies

The NYSE requires that companies listed on the exchange satisfy certain quantitative standards and sign a listing agreement. The NYSE listing standards for US companies requires such companies to have:

(1) pre-tax income of US$2.5 million in the most recent fiscal year and US$2 million in the next two preceding fiscal years, or an aggregate pre-tax income of US$6.5 million in the most recent three fiscal years, with a minimum of US$4.5 million in the most recent fiscal year (all three fiscal years must be profitable);
(2) net tangible assets of US$40 million;
(3) aggregate market value in terms of publicly held shares in the US of US$40 million;
(4) 1.1 million shares publicly held in the US; and
(5) 2,000 holders of round lots (100 shares or more) in the US; or a total of 2,2000 shareholders and average monthly trading volume of 100,000 for the most recent six months.

Although the Nasdaq board of directors has recently adopted changes to its listing criteria, the listing standards and requirements of Nasdaq (and of the AMEX) are less stringent than those of the NYSE.

B) Listing requirements for non-US companies

In order to provide an alternative set of listing standards for companies organised outside the US that meet the normal size and earnings requirements for NYSE listings, the exchange considers the acceptability of such companies' shares and shareholders on a worldwide basis. Nasdaq/NM and regular Nasdaq listing requirements are essentially the same for non-US and US companies.

In view of the widespread use of bearer shares in other countries, in contrast to the use of registered shares in the US, a company would find difficulty certifying the requirements of 5,000 round-lot shareholders on a worldwide basis. Therefore, the NYSE requires that a member firm attests to the liquidity and depth of the market for the company's shares. These standards are met only where a broad liquid market exists for a company's shares in the company's home market.

Non-US companies may elect to qualify for listing on the NYSE under the NYSE's domestic listing criteria or under alternate standards designed to enable major non-US companies to list their shares on the NYSE. The principal criteria of the alternate standard focus on worldwide, rather than US, distribution of a non-US company's shares and apply where there is a broad, liquid market for a company's shares in its country of origin. The NYSE's alternate listing standards for non-US companies require companies to have:

(1) an aggregate pre-tax income of US$100 million in the most recent three years, with a minimum of US$25 million in any one of the three years;
(2) net tangible assets of US$100 million worldwide;
(3) aggregate market value in terms of publicly held shares of US$100 million worldwide;
(4) 2.5 million shares publicly held worldwide; and
(5) 5,000 holders of round lots (100 shares or more) worldwide.

Under AMEX guidelines, foreign issuers face similar listing requirements to domestic concerns. These are three years of operations; either US$4 million in shareholders' equity and pre-tax income of at least US$750,000 in the last fiscal year, or pre-tax income of US$750,000 in two of the last three fiscal years; US$3 million in capitalisation; minimum public distribution of 500,000 shares with 800 public shareholders, or minimum public distribution of one million shares with 400 public shareholders; and minimum market price of US$3 per share. Alternatively, a non-US company that does not meet the share distribution requirements may be considered for listing if it has 800 shareholders worldwide; public distribution of one million shares worldwide; and a market capitalisation of US$3 million. In addition, the NYSE, the AMEX and Nasdaq provide relief from certain corporate governance requirements that may conflict with laws or customs in a company's domicile.

C) Reporting requirements

Securities traded in the US must comply with the registration and periodic reporting requirements of the federal securities laws, regarded as the most stringent among major international markets. If listed on a US stock exchange, issuers must also comply with the reporting requirements imposed by that exchange.

Corporations signing the NYSE listing agreement are bound to notify the exchange of specific facts, such as any change in the general character or nature of their business, any change of officers or directors and any disposal by the corporation or any subsidiary of any property or stock interest in any of its controlled corporations, that will materially affect the financial position of the corporation. A listed corporation must also file copies of certain documents, such as amendments to its certificate of incorporation or by-laws.

The listing agreement also contains requirements concerning disclosure of information in the corporation's annual report to shareholders. According to the agreement, the corporation must publish immediately to all holders of its NYSE-listed securities any action taken with respect to dividends or other rights.

SHAREHOLDER PROTECTION CODES

A) Insider trading

Corporate insiders (directors, officers, and principal stockholders) are presumed to have access to information about their companies that is not available to the rest of the investing public. By trading on this information, these insiders can reap profits at the expense of less well-informed investors. Section 16 of the Securities Exchange Act 1934 and the rules of the SEC promulgated thereunder address the problem of unfair insider trading from three directions. Insiders covered by Section 16 are required to disclose their holdings of, and transactions involving, equity securities of their companies. They are subject to disgorgement of short-swing profits arising from purchases and sales of such securities, and are prohibited from engaging in short sales of their company's equity securities. Corporate insiders of a foreign private issuer are not subject to the provisions of Section 16 with respect to equity securities of such foreign private issuer.

The primary purpose of Section 16 of the 1934 Act is to discourage trading on inside information by subjecting the trades of certain insiders to public scrutiny. Section 16(a) requires insiders to file public reports of their stock ownership and trading activities in equity securities of the issuer with the SEC and any exchange on which the issuer's securities are listed, and to provide copies to the issuer. There are both civil remedies and criminal penalties available to the SEC for the enforcement of Section 16(a), although criminal action for a reporting violation is unlikely.

In 1991, as part of major revisions to the Section 16 rules, transactions by insiders in "derivative securities" (such as options, warrants and convertible securities) became explicitly subject to the reporting obligations, short-swing profit recapture provisions, and short sale prohibitions in Section 16.

Shareholders and public investors at large are protected by Rule 10b-5 (making it unlawful, in connection with the purchase or sale of any security, for any person to employ any device, scheme, or artifice to defraud, or to act in a way that would operate as a fraud or deceit, or to make any untrue statement or to omit to state a material fact necessary to make the statements made, in the light of the circumstances, not misleading) and the various other anti-fraud provisions. Insiders must disclose material facts that are known to them by virtue of their position but that are not known to persons with whom they deal and that, if known, would affect their investment judgement. Failure to disclose in these circumstances constitutes a violation of the anti-fraud provisions. If, on the other hand, disclosure prior to effecting a purchase or sale would be improper or unrealistic under the circumstances, the insider must forego the transaction. A violation of the "disclosure-or-abstain" rule, when combined with a fiduciary duty to disclose, constitutes illegal insider trading. Case law on insider trading is extensive and still evolving.

Outsiders may become fiduciaries of shareholders when they enter into a special confidential relationship in the conduct of a business and are given access to information solely for corporate purposes. As a consequence, they may be held liable under the insider trading rules as constructive insiders. In the *Carpenter (Wall Street Journal)* decision, the Supreme Court held that confidential corporate information can be a property right and, hence, a conspiracy to trade on that information can be within the broad ambit of the federal mail and wire fraud statutes.

The Insider Trading Sanctions Act 1984 added to the Securities Exchange Act 1934 the possibility of seeking civil penalties whenever it appears to the SEC that any person has violated any provision of the Securities Exchange Act or the rules or regulations thereunder by dealing in a security while in possession of material non-public information.

The Insider Trading and Securities Fraud and Enforcement Act 1988 aimed to strengthen and clarify the civil and criminal enforcement provisions of the Insider Trading Sanctions Act 1984. In addition to expanding the sanctions and the scope of liability, the Act creates a private right of action for market purchasers against market sellers when the seller is not an insider with a duty to disclose but is liable solely on a theory of misappropriating inside information. The 1988 Act also expands the SEC's investigative authority to include assistance to foreign governments in pursuing securities violations as a reciprocal means of obtaining foreign governments' support for SEC investigations abroad.

B) Market surveillance

The Private Securities Litigation Reform Act of 1995 was intended to reform portions of the Securities Act 1933 and the Securities Exchange Act 1934 in order to end frivolous lawsuits and to ensure that investors receive the best possible information by reducing the litigation risk to companies that make forward-looking statements. The 1995 Act requires greater specificity in complaints that allege securities law violations and contains a safe harbour provision for both written and oral forward-looking statements, such as projections of revenues, capital expenditures and dividends. The 1995 Act also restores aiding and abetting liability for civil actions brought by the SEC and adopts new rules governing class actions in securities litigation.

The securities laws have been amended to include an exemption from the Freedom of Information Act (FOIA) allowing the SEC to maintain the confidentiality of evidence provided by foreign authorities and authorising the SEC to provide documents and other information to foreign authorities with respect to investigations conducted in the foreign country. These reforms were necessary to implement bilateral enforcement assistance agreements between the SEC and authorities in other countries.

With the SEC's recent successes in "freezing" foreign accounts and the proliferation of international agreements and memoranda of understanding with securities regulators in other countries (such as Japan, Switzerland, the UK and France) as well as a broader recognition of US securities standards by foreign governments, foreign blocking and secrecy statutes are no longer major obstacles. The SEC has become increasingly active and effective in the enforcement of US securities laws on an international basis.

Nasdaq enforces its *Rules of Fair Practice* through a nationwide field inspection programme, carried out by staff in a number of different district offices and by centralised, computer-based monitoring of Nasdaq trading by the market surveillance department at its headquarters in Washington. The major stock exchanges also monitor trading activity in an effort to ensure compliance with SEC and stock exchange rules.

C) Proxy reform

Stockholder meetings depend on proxies – documents giving power or authority to act for another – because of the widespread distribution of corporate securities and the separation of ownership and management. Under Section 14(a) of the Securities and Exchange Act 1934, the solicitation of proxies is governed by SEC rule-making under broad "public interest" standards. The SEC's rules (which exempt foreign private issuers) seek to make the proxy the closest practicable substitute for attendance at the meeting, requiring a brief description of the matters to be considered and the actions proposed to be taken by the proxy holder, facilitating non-management solicitation and prohibiting the making of any materially false or misleading statements.

On 15 October 1992, the SEC adopted a proxy reform package consisting of two sets of rule changes, one aimed at allowing shareholders to communicate with each other more easily about voting matters and the other designed to provide shareholders with clearer information about the compensation of top executives. For example, the shareholder communication rules:

(1) exclude from the definition of solicitation any announcement by a shareholder of his voting intentions (and his reasons) that are made by means of speeches in public forums, press releases, regularly disseminated publications or broadcast media or that are directed to persons to whom the shareholder owes a fiduciary duty;
(2) exempt from the proxy rules, other than the anti-fraud rules, solicitations by any person who is not seeking proxy authority and does not belong to one of the excluded categories (among others, persons who have a substantial interest in the matter other than a pro rata interest as a shareholder), provided that such person, if the beneficial owner of more than US$5 million of the company's securities, files notice of all written solicitations with the SEC within three days; and

(3) eliminate the requirement that the persons solicited by means of speeches in public forums, press releases, or opinions, statements or advertisements published in regularly disseminated publications or broadcast on radio or television, be or have been furnished with a proxy statement, provided that no form or proxy is furnished and a definitive proxy statement is on file with the SEC.

D) Takeovers, tender offers, voting rights

The rules governing takeovers and mergers are found in the regulations of the SEC and state and federal laws, including statutes and judicial decisions. The Supreme Court has held that states may, through takeover laws, regulate voting rights in the corporations they create as long as they do not discriminate against out-of-state interests.

According to Rule 13d-1 under the Securities and Exchange Act 1934, persons who are directly or indirectly the beneficial owners of more than 5% of a company's equity securities must file a statement with the SEC. In addition, such persons must report any material change of the facts set forth in the statement. Persons who acquire the securities in the ordinary course of business without intending to influence the control of the issuer and certain other persons may use the simpler of two forms prescribed for the disclosure of beneficial ownership.

Rule 13e-3 under the Securities Exchange Act 1934 requires issuers and their affiliates to provide material information to shareholders if they propose a private transaction. If there is no firm agreement or formal understanding between the third party and management about management's participation, Rule 13e-3 does not apply. In a management buy-out, management is not a disinterested party because the officers have a personal interest in consummating the proposed buy-out. Management is also not disinterested if a third party offers to take the company private and wants existing management to remain with the company. In order to apply Rule 13e-3 to cases where management's interest in the buy-out is not formally documented, it has been suggested that the rule be extended to all negotiated buy-out transactions, including a third party negotiating a takeover.

E) Compensation fund

The Securities Investor Protection Act 1970 (SIPA) established the Securities Investor Protection Corporation (SIPC), of which every broker or dealer registered with the SEC must be a member, subject to certain limited exceptions. The purpose of SIPA is to provide protection against financial loss to customers (a defined term under SIPA) resulting from financial difficulties of brokers/dealers. Each member pays assessments to the SIPC on a regular basis to establish and maintain a fund. Out of that fund, customers are insured against their broker's insolvency, to the extent of US$500,000 for securities losses and US$100,000 for cash losses.

RESEARCH

Excellent research is provided by Bear Stearns, CSFB, Goldman Sachs, Merrill Lynch, Morgan Stanley, NatWest Markets and Salomon Smith Barney.

NYSE publications

Fact Book
Common Stock Indexes

AMEX publications

AMEX Facts
AMEX Fact Book
AMEX Weekly Bulletin Company Guide

Nasdaq publications

Nasdaq Fact Book and Company Directory
The Nasdaq Handbook

Newspapers and periodicals

The Wall Street Journal (daily)
New York Times (daily)
Washington Post (daily)
Barron's (weekly)
Investment Dealers' Digest
Business Week (weekly)
Fortune (monthly)
Forbes (monthly)
Institutional Investor

CHAPTER

74

Uruguay

Introduction

Total turnover on the Montevideo Stock Exchange (MSE) in 1997 amounted to US$681.8 million, an increase of 13% over 1996, but equity trading accounted for only 0.5% of this. The Electronic Stock Exchange of Uruguay, operating since 1994, has considerably higher turnover (several times that of the MSE), but again trading is almost exclusively confined to forex, money market instruments and bonds.

However, in the past two years some significant events have taken place that may well change the character of Uruguay's capital markets. On 1 April 1996 a new system of state pensions was introduced based on personal accounts managed by both state and private sector investment managers. Secondly, a legal framework has been set up that allows for the establishment of mutual funds. Both these innovations are encouraging for the future of equity trading in Uruguay, especially in the context of the government's continuing programme of fiscal and related reforms, which is designed to provide incentives for companies to tap the capital markets for funding rather than relying exclusively on bank finance.

Uruguay has no foreign exchange controls and capital movement is also unrestricted, as is investment by foreigners (with the exception of investments in the broadcasting sector). There are no personal income taxes or interest rate taxes.

ECONOMIC AND POLITICAL OVERVIEW

President Julio María Sanguinetti's Partido Colorado has been in power since March 1995. The next elections are due in 1999.

The coalition government established with the former ruling party, Partido Nacional (Partido Blanco), has created a majority in Congress that has enabled the implementation of a substantial legislative programme. In the past two years, the Stock Market Act, the Mutual Funds Act and the Social Security Reform Act have all come into operation.

Uruguay's economic performance in 1997 was a considerable improvement on the previous year. GDP growth is estimated at 6.3% (versus 4.9% in 1996). Inflation has been brought under control: the CPI rate has fallen from 24.3% in 1996 to 15% in 1997, and is likely to fall to high single-digit levels in 1998.

Uruguay is a signatory of the Mercosur agreement. The pact aims to establish a common market between Brazil, Argentina, Uruguay and Paraguay, leading to a common tariff structure and free trade among members. Although there is now a common tariff between members, transitional provisions still protect a number of goods.

MARKET PERFORMANCE

A) In 1997

Trading in US dollar-denominated state bonds and bills continued to dominate stock exchange activity. Trading in shares accounts for, at most, 0.5% of MSE turnover. Equity turnover fell by 25% in 1997 to US$3.3 million, and market capitalisation also declined, ending the year down 11% at US$213.3 million.

Since September 1994 Montevideo has had a parallel exchange – the Electronic Stock Market of Uruguay (ESMU) – operated by a consortium of banks. Although trading on this market is also dominated by money market instruments (which account for over 90% of turnover), its volume has been increasing rapidly and could pose a serious competitive threat to the MSE. Attempts to merge the operations of the MSE and ESMU have not proved successful.

Despite the very low participation of equities, the role of the private sector in the MSE has increased quite rapidly since the enactment of the 1996 Stock Market Act.

B) Summary information

Global ranking by market value (US$ terms, end-1997): 75
Market capitalisation (end-1997): US$213.3 million
Growth in market value (local currency terms, 1993–97): 26.04%
Market value as a % of nominal GDP (end-1997E): 1.05%
Number of domestic/foreign companies listed (end-1997): 18/0
Short-term (30-day) interest rate (US$, end-1997): 5.6%
Long term (1-year) interest rate (US$, end-1997): 6.2%
Budget deficit as a % of nominal GDP (end-1997): 1.5%
Inflation rate (1997): 15%
US$ exchange rate (end-1997): NP9.962

C) Market indices and their constituents

There is no formally calculated share index and there are no P/E or other standard ratios publicly available for shares traded. However, the government is examining ways in which the performance of the new pension funds (AFAP) could be measured. This at least should introduce some kind of benchmark return other than US dollar interest rates and yields.

THE STOCK MARKET

A) Brief history and structure

The Montevideo Stock Exchange (MSE), established in 1867, is the only official exchange in Uruguay.

The MSE amended its by-laws in 1992 to allow the purchase of broker titles by legal entities. These reforms were approved by the government in 1993. Previously, banks and other financial institutions were obliged to operate on the exchange through an independent broker. Additional reforms introduced in 1996 cover the legal framework for the securities markets, the formalisation of unit trust trading and the introduction of private pension funds.

B) Opening hours, name and address

The MSE is open from 2.00pm to 3.00pm, Monday to Friday.

BOLSA DE VALORES DE MONTEVIDEO
Misiones 1400, Ground Floor, Montevideo
Tel: (598) 2 965 051
Fax: (598) 2 961 900

MARKET SIZE

A) Number of listings and market value

Exhibit 74.1:
NUMBER OF DOMESTIC COMPANIES LISTED AND MARKET VALUE, MSE, 1993–97

Year-end	*No. of companies listed*	*Market capitalisation (US$ million)*
1993	23	288.41
1994	20	300.32
1995	20	300.29
1996	18	239.32
1997	18	213.30

Source: Montevideo Stock Exchange.

B) Trading volume

Equity turnover on the MSE fell by 25.3% to US$3.33 million in 1997 (following on from a 6.0% fall in 1996). Equity trading only accounts for around 0.5% of total trading value.

Exhibit 74.2:
EQUITY TURNOVER ON THE MSE, 1994–97

	Value traded (US$)
1994	9,885,220
1995	4,749,637
1996	4,460,051
1997	3,334,686

Source: Montevideo Stock Exchange.

Exhibit 74.3:
THE 10 MOST ACTIVELY TRADED SHARES ON THE MSE, 1997

Ranking	*Share*	*Trading value (US$)*
1	Montevideo Refrescos	2,212,198
2	Frigorífico Modelo	522,281
3	Compañía Salus	235,321
4	Fábrica Nacional de Papel	153,103
5	Papetería Mercedes	53,143
6	BCO Comercial Preferidos	52,850
7	Alcan Aluminio Uruguay SA	23,844
8	Fibratex Ord. Series B	19,010
9	Fibratex Ord. Series C	13,510
10	Eternit Uruguay SA	11,409

Source: Montevideo Stock Exchange.

OPERATIONS

Trading system

Since mid-1994 an electronic trading system has been in operation at the MSE.

TAXATION AND REGULATIONS AFFECTING FOREIGN INVESTORS

With the exception of the broadcasting sector, no restrictions of any kind exist on investments by foreigners. There is a system of absolute freedom regarding entrance and remittance of capital and earnings belonging to foreign investors, and foreign and national investments are taxed in the same way.

Act 14.179 provides for a "foreign investment system" that guarantees restitution of capital invested by individuals or corporations domiciled abroad, as well as earnings accrued. Investments under this system must be authorised by the government. The capital to be invested may be in various forms such as foreign currency, machinery, patents, technical processes or trademarks.

Repatriation of investment capital plus earnings is fully guaranteed via a contract signed by the foreign investor and the government which complies with the following legal rules:

(a) capital cannot be repatriated in the three years following the investment;
(b) earnings not transferred abroad within a period of two years shall, for legal purposes, be considered capitalised as of the date of their generation; and
(c) remittances abroad shall be charged first against earnings and subsequently against capital.

The system guarantees the transfer of capital and earnings even in the event of modification of the current system of free remittance of capital. In fact the system is rarely used because of the general freedom to invest, withdraw and remit capital and earnings.

SHAREHOLDER PROTECTION CODES

Several shareholder protection rules are included in Law 16.060 of 1989. This law, commonly known as the "Companies Act", provides that all corporations are subject to government regulation regarding establishment and amendment of their incorporation papers, early dissolution, transformation, merger, division and increase or decrease of capital.

Open corporations (those that invite the public to subscribe for their shares or debentures, or that have shares that are traded on the stock exchange) are subject to government audit during operation and liquidation. Other corporations enjoy a more liberal regime. Internal auditing is optional for private corporations but obligatory for open ones.

There is a system of protection for minority shareholders that translates into recognition of a series of basic rights, such as the right to a minimum dividend (20% of net earnings), the right to preference in increases of capital, the right to vote, the right to information, the right to recess, the right to verification and the right to call shareholders' meetings with a certain percentage of support (20%).

Open corporations are obliged to publish annual balance sheets for approval by the shareholders' meeting. They are also obliged to forward to the government authorities copies of shareholders' meeting minutes and of the corresponding Register of Assistance of Shareholders. They must also inform the government authorities of any changes in the board of directors or auditing committee.

The Stock Market Act 1996 includes various investor protection measures, including outlawing insider trading.

RESEARCH

Sources of information on the Uruguayan equity market include: Banco Santander Uruguay, Citibank, Bank of America, Banco de Montevideo and Banco Comercial.

CHAPTER

75

Venezuela

Introduction

There are three stock exchanges in Venezuela – the Caracas Stock Exchange (CSE), the Maracaibo Stock Exchange (MSE) and the Venezuelan Electronic Stock Exchange (VESE). Trading in exchange-listed equities may be carried out through the relevant exchange or over-the-counter.

Foreign investors have been active in the Venezuelan market since 1990. Almost all equities are common stocks that can be acquired by foreigners and nationals alike. There are no foreign investment restrictions in Venezuela, except in relation to investments in television, radio, transportation, Spanish language newspapers and professional services regulated by national laws.

The Caracas exchange posted encouraging results in 1997, with significant increases in volume, turnover, share price indices and market capitalisation.

Trading in futures contracts began in 1997. Transactions are settled through the Venezuelan Options and Futures Clearing House (CACOFV), which includes mechanisms covering investor and trader risks.

ECONOMIC AND POLITICAL OVERVIEW

Presidential elections are scheduled for the second half of 1998. The AD Party is expected to do best, commanding between 20% and 40% of the popular vote in a four-candidate field.

At the end of 1997, the inflation rate (as measured by the Caracas Price Index) had dropped to 37.6% from 103.2% in 1996, and unemployment was also down at 9%. Foreign investment increased by 171%.

GNP growth was 5.1% in 1997, with the strongest sectors being construction (+12.6%), commerce (+5%) and manufacturing (+2.7%). Growth was underpinned by an increase of 11.2% in petroleum exports and 11.4% in non-petroleum exports. Nevertheless, the final balance of payment figures for 1997 show a surplus of US$5.8 billion, down by almost US$3 billion compared with 1996.

In spite of increased expenditure, the government ended 1997 with a budget surplus of 2.5% of GNP, boosted by revenues up from 20.1% of GNP to 24.5%. Venezuela's international reserves at the end of the year totalled US$17.3 billion, some US$2.07 billion more than at end-1996.

Liberalisation of the petroleum industry continued in 1997, and three rounds of operating agreements were signed. These agreements represent a direct investment of US$64.9 billion between 1997 and 2006, which is expected to increase production capacity from 3.8 million to 6.4 million barrels per day. In 1997 Venezuelan citizens were able to invest in the petroleum industry for the first time, with 35,000 people participating in the first test placement of an issue of fixed-income certificates by the Society for Promotion of Petroleum Investment (SOFIP).

Role of the central bank

Although the central bank is legally an independent entity, it operates under the control of the Ministry of Finance. It is responsible for implementing government monetary, tax and foreign exchange policies. Following the abolition of exchange controls in April 1996, the central bank moved to establish a system of bands for the bolivar based on a central parity.

Monetary policy in 1997 was geared towards ensuring stability in the financial market, and procuring growth in the cash base and monetary liquidity.

MARKET PERFORMANCE

A) In 1997

Total turnover on the CSE reached a record level of Bs2,736 billion (US$5.58 billion), representing an 83.96% increase over 1996. Growth in equity market trading was even more spectacular at 220%.

After a quiet first three months, demand for securities

in the second and third quarters exceeded supply, as new individual and institutional investors were drawn into the market. In the fourth quarter, however, the CSE suffered a setback. Largely due to the Asian crisis and its global repercussions, the Venezuelan stock market fell by 1,019.50 points (9.89%) in one week between the end of October and the start of November. Nevertheless, for the year as a whole, market yield for Caracas was 29.39% (or 26.4% in US dollar terms).

In mid-December the Venezuelan Investment Fund (FIV) organised a public auction of 70% of the stock of Siderúrgica del Orinoco, which was acquired by a consortium of national and foreign firms. Of the remaining 30%, it is planned that 20% will be sold to Sidor employees and 10% to the public.

B) Summary information

Global ranking by market value (US$ terms, end-1997): 45
Market capitalisation (end-1997): US$14.75 billion
Growth in market value (local currency terms, 1993–97): 787.6%
Market value as a % of nominal GNP (end-1997): 16.57%
Number of domestic/foreign companies listed (end-1997): 158/1
Market P/E (all companies listed, Dec 1997): 42.7
MSCI Index (change in US$ terms, 1997): +27.4
Short-term (3-month) interest rate (end-1997): 18.20%
Long-term (5-year) bond yield (end-1997): 17.24%
Budget surplus as a % of nominal GNP (1997): -2.5%
Annual increase in broad money (M3) supply (end-1997): 65.9%
Inflation rate (1997): 37.6%
US$ exchange rate (end-1997): Bs504.25

Exhibit 75.1:
YEAR-END CSE SHARE PRICE INDEX, 1993–97

Year-end	*CSE Capitalisation Equity Index*
1993	1,000.00
1994	1,348.83
1995	2,019.39
1996	6,690.06
1997	8,656.04

Source: Caracas Stock Exchange.

C) Market indices and their constituents

The CSE introduced the Capitalisation Equity Index (end-1993 = 1,000) in December 1994. It comprises 14 of the most actively traded issues and 19 shares in the financial and industrial sectors.

The CSE established a new index – the IBVC – in January 1995. It comprises 19 of the most actively traded shares and is calculated by dividing the market capitalisation of these shares by the capitalisation of the base year (December 1993), and then multiplying by a factor of 1,000. The index includes financial and industrial sub-indices.

THE STOCK MARKET

A) Brief history and structure

The CSE can trace its origins to the middle of the 19th century. Even though the Commercial Code of 1873 contained the legal framework for the workings of an exchange, and in 1917 a special law was approved that regulated its operations, it was not until 1947 that the Bolsa de Comercio de Caracas was founded. It began operations with 18 share issues and six government bonds.

The exchange changed its name to the Bolsa de Valores de Caracas in 1974, and is an active member of the IberoAmerican Federation of Stock Exchanges (FIABV) and the Association of Numbering Agencies (ANNA).

The CSE has 61 members – mostly brokerage houses, although there are some individual members. It is managed by a board of directors, with an independent internal administration for day-to-day operations. The exchange is a profit-making organisation owned by the brokers and supervised by the main regulatory agency, the National Securities Commission (CNV).

B) Different exchanges

There are three exchanges in Venezuela – the Caracas and Maracaibo exchanges, and the Venezuelan Electronic Stock Exchange in Valencia.

C) Opening hours, names and addresses

The Caracas exchange is open Monday to Friday from 8.00am to 12.30pm and 1.30pm to 5.00pm.

BOLSA DE VALORES DE CARACAS
Apartado Postal 62724-A Chacao
Tel: (58) 2 905 5511; Fax: (58) 2 952 2640
E-mail: bvccaracasstock.com

BOLSA DE VALORES DE MARACAIBO
Edif. Banco Central de Venezuela
Ave 5 de Julio y Las Delicias, Piso 9
Maracaibo, Edo. Zulia
Tel: (58) 61 226 833; Fax: (58) 61 226 322

BOLSA ELECTRONICA DE VALORES DE VENEZUELA
Ave. Bolívar, Cámara de Comercio de Valencia
Valencia, Edo. Carabobo
Tel: (58) 41 575 109/115; Fax: (58) 41 575 147

MARKET SIZE

A) Market capitalisation

Total market capitalisation stood at US$14.7 billion at the end of 1997, an increase of 47% relative to 1996's US$10.0 billion.

Exhibit 75.2:
NUMBER OF COMPANIES LISTED AND MARKET VALUE, 1993–97

Year	*No. of companies listed*	*Market value (US$ billion)*
1993	157	7.8
1994	155	5.0
1995	154	4.3
1996	154	10.0
1997	159	14.7

Source: Caracas Stock Exchange.

Exhibit 75.3:
THE 20 LARGEST LISTED SHARES ON THE CSE, END-1997

Ranking	*Company*	*Market value (Bs billion)*
1	Electricidad de Caracas	1,279.8
2	CANTV (D)	1,060.8
3	Banco Provincial	658.9
4	Banco de Venezuela	355.0
5	Sivensa (A)	321.9
6	Vencemos Tip 1	288.6
7	Mercantil S (A)	280.5
8	Mercantil S (B)	191.7
9	Mavesa	190.7
10	Banco Unión	180.0
11	Banco Venezolano de Crédito	170.9
12	Banco Mercantil (A)	168.0
13	Corp Banca	155.6
14	Vencemos Tip 2	155.4
15	Banco Mercantil (B)	147.5
16	Manpa	137.6
17	Fábrica Nacional de Cementos	120.8
18	Fondo de Valores Immobiliarios	113.5
19	ProAgro	93.9
20	Banco Caracas (A)	89.6

Source: Caracas Stock Exchange.

B) Trading volume

Equity turnover on the CSE increased by 220% in 1997 (to Bs1,928.52 billion), while overall turnover (including bonds) increased by 84% to Bs2,736.0 billion.

Exhibit 75.4:
SHARE AND BOND TURNOVER ON THE CSE, 1993–97

Year	*Equity turnover (Bs billion)*	*Total turnover (Bs billion)*
1993	169.2	173.5
1994	161.0	198.9
1995	95.4	838.7
1996	602.5	1,487.5
1997	1,928.5	2,736.0

Source: Caracas Stock Exchange.

Exhibit 75.5:
THE 20 MOST ACTIVELY TRADED SHARES, CSE, 1997

Ranking	*Share*	*Trading value (US$ million)*
1	Electricidad de Caracas	1,107.0
2	CANTV (D)	208.1
3	Banco Provincial	162.0
4	Sivensa (A)	158.1
5	Fondo de Valores Immobiliarios	130.0
6	Vencemos Tip 1	97.4
7	Corimon (B)	95.1
8	Mavesa	62.0
9	Banco Unión	61.2
10	Sudamtex (B)	47.7
11	Vencemos Tip 2	46.6
12	Mantex	46.3
13	Mercantil S (B)	40.0
14	Banco Venezolano de Crédito	34.5
15	Banco de Venezuela	32.5
16	Bancaracas Mercado de Capitales	27.8
17	Banco Mercantil (B)	23.1
18	Banco Fivenez	19.2
19	Banco Consolidado/Corp Banca	14.9
20	Vencred	12.2

Source: Caracas Stock Exchange.

TYPES OF SHARE

Shares traded in Venezuela are regulated by the Capital Markets Act and the Commercial Code.

Two types of shares are traded on the CSE – common/ordinary shares and preferred shares. Shares are issued in registered form only. CNV approval also exists for what it calls a broad menu of combined debt and equity instruments, including bonds as options, floating-rate securities with an option to fix, fixed with an option to float, and others.

Exhibit 75.6:
COUNTRY FUNDS – VENEZUELA

Fund	US$ % change 01/01/97 01/01/98	01/01/93 01/01/98	Fund base currency	Fund size (US$ mil)	Fund volatility	Management group	Opal main sector	Opal subsector
NatWest/IFC LAIF Venezuela Inx	23.39	N/A	US$	0.966	9.335	NatWest Inv M	Open-End	Equity
Ptfl Mercantil en Acciones	9.34	N/A	Bs	N/A	-1	Merinvest	Open-End	Equity

Note: details for some funds may not have been included if the data for the US$ % change for 97/98 is not available

Source: Standard & Poor's Micropal.

Finally, the CNV has adopted rules regarding trading in participation certificates and GDRs:

- *Participation certificates*: the CNV regulates the creation of exchange-traded participation certificates in any type of underlying asset. The certificates must be issued by the trust department of a Venezuelan bank, which in turn must be holding the underlying asset on which the certificate is issued. To date no issue has been made under these rules, although several issues have been studied, including participations in financial assets, real estate and other assets.
- *Global depository receipts (GDRs)* : the rules require notice to the CNV when a GDR programme is adopted by a corporation. Also, GDRs can circulate in the Venezuelan capital markets as long as registration formalities have been completed. Cross-circulation is also allowed – that is, a GDR traded outside of Venezuela can also be traded within Venezuela. Capital gains are taxed if the GDR is traded in the Venezuelan market.

OTHER MARKETS

A futures market was established in Venezuela in September 1997 by the Venezuelan Options and Futures Clearing House (CACOFV). Trading takes place on the CSE. In its first four months of operation, the futures market traded 4,552 contracts. Electricidad de Caracas was the most heavily traded with 2,888 contracts, followed by the Caracas Stock Index (IBC) with 1,398 contracts and CANTV (introduced in November) with 266 contracts.

INVESTORS

Institutional investors such as banks, trust funds, insurance companies and investment firms tend to dominate trading in both shares and bonds. Private individuals have been active during brief periods in the history of the exchange but have generally had only a minor influence on the market.

OPERATIONS

A) Trading system

At the end of 1992, the CSE introduced the Automated System for Stock Transactions (SATB) whereby all transactions are carried out electronically, thus replacing traditional floor trading. Trading takes place from Monday to Friday (except bank holidays) from 9.45am to 2.00pm, with a pre-opening session from 9.00am to 9.45am. There is a pre-closing session from 2.00pm to 2.45pm, which allows brokers to make corrections to transactions already carried out.

B) List of principal brokers

ACTIVALORES SOCIEDAD DE CORRETAJE
Calle Los Chaguaramos, Centro Gerencial Mohedano
P.H.-B, La Castellana – Caracas
Tel: (58) 2 201 7511/7501; Fax: (58) 2 261 7504

BANCARACAS CASA DE BOLSA
la Transversal de Boleíta, Centro Empresarial Boleíta
Edificio Bancaracas, Boleíta – Caracas
Tel: (58) 2 207 2511/4322; Fax: (58) 2 207 2544

BANEX MERCADO DE CAPITALES
Avenida Libertardor, Edificio Banco de Venezuela, Piso 2, Chacao – Caracas
Tel: (58) 2 201 9311/261 8933; Fax: (58) 2 201 9434

CAPITALES NOROCO CASA DE CORETAJE
2a Avenida de Campo Alegre
Torre Cari, Piso 8 y 9, Campo Alegre – Caracas
Tel: (58) 2 953 1853/5933; Fax: (58) 2 953 1078

ESFINCORP CONSULTORES FINANCIEROS AV. LIBERTADOR
Edificio Nuevo Centro, Piso 4, Oficina 4-B, Chacao
P.O. Box 69363, Caracas, 1062-A
Tel: (58) 16 22 37 32

INTERACCIONES MERCADO DE CAPITALES
Centro Plaza – Torre C, Piso 14, Ofc. C
Los Palos Grandes – Caracas
Tel: (58) 2 284 9880/1728; Fax: (58) 2 283 8497/285 0949

INVERWORLD SOCIEDAD DE CORRETAJE
Avenida Guaicaipuro, Torre Banesco 2,
Piso 7, El Rosal – Caracas
Tel: (58) 2 952 4555/6796; Fax: (58) 2 953 4864

MERINVEST SOCIEDAD DE CORRETAJE
Avenida Andrés Bello, Edificio Banco Mercantil,
Piso 14, San Bernardino – Caracas, DF
Tel: (58) 2 503 2700/2724; Fax: (58) 2 503 2768

PABLO GONZALO ARANDA
Avenida Urdaneta, Veroes a Ibarra
Torre Alfa, Piso 10, Letra E, Caracas, DF
Tel: (58) 2 561 9198/2011; Fax: (58) 2 562 4695

PROVINCIAL VALORES CASA DE BOLSA
Avenida Andrés Bello, Edificio Centro Pida, P.H.
San Bernardino – Caracas, DF
Tel: (58) 2 504 6524/5432; Fax: (58) 2 504 5851

VALORES VENCRED
Avenida Universidad, Edificio Centro Mercantil, Piso 4
Oficina 4-7 – Caracas, DF
Tel: (58) 2 806 6841/6837; Fax: (58) 2 806 6859

C) Settlement and transfer

The CSE has a multilateral netting system for shares, which handles financial settlement of transactions carried out by brokers. Physical clearing and custody of securities is ordinarily undertaken by transfer agents. Only banks, insurance companies and institutions authorised by the CNV can act as transfer agents. They are responsible for registering the name of the shareholder within two working days after receiving the relevant documents recording a purchase/sale of a security. The settlement periods are as follows: cash, T to T+3; regular, 5 working days; and forward, from 6 to 60 working days.

In 1995, the Caja Venezolana de Valores (CVV) was established with the CSE taking a majority interest. Other participants include brokerage houses, financial institutions, insurance companies, as well as major corporations. The CVV offers a wide variety of services such as the clearing and settlement of securities listed and traded on the stock exchanges and the over-the-counter market, settlement of funds, and the custody and administration of securities.

D) Commissions and other costs

Brokerage commissions on share transactions are 0.9%, or slightly less depending on the size of the transaction.

TAXATION AND REGULATIONS AFFECTING FOREIGN INVESTORS

In broad terms, foreign investors are subject to the same regulations as domestic investors. However, Decree 2,095, which specifically regulates foreign investment in Venezuela, lists two "sensitive" areas: (a) TV and radio broadcasting and Spanish language newspapers; and (b) professional services regulated by national laws (eg law firms).

Dividends are tax-exempt, but net income from loans granted by financial institutions constituted overseas is taxed at 4.95%. Capital gains tax has been replaced with a tax of 1% which is levied when selling securities on the stock exchange (the tax is higher – up to 34% – for over-the-counter sales).

LISTING AND REPORTING REQUIREMENTS

A) Listing requirements

Companies seeking a listing must have a minimum paid-up capital of Bs20 million. If the company is not registered at the CNV, to secure a listing it will have to make a public offer of at least 20% of its subscribed capital.

B) Reporting requirements

All listed companies must submit quarterly financial statements within the 30 days following the end of the quarter, and audited annual financial statements at least 30 days before the date of the shareholders' general assembly. Companies must also disclose other relevant market information, such as dividend announcements, rights issues and changes in accounting practices.

SHAREHOLDER PROTECTION CODES

A) Substantial shareholdings

CSE listing rules include an obligation that companies must disclose shareholdings of 5% and over.

B) Insider trading

The Securities Act does not forbid insider trading, but the CSE does. The penalty for a trade made with inside information is that a third party may ask to have the trade annulled.

C) Tender offers

Under the Venezuelan Securities Act there are no regulations regarding public offers for the purchase of publicly traded shares, and recently some disputes have occurred concerning potential tender offers for listed companies. The CNV is currently studying a code that would regulate tender offers and would be structured on the system operating in France. Furthermore, recent rulings of the CNV have weakened substantially the position management can take when trying to defend against a tender offer (although these rulings are on appeal before the Venezuelan Supreme Court). Articles 285 and 286 of the Commercial Code and CNV rulings restrict management voting powers at shareholders' meetings.

D) Compensation fund

Individual brokers must have net assets in excess of Bs3 million in cash, securities and/or real estate properties. For brokerage houses, the minimum has been set at Bs20 million.

All CSE members must post a guarantee at the exchange. The amount is set by the board of directors of the CSE and currently stands at Bs50 million.

RESEARCH

The CSE publishes four bulletins (daily, weekly, monthly and annual reports) that provide comprehensive trading information as well as corporate news and announcements. The exchange also has an extensive historic database of all traded securities beginning from 1988. Another major source of information on the stock market is the CNV, as are special bulletins published by large securities firms; those with the best regarded research include Bancaracas, Merinvest and Provincial Valores.

Most newspapers include a financial section, although *Reporte de la Economía* and *Economía Hoy* are the most financially oriented. Also, there are a number of periodicals that provide comprehensive coverage of the capital markets, including *Inversiones*, *Dinero* and *Gerente*.

Venezuela, published by Euromoney Books, provides in-depth information for those wishing to invest or do business in the country. See the order card at the back of this book for details.

PROSPECTIVE CHANGES

The Social Security Macro-Law Reform 1997 will result in the creation of private pension funds. This in turn is likely to encourage an increase in long-term savings, with positive effects for the stock market and the economy.

CHAPTER

76

Vietnam

Introduction

All in all, 1997 was a challenging year for Vietnam, in no small part due to the Asian currency crisis in the second half of the year. Also, little or nothing was achieved in the way of establishment the way of a functioning stock exchange and there has been no progress on privatisation.

Nevertheless, the economy continues to show good growth from a small base and the country's communist leadership appears content to maintain a slow pace of reform in the light of strong economic growth and low inflation.

ECONOMIC AND POLITICAL OVERVIEW

Vietnam is still very much a socialist state with the Vietnam Communist Party (VCP) maintaining its supremacy despite wide-ranging economic reforms. The VCP is the dominant political force, with significant influence over the government, the army and the bureaucracy.

Real economic growth is estimated to have fallen slightly to 9% in 1997, down from 9.5% the previous year. It is important to note, however, that these growth rates are generated by official government sources that do not follow international statistical practices. World Bank estimates suggest that growth might actually be somewhere between 7.2% and 8.5%. Foreign direct investment continued to drive economic growth. In 1997 there was an increase of US$800 million in capital employed at licensed projects, taking the total to US$3 billion. However, the figure for new projects licensed came in much lower, at US$4.5 billion, down from US$8.6 billion in 1996, and this may have a negative impact on foreign direct investment in 1998.

Vietnam's trade deficit fell by 40% in 1997 due to surging exports and new import controls. However, the country is facing increasing competition in its export markets due to the regional currency crisis, and a massive devaluation of the Vietnamese dong may be necessary to redress the country's external balances. The monetary authorities allowed the dong to weaken by 5% in October but some commentators believe that it is still more than 40% overvalued.

Early in December, the central bank signed an agreement to reschedule Vietnam's commercial debt, ending more than a decade of default. The agreement will be supported by the World Bank, which has approved a US$35 million loan to Vietnam to assist in meeting the initial costs of the rescheduling. Vietnam will benefit from a reduction in its debt burden and will also be able to raise funds for expansion on the international capital markets.

Summary information

Nominal GDP (1997): US$25 billion
Inflation rate (average, 1997): 7.0%
US$ exchange rate (end-1997): D12,292

SECURITIES MARKET

The formation of a functioning securities market is still a long way off, despite the establishment of a committee to oversee the development of a stock exchange and associated regulatory bodies and financial institutions.

BANKING

The reform process has been particularly marked in the banking sector. The introduction of new and more reliable banking services and a wider spectrum of financial bodies has done much to facilitate business activity, although the four state-run banks still control the domestic banking sector. Since 1991, 48 joint stock banks and finance companies have been established, and, although of varying quality, these companies are likely to be some of the first to seek a listing on any securities market that may be established.

The State Bank of Vietnam governs the banking indus-

Exhibit 76.1:
COUNTRY FUNDS – VIETNAM

Fund	US$ % change 01/01/97 01/01/98	01/01/93 01/01/98	Fund base currency	Fund size (US$ mil)	Fund volatility	Management group	Opal main sector	Opal subsector
Vietnam Fund	-1.03	13.47	US$	57.422	0.302	Lloyds GSY	Closed-End	Equity
Beta Viet Nam Ltd	-8.63	N/A	US$	71.4	1.254	Beta Funds Lt	Closed-End	Equity
Beta Mekong Fund Ltd	-13.7	N/A	US$	25.8	1.563	Beta Funds Lt	Closed-End	Equity
Vietnam Frontier Fund	-30.36	N/A	US$	61.049	4.339	Frontier Fund	Closed-End	Equity
Templeton Vietnam Opps Inc	-42.72	N/A	US$	110	7.652	Templeton	Closed-End	Equity

Note: details for some funds may not have been included if the data for the US$ % change for 97/98 was not available

Source: Standard & Poor's Micropal.

try and, in tandem with the Ministry of Finance, performs the role of a central bank.

INVESTMENT

Taiwan, Hong Kong, South Korea and Singapore account for a sizeable proportion of what still remains a relatively low level of foreign investment in Vietnam. Direct investment covers all sectors and the level of joint venture participation is equally varied although, in the longer term, Japan and the US are likely to be the dominant investors.

Some country funds have been launched and Vietnam has been included in a number of regional funds. In the absence of a stock exchange, the funds have largely focused on venture capital projects, debt-equity swaps, sovereign debt or investment in foreign listed stocks active in the country.

Vietnam's proximity to the huge markets of China and Hong Kong is clearly in its favour, as is the country's position as an effective staging post for investment into the smaller and less developed markets of Cambodia and Laos.

CHAPTER

77

Zambia

Introduction

The Lusaka Stock Exchange (LSE) is among the new equity markets to have sprung up in sub-Saharan Africa in the 1990s as part of a package of economic reforms that have been adopted by an increasing number of countries across the continent. The stock market opened in February 1994, and is still at an early stage of development. There are seven listed companies that fulfil all the listing requirements (eg, publishing results on a regular basis) and three quoted companies that do not fulfil the listing requirements, but which are traded nevertheless. There are no restrictions on foreign investment in the Lusaka market and there are no exchange controls, which makes the market one of the most liberalised in Africa.

Despite the small number of listed companies, the market is generally representative of Zambia's economy. The largest listed stock is the state-owned Zambia Consolidated Copper Mines (ZCCM), which accounts for the lion's share of the country's exports and government revenues, and is also listed in London and Paris. The other two large companies are Trans Zambezi Industries (TZI), a conglomerate which is also listed on the Luxembourg and Harare exchanges and which joined the main board in Lusaka in 1997, and Zambia Sugar, which had an initial public offering (IPO) in September 1996. Both companies have large interests in Zambia's agricultural sector, which is a mainstay of the country's economy.

Since 1993, the government has been implementing a far-reaching privatisation programme. The unbundling and sale of ZCCM to a number of international mining houses made good progress in 1997 and is now almost complete.

ECONOMIC AND POLITICAL OVERVIEW

Zambia gained independence from British rule in October 1964, when Kenneth Kaunda became the country's first President. He remained in power for 27 years until, following the country's first multi-party elections in November 1991, he was defeated by the Movement for Multi-Party Democracy (MMD), whose leader, Frederick Chiluba, became President. The polls were notable as one of Africa's few free and fair elections resulting in a peaceful handover of power.

Mr Chiluba was re-elected in November 1996, following a controversial campaign in which the constitution was altered to prevent Mr Kaunda from standing as a candidate. Since then, the political scene has remained volatile as shown by a coup attempt by junior officers in October 1997 and a subsequent state of emergency imposed by the government and used to clamp down on opposition. Mr Kaunda was accused of involvement in the coup, arrested in December and court investigations are ongoing.

Until 1975, Zambia was one of sub-Saharan Africa's most prosperous countries on the back of copper exports. With the fall in world copper prices, its fortunes reversed, leaving a legacy of debt (currently US$6.9 billion), foreign exchange shortages and falling output. Over 1991–95, the country experienced a severe drought, on top of its structural economic difficulties, and real GDP contracted by an average of 1% per annum. Since then, the outlook has brightened somewhat and 1996 saw the economy expand by an estimated 6.4%, mainly as a result of the rebound in the agricultural sector. Growth in 1997 is estimated to have slowed to 5% due to cuts in agricultural production and a drop in mining output.

The ZCCM privatisation and attempts to diversify the economy should start paying off in 1998 and produce GDP growth of around 5%. Inflation has come down from an annual average of 46% in 1996 to 18.6% at end-1997, although unemployment is high at an estimated

35%, and total debt/GNP is around 190%. The 1997 budget projects a 1% surplus (as a percentage of GDP) but, in reality, the deficit before foreign aid contributions is close to 7%. Foreign reserves as at mid-1997 covered about eight weeks of imports.

Role of the central bank

The Bank of Zambia is responsible for supervising the commercial banks and ensuring the stability of the financial system. Its policy anchor is price stability and the control of money supply.

MARKET PERFORMANCE

A) In 1997

The LSE stock price index gained 110.7% in local currency terms and 90% in US dollar terms over the year, making it one of the best performing emerging markets in the world. Two new companies joined the exchange – TZI and Zambia Breweries – which helped push market capitalisation up to US$705 million at the end of the year, compared with US$230 million at the end of 1996. Annual turnover increased significantly from US$2.64 million in 1996 to US$8.77 million in 1997.

B) Summary information

Global ranking by market value (US$ terms, end-1997): 72
Market capitalisation (end-1997): US$705 million
Growth in market value (local currency terms, 1995–97): 61.69%
Market value as a % of nominal GDP (end-1997): 18.07%
Number of domestic/foreign companies quoted (end-1997): 9/1
Market P/E (all index companies, end-1997): 9.66
Short-term (3-month) interest rate (end-1997): 21.6%
Budget deficit as a % of nominal GDP (1997): 7%
Annual increase in money (M2) supply (Sept 1997): 27.6%
Inflation rate (1997): 18.6%
US$ exchange rate (end-1997): ZK1,427.5

C) Year-end price/earnings ratios and yields

Exhibit 77.1:
YEAR-END P/E RATIOS AND GROSS DIVIDEND YIELDS, 1994–97

Year-end	*P/E*	*Yield (%)*
1994	N/A	N/A
1995	6.6	2.5
1996	8.4	6.9
1997	9.7	3.9

Source: Lusaka Stock Exchange.

THE STOCK MARKET

A) Brief history and structure

The Lusaka Stock Exchange was opened on 21 February 1994. The market was designed by the International Finance Corporation (IFC) to meet G30 standards. The exchange is owned by six brokers, although there is provision for up to 40 members.

The LSE has a two-tier market structure. The top tier is for companies that meet the criteria for a full listing. The second tier is for companies that do not meet the full listing requirements but in which trading on the exchange is nonetheless permitted. The stock market is regulated by the Securities and Exchange Commission.

B) Different exchanges

The LSE is the only stock exchange in Zambia.

C) Opening hours, names and addresses

The exchange is open Monday to Friday from 10.00am to 11.00am and from 12.00 noon to 1.00pm.

LUSAKA STOCK EXCHANGE
1st Floor, Stock Exchange Building, Cairo Road, Lusaka
Tel: (260) 1 228391; Fax: (260) 1 225969,
E-mail: lusezamnet.zm

MARKET SIZE

A) Number of listings and market value

Total market capitalisation of the 10 companies on the exchange at year-end 1997 was US$705.2 million.

Exhibit 77.2:
NUMBER OF COMPANIES TRADED AND MARKET VALUE, LSE, 1994–97

	No. of companies		*Market value*
Year-end	*Domestic*	*Foreign*	*(US$ million)*
1994	7	0	N/A
1995	8	0	436
1996	8	0	229
1997	10	1	705

Source: Lusaka Stock Exchange.

B) Listed/quoted companies

Exhibit 77.3:
COMPANY RANKINGS BY MARKET VALUE, END-1997

Ranking	*Company*	*Market value (ZK million)*
1	ZCCM	410,764

Exhibit 77.3 continued

2	TZI	282,876
3	ZSUG	173,662
4	SCZ	53,235
5	ZamBrew	32,500
6	CHIL	31,006
7	RTHZ	16,128
8	FH	2,548
9	BATZ	2,143
10	NCBK	1,813

Source: Lusaka Stock Exchange.

C) Trading volume

Turnover increased 232% from US$2.64 million in 1996 to US$8.77 million in 1997.

Exhibit 77.4:
THE FOUR MOST ACTIVELY TRADED SHARES ON THE LSE, 1997

Ranking	*Company*	*Trading value (ZK million)*	*Share volume (million)*
1	ZamSug	5,867.86	170.1
2	Rothmans	1,823.00	30.1
3	Chilanga	1,540.65	13.8
4	TZI	1,450.25	1.3

Source: Lusaka Stock Exchange.

TYPES OF SHARE

Most shares on the LSE are ordinary, although some preferred shares (both with and without voting rights) have been issued.

OPERATIONS

A) Trading system

The LSE trading system is not yet automated and there is no trading floor. Orders are executed manually by staff at the exchange using a single price auction and order matching system. Brokers submit orders by fax. All purchase expenses are paid through the stock exchange and there is a central depository where scrip is held.

Reuters transmits quotations, but not in real time, and prices are available on the Internet.

B) List of principal brokers

CAVMONT SECURITIES
Tel: (260) 1 227763; Fax: (260) 1 227764

EMERGING MARKETS SECURITIES
Tel: (260) 1 229906–10; Fax: (260) 1 237609

FINANCE SECURITIES
Tel: (260) 1 229733–40; Fax: (260) 1 237582

FIRST MERCHANT SECURITIES
Tel: (260) 1 225757; Fax: (260) 1 225764

INTERAFRICA EQUITIES & SECURITIES
Tel: (260) 1 225002; Fax: (260) 1 228233

PANGAEA SECURITIES LTD
Tel: (260) 1 238709; Fax: (260) 1 220925

C) Settlement and transfer

All scrip is immobilised and clearing and settlement are fully automated. Clearing is on T+1 and settlement on T+3 with delivery versus payment. All clearing and settlement is via the central depository.

D) Commissions and other costs

Brokerage rates are negotiable and are generally around 1.25%. There is also a fixed commission of 0.25% on each side of trades payable to the LSE.

TAXATION AND REGULATIONS AFFECTING FOREIGN INVESTORS

A) Ownership restrictions

There are no restrictions on foreign ownership. However, in the privatisation of a parastatal, preference is given to Zambian purchasers.

B) Taxation

There is a 15% withholding tax on dividends but no capital gains tax. For unlisted securities, there is a 2.5% property transfer tax levied on the seller.

C) Exchange controls

There are no exchange controls. The Zambian kwacha is fully convertible and rates of exchange are market determined.

LISTING AND REPORTING REQUIREMENTS

A) Listing requirements

Companies seeking a listing on the LSE must be public shareholding companies. There are also requirements covering minimum size, a minimum track record and the holding of annual general meetings.

B) Reporting requirements

Companies listed on the LSE must publish net operating results and submit them to the public no later than one month before their annual general meeting. A copy of the resolutions approved by a general meeting and a copy of the report of the board of directors must be made public. Companies must also publish interim results, as well as any information that could affect the value of their shares.

RESEARCH

Limited research is available from local brokers on specific stocks and on the market in general.

The LSE releases price data to all the main local newspapers and there is also a monthly newsletter. Publications are available on subscription. The LSE also provides prices and market updates on the Internet as well as via Reuters.

African Equities: A Guide to Markets and Companies, published by Euromoney Books, provides in-depth information for those wishing to invest or do business in Africa. See the order card at the back of this book for details.

CHAPTER

78

Zimbabwe

Introduction

Although small by international standards, the Zimbabwe Stock Exchange (ZSE) is the most developed and active market in southern Africa after the Johannesburg Stock Exchange. Market capitalisation (end-1997) stands at Z$42.5 billion and there are 67 listed companies, although the market remains concentrated, with the five largest companies accounting for 53% of total capitalisation.

Since July 1993, foreign investors have been free to invest on the ZSE and to remit both capital and dividends.

After pressure from the IMF and the World Bank, some progress was made in 1997 as regards the privatisation of public enterprises. Dairibord Zimbabwe and the Cotton Company of Zimbabwe were privatised and listed on the ZSE, while the privatisation of the Commercial Bank of Zimbabwe is expected to be completed in 1998. The momentum towards privatisation is likely to accelerate once a private agency is established to facilitate the implementation of the public sector reform programme.

In addition to the equity counters, government stocks, municipal stocks and Zimbabwe Electricity Supply Authority (ZESA) stocks with an aggregate face value of 12 billion are in issue. Institutions are required to invest 45% of their assets in government or quasi-government stocks.

ECONOMIC AND POLITICAL OVERVIEW

The Zimbabwe African National Union-Patriotic Front (Zanu-PF) Party, which has been in power since independence in 1980, holds 147 of the 150 available seats in the House of Assembly, and Robert Mugabe is President. At no time since independence has a significant opposition emerged, although several other parties have been in existence throughout the period and others have been formed more recently.

Having exhausted its capacity to attract further foreign borrowing, Zimbabwe agreed to work with the IMF and the World Bank in 1990 in order to restructure the economy. An economic structural adjustment programme (ESAP) was introduced in order to change the emphasis of the economy from being highly regulated to being an economy in which market forces have a greater role to play. Many aspects of ESAP have now been implemented, including the removal of most controls on foreign exchange, interest rates, bank credit, investment, prices and wages.

The mainstays of the economy are agriculture, mining and manufacturing, with tourism beginning to play an increasingly important role. These sectors contribute around 50% of GDP which, for 1997, stands at some Z$86.8 billion (US$4.8 billion). After 1996's phenomenal 8.1% growth, which followed a good 1995–96 agricultural season, economic growth slowed down to an estimated 4.5% in 1997. The reduction is mainly due to a cut in agricultural output as a result of excessive rains. In addition, manufacturing sector growth has slowed to an estimated 6%. Due to depressed world mineral prices, the mining sector grew by only an estimated 4%. The price of gold seems likely to remain low well into 1998, while other mineral prices such as those for copper, nickel and ferro-chrome, have also been depressed.

After peaking at 22.4% in April 1997, inflation declined to a 10-month low of 14.4% in September before rising to 16% in October. Currency depreciation, increased indirect taxes, the high budget deficit and general increases in the prices of most basic commodities then boosted the CPI to 19.4% in November and 20.1% in December.

Role of the central bank

The central bank – the Reserve Bank of Zimbabwe (RBZ) – is at the apex of the country's banking system and acts

Exhibit 78.1: ZIMBABWE SE INDUSTRIAL PRICE INDEX (US$), 1993–97

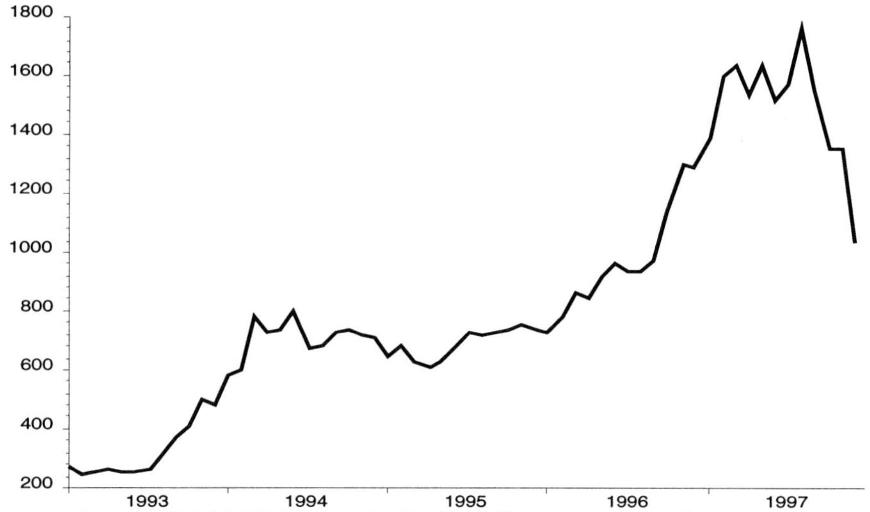

High value 1758.09 1.8.97 Low value 248.66 1.2.93 *Source: Datastream*

as the banks' bank. It is also the lender of last resort and adviser to the government.

The bank is responsible for the implementation of monetary and exchange rate policies. With the removal of direct controls, the bank's conduct of monetary policy has changed to reflect greater reliance on indirect instruments of monetary control, with open market operations assuming a key role. The RBZ's primary responsibility is the achievement of price stability by ensuring low and stable interest and inflation rates, thereby upholding the external and internal value of the Zimbabwean currency.

The RBZ seeks to maintain the stability of the financial sector through supervision of the banks, and is responsible for the preparation of regularly published monetary, financial, balance of payments and exchange rate data.

A new Reserve Bank Bill will be presented to parliament soon. Its aim will be to change the role of the RBZ from that of administrator to that of supervisor and facilitator, and the bank is likely to take on a more interventionist stance in the markets.

MARKET PERFORMANCE

A) In 1997

The ZSE Industrial Index, which accounts for 86.3% of total market capitalisation, reached an all-time high of 12,082 in early August, representing a gain relative to the end of 1996 of 37.5% in local currency terms and 29.5% in US dollar terms. Fears of a possible drought and two large "over-the-counter" privatisations, however, resulted in the market softening and the index stabilising in October at around 10,000. Adverse economic and political developments then began to undermine market sentiment during November and early December and the Industrial Index fell once again, ending the year 18% down at 7,196.43.

Mining stocks had a particularly poor year, largely reflecting sliding international mineral prices. The Mining Index fell from 1,083.60 in December 1996 to 506.38 in December 1997, and mining share prices ended the year at a four-year low.

The National Merchant Bank Ltd arranged a successful dual listing (on the ZSE and the London Stock Exchange) in April, raising Z$333 million, while three parastatals were privatised during the year.

B) Summary information

Global ranking by market value (US$ terms, end-1997): 60
Market capitalisation (end-1997): US$2.3 billion
Growth in market value (local currency terms, 1993–97): 327.7%
Market value as a % of nominal GDP (end-1997): 57%
Number of domestic/foreign companies listed (end-1997): 67/0
Market P/E (end-1997): 9.59
Short-term (90-day) interest rate (end-1997): 31.5%
Long-term (3-year) bond yield (end-1997): 33%
Budget deficit as a % of nominal GDP (1997): 8.5%
Annual increase in broad money (M3) supply (end-1997): 9.52%
Inflation rate (1997): 20.1%
US$ exchange rate (end-1997): Z$18.4

C) Year end share price indices, price/earnings ratios and yields

Exhibit 78.2:
YEAR-END SHARE PRICE INDICES, P/E RATIOS AND DIVIDEND YIELDS, 1993–97

Year-end	*Industrial Index*	*Mining Index*	*P/E*	*Yield (%)*
1993	2,325.26	515.79	8.8	3.6
1994	3,180.60	1,043.06	8.3	5.0
1995	3,972.62	1,329.02	7.4	5.2
1996	8,786.26	1,083.66	14.6	2.9
1997	7,196.43	458.40	9.6	4.4

Sources: Zimbabwe Stock Exchange and Fleming Martin Edwards Securities Limited.

D) Market indices and their constituents

The ZSE has two indices – the Industrial Index and the Mining Index – both based at 1967 = 100. Each index is capitalisation-weighted, comprises all companies in its sector, and tracks daily movement in relation to the base year.

THE STOCK MARKET

A) Brief history and structure

The first stock exchange in Zimbabwe opened in Bulawayo in 1896 and closed six years later. Other exchanges were established in Gwelo and Umatali but both had closed by 1924.

After World War II, a new exchange was founded in Bulawayo and dealings started on 2 January 1946. A second floor was opened in Salisbury in 1951 and these two centres, trading by telephone, continued operating until the Zimbabwe Stock Exchange Act of 1974 required a new exchange to be established. The current exchange therefore dates from the passage of that Act.

The ZSE is controlled by the Ministry of Finance through the Registrar of the Stock Exchange and is governed by a committee of elected members. Members' conduct is regulated by the Zimbabwe Stock Exchange Act in conjunction with the Members' Rules and Regulations.

B) Opening hours, name and address

The ZSE is open from 8.00am to 4.30pm, Monday to Friday, excluding public holidays. Trading takes place during the two daily call-over sessions from 9.00am to 9.45am and 11.45am to 12.30pm.

THE ZIMBABWE STOCK EXCHANGE
5th Floor, Southampton House, c/r Union Avenue / 1st Street
PO Box UA 234, Union Avenue, Harare
Tel: (263) 4 736 861; Fax: (263) 4 791 045
Web site: zse@harare.iafrica.com

MARKET SIZE

At the end of 1997, there were 67 companies listed on the ZSE, with a market capitalisation of Z$42.5 billion (US$2.3 billion). Market turnover increased significantly in 1997 to Z$6.45 billion from Z$2.55 billion.

Exhibit 78.3:
TRADING AND MARKET CAPITALISATION DATA, ZSE, 1993–97

Year	*Number of companies*	*Market turnover (Z$ million)*	*Volume (shares million)*	*Year-end market capitalisation (Z$ million)*
1993	64	347.2	272.30	9,937
1994	65	1,445.4	450.79	14,087
1995	66	1,299.4	649.69	19,849
1996	65	2,554.7	722.67	52,257
1997	67	6,452.4	1,197.20	42,502

Sources: Zimbabwe Stock Exchange and Fleming Martin Edwards Securities Limited.

Exhibit 78.4:
THE 20 LARGEST LISTED COMPANIES, ZSE, END-1997

Ranking	*Company*	*Market value (Z$ million)*
1	Delta	10,117.32
2	Ashanti Goldfields	4,322.38
3	Meikles Africa	3,210.65
4	Barclays Bank of Zimbabwe	3,146.87
5	Hippo Valley Estates	1,730.82
6	TZI	1,484.15
7	Zimbabwe Sun	1,382.43
8	Portland Holdings	1,150.11
9	Zimbabwe Sugar Refinery	1,110.38
10	Edgars Stores	901.65
11	Tobacco Sales	800.32
12	Cottco	789.60
13	Zimbabwe Papers	748.80
14	Wankie Colliery	677.08
15	Border Timbers	652.73
16	First Merchant Bank	636.46
17	M & R	623.50
18	Tedco	503.06
19	Circle Cement	480.00
20	Dairibord Zimbabwe	474.62

Sources: Zimbabwe Stock Exchange and Fleming Martin Edwards Securities Limited.

Exhibit 78.5:
THE 15 MOST ACTIVELY TRADED STOCKS, ZSE, 1997

Ranking	*Company*	*Trading value (Z$ million)*
1	Delta	1,549.64
2	TZI	665.36
3	Meikles Africa	643.73
4	National Merchant Bank	363.20
5	Zimbabwe Papers	301.34
6	Interfresh	181.48
7	Barclays Bank of Zimbabwe	177.71
8	TA Holdings	173.22
9	Zimbabwe Sun	165.70
10	Hippo Valley Estates	154.41
11	CAPS	147.71
12	Wankie Colliery	144.94
13	Seed-co	101.61
14	FMB	97.49
15	DCZ	94.21

Source: Zimbabwe Stock Exchange and Fleming Martin Edwards Securities Limited.

OPERATIONS

A) Trading

Trading takes place using a call-over system.

B) Principal brokers

BARD STOCKBROKERS
3rd Floor, Bard House, 69 Samora Machel Avenue, Harare
PO Box 3321, Harare
Tel: (263) 4 752756/752383/781837
E-mail: bard@harare.iafrica.com

CONTINENTAL SECURITIES TRADING
6th Floor, Fanum House, Samora Machel Avenue, Harare
PO Box CY 255, Harare
Tel: (263) 4 757669/757671-2; Fax: (263) 4 757679

CORPORATE SECURITIES
6th Floor, Livingstone House,
Samora Machel Avenue, Harare,
PO Box 7245, Harare
Tel: (263) 4 702005/728251-2-3; Fax: (263) 4 702006
E-mail: corpsec@harare.iafrica.com

FLEMING, MARTIN EDWARDS SECURITIES LIMITED
Club Chambers, c/r Nelson Mandela Ave/Third Street
PO Box 1475, Harare
Tel: (263) 4 727907-8/707931; Fax: (263) 4 707932
E-mail: edco@id.co.zw

INTERMARKET STOCKBROKERS
5th Floor, UDC Centre,
c/r Union Avenue/1st Street, Harare
PO Box 452, Harare
Tel: (263) 4 750915-5/750922; Fax: (263) 4 759369

KINGDOM STOCKBROKERS
2nd Floor, Karigamombe Centre,
Samora Machel Avenue, Harare
PO Box CY 3205, Causeway
Tel: (263) 4 758857-8/758458-71; Fax: (263) 4 758228
E-mail: persev@kingsec.co.zw

MSASA STOCKBROKERS
2nd Floor, New Africa House,
Union Avenue, Harare
PO Box UA 202, Union Avenue
Tel: (263) 4 772392-4; Fax: (263) 4 749690

QUINCOR JAMES CAPEL
1st Floor, Finsure House,
c/r Union Avenue/2nd Street, Harare
PO Box 1244, Harare
Tel: (263) 4 725421/738656-7; Fax: (263) 4 736043
E-mail: hsbczim@dnet.co.zw

REMO INVESTMENT BROKERS
3rd Floor, Royal Mutual House
45 Nelson Mandela Avenue, Harare
PO Box 3573, Harare
Tel: (263) 4 750717-8/757949; Fax: (263) 4 759804
E-mail: remo@samara.co.zw

SAGIT STOCKBROKERS
20th Floor, Karigomombe Centre,
Samora Machel Avenue, Harare
PO Box 21, Harare
Tel: (263) 4 757869-71/759385-6; Fax: (263) 4 750564
E-mail: sagit@harare.iafrica.com

C) Settlement and transfer

Settlement of all trades takes place on T+7. All scrip is under the control of transfer secretaries, who may work either at the listed company's head office or as professional/institutional bodies that keep the registers on their behalf.

D) Commissions and other costs

Exhibit 78.6:
ORDINARY AND PREFERENCE SHARE COMMISSION RATES

Consideration	*Rate (%)*
On the first Z$50,000	2.0
On the next Z$50,000	1.5
Over Z$100,000	1.0

Source: Zimbabwe Stock Exchange.

All commission is subject to a minimum charge of Z$15, or is at discretion for amounts under Z$100 consideration. The minimum charge on any option is Z$15; the basic charge is Z$20 per transaction.

For registering shares on behalf of a client, a charge of Z$20 per transaction is levied. This charge covers postage but does not include revenue stamps. For scrip held on behalf of a client, a charge per annum or part thereof of Z$50 applies, although brokers have a discretionary right to waive this charge.

Revenue stamps are payable on all transactions at 45 cents per Z$100 charged, rounded up to the nearest 10 cents.

TAXATION AND REGULATIONS AFFECTING FOREIGN INVESTORS

Foreign investors must purchase shares through the ZSE using foreign currency received in Zimbabwe via the normal banking channels. Dividends are fully remittable, after paying withholding tax of 15%. Capital may be repatriated in full on disinvestment, net of capital gains tax of 10% (adjusted by an annual inflation factor of 15%).

Exhibit 78.7:
WITHHOLDING TAXES

Recipient	*Dividends %*	*Interest %*
Resident corporations	Nil	30[1, 2]
Resident individuals	15, 20[3]	30
Non-resident corporations and individuals:		
Non-treaty	15, 20	10
Treaty	15, 20[3-6]	10

Notes:

1. A rate of 30% applies to local interest from any bank, discount house or financial institution.
2. A rate of 30% applies to local interest from building societies.
3. The 15% rate applies to quoted shares, the 20% rate to unquoted shares.
4. A reduced rate of 10% applies to dividends on substantial holdings (25% or more) under the Bulgarian, Canadian, Dutch, French, German, Mauritian and Polish tax treaties.
5. A reduced rate of 15% applies to dividends on substantial holdings (25% or more) under the Norwegian and Swedish tax treaties.
6. A reduced rate of 5% applies to dividends on substantial holdings (25% or more) under the UK tax treaty.

Source: Price Waterhouse.

Foreign shareholdings in listed companies are currently limited to 10% per investor and 40% of the total fully diluted issued share capital in aggregate. This is over and above any foreign holdings in existence on 1 May 1993.

Zimbabwean dual registered shares may now be transferred from a foreign to a local register without prior exchange control approval. The proceeds realised from the sale of such shares qualify for remittance outside Zimbabwe.

SHAREHOLDER PROTECTION CODES

The Minister of Finance is invested with supervisory and regulatory powers under the Zimbabwe Stock Exchange Act. New legislation regarding shareholder protection is currently pending.

A) Mergers and takeovers

Procedures followed are as set out in the London Stock Exchange City Code, except that a takeover bid is triggered when a shareholding reaches 50%.

B) Compensation fund

The Zimbabwe Stock Exchange Security Fund exists for the indemnification/compensation of loss to any investor due to dishonesty or insolvency on the part of a member of the exchange. In addition, all registered stockbrokers must maintain a professional indemnity insurance policy intended to make good any loss resulting from negligence or dishonesty by that stockbroker or its employees.

RESEARCH

African Equities: A Guide to Markets and Companies, published by Euromoney Books, provides in-depth information for those wishing to invest or do business in Africa. See the order card at the back of this book for details.

Regional and global funds

EUROPEAN, AFRICAN AND MIDDLE EASTERN EMERGING MARKET REGIONAL FUNDS

Fund	US$ % change 01/01/97 01/01/98	01/01/93 01/01/98	Fund base currency	Fund size (US$ mil)	Fund volatility	Management group	Opal main sector	Opal subsector
AberdeenProl Frontier Markets	38.95	N/A	£	8.7	-1	ABTRUST	Open-End	Equity
Key BCM Emerging Value Inc	38.35	N/A	US$	93.2	-1	Key Asst Mgt	Open-End	Equity
AIG Europe/Mid East/Africa EM	9.28	N/A	US$	N/A	3.5	AIG Asset Mgt	Open-End	Equity

Note: details for some funds may not have been included if the data for the US$ % change for 97/98 was not available

EMERGING MARKET ASEAN REGIONAL FUNDS

Fund	US$ % change 01/01/97 01/01/98	01/01/93 01/01/98	Fund base currency	Fund size (US$ mil)	Fund volatility	Management group	Opal main sector	Opal subsector
AB Asean Growth	5.13	N/A	US$	16	2.703	Arab Bank Man	Open-End	Equity
Shinwako ASEAN Open	-37.15	N/A	¥	365	6.442	Shinwako	Open-End	Equity
Asean Supreme Fund Ltd	-37.51	N/A	US$	N/A	-1	Jardine Fleming	Open-End	Equity
JF ASEAN	-44.84	34.92	US$	157.4	7.51	Jardine Fleming	Open-End	Equity
Daiwa Original ASEAN Stk	-46.43	N/A	¥	1246	7.599	Daiwa	Open-End	Equity
Nomura ASEAN 4	-48.41	N/A	¥	810	-1	Nomura ITMCo	Open-End	Equity
Nikko Glbl ASEAN	-48.86	N/A	¥	587	7.56	Nikko	Open-End	Equity
Newton UGF South East Asia	-52.06	-12.18	US$	1.6	9.132	Cap House	Open-End	Equity
Fidelity Fds ASEAN	-53.04	-8.5	US$	229.4	9.155	Fidelity	Open-End	Equity
Fidelity ASEAN	-54.6	1.71	£	48	9.633	Fidelity	Open-End	Equity
ASEAN Fund Ltd.	-54.67	-20.58	US$	308.08	8.677	HSBC Asst Mgt	Closed-End	Equity
Guinness Flight ASEAN	-54.97	-10.68	US$	15.8	8.54	Guinness Flight	Open-End	Equity
Thornton SSF ASEAN Growth	-55.25	N/A	US$	3.4	9.66	Thornton	Open-End	Equity
GT ASEAN B	-55.35	-14.9	US$	69.8	9.626	LGT	Open-End	Equity
Nomura Aurora ASEAN	-55.44	N/A	¥	7556	8.074	Nomura ITMCo	Open-End	Equity
GT ASEAN A	-55.57	-16.12	US$	69.8	9.625	LGT	Open-End	Equity
Parvest ASEAN D	-55.89	N/A	US$	27.3	8.866	Paribas Asst	Open-End	Equity
Daiwa Original Emerging ASEAN	-57.1	N/A	¥	116	-1	Daiwa	Open-End	Equity
Jupiter Archipelago	-57.2	N/A	US$	45.4	-1	N/A	Open-End	Equity
Groupe Indosuez ASEAN	-57.95	-15.2	US$	32.3	9.287	Gartmore	Open-End	Equity
Barclays ASF ASEAN	-58.4	N/A	US$	3	-1	Barclays	Open-End	Equity
JPM Inv-ASEAN Equity A	-60.52	N/A	US$	4.7	-1	N/A	Open-End	Equity
INVESCO ASEAN Dev	-64.28	-15.32	US$	18.2	12.513	Invesco Intl	Open-End	Equity
ImPac AP ASEAN	-75.52	N/A	US$	1.5	-1	Impac Asset M	Open-End	Equity

Note: details for some funds may not have been included if the data for the US$ % change for 97/98 was not available

TOP PERFORMING ASIAN REGIONAL FUNDS

Fund	*US$% change*		*Fund base currency*	*Fund size (US$ mil)*	*Fund volatility*	*Management group*	*Opal main sector*	*Opal subsector*
	01/01/97 01/01/98	*01/01/93 01/01/98*						
Regent Pacific Hedge	41.44	N/A	US$	65	4.973	Regent Fd Mgr	Closed-End	Equity
Asian Infrastr Development Fd	13.14	N/A	US$	77.6	4.246	Soros Fund Mgt	Private	Equity
VOC Invest	13.13	N/A	US$	46.789	5.37	Rosenwald Rod	Private	Equity
SCI Asian Hedge Net Prf Ind	10.97	122.78	US$	370	4.215	Sofaer	Open-End	Equity
Discover Asia	9.1	N/A	US$	29.3	3.543	Discover Invest	Open-End	Equity
Taiheiyo Asia Open	7.04	N/A	¥	36	4.484	Taiheiyo ITMC	Open-End	Equity
Winchester Eastern Dragon	2.89	N/A	US$	16	2.726	Olympia Cap I	Open-End	Equity
TR Pacific Investment Trust	-4.03	112.62	£	N/A	7.02	Touche Remnan	Closed-End	Equity
LG Asian Smaller Companies	-6.51	70.73	US$	15.6	6.606	Lloyd George	Open-End	Equity
Five Arrows IMP Asia Cap Gth	-8.58	N/A	US$	0.5	-1	Five Arrows R	Open-End	Equity
Henry Cooke LG Eastern Entpr	-8.59	N/A	£	13.9	8.728	Henry Cooke I	Open-End	Equity
Shaw Greater Asia Fund	-11.45	N/A	US$	6.699	11.324	Shaw Inv Mgt	Private	Equity
S&P Far Eastern Smaller Cos	-13.1	N/A	£	9.4	4.665	Save & Prosper	Open-End	Equity
Tokyo Central Asia Stk Fund	-13.17	N/A	¥	85	4.54	Tokyo	Open-End	Equity
Regent Pacific Arbitrage	-16.14	53.6	US$	32.5	3.494	Regent Fd Mgr	Open-End	Equity
MIM Emerging Asian Strats A	-16.52	N/A	US$	97	4.829	Matthews Intl	Open-End	Equity
Salomon Bros Asia Gth	-17.3	N/A	US$	17	-1	Saloman Bros	Open-End	Equity
JF Asian Emerging Mkts Tst	-19.32	N/A	US$	24.1	5.956	Jardine Fleming	Open-End	Equity
Finepar Orient	-19.76	16.96	Ffr	59	3.862	UE CIC	Open-End	Equity
PDFM Pacific Basin Ex	-20.97	61.44	£	N/A	6.527	N/A	Open-End	Equity
Scudder New Asia Inc	-23.04	10.26	US$	129.9	5.419	Scudder	Closed-End	Equity
Fidelity South East Asia	-23.38	74.59	£	234.3	7.386	Fidelity	Open-End	Equity
IBJ Asian Equity	-23.5	N/A	US$	843.6	-1	IBJ Asia Ltd	Open-End	Equity
GAM East Asia	-24.01	27.03	US$	7.3	8.42	GAM	Open-End	Equity
JF Eastern Smaller Companies	-25.15	106.37	US$	33.2	7.807	Jardine Fleming	Open-End	Equity
N Applegate Asn Smaller Cos	-25.28	N/A	US$	2.4	7.988	Credit Lyonnais	Open-End	Equity
Salomon Bros:Asia Grth/O	-25.33	N/A	US$	1.8	-1	N/A	Open-End	Equity
Asia Pacific Performance	-25.39	N/A	US$	44.7	5.131	Demachy Worms	Open-End	Equity
Salomon Bros:Asia Grth/A	-25.55	N/A	US$	7.7	-1	N/A	Open-End	Equity
Salomon Bros:Asia Grth/C	-25.96	N/A	US$	2.6	-1	N/A	Open-End	Equity
Salomon Bros:Asia Grth/B	-26.05	N/A	US$	7.1	-1	N/A	Open-End	Equity
Newton Oriental	-26.7	39.09	£	6.1	7.137	Cap House	Open-End	Equity
Credit Suisse Orient	-26.82	N/A	£	37.6	8.076	Credit Suisse	Open-End	Equity
Govett Asian Smaller Companies	-26.94	N/A	£	N/A	12.985	Govett & Co	Closed-End	Equity
Worldsec Dynasty	-27.33	43.89	US$	5.2	6.333	Worldsec	Open-End	Equity
Newton UGF Asian Growth	-27.46	27.52	US$	12.4	6.72	Cap House	Open-End	Equity
GAM Asian Developing Mkts	-27.58	N/A	US$	21.6	-1	GAM	Open-End	Equity
F&C PF Emer Asian Equity	-27.59	11.87	US$	7.7	7.978	Hypo For & Co	Open-End	Equity
Morgan Grenfell Asian Sm Cos	-27.67	N/A	US$	16.3	7.264	Morgan Grenfell	Open-End	Equity
DBIM Tigerfund	-27.69	28.21	DM	171.1	6.559	DBIM	Open-End	Equity
Asian Emerging Markets Fund	-27.92	-13.6	US$	15.8	6.677	Emerging Mkts	Open-End	Equity
Colonial Newpt Tgr Cub/Z	-28.05	N/A	US$	0.1	-1	World Funds	Open-End	Equity
Colonial Newpt Tgr Cub/A	-28.22	N/A	US$	7.4	-1	World Funds	Open-End	Equity
Henderson Asian Enterprise	-28.29	54.81	£	34.8	5.634	Henderson	Open-End	Equity
Montgomery Emerg Asia/R	-28.3	N/A	US$	42.7	-1	Montgomery As	Open-End	Equity
Baring Asia Manufacturing Fund	-28.45	N/A	¥	2522	-1	Barings	Open-End	Equity
Stewart Ivory Asia Pacific	-28.51	44.73	£	107.6	5.396	Stewart Ivory	Open-End	Equity

Note: details for some funds may not have been included if the data for the US$ % change for 97/98 was not available

ASIAN SUBCONTINENT REGIONAL FUNDS

Fund	*US$ % change* 01/01/97 01/01/98	01/01/93 01/01/98	Fund base currency	Fund size (US$ mil)	Fund volatility	Management group	Opal main sector	Opal subsector
Regent Moghul	36.18	N/A	US$	12	9.024	Regent Pacific	Closed-End	Equity
Regent South Asia	9.82	N/A	US$	1.8	6.324	Regent Pacific	Open-End	Equity
South Asia Access Fund	9.77	N/A	US$	4.81	-1	Bqe Nationale	Open-End	Equity
EV Medallion Greater India B	5.8	N/A	US$	1.4	6.151	Eaton Vance	Open-End	Equity
Eaton Vance Grtr India/B	5.41	N/A	US$	67.5	6.32	Eaton Vance	Open-End	Equity
Eaton Vance Grtr India/A	4.62	N/A	US$	12.4	6.362	Eaton Vance	Open-End	Equity
South Asia Value Fund	1.69	N/A	US$	8.1	-1	Bqe Nationale	Open-End	Equity
LG India	0.44	N/A	US$	23.5	6.433	Lloyd George	Open-End	Equity
Commonwealth Equity Fund	-2.11	14.61	US$	91.426	5.864	Batterymarch	Private	Equity
N. Applegate Ind S'continent	-2.53	N/A	US$	9.6	7.013	Credit Lyonnais	Open-End	Equity
IS Himalayan Fund NV	-6.19	6.53	US$	200.7	6.351	Indosuez	Closed-End	Equity
MBf Venture Portfolio	-13.52	-32.55	US$	0.3	4.796	MBf	Open-End	Equity

Note: details for some funds may not have been included if the data for the US$ % change for 97/98 was not available

TOP PERFORMING EMERGING EUROPEAN REGIONAL FUNDS

Fund	*US$ % change* 01/01/97 01/01/98	01/01/93 01/01/98	Fund base currency	Fund size (US$ mil)	Fund volatility	Management group	Opal main sector	Opal subsector
Signet New Capital Markets A	75.04	N/A	US$	30	-1	New Cap Mgt	Open-End	Equity
First Russian Frontiers	71.27	N/A	US$	78.911	9.23	Pictet	Closed-End	Equity
Baring Emerging Europe	56.25	N/A	US$	N/A	7.447	Barings	Closed-End	Equity
East Europe Development Ltd	54.48	747.52	US$	N/A	7.053	Invesco CEAM	Closed-End	Equity
Baring GUF Eastern Europe	51.67	N/A	US$	175.7	-1	Barings	Open-End	Equity
Mercury ST Eastern European	41.07	N/A	DM	633.2	-1	Mercury	Open-End	Equity
MCT Eastern Europe Ltd	38.63	N/A	US$	45.7	-1	MC Securities	Open-End	Equity
Fleming FF Eastern European	32.51	N/A	DM	989.7	8.203	Fleming	Open-End	Equity
KB Lux Key Eastern Europe	32.06	N/A	DM	75	-1	Kredietbank	Open-End	Equity
JF Eastern European Trust	31.04	N/A	US$	22.5	-1	Jardine Fleming	Open-End	Equity
Pictet T.F. Eastern Europe	26.99	N/A	DM	280.3	-1	Pictet	Open-End	Equity
State Street Europe Emergente	24.51	N/A	Ffr	37	-1	State Street	Open-End	Equity
Morgan Grenfell Euro Emg Mkts	24.23	N/A	£	8.3	5.449	Morgan Grenfell	Open-End	Equity
Muscovy Frontiers Fund Plc	23.43	N/A	US$	39.2	-1	N/A	Open-End	Equity
Aetna Emerging Europe A	14.89	N/A	US$	36.2	-1	AEtna	Open-End	Equity
HYPO Osteuropa	14.55	N/A	DM	58.1	-1	HCM Cap Mgt	Open-End	Equity
Aetna Emerging Europe B	13.74	N/A	US$	36.2	-1	AEtna	Open-End	Equity
ABN AMRO Eastern Europe Eqty	13.15	N/A	DM	463.2	-1	ABN AMRO	Open-End	Equity
GT Global Eastern Europe	12.9	N/A	US$	N/A	-1	LGT	Closed-End	Equity
Jupiter Tyndall GF E European	12.27	N/A	US$	3.5	-1	Tyndall	Open-End	Equity
EM Osteuropa	11.45	N/A	DM	108.2	6.35	Union Invest	Open-End	Equity
BAI Ost MEF i. WP	11.4	N/A	Sch	N/A	5.119	Bank Austria	Open-End	Equity
Vontobel Eastern Europe Eq A	10.63	N/A	DM	114.5	8.447	Vontobel	Open-End	Equity
Central & Eastern European Fd	10.38	120.36	US$	N/A	5.774	CAFA/Lloyds	Open-End	Equity
Soc Gen C & E European Opps	9.7	N/A	US$	31.1	-1	Société Générale	Closed-End	Equity

Top performing Emerging European regional funds continued

Raiffeisen-Osteuropafonds MEF	9.19	N/A	Sch	N/A	6.405	Raiffeisen	Open-End	Equity
Vontobel Eastern Euro Eq	8.74	N/A	US$	128.5	-1	Vontobel	Open-End	Equity
BBL (F) Emergence Sud	7.85	46.53	Ffr	113	3.645	Bqe Bruxelles	Open-End	Equity
Donau Fonds	7.57	202.04	G	61	5.784	Delta Lloyd F	Open-End	Equity
Schroder Eastern European	6.79	N/A	US$	184.1	7.364	Schroders	Open-End	Equity
ACM/IBA Emerging Europe Ptf	6.6	N/A	DM	21.4	-1	East Fund Mgt	Open-End	Equity
Discover Europe	6.33	N/A	US$	36.5	6.186	Regent Fd Mgr	Open-End	Equity
Central European Growth Fund	6.16	N/A	US$	259.05	7.418	Credit Suisse	Closed-End	Equity
OST-INVEST MEF i.WP	6.14	41.61	Sch	N/A	5.718	Allgemeine Sp	Open-End	Equity
OST AKTIV	4.64	N/A	Sch	N/A	7.326	CA/oig	Open-End	Equity
CA IB Central Europe	4.2	8.02	£	13	6.945	CAFA/Lazard	Open-End	Equity
LOI Eastern Europe	4.05	N/A	DM	88.6	-1	Lombard Odier	Open-End	Equity
Framlington Eastern Europe Fd	2.45	N/A	US$	17.189	5.471	Framlington	Closed-End	Equity
DBIM DB Osteuropa	1.1	N/A	DM	197.3	-1	DBIM	Open-End	Equity
UBS (Lux) Equity I Central Eur	0.76	N/A	Sfr	110.4	-1	UBS (Intrag)	Open-End	Equity
Bankinvest Afd. 9. E.Europe	-2.01	128.77	Dkr	162.24	5.772	Bankinvest	Open-End	Equity
CS Eastern Europe Fund	-4.05	N/A	¥	2402	-1	CS ITMCo	Open-End	Equity
BBL Invest Emerging Europe C	-5.06	N/A	DM	35.5	6.149	Bqe Bruxelles	Open-End	Equity
Nomura Aurora II East Europe	-5.54	N/A	Japanese Yen	9729	-1	Nomura ITMCo	Open-End	Equity
Templeton Central & E Europe	-6.55	N/A	US$	36.2	-1	Templeton	Closed-End	Equity
Groupe Indosuez East European	-8.05	N/A	US$	7	-1	Indosuez	Open-End	Equity
KB Equity Fund East. Europe C	-9.26	N/A	Bfr	570.5	-1	Kredietbank	Open-End	Equity
KB Equity Fund East. Europe D	-9.27	N/A	Bfr	518	-1	Kredietbank	Open-End	Equity
DANUBIA-INVEST MEF i. WP	-88.76	-78.14	Ash	N/A	34.324	Sparinvest Au	Open-End	Equity

Note: details for some funds may not have been included if the data for the US$ % change for 97/98 was not available

LATIN AMERICAN AND CARIBBEAN REGIONAL FUNDS

Fund	*US$ % change 01/01/97 01/01/98*	*01/01/93 01/01/98*	*Fund base currency*	*Fund size (US$ mil)*	*Fund volatility*	*Management group*	*Opal main sector*	*Opal subsector*
Latin American Discovery	43.06	151.68	US$	166.32	8.125	Morgan Stanley	Closed-End	Equity
M Stanley Inst:Latin Am/A	41.16	N/A	US$	73.5	9.951	Morgan Stanley	Open-End	Equity
M Stanley Inst:Latin Am/B	40.5	N/A	US$	8.7	-1	Morgan Stanley	Open-End	Equity
Morgan Stanley Latin Amer I	40.16	N/A	US$	93.1	7.71	Morgan Stanley	Open-End	Equity
M Stanley Fd:Latin Amer/A	39.61	N/A	US$	57.8	8.774	Morgan Stanley	Open-End	Equity
M Stanley Fd:Latin Amer/B	38.89	N/A	US$	28.7	-1	Morgan Stanley	Open-End	Equity
M Stanley Fd:Latin Amer/C	38.74	N/A	US$	20.2	8.801	Morgan Stanley	Open-End	Equity
State Street Amerique Latine	37.75	N/A	Ffr	96	6.719	State Street	Open-End	Equity
NPI Latin American	37.53	N/A	£	9.6	-1	National Prov	Open-End	Equity
Rembrandt:Latin Am Eq/Cmn	35.5	N/A	US$	36.7	-1	Rembrandt	Open-End	Equity
Schroder Latin American	34.17	174.12	US$	958.5	5.867	Schroders	Open-End	Equity
TCW Galileo Latin Amer Eq	33.4	N/A	US$	36.2	6.87	Trust Co	Open-End	Equity
Fidelity Latin America	32.89	N/A	US$	711.9	6.869	Fidelity	Open-End	Equity
T Rowe Price Intl:Lat Am	31.88	N/A	US$	389	7.076	T Rowe Price	Open-End	Equity
Scudder Intl:Latin Amer	31.3	139.98	US$	868.1	6.545	Scudder	Open-End	Equity
Share Latin America	30.91	114.03	US$	6.5	6.59	Bearbull	Open-End	Equity
BT Inv:Latin American Eq	30.8	N/A	US$	28.7	6.436	Bankers Trust	Open-End	Equity
TCW/DW Latin Amer Grth/B	30.56	42.28	US$	279	6.924	Trust Co	Open-End	Equity

Latin American and Caribbean regional funds continued

ABN AMRO Latin American Eqty	30.32	N/A	US$	248.4	6.554	ABN AMRO	Open-End	Equity
Fidelity Latin American Gr	29.97	N/A	C$	36	7.121	Fidelity	Open-End	Equity
Old Mutual Latin Amer Cos	29.9	69.79	£	21.1	6.359	Old Mutual	Open-End	Equity
South America Fund	29.78	144.75	US$	134.78	4.064	BEA Assoc	Closed-End	Equity
Danske Inv Engros Latinamerika	29.56	N/A	Dkr	92.886	6.302	Danske Invest	Open-End	Equity
Fidelity Fds Latin America	29.43	N/A	US$	131.8	6.987	Fidelity	Open-End	Equity
AIG Latin America	29.1	N/A	US$	23.2	6.682	AIG Asset Mgt	Open-End	Equity
Scudder GOF Latin America A-2	28.92	N/A	US$	60.6	6.429	Scudder	Open-End	Equity
Genesis Condor	28.7	145.07	US$	73.1	3.384	Genesis	Closed-End	Equity
Baillie Gifford Latin Amer	28.56	N/A	£	104.2	5.985	Baillie Giffo	Open-End	Equity
Latinvest Fund	28.33	205.92	US$	416.7	7.491	Globalvest Mgt	Open-End	Equity
S&P Latin America	28.29	N/A	£	10.8	6.511	Save & Prosper	Open-End	Equity
Gartmore CSF Latin America	28.22	N/A	US$	12.4	-1	Gartmore	Open-End	Equity
Latinamerika Fonden	28.18	N/A	Skr	242.26	5.851	Handelsbanken	Open-End	Equity
KB Equity Fund Lat America D	28.12	N/A	Bfr	2872.2	6.5	Kredietbank	Open-End	Equity
KB Equity Fund Lat America C	28.11	N/A	Bfr	2794.2	6.499	Kredietbank	Open-End	Equity
Lion Fortune CL Lat Am Eq D	27.93	N/A	US$	28.5	7.07	Credit Lyonnais	Open-End	Equity
Morgan Grenfell Latin Amer	27.93	N/A	£	17.4	6.389	Morgan Grenfell	Open-End	Equity
BBL Invest Latin America Cap	27.83	N/A	US$	105.9	6.629	Bqe Bruxelles	Open-End	Equity
Latinac	27.67	N/A	Sfr	16.3	-1	Gerifonds	Open-End	Equity
Fleming Select Latin American	27.55	N/A	£	39.9	-1	Fleming	Open-End	Equity
NatWest/IFC LAIF Lat Am Index	27.54	N/A	US$	39.555	6.687	NatWest Inv M	Open-End	Equity
Institutioneel Latin Amerika	27.53	N/A	G	83.6	7.06	Robeco	Open-End	Equity
Atlas Latin American Fund	27.3	N/A	C$	15.5	6.502	Fin Atlas	Open-End	Equity
Fleming FF Latin American	27.18	61.6	US$	169.8	6.699	Fleming	Open-End	Equity
BT GAF Latin American Eq Inc	27.02	N/A	US$	37.8	6.267	Bankers Trust	Open-End	Equity
Singer & Fried Aztec	26.62	N/A	£	7.1	6.356	Singer & Fried	Open-End	Equity
Aetna Latin American A	26.47	N/A	US$	21.3	6.411	AEtna	Open-End	Equity
Lloyds IP Latin Am Eq	26.39	N/A	US$	72.3	-1	Lloyds GSY	Open-End	Equity

Note: details for some funds may not have been included if the data for the US$ % change for 97/98 was not available

TOP PERFORMING GLOBAL FUNDS (EMERGING MARKETS)

	US$% change							
	01/01/97	*01/01/93*	*Fund base*	*Fund size*	*Fund*	*Management*	*Opal main*	*Opal*
Fund	*01/01/98*	*01/01/98*	*currency*	*(US$ mil)*	*volatility*	*group*	*sector*	*subsector*
Thornhill Global Equity	403.2	N/A	US$	6	-1	Thornhill AML	Open-End	Equity
SR Emerging	103.38	N/A	US$	513	-1	Sloane Robins	Open-End	Equity
Schwendiman Glb New Mkts LP	69.85	N/A	US$	10.1	5.986	Schwendiman P	Open-End	Equity
Everest Capital Frontier	49.69	N/A	US$	612	5.059	Everest Capital	Open-End	Equity
Trace Glbl Opportunities LP	49.25	N/A	US$	13.5	-1	Trace Capital	Open-End	Equity
Oppenheimer Emg Mkt Int 2	46.01	N/A	US$	234.6	6.665	Oppenheimer	Private	Equity
Globalvest Value	35.75	N/A	US$	8.3	9.724	Alpha Global	Open-End	Equity
Globalvest Value Fund LP	33.77	N/A	US$	15.4	8.319	Globalvest Mgt	Open-End	Equity
Emerging Value Opportunities	30.1	N/A	US$	25.6	-1	MeesPierson M	Open-End	Equity
Croesus EMTR Fund SA	27.64	N/A	US$	27	5.605	Croesus Capital	Open-End	Equity
Olympia Stars Emerging Mkts	26.83	N/A	US$	21.2	3.126	Olympia Cap I	Open-End	Equity
PCP Emerging Markets	23.11	N/A	US$	4.5	-1	PCP Investment	Open-End	Equity
Henderson Emerg Mkts Exempt	21.97	N/A	£	25.9	5.19	Henderson	Open-End	Equity

Top peforming global funds (emerging markets) continued

Deltec Emerging Mkts Eq	20.14	N/A	US$	99.6	5.832	Deltec Secs	Open-End	Equity
GAM Emerging Markets LP	19	N/A	US$	4.32	3.223	GAM	Private	Equity
Global Emerging Mkts Inv Co	17.88	N/A	US$	18.5	5.329	Foreign & Col	Open-End	Equity
Strategos Balanced Fund	17.8	N/A	US$	7.799	-1	VZB Partners	Open-End	Equity
GAM Emerging Mkts Multi-Fund	17.67	123.29	US$	140	4.023	GAM	Open-End	Equity
Emerging Mkts Telecomms	17.02	109.47	US$	177.41	5.431	BEA Assoc	Closed-End	Equity
Permal Emerging Mkts Holdings	16.87	N/A	US$	678.8	3.192	Permal	Open-End	Equity
Syfrets Gl Emerging Mkts	16.7	N/A	US$	2.1	3.2	Syfrets Mgt	Open-End	Equity
Ermitage Emerging Markets	16.33	146.47	US$	26.4	3.329	Ermitage	Open-End	Equity
Kleinwort Emerging Markets IT	15.57	N/A	£	N/A	8.381	Kleinwort Ben	Closed-End	Equity
HYPO New Horizon	14.66	53.25	DM	127.6	5.271	HCM Cap Mgt	Open-End	Equity
C.I. Emerging Markets Fund	14.63	40.2	C$	99	4.179	Canadian Intl	Open-End	Equity
Alpha Global	14.22	61.81	US$	59.4	2.018	N/A	Open-End	Equity
Oppenheimer Devel Mkts/A	14.09	N/A	US$	37.1	-1	Oppenheimer	Open-End	Equity
Evergreen Emerg Mkt Gr/Y	13.74	N/A	US$	64	4.914	Evergreen Ass	Open-End	Equity
Evergreen Emerg Mkt Gr/A	13.48	N/A	US$	5.2	4.934	Evergreen Ass	Open-End	Equity
Oppenheimer Devel Mkts/C	13.18	N/A	US$	4.4	-1	Oppenheimer	Open-End	Equity
Oppenheimer Devel Mkts/B	13.09	N/A	US$	17.7	-1	Oppenheimer	Open-End	Equity
Morgan Stanley Nvgtr EM Eq A	13.08	N/A	US$	235.1	-1	Van Kampen Am	Open-End	Equity
Evergreen Emerg Mkt Gr/C	12.83	N/A	US$	1	4.998	Evergreen Ass	Open-End	Equity
Evergreen Emerg Mkt Gr/B	12.82	N/A	US$	4.2	4.999	Evergreen Ass	Open-End	Equity
Montgomery Emg Communications	12.16	N/A	US$	35.199	5.32	Montgomery As	Closed-End	Equity
F&C Emerging Markets IT (und)	12.08	71.53	£	N/A	6.369	Foreign & Col	Closed-End	Equity
F&C Global Emerging Exempt UT	11.02	N/A	£	29.167	4.999	Foreign & Col	Open-End	Equity
C.I. Sector Emerging Ms Shares	10.94	33.85	C$	51	4.154	Canadian Intl	Open-End	Equity
MFS/Forgn & Col Emg Mkt/A	10.85	N/A	US$	44.1	-1	Massachusetts	Open-End	Equity
Emerging Mkts Trust	10.74	90.81	US$	359.49	4.936	Cap Intl Inc	Private	Equity
Emerging Mkts Brewery	10.58	N/A	US$	13.6	-1	Bank von Erns	Open-End	Equity
Fremont:Emerging Mkts	10.4	N/A	US$	17.1	-1	Fremont MF In	Open-End	Equity
MFS/Forgn & Col Emg Mkt/B	10.29	N/A	US$	47	-1	Massachusetts	Open-End	Equity
FP Umbrella Equity Class	10.27	167.96	US$	20.5	4.44	FP Consult SA	Open-End	Equity
Nicholas-App:Emg Cntry/I	10.12	N/A	US$	82.7	5.851	Nicholas-Appl	Open-End	Equity
Nicholas-App:Emg Cntry/Q	10.03	N/A	US$	39.8	-1	Nicholas-Appl	Open-End	Equity
Emerging Mkts Infrastructure	9.98	N/A	US$	212.09	4.585	BEA Assoc	Closed-End	Equity
Pioneer Emerging Mrkts/A	9.87	N/A	US$	134.2	5.89	Pioneer	Open-End	Equity

Note: details for some funds may not have been included if the data for the US$ % change for 97/98 was not available

TOP PERFORMING GLOBAL FUNDS (DEVELOPED MARKETS)

Fund	*US$ % change 31/12/96 31/12/97*	*31/12/92 31/12/97*	*Fund base currency*	*Fund size (US$ mil)*	*Fund volatility*	*Management group*	*Main sector*	*Class*
Fleming Inc & Gth-Cap (2000)	679.88	395.91	£	10.06	26.33	Fleming Inv Mgmt Ltd	Equity Growth	UK Investment Trusts
Dartmoor Wts	173.06	157.24	£	3.49	20.09	Exeter Asset Mgmt Ltd	Equity Income	UK Investment Trusts
Fleming Inc & Gth -Cap (2000)	104.47	349.03	£	41.71	6.74	Fleming Inv Mgmt Ltd	Equity Growth	UK Investment Trusts
SR International	87.24	N/A	US$	1,040.00	5.33	Sloane Robinson Inv Mgmt	Equity	Offshore Territories
Exmoor Dual-Inc (2001)	68.42	102.65	£	8.71	9.5	Exeter Asset Mgmt Ltd	Equity Income	UK Investment Trusts
Geared Income	60.22	133.48	£	95.28	6.49	Broker Financial Svs Plc	Equity Income	UK Investment Trusts
TR Property Wts	57.96	N/A	£	15.11	14.96	Henderson Investors	Equity Growth	UK Investment Trusts

Top performing global funds (developed markets) continued

British Assets Wts	56.95	N/A	£	13.5	10.37	Friends Ivory & Sime Plc	Equity Income	UK Investment Trusts
Fidelity Sel:Energy Serv	51.87	287.53	US$	920.5	6.93	Fidelity Select Funds	Equity Growth	US Mutuals
GAM Universal USD	49.51	191.01	US$	204.1	4.52	GAM Fund Managers IOM	Equity	Offshore Territories
Overseas Wts	48.35	184.75	£	7.49	7.22	Morgan Grenfell Tst Mngrs Ltd	Equity Growth	UK Investment Trusts
For & Col Enterprise	48.18	389.11	£	277.74	4.67	For & Col Ventures Ltd	Equity Growth	UK Investment Trusts
Momentum Stock Master	47.88	201.19	US$	52.89	4.19	Momentum Asset Mgmt Ltd	Equity	Offshore Territories
Jos Holdings - Cap (2003)	45.66	480.65	£	26.13	4.84	Kleinwort Benson Inv Mgmt Ltd	Equity Growth	UK Investment Trusts
Dartmoor	43.65	273.26	£	143.82	4.91	Exeter Asset Mgmt Ltd	Equity Income	UK Investment Trusts
Exmoor Dual-Ord (2001)	42.47	25.25	£	3.39	14.73	Exeter Asset Mgmt Ltd	Equity	UK Investment Trusts
Gabelli Gl Interactive CP	41.7	N/A	US$	69.5	3.82	Gabelli Funds	Equity Growth	US Mutuals
Henderson HF Gl Technology	39.63	N/A	US$	59.46	N/A	Henderson	Equity	Luxembourg
Deltec Long Distance Equity	38.59	N/A	US$	32.73	N/A	Deltec Securities	Equity	Offshore Territories
GIM World Equity Fund	35.98	79.87	G	1.5	6.05	GIM Fund Management	Equity	Netherlands Unit Trusts
Globalvest Value	35.75	N/A	US$	8.3	8.56	Alpha Global	Equity	Offshore Territories
Jupiter Intl Green-Ord(2001)	35.69	N/A	£	22.18	8.36	Jupiter Asset Mgmt Ltd	Equity Growth	UK Investment Trusts
GAM Global Fund/A	35.02	203.86	US$	84.9	4.23	GAM Funds	Equity Growth	US Mutuals
GAM Global Fund/D	34.77	N/A	US$	5.6	N/A	GAM Funds	Equity Growth	US Mutuals
BBL (L) Invest HealthCare C	34.3	N/A	US$	145.87	N/A	BBL-Banque Brussels Lambert	Equity	Luxembourg
BBL (L) Invest HealthCare D	34.29	N/A	US$	145.87	N/A	BBL-Banque Brussels Lambert	Equity	Luxembourg
Archimedes-Cap (2003)	34.22	121.41	£	15.79	5.17	Guinness Flight Hambro	Equity Growth	UK Investment Trusts
Globalvest Value Fund LP	33.77	N/A	US$	15.39	N/A	Globvest Mgmt Co L.P	Equity	Offshore Territories
Willer Telecom	33.71	N/A	US$	33.92	4.17	Willerfunds Management Co.	Equity	Luxembourg
Framlington Financial	33.54	199.58	£	79.46	3.35	Framlington Group	Equity Growth	UK Unit Trusts/OEICs
Value Realisation	32.58	N/A	£	159.22	N/A	J.Rothschild Cap Mgmt Ltd	Equity Growth	UK Investment Trusts
RBB:BEA Glbl Telcom/Adv	32.35	N/A	US$	0.9	N/A	RBB BEA Funds	Equity Growth	US Mutuals
JRIA/GAM US Dllr Mgd	32.27	N/A	US$	21.89	3.93	J Rothschild Intl Assurance	Equity	Offshore Territories
Skandia/Framlngtn Financial	32.11	191.11	£	12.78	3.31	Skandia/Framlington	Equity Growth	UK Individual Pensions
Gabelli Gl Telecomm	31.87	N/A	US$	135.4	3.58	Gabelli Funds	Equity Growth	US Mutuals
GT Global Fincl Svcs/Adv	30.91	N/A	US$	10	N/A	GT Global Funds	Equity Growth	US Mutuals
GAM Universal DEM Acc	30.74	163	DM	443.25	4.73	GAM Fd Mgt (Ireland)	Equity	Offshore Territories
GAM Universal DEM	30.72	161.9	DM	443.25	4.73	GAM Fd Mgt (Ireland)	Equity	Offshore Territories
Merchants	30.56	121.21	£	580.67	4.02	Kleinwort Benson Inv Mgmt Ltd	Equity Income	UK Investment Trusts
GT Global Fincl Svcs/A	30.32	N/A	US$	34.4	3.76	GT Global Funds	Equity Growth	US Mutuals
INVESCO Splty:Wldwd Comm	30.29	N/A	US$	136.6	3.85	INVESCO Specialty Funds	Equity Growth	US Mutuals
JRIA/GAM Stlg Mgd	30.12	N/A	£	78.7	3.97	J Rothschild Intl Assurance	Equity	Offshore Territories
Dresdner RCM Glbl Health	30	N/A	US$	5	N/A	Dresdnar RCM Funds	Equity Growth	US Mutuals
J Hancock Global Rx/A	29.73	112.87	US$	62.8	4.89	John Hancock Global Funds	Equity Growth	US Mutuals
GT Global Fincl Svcs/B	29.7	N/A	US$	57.6	3.76	GT Global Funds	Equity Growth	US Mutuals
S&P Financial Securities	29.35	231.07	£	448.46	3.34	Save & Prosper Group	Equity Growth	UK Unit Trusts/OEICs
Montgomery Select 50/R	29.27	N/A	US$	245.9	N/A	Montgomery Funds	Equity Growth	US Mutuals

Note: details for some funds may not have been included if the data for the US$ % change for 96/97 was not available

Source: Standard & Poor's Micropal.

MORGAN STANLEY CAPITAL INTERNATIONAL (MSCI) WORLD INDICES*

ARGENTINA MONTHLY INDEX (US$)

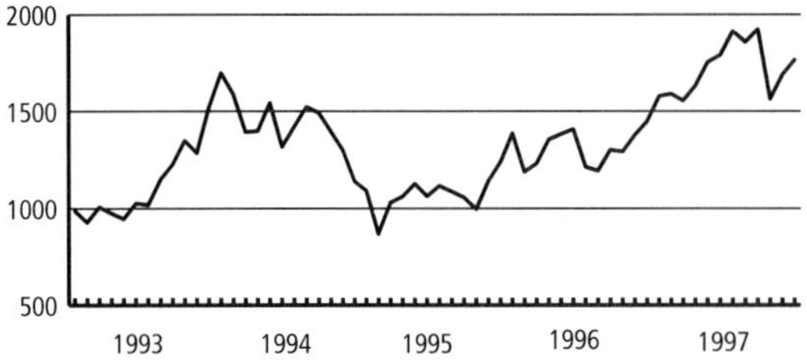

AUSTRALIA MONTHLY INDEX (US$)

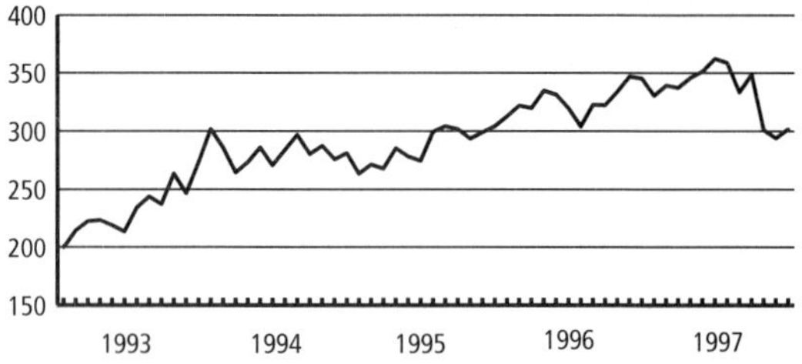

AUSTRIA MONTHLY INDEX (US$)

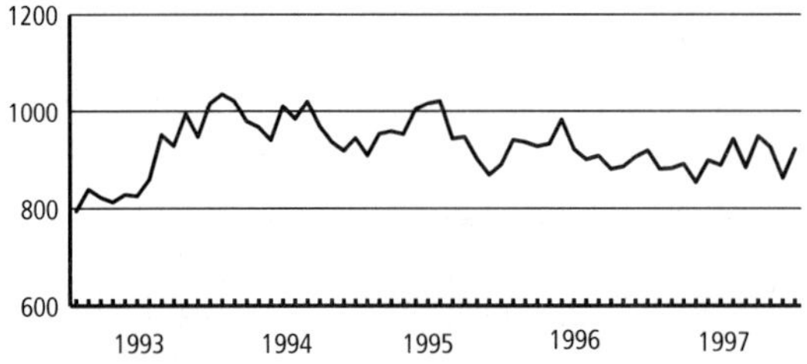

BELGIUM MONTHLY INDEX (US$)

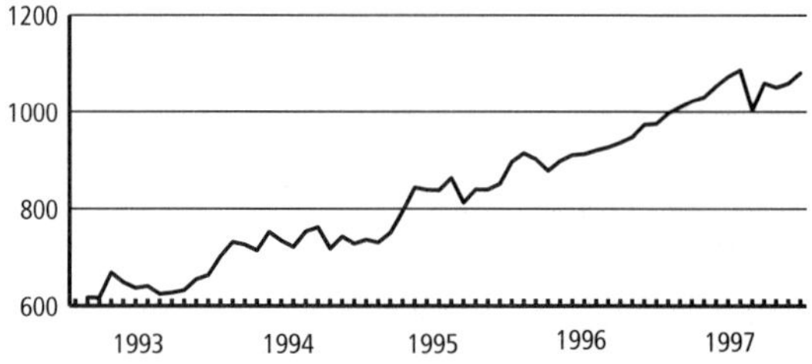

BRAZIL MONTHLY INDEX (US$)

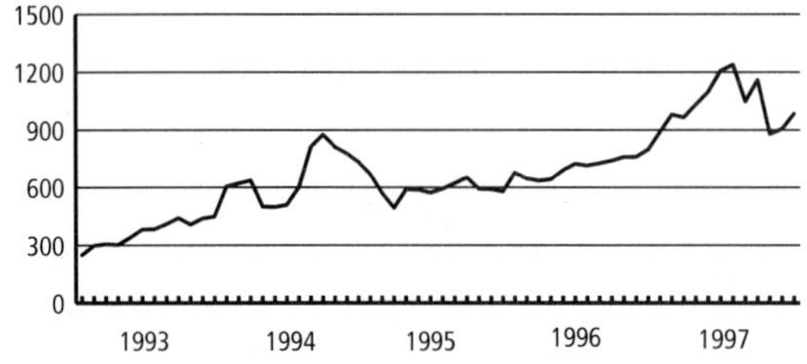

CANADA MONTHLY INDEX (US$)

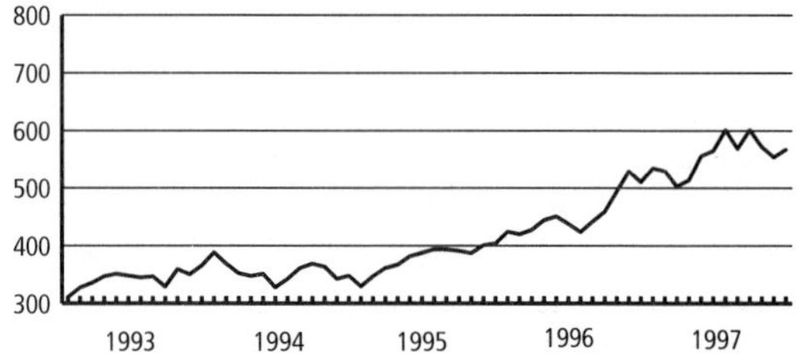

CHILE MONTHLY INDEX (US$)

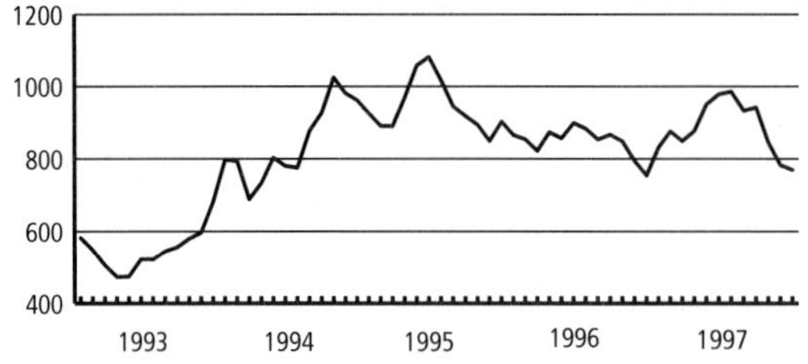

CHINA MONTHLY INDEX (US$)

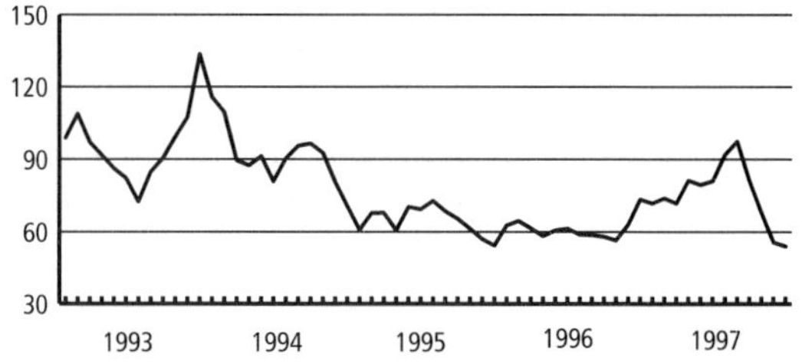

**Excluding dividends*

Source: Morgan Stanley Capital International.

MORGAN STANLEY CAPITAL INTERNATIONAL (MSCI) WORLD INDICES*

COLOMBIA MONTHLY INDEX (US$)

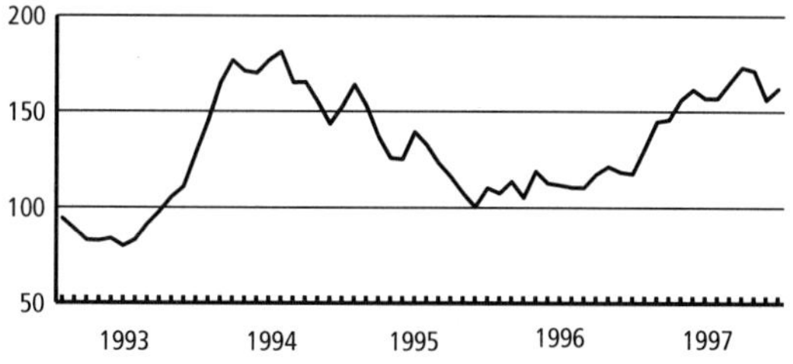

CZECH REPUBLIC MONTHLY INDEX (US$)

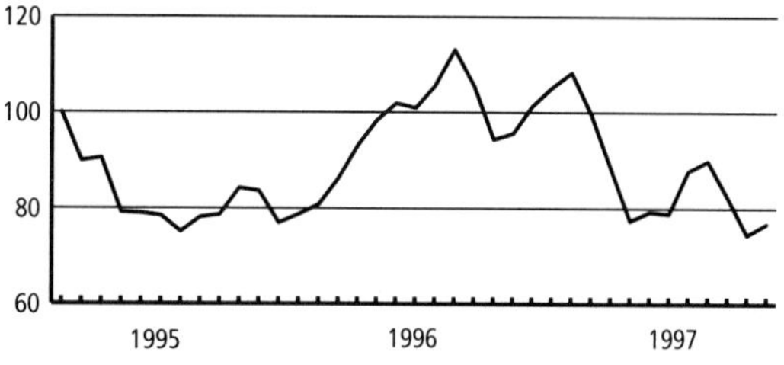

DENMARK MONTHLY INDEX (US$)

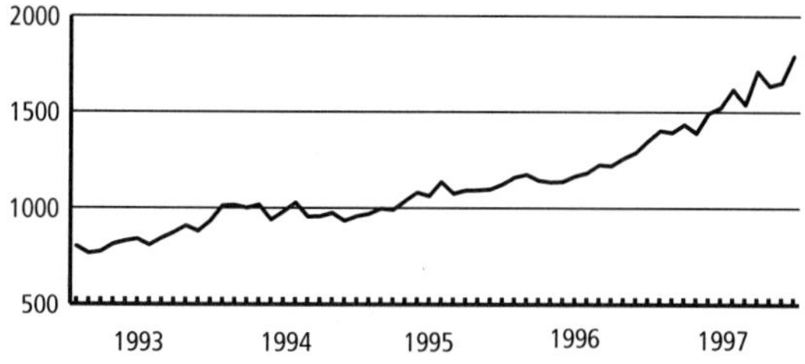

FRANCE MONTHLY INDEX (US$)

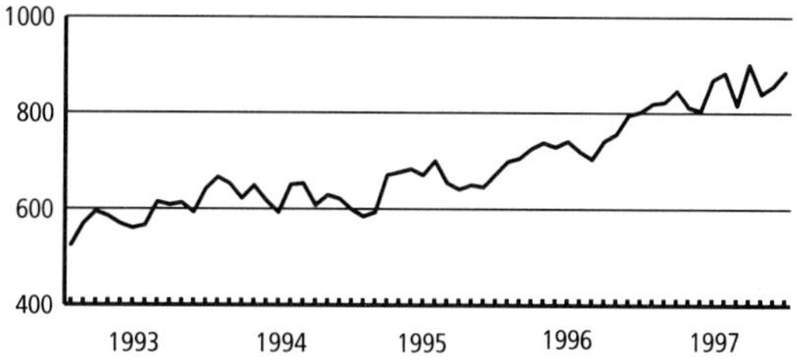

GERMANY MONTHLY INDEX (US$)

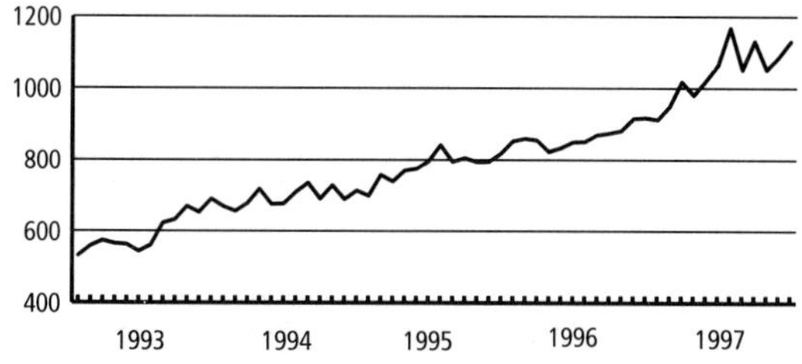

GREECE MONTHLY INDEX (US$)

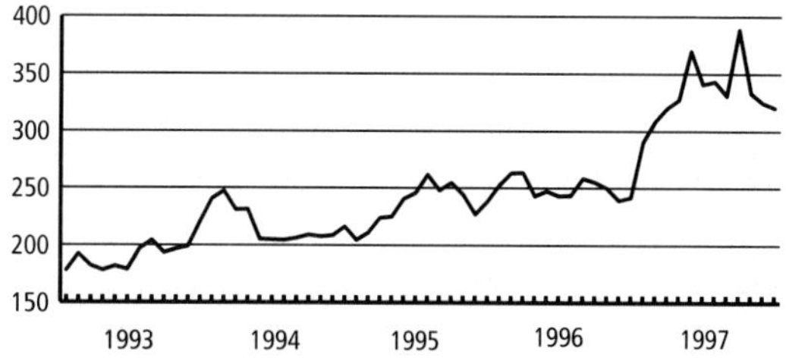

HONG KONG MONTHLY INDEX (US$)

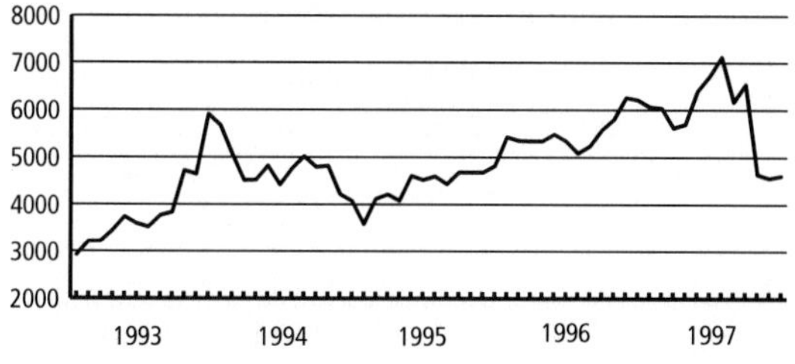

HUNGARY MONTHLY INDEX (US$)

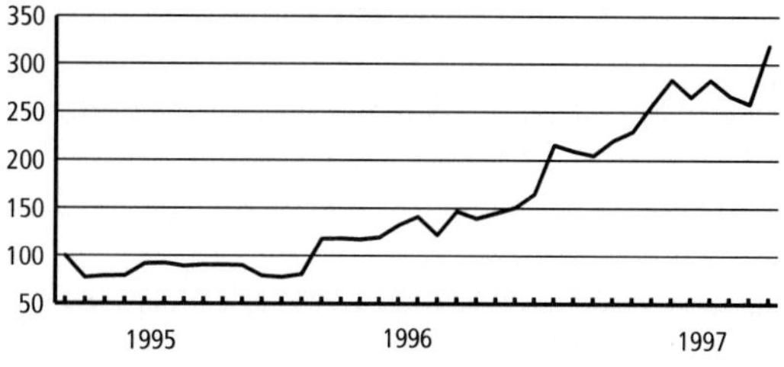

*Excluding dividends

Source: Morgan Stanley Capital International.

MORGAN STANLEY CAPITAL INTERNATIONAL (MSCI) WORLD INDICES*

INDIA MONTHLY INDEX (US$)

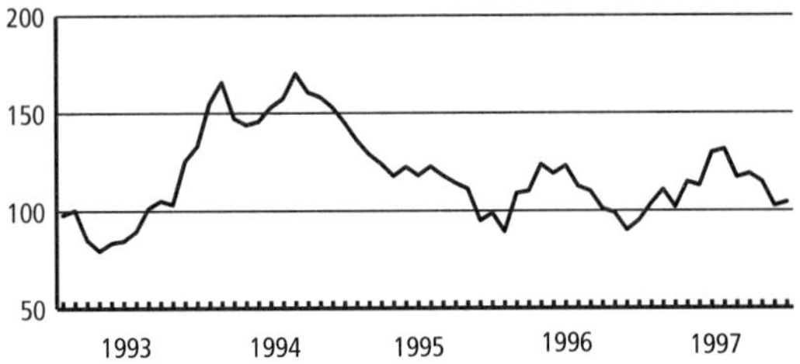

INDONESIA MONTHLY INDEX (US$)

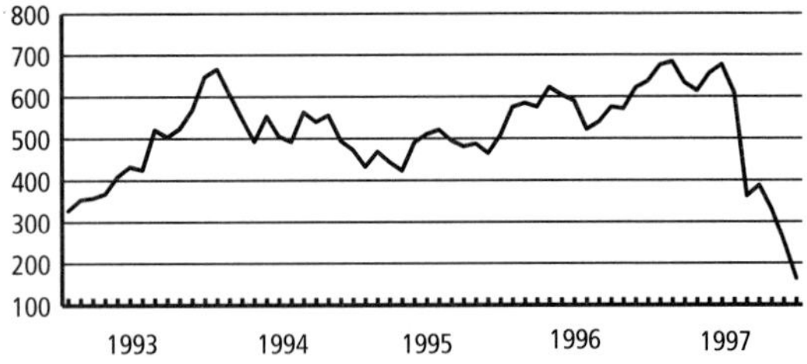

IRELAND MONTHLY INDEX (US$)

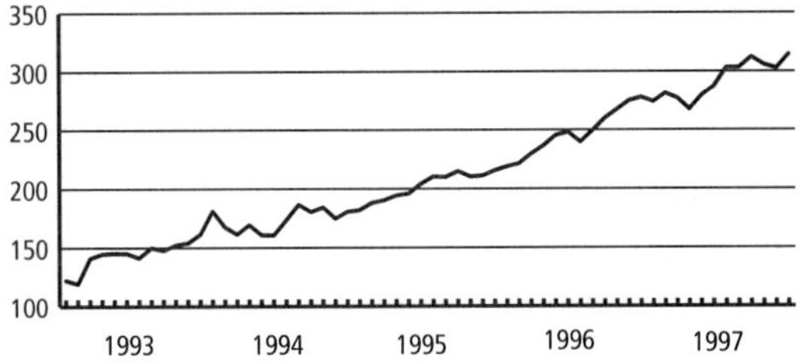

ISRAEL MONTHLY INDEX (US$)

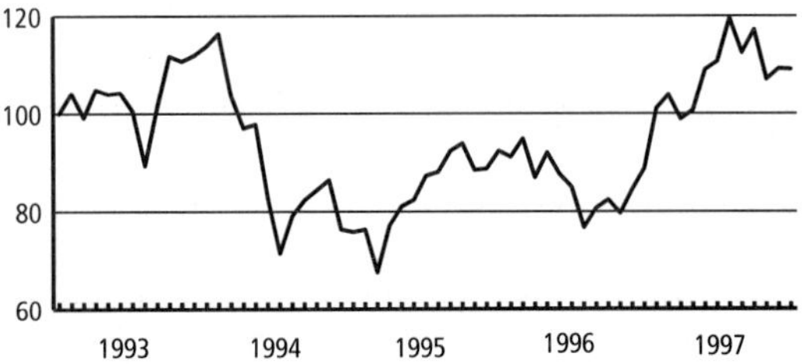

ITALY MONTHLY INDEX (US$)

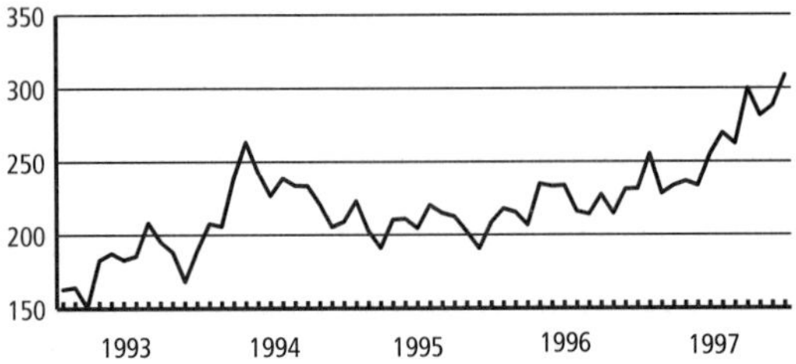

JAPAN MONTHLY INDEX (US$)

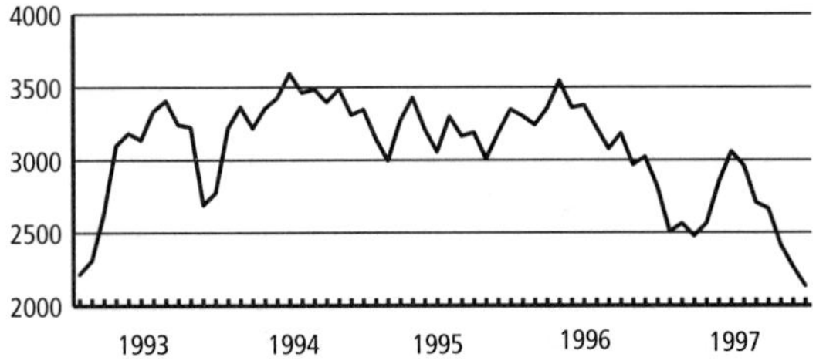

JORDAN MONTHLY INDEX (US$)

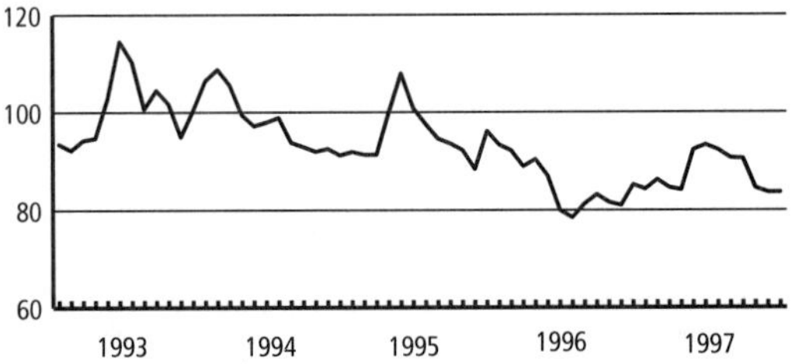

KOREA MONTHLY INDEX (US$)

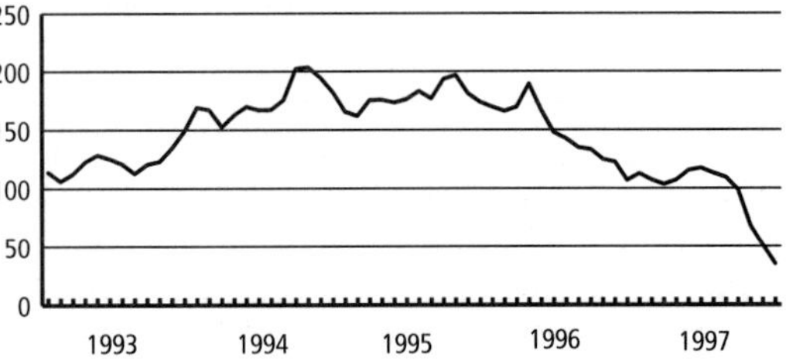

*Excluding dividends

Source: Morgan Stanley Capital International.

MORGAN STANLEY CAPITAL INTERNATIONAL (MSCI) WORLD INDICES*

LUXEMBOURG MONTHLY INDEX (US$)

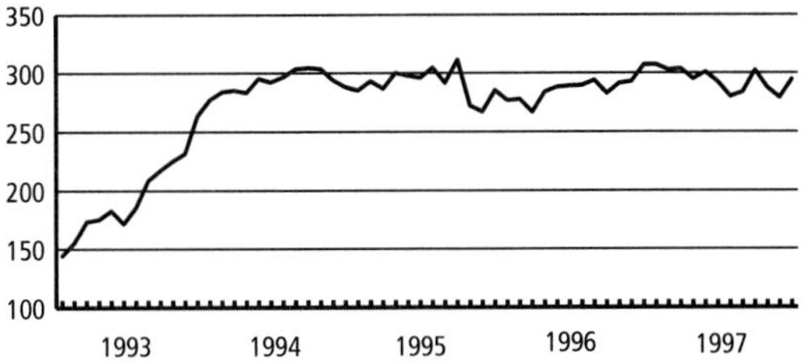

MALAYSIA MONTHLY INDEX (US$)

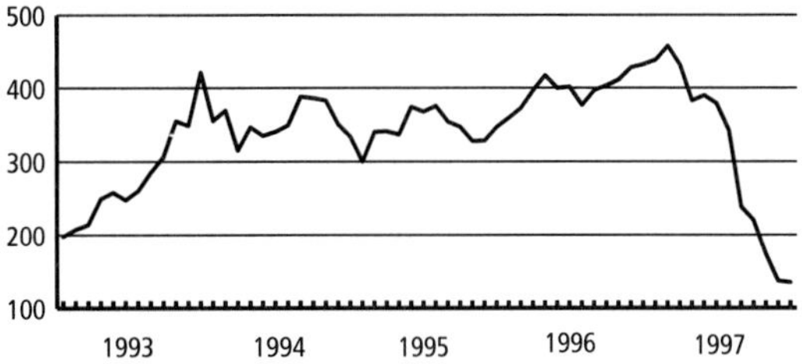

MEXICO MONTHLY INDEX (US$)

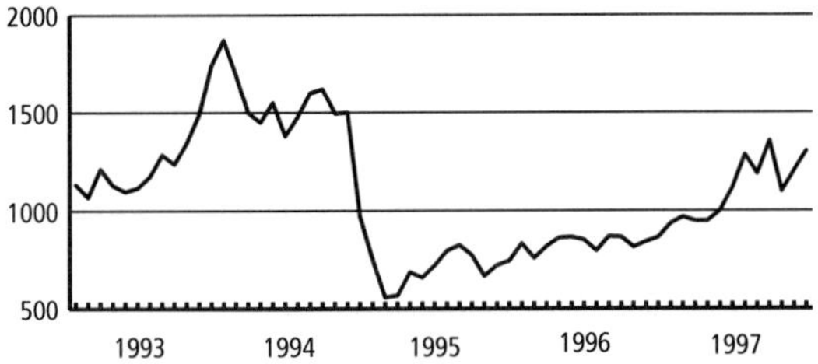

MOROCCO MONTHLY INDEX (US$)

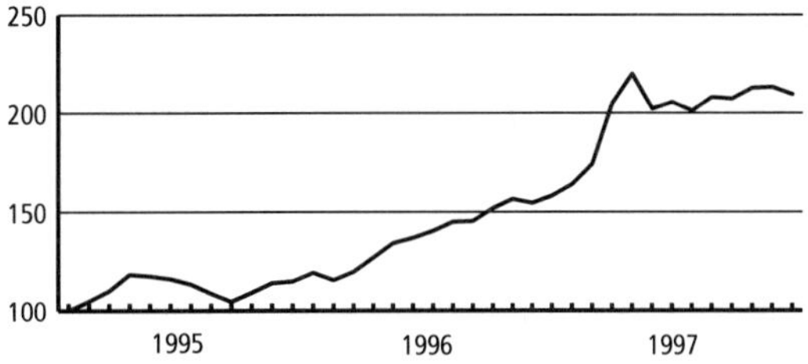

NETHERLANDS MONTHLY INDEX (US$)

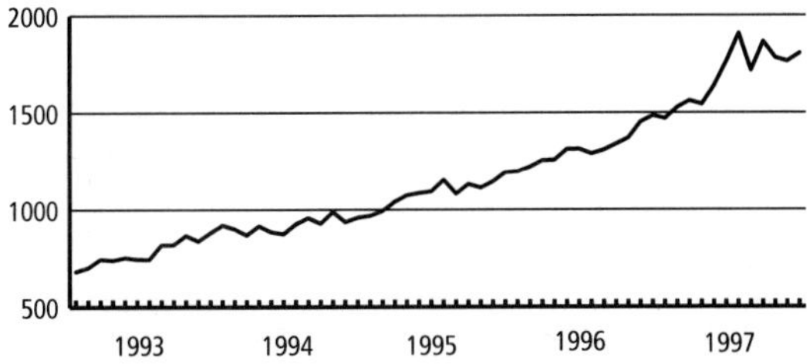

NEW ZEALAND MONTHLY INDEX (US$)

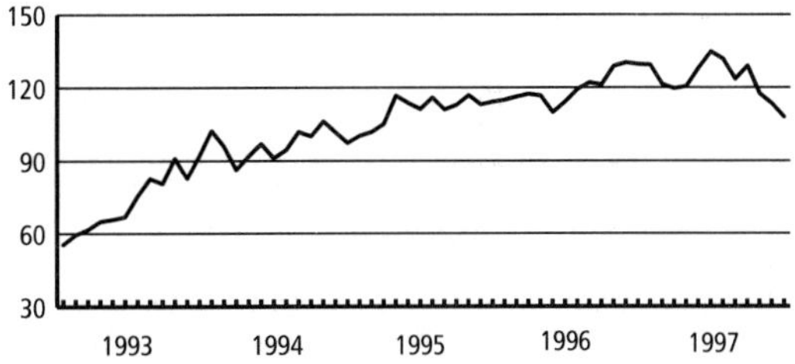

NORWAY MONTHLY INDEX (US$)

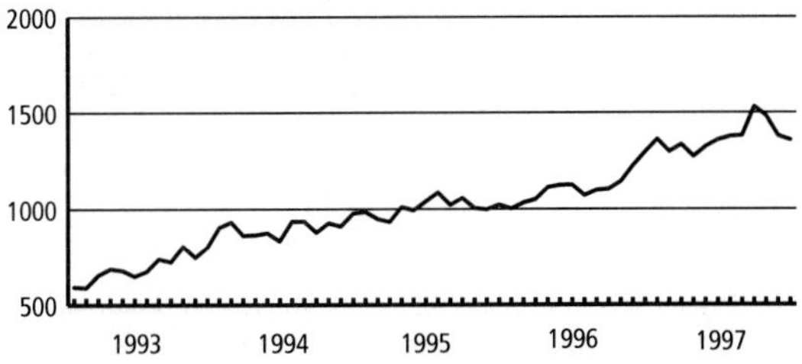

PAKISTAN MONTHLY INDEX (US$)

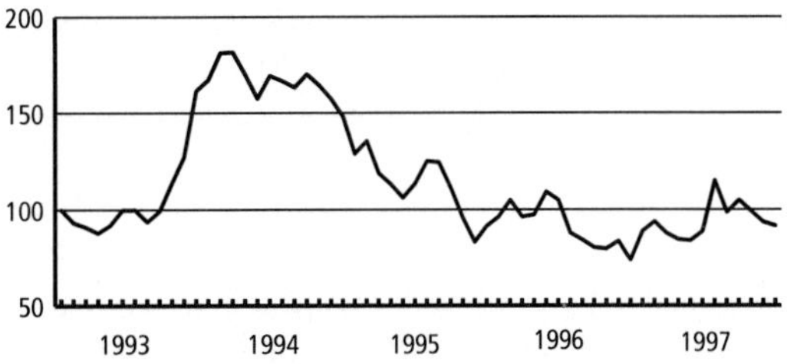

**Excluding dividends*

Source: Morgan Stanley Capital International.

MORGAN STANLEY CAPITAL INTERNATIONAL (MSCI) WORLD INDICES*

PERU MONTHLY INDEX (US$)

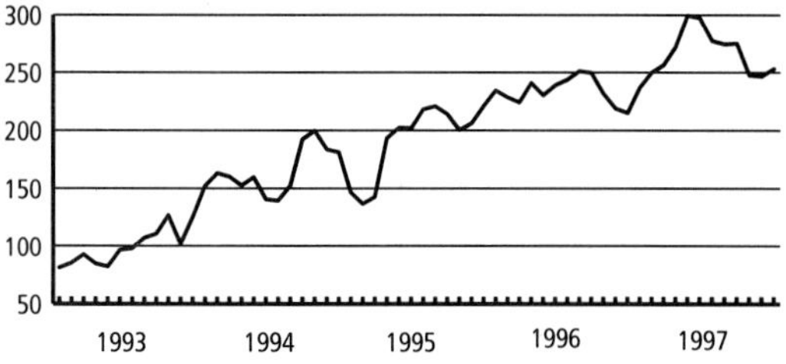

PHILIPPINES MONTHLY INDEX (US$)

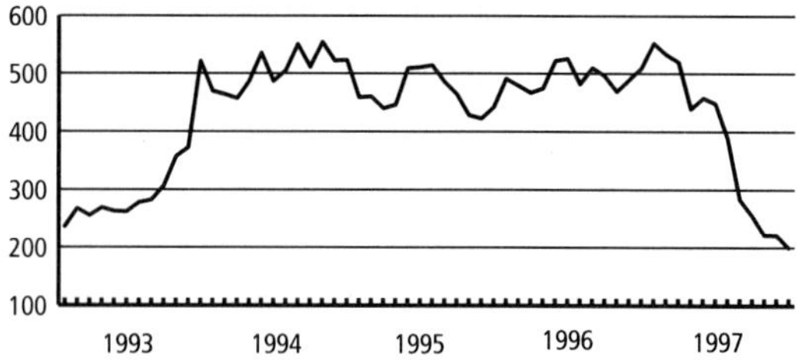

POLAND MONTHLY INDEX (US$)

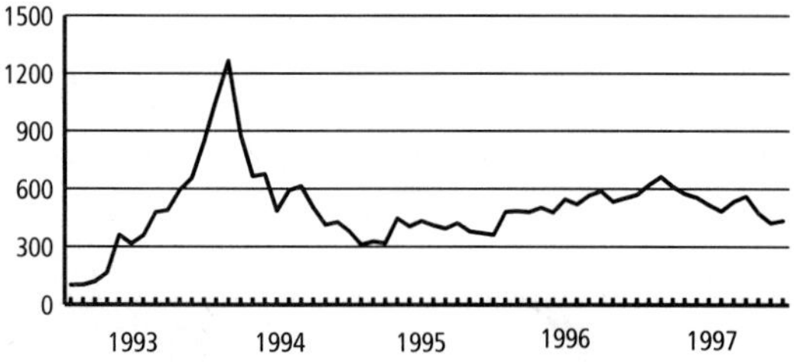

PORTUGAL MONTHLY INDEX (US$)

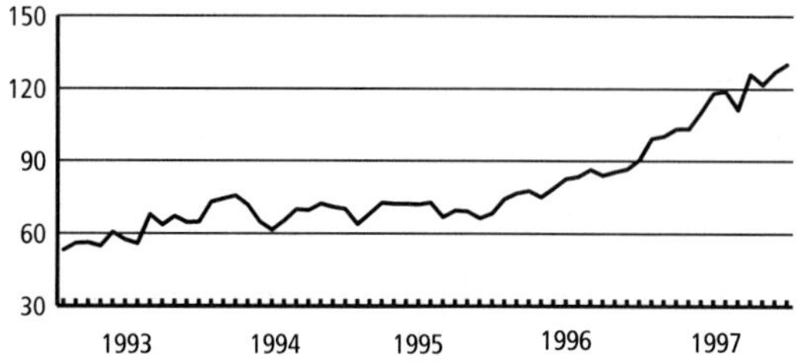

RUSSIA MONTHLY INDEX (US$)

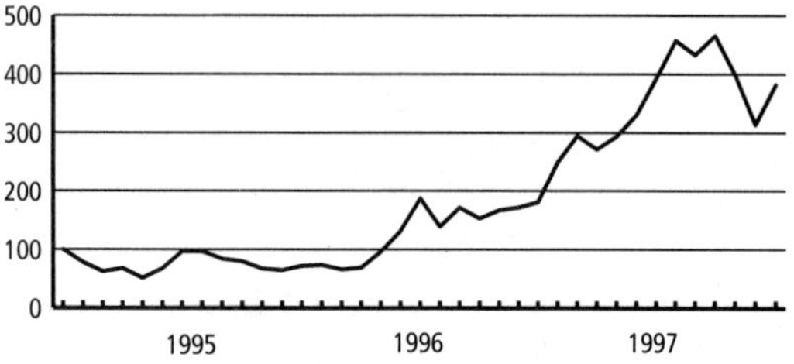

SOUTH AFRICA MONTHLY INDEX (US$)

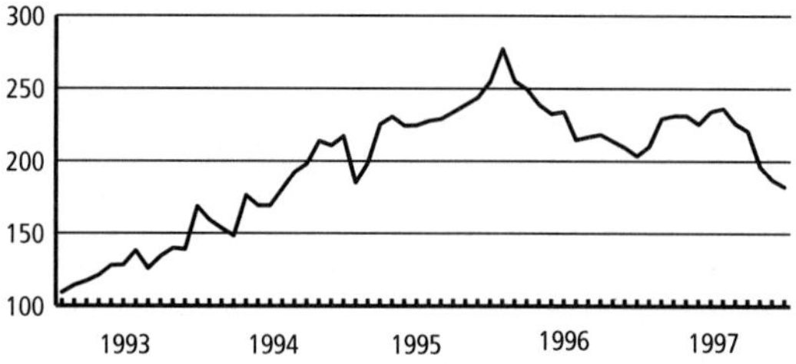

SINGAPORE MONTHLY INDEX (US$)

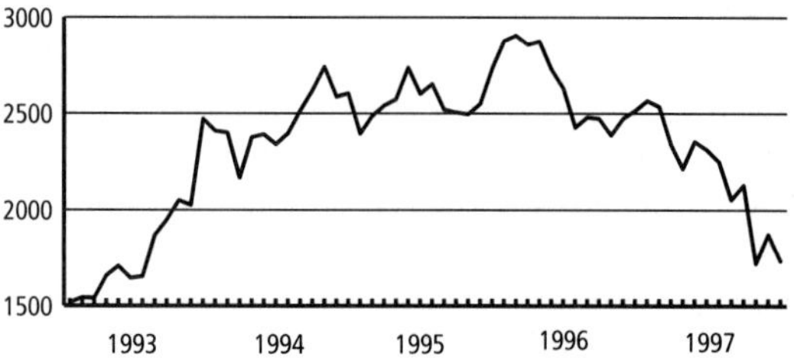

SPAIN MONTHLY INDEX (US$)

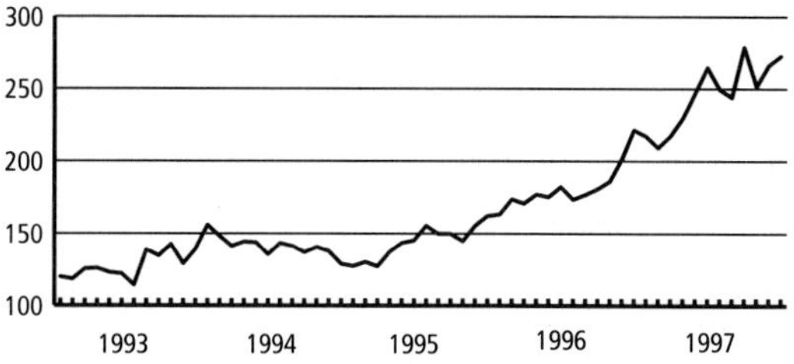

**Excluding dividends*

Source: Morgan Stanley Capital International.

MORGAN STANLEY CAPITAL INTERNATIONAL (MSCI) WORLD INDICES*

SRI LANKA MONTHLY INDEX (US$)

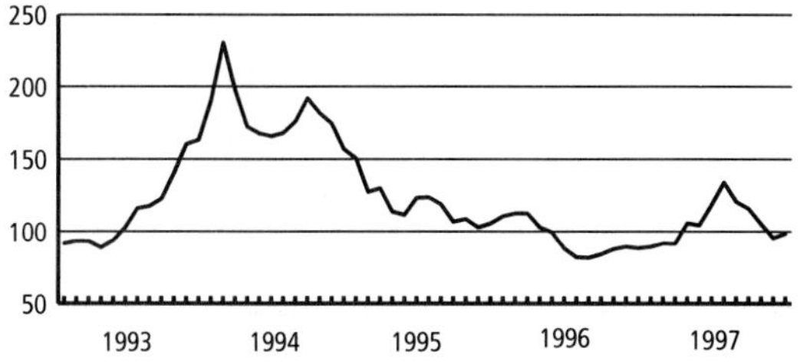

SWEDEN MONTHLY INDEX (US$)

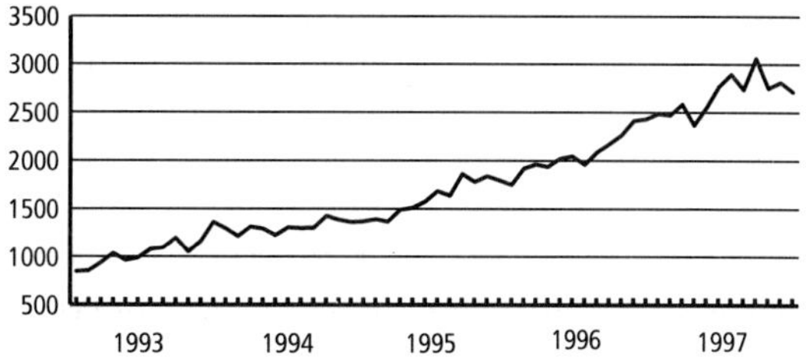

SWITZERLAND MONTHLY INDEX (US$)

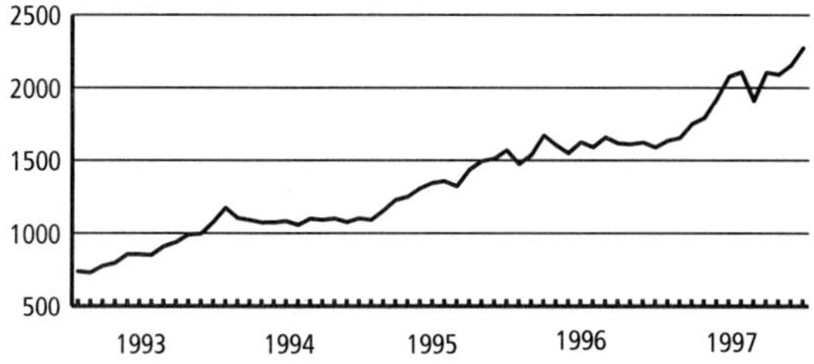

TAIWAN MONTHLY INDEX (US$)

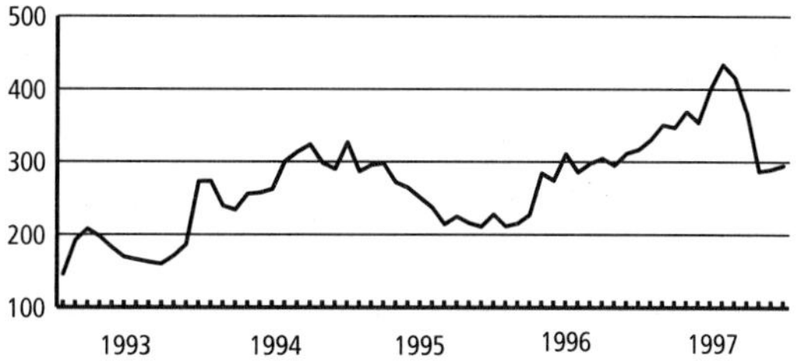

THAILAND MONTHLY INDEX (US$)

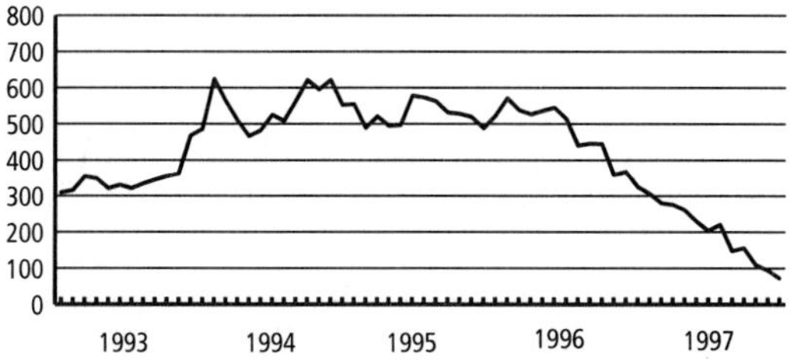

TURKEY MONTHLY INDEX (US$)

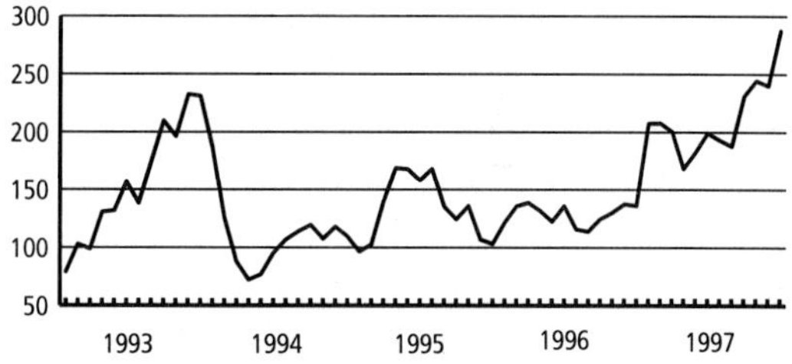

UNITED KINGDOM MONTHLY INDEX (US$)

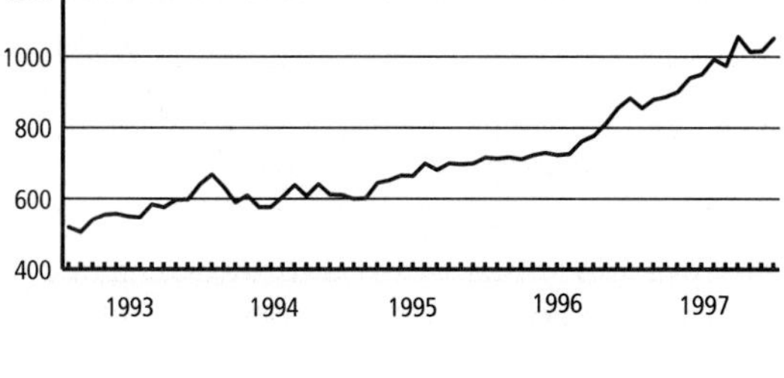

UNITED STATES MONTHLY INDEX (US$)

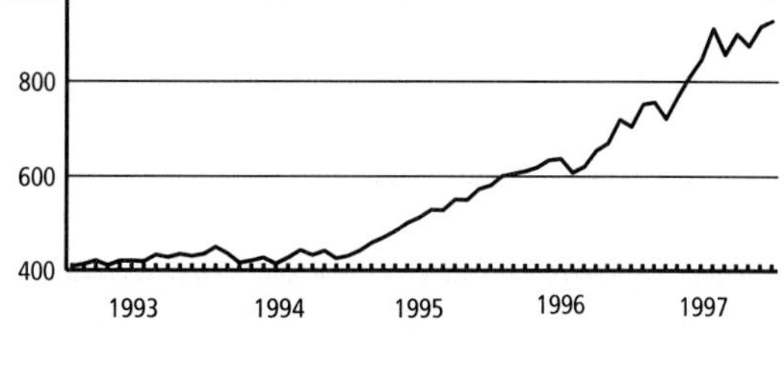

**Excluding dividends*

Source: Morgan Stanley Capital International.

MORGAN STANLEY CAPITAL INTERNATIONAL (MSCI) WORLD INDICES*

VENEZUELA MONTHLY INDEX (US$)

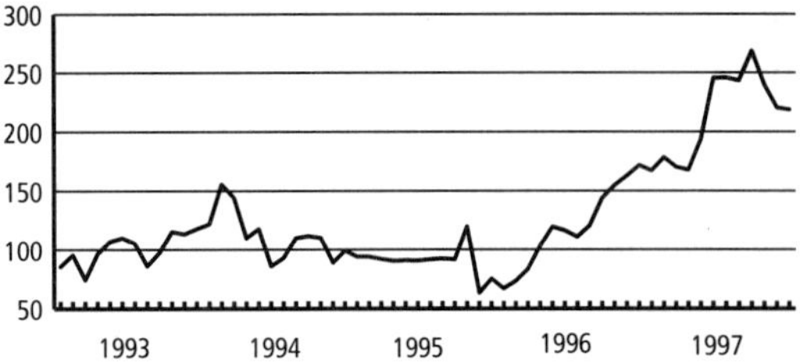

EMERGING MARKETS EUROPE AND MIDDLE EAST MONTHLY INDEX (US$)

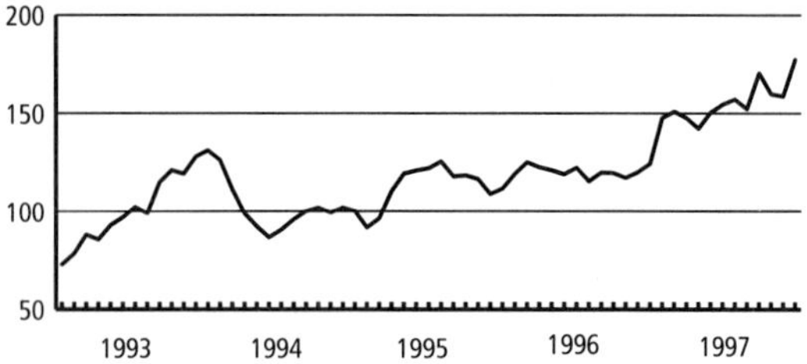

AC FAR EAST FREE EX JAPAN MONTHLY INDEX (US$)

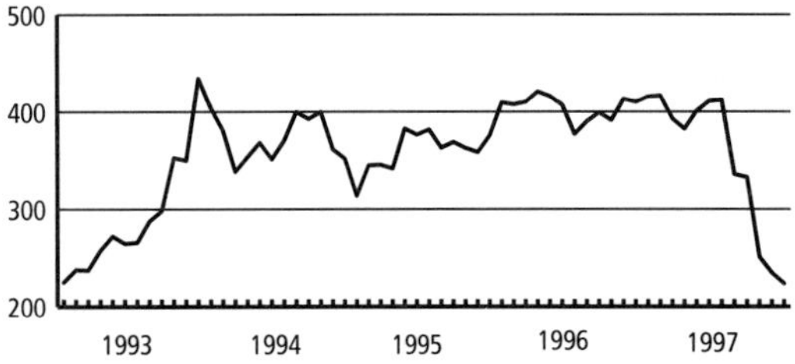

EAFE MONTHLY INDEX (US$)

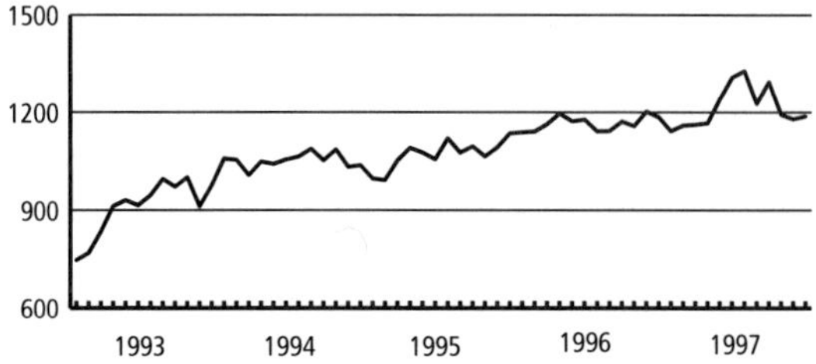

EMERGING MARKETS FREE MONTHLY INDEX (US$)

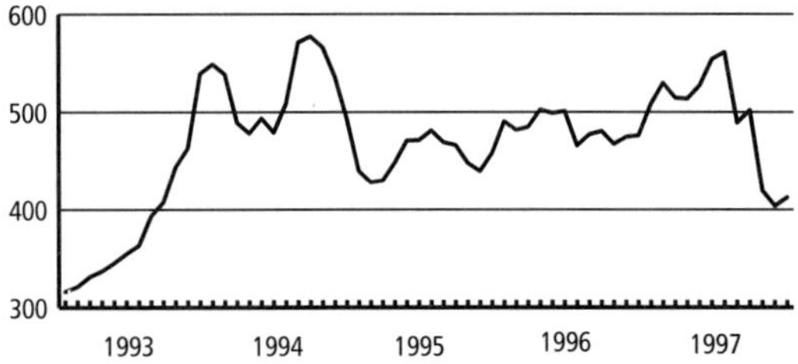

EMERGING MARKETS MONTHLY INDEX (US$)

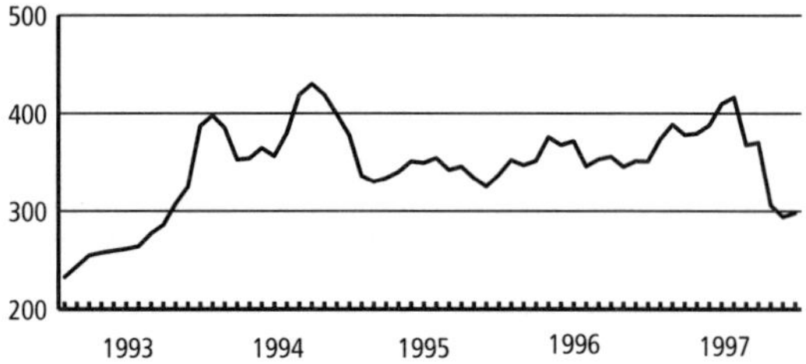

AC WORLD FREE MONTHLY INDEX (US$)

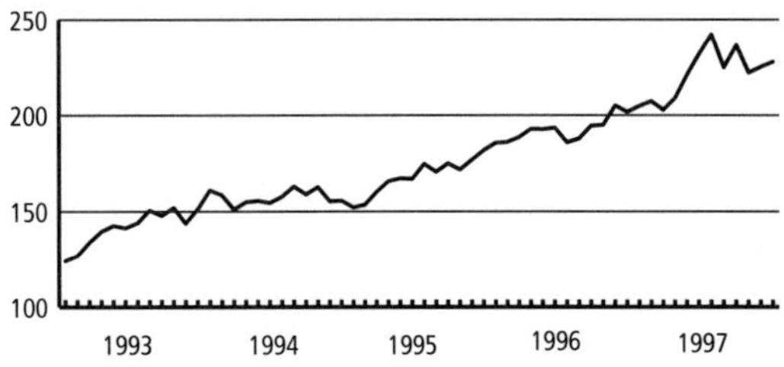

AC WORLD MONTHLY INDEX (US$)

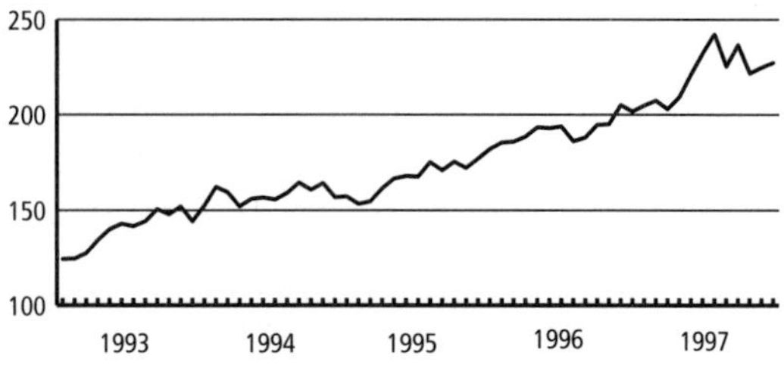

**Excluding dividends*

Source: Morgan Stanley Capital International.

MORGAN STANLEY CAPITAL INTERNATIONAL (MSCI) WORLD INDICES*

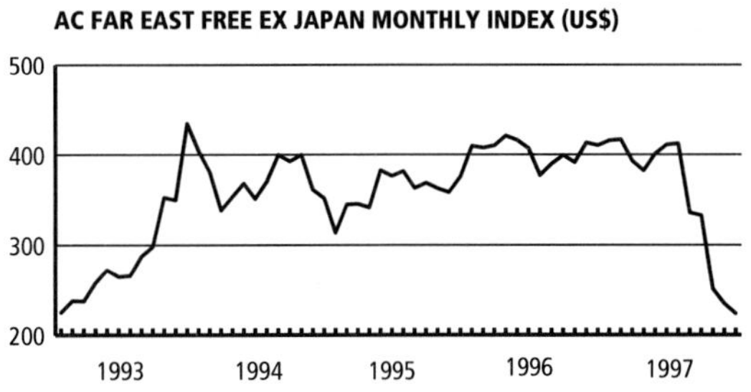

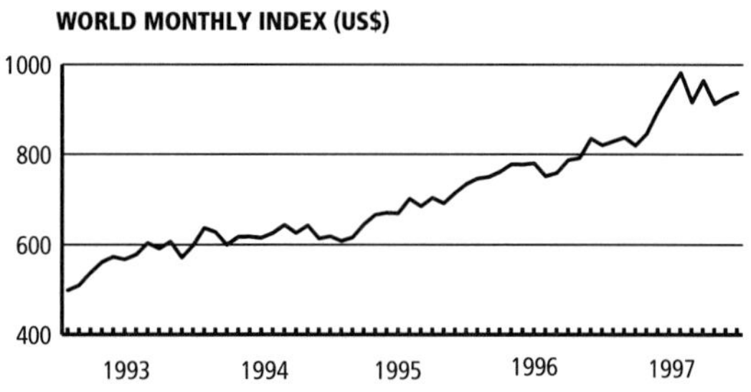

*Excluding dividends

Source: Morgan Stanley Capital International.

SALOMON SMITH BARNEY WORLD EQUITY INDICES

Large capitalisation (Primary Market Index – PMI) versus small capitalisation (Extended Market Index – EMI) total return performance, local currency terms

Australia

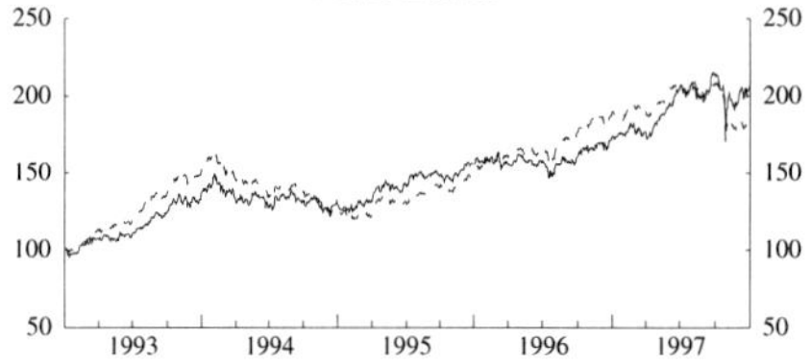

PMI 31DEC92 to 31DEC97 = 109.00%
EMI 31DEC92 to 31DEC97 = 86.01%

Austria

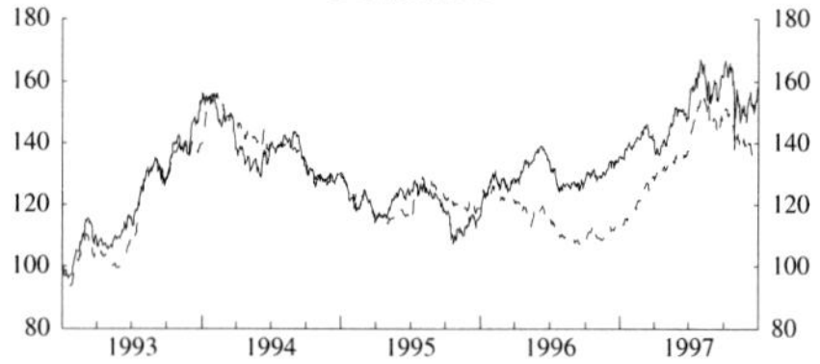

PMI 31DEC92 to 31DEC97 = 58.51%
EMI 31DEC92 to 31DEC97 = 34.57%

Belgium

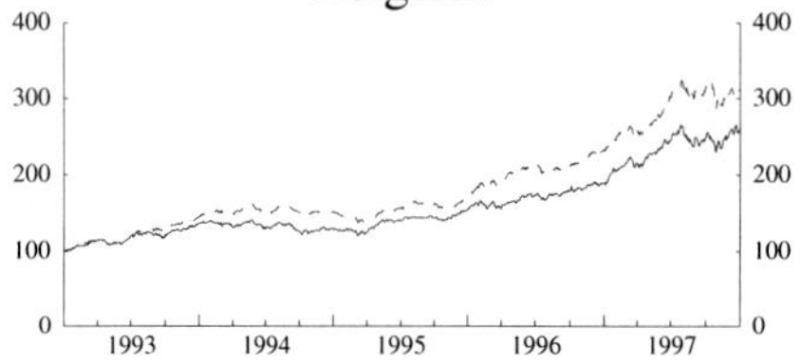

PMI 31DEC92 to 31DEC97 = 161.04%
EMI 31DEC92 to 31DEC97 = 212.72%

Canada

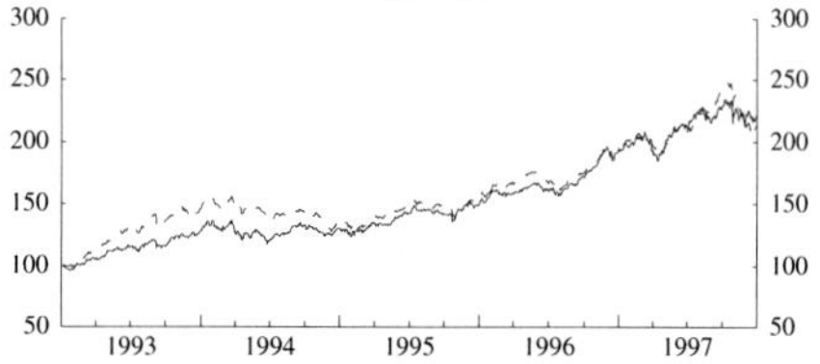

PMI 31DEC92 to 31DEC97 = 122.14%
EMI 31DEC92 to 31DEC97 = 116.17%

Denmark

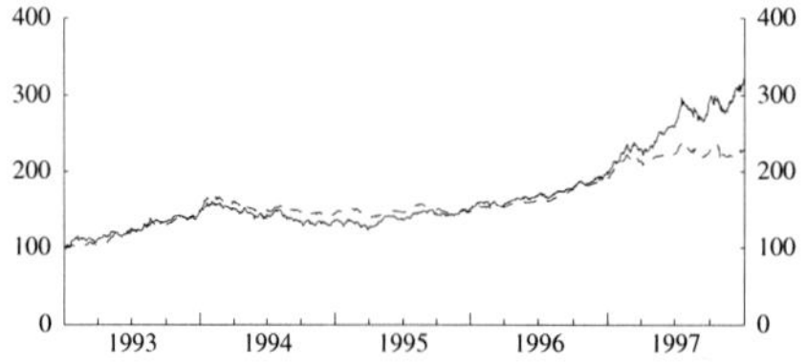

PMI 31DEC92 to 31DEC97 = 222.73%
EMI 31DEC92 to 31DEC97 = 127.03%

Finland

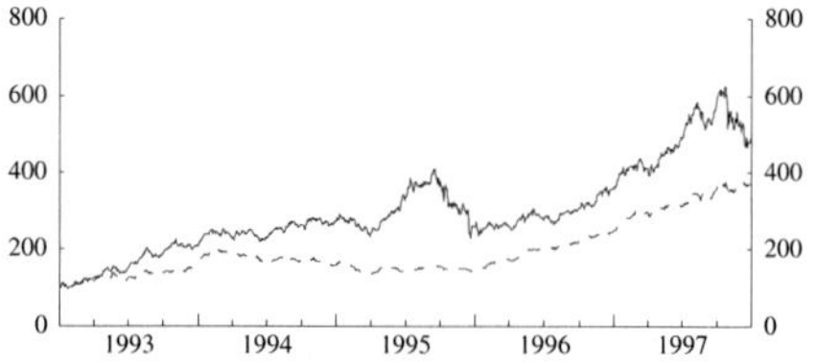

PMI 31DEC92 to 31DEC97 = 395.11%
EMI 31DEC92 to 31DEC97 = 276.49%

France

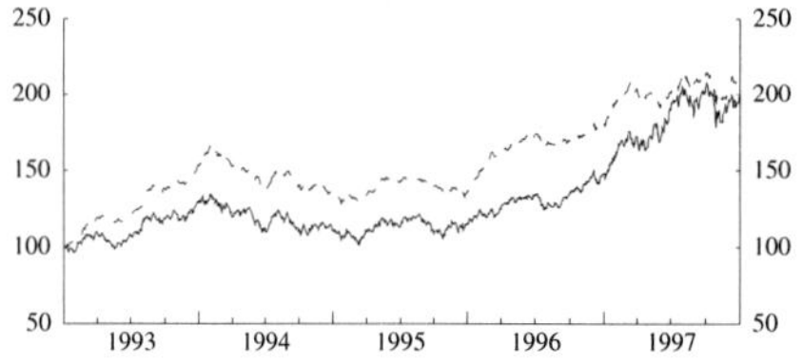

PMI 31DEC92 to 31DEC97 = 102.68%
EMI 31DEC92 to 31DEC97 = 114.98%

Germany

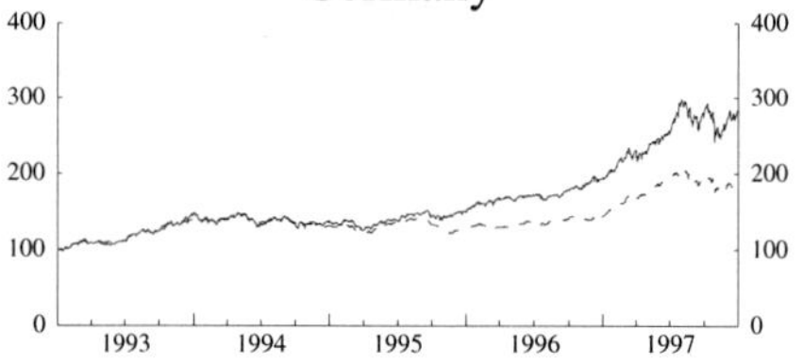

PMI 31DEC92 to 31DEC97 = 185.27%
EMI 31DEC92 to 31DEC97 = 86.09%

Source: Salomon Smith Barney.

SALOMON SMITH BARNEY WORLD EQUITY INDICES

Large capitalisation (Primary Market Index – PMI) versus small capitalisation (Extended Market Index – EMI) total return performance, local currency terms

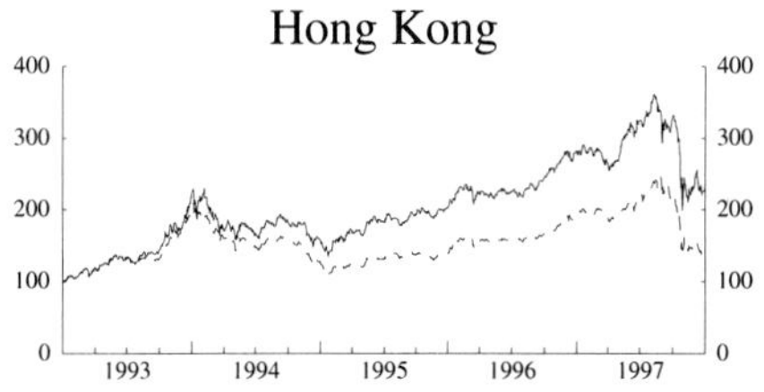

—— PMI 31DEC92 to 31DEC97 = 133.25%
– – EMI 31DEC92 to 31DEC97 = 40.34%

—— PMI 31DEC92 to 31DEC97 = 311.05%
– – EMI 31DEC92 to 31DEC97 = 260.06%

—— PMI 31DEC92 to 31DEC97 = 167.81%
– – EMI 31DEC92 to 31DEC97 = 102.81%

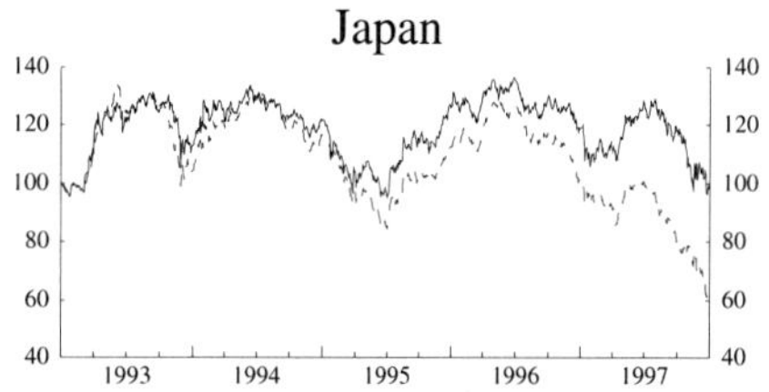

—— PMI 31DEC92 to 31DEC97 = 0.81%
– – EMI 31DEC92 to 31DEC97 = -36.83%

—— PMI 31DEC92 to 31DEC97 = -3.84%
– – EMI 31DEC92 to 31DEC97 = -15.63%

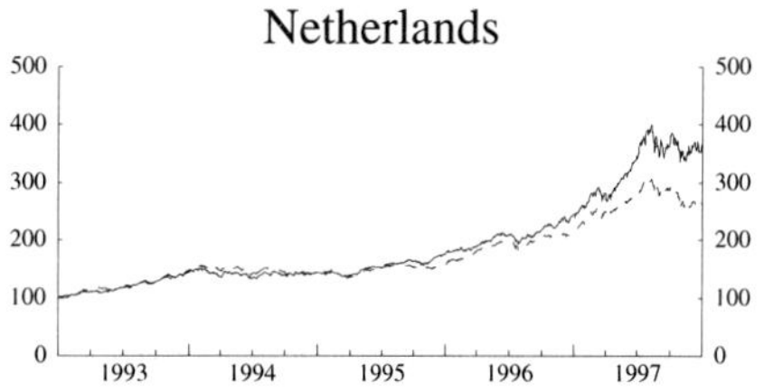

—— PMI 31DEC92 to 31DEC97 = 267.62%
– – EMI 31DEC92 to 31DEC97 = 167.09%

—— PMI 31DEC92 to 31DEC97 = 132.27%
– – EMI 31DEC92 to 31DEC97 = 22.19%

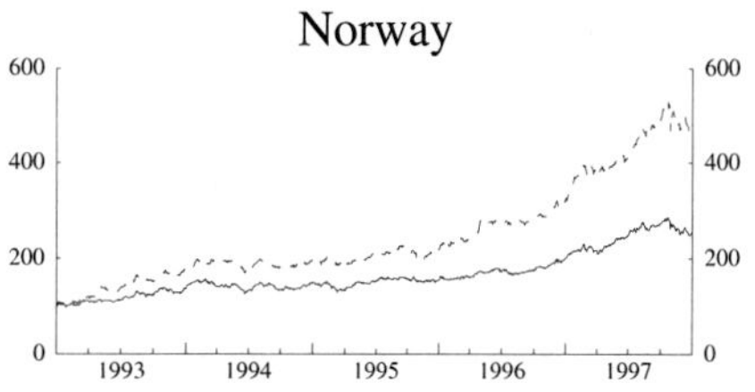

—— PMI 31DEC92 to 31DEC97 = 159.57%
– – EMI 31DEC92 to 31DEC97 = 383.91%

Source: Salomon Smith Barney.

SALOMON SMITH BARNEY WORLD EQUITY INDICES

Large capitalisation (Primary Market Index – PMI) versus small capitalisation (Extended Market Index – EMI) total return performance, local currency terms

—— PMI 31DEC92 to 31DEC97 = 22.27%
– – EMI 31DEC92 to 31DEC97 = -6.40%

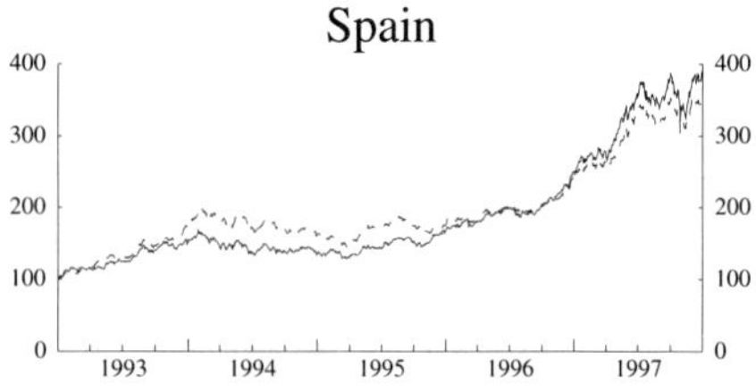

—— PMI 31DEC92 to 31DEC97 = 288.33%
– – EMI 31DEC92 to 31DEC97 = 254.52%

—— PMI 31DEC92 to 31DEC97 = 269.10%
– – EMI 31DEC92 to 31DEC97 = 262.34%

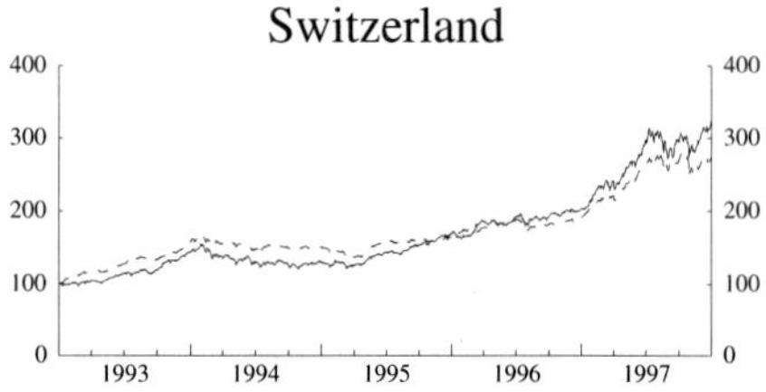

—— PMI 31DEC92 to 31DEC97 = 224.04%
– – EMI 31DEC92 to 31DEC97 = 174.08%

—— PMI 31DEC92 to 31DEC97 = 120.15%
– – EMI 31DEC92 to 31DEC97 = 104.79%

—— PMI 31DEC92 to 31DEC97 = 151.39%
– – EMI 31DEC92 to 31DEC97 = 120.62%

Source: Salomon Smith Barney.

SALOMON SMITH BARNEY WORLD EQUITY INDICES

Large capitalisation (Primary Market Index – PMI) versus small capitalisation (Extended Market Index – EMI) total return performance, US$ terms

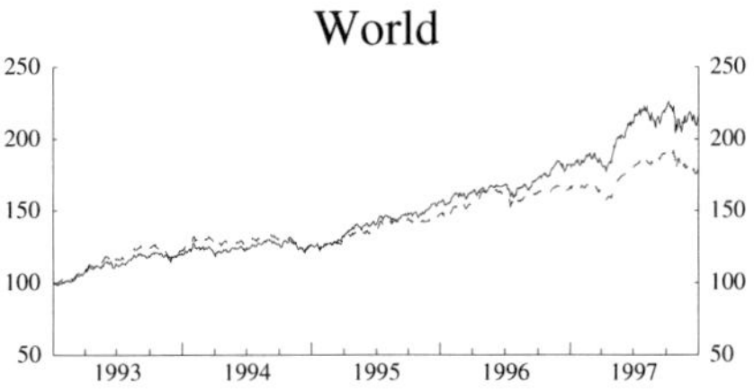

PMI 31DEC92 to 31DEC97 = 116.15%
EMI 31DEC92 to 31DEC97 = 80.35%

PMI 31DEC92 to 31DEC97 = 83.71%
EMI 31DEC92 to 31DEC97 = 45.42%

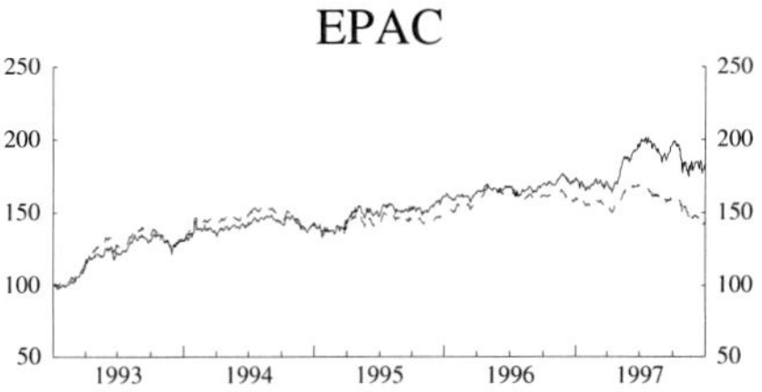

PMI 31DEC92 to 31DEC97 = 82.66%
EMI 31DEC92 to 31DEC97 = 43.13%

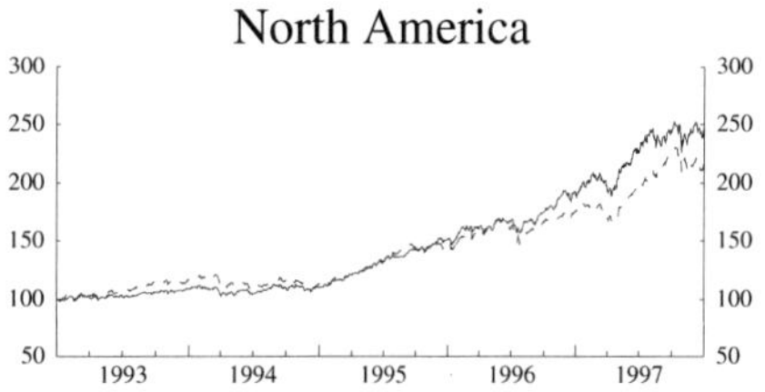

PMI 31DEC92 to 31DEC97 = 148.58%
EMI 31DEC92 to 31DEC97 = 119.11%

PMI 31DEC92 to 31DEC97 = 153.20%
EMI 31DEC92 to 31DEC97 = 124.30%

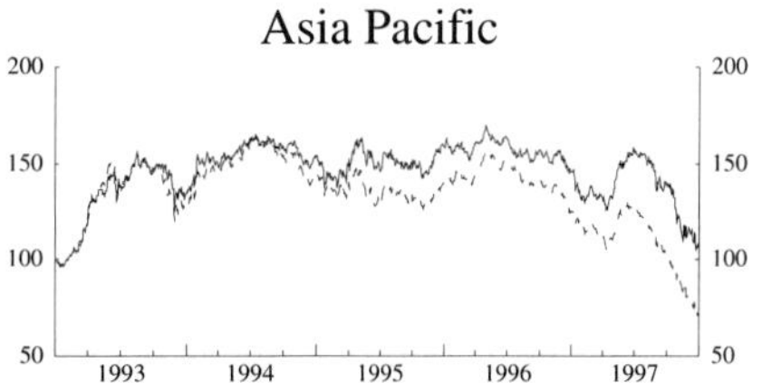

PMI 31DEC92 to 31DEC97 = 9.56%
EMI 31DEC92 to 31DEC97 = -27.58%

PMI 31DEC92 to 31DEC97 = 166.38%
EMI 31DEC92 to 31DEC97 = 126.47%

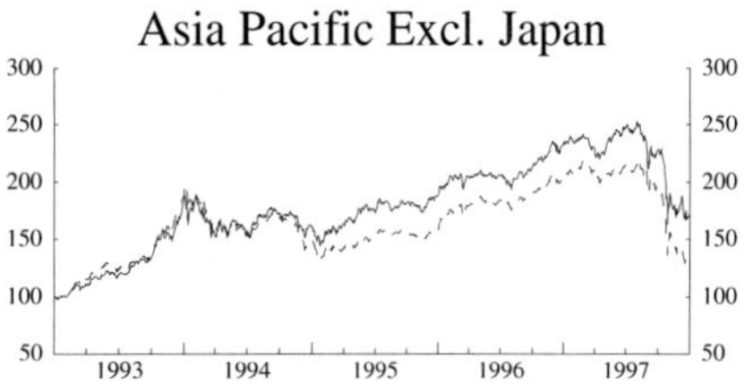

PMI 31DEC92 to 31DEC97 = 73.68%
EMI 31DEC92 to 31DEC97 = 30.86%

Source: Salomon Smith Barney.

SALOMON SMITH BARNEY WORLD EQUITY INDICES

Large capitalisation (Primary Market Index – PMI) versus small capitalisation (Extended Market Index – EMI) total return performance, US$ terms

World Excl. Japan

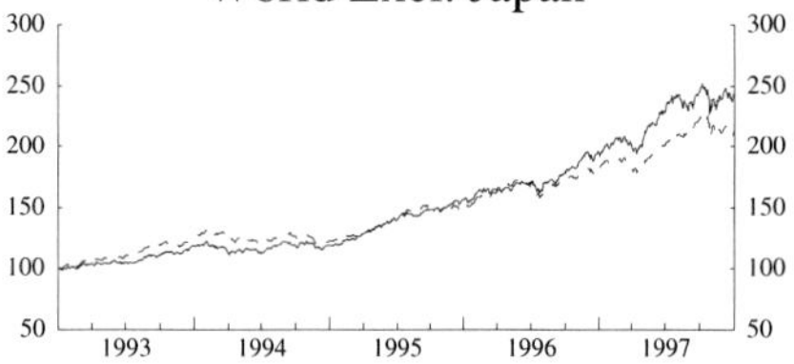

—— PMI 31DEC92 to 31DEC97 = 145.20%
– – EMI 31DEC92 to 31DEC97 = 115.21%

World Excl. U.K.

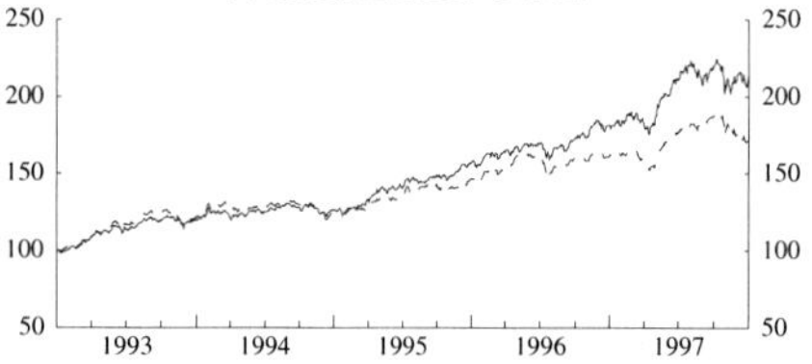

—— PMI 31DEC92 to 31DEC97 = 113.47%
– – EMI 31DEC92 to 31DEC97 = 75.59%

World Excl. U.S. & Japan

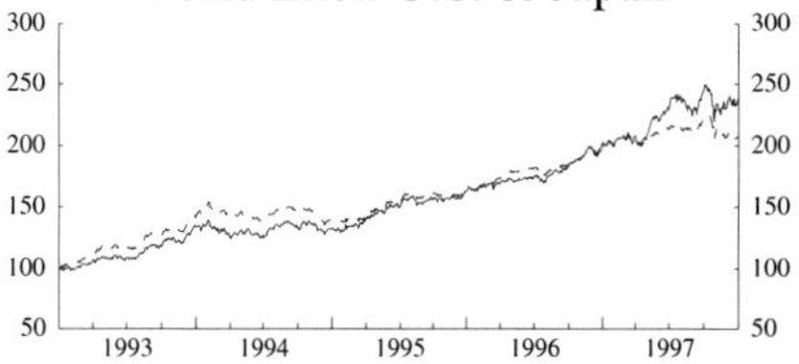

—— PMI 31DEC92 to 31DEC97 = 137.85%
– – EMI 31DEC92 to 31DEC97 = 108.32%

World Excl. U.S. & U.K.

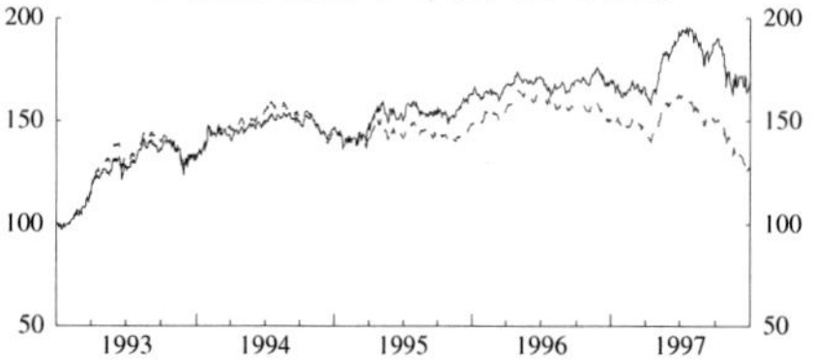

—— PMI 31DEC92 to 31DEC97 = 69.28%
– – EMI 31DEC92 to 31DEC97 = 28.30%

EPAC Excl. Japan

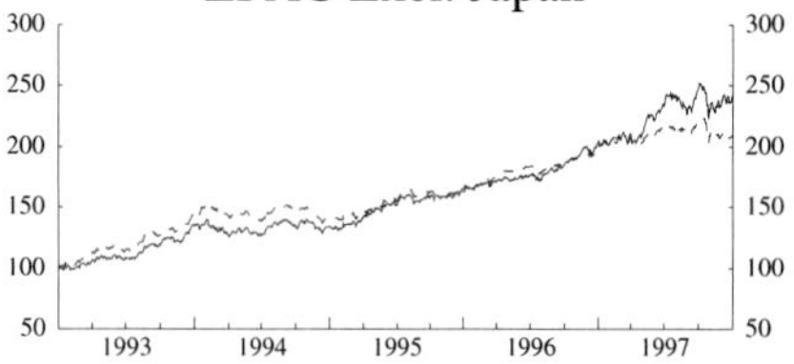

—— PMI 31DEC92 to 31DEC97 = 141.03%
– – EMI 31DEC92 to 31DEC97 = 109.25%

EPAC Excl. U.K.

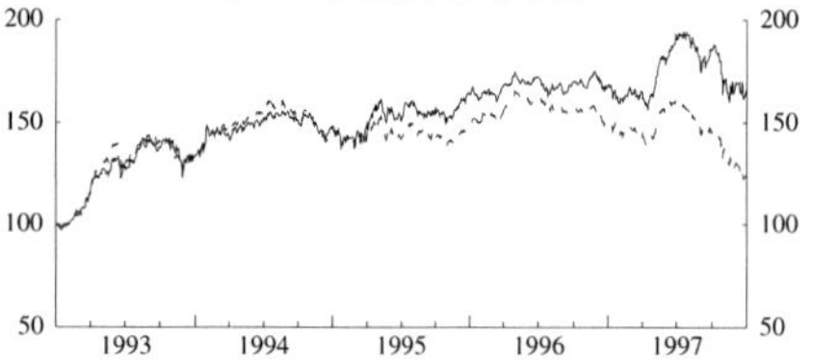

—— PMI 31DEC92 to 31DEC97 = 66.88%
– – EMI 31DEC92 to 31DEC97 = 24.51%

Source: Salomon Smith Barney.